# SOCIAL AND POLITICAL PHILOSOPHY:

## *Classical Western Texts in Feminist and Multicultural Perspectives*

Third Edition

James P. Sterba
*University of Notre Dame*

**THOMSON**

**WADSWORTH**

Australia • Canada • Mexico • Singapore • Spain • United Kingdom • United States

Publisher: Holly J. Allen
Philosophy Editor: Steve Wainwright
Assistant Editor: Lee McCracken
Editorial Assistant: Anna Lustig
Technology Project Manager: Susan DeVanna
Marketing Manager: Worth Hawes
Marketing Assistant: Justine Ferguson
Advertising Project Manager: Bryan Vann
Print/Media Buyer: Judy Inouye

Composition Buyer: Ben Schroeter
Permissions Editor: Joohee Lee
Production Service: Matrix Productions
Copy Editor: Vicki Nelson
Cover Designer: Yvo Riezebos
Cover Image: Stockbyte/PictureQuest
Compositor: G & S Typesetters
Cover and Text Printer: Webcom

Printed in Canada
3  4  5  7  06  05  04

For more information about our products, contact us at: Thomson Learning Academic Resource Center
1-800-423-0563
For permission to use material from this text, contact us by:
Phone: 1-800-730-2214
Fax: 1-800-730-2215
Web: http://www.thomsonrights.com

Library of Congress Cataloging-in-Publication Data

Social and political philosophy : classical Western texts in feminist and multicultural perspectives / [edited by] James P. Sterba.—3rd ed.
    p. cm.
Includes bibliographical references.
    ISBN 0-534-60210-X
    1. Ethics—History.   2. Social ethics—History.
3. Social justice—History.   4. Equality—History.
5. Political science—History.   6. Women's rights—History.
I. Sterba, James P.

HM665.S665 2003
303.3′72′09—dc21                    2002066167

**Wadsworth/Thomson Learning**
10 Davis Drive
Belmont, CA 94002-3098
USA

**Asia**
Thomson Learning
60 Albert Street, #15-01
Albert Complex
Singapore 189969

**Australia**
Nelson Thomson Learning
102 Dodds Street
South Melbourne, Victoria 3205
Australia

**Canada**
Nelson Thomson Learning
1120 Birchmont Road
Toronto, Ontario M1K 5G4
Canada

**Europe/Middle East/Africa**
Thomson Learning
Berkshire House
168-173 High Holborn
London WC1V 7AA
United Kingdom

**Latin America**
Thomson Learning
Seneca, 53
Colonia Polanco
11560 Mexico D.F.
Mexico

**Spain**
Paraninfo Thomson Learning
Calle/Magallanes, 25
28015 Madrid, Spain

# Contents

# Preface to the Third Edition

The third edition of *Social and Political Philosophy: Classical Western Texts in Feminist and Multicultural Perspectives* contains selections from the most recent work of John Rawls (2001) and Alasdair MacIntyre (1999) as well as a new selection on the political theory of Islam. There is also a new section of readings on Augustine and Christine de Puzan. In all, there are eight new readings. There is also a revised Concluding Philosophical Postscript and new recommended readings throughout.

Amid a growing number of feminist anthologies and a growing number of anthologies which either attempt to survey Non-Western philosophies or to introduce a multicultural perspective, *Social and Political Philosophy* remains the only anthology that enables philosophy teachers to put the historical development of Western social and political philosophy into both a feminist and a multicultural perspective. The anthology's aim is:

- To provide an introductory sampling of some of the classical works of the Western tradition in social and political philosophy and

- To situate these readings within a feminist and a multicultural perspective so that they can be better understood and evaluated. No other anthology on the market has this twofold aim.

*Social and Political Philosophy* can also be used in conjunction with either:

1. *Justice: Alternative Political Perspectives* 4th edition (Wadsworth, 2003) which provides opposing readings on the major contemporary conceptions of justice and so continues the discussion of *Social and Political Philosophy* on the contemporary scene, or

2. *Contemporary Social and Political Philosophy* (Wadsworth, 1995) which sets out five contemporary political ideals that have their roots in many of the readings for *Social and Political Philosophy*. These political ideals are also explicitly discussed in the more contemporary readings of the anthology, and *Contemporary Social and Political Philosophy* helps students more fully understand and evaluate that discussion. In *Contemporary Social and Political Philosophy*, I also argue for the controversial thesis that all these political ideals can be reconciled in practice, which is a really challenging idea for students to discuss and evaluate. So, in addition to its intrinsic merits, *Social and Political Philosophy* can also be supplemented nicely by these two other texts.

For help in putting together this third edition, I would like to thank Erin Kelly of Tufts University and my colleague and partner Janet A. Kourany. I would also like to thank the following reviewers: John Anderson, University of Nebraska-Kearney; Kenneth A. Beals, Mary Baldwin College; Richard Bilsker, College of Southern Maryland; Christina Hendricks, University of Wisconsin-Rock County; Michael Howard, The University of Maine; Galen A. Johnson, University of Rhode Island; Randy LeBlanc, University of Texas at Tyler; Joan McGregor, Arizona State University; Mechthild Nagel, SUNY Cortland; Stephen Nathanson, Northeastern University; Robert Porter, Ventura College; George Schedler, Southern Illinois University; Albert Waite, Central Texas, College, as well as Steve Wainright, Philosophy Editor, at Wadsworth Publishing Co., and Merrill Peterson of Matrix Productions Inc. who both assisted me in countless ways. Financial and other support from the National Humanities Center in Research Triangle Park, North Carolina, the University of California at Irvine, and the University of Notre Dame is also greatly appreciated.

# *Acknowledgments*

Selection 1. Reprinted from *The Republic,* Bk II, IV-V Translated by B. Jowett (London: Macmillan, 1892).

Selection 2. Reprinted from "The Function of Equal Education in Plato's *Republic* and *Laws*" by permission of the University of Toronto Press.

Selection 3. Reprinted from *The Four Books,* edited and translated by James Legge. Originally published in *The Chinese Classics,* Volume I (Oxford: Clarendon, 1893).

Selection 4. Reprinted from *Nicomachean Ethics,* Bk I, by permission of Blackwell Publishers.

Selection 5. Reprinted from *The Politics,* Bk I, Oxford University Press.

Selection 6. Reprinted from *Discourses* II-IV by permission of the Department of Classics, Yale University.

Selection 7. Reprinted from "Aristotle and the Politicization of the Soul" by permission of Kluwer Academic Publishers.

Selection 8. Reprinted from *African Proverbs: Guide to Conduct,* by permission of N. K. Dzoba.

Selection 9. Reprinted from the *Works of Aurelius Augustine* Vol. II. Translated by Marcus Dods (Edinburgh: T&T Clark, 1872).

Selection 10. Reprinted from *A Select Library of the Nicene and Post-Nicene Fathers of the Christian Church,* translated by Philip Schaff (Christian Literature Company, 1887).

Selection 11. Reprinted from *The Book of the City of Ladies* by permission of Persea Books (1982).

Selection 12. Reprinted from *Religion and Sexism* (1974) by permission of the author.

Selection 13. Reprinted from *From Africa to Zen* by permission of Rowman and Littlefield (1993).

Selection 14. Reprinted from *Summa Theologica* (London: Burns Oates & Washbourne, 1912).

Selection 15. Reprinted from *The Political Philosophy of St. Thomas Aquinas* by Dino Bigongiari, editor, with permission of Pearson Education, Inc., Upper Saddle River, NJ.

Selection 16. Reprinted from *Summa Theologica* (London: Bains Oates Washbourne, 1912).

Selection 17. Printed by permission of Eileen O'Neill. To appear in *Women Philosophers of the Seventeenth and Eighteenth Centuries,* 2 Vols., tr. and ed. by Eileen O'Neill, Oxford University Press.

Selection 18. Reprinted from *Guide for the Perplexed,* translated by M. Friedlander (London: Routledge and Sons, 1904).

Selection 19. Reprinted from *Leviathan,* Ch. 13-18, 20. First published in 1651.

Selection 20. Reprinted from "Hobbes, Patriarchy and Conjugal Right" by permission of the author.

Selection 21. Reprinted from *The Devastation of the Indies.* Translated by John Phillips and published in London in 1656.

Selection 22. Reprinted from *Two Treatises on Government* (London: Routledge and Sons, 1887).

Selection 23. Reprinted from "Women and John Locke; or Who Owns the Apples in the Garden of Eden?" by permission of *The Canadian Journal of Philosophy.*

Selection 24. Reprinted from John D. Hunter, *Memoirs of a Captivity Among the Indians of North America* (London, 1824).

Selection 25. Reprinted from *Discourse on the Origin of Inequality* by permission of Everyman's Library Limited.

Selection 26. Reprinted from *On the Social Contract* translated by G. D. H. Cole (London: J. M. Dent & Sons Ltd., 1916)

Selection 27. Reprinted from *Emile,* Bk 5, translated by Barbara Foxley (London: Guernsey Press Co., 1911).

Selection 28. Reprinted from *A Vindication of the Rights of Women* (Walter Scott, 1891).

Selection 29. Reprinted from *Struggle for the Land* by permission of the author and Common Courage Press.

Selection 30 and 31. Reprinted from *Theory and Practice,* and *Metaphysic of Morals,* by permission of Cambridge University Press.

Selection 32. Reprinted from *Perceptual Peace* edited by Lewis White Beck by permission of Macmillan Publishing Co. Copyright © 1957. Reprinted by permission of Prentice-Hall, Inc., Upper Saddle River, NJ.

Selection 33. Reprinted from "Kant: 'An Honest but Narrow-Minded Bourgeois'?" Copyright © Ellen Kennedy and Susan Mendus, editors, *Women in Western Political Philosophy.* Reprinted by permission of St. Martin's Press, Incorporated.

Selection 34. Reprinted from "Satyagraha" by permission of Oxford University Press.

Selection 35. Reprinted from *Utilitarianism.* First published in 1863.

Selection 36. Reprinted from *On Liberty.* First published in 1849.

Selection 37. Reprinted from *The Subjection of Women.* First published in 1869.

Selection 38. Reprinted from *The Enfranchisement of Women.* First published in 1851.

Selection 39. Reprinted from "Marital Slavery and Friendship," *Political Theory* (1981) by permission of Sage Publications Inc.

Selection 40. Reprinted from *The Four Books,* edited and translated by James Legge. Originally published in *The Chinese Classics,* Volume II (Oxford: Clarendon, 1895).

Selection 41. Reprinted from *Communist Manifesto.* First published in English by Friedrich Engels in 1888.

Selection 42. Reprinted from *The Critique of the Gotha Program* edited by C. P. Dutt (1966) pp. 5-11 by permission of International Publishers.

Selection 43. Reprinted from *The Origin of the Family, Private Property and the State.* First printed 1884.

Selection 44. Reprinted from "The Unhappy Marriage Between Marxism and Feminism: Toward a More Progressive Union" by permission of South End Press.

Selection 45. Reprinted from pp. 50-58 from *Small Is Beautiful: Economics As If People Mattered* by E. F. Schumacher by permission of HarperCollins Publishers Inc. © 1973 by E. F. Schumacher.

Selection 46. Reprinted from *Justice as Fairness: A Restatement* by John Rawls (2001) by permission of Harvard University Press.

Selection 47. Reprinted from "What Libertarianism Is" by permission of Nelson-Hall.

Selection 48. Reprinted from "Justice as Fairness-For Whom?" from *Justice, Gender and the Family* by Susan Okin. Copyright © 1989 by Basic Books, Inc. Reprinted by permission of Perseus Books.

Selection 49. From *The Islamic Law and Constitution*, translated by Khurshid Ahmad. Copyright © 1955, 1960 by Abu'l A'la Mawdudi. Pages 131–132; 145–161. Reprinted by permission of Islamic Publications.

Selection 50. Reprinted from Jouergen Habermas, "Moral Consciousness and Communicative Action," in Seyla Benhabib and Fred Dallmayr, *The Communicative Ethics Controversy* Copyright © 1990 MIT Press.

Selection 51. Reprinted from *Power/Knowledge* by Michael Foucault. Copyright © 1972, 1975, 1976, 1977 by Michael Foucault. Reprinted by permission of Pantheon Books, a division of Random House, Inc.

Selection 52. Sandra Bartky, "Foucault, Femininity and the Modernization of Patriarchal Power" Reprinted from *Feminism and Foucault: Reflections on Resistance,* edited by Irene Diamond and Lee Quinby. Copyright 1988 by Irene Diamond and Lee Quinby. Reprinted with the permission of Northeastern University Press, Boston.

Selection 53. Reprinted from Cornel West, "Philosophy, Politics and Power: An Afro-American Perspective" in *Philosophy Born of Struggle,* edited by Leonard Harris. Copyright 1983 by Kendall/Hunt Publishing Company. Used with permission.

Selection 54. Reprinted from "The Privatization of Good," *Review of Politics* (1990) by permission.

Selection 55. Reprinted from "Atomism" by permission of the author.

Selection 56. Reprinted from "Feminism and Modern Friendship: Dislocating the Community." Reprinted by permission of *Ethics* and the author.

Selection 57. Reprinted from *Ancient Futures* by permission of Sierra Club Books.

Selection 58. Reprinted from *Post-Analytic Philosophy* edited by John Rajehman and Cornel West by permission of Columbia University Press.

Selection 59. From the speech to Central Division APA presidential address by Martha Nussbaum. Reprinted with permission of the American Philosophical Association.

# General Introduction

THE CENTRAL TASK of social and political philosophy is to provide a justification for coercive institutions. Coercive institutions range in size from the family to the nation-state and world organizations like the United Nations, with their narrower and broader agendas for action. Essentially, they are institutions that, at least sometimes, employ force or the threat of force to control the behavior of their members to achieve either minimal or wide-ranging goals. To justify such coercive institutions, we need to show that the authorities within these institutions have a right to be obeyed and that their members have a corresponding duty to obey them. In other words, we need to show that these institutions have legitimate authority over their members.

Of course, classical social and political philosophers, like Socrates and Plato, were primarily interested in justifying small city-states, like Athens or Sparta. But as larger coercive institutions became both possible and desirable, social and political philosophers sought to justify them. After the seventeenth century, most social and political philosophers focused their attention on justifying the nation-state, whose claim to legitimate authority is restricted by both geography and nationality. But from time to time, and even more frequently in the nineteenth and twentieth centuries, social and political philosophers have sought to justify more wide-ranging coercive institutions, including various forms of world government with more extensive powers than those that are presently exercised by the United Nations.[1] And quite recently, feminist social and political philosophers have raised important challenges to the authority of the family as it is presently constituted.[2]

Obviously, it isn't enough to show that various coercive institutions claim to have legitimate authority over their members or that many or even most of their members accept their claim to such authority. That would show only that these coercive institutions

---

1 See, for example, Frederick Schuman, *International Politics,* 7th ed. (New York: McGraw-Hill, 1969); Finn Laursen, *Federation and World Order* (Copenhagen, 1970); Grenville Clark and Louis Sohn, *World Peace Through World Law,* 3rd ed. (Cambridge, MA: Harvard University Press, 1966).
2 See, for example, Janet Kourany, James Sterba, and Rosemarie Tong, *Feminist Philosophies* (Englewood Cliffs, NJ: Prentice Hall, 1991).

are widely believed to be legitimate authorities, not that they are such. Believing something to be the case never makes it so.

But while coercive institutions that are widely believed to be legitimate authorities may not be such (e.g., Nazi Germany), these institutions can still be effective in controlling the behavior of their members, provided that a sufficient number of their members freely acknowledge their claims to be legitimate authorities. Nevertheless, since the control that these coercive institutions maintain over the behavior of their members, at least to some extent, rests on the credibility of their claims to be legitimate authorities, the central task of social and political philosophy is to show how these claims can be justified.

So the history of social and political philosophy in the Western tradition is the history of attempts to carry out this central task. In each attempt, an appeal is made to one or another social and political ideal. Putting it all too briefly, we can say that Plato appeals to an ideal of justice in the state and in the person; Aristotle to an ideal of happiness or human fulfillment; Augustine to the ideal of eternal life; Thomas Aquinas to an ideal of natural law; Thomas Hobbes to an ideal of self-interested agreement; John Locke to an ideal of consent in a state of nature; Jean-Jacques Rousseau to an ideal of a general will; Immanuel Kant to an ideal of a hypothetical agreement of rational agents; John Stuart Mill and Harriet Taylor to an ideal of the maximization of utility, Karl Marx and Friedrich Engels to an ideal of equality; John Rawls to an ideal of fairness; John Hospers to an ideal of liberty; Jürgen Habermas to an ideal of the normative presuppositions of discourse; Michel Foucault to an ideal of the absence of domination; Alasdair MacIntyre and Charles Taylor to an ideal of a good society; and Martha Nussbaum and Cornel West to a feminist and multicultural ideal.

Although obviously disagreeing about the appropriate grounds of legitimate authority, all of these philosophers agree that submission to coercive institutions as legitimate authorities can be justified in terms of their favored social and political ideal.

Yet despite this general consensus among social and political philosophers concerning the justification of legitimate authority, two problems remain. First, claiming that legitimate authorities can be justified in terms of some ultimate social and political ideal is one thing, but providing that justification is another. Thus, it may turn out that when a justification in terms of some ultimate social and political ideal, like liberty or equality, is finally worked out, no existing coercive institution will be justified because none of them sufficiently conform to that ideal. Second, the authorities who are justified by one of these social and political ideals may not be the same as the authorities justified by another, leaving us in a quandary as to whom to obey, unless the practical differences between what these ideals require can be eliminated or compromised. This is a very difficult problem. In the concluding selection to this anthology, I suggest how it might be possible to resolve this problem for the contemporary scene.

Obviously, the distinctive feature of this anthology is its inclusion of feminist and multicultural perspectives. The inclusion of these two perspectives is actually required by the central task of social and political philosophy. This is because in order to establish that the coercive institutions sanctioned by any social and political ideal are justified as legitimate authorities, the particular ideal must be able to survive in a comparative evaluation with other accessible social and political ideals, including those that are feminist and multicultural. Feminist social and political ideals demand that coercive institutions no longer support the subordination of women by men, surely a reasonable requirement. Multicultural social and political ideals will place a variety of different demands on coercive institutions, some of which will be reasonable while others will not.

What, then, will a curriculum look like that attempts to help carry out the central task of social and political philosophy by including a discussion of feminist and multicultural social and political ideals? Obviously, this text attempts to answer this question. In this text, a survey of some of the greatest works of Western social and political philosophy is combined with some of the greatest related works of non-Western social and political philosophy. Some of these non-Western works are chosen because they parallel the views defended in the Western works (e.g., Confucius's work parallels that of Plato or Aristotle). But other non-Western works are chosen because they challenge the views defended in the Western works (e.g., American Indian works provide an interesting challenge to the Western social contract tradition of Hobbes, Locke, and Rousseau). Obviously, these challenges to Western social and political philosophy could lead to reinterpretations of the Western social and political ideals. For example, an examination of American Indian works might lead us to reinterpret Western social and political ideals to require greater reparations to Native Americans.

In any case, what is clear is that the central task of social and political philosophy, the task of determining when coercive institutions are legitimate authorities, will not be satisfied without a consideration of feminist and multicultural perspectives. The only question that remains is, why has it taken social and political philosophers so long to recognize the need to do so?

# I

# *Plato*

## Introduction

PLATO WAS BORN IN 427 B.C.E. and died at the age of eighty in 347 B.C.E. Both his parents came from distinguished families. On his father's side, his ancestry can be traced to the last king of Athens, and on his mother's side, to the family of Solon, the founder of Athenian law. His birth coincided closely with the death of Pericles, the greatest leader of Athenian democracy, and with the beginning of the Peloponnesian War. As a child of twelve, he had seen the Athenian fleet set sail on the disastrous expedition against Syracuse; he was twenty-three when Athens capitulated and lost its empire to Sparta at the end of the Peloponnesian War. As far as we can tell, he never married.

His family's position and wealth enabled Plato to receive the best education possible for an Athenian youth. In his twenties, he came under the influence of Socrates. By skillful exchanges of questions and answers, Socrates was able to expose people's unexamined beliefs and lead them in the direction of more defensible views. Plato became Socrates' devoted student and faithful defender. However, his genius resided in his ability to construct a philosophical system in which he integrated his own insights with those of Socrates.

The teachings of Socrates were as disturbing to the Athenian populace as they were attractive to his followers. In 399 B.C.E., Socrates was condemned to death on the charge of corrupting the youth. The trial and death of Socrates is described in Plato's *Apology*, *Crito*, and *Phaedon*. Disillusioned with political life in Athens, Plato left the city and traveled for twelve years, spending time in Egypt, Greece, Italy, and Sicily. In his fortieth year, he returned to Athens and founded the first of the great schools of antiquity, the Academy, where he taught with outstanding success and increasing fame. The Academy was to last for over 900 years, until the Christian Emperor Justinian had it closed in 529 C.E. because it was a pagan institution. No other school has existed for so long.

The writings of Plato are in dialogue form, well suited to show the strength of Socrates' question-and-answer way of doing philosophy. Plato himself does not appear as a character in the dialogues, but he speaks through Socrates in almost all of them. As a result, it is not always possible to distinguish with historical accuracy between Socrates' and Plato's views in the dialogues. However, it is generally thought that in the earlier dialogues Plato does not go beyond the teachings of Socrates, whereas in the later ones, such as *The Republic*, he does develop his own positive doctrine.

*The Republic* is an extended discussion of a wide range of moral, social, and metaphysical issues framed as a search for the nature of justice. Our selection opens after Socrates has seemingly demolished Thrasymachus's definition of justice as that which serves the interests of the strongest and has further argued that justice is more profitable than injustice. Glaucon and Adeimantus, both dissatisfied with Socrates' arguments, challenge him to prove that justice is more profitable than injustice.

Socrates responds by suggesting that the nature of justice is more easily discovered in the macrocosm, the state, than in the microcosm, the individual. Socrates offers an account of a just state and then by analogy an account of a just individual, and he tries to show, that in each case, justice is superior to injustice. A just state, he says, will contain three classes—guardians, soldiers, and artisans. After characterizing the selection and education of the guardians, and arguing that both women and men could be guardians, Socrates concludes that a state is just when each class performs well the work for which it is suited. Further, a perfectly just state is not possible unless wisdom and power are united in the person of a philosopher-king.

In "The Function of Equal Education in Plato's *Republic*," Lynda Lange argues that Plato was not a feminist despite the opening of his guardian class to women because his reason for doing so was neither to end women's subordination to men nor to establish equality between the sexes, but rather to make his guardian class more efficient and to promote unity in the state. It might also be questioned whether any political ideal, like Plato's, that is committed to radical inequalities between different classes of people can be appropriately termed feminist. Doesn't equality for women in consistency require equality for other groups discriminated against as well? Nevertheless, whatever its limitation from a feminist perspective, what Plato's work shows is that even in classical times the idea of equality for women was there to be considered.

Kung Fu-Tzu or Confucius, his Latinized name, lived from 551 B.C.E. to 479 B.C.E., about 150 years before Plato. He was not known to the Western world until the late sixteenth century, when Jesuit missionaries, in an effort to convert Chinese rulers, steeped themselves in ancient Confucian literature and were overwhelmed by what they found.[1]

Soon reports made their way back to Europe. Leibniz wrote that the Chinese surpassed Europeans in practical philosophy and recommended that Chinese missionaries be sent to Europe. Voltaire declared that in morality Europeans "ought to become disciples" of the Chinese.[2] Christian Wolff said of the Chinese that "in the Art of Governing, this Nation has ever surpassed all others without exception."[3] Because of all this acclaim, Confucius became known as the patron saint of the Enlightenment.[4]

Confucius was born in the small state of Lu (in modern Shanrung). He traveled to Ch'i and later to Chou, serving in minor government posts. When he was fifty-six, he fell out of favor and spent the next thirteen years traveling and teaching. At sixty-eight, Confucius returned to Lu and taught there until his death eight years later.

---

1 H.G. Creel, *Confucius: The Man and the Myth* (Westport, CT: Greenwood Press, 1972).
2 Ibid.
3 Ibid.
4 Ibid.

The *Analects* is a collection of the sayings of Confucius, probably compiled by his students. Confucius was remarkably successful as a teacher. Of the twenty-two students mentioned in *The Analects,* nine attained important government posts and a tenth turned one down. Moreover, his impact was far-reaching. For 2500 years, he was "the Master" to all of China, and his influence continues today.

Like Plato and later Aristotle, Confucius advocates a virtue ethics, but the list of virtues that he advocates is longer than that advocated by Plato and different in certain respects from the list advocated by Aristotle. One distinctive feature of Confucius' ethics is his stress on filial obligation. For Plato, the just individual is modeled on the just state, but for Confucius, the state is the family writ large. Confucius also advocates meritocracy, various forms of which were incorporated into Chinese society. The British civil service system was actually modeled on the system found in China, and the civil service system in the United States was in turn modeled after the British system, and so ultimately on the Chinese system as well. One also finds in Confucius negative versions of the Golden Rule: "What you do not want done to yourself, do not do to others." No wonder then that one of the Jesuit missionaries, impressed by Confucius' views and seeking to appropriate what he saw, affirmed that if Confucius had lived in the seventeenth century, "he would have been the first to become a Christian."

# 1    The Republic

PLATO

## Book II

WITH THESE WORDS I was thinking that I had made an end of the discussion; but the end, in truth, proved to be only a beginning. For Glaucon, who is always the most pugnacious of men, was dissatisfied at Thrasymachus' retirement; he wanted to have the battle out. So he said to me: Socrates, do you wish really to persuade us, or only to seem to have persuaded us, that to be just is always better than to be unjust?

I should wish really to persuade you, I replied, if I could.

Then you certainly have not succeeded. Let me ask you now:—How would you arrange goods—are there not some which we welcome for their own sakes, and independently of their consequences, as, for example, harmless pleasures and enjoyments, which delight us at the time, although nothing follows from them?

I agree in thinking that there is such a class, I replied.

Is there not also a second class of goods, such as knowledge, sight, health, which are desirable not only in themselves, but also for their results?

Certainly, I said.

And would you not recognize a third class, such as gymnastic, and the care of the sick, and the physician's art; also the various ways of money-making—these do us good but we regard them as disagreeable; and no one would choose them for their own sakes, but only for the sake of some reward or result which flows from them?

There is, I said, this third class also. But why do you ask?

Because I want to know in which of the three classes you would place justice?

In the highest class, I replied,—among those goods which he who would be happy desires both for their own sake and for the sake of their results.

Then the many are of another mind; they think that justice is to be reckoned in the troublesome class, among goods which are to be pursued for the sake of rewards and of reputation, but in themselves are disagreeable and rather to be avoided.

I know, I said, that this is their manner of thinking, and that this was the thesis which Thrasymachus was maintaining just now, when he censured justice and praised injustice. But I am too stupid to be convinced by him.

I wish, he said, that you would hear me as well as him, and then I shall see whether you and I agree. For Thrasymachus seems to me, like a snake, to have been charmed by your voice sooner than he ought to have been; but to my mind the nature of justice and injustice have not yet been made clear. Setting aside their rewards and results, I want to know what they are in themselves, and how they inwardly work in the soul. If you please, then, I will revive the argument of Thrasymachus. And first I will speak of the nature and origin of justice according to the common view of them. Secondly, I will show that all men who practise justice do so against their will, of necessity, but not as a good. And thirdly, I will argue that there is reason in this view, for the life of the unjust is after all far better than the life of the just—if what they say is true, Socrates, since I myself am not of their opinion. But still I acknowledge that I am perplexed when I hear the voices of Thrasymachus and myriads of others dinning in my ears; and, on the other hand, I have never yet heard the superiority of justice to injustice maintained by anyone in a satisfactory way. I want to hear justice praised in respect of itself; then I shall be satisfied, and you are the person from whom I think that I am most

likely to hear this; and therefore I will praise the unjust life to the utmost of my power, and my manner of speaking will indicate the manner in which I desire to hear you too praising justice and censuring injustice. Will you say whether you approve of my proposal?

Indeed I do; nor can I imagine any theme about which a man of sense would oftener wish to converse.

I am delighted, he replied, to hear you say so, and shall begin by speaking, as I proposed, of the nature and origin of justice.

They say that to do injustice is, by nature, good; to suffer injustice, evil; but that the evil is greater than the good. And so when men have both done and suffered injustice and have had experience of both, not being able to avoid the one and obtain the other, they think that they had better agree among themselves to have neither; hence there arise laws and mutual covenants; and that which is ordained by law is termed by them lawful and just. This they affirm to be the origin and nature of justice;—it is a mean or compromise, between the best of all, which is to do injustice and not be punished, and the worst of all, which is to suffer injustice without the power of retaliation; and justice, being at a middle point between the two, is tolerated not as a good, but as the lesser evil, and honoured by reason of the inability of men to do injustice. For no man who is worthy to be called a man would ever submit to such an agreement if he were able to resist; he would be mad if he did. Such is the received account, Socrates, of the nature and origin of justice.

Now that those who practice justice do so involuntarily and because they have not the power to be unjust will best appear if we imagine something of this kind: having given both to the just and the unjust power to do what they will, let us watch and see whither desire will lead them; then we shall discover in the very act the just and unjust man to be proceeding along the same road, following their interest, which all natures deem to be their good, and are only diverted into the path of justice by the force of law. The liberty which we are supposing may be most completely given to them in the form of such a power as is said to have been possessed by Gyges, the ancestor of Croesus the Lydian. According to the tradition, Gyges was a shepherd in the service of the king of Lydia; there was a great storm, and an earthquake made an opening in the earth at the place where he was feeding his flock. Amazed at the sight, he descended into the opening, where, among other marvels, he beheld a hollow brazen horse, having doors, at which he stooping and looking in saw a dead body of stature, as appeared to him, more than human, and having nothing on but a gold ring; this he took from the finger of the dead and reascended. Now the shepherds met together, according to custom, that they might send their monthly report about the flocks to the king; into their assembly he came having the ring on his finger, and as he was sitting among them he chanced to turn the collet of the ring inside his hand, when instantly he became invisible to the rest of the company and they began to speak of him as if he were no longer present. He was astonished at this, and again touching the ring he turned the collet outwards and reappeared; he made several trials of the ring, and always with the same result—when he turned the collet inwards he became invisible, when outwards he reappeared. Whereupon he contrived to be chosen one of the messengers who were sent to the court; where as soon as he arrived he seduced the queen, and with her help conspired against the king and slew him, and took the kingdom. Suppose now that there were two such magic rings, and the just put on one of them and the unjust the other; no man can be imagined to be of such an iron nature that he would stand fast in justice. No man would keep his hands off what was not his own when he could safely take what he liked out of the market, or go into houses and lie with anyone of his pleasure, or kill or release from prison whom he would, and in all respects be like a God among men. Then the actions of the just would be as the actions of the unjust; they would both come at last to the same point. And this we may truly affirm to be a great proof that a man is just, not willingly or because he thinks that justice is any good to him individually, but of necessity,

for wherever anyone thinks that he can safely be unjust, there he is unjust. For all men believe in their hearts that injustice is far more profitable to the individual than justice, and he who argues as I have been supposing, will say that they are right. If you could imagine anyone obtaining this power of becoming invisible, and never doing any wrong or touching what was another's, he would be thought by the lookers-on to be a most wretched idiot, although they would praise him to one another's faces, and keep up appearances with one another from a fear that they too might suffer injustice. Enough of this.

Now, if we are to form a real judgment of the life of the just and unjust, we must isolate them; there is no other way; and how is the isolation to be effected? I answer: Let the unjust man be entirely unjust, and the just man entirely just; nothing is to be taken away from either of them, and both are to be perfectly furnished for the work of the respective lives. First, let the unjust be like other distinguished masters of craft; like the skilful pilot or physician, who knows intuitively his own powers and keeps within their limits, and who, if he fails at any point, is able to recover himself. So let the unjust make his unjust attempts in the right way, and lie hidden if he means to be great in his injustice: (he who is found out is nobody:) for the highest reach of injustice is, to be deemed just when you are not. Therefore I say that in the perfectly unjust man we must assume the most perfect injustice; there is to be no deduction, but we must allow him, while doing the most unjust acts, to have acquired the greatest reputation for justice. If he has taken a false step he must be able to recover himself; he must be one who can speak with effect, if any of his deeds come to light, and who can force his way where force is required by his courage and strength, and command of money and friends. And at his side let us place the just man in his nobleness and simplicity, wishing, as Aeschylus says, to be and not to seem good. There must be no seeming, for if he seems to be just he will be honoured and rewarded, and then we shall not know whether he is just for the sake of justice or for the sake of honours and rewards; therefore, let him be clothed in justice only, and have no other covering; and he must be imagined in a state of life the opposite of the former. Let him be the best of men, and let him be thought the worst; then he will have been put to the proof; and we shall see whether he will be affected by the fear of infamy and its consequences. And let him continue thus to the hour of death; being just and seeming to be unjust. When both have reached the uttermost extreme, the one of justice and the other of injustice, let judgment be given which of them is the happier of the two.

Heavens! my dear Glaucon, I said, how energetically you polish them up for the decision, first one and then the other, as if they were two statues.

I do my best, he said. And now that we know what they are like there is no difficulty in tracing out the sort of life which awaits either of them. This I will proceed to describe; but as you may think the description a little too coarse, I ask you to suppose, Socrates, that the words which follow are not mine.—Let me put them into the mouths of the eulogists of injustice: They will tell you that the just man who is thought unjust will be scourged, racked, bound—will have his eyes burnt out; and, at last, after suffering every kind of evil, he will be impaled: Then he will understand that he ought to seem only, and not to be, just; the words of Aeschylus may be more truly spoken of the unjust than of the just. For the unjust is pursuing a reality; he does not live with a view to appearances—he wants to be really unjust and not to seem only:—

His mind has a soil deep and fertile,
Out of which spring his prudent counsels.[1]

In the first place, he is thought just, and therefore bears rule in the city; he can marry whom he will, and give in marriage to whom he will; also he can trade and deal where he likes, and always to his own advantage, because he has no misgivings about injustice; and at every contest, whether in public or private, he gets the better of his antagonists, and gains at their expense, and is rich, and out of his gains he can benefit his friends, and

harm his enemies; moreover, he can offer sacrifices, and dedicate gifts to the gods abundantly and magnificently, and can honour the gods or any man whom he wants to honour in a far better style than the just, and therefore he is likely to be dearer than they are to the gods. And thus, Socrates, gods and men are said to unite in making the life of the unjust better than the life of the just.

I was going to say something in answer to Glaucon, when Adeimantus, his brother, interposed: Socrates, he said, you do not suppose that there is nothing more to be urged?

Why, what else is there? I answered.

The strongest point of all has not been even mentioned, he replied.

Well, then, according to the proverb, "Let brother help brother"—if he fails in any part do you assist him; although I must confess that Glaucon has already said quite enough to lay me in the dust, and take from me the power of helping justice.

Nonsense, he replied. But let me add something more: There is another side to Glaucon's argument about the praise and censure of justice and injustice, which is equally required in order to bring out what I believe to be his meaning. Parents and tutors are always telling their sons and their wards that they are to be just; but why? Not for the sake of justice, but for the sake of character and reputation; in the hope of obtaining for him who is reputed just some of those offices, marriages, and the like which Glaucon has enumerated among the advantages accruing to the unjust from the reputation of justice. More, however, is made of appearances by this class of persons than by the others; for they throw in the good opinion of the gods, and will tell you of a shower of benefits which the heavens, as they say, rain upon the pious; and this accords with the testimony of the noble Hesiod and Homer, the first of whom says, that the gods make the oaks of the just—

To bear acorns at their summit, and bees in the middle;
And the sheep are bowed down with the weight of their fleeces,[2]

and many other blessings of a like kind are provided for them. And Homer has a very similar strain; for he speaks of one whose fame is—

> As the fame of some blameless king who, like a god,
>> Maintains justice; to whom the black earth brings forth
>> Wheat and barley, whose trees are bowed with fruit,
>> And his sheep never fail to bear, and the sea gives him fish.[3]

Still grander are the gifts of heaven which Musaeus and his son[4] vouchsafe to the just; they take them down into the world below, where they have the saints lying on couches at a feast, everlastingly drunk, crowned with garlands; their idea seems to be that an immortality of drunkenness is the [finest wage] of virtue. Some extend their rewards yet further; the posterity, as they say, of the faithful and just shall survive to the third and fourth generation. This is the style in which they praise justice. But about the wicked there is another strain; they bury them in a slough in Hades, and make them carry water in a sieve; also while they are yet living they bring them to infamy, and inflict upon them the punishments which Glaucon described as the portion of the just who are reputed to be unjust; nothing else does their invention supply. Such is their manner of praising the one and censuring the other.

Once more, Socrates, I will ask you to consider another way of speaking about justice and injustice, which is not confined to the poets, but is found in prose writers. The universal voice of mankind is always declaring that justice and virtue are honourable, but grievous and toilsome; and that the pleasures of vice and injustice are easy of attainment, and are only censured by law and opinion. They say also that honesty is for the most part less profitable than dishonesty; and they are quite ready to call wicked men happy, and to honour them both in public and private when they are rich or in any other way influential, while they despise and overlook those who may be weak and poor, even though acknowledging them to be better than the others. But most extraordinary of all is their mode of speaking about virtue and the gods: they say that the gods apportion calamity and misery to many good men, and good and happiness to the wicked. And mendicant prophets go to rich men's doors and persuade them that they have a power committed to them by the gods of making an atonement for a man's own or his ancestor's sins by sacrifices or charms, with rejoicings and feasts; and they promise to harm an enemy, whether just or unjust, at a small cost; with magic arts and incantations binding heaven, as they say, to execute their will. And the poets are the authorities to whom they appeal, now smoothing the path of vice with the words of Hesiod:—

> Vice may be had in abundance without trouble; the way is smooth and her dwelling-place is near. But before virtue the gods have set toil,[5]

and a tedious and uphill road: then citing Homer as a witness that the gods may be influenced by men; for he also says:—

> The gods, too, may be turned from their purpose; and men pray to them and avert their wrath by sacrifices and soothing entreaties, and by libations and the odour of fat, when they have sinned and transgressed.[6]

And they produce a host of books written by Musaeus and Orpheus, who were children of the Moon and the Muses—that is what they say—according to which they perform their ritual, and persuade not only individuals, but whole cities, that expiations and atonements for sin may be made by sacrifices and amusements which fill a vacant hour, and are equally at the service of the living and the dead; the latter sort they call mysteries, and they redeem us from the pains of hell, but if we neglect them no one knows what awaits us.

He proceeded: And now when the young hear all this said about virtue and vice, and the way in which gods and men regard them, how are their minds likely to be affected, my dear Socrates,—those of them, I mean, who are quickwitted and, like bees on the wing, light on every flower, and from all that they hear are prone to draw conclusions as to what manner of persons they should be and in what way they should walk if they would make the best of life? Probably the youth will say to himself in the words of Pindar—

> Can I by justice or by crooked ways of deceit ascend a loftier tower which may be a fortress to me all my days?

For what men say is that, if I am really just and am not also thought just, profit there is none, but the pain and loss on the other hand are unmistakable. But if, though unjust, I acquire the reputation of justice, a heavenly life is promised to me. Since then, as philosophers prove, appearance tyrannizes over truth and is lord of happiness, to appearance I must devote myself. I will describe around me a picture and shadow of virtue to be the vestibule and exterior of my house; behind I will trail the subtle and crafty fox, as Archilochus, greatest of sages, recommends. But I hear someone exclaiming that the concealment of wickedness is often difficult; to which I answer, Nothing great is easy. Nevertheless, the argument indicates this, if we would be happy, to be the path along which we should proceed. With a view to concealment we will establish secret brotherhoods and political clubs. And there are professors of rhetoric who teach the art of persuading courts and assemblies; and so, partly by persuasion and partly by force, I shall make unlawful gains and not be punished. Still I hear a voice saying that the gods cannot be deceived, neither can they be compelled. But what if there are no gods? or, suppose them to have no care of human things—why in either case should we mind about concealment? And even if there are gods, and they do care about us, yet we know of them only from tradition and the genealogies of the poets; and these are the very persons who say that they may be influenced and turned by "sacrifices and soothing entreaties and by offerings." Let us be consistent then, and believe both or neither. If the poets speak truly, why then we had better be unjust, and offer of the fruits of injustice; for if we are just, although we may escape the vengeance of heaven, we shall lose the gains of injustice; but, if we are unjust, we shall keep the gains, and by our sinning and praying, and praying and sinning, the gods will be propitiated, and we shall not be punished. "But there is a world below in which either we or our posterity will suffer for our unjust deeds." Yes, my friend, will be the [reply], but there are mysteries and atoning deities, and these have great power. That is what mighty cities declare; and the children of the gods, who were their poets and prophets, bear a like testimony. On what principle, then, shall we any longer choose justice rather than the worst injustice? When, if we only unite the latter with a deceitful regard to appearances, we shall fare to our mind both with gods and men, in life and after death, as the most numerous and the highest authorities tell us. Knowing all this, Socrates, how can a man who has any superiority of mind or person or rank or wealth, be willing to honour justice; or indeed to refrain from laughing when he hears justice praised? And even if there should be someone who is able to disprove the truth of my words, and who is satisfied that justice is best, still he is not angry with the unjust, but is very ready to forgive them, because he also knows that men are not just of their own free will; unless, peradventure, there be someone whom the divinity within him may have inspired with a hatred of injustice, or who has attained knowledge of the truth—but no other man. He only blames injustice who, owing to cowardice or age or some weakness, has not the power of being unjust. And this is proved by the fact that when he obtains the power, he immediately becomes unjust as far as he can be.

The cause of all this, Socrates, was indicated by us at the beginning of the argument, when my brother and I told you how astonished we were to find that of all the professing panegyrists of justice—beginning with the ancient heroes of whom any memorial has been preserved to us, and ending with the men of our own time—no one has ever blamed injustice or praised justice except with a view to the glories, honours, and benefits which flow from them. No one has ever adequately described either in verse or prose the true essential nature of either of them abiding in the soul, and invisible to any human or divine eye; or shown that of all the things of a man's soul which he has within him, justice is the greatest good, and injustice the greatest evil. Had this been the universal strain, had you sought to persuade us of this from our youth upwards, we should not have been on the watch to keep one another from doing wrong, but everyone would have been his own watchman, because afraid, if he did wrong, of harbouring in himself the greatest of evils. I dare say that Thrasymachus and others would seriously hold the language which I have been merely repeating, and words even stronger than these about justice and injustice, grossly, as I conceive, perverting their true nature. But I speak in this vehement manner, as I must frankly confess to you, because I want to hear from you the opposite side; and I would ask you to show not only the superiority which justice has over injustice, but what effect they have on the possessor of them which makes the one to be a good and the other an evil to him. And please, as Glaucon requested of you, to exclude reputations; for unless you take away from each of them his true reputation and add on the false, we shall say that you do not praise justice, but the appearance of it; we shall think that you are only exhorting us to keep injustice dark, and that you really agree with Thrasymachus in thinking that justice is another's good and the interest of the stronger, and that injustice is a man's own profit and interest, though injurious to the weaker. Now as you have admitted that justice is one of that highest class of goods which are desired indeed for their results, but in a far greater degree for their own sakes— like sight or hearing or knowledge or health, or any other real and natural and not merely conventional good—I would ask you in your praise of justice to regard one point only: I mean the essential good and evil which justice and injustice work in the possessors of them. Let others praise justice and censure injustice, magnifying the rewards and honours of the one and abusing the other; that is a manner of arguing which, coming from them, I am ready to tolerate, but from you who have spent your whole life in the consideration of this question, unless I hear the contrary from your own lips, I expect something better.

And therefore, I say, not only prove to us that justice is better than injustice, but show what they either of them do to the possessor of them, which makes the one to be a good and the other an evil, whether seen or unseen by gods and men.

I had always admired the genius of Glaucon and Adeimantus, but on hearing these words I was quite delighted, and said: Sons of an illustrious father, that was not a bad beginning of the Elegiac verses which the admirer of Glaucon made in honour of you after you had distinguished yourselves at the battle of Megara:—

"Sons of Ariston," he sang, "divine offspring of an illustrious hero."

The epithet is very appropriate, for there is something truly divine in being able to argue as you have done for the superiority of injustice, and remaining unconvinced by your own arguments. And I do believe that you are not convinced—this I infer from your general character, for had I judged only from your speeches I should have mistrusted you. But now, the greater my confidence in you, the greater is my difficulty in knowing what to say. For I am in a strait between two; on the one hand I feel that I am unequal to the task; and my inability is brought home to me by the fact that you were not satisfied with the answer which I made to Thrasymachus, proving, as I thought, the superiority which justice has over injustice. And yet I cannot refuse to help, while breath and speech remain to me; I am afraid that there would be an impiety in being present when justice is evil spoken of and not lifting up a hand in her defence. And therefore I had best give such help as I can.

Glaucon and the rest entreated me by all means not to let the question drop, but to proceed in the investigation. They wanted to arrive at the truth, first, about the nature of justice and injustice, and secondly, about their relative advantages. I told them, what I really thought, that the enquiry would be of a serious nature, and would require very good eyes. Seeing then, I said, that we are no great wits, I think that we had better adopt a method which I may illustrate thus; suppose that a short-sighted person had been asked by someone to read small letters from a distance; and it occurred to someone else that they might be found in another place which was larger and in which the letters were larger—if they were the same and he could read the larger letters first, and then proceed to the lesser—this would have been thought a rare piece of good fortune.

Very true, said Adeimantus; but how does the illustration apply to our enquiry?

I will tell you, I replied; justice, which is the subject of our enquiry, is, as you know, sometimes spoken of as the virtue of an individual, and sometimes as the virtue of a State.

True, he replied.

And is not a State larger than an individual?

It is.

Then in the larger the quantity of justice is likely to be larger and more easily discernible. I propose therefore that we enquire into the nature of justice and injustice, first as they appear in the State, and secondly in the individual, proceeding from the greater to the lesser and comparing them.

That, he said, is an excellent proposal.

And if we imagine the State in process of creation, we shall see the justice and injustice of the State in process of creation also.

I dare say.

When the State is completed there may be a hope that the object of our search may be more easily discovered.

Yes, far more easily.

But ought we to attempt to construct one? I said; for to do so, as I am inclined to think, will be a very serious task. Reflect therefore.

I have reflected, said Adeimantus, and am anxious that you should proceed.

A State, I said, arises, as I conceive, out of the needs of mankind; no one is self-sufficing, but all of us have many wants. Can any other origin of a State be imagined?

There can be no other.

Then, as we have many wants, and many persons are needed to supply them, one takes a helper for one purpose and another for another; and when these partners and helpers are gathered together in one habitation the body of inhabitants is termed a State.

True, he said.

And they exchange with one another, and one gives, and another receives, under the idea that the exchange will be for their good.

Very true.

Then, I said, let us begin and create in idea a State; and yet the true creator is necessity, who is the mother of our invention.

Of course, he replied.

Now the first and greatest of necessities is food, which is the condition of life and existence.

Certainly.

The second is a dwelling, and the third clothing and the like.

True.

And now let us see how our city will be able to supply this great demand: We may suppose that one man is a [farmer], another a builder, someone else a weaver—shall we add to them a shoemaker, or perhaps some other purveyor to our bodily wants?

Quite right.

The barest notion of a State must include four or five men.

Clearly.

And how will they proceed? Will each bring the result of his labours into a common stock?—the individual [farmer], for example, producing for four, and labouring four times as long and as much as he needs in the provision of food with which he supplies others as well as himself; or will he have nothing to do with others and not be at the trouble of producing for them, but provide for himself alone a fourth of the food in a fourth of the time, and in the remaining three fourths of his time be employed in making a house or a coat or a pair of shoes, having no partnership with others, but supplying himself all his own wants?

Adeimantus thought that he should aim at producing food only and not at producing everything.

Probably, I replied, that would be the better way; and when I hear you say this, I am myself reminded that we are not all alike; there are diversities of natures among us which are adapted to different occupations.

Very true.

And will you have a work better done when the workman has many occupations, or when he has only one?

When he has only one.

Further, there can be no doubt that a work is spoilt when not done at the right time?

No doubt.

For business is not disposed to wait until the doer of the business is at leisure; but the doer must follow up what he is doing, and make the business his first object.

He must.

And if so, we must infer that all things are produced more plentifully and easily and of a better quality when [each person] does one thing which is natural to him and does it at the right time, and leaves other things.

Undoubtedly.

Then more than four citizens will be required; for the [farmer] will not make his own plough or mattock, or other implements of agriculture, if they are to be good for anything. Neither will the builder make his tools—and he too needs many; and in like manner the weaver and shoemaker.

True.

Then carpenters, and smiths, and many other artisans, will be sharers in our little State, which is already beginning to grow?

True.

Yet even if we add [cowherds], shepherds, and other herdsmen, in order that our [farmers] may have oxen to plough with, and builders as well as [farmers] may have draught cattle, and curriers and weavers fleeces and hides,—still our State will not be very large.

That is true; yet neither will it be a very small State which contains all these.

Then, again, there is the situation of the city—to find a place where nothing need be imported is wellnigh impossible.

Impossible.

Then there must be another class of citizens who will bring the required supply from another city?

There must.

But if the trader goes empty-handed, having nothing which they require who would supply his need, he will come back empty-handed.

That is certain.

And therefore what they produce at home must be not only enough for themselves, but such both in quantity and quality as to accommodate those from whom their wants are supplied.

Very true.

Then more [farmers] and more artisans will be required?

They will.

Not to mention the importers and exporters, who are called merchants?

Yes.

Then we shall want merchants?

We shall.

And if merchandise is to be carried over the sea, skilful sailors will also be needed, and in considerable numbers?

Yes, in considerable numbers.

Then, again, within the city, how will they exchange their productions? To secure such an exchange was, as you will remember, one of our principal objects when we formed them into a society and constituted a State.

Clearly they will buy and sell.

Then they will need a market-place, and a money-token for purpose of exchange.

Certainly.

Suppose now that a [farmer], or an artisan, brings some production to market, and he comes at a time when there is no one to exchange with him,—is he to leave his calling and sit idle in the market-place?

Not at all; he will find people there who, seeing the want, undertake the office of salesmen. In well-ordered states they are commonly those who are the weakest in bodily strength, and therefore of little use for any other purpose; their duty is to be in the market, and to give money in exchange for goods to those who desire to sell and to take money from those who desire to buy.

This want, then, creates a class of retail-traders in our State. Is not "retailer" the term which is applied to those who sit in the market-place engaged in buying and selling, while those who wander from one city to another are called merchants?

Yes, he said.

And there is another class of servants, who are intellectually hardly on the level of companionship; still they have plenty of bodily strength for labour, which accordingly they sell, and are called, if I do not mistake, hirelings, hire being the name which is given to the price of their labour.

True.

Then hirelings will help to make up our population?

Yes.

And now, Adeimantus, is our State matured and perfected?

I think so.

Where, then, is justice, and where is injustice, and in what part of the State did they spring up?

Probably in the dealings of these citizens with one another. I cannot imagine that they are more likely to be found any where else.

I dare say that you are right in your suggestion, I said; we had better think the matter out, and not shrink from the enquiry.

Let us then consider, first of all, what will be their way of life, now that we have thus established them. Will they not produce corn, and wine, and clothes, and shoes, and build houses for themselves? And when they are housed, they will work, in summer, commonly, stripped and barefoot, but in winter substantially clothed and shod. They will feed on barley-meal and flour of wheat, baking and kneading them, making noble cakes and loaves; these they will serve up on a mat of reeds or on clean leaves, themselves reclining the while upon beds strewn with yew or myrtle. And they and their children will feast, drinking of the wine which they have made, wearing garlands on their heads, and hymning the praises of the gods, in happy converse with one another. And they will

take care that their families do not exceed their means; having an eye to poverty or war.

But, said Glaucon, interposing, you have not given them a relish to their meal.

True, I replied, I had forgotten; of course they must have a relish—salt and olives, and cheese, and they will boil roots and herbs such as country people prepare; for a dessert we shall give them figs, and peas, and beans; and they will roast myrtle-berries and acorns at the fire, drinking in moderation. And with such a diet they may be expected to live in peace and health to a good old age, and bequeath a similar life to their children after them.

Yes, Socrates, he said, and if you were providing for a city of pigs, how else would you feed the beasts?

But what would you have, Glaucon? I replied.

Why, he said, you should give them the ordinary conveniences of life. People who are to be comfortable are accustomed to lie on sofas, and dine off tables, and they should have sauces and sweets in the modern style.

Yes, I said, now I understand: the question which you would have me consider is, not only how a State, but how a luxurious State is created; and possibly there is no harm in this, for in such a State we shall be more likely to see how justice and injustice originate. In my opinion the true and healthy constitution of the State is the one which I have described. But if you wish also to see a State at fever-heat, I have no objection. For I suspect that many will not be satisfied with the simpler way of life. They will be for adding sofas, and tables, and other furniture; also dainties, and perfumes, and incense, and courtesans, and cakes, all these not of one sort only, but in every variety; we must go beyond the necessaries of which I was at first speaking, such as houses, and clothes, and shoes: the arts of the painter and the embroiderer will have to be set in motion, and gold and ivory and all sorts of materials must be procured.

True, he said.

Then we must enlarge our borders; for the original healthy State is no longer sufficient. Now will the city have to fill and swell with a multitude of callings which are not required by any natural want; such as the whole tribe of hunters and actors, of whom one large class has to do with forms and colours; another will be the votaries of music—poets and their attendant train of rhapsodists, players, dancers, contractors; also makers of divers kinds of articles, including women's dresses. And we shall want more servants. Will not tutors be also in request, and nurses wet and dry, tirewomen and barbers, as well as confectioners and cooks; and swineherds, too, who were not needed and therefore had no place in the former edition of our State, but are needed now? They must not be forgotten: and there will be animals of many other kinds, if people eat them.

Certainly.

And living in this way we shall have much greater need of physicians than before?

Much greater.

And the country which was enough to support the original inhabitants will be too small now, and not enough?

Quite true.

Then a slice of our neighbours' land will be wanted by us for pasture and tillage, and they will want a slice of ours, if, like ourselves, they exceed the limit of necessity, and give themselves up to the unlimited accumulation of wealth?

That, Socrates, will be inevitable.

And so we shall go to war, Glaucon. Shall we not?

Most certainly, he replied.

Then, without determining as yet whether war does good or harm, this much we may affirm, that now we have discovered war to be derived from causes which are also the causes of almost all the evils in States, private as well as public.

Undoubtedly.

And our State must once more enlarge; and this time the enlargement will be nothing short of a whole army, which will have to go out and fight with the invaders for all that we have, as well as for the things and persons whom we were describing above.

Why? he said; are they not capable of defending themselves?

No, I said; not if we were right in the principle which was acknowledged by all of us when we were framing the State: the principle, as you will remember, was that one [person] cannot practice many arts with success.

Very true, he said.

But is not war an art?

Certainly.

And an art requiring as much attention as shoe-making?

Quite true.

And the shoemaker was not allowed by us to be a [farmer], or a weaver, or a builder—in order that we might have our shoes well made; but to him and to every other worker was assigned one work for which he was by nature fitted, and at that he was to continue working all his life long and at no other; he was not to let opportunities slip, and then he would become a good workman. Now nothing can be more important than that the work of a soldier should be well done. But is war an art so easily acquired that a man may be a warrior who is also a [farmer], or shoemaker, or other artisan; although no one in the world would be a good dice or draught player who merely took up the game as a recreation, and had not from his earliest years devoted himself to this and nothing else? No tools will make a man a skilled workman, or master of defence, nor be of any use to him who has not learned how to handle them, and has never bestowed any attention upon them. How then will he who takes up a shield or other implement of war become a good fighter all in a day, whether with heavy-armed or any other kind of troops?

Yes, he said, the tools which would teach men their own use would be beyond price.

And the higher the duties of the guardian, I said, the more time, and skill, and art, and application will be needed by him?

No doubt, he replied.

Will he not also require natural aptitude for his calling?

Certainly.

Then it will be our duty to select, if we can, natures which are fitted for the task of guarding the city?

It will. . . .

## Book IV

But where, amid all this, is justice? son of Ariston, tell me where. Now that our city has been made habitable, light a candle and search, and get your brother and Polemarchus and the rest of our friends to help, and let us see where in it we can discover justice and where injustice, and in what they differ from one another, and which of them the man who would be happy should have for his portion, whether seen or unseen by gods and men.

Nonsense, said Glaucon: did you not promise to search yourself, saying that for you not to help justice in her need would be an impiety?

I do not deny that I said so; and as you remind me, I will be as good as my word; but you must join.

We will, he replied.

Well, then, I hope to make the discovery in this way: I mean to begin with the assumption that our State, if rightly ordered, is perfect.

That is most certain.

And being perfect, is therefore wise and valiant and temperate and just.

That is likewise clear.

And whichever of these qualities we find in the State, the one which is not found will be the residue?

Very good.

If there were four things, and we were searching for one of them, wherever it might be, the one sought for might be known to us from the first, and there would be no further trouble; or we might know the other three first, and then the fourth would clearly be the one left.

Very true, he said.

And is not a similar method to be pursued about the virtues, which are also four in number?

Clearly.

First among the virtues found in the State, wisdom comes into view, and in this I detect a certain peculiarity.

What is that?

The State which we have been describing is said to be wise as being good in counsel?

Very true.

And good counsel is clearly a kind of knowledge, for not by ignorance, but by knowledge, do men counsel well?

Clearly.

And the kinds of knowledge in a State are many and diverse?

Of course.

There is the knowledge of the carpenter; but is that the sort of knowledge which gives a city the title of wise and good in counsel?

Certainly not; that would only give a city the reputation of skill in carpentering.

Then a city is not to be called wise because possessing a knowledge which counsels for the best about wooden implements?

Certainly not.

Nor by reason of a knowledge which advises about brazen pots, he said, nor as possessing any other similar knowledge?

Not by reason of any of them, he said.

Nor yet by reason of a knowledge which cultivates the earth; that would give the city the name of agricultural?

Yes.

Well, I said, and is there any knowledge in our recently-founded State among any of the citizens which advises, not about any particular thing in the State, but about the whole, and considers how a State can best deal with itself and with other States?

There certainly is.

And what is this knowledge, and among whom is it found? I asked.

It is the knowledge of the guardians, he replied, and is found among those whom we were just now describing as perfect guardians.

And what is the name which the city derives from the possession of this sort of knowledge?

The name of good in counsel and truly wise.

And will there be in our city more of these true guardians or more smiths?

The smiths, he replied, will be far more numerous.

Will not the guardians be the smallest of all the classes who receive a name from the profession of some kind of knowledge?

Much the smallest.

And so by reason of the smallest part or class, and of the knowledge which resides in this presiding and ruling part of itself, the whole State, being thus constituted according to nature, will be wise; and this, which has the only knowledge worthy to be called wisdom, has been ordained by nature to be of all classes the least.

Most true.

Thus, then, I said, the nature and place in the State of one of the four virtues has somehow or other been discovered.

And, in my humble opinion, very satisfactorily discovered, he replied.

Again, I said, there is no difficulty in seeing the nature of courage, and in what part that quality resides which gives the name of courageous to the State.

How do you mean?

Why, I said, everyone who calls my State courageous or cowardly, will be thinking of the part which fights and goes out to war on the State's behalf.

No one, he replied, would ever think of any other.

The rest of the citizens may be courageous or may be cowardly, but their courage or cowardice will not, as I conceive, have the effect of making the city either the one or the other.

Certainly not.

The city will be courageous in virtue of a portion of herself which preserves under all circumstances that opinion about the nature of things to be feared and not to be feared in which our legislator educated them; and this is what you term courage.

I should like to hear what you are saying once more, for I do not think that I perfectly understand you.

I mean that courage is a kind of [preservation].

[Preservation] of what?

Of the opinion respecting things to be feared, what they are and of what nature, which the law implants through education; and I mean by the words "under all circumstances" to intimate that in pleasure or in pain, or under the influence of desire or fear, a man preserves, and does not lose this opinion. Shall I give you an illustration?

If you please.

You know, I said, that dyers, when they want to dye wool for making the true sea-purple, begin by selecting their white colour first; this they prepare and dress with much care and pains, in order that the white ground may take the purple hue in full perfection. The dyeing then proceeds; and whatever is dyed in this manner becomes a fast colour, and no washing either with lyes or without them can take away the bloom. But, when the ground has not been duly prepared, you will have noticed how poor is the look wither of purple or of any other colour.

Yes, he said; I know that they have a washed-out and ridiculous appearance.

Then now, I said, you will understand what our object was in selecting our soldiers, and educating them in music and gymnastic; we were contriving influences which would prepare them to take the dye of the laws in perfection, and the colour of their opinion about dangers and of every other opinion was to be indelibly fixed by their nurture and training, not to be washed away by such potent lyes as pleasure—a far mightier agent in washing the soul than any soda or lye; or by sorrow, fear, and desire, the mightiest of all other solvents. And this sort of universal saving power of true opinion in conformity with law about real and false dangers I call and maintain to be courage, unless you disagree.

But I agree, he replied; for I suppose that you mean to exclude mere uninstructed courage, such as that of a wild beast or of a slave—this, in your opinion, is not the courage which the law ordains, and ought to have another name.

Most certainly.

Then I may infer courage to be such as you describe?

Why, yes, said I, you may, and if you add the words "of a citizen," you will not be far wrong;—hereafter, if you like, we will carry the examination further, but at present we are seeking not for courage but justice; and for the purpose of our enquiry we have said enough.

You are right, he replied.

Two virtues remain to be discovered in the State—first, temperance, and then justice which is the end of our search.

Very true.

Now, can we find justice without troubling ourselves about temperance?

I do not know how that can be accomplished, he said, nor do I desire that justice should be brought to light and temperance lost sight of; and therefore I wish that you would do me the favour of considering temperance first.

Certainly, I replied, I should not be justified in refusing your request.

Then consider, he said.

Yes, I replied; I will; and as far as I can at present see, the virtue of temperance has more of the nature of harmony and symphony than the preceding.

How so? he asked.

Temperance, I replied, is the ordering or controlling of certain pleasures and desires; this is curiously enough implied in the saying of "a man being his own master;" and other traces of the same notion may be found in language.

No doubt, he said.

There is something ridiculous in the expression "master of himself;" for the master is also the servant and the servant the master; and in all these modes of speaking the same person is denoted.

Certainly.

The meaning is, I believe, that in the human soul there is a better and also a worse principle; and when the better has the worse under control, then a man is said to be master of himself; and this is a term of praise; but when, owing to evil education or association, the better principle, which is also the smaller, is overwhelmed by the greater mass of the worse—in this case he is blamed and is called the slave of self and unprincipled.

Yes, there is reason in that.

And now, I said, look at our newly-created State, and there you will find one of these two conditions realized; for the State, as you will acknowledge, may be justly called master of itself, if the words "temperance" and "self-mastery" truly express the rule of the better part over the worse.

Yes, he said, I see that what you say is true.

Let me further note that the manifold and complex pleasures and desires and pains are generally found in children and women and servants, and in the freemen so called who are of the lowest and more numerous class.

Certainly, he said.

Whereas the simple and moderate desires which follow reason, and are under the guidance of mind and true opinion, are to be found only in a few, and those the best born and best educated.

Very true.

These two, as you may perceive, have a place in our State; and the meaner desires of the many are held down by the virtuous desires and wisdom of the few.

That I perceive, he said.

Then if there be any city which may be described as master of its own pleasures and desires, and master of itself, ours may claim such a designation?

Certainly, he replied.

It may also be called temperate, and for the same reasons?

Yes.

And if there be any State in which rulers and subjects will be agreed as to the question who are to rule, that again will be our State?

Undoubtedly.

And the citizens being thus agreed among themselves, in which class will temperance be found—in the rulers or in the subjects?

In both, as I should imagine, he replied.

Do you observe that we were not far wrong in our guess that temperance was a sort of harmony?

Why so?

Why, because temperance is unlike courage and wisdom, each of which resides in a part only, the one making the State wise and the other valiant; not so temperance, which extends to the whole, and runs through all the notes of the scale, and produces a harmony of the weaker and the stronger and the middle class, whether you suppose them to be stronger or weaker in wisdom or power or numbers or wealth, or anything else. Most truly then may we deem temperance to be the agreement of the naturally superior and inferior, as to the right to rule of either, both in states and individuals.

I entirely agree with you.

And so, I said, we may consider three out of the four virtues to have been discovered in our State. The last of those qualities which make a state virtuous must be justice, if we only knew what that was.

The inference is obvious.

The time then has arrived, Glaucon, when, like huntsmen, we should surround the cover, and look sharp that justice does not steal away, and pass out of sight and escape us; for beyond a doubt she is somewhere in this country: watch therefore and strive to catch a sight of her, and if you see her first, let me know.

Would that I could! but you should regard me rather as a follower who has just eyes enough to see what you show him—that is about as much as I am good for.

Offer up a prayer with me and follow.

I will, but you must show me the way.

Here is no path, I said, and the wood is dark and perplexing; still we must push on.

Let us push on.

Here I saw something: Halloo! I said, I begin to perceive a track, and I believe that the quarry will not escape.

Good news, he said.

Truly, I said, we are stupid fellows.

Why so?

Why, my good sir, at the beginning of our enquiry, ages ago, there was justice tumbling out at our feet, and we never saw her; nothing could be more ridiculous. Like people who go about looking for what they have in their hands—that was the way with us—we looked not at what we were seeking, but at what was far off in the distance; and therefore, I suppose, we missed her.

What do you mean?

I mean to say that in reality for a long time past we have been talking of justice, and have failed to recognise her.

I grow impatient at the length of your exordium.

Well then, tell me, I said, whether I am right or not: You remember the original principle which we were always laying down at the foundation of the State, that one man should practise one thing only, the thing to which his nature was best adapted;—now justice is this principle or a part of it.

Yes, we often said that one man should do one thing only.

Further, we affirmed that justice was doing one's own business, and not being a busybody; we said so again and again, and many others have said the same to us.

Yes, we said so.

Then to do one's own business in a certain way may be assumed to be justice. Can you tell me whence I derive this inference?

I cannot, but I should like to be told.

Because I think that this is the only virtue which remains in the State when the other virtues of temperance and courage and wisdom are abstracted; and, that this is the ultimate cause and condition of the existence of all of them, and while remaining in them is also their preservative; and we were saying that if the three were discovered by us, justice would be the fourth or remaining one.

That follows of necessity.

If we are asked to determine which of these four qualities by its presence contributes most to the excellence of the State, whether the agreement of rulers and subjects, or the preservation in the soldiers of the opinion which the law ordains about the true nature of dangers, or wisdom and watchfulness in the rulers, or whether this other which I am mentioning, and which is found in children and women, slave and freeman, artisan, ruler, subject,—the quality, I mean, of everyone doing his own work, and not being a busybody, would claim the palm—the question is not so easily answered.

Certainly, he replied, there would be a difficulty in saying which.

Then the power of each individual in the State to do his own work appears to compete with the other political virtues, wisdom, temperance, courage.

Yes, he said.

And the virtue which enters into this competition is justice?

Exactly.

Let us look at the question from another point of view: Are not the rulers in a State those to whom you would entrust the office of determining suits at law?

Certainly.

And are suits decided on any other ground but that a man may neither take what is another's, nor be deprived of what is his own?

Yes, that is their principle.

Which is a just principle?

Yes.

Then on this view also justice will be admitted to be the having and doing what is a man's own, and belongs to him?

Very true. . . .

Very good; and if we were to affirm that we had discovered the just man and the just State, and the nature of justice in each of them, we should not be telling a falsehood?

Most certainly not.

May we say so, then?

Let us say so.

And now, I said, injustice has to be considered.

Clearly.

Must not injustice be a strife which arises among the three principles—a meddlesomeness, and interference, and rising up of a part of the soul against the whole, an assertion of unlawful authority, which is made by a rebellious subject against a true prince, of whom he is the natural vassal,—what is all this confusion and delusion but injustice, and intemperance and cowardice and ignorance, and every form of vice?

Exactly so.

And if the nature of justice and injustice be known, then the meaning of acting unjustly and being unjust, or, again, of acting justly, will also be perfectly clear?

What do you mean? he said.

Why, I said, they are like disease and health; being in the soul just what disease and health are in the body.

How so? he said.

Why, I said, that which is healthy causes health, and that which is unhealthy causes disease.

Yes.

And just actions cause justice, and unjust actions cause injustice?

That is certain.

And the creation of health is the institution of a natural order and government of one by another in the parts of the body; and the creation of disease is the production of a state of things at variance with this natural order?

True.

And is not the creation of justice the institution of a natural order and government of one by another in the parts of the soul, and the creation of injustice the production of a state of things at variance with the natural order?

Exactly so, he said.

Then virtue is the health and beauty and well-being of the soul, and vice the disease and weakness and deformity of the same?

True.

And do not good practices lead to virtue, and evil practices to vice?

Assuredly.

Still our old question of the comparative advantage of justice and injustice has not been answered: Which is the more profitable, to be just and act justly and practise virtue, whether seen or unseen of gods and men, or to be unjust and act unjustly, if only unpunished and unreformed?

In my judgment, Socrates, the question has now become ridiculous. We know that, when the bodily constitution is gone, life is no longer endurable, though pampered with all kinds of meats and drinks, and having all wealth and all power; and shall we be told . . . life is still worth having to a man, if only he be allowed to do whatever he likes with the single exception that he is not to acquire justice and virtue, or to escape from injustice and vice; assuming them both to be such as we have described?

Yes, this is ridiculous. . . .

## Book V

Well, I replied, I suppose that I must retrace my steps and say what I perhaps ought to have said before in the proper place. The part of the men has been played out, and now properly enough comes the turn of the women. Of them I will proceed to speak, and the more readily since I am invited by you.

For men born and educated like our citizens, the only way, in my opinion, of arriving at a right conclusion about the possession and use of women and children is to follow the path on which we originally started, when we said that the men were to be the guardians and watchdogs of the herd.

True.

Let us further suppose the birth and education of our women to be subject to similar or nearly similar regulations; then we shall see whether the result accords with our design.

What do you mean?

What I mean may be put into the form of a question, I said: Are dogs divided into hes and shes, or do they both share equally in hunting and in keeping watch and in the other duties of dogs? or do we entrust to the males the entire and exclusive care of the flocks, while we leave the females at home, under the idea that the bearing and suckling [of] their puppies is labour enough for them?

No, he said, they share alike; the only difference between them is that the males are stronger and the females weaker.

But can you use different animals for the same purpose, unless they are bred and fed in the same way?

You cannot.

Then, if women are to have the same duties as men, they must have the same nurture and education?

Yes.

The education which was assigned to the men was music and gymnastic.

Yes.

Then women must be taught music and gymnastic and also the art of war, which they must practise like the men?

That is the inference, I suppose.

I should rather expect, I said, that several of our proposals, if they are carried out, being unusual, may appear ridiculous.

No doubt of it.

Yes, and the most ridiculous thing of all will be the sight of women naked in the palaestra, exercising with the men, especially when they are no longer young; they certainly will not be a vision of beauty, any more than the enthusiastic old men who in spite of wrinkles and ugliness continue to frequent the gymnasia.

Yes, indeed, he said: according to present notions the proposal would be thought ridiculous.

But then, I said, as we have determined to speak our minds, we must not fear the jests of the wits which will be directed against this sort of innovation; how they will talk of women's attainments both in music and gymnastic, and above all about their wearing armour and riding upon horseback!

Very true, he replied.

Yet having begun we must go forward to the rough places of the law; at the same time begging of these gentlemen for once in their life to be serious. Not long ago, as we shall remind them, the Hellenes were of the opinion, which is still generally received among the barbarians, that the sight of a naked man was ridiculous and improper; and when first the Cretans and then the Lacedaemonians introduced the custom, the wits of that day might equally have ridiculed the innovation.

No doubt.

But when experience showed that to let all things be uncovered was far better than to cover them up, and the ludicrous effect to the outward eye vanished before the better principle which reason asserted, then the man was perceived to be a fool who directs the shafts of his ridicule to any other sight but that of folly and vice, or seriously inclines to weigh the beautiful by any other standard but that of the good.

Very true, he replied.

First, then, whether the question is to be put in jest or in earnest, let us come to an understanding about the nature of woman: Is she capable of sharing either wholly or partially in the actions of men, or not at all? And is the art of war one of those arts in which she can or can not share? That will be the best way of commencing the enquiry, and will probably lead to the fairest conclusion.

That will be much the best way.

Shall we take the other side first and begin by arguing against ourselves; in this manner the adversary's position will not be undefended.

Why not? he said.

Then let us put a speech into the mouths of our opponents. They will say: "Socrates and Glaucon, no adversary need convict you, for you yourselves, at the first foundation of the State, admitted the principle that everybody was to do the one work suited to his own nature." And certainly, if I am not mistaken, such an admission was made by us. "And do not the natures of men and women differ very much indeed?" And we shall reply: Of course they do. Then we shall be asked, "Whether the tasks assigned to men and to women should not be different, and such as are agreeable to their different natures?" Certainly they should. "But if so, have you not fallen into a serious inconsistency in saying that men and women, whose natures are so entirely different, ought to perform the same actions?"—What defence will you make for us, my good Sir, against anyone who offers these objections?

That is not an easy question to answer when asked suddenly; and I shall and I do beg of you to draw out the case on our side.

These are the objections, Glaucon, and there are many others of a like kind, which I foresaw long ago; they made me afraid and reluctant to take in hand any law about the possession and nurture of women and children.

By Zeus, he said, the problem to be solved is anything but easy.

Why yes, I said, but the fact is that when a man is out of his depth, whether he has fallen into a little swimming bath or into mid ocean, he has to swim all the same.

Very true.

And must not we swim and try to reach the shore: we will hope that Arion's dolphin or some other miraculous help may save us?

I suppose so, he said.

Well then, let us see if any way of escape can be found. We acknowledged—did we not?—that different natures ought to have different pursuits, and that men's and women's natures are different. And now what are we saying?—that different natures ought to have the same pursuits,—this is the inconsistency which is charged upon us.

Precisely.

Verily, Glaucon, I said, glorious is the power of the art of contradiction!

Why do you say so!

Because I think that many a man falls into the practice against his will. When he thinks that he is reasoning he is really disputing, just because he cannot define and divide, and so know that of which he is speaking; and he will pursue a merely verbal opposition in the spirit of contention and not a fair discussion.

Yes, he replied, such is very often the case; but what has that to do with us and our argument?

A great deal; for there is certainly a danger of our getting unintentionally into a verbal opposition.

In what way?

Why we valiantly and pugnaciously insist upon the verbal truth, that different natures ought to have different pursuits, but we never considered at all what was the meaning of sameness or difference of nature, or why we distinguished them when we assigned different pursuits to different natures and the same to the same natures.

Why, no, he said, that was never considered by us.

I said: Suppose that by way of illustration we were to ask the question whether there is not an opposition in nature between bald men and hairy men; and if this is admitted by us, then, if bald men are cobblers, we should forbid the hairy men to be cobblers, and conversely?

That would be a jest, he said.

Yes, I said, a jest; and why? because we never meant when we constructed the State, that the opposition of natures should extend to every difference, but only to those differences which affected the pursuit in which the individual is engaged; we should have argued, for example, that a physician and one who is in mind a physician may be said to have the same nature.

True.

Whereas the physician and the carpenter have different natures?

Certainly.

And if, I said, the male and female sex appear to differ in their fitness for any art or pursuit, we should say that such pursuit or art ought to be assigned to one or the other of them; but if the difference consists only in women bearing and men begetting children, this does not amount to a proof that a woman differs from a man in respect to the sort of education she should receive; and we shall therefore continue to maintain that our guardians and their wives ought to have the same pursuits.

Very true, he said.

Next, we shall ask our opponent how, in reference to any of the pursuits or arts of civic life, the nature of a woman differs from that of a man?

That will be quite fair.

And perhaps he, like yourself, will reply that to give a sufficient answer on the instant is not easy; but after a little reflection there is no difficulty.

Yes, perhaps.

Suppose then that we invite him to accompany us in the argument, and then we may hope to show him that there is nothing peculiar in the constitution of women which would affect them in the administration of the State.

By all means.

Let us say to him: Come now, and we will ask you a question:—when you spoke of a nature gifted or not gifted in any respect, did you mean to say that one man will acquire a thing easily, an-

other with difficulty; a little learning will lead the one to discover a great deal; whereas the other, after much study and application, no sooner learns than he forgets; or again, did you mean, that the one has a body which is a good servant to his mind, while the body of the other is a hindrance to him?—would not these be the sort of differences which distinguish the man gifted by nature from the one who is ungifted?

No one will deny that.

And can you mention any pursuit of mankind in which the male sex has not all these gifts and qualities in a higher degree than the female? Need I waste time in speaking of the art of weaving, and the management of pancakes and preserves, in which womankind does really appear to be great, and in which for her to be beaten by a man is of all things the most absurd?

You are quite right, he replied, in maintaining the general inferiority of the female sex: although many women are in many things superior to many men, yet on the whole what you say is true.

And if so, my friend, I said, there is no special faculty of administration in a state which a woman has because she is a woman, or which a man has by virtue of his sex, but the gifts of nature are alike diffused in both; all the pursuits of men are the pursuits of women also, but in all of them a woman is inferior to a man.

Very true.

Then are we to impose all our enactments on men and none of them on women?

That will never do.

One woman has a gift of healing, another not; one is a musician, and another has no music in her nature?

Very true.

And one woman has a turn for gymnastic and military exercises, and another is unwarlike and hates gymnastics?

Certainly.

And one woman is a philosopher, and another is an enemy of philosophy; one has spirit, and another is without spirit?

That is also true.

Then one woman will have the temper of a

guardian, and another not. Was not the selection of the male guardians determined by differences of this sort?

Yes.

Men and women alike possess the qualities which make a guardian; they differ only in their comparative strength or weakness.

Obviously.

And those women who have such qualities are to be selected as the companions and colleagues of men who have similar qualities and whom they resemble in capacity and in character?

Very true.

And ought not the same natures to have the same pursuits?

They ought.

Then, as we were saying before, there is nothing unnatural in assigning music and gymnastic to the wives of the guardians—to that point we come round again.

Certainly not.

The law which we then enacted was agreeable to nature, and therefore not an impossibility or mere aspiration; and the contrary practice, which prevails at present, is in reality a violation of nature.

That appears to be true.

We had to consider, first, whether our proposals were possible, and secondly whether they were the most beneficial?

Yes.

And the possibility has been acknowledged?

Yes.

The very great benefit has next to be established?

Quite so.

You will admit that the same education which makes a man a good guardian will make a woman a good guardian; for their original nature is the same?

Yes.

I should like to ask you a question.

What is it?

Would you say that all men are equal in excellence, or is one man better than another?

The latter.

And in the commonwealth which we were founding do you conceive the guardians who have been brought up on our model system to be more perfect men, or the cobblers whose education has been cobbling?

What a ridiculous question!

You have answered me, I replied: Well, and may we not further say that our guardians are the best of our citizens?

By far the best.

And will not their wives be the best women?

Yes, by far the best.

And can there be anything better for the interests of the State than that the men and women of a State should be as good as possible?

There can be nothing better.

And this is what the arts of music and gymnastic, when present in such manner as we have described, will accomplish?

Certainly.

Then we have made an enactment not only possible but in the highest degree beneficial to the State?

True.

Then let the wives of our guardians strip, for their virtue will be their robe, and let them share in the toils of war and the defence of their country; only in the distribution of labours the lighter are to be assigned to the women, who are the weaker natures, but in other respects their duties are to be the same. And as for the man who laughs at naked women exercising their bodies from the best of motives, in his laughter he is plucking

A fruit of unripe wisdom,

and he himself is ignorant of what he is laughing at, or what he is about;—for that is, and ever will be, the best of savings, *That the useful is the noble and the hurtful is the base.*

Very true.

Here, then, is one difficulty in our law about women, which we may say that we have now escaped; the wave has not swallowed us up alive for enacting that the guardians of either sex should have all their pursuits in common; to the utility and also to the possibility of this arrangement the consistency of the argument with itself bears witness.

Yes, that was a mighty wave which you have escaped.

Yes, I said, but a greater is coming; you will not think much of this when you see the next.

Go on; let me see.

The law, I said, which is the sequel of this and of all that has preceded, is to the following effect,—"that the wives of our guardians are to be common, and their children are to be common, and no parent is to know his own child, nor any child his parent."

Yes, he said, that is a much greater wave than the other; and the possibility as well as the utility of such a law are far more questionable.

I do not think, I said, that there can be any dispute about the very great utility of having wives and children in common; the possibility is quite another matter, and will be very much disputed.

I think that a good many doubts may be raised about both.

You imply that the two questions must be combined, I replied. Now I meant that you should admit the utility; and in this way, as I thought, I should escape from one of them, and then there would remain only the possibility.

But that little attempt is detected, and therefore you will please to give a defence of both.

Well, I said, I submit to my fate. Yet grant me a little favour: let me feast my mind with the dream as day dreamers are in the habit of feasting themselves when they are walking alone; for before they have discovered any means of effecting their wishes—that is a matter which never troubles them—they would rather not tire themselves of thinking about possibilities; but assuming that what they desire is already granted to them, they proceed with their plan, and delight in detailing what they mean to do when their wish has come true—that is a way which they have of not doing much good to a capacity which was never good for much. Now I myself am beginning to lose heart, and I should like, with your permission, to pass over the question of possibility at present. Assuming therefore the possibility of the proposal, I shall now proceed to enquire how the rulers will carry out these arrangements, and I shall demonstrate that our plan, if executed, will be of the greatest benefit to the State and to the guardians. First of all, then, if you have no objection, I will endeavour with your help to consider the advantages of the measure; and hereafter the question of possibility.

I have no objection; proceed.

First, I think that if our rulers and their auxiliaries are to be worthy of the name which they bear, there must be willingness to obey in the one and the power of command in the other; the guardians must themselves obey the laws, and they must also imitate the spirit of them in any details which are entrusted to their care.

That is right, he said.

You, I said, who are their legislator, having selected the men, will now select the women and give them to them;—they must be as far as possible of like natures with them; and they must live in common houses and meet at common meals. None of them will have anything specially his or her own; they will be together, and will be brought up together, and will associate at gymnastic exercises. And so they will be drawn by a necessity of their natures to have intercourse with each other—necessity is not too strong a word, I think?

Yes, he said;—necessity, not geometrical, but another sort of necessity which lovers know, and which is far more convincing and constraining to the mass of mankind.

True, I said; and this, Glaucon, like all the rest, must proceed after an orderly fashion; in a city of the blessed, licentiousness is an unholy thing which the rulers will forbid.

Yes, he said, and it ought not to be permitted.

Then clearly the next thing will be to make matrimony sacred in the highest degree, and what is most beneficial will be deemed sacred?

Exactly.

And how can marriages be made most beneficial?—that is a question which I put to you, because I see in your house dogs for hunting, and of the nobler sort of birds not a few. Now, I beseech you, do tell me, have you ever attended to their pairing and breeding?

In what particulars?

Why, in the first place, although they are all of a good sort, are not some better than others?

True.

And do you breed from them all indifferently, or do you take care to breed from the best only?

From the best.

And do you take the oldest or the youngest, or only those of ripe age?

I choose only those of ripe age.

And if care was not taken in the breeding, your dogs and birds would greatly deteriorate?

Certainly.

And the same of horses and of animals in general?

Undoubtedly.

Good heavens! my dear friend, I said, what consummate skill will our rulers need if the same principle holds of the human species!

Certainly, the same principle holds; but why does this involve any particular skill?

Because, I said, our rulers will often have to practise upon the body corporate with medicines. Now you know that when patients do not require medicines, but have only to be put under a regimen, the inferior sort of practitioner is deemed to be good enough; but when medicine has to be given, then the doctor should be more of a man.

That is quite true, he said; but to what are you alluding?

I mean, I replied, that our rulers will find a considerable dose of falsehood and deceit necessary for the good of their subjects: we were saying that the use of all these things regarded as medicines might be of advantage.

And we were very right.

And this lawful use of them seems likely to be often needed in the regulations of marriages and births.

How so?

Why, I said, the principle has been already laid down that the best of either sex should be united with the best as often, and the inferior with the inferior as seldom as possible; and that they should

rear the offspring of the one sort of union, but not of the other, if the flock is to be maintained in first-rate condition. Now these goings on must be a secret which the rulers only know, or there will be a further danger of our herd, as the guardians may be termed, breaking out into rebellion.

Very true.

Had we not better appoint certain festivals at which we will bring together the brides and bridegrooms, and sacrifices will be offered and suitable [hymns] composed by our poets: the number of weddings is a matter which must be left to the discretion of the rulers, whose aim will be to preserve the average of population? There are many other things which they will have to consider, such as the effects of wars and diseases and any similar agencies, in order as far as this is possible to prevent the State from becoming either too large or too small.

Certainly, he replied.

We shall have to invent some ingenious kind of lots which the less worthy may draw on each occasion of our bringing them together, and then they will accuse their own ill-luck and not the rulers.

To be sure, he said.

And I think that our braver and better youth, besides their other honours and rewards, might have greater facilities of intercourse with women given them; their bravery will be a reason, and such fathers ought to have as many sons as possible.

True.

And the proper officers, whether male or female or both, for offices are to be held by women as well as by men—

Yes—

The proper officers will take the offspring of the good parents to the pen or fold, and there they will deposit them with certain nurses who dwell in a separate quarter; but the offspring of the inferior, or of the better when they chance to be deformed, will be put away in some mysterious, unknown place, as they should be.

Yes, he said, that must be done if the breed of the guardians is to be kept pure.

They will provide for their nurture, and will

bring the mothers to the fold when they are full of milk, taking the greatest possible care that no mother recognises her own child; and other wet-nurses may be engaged if more are required. Care will also be taken that the process of suckling shall not be protracted too long; and the mothers will have no getting up at night or other trouble, but will hand over all this sort of thing to the nurses and attendants.

You suppose the wives of our guardians to have a fine easy time of it when they are having children.

Why, said I, and so they ought. Let us, however, proceed with our scheme. We were saying that the parents should be in the prime of life?

Very true.

And what is the prime of life? May it not be defined as a period of about twenty years in a woman's life, and thirty in a man's?

Which years do you mean to include?

A woman, I said, at twenty years of age may begin to bear children to the State, and continue to bear them until forty; a man may begin at five-and-twenty, then he has passed the point at which the pulse of life beats quickest, and continue to beget children until he be fifty-five.

Certainly, he said, both in men and women those years are the prime of physical as well as of intellectual vigour.

Anyone above or below the prescribed ages who [engages in reproduction] shall be said to have done an unholy and unrighteous thing; the child of which he is the father, if it steals into life, will have been conceived under auspices very unlike the sacrifices and prayers, which at each [wedding] priestesses and priests and the whole city will offer, that the new generation may be better and more useful than their good and useful parents, whereas his child will be the offspring of darkness and strange lust.

Very true, he replied.

And the same law will apply to anyone of those within the prescribed age who forms a connection with any woman in the prime of life without the sanction of the rulers; for we shall say that he is raising up a bastard to the State, uncertified and unconsecrated.

Very true, he replied.

This applies, however, only to those who are within the specified age: after that we allow them to range at will, except that a man may not marry his daughter or his daughter's daughter, or his mother or his mother's mother; and women, on the other hand, are prohibited from marrying their sons or fathers, or son's son or father's father, and so on in either direction. And we grant all this, accompanying the permission with strict orders to prevent any embryo which may come into being from seeing the light; and if any force a way to the birth, the parents must understand that the off-spring of such a union cannot be maintained, and arrange accordingly.

That also, he said, is a reasonable proposition. But how will they know who are fathers and daughters, and so on?

They will never know. The way will be this:— dating from the day [a man becomes a] bride-groom, . . . [he] will call all the male children who are born in the seventh and the tenth month afterwards his sons, and the female children his daughters, and they will call him father, and he will call their children his grandchildren, and they will call the elder generation grandfathers and grandmothers. All who were begotten at the time when their fathers and mothers came together will be called their brothers and sisters, and these, as I was saying, will be forbidden to intermarry. This, however, is not to be understood as an absolute prohibition of the marriage of brothers and sisters; if the lot favours them, and they receive the sanction of the Pythian oracle, the law will allow them.

Quite right, he replied.

Such is the scheme, Glaucon, according to which the guardians of our State are to have their wives and families in common. And now you would have the argument show that this community is consistent with the rest of our polity, and also that nothing can be better—would you not?

Yes, certainly.

Shall we try to find a common basis by asking of ourselves what ought to be the chief aim of the legislator in making laws and in the organization of a State—what is the greatest good, and what is the greatest evil, and then consider whether our previous description has the stamp of the good or of the evil?

By all means.

Can there be any greater evil than discord and distraction and plurality where unity ought to reign? or any greater good than the bond of unity?

There cannot.

And there is unity where there is community of pleasures and pains—where all the citizens are glad or grieved on the same occasions of joy and sorrow?

No doubt.

Yes; and where there is no common but only private feeling a State is disorganized—when you have one half of the world triumphing and the other plunged in grief at the same events happening to the city or the citizens?

Certainly.

Such differences commonly originate in a disagreement about the use of the terms "mine" and "not mine," "his" and "not his."

Exactly so.

And is not that the best-ordered State in which the greatest number of persons apply the terms "mine" and "not mine" in the same way to the same thing?

Quite true.

Or that again which most nearly approaches to the condition of the individual—as in the body, when but a finger of one of us is hurt, the whole frame, down towards the soul as a centre and forming one kingdom under the ruling power therein, feels the hurt and sympathizes all together with the part affected, and we say that the man has a pain in his finger; and the same expression is used about any other part of the body, which has a sensation of pain at suffering or of pleasure at the alleviation of suffering.

Very true, he replied; and I agree with you that in the best-ordered State there is the nearest approach to this common feeling which you describe.

Then when anyone of the citizens experience any good or evil, the whole State will make his case their own, and will either rejoice or sorrow with him?

Yes, he said, that is what will happen in a well-ordered State.

It will now be time, I said, for us to return to our State and see whether this or some other form is most in accordance with these fundamental principles.

Very good.

Our State like every other has rulers and subjects?

True.

All of whom will call one another citizens?

Of course.

But is there not another name which people give to their rulers in other States?

Generally they call them masters, but in democratic States they simply call them rulers.

And in our State what other name besides that of citizens do the people give the rulers?

They are called saviours and helpers, he replied.

And what do the rulers call the people?

Their maintainers and foster-fathers.

And what do they call them in other States?

Slaves.

And what do the rulers call one another in other States?

Fellow-rulers.

And what in ours?

Fellow-guardians.

Did you ever know an example in any other State of a ruler who would speak of one of his colleagues as his friend and of another as not being his friend?

Yes, very often.

And the friend he regards and describes as one in whom he has an interest, and the other as a stranger in whom he has no interest?

Exactly.

But would any of your guardians think or speak of any other guardian as a stranger?

Certainly he would not; for everyone whom they meet will be regarded by them either as a brother or sister, or father or mother, or son or daughter, or as the child or parent of those who are thus connected with him.

Capital, I said; but let me ask you once more: Shall they be a family in name only; or shall they in all their actions be true to the name? For example, in the use of the word "father," would the care of a father be implied and the filial reverence and duty and obedience to him which the law commands; and is the violator of these duties to be regarded as an impious and unrighteous person who is not likely to receive much good either at the hands of God or of man? Are these to be or not to be the strains which the children will hear repeated in their ears by all the citizens about those who are intimated to them to be their parents and the rest of their kinsfolk?

These, he said, and none other; for what can be more ridiculous than for them to utter the names of family ties with the lips only and not to act in the spirit of them?

Then in our city the language of harmony and concord will be more often heard than in any other. As I was describing before, when anyone is well or ill, the universal word will be "with me it is well" or "it is ill."

Most true.

And agreeably to this mode of thinking and speaking, were we not saying that they will have their pleasures and pains in common?

Yes, and so they will.

And they will have a common interest in the same thing which they will alike call "my own," and having this common interest they will have a common feeling of pleasure and pain?

Yes, far more so than in other States.

And the reason of this, over and above the general constitution of the State, will be that the guardians will have a community of women and children?

That will be the chief reason.

And this unity of feeling we admitted to be the greatest good, as was implied in our own comparison of a well-ordered State to the relation of the body and the members, when affected by pleasure or pain?

That we acknowledged, and very rightly.

Then the community of wives and children among our citizens is clearly the source of the greatest good to the State?

Certainly.

And this agrees with the other principle which

we were affirming,—that the guardians were not to have houses or lands or any other property; their pay was to be their food, which they were to receive from the other citizens, and they were to have no private expenses; for we intended them to preserve their true character of guardians.

Right, he replied.

Both the community of property and the community of families, as I am saying, tend to make them more truly guardians; they will not tear the city in pieces by differing about "mine" and "not mine;" each man dragging any acquisition which he has made into a separate house of his own, where he has a separate wife and children and private pleasures and pains; but all will be affected as far as may be by the same pleasures and pains because they are all of one opinion about what is near and dear to them, and therefore they all tend towards a common end.

Certainly, he replies.

And as they have nothing but their persons which they can call their own, suits and complaints will have no existence among them; they will be delivered from all those quarrels of which money or children or relations are the occasion.

Of course they will.

Neither will trials for assault or insult ever be likely to occur among them. For that equals should defend themselves against equals we shall maintain to be honourable and right; we shall make the protection of the person a matter of necessity.

That is good, he said.

Yes; and there is a further good in the law; viz. that if a man has a quarrel with another he will satisfy his resentment then and there, and not proceed to more dangerous lengths.

Certainly.

To the elder shall be assigned the duty of ruling and chastising the younger.

Clearly.

Nor can there be a doubt that the younger will not strike or do any other violence to an elder, unless the magistrates command him; nor will he slight him in any way. For there are two guardians, shame and fear, mighty to prevent him: shame, which makes men refrain from laying hands on those who are to them in the relation of parents; fear, that the injured one will be succoured by the others who are his brothers, sons, fathers.

That is true, he replied.

Then in every way the laws will help the citizens to keep the peace with one another?

Yes, there will be no want of peace.

And as the guardians will never quarrel among themselves there will be no danger of the rest of the city being divided either against them or against one another.

None whatever.

I hardly like even to mention the little meannesses of which they will be rid, for they are beneath notice: such, for example, as the flattery of the rich by the poor, and all the pains and pangs which men experience in bringing up a family, and in finding money to buy necessaries for their household, borrowing and then repudiating, getting how they can, and giving the money into the hands of women and slaves to keep—the many evils of so many kinds which people suffer in this way are mean enough and obvious enough, and not worth speaking of.

Yes, he said, a man has no need of eyes in order to perceive that.

And from all these evils they will be delivered, and their life will be blessed as the life of Olympic victors and yet more blessed.

How so?

The Olympic victor, I said, is deemed happy in receiving a part only of the blessedness which is secured to our citizens, who have won a more glorious victory and have a more complete maintenance at the public cost. For the victory which they have won is the salvation of the whole State; and the crown with which they and their children are crowned is the fulness of all that life needs; they receive rewards from the hands of their country while living, and after death have an honourable burial.

Yes, he said, and glorious rewards they are.

Do you remember, I said, how in the course of the previous discussion someone who shall be nameless accused us of making our guardians un-happy—they had nothing and might have possessed all things—to whom we replied that, if an occasion offered, we might perhaps hereafter consider this question, but that, as at present advised, we would make our guardians truly guardians, and that we were fashioning the State with a view to the greatest happiness, not for any particular class, but of the whole?

Yes, I remember.

And what do you say, now that the life of our protectors is made out to be far better and nobler than that of Olympic victors—is the life of shoemakers, or any other artisans, or of [farmers], to be compared with it?

Certainly not.

At the same time I ought here to repeat what I have said elsewhere, that if any of our guardians shall try to be happy in such a manner that he will cease to be a guardian, and is not content with this safe and harmonious life, which, in our judgment, is of all lives the best, but infatuated by some youthful conceit of happiness which gets up into his head shall seek to appropriate the whole state to himself, then he will have to learn how wisely Hesiod spoke, when he said, "half is more than the whole."

If he were to consult me, I should say to him: Stay where you are, when you have the offer of such a life.

You agree then, I said, that men and women are to have a common way of life such as we have described—common education, common children; and they are to watch over the citizens in common whether abiding in the city or going out to war; they are to keep watch together, and to hunt together like dogs; and always and in all things, as far as they are able, women are to share with the men? And in so doing they will do what is best, and will not violate, but preserve the natural relation of the sexes.

I agree with you, he replied. . . .

Let me begin by reminding you that we found our way hither in the search after justice and injustice.

True, he replied; but what of that?

I was only going to ask whether, if we have discovered them, we are to require that the just man should in nothing fail of absolute justice; or may we be satisfied with an approximation, and the attainment in him of a higher degree of justice than is to be found in other men?

The approximation will be enough.

We were enquiring into the nature of absolute justice and into the character of the perfectly just, and into injustice and the perfectly unjust, that we might have an ideal. We were to look at these in order that we might judge of our own happiness and unhappiness according to the standard which they exhibited and the degree in which we resembled them, but not with any view of showing that they could exist in fact.

True, he said.

Would a painter be any the worse because, after having delineated with consummate art an ideal of a perfectly beautiful man, he was unable to show that any such man could ever have existed?

He would be none the worse.

Well, and were we not creating an ideal of a perfect State?

To be sure.

And is our theory a worse theory because we are unable to prove the possibility of a city being ordered in the manner described?

Surely not, he replied.

That is the truth, I said. But if, at your request, I am to try and show how and under what conditions the possibility is highest, I must ask you, having this in view, to repeat your former admissions.

What admissions?

I want to know whether ideals are ever fully realized in language? Does not the word express more than the fact, and must not the actual, whatever a man may think, always, in the nature of things, fall short of the truth? What do you say?

I agree.

Then you must not insist on my proving that the actual State will in every respect coincide with the ideal: if we are only able to discover how a city may be governed nearly as we proposed, you will admit that we have discovered the possibility which you demand; and will be contented. I am sure that I should be contented—will not you?

Yes, I will.

Let me next endeavour to show what is that fault in States which is the cause of their present maladministration, and what is the least change which will enable a State to pass into the truer form; and let the change, if possible, be of one thing only, or, if not, of two; at any rate, let the changes be as few and slight as possible.

Certainly, he replied.

I think, I said, that there might be a reform of the State if only one change were made, which is not a slight or easy though still a possible one.

What is it? he said.

Now then, I said, I go to meet that which I liken to the greatest of the waves; yet shall the word be spoken, even though the wave break and drown me in laughter and dishonour; and do you mark my words.

Proceed.

I said: *Until philosophers are kings, or the kings and princes of this world have the spirit and power of philosophy, and political greatness and wisdom meet in one, and those commoner natures who pursue either to the exclusion of the other are compelled to stand aside, cities will never have rest from their evils,—no, nor the human race, as I believe,—and then only will this our State have a possibility of life and behold the light of day.* Such was the thought, my dear Glaucon, which I would fain have uttered if it had not seemed too extravagant; for to be convinced that in no other State can there be happiness private or public is indeed a hard thing.

NOTES

1. Aeschylus, *Seven against Thebes*, 574.
2. Hesiod, *Works and Days*, 230.
3. Homer, *Odyssey*, xix. 109.
4. Eumolpus.
5. Hesiod, *Works and Days*, 287.
6. Homer, *Iliad*, ix. 493.

# 2    The Function of Equal Education in Plato's *Republic*

LYNDA LANGE

PLATO APPEARS TO BE INCONSISTENT in his treatment of women. He developed in the *Republic* the idea that males and females should be educated equally for the highest functions, while at the same time he believed that women were ultimately not as good as men. A further difficulty with Plato's views on women occurs as a result of his apparent about-face on the question in the *Laws*. Numerous attempts have been made to resolve these difficulties.

One of the most popular approaches has been to attempt to explain away Plato's so-called feminism. Among those who consider the *Republic* to be purely ideal, and thoroughly impractical, the equality of women and the communal life of the guardians are sometimes considered to be a virtual *reductio ad absurdum* of Plato's views. If *this* is what is required, they argue, obviously such a state could never be and thus Plato could not have intended it as a literal model for the state.[1]

Those who take Plato's position on women seriously have done so on the basis of the arguments in defence of the recommendation that they not be excluded from public life, and that those females showing signs of the capacity to be guardians should be given exactly the same mental and physical education as their male counterparts.[2] It is true that the mere fact that Plato suggested that it was possible that some women have the potential to be guardians distinguishes him markedly from his contemporaries, and indeed from most political thinkers of the past. This is true in spite of the inadequacy of his views from the standpoint of feminism today.

This inadequacy is by no means minor, however. It is apparent, for example, that Plato did not intend that the guardian class be equally divided by sex. According to Plato, women as a class are inferior to men as a class.[3] Therefore, even though some women are superior to some men, proportionately fewer women than men may be expected to attain to the highest level of development that qualifies individuals to be guardians. Indeed, I shall argue below that his recommendations for women do not necessarily imply that *any* of them will become guardians.

There are numerous passages that indicate that Plato did not consider women to be as good as men. For example, in the discussion in Book III of the *Republic* of the best education for those likely to become guardians, Socrates says that if they go in for drama they must imitate only "men . . . who are brave, sober, pious, free," and not be allowed to imitate women or slaves. It appears from this and other passages, that Plato thought that women, in addition to being weaker in everything, were more likely than men to be cowardly, hysterical, and given to luxury.[4]

In spite of this, however, Plato did not believe that women and men had different social and political functions to fulfil as a result of their having different natures. The difference of sex, according to Plato, is a fact about individuals that is not relevant to their political status, as baldness is not relevant to a man's ability to cobble shoes. There is, nevertheless, a de facto correlation between femaleness and inferiority, as we have seen. What Plato appears to have done with women is allow for exceptions, in much the same way as he allows for exceptions to appear in the otherwise inferior artisan class. Assuming that feminism entails at least the belief that women are "as good as" men, though not necessarily "the same as" men, this correlation of femaleness and inferiority is in itself a good reason for saying that Plato is not a feminist, though not my main reason for saying so.[5]

It may be objected that the provision of equal opportunity for education of the sexes is sufficient to earn Plato the ascription of feminist, on the ground that what is wrong with the male supremacist view is not the fact that women are not found in the same numbers as men in every segment of society, from combat training to the judge's bench, but the fact that their exclusion has been arbitrary and unfair. Given rational and fair criteria for the assignment of social functions, the argument runs, women and men will assume functions appropriate to their individual abilities, which may or may not result in equal numbers in a given field of activity. While the application of rational criteria is of major importance in the structure of the *Republic*, Plato's concept of justice involves no idea of fairness. The amount of attention now paid to the arguments in *Republic* V that it is possible for women to be educated in the same way as men may be partly accounted for by the unexamined modern assumption that if it is *possible* for people to function as equals, then it is self-evidently desirable for them to do so. I do not think Plato would have shared this assumption. He thought democracy was possible, for example, but quite undesirable. There is no indication that concern for fairness or equality was his motive for suggesting that women not be excluded from any social function. In other words, it was not equal participation *for women* in the good life he was concerned about, but some other good for the whole city. This interpretation is consistent with his stated position that the good of the city as a whole is the basic criterion for making judgments, and not the good of the guardian class.[6]

I shall argue that his position on women cannot be properly understood as feminist, no matter how inconsistently so it may be. I believe his position to be philosophically interesting, however, because it seems to be addressed to a profound problem of political theory still very much at issue. This is the contradiction between public and private life which exists where there is a social structure and an ideology that separates the two.

I shall argue at the same time that the inadequacy of his position from the standpoint of current feminism is not fatal to his views (from a logical point of view), because his purposes in making the recommendations concerning women do not require unqualified identity of worth between the sexes or strict quantitative equality such as equal numbers in the guardian class. His theoretical concerns are ultimately not those of feminism.

Before proceeding to further examination of Plato, I shall explain my use of the terms "public" and "private," and what is meant by saying that there is a contradiction between them.

The distinction between the public sphere of activity and the private sphere has been present in all political theory which has attempted to be comprehensive, although the terminology for it varies. Whatever is considered distinctively political activity, such as economic or productive activity of a certain type (for example, that paid for by a wage)—is "public." This is contrasted with whatever is deemed non-political, personal, natural, biological, and so on, all of which may be categorized as "private." The delineation of this distinction is a subject for inquiry in itself, and no more than a brief discussion will be presented here.

The concepts "public" and "private" are linked together; they cannot be understood except in relation to each other. Nothing can be understood to be "public," unless something is "private," and *vice versa*. Each concept contains implicit normative prescriptions for behaviour in its realm and the realm of the other, and also implies the reservation of something to itself. There is also assumed to be a difference in value and importance between the two spheres.

In societies where this dichotomy is maintained, there is a constant opposition between the requirements of public life (for example, for a person in pursuit of a career) and private life (for example, for a parent). This opposition occurs on both the practical and conceptual level. The private or family sphere is associated conceptually with what are usually conceived of as the "natural," or even "instinctive," impulses of human beings for companionship, sex, children, emotional expression, and so on. This is in contrast to the structure of civil society, which is usually considered a product of human artifice, and a matter of convention. The "natural" impulses have often been deemed non-rational, if not positively irrational, whereas the ability to fulfill the duties of a citizen has been tied, at least in theory, to the ability either to transcend or to control one's non-rational impulses by means of reason or intelligence.

Most importantly, role differentiation between the sexes has historically always been articulated as a difference in the duties owed to the state or to economic productivity, and those owed to a particular family. The former duties are basic for men, and the latter are basic for women. The supposed superiority of public, and productive activity is the ideological source of the authority of the male within the private family. His authority ensures that the functions of the family are fulfilled in such a way that their tendency to run counter to the functions of the state is well contained. The male head of a family is virtually a representative within the family of the value system of public life. This helps to explain why those who recommend the elimination of private families, such as Plato, usually also recommend a fairly high degree of state authority over sexual relations and reproduction. The heads of families must constantly adjudicate between the rival demands of the two spheres, which to me hints at the explanation of Plato's alleged feminism.

I believe Plato's true philosophical concern in recommending equal education is ultimately derived from his concept of justice, although it is helpful to consider some crucial historical features of Greek society as well. This approach removes both of the apparent inconsistencies in his views on women.

Plato's concept of social justice is briefly defined by Socrates as the performance by each individual of the work for which he is best suited.[7] Equally important, however, if the structure of the city is to be recognizably Plato's, is his hierarchical arrangement of functions. While it is just for each individual to perform the functions, no matter how menial, for which he is best suited, this by no means entails for Plato an equality of value among functions. The functions which are considered by Plato to be noble and worth pursuing for their own sake are only a small portion of the functions that are needed for the existence of a just city. In fact, *all* of the functions needed for the physical maintenance of the city are inferior functions to be done by the inferior artisan class. The physical defence of the city is consigned to a group of medium value.

In the *Republic* the functions of the guardian class are very closely analogous to the functions of the human mind within the framework of strict dualism. The distinctively human virtue of justice can really only be attributed to those whose "work" is a work of the mind, namely philosophic wisdom. This is because justice is initially defined as a property of the whole city insofar as it is ruled by the wisdom of the guardian class, which thereby performs its proper function and ensures that the other parts perform theirs. The analogy between the justice of the city and the justice of the individual only holds for the members of the guardian class. They are the only individuals self-ruled by intelligence in the same manner in which the city is ruled. The members of other classes, while they are exhorted to moderation, are nevertheless dominated by either appetite or spirit, neither of which are said to be uniquely human traits.

The starting position for Socrates' defence of this concept of justice in the *Republic* is the conviction that the division of labour is better than the performance by each individual of the work necessary for his or her own maintenance. One basic criterion appears to be simple efficiency. Socrates says "more things are produced and better and more easily when each person performs one task according to his nature, at the right moment, and at leisure from other occupations."[8] One could grant to Plato that people's natures suit them to different tasks without being compelled to conclude that they ought not to be allowed to work at any other task. For that conclusion, either a criterion of efficiency or some other additional criterion is needed. The application to production of a standard based on the Platonic virtue of performing well the task for which one is best suited would be almost indistinguishable in practice from the criterion of efficiency. It would be interesting to speculate as to whether there were features of the Greek mode of production emerging in Plato's day that prompted him to think in these terms. For the purpose of this paper, however, we need only note that a hierarchical division of labour was an elementary feature of his political philosophy, before we go on to see how he uses that idea.

He projects this idea onto the individual soul, where it takes the form of a hierarchy of functions for the parts of the soul. From this it follows easily enough that the best functioning of these parts requires attention to one of them to the exclusion of the others. Practical concerns, as functions of the appetitive soul, were considered ignoble. As such their performance was a positive obstacle to the highest development of intelligence. Courage as well, though better than appetite, was still subordinate to intelligence. According to Plato, it was desirable to have as complete a division of these functions as possible. This general train of thought also helps to account for Plato's view of ruling as a specialized "craft,"[9] by analogy with the division of labour in production. This view is by no means self-evident.

The division of functions between social classes, such as that among the artisan, soldier, and guardian classes, is a necessary measure for enabling some to be free of the toil of practical concerns. But this division only accounts for the productive requirements of society and not the reproductive requirements. If it is noted that human reproduction requires nurture and socialization of dependent individuals for a long period of time, and not just birth, then it follows that this activity comprises a large percentage of the labour expended by adults in society. Hence, if it is good for "the best" to be free from practical concerns, they must be free from the responsibility and trouble of caring for children.[10]

In the history of political theory, the almost universal response to this question of reproduction is to designate the female companions of such men (and females in general) as the ones who ought rightly to perform this task. But Plato avoids this approach completely. It is perhaps not surprising that the explanation for this anomaly may be found in his equally anomalous concept of justice.

His reasons for believing that the guardians should have absolutely no private property turn out to be the same as his reasons for recommending that women and children be "in common." In Book III of the *Republic* Socrates argues that in addition to a proper education, the guardians should have houses and possessions provided for them in such a way as to avoid the evils of interfering with the best performance of their work as guardians, or inciting them to wrong other citizens. To avoid this, none must have any private property and literally no private place. The ownership of houses and lands, according to Plato, automatically means "hating and being hated, plotting being plotted against"; he goes even farther in declaring that private ownership is positively incompatible with guardianship, and transforms guardians from helpers to "enemies and masters."[11]

The self-governance of the guardians, and their totally disinterested rule of the city, require total dedication to the understanding of eternal truths. All personal and private concerns are obstacles to the attainment of these goals. It is virtually a corollary of this that attachment to other individuals, whether sexual lovers, husbands, wives, parents, or children, is also an impediment to this type of personal development. In addition, the total absence of private places and belongings in itself almost precludes the existence of a "private family." I think Plato was aware of these consequences and this may be why he has Socrates casually mention in the same book (Book IV) that for the guardians women and children will be in common.[12]

When this question is examined in detail in Book V, the challenge to Socrates appears to be the question of whether or not it is possible for selected men and women to have the same education and functions. These are the arguments that have received most of the scholarly attention from persons interested in Plato's apparent "feminism." Yet proof that the performance of these functions by women is possible is merely the first step. There must also be arguments to show that it is feasible for women and children to be in common to the male guardians,[13] and most important, arguments to show that these things are beneficial to the city. Socrates postpones the question of feasibility, never to return to it, and proceeds to argue that the absence of private families is beneficial.

Plato consistently uses the language of property relations in discussing this question.[14] This is further evidence for the view that his philosophical concerns cannot properly be called feminist. If Plato were a feminist but merely inconsistent, it strikes me as unlikely that the inconsistency would be quite that gross, especially since the ethical question of ownership of one person by another was a familiar one to Plato. Women and children, according to Plato, must not be *privately owned* by the guardians, but must be held in common. That he considered the ownership of property and of private wives and children almost identical in nature is apparent from passages such as the following: "these present prescriptions prevent them from distracting the city by referring *mine* not to the same but to different things, one man dragging off to his own house anything he is able to acquire apart from the rest . . . and having women and children apart, thus introducing into the state the pleasures and pains of individuals."[15] His reservations about the actual worth of women are suggested by the passage in which Socrates says the lawgiver will "select to give over to (these men) women *as nearly as possible* of the same nature" (my emphasis).[16] If the equality of the sexes were Plato's theoretical concern, he would not have written such a passage.

The greatest good for the city, according to Plato, is that which promotes unity, and the greatest cause of disunity is "when the citizens do not utter in unison such words as 'mine' and 'not mine.'"[17] Private marriage is a powerful opponent of unity in this sense, being an endless source of particular, individual interests not shared by the citizens as a group. Plato states very clearly the opposition of private and public life when he writes that ideally the citizens should "rejoice and grieve alike at the same births and deaths," and that "the individualization of these feelings is a dissolvent."[18] Plato's opinion that wives and children should be "in common" is therefore partly explained by the very oppression of women in Greek society. To the extent that they were virtually pieces of property, it seemed to Plato that they should be held in common like other property.

Interestingly, only at this point does Socrates offer an answer to the long-postponed question of what makes the guardians happy. Once again he groups together property and family relations: "I hesitate, so unseemly are they, even to mention the pettiest troubles of which they would be rid, the flatterings of the rich, the embarrassments and pains of the poor in the bringing-up of their children and the procuring of money for the necessities of life for their households, . . . and all the indignities that they endure in such matters, which are obvious and ignoble and not deserving of mention."[19] Being free of all these concerns, and having the honour of the city, the guardians are said to lead the happiest of lives.

There is some evidence that Plato regarded particular family attachments among the rulers as even more of a threat to the unity of the city than private property, for he names the community of women and children as *the cause* of the unity of the state.[20] Socrates draws an analogy between the unified state and a single living organism, but it appears that the more accurate analogy is between the state and the biological family. It is logically impossible for the guardians to "have one experience of pleasure and pain," but they can have the feelings of loyalty and identity of interest identified with the family, albeit in a moderated form. In arguing for the benefits of his scheme, Socrates suggests that no guardian could think of another as an outsider, because "no matter whom he meets, he will feel that he is meeting a brother, a sister, a father, a mother, a son, a daughter."[21] Plato has attempted to remove the contradiction between public and private life for the guardians by raising familial impulses from the private to the public sphere, where their effect is to promote unity in the state, rather than disunity. These sentiments are thereby transformed in theory from the particular interests of individuals to the level of generality appropriate for citizens.

Since there are to be no monogamous relationships in the guardian class, and all sexual intercourse is to be strictly controlled for eugenic reasons, there is no need for equal numbers of men and women. The best age (20–40) for females to have children is over before the age of guardianship; for men the best age to reproduce is 30 to 55. Obviously Plato was assuming that male guardians would be mated with promising young females, who might or might not subsequently become guardians. The problem for the state of the private family has been eliminated without necessarily granting equality of worth or the full participation in government to both sexes.

The separation of sex and love which is briefly discussed in *Republic* III 21 also supports this interpretation. It is strikingly appropriate for this scheme that when sex and love are separated they both become non-exclusive. Non-sexual love may plausibly extend to all the members of a small community, especially in the rational form that Plato regarded as "the right" love: "sober and harmonious love of the orderly and the beautiful." And sex, denigrated as a mere pleasure of appetite, also becomes non-exclusive. It is the combination of sex and love that is likely to create the "madness" and "extravagant pleasure," as well as the personal attachments, so inimical to virtue and the good of the state. Their separation, besides rendering them non-exclusive, also makes them more appropriately moderate.

In the *Laws*, Plato's recommendations for marriage, sex, and child-rearing are considerably different. Plato has moved from his extraordinary ideas of communal sexual relations and child care to an insistence of strict monogamous marriage. In spite of this apparent about-face, a common strand of thought may be picked up in the reasons he offers in the *Laws* for these different institutions.

There is a passage in the *Laws* which suggests that Plato had *not* changed his mind on these questions since writing the *Republic*, but for some reason felt impelled to offer a less radical scheme of regulations. In the course of discussing the education of both sexes he writes: "Now if we are going to look for an exact realization of our scheme, as we have styled it, it will perhaps never be found, so long as there are private wives, children, and houses . . . Still, if we can secure the second-best conditions, which we are now describing, we shall indeed come off well enough."[22] As in the *Republic*, Plato has grouped together the having of property and the having of wives and children, and has thus not progressed beyond his earlier intuition that wives and children "belong to" men. The function of the "second-best" conditions of marriage and procreation is to ameliorate as far as possible the destructive effects of private families on the city.

According to the Athenian: "While the right regulation of the private households within a society is neglected, it is idle to expect the foundation of public law to be secure."[23] It appears there are several evils liable to befall a city where a private family life is considered a thing apart from public life. For these evils two sources are named. One is simple privacy in the descriptive sense. "The privacy of home life," he writes, "screens from the general observation many little incidents . . . which are not in keeping with a legislator's recommendations."[24] A private upbringing may produce a character which is not appropriate for citizens. This is important because of the primacy of education in Plato's political philosophy.

The other source of evil is the character of women as a group. According to the Athenian, women are "inclined to secrecy and craft" and ought not to be "left to their disorders."[25] Whereas Hegel regarded women as a permanent "enemy within the gates,"[26] Plato appears to have felt that the enemy could be co-opted by making education and the rewards of public life open to them. The *Laws* contains several passages condemning the luxury and worthlessness of women left to their own devices. There is also the observation that "her native disposition is inferior to man's,"[27] which is offered as a reason why women ought to be included in the public table. Plato once again gives no consideration to the most common opinion about this, which has been the imposition of male authority on the family. The fact that this is not even discussed is even more surprising in the *Laws* than it is in the *Republic,* because so many of the conventional trappings of marriage are left untouched in the *Laws.* For example, there is the "right of valid betrothal" by the father, and the payment of dowries, and so on.[28] But even these activities are somewhat altered in nature by the ubiquitous laws, all of which are intended to direct everything for the general good of the city.

There is a suggestion that Plato still considered it desirable for "the best" to transcend as far as possible the limitations of the "natural" social companionship of the biological family. The Athenian is asked to justify his position that women ought to participate in the public table. To do so, he reverts to the most basic principles, observing that there are three universal needs: food, drink, and sex. These, he says, are "unwholesome" in their uneducated condition, and must be diverted from the pleasurable to the good.[29]

This citing of basic principles, however, is not followed up by the sort of profound argument for the inclusion of women in public life that we had been led to expect. What follows is a prescription for the tight regulation and minute supervision of marriage and procreation, in order to divert sexual desire from the pleasurable to the good. Plato does not make explicit the connection between this and the inclusion of women in public life. Detailed regulation of sexual relations does not in itself entail that women and men should perform the same social functions. However, a massive attempt is being made to redirect the activities which have the greatest tendency to be intensely personal and individual concerns. For example, a man must "court the (marital) tie that is for the city's good, not that which most takes his own fancy."[30] Plato obviously felt that the redirection of these sentiments would not be possible so long

as women were excluded from public life, though the connection is obscure in the *Laws.*

The following argument, which is consistent with the interpretation made of the *Republic* as well, may make this connection coherent. So long as men and women are unequal in society, and women are confined to private, family life, any regulation of the family will inevitably be imposed through the authority of the husband. To the extent that there is public supervision of the family, the authority of the husband and father is undermined. By the same token, so long as he is the enforcer, he retains the authority, with its accompanying benefits to him within the private sphere, and his family concerns are an individual pursuit. Such authority requires some material base, which means economic responsibility on his part for the needs of the family. This further reinforces the separation of public and private duties between the sexes. This introduces all the contradictions which Plato has attempted to avoid in connection with reproduction.

Plato has replaced the total elimination of private life for the guardians recommended in the *Republic* by tight regulation of it in the *Laws,* but the desired effect seems to me to be the same. Whereas in the *Republic* he was prepared to insist on the complete absence of contradictory tendencies between public and private life in the city, in the *Laws* he attempts rather to ameliorate them and control them.

NOTES

1. Allan Bloom, for example, takes this position in his Interpretive Essay which prefaces his translation of Plato's *Republic* (New York 1968), following Leo Strauss in *The City and Man* (Chicago 1964). I. M. Crombie, in *An Examination of Plato's Doctrines* I (New York 1962), writes that Plato's discussion of the equality of women "should be read by connoisseurs of *a priori* absurdity" (100).

2. For example, Christine Garside Allen "Plato on Women" *Feminist Studies* II 2/3 (1975), and "Can a Woman be Good in the Same Way as a Man?" *Dialogue* X 3 (1971); Christine Pierce 'Equality: *Republic* v' *Monist* LVII (Jan. 1973).

3. Edith Hamilton and Huntington Cairns eds. *Plato: The Collected Dialogues* (Princeton 1973) 455, 781a

4. Ibid 395c–e, 455c–e, 469d

5. See Julia Annas "Plato's *Republic* and Feminism" *Philosophy* LI (1976) 307–21. She observes "Now it is hardly a feminist argument to claim that women do not have a special sphere because men can outdo them at absolutely everything" (307).

6. *Dialogues: Republic* 466a

7. Ibid 433a

8. Ibid 370c

9. Ibid 421c

10. The analysis here is based on the theory of reproduction outlined in Lynda Lange "Reproduction in Democratic Theory" in J. King-Farlow and W. Shea eds *Contemporary Issues in Political Philosophy* (New York 1976).

11. *Republic* 416d, 417b

12. Ibid 424a

13. Ibid 457d

14. Ibid 424a, 453d, 457d, 458c

15. Ibid 464c–d

16. Ibid 458c

17. Ibid 462c

18. Ibid 462b

19. Ibid 465c

20. Ibid 463c, 464b and d

21. Ibid 403a–c

22. *Dialogues: Laws* 807b

23. Ibid 790b

24. Ibid 788a

25. Ibid 781a

26. Hegel *The Phenomenology of Mind* tr J. B. Baillie (New York 1967) 468

27. *Laws* 781a

28. Ibid 774d–e

29. Ibid 782d–783a

30. Ibid 773b

# 3    The Analects

## CONFUCIUS

1:2. The philosopher Yu said, "They are few who, being filial and fraternal, are fond of offending against their superiors. There have been none who, not liking to offend against their superiors, have been fond of stirring up confusion.

"The superior man bends his attention to what is radical. That being established, all practical courses naturally grow up. Filial piety and fraternal submission!—are they not the root of all benevolent actions?"

1:4. The philosopher Tsang said, "I daily examine myself on three points:— whether, in transacting business for others, I may have been not faithful;— whether, in intercourse with friends, I may have been not sincere;—whether I may have not mastered and practiced the instructions of my teacher."

1:6. The master said, "A youth, when at home, should be filial, and, abroad, respectful to his elders. He should be earnest and truthful. He should overflow in love to all, and cultivate the friendship of the good. When he has time and opportunity, after the performance of these things, he should employ them in polite studies."

1:7. Tsze-hsia said, "If a man withdraws his mind from the love of beauty, and applies it as sincerely to the love of the virtuous; if, in serving his parents, he can exert his utmost strength; if, in serving his prince, he can devote his life; if, in his intercourse with his friends, his words are sincere:—although men say that he has not learned, I will certainly say that he has."

1:11. The Master said, "While a man's father is alive, look at the bent of his will; when his father is dead, look at his conduct. If for three years he does not alter from the way of his father, he may be called filial."

2:4. The Master said, "At fifteen, I had my mind bent on learning.

"At thirty, I stood firm.

"At forty, I had no doubts.

"At fifty, I knew the decrees of Heaven.

"At sixty, my ear was an obedient organ *for the reception of truth.*

"At seventy, I could follow what my heart desired, without transgressing what was right."

4:15. The Master said, "Shan, my doctrine is that of an all-pervading unity." The disciple Tsang replied, "Yes."

The Master went out, and the other disciples asked, saying, "What do his words mean?" Tsang said, "The doctrine of our master is to be true to the principles of our nature and the benevolent exercise of them to others,—this and nothing more."

4:16. The Master said, "The mind of the superior man is conversant with righteousness; the mind of the mean man is conversant with gain."

4:17. The Master said, "When we see men of worth, we should think of equaling them; when we see men of a contrary character, we should turn inwards and examine ourselves."

4:18. The Master said, "In serving his parents, a son may remonstrate with them, but gently; when he sees that they do not incline to follow his advice, he shows an increased degree of reverence, but does not abandon his purpose; and should they punish him, he does not allow himself to murmur."

4:23. The Master said, "The cautious seldom err."

4:24. The Master said, "The superior man wishes to be slow in his speech and earnest in his conduct."

4:25. The Master said, "Virtue is not left to stand alone. He who practices it will have neighbors."

5:11. Tsze-kung said, "What I do not wish men to do to me, I also wish not to do to men." The Master said, "Tsze, you have not attained that."

5:12. Tsze-kung said, "The Master's personal displays of his principles and ordinary descriptions of them may be heard. His discourses about man's nature, and the way of Heaven, cannot be heard."

6:18. The Master said, "They who know the truth are not equal to those who love it, and they who love it are not equal to those who delight in it."

6:20. Fan Ch'ih asked what constituted wisdom. The Master said, "To give one's self earnestly to the duties due to men, and, while respecting spiritual beings, to keep aloof from them, may be called wisdom." He asked about perfect virtue. The Master said, "The man of virtue makes the difficulty to be overcome his first business, and success only a subsequent consideration;—this may be called perfect virtue."

6:25. The Master said, "The superior man, extensively studying all learning, and keeping himself under the restraint of the rules of propriety may thus likewise not overstep what is right."

6:27. The Master said, "Perfect is the virtue which is according to the Constant Mean! Rare for a long time has been its practice among the people."

6:28. Tsze-kung said, "Suppose the case of a man extensively conferring benefits on the people, and able to assist all, what would you say of him? Might he be called perfectly virtuous?" The Master said, "Why speak only of virtue in connection with him? Must he not have the qualities of a sage? Even Yao and Shun were still solicitous about this.*

"Now the man of perfect virtue, wishing to be established himself, seeks also to establish others; wishing to be enlarged himself, he seeks also to enlarge others.

"To be able to judge of others by what is nigh in ourselves;—this may be called the art of virtue."

7:27. The Master said, "There may be those who act without knowing why. I do not do so. Hearing much and selecting what is good and following it; seeing much and keeping it in memory—this is the second style of knowledge."

7:36. The Master said, "The superior man is satisfied and composed; the mean man is always full of distress."

7:37. The Master was mild, and yet dignified; majestic, and yet not fierce; respectful, and yet easy.

8:2. The Master said, "Respectfulness, without the rules of propriety, becomes laborious bustle; carefulness, without the rules of propriety, becomes timidity; boldness, without the rules of propriety, becomes insubordination; straightforwardness, without the rules of propriety, becomes rudeness.

"When those who are in high stations perform well all their duties to their relations, the people are aroused to virtue. When old friends are not neglected by them, the people are preserved from meanness."

8:8. The Master said, "It is by Odes that the mind is aroused.

"It is by the Rules of Propriety that the character is established.

"It is from Music that the finish is received."

8:13. The Master said, "With sincere faith he unites the love of learning; holding firm to death, he is perfecting the excellence of his course.

"Such a one will not enter a tottering state, nor dwell in a disorganized one. When right principles of government prevail in the kingdom, he will show himself; when they are prostrated, he will keep concealed.

"When a country is well governed, poverty and a mean condition are things to be ashamed of. When a country is ill governed, riches and honor are things to be ashamed of."

9:4. There were four things from which the Master was entirely free. He had no foregone conclusions, no arbitrary predetermination, no obstinacy and no egoism.

9:24. The Master said, "Hold faithfulness and sincerity as first principles. Have no friends not equal to yourself. When you have faults, do not fear to abandon them."

11:11. Chi Lu asked about serving the spirits of the dead. The Master said, "While you are not able to serve men, how can you serve their spirits?" Chi Lu added, "I venture to ask about death?" He was answered, "While you do not know life, how can you know about death?"

12:1. Yen Yüan asked about perfect virtue. The Master said, "To subdue one's self and return to propriety, is perfect virtue. If a man can for one day subdue himself and return to propriety, all under heaven will ascribe perfect virtue to him. Is the practice of perfect virtue from a man himself, or is it from others?"

---

* Confucius, Mencius, and other Chinese philosophers refer to Yao, Shun, and Duke Chou as ideal rulers and sages. Yao and Shun were legendary, successive rulers of the third millenium B.C.E. Duke Chou helped to establish the Chou dynasty in 1111 B.C.E.—ED.

Yen Yüan said, "I beg to ask the steps of that process." The Master replied, "Look not at what is contrary to propriety; listen not to what is contrary to propriety; speak not what is contrary to propriety; make no movement which is contrary to propriety." Yen Yüan then said, "Though I am deficient in intelligence and vigor, I will make it my business to practice this lesson."

12:2. Chung-kung asked about perfect virtue. The Master said, "It is, when you go abroad, to behave to everyone as if you were receiving a great guest; to employ the people as if you were assisting at a great sacrifice; not to do to others as you would not wish done to yourself; to have no murmuring against you in the country, and none in the family." Chung-kung said, "Though I am deficient in intelligence and vigor, I will make it my business to practice this lesson."

12:9. The duke Ai inquired of Yu Zo, saying, "The year is one of scarcity, and the returns for expenditure are not sufficient;—what is to be done?"

Yu Zo replied to him, "Why not simply tithe the people?"

"With two tenths," said the duke, "I find them not enough;—how could I do with that system of one tenth?"

Yu Zo answered, "If the people have plenty, their prince will not be left to want alone. If the people are in want, their prince cannot enjoy plenty alone."

12:15. The Master said, "By extensively studying all learning, and keeping himself under the restraint of the rules of propriety, *one* may thus likewise not err from what is right."

12:17. Chi K'ang asked Confucius about government. Confucius replied, "To govern means to rectify. If you lead on the people with correctness, who will dare not to be correct?"

12:22. Fan Ch'ih asked about benevolence. The Master said, "It is to love all men." He asked about knowledge. The Master said, "It is to know all men."

Fan Ch'ih did not immediately understand these answers.

The Master said, "Employ the upright and put aside all the crooked; in this way the crooked can be made to be upright."

Fan Ch'ih retired, and, seeing Tszehsia, he said to him, "A little while ago, I had an interview with our Master, and asked him about knowledge. He said, 'Employ the upright and put aside all the crooked;—in this way, the crooked will be made to be upright.' What did he mean?"

13:6. The Master said, "When a prince's personal conduct is correct, his government is effective without the issuing of orders. If his personal conduct is not correct, he may issue orders, but they will not be followed."

13:9. When the Master went to Wei, Zan Yu acted as driver of his carriage.

The Master observed, "How numerous are the people!"

Yu said, "Since they are thus numerous, what more shall be done for them?" "Enrich them," was the reply.

"And when they have been enriched, what more shall be done?" The Master said, "Teach them."

13:11. The Master said, "'If good men were to govern a country in succession for a hundred years, they would be able to transform the violently bad, and dispense with capital punishments.' True indeed is this saying!"

13:13. The Master said, "If a minister make his own conduct correct, what difficulty will he have in assisting in government? If he cannot rectify himself, what has he to do with rectifying others?"

13:16. The duke of Sheh asked about government.

The Master said, "Good government obtains when those who are near are made happy, and those who are far off are attracted."

13:18. The duke of Sheh informed Confucius, saying, "Among us here are those who may be styled upright in their conduct. If their fathers have stolen a sheep, they will bear witness to the fact."

Confucius said, "Among us, in our part of the country, those who are upright are different from this. The father conceals the misconduct of the son, and the son conceals the misconduct of the father. Uprightness is to be found in this."

13:19. Fan Ch'ih asked about perfect virtue. The Master said, "It is, in retirement, to be sedately grave; in the management of business, to be reverently attentive; in intercourse with others, to be strictly sincere. Though a man go among rude, uncultivated tribes, these qualities may not be neglected."

14:30. The Master said, "The way of the superior man is threefold, but I am not equal to it. Virtuous, he is free from anxieties; wise, he is free from perplexities; bold, he is free from fear."

Tsze-kung said, "Master, that is what you yourself say."

14:36. Someone said, "What do you say concerning the principle that injury should be recompensed with kindness?"

The Master said, "With what then will you recompense kindness?"

"Recompense injury with justice, and recompense kindness with kindness."

15:17. The Master said, "The superior man in everything considers righteousness to be essential. He performs it according to the rules of propriety. He brings it forth in humility. He completes it with sincerity. This is indeed a superior man."

15:18. The Master said, "The superior man is distressed by his want of ability. He is not distressed by men's not knowing him."

15:19. The Master said, "The superior man dislikes the thought of his name not being mentioned after his death."

15:20. The Master said, "What the superior man seeks, is in himself. What the mean man seeks, is in others."

15:21. The Master said, "The superior man is dignified, but does not wrangle. He is sociable, but not a partisan."

15:22. The Master said, "The superior man does not promote a man simply on account of his words, nor does he put aside good words because of the man."

15:23. Tsze-kung asked, saying, "Is there one word which may serve as a rule of practice for all one's life?" The Master said, "Is not RECIPROCITY such a word? What you do not want done to yourself, do not do to others."

15:38. The Master said, "In teaching there should be no distinction of classes."

16:10. Confucius said, "The superior man has nine things which are subjects with him of thoughtful consideration. In regard to the use of his eyes, he is anxious to see clearly. In regard to his ears, he is anxious to hear distinctly. In regard to his countenance, he is anxious that it should be benign. In regard to his demeanor, he is anxious that it should be respectful. In regard to his speech, he is anxious that it should be sincere. In regard to his doing business, he is anxious that it should be reverently careful. In regard to what he doubts about, he is anxious to question others. When he is angry, he thinks of the difficulties [his anger may involve him in]. When he sees gain to be got, he thinks of righteousness."

17:2. The Master said, "By nature, men are nearly alike; by practice, they get to be wide apart."

17:6. Tsze-chang asked Confucius about

perfect virtue. Confucius said, "To be able to practice five things everywhere under heaven constitutes perfect virtue." He begged to ask what they were, and was told, "Gravity, generosity of soul, sincerity, earnestness, and kindness. If you are grave, you will not be treated with disrespect. If you are generous, you will win all. If you are sincere, people will repose trust in you. If you are earnest, you will accomplish much. If you are kind, this will enable you to employ the services of others."

## Recommended Readings

TEXT

Annas, Julia. *An Introduction to Plato's Republic*. Oxford: Oxford University Press, 1981.
Cropsey, Joseph. *Plato's World*. Chicago: University of Chicago Press, 1995.
Cross, R. C., and A. D. Woozley. *Plato's Republic: A Philosophical Commentary*. London: Macmillan, 1964.
Irwin, T. H. *Plato's Ethics*. Oxford: Oxford University Press, 1995.
Kraut, Richard. *Socrates and the State*. Princeton: Princeton University Press, 1984.
Zeitin, Irving, *Plato's Vision*. Englewood Cliffs: Prentice Hall, 1993

FEMINIST PERSPECTIVE

Canto, Monique. "The Politics of Women's Bodies: Reflections on Plato." In *The Female Body in Western Culture: Contemporary Perspectives,* edited by Susan Rubin Suleiman, 339–353. Cambridge, MA: Harvard University Press, 1986.
Dickason, Anna. "Anatomy and Destiny: The Role of Biology in Plato's View of Women." In *Women and Philosophy,* edited by C. Gould and M. Wartofsky, 45–53. New York: Putnam, 1976.
Saxonhouse, Arlene. "The Philosopher and the Female in the Political Thought of Plato." *Political Theory* 4, no.2 (1976).

MULTICULTURAL PERSPECTIVE

Dawson, Raymond. *Confucius*. New York: Hill and Wang, 1981.
Hsu, Leanard. *The Political Philosophy of Confucius*. London: Routledge and Sons, 1932.

# II

---

# *Aristotle and Musonius Rufus*

## Introduction

ARISTOTLE WAS BORN in 384 B.C.E. in the northern Greek city of Stagira in Macedonia. His father, Nicomachus, held the post of physician to Amnytas II, King of Macedonia and father of Philip the Great. When he was eighteen, he entered Plato's Academy, where he studied and taught for approximately twenty years. Plato is said to have considered him "the mind of the school." Nevertheless, after Plato's death, Aristotle was not named to head the Academy, and he decided to leave Athens. He went to Assos in Asia Minor, where he married Pythias. They had a daughter, but after Pythias died, Aristotle took Herpyllis as a mistress and had a son with her, Nicomachus. In 353 B.C.E., Philip of Macedon invited Aristotle to tutor his thirteen-year-old son, Alexander, who was to become Alexander the Great.

During this period, Aristotle renewed his interest in politics, collecting and studying constitutions from around the world. Soon after the death of Philip, Aristotle returned to Athens and began his own school, the Lyceum. In adjacent buildings, Aristotle assembled a large library and a museum of natural history with the help of a grant of money from Alexander and specimens that Alexander had sent in from around his empire. There Aristotle worked for twelve or thirteen years, producing most of the works that survive to this day in the form of lecture notes.

In response to the anti-Macedonian feeling that swept through Greece after the death of Alexander, Aristotle left Athens, lest, as he is said to have put it, the Athenians sin twice against philosophy. He died in Chalis one year later in 322 B.C.E. at the age of sixty-two, leaving behind a will in which he provided for Herpyllis, their son, and his daughter by Pythias, and for the emancipation of his four slaves and their children. He also requested to be buried beside his wife Pythias.

The first selection is from Aristotle's *Nicomachean Ethics* (named after his son, who is supposed to have edited these notes). In this selection, Aristotle tries to provide ethics with a firm foundation. He begins by noting that all human activity aims at some good.

He then argues that for humans, happiness is the ultimate good. Happiness, he claims, is wrongly thought to consist simply in pleasure, wealth, and honor. Rightly understood, Aristotle argues, happiness is the activity of the soul exhibiting the best and most complete excellence or virtue. He further argues that happiness also requires certain external goods like friends, wealth, political power, good birth, children, and beauty.

In this selection, Aristotle identifies happiness with virtuous activity. But is it clear how these two things can or should be identified? Imagine that you are engaged in the following dialogue with Aristotle:

*You:* Why should I be virtuous?

*A:* Well, we agree, don't we, that it is a good thing to be happy?

*You:* Suppose we do.

*A:* It turns out that being virtuous will make you happy. So that is why you should be virtuous.

*You:* But according to the ordinary notion of happiness, it seems possible to be happy without always being virtuous.

*A:* But as I define happiness, being happy is the same as being virtuous.

*You:* But, then, doesn't my original question return in a different form? Why should I seek happiness in your sense and thereby always be virtuous rather than seek happiness in the ordinary sense and only sometimes be virtuous?

*A:* That is an interesting objection.

*You:* Things are even more complicated than I have indicated so far. With respect to the ordinary notion of happiness, what makes you happy can make other people unhappy, and so the question arises: Whose happiness should you pursue, yours or theirs?

*A:* But, as I define happiness, this can never happen. When happiness and virtue are interdefined, there are no conflicts between one person's happiness and the happiness of others.

*You:* But given your definition of happiness, we can still ask the question: Why should I strive to be happy/virtuous in your sense of the term, when it may not make me happy or may not make others happy in the ordinary sense of the term?

*A:* That is another interesting objection.

Does Aristotle have adequate responses to these objections? What do you think?

The second selection is from Aristotle's *Politics*. Here Aristotle begins by noting that the state is a political association that aims at the highest good. He argues that the state arises by nature. So human beings are political animals, and the state is prior to the individual. He then argues that in nature, it is proper for one's soul to rule over one's body, for humans to rule over other animals, and for males to rule over females. In all these cases, the ruler/ruled relationship is for the common good, claims Aristotle. It follows for Aristotle that since natural slaves participate in reason only insofar as they recognize it but do not possess it, they can be properly ruled. Here too the ruler/ruled relationship is supposedly for the common good. The justification for ruling, then, is that the deliberative faculty is not present at all in slaves, in females it is present but ineffective, and in children it is present but undeveloped.

Aristotle's views about women and slaves were very widely held in the classical world; still, there were well-known exceptions, and one of these was Musonius Rufus. Born of an Etruscan family in the town of Volsinii probably sometime before 30 C.E. Rufus is considered one of the founders of Stoic philosophy. In his time, he was compared to Socrates, both in his life and work; modern scholars sometimes refer to him as "the Roman Socrates."[1] As a prominent Stoic philosopher, he fell out of favor with Nero and was executed sometime before 101 C.E.

One of the stories that has come down to us is that when Rufus was lying chained in the prison of Nero, a friend communicated with him, inquiring what he might do to secure his release. Rufus acknowledged his friend's thoughtfulness yet politely but firmly refused assistance. His friend replied, "Socrates the Athenian refused to be released by his friends, and consequently went to trial and was put to death." Rufus answered, "Socrates was put to death because he did not take the trouble to defend himself, but I intend to make my defense. Farewell."[2]

Like Socrates, Rufus left no writings of his own. His views, as we have them, come from reports of his discussions written down many years later by his students. A distinctive feature of Rufus's views is his argument for equality between women and men, found in the selection excerpted here. Obviously, from a feminist perspective, there is much to appreciate in Musonius Rufus's views.

In "Aristotle and the Politicization of the Soul," Elizabeth Spelman argues that Aristotle's attempt to give his political views about the authority of men over women a metaphysical grounding by basing it on the authority of the rational over the irrational parts of the soul is, in fact, circular because the authority of the rational over the irrational parts of the soul is itself explicated in terms of the authority of men over women. However, if we assume that what Aristotle was trying to do here is simply show that natural slavery is justified, using as support for this the authority of men over women and the authority of the rational over the irrational, then his argument would not be circular. Aristotle would simply be assuming what Spelman thought he was trying to prove. Of course, this interpretation would not make Aristotle's argument any more acceptable from a feminist perspective.

The Ewe proverbs selected here are compiled and explained by N. K. Dzobo, a professor of education in Ghana and a member of the Ewe tribe. The Ewe tribe lives in what are now southern Ghana, Togo, and Benin. As one reads these proverbs, one cannot but be impressed by the universality of the moral experience they convey. Obviously, those who think that all morality is relative need to explain why these proverbs seem to have such universal moral authority.

---

1 Cora E. Lutz, "Musonius Rufus: 'The Roman Socrates,'" *Yale Classical Studies* (1947), 3–117; R. Hirzel, *Der Dialog* (Leipzig, 1985), 2:239.
2 Lutz, 3.

# 4          Nicomachean Ethics

ARISTOTLE

*Book I*
CHAPTER I

EVERY SCIENCE and every investigation, and likewise every practical pursuit and undertaking, appears to aim at some good: and consequently the good has been well defined as the object at which all things aim. It is true that a certain variety can be observed among the ends aimed at; sometimes the mere activity of practicing the pursuit is the object of pursuing it, whereas in other cases the end aimed at is some product over and above the pursuit itself; and in the pursuits that aim at certain objects besides their mere practice, those products are essentially superior in value to the activities that produce them. But as there are numerous pursuits and sciences and branches of knowledge, it follows that the ends at which they aim are correspondingly numerous. Medicine aims at producing health, naval architecture at building ships, strategic science at winning victories, economics at acquiring wealth. And many pursuits of this sort are subordinate to some single faculty—for instance bit-making and the other departments of the harness trade are subordinate to the art of horsemanship, and the latter together with every other military activity to the science of strategics, and similarly other arts to different arts again. Now in all these cases the ends of the master sciences are of higher value than the objects of the subordinate ones, the latter being only pursued for the sake of the former. Nor does it make any difference whether the end aimed at by the pursuit is the mere activity of pursuing it or something else besides this, as in the case of the sciences mentioned.

If, therefore, among the ends at which our conduct aims there is one which we will for its own sake, whereas we will the other ends only for the sake of this one, and if we do not choose everything for the sake of some other thing—that would clearly be an endless process, making all desire futile and idle—it is clear that this one ultimate end will be good, and the greatest good. Then will not a knowledge of this ultimate end be of more than theoretic interest? Will it not also have great practical importance for the conduct of life? Shall we not be more likely to attain our needs if like archers we have a target before us to aim at? If this be so, an attempt must be made to ascertain at all events in outline what precisely this supreme good is, and under which of the theoretical or practical sciences it falls.

Now it would be agreed that it must be the subject of the most authoritative of the sciences—the one that is in the fullest sense of the term a master-craft. This term clearly describes the science of politics, since it is that which ordains which of the sciences ought to exist in states and what branches of knowledge the various classes of citizens must study and up to what point; we observe that even the most highly esteemed faculties, such as strategics and domestic economy and oratory, are subordinate to political science. As then this science employs the rest of the sciences, and as it moreover lays down laws prescribing what people are to do and what things they are to abstain from, the end of political science must comprise the ends of the other sciences. Consequently the good of man must be the subject pursued by the science of politics. No doubt it is true that the good is the same for the individual and for the state; but still the good of the state is manifestly a greater and more perfect object both to ascertain and to secure. To procure the good of only a single individual is better than nothing; but to effect the good of a nation or a state is a nobler and more divine achievement.

This then being the object of our present investigation, it is in a sense the science of politics.

The present investigation therefore, as directed to these objects, may be termed political science.

Our treatment of this science will be adequate if it achieves the degree of accuracy that is appropriate to the subject. The same amount of precision is not requisite in every department of philosophy, any more than in every product of the arts and crafts. Questions of right and of justice, which are the matters investigated by political science, involve much difference of opinion and much uncertainty; indeed this has given rise to the view that such things are mere conventions, and not realities in the order of nature. There is a similar uncertainly as to the meaning of the term "good," owing to the fact that good things may often lead to harmful consequences; before now people have been ruined by wealth, and courage has been the undoing of others. Therefore in dealing with subjects and starting from conceptions so indefinite we must be content to obtain not more than a rough outline of the truth, and to reach conclusions which, like the matters dealt with and the principles postulated, have merely a general validity. And accordingly the reader likewise must accept the various views propounded in the same spirit. It is the mark of an educated mind to expect that degree of precision in each department which the nature of the subject allows: to demand rigorous demonstration from a political orator is on a par with accepting plausible probabilities from a mathematician. Also a man judges correctly about matters that are within his personal knowledge, and of these he is a competent student. Consequently while a specialist can make judgements as to his own particular subject it requires a person of all-round education to form competent judgements about things in general. That is why a young man is not a competent student of political science,[1] because he has had no practical experience of the affairs of life, which supply the premises and form the subjects of political theory. Moreover, as he is liable to be guided by his emotions it will be a waste of time for him to attend lectures on Ethics. He will get no profit from them, inasmuch as the real object of ethical instruction is not to impart knowledge but to influence conduct. Nor does it make any difference whether the student is young in years or immature in character; his deficiency is not a matter of age but is due to his living his life and pursuing his various aims under the guidance of emotion. For the immature ethical study is of no value, any more than it is for persons deficient in self-control; but those who regulate their aims and guide their conduct by principle may derive great benefit from the science.

So much by way of preface in regard to the student and to the manner in which our discourse is to be received and the object which we have in view.

To resume: inasmuch as all study and all deliberate action is aimed at some good object, let us state what is the good which is in our view the aim of political science, and what is the highest of the goods obtainable by action.

Now as far as the name goes there is virtual agreement about this among the vast majority of [humankind]. Both ordinary people and persons of trained mind define the good as happiness. But as to what constitutes happiness opinions differ; the answer given by ordinary people is not the same as the verdict of the philosopher. Ordinary men identify happiness with something obvious and visible, such as pleasure or wealth or honour—everybody gives a different definition, and sometimes the same person's own definition alters: when a man has fallen ill he thinks that happiness is health, if he is poor he thinks it is wealth. And when people realise their own ignorance they regard with admiration those who propound some grand theory that is above their heads. The view has been held by some thinkers[2] that besides the many good things alluded to above there also exists something that is good in itself, which is the fundamental cause of the goodness of all the others.

Now to review the whole of these opinions would perhaps be a rather thankless task. It may be enough to examine those that are most widely held, or that appear to have some considerable argument in their favour.

But it is important for us to realise that there is a difference between lines of argument which proceed *from* first principles and those that lead *to* first principles. This was a point properly raised by Plato, who used to ask the question whether the right method is to work down from, or work up to, first principles—just as on a racecourse the runners are either going out from the start to the turning-point at the end of the track or coming back to the finish. A line of argument necessarily starts from something known; but the term "known" has two meanings: some things are known to us, other things are known absolutely. Now presumably we for our part are bound to start from things known to us. Consequently in order to be a competent student of questions of right and justice and of political matters in general, the pupil must himself have been trained in good habits of conduct; for one has to start from facts; and if these be sufficiently clear there will be no need for reasons in addition. The student trained in right conduct knows the principles already, or can easily acquire them. As for one who has neither qualification, let him listen to the verses of Hesiod:

> Best is the man who can himself advise;
> He too is good who hearkeneth to the wise.
> But whoso, being witless, cannot heed
> Another's wisdom, is a dolt indeed![3]

But to resume. To judge by men's mode of living, the mass of [humankind] think that good and happiness consist in pleasure, and consequently are content with a life of mere enjoyment. There are in fact three principle modes of life—the one just mentioned, the life of active citizenship and the life of contemplation. The masses, being utterly servile, obviously prefer the life of mere cattle; and indeed they have some reason for this, inasmuch as many men of high station share the tastes of Sardanapallus.[4] The better people, on the other hand, and men of action, give the highest value to honour, since honour may be said to be the object aimed at in a public career. Neverthe-

less, it would seem that honour is a more superficial thing than the good which we are in search of, because honour seems to depend more on the people who render it than on the person who receives it, whereas we dimly feel that good must be something inherent in oneself and inalienable. Moreover men's object in pursuing honour appears to be to convince themselves of their own worth; at all events they seek to be honoured by persons of insight and by people who are well acquainted with them, and to be honoured for their merit. It therefore seems that at all events in the opinions of these men goodness is more valuable than honour, and probably one may suppose that it has a better claim than honour to be deemed the end at which the life of politics aims. But even virtue appears to lack completeness as an end, inasmuch as it seems to be possible to possess it while one is asleep or living a life of perpetual inactivity, and moreover one can be virtuous and yet suffer extreme sorrow and misfortune; but nobody except for the sake of maintaining a paradox would call a man happy in those circumstances.

However, enough has been said on this topic, which has indeed been sufficiently discussed in popular treatises.[5]

The third life is the life of contemplation, which we shall consider later.

The life of money-making is a cramped way of living, and clearly wealth is not the good we are in search of, as it is only valuable as a means to something else. Consequently a stronger case might be made for the objects previously specified, because they are valued for their own sake; but even they appear to be inadequate, although a great deal of discussion has been devoted to them.

What then is the precise nature of the practicable good which we are investigating? It appears to be one thing in one occupation or profession and another in another: the object pursued in medicine is different from that of military science, and similarly in regard to the other activities. What definition of the term "good" then is applicable to all of them? Perhaps "the object for the sake of attaining which all the subsidiary activities are undertaken." The object pursued in the practice of medicine is health, in a military career victory, in architecture a building—one thing in one pursuit and another in another, but in every occupation and every pursuit it is the end aimed at, since it is for the sake of this that the subsidiary activities in all these pursuits are undertaken. Consequently if there is some one thing which is the end and aim of all practical activities whatsoever, that thing, or if there are several, those things, will constitute the practicable good.

Our argument has therefore come round again by a different route to the point reached before. We must endeavour to render it yet clearer.

Now the objects at which our actions aim are manifestly several, and some of these objects, for instance, money, and instruments in general, we adopt as means to the attainment of something else. This shows that not all the objects we pursue are final ends. But the greatest good manifestly is a final end. Consequently if there is only one thing which is final, that will be the object for which we are now seeking, or if there are several, it will be that one among them which possesses the most complete finality.

Now a thing that is pursued for its own sake we pronounce to be more final than one pursued as a means to some other thing, and a thing that is never desired for the sake of something else we call more final than those which are desired for the sake of something else as well as for their own sake. In fact the absolutely final is something that is always desired on its own account and never as a means for obtaining something else. Now this description appears to apply in the highest degree to happiness, since we always desire happiness for its own sake and never on account of something else; whereas honour and pleasure and intelligence and each of the virtues, though we do indeed desire them on their own account as well, for we should desire each of them even if it produced no external result, we also desire for the sake of happiness, because we believe that they will bring it to us, whereas nobody desires happiness for the sake of those things, nor for anything else but itself.

The same result seems to follow from a consideration of the subject of self-sufficiency, which is felt to be a necessary attribute of the final good. The term self-sufficient denotes not merely being sufficient for oneself alone, as if one lived the life of a hermit, but also being sufficient for the needs of one's parents and children and wife, and one's friends and fellow-countrymen in general, inasmuch as man is by nature a social being.

Yet we are bound to assume some limit in these relationships, since if one extends the connexion to include one's children's children and friends' friends, it will go on *ad infinitum*. But that is a matter which must be deferred for later consideration. Let us define self-sufficiency as the quality which makes life to be desirable and lacking in nothing even when considered by itself; and this quality we assume to belong to happiness. Moreover when we pronounce happiness to be the most desirable of all things, we do not mean that it stands as one in a list of good things—were it so, it would obviously be more desirable in combination with even the smallest of the other goods, inasmuch as that addition would increase the total of good, and of two good things the larger must always be the more desirable.

Thus it appears that happiness is something final and complete in itself, as being the aim and end of all practical activities whatever.

Possibly, however, the student may feel that the statement that happiness is the greatest good is a mere truism, and he may want a clearer explanation of what the precise nature of happiness is. This may perhaps be achieved by ascertaining what is the proper function of man. In the case of flute-players or sculptors or other artists, and generally of all persons who have a particular work to perform, it is felt that their good and their well-being are found in that work. It may be supposed that this similarly holds good in the case of a human being, if we may assume that there is some work which constitutes the proper function of a human being as such. Can it then be the case that whereas a carpenter and a shoemaker have definite functions or businesses to perform, a man as such has none, and is not designed by nature to perform any function? Should we not rather assume that, just as the eye and hand and foot and every part of the body manifestly have functions assigned to them, so also there is a function that belongs to a man, over and above all the special functions that belong to his members? If so, what precisely will that function be? It is clear that the mere activity of living is shared by man even with the vegetable kingdom, whereas we are looking for some function that belongs specially to man. We must therefore set aside the vital activity of nutrition and growth. Next perhaps comes the life of the senses; but this also is manifestly shared by the horse and the ox and all the animals. There remains therefore what may be designated the practical life of the rational faculty.

But the term "rational" life has two meanings: it denotes both the mere possession of reason, and its active exercise. Let us take it that we here mean the latter, as that appears to be the more proper signification of the term. Granted then that the special function of man is the active exercise of the mind's faculties in accordance with rational principle, or at all events not in detachment from rational principle, and that the function of anything, for example, a harper, is generally the same as the function of a good specimen of that thing, for example a good harper (the specification of the function merely being augmented in the latter case with the statement of excellence—a harper is a man who plays the harp, a good harper one who plays the harp well)—granted, I say, the truth of these assumptions, it follows that the good of man consists in the active exercise of the faculties in conformity with excellence or virtue, or if there are several virtues, in conformity with the best and most perfect among them.

Moreover, happiness requires an entire lifetime. One swallow does not make a summer, nor does a single fine day; and similarly one day or a brief period of prosperity does not makes a man supremely fortunate and happy.

Let this then stand as a first sketch of the good, since perhaps our right procedure is to begin by drawing a preliminary outline, and then to fill in the details later on. Given a good outline to start with, it would seem to be within anybody's capac-ity to carry on, and to put in all the details. In discovering these times is a good collaborator; and that is in fact the way in which advances in the arts and crafts have actually been achieved, as anybody is capable of filling in the gaps.

It is also important to bear in mind the warning already given, that we must not expect the same degree of accuracy in every department of study but only so much precision as corresponds with the nature of the particular subject and is proper to the enquiry in hand. A carpenter and a mathematician employ different methods of finding a right angle; the carpenter only aims at such degree of accuracy as is necessary for his work, but the mathematician must arrive at the essential nature and qualities of a right angle, inasmuch as he is a student of truth. In other matters also therefore one must follow the same method, in order that the main task in hand may not be outbalanced by side issues. Nor should we in the case of everything alike expect a statement of the cause *why* the thing is so; in some cases it is enough if we achieve a satisfactory demonstration of the fact *that* it is so. This holds good in regard to first principles: the fact *is* a first principle, a point to start from.

Moreover, first principles are apprehended in various ways, some by the method of induction, some by direct intuition and some by a sort of familiarisation: different methods are used in different cases, and we must endeavour to arrive at each first principle by the method appropriate to its particular nature. Also extreme care must be taken to define the first principles correctly, as they have a most important influence on the subsequent course of the argument. To make a right beginning is more than half the battle, and to start from the right first principle throws light straight away on many of the problems under investigation.

Accordingly, we must examine our first principle[6] not only as a logical conclusion deduced from given premises but also in the light of the opinions currently put forward with regard to it, inasmuch as if a theory is correct, all the data of experience will be in harmony with it, but if it is false they are quickly found to clash with it.

Goods then have been classified in three groups—external goods, goods of the body and goods of the mind; and of these we pronounce the goods of the mind to be good in the most important sense and in the highest degree. But our definition of happiness identifies it with goods of the mind, and so is at all events supported by the classification of goods referred to, which has held the field for a long time and is accepted by philosophers.

Our theory is also correct in speaking of the aim and end as consisting in particular modes of conduct or activities, since this classes happiness among the goods of the mind and not among external goods. And it is in agreement with the popular phrase describing the happy man as a man who "lives well" or "does well," since our formula virtually defines happiness as a form of good living and good conduct.

Indeed the happy man as we describe him appears to possess all the qualifications that are deemed requisite for happiness. Some people identify happiness with virtue, others with prudence or wisdom of some kind, and others with these things or one of them accompanied by pleasure, or not devoid of pleasure; others also include material prosperity. Some of these definitions are widely held and have been current for a long time; others are put forward by a few eminent thinkers. It is not reasonable to suppose that either can be entirely mistaken, but it is probable that the accepted definitions are at least partly, or indeed mainly, correct.

Now our formula agrees with the view that identifies happiness with excellence, or with some particular virtue, inasmuch as activity conforming with excellence presupposes excellence in the agent. Perhaps however it makes an important difference whether the greatest good is judged to consist in possessing excellence or in employing it—whether it is classed as a quality of character or as the exercise of a quality in action. A man may possess a good quality without its producing any good effect, for instance when he is asleep or as in some other way ceased to function; but active virtue cannot be inoperative, since if present it will necessarily be exercised in action, and in good action. The garlands at the Olympic games are not awarded to the handsomest and strongest men present but to the handsomest and strongest who enter for the competitions, as it is among these that the winners are found. Similarly it is people who act rightly that win distinction and credit in life.

Moreover the life of active virtue is intrinsically pleasant. To feel pleasure is a psychological, not a physical experience; and when a man is described as being a "lover" of so and so, it means that the thing in question gives him pleasure: for instance a lover of horses derives pleasure from a horse, and a lover of the theatre from a play; and similarly a lover of justice derives pleasure from just actions, and a lover of virtue from good actions in general. In most cases people's pleasures conflict with one another, because they are not natural pleasures; but lovers of what is noble take pleasure in things that are by nature pleasant, and such is virtuous conduct, so that it is intrinsically pleasant as well as pleasant to them.

In consequence of this their life has no need of pleasure as an external appendage; it contains pleasures within itself. For in addition to what has been said, if a man does not enjoy performing noble actions he is not a good man at all. Nobody would call a man just who did not enjoy acting justly, nor liberal if he did not enjoy acting liberally, and similarly with the other virtues. But if this is so, actions in conformity with virtue will be intrinsically pleasant. Moreover, they are also good and noble; and good and noble in the highest degree, inasmuch as the virtuous man must be a good judge of these matters, and his judgement is as we have said.

Consequently happiness is at once the best and the noblest and the pleasantest thing there is, and these qualities do not exist in separate compartments, as is implied by the inscription at Delos:

> The noblest thing is justice, health the best,
> But getting your desire the pleasantest.

For all these qualities are combined in the highest activities, and it is these activities or the best one among them which according to our definition constitutes happiness. All the same it is manifest that happiness requires external goods in addition, since it is impossible, or at all events difficult, to perform noble actions without resources. Many of them require the aid of friends and of wealth and power in the state. Also a lack of such advantages as good birth or a fine family of children or good looks is a blot on a man's supreme felicity. A very ugly man or one of low birth or without children cannot be classed as completely happy; and still less perhaps can a man whose children or friends are utterly base, or though worthy have died.

As we said then, happiness seems to require prosperity of this kind in addition; and this has led some people to identify happiness with good fortune.

This leads to the question whether happiness is something that can be acquired by study or by a course of training, or whether it comes to us by divine dispensation, or merely by chance.

Now if there is any other thing that comes to men as a gift of providence, it is reasonable to hold that happiness is given us by the gods, and more so than any other of man's possessions inasmuch as it is the best of them all. This however is perhaps a matter that belongs more properly to another line of enquiry. But even if happiness is not sent by the gods but acquired by virtue or by some process of study or training, it is nevertheless among the most divine things that exist; for it would seem that the prize of virtue must be the highest aim and end, and something divine and supremely felicitous.

It would also be something that is widely distributed, since everybody not incapable of virtue could acquire it by means of study and by effort. And if happiness thus acquired is a better thing than prosperity due to fortune, it is reasonable to assume that it can be won in this way, inasmuch as nature's order is planned on the best lines possible, as likewise are works of art and the various products of design, and especially those of the highest form of design. For the greatest and noblest of all matters to be attributable to mere

chance would seem too great a violation of the harmony of things.

This definition of happiness also throws light on our question how happiness may be attained. We pronounced it to be the active exercise of the faculties on certain lines; whereas goods of the other kinds are only requisite as a foundation, or else serviceable as auxiliaries and for their utility as instruments.

Moreover this would be in agreement with what we said at the outset, when we laid it down that the end at which statesmanship aims is the highest good, and that the statesman's chief concern is to produce a certain type of character in the citizens, namely to make them good men and capable of noble action. This justifies our refusal to apply the term "happy" to an ox, or a horse or any other animal, inasmuch as no animal is capable of taking part in activity of the kind indicated. For this reason a child also cannot be happy in the proper sense, as he is not old enough to engage in conduct of this nature. When we speak of children as happy we are merely congratulating them on their promise for the future. For happiness, as we said, complete excellence is requisite; and also a life prolonged to its full limit, inasmuch as in the course of a lifetime a great many reverses and accidents of all sorts may occur, and it is possible that the most prosperous man may encounter severe misfortunes in old age, as legend tells us was the case with Priam in the tale of Troy. No one applies the term happy to one who encounters such disasters and comes to such a miserable end as Priam.

Must we then pronounce no other human being either to be happy as long as he is alive? Must we, as Solon[7] puts it, "first see the end"? And if we are indeed to make that rule, is it really true that a man can be happy when he is dead? Is not that a very curious thing to assert, especially for us who define happiness as a form of activity? If on the other hand we refuse to speak of a dead man as happy, and if Solon does not mean this, but that only when a man is dead, and not before, is it safe to congratulate him as finally beyond the reach of evils and misfortunes, yet even this is open to question. It is generally believed that both good and evil can befall a man when he is dead, just as they can happen to one who is still alive without his being aware of them—for instance, the bestowal of honour and of dishonour, and the successes and misfortunes of his children and descendants. In regard to these moreover a difficulty arises; it is possible that a man may have lived in complete happiness till old age and have made an equally happy end, but that then a number of reverses may befall his descendants, some of whom may be good men and may enjoy a life in accordance with their deserts, but others the contrary; and these descendants may obviously stand in any degree of proximity to the ancestor in question. Now it would be strange if a dead man's condition altered together with that of his descendants, and if he became happy and miserable in turn; but it would also be strange if no cognizance at all of people's fortunes reached their forebears, even over a limited period.

However, we must return to the previous question raised, whether it is possible to pronounce a man happy before his death, as that may perhaps throw light on the problem before us now. It may be essential to see how a man's life ends, and perhaps even then he cannot be congratulated as being happy but only as having been happy previously. Yet surely it is paradoxical to say that happiness does not really belong to him at the time when he is in fact happy, and to refuse to call people happy while they are alive, on the ground that fortune may change, but we think of happiness as something stable and not easily liable to change, whereas the wheel of fortune often turns full circle in the same person's experience. It is clear that if we are to wait attendance on the changes of fortune we shall frequently apply the terms happy and miserable to the same person by turns, and so make out our happy man to be

Chameleon-hued, built on no firm foundation.

Or is it a complete mistake merely to wait in attendance on fortune? Good and evil do not con-sist in fortune's vicissitudes, although these do form a part of life, as we said. Happiness is controlled by activities in conformity with virtue and unhappiness by their opposite.

Moreover the difficulty now raised affords further support to our definition. No human actions possess such a degree of permanence as the active exercise of virtue. This appears to be more permanent than our possession of the various branches of knowledge; and even of these the most permanent are the more honourable, because men blest by fortune find their life in them most fully and most continuously. This indeed seems to be the reason why knowledge of this kind when once acquired is not easily forgotten. . . .

May we not then confidently define the happy man as "the man who is engaged in virtuous activities and who is adequately equipped with external goods"? Or ought we to add, "and who is destined to continue to live thus not for some chance period but throughout his whole lifetime, and to end his life correspondingly"? We must add this proviso because the future is hidden from us, and happiness as we define it is an aim and end, something possessing complete finality of every sort and kind. If this is so, it will be possible to ascribe felicity to persons still living who possess and are destined to continue to possess the blessings specified above—though of course we mean felicity on the human level. . . .

Happiness then we define as the active exercise of the mind in conformity with perfect goodness or virtue. It will therefore be necessary to investigate the nature of virtue, as to do so will contribute to our understanding the nature of happiness. Moreover it appears that the true statesman must have made a special study of virtue, because it is his aim to make the citizens good and law-abiding men. As an example of this we have the law-givers of Crete and of Sparta, and the other founders of constitutions recorded in history. But if the investigation of the nature of virtue is a duty of statesmanship, that investigation will clearly fit in with the original plan of this treatise.

Now obviously the virtue which we have to investigate is human virtue, inasmuch as the good and the happiness which we set out to discover were human good and human happiness. And by human virtue we mean not bodily excellence but goodness of the mind; and happiness also we define as an activity of the mind. This being so, it is clearly necessary for the statesman to have some acquaintance with psychology—just as the doctor in order to cure an affection of the eye or any other part of the body must know their anatomical structure. This background of science is even more essential for the statesman, inasmuch as statesmanship is a higher and more honourable profession than medicine; and even physicians of a high standard give a great deal of time to studying anatomy and physiology. Consequently the student of politics must study psychology, though he must study it for its bearing on politics, and only so far as is sufficient to throw light on the matters which fall to him to consider. To pursue it to a greater degree of precision would be a more laborious task than his purpose requires.

NOTES

1. This dictum floated down to Shakespeare, *Troilus and Cressida* II, ii, 165:

> Most like young men, whom Aristotle thought unfit to hear moral philosophy.

2. Plato and the Academy.
3. From *Works and Days,* an early agricultural epic.
4. A mythical Assyrian king; two versions of his epitaph are recorded, one containing the words "Eat, drink, play, since all else is not worth that snap of the fingers," the other ending "I have what I ate, and the delightful deeds of wantonness and love in which I shared; but all my wealth is vanished."
5. There follows a technical refutation, omitted in this version, of Plato's Theory of Ideas as a basis for ethics.
6. I.e., the definition of happiness given above.
7. Herodotus I, 30–33. The famous sage visited Croesus, king of Sardis, and was shown his treasures, but refused to call him the happiest of [humankind] while he was still alive and therefore still liable to misfortune. "It is necessary to see the end of every matter, and to discover how it is going to turn out; for to many men God has given a glimpse of prosperity and then has destroyed them root and branch."

# 5          The Politics

ARISTOTLE

## Book I

I

EVERY STATE IS A COMMUNITY of some kind, and every community is established with a view to some good; for everyone always acts in order to obtain that which they think good. But, if all communities aim at some good, the state or political community, which is the highest of all, and which embraces all the rest, aims at good in a greater degree than any other, and at the highest good.

Some people think that the qualifications of a statesman, king, householder, and master are the same, and that they differ, not in kind, but only in the number of their subjects. For example, the rule over a few is called a master; over more, the manager of a household; over a still larger number, a statesman or king, as if there were no difference between a great household and a small state. The distinction which is made between the king and the statesman is as follows: When the government is personal, the ruler is a king; when, according to the rules of the political science, the citizens rule and are ruled in turn, then he is called a statesman.

But all this is a mistake, as will be evident to

anyone who considers the matter according to the method which has hitherto guided us. As in other departments of science, so in politics, the compound should always be resolved into the simple elements or least parts of the whole. We must therefore look at the elements of which the state is composed, in order that we may see in what the different kinds of rule differ from one another, and whether any scientific result can be attained about each one of them.

## 2

He who thus considers things in their first growth and origin, whether a state or anything else, will obtain the clearest view of them. In the first place there must be a union of those who cannot exist without each other; namely, of male and female, that the race may continue (and this is a union which is formed, not of choice, but because, in common with other animals and with plants, [humankind] have a natural desire to leave behind them an image of themselves), and of natural ruler and subject, that both may be preserved. For that which can foresee by the exercise of mind is by nature lord and master, and that which can with its body give effect to such foresight is a subject, and by nature a slave; hence master and slave have the same interest. Now nature has distinguished between the female and the slave. For she is not . . . like the smith who fashions the Delphian knife for many uses; she makes each thing for a single use, and every instrument is best made when intended for one and not for many uses. But among barbarians no distinction is made between women and slaves, because there is no natural ruler among them: they are a community of slaves, male and female. That is why the poets say,—

> It is meet that Hellenes should rule over barbarians;

as if they thought that the barbarian and the slave were by nature one.

Out of these two relationships the first thing to arise is the family, and Hesiod is right when he says,—

> First house and wife and an ox for the plough,

for the ox is the poor man's slave. The family is the association established by nature for the supply of men's everyday wants, and the members of it are called by Charondas, "companions of the cupboard," and by Epimenides the Cretan, "companions of the manger." But when several families are united, and the association aims at something more than the supply of daily needs, the first society to be formed is the village. And the most natural form of the village appears to be that of a colony from the family, composed of the children and grandchildren, who are said to be "suckled with the same milk." And this is the reason why Hellenic states were originally governed by kings; because the Hellenes were under royal rule before they came together, as the barbarians still are. Every family is ruled by the eldest, and therefore in the colonies of the family the kingly form of government prevailed because they were of the same blood. As Homer says:

> Each one gives law to his children and to his wives.

For they lived dispersedly, as was the manner in ancient times. That is why men say that the Gods have a king, because they themselves either are or were in ancient times under the rule of a king. For they imagine not only the forms of the Gods but their ways of life to be like their own.

When several villages are united in a single complete community, large enough to be nearly or quite self-sufficing, the state comes into existence, originating in the bare needs of life, and continuing in existence for the sake of a good life. And therefore, if the earlier forms of society are natural, so is the state, for it is the end of them, and the nature of a thing is its end. For what each thing is when fully developed, we call its nature, whether we are speaking of a man, a horse, or a family. Besides, the final cause and end of a thing is the best, and to be self-sufficing is the end and the best.

Hence it is evident that the state is a creation of nature, and that man is by nature a political animal. And he who by nature and not be mere accident is without a state, is either a bad man or above humanity; he is like the

Tribeless, lawless, heartless one,

whom Homer denounces—the natural outcast is forthwith a lover of war; he may be compared to an isolated piece at draughts.

Now, that man is more of a political animal than bees or any other gregarious animals is evident. Nature, as we often say, makes nothing in vain, and man is the only animal who has the gift of speech. And whereas mere voice is but an indication of pleasure or pain, and is therefore found in other animals (for their nature attains to the perception of pleasure and pain and the intimation of them to one another, and no further), the power of speech is intended to set forth the expedient and inexpedient, and therefore likewise the just and the unjust. And it is a characteristic of man that he alone has any sense of good and evil, of just and unjust, and the like, and the association of living being who have this sense makes a family and a state.

Further, the state is by nature clearly prior to the family and to the individual, since the whole is of necessity prior to the part; for example, if the whole body be destroyed, there will be no foot or hand, except homonymously, as we might speak of a stone hand; for when destroyed the hand will be no better than that. But things are defined by their function and power; and we ought not to say that they are the same when they no longer have their proper quality, but only that they are homonymous. The proof that the state is a creation of nature and prior to the individual is that the individual, when isolated, is not self-sufficing; and therefore he is like a part in relation to the whole. But he who is unable to live in society, or who has no need because he is sufficient for himself, must be either a beast or a god: he is no part of a state. A social instinct is implanted in all men by nature, and yet he who first founded the state was the greatest of benefactors. For man, when perfected, is the best of animals, but, when separated from

law and justice, he is the worst of all; since armed injustice is the more dangerous, and he is equipped at birth with arms, meant to be used by intelligence and excellence, which he may use for the worst ends. That is why, if he has not excellence, he is the most unholy and the most savage of animals, and the most full of lust and gluttony. But justice is the bond of men in states; for the administration of justice, which is the determination of what is just, is the principle of order in political society.

### 3

Seeing then that the state is made up of households, before speaking of the state we must speak of the management of the household. The parts of household management correspond to the persons who compose the household, and a complete household consists of slaves and freemen. Now we should begin by examining everything in its fewest possible elements; and the first and fewest possible parts of a family are master and slave, husband and wife, father and children. We have therefore to consider what each of these three relations is and ought to be:—I mean the relation of master and servant, the marriage relation (the conjunction of man and wife has no name of its own), and thirdly, the paternal relation (this also has no proper name). And there is another element of a household, the so-called art of getting wealth, which, according to some, is identical with household management, according to others, a principal part of it; the nature of this art will also have to be considered by us.

Let us first speak of master and slave, looking to the needs of practical life and also seeking to attain some better theory of their relation than exists at present. For some are of the opinion that the rule of a master is a science, and that the management of a household, and the mastership of slaves, and the political and royal rule, as I was saying at the outset, are all the same. Others affirm that the rule of a master over slaves is contrary to nature, and that the distinction between slave and freeman exists by convention only, and not by nature; and being an interference with nature is therefore unjust.

## 4

Property is a part of the household, and the art of acquiring property is a part of the art of managing the household; for no man can live well, or indeed live at all, unless he is provided with necessaries. And as in the arts which have a definite sphere the workers must have their own proper instruments for the accomplishment of their work, so it is in the management of a household. Now instruments are of various sorts; some are living, others lifeless; in the rudder, the pilot of a ship has a lifeless, in the look-out man, a living instrument; for in the arts the servant is a kind of instrument. Thus, too, a possession is an instrument for maintaining life. And so, in the arrangement of the family, a slave is a living possession, and property a number of such instruments; and the servant is himself an instrument for instruments. For if every instrument could accomplish its own work, obeying or anticipating the will of others, like the statues of Daedalus, or the tripods of Hephaestus, which, says the poet,

> of their own accord entered the assembly of the Gods;

if, in like manner, the shuttle would weave and the plectrum touch the lyre, chief workmen would not want servants, nor masters slaves. Now the instruments commonly so called are instruments of production, whilst a possession is an instrument of action. From a shuttle we get something else besides the use of it, whereas of a garment or of a bed there is only the use. Further, as production and action are different in kind, and both require instruments, the instruments which they employ must likewise differ in kind. But life is action and not production, and therefore the slave is the minister of action. Again, a possession is spoken of as a part is spoken of; for the part is not only a part of something else, but wholly belongs to it; and this is also true of a possession. The master is only

the master of the slave; he does not belong to him, whereas the slave is not only the slave of his master, but wholly belongs to him. Hence we see what is the nature and office of a slave; he who is by nature not his own but another's man, is by nature a slave; and he may be said to be another's man who, being a slave, is also a possession. And a possession may be defined as an instrument of action, separable from the possessor.

## 5

But is there anyone thus intended by nature to be a slave, and for whom such a condition is expedient and right, or rather is not all slavery a violation of nature?

There is no difficulty in answering this question, on grounds both of reason and of fact. For that some should rule and others be ruled is a thing not only necessary, but expedient; from the hour of their birth, some are marked out for subjection, others for rule. And there are many kinds both of rulers and subjects (and that rule is the better which is exercised over better subjects—for example, to rule over men is better than to rule over wild beasts; for the work is better which is executed by better workmen, and where one man rules and another is ruled, they may be said to have a work); for in all things which form a composite whole and which are made up of parts, whether continuous or discrete, a distinction between the ruling and the subject element comes to light. Such a duality exists in living creatures, originating from nature as a whole; even in things which have no life there is a ruling principle, as in a musical mode. But perhaps this is matter for a more popular investigation. A living creature consists in the first place of soul and body, and of these two, the one is by nature the ruler and the other the subject. But then we must look for the intentions of nature in things which retain their nature, and not in things which are corrupted. And therefore we must study the man who is in the most perfect state both of body and soul, for in him we shall see the true relation of the two; although in bad or corrupted natures the body will often appear to rule over the soul, because they are in an evil and unnatural condition. At all events we may firstly observe in living creatures both a despotical and a constitutional rule; for the soul rules the body with a despotical rule, whereas the intellect rules the appetites with a constitutional and royal rule. And it is clear that the rule of the soul over the body, and of the mind and the rational element over the passionate, is natural and expedient; whereas the equality of the two or the rule of the inferior is always hurtful. The same holds good of animals in relation to men; for tame animals have a better nature than wild and all tame animals are better off when they are ruled by man; for then they are preserved. Again, the male is by nature superior, and the female inferior; and the one rules, and the other is ruled; this principle, of necessity, extends to all mankind. Where then there is such a difference as that between soul and body, or between men and animals (as in the case of those whose business is to use their body, and who can do nothing better), the lower sort are by nature slaves, and it is better for them as for all inferiors that they should be under the rule of a master. For he who can be, and therefore is, another's, and he who participates in reason enough to apprehend, but not to have, is a slave by nature. Whereas the lower animals cannot even apprehend reason; they obey their passions. And indeed the use made of slaves and of tame animals is not very different; for both with their bodies minister to the needs of life. Nature would like to distinguish between the bodies of freemen and slaves, making the one strong for servile labour, the other upright, and although useless for such services, useful for political life in the arts both of war and peace. But the opposite often happens—that some have the souls and others have the bodies of freemen. And doubtless if men differed from one another in the mere forms of their bodies as much as the statues of the Gods do from men, all would acknowledge that the inferior class should be slaves of the superior. And if this is true of the body, how much more just that a similar distinction should exist in the soul? But the beauty of the body is seen, whereas the beauty of the soul is not seen. It is clear, then, that some men are by nature free, and others slaves, and that for these latter slavery is both expedient and right.

## 6

But that those who take the opposite view have in a certain way right on their side, may be easily seen. For the words slavery and slave are used in two senses. There is a slave or slavery by convention as well as by nature. The convention is a sort of agreement—the convention by which whatever is taken in war is supposed to belong to the victors. But this right many jurists impeach, as they would an orator who brought forward an unconstitutional measure: they detest the notion that, because one man has the power of doing violence and is superior in brute strength, another shall be his slave and subject. Even among philosophers there is a difference of opinion. The origin of the dispute, and what makes the views invade each other's territory, is as follows: in some sense excellence, when furnished with means, has actually the greatest power of exercising force: and as superior power is only found where there is superior excellence of some kind, power seems to imply excellence, and the dispute to be simply one about justice (for it is due to one party identifying justice with goodwill, while the other identifies it with the mere rule of the stronger). If these views are thus set out separately, the other views have no force or plausibility against the view that the superior in excellence ought to rule, or be master. Others, clinging, as they think, simply to a principle of justice (for convention is a sort of justice), assume that slavery in accordance with the custom of war is just, but at the same moment they deny this. For what if the cause of the war be unjust? And again, no one would ever say that he is a slave who is unworthy to be a slave. Were this the case, men of the highest rank would be slaves and the children of slaves if they or their parents chanced to have been taken captive and sold. That is why people do not like to call themselves slaves, but confine the term to foreigners. Yet, in using this language, they really mean the natural slave of whom we spoke at first; for it must be admitted that some are slaves everywhere, others nowhere.

The same principle applies to nobility. People regard themselves as noble everywhere, and not only in their own country, but they deem foreigners noble only when at home, thereby implying that there are two sorts of nobility and freedom, the one absolute, the other relative. The Helen of Theodectes says:

> Who would presume to call me servant who am
> on both sides sprung from the stem of the Gods?

What does this mean but that they distinguish freedom and slavery, noble and humble birth, by the two principles of good and evil? They think that as men and animals beget men and animals, so from good men a good man springs. Nature intends to do this often but cannot.

We see then that there is some foundation for this difference of opinion, and that all are not either slaves by nature or freemen by nature, and also that there is in some cases a marked distinction between the two classes, rendering it expedient and right for the one to be slaves and the others to be masters: the one practising obedience, the others exercising the authority and lordship which nature intended them to have. The abuse of this authority is injurious to both: for the interests of part and whole, of body and soul, are the same, and the slave is a part of the master, a living but separated part of his bodily frame. Hence, where the relation of master and slave between them is natural they are friends and have a common interest, but where it rests merely on convention and force the reverse is true.

7

The previous remarks are quite enough to show that the rule of a master is not a constitutional rule, and that all the different kinds of rule are not, as some affirm, the same as each other. For there is one rule exercised over subjects who are by nature free, another over subjects who are by nature slaves. The rule of a household is a monarchy, for every house is under one head: whereas constitutional rule is a government of freemen and equals. The master is not called a master because he has science, but because he is of a certain character, and the same remark applies to the slave and the freeman. Still there may be a science for the master and a science for the slave. The science of the slave would be such as the man of Syracuse taught, who made money by instructing slaves in their ordinary duties. And such a knowledge may be carried further, so as to include cookery and similar menial arts. For some duties are of the more necessary, others of the more honourable sort; as the proverb says, "slave before slave, master before master." But all such branches of knowledge are servile. There is likewise a science of the master, which teaches the use of slaves; for the master as such is concerned, not with the acquisition, but with the use of them. Yet this science is not anything great or wonderful; for the master need only know how to order that which the slave must know how to execute. Hence those who are in a position which places them above toil have stewards who attend to their households while they occupy themselves with philosophy or with politics. But the art of acquiring slaves, I mean of justly acquiring them, differs both from the art of the master and the art of slave, being a species of hunting or war. Enough of the distinction between master and slave.

8

Let us now inquire into property generally, and into the art of getting wealth, in accordance with our usual method, for a slave has been shown to be a part of property. The first question is whether the art of getting wealth is the same as the art of managing a household or a part of it, or instrumental to it; and if the last, whether in the way that the art of making shuttles is instrumental to the art of weaving, or in the way that the casting of bronze is instrumental to the art of the statuary, for they are not instrumental in the same way, but the one provides tools and the other material; and by material I mean the substratum out of which any work is made; thus wool is the material of the weaver, bronze of the statuary. Now it is easy to see that the art of household management is not identical with the art of getting wealth, for the one uses the material which the other provides. For the art which uses household stores can be no other than the art of household management. There is, however, a doubt whether the art of getting wealth is a part of household management or a distinct art. If the getter of wealth has to consider whence wealth and property can be procured, but there are many sorts of property and riches, then are [farming], and the care and provision of food in general, parts of the art of household management or distinct arts? Again, there are many sorts of foods, and therefore there are many kinds of lives both of animals and men; they must all have food, and the differences in their food have made differences in their ways of life. For of beasts, some are gregarious, others are solitary; they live in the way which is best adapted to sustain them, accordingly as they are carnivorous or herbivorous or omnivorous: and their habits are determined for them by nature with regard to their ease and choice of food. But the same things are not naturally pleasant to all of them; and therefore the lives of carnivorous or herbivorous animals further differ among themselves. In the lives of men too there is a great difference. The laziest are shepherds, who lead an idle life, and get their subsistence without trouble from tame animals; their flocks having to wander from place to place in search of pasture, they are compelled to follow them, cultivating a sort of living farm. Others support themselves by hunting, which is of different kinds. Some, for example, are brigands, others, who dwell near lakes or marshes or rivers or a sea in which there are fish, are fishermen, and others live by the pursuit of birds or wild beasts. The greater number obtain a living from the cultivated fruits of the soil. Such are the modes of subsistence which prevail among those whose industry springs up of itself, and whose food is not acquired by exchange and retail trade—there is the shepherd, the [farmer], the brigand, the fisherman, the hunter. Some gain a comfortable maintenance out of two employments, eking out the deficiencies of one of them by another: thus the life of a shepherd may be combined with that of a brigand, the life of a farmer with that of a hunter. Other modes of life are similarly combined in any way which the needs of men may require. Property, in the sense of a bare livelihood, seems to be given by nature herself to all, both when they are first born, and when they are grown up. For some animals bring forth, together with their offspring, so much food as will last until they are able to supply themselves: of this the vermiparous or oviparous animals are an instance; and the viviparous animals have up to a certain time a supply of food for their young in themselves, which is called milk. In like manner we may infer that, after the birth of animals, plants exist for their sake, and that the other animals exist for the sake of man, the tame for use and food, the wild, if not all, at least the greater part of them, for food, and for the provision of clothing and various instruments. Now if nature makes nothing incomplete, and nothing in vain, the inference must be that she has made all animals for the sake of man. And so, from one point of view, the art of war is a natural art of acquisition, for the art of acquisition includes hunting, an art which we ought to practise against wild beasts, and against men who, though intended by nature to be governed, will not submit; for war of such a kind is naturally just.

Of the art of acquisition then there is one kind which by nature is a part of the management of a household, in so far as the art of household management must either find ready to hand, or itself provide, such things necessary to life, and useful for the community of the family or state, as can be stored. They are the elements of true riches; for the amount of property which is needed for a good life is not unlimited, although Solon in one of his poems says that

No bound of riches has been fixed for man.

But there is a boundary fixed, just as there is in the other arts; for the instruments of any art are never unlimited, either in number or size, and riches may be defined as a number of instruments to be used in a household or in a state. And so we see that there is a natural art of acquisition which is practised by managers of households and by statesmen, and the reason for this.

9

There is another variety of the art of acquisition which is commonly and rightly called an art of wealth-getting, and has in fact suggested the notion that riches and property have no limit. Being nearly connected with the preceding, it is often identified with it. But though they are not very different, neither are they the same. The kind already described is given by nature, the other is gained by experience and art.

Let us begin our discussion of the question with the following considerations. Of everything which we possess there are two uses: both belong to the thing as such, but not in the same manner, for one is the proper, and the other the improper use of it. For example, a shoe is used for wear, and is used for exchange; both are uses of the shoe. He who gives a shoe in exchange for money or food to him who wants one, does indeed use the shoe as a shoe, but this is not its proper use, for a shoe is not made to be an object of barter. The same may be said of all possessions, for the art of exchange extends to all of them, and it arises at first from what is natural, from the circumstance that some have too little, others too much. Hence we may infer that retail trade is not a natural part of the art of getting wealth; had it been so, men would have ceased to exchange when they had enough. In the first community, indeed, which is the family, this art is obviously of no use, but it begins to be useful when the society increases. For the members of the family originally had all things in common; later, when the family divided into parts, the parts shared in many things, and different parts in different things, which they had to give in exchange for what they wanted, a kind of barter which is still practised among barbarous nations who exchange with one another the necessaries of life and nothing more; giving and receiving wine, for example, in exchange for corn, and the like. This sort of barter is not part of the wealth-getting art and is not contrary to nature, but is needed for the satisfaction of men's natural wants. The other form of exchange grew, as might have been inferred, out of this one. When the inhabitants of one country became more dependent on those of another, and they imported what they needed, and exported what they had too much of, money necessarily came into use. For the various necessaries of life are not easily carried about, and hence men agreed to employ in their dealings with each other something which was intrinsically useful and easily applicable to the purposes of life, for example, iron, silver, and the like. Of this the value was at first measured simply by size and weight, but in process of time they put a stamp upon it, to save the trouble of weighing and to mark the value.

When the use of coin had once been discovered, out of the barter of necessary articles arose the other art of wealth-getting, namely, retail trade; which was at first probably a simple matter, but became more complicated as soon as men learned by experience whence and by what exchanges the greatest profit might be made. Originating in the use of coin, the art of getting wealth is generally thought to be chiefly concerned with it, and to be the art which produces riches and wealth, having to consider how they may be accumulated. Indeed, riches is assumed by many to be only a quantity of coin, because the arts of getting wealth and retail trade are concerned with coin. Others maintain that coined money is a mere sham, a thing not natural, but conventional only, because, if the users substitute another commodity for it, it is worthless, and because it is not useful as a means to any of the necessities of life, and, indeed, he who is rich in coin may often be in want of necessary food. But how can that be wealth of which a man may have a great abundance and yet perish with hunger, like Midas in the fable, whose insatiable prayer turned everything that was set before him into gold?

Hence men seek after a better notion of riches and of the art of getting wealth, and they are right. For natural riches and the natural art of wealth-getting are a different thing; in their true form they are part of the management of a household; whereas retail trade is the art of producing wealth, not in every way, but by exchange. And it is thought to be concerned with coin; for coin is the unit of exchange and the limit of it. And there is no bound to the riches which spring from this art of wealth-getting. As in the art of medicine there is no limit to the pursuit of health, and as in the other arts there is no limit to the pursuit of their several ends, for they aim at accomplishing their ends to the uttermost (but of the means there is a limit, for the end is always the limit), so, too, in this art of wealth-getting there is no limit of the end, which is riches of the spurious kind, and the acquisition of wealth. But the art of wealth-getting which consists in household management, on the other hand, has a limit; the unlimited acquisition of wealth is not its business. And, therefore, from one point of view, all riches must have a limit; nevertheless, as a matter of fact, we find the opposite to be the case; for all getters of wealth increase their hoard of coin without limit. The source of the confusion is the near connexion between the two kinds of wealth-getting; in both, the instrument is the same, although the use is different, and so they pass into one another; for each is a use of the same property, but with a difference: accumulation is the end in the one case, but there is a further end in the other. Hence some persons are led to believe that getting wealth is the object of household management, and the whole idea of their lives is that they ought either to increase their money without limit, or at any rate not to lose it. The origin of this disposition in men is that they are intent upon living only, and not upon living well; and, as their desires are unlimited, they also desire that the means of gratifying them should be without limit. Those who do aim at a good life seek the means of obtaining bodily pleasures; and, since the enjoyment of these appears to depend on property, they are absorbed in getting wealth: and so there arises the second species of wealth-getting. For, as their enjoyment is in excess, they seek an art which produces the excess of enjoyment; and, if they are not able to supply their pleasures by the art of getting wealth, they try other causes, using in turn every faculty in a manner contrary to nature. The quality of courage, for example, is not intended to make wealth, but to inspire confidence; neither is this the aim of the general's or of the physician's art; but the one aims at victory and the other at health. Nevertheless, some men turn every quality or art into a means of getting wealth; this they conceive to be the end, and to the promotion of the end they think all things must contribute.

Thus, then, we have considered the art of wealth-getting which is unnecessary, and why men want it; and also the necessary art of wealth-getting, which we have seen to be different from the other, and to be a natural part of the art of managing a household, concerned with the provision of food, not, however, like the former kind, unlimited, but having a limit.

10

And we have found the answer to our original question, Whether the art of wealth-getting is the business of the manager of a household and of the statesman or not their business?—viz. that it is an art which is presupposed by them. For political science does not make men, but takes from nature and uses them; and nature provides them with food from the element of earth, air, or sea. At this stage begins the duty of the manager of a household, who has to order the things which nature supplies;—he may be compared to the weaver who has not to make but to use wool, and to know what sort of wool is good and serviceable or bad and unserviceable. Were this otherwise, it would be difficult to see why the art of wealth-getting is a part of the management of a household and the art of medicine not; for surely the members of a household must have health just as they must have life or any other necessary. And as from one point of view the master of the house and the ruler of the state have to consider about health, from another point of view not they but the physician; so in one way the art of household management, in another way the subordinate art, has to consider about money. But, strictly speaking, as I have already said, the means of life must be provided beforehand by nature; for the business of nature is to furnish food to that which is born, and the food of the offspring always remains over in the parent. Wherefore the art of making money out of fruits and animals is always natural.

Of the two sorts of money-making one, as I have just said, is a part of household management, the other is retail trade: the former necessary and honourable, the latter a kind of exchange which is justly censured; for it is unnatural, and a mode by which men gain from one another. The most hated sort, and with the greatest reason, is usury, which makes a gain out of money itself, and not from the natural use of it. For money was intended to be used in exchange, but not to increase at interest. And this term usury, which means the birth of money because the offspring resembles the parent. Wherefore of all modes of making money this is the most unnatural. . . .

## 12

Of household management we have seen that there are three parts—one is the rule of a master over slaves, which has been discussed already, another of a father, and the third of a husband. A husband and father rules over wife and children, both free, but the rule differs, the rule over his children being a royal, over his wife a constitutional rule. For although there may be exceptions to the order of nature, the male is by nature fitter for command than the female, just as the elder and full-grown is superior to the younger and more immature. But in most constitutional states the citizens rule and are ruled by turns, for the idea of a constitutional state implies that the natures of the citizens are equal, and do not differ at all. Nevertheless, when one rules and the other is ruled we endeavour to create a difference of outward forms and names and titles of respect, which may be illustrated by the saying of Amasis about his foot-pan. The relation of the male to the female is of this kind, but there the inequality is permanent. The rule of a father over his children is royal, for he receives both love and the respect due to age, exercising a kind of royal power. And therefore Homer has appropriately called Zeus "father of Gods and men," because he is the king of them all. For a king is the natural superior of his subjects, but he should be of the same kin or kind with them, and such is the relation of elder and younger, of father and son.

## 13

Thus it is clear that household management attends more to men than to the acquisition of inanimate things, and to human excellence more than to the excellence of property which we call wealth, and to the virtue of freemen more than to the virtue of slaves. A question may indeed be raised, whether there is any excellence at all in a slave beyond merely instrumental and ministerial qualities—whether he can have the virtues of temperance, courage, justice, and the like; or whether slaves possess only bodily and ministerial qualities. And, whichever way we answer the question, a difficulty arises; for, if they have virtue, in what will they differ from freemen? On the other hand, since they are men and share in reason, it seems absurd to say that they have no virtue. A similar question may be raised about women and children, whether they too have virtues: ought a woman to be temperate and brave and just, and is a child to be called temperate, and intemperate, or not? So in general we may ask about the natural ruler, and the natural subject, whether they have the same or different virtues. For a noble nature is equally required in both, but if so, why should one of them always rule, and the other always be ruled? Nor can we say that this is a question of degree, for the difference between ruler and subject is a difference of kind, and therefore not of degree; yet how strange is the supposition that the one ought, and that the other ought not, to have virtue! For if the ruler is intemperate and unjust, how can he rule well? If the subject, how can he obey well? If he be licentious and cowardly, he will certainly not do his duty. It is evident, therefore, that both of them must have a share of virtue, but varying according to their various natures. And this is at once indicated by the soul, in which one part naturally rules, and the other is subject, and the virtue of the ruler we maintain to be different from that of the subject;—the one being the virtue of the rational, and the other of the irrational part. Now, it is obvious that the same principle applies generally, and therefore almost all things rule and are ruled according to nature. But the kind of rule differs;—the freeman rules over the slave after another manner from that in which the male rules over the female, or the man over the child; although the parts of the soul are present in all of them, they are present in different degrees. For the slave has no deliberative faculty at all; the woman has, but it is without authority,[1] and the child has, but it is immature. So it must necessarily be with the moral virtues also; all may be supposed to partake of them, but only in such manner and degree as is required by each for the fulfilment of his duty. Hence the ruler ought to have moral virtue in perfection, for his duty is entirely that of a master artificer, and the master artificer is reason; the subjects, on the other hand, require only that measure of virtue which is proper to each of them. Clearly, then, moral virtue belongs to all of them; but the temperance of a man and of a woman, or the courage and justice of a man and of a woman, are not, as Socrates maintained, the same; the courage of a man is shown in commanding, of a woman in obeying. And this holds of all other virtues, as will be more clearly seen if we look at them in detail, for those who say generally that virtue consists in a good disposition of the soul, or in doing rightly, or the like, only deceive themselves. Far better than such definitions is their mode of speaking, who, like Gorgias, enumerate the virtues. All classes must be deemed to have their special attributes; as the poet says of women,

Silence is a woman's glory,

but this is not equally the glory of man. The child is imperfect, and therefore obviously his virtue is not relative to himself alone, but to the perfect man and to his teacher,[2] and in like manner the virtue of the slave is relative to a master. Now we determined that a slave is useful for the wants of life, and therefore he will obviously require only so much virtue as will prevent him from failing in his duty through cowardice and intemperance. Someone will ask whether, if what we are saying is true, virtue will not be required also in the artisans, for they often fail in their work through misconduct? But is there not a great difference in the two cases? For the slave shares in his master's life; the artisan is less closely connected with him, and only attains excellence in proportion as he becomes a slave, [i.e., is under the direction of a master]. The meaner sort of mechanic has a special and separate slavery; and whereas the slave exists by nature, not so the shoemaker or other artisan. It is manifest, then, that the master ought to be the source of excellence in the slave; but not merely because he possesses the art which trains him in his duties. Wherefore they are mistaken who forbid us to converse with slaves and say that we should employ command only,[3] for slaves stand even more in need of admonition than children.

The relations of husband and wife, parent and child, their several virtues, what in their intercourse with one another is good, and what is evil, and how we may pursue the good and escape the evil, will have to be discussed when we speak of the different forms of government. For, inasmuch as every family is a part of a state, and these relationships are the parts of a family, the virtue of the part must have regard to the virtue of the whole. And therefore women and children must be trained by education with an eye to the state, if the virtues of either of them are supposed to make any difference in the virtues of the state. And they must make a difference: for the children grow up to be citizens, and half the free persons in a state are women.[4]

Of these matters, enough has been said; of what remains, let us speak at another time. Regarding, then, our present enquiry as complete, we will make a new beginning. And, first, let us examine the various theories of a perfect state.

NOTES

1. Or, ineffective.
2. "His father who guides him" (Bernays).
3. Plato Laws, vi. 777.
4. Plato Laws, vi. 781 B.

# 6    Discourses

MUSONIUS RUFUS

## That Man is Born with an Inclination toward Virtue

ALL OF US, HE USED TO SAY, are so fashioned by nature that we can live our lives free from error and nobly; not that one can and another cannot, but all. The clearest evidence of this is the fact that lawgivers lay down for all alike what may be done and forbid what may not be done, exempting from punishment no one who disobeys or does wrong, not the young nor the old, not the strong nor the weak, not anyone whomsoever. And yet if the whole notion of virtue were something that came to us from without, and we shared no part of it by birth, just as in activities pertaining to the other arts no one who has not learned the art is expected to be free from error, so in like manner in things pertaining to the conduct of life it would not be reasonable to expect anyone to be free from error who had not learned virtue, seeing that virtue is the only thing that saves us from error in daily living. Now in the care of the sick we demand no one but the physician to be free from error, and in handling the lyre no one but the musician, and in managing the helm no one but the pilot, but in the conduct of life it is no longer only the philosopher whom we expect to be free from error, though he alone would seem to be the only one concerned with the study of virtue, but all men alike, including those who have never given any attention to virtue. Clearly, then, there is no explanation for this other than that the human being is born with an inclination toward virtue. And this indeed is strong evidence of the presence of goodness in our nature, that all speak of themselves as having virtue and being good. For take the common man; when asked whether he is stupid or intelligent, not one will confess to being stupid; or again, when asked whether he is just or

unjust, not one will say that he is unjust. In the same way, if one asks him whether he is temperate or intemperate, he replies at once that he is temperate; and finally, if one asks whether he is good or bad, he would say that he is good, even though he can name no teacher of virtue or mention any study or practice of virtue he has ever made. Of what, then, is this evidence if not of the existence of an innate inclination of the human soul toward goodness and nobleness, and of the presence of the seeds of virtue in each one of us? Moreover, because it is entirely to our advantage to be good, some of us deceive ourselves into thinking that we are really good, while others of use are ashamed to admit that we are not. Why then pray, when one who has not learned letters or music or gymnastics never claims to have knowledge of these arts nor makes any pretence of knowing them, and is quite unable even to name a teacher to whom he went, why, I say, does everyone profess that he has virtue? It is because none of those other skills is natural to man, and no human being is born with a natural facility for them, whereas an inclination toward virtue is inborn in each one of us.

## That Women Too Should Study Philosophy

When someone asked him if women too should study philosophy, he began to discourse on the theme that they should, in somewhat the following manner. Women as well as men, he said, have received from the gods the gift of reason, which we use in our dealings with one another and by which we judge whether a thing is good or bad, right or wrong. Likewise the female has the same senses as the male; namely sight, hearing, smell, and the others. Also both have the same parts of the body, and one has nothing more than the other. Moreover, not men alone, but women too, have a natural inclination toward virtue and the capacity for acquiring it, and it is the nature of women no less than men to be pleased by good and just acts and to reject the opposite of these. If this is true, by what reasoning would it ever be appropriate for men to search out and consider how they may lead good lives, which is exactly the study of philosophy, but inappropriate for women? Could it be that it is fitting for men to be good, but not for women? Let us examine in detail the qualities which are suitable for a woman who would lead a good life, for it will appear that each one of them would accrue to her most readily from the study of philosophy. In the first place, a woman must be a good housekeeper; that is a careful accountant of all that pertains to the welfare of her house and capable of directing the household slaves. It is my contention that these are the very qualities which would be present particularly in the woman who studies philosophy, since obviously each of them is a part of life, and philosophy is nothing other than knowledge about life, and the philosopher, as Socrates said, quoting Homer, is constantly engaged in investigating precisely this: "Whatsoever of good and of evil is wrought in thy halls." But above all a woman must be chaste and self-controlled; she must, I mean, be pure in respect of unlawful love, exercise restraint in other pleasures, not be a slave to desire, not be contentious, not lavish in expense, nor extravagant in dress. Such are the works of a virtuous woman, and to them I would add yet these: to control her temper, not to be overcome by grief, and to be superior to uncontrolled emotion of every kind. Now these are the things which the teachings of philosophy transmit, and the person who has learned them and practices them would seem to me to have become a well-ordered and seemly character, whether man or woman. Well then, so much for self-control. As for justice, would not the woman who studies philosophy be just, would she not be a blameless life-partner, would she not be a sympathetic helpmate, would she not be an untiring defender of husband and children, and would she not be entirely free of greed and arrogance? And who better than the

woman trained in philosophy—and she certainly of necessity if she has really acquired philosophy—would be disposed to look upon doing a wrong as worse than suffering one (as much worse as it is the baser), and to regard being worsted as better than gaining an unjust advantage? Moreover, who better than she would love her children more than life itself? What women would be more just than such a one? Now as for courage, certainly it is to be expected that the educated woman will be more courageous than the uneducated, and one who has studied philosophy than one who has not; and she will not therefore submit to anything shameful because of fear of death or unwillingness to face hardship, and she will not be intimidated by anyone because he is of noble birth, or powerful, or wealthy, no, not even if he be the tyrant of her city. For in fact she has schooled herself to be high-minded and to think of death not as an evil and life not as a good, and likewise not to shun hardship and never for a moment to seek ease and indolence. So it is that such a woman is likely to be energetic, strong to endure pain, prepared to nourish her children at her own breast, and to serve her husband with her own hands, and willing to do things which some would consider no better than slaves' work. Would not such a woman be a great help to the man who married her, an ornament to her relatives, and a good example for all who know her? Yes, but I assure you, some will say, that women who associate with philosophers are bound to be arrogant for the most part and presumptuous, in that abandoning their own households and turning to the company of men they practice speeches, talk like sophists, and analyze syllogisms, when they ought to be sitting at home spinning. I should not expect the women who study philosophy to shirk their appointed tasks for mere talk any more than men, but I maintain that their discussions should be conducted for the sake of their practical application. For as there is no merit in the science of medicine unless it conduces to the healing of man's body, so if a philosopher has or teaches reason, it is of no use if it does not contribute to the virtue of man's soul. Above all, we ought to examine the doctrine which we think women who study philosophy ought to follow; we ought to see if the study which presents modesty as the greatest good can make them presumptuous, if the study which is a guide to the greatest self-restraint accustoms them to live heedlessly, if what sets forth intemperance as the greatest evil does not teach self-control, if what represents the management of a household as a virtue does not impel them to manage well their homes. Finally, the teachings of philosophy exhort the woman to be content with her lot and to work with her own hands.

## Should Daughters Receive the Same Education as Sons?

Once when the question arose as to whether or not sons and daughters ought to be given the same education, he remarked that trainers of horses and dogs make no distinction in the training of the male and the female; for female dogs are taught to hunt just as the males are, and one can see no difference in the training of mares, if they are expected to do a horse's work, and the training of stallions. In the case of man, however, it would seem to be felt necessary to employ some special and exceptional training and education for males over females, as if it were not essential that the same virtues should be present in both alike, in man and woman, or as if it were possible to arrive at the same virtues, not through the same, but through different instruction. And yet that there is not one set of virtues for a man and another for a woman is easy to perceive. In the first place, a man must have understanding and so must a woman, or what pray would be the use of a foolish man or woman? Then it is essential for one no less than the other to live justly, since the man who is not just would not be a good citizen, and the woman would not manage her household well if she did not do it justly; but if she is unjust she will wrong her husband like Eriphyle in the story. Again, it is recognized as right for a woman in wedlock to be chaste, and so it is likewise for a man; the law, at all events, decrees the same punishment for com-

mitting adultery as for being taken in adultery. Gluttony, drunkenness, and other related vices, which are vices of excess and bring disgrace upon those guilty of them, show that self-control is most necessary for every human being, male and female alike; for the only way of escape from wantonness is through self-control; there is no other. Perhaps someone may say that courage is a virtue appropriate to men only. That is not so. For a woman too of the right sort must have courage and be wholly free of cowardice, so that she will neither be swayed by hardships nor by fear; otherwise, how will she be said to have self-control, if by threat or force she can be constrained to yield to shame? Nay more, it is necessary for women to be able to repel attack, unless indeed they are willing to appear more cowardly than hens and other female birds which fight with creatures much larger than themselves to defend their young. How then should women not need courage? That women have some prowess in arms the race of the Amazons demonstrated when they defeated many tribes in war. If, therefore, something of this courage is lacking in other women, it is due to lack of use and practice rather than because they were not endowed with it. If then men and women are born with the same virtues, the same type of training and education must, of necessity, befit both men and women. For with every animal and plant whatsoever, proper care must be bestowed upon it to produce the excellence appropriate to it. Is it not true that, if it were necessary under like circumstances for a man and a woman to be able to play the flute, and if, furthermore, both had to do so in order to earn a living, we should give them both exactly the same thorough training in flute playing; and similarly if it were necessary for either to play the harp? Well then, if it is necessary for both to be proficient in the virtue which is appropriate to a human being, that is for both to be able to have understanding, and self-control, and courage, and justice, the one no less than the other, shall we not teach them both alike the art by which a human being becomes good? Yes, certainly we must do that and nothing else. "Come now," I suppose someone will say "do you expect that men should learn spinning the same as women, and that women should take part in gymnastic exercises the same as men?" No, that I should not demand. But I do say that, since in the human race man's constitution is stronger and woman's weaker, tasks should be assigned which are suited to the nature of each; that is the heavier tasks should be given to the stronger and lighter ones to the weaker. Thus spinning and indoor work would be more fitting for women than for men, while gymnastics and outdoor work would be more suitable for men. Occasionally, however, some men might more fittingly handle certain of the lighter tasks and what is generally considered women's work, and again, women might do heavier tasks which seem more appropriate for men whenever conditions of strength, need, or circumstance warranted. For all human tasks, I am inclined to believe, are a common obligation and are common for men and women, and none is necessarily appointed for either one exclusively, but some pursuits are more suited to the nature of one, some to the other, and for this reason some are called men's work and some women's. But whatever things have reference to virtue, these one would properly say are equally appropriate to the nature of both, inasmuch as we agree that virtues are in no respect more fitting for the one than the other. Hence I hold it reasonable that the things which have reference to virtue ought to be taught to male and female alike; and furthermore that straight from infancy they ought to be taught that this is right and that is wrong, and that it is the same for both alike; that this is helpful, that is harmful, that one must do this, one must not do that. From this training understanding is developed in those who learn, boys and girls alike, with no difference. Then they must be inspired with a feeling of shame toward all that is base. When these two qualities have been created within them, man and woman are of necessity self-controlled. And most of all the child who is trained properly, whether boy or girl, must be accustomed to endure hardship, not to fear death, not to be disheartened in the face of any misfortune; he must in short be accustomed to every situation which calls for courage. Now courage, it was demonstrated above, should be present in women too. Furthermore to shun selfishness and to have high regard for fairness and, being a human being, to wish to help and to be unwilling to harm one's fellow men is the noblest lesson, and it makes those who learn it just. What reason is there why it is more appropriate for a man to learn this? Certainly if it is fitting for women to be just, it is necessary for both to learn the same lessons which are in the highest degree appropriate to the character of each and supremely important. If it happens that a man knows a little something about a certain skill and a woman not, or again she knows something and he not, that suggests no difference in the education of either. But about the all-important things let not one know and the other not, but let them know the same things. If you ask me what doctrine produces such an education, I shall reply that as without philosophy no man would be properly educated, so no woman would be. I do not mean that women should possess technical skill and acuteness in argument. It would be quite superfluous, since they will use philosophy for the ends of their life as women. Even in men I do not prize this accomplishment too highly. I only urge that they should acquire from philosophy goodness in conduct and nobility of character. Now in very truth philosophy is training in nobility of character and nothing else.

# 7    Aristotle and the Politicization of the Soul

ELIZABETH V. SPELMAN

IN BOOK I OF THE *Politics* Aristotle argues that men are by nature the rulers of women. The conclusion of the argument, which has to do with relationships *between* people—in particular, political relationships between men and women—is said to be based on what is known about relationships *within* people: in particular, relationships between the rational and irrational elements of the human soul. That is, this part of Aristotle's political theory is said to rest on his metaphysics or theory of the soul. I hope to show that not the least of the reasons for examining Aristotle's argument is that doing so sheds light on the question of whether metaphysical positions are politically innocent. To ask this question is a defining if not necessarily a distinguishing characteristic of a feminist perspective in philosophy.

Aristotle's argument is outlined briefly in Part I. In Part II I begin examination of the argument by describing Aristotle's theory of the soul, noting especially the kind of authority which, according to Aristotle, the rational part of the soul has over the irrational part. In Part III I observe that when he tries to make use of his view about the authority of the rational part of the soul over the irrational part, to defend his view about the authority of men over women, Aristotle ends up contradicting his view about the authority of the rational part. In Part IV I argue that Aristotle's attempt to justify the authority of men over women by reference to the authority of the rational part over the irrational part is in any event circular: a close reading of the texts shows that both understanding what it means to talk about relations of authority between parts of the soul, and establishing that one part has authority over another, depends on understanding what it means to talk about relations of authority between classes of persons (including those between men and women), and on

establishing or assuming that certain classes do have authority over others—in particular, that men have authority over women. Aristotle makes clear to us what the relation between the rational and irrational parts of the soul is, by reference to the very same political relationships he hopes to justify by reference to the soul. Part V concludes with some comments on the nature of Aristotle's argument and the nature of my response to him.

Aristotle's argument about the natural authority of men over women is very close to his arguments about the natural authority of masters over slaves, fathers over children, "intellectuals" over laborers, and is offered simultaneously with those arguments in the *Politics*. Though my examination focuses mainly on Aristotle's view of women, the scope of Aristotle's argument is a reminder that oppressive attitudes towards women have close connections to oppressive attitudes towards other groups or classes, that the oppression of women is related in theory as well as in practice to the oppression of other groups.

## I

One of the requirements of a state is that some rule and some be ruled:

> there must be a union of those who cannot exist without each other; . . . of natural ruler and subject, that both may be preserved. (P 1252a25–32)

And this means in particular, Aristotle says, that men are to rule women, masters are to rule slaves, fathers are to rule children. But why? The mere principle that some are to rule and some are to be ruled doesn't itself tell us who is to rule whom. Aristotle is untroubled by the ideas that humans are to rule animals, because he believes that animals' lack of reason establishes their inferiority to humans and disqualifies them from eligibility to rule. But all humans *qua* humans have reason and "share in the rational principle" (P 1259b27). So to what grounds must one move in order to establish the inferior and subordinate status of women vis-à-vis men, slaves vis-à-vis masters, children vis-à-vis fathers?

Well, says Aristotle, fortunately, "the very constitution of the soul has shown us the way" (P 1260a5). The soul has two main parts or elements, the rational and the irrational, and it is "natural and expedient" for the rational to rule over the irrational (P 1254b4ff.).[1] Just so, men are to rule women, for in women the deliberative capacity of the rational element is without authority—it is easily overruled by the irrational element. In similar fashion, masters are to rule slaves, for while slaves, in virtue of the rational element in their souls, can hear and obey orders, they really don't have the capacity to deliberate. Indeed all that distinguishes slaves from nonhuman beasts of burden is that they, unlike beasts, have just enough reason to understand the results of the masters' deliberations; otherwise their capacities are identical to those of the beasts (P 1254b19ff.). Fathers are to rule children, because although children have the capacity to deliberate that is associated with the rational element of the soul, this capacity is immature (P 1260a6–15).

It is, then, by reference to the relationships between the rational parts of the soul that Aristotle tries to justify his view that certain classes of beings are naturally subordinate to others. Just as one part of the soul stands in a certain relationship to another, so one class of beings stands in a certain relationship to another class. But this is a bare outline of the argument. In order to understand Aristotle's argument thoroughly, we have to understand in more detail how he describes the workings of the parts of the soul and their relationship to one another (Part II). We also have to understand just how he moves from a description of the parts of the soul to a description of the parts of the state (Part III).

## II

We have to turn to the *Nicomachean Ethics* as well as to parts of the *Politics* to fill in the details of Aristotle's description of the relationship between the rational and irrational parts of the soul. A central feature of his depiction of that relationship is that it is a relationship of authority. The rational part is supposed to rule the irrational part. This is an authority intended for it and vested in it by nature (P 1254b7–8), though Aristotle both explicitly and implicitly allows that the rational part is not always fully empowered to exercize that authority: as we've seen, Aristotle says that in the case of women, slaves and children, the rational part does *not* rule the irrational part (as we shall soon see, we have to ask whether it is even *supposed* to, in the case of women, slaves, and children). Even in adult male masters, sometimes the irrational part is not ruled by the rational part; if that weren't so, Aristotle presumably would not have thought it necessary, as he does in the *Ethics* and the *Politics,* to give instructions about the importance of the rational part remaining in control and command. Hence when Aristotle talks about the rule of the rational part of the soul over the irrational part, he cannot be said to be merely pointing out that what happens in one part of the soul determines what happens in another part in some mechanical fashion. In fact, if this is what Aristotle meant by the rule of the rational over the irrational part, then he would have to say that the irrational part sometimes rules over the irrational part; but he explicitly resists this when he suggests that sometimes the irrational part "appears" to rule over the rational part even when it really doesn't (P 1254b). So the rule or authority he ascribes to the rational part must have to do with entitlement: the rational part has the right to, or ought to, or is intended by nature to, rule the irrational part, even if that isn't always what happens.

The first thing, then, to note about Aristotle's description of the relation between the rational and irrational parts of the soul is that it is a relationship of ruler and subject. But, again, this relationship is not described in merely mechanical terms, as if something in one part of us moves or clicks or fires. As soon as he begins to characterize the rule of the soul over the body, or of the rational part of the soul over the irrational part, Aristotle turns to the language of persons and politics: such rule is despotical, or constitutional, or royal (P 1254b3–5; when the parts of the soul are properly aligned, the rational part dictates or commands, and the irrational part obeys—in the way in which a child obeys its father (NE 1102b30–1103a4). Indeed the relationship between the parts of the soul is treated by Aristotle in most of the *Nicomachean Ethics* and the *Politics* as if it were a relationship between political entities, not as if it were between impersonal, quasi-organic parts. He not only describes the parts of the soul in language applicable to persons or agents; he sometimes speaks of the parts of the soul by analogy to *particular* persons or kinds of persons:

> as the child should live according to the direction of his tutor, so the appetitive element should live according to rational principle (NE 1119b14) the nature of appetite is illustrated by what the poets call Aphrodite, "guile-weaving daughter of Cyprus." (NE 1149b17)

The relationship of master and servant or that of husband and wife show us

> the ratios in which the part of the soul that has a rational principle stands to the irrational part. (NE 1138b5–12)

In fact Aristotle goes so far as to suggest the *identification* of the person with a part of the soul:

> the things men have done on a rational principle are thought most properly their own acts and voluntary acts. That this is the man himself, then, or is so more than anything else, is plain . . . (NE 1168b35ff.; cf. 1166a17ff.)

Indeed, sometimes he depicts reason as another person to whom the person owes obedience:

> reason in each of its possessors chooses what is best for itself and the good man obeys his reason. (NE 1169a17–18)

In sum, Aristotle's depiction of the relationship between the parts of the soul is a highly personal-

ized (or anthropomorphized) and politicized one. One reason this is so noticeable is that Aristotle here fails to respect his own admonitions in the *De Anima*[2] about not personalizing the parts or functions of the soul. There, in a manner familiar to students of 20th-century Anglo-American philosophy, Aristotle suggests we remember that predicates which apply to persons in virtue of having souls nevertheless apply to the *persons* and not to their souls: the person is angry, not the soul or a part of the soul; the person thinks, not the soul or a part of it (*De Anima*, 408b14, 408b27). But his own warning is not heeded here, for Aristotle treats the parts of the soul as if they were persons or agents themselves, and in particular as if they were persons standing in political relations to one another: relations apparently best described in terms such as constitutional or royal ruler; obedient or resistant subject; master and slave.

Having looked at Aristotle's description of the soul, we must now look at the way in which he makes use of this description to justify his view that women are naturally subordinate to men.

### III

As we have seen, in the *Politics* Aristotle turns to the constitution of the soul in order to justify his view that certain classes of beings are by nature to rule over other classes. He wants us to see that just as the irrational part of the soul is subordinate by nature to the rational part, so women are subordinate by nature to men.

We must remember here that Aristotle's claim about the natural subordination of the irrational part to the rational part, about the authority of the rational part over the irrational part, can only be understood as a claim about entitlement, for sometimes, even in free men, the irrational part in fact is not controlled by the rational part. It is unnatural for the irrational part not to listen to and obey the rational part, for it is intended by nature to do so (P 1254b4ff.). With this in mind, let's spell out Aristotle's argument.

Aristotle's claim about the soul is that

(a) In the soul, the rational part by nature rules or has authority over (but does not always control) the irrational part.

Now Aristotle wants to use (a) to argue that understanding the nature of the authority of the rational part over the irrational part shows us the nature of the authority of men over women. So he wants to argue, on the basis of (a), that

(b) In the state, men by nature rule or have authority over women.

But why does Aristotle associate men with the rational part and women with the irrational part of the soul? Because, he holds,

(c) In men's souls, the rational part by nature rules or has authority over the irrational part.

while

(d) In women's souls, the rational part by nature does not rule or have authority over the irrational part.

Or is it that

(e) In women's souls, the irrational part by nature rules or has authority over the rational part?

While (c) seems straightforward, both (d) and (e) seem to be uninvited guests, given Aristotle's insistence and dependence on (a). Does Aristotle hold that in the case of women, the lack of authority in the rational part is tantamount to the assumption of authority in the irrational part (as in (e))? Aristotle certainly must hold at least (d), for in the case of women, he says, the deliberative capacity is without authority and the irrational part actually controls or overwhelms the rational part. So even if Aristotle is not committed here to the view (e) that in women the irrational part is supposed to rule (parallel to his claim that in free men the rational part is supposed to rule), he must by saying (d) that in the case of women the rational part is not supposed to rule, it is not supposed to have authority. For his claim is not just that women *happen* to be subordinate to men; they are intended by nature to be subordinate to men. (Just as those who are to rule are rulers by nature,

so those who are to be ruled are subjects by nature.) And nature could not succeed in this intention with respect to those who are subordinate unless nature at least intended the rational part to be without authority in women. On Aristotle's own reckoning, women are subordinate to men by nature; that by virtue of which women are naturally subordinate to men must be, of course, something intended by nature; so the lack of authority in women's rational element must be intended by nature. In short, women are by nature unnatural.

In light of this, the eager remark by some Aristotelian scholars,[3] that Aristotle's view about the relation between men and women is not merely a comment on or reflection on the *status quo*, takes on special significance. For in one sense that is quite right: in saying that women are subordinate to men, Aristotle was not merely making an observation on the world around him. For insofar as that observation is correct, nature, according to Aristotle, has gotten her way (recall that Aristotle doesn't think this always happens, e.g., P 1254a–b). The rational element in women doesn't just happen to be without authority; for if that were the case, there would be no way to distinguish between the natural condition of a woman and the unnatural condition of a free man who is, for example, overindulgent: in the latter case, the rational part of the man's soul doesn't happen to exercise its authority, though it is intended to have authority; while in the former case, the rational part of the woman's soul is without authority but is not intended to have authority; if it were intended to have authority it wouldn't be in a woman!

But now Aristotle's argument is in deep trouble. For he *begins* his argument by saying that nature intends the rational part of the soul to have authority over the irrational part. But in order to get from there to the claim that nature intends men to rule over women, he has *also* to say that nature intends the rational part of the soul not to have authority over the irrational part, in the case of women. The merely contingent lack of authority of the rational part of someone's soul would not establish the claim that the person is naturally subordinate to someone else. Those who are naturally subordinate must be, on Aristotle's own reckoning, those in whom we can say that nature intended their rational part not to have authority.

Aristotle's problem is not merely that in order to generate the conclusion he wishes to reach, he has to deny one of his central premises. That is, the problem is not merely that in order to reach the conclusion that women are by nature subordinate to men, he has to deny that the rational part of the soul by nature rules over the irrational part. Let us look at the argument once again. He says that just as the rational part of the soul is to rule the irrational part, so men are to rule women. As we've seen, this requires the association of rationality with men and irrationality with women. But on what grounds does he make these associations? Well, as we noted, he makes them on the grounds that nature intended rationally to rule in men, and intended rationality not to rule in women. But this is merely begging the question, unless he can explain how he knows that nature intended this. His only possible reply to this is that in men rationality prevails and in women it does not. But even if true this wouldn't justify the view that is what nature intends—for as we've seen, Aristotle himself points out that the mere fact of the dominance of one part of the soul over the other, or of one group of people over another, is never proof that this is the way things ought to be according to nature.

So Aristotle's argument for the natural subordination of women to men is, to put it charitably, wobbly: he holds an inconsistent view about the natural relationship between the rational and irrational parts of the soul, and he begs the question when he claims that the rational element by nature rules in men but does not in women.

## IV

What I've been analyzing above is Aristotle's attempt to come to a position in political theory on the basis of a metaphysical position. As noted in Part II, that metaphysical position is itself a politicized one insofar as it is deeply etched in the language of political theory. The *dramatis personae* of the soul, and the drama itself, are modelled on the human persons and the human drama found in the political realm. If this is so, then we have to ask what business Aristotle has referring to the kind of relation that exists between metaphysical entities to clarify the kind of relation existing between political entities, if the relationship between the metaphysical entities itself is modelled on the relationship between political entities. In short, is Aristotle's argument from metaphysics to politics circular?

As we saw in Part II, Aristotle refers to relationships between kinds of persons to describe by analogy the relationships that hold between parts of the soul. And on more than one occasion, Aristotle explains why we need analogies to describe intra-psychic relationships. For example, in explaining the kind of relationship there is between the irrational element and the rational element, he says:

> while in the body we see that which moves astray, in the soul we do not. No doubt, however, we must none the less suppose that in the soul too there is something contrary to the rational principle, resisting and opposing it. . . . Now even this seems to have a share in a rational principle, as we said; at any rate in the continent man it obeys the rational principle—and presumably in the temperate and brave man it is still more obedient; for in him it speaks, on all matters, with the same voice as the rational principle. (NE 1102b27–30)

Aristotle says it is hard to tell what kind of soul a man has—whether that of a freeman or slave—because it doesn't always happen that a man with a freeman's soul also has a freeman's body and we cannot view the soul directly.

> And doubtless if men differed from one another in the mere forms of their bodies as much as the statues of the Gods do from men, all would acknowledge that the inferior class should be slaves of the superior. And if this is true of the body, how much more just that a similar distinction should exist in the soul? but the beauty of the body is seen, whereas the beauty of the soul is not seen. (P 1254b32–1255a2)

As he also says, "to gain light on things imperceptible we must use the evidence of sensible things" (NE 1104a13).[4] So Aristotle seems to take it as a given that in order to describe the soul, in order to make sense of relationships among parts of the soul, he has to rely on reference to and analogy to visible things. The particular visible things he relies on, as we've seen, are human beings standing in relationships of power and authority.

To point this out is not to ignore the fact that in general Aristotle's descriptions of the many parts of the world are in hierarchial terms. For example, Aristotle refers to ruler/subject relations as existing not only in the soul and in the state:[5]

> in all things which form a composite whole and which are made up of parts, whether continuous or discrete, a distinction between ruling and subject element comes to light. Such a duality exists in living creatures, but not in them only; it originates in the constitution of the universe; even in things which have no life there is a ruling principle, as in a musical mode. (P 1254a29–34)

However, not all ruling and subject elements need be conceived of as being like persons in political relationships. For example, although Aristotle spends a good bit of time in the *De Anima* discussing the hierarchy of functions in the soul, one is hard put to find evidence of the highly personalized and politicized language that appears both in the NE and the *Politics*. Indeed, as mentioned above (p. 74), he explicitly discourages his readers from thinking of the parts or functions of the soul as if they were themselves persons.[6] In a somewhat similar fashion in the *Metaphysics* he advises us not to take seriously the myths according to which the gods are thought of in anthropomorphic terms (*Meta.* 1074b6ff.). But when he describes the ruling and subject elements in the soul, he immediately recurs to the language of persons and politics. He speaks of the kind of rule of the rational part over the irrational part in terms that have to do with the rule of a person or persons over other persons—"constitutional" or "royal" rule (P 1254b5; cf. NE 1138b5ff.). This fact is very significant. For presumably Aristotle is "bringing

to light" the distinction between the ruling and subject elements among humans by pointing to the distinction between ruling and subject elements in the soul. But the kind of distinction between ruling and subject elements in the soul itself "comes to light" only through relationship of authority among human beings. As described in Part II, Aristotle brings to light what he takes to be the appropriate relationship—the relationship intended by nature—between parts of the soul, by analogy to relationships of authority among humans:

> as the child should live according to the direction of his tutor, so the appetitive element should live according to rational principle. (NE 1119b14)

> Metaphorically and in virtue of a certain resemblance there is a justice, not indeed between a man and himself, but between certain parts of him; yet not every kind of justice but that of master and servant or that of husband and wife. For these are the ratios in which the part of the soul that has a rational principle stands to the irrational part. (NE 1138b5–12)

We have to note that Aristotle does *not* try to justify his view about the natural rule of men over women by reference to a general principle about ruling and subject elements, for he quite explicitly refers us in particular to the constitution of the soul. There we find ruling and subject elements, but they are highly personalized entities whose relationships are described in terms of political relationships among human beings. In light of this, we must conclude that Aristotle's argument for the natural rule of men over women is circular. He argues for the position that men by nature rule women. How do we know that they do? We know this because the rational element of the soul by nature rules the irrational element. And how do we know this? This is where we come full circle: Because men rule women (and also because masters rule slaves, because tutors rule children). In fact the rule of men over women provides us with a means of understanding the kind of relationship among parts of the soul; and, coupled with the assumption that men represent the rational element and women represent the irrational element, it provides us with a means of establishing that in the soul the rational element rules the irrational.

Aristotle took a short-cut in his journey from his metaphysics, from his philosophical psychology, to his political theory: he built the particular relationships of authority he wished to justify on the basis of the metaphysics, into the metaphysics itself. For first of all, the terms used to describe the kind of authority the rational part has over the irrational part are unapologetically borrowed from the terminology of political relationships; yet presumably we are supposed to be relying on an understanding of the kind of authority the rational part has over the irrational part to understand the kind of authority men in the *polis* have over women. And secondly, the location of authority in the soul is supposed to tell us about the location of authority in the *polis*. Yet we are told that the clue that such authority is located in the rational part of the soul over against the irrational part, is that authority is located in men over against women, masters over against slaves, etc.

None of this is to say that if Aristotle hadn't thought men were naturally the rulers of women, he never would have suggested that the rational part of the soul rules the irrational part. Had he believed—ah, the power of counterfactuals to stretch the imagination—had he believed and wished to justify the belief that women were by nature the rulers of men, he might have used such a relationship between them as a model for the relationship between parts of the soul, and have ended up with the same problems of circularity.

I've said that Aristotle's political conclusion is built into his metaphysics. The political conclusion is sexist. Does that mean the metaphysics is sexist? Is the view that the rational part of the soul by nature rules over the irrational part a sexist view? No. What is sexist is not the assertion of the authority of the rational part over the irrational part, but his association of rationality with men and irrationality with women.[7] The metaphysics *is* politicized, however, and this primes it for use to defend political positions that are sexist.

## V

There are several reasons why I've thought it important to focus on Aristotle's argument for the natural subordination of women to men. It is not just that the argument doesn't work.

First of all, in taking a close look at the metaphysical position Aristotle relies on, we begin to see how thoroughly drenched it is with political language and imagery. Even if this were all we could say it would be important to say it, because according to what might be called the theory of philosophical cleanliness, metaphysics and philosophical psychology are supposed to be separate from and cleansed of political considerations: we may be entitled to draw political conclusions from metaphysics or psychology, but particular conclusions are not supposed to shape the metaphysics and psychology itself. So we see Aristotle wanting us to draw conclusions about politics from his psychology—a disingenuous request, and an absurd operation, if he believed that the psychology really was a version of politics to begin with. In a very similar way, I take it, we are nowadays asked to think about what consequences for social and political relations might be drawn, for example, from the studies called sociobiology, and from studies on intelligence: what do studies of human biology, or the animal kingdom, or the human psyche, have to tell us about the appropriateness or inappropriateness of particular social and political relations? ("Dear Dr. Freud, tell us what women's psyches are like so we'll know what to do with their lives!") We are expected to assume, however, that these studies are not themselves influenced by the political or social conclusions which will be said to follow from them. I leave it to students of sociobiology, psychology, and intelligence theory to judge whether and how such studies are biased by political considerations; for example, is it true, as Marshall Sahlins suggests, that "the theory of sociobiology has an intrinsic ideological dimension"; is it true that sociobiology involves "the grounding of human social behaviour in an advanced or scientific notion of organic evolution, which is in its own terms the representation of a cultural form of economic action"?[8] What I hope to have shown here is just how Aristotle's psychology is infused with the language and imagery of politics and how the political conclusions Aristotle wished to draw from his psychology get attached to his psychological premises.

It is important to note in this connection that this paper is not written from the viewpoint of a social historian or an historian of ideas. I have not been attempting here to try to show the connection between Aristotle's philosophical views, on the one hand, and the historical and political context in which he lived, on the other. Rather, I have been trying to show the conceptual and logical connections between Aristotle's political theory and his psychological theory. As mentioned above, the question of their relative dependence on one another has been raised before. Most recently a version of the question has been raised by W. W. Fortenbaugh, in an article called "Aristotle on Women and Slaves."[9] I shall conclude this essay with a response to Fortenbaugh.

Fortenbaugh holds that Aristotle's argument about women and slaves is a "political application of . . . philosophical psychology" (p. 135). He considers the possible charge that Aristotle's use of his psychology to defend a political position is merely an *ad hoc* device to defend the status quo. In response to this, Fortenbaugh represents Aristotle as holding *not* that women are subordinate to men, and that's how we know their deliberative capacity is without authority; but *rather* that women's deliberative capacity is without authority and that is how we know they are subordinate to men. According to Fortenbaugh, Aristotle's claim about the lack of authority which characterizes women's deliberative capacity is based not on "inter-personal relationships" but on "an intra-personal relationship" (*ibid.*): Aristotle "looks within the slave to explain his social position . . . [and] looks within the woman to explain her role and her virtues" (p. 138).

Now since, as we've seen, Aristotle himself said that we can't "look within" to see the soul, we have to ask how, according to Fortenbaugh, we know that in women's soul the deliberative capacity lacks authority. Fortenbaugh's answer would seem to be, "because it is often overruled by her emotions or a logical side" (p. 138). But doesn't that happen in the case of free men also? Yes, the reply must go (see p. 66 above), but that doesn't mean that free men are to occupy subordinate roles, for in them the deliberative capacity is by nature with authority even if it doesn't always exercise it. So it must be that in women, on the other hand, the deliberative capacity is by nature without authority. But how do we know that? Psychology can't tell us that, because it tells us—that is the foundation for Aristotle's political argument, according to Fortenbaugh—that the rational part by nature *does* have such authority. The only reason we've been given for believing not just that women's deliberative capacity lacks authority, but *by nature* lacks this authority, is that if it weren't true women would not be by nature subordinate to men (at least not in terms of the argument of the *Politics*). Hence it is a requirement of Aristotle's politics that in women the deliberative capacity be without authority; it is not a conclusion of his psychology. In fact Fortenbaugh himself says this repeatedly throughout his short article without realizing the damaging import of it for his argument: e.g., he says that Aristotle "demands of women a virtue which reflects their domestic role" (p. 137); "it also seems proper to assign slaves [this applies to women as well] a virtue limited by the demands of their subordinate role" (p. 136). Fortenbaugh is saying here that Aristotle has a certain role in mind for women and slaves, and must thus posit for them and in them a psychological condition befitting their position. This isn't, however, what Fortenbaugh describes his own view as proposing!

Fortenbaugh fails to consider what gets built into Aristotle's psychological theory to make it seem even a plausible basis from which to argue for a political conclusion. He does not here consider the *kind* of authority the rational part is supposed to have over the irrational part. He also

seems to think that the question of the role of irrationality in women is an empirical one (p. 139);
but if it were treated by Aristotle as an empirical
question, then it would have to be conceivable
that women's souls could be like what Aristotle
calls the souls for free men. But if that is conceivable, women could not be said to be *by nature*
subordinate to men.

Aristotle's argument deserves far more serious
attention than Fortenbaugh has given it. I hope to
have provided some of that attention—not only
to show that the argument suffers from difficulties
Fortenbaugh doesn't even imagine, but to point
out that the movement from a metaphysical position to a political position is not always as innocent as it seems.

## NOTES

1. Cf. *Nicomachean Ethics,* Bk. I, Ch. 13.
2. Even in the *De Anima,* as Hamlyn has pointed
out, "Aristotle does not often live up to this remark."
D. W. Hamlyn, *Aristotle's De Anima* (Oxford: Clarendon Press, 1968), p. 81.
3. Most recently, in W. W. Fortenbaugh's "Aristotle
on Slaves and Women," in *Articles on Aristotle: 2. Ethics
and Politics,* eds. Jonathan Barnes, Malcolm Schofield,
Richard Sorabji (London: Duckworth, 1977), pp. 135–
139.
4. I think the view adumbrated here by Aristotle,
about the necessity of referring to publicly observable
beings or things or activities to describe things or activities that are not publicly observable, is complemented
by fairly recent developments in the philosophy of
mind—in particular, by the view roughly associated
with Wittgenstein and with Strawson according to
which the concept of mind or soul is parasitic upon concepts of publicly observable things. I shall not elaborate
on that view here, but wish to point out that it may enable us to see how easily it may happen that we use anthropomorphized language to describe the soul or
mind.
5. Barker thinks that the fact that Aristotle refers to
"a general principle of rule and subordination" saves
him from the charge that he appears to argue in a circle.
Ernest Barker, *The Politics of Aristotle* (Oxford: Clarendon Press, 1952), p. 35, fn. 1. In what follows I explain
why I don't think Barker's view can be sustained.
6. As mentioned in fn. 2 above, Aristotle sometimes
uses personalized language in the *De Anima.* But interestingly it is not also politicized language.
7. That association, as we saw in Section II, is perfectly arbitrary. Moreover, to maintain it, Aristotle has
to hold that in one class, the class of men, the rational
by nature rules, and in another class, that of women, the
rational by nature does not rule. But if there is any class
in whom the rational by nature does not rule, then the
original premise of Aristotle's argument—that the rational by nature rules the irrational—is contradicted.
8. Marshall Sahlins, *The Use and Abuse of Biology:
An Anthropological Critique of Sociobiology* (Ann Arbor:
University of Michigan Press, 1977), pp. xii and xv. See
also Donna Haraway, "Animal Sociology and a Natural
Economy of the Body Politic" (two parts), *Signs* 4
(1978), 21–60, and "The Biological Enterprise: Sex,
Mind and Profit from Human Engineering to Sociobiology," *Radical History Review* 20 (1979), 206–237;
Paul Thom, "Stiff Cheese for Women," *Philosophical Forum* 8 (1976), 94–107.
9. Fortenbaugh, *op. cit.* Further page references in
text are to this article.

# 8          Ewe Proverbs

"The child who breaks a snail's shell cannot break
a tortoise's shell."

*Moral Teaching:* There are certain things any human being can do and others he cannot because
his powers are limited; therefore you must know
the limit of your powers and keep your ambitions
within them. Do not be overambitious. . . .

"The game that you miss, i.e. runs away from a
hunter, is always a big one."

*Moral Teaching:* There is always a tendency to overvalue things that we want but we do not have, and so this proverb is warning against the danger of overvaluing the real worth of what we want badly but cannot get. We must rather learn to appreciate whatever we have.

"Suffering and happiness are twins."

*Moral Teaching:* Life is a mixture of joy and suffering and so we must learn to accept both, and the acceptance of both is a sign of maturity.

"The crab says that when you see it walking clumsily it does not mean that it has lost its way."

*Moral Teaching:* This proverb can be used by anybody whose actions are misunderstood, to warn those who judge him that he had not forgotten the essential principles that guide his behaviour. The proverb warns against the practice of misjudging the basic principles that guide the behaviour of people. . . .

"The virtue cannot cure baldness" (because if it can it would have cured its own baldness).

*Moral Teaching:* In the traditional society some people lay claim to certain powers to cure diseases, to make others wealthy or to make barren women productive. The problem is, how do you test the validity of the claims that they make? This proverb establishes a standard for evaluating such claims. Whatever powers a person claims to have, such powers must be seen to make a practical difference to his own life before his claims could be accepted as valid, and so anybody who accepts such claims without this test of their validity will be considered gullible. The proverb is counselling against the tendency to be gullible in such matters and recommends critical assessment and discernment instead of gullibility. . . .

"There is no rain whose flood can submerge all mountains," i.e., there is an end to every fall of rain.

*Moral Teaching:* There is an end to everything and people are supposed to use this knowledge to guide their behaviour or to comfort themselves in their sufferings. . . .

"A lazy man's farm is a breeding ground for snakes."

*Explanation:* A lazy farmer does not keep his farm clear of weeds and so snakes can easily live there and he may be bitten by them, and this will be regarded as a punishment for his laziness.

*Moral Teaching:* Laziness has its own appropriate punishment and so people must learn to be hardworking so as to avoid the inevitable punishment for laziness.

"The person who goes to draw water does not drink mud."

*Explanation:* In many African homes women and children go out to draw water from common wells or from nearby streams, and in the big towns from public hydrants. Since water-drawers provide water for their homes they themselves will get good water to drink at all cost.

*Moral Teaching:* Those who work will always eat the fruits of their labour. Every just toil will be rewarded and the traditional society uses the truth of the saying as a motivation for hard work. . . .

"A child who resembles his father does not necessarily take after his father."

*Moral Teaching:* Children must *learn to behave* themselves because any physical resemblances between them and their parents will not automatically help them maintain the good name of their parents.

"The antelope does not wear the shoes of an elephant."

*Moral Teaching:* Accept your humble status and do not aspire after greatness that is beyond your reach. This proverb offers a lesson also in the importance of self-acceptance and warns against unrealistic and inordinate aspirations. . . .

"The salt does not praise itself." (It is others who say that salt is good.)

*Moral Teaching:* Do not brag about your goodness but be modest about it. This proverb therefore teaches people to have a humble estimate about their merits.

"However good the hair may be a hat is worn on it."

*Moral Teaching:* This proverb again emphasises the importance of submission to authority. No individual is so good that he cannot be subjected to some kind of authority. Every individual must be prepared to submit himself to one form of authority or another, be it human or divine.

"When you are carrying beef on your head you do not use your feet to catch grasshoppers."

*Explanation:* Beef is a better meat than grasshopper and so if you have beef you do not go after a grasshopper.

*Moral Teaching:* Be able to tell the relative value of things you have and do not spend your energy on less valuable things. This proverb teaches the importance of the right judgment of the relative value of things. . . .

"You clean the ceiling before you clean the floor."

*Moral Teaching:* The simple truth of this statement is used to teach the need for doing things according to a specific form of procedure. Orderly procedure is a social value.

"You do not take a big gourd to a farm that is close by."

*Explanation:* Farmers take water pots or gourds to their farms and usually the size of the pot will depend upon how far the farm is from the village. If the farm is close by you take a small pot of water and if not you take a big one.

*Moral Teaching:* The ability to size up the seriousness of a problem and to work out the appropriate solution to it is at a premium in a society where nothing is allowed to disrupt human relationships. Members of a traditional society are expected to learn to assess accurately the seriousness of a problem, and work out an appropriate solution to it. Over-estimation or under-estimation is considered as a serious defect in an assessment of problems.

"If you are patient enough you can cook a stone and it will become soft."

*Moral Teaching:* With patience you can achieve seemingly impossible tasks. . . .

"A stump that stays in a river for a hundred years does not become a crocodile."

*Moral Teaching:* The Ewe on the whole are very patriotic and they teach their children to love their places of birth. This proverb . . . warns people who go to live in foreign lands that they will never become real citizens of those lands. Even if they stay abroad for a long time they will be regarded as "strangers" and because of this they must learn to love and honour their homelands. . . .

"Knowledge is like a baobab tree (monkey-bread tree) and no one person can embrace it with both arms."

*Explanation:* The baobab tree usually has a very huge base stem and cannot be embraced by the two arms of any human being.

*Moral Teaching:* Knowledge and truth are like the unbounded ocean and so no one individual can claim to have a corner on them. Individuals must therefore be humble in their claims to knowledge and in such a humble frame of mind they can always acquire more knowledge since there is no limit to what any man can know. . . .

"Love is like an egg, it breaks easily" (and so it should be handled carefully).

*Moral Teaching:* The loving relationship is very vulnerable and so must be carefully handled otherwise it will turn into hate or indifference. . . .

"You do not grumble about self-imposed or self-chosen tasks."

*Moral Teaching:* This proverb also teaches cheerfulness and endurance in discharging self-chosen projects. . . .

"The chicken is never declared innocent in the court of hawks" (because the chicken is a prey to hawks).

*Moral Teaching:* This proverb is advising on how to relate to one's enemies and the relationship should be one of non-interference in their affairs. . . .

"The new is woven on to the old."

*Moral Teaching:* In this proverb "the old" stands for the "traditions of the past," and it is maintained that the traditions of the past form the foundation of the present and so traditions should be respected. The proverb is meant to develop a positive attitude to and respect for traditional practices. . . .

"The cotton thread says that it is only as a team that you carry a stone."

*Explanation:* This proverb comes from the practice of kente weavers who, to straighten their cotton threads, make them into a loop and hang them down with a heavy stone from a transverse wooden bar. The loop of many threads can stand the weight of a heavy stone while one single thread cannot.

*Moral Teaching:* There is strength in unity, therefore learn to work together with others.

"One hand cannot hold a bull's horns."

*Explanation:* The "bull's horn" represents any difficult task which cannot be done by one man alone but as he teams up with others they could do it.

*Moral Teaching:* This proverb stresses the need for a united effort in solving difficult problems, and it also advises individuals who trust too much in their own strengths to learn to co-operate with others in solving difficult tasks. The two virtues commended by the two preceding proverbs are—*unity* and *cooperation*. . . .

## Recommended Readings

TEXTS

Broadie, Sarah. *Ethics with Aristotle*. Oxford: Oxford University Press, 1991.

Cooper, John. *Reason and Human Good in Aristotle*. Cambridge, MA: Harvard University Press, 1975; Indianapolis: Hackett, 1986.

Irwin, T. H. *Aristotle's First Principles*. Oxford: Oxford University Press, 1988.

Keyt, David, and Fred Miller, eds. *Essays on Aristotle's Politics*. Oxford: Blackwell's, 1991.

Kraut, Richard. *Aristotle on the Human Good*. Princeton: Princeton University Press, 1989.

Lutz, Cora. "Musonius Rufus: The Roman Socrates." *Yale Classical Studies* (1947):3–117.

Meikle, Scott. Aristotle's *Economic Thought* Oxford: Clarendon Press, 1995.

Miller, Fred. *Nature, Justice, and Rights in Aristotle's Politics* Oxford: Oxford University Press, 1997.

Mulgan, R. G. *Aristotle's Political Theory*. Oxford: Oxford University Press, 1977.

Nussbaum, Martha C. *The Fragility of Goodness*. Cambridge: Cambridge University Press, 1986.

FEMINIST PERSPECTIVE

Allen, Prudence. *The Concept of Woman: The Aristotelian Revolution 750 B.C.–A.D. 1250*. Montreal: Eden Press, 1985.

Fortenbaugh, W. W. "Aristotle on Slaves and Women." In *Articles on Aristotle,* edited by Jonathan Barnes, Malcolm Schofield, and Richard Sorabji, 2:135–139. New York: St. Martin's Press, 1977.

Matthews, Gareth B. "Gender and Essence in Aristotle." In *Women and Philosophy,* edited by Janna L. Thompson. Bundoora, Australia: Australian Association of Philosophy, 1986.

MULTICULTURAL PERSPECTIVE

Appiah, Anthony Kwame. *In My Father's House.* Oxford: Oxford University Press, 1992.
Serequeberhan, Tsenay. *African Philosophy.* New York: Paragon, 1991.

# III

# *Augustine and Christine de Pizan*

## Introduction

AUGUSTINE (AURELIUS AUGUSTINAS) was born in 353 in the north African town of Thagaste (located in what is now Algeria). His mother Monica was a Christian, but his father Patricius remained a pagan until shortly before his death. Augustine and his brother and sister were brought up as Christians, but Augustine, as he describes in his *Confessions,* soon strayed from the fold. Sent to school in Carthage—"a hissing cauldron of lust," as he subsequently described it—he found his boyhood faith giving way to worldly impulses and non-Christian ideas. He lived with a mistress and fathered a son by her whom they named Adeodatus (literally meaning "given by God").

Inspired by reading Cicero to search for wisdom, Augustine joined the sect of Manichaeans, who believed that the world is a scene of perpetual conflict between two forces—one of light and goodness, the other of darkness and evil. But Augustine soon become dissatisfied with their answers to the questions that troubled him, and he turned to Neoplatonism. Later, in rereading St. Paul, he discovered that "whatever truth I had found in the Platonists was set down here as well." Having come to Milan to take up a chair as professor of rhetoric, he happened to hear Bishop Ambrose preach and was impressed by the style and content of his sermons. Monica had also followed Augustine to Milan and urged him to give up his mistress and marry someone respectable. Marriage plans were made, and his mistress was sent back to Africa, leaving Adeodatus with Augustine. But Augustine could not wait for the marriage and took another mistress.

The turning point of Augustine's life came in his thirty-second year. Intellectually reconciled to Christianity yet lacking the strength of will to break with his lustful habits, one summer day in the garden of the house where he was staying, he flung himself beneath a tree and wept. Then from a neighboring house came the voice of a child chanting the words, "Take and read: take and read." He understood this to mean the *New Testament,* and opening it at random he read the first passage on which his eyes fell (Romans 13:13–14):

> Not in reveling or drunkenness, not in debauchery or vice, not in quarrelling or jealousy, but put on the Lord Jesus Christ, and make no provision for the flesh, to gratify its desires.

Suddenly, Augustine's conversion was complete: "In an instant, as I came to the end of the sentence, it was as though the light of confidence flooded into my heart. . . ." Augustine now believed that God had given him the strength to subdue his wayward inclinations: "O Lord . . . it was your power that drained dry the well of corruption in the depths of my heart." So in 387, Augustine and his son were baptized by Ambrose.

In 388, Augustine, Monica, and Adeodatus left Milan to return to Africa, but Monica contracted a fever and died along the way. Augustine established a small monastic community in Tagaste with a plan of devoting himself to writing. But in 391, his bishop, Valerius, prevailed upon him to accept ordination and move to Hippo. When Valerius died in 396, Augustine succeeded him as bishop of Hippo and remained in that post for the rest of his life. Augustine was a prolific writer, and he left us an enormous body of books and pamphets. His *Confessions* and *The City of God* still rank as classic works of Western civilization.

In 430, Hippo was besieged by the Vandals. Choosing to remain in the city to carry out his duties, Augustine died at the age of seventy-six just before the Vandals broke through the city's defenses. When the Vandals burned the city, out of respect for Augustine they left his cathedral and library unscathed.

Augustine wrote *The City of God* against those who blamed Christianity for the sacking of Rome by the Goths in 410 and for the general crumbling of the Roman empire. *The City of God* records the careers of two "cities"—the earthly city, which is composed of the nonsaved, whose eternal destiny is damnation in hell, and the city of God, which is composed of the saved, whose eternal destiny is the beatific vision of God in heaven.

In our selection, Augustine contrasts the perspectives of the two cities regarding the supreme good and evil. Those of the city of God contend that life eternal is the supreme good and death eternal the supreme evil, and those of the earthly city contend that the supreme good and the supreme evil is found in this world. Augustine, however, argues that the occupants of both cities commonly desire peace and that conflict only arises between them when those of the earthly city seek to impose laws of religion that conflict with the divine teachings of the city of God. Yet while Augustine objects to imposing laws of religion on those of the city of God that conflict with Christian teachings, would he similarly object to imposing laws based on Christian teachings on those of the earthly city when they have no grounds for accepting those laws?

In the selection from his *Confessions,* Augustine argues for the subordination of women to men. The most relevant passage from the Bible is *Genesis* 1:27–28:

> God made man in the image of God. God made him; male and female He made them, and blessed them.

This passage strongly implies that woman as well as man reflects the divine image. But Paul implies the contrary, calling man the glory of God, woman the glory of man, and prescribing on that basis different rules of conduct for the two sexes:

> For man indeed ought not to cover his head, forasmuch as he is the image and glory of God; but the woman is the glory of man. (I Corinthians 11:7)

Christine de Pizan was born in 1365 in Venice. Shortly after her birth, her father Tommaso di Benvenuto de Pizzano found favor with Charles V and was invited to join his court in Paris. Encouraged by her father, Christine used her family's close ties to the court to obtain a good education. At the age of fifteen, she married Estienne de Castel, a court notary who also encouraged Christine's learning and literary activity. When her husband died, leaving her at the age of twenty-five with three small children to support, Christine turned to writing to earn her living. She became recognized as an accomplished lyric poet and served as the official biographer of Charles V. She was also the chief correspondent in the quarrel over *The Romance of the Rose,* attacking this central work of medieval literature for being immoral and for slandering women. She produced a vast corpus of works in verse and prose and wrote *The Book of the City of the Ladies* in 1405. Christine's title alludes to Augustine's *City of God,* not to rival that work, but to indicate that she, too, like Augustine, was working within a Christian tradition of political philosophy. The book portrays a walled city constructed for the protection of women from both physical and moral harm. In it, Reason, Justice and Duty, personified as Ladies, offer guidance to women.

In our selection from *The Book of the City of the Ladies,* Christine asks Reason whether God has ever wished to ennoble the mind of woman with the loftiness of the sciences. Reason replies affirmatively, citing examples of such women. Reason further explains that if women happen to know less than men, it is because they lack the opportunities that men have to learn. Similarly, men who live relatively isolated in the mountains might seem savage or simple minded compared to men who have more cultural and educational advantages. When Christine asks Reason whether prudence is found in the natural sensibility of women, Reason again answers affirmatively but then points out that sometimes husbands take offense when their wives demonstrate this virtue because it shows up their own deficiencies.

In her "Misogynism and Virginal Feminism in the Fathers of the Church," Rosemary Radford Ruether shows how Augustine tried to reconcile the apparent conflict between the two passages by arguing that while man alone reflects the divine image and woman alone does not, man and woman considered together also reflect the divine image. In his reconciliation, Augustine takes woman to stand in her relationship to man as body to soul. Thus, women are associated with the body in a way that men are not. Still, Augustine, along with the other Church Fathers, allowed that there was one way that women could escape their lesser status; they could become virgins and live the monistic, angelic life. Not surprisingly, Reuther hopes some way will be found to introduce a full-bodied equality into this Augustinian perspective on the relationship between men and women.

Of course, a more egalitarian interpretation of the relationship between men and women would surely have been easier to come by if the religious texts themselves had portrayed the Godhead in feminine as well as masculine terms. As Jorge Valadez points out in his "Pre-Columbian Philosophical Perspectives," that is exactly how the Aztecs conceived of their supreme diety Ometeotl. Ometeotl was referred to as 'the lord and lady of our maintainance" and as "our mother, our father." Valadez also points out that the Mayans saw themselves not as standing against nature but rather as an integral part of it, which led them to be more respectful of nature than eurocentric societies have been. Is it possible, then, that these pre-Columbian societies possessed a wisdom that has yet to take hold in eurocentric societies like our own?

# 9    The City of God

AUGUSTINE

*What the Christians believe regarding the supreme good and evil, in opposition to the philosophers, who have maintained that the supreme good is in themselves.*

If, then, we be asked what the city of God has to say upon these points, and, in the first place, what its opinion regarding the supreme good and evil is, it will reply that life eternal is the supreme good, death eternal the supreme evil, and that to obtain the one and escape the other we must live rightly. And thus it is written, "The just lives by faith,"[1] for against which the spirit may lust? And as we cannot attain to this in the present life, however ardently we desire it, (let us by God's help accomplish at least this, to preserve the soul from succumbing and yielding to the flesh that lusts against it, and to refuse our consent to the perpetration of sin.) Far be it from us, then, to fancy that while we are still engaged in this intestine war, we have already found the happiness which we seek to reach by victory. And who is there so wise that he has no conflict at all to maintain against his vices?

What shall I say of that virtue which is called prudence. Is not all its vigilance spent in the discernment of good from evil things, so that no mistake may be admitted about what we should desire and what avoid? And thus it is itself a proof that we are in the midst of evils, or that evils are in us; for it teaches us that it is an evil to consent to sin, and a good to refuse this consent. And yet this evil, to which prudence teaches and temperance enables us not to consent, is removed from this life neither by prudence nor by temperance. And justice, whose office it is to render to every man his due, whereby there is in man himself a certain just order of nature, so that the soul is subjected to God, and the flesh to the soul, and consequently both soul and flesh to God,—does not this virtue demonstrate that it is as yet rather labouring towards its end than resting in its finished work? For the soul is so much the less subjected to God as it is less occupied with the thought of God; and the flesh is so much the less subjected to the spirit as it lusts more vehemently against the spirit. So long, therefore, as we are beset by this weakness, this plague, this disease, how shall we dare to say that we are safe? and if not safe, then how can we be already enjoying our final beatitude? Then that virtue which goes by the name of fortitude is the plainest proof of the ills of life, for it is these ills which it is compelled to bear patiently. And this holds good, no matter though the ripest wisdom co-exists with it. And I am at a loss to understand how the Stoic philosophers can presume to say that these are no ills, though at the same time they allow the wise man to commit suicide and pass out of this life if they become so grievous that he cannot or ought not to endure them. But such is the stupid pride of these men who fancy that the supreme good can be found in this life, and that they can become happy by their own resources, that their wise man, or at least the man whom they fancifully depict as such, is always happy, even though he become blind, deaf, dumb, mutilated, racked with pains, or suffer any conceivable calamity such as may compel him to make away with himself and they are not ashamed to call the life that is beset with these evils happy. O happy life, which seeks the aid of death to end it! If it is happy, let the wise man remain in it; but if these ills drive him out of it, in what sense is it happy? Or how can they say that these are not evils which conquer the virtue of fortitude, and force it not only to yield, but so to rave that it in one breath calls life happy and recommends it to be given up? For who is so blind as not to see that if it were happy it would not be fled from? And if they say we should flee from it on account of the infirmities that beset it, why then do they not lower their pride and acknowledge that it is miserable? Was it, I would ask, fortitude or weakness which prompted Cato to kill himself? for he would not have done so had he not been too weak to endure Cæsar's victory. Where, then, is his fortitude? It has yielded, it has succumbed, it has been so thoroughly overcome as to abandon, forsake, flee this happy life. Or was it no longer happy? Then it was miserable. How, then, were these not evils which made life miserable, and a thing to be escaped from?

And therefore those who admit that these are evils, as the Peripatetics do, and the Old Academy, the sect which Varro advocates, express a more intelligible doctrine; but theirs also is a surprising mistake, for they contend that this is a happy life which is beset by these evils, even though they be so great that he who endures them should commit suicide to escape them. "Pains and anguish of body," says Varro, "are evils, and so much the worse in proportion to their severity; and to escape them you must quit this life." What life, I pray? This life, he says, which is oppressed by such evils. Then it is happy in the midst of these very evils on account of which you say we must quit it? Or do you call it happy because you are at liberty to escape these evils by death? What, then, if by some secret judgment of God you were held fast and not permitted to die, nor suffered to live without these evils? In that case, at least, you would say that such a life was miserable. It is soon relinquished, no doubt, but this does not make it not miserable; for were it eternal, you yourself would pronounce it miserable. Its brevity, therefore, does not clear it of misery, . . . neither ought it to be called happiness because it is a brief misery. Certainly there is a mighty force in these evils which compel a man—according to them, even a wise man—to cease to be a man that he may escape them, though they say, and say truly, that it is as it were the first and strongest demand of nature that a man cherish himself, and naturally therefore avoid death, and should so stand his own friend as to wish and vehemently aim at continuing to exist as a living creature, and subsisting in this union of soul and body. There is a mighty force in these evils to overcome this natural instinct by which death is by every means and with all a man's efforts avoided, and to overcome it so completely (that what was avoided is desired, sought after) and if it cannot in any other way be obtained, is inflicted by the man on himself. There is a mighty force in these evils which make fortitude a homicide,—if, indeed, that is to be called fortitude which is so thoroughly overcome by these evils, that it not only cannot preserve by patience the man whom it undertook to govern and defend, but is itself obliged to kill him. The wise man, I admit, ought to bear death with patience, but when it is inflicted by another. If, then, as these men maintain, he is obliged to inflict it on himself, certainly it must be owned that the ills which compel him to this are not only evils, but intolerable evils. The life, then, which is either subject to accidents, or environed with evils so considerable and grievous, could never have been called happy, if the men who give it this name had condescended to yield to the truth, and to be conquered by valid arguments, when they inquired after the happy life, as they yield to unhappiness, and are overcome by overwhelming evils, when they put themselves to death, and if they had not fancied that the supreme good was to be found in this mortal life; for the very virtues of this life, which are certainly its best and most useful possessions, are all the more telling proofs of its miseries in proportion as they are helpful against the violence of its dangers, toils, and woes. For if these are true virtues,—and such cannot exist save in those who have true piety,—they do not profess to be able to deliver the men who possess them from all miseries; for true virtues tell no such lies, but they profess that by the hope of the future world this life, which is miserably involved in the many and great evils of this world, is happy as it is also safe. For if not yet safe, how could it be happy? And therefore the Apostle Paul, speaking not of men without prudence, temperance, fortitude, and justice, but of those whose lives were regulated by true piety, and whose virtues were therefore true, says,

For we are saved by hope: now hope which is seen is not hope; for what a man seeth, why doth he yet hope for? But if we hope for that we see not, then do we with patience wait for it.[2]

As, therefore, we are saved, so we are made happy by hope. And as we do not as yet possess a present, but look for a future salvation, so is it with our happiness, and this "with patience"; for we are encompassed with evils, which we ought patiently to endure, until we come to the ineffable enjoyment of unmixed good; for there shall be no longer anything to endure. Salvation, such as it shall be in the world to come, shall itself be our final happiness. And this happiness these philosophers refuse to believe in, because they do not see it, and attempt to fabricate for themselves a happiness in this life; based upon a virtue which is as deceitful as it is proud. . . .

*Of the happiness of the eternal peace, which constitutes the end or true perfection of the saints.*

And thus we may say of peace, as we have said of eternal life, that it is the end of our good; and the rather because the Psalmist says of the city of God, the subject of this laborious work,

> Praise the Lord, O Jerusalem; praise thy God, O Zion: for He hath strengthened the bars of thy gates; He hath blessed thy children within thee; who hath made thy borders peace.[3]

For when the bars of her gates shall be strengthened, none shall go in or come out from her; consequently we ought to understand the peace of her borders as that final peace we are wishing to declare. For even the mystical name of the city itself, that is, *Jerusalem,* means, as I have already said, "Vision of Peace." But as the word peace is employed in connection with things in this world in which certainly life eternal has no place, we have preferred to call the end or supreme good of this city life eternal rather than, peace. Of this end the apostle says, "But now, being freed from sin, and become servants to God, ye have your fruit unto holiness, and the end life eternal."[4] But, on the other hand, as those who are not familiar with Scripture may suppose that the life of the wicked is eternal life, either because

of the immortality of the soul, which some of the philosophers even have recognised, or because of the endless punishment of the wicked, which forms a part of our faith, and which seems impossible unless the wicked live for ever, it may therefore be advisable, in order that every one may readily understand what we mean, to say that the end or supreme good of this city is either peace in eternal life, or eternal life in peace. For peace is a good so great, that even in this earthly and mortal life there is no word we hear with such pleasure, nothing we desire with such zest, or find to be more thoroughly gratifying. So that if we dwell for a little longer on this subject, we shall not, in my opinion, be wearisome to our readers, who will attend both for the sake of understanding what is the end of this city of which we speak, and for the sake of the sweetness of peace which is dear to all.

> That even the fierceness of war and all the disquietude of men make towards this one end of peace, which every nature desires.

Whoever gives even moderate attention to human affairs and to our common nature, will recognise that if there is no man who does not wish to be joyful, neither is there any one who does not wish to have peace. For even they who make war desire nothing but victory,—desire, that is to say, to attain to peace with glory. For what else is victory than the conquest of those who resist us? and when this is done there is peace. It is therefore with the desire for peace that wars are waged, even by those who take pleasure in exercising their warlike nature in command and battle. And we do not as yet see our good, and must therefore live by faith; neither have we in ourselves power to live rightly, but can do so only if He who has given us faith to believe in His help do help us when we believe and pray. As for those who have supposed that the sovereign good and evil are to be found in this life, and have placed it either in the soul or the body, or in both, or, to speak more explicitly, either in pleasure or in virtue, or in both; in repose or in virtue, or in both; in pleasure and repose, or in virtue, or in all combined; in the primary objects of nature, or in virtue, or in both,—all these have, with a marvellous shallowness, sought to find their blessedness in this life and in themselves. Contempt has been poured upon such ideas by the Truth, saying by the prophet, "The Lord knoweth the thoughts of men" (or, as the Apostle Paul cites the passage, "The Lord knoweth the thoughts of the *wise*") "that they are vain."[5]

For what flood of eloquence can suffice to detail the miseries of this life? Cicero, in the *Consolation* on the death of his daughter, has spent all his ability in lamentation; but how inadequate was even his ability here? For when, where, how, in this life can these primary objects of nature be possessed so that they may not be assailed by unforeseen accidents? Is the body of the wise man exempt from any pain which may dispel pleasure, from any disquietude which may banish repose? The amputation or decay of the members of the body puts an end to its integrity, deformity blights its beauty, weakness its health, lassitude its vigour, sleepiness or sluggishness its activity,—and which of these is it that may not assail the flesh of the wise man? Comely and fitting attitudes and movements of the body are numbered among the prime natural blessings; but what if some sickness makes the members tremble? what if a man suffers from curvature of the spine, to such an extent that his hands reach the ground, and he goes upon all-fours like a quadruped? Does not this destroy all beauty and grace in the body, whether at rest or in motion? What shall I say of the fundamental blessings of the soul, sense and intellect, of which the one is given for the perception, and the other for the comprehension of truth? But what kind of sense is it that remains when a man becomes deaf and blind? where are reason and intellect when disease makes a man delirious? We can scarcely, or not at all, refrain from tears, when we think of or see the actions and words of such frantic persons, and consider how different from and even opposed to their own sober judgment and ordinary conduct their present demeanour is. And what shall I say of those who suffer from demoniacal possession? Where is their own intelligence hidden and buried while the malignant spirit is using their body and soul according to his own will?

And who is quite sure that no such thing can happen to the wise man in this life? Then, as to the perception of truth, what can we hope for even in this way while in the body, as we read in the true book of Wisdom.

> The corruptible body weigheth down the soul, and the earthly tabernacle presseth down the mind that museth upon many things?[6]

And eagerness, or desire of action, if this is the right meaning to put upon the Greek ὁρμή is also reckoned among the primary advantages of nature; and yet is it not this which produces those pitiable movements of the insane, and those actions which we shudder to see, when sense is deceived and reason deranged?

In fine, virtue itself, which is not among the primary objects of nature, but succeeds to them as the result of learning, though it holds the highest place among human good things, what is its occupation save to wage perpetual war with vices,—not those that are outside of us, but within; not other men's, but our own,—a war which is waged especially by that virtue which the Greeks call σωφροσύνη, and we temperance[7] and which bridles carnal lusts, and prevents them from winning the consent of the spirit to wicked deeds? For we must not fancy that there is no vice in us, when, as the apostle says, "The flesh lusteth against the spirit;"[8] for to this vice there is a contrary virtue, when, as the same writer says, "The spirit lusteth against the flesh." "For these two," he says, "are contrary one to the other, so that you cannot do the things which you would." But what is it we wish to do when we seek to attain the supreme good, unless that the flesh should cease to lust against the spirit, and that there be no vice in us hence it is obvious that peace is the end sought for by war. For every man seeks peace by waging war, but no man seeks war by making peace. For even they who intentionally interrupt the peace in which they are living have no hatred of peace, but only wish it changed into a peace that suits them better. They do not, therefore, wish to have no peace, but only one more to their mind. And in the case of sedition, when men have separated themselves from the community, they yet do not effect what they wish, unless they maintain some kind of peace with their fellow-conspirators. And therefore even robbers take care to maintain peace with their comrades, that they may with greater effect and greater safety invade the peace of other men. And if an individual happen to be of such unrivalled strength, and to be so jealous of partnership, that he trusts himself with no comrades, but makes his own plots, and commits depredations and murders on his own account, yet he maintains some shadow of peace with such persons as he is unable to kill, and from whom he wishes to conceal his deeds. In his own home, too, he makes it his aim to be at peace with his wife and children, and any other members of his household; for unquestionably their prompt obedience to his every look is a source of pleasure to him. And if this be not rendered, he is angry, he chides and punishes; and even by this storm he secures the calm peace of his own home, as occasion demands. For he sees that peace cannot be maintained unless all the members of the same domestic circle be subject to one head, such as he himself is in his own house. And therefore if a city or nation offered to submit itself to him, to serve him in the same style as he had made his household serve him, he would no longer lurk in a brigand's hiding-places, but lift his head in open day as a king, though the same covetousness and wickedness should remain in him. And thus all men desire to have peace with their own circle whom they wish to govern as suits themselves. For even those whom they make war against they wish to make their own, and impose on them the laws of their own peace.

But let us suppose a man such as poetry and mythology speak of,—a man so insociable and savage as to be called rather a semi-man than a man:[9] Although, then, his kingdom was the solitude of a dreary cave, and he himself was so singularly bad-hearted that he was named Κακός, which is the Greek word for *bad;* though he had no wife to soothe him with endearing talk, no children to play with, no sons to do his bidding, no friend to enliven him with intercourse, not

even his father Vulcan (though in one respect he was happier than his father, not having begotten a monster like himself); although he gave to no man, but took as he wished whatever he could, from whomsoever he could, when he could; yet in that solitary den, the floor of which, as Virgil[10] says, was always reeking with recent slaughter, there was nothing else than peace sought, a peace in which no one should molest him, or disquiet him with any assault or alarm. With his own body he desired to be at peace; and he was satisfied only in proportion as he had this peace. For he ruled his members, and they obeyed him; and for the sake of pacifying his mortal nature, which rebelled when it needed anything, and of allaying the sedition of hunger which threatened to banish the soul from the body, he made forays, slew, and devoured, but used the ferocity and savageness he displayed in these actions only for the preservation of his own life's peace. So that, had he been willing to make with other men the same peace which he made with himself in his own cave, he would neither have been called bad, nor a monster, nor a semiman. Or if the appearance of his body and his vomiting smoky fires frightened men from having any dealings with him, perhaps his fierce ways arose not from a desire to do mischief, but from the necessity of finding a living. But he may have had no existence, or, at least, he was not such as the poets fancifully describe him, for they had to exalt Hercules, and did so at the expense of Cacus. It is better, then, to believe that such a man or semi-man never existed, and that this, in common with many other fancies of the poets, is mere fiction. For the most savage animals (and he is said to have been almost a wild beast) encompass their own species with a ring of protecting peace. They cohabit, beget, produce, suckle, and bring up their young, though very many of them are not gregarious, but solitary,—not like sheep, deer, pigeons, starlings, bees, but such as lions, foxes, eagles, bats. For what tigress does not gently purr over her cubs, and lay aside her ferocity to fondle them? What kite, solitary as he is when circling over his prey, does not seek a mate, build a nest, hatch the eggs, bring up the young birds, and maintain with the mother of his family as peaceful a domestic alliance as he can? How much more powerfully do the laws of man's nature move him to hold fellowship and maintain peace with all men so far as in him lies, since even wicked men wage war to maintain the peace of their own circle, and wish that, if possible, all men belonged to them, that all men and things might serve but one head, and might, either through love or fear, yield themselves to peace with him! It is thus that pride in its perversity apes God. It abhors equality with other men under Him; but, instead of His rule, it seeks to impose a rule of its own upon its equals. It abhors, that is to say, the just peace of God, and loves its own unjust peace; but it cannot help loving peace of one kind or other. For there is no vice so clean contrary to nature that it obliterates even the faintest traces of nature.

He, then, who prefers what is right to what is wrong, and what is well-ordered to what is perverted, sees that the peace of unjust men is not worthy to be called peace in comparison with the peace of the just. And yet even what is perverted must of necessity be in harmony with, and in dependence on, and in some part of the order of things, for otherwise it would have no existence at all. Suppose a man hangs with his head downwards, this is certainly a perverted attitude of body and arrangement of its members; for that which nature requires to be above is beneath, and *vice versâ*. This perversity disturbs the peace of the body, and is therefore painful. Nevertheless the spirit is at peace with its body, and labours for its preservation, and hence the suffering; but if it is banished from the body by its pains, then, so long as the bodily framework holds together, there is in the remains a kind of peace among the members, and hence the body remains suspended. And inasmuch as the earthy body tends towards the earth, and rests on the bond by which it is suspended, it tends thus to its natural peace, and the voice of its own weight demands a place for it to rest; and though now lifeless and without feeling, it does not fall from the peace that is natural to its place in creation, whether it already has it, or is tending towards it. For if you apply embalming prepara-

tions to prevent the bodily frame from mouldering and dissolving, a kind of peace still unites part to part, and keeps the whole body in a suitable place on the earth,—in other words, in a place that is at peace with the body. If, on the other hand, the body receive no such care, but be left to the natural course, it is disturbed by exhalations that do not harmonize with one another, and that offend our senses; for it is this which is perceived in putrefaction until it is assimilated to the elements of the world, and particle by particle enters into peace with them. Yet throughout this process the laws of the most high Creator and Governor are strictly observed, for it is by Him the peace of the universe is administered. For although minute animals are produced from the carcase of a larger animal, all these little atoms, by the law of the same Creator, serve the animals they belong to in peace. And although the flesh of dead animals be eaten by others, no matter where it be carried, nor what it be brought into contact with, nor what it be converted and changed into, it still is ruled by the same laws which pervade all things for the conservation of every mortal race, and which bring things that fit one another into harmony. . . .

*What produces peace, and what discord, between the heavenly and earthly cities.*

But the families which do not live by faith seek their peace in the earthly advantages of this life; while the families which live by faith look for those eternal blessings which are promised, and use as pilgrims such advantages of time and of earth as do not fascinate and divert them from God, but rather aid them to endure with greater ease, and to keep down the number of those burdens of the corruptible body which weigh upon the soul. Thus the things necessary for this mortal life are used by both kinds of men and families alike, but each has its own peculiar and widely different aim in using them. The earthly city, which does not live by faith, seeks an earthly peace, and the end it proposes, in the well-ordered concord of civic obedience and rule, is the combination of men's wills to attain the things which are helpful to this life. The heavenly city, or rather the part of it which sojourns on earth and lives by faith, makes use of this peace only because it must, until this mortal condition which necessitates it shall pass away. Consequently, so long as it lives like a captive and a stranger in the earthly city, though it has already received the promise of redemption, and the gift of the Spirit as the earnest of it, it makes no scruple to obey the laws of the earthly city, whereby the things necessary for the maintenance of this mortal life are administered; and thus, as this life is common to both cities, so there is a harmony between them in regard to what belongs to it. But, as the earthly city has had some philosophers whose doctrine is condemned by the divine teaching, and who, being deceived either by their own conjectures or by demons, supposed that many gods must be invited to take an interest in human affairs, and assigned to each a separate function and a separate department,—to one the body, to another the soul; and in the body itself, to one the head, to another the neck, and each of the other members to one of the gods; and in like manner, in the soul, to one god the natural capacity was assigned, to another education, to another anger, to another lust; and so the various affairs of life were assigned,—cattle to one, corn to another, wine to another, oil to another, the woods to another, money to another, navigation to another, wars and victories to another, marriages to another, births and fecundity to another, and other things to other gods: and as the celestial city, on the other hand, knew that one God only was to be worshipped, and that to Him alone was due that service which the Greeks call λατρεία, and which can be given only to a god, it has come to pass that the two cities could not have common laws of religion, and that the heavenly city has been compelled in this matter to dissent, and to become obnoxious to those who think differently, and to stand the brunt of their anger and hatred and persecutions, except in so far as the minds of their enemies have been alarmed by the multitude of the Christians and quelled by the manifest protection of God accorded to them. This heavenly city, then, while it sojourns on earth, calls citizens out of all nations, and gathers together a society of pilgrims of all languages, not scrupling about diversities in the manners, laws, and institutions whereby earthly peace is secured and maintained, but recognising that, however various these are, they all tend to one and the same end of earthly peace. It therefore is so far from rescinding and abolishing these diversities, that it even preserves and adopts them, so long only as no hindrance to the worship of the one supreme and true God is thus introduced. Even the heavenly city, therefore, while in its state of pilgrimage, avails itself of the peace of earth, and, so far as it can without injuring faith and godliness, desires and maintains a common agreement among men regarding the acquisition of the necessaries of life, and makes this earthly peace bear upon the peace of heaven; for this alone can be truly called and esteemed the peace of the reasonable creatures, consisting as it does in the perfectly ordered and harmonious enjoyment of God and of one another in God. When we shall have reached that peace, this mortal life shall give place to one that is eternal, and our body shall be no more this animal body which by its corruption weighs down the soul, but a spiritual body feeling no want, and in all its members subjected to the will. In its pilgrim state the heavenly city possesses this peace by faith; and by this faith it lives righteously when it refers to the attainment of that peace every good action towards God and man; for the life of the city is a social life.

NOTES

1. Hab. ii. 4.
2. Both. viii. 24.
3. Ps. cxlvii. 12–14.
4. Rom. vi. 22.
5. Ps. xciv. 11, and 1 Cor. iii. 20.
6. Wisdom ix. 15.
7. Cicero, *Tusc. Quæst*. iii. 8.
8. Gal. v. 17.
9. He refers to the giant Cacus.
10. *Æneid*, viii. 195.

# 10     Confessions

AUGUSTINE

THANKS TO THEE, O Lord. We behold the heaven and the earth, whether the corporeal part, superior and inferior, or the spiritual and corporeal creature; and in the embellishment of these parts, whereof the universal mass of the world or the universal creation consisteth, we see light made, and divided from the darkness. We see the firmament of heaven, whether the primary body of the world between the spiritual upper waters and the corporeal lower waters, or—because this also is called heaven—this expanse of air, through which wander the fowls of heaven, between the waters which are in vapours borne above them, and which in clear nights drop down in dew, and those which being heavy flow along the earth. We behold the waters gathered together through the plains of the sea; and the dry land both void and formed, so as to be visible and compact, and the matter of herbs and trees. We behold the lights shining from above—the sun to serve the day, the moon and the stars to cheer the night; and that by all these, times should be marked and noted. We behold on every side a humid element, fruitful with fishes, beasts, and birds; because the density of the air, which bears up the flights of birds, is increased by the exhalation of the waters. We behold the face of the earth furnished with terrestrial creatures, and man, created after Thy image and likeness, in that very image and likeness of Thee (that is, the power of reason and understanding) on account of which he was set over all irrational creatures. And as in his soul there is one power which rules by directing, another made subject that it might obey, so also for the man was corporeally made a woman, who, in the mind of her rational understanding should also have a like nature, in the sex, however, of her body should be in like manner subject to the sex of her husband, as the appetite of action is subjected by reason of the mind, to conceive the skill of acting rightly. These things we behold, and they are severally good, and all very good.

# 11     The Book of the City of Ladies

CHRISTINE DE PIZAN

*27. Christine asks reason whether God has ever wished to ennoble the mind of woman with the loftiness of the sciences; and reason's answer.*

[1.27.1] After hearing these things, I replied to the lady who spoke infallibly: "My lady, truly has God revealed great wonders in the strength of these women whom you describe. But please enlighten me again, whether it has ever pleased this God, who has bestowed so many favors on women, to honor the feminine sex with the privilege of the virtue of high understanding and great learning, and whether women ever have a clever enough mind for this. I wish very much to know this because men maintain that the mind of women can learn only a little."

She answered, "My daughter, since I told you before, you know quite well that the opposite of their opinion is true, and to show you this even more clearly, I will give you proof through examples. I tell you again—and don't doubt the contrary—if it were customary to send daughters to school like sons, and if they were then taught the natural sciences, they would learn as thoroughly and understand the subtleties of all the arts and sciences as well as sons. And by chance there happen to be such women, for, as I touched on before, just as women have more delicate bodies than men, weaker and less able to perform many tasks, so do they have minds that are freer and sharper whenever they apply themselves."

"My lady, what are you saying? With all due respect, could you dwell longer on this point, please. Certainly men would never admit this answer is true, unless it is explained more plainly, for they believe that one normally sees that men know more than women do."

She answered, "Do you know why women know less?"

"Not unless you tell me, my lady."

"Without the slightest doubt, it is because they are not involved in many different things, but stay at home, where it is enough for them to run the household, and there is nothing which so instructs a reasonable creature as the exercise and experience of many different things."

"My lady, since they have minds skilled in conceptualizing and learning, just like men, why don't women learn more?"

She replied, "Because, my daughter, the public does not require them to get involved in the affairs which men are commissioned to execute, just as I told you before. It is enough for women to perform the usual duties to which they are ordained. As for judging from experience, since one sees that women usually know less than men, that therefore their capacity for understanding is less, look at men who farm the flatlands or who live in the mountains. You will find that in many coun-

tries they seem completely savage because they are so simple-minded. All the same, there is no doubt that Nature provided them with the qualities of body and mind found in the wisest and most learned men. All of this stems from a failure to learn, though, just as I told you, among men and women, some possess better minds than others. Let me tell you about women who have possessed great learning and profound understanding and treat the question of the similarity of women's minds to men's."

### 28. She begins to discuss several ladies who were enlightened with great learning, and first speaks about the noble maiden Cornificia.

[1.28.1] "Cornificia, the noble maiden, was sent to school by her parents along with her brother Cornificius when they were both children, thanks to deception and trickery. This little girl so devoted herself to study and with such marvelous intelligence that she began to savor the sweet taste of knowledge acquired through study. Nor was it easy to take her away from this joy to which she more and more applied herself, neglecting all other feminine activities. She occupied herself with this for such a long period of time that she became a consummate poet, and she was not only extremely brilliant and expert in the learnedness and craft of poetry but also seemed to have been nourished with the very milk and teaching of perfect philosophy, for she wanted to hear and know about every branch of learning, which she then mastered so thoroughly that she surpassed her brother, who was also a very great poet, and excelled in every field of learning. Knowledge was not enough for her unless she could put her mind to work and her pen to paper in the compilation of several very famous books. These works, as well as her poems, were much prized during the time of Saint Gregory and he himself mentions them. The Italian, Boccaccio, who was a great poet, discusses this fact in his work and at the same time praises this woman: 'O most great honor for a woman who abandoned all feminine activities and applied and devoted her mind to the study of the greatest scholars!' As further proof of what I am telling you, Boccaccio also talks about the attitude of women who despise themselves and their own minds, and who, as though they were born in the mountains totally ignorant of virtue and honor, turn disconsolate and say that they are good and useful only for embracing men and carrying and feeding children. God has given them such beautiful minds to apply themselves, if they want to, in any of the fields where glorious and excellent men are active, which are neither more nor less accessible to them as compared to men if they wished to study them, and they can thereby acquire a lasting name, whose possession is fitting for most excellent men. My dear daughter, you can see how this author Boccaccio testifies to what I have told you and how he praises and approves learning in women." . . .

## 43. Christine asks reason where prudence is found in the natural sensibility of women; and reason's answer to her.

[1.43.1] Then I, Christine, said to her, "My lady, I can truly and clearly see that God—may He be praised for it—has granted that the mind of an intelligent woman can conceive, know, and retain all perceptible things. Even though there are so many people who have such subtle minds that they understand and learn everything which they are shown and who are so ingenious and quick to conceptualize everything that every field of learning is open to them, with the result that they have acquired extraordinary knowledge through devotion to study, I am baffled when eminent scholars—including some of the most famous and learned—exhibit so little prudence in their morals and conduct in the world. Certainly scholarship teaches and provides an introduction to morals. If you please, my lady, I would gladly learn from you whether a woman's mind (which, as it seems to me

from your proofs as well as from what I myself see, is quite understanding and retentive in subtle questions of scholarship and other subjects) is equally prompt and clever in those matters which prudence teaches, that is, whether women can reflect on what is best to do and what is better to be avoided, and whether they remember past events and become learned from the examples they have seen, and, as a result, are wise in managing current affairs, and whether they have foresight into the future. Prudence, it seems to me, teaches those lessons."

"You speak correctly, my daughter," she replied, "but this prudence of which you speak is bestowed by Nature upon men and women, and some possess more, others less. But Nature does not impart knowledge of everything, as much as it simultaneously perfects in those who are naturally prudent, for you realize that two forces together are stronger and more resistant than one force alone. For this reason I say that the person who, from Nature, possesses prudence (which is called 'natural sense'), as well as acquired knowledge along with this prudence, deserves special praise for remarkable excellence. Yet just as you yourself have said, some who possess the one do not possess the other, for the one is the gift of God thanks to the influence of Nature, and the other is acquired through long study, though both are good. But some people prefer natural sense without acquired knowledge rather than a great deal of acquired knowledge with little natural sense. All the same, many opinions can be based upon this proposition, from which many questions can arise. For one could say that one achieves more good by choosing what is more useful for the profit and the utility of the general public. Therefore, one person's knowing the different fields of learning is more profitable for everyone than all the natural sense which he might possess which he could demonstrate to all: for this natural sense can only last as long as the lifetime of the person who has it, and when he dies, his sense dies with him. Acquired learning, on the other hand, lasts forever for those who have it, because of their fame, and it is useful for many people insofar as it can be taught to others and recorded in books for the sake of future generations. In this way their learning does not die with them, and therefore I can show you, using the example of Aristotle and others through whom learning has been transmitted to the world, that their acquired knowledge was more useful to the world than all the prudence without acquired knowledge possessed by all men, past and present, although thanks to the prudence of many, several kingdoms and empires have been well-governed and directed. All of these things are transitory, however, and disappear with time, while learning endures forever.

[1.43.2]"Nevertheless, I will leave these questions unanswered and for others to solve, for they do not pertain to the problem of building our City, and I will come back to the question you raised,

that is, whether women possess natural prudence. Of course they do. You know this already from what I have said to you before, just as, in general, you can see from women's conduct in those duties assigned to them to perform. But be careful if you find this good, for you will see that all women, or the vast majority, are so very attentive, careful, and diligent in governing their households and in providing everything for them, according to their capacities, that sometimes some of their negligent husbands are annoyed; they think their wives are pushing and pressuring them too much to do what they are supposed to and they say their wives want to run everything and be smarter than they are. In this way, what many women tell their husbands with good intentions turns out to their disadvantage.

# 12    Misogynism and Virginal Feminism in the Fathers of the Church

ROSEMARY RADFORD RUETHER

THE USUAL IMAGE OF the Fathers of the Church, especially among those promoting women's liberation, is that of fanatical ascetics and woman haters. Hatred of sex and hatred of women are identified.[1] But this view tends to ignore the high praise of women, in their new role as "virgins," in patristic theology. It also fails to explain the rise of that veneration of Mary that is characteristic of patristic thought in the fourth century A.D. In this chapter I wish to show that this ambivalence between misogynism and the praise of the virginal woman is not accidental. One view is not more "characteristic" than the other. Both stand together as two sides of a dualistic psychology that was the basis of the patristic doctrine of man.

. . .

. . . The crucial biblical text for the creation of man was Genesis 1:27:

> God created man in His own image; in the image of God he created him; male and female He created them.

If the Fathers could have had the first part of the text without the final phrase, they would have been happier. Indeed, they often quote only the first part of this text without alluding to the second.[2] About the character of the image of God in man they had no doubts. This referred to man's soul or reason. The Hellenistic Jew Philo had already established this interpretation by the first century A.D.[3] The problem came with reconciling this spiritual interpretation of the image of God with the subsequent reference to bisexuality, which they saw as a bodily characteristic. Since God was wholly spiritual and noncorporeal, this appeared to mix contraries and imply either a sexed spirituality or a bodily God. Since it was anathema to think of God as bodily, with male and female characteristics, the two parts of the text must be separated so that the "image" could be defined in a monistic, spiritual way, and bisexuality could refer to something other than the nature of God as reflected in man.

For Greek thought it was axiomatic that spiritual reality was unitary (*monistic,* from which the words "monk" and "monastic" derive). Duality appears only with matter. So God cannot be dual, nor can man's spiritual image be bisexual. This does not mean an "androgynous" view of God and the original humanity, as some recent commentators have thought. The guiding view of the Fathers was not an androgyny that preserved bisexuality on a psychic level, but rather that monism which, alone, is appropriate to spirit.[4] This could be stated by identifying maleness with monism, making femaleness secondary, or else by a nonsexual monism, but not by a true androgyny. Gregory Nyssa chose the latter course, and Augustine the former.

. . .

. . . For Augustine, man as the image of God was summed up in Adam, the unitary ancestor of humanity. But Adam is compound, containing both male spirit and female corporeality. When Eve is taken from Adam's side, she symbolizes this corporeal side of man, taken from him in order to be his helpmate. But she is a helpmate solely for the corporeal task of procreation, for which alone she is indispensable.[5] For any spiritual task another male would be more suitable than a female as a helpmate.

Inexplicably, Augustine must also affirm that Eve, too, has a rational nature, being likewise a compound of spirit and body. Yet in relation to man she stands for body *vis-à-vis* male spirit.[6] Moreover, Augustine persists in calling this latter her "nature," not only with a view to sin but in the order of nature as well. Augustine defines the male as, alone, the full image of God Woman, by her-

self, is not this image, but only when taken together with the male, who is her "head." Augustine justifies this view by fusing the Genesis text with I Corinthians 11:3–12.

> How then did the apostle tell us that the man is the image of God and therefore he is forbidden to cover his head, but that the woman is not so, and therefore she is commanded to cover hers? Unless forsooth according to that which I have said already, when I was treating of the nature of the human mind, that the woman, together with her own husband, is the image of God, so that the whole substance may be one image, but when she is referred to separately in her quality as a helpmeet, which regards the woman alone, then she is not the image of God, but, as regards the man alone, he is the image of God as fully and completely as when the woman too is joined with him in one.[7]

This assimilation of male–female dualism into soul–body dualism in patristic theology conditions basically the definition of woman, both in terms of her subordination to the male in the order of nature and her "carnality" in the disorder of sin. The result of this assimilation is that woman is not really seen as a self-sufficient, whole person with equal honor, as the image of God in her own right, but is seen, ethically, as dangerous to the male. Augustine works this out explicitly, but patristic theology makes use of the same assumptions of woman's subordination to man in the order of nature, and her special "carnality" in the disorder of sin, which imply the same attitudes, however unjustified by the contrary assumption of the equivalence of male and female in the original creation. This definition of femaleness as body decrees a natural subordination of female to male, *as flesh must be subject to spirit in the right ordering of nature.*[8] It also makes her peculiarly the symbol of the Fall and sin, since sin is defined as the disordering of the original justice wherein the bodily principle revolts against its ruling spirit and draws the reason down to its lower dictates.

This double definition of woman, as submissive body in the order of nature and "revolting" body in the disorder of sin, allows the Fathers to slide somewhat inconsistently from the second to the first and attribute woman's inferiority first to sin and then to nature. In Augustine the stress falls decidedly on the side of woman's natural inferiority as body in relation to mind in the right ordering of nature, and thus he is somewhat temperate in his polemics against Eve as the original cause of the Fall. For him, the Fall could only occur, not when the body tempts, but when the male ruling principle agrees to "go along." This, however, does not imply a milder view of sin, only a more contemptuous view of Eve's capacity to cause the Fall "by herself."[9] In other Fathers, . . . Eve is made to sound as though she bore the primary responsibility.

. . .

This assimilation of woman into bodiliness allows Augustine to explain why woman's subjugation is "natural" within the order of creation, but it makes for some contradiction when it comes time to defend woman's redeemability and her ability, like that of the man, to become "virgin" and return to the monistic incorporeal nature. This conflict does not appear in Nyssa in the same way, because he makes bisexuality, rather than femaleness, the symbol of corporeality, and thus makes woman and man equivalent, both in their spiritual natures and in their sexed bodily natures. But, then, the Greeks had the corresponding conflict of an inexplicable use of language which suggested that woman was subordinate to man in nature and peculiarly identified with "carnality"— a language to which they, too, were addicted.

Augustine attempts to explain this contradiction by distinguishing between what woman is, as a rational spirit (in which she is equivalent to the male), and what she "symbolizes" in her bodily nature, where she stands for the subjection of body to spirit in nature and that debasing carnality that draws the male mind down from its heavenly heights. But he thinks that what she thus symbolizes, in the eye of male perception, is also what she "is" in her female nature! It never occurs to him that defining woman as something other than what she is, and placing her in subjugation in the order of nature *from the perspective of the male*

*visual impression of her as a "body"* is nothing else than an expression, in the male himself, of that disorder of sin, and thus, in no way a stance for the definition of woman's nature! For Augustine, however, this androcentric perspective is never questioned, but presupposed. Yet he, too, must admit that woman has "another" possibility beyond this androcentrically conceived bodiliness. She, too, has a rational nature and can be saved by overcoming the body and living according to the spirit. Augustine cannot deny this since he, along with all the Church Fathers, believes that woman can become "virgin" and live the monistic, angelic life.

. . .

In this twilight period of antiquity, we see . . . the image of the virginal woman appearing as a new cultural ideal, raising up the possibility of woman as capable of the highest spiritual development, which could lead to the *summum bonum* of communion with the divine, intellectual nature of the Divine itself. Such heights had previously been reserved for men in antiquity . . .

. . . Virginal woman was thus bound for heaven, and her male ascetic devotees would stop at nothing short of this prize for her. But they paid the price of despising all real physical women, sex and fecundity, and wholly etherealizing women into incorporeal phantasms in order to provide love objects for the sublimated libido and guard against turning back to any physical expression of love with the dangerous daughters of Eve.

Perhaps the task of Christians today, as they take stock of this tradition and its defects, is not merely to vilify its inhumanity but rather to cherish the hard-won fruits of transcendence and spiritual personhood, won at such a terrible price of the natural affections of men and the natural humanity of women. Without discarding these achievements, we must rather find out how to pour them back into a full-bodied Hebrew sense of creation and incarnation, as male and female, but who can now be fully personalized autonomous selves and also persons in relation to each other, not against the body, but in and through the body.

NOTES

1. William Phipps, *Was Jesus Married?* (New York: Harper & Row, 1970), pp. 142–163.

2. For example, Athanasius' *De Incarnatione* and Origen's *De Principiis* develop an anthropology built on the doctrine of the "image" without any mention of bisexuality.

3. Philo, *Leg. All.* J, 31–32; *De Conf.* 62–63; also see *De Migr. Abr.* 174.

4. M. N. Maxey, "Beyond Eve and Mary," *Dialog.* X (Spring 1971), 112 ff.

5. Augustine, *De Grat. Ch. et de Pecc. Orig.* II, 40.; *De Genesi ad Lit.* 9.5.

6. Augustine, *Confessiones* 13.32; *De Opere Monach,* 40.

7. Augustine, *De Trinitate* 7.7, 10.

8. Augustine, *De Contin.* 1.23; Augustine parallels the supra- and subordinations of Christ and the Church; man and woman and the soul and the body. On the ambivalence between an equivalent and a subordinate view of women in the Fathers, especially Augustine, see Kari Elizabeth Børresen, *Subordination et Équivalence; Nature et rôle de la femme d'après Augustin et Thomas d'Aquin* (Oslo: Universitets-forlaget, 1968).

9. Augustine, *De Civitate Dei* 14, 11; *De Genesi ad Lit.* 11, 42.

# 13    Pre-Columbian Philosophical Perspectives

JORGE VALADEZ

## *Complementary Dualities*

DUALITIES SUCH AS life/death, celestial world/underworld, male/female, night/day, and so forth were of central importance in the Mesoamerican worldview. These dualities were not conceived as being oppositional in nature; instead, they were understood as being different and necessary aspects of reality. One of the clearest examples of this type of nonoppositional duality was the supreme dual god of the Aztecs, Ometeotl. This supreme deity, who was the ultimate originator of all that exists, had a dual male and female nature. Ometeotl was sometimes called Tonacatecuhtli-Tonacacihuatl, which means "lord and lady of our maintenance," and often he/she was referred to as "our mother, our father."[1] The dual nature of Ometeotl enabled him/her to beget other beings and the universe from his/her own essence. It is clear that the Aztecs wanted to incorporate both the male and the female principle within a single supreme entity and that they saw no contradiction in a deity who was simultaneously male and female.

It is interesting and instructive to compare the conception of a male/female dual god with the monotheistic God of the Judeo-Christian tradition. Traditionally, the Christian god has been characterized primarily as having male qualities and has been referred to in explicitly male terms. For example, the first two substantive terms in the expression "the father, the son, and the holy ghost" refer to God in terms that are unequivocally male, while the third substantive term, "the holy ghost," has traditionally never been spoken of in female terms. And historically, rarely if ever have we heard the Christian God referred to by the female pronoun "she" or by the phrase "holy mother." He is usually characterized by predominantly male qualities that emphasized his power and authority instead of, say, his nurturance and unconditional acceptance. Some contemporary theologians have argued that these gender-specific characterizations of the Christian God deny women full spiritual participation in the Christian religious tradition. In any case, we can see that the Aztec conceptualization of the supreme deity Ometeotl incorporates the two aspects of the male/female duality into a single divine entity. . . .

## The Ecological Culture of the Maya

. . . The Mayans had what we might call an ecological culture, that is, a culture whose basic metaphysical perspective reflected the idea of the cyclical regeneration of the earth. Their agricultural orientation was manifested in several ways. First, they were an agriculturally advanced culture: They built canal systems for crop irrigation, practiced slope-field and raised-field farming, and cultivated corn, squash, beans, cotton, cacao, chili peppers, and other crops. Second, they recognized that the cultivation of maize and other crops had made possible the development of the permanent communities where the temples and pyramids that were important to the evolution of their culture and religion were built. Third, their rituals and their dominant metaphors indicated that they were intimately in tune with the seasonal and agricultural cycles of their rich vegetative environment.

The predominance of the ecological orientation in the Mayan world can be seen in the rich symbolism of the "cosmic tree." The cosmic tree is a symbol, used by many cultures throughout the world, of the earth as a fertile, living totality. In the Mayan culture this tree represents the earth as a living entity capable of periodic regeneration. Thus, according to the traditions of the present-day Tzutujil Mayas, the earth (and all that it contains) is seen as a tree or a maize plant that periodically sprouts, blossoms, dies, and is regenerated.[2] The significance of this metaphor in which the world is seen as a biological unit is twofold: First, there is recognition of the fact that just as there is an interconnection between the different parts of a plant, so there is an interconnection between the different biological units of the earth; second, there is the conviction that just as plants need nurturance from the sun, the soil, and

water in order to live, so there is corresponding need for the world to be nurtured and renewed in order for it to continue to exist. This renewal was achieved by religious rituals performed at specific times as determined by the temporal cycles that were measured by Mayan calendars.[3] It is interesting to note here that the Mayan view of the earth as a regenerating biological unit is remarkably similar to the modern-day "Gaia hypothesis," which states that the earth consists of many complex, interacting ecological systems. Some biologists and ecologists have argued that by adopting this view of the earth we will be more aware of the need to maintain and protect the earth's own ecological balance.

One of the implications of the Mayan view of the earth is that because nature does not belong to human beings, they do not have the right to do with it as they please. Nature is not something to be "mastered" and controlled for human purposes. In the Mayan perspective people do not stand against nature, but are rather an integral part of it. Humans should take care of nature and nurture it, because they depend on the earth for their nourishment and survival, and because, as biological entities that are born, reproduce, and die, humans are also part of the natural life cycles that permeate the earth. Even among the contemporary Maya of Guatemala there is still a deep sense of respect for the earth because of the belief that ultimately it belongs to the gods and not to mortal man. People are the caretakers, not the owners, of the earth. This accounts for the traditional belief among members of such communities that it is not correct to partition tracts of land and sell them. The earth should be nurtured and cultivated for the good of the whole community; it is not something to be bought and sold for profit. The ancient Maya believed that it was not possible to buy and sell the earth in that it did not belong to them in the first place. This belief is maintained, though perhaps to a lesser degree, by some contemporary Mayan communities.

By contrast, Western culture has elevated the individual's right to own private property into a fundamental human right. We see this "right" as so basic that we consider it more important than the right of an individual to have enough to eat or to have adequate shelter. Nevertheless, despite the importance in the Western tradition of the individual right to own private property, it seems plausible to say that, as far as basic individual human rights are concerned, the individual right to have adequate nourishment or shelter is more basic or primary than the individual right to own private property. But perhaps even more important, an analysis of the ecological orientation of the Maya reminds us that it is only recently that Western societies have realized that a fundamental change in our attitude toward nature is necessary to ensure our ecological survival. We have used and abused nature to such an extent—through air pollutants, the use of toxic chemicals, the production of non-biodegradable materials, and so forth—that we have placed our own survival, and the survival of other people in the world, in jeopardy. Our view of our relationship to the earth is starting to change so that we are beginning to see the world as an integrated ecological system that may be deeply affected by our actions.

NOTES

1. Miguel Yeon-Portilla, *Aztec Thought and Culture* (Norman: University of Oklahoma Press, 1963), p. 84.

2. David Carrasco, *Religions of Mesoamerica* (San Francisco, Harpes and Row 1990).

3. I do not have the space here to go into a detailed explanation of the complex Mayan system of interlocking calendars. Suffice it to say that they developed their calendar system, which consisted of at least six different calendars, in order to pinpoint and keep track of the important events in their history. For an excellent explanation of their calendar system, see Schele and Miller, pp. 317–21.

## Recommended Readings

TEXTS

Chadwick, Henry. *Augustine*. Oxford: Oxford University Press, 1986.

Clark, Mary T., trans. *Augustine of Hippo: Selected Writings*. New York: Paulist Press, 1984.

D'Arcy, M. C. *St. Augustine*. New York: Meridian Books, 1957.

Markus, R. A., ed. *Augustine: A Collection of Critical Essays*. Garden City, NY: Doubleday & Co., 1972.

Marron, Henri. *Saint Augustine*. Trans. Patrick Hepburne-Scott. London: Longmans, Green and Co., 1957.

Meagher, Robert. *Augustine: An Introduction*. New York: Harper & Row, 1979.

O'Meara, John J, ed. *An Augustine Reader*. Garden City, NY: Image Books, 1973.

FEMINIST PERSPECTIVE

Lucas, Angela. *Women in the Middle Ages: Religion, Marriage and Letters*. Brighton: Harvester Press, 1984.

Pierce, Christine. "Natural Law Language and Women." In *Women in Sexist Society,* edited by Vivian Gornick and Barbara K. Moran. New York: Basic Books, 1971.

MULTICULTURAL PERSPECTIVE

Jorrin, Miguel and Martz, John, *Latin-American Political Thought and Ideology,* Chapel Hill: University of North Carolina Press, 1970.

Leon-Portilla, Leon, *Aztec Thought and Culture,* Norman: University of Oklahoma Press, 1963.

# IV

---

# *Aquinas*

## Introduction

THOMAS AQUINAS WAS BORN IN 1224 or 1225 in the castle of Roccaecca near Aquino, between Naples and Rome. His family belonged to the lesser nobility of the area. When Aquinas was five, he was placed in the Benedictine monastery of Monte Cassino. At fourteen, he entered the University of Naples, which had been founded by Emperor Frederick II in 1224. There he became acquainted with a new monastic order, the Dominicans, and in 1244 he decided to join the order. His family objected to this decision because they had hoped that he would join the local Benedictine order and someday become abbot of Monte Cassino. To change his mind, Aquinas's brothers kidnapped him and imprisoned him in one of the family castles. After a year, however, his mother relented and arranged his escape. Aquinas then went to Paris to begin his Dominican novitiate and study with Albert the Great, the greatest teacher of the day. In 1248, Aquinas followed Albert to Cologne and later, on Albert's recommendation, returned to Paris to complete his master (professor) of theology degree in 1256.

Aquinas was a highly successful teacher and attracted many students. In addition to teaching and traveling extensively on ecclesiastical business, in the space of twenty years, he wrote seventeen volumes on philosophy and theology. It is reported that he could dictate simultaneously to four secretaries, each on different topics.

In 1264 he completed his *Summa Contra Gentiles,* and in 1265 he began *On Kingship,* which he never completed. In 1266, he began work on what was to be his most important work, his *Summa Theologica,* which was intended to be a systematic introduction to theology for Dominican novices.

Called to Lyons, in 1274, by Pope Gregory X to participate in a council, en route he struck his head and died of complications. Fifty years later, he was canonized by the Church.

Aquinas's overall goal was to reconcile reason, particularly as reflected in the work of Aristotle, with Christian faith. In our first selection from the *Summa Theologica,* Aquinas pursues that goal by defining law in general as the rule or measure of human acts, a rule or measure determined by reason and promulgated with a view to the common good by whoever has care of the community. Aquinas then distinguishes several kinds of law—

eternal law, natural law, human law, and divine law—on the basis of their origins. Eternal law is God's plan directing all things to their ends. Natural law is that part of the eternal law that is knowable by human beings through reason alone. Human law is the determination of natural law by human reason. Divine law is a special revelation from God, directing human behavior.

Aquinas argues that the first precept of the natural law is that good is to be done and pursued and evil to be avoided, and that from this precept all other precepts are derived. Aquinas then discusses the respects in which natural law is the same and not the same for all humans, the respects in which natural law can be changed and not changed, and the respects in which natural law can be abolished and not abolished from the human heart.

As a component of his attempt to reconcile faith and reason, it is difficult to object to Aquinas's general accounts of law and natural law. It is much easier to object to what are taken to be particular requirements of natural law.

Presumably, Aquinas takes the recommendations that he makes in *On Kingship* to be particular requirements of natural law. Yet obviously, Aquinas's argument in favor of kings would not be given much credence today. Aquinas's views about women set out in the second selection from the *Summa Theologica* are also outrageous from a feminist standpoint. Aquinas accepts Aristotle's view that a woman is a misbegotten man. He also claims that a woman is a helpmate to man only with respect to procreation and the care of children. For all other things, Aquinas contends, men are better served by other men.

In *The Equality of Men and Women*, written in 1622, Marie le Jars de Gournay defends the equality of women, working within much the same philosophical and religious traditions as Aquinas. Thus, she appeals to the authority of scripture (the writings of St. Paul, St. Peter, and St. John the Evangelist), the pillars of the Church (Theodoret, Jerome), and great men who have served as guiding lights of the world (Plato, Socrates, Antisthenes, Plutarch, and Seneca). She also advances a number of arguments of her own. She does, however, misrepresent Aristotle's view, claiming that he does not "hold an unfavorable opinion of the ladies."

Maimonides, in our selection from *Guide for the Perplexed*, like Aquinas yet writing before him, sought to reconcile reason, particularly as reflected in the work of Aristotle, with faith, but in his case, it is Judaism, not Christianity, that is to be reconciled with reason. Maimonides claims that it is possible to reconcile all 613 commandments of the Jewish law with reason, on the grounds that they all serve the general welfare. However, most people today would have difficulty believing that putting a stubborn and rebellious son to death or renouncing sexual intercourse would serve the general welfare or in any other way be a requirement of reason.

# 14     Summa Theologica

## THOMAS AQUINAS

*Part II*
*First Part*

## QUESTION 90.
## OF THE ESSENCE OF LAW.

*First Article.*
*Whether Law Is Something*
*Pertaining to Reason?*

*We proceed thus to the First Article:*—

*Objection* 1. It seems that law is not something pertaining to reason. For the Apostle says (Rom. vii. 23): *I see another law in my members,* etc. But nothing pertaining to reason is in the members; since the reason does not make use of a bodily organ. Therefore law is not something pertaining to reason.

*Obj.* 2. Further, in the reason there is nothing else but power, habit, and act. But law is not the power itself of reason. In like manner, neither is it a habit of reason: because the habits of reason are the intellectual virtues of which we have spoken . . . (Q. LVII.). Nor again is it an act of reason: because then law would cease, when the act of reason ceases, for instance, while we are asleep. Therefore law is nothing pertaining to reason.

*Obj.* 3. Further, the law moves those who are subject to it to act aright. But it belongs properly to the will to move to act, as is evident from what has been said . . . (Q. IX., A. I). Therefore law pertains, not to the reason, but to the will; according to the words of the Jurist (*Lib.* i. *ff., De Const. Prin.*): *Whatsoever pleaseth the sovereign, has force of law.*

*On the contrary,* It belongs to the law to command and to forbid. But it belongs to reason to command, as stated . . . (Q. XVII., A. r). Therefore law is something pertaining to reason.

*I answer that,* Law is a rule and measure of acts, whereby man is induced to act or is restrained from acting: for *lex* (law) is derived from *ligare* (to bind), because it binds one to act. Now the rule and measure of human acts is the reason, which is the first principle of human acts, as is evident from what has been stated . . . (Q I., A., 1 *ad* 3); since it belongs to the reason to direct to the end, which is the first principle in all matters of action, according to the Philosopher (*Phys.* ii.). Now that which is the principle in any genus, is the rule and measure of the genus: for instance, unity in the genus of numbers, and the first movement in the genus of movements. Consequently it follows that law is something pertaining to reason.

*Reply Obj.* 1. Since law is a kind of rule and measure, it may be in something in two ways. First, as in that which measures and rules: and since this is proper to reason, it follows that, in this way, law is in the reason alone.—Secondly, as in that which is measured and ruled. In this way, law is in all those things that are inclined to something by reason of some law: so that any inclination arising from a law, may be called a law, not essentially but by participation as it were. And thus the inclination of the members to concupiscence is called *the law of the members.*

*Reply Obj.* 2. Just as, in external action, we may consider the work and the work done, for instance the work of building and the house built; so in the acts of reason, we may consider the act itself of reason, i.e., to understand and to reason, and something produced by this act. With regard to the speculative reason, this is first of all the definition; secondly, the proposition; thirdly, the syllogism or argument. And since also the practical reason makes use of a syllogism in respect of the work to be done, . . . (Q. XIII., A. 3; Q. LXXVI., A. I) and as the Philosopher teaches (*Ethic.* vii.); hence we find in the practical reason something that holds the same position in regard to operations, as, in the speculative intellect, the proposition holds in regard to conclusions. Suchlike universal propositions of the practical intellect that are directed to actions have the nature of law. And these propositions are sometimes under our actual consideration, while sometimes they are retained in the reason by means of a habit.

*Reply Obj.* 3. Reason has its power of moving from the will, . . . (Q. XVII., A. I): for it is due to the fact that one wills the end, that the reason issues its commands as regards things ordained to the end. But in order that the volition of what is commanded may have the nature of law, it needs to be in accord with some rule of reason. And in this sense is to be understood the saying that the will of the sovereign has the force of law; otherwise the sovereign's will would savour of lawlessness rather than of law.

## Second Article.
### Whether the Law is Always Directed to the Common Good?

*We proceed thus to the Second Article:—*

*Objection* 1. It seems that the law is not always directed to the common good as to its end. For it belongs to law to command and to forbid. But commands are directed to certain individual goods. Therefore the end of the law is not always the common good.

*Obj.* 2. Further, the law directs man in his actions. But human actions are concerned with particular matters. Therefore the law is directed to some particular good.

*Obj.* 3. Further, Isidore says (*Etym.* ii.): *If the law is based on reason, whatever is based on reason will be a law.* But reason is the foundation not only of what is ordained common good, but also of that which is directed to private good. Therefore that law is not only directed to the good of all, but also to the private good of an individual.

*On the contrary,* Isidore says (*Etym.* v.) that *laws are enacted for no private profit, but for the common benefit of the citizens.*

*I answer that,* As stated above (A. 1), the law belongs to that which is a principle of human acts, because it is their rule and measure. Now as reason is a principle of human acts, so in reason itself there is something which is the principle in respect of all the rest: wherefore to this principle chiefly and mainly law must needs be referred.—Now the first principle in practical matters, which are the object of the practical reason, is that last end: and the last end of human life is bliss or happiness . . . (Q. II., A. 7; Q. III., A. 1). Consequently the law must needs regard principally the relationship to happiness. Moreover, since every part is ordained to the whole, as imperfect to perfect; and since one man is a part of the perfect community, the law must needs regard properly the relationship to universal happiness. Wherefore the Philosopher, in the above definition of legal matters mentions both happiness and the body politic: for he says (*Ethic.* v.) that we call those legal matters *just, which are adapted to produce and preserve happiness and its parts for the body politic:* since the state is a perfect community, as he says in *Polit.* i.

Now in every genus, that which belongs to it chiefly is the principle of the others, and the others belong to that genus in subordination to that thing: thus fire, which is chief among hot things, is the cause of heat in mixed bodies, and these are said to be hot in so far as they have a share of fire. Consequently, since the law is chiefly ordained to the common good, any other precept in regard to some individual work, must needs be devoid of the nature of a law, save in so far as it regards the common good. Therefore every law is ordained to the common good.

*Reply Obj.* 1. A command denotes an application of a law to matters regulated by the law. Now the order to the common good, at which the law aims, is applicable to particular ends. And in this way commands are given even concerning particular matters.

*Reply Obj.* 2. Actions are indeed concerned with particular matters: but those particular matters are referable to the common good, not as to a common genus or species, but as to a common final cause, according as the common good is said to be the common end.

*Reply Obj.* 3. Just as nothing stands firm with regard to the speculative reason except that which is traced back to the first indemonstrable principles, so nothing stands firm with regard to the practical reason, unless it be directed to the last end which is the common good: and whatever stands to reason in this sense, has the nature of a law.

## Third Article.
### Whether the Reason of Any Man Is Competent to Make Laws?

*We proceed thus to the Third Article:—*

*Objection* 1. It seems that the reason of any man is competent to make laws. For the Apostle says (Rom. ii 14) that *when the Gentiles, who have not the law, do by nature those things that are of the law, . . . they are a law to themselves.* Now he says this of all in general. Therefore anyone can make a law for himself.

*Obj.* 2. Further, as the Philosopher says (*Ethic.* ii.), *the intention of the lawgiver is to lead men to virtue.* But every man can lead another to virtue. Therefore the reason of any man is competent to make laws.

*Obj.* 3. Further, just as the sovereign of a state governs the state, so every father of a family governs his household. But the sovereign of a state can make laws for the state. Therefore every father of a family can make laws for his household.

*On the contrary,* Isidore says (*Etym.* v.; and the passage is quoted in *Decretals, Dist.* 2): *A law is an ordinance of the people, whereby something is sanctioned by the Elders together with the Commonalty.*

*I answer that,* A law, properly speaking, regards first and foremost the order to the common good. Now to order anything to the common good, belongs either to the whole people, or to someone who is the viceregent of the whole people. And therefore the making of a law belongs either to the whole people or to a public personage who has care of the whole people: since in all other matters the directing of anything to the end concerns him to whom the end belongs.

*Reply Obj.* 1. As stated above (*A.* 1 *ad* 1), a law

is in a person not only as in one that rules, but also by participation as in one that is ruled. In the latter way each one is a law to himself, in so far as he shares the direction that he receives from one who rules him. Hence the same text goes on: *Who show the work of the law written in their hearts.*

*Reply Obj.* 2. A private person cannot lead another to virtue efficaciously: for he can only advise, and if his advice be not taken, it has no coercive power, such as the law should have, in order to prove an efficacious inducement to virtue, as the Philosopher says (*Ethic.* x.). But this coercive power is vested in the whole people or in some public personage, to whom it belongs to inflict penalties . . . (Q. XCII., A. 2 *ad* 3; II. -II., Q. LXIV., A. 3). Wherefore the framing of laws belongs to him alone.

*Reply Obj.* 3. As one man is a part of the household, so a household is a part of the state: and the state is a perfect community, according to *Polit.* i. And therefore, as the good of one man is not the last end, but is ordained to the common good; so too the good of one household is ordained to the good of a single state, which is a perfect community. Consequently he that governs a family, can indeed make certain commands or ordinances, but not such as to have properly the force of law.

## Fourth Article.
### Whether Promulgation Is Essential to a Law?

*We proceed thus to the Fourth Article:—*

*Objection* 1. It seems that promulgation is not essential to a law. For the natural law above all has the character of law. But the natural law needs no promulgation. Therefore it is not essential to a law that it be promulgated.

*Obj.* 2. Further, it belongs properly to a law to bind one to do or not to do something. But the obligation of fulfilling a law touches not only those in whose presence it is promulgated, but also others. Therefore promulgation is not essential to a law.

*Obj.* 3. Further, the binding force of a law extends even to the future, since *laws are binding in matters of the future,* as the jurists say (*Cod.* i., tit. *De lege et constit.*). But promulgation concerns those who are present. Therefore it is not essential to a law.

*On the contrary,* It is laid down in the *Decretals* (*Append. Grat.*) that *laws are established when they are promulgated.*

*I answer that,* As stated above (A. 1), a law is imposed on others by way of a rule and measure. Now a rule or measure is imposed by being applied to those who are to be ruled and measured by it. Wherefore, in order that a law obtain the binding force which is proper to a law, it must needs be applied to the men who have to be ruled by it. Such application is made by its being notified to them by promulgation. Wherefore promulgation is necessary for the law to obtain its force.

Thus from the four preceding articles, the definition of law may be gathered; and it is nothing else than an ordinance of reason for the common good, made by him who has care of the community, and promulgated.

*Reply Obj.* 1. The natural law is promulgated by the very fact that God instilled it into man's mind so as to be known by him naturally.

*Reply Obj.* 2. Those who are not present when a law is promulgated, are bound to observe the law, in so far as it is notified or can be notified to them by others, after it has been promulgated.

*Reply Obj.* 3. The promulgation that takes place now, extends to future time by reason of the durability of written characters, by which means it is continually promulgated. Hence Isidore says (*Etym.* ii.) that *lex* (law) *is derived from legere* (to read) *because it is written.*

## QUESTION 91.
## OF THE VARIOUS KINDS OF LAW.

*First Article.*
## Whether There Is an Eternal Law?

*We proceed thus to the First Article:—*

*Objection* 1. It seems that there is no eternal law. Because every law is imposed on someone. But there was not someone from eternity on whom a law could be imposed: since God alone was from eternity. Therefore no law is eternal.

*Obj.* 2. Further, promulgation is essential to law. But promulgation could not be from eternity: because there was no one to whom it could be promulgated from eternity. Therefore no law can be eternal.

*Obj.* 3. Further, a law implies order to an end. But nothing ordained to an end is eternal: for the last end alone is eternal. Therefore no law is eternal.

*On the contrary,* Augustine says (*De Lib. Arb.* i.): *That Law which is the Supreme Reason cannot be understood to be otherwise than unchangeable and eternal.*

*I answer that,* As stated above (Q. XC., A. 1 *ad* 2; AA. 3, 4), a law is nothing else but a dictate of practical reason emanating from the ruler who governs a perfect community. Now it is evident, granted that the world is ruled by Divine Providence . . . (Q. XXII., AA., 1, 2), that the whole community of the universe is governed by Divine Reason. Wherefore the very Idea of the government of things in God the Ruler of the universe, has the nature of a law. And since the Divine Reason's conception of things is not subject to time but is eternal, according to Prov. viii. 23, therefore it is that this kind of law must be called eternal.

*Reply Obj.* 1. Those things that are not in themselves, exist with God, inasmuch as they are foreknown and preordained by Him, according to Rom. iv. 17: *Who calls those things that are not, as those that are.* Accordingly the eternal concept of the Divine law bears the character of an eternal law, in so far as it is ordained by God to the government of things foreknown by Him.

*Reply Obj.* 2. Promulgation is made by word of mouth or in writing; and in both ways the eternal law is promulgated: because both the Divine Word and the writing of the Book of Life are eternal. But the promulgation cannot be from eternity on the part of the creature that hears or reads.

*Reply Obj.* 3. The law implies order to the end actively, in so far as it directs certain things to the end; but not passively,—that is to say, the law itself is not ordained to the end,—except accidentally, in a governor whose end is extrinsic to him, and to which end his law must needs be ordained. But the end of the Divine government is God Himself, and His law is not distinct from Himself. Wherefore the eternal law is not ordained to another end.

## Second Article.
### Whether There Is in Us a Natural Law?

*We proceed thus to the Second Article:—*

*Objection* 1. It seems that there is no natural law in us. Because man is governed sufficiently by the eternal law: for Augustine says (*De Lib. Arb.* i.) that *the eternal law is that by which it is right that all things should be most orderly.* But nature does not abound in superfluities as neither does she fail in necessaries. Therefore no law is natural to man.

*Obj.* 2. Further, by the law man is directed, in his acts, to the end, as stated above (Q. XC., A. 2). But the directing of human acts to their end is not a function of nature, as is the case in irrational creatures, which act for an end solely by their natural appetite; whereas man acts for an end by his reason and will. Therefore no law is natural to man.

*Obj.* 3. Further, the more a man is free, the less is he under the law. But man is freer than all the animals, on account of his free-will, with which he is endowed above all other animals. Since therefore other animals are not subject to a natural law, neither is man subject to a natural law.

*On the contrary,* The gloss on Rom. ii. 14: *When the Gentiles, who have not the law, do by nature those things that are of the law,* comments as follows: *Although they have no written law, yet they have the natural law, whereby each one knows, and is conscious of, what is good and what is evil.*

*I answer that,* As stated above (Q. XC., A. 1 *ad* 1), law, being a rule and measure, can be in a person in two ways: in one way, as in him that rules and measures; in another way, as in that which is ruled and measured, since a thing is ruled and measured, in so far as it partakes of the rule or measure. Wherefore, since all things subject to Divine providence are ruled and measured by the

eternal law, as was stated above (A. 1); it is evident that all things partake somewhat of the eternal law, in so far as, namely, from its being imprinted on them, they derive their respective inclinations to their proper acts and ends. Now among all others, the rational creature is subject to Divine providence in the most excellent way, in so far as it partakes of a share of providence, by being provident both for itself and for others. Wherefore it has a share of the Eternal Reason, whereby it has a natural inclination to its proper act and end: and this participation of the eternal law in the rational creature is called the natural law. Hence the Psalmist after saying (Ps. iv. 6): *Offer up the sacrifice of justice,* as though someone asked what the works of justice are, adds: *Many say, Who showeth us good things?* in answer to which question he says: *The light of Thy countenance, O Lord, is signed upon us:* thus implying that the light of natural reason, whereby we discern what is good and what is evil, which is the function of the natural law, is nothing else than an imprint on us of the Divine light. It is therefore evident that the natural law is nothing else than the rational creature's participation of the eternal law.

*Reply Obj.* 1. This argument would hold, if the natural law were something different from the eternal law: whereas it is nothing but a participation thereof, as stated above.

*Reply Obj.* 2. Every act of reason and will in us is based on that which is according to nature . . . (Q. X., A. 1): for every act of reasoning is based on principles that are known naturally, and every act of appetite in respect of the means is derived from the natural appetite in respect of the last end. Accordingly the first direction of our acts to their end must needs be in virtue of the natural law.

*Reply Obj.* 3. Even irrational animals partake in their own way of the Eternal Reason, just as the rational creature does. But because the rational creature partakes thereof in an intellectual and rational manner, therefore the participation of the eternal law in the rational creature is properly called a law, since a law is something pertaining to reason, as stated above (Q. XC., A. 1). Irrational creatures, however, do not partake thereof in a rational manner, wherefore there is no participation of the eternal law in them, except by way of similitude.

## Third Article.
## Whether There Is a Human Law?

*We proceed thus to the Third Article:—*

*Objection* 1. It seems that there is not a human law. For the natural law is a participation of the eternal law, as stated above (A. 2). Now through the eternal law *all things are most orderly*, as Augustine states (*De Lib. Arb.* i.). Therefore the natural law suffices for the ordering of all human affairs. Consequently there is no need for a human law.

*Obj.* 2. Further, a law bears the character of a measure, as stated above (Q. XC., A. 1). But human reason is not a measure of things, but vice versa (*cf. Metaph.* x.). Therefore no law can emanate from human reason.

*Obj.* 3. Further, a measure should be most certain, as stated in *Metaph.* x. But the dictates of human reason in matters of conduct are uncertain, according to Wis. ix. 14: *The thoughts of mortal man are fearful, and our counsels uncertain.* Therefore no law can emanate from human reason.

*On the contrary,* Augustine *De Lib. Arb.* i.) distinguishes two kinds of law, the one eternal, the other temporal, which he calls human.

*I answer that,* As stated above (Q. XC., A. 1, *ad* 2), a law is a dictate of the practical reason. Now it is to be observed that the same procedure takes place in the practical and in the speculative reason: for each proceeds from principles to conclusions, as stated above (*ibid.*). Accordingly we conclude that just as, in the speculative reason, from naturally known indemonstrable principles, we draw the conclusions of the various sciences, the knowledge of which is not imparted to us by nature, but acquired by the efforts of reason, so too it is from the precepts of the natural law, as from general and indemonstrable principles, that the human reason needs to proceed to the more particular determination of certain matters. These particular determinations, devised by human reason, are called human laws, provided the other essential conditions

of law be observed, as stated above (Q. XC., AA. 2, 3, 4). Wherefore Tully says in his *Rhetoric* (*De Invent. Rhet.* ii.) that *justice has its source in nature; thence certain things came into custom by reason of their utility; afterwards these things which emanated from nature and were approved by custom, were sanctioned by fear and reverence for the law.*

*Reply Obj.* 1. The human reason cannot have a full participation of the dictate of the Divine Reason, but according to its own mode, and imperfectly. Consequently, as on the part of the speculative reason, by a natural participation of Divine Wisdom, there is in us the knowledge of certain general principles, but not proper knowledge of each single truth, such as that contained in the Divine Wisdom; so too, on the part of the practical reason, man has a natural participation of the eternal law, according to certain general principles, but not as regards the particular determinations of individual cases, which are, however, contained in the eternal law. Hence the need for human reason to proceed further to sanction them by law.

*Reply Obj.* 2. Human reason is not, of itself, the rule of things: but the principles impressed on it by nature, are general rules and measures of all things relating to human conduct, whereof the natural reason is the rule and measure, although it is not the measure of things that are from nature.

*Reply Obj.* 3. The practical reason is concerned with practical matters, which are singular and contingent: but not with necessary things, with which the speculative reason is concerned. Wherefore human laws cannot have that inerrancy that belongs to the demonstrated conclusions of sciences. Nor is it necessary for every measure to be altogether unerring and certain, but according as it is possible in its own particular genus.

## Fourth Article.
## Whether There Was Any Need for a Divine Law?

*We proceed thus to the Fourth Article:—*

*Objection* 1. It seems that there was no need for a Divine law. Because, as stated above (A. 2), the natural law is a participation in us of the eternal law. But the eternal law is a Divine law, as stated above (A. 1). Therefore there is no need for a Divine law in addition to the natural law, and human laws derived therefrom.

*Obj.* 2. Further, it is written (Ecclus. xv. 14) that *God left man in the hand of his own counsel.* Now counsel is an act of reason . . . (Q. XIV., A. 1). Therefore man was left to the direction of his reason. But a dictate of human reason is a human law, as stated above (A. 3). Therefore there is no need for man to be governed also by a Divine law.

*Obj.* 3. Further, human nature is more self-sufficing than irrational creatures. But irrational creatures have no Divine law besides the natural inclination impressed on them. Much less, therefore, should the rational creature have a Divine law in addition to the natural law.

*On the contrary,* David prayed God to set His law before him, saying: *Set before me for a law the way of Thy justifications, O Lord.*

*I answer that,* Besides the natural and the human law it was necessary for the directing of human conduct to have a Divine law. And this for four reasons. First, because it is by law that man is directed how to perform his proper acts in view of his last end. And indeed if man were ordained to no other end than that which is proportionate to his natural faculty, there would be no need for man to have any further direction on the part of his reason, besides the natural law and human law which is derived from it. But since man is ordained to an end of eternal happiness which is inproportionate to man's natural faculty . . . (Q. V., A. 5), therefore it was necessary that, besides the natural and the human law, man should be directed to his end by a law given by God.

Secondly, because, on account of the uncertainty of human judgment, especially on contingent and particular matters, different people form different judgments on human acts; whence also different and contrary laws result. In order, therefore, that man may know without any doubt what he ought to do and what he ought to avoid, it was necessary for man to be directed in his proper acts by a law given by God, for it is certain that such a law cannot err.

Thirdly, because man can make laws in those matters of which he is competent to judge. But man is not competent to judge of interior movements, that are hidden, but only of exterior acts which appear: and yet for the perfection of virtue it is necessary for man to conduct himself aright in both kinds of acts. Consequently human law could not sufficiently curb and direct interior acts; and it was necessary for this purpose that a Divine law should supervene.

Fourthly, because, as Augustine says (*De Lib. Arb.* i.), human law cannot punish or forbid all evil deeds: since while aiming at doing away with all evils, it would do away with many good things, and would hinder the advance of the common good, which is necessary for human intercourse. In order, therefore, that no evil might remain unforbidden and unpunished, it was necessary for the Divine law to supervene, whereby all sins are forbidden.

And these four causes are touched upon in Ps. cxviii. 8, where it is said: *The law of the Lord is unspotted,* i.e., allowing no foulness of sin; *converting souls,* because it directs not only exterior, but also interior acts; *the testimony of the Lord is faithful,* because of the certainty of what is true and right; *giving wisdom to little ones,* by directing man to an end supernatural and Divine.

*Reply Obj.* 1. By the natural law the eternal law is participated proportionately to the capacity of human nature. But to his supernatural end man needs to be directed in a yet higher way. Hence the additional law given by God, whereby man shares more perfectly in the eternal law.

*Reply Obj.* 2. Counsel is a kind of inquiry: hence it must proceed from some principles. Nor is it enough for it to proceed from principles imparted by nature, which are the precepts of the natural law, for the reasons given above: but there is need for certain additional principles, namely the precepts of the Divine law.

*Reply Obj.* 3. Irrational creatures are not ordained to an end higher than that which is proportionate to their natural powers: consequently the comparison fails. . . .

# QUESTION 94.
## OF THE NATURAL LAW.

## First Article.
### Whether the Natural Law Is a Habit?

*We proceed thus to the First Article:—*

*Objection* 1. It seems that the natural law is a habit. Because, as the Philosopher says (*Ethic.* ii.), *there are three things in the soul, power, habit and passion.* But the natural law is not one of the soul's powers: nor is it one of the passions; as we may see by going through them one by one. Therefore the natural law is a habit.

*Obj.* 2. Further, Basil (Damascene, *De Fide Orthod.* iv.) says that the conscience or *synderesis is the law of our mind;* which can only apply to the natural law. But the *synderesis* is a habit . . . (Q. LXXIX., A. 12). Therefore the natural law is a habit.

*Obj.* 3. Further, the natural law abides in man always, as will be shown further on (A. 6). But man's reason, which the law regards, does not always think about the natural law. Therefore the natural law is not an act, but a habit.

*On the contrary,* Augustine says (*De Bono Conjug.* xxi.) that *a habit is that whereby something is done when necessary.* But such is not the natural law: since it is in infants and in the damned who cannot act by it. Therefore the natural law is not a habit.

*I answer that,* A thing may be called a habit in two ways. First, properly and essentially: and thus the natural law is not a habit. For it has been stated above (Q. XC., A. 1 *ad* 2) that natural law is something appointed by reason, just as a proposition is a work of reason. Now that which a man does is not the same as that whereby he does it: for he makes a becoming speech by the habit of grammar. Since then a habit is that by which we act, a law cannot be a habit properly and essentially.

Secondly, the term habit may be applied to that which we hold by a habit: thus faith may mean that which we hold by faith. And accordingly, since the precepts of the natural law are sometimes considered by reason actually, while sometimes they are in the reason only habitually, in this way the natural law may be called a habit. Thus, in speculative matters, the indemonstrable principles are not the habit itself whereby we hold those principles, but are the principles the habit of which we possess.

*Reply Obj.* 1. The Philosopher proposes there to discover the genus of virtue; and since it is evident that virtue is a principle of action, he mentions only those things which are principles of human acts, viz., powers, habits and passions. But there are other things in the soul besides these three: there are acts; thus *to will* is in the one that wills; again, things known are in the knower; moreover its own natural properties are in the soul, such as immortality and the like.

*Reply Obj.* 2. *Synderesis* is said to be the law of our mind, because it is a habit containing the precepts of the natural law, which are the first principles of human actions.

*Reply Obj.* 3. This argument proves that the natural law is held habitually: and this is granted.

*To the argument advanced in the contrary sense* we reply that sometimes a man is unable to make use of that which is in him habitually, on account of some impediment: thus, on account of sleep, a man is unable to use the habit of science. In like manner, through the deficiency of his age, a child cannot use the habit of understanding of principles, or the natural law, which is in him habitually.

## Second Article.
### Whether the Natural Law Contains Several Precepts, or One Only?

*We proceed thus to the Second Article:—*

*Objection* 1. It seems that the natural law contains, not several precepts, but one only. For law is a kind of precept . . . (Q. XCII., A. 2). If therefore there were many precepts of the natural law, it would follow that there are also many natural laws.

*Obj.* 2. Further, the natural law is consequent to human nature. But human nature, as a whole, is one; though, as to its parts, it is manifold.

Therefore, either there is but one precept of the law of nature, on account of the unity of nature as a whole; or there are many, by reason of the number of parts of human nature. The result would be that even things relating to the inclination of the concupiscible faculty belong to the natural law.

*Obj.* 3. Further, law is something pertaining to reason, as stated above (Q. XC., A. 1). Now reason is but one in man. Therefore there is only one precept of the natural law.

*On the contrary,* The precepts of the natural law in man stand in relation to practical matters, as the first principles to matters of demonstration. But there are several first indemonstrable principles. Therefore there are also several precepts of the natural law.

*I answer that,* As stated above (Q. XCI., A. 3), the precepts of the natural law are to the practical reason, what the first principles of demonstrations are to the speculative reason; because both are self-evident principles. Now a thing is said to be self-evident in two ways: first, in itself; secondly, in relation to us. Any proposition is said to be self-evident in itself, if its predicate is contained in the notion of the subject: although, to one who knows not the definition of the subject, it happens that such a proposition is not self-evident. For instance, this proposition, *Man is a rational being,* is, in its very nature, self-evident, since who says *man,* says a *rational being:* and yet to one who knows not what a man is, this proposition is not self-evident. Hence it is that, as Boethius says (*De Hebdom.*), certain axioms or propositions are universally self-evident to all; and such are those propositions whose terms are known to all, as, *Every whole is greater than its part,* and, *Things equal to one and the same are equal to one another.* But some propositions are self-evident only to the wise, who understand the meaning of the terms of such propositions: thus to one who understands that an angel is not a body, it is self-evident that an angel is not circumscriptively in a place: but this is not evident to the unlearned, for they cannot grasp it.

Now a certain order is to be found in those things that are apprehended universally. For that which, before aught else, falls under apprehension, is *being,* the notion of which is included in all things whatsoever a man apprehends. Wherefore the first indemonstrable principle is that *the same thing cannot be affirmed and denied at the same time,* which is based on the notion of *being* and *not-being:* and on this principle all others are based, as is stated in *Metaph.* iv. Now as *being* is the first thing that falls under the apprehension simply, so *good* is the first thing that falls under the apprehension of the practical reason, which is directed to action: since every agent acts for an end under the aspect of good. Consequently the first principle in the practical reason is one founded on the notion of good, viz., that *good is that which all things seek after.* Hence this is the first precept of law, that *good is to be done and ensued, and evil is to be avoided.* All other precepts of the natural law are based upon this: so that whatever the practical reason naturally apprehends as man's good (or evil) belongs to the precepts of the natural law as something to be done or avoided.

Since, however, good has the nature of an end, and evil, the nature of a contrary, hence it is that all those things to which man has a natural inclination, are naturally apprehended by reason as being good, and consequently as objects of pursuit, and their contraries as evil, and objects of avoidance. Wherefore according to the order of natural inclinations, is the order of the precepts of the natural law. Because in man there is first of all an inclination to good in accordance with the nature which he has in common with all substances: inasmuch as every substance seeks the preservation of its own being, according to its nature: and by reason of this inclination, whatever is a means of preserving human life, and of warding off its obstacles, belongs to the natural law. Secondly, there is in man an inclination of things that pertain to him more specially, according to that nature which he has in common with other animals: and in virtue of this inclination, those things are said to belong to the natural law, *which nature has taught to all animals* (*Pandect. Just.* I., Tit. I.), such as sexual intercourse, education of offspring and so forth. Thirdly, there is in man an inclination to good, according to the nature of his reason, which nature is proper to him: thus man has a natural inclination to know the truth about God, and to live in society: and in this respect, whatever pertains to this inclination belongs to the natural law; for instance, to shun ignorance, to avoid offending those among whom one has to live, and other such things regarding the above inclination.

*Reply Obj.* 1. All these precepts of the law of nature have the character of one natural law, inasmuch as they flow from one first precept.

*Reply Obj.* 2. All the inclinations of any parts whatsoever of human nature, *e.g.,* of the concupiscible and irascible parts, in so far as they are ruled by reason, belong to the natural law, and are reduced to one first precept, as stated above: so that the precepts of the natural law are many in themselves, but are based on one common foundation.

*Reply Obj.* 3. Although reason is one in itself, yet it directs all things regarding man; so that whatever can be ruled by reason, is contained under the law of reason.

## Third Article.
## Whether All Acts of Virtue Are Prescribed by the Natural Law?

*We proceed thus to the Third Article:—*

*Objection* 1. It seems that not all acts of virtue are prescribed by the natural law. Because, as stated above (Q. XC., A. 2) it is essential to a law that it be ordained to the common good. But some acts of virtue are ordained to the private good of the individual, as is evident especially in regard to acts of temperance. Therefore not all acts of virtue are the subject of natural law.

*Obj.* 2. Further, every sin is opposed to some virtuous act. If therefore all acts of virtue are prescribed by the natural law, it seems to follow that all sins are against nature: whereas this applies to certain special sins.

*Obj.* 3. Further, those things which are according to nature are common to all. But acts of virtue are not common to all: since a thing is virtuous in

one, and vicious in another. Therefore not all acts of virtue are prescribed by the natural law.

*On the contrary,* Damascene says (*De Fide Orthod.* iii.) that *virtues are natural.* Therefore virtuous acts also are a subject of the natural law.

*I answer that,* We may speak of virtuous acts in two ways: first, under the aspect of virtuous; secondly, as such and such acts considered in their proper species. If then we speak of acts of virtue, considered as virtuous, thus all virtuous acts belong to the natural law. For it has been stated (A. 2) that to the natural law belongs everything to which a man is inclined according to his nature. Now each thing is inclined naturally to an operation that is suitable to it according to its form: thus fire is inclined to give heat. Wherefore, since the rational soul is the proper form of man, there is in every man a natural inclination to act according to reason: and this is to act according to virtue. Consequently, considered thus, all acts of virtue are prescribed by the natural law: since each one's reason naturally dictates to him to act virtuously. But if we speak of virtuous acts, considered in themselves, i.e., in their proper species, thus not all virtuous acts are prescribed by the natural law: for many things are done virtuously, to which nature does not incline at first; but which, through the inquiry of reason, have been found by men to be conducive to well-living.

*Reply Obj.* 1. Temperance is about the natural concupiscence of food, drink and sexual matters, which are indeed ordained to the natural common good, just as other matters of law are ordained to the moral common good.

*Reply Obj.* 2. By human nature we may mean either that which is proper to man—and in this sense all sins, as being against reason, are also against nature, as Damascene states (*De Fide Orthod.* ii.): or we may mean that nature which is common to man and other animals; and in this sense, certain special sins are said to be against nature; thus contrary to sexual intercourse, which is natural to all animals, is unisexual lust, which has received the special name of the unnatural crime.

*Reply Obj.* 3. This argument considers acts in themselves. For it is owing to the various conditions of men, that certain acts are virtuous for some, as being proportionate and becoming to them, while they are vicious for others, as being out of proportion to them.

## Fourth Article.
## Whether the Natural Law Is the Same in All Men?

*We proceed thus to the Fourth Article.—*

*Objection* 1. It seems that the natural law is not the same in all. For it is stated in the Decretals (*Dist.* i. (that *the natural law is that which is contained in the Law and the Gospel.* But this is not common to all men; because, as it is written (Rom. x. 16), *all do not obey the gospel.* Therefore the natural law is not the same in all men.

*Obj.* 2. Further, *Things which are according to the law are said to be just,* as stated in *Ethic.* v. But it is stated in the same book that nothing is so universally just as not to be subject to change in regard to some men. Therefore even the natural law is not the same in all men.

*Obj.* 3. Further, as stated above (AA. 2, 3), to the natural law belongs everything to which a man is inclined according to his nature. Now different men are naturally inclined to different things; some to the desire of pleasures, others to the desire of honours, and other men to other things. Therefore there is not one natural law for all.

*On the contrary,* Isidore says (*Etym.* v.); *The natural law is common to all nations.*

*I answer that,* As stated above (AA. 2, 3), to the natural law belongs those things to which a man is inclined naturally: and among these it is proper to man to be inclined to act according to reason. Now the process of reason is from the common to the proper, as stated in *Phys.* i. The speculative reason, however, is differently situated in this matter, from the practical reason. For, since the speculative reason is busied chiefly with necessary things, which cannot be otherwise than they are, its proper conclusions, like the universal principles, contain the truth without fail. The practical reason, on the other hand, is busied with contingent matters, about which human actions are concerned: and consequently, although there is necessity in the general principles, the more we descend to matters of detail, the more frequently we encounter defects. Accordingly then in speculative matters truth is the same in all men, both as to principles and as to conclusions: although the truth is not known to all as regards the conclusions, but only as regards the principles which are called common notions. But in matters of action, truth or practical rectitude is not the same for all, as to matters of detail, but only as to the general principles: and where there is the same rectitude in matters of detail, it is not equally known to all.

It is therefore evident that, as regards the general principles whether of speculative or of practical reason, truth or rectitude is the same for all, and is equally known by all. As to the proper conclusions of the speculative reason, the truth is the same for all, but is not equally known to all: thus it is true for all that the three angles of a triangle are together equal to two right angles, although it is not known to all. But as to the proper conclusions of the practical reason, neither is the truth or rectitude the same for all, nor, where it is the same, is it equally known by all. Thus it is right and true for all to act according to reason: and from this principle it follows as a proper conclusion, that goods entrusted to another should be restored to their owner. Now this is true for the majority of cases: but it may happen in a particular case that it would be injurious, and therefore unreasonable, to restore goods held in trust; for instance if they are claimed for the purpose of fighting against one's country. And this principle will be found to fail the more, according as we descend further into detail, *e.g.,* if one were to say that goods held in trust should be restored with such and such a guarantee, or in such and such a way; because the greater the number of conditions added, the greater the number of ways in which the principle may fail, so that it be not right to restore or not to restore.

Consequently we must say that the natural law, as to general principles, is the same for all, both as to rectitude and as to knowledge. But as to certain matters of detail, which are conclusions, as it were, of those general principles, it is the same for all in the majority of cases, both as to rectitude and as to knowledge; and yet in some few cases it may fail, both as to rectitude, by reason of certain obstacles (just as natures subject to generation and corruption fail in some few cases on account of some obstacle), and as to knowledge, since in some the reason is perverted by passion, or evil habit, or an evil disposition of nature; thus formerly, theft, although it is expressly contrary to the natural law, was not considered wrong among the Germans, as Julius Caesar relates (*De Bello Gall.* vi.).

*Reply Obj.* 1. The meaning of the sentence quoted is not that whatever is contained in the Law and the Gospel belongs to the natural law, since they contain many things that are above nature; but that whatever belongs to the natural law is fully contained in them. Wherefore Gratian, after saying that *the natural law is what is contained in the Law and the Gospel*, adds at once, by way of example, *by which everyone is commanded to do to others as he would be done by.*

*Reply Obj.* 2. The saying of the Philosopher is to be understood of things that are naturally just, not as general principles, but as conclusions drawn from them, having rectitude in the majority of cases, but failing in a few.

*Reply Obj.* 3. As, in man, reason rules and commands the other powers, so all the natural inclinations belonging to the other powers must needs be directed according to reason. Wherefore it is universally right for all men, that all their inclinations should be directed according to reason.

## Fifth Article.
## Whether the Natural Law Can Be Changed?

*We proceed thus to the Fifth Article:—*

*Objection* 1. It seems that the natural law can be changed. Because on Ecclus. vxii. 9, *He gave them instructions, and the law of life*, the gloss says: *He wished the law of the letter to be written, in order to correct the law of nature.* But that which is corrected is changed. Therefore the natural law can be changed.

*Obj.* 2. Further, the slaying of the innocent, adultery, and theft are against the natural law. But we find these things changed by God: as when God commanded Abraham to slay his innocent son (Gen. xxii. 2); and when He ordered the Jews to borrow and purloin the vessels of the Egyptians (Exod. xii. 35); and when He commanded Osee to take to himself *a wife of fornications* (*Osee* i. 2). Therefore the natural law can be changed.

*Obj.* 3. Further, Isidore says (*Etym.* v.) that *the possession of all things in common, and universal freedom, are matters of natural law.* But these things are seen to be changed by human laws. Therefore it seems that the natural law is subject to change.

*On the contrary,* It is said in the Decretals (*Dist.* v.): *The natural law dates from the creation of the rational creature. It does not vary according to time, but remains unchangeable.*

*I answer that,* A change in the natural law may be understood in two ways. First, by way of addition. In this sense nothing hinders the natural law from being changed: since many things for the benefit of human life have been added over and above the natural law, both by the Divine law and by human laws.

Secondly, a change in the natural law may be understood by way of subtraction, so that what previously was according to the natural law, ceases to be so. In this sense, the natural law is altogether unchangeable in its first principles: but in its secondary principles, which, as we have said (A. 4), are certain detailed proximate conclusions drawn from the first principles, the natural law is not changed so that what it prescribes be not right in most cases. But it may be changed in some particular cases of rare occurrence, through some special causes hindering the observance of such precepts, as stated above (A. 4).

*Reply Obj.* 1. The written law is said to be given for the correction of the natural law, either because it supplies what was wanting to the natural law; or because the natural law was perverted in the hearts of some men, as to certain matters, so that they esteemed those things good which are naturally evil; which perversion stood in need of correction.

*Reply Obj.* 2. All men alike, both guilty and innocent, die the death of nature: which death of nature is inflicted by the power of God on account of original sin, according to I Kings ii. 6: *The Lord killeth and maketh alive.* Consequently, by the command of God, death can be inflicted on any man, guilty or innocent, without any injustice whatever.—In like manner adultery is intercourse with another's wife; who is allotted to him by the law emanating from God. Consequently intercourse with any woman, by the command of God, is neither adultery nor fornication.—The same applies to theft, which is the taking of another's property. For whatever is taken by the command of God, to Whom all things belong, is not taken against the will of its owner, whereas it is in this that theft consists.—Nor is it only in human things, that whatever is commanded by God is right; but also in natural things, whatever is done by God is, in some way, natural . . . (Q. CV., A. 6 *ad* 1).

*Reply Obj.* 3. A thing is said to belong to the natural law in two ways. First, because nature inclines thereto: *e.g.*, that one should not do harm to another. Secondly, because nature did not bring in the contrary: thus we might say that for man to be naked is of the natural law, because nature did not give him clothes, but art invented them. In this sense, *the possession of all things in common and universal freedom* are said to be of the natural law, because, to wit, the distinction of possessions and slavery were not brought in by nature, but devised by human reason for the benefit of human life. Accordingly the law of nature was not changed in this respect, except by addition.

## Sixth Article.
## Whether the Law of Nature Can Be Abolished from the Heart of Man?

*We proceed thus to the Sixth Article:—*

*Objection* 1. It seems that the natural law can be abolished from the heart of man. Because on Rom. ii. 14, *When the Gentiles who have not the law,* etc., the gloss says that *the law of righteousness, which sin had blotted out, is graven on the heart of man when he is restored by grace.* But the law of righteousness is the law of nature. Therefore the law of nature can be blotted out.

*Obj.* 2. Further, the law of grace is more efficacious than the law of nature. But the law of grace is blotted out by sin. Much more therefore can the law of nature be blotted out.

*Obj.* 3. Further, that which is established by law is made just. But many things are enacted by men, which are contrary to the law of nature. Therefore the law of nature can be abolished from the heart of man.

*On the contrary,* Augustine says (*Conf.* ii.): *Thy law is written in the hearts of men, which iniquity itself effaces not.* But the law which is written in men's hearts is the natural law. Therefore the natural law cannot be blotted out.

*I answer that,* As stated above (AA. 4, 5), there belong to the natural law, first, certain most general precepts, that are known to all; and secondly, certain secondary and more detailed precepts, which are, as it were, conclusions following closely from first principles. As to those general principles, the natural law, in the abstract, can nowise be blotted out from men's hearts. But it is blotted out in the case of a particular action, in so far as reason is hindered from applying the general principle to a particular point of practice, on account of concupiscence or some other passion . . . (Q. LXXVII., A. 2).—But as to the other, *i. e.*, the secondary precepts, the natural law can be blotted out from the human heart, either by evil persuasions, just as in speculative matters errors occur in respect of necessary conclusions; or by vicious customs and corrupt habits, as among some men, theft, and even unnatural vices, as the Apostle states (Rom. i.), were not esteemed sinful.

*Reply Obj.* 1. Sin blots out the law of nature in particular cases, not universally, except perchance in regard to the secondary precepts of the natural law, in the way stated above.

*Reply Obj.* 2. Although grace is more efficacious than nature, yet nature is more essential to man, and therefore more enduring.

*Reply Obj.* 3. This argument is true of the secondary precepts of the natural law, against which some legislators have framed certain enactments which are unjust. . . .

# 15          On Kingship

THOMAS AQUINAS

*Chapter Two: Whether It Is More
Expedient for a City or Province to Be
Ruled by One Man or by Many*

[16] HAVING SET FORTH these preliminary points we must now inquire what is better for a province of a city: whether to be ruled by one man or by many.

[17] This question may be considered first from the viewpoint of the purpose of government. The aim of any ruler should be directed toward securing the welfare of that which he undertakes to rule. The duty of the pilot, for instance, is to preserve his ship amidst the perils of the sea and to bring it unharmed to the port of safety. Now the welfare and safety of a multitude formed into a society lies in the preservation of its unity which is called peace. If this is removed, the benefit of social life is lost and, moreover, the multitude in its disagreement becomes a burden to itself. The chief concern of the ruler of a multitude, therefore, is to procure the unity of peace.[1] It is not even legitimate for him to deliberate whether he shall establish peace in the multitude subject to him, just as a physician does not deliberate whether he shall heal the sick man encharged to him;[2] for no one should deliberate about an end which he is obliged to seek, but only about the means to attain that end. Wherefore the Apostle, having commended the unity of the faithful people, says: "Be ye careful to keep the unity of the spirit in the bond of peace."[3] Thus, the more efficacious a government is in keeping the unity of peace, the more useful it will be. For we call that more useful which leads more directly to the end. Now it is manifest that what is itself one can more efficaciously bring about unity than several–just as the most efficacious cause of heat is that which is by its nature hot.[4] Therefore the rule of one man is more useful than the rule of many.

[18] Furthermore, it is evident that several persons could by no means preserve that stability of the community if they totally disagreed. For union is necessary among them if they are to rule at all; several men, for instance, could not pull a ship in one direction unless joined together in some fashion. Now several are said to be united according as they come closer to being one. So one man rules better than several who come near being one.[5]

[19] Again, whatever is in accord with nature is best, for in all things nature does what is best. Now every natural governance is governance by one. In the multitude of bodily members there is one which is the principal mover, namely, the heart; and among the powers of the soul one power presides as chief, namely, the reason. Among bees there is one king bee,[a] and in the whole universe there is One God, Maker and Ruler of all things. And there is a reason for this. Every multitude is derived from unity. Wherefore, if artificial things are an imitation of natural things and a work of art is better according as it attains a closer likeness to what is in nature, it follows that it is best for a human multitude to be ruled by one person.[6]

[20] This is also evident from experience. For provinces or cities which are not ruled by one person are torn with dissensions and tossed about without peace, so that the complaint seems to be fulfilled which the Lord uttered through the Prophet: "Many pastors have destroyed my vineyard."[7] On the other hand, provinces and cities which are ruled under one king enjoy peace, flourish in justice, and delight in prosperity. Hence, the Lord by His prophets promises to His people as a

a In popular ancient and medieval opinion, the chief bee was considered to be a male. Aristotle, *Hist. Anim.* V, 21:553a25.

great reward that He will give them one head and that "one Prince will be in the midst of them."[8]

## Chapter Three: That the Dominion of a Tyrant Is the Worst

[21] Just as the government of a king is the best, so the government of a tyrant is the worst.[9]

[22] For democracy stands in contrary opposition to polity, since both are governments carried on by many persons, as is clear from what has already been said;[b] while oligarchy is the opposite of aristocracy, since both are governments carried on by a few persons; and kingship is the opposite of tyranny, since both are carried on by one person. Now, as has been shown above,[c] monarchy is the best government. If, therefore, "it is the contrary of the best that is worst,"[10] it follows that tyranny is the worst kind of government.

[23] Further, a united force is more efficacious in producing its effect than a force which is scattered or divided. Many persons together can pull a load which could not be pulled by each one taking his part separately and acting individually. Therefore, just as it is more useful for a force operating for a good to be more united, in order that it may work good more effectively, so a force operating for evil is more harmful when it is one than when it is divided. Now, the power of one who rules unjustly works to the detriment of the multitude, in that he diverts the common good of the multitude to his own benefit. Therefore, for the same reason that, in a just government, the government is better in proportion as the ruling power is one—thus monarchy is better than aristocracy, and aristocracy better than polity—so the contrary will be true of an unjust government, namely, that the ruling power will be more harmful in proportion as it is more unitary. Consequently, tyranny is more harmful than oligarchy and oligarchy more harmful than democracy.

[24] Moreover, a government becomes unjust by the fact that the ruler, paying no heed to the

common good, seeks his own private good. Wherefore the further he departs from the common good the more unjust will his government be. But there is a greater departure from the common good in an oligarchy, in which the advantage of a few is sought, than in a democracy, in which the advantage of many is sought; and there is a still greater departure from the common good in a tyranny, where the advantage of only one man is sought. For a large number is closer to the totality than a small number, and a small number than only one. Thus, the government of a tyrant is the most unjust.

[25] The same conclusion is made clear to those who consider the order of divine providence, which disposes everything in the best way. In all things, good ensues from one perfect cause, i.e., from the totality of the conditions favorable to the production of the effect, while evil results from any one partial defect.[11] There is beauty in a body when all its members are fittingly disposed; ugliness, on the other hand, arises when any one member is not fittingly disposed. Thus ugliness results in different ways from many causes, beauty in one way from one perfect cause. It is thus with all good and evil things, as if God so provided that good, arising from one cause, be stronger, and evil, arising from many causes, be weaker. It is expedient therefore that a just government be that of one man only in order that it may be stronger; however, if the government should turn away from justice, it is more expedient that it be a government by many, so that it may be weaker and the many may mutually hinder one another. Among unjust governments, therefore, democracy is the most tolerable, but the worst is tyranny.

[26] This same conclusion is also apparent if one considers the evils which come from tyrants. Since a tyrant, despising the common good, seeks his private interest, it follows that he will oppress his subjects in different ways according as he is dominated by different passions to acquire certain goods. The one who is enthralled by the passion of cupidity seizes the good of his subjects; whence Solomon says: "A just king setteth up the land; a covetous man shall destroy it."[12] If he is dominated by the passion of anger, he sheds blood for

b Bk. I, Ch. I, §§11–12.
c Bk. I, Ch. II.

nothing; whence it is said by Ezechiel: "Her princes in the midst of her are like wolves ravening the prey to shed blood."[13] Therefore this kind of government is to be avoided as the Wise man admonishes: "Keep thee far from the man who has the power to kill,"[14] because, forsooth, he kills not for justice's sake but by his power, for the lust of his will. Thus there can be no safety. Everything is uncertain when there is a departure from justice. Nobody will be able firmly to state: This thing is such and such, when it depends upon the will of another, not to say upon his caprice. Nor does the tyrant merely oppress his subjects in corporal things but he also hinders their spiritual good. Those who seek more to use than to be of use to their subjects prevent all progress, suspecting all excellence in their subjects to be prejudicial to their own evil domination. For tyrants hold the good in greater suspicion than the wicked, and to them the valor of others is always fraught with danger.[d]

[27] So the above-mentioned[15] tyrants strive to prevent those of their subjects who have become virtuous from acquiring valor and high spirit in order that they may not want to cast off their iniquitous domination. They also see to it that there be no friendly relations among these so that they may not enjoy the benefits resulting from being on good terms with one another, for as long as one has no confidence in the other, no plot will be set up against the tyrant's domination. Wherefore they sow discords among the people, foster any that have arisen, and forbid anything which furthers society and co-operation among men, such as marriage, company at table, and anything of like character, through which familiarity and confidence are engendered among men. They moreover strive to prevent their subjects from becoming powerful and rich since, suspecting these to be as wicked as themselves, they fear their power and wealth; for the subjects might become

harmful to them even as they are accustomed to use power and wealth to harm others.[16] Whence in the Book of Job it is said of the tyrant: "The sound of dread is always in his ears, and when there is peace (that is, when there is no one to harm him) he always suspects treason."[17]

[28] It thus results that when rulers, who ought to induce their subjects to virtue,[18] are wickedly jealous of the virtue of their subjects and hinder it as much as they can, few virtuous men are found under the rule of tyrants. For, according to Aristotle's sentence, brave men are found where brave men are honored.[19] And as Cicero says: "Those who are despised by everybody are disheartened and flourish but little."[20] It is also natural that men brought up in fear should become mean of spirit and discouraged in the face of any strenuous and manly task. This is shown by experience in provinces that have long been under tyrants. Hence the Apostle says to the Colossians: "Fathers, provoke not your children to indignation, lest they be discouraged."[21]

[29] So, considering these evil effects of tyranny, King Solomon says, "When the wicked reign, men are ruined,"[22] because, forsooth, through the wickedness of tyrants, subjects fall away from the perfection of virtue. And again he says: "When the wicked shall bear rule the people shall mourn, as though led into slavery."[23] And again: "When the wicked rise up men shall hide themselves,"[24] that they may escape the cruelty of the tyrant. It is no wonder, for a man governing without reason, according to the lust of his soul, in no way differs from the beast. Whence Solomon says: "As a roaring lion and a hungry bear, so is a wicked prince over the poor people."[25] Therefore men hide from tyrants as from cruel beasts, and it seems that to be subject to a tyrant is the same thing as to lie prostrate beneath a raging beast.

---

d This sentence occurs word for word in Sallust, *Bel. Cat.* VII, 2, where, however, it is said of kings. It is the sentence immediately preceding the one quoted below in §31, Ch. 111. This plagiarism is most unusual in St. Thomas' writings.—ED.

NOTES

1. *C. G.* i. 42; iv. 76; *S.* I, Q. 103, A. 3. This idea is characteristic of Hellenistic political philosophy, according to which the main function of the King-Saviour is considered to be the establishment of order and peace. . . .

2. *Eth*. iii. 5; *In Eth*. iii. 8; *C. G.* iii. 146; *In Matth.* xii. 2. In thus tracing back to Aristotle the idea that peace is the chief social good, St. Thomas was misled by the fact that the Latin text of *Ethics* translated the Greek *eunomia* (good laws well obeyed) by *peace*.

3. Ephes. iv. 3.

4. *C. G.* iv. 76; *S.* I, Q. 103, A. 3.

5. *In Eth*. viii. 10.

6. *Phys*. ii. 2.

7. Jerem. xii. 10.

8. Ezech. xxxiv. 24; Jerem. xxx, 21.

9. *Eth*. viii. 12; *In Eth*. viii. 10.

10. *Eth*. viii. 12.

11. *De div. nom*. iv. 30; *R. P.* iii. 22.

12. Prov. xxix. 4.

13. Ezech. xxii. 27.

14. Ecclus. ix. 18.

15. In Latin: *praedicti tyranni*. §27 is a reproduc-

tion of Aristotle's account of the traditional tyrant's policy of repression, "many of whose characteristics are supposed to have been instituted by Periander of Corinth; but many may also be derived from the Persian government" (*Pol* v. 11). . . .

16. Although there is no doubt about the fact that *Pol*. v. 11 is the source of this section, yet the text cannot be shown to depend literally on this source. . . .

17. Job xv. 21.

18. *Eth*. ii. 1; *In Eth*. ii. 1; *S*, 1–11, Q. 95, A. 1, pp. 55 ff.

19. *Eth*. iii. 11; *In Eth*. iii. 16.

20. *Tusc. disp*. 1, 2, 4.

21. Coloss. iii. 21.

22. Prov. xxviii. 12.

23. *Ibid*., xxix. 2.

24. *Ibid*., xxviii. 28.

25. *Ibid*., 15.

# 16    Summa Theologica

## THOMAS AQUINAS

*Part I*

### QUESTION 92.
### THE PRODUCTION OF THE WOMAN.

*First Article.*
*Whether the Woman Should Have Been Made in the First Production of Things?*

*We proceed thus to the First Article:—*

*Objection* 1. It would seem that the woman should not have been made in the first production of things. For the Philosopher says (*De Gener. Animal*. ii. 3), that the *female is a misbegotten male*. But nothing misbegotten or defective should have been in the first production of things. Therefore woman should not have been made at that first production.

*Obj.* 2. Further, subjection and limitation were a result of sin, for to the woman was it said after sin (Gen. iii. 16): *Thou shalt be under the man's power;* and Gregory says that, *Where there is no sin, there is no inequality*. But woman is naturally of less strength and dignity than man; *for that agent is always more honourable than the patient*, as Augustine says (*Gen. ad lit*. xii. 16). Therefore woman should not have been made in the first production of things before sin.

*Obj.* 3. Further, occasions of sin should be cut off. But God foresaw that the women would be an occasion of sin to man. Therefore He should not have made woman.

*On the contrary,* It is written (Gen. ii, 18): *It is not good for man to be alone; let us make him a helper like to himself.*

*I answer that,* It was necessary for woman to be made, as the Scripture says, as *a helper* to man; not, indeed, as a helpmate in other works, as some say, since man can be more efficiently helped by another man in other works; but as a helper in the work of generation. This can be made clear if we observe the mode of generation carried out in various living things. Some living things do not possess in themselves the power of generation, but are generated by some other specific agent, such as some plants and animals by the influence of the heavenly bodies, from some fitting matter and not from seed: others possess the active and passive generative power together; as we see in plants which are generated from seed; for the noblest vital function in plants is generation. Wherefore we observe that in these the active power of generation invariably accompanies the passive power. Among perfect animals the active power of generation belongs to the male sex, and the passive power to the female. And as among animals there is a vital operation nobler than generation, to which their life is principally directed; therefore the male sex is not found in continual union with the female in perfect animals, but only at the time of coition; so that we may consider that by this means the male and female are one, as in plants they are always united; although in some cases one of them preponderates, and in some the other. But man is yet further ordered to a still nobler vital action, and that is intellectual operation. Therefore there was greater reason for the distinction of these two forces in man; so that the female should be produced separately from the male; although they are carnally united for generation. Therefore directly after the formation of woman, it was said: *And they shall be two in one flesh* (Gen. ii. 24).

*Reply Obj.* 1. As regards the individual nature, woman is defective and misbegotten, for the active force in the male seed tends to the production of a perfect likeness in the masculine sex; while the production of woman comes from defect in the active force or from some material indisposition, or even from some external influence; such as that of a south wind, which is moist, as the Philosopher observes (*De Gener. Animal.* iv. 2). On the other hand, as regards human nature in general, woman is not misbegotten, but is included in nature's intention as directed to the work of generation. Now the general intention of nature depends on God, Who is the universal Author of nature.

Therefore, in producing nature, God formed not only the male but also the female.

*Reply Obj.* 2. Subjection is twofold. One is servile, by virtue of which a superior makes use of a subject for his own benefit; and this kind of subjection began after sin. There is another kind of subjection, which is called economic or civil, whereby the superior makes use of his subjects for their own benefit and good; and this kind of subjection existed even before sin. For good order would have been wanting in the human family if some were not governed by others wiser than themselves. So by such a kind of subjection woman is naturally subject to man, because in man the discretion of reason predominates. Nor is inequality among men excluded by the state of innocence . . . (Q. XCVI., A. 3).

*Reply Obj.* 3. If God had deprived the world of all those things which proved an occasion of sin, the universe would have been imperfect. Nor was it fitting for the common good to be destroyed in order that individual evil might be avoided; especially as God is so powerful that He can direct any evil to a good end.

## Second Article.
### Whether Woman Should Have Been Made from Man?

*We proceed thus to the Second Article:—*

*Objection* 1. It would seem that woman should not have been made from man. For sex belongs both to man and animals. But in the other animals the female was not made from the male. Therefore neither should it have been so with man.

*Obj.* 2. Further, things of the same species are of the same matter. But male and female are of the same species. Therefore, as man was made of the slime of the earth, so woman should have been made of the same, and not from man.

*Obj.* 3. Further, woman was made to be a helpmate to man in the work of generation. But close relationship makes a person unfit for that office; hence near relations are debarred from intermarriage, as is written (Lev. xviii. 6). Therefore woman should not have been made from man.

*On the contrary,* It is written (Ecclus. xvii. 5): *He created of him,* that is, out of man, *a helpmate like himself,* that is, woman.

*I answer that,* When all things were first formed, it was more suitable for the woman to be made from the man than (for the female to be from the male) in other animals. First, in order thus to give the first man a certain dignity consisting in this, that as God is the principle of the whole universe, so the first man, in likeness to God, was the principle of the whole human race. Wherefore Paul says that *God made the whole human race from one* (Acts xvii. 26). Secondly, that man might love woman all the more, and cleave to her more closely, knowing her to be fashioned from himself. Hence it is written (Gen. ii. 23, 24): *She was taken out of man, wherefore a man shall leave father and mother, and shall cleave to his wife.* This was not necessary as regards the human race, in which the male and female live together for life, which is not the case with other animals. Thirdly, because, as the Philosopher says (*Ethic.* viii. 12), the human male and female are united, not only for generation, as with other animals, but also for the purpose of domestic life, in which each has his or her particular duty, and in which the man is the head of the woman. Wherefore it was suitable for the woman to be made out of man, as out of her principle. Fourthly, there is a sacramental reason for this. For by this is signified that the Church takes his origin from Christ. Wherefore the Apostle says (Eph. v. 32): *This is a great sacrament; but I speak in Christ and in the Church.*

*Reply Obj.* 1. is clear from the foregoing.

*Reply Obj.* 2. Matter is that from which something is made. Now created nature has a determinate principle; and since it is determined to one thing, it has also a determinate mode of proceeding. Wherefore from determinate matter it produces something in a determinate species. On the other hand, the Divine Power, being infinite, can produce things of the same species out of any matter, such as a man from the slime of the earth, and a woman from a man.

*Reply Obj.* 3. A certain affinity arises from natural generation, and this is an impediment to matrimony. Woman, however, was not produced from man by natural generation, but by the Divine Power alone. Wherefore Eve is not called the daughter of Adam; and so this argument does not prove.

## Third Article.
## Whether the Woman Was Fittingly Made from the Rib of Man?

*We proceed thus to the Third Article:—*

*Objection* 1. It would seem that the woman should not have been formed from the rib of man. For the rib was much smaller than the woman's body. Now from a smaller thing a larger thing can be made only—either by addition (and then the woman ought to have been described as made out of that which was added, rather than out of the rib itself);—or by rarefaction, because, as Augustine says (*Gen. ad lit.* x.): *A body cannot increase in bulk except by rarefaction.* But the woman's body is not more rarefied than man's—at least, not in the proportion of a rib to Eve's body. Therefore Eve was not formed from a rib of Adam.

*Obj.* 2. Further, in those things which were first created there was nothing superfluous. Therefore a rib of Adam belonged to the integrity of his body. So, if a rib was removed, his body remained imperfect; which is unreasonable to suppose.

*Obj.* 3. Further, a rib cannot be removed from man without pain. But there was no pain before sin. Therefore it was not right for a rib to be taken from the man, that Eve might be made from it.

*On the contrary,* It is written (Gen. ii. 22): *God built the rib, which He took from Adam, into a woman.*

*I answer that,* It was right for the woman to be made from a rib of man. First, to signify the social union of man and woman, for the woman should neither *use authority over man,* and so she was not made from his head; nor was it right for her to be subject to man's contempt as his slave, and so she was not made from his feet. Secondly, for the sacramental signification; for from the side of Christ sleeping on the Cross the Sacraments flowed—namely, blood and water—on which the Church was established.

*Reply Obj.* 1. Some say that the woman's body was formed by a material increase, without anything being added; in the same way as our Lord multiplied the five loaves. But this is quite impossible. For such an increase of matter would either be by a change of the very substance of the matter itself, or by a change of its dimensions. Not by change of the substance of the matter, both because matter, considered in itself, is quite unchangeable, since it has a potential existence, and has nothing but the nature of a subject, and because quantity and size are extraneous to the essence of matter itself. Wherefore multiplication of matter is quite unintelligible, as long as the matter itself remains the same without anything added to it; unless it receives greater dimensions. This implies rarefaction, which is for the same matter to receive greater dimensions, as the Philosopher says (*Phys.* iv.). To say, therefore, that the same matter is enlarged, without being rarefied, is to combine contradictories—viz., the definition with the absence of the thing defined.

Wherefore, as no rarefaction is apparent in such multiplication of matter, we must admit an addition of matter: either by creation or, which is more probable, by conversion. Hence Augustine says (*Tract.* xxiv., *in Joan*) that *Christ filled five thousand men with five loaves, in the same way as from a few seeds He produces the harvest of corn*—that is, by transformation of the nourishment. Nevertheless, we say that the crowds were fed with five loaves, or that woman was made from the rib, because an addition was made to the already existing matter of the loaves and of the rib.

*Reply Obj.* 2. The rib belonged to the integral perfection of Adam, not as an individual, but as the principle of the human race; just as the semen belongs to the perfection of the begetter, and is released by a natural and pleasurable operation. Much more, therefore, was it possible that by the Divine power the body of the woman should be produced from the man's rib.

From this it is clear how to answer the third objection. . . .

# 17     The Equality of Men and Women

MARIE LE JARS DE GOURNAY

MOST OF THOSE who take up the cause of women against the arrogant way men confer superiority upon themselves pay them back in full. For, they claim superiority for the women.[1] I flee from all extremes and am content with the equality of women and men, for Nature is as much opposed to superiority as to inferiority, in this respect. Indeed, for some it isn't sufficient to confer superiority on the masculine sex; they also want to confine women to their indisputable and necessary place, namely at the distaff and at the distaff alone.[2] But women may console themselves in the fact that this contempt comes only from those

men whom they would least want to resemble—people who, if they were women, would increase the reproofs which could be spewed upon the feminine sex, and who feel in their heart that they have nothing to recommend themselves except the prestige of their masculine sex. This is true all the more so since they have heard it trumpeted through the streets that women lack dignity and intellectual ability, even the temperament and organs requisite for acquiring intellectual ability; their eloquence triumphs when preaching these maxims, most of all since "dignity," "intellectual ability," "organs" and "temperament" are such fashionable words. These men have not learned, on the other hand, that the foremost quality of an incompetent person is to support those things based on popular opinion and hearsay. See how such minds compare the two sexes: in their opinion the height of ability which women can attain is to resemble the common run of men. It is as difficult to imagine that a great woman can call herself a great human being, as it is to grant that a man can rise to the level of a God. These people are even braver than Hercules, who defeated only twelve monsters in twelve battles, while with a single word they defeat half of the human race. Who will believe, however, that those who want to improve and strengthen their own position out of the weakness of others, can improve and strengthen themselves by their own power? And it is ridiculous that they think they are free of the audacity of vilifying the feminine sex, when at the same time they praise themselves and give themselves a specious brilliance, sometimes in particular or in general, however wrong or false it may be, as if the truth of their bragging got its measure and quality from their impudence. God knows that I am acquainted with these joyful braggarts, whose boasts soon become proverbial among the most inflammatory claims that are contemptuous of women. But if they turn out to be the gallant and intelligent men that they declare themselves to be—as if by Edict—then why don't they turn women into mindless brutes by another, counterpoised Edict? And while I think very highly of both the dignity and intellectual capacities of the ladies, I do not claim, at this time, to be able to prove this by means of ratiocination since the tenacious can always dispute this, nor by examples, since they are too common, thus only by the authority of God himself and of the pillars of his Church and of the great men who have served as the guiding light of the World. Let us place these glorious witnesses right at the start and reserve God and the holy Church Fathers for further on, like a treasure.

Plato, whose title as "divine" has never been disputed, and consequently Socrates, his exponent and Mouth Piece in his Writings (if these works are not those of his most divine preceptor, Socrates himself), assign to women the same rights, faculties and functions as men in the *Republic* and elsewhere. They maintain, moreover, that many a time the women have surpassed the men of their Country. Indeed, women have invented some of the finest arts and have taken precedence over men, as monumental and sovereign exemplars even, in all sorts of perfections and virtues in the most famous of the ancient cities, among others, Alexandria, the first city of the Empire after Rome.[3]* In consequence, it so happened that these two Philosophers, miracles of Nature, thought they could add brilliance to the truly weighty arguments in their books by putting them in the mouths of Diotima and Aspasia.[4] Socrates does not shrink from calling Diotima his mistress and Tutor in the highest reaches of learning, while he himself is the Tutor and Master of the human race. Theodoret[5] points this out so readily in his Oration of Faith that it seems to me that it is very plausible that he had a favorable opinion of our sex. After this evidence of Socrates' opinion of women, one sees well enough that if in Xenophon's *Symposium*[6] he comes out with some words against their wisdom in comparison with that of men, he sees them in light of the ignorance and inexperience in which they were reared, or else, in the worst case, he takes this to be so of women in general, leaving frequent and ample place for exceptions—a thing which the chatterboxes in question in no way propose. Women surely achieve a high degree of excellence less often than men do, but it is a marvel that the lack of good instruction, even the abundance of bad speech and teaching, does not make matters worse by keeping them from achieving excellence at all. Is there a greater difference between men and women than among women themselves, depending on the education they have had, depending on whether they were reared in the city or in a village, or depending on their National origin? And why couldn't an education or healthy diet of practical affairs and Letters, equal to that of men, fill in the

*Hypatia.—ED.

gap which usually appears between the minds of men and their own? For, such a well-rounded education is as important as any single branch of culture, for example, social interaction, which French and English women have abundant opportunities to engage in, which Italian women have none, so that the latter are, by and large, far surpassed by the former in this. I say "by and large" because in particular cases Italian ladies sometimes prevail: we did take from them two Queens,[7] to whose wisdom France is greatly obliged. Why, really, couldn't a well-rounded education make a decisive contribution to filling in the gap that we perceive between the intellectual faculties of men and of women, considering that in this example the worst surpasses the best with the assistance of a single part, namely, as I said, social interaction and conversation? For, the appearance of Italian women is more subtle and suitable for refining the mind, as is clear in the case of their men when compared with Frenchmen and Englishmen. Plutarch maintains, in his Treatise about the virtuous deeds of women,[8] that the virtue of man is the same thing as the virtue of woman. Seneca, on the other hand, announces in his *Consolations*[9] that we must not suppose that Nature has treated ladies ungratefully, or restricted and diminished their virtues and minds more than the virtues and minds of men; instead, she has endowed them with a matching vigor and with a matching capacity for everything that is honorable and praiseworthy. Having examined these two, let us see what the third master of the Triumvirate of humane and moral wisdom thinks of this issue in his *Essays.*[10] It seems to him, he says, though he does not know why, that one rarely finds women worthy of dominating men. Isn't he taking women in particular cases to be the equals of men, and claiming that if he can't hold this view in general it is for fear of being wrong, even though he could blame the limited scope of his view on the poor and disgraceful educational fare allotted to our sex? Moreover, in other places in the same book, he cites and focuses on the authority that Plato assigns to women in his *Republic,* and on Antisthenes' denial of any difference in the talent and

virtue of the two sexes.[11] As for the Philosopher, Aristotle, since we are leaving no stone unturned, he did not, in general—as far as I know—hold an unfavorable opinion of the ladies. He rather supported this view, relying no doubt on the decisions of his spiritual father and grandfather, Plato and Socrates, as on something constant and fixed by the influence of such persons through whose mouths, one cannot deny, the entire human race, and reason itself, have pronounced their judgment. Is it necessary to cite numerous other ancient and modern writers of illustrious renown, among the latter, Erasmus, Politian, Agrippa,* or the honorable and discerning Tutor of the courtiers,† and so many other famous Poets who all serve as a counterpoise to those contemptuous of the female sex, and as partisans of women's interests, aptitude and propensity for every function and every laudable and worthy activity?[12] In truth, women console themselves with the thought that these detractors of their merit cannot give evidence that they are intelligent people, if all these minds are. And a clever man will not say, even if he believes it, that worthiness and privilege in women falls short of that in men, until he first has all these writers declared dumb brutes by decree in order to invalidate their testimony which is at odds with his own disparaging view. But then it would be necessary to declare whole Populations, even the most sublime, to be dumb animals, like the people of Smyrna in Tacitus, who in the olden days in Rome alleged that they were descendants of Tantalus, son of Jupiter, or of Theseus, grandson of Neptune or of an Amazon, whom they hence compared to these Gods, in order to obtain precedence in nobility over their neighbors. In regard to Salic law,[13] which deprives women of the crown, it exists only in France. It was invented at the time of Pharamond solely because of the wars against the Empire, whose yoke our Fathers shook off: the female sex was probably physically less fit to bear arms by reason that we have to bear and

*Erasmus, *Letters;* Politian, *Colloquies;* Agrippa, *On the Nobility and Excellence of Women.*—ED.
†Courtier.—ED.

nourish children.[14]* Nevertheless, we must also note that while the Peers of France, as they were originally conceptualized,[15] were created as a species of associates of the King, as their name indicates, the wives of the Peers, taken on their own, have the same ranking, privilege and vote as the Peers. Similarly, the Lacedemonians, a decent and generous People, consulted their wives on all private and public matters.† At the same time the French have been well served by the creation of Regents who are as equally empowered as the Kings. For, without that, how many times might the State have been forfeited? Today we know by experience how necessary such a remedy is during the minority of kings. The Teutons, a bellicose Peoples, who, says Tacitus, after more than two hundred years of war were triumphant rather than vanquished, brought dowries to their wives and not the other way around. There were, moreover, some tribes which were always ruled by our sex. And when Aeneas presented the scepter of Ilion to Dido, the scholiasts say that this was due to the fact that in the days of yore the eldest daughters, such as this Princess, ruled over the Royal Houses. Could one wish for two more beautiful reversals of Salic law, if the law can endure two such reversals? Of course neither our old Gauls nor the Carthaginians had contempt for women; when they were united in Hannibal's army for the purpose of crossing the Alps, they established the ladies of Gaul as arbiters of their disputes. And when men in many places would rob our sex of its share of the best advantages, inequality in physical force, rather than in spiritual powers or moral worth, can easily be the cause of the larceny and suffering. Physical force is such a low virtue that while men surpass women in this respect, animals far surpass men in the same respect. And if this same Latin Historiographer[16] teaches us that where force reigns, equity, probity and modesty itself are the attributes of the conqueror, will we be surprised to see that intellectual ability and the virtues in general are those of our men, thus depriving women of them?

To be exact, moreover, the human animal is neither man nor woman, the sexes having been created not as ends in themselves but *secundum quid*, as the School says, that is to say, solely for the purpose of propagation. The unique form and differentia of this animal, consists only in the human soul. And if we are permitted to jest in passing, the little joke will not be outside of our concerns: nothing resembles a male cat on the window ledge more than a female cat. Man and woman are one to such a degree that if man is more than woman, then woman is more than man. Man was created male and female, the Scriptures say, reckoning the two as only one. For which reason Jesus Christ is called "the Son of Man," even though he is only the son of a woman. Thus, the great Saint Basil later said: "Virtue in man and in woman is the same, since God has bestowed upon them the same creation and the same honor; *masculum et foeminam fecit eos.*"[17]* Now in those who have the same Nature, their actions are likewise the same, and whenever their works are the same, they will be esteemed and valued the same in consequence. That, then, is the opinion of this powerful pillar and venerable witness of the Church. Concerning this point, it is timely to remember that certain ancient quibblers went so far with this foolish arrogance as to contest that the female sex, as opposed to the male sex, is made in the image of God, which image they must have taken to be in the beard, according to my understanding. In addition, and as a consequence, they had to deny that woman is made in the image of man, since women cannot resemble men without resembling Him whom man resembles. God Himself has distributed the gifts of Prophecy indifferently to both men and women, and has also made them Judges, instructors, leaders of his People, faithful in peace and in war. And, what is more, He has made them triumph in the noble victories that women have also many a time won, bearing the standard in divers parts of the World.

*See Hotman for the etymology of "Peers" and du Tillet and Math, *History of the Kings for the Lady Peers.*—ED.

†Plutarch.—ED.

* *Homilies,* I.—ED.

And over which people, do you think? Over Cyrus and Theseus, and, one should add, Hercules whom they thoroughly thrashed even if they did not vanquish him. Also the fall of Penthesilea was the crowning-act of Achilles' glory.[18] Hear how Seneca and Ronsard speak of him:

> The Amazon, last terror of the Greeks, he vanquished.
> Penthesilea he hurled into the dust.

Have women, moreover, (this is just a remark in passing) excelled less in trustworthiness, which encompasses all of the principal virtues, than in magnanimity and in fighting power? Paterculus[19] tells us that during the period of the Roman proscriptions, the trustworthiness of children was non-existent, that of the freedmen slight, and that of the women great. If Saint Paul, to continue my journey along the path of holy testimony, prohibits women from entering the ministry and commands them to be silent in Church,[20] it is evident that this is not out of contempt for women, but surely only out of fear that they may lead men into temptation by showing so clearly and publicly, which would be inevitable when ministering and preaching, that they are more graceful and beautiful than men. I say that the lack of contempt is clear, since this Apostle speaks of Thesbé as his coadjutor in the service of Our Lord, not even to touch upon Saint Petronella's strong influence on Saint Peter.[21] And, then, in the church Magdalene is called "*par Apostolis*," the equal of the Apostles. Indeed, the Church and the Apostles themselves have allowed an exception from this rule of silence for the woman who was known by all of Provence to preach for thirty years in the St. Baume cave near Marseilles.[22] And if someone should call into question this evidence concerning the woman's preaching, we will ask him what the Sibyls did if not preach to the Universe, through divine inspiration, about the future coming of Jesus Christ? All the ancient Nations allowed women to be Priestesses, just as men could be priests. And Christians are at least forced to admit that women are capable of administering the Sacrament of Baptism. But then which faculty needed to administer the other sacraments can be justly denied to exist in women, if we were justly accorded what is needed for Baptism? While one might say that the necessity of Baptism for dying infants has forced the ancient Fathers to establish this practice in spite of themselves, it is certain that they would never have believed that necessity could excuse them from doing wrong to the point of allowing them to desecrate and dishonor the administering of a Sacrament. And consequently, this power to administer the Sacrament having been granted to women, one sees clearly that men have only forbidden them to administer the other Sacraments so that the authority of men will always be more thoroughly maintained, either because these men share the same sex, or so that, rightly or wrongly, peace may be assured between the two sexes, by means of the weakening and disparaging of one. Certainly Saint Jerome wrote wisely on our topic:* in the matters of service to God, a person's religious sentiment and doctrinal knowledge ought to be considered, not one's sex. This judgment ought to be generalized in order, with all the more reason, to allow women to engage in all honorable activities and intellectual disciplines. And this precisely follows the intention of this very saint, who, for his part, gives women credit and has much respect for them. Furthermore, Saint John the Eagle, the most beloved of the Evangelists, did not have contempt for women any more than did Saint Peter, Saint Paul and those two Church Fathers, namely Saint Basil and Saint Jerome,† since he addresses his Epistles especially to them. This is all without even mentioning the numerous other Saints and Church Fathers who make a similar suggestion in their Writings. As for Judith, I would not consider mentioning her if this were a special case, namely one that simply depended on the impulses and will of the agent, any more than I would speak of other cases of this caliber, even though there are a vast number of them, all as heroic in all sorts of ways as those which add the crowning touch to the most illustrious of men. I will not record isolated deeds for fear that they will

* *Epistles.*—Ed.
†Electra.—Ed.

not appear as honors and talents of our sex, but as the mere froth of a peculiar and over-stimulated imagination. But the case of Judith merits a place here. For, her project, issued from the heart of a young woman, in the midst of so many feeble-hearted men that lacked courage, and in such a critical situation.[23] It was such an eminent and difficult undertaking, for such an important end as the safety of a People and a City faithful to God, that it seems rather to be a matter of divine inspiration and advantage bestowed upon women than a purely voluntary act. This also seems to be the case for the deeds of the Maid of Orleans,[24] which arose out of roughly the same circumstances, but which were useful in a wider and more extensive variety of ways, including the safety of a great Kingdom and its Prince.*

> The illustrious Amazon skilled in arts of War,
> Mowed down squadrons and much danger bore,
> A hard breastplate her rounded breast did wear,
> The purple tip glowed with a graceful air,
> Her Sire with laurel and glory for to crown,
> The Virgin braved the warriors of renown.

Let us add that Magdalene is the only soul to whom the Redeemer had ever pronounced these words and promised this august favor: "In all places where the Gospel is preached, they shall speak of you."[25] Jesus Christ, moreover, revealed his joyous and glorious resurrection to women first, in order to make them, as a venerable Father of the Church says, Apostles to his own Apostles, and in order, as we know, to give them an express mission: "Go, He said, to the Apostles and to Peter and tell them what you have seen."[26] Concerning this I must note that He revealed His new birth to women and men equally in the person of Anna, daughter of Phanuel, who recognized him at the same moment as good, old Saint Simon.[27] This birth, in addition, was predicted among the Gentiles only by the Sibyls cited above—a special privilege of the female sex. What an honor was also given to women in the incident concerning Pilate, when an unexpected dream was had by one

of us, at the exclusion of all the men, and on such an exalted occasion.[28] And if men pride themselves on the fact that Jesus Christ was of their sex, I reply that it was necessary for the sake of decorum. For, if He had been of the female sex, He would not have been able to mingle among the crowds, at all hours of the day and night, in order to convert them, to help them and to save the human race, without creating a scandal, particularly in the face of the malice of the Jews. Besides, if someone is so dull-witted as to imagine God as being masculine or feminine, he shows as plain as day that he is as bad a philosopher as he is a theologian. For, although God's name has a masculine ring to it, accepting one sex rather than the other does not necessarily follow. Moreover, the advantage that men have through His incarnation as one from their sex (if they can derive any advantage from this, considering the lack of reasoning just pointed out) is compensated for by the fact that he was conceived in the body of a woman, by the complete perfection of this woman—the sole one among all the purely human creatures to carry the title of "perfect" since the fall of our first parents—and by her assumption into heaven, which was also a unique event for a human being. Finally, if the Scriptures have declared the husband as the master of his wife, the most stupid thing a man can do is to take this as a privilege signifying he is worthy to be his wife's master.[29] For, considering the examples, authorities, and reasons noted in this discourse, by which the equality of God's favors and kindness toward the two species or sexes, indeed their very unity, has been proven, and considering that God declares: "The two will be but one," and also declares: "A man will leave his father and mother to follow his wife,"[30] it seems that this statement was motivated only by the express need to maintain peace within marriage. This need would require, no doubt, that one of the parties submit to the other, and the male with his physical force could not bear the thought that submission come from his side. But even if it were true, as some maintain, that this submission were imposed on woman as a punishment for Eve's sin, it would still be a far cry

---

*Allusion to *Aeneid*.—ED.

from concluding in favor of the alleged superiority of man. If we believed that the Scriptures command woman to submit to man, as unworthy to oppose him, see the absurdity that follows: woman would be worthy of having been made in the image of the Creator, worthy of enjoying the most holy Eucharist, the mysteries of the Redemption, Paradise and the vision of, indeed the union with, God, but not of the honors and privileges of man. Would this not be to declare man more precious and exalted than these things and consequently to commit the most grievous blasphemy?

NOTES

1. The reference here is to the long literary tradition of the *querelle des femmes* or "quarrel about women," which includes, for example Henricus Cornelius Agrippa (von Nettesheim), *Declamation on the Nobility and Excellence of the Female Sex* . . . (Antwerp, 1529) and Lucrezia Marinella, *The Nobility and Excellence of Women* . . . (Venice, 1600).

2. There is a long tradition of setting philosophy at odds with work "fitting for women." Diogenes Laertius reports that Theodorus attacked the ancient Cynic, Hipparchia, for not attending to her domestic duties by saying "Who is the woman who has left the shuttle so near the warp?" Hipparchia replied, "I, Theodorus, am that person, but do I appear to you to have come to a wrong decision, if I devote that time to philosophy, which I otherwise should have spent at the loom?"

Later, Gournay's contemporary, the philosopher Anna Maria van Schurman (1607–1678), would say in her feminist treatise, *Question célèbre* (1646): "I know that in order for us not to be left useless, they give us for our share the needle and the spindle, and they tell us that these ought to be the occupation of our sex." Cited in Mario Schiff, *La Fille D'Alliance de Montaigne: Marie de Gournay* (Paris, 1910), p. 62.

3. In the 1634 and 1641 editions of this work, Marie de Gournay includes, at this point, a long paragraph with examples of illustrious women. She begins with Hypatia of Alexandria and adds Themistoclea, Theano, Damo, Cornelia, Laelis, and Arete, as well as a contemporary, the 17th century "Star of Utrecht," Anna Maria van Schurman.

4. Diotima, a priestess from Mantinea described in Plato's *Symposium* as meeting with Socrates in Athens about 440 B.C. and discussing with him the concepts of beauty, immortality and love. She is mentioned in Lucian's *Eunuch* and *The Portraits*, Aristedes' *Orations*, Maximus Tyrius's *Dissertation*, Clement of Alexandria's *Stromates*, Themistius' *Orationes* and in some of Proclus's commentaries on Plato. It is still debated whether she was a historical personage or a fictitious character.

Aspasia of Miletus (d. circa 401 B.C.), a rhetorician and member of the sophist circle of Pericles. The *Epitaphia*, discussed in Plato's *Menexenus*, is believed to have been co-written by her and her husband, Pericles. She was tried for impiety, but acquitted.

5. St. Theodoret (c. 393–466 A.D.), bishop of Cyrrhus, Syria, theologian and church historian.

6. Xenophon (c. 428/7–354 B.C.), associate of Socratic circles, historian, general, writer on economics and public policy. His *Symposium* describes a fictitious party at the house of Callias c. 422 and Socrates' participation in the discussions.

7. This is probably a reference to Catherine de' Medici (1519–1589) and Marie de' Medici (1573–1642).

8. L. Mestrius Plutarch of Chaeronea (c. 50 A.D.–120 A.D), philosopher and biographer, whose works are divided into two main collections: *Moralia* and *Parallel Lives*. In the former collection, in his essay on the *Bravery of Women*, he states that "man's virtues and woman's virtues are one and the same." (242 F)

9. Lucius Annaeus Seneca (c. 5/4 B.C.–65 A.D.), moral philosopher, dramatist, as well as tutor and minister to Nero. In his *To Marcia, On Consolation*, he writes: "Who, however, said that Nature acted stingily with women's natural capacities [ingeniis] and narrowly restricted their virtues? Believe me, their strength is equal; their capacity for virtue, if they like, is equal. They equally endure suffering and toil, whenever they are accustomed to it." (XVI, 1–2).

10. The "third master" is Michel Eyquem de Montaigne (1533–1592), whose *Essais* was first published in its entirety in 1595 under the editorial direction of his "adopted daughter," Marie de Gournay herself.

11. Antisthenes (c. 445–c. 360 B.C.), considered the founder of the Cynic sect. He wrote dialogues, including one on Aspasia (see fn. 4), interpretations of Homer and orations. His views were reported by Diogenes Laertius, Seneca, Xenophon, and Aristotle.

12. Erasmus (1466?–1536) of Rotterdam, Dutch humanist, Catholic priest, classics scholar, who published editions of ancient texts, as well as those of the Fathers of the Church, and a Latin edition of the New Testament based on the original Greek Text. His own original satirical and critical works included *In Praise of Folly* (1509).

Angelo Poliziano, or Politian, (1454–1494), Italian poet and humanist, classics scholar and protégé of Lorenzo de' Medici.

Henricus Cornelius Agrippa von Nettesheim (1486–1535), German physician, occultist, and philosopher. See fn. 1.

The "tutor of the courtiers" is Baldassare Castiglione (1478–1529), Italian count and statesman attached to the courts of Milan and Urbino. His famous book, *The Courtier* (1528), is a treatise on the etiquette, intellectual and social life and problems of the courtiers and courtesans of 15th and 16th century Italy.

13. Salic Law is an alleged fundamental law of French monarchy, deriving from Merovingian and Carolingian times, which excludes women from dynastic succession.

14. François de Villiers-Saint-Paul Hotman (1524–1590), Protestant jurist and author of *Franco-Gallia* (1573), which showed the Germanic origins of early Frankish institutions, argued for an elective monarchy in France and discussed Salic law; his brother Antoine wrote *Treatise on Salic Law* (1593).

Jean du Tillet, *The Chronicle of the Kings of France from Pharamond to Henry II* (1549).

Pharamond, legendary Frankish leader of the 5th Century, descended from Priam.

15. Peers of France are the members of the "first estate," or noble class.

16. Namely, Tacitus.

17. "He made them both—the male and the female."

18. Penthesilea, mythological Queen of the Amazons, slain by Achilles and immortalized in such works as Virgil's *Aeneid*.

19. Paterculus (1st Cent. A.D.), Latin historian and author of *Compendium of Roman History*.

20. Saint Paul's dictum: "Let the women keep silence in the churches, for it is not permitted to them to speak" [*Mulieres in Ecclesiis taceant non enim permittitur eis loqui*] (1 Cor. 14:34).

21. Saint Petronella (1st Cent. A.D.), legendary spiritual daughter of Saint Peter and patron saint of the kings of France.

22. Eastern and Western liturgists hold different views on the identity of Mary Magdalene. The Eastern liturgists distinguish three persons: Mary of Bethanay, sister of Martha and Lazarus, who anointed Jesus' head and feet (Mark xiv, Matt. xxvi, John xii. See also Luke 10; John 11), the unnamed harlot at the house of Simon, who anointed Jesus' feet with perfume (Luke vii), and Mary of Magdala, out of whom Jesus had cast seven devils, and who witnessed Calvary and the burial and resurrection of Jesus (Matt. xxviii, Mark xvi, Luke xxiv, John xx). On this view Mary Magdalene is not a former sinner. On the other hand, many Western exegetes identify the harlot with Magdalene. See Omer Englebert, *The Lives of the Saints* (New York: Collier Books, 1964). According to Gnostic scriptures, Jesus had called Magdalene the "Apostle to the Apostles" and had said that she would excel above all his other disciples and rule in the future Kingdom of Light. See Elaine Pagels, *The Gnostic Gospels* (New York: Random House, 1979). According to some Christian myths, Magdalene and the Virgin Mary lived for a time in Ephesus. Magdalene later went to Marseilles and lived for thirty years in a former pagan cave at St. Baume, where she lived on nothing but the songs of angels. See Barbara Walker, *The Woman's Encyclopedia of Myths and Secrets* (New York: Harper & Row, 1983).

23. In the Apocrypha, Judith is described as the young widow who saved her people by beheading the Assyrian general, Holofernes, who had invaded her town of Bethulia.

24. That is, Saint Joan of Arc (1412–1431).

25. Matt. 26:13; Mark 14:9.

26. John 20: 11–18.

27. Luke 2:29–30.

28. Matt. 27:19.

29. Gen. 3:16; Eph. 5:23.

30. Gen. 2:24; Eph. 5:31.

# 18    Guide for the Perplexed

## MAIMONIDES

## *Book III*

### CHAPTER XXVII

THE GENERAL OBJECT of the Law is twofold: the well-being of the soul, and the well-being of the body. The well-being of the soul is promoted by correct opinions communicated to the people according to their capacity. Some of these opinions are therefore imparted in a plain form, others allegorically; because certain opinions are in their plain form too strong for the capacity of the common people. The well-being of the body is established by a proper management of the relations in which we live one to another. This we can attain in two ways: first by removing all violence from our midst; that is to say, that we do not do everyone as he pleases, desires, and is able to do; but everyone of us does that which contributes towards the common welfare. Secondly, by teaching everyone of us such good morals as must produce a good social state. Of these two objects, the one, the well-being of the soul, or the communication of correct opinions, comes undoubtedly first in rank, but the other, the well-being of the body, the government of the state, and the establishment of the best possible relations among men, is anterior in nature and time. The latter object is required first; it is also treated [in the Law] most carefully and most minutely, because the well-being of the soul can only be obtained after that of the body has been secured. For it has already been found that man has a double perfection: the first perfection is that of the body, and the second perfection is that of the soul. The first consists in the most healthy condition of his mental relations, and this is only possible when man has all his wants supplied, as they arise; if he has his food, and other things needful for his body, e.g., shelter, bath, and the like. But one man alone cannot procure all this; it is impossible for a single man to obtain this comfort; it is only possible in society, since man, as is well known, is by nature social.

The second perfection of man consists in his becoming an actually intelligent being; i.e., he knows about the things in existence all that a person perfectly developed is capable of knowing. This second perfection certainly does not include any action or good conduct, but only knowledge, which is arrived at by speculation, or established by research.

It is clear that the second and superior kind of perfection can only be attained when the first perfection has been acquired; for a person that is suffering from great hunger, thirst, heat, or cold, cannot grasp an idea even if communicated by others, much less can he arrive at it by his own reasoning.

But when a person is in possession of the first perfection, then he may possibly acquire the second perfection, which is undoubtedly of a superior kind, and is alone the source of eternal life. The true Law, which as we said is one, and beside which there is no other Law, viz., the Law of our teacher Moses, has for its purpose to give us the twofold perfection. It aims first at the establishment of good mutual relations among men by removing injustice and creating the noblest feelings. In this way the people in every land are enabled to stay and continue in one condition, and everyone can acquire his first perfection. Secondly, it seeks to train us in faith, and to impart correct and true opinions when the intellect is sufficiently developed. . . .

## CHAPTER XXVIII

. . . The result of all these preliminary remarks is this: The reason of a commandment, whether positive or negative, is clear, and its usefulness evident, if it directly tends to remove injustice, or to teach good conduct that furthers the well-being of society, or to impart a truth which ought to be believed either on its own merit or as being indispensable for facilitating the removal of injustice or the teaching of good morals. There is no occasion to ask for the object of such commandments; for no one can, e.g., be in doubt as to the reason why we have been commanded to believe that God is one; why we are forbidden to murder, to steal, and to take vengeance, or to retaliate, or why we are commanded to love one another. But there are precepts concerning which people are in doubt, and of divided opinions, some believing that they are mere commands, and serve no purpose whatever, whilst others believe that they serve a certain purpose, which, however, is unknown to man. Such are those precepts which in their literal meaning do not seem to further any of the three above-named results: to impart some truth, to teach some moral, or to remove injustice. They do not seem to have any influence upon the well-being of the soul by imparting any truth, or upon the well-being of the body by suggesting such ways and rules as are useful in the government of a state, or in the management of a household.

Such are the prohibitions of wearing garments containing wool and linen; of sowing divers seeds, or of boiling meat and milk together; the commandment of covering the blood [of slaughtered beasts and birds], the ceremony of breaking the neck of a calf [in case of a person being found slain, and the murderer being unknown]; the law concerning the firstborn of an ass, and the like. I am prepared to tell you my explanation of all these commandments, and to assign for them a true reason supported by proof, with the exception of some minor rules, and of a few commandments, as I have mentioned above. I will show that all these and similar laws must have some bearing upon one of the following three things, viz., the regulation of our opinions, or the improvement of our social relations, which implies two things, the removal of injustice, and the teaching of good morals. . . .

## CHAPTER XXXI

There are persons who find it difficult to give a reason for any of the commandments, and consider it right to assume that the commandments and prohibitions have no rational basis whatever. They are led to adopt this theory by a certain disease in their soul, the existence of which they perceive, but which they are unable to discuss or to describe. For they imagine that these precepts, if they were useful in any respect, and were commanded because of their usefulness, would seem to originate in the thought and reason of some intelligent being. But as things which are not objects of reason and serve no purpose, they would undoubtedly be attributed to God, because no thought of man could have produced them. According to the theory of those weak-minded persons, man is more perfect than his Creator. For what man says or does has a certain object, whilst the actions of God are different; He commands us to do what is of no use to us, and forbids us to do what is harmless. Far be this! On the contrary, the sole object of the Law is to benefit us. . . . But if no reason could be found for these statutes, if they produced no advantage and removed no evil, why then should he who believes in them and follows them be wise, reasonable, and so excellent as to raise the admira-

tion of all nations? But the truth is undoubtedly as we have said, that every one of the six hundred and thirteen precepts serves to inculcate some truth, to remove some erroneous opinion, to establish proper relations in society, to diminish evil, to train in good manners, or to warn against bad habits. All this depends on three things: opinions, morals, and social conduct. . . . Thus these three principles suffice for assigning a reason for everyone of the Divine commandments.

## CHAPTER XXXIII

It is also the object of the perfect Law to make man reject, despise, and reduce his desires as much as is in his power. He should only give way to them when absolutely necessary. It is well known that it is intemperance in eating, drinking, and sexual intercourse that people mostly rave and indulge in; and these very things counteract the ulterior perfection of man, impede at the same time the development of his first perfection, and generally disturb the social order of the country and the economy of the family. For by following entirely the guidance of lust, in the manner of fools, man loses his intellectual energy, injures his body, and perishes before his natural time; sighs and cares multiply; there is an increase of envy, hatred, and warfare for the purpose of taking what another possesses. The cause of all this is the circumstance that the ignorant considers physical enjoyment as an object to be sought for its own sake. God in His wisdom has therefore given us such commandments as would counteract that object, and prevent us altogether from directing our attention to it, and has debarred us from everything that leads only to excessive desire and lust. This is an important thing included in the objects of our Law. See how the Law commanded to slay a person from whose conduct it is evident that he will go too far in seeking the enjoyment of eating and drinking. I mean "the rebellious and stubborn son"; he is described as "a glutton and a drunkard" (Deut. xxi. 20). The Law commands to stone him and to remove him from society lest he grow up in this character, and kill many, and injure the condition of good men by his great lust. . . .

Similarly one of the intentions of the Law is purity and sanctification; I mean by this renouncing and avoiding sexual intercourse and causing it to be as infrequent as possible, as I shall make clear. Thus, when He, may He be exalted, commanded the religious community to be sanctified with a view to receiving the Torah, and He said: *And sanctify them today and tomorrow*—He said; *Come not near a woman.* Consequently He states clearly that sanctity consists in renouncing sexual intercourse, just as He also states explicitly that the giving-up of the drinking of wine constitutes sanctity, in what He says about the Nazarite: *He shall be saintly.* . . .

## CHAPTER XXXIV

It is also important to note that the Law does not take into account exceptional circumstances; it is not based on conditions which rarely occur. Whatever the Law teaches, whether it be of an intellectual, a moral, or a practical character, is founded on that which is the rule and not on that which is the exception; it ignores the injury that might be caused to a single person through a certain maxim or a certain divine precept. . . . If the Law depended on the varying conditions of man, it would be imperfect in its totality, each precept being left indefinite. For this reason it would not be right to make the fundamental principles of the Law dependent on a certain time or a certain place; on the contrary, the statutes and the judgments must be definite, unconditional, and general. . . .

After having premised these introductory remarks I will now proceed to the exposition of that which I intended to explain.

## CHAPTER XXXV

In accordance with this intention I find it convenient to divide all precepts into fourteen classes.

The first class comprises those precepts which form fundamental principles. . . .

The second class comprises the precepts which are connected with the prohibition of idolatry. . . .

The third class is formed by commandments which are connected with the improvement of the moral condition [of mankind]. . . .

The fourth class includes precepts relating to charity, loans, gifts, and the like. . . . The object of these precepts is clear; their benefit concerns all people by turns; for he who is rich to-day may one day be poor—either he himself or his descendants; and he who is now poor, he himself or his son may be rich to-morrow.

The fifth class contains those precepts which relate to the prevention of wrong and violence. . . . Their beneficial character is evident.

The sixth class is formed of precepts respecting fines, e.g., the laws on the theft and robbery, on false witnesses. . . . Their benefit is apparent; for if sinners and robbers were not punished, injury would not be prevented at all: and persons scheming evil would not become rarer. They are wrong who suppose that it would be an act of mercy to abandon the laws of compensation for injuries; on the contrary, it would be perfect cruelty and injury to the social state of the country. It is an act of mercy that God commanded "judges and officers thou shalt appoint to thee in all thy gates" (Deut. xvi. 18).

The seventh class comprises those laws which regulate the business transactions of men with each other; e.g., laws about loans, hire, trust, buying, selling, and the like; the rules about inheritance belong to this class. . . . The object of these precepts is evident, for monetary transactions are necessary for the peoples of all countries, and it is impossible to have these transactions without a proper standard of equity and without useful regulations.

The eighth class includes those precepts which relate to certain days, as Sabbaths and holydays. . . .

The ninth class comprises the general laws concerning religious rites and ceremonies. . . .

The object of these laws is apparent; they all prescribe actions which firmly establish the love of God in our minds, as also the right belief concerning Him and His attributes.

The tenth class is formed of precepts which relate to the Sanctuary, its vessels, and its ministers. . . .

The eleventh class includes those precepts which related to Sacrifices. . . .

The twelfth class comprises the laws concerning things unclean and clean. . .

The thirteenth class includes the precepts concerning forbidden food and the like . . .

The fourteenth class comprises the precepts concerning forbidden sexual intercourse; they are given in the section *Nashim* and *Hilkot issurebiah*. The laws concerning the intermixture of cattle belong to this class. The object of these precepts is likewise to diminish sexual intercourse, to restrain as much as possible indulgence in lust, and [to teach] that this enjoyment is not, as foolish people think, the final cause of man's existence. . . .

As is well known, the precepts are also divided into two classes, viz., precepts concerning the relation between man and God, and precepts concerning the relation between man and man. Of the classes into which we divide the precepts and which we have enumerated, the fifth, sixth, and seventh, and part of the third, include laws concerning the relation of man to man. The other classes contain the laws about the relation of man to God, i.e., positive or negative precepts, which tend to improve the moral or intellectual condition of mankind, or to regulate such of each man's actions which [directly] only concern him and lead him to perfection. For these are called laws concerning man's relation to God, although in reality they lead to results which concern also his fellow-men; because these results become only apparent after a long series of intermediate links, and from a general point of view; whilst directly these laws are not intended to prevent man from injuring his fellow-man. Note this. . . .

## CHAPTER XL

The precepts of the fifth class, enumerated in the Section "On Damages" (*Sepher nezikin*), aim at the removal of wrong and the prevention of injury. As we are strongly recommended to prevent damage, we are responsible for every damage caused by our property or through our work in so far as it is in our power to take care and to guard it from becoming injurious. We are, therefore, responsible for all damage caused by our cattle; we must guard them. The same is the case with fire and pits; they are made by man, and he can be careful that they do not cause damage. . . .

This class includes also the duty of killing him who pursues another person; that is to say, if a person is about to commit a crime we may prevent it by killing him. Only in two cases is this permitted; viz., when a person runs after another in order to murder him, or in order to commit fornication; because in these two cases the crime, once committed; cannot be remedied. . . .

The beneficial character of the law concerning "the breaking of the neck of a heifer" (Deut. xxi. 1–8) is evident. For it is the city that is nearest to the slain person that brings the heifer, and in most cases the murderer comes from that place. The elders of the place call upon God as their witness, according to the interpretation of our Sages, that they have always kept the roads in good condition, have protected them, and have directed everyone that asked his way; that the person has not been killed because they were careless in these general provisions, and they do not know who has slain him. As a rule the investigation, the procession of the elders, the measuring, and the taking of the heifer, make people talk about it, and by making the event public, the murdered may be found out, and he who knows of him, or has heard of him, or has discovered him by any clue, will now name the person that is the murderer, and as soon as a man, or even a woman or handmaid, rises up and names a certain person as having committed the murder, the heifer is not killed. It is well known that it is considered great wickedness and guilt on the part of a person who knows the murderer, and is silent about him whilst the elders call upon God as witness that they know nothing about the murderer. Even a woman will, therefore, communicate whatever knowledge she has of him. When the murderer is discovered, the benefit of the law is apparent. . . . Force is added to the law by the rule that the place in which the neck of the heifer is broken should never be cultivated or sown. The owner of the land will therefore use all means in his power to search and to find the murderer, in order that the heifer be not killed and his land be not made useless to him.

## CHAPTER XLI

The precepts of the sixth class comprise the different ways of punishing the sinner. Their general usefulness is known and has also been mentioned by us. . . .

The law concerning false witnesses (Deut. xix. 19) prescribes that they shall suffer exactly the same loss which they intended to inflict upon another. If they intended to bring a sentence of death against a person, they are killed; if they aimed at the punishment of stripes, they receive stripes; and if they desire to make a person pay money, they are sentenced to pay exactly the same sum. The object of all these laws is to make the punishment equal to the crime; and it is also on this account that the judgments are "righteous" (Deut. iv. 8). . . . .—Whether the punishment is great or small, the pain inflicted intense or less intense, depends on the following four conditions.

1. The greatness of the sin. Actions that cause great harm are punished severely, whilst actions that cause little harm are punished less severely.
2. The frequency of the crime. A crime that is frequently committed must be put down by severe punishment; crimes of rare occurrence may be suppressed by a lenient punishment considering that they are rarely committed.
3. The amount of temptation. Only fear of a severe punishment restrains us from actions for which there exists a greater temptation, either because we have a great desire for these actions, or are accustomed to them, or feel unhappy without them.
4. The facility of doing the thing secretly, and unseen and unnoticed. From such acts we are deterred only by the fear of a great and terrible punishment. . . .

Death by the court of law is decreed in important cases: when faith is undermined, or a great crime is committed, viz., idolatry, incest, murder, or actions that lead to these crimes. It is further decreed for breaking the Sabbath (Exod. xxxi. 15); because the keeping of Sabbath is a confirmation of our belief in the Creation; a false prophet and a rebellious elder are put to death on account of the mischief which they cause; he who strikes his father or his mother is killed on account of his great audacity, and because he undermines the constitution of the family, which is the foundation of the state. A rebellious and disobedient son is put to death (Deut. xxi. 18 *seq.*) on account of what he might become, because he will likely be a murderer; he who steals a human being is killed, because he is also prepared to kill him whom he steals (Exod. xxi. 16). Likewise he who is found breaking into a house is prepared for murder (*ibid.* xxii. 1), as our Sages stated. These three, the rebellious and disobedient son, he who steals and sells a human being, and he who breaks into a house, become murderers in the course of time, as is well known. Capital punishment is only decreed for these serious crimes, and in no other case. Not all forbidden sexual intercourse is visited with the penalty of death, but only in those cases in which the criminal act can easily be done, is of frequent occurrence, is base and disgraceful, and of a tempting character; otherwise excision is the punishment. Likewise not all kinds of idolatry are capital crimes, but only the principal acts of idolatry, such as praying to an idol, prophesying in its name, passing a child through the fire, consulting with familiar spirits, and acting as a wizard or witch. . . .

## Recommended Readings

### TEXTS

Bigongiari, Dino. *The Political Ideas of St. Thomas Aquinas.* New York: Hafner, 1953.

Burns, James, ed. *Cambridge History of Medieval Political Thought, 350–1450.* Cambridge: Cambridge University Press, 1989.

Coppleston, Frederick. *Aquinas*. London: Penguin, 1955.

Finnis, John. *Natural Law and Natural Rights*. Oxford: Oxford University Press, 1982.

Gilby, Thomas. *The Political Thought of Thomas Aquinas*. Chicago: University of Chicago Press, 1958.

Gilson, Etienne. *The Christian Philosophy of St. Thomas Aquinas*. New York: Random House, 1956.

Kenny, Anthony, ed. *Aquinas*. Notre Dame, IN: Notre Dame Press, 1976.

Lisska, Anthony, *Aquinas's Theory of Natural Law*. Oxford: Oxford University Press, 1996.

McInerny, R. *St. Thomas Aquinas*. Notre Dame, IN: Notre Dame Press, 1982.

Sigmund, Paul, ed. *St. Thomas Aquinas on Politics and Ethics*. New York: W. W. Norton, 1988.

## FEMINIST PERSPECTIVE

Lucas, Angela. *Women in the Middle Ages: Religion, Marriage and Letters*. Brighton: Harvester Press, 1984.

Pierce, Christine. "Natural Law Language and Women." In *Woman in Sexist Society,* edited by Vivian Gornick and Barbara K. Moran. New York: Basic Books, 1971.

## MULTICUTURAL PERSPECTIVE

Kraemer, Joel. *Perspectives on Maimonides*. Oxford: Oxford University Press, 1991.

Weiss, Raymond. *Maimonides' Ethics: The Encounter of Philosophic and Religious Morality*. Chicago: University of Chicago Press, 1991.

# V

# *Hobbes*

## Introduction

THOMAS HOBBES WAS born at Malmesbury in Wiltshire, England, in 1588 and died in 1679 at the age of 91. He was educated at Oxford University, where he found Aristotelian and Scholastic philosophy boring and devoted much of his time to reading classical literature. After receiving his bachelor's degree, he secured the position of tutor and companion to William Cavendish, the future earl of Devonshire. Hobbes, who never married, lived and worked with the Cavendish family for most of his life. During this period, he pursued his own liberal studies and wrote a translation of Thucydide's *History of the Peloponnesian War,* admiring him for his sense of prudence and his sensitivity to the dangers of democracy. He also served for a few years as mathematics tutor to the future King Charles II. His tutoring posts gave him the opportunity to travel, to correspond, and to meet with such Enlightenment figures as Galileo, René Descartes, Francis Bacon, and Pierre Gassendi. During this time, Hobbes developed an interest in the deductive form of geometry and the materialism of physics. Hobbes's chief work, *Leviathan or the Matter, Forme and Power of a Commonwealth Eclesiastical and Civil,* was published in 1651. Hobbes translated it into Latin in 1670.

In the selection taken from *Leviathan,* Hobbes begins with the assumption that all people are by nature self-seeking and hostile toward one another. But finding the constant hostility of a state of nature ("a war of all against all") intolerable, people form contracts and turn over the enforcement of them to sovereign powers, to which they are thereafter irrevocably bound to be loyal in virtually all circumstances. It is through such social contracts that the state of nature is transformed into civil societies. Hobbes allows that people can contract into various forms of government, although he clearly favors monarchy as providing the most security with the least possibility of mischief brought by faction.

One problem with Hobbes's justification for civil society is that it is doubtful that people who are motivated only by self-interest would be able to form stable civil societies. This is because people so motivated would have reason to break the law when doing so is to their advantage. State officials whose task it is to enforce the law would also look for ways to bend the law to their own advantage. So, given his assumption that all people are motivated only by self-interest, Hobbes cannot derive a justification for everyone obeying even those laws of civil society that are for the common good.

But why assume that it is rational only to be motivated by self-interest? Why not assume that it is equally rational to be altruistically motivated or that what is most rational or reasonable is to be motivated partly by self-interest and partly altruistically? An advantage of adopting these latter assumptions is that it would then seem possible to justify a civil society where the laws are for the common good.[1]

There are further problems with Hobbes's theory from a feminist perspective. Carole Pateman, in "Hobbes, Patriarchy and Conjugal Right," draws attention to some little-recognized aspects of Hobbes's theory. (See chapter 20 in the selection from *Leviathan*.) First, women in the state of nature are as free as men. Second, women in the state of nature become both mothers and lords to their children. So, in the state of nature only women have dominion over children. Third, all this changes when men begin to form families by conquest and women become the servants of men. What Hobbes does not explain, as Pateman indicates, is why women who are as free as men in the state of nature should not oppose this conquest by men at every possible turn.

In the selection from Bartolomé de Las Casas's "The Devastation of the Indies," Las Casas describes the various practices by which the Spanish conquered the West Indies. Beginning in 1514, Las Casas spent fifty years crusading for Indian rights. In 1542, he helped secure the passage of new reform laws, and in 1550, he brought the Spanish conquest itself to a halt while Emperor Charles V considered his charges of injustice.

In connection with Hobbes's theory, we could raise the question: Whose side would Hobbes be on in the conflict between the Indians and their Spanish conquerors? Hobbes seems to have viewed the relations between various Indian tribes in the Americas, even before the arrival of white settlers, as a state of war, nasty and brutish (see chapter 13), although probably few Indians would have so viewed them. What then happens on the arrival of Spaniards? Is the use of force to enslave them in the land they had long inhabited justified on Hobbes's theory, and if it is, what would this show, if anything, about the validity of his theory? These are not the kind of questions that are usually asked about Hobbes's theory, but maybe they should be.

1 For development of this line of argument, see my *How to Make People Just* (Totowa, NJ: Rowman & Littlefield, 1988), chap. 11.

# 19    Leviathan

THOMAS HOBBES

CHAPTER 13

OF THE NATURAL CONDITION OF
MANKIND AS CONCERNING THEIR
FELICITY, AND MISERY

NATURE HATH MADE MEN so equal, in the faculties of body, and mind; as that though there be found one man sometimes manifestly stronger in body, or of quicker mind than another; yet when all is reckoned together, the difference between man, and man, is not so considerable, as that one man can thereupon claim to himself any benefit, to which another may not pretend, as well as he. For as to the strength of body, the weakest has strength enough to kill the strongest, either by secret machination, or by confederacy with others, that are in the same danger with himself.

And as to the faculties of the mind, (setting aside the arts grounded upon words, and especially that skill of proceeding upon general, and infallible rules, called science; which very few have, and but in few things; as being not a native faculty, born with us; nor attained, (as prudence,) while we look after somewhat else,) I find yet a greater equality amongst men, than that of strength. For prudence, is but experience; which equal time, equally bestows on all men, in those things they equally apply themselves unto. That which may perhaps make such equality incredible, is but a vain conceit of one's own wisdom, which almost all men think they have in a greater degree, than the vulgar; that is, than all men but themselves, and a few others, whom by fame, or for concurring with themselves, they approve. For such is the nature of men, that howsoever they may acknowledge many others to be more witty, or more eloquent, or more learned; yet they will hardly believe there be many so wise as themselves: For they see their own wit at hand, and other men's at a dis-

tance. But this proveth rather that men are in that point equal, than unequal. For there is not ordinarily a greater sign of the equal distribution of any thing, than that every man is contented with his share.

From this equality of ability, ariseth equality of hope in the attaining of our ends. And therefore if any two men desire the same thing, which nevertheless they cannot both enjoy, they become enemies; and in the way to their end, (which is principally their own conservation, and sometimes their delectation only,) endeavour to destroy, or subdue one another. And from hence it comes to pass, that where an invader hath no more to fear, than another man's single power; if one plant, sow, build, or possess a convenient seat, others may probably be expected to come prepared with forces united, to dispossess, and deprive him, not only of the fruit of his labour, but also of his life, or liberty. And the invader again is in the like danger of another.

And from this diffidence of one another, there is no way for any man to secure himself, so reasonable, as anticipation; that is, by force, or wiles, to master the persons of all men he can, so long, till he see no other power great enough to endanger him: and this is no more than his own conservation requireth, and is generally allowed. Also because there be some, that taking pleasure in contemplating their own power in the acts of conquest, which they pursue farther than their security requires; if others, that otherwise would be glad to be at ease within modest bounds, should not by invasion increase their power, they would not be able, long time, by standing only on their defence, to subsist. And by consequence, such augmentation of dominion over men, being necessary to a man's conservation, it ought to be allowed him.

Again, men have no pleasure, (but on the contrary a great deal of grief) in keeping company, where there is no power able to over-awe them all. For every man looketh that his companion should value him, at the same rate he sets upon himself: and upon all signs of contempt, or undervaluing, naturally endeavours, as far as he dares (which amongst them that have no common power to keep them in quiet, is far enough to make them destroy each other), to extort a greater value from his contemners, by damage; and from others, by the example.

So that in the nature of man, we find three principal causes of quarrel. First, competition; secondly, diffidence; thirdly, glory.

The first, maketh men invade for gain; the second, for safety; and the third, for reputation. The first use violence, to make themselves masters of other men's persons, wives, children, and cattle; the second, to defend them; the third, for trifles, as a word, a smile, a different opinion, and any other sign of undervalue, either direct in their persons, or by reflection in their kindred, their friends, their nation, their profession, or their name.

Hereby it is manifest, that during the time men live without a common power to keep them all in awe, they are in that condition which is called war; and such a war, as is of every man, against every man. For WAR, consisteth not in battle only, or that act of fighting; but in a tract of time, wherein the will to contend by battle is sufficiently known: and therefore the notion of *time,* is to be considered in the nature of war; as it is in the nature of weather. For as the nature of foul weather, lieth not in a shower or two of rain; but in an inclination thereto of many days together: so the nature of war, consisteth not in actual fighting; but in the known disposition thereto, during all the time there is no assurance to the contrary. All other time is PEACE.

Whatsoever therefore is consequent to a time of war, where every man is enemy to every man; the same is consequent to the time, wherein men live without other security, than what their own strength, and their own invention shall furnish them withal. In such condition, there is no place for industry; because the fruit thereof is uncertain: and consequently no culture of the earth; no navigation, nor use of the commodities that may be imported by sea; no commodious building; no instruments of moving, and removing such things as require much force; no knowledge of the face of the earth; no account of time; no arts; no letters; no society; and which is worst of all, continual fear, and danger of violent death; and the life of man, solitary, poor, nasty, brutish, and short.

It may seem strange to some man, that has not well weighed these things: that nature should thus dissociate, and render men apt to invade, and destroy one another: and he may therefore, not trusting to this inference, made from the passions, desire perhaps to have the same confirmed by experience. Let him therefore consider with himself, when taking a journey, he arms himself, and seeks to go well accompanied; when going to sleep, he locks his doors; when even in his house he locks his chests; and this when he knows there be laws, and public officers, armed, to revenge all injuries shall be done him; what opinion he has of his fellow subjects, when he rides armed; of his fellow citizens, when he locks his doors; and of his children, and servants, when he locks his chests. Does he not there as much accuse mankind by his actions, as I do by my words? But neither of us accuse man's nature in it. The desires, and other passions of man, are in themselves no sin. No more are the actions, that proceed from those passions, till they know a law that forbids them: which till laws be made they cannot know: nor can any law be made, till they have agreed upon the person that shall make it.

It may peradventure be thought, there was never such a time, nor condition of war as this; and I believe it was never generally so, over all the world: but there are many places, where they live so now. For the savage people in many places of *America,* except the government of small families, the concord whereof dependeth on natural lust, have no government at all; and live at this day in that brutish manner, as I said before. Howsoever, it may be perceived what manner of life there would be, where there were no common power to fear; by the manner of life, which men that have formerly lived under a peaceful government, use to degenerate into, in a civil war.

But though there had never been any time, wherein particular men were in a condition of war one against another; yet in all times, kings, and persons of sovereign authority, because of their independency, are in continual jealousies, and in the state and posture of gladiators; having their weapons pointing, and their eyes fixed on one another; that is, their forts, garrisons, and guns upon the frontiers of their kingdoms; and continual spies upon their neighbours; which is a posture of war. But because they uphold thereby, the industry of their subjects; there does not follow from it, that misery, which accompanies the liberty of particular men.

To this war of every man against every man, this also is consequent; that nothing can be unjust. The notions of right and wrong, justice and injustice have there no place. Where there is no common power, there is no law: where no law, no injustice. Force, and fraud, are in war the two cardinal virtues. Justice, and injustice are none of the faculties neither of the body, nor mind. If they were, they might be in a man that were alone in the world, as well as his senses, and passions. They are qualities, that relate to men in society, not in solitude. It is consequent also to the same condition, that there be no propriety, no dominion, no *mine* and *thine* distinct; but only that to be every man's, that he can get; and for so long, as he can keep it. And thus much for the ill condition, which man by mere nature is actually placed in; though with a possibility to come out of it, consisting partly in the passions, partly in his reason.

The passions that incline men to peace, are fear of death; desire of such things as are necessary to commodious living; and a hope by their industry to obtain them. And reason suggesteth convenient articles of peace, upon which men may be drawn to agreement. These articles, are they, which otherwise are called the Laws of Nature: where of I shall speak more particularly, in the two following chapters.

# CHAPTER 14

## OF THE FIRST AND SECOND NATURAL LAWS, AND OF CONTRACTS

The RIGHT OF NATURE, which writers commonly call *jus naturale,* is the liberty each man hath, to use his own power, as he will himself, for the preservation of his own nature; that is to say, of his own life; and consequently, of doing any thing, which in his own judgment, and reason, he shall conceive to be the aptest means thereunto.

By LIBERTY, is understood, according to the proper signification of the word, the absence of external impediments: which impediments, may oft take away part of a man's power to do what he would; but cannot hinder him from using the power left him, according as his judgment, and reason shall dictate to him.

A LAW OF NATURE, (*lex naturalis,*) is a precept, or general rule, found out by reason, by which a man is forbidden to do that, which is destructive of his life, or taketh away the means of preserving the same; and to omit that, by which he thinketh it may be best preserved. For though they that speak of this subject, use to confound *jus,* and *lex, right,* and *law;* yet they ought to be distinguished; because RIGHT, consisteth in liberty to do, or to forbear; whereas LAW, determineth, and bindeth to one of them: so that law, and right, differ as much, as obligation, and liberty; which in one and the same matter are inconsistent.

And because the condition of man, (as hath been declared in the precedent chapter) is a condition of war of everyone against everyone; in which case everyone is governed by his own reason; and there is nothing he can make use of that may not be a help unto him, in preserving his life against his enemies; it followeth, that in such a condition, every man has a right to every thing; even to one another's body. And therefore, as long as this natural right of every man to every thing endureth, there can be no security to any man, (how strong or wise soever he be,) of living out the time, which nature ordinarily alloweth men to live. And consequently it is a precept, or general rule of reason, *that every man, ought to endeavour peace, as far as he has hope of obtaining it; and when he cannot obtain it, that he may seek, and use, all helps, and advantages of war.* The first branch of which rule, containeth the first, and fundamental law of nature; which is, *to seek peace, and follow it.* The second, the sum of the right of nature; which is, *by all means we can, to defend ourselves.*

From this fundamental law of nature, by which men are commanded to endeavour peace, is derived this second law; *that a man be willing, when others are so too, as farforth, as for peace, and defence of himself he shall think it necessary, to lay down this right to all things; and be contented with so much liberty against other men, as he would allow other men against himself.* For as long as every man holdeth this right, of doing any thing he liketh; so long are all men in the condition of war. But if other men will not lay down their right, as well as he; then there is no reason for anyone, to divest himself of his: for that were to expose himself to prey, (which no man is bound to) rather than to dispose himself to peace. This is that law of the Gospel; *whatsoever you require that others should do to you, that do ye to them.* And that law of all men, *quod tibi fieri non vis, alteri ne feceris.*

To *lay down* a man's *right* to anything, is to *divest* himself of the *liberty,* of hindering another of the benefit of his own right to the same. For he that renounceth, or passeth away his right, giveth not to any other man a right which he had not before; because there is nothing to which every man had not right by nature: but only standeth out of his way, that he may enjoy his own original right, without hindrance from him; not without hindrance from another. So that the effect which redoundeth to one man, by another man's defect of right, is but so much diminution of impediments to the use of his own right original.

Right is laid aside, either by simply renouncing it; or by transferring it to another. By *simply* RENOUNCING; when he cares not to whom the benefit thereof redoundeth. By TRANSFERRING; when he intendeth the benefit thereof to some certain person, or persons. And when a man hath in either manner abandoned, or granted away his right; then is he said to be OBLIGED, or

BOUND, not to hinder those, to whom such right is granted, or abandoned, from the benefit of it: and that he *ought*, and it is his DUTY, not to make void that voluntary act of his own: and that such hindrance is INJUSTICE, and INJURY, as being *sine jure;* the right being before renounced, or transferred. So that *injury,* or *injustice,* in the controversies of the world, is somewhat like to that, which in the disputations of scholars is called *absurdity.* For as it is there called an absurdity, to contradict what one maintained in the beginning: so in the world, it is called injustice, and injury, voluntarily to undo that, which from the beginning he had voluntarily done. The way by which a man either simply renounceth, or transferreth his right, is a declaration, or signification, by some voluntary and sufficient sign, or signs, that he doth so renounce, or transfer; or hath so renounced, or transferred the same, to him that accepteth it. And these signs are either words only, or actions only; or (as it happeneth most often) both words, and actions. And the same are the BONDS, by which men are bound, and obliged: bonds, that have their strength, not from their own nature, (for nothing is more easily broken than a man's word,) but from fear of some evil consequence upon the rupture.

Whensoever a man transferreth his right, or renounceth it; it is either in consideration of some right reciprocally transferred to himself; or for some other good he hopeth for thereby. For it is a voluntary act: and of the voluntary acts of every man, the object is some *good to himself.* And therefore there be some rights, which no man can be understood by any words, or other signs, to have abandoned, or transferred. As first a man cannot lay down the right of resisting them, that assault him by force, to take away his life; because he cannot be understood to aim thereby, at any good to himself. The same may be said of wounds, and chains, and imprisonment; both because there is no benefit consequent to such patience; as there is to the patience of suffering another to be wounded, or imprisoned: as also because a man cannot tell, when he seeth men proceed against him by violence, whether they intend his death or not. And lastly the motive, and end for which this renouncing, and transferring of right is introduced, is nothing else but the security of a man's person, in his life, and in the means of so preserving life, as not to be weary of it. And therefore if a man by words, or other signs, seems to despoil himself of the end, for which those signs were intended; he is not to be understood as if he meant it, or that it was his will; but that he was ignorant of how such words and actions were to be interpreted.

The mutual transferring of right, is that which men call CONTRACT.

There is difference between transferring of right to the thing; and transferring, or tradition, that is, delivery of the thing it self. For the thing may be delivered together with the translation of the right; as in buying and selling with ready money; or exchange of goods, or lands: and it may be delivered some time after.

Again, one of the contractors, may deliver the thing contracted for on his part, and leave the other to perform his part at some determinate time after, and in the mean time be trusted; and then the contract on his part, is called PACT, or COVENANT: or both parts may contract now, to perform hereafter: in which cases, he that is to perform in time to come, being trusted, his performance is called *keeping of promise,* or faith; and the failing of performance (if it be voluntary) *violation of faith.*

When the transferring of right, is not mutual; but one of the parties transferreth, in hope to gain thereby friendship, or service from another, or from his friends; or in hope to gain the reputation of charity, or magnanimity; or to deliver his mind from the pain of compassion; or in hope of reward in heaven; this is not contract, but GIFT, FREE-GIFT, GRACE: which words signify one and the same thing.

Signs of contract, are either *express,* or *by inference.* Express, are words spoken with understanding of what they signify: and such words are either of the time *present,* or *past;* as, *I give, I grant, I have given, I have granted, I will that this be yours:* or of the future; as, *I will give, I will grant:* which words of the future are called PROMISE.

Signs by inference, are sometimes the consequence of words; sometimes the consequence of silence; sometimes the consequence of actions; sometimes the consequence of forbearing an action: and generally a sign by inference, of any contract, is whatsoever sufficiently argues the will of the contractor.

Words alone, if they be of the time to come, and contain a bare promise, are an insufficient sign of a free-gift and therefore not obligatory. For if they be of the time to come, as, *tomorrow I will give,* they are a sign I have not given yet, and consequently that my right is not transferred, but remaineth till I transfer it by some other act. But if the words be of the time present, or past, as *I have given, or do give to be delivered tomorrow,* then is my tomorrow's right given away to day; and that by the virtue of the words, though there were no other argument of my will. And there is a great difference in the signification of these words, *volo hoc tuum esse cras,* and *cras dabo;* that is, between *I will that this be thine tomorrow,* and, *I will give it thee tomorrow:* for the word *I will,* in the former manner of speech, signifies an act of the will present; but in the latter, it signifies a promise of an act of the will to come: and therefore the former words, being of the present, transfer a future right; the latter, that be of the future, transfer nothing. But if there be other signs of the will to transfer a right, besides words; then, though the gift be free, yet may the right be understood to pass by words of the future: as if a man propound a prize to him that comes first to the end of a race, the gift is free; and though the words be of the future, yet the right passeth: for if he would not have his words so be understood, he should not have let them run.

In contracts, the right passeth, not only where the words are of the time present, or past, but also where they are of the future: because all contract is mutual translation, or change of right; and therefore he that promiseth only, because he hath already received the benefit for which he promiseth, is to be understood as if he intended the right should pass: for unless he had been content to have his words so understood, the other would not have performed his part first. And for that cause, in buying, and selling, and other acts of contract, a promise is equivalent to a covenant; and therefore obligatory.

He that performeth first in the case of a contract, is said to MERIT that which he is to receive by the performance of the other; and he hath it as *due*. Also when a prize is propounded to many, which is to be given to him only that winneth; or money is thrown amongst many, to be enjoyed by them that catch it; though this be a free gift; yet so to win, or so to catch, is to *merit*, and to have it as DUE. For the right is transferred in the propounding of the prize, and in throwing down the money; though it be not determined to whom, but by the event of the contention. But there is between these two sorts of merit, this difference, that in contract, I merit by virtue of my own power, and the contractor's need; but in this case of free gift, I am enabled to merit only by the benignity of the giver: in contract, I merit at the contractor's hand that he should depart with his right; in this case of gift, I merit not that the giver should part with this right; but that when he has parted with it, it should be mine, rather than another's. And this I think to be the meaning of that distinction of the Schools, between *meritum congrui,* and *meritum condigni.* For God Almighty, having promised Paradise to those men (hoodwinked with carnal desires,) that can walk through this world according to the precepts, and limits prescribed by him; they say, he that shall so walk, shall merit Paradise *ex congruo.* But because no man can demand a right to it, by his own righteousness, or any other power in himself, but by the free grace of God only; they say, no man can merit Paradise *ex condigno.* This I say, I think is the meaning of that distinction; but because disputers do not agree upon the signification of their own terms of art, longer than it serves their turn; I will not affirm any thing of their meaning: only this I say; when a gift is given indefinitely, as a prize to be contended for, he that winneth meriteth, and may claim the prize as due.

If a covenant be made, wherein neither of the parties perform presently, but trust one another; in the condition of mere nature, (which is a condition of war of every man against every man,) upon any reasonable suspicion, it is void: but if there be a common power set over them both, with right and force sufficient to compel performance, it is not void. For he that performeth first, has no assurance the other will perform after; because the bonds of words are too weak to bridle men's ambition, avarice, anger, and other passions, without the fear of some coercive power; which in the condition of mere nature, where all men are equal, and judges of the justness of their own fears, cannot possibly be supposed. And therefore he which performeth first, does but betray himself to his enemy; contrary to the right (he can never abandon) of defending his life, and means of living.

But in a civil estate, where there is a power set up to constrain those that would otherwise violate their faith, that fear is no more reasonable; and for that cause, he which by the covenant is to perform first, is obliged so to do.

The cause of fear, which maketh such a covenant invalid, must be always something arising after the covenant made; as some new fact, or other sign of the will not to perform: else it cannot make the covenant void. For that which could not hinder a man from promising, ought not to be admitted as a hinderance of performing.

He that transferreth any right, transferreth the means of enjoying it, as far as lieth in his power. As he that selleth land, is understood to transfer the herbage, and whatsoever grows upon it; nor can he that sells a mill turn away the stream that drives it. And they that give to a man the right of government in sovereignty, are understood to give him the right of levying money to maintain soldiers: and of appointing magistrates for the administration of justice.

To make covenants with brute beasts, is impossible; because not understanding our speech, they understand not, nor accept of any translation of right; nor can translate any right to another: and without mutual acceptation, there is no covenant.

To make covenant with God, is impossible, but by mediation of such as God speaketh to, either by revelation supernatural, or by his lieutenants that govern under him, and in his name: for otherwise we know not whether our covenants be accepted, or not. And therefore they that vow any thing contrary to any law of nature, vow in vain; as being a thing unjust to pay such vow. And if it be a thing commanded by the law of nature, it is not the vow, but the law that binds them.

The matter, or subject of a covenant, is always something that falleth under deliberation; (for to covenant, is an act of the will; that is to say an act, and the last act, of deliberation;) and is therefore always understood to be something to come; and which is judged possible for him that covenanteth, to perform.

And therefore, to promise that which is known to be impossible, is no covenant. But if that prove impossible afterwards, which before was thought possible, the covenant is valid, and bindeth, (though not to the thing it self,) yet to the value; or, if that also be impossible, to the unfeigned endeavour of performing as much as is possible: for to more no man can be obliged.

Men are freed of their covenants two ways; by performing; or by being forgiven. For performance, is the natural end of obligation; and forgiveness, the restitution of liberty; as being a retransferring of that right, in which the obligation consisted.

Covenants entered into by fear, in the condition of mere nature, are obligatory. For example, if I covenant to pay a ransom, or service for my life, to an enemy; I am bound by it. For it is a contract, wherein one receiveth the benefit of life; the other is to receive money, or service for it; and consequently, where no other law (as in the condition, of mere nature) forbiddeth the performance, the covenant is valid. Therefore prisoners of war, if trusted with the payment of their ransom, are obliged to pay it: and if a weaker prince, make a disadvantageous peace with a stronger, for fear; he is bound to keep it; unless (as hath been said before) there ariseth some new, and just cause of fear, to renew the war. And even in commonwealths, if I be forced to redeem myself for a thief by promising him money, I am bound to pay it, till the civil law discharge me. For whatsoever I may lawfully do without obligation, the same I may lawfully covenant to do through fear: and what I lawfully covenant, I cannot lawfully break.

A former covenant, makes void a later. For a man that hath passed away his right to one man today, hath it not to pass tomorrow to another: and therefore the later promise passeth no right, but is null.

A covenant not to defend myself from force, by force, is always void. For (as I have showed before) no man can transfer, or lay down his right to save himself from death, wounds, and imprisonment, the avoiding whereof is the only end of laying down any right, and therefore the promise of not resisting force, in no covenant transferreth any right; nor is obliging. For though a man may covenant thus, *unless I do so, or so, kill me;* he cannot covenant thus, *unless I do so, or so, I will not resist you, when you come to kill me.* For man by nature chooseth the lesser evil, which is danger of death in resisting; rather than the greater, which is certain and present death in not resisting. And this is granted to be true by all men, in that they lead criminals to execution, and prison, with armed men, notwithstanding that such criminals have consented to the law, by which they are condemned.

A covenant to accuse oneself, without assurance of pardon, is likewise invalid. For in the condition of nature, where every man is judge, there is no place for accusation: and in the civil state, the accusation is followed with punishment; which being force, a man is not obliged not to resist. The same is also true, of the accusation of those, by whose condemnation a man falls into misery; as of a father, wife, or benefactor. For the testimony of such an accuser, if it be not willingly given, is presumed to be corrupted by nature; and therefore not to be received: and where a man's testimony is not to be credited, he is not bound to give it. Also accusations upon torture, are not to be reputed as testimonies. For torture is to be used but as means of conjecture, and light, in the further examination, and search of truth: and what is in that case confessed, tendeth to the ease of him that is tortured, not to the informing of the torturers: and therefore ought not to have the credit of a sufficient testimony: for whether he deliver himself by true, or false accusation, he does it by the right of preserving his own life.

The force of words, being (as I have formerly noted) too weak to hold men to the performance of their covenants; there are in man's nature, but two imaginable helps to strengthen it. And those are either a fear of the consequence of breaking their word; or a glory, or pride in appearing not to need to break it. This latter is a generosity too rarely found to be presumed on, especially in the pursuers of wealth, command, or sensual pleasure; which are the greatest part of mankind. The passion to be reckoned upon, is fear; whereof there be two very general objects: one, the power of spirits invisible; the other, the power of those men they shall therein offend. Of these two, though the former be the greater power, yet the fear of the latter is commonly the greater fear. The fear of the former is in every man, his own religion: which hath place in the nature of man before civil society. The latter hath not so; at least not place enough, to keep men to their promises; because in the condition of mere nature, the inequality of power is not discerned, but by the event of battle. So that before the time of civil society, or in the interruption thereof by war, there is nothing can strengthen a covenant of peace agreed on, against the temptations of avarice, ambition, lust, or other strong desire, but the fear of that invisible power, which they everyone worship as God; and fear as a revenger of their perfidy. All therefore that can be done between two men not subject to civil power, is to put one another to swear by the God he feareth: which *swearing*, or OATH, is a *form of speech, added to a promise; by which he that promiseth, signifieth, that unless he perform, he renounceth the mercy of his God, or calleth to him for vengeance on himself.* Such was the heathen form, *Let* Jupiter *kill me else, as I kill this beast.* So is our form, *I shall do thus, and thus, so help me God.* And this, with the rites and ceremonies, which everyone useth in his own religion, that the fear of breaking faith might be the greater.

By this it appears, that an oath taken according to any other form, or rite, than his, that sweareth, is in vain; and no oath: and that there is no swearing by any thing which the swearer thinks not God. For though men have sometimes used to swear by their kings, for fear, or flattery; yet they would have it thereby understood, they attributed to them divine honour. And that swearing unnecessarily by God, is but prophaning of his name: and swearing by other things, as men do on common discourse, is not swearing, but an impious custom, gotten by too much vehemence of talking.

It appears also, that the oath adds nothing to the obligation. For a covenant, if lawful, binds in the sight of God, without the oath, as much as with it: if unlawful, bindeth not at all; though it be confirmed with an oath.

## CHAPTER 15
## OF OTHER LAWS OF NATURE

From that law of nature, by which we are obliged to transfer to another, such rights, as being retained, hinder the peace of mankind, there followeth a third; which is this, *that men perform their covenants made:* without which, covenants are in vain, and but empty words; and the right of all men to all things remaining, we are still in the condition of war.

And in this law of nature, consisteth the fountain and original of JUSTICE. For where no covenant hath preceded, there hath no right been transferred, and every man has right to every thing; and consequently, no action can be unjust. But when a covenant is made, then to break it is *unjust:* and the definition of INJUSTICE, is no other than *the not performance of covenant.* And whatsoever is not unjust, is *just.*

But because covenants of mutual trust, where there is a fear of not performance on either part, (as hath been said in the former chapter,) are invalid; though the original of justice be the making of covenants; yet injustice actually there can be none, till the cause of such fear be taken away; which while men are in the natural condition of war, cannot be done. Therefore before the names of just, and unjust can have place, there must be some coercive power, to compel men equally to the performance of their covenants, by the terror of some punishment, greater than the benefit they expect by the breach of their covenant; and to make good that propriety, which by mutual contract men acquire, in recompense of the universal right they abandon: and such power there is none before the erection of a commonwealth. And this is also to be gathered out of the ordinary definition of justice in the Schools: for they say, that *justice is the constant will of giving to every man his own*. And therefore where there is no *own*, that is, no propriety, there is no injustice; and where there is no coercive power erected, that is, where there is no commonwealth, there is no propriety; all men having right to all things: therefore where there is no commonwealth, there nothing is unjust. So that the nature of justice, consisteth in keeping of valid covenants: but the validity of covenants begins not but with the constitution of a civil power, sufficient to compel men to keep them: and then it is also that propriety begins.

The fool hath said in his heart, there is no such thing as justice; and sometimes also with his tongue; seriously alleging, that every man's conservation, and contentment, being committed to his own care, there could be no reason, why every man might not do what he thought conduced thereunto: and therefore also to make, or not make; keep, or not keep covenants, was not against reason, when it conduced to one's benefit. He does not therein deny, that there be covenants; and that they are sometimes broken, sometimes kept; and that such breach of them may be called injustice, and the observance of them justice: but he questioneth, whether injustice, taking away the fear of God, (for the same fool hath said in his heart there is no God,) may not sometimes stand with that reason, which dictateth to every man his own good; and particularly then, when it conduceth to such a benefit, as shall put a man in a condition, to neglect not only the dispraise, and revilings, but also the power of other men. The kingdom of God is gotten by violence: but what if it could be gotten by unjust violence? were it against reason so to get it, when it is impossible to receive hurt by it? and if it be not against reason, it is not against justice; or else justice is not to be approved for good. From such reasoning as this, successful wickedness hath obtained the name of virtue: and some that in all other things have disallowed the violation of faith; yet have allowed it, when it is for the getting of a kingdom. And the heathen that believed, that *Saturn* was deposed by his son *Jupiter*, believed nevertheless the same *Jupiter* to be the avenger of injustice: somewhat like

to a piece of law in *Coke's Commentaries on Littleton;* where he says, if the right heir of the crown be attained of treason; yet the crown shall descend to him, and *eo instante* the attainder be void: from which instances a man will be very prone to infer; that when the heir apparent of a kingdom, shall kill him that is in possession, though his father; you may call it injustice, or by what other name you will; yet it can never be against reason, seeing all the voluntary actions of men tend to the benefit of themselves; and those actions are most reasonable, that conduce most to their ends. This specious reasoning is nevertheless false.

For the question is not of promises mutual, where there is no security of performance on either side; as when there is no civil power erected over the parties promising; for such promises are no covenants: but either where one of the parties has performed already; or where there is a power to make him perform; there is the question whether it be against reason, that is, against the benefit of the other to perform, or not. And I say it is not against reason. For the manifestation whereof, we are to consider; first, that when a man doth a thing, which notwithstanding any thing can be foreseen, and reckoned on, tendeth to his own destruction, howsoever some accident which he could not expect, arriving may turn it to his benefit; yet such events do not make it reasonably or wisely done. Secondly, that in a condition of war, wherein every man to every man, for want of a common power to keep them all in awe, is an enemy, there is no man can hope by his own strength, or wit, to defend himself from destruction, without the help of confederates; where everyone expects the same defence by the confederation, that anyone else does: and therefore he which declares he thinks it reason to deceive those that help him, can in reason expect no other means of safety, than what can be had from his own single power. He therefore that breaketh his covenant, and consequently declareth that he thinks he may with reason do so, cannot be received into any society, that unite themselves for peace and defence, but by the error of them that receive him; nor when he is received, be retained in it, without seeing the danger of their error;

which errors a man cannot reasonably reckon upon as the means of his security: and therefore if he be left, or cast out of society, he perisheth; and if he live in society, it is by the errors of other men, which he could not foresee, nor reckon upon; and consequently against the reason of his preservation; and so, as all men that contribute not to his destruction, forbear him only out of ignorance of what is good for themselves.

As for the instance of gaining the secure and perpetual felicity of heaven, by any way; it is frivolous: there being but one way imaginable; and that is not breaking, but keeping of covenant.

And for the other instance of attaining sovereignty by rebellion; it is manifest, that though the event follow, yet because it cannot reasonably be expected, but rather the contrary; and because by gaining it so, others are taught to gain the same in like manner, the attempt thereof is against reason. Justice therefore, that is to say, keeping of covenant, is a rule of reason, by which we are forbidden to do any thing destructive to our life; and consequently a law of nature.

There be some that proceed further; and will not have the law of nature, to be those rules which conduce to the preservation of man's life on earth; but to the attaining of an eternal felicity after death; to which they think the breach of covenant may conduce; and consequently be just and reasonable (such are they that think it a work of merit to kill, or depose, or rebel against, the sovereign power constituted over them by their own consent). But because there is no natural knowledge of man's estate after death; much less of the reward that is then to be given to breach of faith; but only a belief grounded upon other men's saying, that they know it supernaturally, or that they know those, that knew them, that knew others, that knew it supernaturally; breach of faith cannot be called a precept of reason, or nature.

Others, that allow for a law of nature, the keeping of faith, do nevertheless make exception of certain persons; as heretics, and such as use not to perform their covenant to others: and this also is against reason. For if any fault of a man, be sufficient to discharge our covenant made; the same ought in reason to have been sufficient to have hindered the making of it.

The names of just, and injust, when they are attributed to men, signify one thing; and when they are attributed to actions, another. When they are attributed to men, they signify conformity, or inconformity of manners, to reason. But when they are attributed to actions, they signify the conformity, or inconformity to reason, not of manners, or manner of life, but of particular actions. A just man therefore, is he that taketh all the care he can, that his actions may be all just: and an unjust man, is he that neglecteth it. And such men are more often in our language styled by the names of righteous, and unrighteous; than just, and unjust; though the meaning be the same. Therefore a righteous man, does not lose that title, by one, or a few unjust actions, that proceed from sudden passion, or mistake of things, or persons: nor does an unrighteous man, lose his character, for such actions, as he does, or forbears to do, for fear: because his will is not framed by the justice, but by the apparent benefit of what he is to do. That which gives to human actions the relish of justice, is a certain nobleness or gallantness of courage, (rarely found), by which a man scorns to be beholding for the contentment of his life, to fraud, or breach of promise. This justice of the manners, is that which is meant, where justice is called a virtue; and injustice a vice.

But the justice of actions denominates men, not just, but *guiltless:* and the injustice of the same, (which is also called injury,) gives them but the name of *guilty.*

Again, the injustice of manners, is the disposition, or aptitude to do injury; and is injustice before it proceeds to act; and without supposing any individual person injured. But the injustice of an action, (that is to say injury,) supposeth an individual person injured; namely him, to whom the covenant was made: and therefore many times the injury is received by one man, when the damage redoundeth to another. As when the master commandeth his servant to give money to a stranger; if it be not done, the injury is done to the master, whom he had before covenanted to obey; but the damage redoundeth to the stranger, to whom he had no obligation; and therefore could not injure him. And so also in commonwealths, private men may remit to one another their debts; but not robberies or other violences, whereby they are endamaged; because the detaining of debt, is an injury to themselves; but robbery and violence, are injuries to the person of the commonwealth.

Whatsoever is done to a man, conformable to his own will signified to the doer, is no injury to him. For if he that doeth it, hath not passed away his original right to do what he please, by some antecedent covenant, there is no breach of covenant; and therefore no injury done him. And if he have; then his will to have it done being signified, is a release of that covenant: and so again there is no injury done him.

Justice of actions, is by writers divided into *commutative,* and *distributive:* and the former they say consisteth in proportion arithmetical; the latter in proportion geometrical. Commutative therefore, they place in the equality of value of the things contracted for; and distributive, in the distribution of equal benefit, to men of equal merit. As if it were injustice to sell dearer than we buy; or to give more to a man than he merits. The value of all things contracted for, is measured by the appetite of the contractors: and therefore the just value, is that which they be contented to give. And merit, (besides that which is by covenant, where the performance on one part, meriteth the performance of the other part, and falls under justice commutative, not distributive,) is not due by justice; but is rewarded of grace only. And therefore this distinction, in the sense wherein it useth to be expounded, is not right. To speak properly, commutative justice, is the justice of a contractor; that is, a performance of covenant, in buying, and selling; hiring, and letting to hire; lending, and borrowing; exchanging, bartering, and other acts of contract.

And distributive justice, the justice of an arbitrator; that is to say, the act of defining what is just. Wherein, (being trusted by them that make him arbitrator,) if he perform his trust, he is said to distribute to every man his own: and this is indeed just distribution, and may be called, (though improperly,) distributive justice; but more properly equity; which also is a law of nature, as shall be shown in due place.

As justice dependeth on antecedent covenant; so does GRATITUDE depend on antecedent grace; that is to say, antecedent free-gift: and is the fourth law of nature; which may be conceived in this form, *that a man which receiveth benefit from another of mere grace, endeavour that he which giveth it, have no reasonable cause to repent him of his good will.* For no man giveth, but with intention of good to himself; because gift is voluntary; and of all voluntary acts, the object is to every man his own good; of which if men see they shall be frustrated, there will be no beginning of benevolence, or trust; nor consequently of mutual help; nor of reconciliation of one man to another; and therefore they are to remain still in the condition of *war;* which is contrary to the first and fundamental law of nature, which commandeth men to *seek peace.* The breach of this law, is called *ingratitude;* and hath the same relation to grace, that injustice hath to obligation by covenant.

A fifth law of nature, is COMPLAISANCE; that is to say, *that every man strive to accommodate himself to the rest.* For the understanding whereof, we may consider, that there is in men's aptness to society, a diversity of nature, rising from their diversity of affections; not unlike to that we see in stones brought together for building of an edifice. For as that stone which by the asperity, and irregularity of figure, takes more room from others, that itself fills; and for the hardness, cannot be easily made plain, and thereby hindereth the building, is by the builders cast away as unprofitable, and troublesome: so also, a man that by asperity of nature, will strive to retain those things which to himself are superfluous, and to others necessary; and for the stubbornness of his passions, cannot be corrected, is to be left, or cast out of society, as cumbersome thereunto. For seeing every man, not only by right, but also by necessity of nature, is supposed to endeavour all he can, to obtain that which is necessary for his conservation; he that shall oppose himself against it, for things superfluous, is guilty of the war that thereupon is to follow; and therefore doth that, which is contrary to the fundamental law of nature, which commandeth *to seek peace*. The observers of this law, may be called SOCIABLE, (the Latins call them *commodi;*) the contrary, *stubborn, insociable, froward, intractable.*

A sixth law of nature, is this, *that upon caution of the future time, a man ought to pardon the offences past of them that repenting, desire it.* For PARDON, is nothing but granting of peace; which though granted to them that persevere in their hostility, be not peace, but fear; yet not granted to them that give caution of the future time, is sign of an aversion to peace; and therefore contrary to the law of nature.

A seventh is, *that in revenges,* (that is, retribution of evil for evil), *men look not at the greatness of the evil past, but the greatness of the good to follow.* Whereby we are forbidden to inflict punishment with any other design, that for correction of the offender, or direction of others. For this law is consequent to the next before it, that commandeth pardon, upon security of the future time. Besides, revenge without respect to the example, and profit to come, is a triumph, or glorying in the hurt of another, tending to no end; (for the end is always somewhat to come;) and glorying to no end, is vain-glory, and contrary to reason; and to hurt without reason, tendeth to the introduction of war; which is against the law of nature; and is commonly styled by the name of *cruelty.*

And because all signs of hatred, or contempt, provoke to fight; insomuch as most men choose rather to hazard their life, than not to be revenged: we may in the eighth place, for a law of nature, set down this precept, *that no man by deed, word, countenance, or gesture, declare hatred, or contempt of another.* The breach of which law, is commonly called *contumely.*

The question who is the better man, has no place in the condition of mere nature; where, (as has been shewn before,) all men are equal. The inequality that now is, has been introduced by the laws civil. I know that *Aristotle* in the first book of his *Politics,* for a foundation of his doctrine,

maketh men by nature, some more worthy to command, meaning the wiser sort, (such as he thought himself to be for his philosophy;) others to serve, (meaning those that had strong bodies, but were not philosophers as he;) as if master and servant were not introduced by consent of men, but by difference of wit: which is not only against reason; but also against experience. For there are very few so foolish, that had not rather govern themselves, than be governed by others: nor when the wise in their own conceit, contend by force, with them who distrust their own wisdom, do they always, or often, or almost at any time, get the victory. If nature therefore have made men equal, that equality is to be acknowledged: or if nature have made men unequal; yet because men that think themselves equal, will not enter into conditions of peace, but upon equal terms, such equality must be admitted. And therefore for the ninth law of nature, I put this, *that every man acknowledge other for his equal by nature.* The breach of this precept is *pride.*

On this law, dependeth another, *that at the entrance into conditions of peace, no man require to reserve to himself any right, which he is not content should be reserved to everyone of the rest.* As it is necessary for all men that seek peace, to lay down certain rights of nature; that is to say, not to have liberty to do all they list: so is it necessary for man's life, to retain some; as right to govern their own bodies; enjoy air, water, motion, ways to go from place to place; and all things else without which a man cannot live, or not live well. If in this case, at the making of peace, men require for themselves, that which they would not have to be granted to others, they do contrary to the precedent law, that commandeth the acknowledgment of natural equality, and therefore also against the law of nature. The observers of this law, are those we call *modest,* and the breakers *arrogant* men. The Greeks call the violation of this law πλεονεξια; that is, a desire of more than their share.

Also if *a man be trusted to judge between man and man,* it is a precept of the law of nature, *that he deal equally between them.* For without that, the controversies of men cannot be determined but by war. He therefore that is partial in judgment, doth what in him lies, to deter men from the use of judges, and arbitrators; and consequently, (against the fundamental law of nature,) is the cause of war.

The observance of this law, from the equal distribution to each man, of that which in reason belongeth to him, is called EQUITY, and (as I have said before) distributive justice: the violation, *acception of persons, προσωποληψία*.

And from this followeth another law, *that such things as cannot be divided, be enjoyed in common, if it can be; and if the quantity of the thing permit, without stint; otherwise proportionably to the number of them that have right*. For otherwise the distribution is unequal, and contrary to equity.

But some things there be, that can neither be divided, nor enjoyed in common. Then, the law of nature, which prescribeth equity, requireth, *that the entire right; or else, (making the use alternate,) the first possession, be determined by lot*. For equal distribution, is of the law of nature; and other means of equal distribution cannot be imagined.

Of *lots* there be two sorts, *arbitrary*, and *natural*. Arbitrary, is that which is agreed on by the competitors: natural, is either *primogeniture*, (which the Greek calls *κληρονομία*, which signifies, *given by lot;*) or *first seizure*.

And therefore those things which cannot be enjoyed in common, nor divided, ought to be adjudged to the first possessor; and in some cases to the first-born, as acquired by lot.

It is also a law of nature, *that all men that mediate peace, be allowed safe conduct*. For the law that commandeth peace, as the *end*, commandeth intercession, as the *means;* and to intercession the means is safe conduct.

And because, though men be never so willing to observe these laws, there may nevertheless arise questions concerning a man's action; first, whether it were done, or not done; secondly, (if done,) whether against the law, or not against the law, the former whereof, is called a question *of fact;* the latter a question *of right;* therefore unless the parties to the question, covenant mutually to stand to the sentence of another, they are as far from peace as ever. This other, to whose sentence they submit, is called an ARBITRATOR. And therefore it is of the law of nature, *that they that are at controversy, submit their right to the judgment of an arbitrator.*

And seeing every man is presumed to do all things in order to his own benefit, no man is a fit arbitrator in his own cause: and if he were never so fit; yet equity allowing to each party equal benefit, if one be admitted to be judge, the other is to be admitted also; and so the controversy, that is, the cause of war, remains, against the law of nature.

For the same reason no man in any cause ought to be received for arbitrator, to whom greater profit, or honour, or pleasure apparently ariseth out of the victory of one party, than of the other: for he hath taken (though an unavoidable bribe, yet) a bribe; and no man can be obliged to trust him. And thus also the controversy, and the condition of war remaineth, contrary to the law of nature.

And in a controversy of *fact*, the judge being to give no more credit to one, than to the other, (if there be no other arguments,) must give credit to a third; or to a third and fourth; or more: for else the question is undecided, and left to force, contrary to the law of nature.

These are the laws of nature, dictating peace, for a means of the conservation of men in multitudes; and which only concern the doctrine of civil society. There be other things tending to the destruction of particular men; as drunkenness, and all other parts of intemperance; which may therefore also be reckoned amongst those things which the law of nature hath forbidden; but are not necessary to be mentioned, nor are pertinent enough to this place.

And though this may seem too subtle a deduction of the laws of nature, to be taken notice of by all men; whereof the most part are too busy in getting food, and the rest too negligent to understand; yet to leave all men inexcusable, they have been contracted into one easy sum, intelligible, even to the meanest capacity; and that is, *Do not that to another, which thou wouldest not have done to thyself;* which sheweth him, that he has no more to do in learning the laws of nature, but, when weighing the actions of other men with his own, they seem too heavy, to put them into the other part of the balance, and his own into their place, that his own passions, and self-love, may add nothing to the weight; and then there is none of these laws of nature that will not appear unto him very reasonable.

The laws of nature oblige *in foro interno;* that is to say, they bind to a desire they should take place: but *in foro externo;* that is, to the putting them in act, not always. For he that should be modest, and tractable, and perform all he promises, in such time, and place, where no man else should do so, should but make himself a prey to others, and procure his own certain ruin, contrary to the ground of all laws of nature, which tend to nature's preservation. And again, he that having sufficient security, that others shall observe the same laws towards him, observes them not himself, seeketh not peace, but war; and consequently the destruction of his nature by violence.

And whatsoever laws bind *in foro interno,* may be broken, not only by a fact contrary to the law, but also by a fact according to it, in case a man think it contrary. For though his action in this case, be according to the law; yet his purpose was against the law; which, where the obligation is *in foro interno,* is a breach.

The laws of nature are immutable and eternal; for injustice, ingratitude, arrogance, pride, iniquity, acception of persons, and the rest, can never be made lawful. For it can never be that war shall preserve life, and peace destroy it.

The same laws, because they oblige only to a desire, and endeavour, I mean an unfeigned and constant endeavour, are easy to be observed. For in that they require nothing but endeavour; he that endeavoureth their performance, fulfilleth them; and he that fulfilleth the law, is just.

And the science of them, is true and only moral philosophy. For moral philosophy is nothing else but the science of what is *good,* and *evil,* in the conservation, and society of mankind. *Good* and *evil,* are names that signify our appetites, and aversions; which in different tempers, customs, and doctrines of men, are different: and divers men,

differ not only in their judgment, on the senses of what is pleasant, and unpleasant to the taste, smell, hearing, touch, and sight; but also of what is conformable, or disagreeable to reason, in the actions of common life. Nay, the same man, in divers times, differs from himself; and one time praiseth, that is, calleth good, what another time he dispraiseth, and calleth evil: from whence arise disputes, controversies, and at last war. And therefore so long a man is in the condition of mere nature, (which is a condition of war,) as private appetite is the measure of good, and evil: and consequently all men agree on this, that peace is good, and therefore also the way, or means of peace, which, (as I have shewed before) are *justice, gratitude, modesty, equity, mercy,* and the rest of the laws of nature, are good; that is to say, *moral virtues;* and their contrary *vices,* evil. Now the science of virtue and vice, is moral philosophy; and therefore the true doctrine of the laws of nature, is the true moral philosophy. But the writers of moral philosophy, though they acknowledge the same virtues and vices; yet not seeing wherein consisted their goodness; nor that they come to be praised, as the means of peaceable, sociable, and comfortable living; place them in a mediocrity of passions: as if not the cause, but the degree of daring, made fortitude; or not the cause, but the quantity of a gift, made liberality.

These dictates of reason, men use to call by the name of laws; but improperly: for they are but conclusions, or theorems concerning what conduceth to the conservation and defence of themselves; whereas law, properly, is the word of him, that by right hath command over others. But yet if we consider the same theorems, as delivered in the word of God, that by right commandeth all things; then are they properly called laws.

## CHAPTER 16
## OF PERSONS, AUTHORS, AND THINGS PERSONATED

A person, is he, *whose words or actions are considered, either as his own, or as representing the words or actions of another man, or of any other thing to whom they are attributed, whether truly or by fiction.*

When they are considered as his own, then is he called a *natural person:* and when they are considered as representing the words and actions of another, then is he a *feigned* or *artificial person.*

The word person is Latin: instead of whereof the Greeks have πρόσωπον, which signifies the *face,* as *persona* in Latin signifies the *disguise,* or *outward appearance* of a man, counterfeited on the stage; and sometimes more particularly that part of it, which disguiseth the face, as a mask or vizard: and from the stage, hath been translated to any representer of speech and action, as well in tribunals, as theatres. So that a *person,* is the same that an *actor* is, both on the stage and in common conversation; and to *personate,* is to *act,* or *represent* himself, or another; and he that acteth another, is said to bear his person, or act in his name; (in which sense Cicero useth it where he says, *Unus sustineo tres personas; mei, adversarii, et judicis,* I bear three persons; my own, my adversary's, and the judge's;) and is called in divers occasions, diversly; as a *representer,* or *representative,* a *lieutenant,* a *vicar,* an *attorney,* a *deputy,* a *procurator,* an *actor,* and the like.

Of persons artificial, some have their words and actions *owned* by those whom they represent. And then the person is the *actor;* and he that owneth his words and actions, is the AUTHOR: in which case the actor acteth by authority. For that which in speaking of goods and possessions, is called an *owner,* and in Latin *dominus,* in Greek κύριος; speaking of actions, is called author. And as the right of possession, is called dominion; so the right of doing any action, is called AUTHORITY. So that by authority, is always understood a right of doing any act: and *done by authority,* done by commission, or licence from him whose right it is.

From hence it followeth, that when the actor maketh a covenant by authority, he bindeth thereby the author, no less than if he had made it himself; and no less subjecteth him to all the consequences of the same. And therefore all that hath been said formerly, (*chap.* 14) of the nature of covenants between man and man in their natural capacity, is true also when they are made by their actors, representers, or procurators, that have authority from them, so far forth as is in their commission, but no farther.

And therefore he that maketh a covenant with the actor, or representer, not knowing the authority he hath, doth it at his own peril. For no man is obliged by a covenant, whereof he is not author; nor consequently by a covenant made against, or beside the authority he gave.

When the actor doth any thing against the law of nature by command of the author, if he be obliged by former covenant to obey him, not he, but the author breaketh the law of nature: for though the action be against the law of nature; yet it is not his: but contrarily, to refuse to do it, is against the law of nature, that forbiddeth breach of covenant.

And he that maketh a covenant with the author, by mediation of the actor, not knowing what authority he hath, but only takes his word; in case such authority be not made manifest unto him upon demand, is no longer obliged: for the covenant made with the author, is not valid, without his counter-assurance. But if he that so covenanteth, knew beforehand he was to expect no other assurance, than the actor's word; then is the covenant valid; because the actor in this case maketh himself the author. And therefore, as when the authority is evident, the covenant obligeth the author, not the actor; so when the authority is feigned, it obligeth the actor only; there being no author but himself.

There are few things, that are incapable of being represented by fiction. Inanimate things, as a church, a hospital, a bridge, may be personated by a rector, master, or overseer. But things inanimate, cannot be authors, nor therefore give authority to their actors: yet the actors may have authority to procure their maintenance, given them by those that are owners, or governors of those things. And therefore, such things cannot be personated, before there be some state of civil government.

Likewise children, fools, and madmen that have no use of reason, may be personated by guardians, or curators; but can be no authors, (during that time) of any action done by them, longer than (when they shall recover the use of reason) they shall judge the same reasonable. Yet during the folly, he that hath right of governing them, may give authority to the guardian. But this again has no place but in a state civil, because before such estate, there is no dominion of persons.

An idol, or mere figment of the brain, may be personated; as were the gods of the heathen; which by such officers as the state appointed, were personated, and held possessions, and other goods, and rights, which men from time to time dedicated, and consecrated unto them. But idols cannot be authors: for an idol is nothing. The authority proceeded from the state: and therefore before introduction of civil government, the gods of the heathen could not be personated.

The true God may be personated. As he was; first, by Moses; who governed the Israelites, (that were not his, but God's people,) not in his own name, with *hoc dicit Moses;* but in God's name, with *hoc dicit Dominus.* Secondly, by the Son of man, his own Son, our blessed Saviour Jesus Christ, that came to reduce the Jews, and induce all nations into the kingdom of his father; not as of himself, but as sent from his father. And thirdly, by the Holy Ghost, or Comforter, speaking, and working in the Apostles: which Holy Ghost, was a Comforter that came not of himself; but was sent, and proceeded from them both.

A multitude of men, are made *one* person, when they are by one man, or one person, represented; so that it be done with the consent of everyone of that multitude in particular. For it is the *unity* of the represented; that maketh the person *one.* And it is the representer that beareth the person, and but one person: and *unity,* cannot otherwise be understood in multitude.

And because the multitude naturally is not *one,* but *many;* they cannot be understood for one; but many authors, of every thing their representative saith, or doth in their name; every man giving their common representer, authority from himself in particular; and owning all the actions the representer doth, in case they give him authority without stint: otherwise, when they limit him in what, and how far he shall represent them, none of them owneth more, than they gave him commission to act.

And if the representative consist of many men, the voice of the greater number, must be considered as the voice of them all. For if the lesser number pronounce (for example) in the affirmative, and the greater in the negative, there will be negatives more than enough to destroy the affirmatives; and thereby the excess of negatives, standing uncontradicted, are the only voice the representative hath.

And a representative of even number, especially when the number is not great, whereby the contradictory voices are oftentimes equal, is therefore oftentimes mute, and incapable of action. Yet in some cases contradictory voices equal in number, may determine a question; as in condemning, or absolving, equality of votes, even in that they condemn not, do absolve; but not on the contrary condemn, in that they absolve not. For when a cause is heard; not to condemn, is to absolve: but on the contrary, to say that not absolving, is condemning, is not true. The like it is in a deliberation of executing presently, or deferring till another time: for when the voices are equal, the not decreeing execution, is a decree of dilation.

Or if the number be odd, as three, or more, (men, or assemblies;) whereof everyone has by a negative voice, authority to take away the effect of all the affirmative voices of the rest, this number is no representative; because by the diversity of opinions, and interests of men, it becomes oftentimes, and in cases of the greatest consequence, a mute person, and unapt, as for many things else, so for the government of a multitude, especially in time of war.

Of authors there be two sorts. The first simply so called; which I have before defined to be him, that owneth the action of another simply. The second is he, that owneth an action, or covenant of another conditionally; that is to say, he undertaketh to do it, if the other doth it not, at, or before a certain time. And these authors conditional, are generally called SURETIES, in Latin *fidejus-*

*sores,* and *sponsores;* and particularly for debt, *praedes;* and for appearance before a judge, or magistrate, *vades.*

## Part 2 of Commonwealth

### CHAPTER 17

### OF THE CAUSES, GENERATION, AND DEFINITION OF A COMMONWEALTH

The final cause, end, or design of men, (who naturally love liberty, and dominion over others,) in the introduction of that restraint upon themselves, (in which we see them live in commonwealths,) is the foresight of their own preservation, and of a more contented life thereby; that is to say, of getting themselves out from that miserable condition of war, which is necessarily consequent (as hath been shown), to, the natural passions of men, when there is no visible power to keep them in awe, and tie them by fear of punishment to the performance of their covenants, and observation of those laws of nature set down in the fourteenth and fifteenth chapters.

For the laws of nature (as *justice, equity, modesty, mercy,* and (in sum) *doing to others, as we would be done to,*) of themselves, without the terror of some power, to cause them to be observed, are contrary to our natural passions, that carry us to partiality, pride, revenge, and the like. And covenants, without the sword, are but words, and of no strength to secure a man at all. Therefore notwithstanding the laws of nature, (which everyone hath then kept, when he has the will to keep them, when he can do it safely,) if there be no power erected, or not great enough for our security; every man will, and may lawfully rely on his own strength and art, for caution against all other men. And in all places, where men have lived by small families, to rob and spoil one another, has been a trade, and so far from being reputed against the law of nature, that the greater spoils they gained, the greater was their honour; and men observed no other laws therein, but the laws of honour; that is, to abstain from cruelty, leaving to men their lives, and instruments of husbandry.

And as small families did then; so now do cities and kingdoms which are but greater families (for their own security) enlarge their dominions, upon all pretences of danger, and fear of invasion, or assistance that may be given to invaders, endeavour as much as they can, to subdue, or weaken their neighbours, by open force, and secret arts, for want of other caution, justly; and are remembered for it in after ages with honour.

Nor is it the joining together of a small number of men, that gives them this security; because in small numbers, small additions on the one side or the other, make the advantage of strength so great, as is sufficient to carry the victory; and therefore, gives encouragement to an invasion. The multitude sufficient to confide in for our security, is not determined by any certain number, but by comparison with the enemy we fear; and is then sufficient, when the odds of the enemy is not of so visible and conspicuous moment, to determine the event of war, as to move him to attempt.

And be there never so great a multitude; yet if their actions be directed according to their particular judgments, and particular appetites, they can expect thereby no defence, nor protection, neither against a common enemy, nor against the injuries of one another. For being distracted in opinions concerning the best use and application of their strength, they do not help, but hinder one another; and reduce their strength by mutual opposition to nothing: whereby they are easily, not only subdued by a very few that agree together; but also when there is no common enemy, they make war upon each other, for their particular interests. For if we could suppose a great multitude of men to consent in the observation of justice, and other laws of nature, without a common power to keep them all in awe; we might as well suppose all mankind to do the same; and then there neither would be, nor need to be any civil government, or commonwealth at all; because there would be peace without subjection.

Nor is it enough for the security, which men desire should last all the time of their life, that they be governed, and directed by one judgment, for a limited time; as in one battle, or one war. For though they obtain a victory by their unanimous endeavour against a foreign enemy; yet afterwards, when either they have no common enemy, or he that by one part is held for an enemy, is by another part held for a friend, they must needs by the difference of their interests dissolve, and fall again into a war amongst themselves.

It is true, that certain living creatures, as bees, and ants, live sociably one with another, (which are therefore by *Aristotle* numbered amongst political creatures;) and yet have no other direction, than their particular judgments and appetites; nor speech, whereby one of them can signify to another, what he thinks expedient for the common benefit: and therefore some man may perhaps desire to know, why mankind cannot do the same. To which I answer,

First, that men are continually in competition for honour and dignity, which these creatures are not; and consequently amongst men there ariseth on that ground, envy and hatred, and finally war; but amongst these not so.

Secondly, that amongst these creatures, the common good differeth not from the private; and being by nature inclined to their private, they procure thereby the common benefit. But man, whose joy consisteth in comparing himself with other men, can relish nothing but what is eminent.

Thirdly, that these creatures, having not, (as man) the use of reason, do not see, nor think they see any fault, in the administration of their common business; whereas amongst men, there are very many, that think themselves wiser, and abler to govern the public, better than the rest; and these strive to reform and innovate, one this way, another that way; and thereby bring it into distraction and civil war.

Fourthly, that these creatures, though they have some use of voice, in making known to one another their desires, and other affections; yet they want that art of words, by which some men can represent to others, that which is good, in the likeness of evil; and evil, in the likeness of good; and augment, or diminish the apparent greatness of good and evil; discontenting men, and troubling their peace at their pleasure.

Fifthly, irrational creatures cannot distinguish between *injury*, and *damage;* and therefore as long as they be at ease, they are not offended with their fellows: whereas man is then most troublesome, when he is most at ease: for then it is that he loves to shew his wisdom, and control the actions of them that govern the commonwealth.

Lastly, the agreement of these creatures is natural; that of men, is by covenant only, which is artificial: and therefore it is no wonder if there be somewhat else required (besides covenant) to make their agreement constant and lasting; which is a common power, to keep them in awe, and to direct their actions to the common benefit.

The only way to erect such a common power, as may be able to defend them from the invasion of foreigners, and the injuries of one another, and thereby to secure them in such sort, as that by their own industry, and by the fruits of the earth, they may nourish themselves and live contentedly; is, to confer all their power and strength upon one man, or upon one assembly of men, that may reduce all their wills, by plurality of voices, unto one will: which is as much as to say, to appoint one man, or assembly of men, to bear their person; and everyone to own, and acknowledge himself to be author of whatsoever he that so beareth their person, shall act, or cause to be acted, in those things which concern the common peace and safety; and therein to submit their wills, everyone to his will, and their judgments, to his judgments. This is more than consent, or concord; it is a real unity of them all, in one and the same person, made by covenant of every man with every man, in such manner, as if every man should say to every man, *I authorize and give up my right of governing myself, to this man, or to this assembly of men, on this condition, that thou give up thy right to him, and authorize all his actions in like manner.* This done, the multitude so united in one person, is called a COMMONWEALTH, in Latin CIVITAS. This is the generation of that great LEVIATHAN, or rather (to speak more reverently) of that *mortal god,* to which we owe under the *immortal God,* our peace and defence. For by this authority, given him by every particular man in the commonwealth, he hath the use of so much power and strength conferred on him, that by terror thereof, he is enabled to form the wills of them all, to peace at home, and mutual aid against their enemies abroad. And in him consisteth the essence of the commonwealth; which (to define it,) is *one person, of whose acts a great multitude, by mutual covenants one with another, have made themselves every-one the author, to the end he may use the strength and means of them all, as he shall think expedient, for their peace and common defence.*

And he that carrieth this person, is called SOV-EREIGN, and said to have sovereign power; and every one besides, his SUBJECT.

The attaining to this sovereign power, is by two ways. One, by natural force; as when a man maketh his children, to submit themselves, and their children to his government, as being able to destroy them if they refuse; or by war subdueth his enemies to his will, giving them their lives on that condition. The other, is when men agree amongst themselves, to submit to some man, or assembly of men, voluntarily, on confidence to be protected by him against all others. This latter, may be called a political commonwealth, or commonwealth by *institution;* and the former, a commonwealth by *acquisition.* And first, I shall speak of a commonwealth by institution.

## CHAPTER 18
## OF THE RIGHTS OF SOVEREIGNS BY INSTITUTION

A *commonwealth* is said to be *instituted,* when a *multitude* of men do agree, and *covenant, every-one, with everyone,* that to whatsoever *man,* or *assembly of men,* shall be given by the major part, the *right* to *present* the person of them all, (that is to say, to be their *representative;*) everyone, as well he that *voted for it,* as he that *voted against it,* shall *authorize* all the actions and judgments, of that man, or assembly of men, in the same manner, as if they were his own, to the end, to live peaceably amongst themselves, and be protected against other men.

From this institution of a commonwealth are derived all the *rights,* and *faculties* of him, or them, on whom the sovereign power is conferred by the consent of the people assembled.

First, because they covenant, it is to be understood, they are not obliged by former covenant to any thing repugnant hereunto. And consequently they that have already instituted a commonwealth, being thereby bound by covenant, to own the actions, and judgments of one, cannot lawfully make a new covenant, amongst themselves, to be obedient to any other, in any thing whatsoever, without his permission. And therefore, they that are subjects to a monarch, cannot without his leave cast off monarchy, and return to the confusion of a disunited multitude; nor transfer their person from him that beareth it, to another man, or other assembly of men: for they are bound, every man to every man, to own, and be reputed author of all, that he that already is their sovereign, shall do, and judge fit to be done: so that any one man dissenting, all the rest should break their covenant made to that man, which is injustice: and they have also every man given the sovereignty to him that beareth their person; and therefore if they depose him, they take from him that which is his own, and so again it is injustice. Besides, if he that attempteth to depose his sovereign, be killed, or punished by him for such attempt, he is author of his own punishment, as being by the institution, author of all his sovereign shall do: and because it is injustice for a man to do any thing, for which he may be punished by his own authority, he is also upon that title, unjust. And whereas some men have pretended for their disobedience to their sovereign, a new covenant, made, not with men, but with God; this also is unjust: for there is no covenant with God, but by mediation of somebody that representeth God's person: which none doth but God's lieutenant, who hath the sovereignty under God. But this pretence of covenant with God, is so evident a lie, even in the pretenders' own consciences, that it is not only an act of an unjust, but also of a vile, and unmanly disposition.

Secondly, because the right of bearing the person of them all, is given to him they make sovereign, by covenant only of one to another, and not of him to any of them; there can happen no breach of covenant on the part of the sovereign; and consequently none of his subjects, by any pretence of forfeiture, can be freed from his subjection. That he which is made sovereign maketh no covenant with his subjects beforehand, is manifest; because either must make it with the whole multitude, as one party to the covenant; or he must make several covenants with every man. With the whole, as one party, it is impossible; because as yet they are not one person: and if he make so many several covenants as there be men, those covenants after he hath the sovereignty are void, because what act soever can be pretended by anyone of them for breach thereof, is that act both of himself, and of all the rest, because done in the person, and by the right of everyone of them in particular. Besides, if anyone, or more of them, pretend a breach of the covenant made by the sovereign at his institution; and others, or one other of his subjects, or himself alone, pretend there was no such breach, there is in this case, no judge to decide the controversy; it returns therefore to the sword again; and every man recovereth the right of protecting himself by his own strength, contrary to the design they had in the institution. It is therefore in vain to grant sovereignty by way of precedent covenant. The opinion that any monarch receiveth his power by covenant, that is to say, on condition, proceedeth from want of understanding this easy truth, that covenants being but words and breath, have no force to oblige, contain, constrain, or protect any man, but what it has from the public sword; that is, from the untied hands of that man, or assembly of men that hath the sovereignty, and whose actions are avouched by them all, and performed by the strength of them all, in him united. But when an assembly of men is made sovereign; then no man imagineth any such covenant to have passed in the institution; for no man is so dull as to say, for example, the people of Rome made a covenant with the Romans, to hold the sovereignty on such or such conditions; which not performed, the Romans might lawfully depose the Roman people. That men see not the reason to be alike in a monarchy, and in a popular government, proceedeth from the ambition of some, that are kinder to the government of an assembly, whereof they may hope to participate, than of monarchy, which they despair to enjoy.

Thirdly, because the major part hath by consenting voices declared a sovereign; he that dissented must now consent with the rest; that is, be contented to avow all the actions he shall do, or else justly be destroyed by the rest. For if he voluntarily entered into the congregation of them that were assembled, he sufficiently declared thereby his will, (and therefore tacitly covenanted) to stand to what the major part should ordain: and therefore if he refuse to stand thereto, or make protestation against any of their decrees, he does contrary to his covenant, and therefore unjustly. And whether he be of the congregation, or not; and whether his consent be asked, or not, he must either submit to their decrees, or be left in the condition of war he was in before; wherein he might without injustice be destroyed by any man whatsoever.

Fourthly, because every subject is by this institution author of all the actions, and judgments of the sovereign instituted; it follows, that whatsoever he doth, it can be no injury to any of his subjects; nor ought he to be by any of them accused of injustice. For he that doth any thing by authority from another, doth therein no injury to him by whose authority he acteth: but by this institution of a commonwealth, every particular man is author of all the sovereign doth; and consequently he that complaineth of injury from his sovereign, complaineth of that whereof he himself is author; and therefore ought not to accuse any man but himself; no nor himself of injury; because to do injury to one's self, is impossible. It is true that they that have sovereign power, may commit iniquity; but not injustice, or injury in the proper signification.

Fifthly, and consequently to that which was said last, no man that hath sovereign power can justly be put to death, or otherwise in any manner by his subjects punished. For seeing every subject is author of the actions of his sovereign; he punisheth another, for the actions committed by himself.

And because the end of this institution, is the peace and defence of them all; and whosoever has right to the end, has right to the means; it belongeth of right, to whatsoever man, or assembly that hath the sovereignty, to be judge both of the means of peace and defence; and also of the hindrances, and disturbances of the same; and to do whatsoever he shall think necessary to be done, both beforehand, for the preserving of peace and security, by prevention of discord at home, and hostility from abroad; and, when peace and security are lost, for the recovery of the same. And therefore,

Sixthly, it is annexed to the sovereignty, to be judge of what opinions and doctrines are averse, and what conducing to peace; and consequently, on what occasions, how far, and what, men are to be trusted withal, in speaking to multitudes of people; and who shall examine the doctrines of all books before they be published. For the actions of men proceed from their opinions; and in the well-governing of opinions, consisteth the well-governing of men's actions, in order to their peace, and concord. And though in matter of doctrine, nothing ought to be regarded but the truth; yet this is not repugnant to regulating of the same by peace. For doctrine repugnant to peace, can no more be true, than peace and concord can be against the law of nature. It is true, that in a commonwealth, where by the negligence, or unskilfulness of governors, and teachers, false doctrines are by time generally received; the contrary truths may be generally offensive: Yet the most sudden, and rough busling in of a new truth, that can be, does never break the peace, but only sometimes awake the war. For those men that are so remissly governed, that they dare take up arms, to defend, or introduce an opinion, are still in war; and their condition not peace, but only a cessation of arms for fear of one another; and they live as it were, in the precincts of battle continually. It belongeth therefore to him that hath the sovereign power, to be judge, or constitute all judges of opinions and doctrines, as a thing necessary to peace; thereby to prevent discord and civil war.

Seventhly, is annexed to the sovereignty, the whole power of prescribing the rules, whereby every man may know, what goods he may enjoy, and what actions he may do, without being molested by any of his fellow-subjects; and this is it

men call *propriety*. For before constitution of sovereign power (as hath already been shown) all men had right to all things; which necessarily causeth war: and therefore this propriety, being necessary to peace, and depending on sovereign power, is the act of that power, in order to the public peace. These rules of propriety (or *meum* and *tuum*) and of *good, evil, lawful,* and *unlawful* in the actions of subjects, are the civil laws; that is to say, the laws of each commonwealth in particular; though the name of civil law be now restrained to the ancient civil laws of the city of *Rome;* which being the head of a great part of the world, her laws at that time were in these parts the civil law.

Eighthly, is annexed to the sovereignty, the right of judicature; that is to say, of hearing and deciding all controversies, which may arise concerning law, either civil, or natural; or concerning fact. For without the decision of controversies, there is no protection of one subject, against the injuries of another; the laws concerning *meum* and *tuum* are in vain; and to every man remaineth, from the natural and necessary appetite of his own conservation, the right of protecting himself by his private strength, which is the condition of war; and contrary to the end for which every commonwealth is instituted.

Ninthly, is annexed to the sovereignty, the right of making war and peace with other nations, and commonwealths; that is to say, of judging when it is for the public good, and how great forces are to be assembled, armed, and paid for that end; and to levy money upon the subjects, to defray the expenses thereof. For the power by which the people are to be defended, consisteth in their armies; and the strength of an army, in the union of their strength under one command; which command the sovereign instituted, therefore hath; because the command of the *militia*, without other institution, maketh him that hath it sovereign. And therefore whosoever is made general of an army, he that hath the sovereign power is always generalissimo.

Tenthly, is annexed to the sovereignty, the choosing of all counsellors, ministers, magistrates, and officers, both in peace, and war. For seeing the sovereign is charged with the end, which is the common peace and defence, he is understood to have power to use such means, as he shall think most fit for his discharge.

Eleventhy, to the sovereign is committed the power of rewarding with riches, or honour; and of punishing with corporal, or pecuniary punishment, or with ignominy every subject according to the law he hath formerly made; or if there be no law made, according as he shall judge most to conduce to the encouraging of men to serve the commonwealth, or deterring of them from doing disservice to the same.

Lastly, considering what values men are naturally apt to set upon themselves; what respect they look for from others; and how little they value other men; from whence continually arise amongst them, emulation, quarrels, factions, and at last war, to the destroying of one another, and diminution of their strength against a common enemy; it is necessary that there be laws of honour, and a public rate of the worth of such men as have deserved, or are able to deserve well of the commonwealth; and that there be force in the hands of some or other, to put those laws in execution. But it hath already been shown, that not only the whole *militia*, or forces of the commonwealth; but also the judicature of all controversies, is annexed to the sovereignty. To the sovereign therefore it belongeth also to give titles of honour; and to appoint what order of place, and dignity, each man shall hold; and what signs of respect, in public or private meetings, they shall give to one another.

These are the rights, which make the essence of sovereignty; and which are the marks, whereby a man may discern in what man, or assembly of men, the sovereign power is placed, and resideth. For these are incommunicable, and inseparable. The power to coin money; to dispose of the estate and persons of infant heirs; to have praeemption in markets; and all other statute prerogatives, may be transferred by the sovereign; and yet the power to protect his subjects be retained. But if he transfer the *militia*, he retains the judicature in vain, for want of execution of the laws: or if he grant away the power of raising money; the *militia* is in vain: or if he give away the government of doctrines,

men will be frightened into rebellion with the fear of spirits. And so if we consider anyone of the said rights, we shall presently see, that the holding of all the rest will produce no effect, in the conservation of peace and justice, the end for which all commonwealths are instituted. And this division is it, whereof it is said, *a kingdom divided in itself cannot stand:* for unless this division precede, division into opposite armies can never happen. If there had not first been an opinion received of the greatest part of England, that these powers were divided between the King, and the Lords, and the House of Commons, the people had never been divided and fallen into this civil war; first between those that disagreed in politics; and after between the dissenters about the liberty of religion; which have so instructed men in this point of sovereign right, that there be few now (in *England,*) that do not see, that these rights are inseparable, and will be so generally acknowledged at the next return of peace; and so continue, till their miseries are forgotten; and no longer, except the vulgar be better taught than they have hitherto been.

And because they are essential and inseparable rights, it follows necessarily, that in whatsoever words any of them seem to be granted away, yet if the sovereign power itself be not in direct terms renounced, and the name of sovereign no more given by the grantees to him that grants them, the grant is void: for when he has granted all he can, if we grant back the sovereignty, all is restored, as inseparably annexed thereunto.

This great authority being indivisible, and inseparably annexed to the sovereignty, there is little ground for the opinion of them, that say of sovereign kings, though they be *singulis majores*, of greater power than every one of their subjects, yet they be *universis minores*, of less power than them all together. For if by *all together*, they mean not the collective body as one person, then *all together*, and *everyone*, signify the same; and the speech is absurd. But if by *all together*, they understand them as one person, (which person the sovereign bears,) then the power of all together, is the same with the sovereign's power; and so again the speech is absurd: which absurdity they see well enough, when the sovereignty is in an assembly of the people; but in a monarch they see it not; and yet the power of sovereignty is the same in whomsoever it be placed.

And as the power, so also the honour of the sovereign, ought to be greater, than that of any, or all the subjects. For in the sovereignty is the fountain of honour. The dignities of lord, earl, duke, and prince are his creatures. As in the presence of the master, the servants are equal, and without any honour at all; so are the subjects, in the presence of the sovereign. And though they shine some more, some less, when they are out of his sight; yet in his presence, they shine no more than the stars in presence of the sun.

But a man may here object, that the condition of subjects is very miserable; as being obnoxious to the lusts, and other irregular passions of him, or them that have so unlimited a power in their hands. And commonly they that live under a monarch, think it the fault of monarchy; and they that live under the government of democracy, or other sovereign assembly, attribute all the inconvenience to that form of commonwealth: whereas the power in all forms, if they be perfect enough to protect them, is the same; not considering that the estate of man can never be without some incommodity or other; and that the greatest, that in any form of government can possibly happen to the people in general, is scarce sensible, in respect of the miseries, and horrible calamities, that accompany a civil war, or that dissolute condition of masterless men, without subjection to laws, and a coercive power to tie their hands from rapine and revenge: nor considering that the greatest pressure of sovereign governors, proceedeth not from any delight, or profit they can expect in the damage or weakening of their subjects, in whose vigour, consisteth their own strength and glory; but in the restiveness of themselves, that unwillingly contributing to their own defence, make it necessary for their governors to draw from them what they can in time of peace, that they may have means on any emergent occasion, or sudden need, to resist, or take advantage on their enemies. For all men are by nature provided of notable multiplying glasses, (that is their passions and self-love,) through which, every little payment appeareth a great grievance; but are destitute of those prospective glasses, (namely moral and civil science,) to see afar off the miseries that hang over them, and cannot without such payments be avoided. . . .

# CHAPTER 20

## OF DOMINION PATERNAL, AND DESPOTICAL

A *commonwealth by acquisition*, is that, where the sovereign power is acquired by force; and it is acquired by force, when men singly, or many together by plurality of voices, for fear of death, or bonds, do authorize all the actions of that man, or assembly, that hath their lives and liberty in his power.

And this kind of dominion, or sovereignty, differeth from sovereignty by institution, only in this, that men who choose their sovereign, do it for fear of one another, and not of him whom they institute: but in this case, they subject themselves, to him they are afraid of. In both cases they do it for fear: which is to be noted by them, that hold all such covenants, as proceed from fear of death, or violence, void: which if it were true, no man, in any kind of commonwealth, could be obliged to obedience. It is true, that in a commonwealth once instituted, or acquired, promises proceeding from fear of death or violence, are no covenants, nor obliging, when the thing promised is contrary to the laws; but the reason is not, because it was made upon fear, but because he that promiseth, hath no right in the thing promised. Also, when he may lawfully perform, and doth not, it is not the invalidity of the covenant, that absolveth him, but the sentence of the sovereign. Otherwise, whensoever a man lawfully promiseth, he unlawfully breaketh: but when the sovereign, who is the actor, acquitteth him, then he is acquitted by him that extorted the promise, as by the author of such absolution.

But the rights, and consequences of sovereignty, are the same in both. His power cannot, without his consent, be transferred to another: he cannot forfeit it: he cannot be accused by any of his subjects, of injury: he cannot be punished by them: he is judge of what is necessary for peace;

and judge of doctrines: he is sole legislator; and supreme judge of controversies; and of the times, and occasions of war, and peace: to him it belongeth to choose magistrates, counsellors, commanders, and all other officers, and ministers; and to determine of rewards, and punishments, honour, and order. The reasons whereof, are the same which are alleged in the precedent chapter, for the same rights, and consequences of sovereignty by institution.

Dominion is acquired two ways; by generation, and by conquest. The right of dominion by generation, is that, which the parent hath over his children; and is called PATERNAL. And is not so derived from the generation, as if therefore the parent had dominion over his child because he begat him; but from the child's consent, either express, or by other sufficient arguments declared. For as to the generation, God hath ordained to man a helper; and there by always two that are equally parents: the dominion therefore over the child, should belong equally to both; and he be equally subject to both, which is impossible; for no man can obey two masters. And whereas some have attributed the dominion to the man only, as being of the more excellent sex; they misreckon in it. For there is not always that difference of strength, or prudence between the man and the woman, as that the right can be determined without war. In commonwealths, this controversy is decided by the civil law: and for the most part, (but not always) the sentence is in favour of the father; because for the most part commonwealths have been erected by the fathers, not by the mothers of families. But the question lieth now in the state of mere nature; where there are supposed no laws of matrimony; no laws for the education of children; but the law of nature, and the natural inclination of the sexes, one to another, and to their children. In this condition of mere nature, either the parents between themselves dispose of the dominion over the child by contract; or do not dispose thereof at all. If they dispose thereof, the right passeth according to the contract. We find in history that the *Amazons* contracted with the men of the neighbouring countries, to whom they had

recourse for issue, that the issue male should be sent back, but the female remain with themselves: so that the dominion of the females was in the mother.

If there be no contract, the dominion is in the mother. For in the condition of mere nature, where there are no matrimonial laws, it cannot be known who is the father, unless it be declared by the mother: and therefore the right of dominion over the child dependeth on her will, and is consequently hers. Again, seeing the infant is first in the power of the mother, so as she may either nourish, or expose it; if she nourish it, it oweth its life to the mother; and is therefore obliged to obey her, rather than any other; and by consequence the dominion over it is hers. But if she expose it, and another find and nourish it, the dominion is in him that nourisheth it. For it ought to obey him by whom it is preserved; because preservation of life being the end, for which one man becomes subject to another, every man is supposed to promise obedience, to him, in whose power it is to save, or destroy him.

If the mother be the father's subject, the child, is in the father's power: and if the father be the mother's subject, (as when a sovereign queen marrieth one of her subjects,) the child is subject to the mother; because the father also is her subject.

If a man and woman, monarchs of two several kingdoms, have a child, and contract concerning who shall have the dominion of him, the right of the dominion passeth by the contract. If they contract not, the dominion followeth the dominion of the place of his residence. For the sovereign of each country hath dominion over all that reside therein.

He that hath the dominion over the child, hath dominion also over the children of the child; and over the children's children. For he that hath dominion over the person of a man, hath dominion over all that is his; without which, dominion were but a title, without the effect.

The right of succession to paternal dominion, proceedeth in the same manner, as doth the right of succession to monarchy; of which I have already sufficiently spoken in the precedent chapter.

Dominion acquired by conquest, or victory in war, is that which some writers call DESPOTICAL, from Δεσπότης, which signifieth a *lord,* or *master;* and is the dominion of the master over his servant. And this dominion is then acquired to the victor, when the vanquished, to avoid the present stroke of death, covenanteth either in express words, or by other sufficient signs of the will, that so long as his life, and the liberty of his body is allowed him, the victor shall have the use thereof, at his pleasure. And after such covenant made, the vanquished is a SERVANT, and not before: for by the word *servant,* (whether it be derived from *servire,* to serve, or from *servare,* to save, which I leave to grammarians to dispute) is not meant a captive, which is kept in prison, or bonds, till the owner of him that took him, or bought him of one that did, shall consider what to do with him: (for such men, (commonly called slaves,) have no obligation at all; but may break their bonds, or the prison; and kill, or carry away captive their master, justly:) but one, that being taken, hath corporal liberty allowed him; and upon promise not to run away, nor to do violence to his master, is trusted by him.

It is not therefore the victory, that giveth the right of dominion over the vanquished, but his own covenant. Nor is he obliged because he is conquered; that is to say, beaten, and taken, or put to flight; but because he cometh in, and submitteth to the victor; nor is the victor obliged by an enemy's rendering himself, (without promise of life,) to spare him for this his yielding to discretion; which obliges not the victor longer, than in his own discretion he shall think fit.

And that which men do, when they demand (as it is now called) *quarter,* (which the Greeks called Ζωγρία, *taking alive,*) is to evade the present fury of the victor, by submission, and to compound for their life, with ransom, or service: and therefore he that hath quarter, hath not his life given, but deferred till farther deliberation; for it is not a yielding on condition of life, but to discretion. And then only is his life in security, and his service due, when the victor hath trusted him with his corporal liberty. For slaves that work in prisons, or fet-

ters, do it not of duty, but to avoid the cruelty of their task-masters.

The master of the servant, is master also of all he hath; and may exact the use thereof; that is to say, of his goods, of his labour, of his servants, and of his children, as often as he shall think fit. For he holdeth his life of his master, by the covenant of obedience; that is, of owning, and authorizing whatsoever the master shall do. And in case the master, if he refuse, kill him, or cast him into bonds, or otherwise punish him for disobedience, he is himself the author of the same; and cannot accuse him of injury.

In sum, the rights and consequences of both *paternal* and *despotical* dominion, are the very same with those of a sovereign by institution; and for the same reasons: which reasons are set down in the precedent chapter. So that for a man that is monarch of divers nations, whereof he hath, in one the sovereignty by institution of the people assembled, and in another by conquest, that is by the submission of each particular, to avoid death or bonds; to demand of one nation more than of the other, from the title of conquest, as being a conquered nation, is an act of ignorance of the rights of sovereignty. For the sovereign is absolute over both alike; or else there is no sovereignty at all; and so every man may lawfully protect himself, if he can, with his own sword, which is the condition of war.

By this it appears; that a great family if it be not part of some commonwealth, is of itself, as to the rights of sovereignty, a little monarchy; whether that family consist of a man and his children; or of a man and his servants; or of a man, and his children, and servants together: wherein the father or master is the sovereign. But yet a family is not properly a commonwealth; unless it be of that power by its own number, or by other opportunities, as not to be subdued without the hazard of war. For where a number of men are manifestly too weak to defend themselves united, everyone may use his own reason in time of danger, to save his own life, either by flight, or by submission to the enemy, as he shall think best; in the same manner as a very small company of soldiers, surprised by an army, may cast down their arms, and demand quarter, or run away, rather than be put to the sword, And thus much shall suffice; concerning what I find by speculation, and deduction, of sovereign rights, from the nature, need, and designs of men, in erecting of commonwealths, and putting themselves under monarchs, or assemblies, entrusted with power enough for their protection.

Let us now consider what the Scripture teacheth in the same point. To Moses, the children of *Israel* say thus: *Speak thou to us, and we will hear thee; but let not God speak to us, lest we die.* (*Exod.* 20. 19.) This is absolute obedience to Moses. Concerning the right of kings, God himself by the mouth of Samuel, saith, (1 *Sam.* 8. 11, 12, &c.) *This shall be the right of the king you will have to reign over you. He shall take your sons, and set them to drive his chariots, and to be his horsemen, and to run before his chariots; and gather in his harvest; and to make his engines of war, and instruments of his chariots; and shall take your daughters to make perfumes, to be his cooks, and bakers. He shall take your fields, your vine-yards, and your olive-yards, and give them to his servants. He shall take the tithe of your corn and wine, and give it to the men of his chamber, and to his other servants. He shall take your man-servants, and your maid-servants, and the choice of your youth, and employ them in his business. He shall take the tithe of your flocks; and you shall be his servants.* This is absolute power, and summed up in the last words, *you shall be his servants.* Again, when the people heard what power their king was to have, yet they consented thereto, and say thus, (*verse* 19) *we will be as all other nations, and our king shall judge our causes, and go before us, to conduct our wars.* Here is confirmed the right that sovereigns have, both to the *militia,* and to all *judicature;* in which is contained as absolute power, as one man can possibly transfer to another. Again, the prayer of king Solomon to God, was this (1 *Kings,* 3. 9): *Give to thy servant understanding, to judge thy people, and to discern between good and evil.* It belongeth therefore to the sovereign to be judge, and to prescribe the rules of *discerning good* and *evil:* which rules

are laws; and therefore in him is the legislative power. Saul sought the life of *David;* yet when it was in his power to slay *Saul,* and his servants would have done it. *David* forbad them, saying, (1 *Sam.* 24. 9). *God forbid I should do such an act against my Lord, the anointed of God.* For obedience of servants St. *Paul* saith; (*Col.* 3. 20) *Servants obey your masters in all things;* and, (*Verse* 22) *children obey your parents in all things.* There is simple obedience in those that are subject to paternal, or despotical dominion. Again, (*Matt.* 23. 2, 3) *The Scribes and Pharisees sit in Moses' chair, and therefore all that they shall bid you observe, that observe and do.* There again is simple obedience. And St. *Paul,* (*Titus* 3. 2) *Warn them that they subject themselves to princes, and to those that are in authority, and obey them.* This obedience is also simple. Lastly, our Saviour himself acknowledges, that men ought to pay such taxes as are by kings imposed, where he says, *Give to Caesar that which is Caesar's;* and paid such taxes himself. And that the king's word, is sufficient to take any thing from any subject, when there is need; and that the king is judge of that need: for he himself, as king of the Jews, commanded his disciples to take the ass, and ass's colt to carry him into Jerusalem, saying, (*Matth.* 21. 2, 3) *Go into the village over against you, and you shall find a she ass tied, and her colt with her; untie them, and bring them to me. And if any man ask you, what you mean by it, say the Lord hath need of them: and they will let them go.* They will not ask whether his necessity be a sufficient title; nor whether he be judge of that necessity; but acquiesce in the will of the Lord.

To these places may be added also that of *Genesis,* (*Genesis* 3. 5). *Ye shall be as gods, knowing good and evil.* And *verse* 11. *Who told thee that thou wast naked? hast thou eaten of the tree, of which I commanded thee thou shouldest not eat?* For the cognizance or judicature of good and evil, being forbidden by the name of the fruit of the tree of knowledge, as a trial of *Adam's* obedience; the devil to inflame the ambition of the woman, to whom that fruit already seemed beautiful, told her that by tasting it, they should be as gods, knowing *good* and *evil.* Whereupon having both eaten, they did indeed take upon them God's office, which is judicature of good and evil; but acquired no new ability to distinguish between them aright. And whereas it is said, that having eaten, they saw they were naked; no man hath so interpreted that place, as if they had been formerly blind, and saw not their own skins: the meaning is plain, that it was then they first judged their nakedness (wherein it was God's will to create them) to be uncomely; and by being ashamed, did tacitly censure God himself. And thereupon God saith, *Hast thou eaten, &c.* as if he should say, doest thou that owest me obedience, take upon thee to judge of my commandments? Whereby it is clearly, (though allegorically,) signified, that the commands of them that have the right to command, are not by their subjects to be censured, nor disputed.

So that it appeareth plainly, to my understanding, both from reason, and Scripture, that the sovereign power, whether placed in one man, as in monarchy, or in one assembly of men, as in popular, and aristocractical commonwealths, is as great, as possibly men can be imagined to make it. And though of so unlimited a power, men may fancy many evil consequences, yet the consequences of the want of it, which is perpetual war of every man against his neighbour, are much worse. The condition of man in this life shall never be without inconveniences; but there happeneth in no commonwealth any great inconvenience, but what proceeds from the subject's disobedience, and breach of those covenants, from which the commonwealth hath its being. And whosoever thinking sovereign power too great, will seek to make it less, must subject himself, to the power, that can limit it; that is to say, to a greater.

The greatest objection is, that of the practice; when men ask, where, and when, such power has by subjects been acknowledged. But one may ask them again, when, or where has there been a kingdom long free from sedition and civil war. In those nations, whose commonwealths have been long-lived, and not been destroyed but by foreign war, the subjects never did dispute of the sovereign power. But howsoever, an argument from the practice of men, that have not sifted to the bottom, and with exact reason weighed the causes, and nature of commonwealths, and suffer daily those miseries, that proceed from the ignorance thereof, is invalid. For though in all places of the world, men should lay the foundation of their houses on the sand, it could not thence be inferred, that so it ought to be. The skill of making, and maintaining commonwealths, consisteth in certain rules, as doth arithmetic and geometry; not (as tennis-play) on practice only: which rules, neither poor men have the leisure, nor men that have had the leisure, have hitherto had the curiosity, or the method to find out.

# 20    Hobbes, Patriarchy and Conjugal Right

CAROLE PATEMAN

MOST STUDIES OF HOBBES have nothing to say about the relation of his political theory to seventeenth-century patriarchalism. Writers who have thought it worthwhile to consider the question have almost all agreed that Hobbes's argument is patriarchal, although more recently the claim has been made that, for example, Hobbes's views were subversive of "patriarchal attitudes," or that his theory is free from patriarchal assumptions.[1] More strongly, in a rational choice interpretation of Hobbes (which shares Hobbes's radical individualism) the implicit assumption is that Hobbes's theory is so far opposed to patriarchalism that his sovereign can be referred to as "she."[2] Despite such differences, political theorists are united on one point; they agree that to argue about patriarchy is to argue about the family and paternal power. Hobbes is assumed to be a patriarchal theorist in the same sense that his adversary Sir Robert Filmer is a patriarchalist; or, conversely, Hobbes is assumed to be opposed to patriarchalism because his theory is antithetical to Filmer's on some crucial issues.

The major debates about patriarchy over the past two decades have been conducted by feminists, not mainstream political theorists, but feminists have paid remarkably little attention to political theory in the controversy over the meaning and usefulness of the term "patriarchy." The predominant assumption among feminists, or, at least, among those engaged in the theoretically informed controversies over patriarchy, is also that patriarchal relations are familial relations and that patriarchal political right is paternal right.[3] To be sure, many feminists also use "patriarchy" to mean the power that men exercise over women more generally—what I shall call masculine right—but, notwithstanding the copious empirical evidence available to support this interpretation, the usage has not yet been given a great deal of theoretical substance. A major reason for this lack of theoretical robustness is feminist neglect of the arguments among political theorists about patriarchy in the seventeenth century. Feminist scholars have undertaken some very revealing and exciting work on the classic texts of political theory, but little attention has been paid to Hobbes, whose writings are of fundamental importance for an understanding of patriarchy as masculine right. Hobbes is a patriarchal theorist—but the possibility that is considered by neither conventional political theorists nor feminists is that he is a patriarchalist who rejects paternal right.

Both feminism and political theory are dogged by an anachronistic, although literal, interpretation of patriarchy as father-right. Patriarchy is assumed to be about fathers and mothers. For example, Di Stefano has argued that Hobbes is a masculinist theorist, but her reading of Hobbes is that his arguments rest on a denial of the mother. His picture of natural, atomized individuals, who spring up like mushrooms—"consider men as if but even now sprung out of the earth, and suddenly, like mushrooms, come to full maturity, without all kind of engagement to each other"[4]—denies any significance to the mother–child relationship and the dependence on the mother that provides the first intersubjective context for the development of human capacities. Di Stefano claims that there is no room for nurture within the family in Hobbes's state of nature; "men are not born of, much less nurtured by, women, or anyone else for that matter."[5] Hobbes's family is certainly very peculiar, but the problem with Di Stefano's argument is that, in the state of nature, mothers, far from being denied, are enthroned. For Hobbes, political right in the natural condition is mother-right. Hobbes goes to great lengths to deny that father-right is the origin of political right, yet he is still seen as a patriarchalist in the same sense as Filmer for whom political and paternal power were one and the same.

A different problem confronts the writers who argue that Hobbes subverts patriarchalism, or merely tacitly assume that the terms "men" and "individual" in Hobbes's texts are used generically; they fail to explain why Hobbes's writings contain so many references to the rightful power of fathers—or why he endorses the subjection of wives to husbands. Commentators on Hobbes, like almost all political theorists of the recent past, see no problems of political interest arising from the subordination of wives to husbands. Conjugal right, the right exercised by men, as husbands, over their wives, is not a matter that falls within their scholarly purview. The standard interpretations of the theoretical battle between the classic contract theorists, including Hobbes, and the patriarchalists of the seventeenth century is that the engagement concerned the political right of fathers and the natural liberty of sons. That the father was a master, exercising jurisdiction over servants and apprentices, is acknowledged, but another inhabitant of the family is usually ignored. The father is also a husband, and as a husband is a master over his wife. In discussions of Hobbes and patriarchy, the position of the *wife* in the family is rarely mentioned. She appears, if at all, in another capacity, as a *mother*. When a problem about women is admitted to exist, it is taken to be that of maternal jurisdiction over children.

The failure to distinguish marriage from the family and to recognize the existence of conjugal right means that the most distinctive aspect of Hobbes's political theory is disregarded. Hobbes is the only contract theorist (and almost the only writer admitted into the "tradition" of Western political theory) who begins from the premise that there is no natural dominion of men over women. In his natural condition female individuals are as free as, and equal to, male individuals. The remarkable starting point of his political theory is usually passed over extremely quickly. Even in discussions that focus on patriarchy no questions are asked or explanations offered about why and how it is, in the absence of sexual dominion in the state of nature, that marriage and the family take a patriarchal form. Nor is anything odd seen in the fact that Hobbes argues both that women are naturally free and always subject to men through (the marriage) contract.

There are also other problems about Hobbes, patriarchy and contract when "patriarchy" is interpreted literally. Some commentators have noted certain tensions in Hobbes's arguments between contract and patriarchy; one earlier scholar, for instance, took the logical position that if Hobbes is interpreted as a patriarchalist then the original contract is superfluous.[6] Another commentator has attributed a consensual form of patriarchy to Hobbes and argued that his patriarchalism is, therefore, the strongest form—and even a more typically English variety.[7] Hobbes took contract much further than most other classic contract theorists and claimed that even infants (could be said to have) contracted themselves into subjection to mothers. To posit a contract by an infant is to reject outright any suggestion that political subjec-

tion is natural and to confirm in the most emphatic possible manner that all dominion is conventional in origin. Yet it was precisely the doctrine of the natural freedom of mankind and its corollary, contract and consent, that Sir Robert Filmer saw as the major cause of sedition and political disorder. Why, then, should a purported advocate of patriarchy as paternal right, and a writer who, in his own way, was as absolutist as his opponent, take so many pains to deny the assumptions of Filmer's theory? More generally, if political right has a natural origin in fatherhood and contract is thus superfluous—and, according to Filmer, politically dangerous—why should Hobbes argue that civil society was created through an original contract?

To remain within the standard, patriarchal interpretation of "patriarchy" as fatherly power is to remain within a patriarchal reading of Hobbes's texts, a reading that ignores the subjection of women. Hobbes's patriarchalism is a new, *specifically modern* form, that is conventional, contractual and originates in conjugal right, or, more accurately, sex-right; that is, in men's right of sexual access to women, which in its major institutional form in modern society, is exercised as conjugal right (a term also providing a polite locution in, say, a discussion of Adam and Eve). To appreciate the character of Hobbes's patriarchal theory the distinctive features of his natural condition—mother-right and the absence of natural dominion of male over female individuals—have to be taken seriously as fundamental premises of his political theory. In addition, Hobbes's extraordinary conception of the "family" needs to be emphasized. Hobbes did not merely leave no room for nurture or argue that the family was conventional, a political rather than a natural social form. For Hobbes, a "family" was solely composed of a master and servants of various kinds and had its origins in conquest.

## I

Before looking in greater detail at Hobbes's arguments it is necessary to say something more about patriarchy and to look again at Filmer's patriarchalism.[8] A good deal of confusion over the term "patriarchy" has arisen because of the failure to distinguish between three different historical forms of patriarchal theory: traditional, classic and modern. Traditional patriarchal argument assimilates all power relations to paternal rule. For centuries the family and the authority of the father at its head provided the model and metaphor for political society and political right. The traditional form is also full of stories, of conjectural histories, about the emergence or creation of political society from the family or the coming together of many families. Such stories are also to be found in the writings of the classic contract theorists, even though they defeated and eliminated the second, short-lived form of classic patriarchalism. Classic patriarchy was formulated and died in the seventeenth century and is exemplified by Sir Robert Filmer's arguments. Schochet shows in *Patriarchalism in Political Thought* that Sir Robert broke with the traditional form by insisting that paternal and political rule were not merely analogous but identical. In the 1680s and 1690s, "the Filmerian position very nearly became the official state ideology."[9] The classic form was a fully developed theory of political right and political obedience and was the first of its kind; "there was no patriarchal theory of obligation prior to 1603."[10] The standard claim in political theory is that patriarchalism was dead and buried by 1700—but the form that passed away was Filmer's classic patriarchy.

Filmer wrote in response to the challenge posed by the doctrine of the natural freedom of mankind. If men were born free and equal then, necessarily, political right or the dominion of one man over another could be established in one way only; through an agreement (contract) between those concerned that such a relation should be brought into being. According to Filmer, acknowledgement that Adam had been granted monarchial power by God by virtue of his fatherhood cut the ground from under the feet of the contract theorists. At the birth of his first son, Adam became the first king and his political right passed to all subsequent fathers and kings, who were one and the same: all kings ruled as fathers in consequence of their procreative power, and all fathers were monarchs in their families. Sons were born into political subjection to their fathers and hence to the monarch: no such political nonsense as talk of contracts was required to justify political subjection. Filmer's account of the natural origin of political right appears straightforward enough, and no hint is given in discussions of the relation between the theories of Hobbes and Filmer that patriarchy is more complicated.

Paternal right is only one dimension of patriarchy—as Filmer himself reveals. Filmer's apparently straightforward statements obscure the original foundation of political right. Paternal power is not the origin of political right. Father-right is established only after political right has been brought into being. Another act of political genesis is required before a man can acquire the natural right of fatherhood. Sons do not spring up like mushrooms, as Filmer was quick to remind Hobbes. Adam's political title is granted *before* he becomes a father. If he is to be a father, Eve has to become a mother. In other words, *sex-right or conjugal right must necessarily precede the right of fatherhood*. The genesis of political dominion lies in Adam's sex-right, *not* in his fatherhood.

Filmer makes clear that Adam's political right is originally established in his right as a husband over Eve: "God gave to Adam . . . the dominion over the woman," and, citing Genesis 3:16, "God ordained Adam to rule over his wife, and her desires were to be subject to his."[11] (Genesis states that Eve's "desires shall be to thy husband, and he shall rule over thee.") Adam's desire is to become a father, but in no ordinary sense of "father." He desires to obtain the remarkable powers of a patriarchal father. Filmer briefly mentions Adam's original, divine grant of political right over Eve at various points, but it has a shadowy presence in his writings. In recent (patriarchal) commentaries on his texts, sex-right has completely disappeared. And, to be sure, when reading Filmer from the perspective of only one dimension of patriarchalism, conjugal right is not easy to discern under the cloak of Adam's fatherhood.

The biblical patriarchal image (here in Locke's words) is of "nursing Fathers tender and carefull of the publick weale."[12] The patriarchal story is about the procreative power of a father who is complete in himself, who embodies the creative power of both female and male. His procreative power both gives and animates physical life and creates and maintains political right. Filmer is able to refer to Adam's power over Eve so casually because classic patriarchalism declares women to be procreatively and politically irrelevant. The reason that Adam has dominion over "the woman" is, according to Filmer (here following the patriarchal idea of fatherhood, which is very ancient), that "the man . . . [is] the nobler and principal agent in generation."[13] Women are merely empty vessels for the exercise of men's sexual and procreative power. The original political right that God gives to Adam is the right, so to speak, to fill the empty vessel. Adam, and all men, must do this if they are to become fathers. But men's generative power has a dual aspect. The genesis of new physical life belongs in their hands, not in the empty vessel. Men are the "principal agents in generation," and "generation" includes political creativity. Men's generative power includes the ability to create new political life, or to give birth to political right.

In view of the character of the extraordinary powers that classic patriarchalism arrogates to men, it is appropriate that the powers are contained in the name of "father" and encompassed under the writ of "fatherhood." The presence of conjugal right is very faint in Filmer's writings because (although at one level he must acknowledge it) Adam's original political right is subsumed under the power of fatherhood. For instance, after stating that Eve and her desires are subject to Adam, Filmer continues in the next sentence, "here we have the original grant of government, and the fountain of all power placed in the Father of all mankind." Moreover, Adam is also Eve's father. In the story of the Book of Genesis, Eve is created only after Adam and the animals have been placed on earth. God creates and names the animals and Adam but, we are told in Genesis 2:20, "for Adam there was not found an help meet for him." Eve is then created, but she in not created *ab initio* but *from* Adam, who is, in a sense, her parent, and Adam, not God, gives Eve

her name. Filmer is therefore able to treat all political right as the right of a father. Eve is not only under the dominion of Adam, but he is (with God's help) the "principal agent" in her generation. The father in classic patriarchal theory is not just one of two parents—he is *the* parent, and the being able to generate political right.

The greatest story of masculine political birth is the story of an original contract that creates civil freedom and civil society. The classic patriarchalists lost the battle over fathers and sons and the natural origin of political right. Patriarchalism, in the sense of paternal right, ceased to be politically relevant by the end of the seventeenth century. Civil society is constituted by the (ostensibly) universal, conventional bonds of contract not the particular, natural bonds of kinship and fatherhood. However, the standard account of the defeat of patriarchy ignores the fact that the contract theorists had no quarrel with classic patriarchalism over the true origin of political right; they fought against paternal right but had no wish to disturb the other dimension of patriarchy, conjugal right.

The "freedom of mankind" in contract argument means what it says, the freedom of *men*. The victory of contract doctrine over the classic form of patriarchal argument was, rather, the *transformation* of classic patriarchy into a new form. The contract theorists constructed their own, modern patriarchal argument—the third of the historical forms. Modern patriarchy is contractual not natural and embodies masculine right not the right of fatherhood. Hobbes, the most brilliant and bold of contract theorists, is a patriarchal theorist in the modern sense, but his arguments differ in some significant respects from those of his fellow contract theorists and, in the end, it was they, not Hobbes, who provided the necessary theoretical framework for patriarchal civil society.

## II

On the face of it, Hobbes's writings seem unequivocally opposed to both dimensions of classic patriarchy. Hobbes's theory rests on mother-right and the absence of natural sexual dominion; how, then, does Hobbes transform natural maternal power and women's natural freedom into patriarchal right, and why have scholars been able to identify so many passages in Hobbes's writings where he apparently falls back on the traditional form of patriarchal argument? The appropriate place to begin to consider the conjuring tricks is with Hobbes's picture of the natural condition. Hobbes's imaginative resolution of civil society into its most fundamental ("natural") parts was much more rigorous than the similar undertakings of the other contract theorists. Hobbes was willing to take the logic of individualism to its most radical conclusions in this as in other respects. When Hobbes reconstitutes natural entities in perpetual motion into something recognizably human, the result is that humans interact in a natural condition that can barely be recognized as social. Hobbes's state of nature is the famous war of all against all, and, in a statement which is rarely seen as of political significance, Hobbes writes that in the natural condition there are "no matrimonial laws."[14] Marriage—that is to say, a long-term relation between the sexes—must be brought about in exactly the same way as any other relation between the inhabitants of the state of nature where there is no natural order of dominion, and no politically significant difference in strength or prudence between individuals. Relations can arise in two ways only: either individuals contract themselves into a given relationship; or one, by some stratagem, is able to coerce another into the desired arrangement. This is also true of relations between a man and a woman. In the natural condition women face men as free equals; Hobbes writes that "whereas some have attributed the dominion to the man only, as being of the more excellent sex; they misreckon in it. For there is not always that difference of strength or prudence between the man and the woman, as that the right can be determined without war."[15]

In the state of nature there is no law to regulate marriage—and no marriage. Marriage does not exist because marriage is a long-term arrangement, and long-term sexual relationships, like other such relationships, are very difficult to establish and maintain in Hobbes's natural condi-

tion. The boundaries separating the inhabitants one from another are so tightly drawn by Hobbes that each one can judge the rest only from a subjective perspective, or from the perspective of pure self-interest. Natural individuals will, therefore, always break an agreement, or refuse to play their part in a contract, if it appears in their interest to do so. To enter a contract or to signify agreement to do so is to leave oneself open to betrayal. Hobbes's natural state suffers from an endemic problem of keeping contracts and of "performing second"; "If a covenant be made, wherein neither of the parties perform presently, but trust one another; . . . upon any reasonable suspicion, it is void: . . . And . . . he which performeth first, does but betray himself to his enemy."[16] The only contract that an individual, of his or her own volition, can enter into in safety is one in which agreement and performance take place at the same time. An agreement to perform an act of coitus provides an example of a contract that comes close to meeting this criterion, but an agreement to marry, to enter into a long-term sexual relationship, would founder in the same manner as contracts to create other relations that endure over time.

The women and men in Hobbes's state of nature can engage in sexual intercourse and, therefore, children can be born. A child, however, is born a long time after any act of intercourse. As Hobbes notes, in the absence of matrimonial laws proof of fatherhood rests on the testimony of the mother. Since there is no way of establishing paternity with any certainty, the child belongs to the mother. Hobbes's argument is all the more striking since he, too, suggests that men are the "principal agents" in generation. Echoing the classic patriarchal view of fatherhood, Hobbes writes that "as to the generation, God hath ordained to man a helper"[17]—but the female "helper" in the state of nature becomes much more than an auxiliary once the birth takes place. Hobbes insists that no man can have two masters and so only one parent can have dominion over the child. In the natural condition the mother, not the father, enjoys this right. In direct contradiction of Sir Robert Filmer and the patriarchal doctrine that political right originates in the father's generative power, Hobbes proclaims that "every woman that bears children, becomes both a *mother* and a *lord*."[18] At birth, the infant is in the mother's power. She makes the decision whether to expose or to nourish the child. To have the power to preserve life is, according to Hobbes, to exercise rightful dominion, whether the subject is a newly born infant or a vanquished adult. If the mother preserves the infant, she thereby becomes a lord; "because preservation of life being the end, for which one man [or infant] becomes subject to another, every man is supposed to promise obedience, to him [or her], in whose power it is to save, or destroy him."[19]

From 1861 for a half century or more (following the publication of Sir Henry Maine's *Ancient Law* and Johann Bachofen's *Mother Right*) another controversy raged about political origins, matriarchy and patriarchy. The proponents were all reluctant to admit that matriarchy in the literal sense—rule by women as mothers—ever existed, even hypothetically.[20] Similarly, some contemporary theorists still find it necessary to take issue with Hobbes's logic on mother-right. The rather amusing objection has been raised that Hobbes is mistaken; a mother "simply does not wield" the power Hobbes ascribes to her.[21] The "helper" herself always requires another helper. In Hobbes's day, the objection continues, the mother was attended by a midwife or male physician, and it is the latter who, at the moment of birth, has power over the child in her or his hands. Hobbes should have concluded that neither fathers nor mothers possessed an original political power in the natural condition, but then his argument against natural paternal right would have been "more absurd still." In his eagerness to combat Filmer, Hobbes "overlooked the defects attached to an argument which would transfer this power to a party—the mother—whom no one supposed ever had a proper right or even opportunity to exercise it (given the establishment of a civil society.)"[22] Precisely; in patriarchal civil society, past or present, political theorists rarely are willing to contemplate that mothers (women) could legitimately exercise

political right, even in an hypothetical state of nature or as a matter of mere logic. The other social contract theorists, unlike Hobbes, built masculine sexual dominion as a natural fact of human existence into their political theories and so demonstrated in a straightforward fashion that, for all that their arguments are couched in universal terms, equality, freedom and contract are a male privilege—although contemporary political theorists still manage to avoid noticing the fact.[23] Hobbes's logic is impeccable. In his natural condition (whatever the facts of childbirth in the seventeenth century) a pregnant woman would not give herself up as a hostage to fortune by enlisting helpers in her labors; no free, strong woman would place her right of dominion at risk with such assistance.

By nature, a mother is a lord who can do as she wills with her infant. If she decides to "breed him," the condition on which she does so, Hobbes states, is that "being grown to full age he become not her enemy."[24] That is to say, the infant must contract to obey her. The mother's political right over her child originates in contract, and gives her absolute power. A woman can contract away her right over her child to the father, but, when the premise of Hobbes's argument is that women naturally stand as equals to men, there is no reason why a woman should do this, and, least of all, why she should *always* do so. To argue that a tiny infant can contract, or should be regarded as if it had contracted, with its mother is, as Filmer insisted, anthropological nonsense. In terms of Hobbes's understanding of "contract," however, this agreement is as convincing an example of a contract as any other in Hobbes's writings. Scholars have drawn attention to Hobbes's claim that the reasons and circumstances under which agreement are given are irrelevant to the validity of the contract; for Hobbes, it makes no difference whether a contract is entered into after due deliberation or with the conqueror's sword at one's breast. Submission to overwhelming power in return for protection, whether the power is that of the conqueror's sword or the mother's power over her newly born infant, is always a valid sign of agreement for Hobbes. Hobbes's assimilation of conquest to contract, enforced submission to consent, is often remarked upon, but the political significance of this peculiar notion of contract for the origin of the family in the state of nature and for the making of the original pact is less often appreciated.

## III

The logical conclusion of Hobbes's resolution of civil society into its natural parts of rational entities in motion, and his reconstitution of the natural condition, is that the sexes come together only fleetingly and that the original political right is mother-right. Yet Hobbes also writes in a passage (cited by Richard Chapman and Gordon Schochet, for example), "that the beginning of all dominion amongst men was in families. In which, . . . the father of the family by law of nature was absolute lord of his wife and children: [and] made what laws amongst them he pleased."[25] And he also refers to familial government or a "patrimonial kingdom" in which the family:

> if it grow by multiplication of children, either by generation, or adoption; or of servants, either by generation, conquest, or voluntary submission, to be so great and numerous, as in probability it may protect itself, then is that family called a *patrimonial kingdom,* or monarchy by acquisition, wherein the sovereignty is in one man, as it is in a monarch made by *political institution.* So that whatsoever rights be in the one, the same also be in the other.[26]

Moreover, Hobbes also makes statements such as "cities and kingdoms . . . are but greater families,"[27] and "a great family is a kingdom, and a little kingdom a family."[28] He also remarks that Germany, like other countries "in their beginnings," was divided between a number of masters of families, all at war with each other.[29] Such statements have been treated as evidence that Hobbes was a patriarchalist like Filmer and that his natural condition was composed of families not individuals. Such an interpretation leaves unanswered the

questions of how the transformation comes about from mother-right to the patriarchal family in the state of nature and how the family is generated.

Chapman has stressed that Hobbes's family is an artificial, political institution rather than a natural social form, but its extraordinary character consists in more than a conventional, political origin. No attention is paid to the most bizarre aspect of Hobbes's account of the family because conjugal right and the position of a wife are ignored. Indeed, the scholars involved in the debate about Hobbes and the family have not paused to wonder how there can be wives in the state of nature where there is no law of matrimony. Nor have they asked how families can come into existence when marriage does not exist and yet marriage is the "origin" of the family. Hobbes's "family" is very curious and has nothing in common with the families of Filmer's pages, the family as found in the writings of the other classical social contract theorists, or as popularly understood today. Consider Hobbes's definition: in *Leviathan* he states that a family "consist[s] of a man and his children; or of a man and his servants; or of a man, and his children, and servants together; wherein the father or master is the sovereign."[30] In *De Cive* we find "a *father* with his *sons* and *servants,* grown into a civil person by virtue of his paternal jurisdiction, is called a *family.*"[31] What has happened to the wife and mother? Only in *Elements of Law* does he write that "the father or mother of the family is sovereign of the same."[32] But the sovereign cannot be the mother, given the conjectural history of the origin of the family implicit in Hobbes's argument.

The "natural" characteristics postulated by Hobbes mean that long-term relationships are very unlikely in his state of nature. However, Hobbes states in *Leviathan* that, in the war of all against all, "there is no man who can hope by his own strength, or wit, to defend himself from destruction, without the help of confederates."[33] But how can such a protective confederation be formed in the natural condition when there is an acute problem of keeping agreements? The answer is that confederations are formed by conquest. If one male individual manages to conquer another in the state of nature the conqueror will have obtained a servant. Hobbes assumes that no one would willfully give up his life, so, faced with the conqueror's sword, the defeated man will make a (valid) contract to obey his victor. Hobbes defines dominion or political right acquired through force as "the dominion of the master over his servant."[34] Conqueror and conquered then constitute "a little body politic, which consisteth of two persons, the one sovereign, which is called the *master,* or lord; the other subject, which is called the *servant.*"[35] Hobbes distinguishes a servant from a slave, but his definition of a servant makes it hard to maintain the distinction: "the master of the servant, is master also of all he hath: and may exact the use thereof; that is to say, of his goods, of his labour, of his servants, and of his children, as often as he shall think fit."[36]

The master and his slave-servant form the little body politic of a defensive confederation against the rest of the inhabitants of the state of nature. That is to say, according to Hobbes's definition of a "family," the master and his servant form a family. For Hobbes, the origin of the family is entirely conventional. A "family" is created not through procreation but by conquest, and a family consists of a master and his servants; that is, all those, whatever their age or sex, who fall under his absolute jurisdiction. A "family" composed only of a master and his male servants is a singular institution and it becomes more singular still if this male household contains children. Hobbes remarks at one point that sovereignty can be established "by natural force; as when a man maketh his children, to submit themselves, and their children to his government."[37] Children have again sprung up like mushrooms, ready to submit to (contract with) their families. And what of their mothers; how are they included in the "family"? In the natural condition there are two ways only in which sexual relations between free, equal women and men can take place. Either a woman freely contracts to engage in intercourse or she is outwitted and taken by force. There is no reason why a woman should contract of her own free will to enter into a long-term sexual relationship and become a "wife," that is, to be in servitude to—to become the servant (slave) of—a man. In the state of nature a woman is as able as a man to defend herself or to conquer another to form a protective confederation of master and servant. Why then does Hobbes assume that only men become masters of servants?

The answer is that, by the time the original contract is entered into, *all* the women in the natural condition have been conquered by men and become servants. Hobbes is explicit that "dominion amongst men" begins in the defensive confederation or small body politic he calls a family, but he does not spell out that men also gain dominion over women by creating "families." A conjectural history of how this comes about might run as follows. At first, women, who are as strong and as capable as men, are able to ensure that sexual relations are consensual. When a woman becomes a mother and decides to become a lord and raise her child, her position changes; she is put at a slight disadvantage against men, since now she has her infant to defend too. Conversely, a man obtains a slight advantage over her and is then able to defeat the woman he had initially to treat with as an equal. Mothers are lords in Hobbes's state of nature, but paradoxically, for a woman to become a mother and a lord is her downfall. She has then given an opening for a male enemy to outwit and vanquish her in the ceaseless natural conflict. Mother-right can never be more than fleeting.

The original political dominion of maternal lordship is quickly overcome and replaced by masculine right. Each man can obtain a "family" of a woman servant and her child. Thus mother-right is overturned and the state of nature becomes filled with patriarchal "families." All the women in the natural condition are forcibly incorporated (which for Hobbes, is to say contract themselves) into "families" and become the permanent servants of male masters. The "help" given by women to men in procreation then becomes the unending help of domestic servitude. The "wife" is relegated to the status of a helper too politically insignificant to be worthy of listing as a member of this peculiar protective association. A story along these lines is necessary to explain the existence of patriarchal "families" in the state of nature, and also to explain why a patriarchal law of matrimony is instituted through the original contract.

But it is hard to tell a consistent and convincing story about women's subjection when beginning from the postulate of natural freedom and equality between women and men.[38] The conquest of women would surely take more than one generation. Some women, either by choice or the accident of nature, would be childless and so would remain free. Indeed, once childless women saw the fate of women who decided to exercise maternal lordship they would, as rational beings, choose to remain childless and conserve their natural freedom. Free women would, however, be found only in the first generation in the natural condition. Childless women would die, and all subsequent generations of women would be born into servitude (and so, according to Hobbes's definition of servitude, would be under the jurisdiction of the master). The problem with this version of the conjectural history is that, if there are free childless women in the first generation in the natural condition, there is no reason why they should not form protective confederations of their own by conquering men, or each other, and so obtaining servants. Women and men would then wage the war of all against all as masters of "families"—and who knows who might win in the end? But in Hobbes's theory we do know who wins, and thus there is only one story that can be told. Women must all be conquered in the first generation; there can be no female masters in the state of nature or there will be no original contract and no law of matrimony.

## IV

The method through which Hobbes constructed his picture of the state of nature meant that, as a ruthlessly consistent theorist, he had to begin from the logical but shocking premise of an absence of sexual dominion and original mother-right. But Hobbes was well aware, as indicated in the passages that I cited above, that, historically, paternal right and the subjection of wives was the established custom. In the *logical* beginning, all political right is maternal right. In the *historical* beginning, masculine or "paternal" right holds sway. The story of the defeat of women in the state of nature explains how patriarchal "families," incorporating all the women, are formed through conquest and ruled by "fathers." This stage of the history of the natural condition must be reached if men are to enter the original contract, exercise their political creativity and create a new phase of history in the form of modern patriarchal society. Commentators on contract theory generally take it for granted that there are no problems in referring to "individuals" entering into the original contract, so implying that any or all of the inhabitants of the state of nature can participate. Some commentators are more careful, and Schochet, for example, notes that in the seventeenth century fathers of families were assumed to have sealed the original pact. He argues that Hobbes shared this assumption. Despite Hobbes's use of traditional patriarchal language, his "families" are not ruled by men as fathers but by men as masters. Masters of families rule by virtue of contract (conquest) not their paternal, procreative capacity. Men as masters—or as free and equal men—enter into the original contract that constitutes civil society. Women, now in subjection, no longer have the necessary standing (they are no longer free and equal or "individuals") to take part in creating a new civil society.

The civil law of matrimony, which upholds conjugal right, is created through the original pact. Political theorists consistently omit to mention one of the most remarkable features of Hobbes's political theory. Hobbes makes it quite clear that conjugal right is not natural. Conjugal right is created through the original contract and so is a *political* right. The right is deliberately created by the men who bring civil society into being. The other classic contract theorists presuppose that the institution of marriage exists naturally and that conjugal relations are nonpolitical relations, carried over into civil society. In Hobbes's theory, the law of matrimony is created as part of the civil law. Contemporary political theorists, too, take for granted that the structure of the institution of marriage is nonpolitical and so they pay no attention to conjugal right. Hobbes's political theory makes clear what the other classic contract stories, and contemporary commentaries on contract theory, leave implicit: that the original contract is not only a *social* contract that constitutes the civil law and political right in the sense of (state) government; it is also a *sexual* contract that institutes political right in the form of patriarchal—masculine—power, or government by men, a power exercised in large part as conjugal right.

Hobbes states that in civil society the husband has dominion "because for the most part commonwealths have been erected by the fathers, not by the mothers of families."[39] Or again, "in all cities . . . constituted of *fathers,* not *mothers* governing their families, the domestical command belongs to the man; and such a contract, if it be made according to the civil laws, is called matrimony."[40] If free and equal women could enter the original contract there is no reason whatsoever why they would agree to create a civil law that secures their permanent subjection as wives. Matrimonial law takes a patriarchal form because *men* have made the original contract. The fact that the law of matrimony is part of the civil law provides another reason for self-interested individual men to make a collective agreement. In addition to securing their natural liberty, *men as a sex* have an interest in a political mechanism which secures for them collectively the fruits of the conquests made severally by each man in the natural condition. Through the civil institution of marriage they can all lawfully obtain the familiar "helpmeet" and gain the sexual and domestic services of a wife, whose permanent servitude is now guaranteed by the law and sword of Leviathan.

Hobbes had no wish to challenge the law of matrimony of his own day, embodied in the common law doctrine of coverture. The law of coverture was given classic expression by Sir William Blackstone in his *Commentaries on the Laws of England* in the eighteenth century. Under coverture, a wife had no independent juridical existence; she was a civilly dead being, absorbed into the person of her husband. No one, it would seem, could fail to be struck by the legal powers given to husbands, whether in Blackstone's gloss on the law or in marital practice—powers that can only be compared, as they were regularly compared by feminists in the nineteenth century, to those of slave-masters.[41] Yet patriarchy runs so deeply in the contemporary theoretical consciousness that Chapman comments (echoing Blackstone) that "the most striking feature of the common law family is the liabilities attached to the man, particularly regarding the acts of his wife and servants."[42] Now, if women had made the original contract, civil law might well reflect the fact and attach all manner of "liabilities" to men. But we did not make it, and could not have made it, and so "the most striking feature" of coverture is the juridical nonexistence of a wife (just as she disappears in Hobbes's definition of the "family" in the state of nature). The liabilities of the husband that impress Chapman are the other side of the wife's subjection. "Liabilities" are the price the husband pays for being a master, that is, a protector. The most fundamental premise of Hobbes's political theory is that no individual will give up the right of self-protection.[43] In the state of nature women too have this right, but in civil society women as wives have given up (been forced to give up) this right in favour of the "protection" of their husband—and husbands are now protected by the sword of Leviathan.

Students of Hobbes do not usually make a connection between the original overthrow of mother-right and the establishment of Leviathan. The crucial political significance of the conquest of women in the natural condition is that, unless the defeat occurs, Leviathan is impossible to envisage. The conjuror Hobbes is far too clever a wizard for his patriarchal successors and the trick is never remarked on in discussions of his theory. If women took part in the original contract the awesome figure of the mortal god Leviathan could not be created. Leviathan can be brought into being only if participation in his generation is confined to men. The creation of civil society is an act of masculine political birth; men have no need of a "helper" in *political* generation. In the state of nature, individuals are differentiated only by their sex; that is to say, by their bodily form (in strength, rationality and prudence there is no politically significant difference between individuals with female bodies and individuals with male bodies). Hobbes's account of the institution of Leviathan makes sense only if the participants in the original contract all have the same bodily form.

The creation of Leviathan, Hobbes tells us, involves "more than consent, or concord; it is a real unity of them all, in one and the same person."[44] When men cease to be a mere natural multitude and transform themselves through the act of contract into a unified body, or body politic, bound together through the conventional bonds of contract and civil law, their unity is represented in a very literal sense by the person of their (absolute) master and ruler, Leviathan. They create him "to bear their person," and, Hobbes states, "it is the *unity* of the representer, not the *unity* of the represented, that maketh the person *one*."[45] No such unity would be possible if both sexes took part in the constitution of Leviathan—there could be no representative figure who could represent the "person," the bodily form, of both sexes. Men must be represented and their civil unity given literal symbolic personification by one of their own kind. Similarly, "private bodies" are also represented by one person, and Hobbes uses the example of "all families, in which the father, or master ordereth the whole family." Husband and wife cannot govern jointly in the family; there can be one master only, and the husband is the necessary "one person representative" of the family in civil society.[46] An act of masculine political birth creates civil beings and their sovereign in the image of their makers (only Adam, the first man, through the hand of God, could generate a woman). If the representer is to be unified, he must be *he*. To attempt to represent both sexes within the figure of one master would be to dissolve his unity and oneness and to shatter political order.

## V

Hobbes turned classic into modern patriarchy but several features of his argument worked against

him becoming a founding father of modern patriarchal theory. For example, Hobbes negated Filmer's arguments but that was not sufficient to create the theory required for civil patriarchy. Hobbes turned Filmer's social bonds into their opposite. Filmer saw families and kingdoms as homologous and bound together through the natural, procreative power of the father. Hobbes saw families and kingdoms as homologous, but as bound together through the conventional tie of contract, or, what for Hobbes is the same thing, the force of the sword. Hobbes also agreed with Filmer that sovereignty must be absolute—but sovereignty in the state, not in private bodies. Civil fathers and masters are not miniature Leviathans. Their powers run only so far as permitted by Leviathan's laws and his sword. Leviathan thus enabled Hobbes to offer a solution to the problem that dogged Filmer's classic patriarchalism. Hinton has noted that if fathers were kings then there could be no king with true monarchial power.[47] Hobbes's civil masters cannot detract from the absolute mastery of Leviathan. Hobbes's solution, however, retained absolutism in the state, the form of political right that, as Locke argued, had to be replaced by limited, constitutional government in a properly *civil* order.

The absolute power of Leviathan's sword was not the only problem with Hobbes's patriarchalism. Hobbes was too revealing about civil society. The political character of conjugal right was expertly concealed in Locke's separation of what he called "paternal" power from political power and, ever since, most political theorists, whatever their views about other forms of subordination, have accepted that the powers of husbands derive from nature and, hence, are not political. Not only are a range of important questions about domination and subjection in our own society thus suppressed, but some other important questions about the "origin" of civil society are also nearly avoided. In the past two decades, individualism of a radical, Hobbesian kind has become very influential, although the absolutist conclusions that Hobbes drew from his individualist premises are rejected in favour of a view of the state as a minimal, protective association.[48] The association is held to have a legitimate origin in voluntary transactions between individuals in the state of nature. In the final chapter of *Leviathan,* Hobbes writes that "there is scarce a commonwealth in the world, whose beginnings can in conscience be justified."[49] Hobbes's "beginning" of the original contract between men can only be justified if, as he believed, political order depended on the erection of Leviathan. Without Leviathan, and from Hobbes's starting point of free and equal women and men, a voluntary beginning might be possible. Such a story could not be told by political theorists who acknowledge only half the original contract (the social contract) and thus endorse patriarchal right. The origin of the patriarchal protective state in Hobbes's theory lies in the conquest and servitude of women in the state of nature and in their civil subjection and domestication as wives.

Hobbes's theory is an early version of the argument, presented in the later nineteenth and early twentieth centuries in elaborate detail and with reference to much ethnographic data, that civilization and political society resulted from the overthrow of mother-right and the triumph of patriarchy. The silences and omissions of contemporary political theory and the standard readings of Hobbes's texts do nothing to question that argument. Scholars do not mention the problems about women and the civil order arising from Hobbes's theory and the subsequent development of contract theory. For example, why has conjugal right never been seen as political when every other form of power has been subjected to the closest scrutiny and judgment? Why is women's exclusion from the original pact not mentioned in most discussions of contract theory? If women can take no part in the original contract what is their status as parties to the marriage contract? Has Hobbes's identification of enforced submission with consent (contract) any relevance to present-day sexual relations? By the beginning of the eighteenth century, when, according to political theorists today, patriarchalism had come to an end, Mary Astell asked, "if *all Men are born Free,* how is it that all Women are born Slaves?"[50] Most political theorists have yet to recognize the existence or relevance of Astell's question—or the political significance of the fact that Hobbes did not think that we were so born.

NOTES

1. The arguments are those, respectively, of Richard A. Chapman, "*Leviathan* Writ Small: Thomas Hobbes on the Family," *American Political Science Review,* 69, 1975, p. 77; and John Zvesper, "Hobbes' Individualistic Analysis of the Family," *Politics,* 5, 1985, p. 33. For references to other discussions of Hobbes and patriarchy see Chapman, nn. 2–14 on p. 76.

2. Jean Hampton, *Hobbes and the Social Contract Tradition* (Cambridge: Cambridge University Press, 1986).

3. Contemporary feminist arguments about patriarchy are discussed in Carole Pateman, *The Sexual Contract* (Cambridge: Polity; Stanford: Stanford University Press, 1988), ch. 2.

4. Thomas Hobbes, *Philosophical Rudiments Concerning Government and Society,* the English version of *De Cive,* in *The English Works of Thomas Hobbes of Malmesbury* (London: John Bohn, 1841), vol. 2, ch. 8, p. 109.

5. Christine Di Stefano, "Masculinity as Ideology in Political Theory: Hobbesian Man Considered," *Women's Studies International Forum,* 6, 1983, p. 638.

6. Leslie Stephen in 1904; cited by Gordon Schochet, *Patriarchalism in Political Thought* Oxford: Basil Blackwell, 1975), p. 234.

7. R. W. K. Hinton, "Husbands, Fathers, and Conquerors," *Political Studies,* 16, 1968, p. 57.

8. This section draws on Pateman, *Sexual Contract,* ch. 4.

9. Schochet, *Patriarchalism,* p. 193.

10. Ibid., p. 16.

11. Sir Robert Filmer, *Patriarcha or the Natural Powers of the Kings of England Asserted and Other Political Works,* ed. Peter Laslett (Oxford: Basil Blackwell, 1949). pp. 241, 283. Genesis, too, can be interpreted in more than one way, and equality of men and women in the sight of God is not incompatible with male supremacy in human affairs; e.g. Calvin argued from both the perspective of *cognitio dei* (the eternal, divine perspective in which all things are equal) and the perspective of *cognitio hominis* (the wordly perspective in which humans are hierarchically ordered). See Mary Potter, "Gender Equality and Gender Hierarchy in Calvin's Theology," *Signs,* 11, 1986, pp. 725–39.

12. John Locke, *Two Treatises of Government,* 2nd edn, ed. Peter Laslett (Cambridge: Cambridge University Press, 1967), II, §2.

13. Filmer, *Patriarcha,* p. 245.

14. Hobbes, *Leviathan*, in *English Works*, vol. 3, ch. 20, p. 187.

15. Ibid., pp. 186–7.

16. Ibid., ch. 14, pp. 124–5.

17. Ibid., ch. 20, p. 186.

18. Hobbes, *Philosophical Rudiments*, ch. 9, p. 116.

19. Hobbes, *Leviathan*, p. 188.

20. For an account of the controversy, see Rosalind Coward, *Patriarchal Precedents* (London: Routledge and Kegan Paul, 1983), ch. 2. See also Pateman, *Sexual Contract*, ch. 2.

21. Preston King, *The Ideology of Order* (London: Allen and Unwin, 1974), p. 203.

22. King, *Ideology of Order*, pp. 205, 206. Hobbes's most recent biographer suggests that his argument about mother-right derives from his own experience as a child. Hobbes's views perhaps "owed much to that occasion during those years when the curate [Hobbes's father], possibly long before his disappearance, was forced by his character and circumstances to yield the government to Hobbes's mother." Arnold A. Rogow, *Thomas Hobbes: Radical in the Service of Reaction* (New York and London: W. W. Norton, 1986), p. 132. Hobbes's father, rather fond of drink and neglectful of his parish, fled after being accused of assaulting a rector of a neighboring parish. Ironically Rogow was unable to find any new information about Hobbes's mother. Even her maiden name remains uncertain.

23. The other classic contract theorists are discussed in Pateman, *Sexual Contract*, chs. 3 and 4.

24. Hobbes, *Philosophical Rudiments*, ch. 9, p. 116.

25. Thomas Hobbes's *A Dialogue between a Philosopher and a Student of the Common Laws of England*, in *English Works*, vol. 6, p. 147.

26. Thomas Hobbes, *De Corpore Politico, or The Elements of Law*, in *English Works*, vol. 4, ch. 4, pp. 158–9 (Hobbes's emphasis here and below).

27. Hobbes, *Leviathan*, ch. 17, p. 154.

28. Hobbes, *Philosophical Rudiments*, ch. 8, p. 108.

29. Hobbes, *Leviathan*, ch. 10, p. 82.

30. Ibid., ch. 20, p. 191.

31. Hobbes, *Philosophical Rudiments*, ch. 9, p. 121.

32. Hobbes, *De Corpore Politico*, ch. 4, p. 158.

33. Hobbes, *Leviathan*, ch. 15, p. 133.

34. Ibid., ch. 20, p. 189.

35. Hobbes, *De Corpore Politico*, ch. 3, pp. 149–50.

36. Hobbes, *Leviathan*, ch. 20, p. 190.

37. Ibid., ch. 17, p. 159.

38. I am grateful to Peter Morriss for raising the question of generations and for other helpful criticisms.

39. Hobbes, *Leviathan*, ch. 15, p. 187.

40. Hobbes, *Philosophical Rudiments*, ch. 9, p. 118.

41. On the implications of coverture, see Pateman, *Sexual Contract*, chs. 5 and 6.

42. Chapman, "*Leviathan* Writ Small," n. 90 on p. 84.

43. Hampton, *Hobbes*, pp. 197–207, argues that his deduction of absolute sovereignty fails precisely because Hobbes makes self-protection an absolute right. But because she takes no account of Hobbes's patriarchalism, she fails to mention that, if the argument about sovereignty in the state is correct, then conjugal sovereignty fails too.

44. Hobbes, *Leviathan*, ch. 17, p. 158.

45. Ibid., ch. 16, p. 151.

46. Ibid., ch. 22, pp. 221–2.

47. R. W. K. Hinton, "Husbands, Fathers and Conquerors," *Political Studies*, 15, 1967, pp. 294, 299.

48. For an argument that absolutist conclusions are ultimately unavoidable, see Carole Pateman, *The Problem of Political Obligation*, 2nd edn (Cambridge: Polity; Berkeley and Los Angeles: University of California Press, 1985), ch. 3. Hampton, *Hobbes*, interprets Hobbes's commonwealth as a union of slaves within the will of a master.

49. Hobbes, *Leviathan*, part IV, p. 706.

50. Mary Astell, *Some Reflections Upon Marriage*, from the 4th edn of 1730 (New York: Source Book Press, 1970), p. 107 (emphasis in the original).

# 21    The Devastation of the Indies

## BARTOLOMÉ DE LAS CASAS

IN THE YEAR 1523, at the end of the year, this same tyrant [Pedro Arias de Avila or Pedrarias] went into Nicaragua to subjugate that most flourishing province and a sorrowful hour it was when he entered that land. Who could exaggerate the felicity, the good health, the amenities of that prosperous and numerous population? Verily it was a joy to behold that admirable province with its big towns, some of them extending three or four leagues, full of gardens and orchards and prosperous people. But because this land is a great plain without any mountains where the people could take refuge, they had to allow, with great anguish, the Christians to remain in the province and to suffer cruel persecutions from them. And since these Indians were by nature very gentle and peace-loving, the tyrant and his comrades (all of whom had aided him in destroying other kingdoms) inflicted such damage, carried out such slaughters, took so many captives, perpetrated so many unjust acts that no human tongue could describe them.

He once sent fifty horsemen with pikes to destroy an entire province. Not a single human being survived that massacre, neither women nor children nor aged and infirm. And that province was larger than the county of Rusellón in Spain. This terrible massacre was punishment for a trifling offense: some Indians had not responded to a summons promptly enough when the tyrant had commanded that they bring him a load of maize (that grain taking the place of wheat in this region), or else had asked for more Indians to be assigned to serve him or his comrades. And there was no place where the Indians could take refuge from the tyrant-Governor's wrath.

He sent companies of Spaniards to open up other provinces—that is to say, to attack and pillage the peoples in those provinces. They were allowed to capture as many Indians as they liked in peaceful settlements, to become their slaves. And they put the captives in chains and made them carry heavy loads, weighing as much as three arrobas.* And they had to carry these cargoes on their backs for long marches. The result was that the number of captives soon dwindled, most of them dying from exhaustion, so that from four thousand captives there remained only six. They

left the dead bodies on the trail. They were decapitated corpses, for when a captive sank under the heavy load, the Spaniards cut off his head, which fell to one side while the body fell to the other while the captives chained together continued their march without interruption. When commanded to do similar labor, with this experience behind them, the surviving Indians went off weeping and saying, "These are the roads down which we went to serve the Christians. In the past, even when we worked hard we could return to our houses, our wives, and children. But now we go without hope of ever again seeing them."

This tyrant once took it into his head to make a new *repartimiento* (distribution of captives among the Spaniards), this being either a caprice of his or, as was rumored, to rid himself of some Indians he disliked and pass them on to someone else. This occurred at the time of year when grain should be sowed and it kept the Indians from their usual tasks at seed-time. Later on, as a result, the Christians lacked grain, whereupon they seized the stores of grain the Indians kept for themselves and their families. In the famine that followed, more than thirty thousand Indians perished of starvation and there were cases when a woman would kill and eat her own child, in desperation.

Since all the settlements of the Indians in this fertile land were situated in the midst of gardens and orchards, the Christians resided in them, each Christian taking over the houses of the Indians who had been allocated to him according to the royal grant known as the *encomienda*. The Indian who had owned the house now worked for the Christian as his servant, cooking his meals, tilling the soil, working without rest. Oh, the pitiful Indians! Men and women, the aged and the children all worked for this Spanish Christian. For the children, as soon as they could stand on their legs, were put to work. And thus the Indians have been used up and consumed, and the few who survive are still being wasted away. Nor are these hardworking Indians allowed to own a house or anything of their own, and in this respect the Spaniards in Nicaragua have gone beyond the excesses

* An *arroba* equals roughly 22 pounds. —ED.

of injustice that have prevailed on the island of Hispaniola.

The greatest and most horrible pestilence that has laid waste the province of Nicaragua was the freedom given by the Governor to his subordinates in the matter of petitioning slaves from the caciques of the towns. They petitioned every four or five months and each time a new allotment. The Governor could obtain fifty slaves at a time by threatening the cacique with being burned at the stake, or thrown to the fierce dogs if he refused. Since the Indians do not commonly have slaves, at the most a cacique may have two or three or four, he simply went through the settlement, taking to begin with all the orphans, then taking one son from those who had two, and two sons from those who had three. In this way the cacique completed the number demanded by the tyrant, with loud lamentations and weeping by the people, for it seems they most greatly love their sons. And since this act was repeated many times, that whole kingdom became depopulated during the twenties and until the year thirty-three.

For this transaction was aided by six or seven ships voyaging along the coast to take on board and sell the surplus requisitioned slaves in Panama and Peru. And all of those captives soon died for as it has been ascertained from experience repeated a thousand times, the Indians when uprooted from their native land very soon perish. Then, too, they are never given enough to eat and their labor is never lightened in any way, since they are bought and sold to do only heavy work.

Thus more than five hundred thousand Indians were torn out of this province and sold into slavery. And those Indians had been as free as I am. In the infernal wars waged by the Spaniards another five or six hundred thousand souls have perished up to the present time. And these ravages continue. In a matter of fourteen years this province has undergone these things. There must now be in Nicaragua four or five thousand Spaniards who kill, each day, through acts of violence, oppression, and servitude, numerous Indians, and they boast that they have established one of the great population centers in the world. It was more than

enough what those Spaniards did in the province of Cuzocatán where the Villa San Salvador is situated, or is at least in the vicinity. It was a felicitous land bordering the coast of the southern sea, extending a distance of forty or fifty leagues,* and in the capital city of Cuzocatán the Indians gave the Spaniards a great welcome, more than twenty or thirty thousand coming out with gifts of live chickens and cooked foods. In response to this welcome, the captain-general ordered each of his officers to take as many Indians as they liked to serve them as cargo bearers. Each Spaniard then took one to five hundred Indians they needed to be well served, and the innocent Indians endured being allocated in this way and they served the Spaniards faultlessly, whole-heartedly, revering them.

Meanwhile the captain-general commanded the Indians to bring him gold, much gold, for that was mainly what he had come there for. The Indians replied that they would gladly provide the Spaniards with all the gold they possessed, and they gathered together a large quantity of copper axes overlaid with a coating of gold, giving them the aspect of solid gold. The captain then had the gold assayed and when it was found that the axes were of copper, he exclaimed: "To the devil with this land! There is no gold here," and he commanded his men to put the Indians that served them in chains and branded as slaves. This was done and to all the Indians they could lay hands on, and I saw one of the sons of the ruler of that city being chained and branded. Some Indians escaped, and when the Indians of the land heard of this great misfortune, they gathered together and took up arms and in the battle that followed, the Spaniards massacred and tortured a great number of Indians. Then they built a city which has now, by divine justice, been destroyed in three deluges, one of water, another of muddy earth, the third of stones larger than thirteen oxen.

When the Spaniards had killed all the chieftains and all the Indians capable of making war, they cast all the others into infernal servitude. And

* A Spanish *legua* equals roughly 3½ miles. —ED.

when the Spaniards demanded tribute-slaves, they gave them their sons and daughters, the only slaves they had. These the Spaniards sent by shiploads down the coast to be sold in Peru.

Thus, with massacres and other outrages they laid waste a kingdom extending for more than one hundred square leagues, a land that had been among the most flourishing and populous in the whole world.

## Recommended Readings

### TEXTS

Baumgold, Deborah. *Hobbes's Political Theory*. Cambridge: Cambridge University Press, 1988.

Burns, James, ed. *Cambridge History of Political Thought, 1450–1700*. Cambridge: Cambridge University Press, 1991.

Dietz, Mary G., ed. *Thomas Hobbes and Political Theory*. Lawrence: University of Kansas Press, 1990.

Gauthier, David. *The Logic of Leviathan*. Oxford: Oxford University Press, 1969.

Johnston, David. *The Rhetoric of Leviathan*. Princeton: Princeton University Press, 1986.

Kavka, Gregory. *Hobbesian Moral and Political Theory*. Princeton: Princeton University Press, 1986.

Macpherson, C. B. *The Political Theory of Possessive Individualism*. Oxford: Oxford University Press, 1962.

Strauss, Leo. *The Political Philosophy of Hobbes*. Oxford: Oxford University Press, 1936.

Warrender, Richard. *The Political Philosophy of Hobbes*. Oxford: Oxford University Press, 1957.

### FEMINIST PERSPECTIVE

Di Stefano, Christine. "Masculinity as Ideology in Political Theory: Hobbesian Man Considered." *Women's Studies International Forum* 6, no. 6 (1983).

Schochet, Gordon. "Thomas Hobbes on the Family and the States of Nature." *Political Science Quarterly* 82, no. 3 (1967): 427–445.

Zvesper, John. "Hobbes' Individualistic Analysis of the Family." *Politics* 5, no. 2 (October 1985).

### MULTICULTURAL PERSPECTIVE

Boff, Leonardo, and Virgil Elizondo. *The Voice of the Victims*. Philadelphia: Trinity Press International, 1990.

Las Casas, Bartolome de. *History of the Indies*. New York: Harper & Row, 1971.

# VI

---

## *Locke*

## Introduction

JOHN LOCKE WAS BORN IN SOMERSET IN 1632. He attended Westminster, an excellent school near London, and then Oxford University, where he earned bachelor's and master's degrees and taught for a period. In 1666, Locke met Lord Ashley, later to become the first Earl of Shaftesbury. Locke, who was then studying medicine, saved his life by persuading him to undergo an operation for an abscess of the liver. Locke took up residence in the Ashley household, serving both as a political secretary to Shaftesbury and as a tutor to his son. Shaftesbury held office during the 1679 national scare over the Popish Plot. He used this crisis to force King Charles II to exclude his brother James, a Catholic, from succession to the throne. It is certain that Locke had knowledge of the behind-the-scenes tactics—the forced confessions, the judicial murders, the mob oratory and agitation—but he never criticized Shaftesbury's actions in any way. He was always a faithful supporter.

Shaftesbury's political activities ended in a trial for treason, and, although he was acquitted, he thought it best to flee to Holland. Locke also came under suspicion for writing against the government and followed Shaftesbury to Holland. Recent scholarship has shown that by this time Locke had, in fact, been writing against the government; he had written at least the first part of his *Two Treatises of Government*. Locke stayed in Holland until 1689, returning when William and Mary, to whom he had been an adviser, came to the English throne.

On his return, Locke published most of the works on philosophy, education, and religion for which he is known. In 1690, he published *Two Treatises of Government*, anonymously. Not until his will was revealed at his death in 1704 did he publicly claim authorship of this volume. He died at the home of his closest friend, Damiris Cudworth, who cared for him during the last twelve years of his life.

Locke's *Two Treatises of Government* was written partly in response to the royalist view of Sir Robert Filmer and partly in support of the opposition movement against Charles II. In our selection, Locke, like Hobbes, defends a social contract theory of political obligation, but unlike Hobbes, Locke considers those in a state of nature as bound by natural laws that restrict their pursuit of self-interest. In a state of nature, Locke says, persons have a natural duty to preserve themselves, and where there is no conflict, they have a natural duty to preserve the rest of humankind. He also claims that persons in this state have a natural right to punish wrongdoers as much as reparation and restraint require, and a natural right to appropriate the earth's resources. Whatever people remove from a state of nature and mix their labor with is their property as long as there is enough and as good left for others and nothing is allowed to spoil or go to waste. Locke argues that the problems that would arise with the exercise of these natural rights in a state of nature, where each person could judge in his own case, leads to the formation of a civil society.

According to Locke, people are obligated to obey a particular government if they consent to obey that government. Here Locke distinguishes between express and tacit consent. Express consent is a deliberative and voluntary promise to obey. Tacit consent is given in a number of ways, such as owning property, lodging for a week, or walking freely on a highway. But given Locke's definition of tacit consent, it would seem impossible for anyone residing in a country not to be tacitly consenting to its government, even those who were actually planning to overthrow it! Yet despite the seeming inescapability of tacitly consenting to a government and hence becoming bound to obey it, Locke still goes on to lay out a number of conditions under which he thinks revolution would be justified, such as when a government invades property rights, seeks absolute power, or seeks to corrupt the representatives of the people.

In chapter 5 of the *First Treatise* and chapter 7 of the *Second Treatise*, selected here, Locke addresses the question of the relationship between the sexes, relying heavily on biblical authority. In chapter 5, Locke, like Filmer, begins with the punishment inflicted on Eve according to the Genesis account: "he shall rule over thee." But unlike Filmer, Locke takes this claim as a prediction of the hardship that women would ordinarily suffer rather than a grant of authority to husbands to rule over their wives. Nevertheless, in chapter 7, Locke does maintain that when husbands and wives have conflicting wills, "the last determination . . . falls to the man's share as the abler and the stronger." However, Locke points out that this does not represent any absolute authority of husbands over their wives since, in many cases, wives have the right to separate themselves from their husbands.

In "Women and John Locke; Or, Who Owns the Apples in the Garden of Eden?" Lorenne M. G. Clark argues that Locke's reason for maintaining the natural superiority of men over women based on women's procreative role is that he wanted to uphold a system of individually held private property under the exclusive control of male heads of households. To maintain this male-controlled private property system, Clarke argues, Locke had to deny women an equal right to the disposition of family property that they helped create. And to justify this denial, Locke appealed to the natural superiority of men over women based on women's procreative role. But how could any natural differences between men and women be grounds for denying women a right to what they produce, or, put another way, why shouldn't women own the apples they produce both inside and outside the Garden of Eden?

Tecumseh, considered by some to be one of the most effective Indian opponents of the United States, was born into the Crouching Panther clan of the Shawnee on the Mad River near what is now Springfield, Ohio, in 1769. He earned his warrior's reputation fighting in the defeats of General Harmer at Fort Wayne (1790) and General St. Clair on the Wabash River (1791).

In the late 1790s, he met a white woman, Rebecca Galloway, who taught him English and read to him from various history books, including the Bible. These studies and his own reflections led Tecumseh to endorse the view that all Indian land belonged to Indians as a whole and not to any particular tribe. This position brought Tecumseh into direct conflict with William Henry Harrison, who as governor of Indiana Territory was negotiating treaties with various tribes at bargain prices, sometimes with the threat of force. When after meeting with Tecumseh, Harrison refused to tear up a treaty he had recently made with the Miamies, ceding a large tract of land on both sides of the Wabash River, Tecumseh set out on the first of several journeys to visit tribes as far removed as the Cherokees, Choctaws, and Creeks in the South and the Sacs and the Sioux along the upper Mississippi, seeking to unite them against the Americans. Although he was rejected by some, he nevertheless succeeded in rallying many groups to his cause. In our selection, *We Must Be United*, Tecumseh is speaking to the Osaga.

Here the questions for Locke's theory are: What side would Locke be on in the conflict between Tecumseh and Harrison, and what, if anything, would this show about the validity of his theory?

# 22    Two Treatises of Government

JOHN LOCKE

*Book II*

## CHAPTER II
## OF THE STATE OF NATURE

4. TO UNDERSTAND POLITICAL POWER ARIGHT, and derive it from its original, we must consider what estate all men are naturally in, and that is, a state of perfect freedom to order their actions, and dispose of their possessions and persons as they think fit, within the bounds of the law of Nature, without asking leave or depending upon the will of any other man.

A state also of equality, wherein all the power and jurisdiction is reciprocal, no one having more than another, there being nothing more evident than that creatures of the same species and rank, promiscuously born to all the same advantages of Nature, and the use of the same faculties,

should also be equal one amongst another, without subordination or subjection, unless the lord and master of them all should, by any manifest declaration of his will, set one above another, and confer on him, by an evident and clear appointment, an undoubted right to dominion and sovereignty. . . .

6. But though this be a state of liberty, yet it is not a state of license; though man in that state have an uncontrollable liberty to dispose of his person or possessions, yet he has not liberty to destroy himself, or so much as any creature in his possession, but where some nobler use than its bare preservation calls for it. The state of Nature has a law of Nature to govern it, which obliges everyone, and reason, which is that law, teaches all mankind who will but consult it, that being all equal and independent, no one ought to harm another in his life, health, liberty or possessions;

for men being all the workmanship of one om-
nipotent and infinitely wise Maker; all the servants
of one sovereign Master, sent into the world by
His order and about His business; they are His
property, whose workmanship they are made to
last during His, not one another's pleasure. And,
being furnished with like faculties, sharing all in
one community of Nature, there cannot be supposed any such subordination among us that may
authorize us to destroy one another, as if we were
made for one another's uses, as the inferior ranks
of creatures are for ours. Everyone as he is bound
to preserve himself, and not to quit his station wil-
fully, so by the like reason, when his own preservation comes not in competition, ought he as
much as he can to preserve the rest of mankind,
and not unless it be to do justice on an offender,
take away, or impair the life, or what tends to the
preservation of the life, the liberty, health, limb, or
goods of another.

7. And that all men may be restrained from invading other's rights, and from doing hurt to one
another, and the law of Nature be observed, which
willeth the peace and preservation of all mankind,
the execution of the law of Nature is in that state
put into every man's hands, whereby everyone has
a right to punish the transgressors of that law to
such a degree as may hinder its violation. For the
law of Nature would, as all other laws that concern
men in this world, be in vain if there were nobody
that in the state of Nature had a power to execute
that law, and thereby preserve the innocent and
restrain offenders; and if anyone in the state of Nature may punish another for any evil he has done,
everyone may do so. For in that state of perfect
equality, where naturally there is no superiority or
jurisdiction of one over another, what any may do
in prosecution of that law, everyone must needs
have a right to do.

8. And thus, in the state of Nature, one man
comes by a power over another, but yet no absolute or arbitrary power to use a criminal when
he has got him in his hands, according to the passionate heats, or boundless extravagancy of his
own will, but only to retribute to him so far as
calm reason and conscience dictate, what is proportionate to his transgression, which is so much
as may serve for reparation and restraint. For these
two are the only reasons why one man may lawfully do harm to another, which is that we call
punishment. In transgressing the law of Nature,
the offender declares himself to live by another
rule than that of reason and common equity,
which is that measure God has set to the actions
of men for their mutual security, and so he becomes dangerous to mankind; the tie which is
to secure them from injury and violence being
slighted and broken by him, which being a trespass against the whole species, and the peace and
safety of it, provided for by the law of Nature,
every man upon this score, but the right he hath
to preserve mankind in general, may restrain, or
where it is necessary, destroy things noxious to
them, and so may bring such evil on anyone who
hath transgressed that law, as may make him repent the doing of it, and thereby deter him, and,
by his example, others from doing the like mischief. And in this case, and upon this ground,
every man hath a right to punish the offender, and
be executioner of the law of Nature.

9. I doubt not but this will seem a very strange
doctrine to some men; but before they condemn
it, I desire them to resolve me by what right any
prince or state can put to death or punish an alien
for any crime he commits in their country? It is
certain their laws, by virtue of any sanction they
receive from the promulgated will of the legislature, reach not a stranger. They speak not to him,
nor, if they did, is he bound to hearken to them.
The legislative authority by which they are in force
over the subjects of that commonwealth hath no
power over him. Those who have the supreme
power of making laws in England, France, or Holland are, to an Indian, but like the rest of the
world—men without authority. And therefore, if
by the law of Nature every man hath not a power
to punish offences against it, as he soberly judges
the case to require, I see not how the magistrates
of any community can punish an alien of another
country, since, in reference to him, they can have
no more power than what every man naturally
may have over another.

10. Besides the crime which consists in violating the laws, and varying from the right rule of reason, whereby a man so far becomes degenerate, and declares himself to quit the principles of human nature and to be a noxious creature, there is commonly injury done, and some person or other, some other man, receives damage by his transgression; in which case, he who hath received any damage has (besides the right of punishment common to him, with other men) a particular right to seek reparation from him that hath done it. And any other person who finds it just may also join with him that is injured, and assist him in recovering from the offender so much as may make satisfaction for the harm he hath suffered.

11. From these two distinct rights (the one of punishing the crime, for restraint and preventing the like offence, which right of punishing is in everybody, the other of taking reparation, which belongs only to the injured party) comes it to pass that the magistrate, who by being magistrate hath the common right of punishing put into his hands, can often, where the public good demands not the execution of the law, remit the punishment of criminal offences by his own authority, but yet cannot remit the satisfaction due to any private man for the damage he has received. That he who hath suffered the damage has a right to demand in his own name, and he alone can remit. The damnified person has this power of appropriating to himself the goods or service of the offender by right of self-preservation, as every man has a power to punish the crime to prevent its being committed again, by the right he has of preserving all mankind, and doing all reasonable things he can in order to that end. And thus it is that every man in the state of Nature has a power to kill a murderer, both to deter others from doing the like injury (which no reparation can compensate) by the example of the punishment that attends it from everybody, and also to secure men from the attempts of a criminal who, having renounced reason, the common rule and measure God hath given to mankind, hath, by the unjust violence and slaughter he hath committed upon one, declared war against all mankind, and therefore may be destroyed as a lion or a tiger, one of those wild savage beasts with whom men can have no society nor security. And upon this is grounded that great law of Nature, "Whoso sheddeth man's blood by man shall his blood be shed." And Cain was so fully convinced that everyone had a right to destroy such a criminal, that, after the murder of his brother, he cries out, "Everyone that findeth me shall slay me," so plain was it writ in the hearts of all mankind.

12. By the same reason may a man in the state of Nature punish the lesser breaches of that law, it will, perhaps, be demanded, with death? I answer: Each transgression may be punished to that degree, and with so much severity, as will suffice to make it an ill bargain to the offender, give him cause to repent, and terrify others from doing the like. Every offence that can be committed in the state of Nature may, in the state of Nature, be also punished equally, and as far forth, as it may, in a commonwealth. For though it would be beside my present purpose to enter here into the particulars of the law of Nature, or its measures of punishment; yet it is certain there is such a law, and that too as intelligible and plain to a rational creature and a studier of that law as the positive laws of commonwealths, nay, possibly plainer; as much as reason is easier to be understood than the fancies and intricate contrivances of men, following contrary and hidden interests put into words; for truly so are a great part of the municipal laws of countries, which are only so far right as they are founded on the law of Nature, by which they are to be regulated and interpreted.

13. To this strange doctrine—viz., That in the state of Nature everyone has the executive power of the law of Nature, I doubt not but it will be objected that it is unreasonable for men to be judges in their own cases, that self-love will make men partial to themselves and their friends; and, on the other side, ill-nature, passion, and revenge will carry them too far in punishing others, and hence nothing but confusion and disorder will follow, and that therefore God hath certainly appointed government to restrain the partiality and violence of men. I easily grant that civil government is the

proper remedy for the inconveniences of the state of Nature, which must certainly be great where men may be judges in their own case, since it is easy to be imagined that he who was so unjust as to do his brother an injury will scarce be so just as to condemn himself for it. But I shall desire those who make this objection to remember that absolute monarchs are but men; and if government is to be the remedy of those evils which necessarily follow from men being judges in their own cases, and the state of Nature is therefore not to be endured, I desire to know what kind of government that is, and how much better it is than the state of Nature, where one man commanding a multitude has the liberty to be judge in his own case, and may do to all his subjects whatever he pleases without the least question or control of those who execute his pleasure? and in whatsoever he doth, whether led by reason, mistake, or passion, must be submitted to? which men in the state of Nature are not bound to do one to another. And if he that judges, judges amiss in his own or any other case, he is answerable for it to the rest of mankind.

14. It is often asked as a mighty objection, where are, or ever were, there any men in such a state of Nature? To which it may suffice as an answer at present, that since all princes and rulers of "independent" governments all through the world are in a state of Nature, it is plain the world never was, nor never will be, without numbers of men in that state. I have named all governors of "independent" communities, whether they are, or are not, in league with others; for it is not every compact that puts an end to the state of Nature between men, but only this one of agreeing together mutually to enter into one community, and make one body politic; other promises and compacts men may make one with another, and yet still be in the state of Nature. The promises and bargains for truck,* &c., between the two men in Soldania, or between a Swiss and an Indian, in the woods of America, are binding to them, though they are perfectly in a state of Nature in reference to one another for truth, and keeping of faith

belongs to men as men, and not as members of society. . . .

## CHAPTER III
## OF THE STATE OF WAR

16. THE state of war is a state of enmity and destruction; and therefore declaring by word or action, not a passionate and hasty, but sedate, settled design upon another man's life puts him in a state of war with him against whom he has declared such intention, and so has exposed his life to the other's power to be taken away by him, or anyone that joins with him in his defence, and espouses his quarrel; it being reasonable and just I should have a right to destroy that which threatens me with destruction; for by the fundamental law of Nature, man being to be preserved as much as possible, when all cannot be preserved, the safety of the innocent is to be preferred, and one may destroy a man who makes war upon him, or has discovered an enmity to his being, for the same reason he may kill a wolf or a lion, because they are not under the ties of the common law of reason, have no other rule but that of force and violence, and so may be treated as a beast of prey, those dangerous and noxious creatures that will be sure to destroy him whenever he falls into their power.

17. And hence it is that he who attempts to get another man into his absolute power does thereby put himself into a state of war with him; it being to be understood as a declaration of a design upon his life. For I have reason to conclude that he who would get me into his power without my consent would use me as he pleased when he had got me there, and destroy me too when he had a fancy to it; for nobody can desire to have me in his absolute power unless it be to compel me by force to that which is against the right of my freedom—*i.e.,* make me a slave. To be free from such force is the only security of my preservation, and reason bids me look on him as an enemy to my preservation who would take away that freedom which is the fence to it; so that he who makes an attempt to enslave me thereby puts himself into a state of war with me. He that in the state of Nature would take

*Exchange.—ED.

away the freedom that belongs to anyone in that state must necessarily be supposed to have a design to take away everything else, that freedom being the foundation of all the rest; as he that in the state of society would take away the freedom belonging to those of that society or commonwealth must be supposed to design to take away from them everything else, and so be looked on as in a state of war.

18. This makes it lawful for a man to kill a thief who has not in the least hurt him, nor declared any design upon his life, any further than by the use of force, so to get him in his power as to take away his money, or what he pleases, from him; because using force, where he has no right to get me into his power, let his pretence be what it will, I have no reason to suppose that he would take away my liberty would not, when he had me in his power, take away everything else. And, therefore, it is lawful for me to treat him as one who has put himself into a state of war with me—*i.e.*, kill him if I can; for to that hazard does he justly expose himself whoever introduces a state of war, and is aggressor in it.

19. And here we have the plain difference between the state of Nature and the state of war, which however some men have confounded, are as far distant as a state of peace, goodwill, mutual assistance, and preservation; and a state of enmity, malice, violence, and mutual destruction are one from another. Men living together according to reason without a common superior on earth, with authority to judge between them, is properly the state of Nature. But force, or a declared design of force upon the person of another, where there is no common superior on earth to appeal to for relief, is the state of war; and it is the want of such an appeal gives a man the right of war even against an aggressor, though he be in society and a fellow-subject. Thus, a thief whom I cannot harm, but by appeal to the law, for having stolen all that I am worth, I may kill when he sets on me to rob me but of my horse or coat, because the law, which was made for my preservation, where it cannot interpose to secure my life from present force, which if lost is capable of no reparation, permits me my

own defence and the right of war, a liberty to kill the aggressor, because the aggressor allows not time to appeal to our common judge, nor the decision of the law, for remedy in a case where the mischief may be irreparable. Want of a common judge with authority puts all men in a state of Nature; force without right upon a man's person makes a state of war both where there is, and is not, a common judge.

20. But when the actual force is over, the state of war ceases between those that are in society and are equally on both sides subject to the judge; and, therefore, in such controversies, when the question is put, "Who shall be judge?" it cannot be meant who shall decide the controversy; everyone knows what Jephtha here tells us, that "the Lord the Judge" shall judge. Where there is no judge on earth the appeal lies to God in Heaven. That question then cannot mean who shall judge, whether another hath put himself in a state of war with me, and whether I may, as Jephtha did, appeal to Heaven in it? Of that I myself can only be judge in my own conscience, as I will answer it at the great day to the Supreme Judge of all men. . . .

## CHAPTER V
## OF PROPERTY

25. WHETHER we consider natural reason, which tells us that men, being once born, have a right to their preservation, and consequently to meat and drink and such other things as Nature affords for their subsistence, or "revelation," which gives us an account of those grants God made of the world to Adam, and to Noah and his sons, it is very clear that God, as King David says (Psalm cxv.16), "has given the earth to the children of men," given it to mankind in common. But, this being supposed, it seems to some a very great difficulty how anyone should ever come to have a property in anything, I will not content myself to answer, that, if it be difficult to make out "property" upon a supposition that God gave the world to Adam and his posterity in common, it is impossible that any man but one universal monarch should have "property" upon a supposition that

God gave the world to Adam and his heirs in succession, exclusive of all the rest of his posterity; but I shall endeavour to show how men might come to have a property in several parts of that which God gave to mankind in common, and that without any express compact of all the commoners.

26. God, who hath given the world to men in common, hath also given them reason to make use of it to the best advantage of life and convenience. The earth and all that is therein is given to men for the support and comfort of their being. And though all the fruits it naturally produces and beasts it feeds, belong to mankind in common, as they are produced by the spontaneous hand of Nature, and nobody has originally a private dominion exclusive of the rest of mankind in any of them, as they are thus in their natural state, yet being given for the use of men, there must of necessity be a means to appropriate them some way or other before they can be of any use, or at all beneficial to any particular men. The fruit or venison which nourishes the wild Indian, who knows no enclosure, and is still a tenant in common, must be his, and so his — *i.e.,* a part of him, that another can no longer have any right to it before it can do him any good for the support of his life.

27. Though the earth and all inferior creatures be common to all men, yet every man has a "property" in his own "person." This nobody has any right to but himself. The "labour" of his body and the "work" of his hands, we may say, are properly his. Whatsoever, then, he removes out of the state that Nature hath provided and left it in, he hath mixed his labour with it, and joined to it something that is his own, and thereby makes it his property. It being by him removed from the common state Nature placed it in, it hath by this labour something annexed to it that excludes the common right of other men. For this "labour" being the unquestionable property of the labourer, no man but he can have a right to what that is once joined to, at least where there is enough, and as good left in common for others.

28. He that is nourished by the acorns he picked up under an oak, or the apples he gathered from the trees in the wood, has certainly appropriated them to himself. Nobody can deny but the nourishment is his. I ask, then, when did they begin to be his? when he digested? or when he ate? or when he boiled? or when he brought them home? or when he picked them up? And it is plain, if the first gathering made them not his, nothing else could. That labour put a distinction between them and common. That added something to them more than Nature, the common mother of all, had done, and so they became his private right. And will anyone say he had no right to those acorns or apples he thus appropriated because he had not the consent of all mankind to make them his? Was it a robbery thus to assume to himself what belonged to all in common? If such a consent as that was necessary, man had starved, notwithstanding the plenty God had given him. We see in commons, which remain so by compact, that it is the taking any part of what is common, and removing it out of the state Nature leaves it in, which begins the property, without which the common is of no use. And the taking of this or that part does not depend on the express consent of all the commoners. Thus, the grass my horse has bit, the turfs my servant has cut, and the ore I have digged in anyplace, where I have a right to them in common with others, become my property without the assignation or consent of anybody. The labour that was mine, removing them out of that common state they were in, hath fixed my property in them.

29. By making an explicit consent of every commoner necessary to anyone's appropriating to himself any part of what is given in common. Children or servants could not cut the meat which their father or master had provided for them in common without assigning to everyone his peculiar part. Though the water running in the fountain be everyone's, yet who can doubt but that in the pitcher is his only who drew it out? His labour hath taken it out of the hands of Nature where it was common, and belonged equally to all her children, and hath thereby appropriated it to himself.

30. Thus this law of reason makes the deer that Indian's who hath killed it; it is allowed to be his goods who hath bestowed his labour upon it,

though, before, it was the common right of everyone. And amongst those who are counted the civilized part of mankind, who have made and multiplied positive laws to determine property, this original law of Nature for the beginning of property, in what was before common, still takes place, and by virtue thereof, what fish anyone catches in the ocean, that great and still remaining common of mankind; or what ambergris anyone takes up here is by the labour that removes it out of that common state Nature left it in, made his property who takes that pains about it. And even amongst us, the hare that anyone is hunting is thought his who pursues her during the chase. For being a beast that is still looked upon as common, and no man's private possession, whoever has employed so much labour about any of that kind as to find and pursue her has thereby removed her from the state of Nature wherein she was common, and hath began a property.

31. It will, perhaps, be objected to this, that if gathering the acorns or other fruits of the earth, &c., makes a right to them, then anyone may engross as much as he will. To which I answer, Not so. The same law of Nature that does by this means give us property, does also bound that property too. "God has given us all things richly" (I Tim. vi. 12). Is the voice of reason confirmed by inspiration? But how far has He given it us—"to enjoy?" As much as anyone can make use of to any advantage of life before it spoils, so much he may by his labour fix a property in. Whatever is beyond this is more than his share, and belongs to others. Nothing was made by God for man to spoil or destroy. And thus considering the plenty of natural provisions there was a long time in the world, and the few spenders, and to how small a part of that provision the industry of one man could extend itself and engross it to the prejudice of others, especially keeping within the bounds set by reason of what might serve for his use, there could be then little room for quarrels or contentions about property so established.

32. But the chief matter of property being now not the fruits of the earth and the beasts that subsist on it, but the earth itself, as that which takes in and carries with it all the rest; I think it is plain that property in that too is acquired as the former. As much land as a man tills, plants, improves, cultivates, and can use the product of, so much is his property. He by his labour does, as it were, enclose it from the common. Nor will it invalidate his right to say everybody else has an equal title to it, and therefore he cannot appropriate, he cannot enclose, without the consent of all his fellow-commoners, all mankind. God, when He gave the world in common to all mankind, commanded man also to labour, and the penury of his condition required it of him. God and his reason commanded him to subdue the earth—*i.e.,* improve it for the benefit of life and therein lay out something upon it that was his own, his labour. He that, in obedience to this command of God, subdued, tilled, and sowed any part of it, thereby annexed to it something that was his property, which another had no title to, nor could without injury take from him.

33. Nor was this appropriation of any parcel of land, by improving it, any prejudice to any other man, since there was still enough and as good left, and more than the yet unprovided could use. So that, in effect, there was never the less left for others because of his enclosure for himself. For he that leaves as much as another can make use of does as good as take nothing at all. Nobody could think himself injured by the drinking of another man, though he took a good draught, who had a whole river of the same water left him to quench his thirst. And the case of land and water, where there is enough of both, is perfectly the same.

34. God gave the world to men in common, but since He gave it them for their benefit and the greatest conveniencies of life they were capable to draw from it, it cannot be supposed he meant it should always remain common and uncultivated. He gave it to the use of the industrious and rational (and labour was to be his title to it); not to the fancy or covetousness of the quarrelsome and contentious. He that had as good left for his improvement as was already taken up needed not

complain, ought not to meddle with what was already improved by another's labour; if he did it is plain he desired the benefit of another's pains, which he had no right to, and not the ground which God had given him, in common with others, to labour on, and whereof there was as good left as that already possessed; and more than he knew what to do with, or his industry could reach to. . . .

37. This is certain, that in the beginning, before the desire of having more than men needed had altered the intrinsic value of things, which depends only on their usefulness to the life of man, or had agreed that a little piece of yellow metal, which would keep without wasting or decay, should be worth a great piece of flesh or a whole heap of corn, though men had a right to appropriate by their labour, each one to himself, as much of the things of Nature as he could use, yet this could not be much, nor to the prejudice of others, where the same plenty was still left, to those who would use the same industry.

Before the appropriation of land, he who gathered as much of the wild fruit, killed, caught, or tamed as many of the beasts as he could—he that so employed his pains about any of the spontaneous products of Nature as any way to alter them from the state Nature put them in, by placing any of his labour on them, did thereby acquire a propriety in them; but if they perished in his possession without their due use—if the fruits rotted or the venison putrefied before he could spend it, he offended against the common law of Nature, and was liable to be punished: he invaded his neighbour's share, for he had no right farther than his use called for any of them, and they might serve to afford him conveniencies of life. . . .

39. And thus, without supposing any private dominion and property in Adam over all the world, exclusive of all other men, which can no way be proved, nor anyone's property be made out from it, but supposing the world, given as it was to the children of men in common, we see how labour could make men distinct titles to several parcels of it for their private uses, wherein

there could be no doubt of right, no room for quarrel.

40. Nor is it so strange as, perhaps, before consideration, it may appear, that the property of labour should be able to overbalance the community of land, for it is labour indeed that puts the difference of value on everything; and let anyone consider what the difference is between an acre of land planted with tobacco or sugar, sown with wheat or barley, and an acre of the same land lying in common without any husbandry upon it, and he will find that the improvement of labour makes the far greater part of the value. I think it will be but a very modest computation to say, that of the products of the earth useful to the life of man, nine-tenths are the effects of labour. Nay, if we will rightly estimate things as they come to our use, and cast up the several expenses about them— what in them is purely owing to Nature and what to labour—we shall find that in most of them ninety-nine hundredths are wholly to be put on the account of labour.

41. There cannot be a clearer demonstration of anything than several nations of the Americans are of this, who are rich in land and poor in all the comforts of life; whom Nature, having furnished as liberally as any other people with the materials of plenty—*i.e.,* a fruitful soil, apt to produce in abundance what might serve for food, raiment, and delight; yet, for want of improving it by labour, have not one hundredth part of the conveniences we enjoy, and a king of a large and fruitful territory there feeds, lodges, and is clad worse than a day labourer in England. . . .

42. To make this a little clearer, let us but trace some of the ordinary provisions of life, through their several progresses, before they come to our use, and see how much they receive of their value from human industry. Bread, wine, and cloth are things of daily use and great plenty; yet notwithstanding acorns, water, and leaves, or skins must be our *bread, drink and clothing,* did not labour furnish us with these more useful commodities. For whatever bread is more worth than acorns, wine than water, and cloth or silk than leaves,

skins or moss, that is wholly owing to labour and industry. The one of these being the food and raiment which unassisted Nature furnishes us with; the other provisions which our industry and pains prepare for us, which how much they exceed the other in value, when anyone hath computed, he will then see how much labour makes the far greatest part of the value of things we enjoy in this world; and the ground which produces the materials is scarce to be reckoned in as any, or at most, but a very small part of it; so little, that even amongst us, land that is left wholly to Nature, that hath no improvement of pasturage, tillage, or planting, is called, as indeed it is, waste; and we shall find the benefit of it amount to little more than nothing.

43. An acre of land that bears here twenty bushels of wheat, and another in America, which, with the same husbandry, would do the like, are, without doubt, of the same natural, intrinsic value. But yet the benefit mankind receives from one in a year is worth £5, and the other possibly not worth a penny; if all the profit an Indian received from it were to be valued and sold here, at least I may truly say, not one thousandth. It is labour, then, which puts the greatest part of value upon land, without which it would scarcely be worth anything; it is to that we owe the greatest part of all its useful products; for all that the straw, bran, bread, of that acre of wheat, is more worth than the product of an acre of as good land which lies waste is all the effect of labour. For it is not barely the ploughman's pains, the reaper's and thresher's toil, and the baker's sweat, is to be counted into the bread we eat; the labour of those who broke the oxen, who digged and wrought the iron and stones, who felled and framed the timber employed about the plough, mill, oven, or any other utensils, which are a vast number, requisite to this corn, from its sowing to its being made bread, must all be charged on the account of labour, and received as an effect of that; Nature and the earth furnished only the almost worthless materials as in themselves. It would be a strange catalogue of things that industry provided and made use of

about every loaf of bread before it came to our use if we could trace them; iron, wood, leather, bark, timber, stone, bricks, coals, lime, cloth, dyeing-drugs, pitch, tar, masts, ropes, and all the materials made use of in the ship that brought any of the commodities made use of by any of the workmen, to any part of the work, all which it would be almost impossible, at least too long, to reckon up. . . .

45. Thus labour, in the beginning, gave a right of property, wherever anyone was pleased to employ it, upon what was common, which remained a long while, the far greater part, and is yet more than mankind makes use of. Men at first, for the most part, contented themselves with what unassisted Nature offered to their necessities; and though afterwards, in some parts of the world, where the increase of people and stock, with the use of money, had made land scarce, and so of some value, the several communities settled the bounds of their distinct territories, and, by laws, within themselves, regulated the properties of the private men of their society, and so, by compact and agreement, settled the property which labour and industry began. And the leagues that have been made between several states and kingdoms, either expressly or tacitly disowning all claim and right to the land in the other's possession, have, by common consent, given up their pretences to their natural common right, which originally they had to those countries; and so have, by positive agreement, settled a property amongst themselves, in distinct parts of the world; yet there are still great tracts of ground to be found, which the inhabitants thereof, not having joined with the rest of mankind in the consent of the use of their common money, lie waste, and are more than the people who dwell on it, do, or can make use of, and so still lie in common; though this can scarce happen amongst that part of mankind that have consented to the use of money.

46. The greatest part of things really useful to the life of man, and such as the necessity of subsisting made the first commoners of the world look after—as it doth the Americans now—are

generally things of short duration, such as—if they are not consumed by use—will decay and perish of themselves. Gold, silver, and diamonds are things that fancy or agreement hath put the value on, more than real use and the necessary support of life. Now of those good things which Nature hath provided in common, everyone hath a right (as hath been said) to as much as he could use, and had a property in all he could effect with his labour; all that his industry could extend to, to alter from the state Nature had put it in, was his. He that gathered a hundred bushels of acorns or apples had thereby a property in them; they were his goods as soon as gathered. He was only to look that he used them before they spoiled, else he took more than his share, and robbed others. And, indeed, it was a foolish thing, as well as dishonest, to hoard up more than he could make use of. If he gave away a part to anybody else, so that it perished not uselessly in his possession, these he also made use of. And if he also bartered away plums that would have rotted in a week, for nuts that would last good for his eating a whole year, he did no injury; he wasted not the common stock; destroyed no part of the portion of goods that belonged to others, so long as nothing perished uselessly in his hands. Again, if he would give his nuts for a piece of metal, pleased with its colour, or exchange his sheep for shells, or wool for sparkling pebble or a diamond, and keep those by him all his life, he invaded not the right of others; he might heap up as much of these durable things as he pleased; the exceeding of the bounds of his just property not lying in the largeness of his possession, but the perishing of anything uselessly in it.

47. And thus came in the use of money; some lasting thing that men might keep without spoiling, and that, by mutual consent, men would take in exchange for the truly useful but perishable supports of life.

48. And as different degrees of industry were apt to give men possessions in different proportions, so this invention of money gave them the opportunity to continue and enlarge them. For

supposing an island, separate from all possible commerce with the rest of the world, wherein there were but a hundred families, but there were sheep, horses, and cows, with other useful animals, wholesome fruits, and land enough for corn for a hundred thousand times as many, but nothing in the island, either because of its commonness or perishableness, fit to supply the place of money. What reason could anyone have there to enlarge his possessions beyond the use of his family, and a plentiful supply to its consumption, either in what their own industry produced, or they could barter for like perishable, useful commodities with others? Where there is not something both lasting and scarce, and so valuable to be hoarded up, there men will not be apt to enlarge their possessions of land, were it never so rich, never so free for them to take. For I ask, what would a man value ten thousand or an hundred thousand acres of excellent land, ready cultivated and well stocked, too, with cattle, in the middle of the inland parts of America, where he had no hopes of commerce with other parts of the world, to draw money to him by the sale of the product? It would not be worth the enclosing, and we should see him give up again to the wild common of Nature whatever was more than would supply the conveniences of life, to be had there for him and his family.

49. Thus, in the beginning, all the world was America, and more so than that is now; for no such thing as money was anywhere known. Find out something that hath the use and value of money amongst his neighbours, you shall see the same man will begin presently to enlarge his possessions.

50. But since gold and silver, being little useful to the life of man, in proportion to food, raiment, and carriage, has its value only from the consent of men—whereof labour yet makes in great part the measure—it is plain that the consent of men have agreed to a disproportionate and unequal possession of the earth—I mean out of the bounds of society and compact; for in governments the laws regulate it; they having, by consent, found out and agreed in a way how a man may, rightfully and

without injury, possess more than he himself can make use of by receiving for the overplus gold and silver, which may continue long in a man's possession without decaying, and agreeing those metals should have a value. . . .

## CHAPTER VII
## OF POLITICAL OR CIVIL SOCIETY

. . . 87. Man being born, as has been proved, with a title to perfect freedom and an uncontrolled enjoyment of all the rights and privileges of the law of Nature, equally with any other man, or number of men in the world, hath by nature a power not only to preserve his property—that is, his life, liberty, and estate against the injuries and attempts of other men, but to judge of and punish the breaches of that law in others, as he is persuaded the offence deserves, even with death itself, in crimes where the heinousness of the fact, in his opinion, requires it. But because no political society can be, nor subsist, without having in itself the power to preserve the property, and in order thereunto punish the offences of all those of that society, there, and there only, is political society where every one of the members hath quitted this natural power, resigned it up into the hands of the community in all cases that exclude him not from appealing for protection to the law established by it. And thus all private judgment of every particular member being excluded, the community comes to be umpire, and by understanding indifferent rules and men authorized by the community for their execution, decides all the differences that may happen between any members of that society concerning any matter of right, and punishes those offences which any member hath committed against the society with such penalties as the law has established; whereby it is easy to discern who are, and are not, in political society together. Those who are united into one body, and have a common established law and judicature to appeal to, with authority to decide controversies between them and punish offenders, are in civil society one with another; but those who have no such common appeal, I mean on earth, are still in the state

of Nature, each being where there is no other, judge for himself and executioner; which is, as I have before showed it, the perfect state of Nature.

88. And thus the commonwealth comes by a power to set down what punishment shall belong to the several transgressions they think worthy of it, committed amongst the members of that society (which is the power of making laws) as well as it has the power to punish any injury done unto any of its members by anyone that is not of it (which is the power of war and peace); and all this for the preservation of the property of all the members of that society, as far as is possible. But though every man entered into society has quitted his power to punish offences against the law of Nature in prosecution of his own private judgment, yet with the judgment of offences which he has given up to the legislative, in all cases where he can appeal to the magistrate, he has given up a right to the commonwealth to employ his force for the execution of the judgments of the commonwealth whenever he shall be called to it, which, indeed, are his own judgments, they being made by himself or his representative. And herein we have the original of the legislative and executive power of civil society, which is to judge by standing laws how far offences are to be punished when committed within the commonwealth; and also by occasional judgments founded on the present circumstances of the fact, how far injuries from without are to be vindicated, and in both these to employ all the force of all the members when there shall be need.

89. Wherever, therefore, any number of men so unite into one society as to quit everyone his executive power of the law of Nature, and to resign it to the public, there and there only is a political or civil society. And this is done wherever any number of men, in the state of Nature, enter into society to make one people one body politic under one supreme government; or else when anyone joins himself to, and incorporates with any government already made. For hereby he authorizes the society, of which is all one, the legislative thereof, to make laws for him as the public good of the society shall require, to the execution

whereof his own assistance (as to his own decrees) is due. And this puts men out of a state of Nature into that of a commonwealth, by setting up a judge on earth with authority to determine all the controversies and redress the injuries that may happen to any member of the commonwealth, which judge is the legislative or magistrates appointed by it. And wherever there are any number of men, however associated, that have no such decisive power to appeal to, there they are still in the state of Nature.

90. And hence it is evident that absolute monarchy, which by some men is counted for the only government in the world, is indeed inconsistent with civil society, and so can be no form of civil government at all. For the end of civil society being to avoid and remedy those inconveniencies of the state of Nature which necessarily follow from every man's being judge in his own case by setting up a known authority to which everyone of that society may appeal upon any injury received, or controversy that may arise, and which everyone of the society ought to obey.[1] Wherever any persons are who have not such an authority to appeal to, and decide any difference between them there, those persons are still in the state of Nature. And so is every absolute prince in respect of those who are under his dominion. . . .

93. In absolute monarchies, indeed, as well as other governments of the world, the subjects have an appeal to the law, and judges to decide any controversies, and restrain any violence that may happen betwixt the subjects themselves, one amongst another. This everyone thinks necessary, and believes; he deserves to be thought a declared enemy to society and mankind who should go about to take it away. But whether this be from a true love of mankind and society, and such a charity as we owe all one to another, there is reason to doubt. For this is no more than what every man, who loves his own power, profit, or greatness, may, and naturally must do, keep those animals from hurting or destroying one another, who labour and drudge only for his pleasure and advantage; and so are taken care of, not out of any love the master has for them, but love of himself, and the profit they bring him. For if it be asked what security, what fence is there in such a state against the violence and oppression of this absolute ruler, the very question can scarce be borne. They are ready to tell you that it deserves death only to ask after safety. Betwixt subject and subject, they will grant, there must be measures, laws, and judges for their mutual peace and security. But as for the ruler, he ought to be absolute, and is above all such circumstances; because he has a power to do more hurt and wrong, it is right when he does it. To ask how you may be guarded from harm or injury on that side, where the strongest hand is to do it, is presently the voice of faction and rebellion. As if when men, quitting the state of Nature, entered into society, they agreed that all of them but one should be under the restraint of laws; but that he should still retain all the liberty of the state of Nature, increased with power, and made licentious by impunity. This is to think that men are so foolish that they take care to avoid what mischiefs may be done them by polecats or foxes, but are content, nay, think it safety, to be devoured by lions. . . .

CHAPTER VIII

OF THE BEGINNING OF POLITICAL SOCIETIES

95. Men being, as has been said, by nature all free, equal, and independent, no one can be put out of this estate and subjected to the political power of another without his own consent, which is done by agreeing with other men, to join and unite into a community for their comfortable, safe, and peaceable living, one amongst another, in a secure enjoyment of their properties, and a greater security against any that are not of it. This any number of men may do, because it injures not the freedom of the rest; they are left, as they were, in the liberty of the state of Nature. When any number of men have so consented to make one community or government, they are thereby presently incorporated, and make one body politic, wherein the majority have a right to act and conclude the rest.

96. For, when any number of men have, by the consent of every individual, made a community, they have thereby made that community one body, with a power to act as one body, which is only by the will and determination of the majority. For that which acts any community, being only the consent of the individuals of it, and it being one body, must move one way, it is necessary the body should move that way whither the greater force carries it, which is the consent of the majority, or else it is impossible it should act or continue one body, one community, which the consent of every individual that united into it agreed that it should; and so everyone is bound by that consent to be concluded by the majority. And therefore we see that in assemblies empowered to act by positive laws where no number is set by that positive law which empowers them, the act of the majority passes for the act of the whole, and of course determines as having, by the law of Nature and reason, the power of the whole.

97. And thus every man, by consenting with others to make one body politic under one government, puts himself under an obligation to everyone of that society to submit to the determination of the majority, and to be concluded by it; or else this original compact, whereby he with others incorporates into one society, would signify nothing, and be no compact if he be left free and under no other ties than he was in before in the state of Nature. For what appearance would there be of any compact? What new engagement if he were no farther tied by any decrees of the society than he himself thought fit and did actually consent to? This would be still as great a liberty as he himself had before his compact, or anyone else in the state of Nature, who may submit himself and consent to any acts of it if he thinks fit.

98. For if the consent of the majority shall not in reason be received as the act of the whole, and conclude every individual; nothing but the consent of every individual can make anything to be the act of the whole, which, considering the infirmities of health and avocations of business, which in a number though much less than that of a commonwealth, will necessarily keep many away from the public assembly; and the variety of opinions and contrariety of interests which unavoidably happen in all collections of men, it is next impossible ever to be had. And, therefore, if coming into society be upon such terms it will be only like Cato's coming into the theatre, *tantum ut exiret.* Such a constitution as this would make the mighty leviathan of a shorter duration than the feeblest creatures, and not let it outlast the day it was born in, which cannot be supposed till we can think that rational creatures should desire and constitute societies only to be dissolved. For where the majority cannot conclude the rest, there they cannot act as one body, and consequently will be immediately dissolved again.

99. Whosoever, therefore, out of a state of Nature unite into a community, must be understood to give up all the power necessary to the ends for which they unite into society to the majority of the community, unless they expressly agreed in any number greater than the majority. And this is done by barely agreeing to unite into one political society, which is all the compact that is, or needs be, between the individuals that enter into or make up a commonwealth. And thus, that which begins and actually constitutes any political society is nothing but the consent of any number of freemen capable of majority, to unite and incorporate into such a society. And this is that, and that only, which did or could give beginning to any lawful government in the world.

100. To this I find two objections made:
1. That there are no instances to be found in story of a company of men, independent and equal one amongst another, that met together, and in this way began and set up a government.
2. It is impossible of right that men should do so, because all men, being born under government, they are to submit to that, and are not at liberty to begin a new one.

101. To the first there is this to answer: That it is not at all to be wondered that history gives us but a very little account of men that lived together in the state of Nature. The inconveniencies of that condition, and the love and want of society, no sooner brought any number of them together, but

they presently united and incorporated if they designed to continue together. And if we may not suppose men ever to have been in the state of Nature, because we hear not much of them in such a state, we may as well suppose the armies of Salmanasser or Xerxes were never children, because we hear little of them till they were men and embodied in armies. Government is everywhere antecedent to records, and letters seldom come in amongst a people till a long continuation of civil society has, by other more necessary arts, provided for their safety, ease, and plenty. And then they begin to look after the history of their founders, and search into their original when they have outlived the memory of it. For it is with commonwealths as with particular persons, they are commonly ignorant of their own births and infancies; and if they know anything of it, they are beholding for it to the accidental records that others have kept of it, and those that we have of the beginning of any polities in the world, excepting that of the Jews, where God Himself immediately interposed, and which favours not at all paternal dominion; are all either plain instances of such a beginning as I have mentioned, or at least have manifest footsteps of it. . . .

. . . The other objection, I find, urged against the beginning of polities, in the way I have mentioned, is this, viz.:—

113. "That all men being born under government, some or other, it is impossible any of them should ever be free and at liberty to unite together and begin a new one, or ever be able to erect a lawful government." If this argument be good, I ask, How came so many lawful monarchies into the world? For if anybody, upon this supposition, can show me any one man, in any age of the world, free to begin a lawful monarchy, I will be bound to show him ten other free men at liberty, at the same time, to unite and begin a new government under a regal or any other form. It being demonstration that if anyone born under the dominion of another may be so free as to have a right to command others in a new and distinct empire, everyone that is born under the dominion of another may be so free too, and may become a ruler

or subject of a distinct separate government. And so, by this their own principle, either all men, however born, are free, or else there is but one lawful prince, one lawful government in the world; and then they have nothing to do but barely to show us which that is, which, when they have done, I doubt not but all mankind will easily agree to pay obedience to him.

114. Though it be a sufficient answer to their objection to show that it involves them in the same difficulties that it doth those they use it against, yet I shall endeavour to discover the weakness of this argument a little farther.

"All men," say they, "are born under government, and therefore they cannot be at liberty to begin a new one. Everyone is born a subject to his father or his prince, and is therefore under the perpetual tie of subjection and allegiance." It is plain mankind never owned nor considered any such natural subjection that they were born in, to one or to the other, that tied them, without their own consents, to a subjection to them and their heirs.

115. For there are no examples so frequent in history, both sacred and profane, as those of men withdrawing themselves and their obedience from the jurisdiction they were born under, and the family or community they were bred up in, and setting up new governments in other places, from whence sprang all that number of petty commonwealths in the beginning of ages, and which always multiplied as long as there was room enough, till the stronger or more fortunate swallowed the weaker; and those great ones, again breaking to pieces, dissolved into lesser dominions; all which are so many testimonies against paternal sovereignty, and plainly prove that it was not the natural right of the father descending to his heirs that made governments in the beginning; since it was impossible, upon that ground, there should have been so many little kingdoms but only one universal monarchy if men had not been at liberty to separate themselves from their families and their government, be it what it will that was set up in it, and go and make distinct commonwealths and other governments as they thought fit. . . .

119. Every man being, as has been showed, naturally free, and nothing being able to put him into subjection to any earthly power, but only his own consent, it is to be considered what shall be understood to be a sufficient declaration of a man's consent to make him subject to the laws of any government. There is a common distinction of an express and a tacit consent, which will concern our present case. Nobody doubts but an express consent of any man, entering into any society, makes him a perfect member of that society, a subject of that government. The difficulty is, what ought to be looked upon as a tacit consent, and how far it binds—*i.e.*, how far anyone shall be looked on to have consented, and thereby submitted to any government, where he has made no expressions of it at all. And to this I say, that every man that hath any possession or enjoyment of any part of the dominions of any government doth hereby give his tacit consent, and is as far forth obliged to obedience to the laws of that government, during such enjoyment, as anyone under it, whether this his possession be of land to him and his heirs for ever, or a lodging only for a week; or whether it be barely travelling freely on the highway; and, in effect, it reaches as far as the very being of anyone within the territories of that government. . . .

122. But submitting to the laws of any country, living quietly and enjoying privileges and protection under them, makes not a man a member of that society; it is only a local protection and homage due to and from all those who, not being in a state of war, come within the territories belonging to any government, to all parts whereof the force of its law extends. But this no more makes a man a member of that society, a perpetual subject of that commonwealth, than it would make a man a subject to another in whose family he found it convenient to abide for some time, though, whilst he continued in it, he were obliged to comply with the laws and submit to the government he found there. And thus we see that foreigners, by living all their lives under another government, and enjoying the privileges and protection of it, though they are bound, even in conscience, to submit to

its administration as far forth as any denizen, yet do not thereby come to be subjects or members of that commonwealth. Nothing can make any man so, but his actually entering into it by positive engagement and express promise and compact. This is that which, I think, concerning the beginning of political societies, and that consent which makes anyone a member of any commonwealth.

## CHAPTER IX
## OF THE ENDS OF POLITICAL SOCIETY AND GOVERNMENT

123. If man in the state of Nature be so free as has been said, if he be absolute lord of his own person and possessions, equal to the greatest and subject to nobody, why will he part with his freedom, this empire, and subject himself to the dominion and control of any other power? To which it is obvious to answer, that though in the state of Nature he hath such a right, yet the enjoyment of it is very uncertain and constantly exposed to the invasion of others; for all being kings as much as he, every man his equal, and the greater part no strict observers of equity and justice, the enjoyment of the property he has in this state is very unsafe, very insecure. This makes him willing to quit this condition which, however free, is full of fears and continual dangers; and it is not without reason that he seeks out and is willing to join in society with others who are already united, or have a mind to unite for the mutual preservation of their lives, liberties and estates, which I call by the general name—property.

124. The great and chief end, therefore, of men uniting into commonwealths, and putting themselves under government, is the preservation of their property; to which in the state of Nature there are many things wanting.

Firstly, There wants an established, settled, known law, received and allowed by common consent to be the standard of right and wrong, and the common measure to decide all controversies between them. For though the law of Nature be plain and intelligible to all rational creatures, yet men, being biased by their interest, as well as ignorant for want of study of it, are not apt to allow of it as a law binding to them in the application of it to their particular cases.

125. Secondly: in the state of Nature there wants a known and indifferent judge, with authority to determine all differences according to the established law. For everyone in that state being both judge and executioner of the law of Nature, men being partial to themselves, passion and revenge is very apt to carry them too far, and with too much heat in their own cases, as well as negligence and unconcernedness, make them too remiss in other men's.

126. Thirdly: in the state of Nature there often wants power to back and support the sentence when right, and to give it due execution. They who by any injustice offended will seldom fail where they are able by force to make good their injustice. Such resistance many times makes the punishment dangerous, and frequently destructive to those who attempt it.

127. Thus mankind, notwithstanding all the privileges of the state of Nature, being but in an ill condition while they remain in it are quickly driven into society. Hence it comes to pass, that we seldom find any number of men live any time together in this state. The inconveniencies that they are therein exposed to by the irregular and uncertain exercise of the power every man has of punishing the transgressions of others, make them take sanctuary under the established laws of government, and therein seek the preservation of their property. It is this which makes them so willingly give up everyone his single power of punishing to be exercised by such alone as shall be appointed to it amongst them, and by such rules as the community, or those authorized by them to that purpose, shall agree on. And in this we have the original right and rise of both the legislative and executive power as well as of the governments and societies themselves.

128. For in the state of Nature to omit the liberty he has of innocent delights, a man has two powers. The first is to do whatsoever he thinks fit for the preservation of himself and others within the permission of the law of Nature; by which law, common to them all, he and all the rest of man-kind are one community, make up one society distinct from all other creatures, and were it not for the corruption and viciousness of degenerate men, there would be no need of any other, no necessity that men should separate from this great and natural community, and associate into lesser combinations. The other power a man has in the state of Nature is the power to punish the crimes committed against that law. Both these he gives up when he joins in a private, if I may so call it, or particular political society, and incorporates into any commonwealth separate from the rest of mankind.

129. The first power—viz., of doing whatsoever he thought fit for the preservation of himself and the rest of mankind, he gives up to be regulated by laws made by the society, so far forth as the preservation of himself and the rest of that society shall require; which laws of the society in many things confine the liberty he had by the law of Nature.

130. Secondly. The power of punishing he wholly gives up, and engages his natural force, which he might before employ in the execution of the law of Nature, by his own single authority, as he thought fit, to assist the executive power of the society as the law thereof shall require. For being now in a new state, wherein he is to enjoy many conveniencies from the labour, assistance, and society of others in the same community, as well as protection from its whole strength, he is to part also with as much of his natural liberty, in providing for himself, as the good, prosperity, and safety of the society shall require, which is not only necessary but just, since the other members of the society do the like.

131. But though men when they enter into society give up the equality, liberty, and executive power they had in the state of Nature into the hands of the society, to be so far disposed of by the legislative as the good of the society shall require, yet it being only with an intention in everyone the better to preserve himself, his liberty and property (for no rational creature can be supposed to change his condition with an intention to be worse), the power of the society or legislative constituted by

them can never be supposed to extend farther than the common good, but is obliged to secure everyone's property by providing against those three defects above mentioned that made the state of Nature so unsafe and uneasy. And so, whoever has the legislative or supreme power of any commonwealth, is bound to govern by established standing laws, promulgated and known to the people, and not by extemporary decrees, by indifferent and upright judges, who are to decide controversies by those laws; and to employ the force of the community at home only in the execution of such laws, or abroad to prevent or redress foreign injuries and secure the community from inroads and invasion. And all this to be directed to no other end but the peace, safety, and public good of the people.

## CHAPTER XIX
## OF THE DISSOLUTION
## OF GOVERNMENTS

211. HE that will, with any clearness, speak of the dissolution of government, ought in the first place to distinguish between the dissolution of the society and the dissolution of the government. That which makes the community, and brings men out of the loose state of Nature into one politic society, is the agreement which everyone has with the rest to incorporate and act as one body, and so be one distinct commonwealth. The usual, and almost only way whereby this union is dissolved, is the inroad of foreign force making a conquest upon them. For in that case (not being able to maintain and support themselves as one entire and independent body) the union belonging to that body, which consisted therein, must necessarily cease, and so everyone returns to the state he was in before, with a liberty to shift for himself and provide for his own safety, as he thinks fit, in some other society. Whenever the society is dissolved, it is certain the government of that society cannot remain. Thus conquerors' swords often cut up governments by the roots, and mangle societies to pieces, separating the subdued or scattered multitude from the protection of and dependence on that society which ought to have preserved them

from violence. The world is too well instructed in, and too forward to allow of this way of dissolving of governments, to need any more to be said of it; and there wants not much argument to prove that where the society is dissolved, the government cannot remain; that being as impossible as for the frame of a house to subsist when the materials of it are scattered and displaced by a whirlwind, or jumbled into a confused heap by an earthquake.

212. Besides this overturning from without, governments are dissolved from within:

First. When the legislative is altered, civil society being a state of peace amongst those who are of it, from whom the state of war is excluded by the umpirage which they have provided in their legislative for the ending all differences that may arise amongst any of them; it is in their legislative that the members of a commonwealth are united and combined together into one coherent living body. This is the soul that gives form, life, and unity to the commonwealth; from hence the several members have their mutual influence, sympathy, and connection; and therefore when the legislative is broken, or dissolved, dissolution and death follows. For the essence and union of the society consisting in having one will, the legislative, when once established by the majority has the declaring and, as it were, keeping of that will. The constitution of the legislative is the first and fundamental act of society, whereby provision is made for the continuation of their union under the direction of persons and bonds of laws, made by persons authorized thereunto, by the consent and appointment of the people, without which no one man, or number of men, amongst them can have authority of making laws that shall be binding to the rest. When anyone, or more, shall take upon them to make laws whom the people have not appointed so to do, they make laws without authority, which the people are not therefore bound to obey; by which means they come again to be out of subjection, and may constitute to themselves a new legislative, as they think best, being in full liberty to resist the force of those who, without authority, would impose anything upon them. Everyone is at the disposure of his own will, when those who had, by the delegation of the society, the declaring of the public will, are excluded from it, and others usurp the place, who have no such authority or delegation.

213. This being usually brought about by such in the commonwealth, who misuse the power they have, it is hard to consider it aright, and know at whose door to lay it, without knowing the form of government in which it happens. Let us suppose, then, the legislative placed in the concurrence of three distinct persons:—First, a single hereditary person having the constant, supreme, executive power, and with it the power of convoking and dissolving the other two within certain periods of time. Secondly, an assembly of hereditary nobility. Thirdly, an assembly of representatives chosen, *pro tempore,* by the people. Such a form of government supposed, it is evident—

214. First, that when such a single person or prince sets up his own arbitrary will in place of the laws which are the will of the society declared by the legislative, then the legislative is changed. For that being, in effect, the legislative whose rules and laws are put in execution, and required to be obeyed when other laws are set up, and other rules pretended and enforced than what the legislative, constituted by the society, have enacted, it is plain that the legislative is changed. Whoever introduces new laws, not being there unto authorized, by the fundamental appointment of the society, or subverts the old, disowns and overturns the power by which they were made, and so sets up a new legislative.

215. Secondly, when the prince hinders the legislative from assembling in its due time, or from acting freely, pursuant to those ends for which it was constituted, the legislative is altered. For it is not a certain number of men—no, nor their meeting, unless they have also freedom of debating and leisure of perfecting what is for the good of the society wherein the legislative consists; when these are taken away, or altered, so as to deprive the society of the due exercise of their power, the legislative is truly altered. For it is not names that constitute governments, but the use and exercise of those powers that were intended to accompany them; so that he who takes away the freedom, or hinders the acting of the legislative in its due seasons, in effect takes away the legislative, and puts an end to the government.

216. Thirdly, when, by the arbitrary power of the prince, the electors or ways of election are altered without the consent and contrary to the common interest of the people, there also the legislative is altered. For if others than those whom the society hath authorized thereunto do choose, or in another way than what the society hath prescribed, those chosen are not the legislative appointed by the people.

217. Fourthly, the delivery also of the people into the subjection of a foreign power, either by the prince or by the legislative, is certainly a change of the legislative, and so a dissolution of the government. For the end why people entered into society being to be preserved one entire, free, independent society, to be governed by its own laws, this is lost whenever they are given up into the power of another.

218. Why, in such a constitution, as this, the dissolution of the government in these cases is to be imputed to the prince is evident, because he, having the force, treasure, and offices of the State to employ, and often persuading himself or being flattered by others, that, as supreme magistrate, he is incapable of control; he alone is in a condition to make great advances towards such changes under pretence of lawful authority, and has it in his hands to terrify or suppress opposers as factious, seditious, and enemies to the government; whereas no other part of the legislative, or people, is capable by themselves to attempt any alteration of the legislative without open and visible rebellion, apt enough to be taken notice of, which, when it prevails, produces effects very little different from foreign conquest. Besides, the prince, in such a form of government, having the power of dissolving the other parts of the legislative, and thereby rendering them private persons, they can never, in opposition to him, or without his concurrence, alter the legislative by a law, his consent being necessary to give any of their decrees that sanction. But yet so far as the other parts of the

legislative any way contribute to any attempt upon the government, and do either promote, or not, what lies in them, hinder such designs, they are guilty, and partake in this, which is certainly the greatest crime men can be guilty of one towards another.

219. There is one way more whereby such a government may be dissolved, and that is: When he who has the supreme executive power neglects and abandons that charge, so that the laws already made can no longer be put in execution; this is demonstratively to reduce all the anarchy, and so effectually to dissolve the government. For laws not being made for themselves, but to be, by their execution, the bonds of the society to keep every part of the body politic in its due place and function. When that totally ceases, the government visibly ceases, and the people become a confused multitude without order or connection. Where there is no longer the administration of justice for the securing of men's rights, nor any remaining power within the community to direct the force, or provide for the necessities of the public, there certainly is no government left. Where the laws cannot be executed it is all one as if there were no laws, and a government without laws is, I suppose, a mystery in politics inconceivable to human capacity, and inconsistent with human society.

220. In these, and the like cases, when the government is dissolved, the people are at liberty to provide for themselves by erecting a new legislative differing from the other by the change of persons, or form, or both, as they shall find it most for their safety and good. For the society can never, by the fault of another, lose the native and original right it has to preserve itself, which can only be done by a settled legislative and a fair and impartial execution of the laws made by it. But the state of mankind is not so miserable that they are not capable of using this remedy till it be too late to look for any. To tell people they may provide for themselves by erecting a new legislative, when, by oppression, artifice, or being delivered over to a foreign power, their old one is gone, is only to tell them they may expect relief when it is too late, and

the evil is past cure. This is, in effect, no more than to bid them first be slaves, and then to take care of their liberty, and, when their chains are on, tell them they may act like free men. This, if barely so, is rather mockery than relief, and men can never be secure from tyranny if there be no means to escape it till they are perfectly under it; and, therefore, it is that they have not only a right to get out of it, but to prevent it. . . .

224. But it will be said this hypothesis lays a ferment for frequent rebellion. To which I answer:

First: no more than any other hypothesis. For when the people are made miserable, and find themselves exposed to the ill usage of arbitrary power, cry up their governors as much as you will for sons of Jupiter, let them be sacred and divine, descended or authorized from Heaven; give them out for whom or what you please, the same will happen. The people generally ill treated, and contrary to right, will be ready upon any occasion to ease themselves of a burden that sits heavy upon them. They will wish and seek for the opportunity, which in the change, weakness, and accidents of human affairs, seldom delays long to offer itself. He must have lived but a little while in the world, who has not seen examples of this in his time; and he must have read very little who cannot produce examples of it in all sorts of governments in the world.

225. Secondly: I answer, such revolutions happen not upon every little mismanagement in public affairs. Great mistakes in the ruling part, many wrong and inconvenient laws, and all the slips of human frailty will be borne by the people without mutiny or murmur. But if a long train of abuses, prevarications, and artifices, all tending the same way, make the design visible to the people, and they cannot but feel what they lie under, and see whither they are going, it is not to be wondered that they should then rouse themselves, and endeavour to put the rule into such hands which may secure to them the ends for which government was at first erected, and without which, ancient names and specious forms are so far from being better, that they are much worse than the state

of Nature or pure anarchy; the inconveniencies being all as great and as near, but the remedy farther off and more difficult.

226. Thirdly: I answer, that this power in the people of providing for their safety anew by a new legislative when their legislators have acted contrary to their trust by invading their property, is the best fence against rebellion, and the probablest means to hinder it. For rebellion being an opposition, not to persons, but authority, which is founded only in the constitutions and laws of the government; those, whoever they be, who, by force, break through, and, by force, justify their violation of them, are truly and properly rebels. For when men, by entering into society and civil government, have excluded force, and introduced laws for the preservation of property, peace, and unity amongst themselves, those who set up force again in opposition to the laws, do *rebellare*—that is, bring back again the state of war, and are properly rebels, which they who are in power, by the pretence they have to authority, the temptation of force they have in their hands, and the flattery of those about them being likeliest to do, the properest way to prevent the evil is to show them the danger and injustice of it who are under the greatest temptation to run into it. . . .

## Book I

### CHAPTER V

### OF ADAM'S TITLE TO SOVEREIGNTY BY THE SUBJECTION OF EVE

44. . . . [W]e find our author build[s] his monarchy of Adam on Gen. iii. 26: "And thy desire shall be to thy husband, and he shall rule over thee." "Here we have," says he, "the original grant of government," from whence he concludes, in the following part of the page "that the supreme power is settled in the fatherhood, and limited to one kind of government—that is to monarchy"; for let his premises be what they will, this is always the conclusion; let but "rule" in any text be but once named, and presently "absolute monarchy"

is by Divine right established. If anyone will but carefully read our author's own reasoning from these words, and consider, among other things, "the line and posterity of Adam," as he there brings them in, he will find some difficulty to make sense of what he says; but we will allow this at present to his peculiar way of writing, and consider the force of the text in hand. The words are the curse of God upon the woman for having been the first and forwardest in the disobedience; and if we will consider the occasion of what God says here to our first parents, that He was denouncing judgment and declaring his wrath against them both for their disobedience, we cannot suppose that this was the time wherein God was granting Adam prerogatives and privileges, investing him with dignity and authority. Elevating him to dominion and monarchy; for though as a helper in the temptation as well as a partner in the transgression, Eve was laid below him, and so he had accidentally a superiority over her for her greater punishment; yet he, too, had his share in the Fall as well as the sin, and was laid lower, as may be seen in the following verses; and it would be hard to imagine that God, in the same breath, should make him universal monarch over all mankind, and a day-labourer for his life. Turn him out of Paradise "to till the ground" (ver. 23), and at the same time advance him to a throne and all the privileges and ease of absolute power.

45. This was not a time when Adam could expect any favours, any grant of privileges from his offended Maker. If this be the "original grant of government," as our author tells us, and Adam was now made monarch, whatever Sir Robert [Filmer] would have him, it is plain God made him but a very poor monarch, such a one as our author himself would have counted it no great privilege to be. God sets him to work for his living, and seems rather to give him a spade into his hand to subdue the earth, than a sceptre to rule over its inhabitants. "In the sweat of thy face thou shalt eat thy bread," says God to him (ver. 19). This was unavoidable, may it perhaps be answered, because he was yet without subjects, and

had nobody to work for him; but afterwards, living as he did above 900 years, he might have people enough whom he might command to work for him. "No," says God, "not only whilst thou art without other help save thy wife, but as long as thou livest shalt thou live by thy labour." "In the sweat of thy face shalt thou eat thy bread, till thou return unto the ground, for out of it wast thou taken; for dust thou art, and unto dust shalt thou return" (ver. 19). It will perhaps be answered again in favour of our author, that these words are not spoken personally to Adam, but in him, as their representative to all mankind, this being a curse upon mankind because of the Fall.

46. God, I believe, speaks differently from men, because He speaks with more truth, more certainty; but when He vouchsafes to speak to men, I do not think He speaks differently from them in crossing the rules of language in use amongst them; this would not be to condescend to their capacities, when He humbles Himself to speak to them, but to lose His design in speaking what, thus spoken, they could not understand. And yet thus must we think of God, if the interpretations of Scripture necessary to maintain our author's doctrine must be received for good; for, by the ordinary rules of language, it will be very hard to understand what God says; if what He speaks here, in the singular number, to Adam, must be understood to be spoken to all mankind, and what He says in the plural number (Gen. i. 26 and 28), must be understood of Adam alone, exclusive of all others; and what He says to Noah and his sons jointly must be understood to be meant to Noah alone (Gen. ix.).

47. Further, it is to be noted, that these words here of Gen. iii. 16, which our author calls "the original grant of government," were not spoken to Adam, neither, indeed, was there any grant in them made to Adam, but a punishment laid upon Eve; and if we will take them as they were directed in particular to her, or in her, as a representative to all other women, they will at most concern the female sex only, and import no more but that subjection they should ordinarily be in to their husbands; but there is here no more law to oblige a woman to such a subjection, if the circumstances either of her condition or contract with her husband should exempt her from it, than there is that she should bring forth her children in sorrow and pain if there could be found a remedy for it, which is also part of the same curse upon her, for the whole verse runs thus: "Unto the woman He said, I will greatly multiply thy sorrow and thy conception; in sorrow thou shalt bring forth children, and thy desire shall be to the husband, and he shall rule over thee." It would, I think, have been a hard matter for anybody but our author to have found out a grant of "monarchical government to Adam" in these words, which were neither spoke to nor of him; neither will anyone, I suppose, by these words think the weaker sex, as by a law so subjected to the curse contained in them, that it is their duty not to endeavour to avoid it. And will anyone say that Eve, or any other woman, sinned if she were brought to bed without those multiplied pains God threatens her here with, or that either of our Queens, Mary or Elizabeth, had they married any of their subjects, had been by this text put into a political subjection to him, or that he thereby should have had "monarchical rule" over her? God in this text gives not, that I see, any authority to Adam over Eve, or men over their wives, but only foretells what should be the woman's lot, how by His Providence He would order it so that she should be subject to her husband, as we see that generally the laws of mankind and customs of nations have ordered it so, and there is, I grant, a foundation in Nature for it.

48. Thus when God says of Jacob and Esau that "the elder should serve the younger" (Gen. xxv. 23), nobody supposes that God hereby made Jacob Esau's sovereign, but foretold what should *de facto* come to pass.

But if these words here spoke to Eve must needs be understood as a law to bind her and all other women to subjection, it can be no other subjection than what every wife owes her husband, and then if this be the "original grant of government" and the "foundation of monarchical power," there will be as many monarchs as there are husbands. If therefore these words give any power to Adam, it can be only a conjugal power, not a political—the power that every husband hath to order the things of private concernment in his family, as proprietor of the goods and land there, and to have his will take place in all things of their common concernment before that of his wife; but not a political power of life and death over her, much less over anybody else. . . .

NOTE

1. "The public power of all society is above every soul contained in the same society, and the principal use of that power is to give laws unto all that are under it, which laws in such cases we must obey, unless there be reason showed which may necessarily enforce that the law of reason or of God doth enjoin the contrary."—Hooker. Eccl. Pol. lib. i. sect. 16.

# 23    Women and John Locke; Or, Who Owns the Apples in the Garden of Eden?

LORENNE M. G. CLARK

THE IDEA OF CREATING a society guaranteeing equality between the sexes has never been considered by most political theorists. They have either endorsed, or simply accepted, the assumption that there is a natural inequality of the sexes which ought to be preserved in civil society.[1] This same presupposition has excluded the family from the theorists' framework of what are thought to be distinctively *political* institutions. Despite the centrality of the family to human life, it has been consigned to the domain of purely natural phenomena. The related belief that women and children must be relegated for theoretical purposes to the family, to be safely ignored in a realm of brute nature, suffices to allow such theorists to exclude women from the ontology of politics.[2]

In looking at major theorists from this perspective, the task is not simply to show that they display sexist attitudes. The main purpose is to demonstrate that their theories rest on these assumptions and that they would be vastly different theories if these assumptions were not made. The point of such a demonstration is to establish that the theories which have been advanced on these foundations are not workable as blueprints for political institutions guaranteeing sexual equality. It remains to show how major political theorists demonstrate these assumptions, what use is made by them of these premises, either explicitly or implicitly, and what problems this causes in their theories, whether recognized or not. I wish to examine Locke from this point of view. To what extent does Locke illustrate the basic sexist assumptions which I have argued lie at the foundation of western political theory? The specific premises I take to be central to this argument are, first, that there is a "natural" inequality of the sexes and a "natural" superiority of the male; second, that reproduction is not a central fact of political life and is of no value in creating a significant life for man; and, third, that the family is not a political, but a "natural" institution which remains outside the political framework in an ahistorical state of nature.

In addition to these major assumptions, there are further minor, or derivative hypotheses, which require examination. Among these, and of particular relevance to Locke, are questions relating to inheritance and the ownership of property. How do the major premises function to justify ownership and inheritance of private property in order to preserve dominant sex and class position? Is ownership of the means and products of reproduction, as well as those of production, what is really needed to generate the kind of political society which Locke thinks is needed to secure "the peace, safety, and public good of the people" which is, he argues, the end of government?[3]

The first assumption, that there is an inequality of the sexes and that the male is superior, is both implicit and explicit in Locke. In *The First Treatise*, in attempting to refute Filmer's claim that Adam rules over Eve by dint of the law of God, Locke is at great pains to show that the source of the condition in which women are subjugated to men does not lie in law, but in nature:

> Farther it is to be noted, that these words here of 3 *Gen.* 16 which our A. calls the Original Grant of Government were not spoken to Adam, neither indeed was there any Grant in them made to Adam, but a Punishment laid upon Eve; and if we will take them as they were directed in particular to her, or in her, as their representative to all other Women, they will at most concern the Female Sex only, and import no more but that Subjection they should ordinarily be in to their Husbands: But there is here no more Law to oblige a Woman to such a Subjection, if the Circumstances either of her Condition or Contract with her Husband should exempt her from it, than there is, that she should bring forth her Children in Sorrow and Pain, if there could be found a Remedy for it, which is also a part of the same Curse upon her:[4]

Thus, the subjection in which most women are ordinarily found with respect to men is explicitly not the result of law, or any sort of arbitrary convention, not even that most Divine convention established by the will and authority of God. Rather it lies in the punishment laid on her, and on her alone, which consists in her being, as he says later in the same passage, "the weaker Sex," and forced to bring forth children in pain and sorrow. Women are, then, by nature weaker than men, and this weakness is itself a direct result of the unique capacities women have with respect to reproduction. The Curse of God laid on women consists in her being by nature disadvantaged, and the disad-

vantage is clearly considered to be her reproductive capacities. The fact that women and women alone can bear children is a natural disadvantage which leads to a natural inequality between the sexes. Despite the fact that Locke believes that the inequality of the sexes is contingent, grounded in natural differences between the sexes with respect to reproduction, this nonetheless establishes the superiority of the male:

> For though as a helper in the Temptation, as well as a Partner in the Transgression, Eve was laid below him, and so he had accidentally a Superiority over her. . . .[5]

But given that there is this natural inequality, the common condition of women is to be under the subjection of men. However, precisely because this is a natural inequality, it is one which can, on rare occasions, be overcome. Should she be of noble birth, or ample means, these qualities compensate for her natural disadvantages, and she can, by means of these qualities, escape the condition of subjugation to which she would otherwise be liable:

> And will anyone say, that Eve, or any other Woman sinn'd, if she were brought to Bed without those multiplied Pains God threatens her here with? Or that either of our Queens Mary or Elizabeth, had they Married any of their Subjects, had been by this Text put into a Political Subjection to him? Or that he thereby should have had Monarchical Rule over her? God, in this Text gives not, that I see, any Authority to Adam over Eve, or to Men over their Wives, but only foretells what should be Woman's Lot, how by his Providence he would order it so, that she should be subject to her husband, as we see that generally the laws of Mankind and customs of Nations have ordered it so; and there is, I grant, a Foundation in Nature for it.[6]

Locke explicitly here acknowledges that the subjection of women to men is codified in law and custom. But he finds its source in nature and is, by this means, able to argue that in some few instances, it is a natural liability which can be overcome.

Locke's objective in Chapter V of the *First Treatise* "Of Adam's Title to Sovereignty by the Subjection of Eve," is to show that, from the fact that God created a natural basis for inequality between the sexes, the superiority of the male, and the subjection of wife to husband, this does not establish any basis, natural or otherwise, for Absolute Sovereignty and the absolute duty of obedience Filmer alleges to exist between subjects and monarch. The most Genesis 1:28 and 3:16 establish says Locke, is, in the first, "the Subjection of the Inferior Ranks of Creatures to Mankind," and, in the other, "the Subjection that is due from a Wife to her Husband."[7] Thus he neither questions nor criticizes the alleged basis of the inequality and endorses the assumption that the natural difference between the sexes leads to the creation of an obligation on the part of a wife to be subjected to the will and authority of her husband: it is what is *due* from her to him.

In *The Second Treatise,* in "Of Paternal Power," he states that "though I have said above that all men by nature are equal, I cannot be supposed to understand all sorts of equality," he cites age, virtue, excellence of parts and merit, birth, alliance, and benefits, as differences in respect of which some men gain a precedence over others. He goes on to say that none of these differences in respect of which men are not in some sense equal, conflict with the way in which they are equal, namely, "in respect of jurisdiction or dominion one over another . . . that equal right that every man has to his natural freedom, without being subjected to the will or authority of any other man."[8] Thus, Locke does not deny that there are differences between men.[9] He argues instead that men are equal with respect to the right to autonomy *despite* these differences. However, as we have already seen, the allegedly "natural" differences between the sexes do justify the natural domination of women by men. His explicit statement on this issue in *The Second Treatise* is as follows:

> . . . it therefore being necessary that the last determination—i.e., the rule—should be somewhere, it naturally falls to the man's share, as the abler and the stronger.[10]

It *naturally* falls to the man's share. Here he stresses that it is man's natural superiority, by virtue of his being "abler and the stronger," which

gives rise to men's rightful rule over women, rather than tracing this to woman's natural disadvantage. We agree here with Elrington, who says that this implies that the right of the husband arises solely from superior power. There are more similarities between Locke and Hobbes than are sometimes assumed.[11]

Two things are immediately obvious from this. In *The First Treatise* Locke appeared to argue that it is simply as a consequence of women's natural disadvantage that men do, as a matter of fact, ordinarily rule over women, but in the end he concludes that wives have a duty to obey. Thus there is a curious asymmetry between the sexes with respect to the consequences which follow from the fact that there are differences, natural and otherwise, between one person and another. The presupposition of a fundamental right to autonomy overrides any differences which may exist between individual men. The natural differences between the sexes, on the other hand, do override any presupposition of an equal right to autonomy as between men and women. Here, and only here, a natural difference creates a justified domination of one person by another. However, the existence of clearly non-natural differences between one woman and another may sometimes override the presumption of female inferiority which explains and justifies the general subjugation of women by men. Thus, exceptional women may, because of the presence of social differences, overcome their natural disadvantage and so escape subjection. But the general rule is that the natural differences between men and women negative any presupposition to equality between the sexes with respect to autonomy, differences between individual men do not negative this presupposition, and differences between individual women may negative the presumption of inferiority and so create a right to autonomy in some cases. What seems abundantly clear, however, is that Locke believed that there was a natural inequality between the sexes, that men were superior, and that this superiority ordinarily gave them a right to the obedience of their wives. It also seems clear that he believed that the source of women's inferiority lay in her reproductive capacities, and that he regarded this as a natural rather than a conventional disadvantage, though it must be pointed out that it is somewhat difficult to say that this was all that Locke saw as the source and nature of women's inferior status since it is far from clear what her reproductive disadvantage has to do with the "greater strength" and being "abler" he attributes to man and which he uses to justify the authority of husband over wife in the *Second Treatise*.

How these assumptions affected the development of his theory can best be seen by considering how they shaped his assumptions about the family and about the relation of the family to other political institutions. Throughout both *Treatises* Locke assumes that the natural condition of women is to be in the family. The subjection of women by men is the subjection of Wife by Husband. He nowhere discusses the status of the single woman. Women are, for Locke, married women, and, hence, most women are under the subjection of men. And most women are married women, because it is woman's nature to reproduce children which she is incapable of providing for on her own.[12] When he discusses the role of women, he explicitly states that they were created as companions for men and that they are incapable of bearing and rearing children without the assistance of men at least until all of the children are, as he says, "out of a dependency for support." Thus, it is the natural fate of women to be married as a consequence of their reproductive capacities, and to be under the subjection of their husbands because they are dependent on him for support of their offspring. Locke thus assumes that the family, and the structure of authority within it, is a natural association created in the state of nature.

The problem for Locke was then to distinguish political authority from natural authority. Political authority must rest on consent, and, hence, must be distinguished and distinguishable from natural familial authority which rests on a natural superiority of the male over the female which is itself grounded in a natural difference between them with respect to their reproductive roles.

In discussing the beginning of political societies, Locke admits that historically most civil societies began under the government and administration of one man:

> . . . the government commonly began in the father, for the father, having by the law of nature the same power with every man else to punish as he thought fit any offenses against that law, might thereby punish his transgressing children even when they were men.[13]

This is an *admission* for Locke because, for other reasons which we know very well, he was out to attack the concept of patriarchal government, but nonetheless had to acknowledge the historical fact that most governments began as forms of paternal power and were, therefore, patriarchal governments. He did not want legitimate government to hang on the natural dominion man has in the family. The interesting and important point to be seen is that since he himself assumes that male dominion in the family is natural, he must show that paternal power is to be distinguished from political power in order to argue that the basis for legitimate government is consent. Since he assumed that in the state of nature men exercised a natural dominion over women, he could hardly argue against patriarchal concepts of government that even patriarchal dominion in the family is artificial and so cannot be used to justify patriarchal concepts of government. This would have been the most plausible argument to advance to effect that conclusion. But he did not use it, and that is just the point. So far as he is concerned, that position is a non-starter. He simply assumes that the family, and the division of power within it, is a natural and not a political creation. As will become apparent, what is even more important is that he *must* assume this in order to arrive at a theory of society which conforms to the principles he thinks it must.

In the state of nature, women are naturally disadvantaged, men are naturally superior, and the family arises as a natural institution based on these natural differences between the sexes.[14] Thus, everything he says about equality in the state of nature pertains only to men. It is men, and men only, who are naturally free from the dominion of one over another, though this is consistent with his belief that some women do manage to maintain some measure of control over their lives and their property.[15] The vast majority of women are already under the domination of individual men because they are "naturally" weaker and less able; they share the common natural disadvantage to which all women are subject, and have none of the compensating virtues which can be used to offset their natural liability and so place them in a position where they do not have to accept the will and authority of men in order to survive. Thus, Locke's hypothetical state of nature is as full of presumptions about the differential reproductive natures and relations of the sexes as it is about the differential productive natures and relations of men, which have been so often and so thoroughly dealt with by others.[16] It is simply seventeenth century England devoid of legitimate Lockean law and authority.

However, in his attempts to undermine the concept of patriarchal government Locke was forced to take a somewhat less conservative view of the relations between the sexes in the family than might otherwise have been the case. He also cites anthropological evidence which in fact challenges his unrecognized assumptions about sexual inequality in the state of nature. But of course he did not draw from these the conclusions he ought to have as to the conventional nature of existing familial relationships. His basic argument in Ch. IV, "Of Paternal Power," in *The Second Treatise,* is that no support for patriarchal government can be derived from the existence of paternal power in the family because the power in the family, which consists in the exercise of parental authority over children, is equally shared between father and mother. He argues that "paternal" power is really a misnomer, and should be replaced with "parental" power, because "paternal"

> . . . seems so to place the power of parents over their children wholly in the father, as if the mother had no share in it; whereas, if we consult reason or revelation, we shall find she has an equal title.[17]

He hardly mentions the dominion of husband over wife. He did not see that this was relevant so far as his attack on patriarchal government was concerned. All he wanted to establish was that no one man, by right independent of consent, could rule over another, not that no one man by right could rule over a woman. He assumed that men would continue to exercise dominion over women in the political as well as the familial sphere, and so there was no need to question the authority of husband over wife. But it was important to him to show that the father did not have absolute authority over his children. As he puts the case himself:

> . . . it will but very ill serve the turn of those men who contend so much for the absolute power and authority of the fatherhood, as they call it, that the mother should have any share in it; and it would have but ill supported the monarchy they contend for, when by the very name it appeared that the fundamental authority from whence they would derive their government of a single person only was not placed in one but two persons jointly.[18]

Thus, the family provides no justification for one-man rule in government because the authority over children devolves on two persons. The joint authority of parents is, however, a theme he relentlessly repeats, and in fact, he goes as far as he can in denigrating the authority over children which paternity legitimizes, in order to undermine as far as possible patriarchal concepts of what constitutes legitimate government:

> But what reason can hence advance this care of the parents due to their offspring into an absolute arbitrary dominion of the father, whose power reaches no farther than. . . . to give such strength and health to their bodies . . . as may best fit his children to be most useful to themselves and others . . . But in this power the mother, too, has her share with the father. Nay, this power so little belongs to the father by any peculiar right of nature, but only as he is guardian of his children, that when he quits his care of them he loses his power over them . . . so little power does the bare act of begetting give a man over his issue. . . .[19]

Mere fatherhood establishes nothing, says Locke. Authority, in this case, proceeds not from simple paternity but from the acceptance of responsibility. And so, of course he wants to say, in government. Notice, too, that he here wishes to construe the parental role as one of *guardianship,* which is certainly more applicable to civil than to natural relationships. In his enthusiasm to denaturalize politics, he verges on politicizing the family.

One could, in fact, push this somewhat further. While he has said elsewhere that the power of a husband over his wife is one form of power a man can have,[20] he wants to distinguish it both from the power a father has over his children, and the power a magistrate has over his subjects. Only the latter is *political* power. But more importantly for our point here, only the case of a father's power over his children presents us with a relationship which is in any way relevant to a consideration of the nature and limits of political power. The relationship between husband and wife, in which the husband is in the superior position, does not even have to be justified as does the power of a father over his children. That form of power simply comes about as a result of a natural inequality which, unlike that between parents and children, does not disappear through time and tutelage. This is a natural dominion of one sex over the other. Thus, the relationship between parents and children is more like the relationship between a legitimate sovereign and his subjects, in that it is a limited power in which the period of domination is grounded on natural inequalities which disappear over time. Of course, it is unlike legitimate sovereignty in that the latter never licenses an absolute authority since there are no natural inequalities of even a temporary sort between the persons so organized.

> But these two powers, political and paternal, are so perfectly distinct and separate, are built upon so different foundations, and given to so much different ends, that every subject that is a father has as much a paternal power over his children as the prince has over his, and every prince that has parents owes them as much filial duty and obedience as the meanest of his subjects do theirs, and cannot therefore contain any part or degree of that kind of dominion which a prince or magistrate has over his subjects.[21]

Thus, while Locke rejects "paternal" in favour of "parental," he is deliberately distinguishing "paternal" power from the power of husband over wife. While we may now have a better name for the relationship existing between father and children, we now have no name to refer to the relationship between husband and wife! It almost ceases to be a power relationship, since it is not seen as a species of power deserving a unique *nominatum.* In any case, both the power of a father over his children and political power are to be contrasted with the power of husband over wife, which, clearly, does not change. This is not, of course, an argument which Locke makes. But it is obviously what must lie behind his thinking or he would not have concentrated his attack on patriarchal government by an analysis of the parent role of a father *vis-a-vis* his children. He would not have construed patriarchal power to be exclusively parental power, rather than as involving as well the relation of husband and wife.

In his zeal to find arguments against patriarchal government his rudimentary anthropology almost gets him too far, however:

> And what will become of this paternal power in that part of the world where one woman has more than one husband at a time, or in those parts of America where, when the husband and wife part, which happens frequently, the children are all left to the mother, follow her, and are wholly under her care and provision?[22]

He does not go the whole way here and begin to question the assumed naturalness of monogamy and male dominance, but the implications are clear that he believes that there are some real "states of nature" in which even the dominion of male over female does not exist.

However, it must be said that he does at times seem to be aware that the dominion of husband over wife poses something of a problem for his arguments against patriarchal government. He does, for example, argue that marriage is a contractual relationship:

> Conjugal society is made by a voluntary compact between man and woman. . . .[23]

Thus, he is trying to make it as analogous to his view of legitimate government as is possible. Just as legitimate authority rests on the consent of the governed, so the authority of husband over wife is legitimized by her consent. And he allows that the power of a husband over a wife is not unlimited:

> . . . the power of the husband being so far from that of an absolute monarch that the wife has in many cases a liberty to separate from him where natural right or their contract allows it, whether that contract be made by themselves in the state of nature, or by the customs or laws of the country they live in; and the children upon such separation fall to the father's or mother's lot, as such contract does determine.[24]

He also stresses that it is the obligation of both parents to care for their offspring:

> God having made the parents instruments in his great design of continuing the race of mankind and the occasion of life to their children, as he has laid on them an obligation to nourish, preserve, and bring up their offspring. . . .[25]

He explains monogamy on the basis of the fact that infant human beings require more nurturing than the offspring of other animals:

> . . . the father, who is bound to take care for those he has begot, is under an obligation to continue in conjugal society with the same woman longer than other creatures whose young being able to subsist of themselves before the time of procreation returns again, the conjugal bond dissolves of itself and they are at liberty. . . .[26]

Thus, it is apparently a natural duty that a father should provide for those he has helped to create, and, hence, it could plausibly be maintained that it is a natural right of women to be assisted in the nurturing of the young they bear. But since he also believes that women, like the females of other carnivorous vivipores, are incapable of providing on their own for their offspring,[27] it is clear that they do not have much option but to get married if they desire to have children, or if they find they are going to have a child whether they desire it or not. It certainly did not occur to him that they

could avoid the problem of having yet another child before the others are "out of a dependency for support"[28] by simply refusing, by right, the conjugality of the marriage bed. His view is simply that it is women's lot to be "companions" for men who would otherwise be lonely.[29] But clearly it isn't loneliness that he thought would be the problem, however piously he may paper it over with talk about God's grand design for the continuity of the species and the innate perfection of man to care for himself.[30] He realized that, as an unavoidable consequence of men's appetite for more than dialogue, women would be with child.[31] At least he had the good grace to insist on the duty of a biological father to look after his own, but how he could construe this to be a voluntary compact, given his own strong beliefs about what it means for something to be truly consented to in the sense that it creates a binding obligation escapes me.

> It remains only to be considered whether promises extorted by force, without right, can be thought "consent," and how far they bind. To which I shall say they bind not at all, because whatsoever another gets from me by force I still retain the right of. . . . By the same reason, he that forced a promise from me ought presently to restore it; i.e., quit me of the obligations of it, or I may resume it myself; i.e., choose whether I will perform it. . . .

And:

> . . . for what compact can be made with a man that is not master of his own life? What condition can he perform? And if he be once allowed to be master of his own life, the despotical arbitrary power of his master ceases. He that is master of himself and his own life has a right, too, to the means of preserving it; so that, as soon as compact enters, slavery ceases. . . .[32]

The consent necessary to create a binding compact can be given only by those who are in control, who are *masters,* of their own lives. But what of women with child? Given the belief, false though it may be, that women cannot on their own provide for their offspring, how could he have believed them to be in a position to make the kind of contract which he himself believed to be necessary to create binding obligations? Such contracts, flowing from voluntary agreement, can be made only between equals, where both parties bargain from positions of equal strength. But how, in such circumstances, could women not be bargaining from a position of weakness? And if the promise of the mother is extracted under threat that unless she makes it, she will not have that required support for their offspring, regardless of the fact that it may be her natural right, then in what sense does this create a binding promise? It is surely the sort of thing which someone with even an elementary knowledge of contract theory would know to fall dangerously close, if not well within, the bounds of an unconscionable transaction.

However, leaving aside the question of how Locke thinks he can argue that marriage is in fact contractual given what he says about the elements necessary to create a binding agreement, it is to Locke's credit that he saw even the possibility of contractual marriage, which at least opens up the possibility of mutuality between husband and wife. In paragraph 83 of the *Second Treatise* he even goes so far as to suggest that the absolute authority of husband over wife is not in fact necessary to the chief end of marriage, namely, procreation, and, therefore, that conjugal society "might be varied and regulated by that Contract, which unites Man and Wife." Note, he does not say that it *ought* to be regulated by a contract which establishes a mutuality of authority, merely that it *might* be since this is not incompatible with the reproduction and rearing of children.[33]

Unfortunately, however, this possibility is an apparent credit to Locke only because he fails to mention that procreation is at most only one of the objectives of marriage, and while mutuality as between husband and wife may be compatible with this function, it is incompatible with the major function of marriage which is to provide the mechanism for the transfer of property across generations. However much Locke may have tried to make out that marriage is a voluntary contractual arrangement, which might even be varied to wrest

absolute authority from the hands of the husband, the husband had a power over his wife that she did not have over him. In the final analysis he is the ruler because he, and he alone, has exclusive ability to control and to dispose of property. This was certainly the case under the marriage "contracts" with which Locke was familiar and is, indeed, assumed throughout his own discussion. One of Locke's major objectives was to provide the theoretical basis for the absolute right of the male to pass his property to his rightful heirs. Clearly any variation in marriage contracts which moved toward any real substantive equality between husband and wife would have to include equal right to the disposition of familial property and this obviously is incompatible with Locke's objective of legitimizing exclusive male control of inheritable property.

Throughout the *Second Treatise* family property is always referred to as *his* property, even though for other purposes, he is at pains to show that the wife has a legitimate share in "his" property. *Vis-a-vis* strangers, in the technical sense of strangers to their alleged marriage contract, she has a right to a share of his property. Locke, in fact, makes a great deal of this, but the reason he does so is certainly not to ensure the equality of women either in or out of marriage. It is to ensure that no absolute monarch, tyrant, or victor in conquest or usurpation, could alienate the male's property from his legitimate heirs. Locke says anything, advances any argument he can lay his hands on, to establish the principle that a man's legitimate heirs have a right to inherit his property, regardless even of the father's transgressions. So concerned is Locke to ensure the certainty and legitimacy of inheritance that he will allow even a wife a rightful share in property, but only *as against strangers*. Locke is not concerned to ensure that either a wife or a man's children will inherit—that is, that they have a right to inherit which can be enforced against the husband/father. Whether or not they do inherit depends on the arbitrary will of the male. Locke's point is to ensure that no government can have the right to dispossess a man eternally of his rightful property. He is not at all concerned to lay the basis for inheritance rights of the wife and heirs against the husband/father, but rather to lay as firm a foundation as possible for the right of wives and heirs to inherit *as against strangers,* and the point of this is not simply to ensure that his dependents are taken care of, but to establish the integrity of the male right to absolute dominion over the use and future disposition of his private property.

In "Of Paternal Power" Locke clearly assumes the exclusive right of the male to dispose of familial property.[34] So far as is consistent with fulfilling his obligation to provide support for his offspring, his right to dispose of his property is unlimited:

> . . . a father may dispose of his own possessions as he pleases when his children are out of danger of perishing for want. . . .[35]

> . . . there is another power ordinary in the father whereby he has a tie on the obedience of his children; which, though it be common to him with other men, yet, the occasions of showing it almost constantly happening to fathers in their private families, and the instances of it elsewhere being rare and less taken notice of, it passes in the world for a part of paternal jurisdiction. And this is the power men generally have to bestow their estates on those who please them best; the possession of the father being the expectation and inheritance of the children, ordinarily in certain proportions according to the law and custom of each country, yet it is commonly in the father's power to bestow it with a more sparing or liberal hand, according as the behaviour of this or that child has comported with his will and humor.[36]

In the passage earlier cited in which he gives ultimate rule to husband over wife, by dint of his being naturally abler and stronger, he says that this does not give him dominion over what "by contract is her peculiar right," which sounds marvellously egalitarian, but what is more important is that it *does* extend to "the things of their common interest and *property*"[37] (emphasis mine). He makes it sound as if this is a limitation of male prerogative, when in fact it is just the reverse. By what earthly, or even heavenly, principles of fairness, should she be entitled, on dissolution of the marriage contract, only to what she brought with her

into it? and then only if she was smart enough to get it covered in the contract and he willing to accept the contract on those terms? Besides, as Locke well knew, the customs of the country he had in mind certainly did not allow women any control over the disposition of property, whether they owned it previously as *feme sole,* or acquired it after marriage. The situation up to 1882 and the passing of the first *Married Woman's Property Act* is well summed up by Megarry:

> . . . the wife had no power to dispose of her property *inter vivos,* and even with her husband's concurrence, had no power of disposition by will. The husband acting by himself, could dispose of an estate for his own lifetime, but no longer. . . . Leaseholds vested in the husband alone, and he could dispose of them in his lifetime without the concurrence of his wife. He could not, however, dispose of them by will, and on his death the wife's rights revived. . . . Pure personality vested in the husband absolutely and passed under any disposition by him whether *inter vivos* or by will, or on his intestacy.[38]

Thus, the husband certainly has the real power. One might well ask what woman in her right mind would marry unless she had to, given her dependent status once she did. The idea that they were in any way mistresses of their own destiny and so in a position to bargain from positions of equality is surely a fiction of the first order. At least Locke suggests that the husband has some sort of moral, natural, duty to provide for his dependents, which, presumably, he would have been willing to see incorporated into the property laws for which his civil society was needed, and this is something of an advance on the situation as it existed in England at the time, where, again to quote Megarry:

> From the Fourteenth century to 1939 there was in general no restriction upon a testator's power to dispose of property as he thought fit: for good reasons or bad, he might give all his property to a mistress or to charities and leave his family penniless.[39]

Even on intestacy of the male; i.e., the only legally possible testators, the wife had no rights of inheritance at all, except those minor ones of dower,[40]

. . . the issue were preferred to other relatives, the male issue being preferred to the female issue.[41]

But this is scant remedy for the clear injustices of the existing situation, and there is nothing in Locke to suggest that he thought his theory necessitated any sweeping changes, in this particular respect.

This is all the more paradoxical in view of the fact that Locke believed marriage to be as much a fact of life in the state of nature as in civil society. The moral obligation to honour one's parents exists, says Locke, whether the child lives still under "the law of nature or municipal law of their country."[42] But more importantly, reproduction has no, and ought not to have any, civil consequences. The law, says Locke, has no right to make laws respecting filial duty.[43] The husband/father rules in the family by dint of that "executive power of the law of nature which every free man naturally has,"[44] "by virtue of the executive power of the law of nature which, as a man, he had a right to."[45] Men are "the natural fathers of families."[46] And, the grouping of man and wife, which gave rise to parents and children, and even to master and servant, still, he says, "came short of political society."[47] Thus, all of this takes place in the state of nature, and must remain unchanged in civil society, despite Locke's suggestion that it might be arranged otherwise.

But how could it in fact be changed and still preserve the function the family had of ensuring inheritance under control of the husband/father? Locke says nothing whatsoever about the effects different marriage contracts would have on the distribution of familial property. In fact, he does not even acknowledge that this is in fact one, much less the primary, objective of marriage law. Until well into the eighteenth century, the chief function of marriage was the preservation of family property across generations, and the formality of a full marriage ceremony was, on the whole, reserved for the propertied classes. One's choice of a marriage partner was dictated by the demands of interest, not affection, and what held it together were considerations of property and lineage.[48] Property passed through blood lines and blood lines were determined by the father. Thus the authority of the father is essential in order to facilitate the regulation of property distribution within the framework Locke envisions.

As we have seen, Locke sees marriage as a natural association which occurs in the state of nature. But he says nothing whatsoever about how the authority of the husband *vis-a-vis* family property occurs in the state of nature, tracing the formation of the family as he does only in terms of its procreative function. Thus he provides no explicit argument as to why familial property is under the control of the husband/father but that it is so is certainly implicit throughout his argument. And though he appears to disavow that the inequality of marriage necessarily must continue in civil society, it is clear that it must if control of familial property is to remain under the control of the husband/father. Marriage is already assumed at the point at which civil society begins, and so also is patriarchal control of family property. It is highly significant that Locke discusses the possibility of marriage contracts based on mutuality only in relation to the rearing of children and says not a word about this in relation to the distribution of property. And the reason he did not is clear. Mutuality in marriage is not compatible with a system of property distribution accomplished through blood lines determined by the father. The exclusive male "right" to dispose of family property can be established and maintained only by non-mutuality in marriage relations at least in relation to property. And surely no one would be inclined to argue that there is true mutuality in the marriage contract unless it applies to the right to control and dispose of familial property as well as to authority over children. Indeed, what could equal authority over children amount to unless it entailed the equal right of mother and father to determine the inheritance of each of the children? Thus, for Locke, the inequality of property as between husband and wife is as firmly rooted in the state of nature and is as necessary within civil society as is the inequality of property between one man and another.

The inequality of power with respect to the control of property as between husband and wife is not a product of civil society and could not be changed in civil society without disrupting the "natural" method of property transfer accomplished by means of traditional marriage in which absolute authority over the disposition of property vested in the husband alone. And that this authority should continue is assumed throughout Locke's argument. The inequality in the distribution of property as between one man and another is, as we know, justified by reference to the greater industry and rationality of some men. It is for this reason that the resulting unequal distribution should be protected by means of the coercive resources of civil society. But what could possibly justify the inequality in control and disposition of familial property as between husband and wife? This is not even mentioned. And yet are not women as able to labour as men? Why ought not they to have a right to the products of their labour, and to that with which they have mixed their labour?

The question of the right of women to the products of their labour is mentioned only once. In "Of Conquest" Locke settles in to establish that no monarch has the right to alienate eternally a man's private property, even when that man has acted on the side of injustice:

> Let the conqueror have as much justice on his side as could be supposed, he has no right to seize more than the vanquished could forfeit; his life is at the victor's mercy, and his service and goods he may appropriate to make himself reparation; but he cannot take the goods of his wife and children; they, too, had a title to the goods he enjoyed, and their shares in the estate he possessed. . . . I am conquered; my life, it is true, as forfeit, is at mercy, but not my wife's and children's. They made not the war nor assisted in it. I could not forfeit their lives; they were not mine to forfeit. My wife had a share in my estate; that neither could I forfeit. And my children also, being born of me, had a right to be maintained out of my labor or substance. Here then is the case: the conqueror has a title to reparation for damages received, and the children have a title to their father's estate for their subsistence.[49]

He then goes on in the same passage to remark,

> For as to the wife's share, whether her own labour or compact gave her title to it, it is plain her husband could not forfeit what was hers.[50]

From this one can certainly conclude that woman's labour gives her title to possession. We have already seen that on dissolution of a marriage she can regain control of what she brings into the marriage by compact. But what is the relation of these things? Does she automatically retain control, by means of the marriage contract, over those things she has previously come to own by means of her labour? Does she have a claim to all things she gains by means of her labour during the marriage? If labour gives absolute title, why should it have to be further protected by means of an explicit contract? Most pressing of all, if she has absolute title through labour, by what principle does the husband gain control over her property *whether there is a contract or not*? And, why should not her labour during marriage give her equal title to control, whether *inter vivos* or by testament, over their joint holdings? Even if it can be argued that women, like men, are in the state of nature, at liberty to appropriate and come to own property, how is it that they come to lose it by marriage, and why is it that during marriage their right to the product of their labour is extinguished? None of these questions are, of course, discussed, much less answered by Locke. He simply assumes the *status quo* with respect to the property rights of married women and the dependent status for women that marriage creates. But what natural principles *could* possibly be advanced for this, since this is a situation which arises in the state of nature and must continue unchanged in civil society?

The answer, I suggest, is only too obvious. Because women are less able, and are weaker than men, they either do not appropriate, or, even if they do, have no claim to ownership. They are naturally inferior because [they are] weaker than men and are, therefore, naturally subject to their dominion. Even the arguments advanced for their rights *vis-a-vis* strangers are rights which *revive* when their husbands do something by which they forfeit some measure of their rights. Thus, the best light that can be put on things is that women's rights are dependent on men's rights. They do not have independent rights, and the reason for this is that they could not be regarded as independent persons with full property rights if the exclusive right of the male to dispose of property is to be maintained. They are not men and hence are not under the law of nature with respect to their equal right to be free of the dominion of any other person. That is assumed at the outset and is never challenged.

Nor is it to the point to argue in Locke's defence that it would be too much to expect him to challenge the existing *status quo* with respect to property and ownership within marriage. Locke was quite prepared to challenge the deepest principles of English land law, and, indeed, he did so.[51] But so far as the rights of women were concerned, he said not a word. He leaves them in the family, born in the state of nature and necessarily left unchanged in civil society, for even their rights as against strangers are grounded in the alleged natural law and principles applying to the state of nature. Thus he clearly accepted the premiss that there is a natural inequality of the sexes and that the male is by nature superior. He does not allow the reproductive function any place in political life; indeed, the facts of reproduction create no more rights or duties in civil society than exist in the state of nature with respect either to women or to children. Certainly no value is attached to it as even part of that which gives significance to a life for man. At best it is regarded as a natural inevitability which creates natural obligations for men, with respect both to support of their offspring and continued cohabitation with their wives.

There is, of course, an implicit significance for men in the conjugal relation which Locke regards as "natural." While he explains monogamy on the basis of the need for continued support of human offspring, and the natural obligation of human males to accept responsibility for the offspring they help to create, it is obvious that only monogamy ensures control over certainty of paternity. Only if one man does control one woman can he be sure that the offspring she brings forth

are equally his. This is deeply significant for Locke because of the value he attaches to private property and the absolute natural right a man has to pass his rightful property on to his legitimate heirs. While he did not want this natural right to account for the creation of government, since that would further serve the interests of patriarchal theories of government, that there was such a natural right is never questioned:

> All which are so many testimonies against paternal sovereignty, and plainly prove that it was not the natural right of the father descending to his heirs that made governments in the beginning, since it was impossible, upon that ground, there should have been so many little kingdoms. . . .[52]

If significance for man is achieved through embodying himself in property which can persist through time, this significance can be achieved only if he can also ensure that those to whom such property passes are also "his." Thus certainty of paternity is as important for a significant life for man as is control of the future disposition of private property.[53]

In regarding marriage as he does, Locke is clearly making the relation between men and women subservient to the needs of ensured certainty of ownership under male control. The whole point of the theory is to guarantee absolute male ownership of private property, determinable over time. The limited discussion he gives of marriage and of the relation between parents and children focuses only on the need for such relations because of the need for continuation of the species. It is a right to each other's bodies, about as materialistic as one can get. In discussing the relation of parents and children he stresses only the responsibilities the parental role imposes, its necessity in order to ensure that sons will grow up properly tutored, their reason sufficiently developed to enable them to take over, and to exercise responsibly, the incidents of ownership.

The interesting point to be seen in this is that Locke's view of marriage as essentially concerned to preserve lineage is precisely to articulate the function marriage had historically at least up to the eighteenth century. Thus Locke is, here as elsewhere, defending the *status quo:* he is endorsing a view of marriage which sees it primarily as a mechanism for regulating the distribution of property along blood lines determined by the father. But it is significant that he does not articulate this as its function, but holds instead that it is a necessary institution because of the need for continuation of the species. He never even hints that it isn't continuity of the *species* which is important but ensured continuity of *individual* male heirs capable of functioning as the determinate future individuals on whom property held by individual men may devolve. If one simply takes him at his word, and sees him as promulgating the view that marriage ought centrally to be concerned with the relations between husband and wife, and between parents and children, where the rearing of children ought to be the real focus and purpose of marriage, one could see him as paving the way for the "companionate" marriage which began to emerge all across Western Europe by about 1750.[54] But it is impossible to see in him the precursor of a more "liberal" attitude toward marriage and the relation of the sexes because he clearly endorsed the view that patriarchal control of family property ought to continue in civil society, and he consistently made the procreative responsibilities of marriage subservient to the needs of a system of individually held private property under the exclusive control of male "heads of households." It isn't just that he assumed that this method of property disposition would continue, which could perhaps be explained by his failure of imagination with respect to alternative methods of property transfer across generations. His theory had two major objectives, the legitimizing of inequality in the distribution of property as between one man and another (or, more accurately, as between one family and another), and the legitimizing of an exclusive male right to control and dispose of familial property. Thus, it isn't simply that he thought patriarchal control of family property was the only available mechanism for ensuring the determination of property over time, but that it was in fact the only possible mechanism for ensuring one of the theoretical objectives.

Thus marriage and parenthood are not, for Locke, intrinsic goods. They are simply instrumental goods necessary for ensured male ownership of property determinable over time. But even though according to Locke, nothing but bare obligation, mutual right, holds husband to wife, this can hardly be reckoned a bad bargain when one considers the benefits with respect to property that then accrue to him. He gets everything the wife owned when she came into it, unless she can get it expressly excluded by contract. But then the terms of the contract come into effect only if there is a dissolution of the marriage or indiscretion on the part of the husband, and he can claim her labour as his own during the time of the marriage. All that and companionship too. I conclude, therefore, that Locke's theory does display, unequivocally, those sexist assumptions which I am alleging lie at the heart of western political theory. What remains now is to show that the sexism cannot be expunged while leaving the theory defensible. What consequences follow if we take what he says about the state of nature and civil society and assume that his ontology included both males and females? First of all, there is no marriage in the state of nature and women retain control over that with which they have mixed their labour. Or, even if they do become parties to (unenforceable) marriage contracts, they retain control over whatever property they already have and will continue to have the right both to appropriate and to control the property of their future labour. Thus, men do not have exclusive right to the disposition of familial property. Children or anyone else will be able to inherit directly from the mother.

But the serious consequence for the theory is over the issue of control over the means and products of *reproduction,* of reproductive, rather than productive, labour. Who owns the children? If women are independently able to provide for themselves because they have the right to garner and control property, why should they care whose children they have, and why will it matter? And since children are the products of women's unique labour of reproduction, surely they alone are entitled to own them (assuming, of course, that anyone should). What reason will women have to ensure any particular man that the child they bear is his as well as theirs? And if anything does hang on it, how will the men be able to ensure that the child she says is theirs is theirs? And without the certainty of paternity, what about the certainty of inheritance? In the final analysis, what point is there to a theory whose sole object is to ensure the individual right of men to appropriate, own, and control the future disposition of property if they cannot be sure of the paternity of their potential inheritors? The theory which has this objective is inherently sexist because the chief end of it can be achieved only by keeping women in an inferior and dependent position in order to ensure certainty of paternity, and, hence, certainty of inheritance. Exclusively male control of the means and products of productive labour requires control of the means and products of reproductive labour. Thus, in so far as the peace, safety, and public good of the people consists in protecting the private property of individual men, then ownership of the means and products of reproduction is as necessary for this end as is protected ownership of the means and products of productive labour.

Locke appears to argue that because most women will be in need of support as a result of their biological liability with respect to reproduction, most women will therefore be married, and, hence, subject to the will and authority of their husbands. The real argument, however, is that women's unique capacities with respect to reproduction *must be transformed into economic and social disadvantages* in order to ensure that they will be forced into a position of dependence on men. Thus, a system of private property owned and controlled by males necessitates transforming a mere biological difference into an economic and social disadvantage in order to ensure the continuation of that system. Locke's theory is fundamentally sexist because it must treat a biological, "natural," difference between the sexes as a source of "natural" inequality which licenses enshrining it as an economic and social disadvantage. Within Locke's theory women must *necessarily* be regarded as naturally disadvantaged. For unless they are so placed, they need not be dependent on men. And if they are not dependent on men, men

would be unable to be sole owners of private property and would have no determinable heirs on whom to devolve the accumulated fruits of their labours. Thus, the cornerstone of Locke's theory is the assumed natural disadvantage of women, and the ultimate objection to his theory is that it must convert a biological difference between the sexes into a socioeconomic liability. There is absolutely no reason why the biological difference between the sexes with respect to reproduction need lead to an inferior and dependent status for women. Indeed, this is acknowledged by Locke himself in allowing that women of means are not subject to the will and authority of their husbands. The difference between the sexes with respect to their role in relation to reproduction is no more a "natural" disadvantage than is any other difference between persons. That it is a disadvantage is a result of convention and not nature. Thus, in arguing against its being the product of law or convention, Locke's theory is, in the end, far more objectionable than that of Filmer, for Locke must insist on the natural inferiority of women due to their naturally disadvantaged position with respect to reproduction, while it is quite clear that that disadvantaged position can be brought about only by denying women access to the ownership and control of private property and thereby gaining the means to ensure their own survival and that of any children they might bear.

That the female role in relation to reproduction is a socioeconomic disadvantage is obvious. But that it is a purely social disadvantage, a liability created not by "nature" but by convention, is nowhere acknowledged by Locke, and indeed must be denied by him in order to generate the society he believes to be the only justifiable one. Since he says over and over again that the chief end of government is the protecting of private property, and since it is assumed throughout that ownership and control of that property is in the hands of individual men, the conclusion I have advanced is unavoidable. To assume that women as well as men, whether married or single, could own and control property independently of men would destroy the allegedly natural domination of husband over wife and would destroy the necessity of a protected right to property disposition since it would lead to uncertainty of paternity. Thus, women's reproductive capacity must be embedded within a system of conventions whereby it creates an economic dependence, and that can be accomplished only by denying women rights to ownership and control of property as a consequence of their reproductive function. Locke's argument is basically very simple. The role of women is to bear men's children; the price of bearing children is loss of autonomy with respect to the acquisition, ownership, and control of property. Thus, women who bear children are and must be dependent on men for their survival and for the survival of their offspring. But as is clear, there is absolutely no reason why reproduction should negate rights of ownership, indeed no reason why it should not generate such rights. What is just as clear, however, is that it must necessarily negate any such rights if the system is to be maintained in which men alone have the ability to accumulate forms of private property other than women and children. If Adam does not own Eve, how can he be sure who his descendants are, and, hence, on whom his apples ought properly to devolve? And if Eve owns her own apples, why should she obey Adam?

NOTES

1. See my "Rights of Women—Politics and Law: The Theory and Practice of the Ideology of Male Supremacy," in *Contemporary Issues in Political Philosophy*, J. King-Farlow and W. Shea, eds., Neal Watson Academic Publications, New York, 1976.

2. This is to say that, in so far as women are exclusively relegated to the family, in so far as their basic and primary function is regarded as reproductive rather than productive, women are not members of political society. In so far as they are producers rather than reproducers, they do gain visibility within the framework assumed by traditional political theory. This point is elaborated *ibid*.

3. John Locke, *The Second Treatise of Government*, Liberal Arts Press, New York, 1952, T. P. Peardon, ed, p. 73. All further references to this work are to this edition. References to *The First Treatise of Government* are to *Two Treatises of Government*, Mentor Books, 1963, P. Laslett ed. Though much has been written about Locke's influence on the founding fathers of the American Constitution, it is interesting to note how close this phrasing and sentiment is to the feelings expressed in

the famous phrase of the major document determining Canada's constitutional future, the preamble to Section 91 of the British North America Act, in which the powers and ends of the Federal Government are said to be the "peace, order, and good government" of the nation.

4. *The First Treatise, op. cit.*, p. 209.

5. *Ibid.*, p. 208.

6. *Ibid.*, pp. 209–210.

7. *Ibid.*, p. 212, and see also p. 211: ". . . this Text gave not Adam that Absolute *Monarchical Power* our A. Supposes, . . . but the Subjection of Eve to Adam, a Wife to her Husband."

8. *The Second Treatise, op. cit.*, p. 31.

9. He is singularly silent, however, on the issue of whether these are "natural" differences. Given the things he cites, it hardly seems possible to construe all of them as in any way "natural." Thus, the differences between individual women, which can compensate for their "natural" disadvantage, are likewise social and not natural.

10. *The Second Treatise, op. cit.*, p. 46.

11. See Hobbes, *Leviathan*, Ch. 20, and Laslett's footnote to p. 364, *Two Treatises of Government, op. cit.*

12. *Ibid.*, p. 45.

13. *Ibid.*, p. 59.

14. If anything lies at the heart of traditional political theory's inability to devise a theory which does guarantee sexual equality it is the assumption that women's unique capacities with respect to reproduction are natural, rather than social or conventional, disadvantages. Reproduction is consistently regarded as a natural *liability*. The point of the present paper is to show the centrality and necessity of this assumption within Locke's theoretical perspective.

15. I am much indebted to Professor John King-Farlow for many helpful comments he made on an earlier draft of this paper, particularly with respect to the conditions under which women's "natural" inferiority may be overcome.

16. Most notably by Professor C. B. MacPherson in *The Political Theory of Possessive Individualism*, Clarendon Press, Oxford, 1962. I am in complete agreement with MacPherson's view of what Locke was about and my own work has been greatly influenced by his views. Like MacPherson, I see Locke as beginning from certain assumptions, which he designates "natural," which he then uses to justify gross inequality, when the reality of the case is that he must arrange social affairs to create the allegedly "natural" state of affairs which is in fact necessary to bring about the state of inequality which he considers desirable.

17. *The Second Treatise, op. cit.*, p. 30.

18. *Ibid.*, p. 31.

19. *Ibid.*, p. 36.

20. *Ibid.*, pp. 3–4.

21. *Ibid.*, p. 40.
22. *Ibid.*, p. 36.
23. *Ibid.*, p. 44.
24. *Ibid.*, p. 46.
25. *Ibid.*, p. 37.
26. *Ibid.*, p. 45.
27. *Ibid.*
28. *Ibid.*
29. *Ibid.*, p. 44.
30. *Ibid.*, p. 32.
31. I do not mean to suggest here that only males have sexual desires, or that it is a regrettable that they do. I mean to point out only that Locke did not acknowledge that men had any such desires.
32. *The Second Treatise, op. cit.*, pp. 106 and 98.
33. *Ibid.*, p. 47.
34. *Ibid.*, pp. 33–34.
35. *Ibid.*, p. 37.
36. *Ibid.*, p. 41.
37. *Ibid.*, p. 46.
38. Megarry, R. E., *A Manual of the Law of Real Property*, 2nd Edition, London, Stevens & Sons, Ltd., 1955, p. 538.
39. *Ibid.*, p. 291.
40. It is interesting that the dower rights of a widow entitled her to a life-estate in one-third of her husband's estate, whereas the courtesy rights of the widower entitled him to a life-estate in the whole of the real property of his deceased wife. Women in England were worse off than black men in America. While black men were declared to be 3⁄5 of a white man, English women were clearly only 1⁄3 of an Englishman.
41. Megarry, *op. cit.*, p. 316.
42. *The Second Treatise, op. cit.*, p. 37.
43. *Ibid.*, p. 40.
44. *Ibid.*, p. 42.
45. *Ibid.*, p. 43.

46. *Ibid.*
47. *Ibid.*, p. 44.
48. Shorter, E. *The Making of the Modern Family*, Basic Books, New York, 1975, Chs. Two and Six particularly.
49. *The Second Treatise, op. cit.*, p. 104.
50. *Ibid.*
51. The basis of English land law from the Norman conquest on was that all land was owned by the Crown, and was held by individuals only on sufferance. By the 17th century, this was, of course, being eroded. For all practical purposes, land was owned by individuals, in the sense that it was individuals who had exclusive right to the disposition of property they held, at least under some forms of holding. But the legal principle continued, and, indeed, continues to the present. Legally speaking, all land is held by the Crown. Locke attacked that fundamental conception of the basis of English land law at its very root in arguing that the land was given by God to all men in common. He is thus attempting to provide an alternative basis of individual rights of ownership, and to trace rights of ownership from God rather than from the Monarch. No doubt it was his strong desire to wrest rights with respect to land away from the monarchy which lies at the heart of his strong distaste for monarchy.
52. *The Second Treatise, op. cit.*, p. 66.
53. The idea that the certainty of paternity and the need for continuity through time are basic issues motivating the direction of western political theory is discussed and developed by Mary O'Brien in "The Politics of Impotence" in *Contemporary Issues in Political Philosophy, op. cit.* The issue of the relation between control of the means and products of production and control of the means and products of reproduction is discussed further in my paper "Politics and Law," *op. cit.*
54. Shorter, *op. cit.*, Chs. Four, Five, and Six.

# 24    We Must Be United

TECUMSEH

BROTHERS—We all belong to one family; we are all children of the Great Spirit; we walk in the same path; slake our thirst at the same spring; and now affairs of the greatest concern lead us to smoke the pipe around the same council fire!

Brothers—We are friends; we must assist each

other to bear our burdens. The blood of many of our fathers and brothers has run like water on the ground, to satisfy the avarice of the white men. We, ourselves are threatened with a great evil; nothing will pacify them but the destruction of all the red men.

Brothers—When the white men first set foot on our grounds, they were hungry; they had no place on which to spread their blankets, or to kindle their fires. They were feeble; they could do nothing for themselves. Our fathers commiserated their distress, and shared freely with them whatever the Great Spirit had given his red children. They gave them food when hungry, medicine when sick, spread skins for them to sleep on, and gave them grounds, that they might hunt and raise corn.

Brothers—The white people are like poisonous serpents: when chilled, they are feeble, and harmless, but invigorate them with warmth, and they sting their benefactors to death.

The white people came among us feeble; and now we have made them strong, they wish to kill us, or drive us back, as they would wolves and panthers.

Brothers—The white men are not friends to the Indians: at first, they only asked for land sufficient for a wigwam; now, nothing will satisfy them but the whole of our hunting grounds, from the rising to the setting sun.

Brothers—The white men want more than our hunting grounds; they wish to kill our warriors; they would even kill our old men, women, and little ones.

Brothers—Many winters ago, there was no land; the sun did not rise and set: all was darkness. The Great Spirit made all things. He gave the white people a home beyond the great waters. He supplied these grounds with game, and gave them to his red children; and he gave them strength and courage to defend them.

Brothers—My people wish for peace; the red men all wish for peace; but where the white people are, there is no peace for them, except it be on the bosom of our mother.

Brothers—The white men despise and cheat the Indians; they abuse and insult them; they do not think the red men sufficiently good to live.

The red men have borne many and great injuries; they ought to suffer them no longer. My people will not; they are determined on vengeance; they have taken up the tomahawk; they will make it fat with blood; they will drink the blood of the white people.

Brothers—My people are brave and numerous; but the white people are too strong for them alone. I wish you to take up the tomahawk with them. If we all unite, we will cause the rivers to stain the great waters with their blood.

Brothers—If you do not unite with us, they will first destroy us, and then you will fall an easy prey to them. They have destroyed many nations of red men because they were not united, because they were not friends to each other.

Brothers—The white people send runners amongst us; they wish to make us enemies, that they may sweep over and desolate our hunting grounds, like devastating winds, or rushing waters.

Brothers—Our Great Father over the great waters [the king of England] is angry with the white people, our enemies. He will send his brave warriors against them; he will send us rifles, and whatever else we want—he is our friend, and we are his children.

Brothers—Who are the white people that we should fear them? They cannot run fast, and are good marks to shoot at: they are only men; our fathers have killed many of them; we are not squaws, and we will stain the earth red with their blood.

Brothers—The Great Spirit is angry with our enemies; he speaks in thunder, and the earth swallows up villages, and drinks up the Mississippi. The great waters will cover their lowlands; their corn cannot grow; and the Great Spirit will sweep those who escape to the hills from the earth with his terrible breath.

Brothers—We must be united; we must smoke the same pipe; we must fight each other's battles; and more than all, we must love the Great Spirit; he is for us; he will destroy our enemies, and make his red children happy.

## Recommended Readings

TEXTS

Ashcraft, Richard. *Revolutionary Politics and Locke's Two Treatises of Government.* Princeton: Princeton University Press, 1986.

Dunn, John. *The Political Thought of John Locke.* Cambridge: Cambridge University Press, 1969.

Gough, J. W. *John Locke's Political Philosophy.* 2nd ed. Oxford: Clarendon Press, 1973.

Macpherson, C. B. *The Political Theory of Possessive Individualism.* Oxford: Oxford University Press, 1962.

Schochet, Gordon, ed. *Life, Liberty and Property: Essays on Locke's Political Ideas.* Belmont, CA: Wadsworth, 1971.

Simmons, John. *The Lockean Theory of Rights.* Princeton: Princeton University Press, 1992.

Tuck, Richard. *Natural Rights Theories.* Cambridge: Cambridge University Press, 1979.


FEMINIST PERSPECTIVE

Butler, Melissa. "Early Liberal Roots of Feminism: John Locke and the Attack on Patriarchy." *American Political Science Review* 72 (1978).

Squadrito, Kathy. "Locke on the Equality of the Sexes." *Journal of Social Philosphy* 10 (1979): 6–11.


MULTICULTURAL PERSPECTIVE

Dockstader, Frederick. *Great North American Indians: Profiles in Life and Leadership.* New York: Van Nostrand Reinhold, 1977.

Eckert, Allan. *A Sorrow in Our Heart: The Life of Tecumseh.* New York: Bantam Books, 1992.

# VII

# *Rousseau*

## Introduction

J EAN-JACQUES ROUSSEAU WAS BORN IN GENEVA IN 1712. His mother died a week after his birth. His father, who combined the professions of watchmaker and dancing master, left him when he was ten to be brought up by an aunt. He was educated at home. At thirteen, he was apprenticed to an engraver who often beat him; he fled from Geneva to Savoy when he was sixteen. Having no means of subsistence, he went to a Catholic priest and represented himself as a Protestant wishing to be converted. The formal conversion took place in Turin, at an institution for catechumens. As a convert to Catholicism, Rousseau was given twenty francs. Later, in his *Confessions* he represented his motives as wholly mercenary: "I could not dissemble from myself that this holy deed I was about to do was at bottom the act of a bandit."

Returning to Savoy, Rousseau was befriended by Madame de Warens, a convert from Protestantism like himself, with whom he lived as a guest and later as a lover. De Warens also had another lover, her handyman, and all lived together harmoniously. When the handyman died, Rousseau said he felt grief but then consoled himself with the thought, "Well, at any rate I shall get his clothes."

In 1745, Rousseau took up with Therese Lelasseur, who was a servant at the boardinghouse where he was staying in Paris. He lived with her for the rest of his life (not to the exclusion of other affairs). They had five children, each of which he took to the foundling hospital. Twenty-five years later, near the end of his life, he married her.

In 1749, Rousseau entered an essay contest sponsored by the Academy of Dijon on the question: Have the arts and sciences conferred benefits on humankind? Rousseau maintained the negative and won the prize. The ideas of this essay were developed in *Discourse on Inequality,* in which Rousseau argued that humans are inherently good but have been made bad by society. Rousseau sent this essay to Voltaire, but it did not meet with his approval. Later, the two quarreled publicly over the significance of the earthquake of Lisbon that killed 30,000 in 1755. Reflecting on this earthquake, Voltaire wrote a poem throwing doubt on the existence of a provident God. Rousseau, in contrast, saw no reason to make such a fuss about the earthquake, regarding it as a good thing that a certain number of people should get killed now and then.

Rousseau's publication of *Emile* and *The Social Contract* in 1762 met with a storm of official condemnation, mostly for a chapter in *Emile* on natural religion. Rousseau was obliged to flee Paris. Geneva would not have him. Finally, Frederick the Great allowed him to enter Prussia, but after three years the persecution of local officials forced him to flee. He went to England at the invitation of David Hume. At first all went well, but by this time Rousseau had come to suffer from a persecution mania, and he suspected Hume of plotting against his life. So he fled to Paris, where he spent his last years, dying in poverty in 1778.

In *The Social Contract,* Rousseau begins with the observation that people are born free, yet everywhere they are found in chains. But rather than removing all the chains, Rousseau proposes to justify the existence of chains—of a certain sort. According to Rousseau, the sort of chains that are justified make people as free as they would be in a state of nature. In such a society, people's moral freedom (obedience to the general will) and their civil liberty (freedom to do what the general will does not forbid) must be greater than their natural freedom (freedom they would have to do whatever they want in a state of nature).

According to Rousseau, everyone has two wills: a particular will and a general will. While one's particular will may or may not conflict with one's general will, one's general will always regards the common interest. If one fails to obey one's general will, Rousseau claims that one can be forced to do so, because that would only entail forcing one to be free. And who could object to being free? Nevertheless, a main problem with Rousseau's social contract theory is that it is difficult to know what one's general will is—that is, it is difficult to know what is truly for the common interest.

The selection from *Emile* is taken from the chapter on the education of Sophy, the ideal woman. According to Rousseau, women are intended by their nature to serve as helpmates for men. To achieve this goal, they must realize their two natural functions: to attract men and to control or restrain men's passions—to be seductive, arousing, and flirtatious (a sex object) and at the same time controlled, chaste, modest, and virtuous (not a sex object). Or as Susan Okin has aptly put it, they must combine the traits of a concubine and a nun.[1] In general, Rousseau sees women as having different traits and virtues from men. Women are weak and passive, modest, retiring, controlled by what people think, coquettish, docile, good at practical thinking, willing to suffer wrongs without complaint, and obedient. By contrast, men are strong and active, not controlled by what people think, and good at abstract thinking.

In *A Vindication of the Rights of Woman,* published in 1792, Mary Wollstonecraft responds directly to Rousseau, arguing that the same virtues and desirable traits should be open to women and men. She argues that there is no good reason why women and men should not be judged by the same standard of virtue. Many of the differences that do exist between the sexes, she argues, are not natural but acquired, given our radically different way of bringing up boys and girls. To the question, Why have women throughout human history submitted themselves to (inferior) men as their masters, Wollstonecraft responds with a question, Why have men submitted themselves to (inferior) other men who happen to be their masters?

---

1 Susan Okin, *Women in Western Political Thought* (Princeton: Princeton University Press, 1979).

In "Perversions of Justice: A Native-American Examination of the Doctrine of U.S. Rights to Occupancy in North America," Ward Churchill argues that the United States does not now possess, nor has it ever possessed, a legitimate right to occupancy in at least half the territory it claims as its own on this continent. He argues that the Supreme Court through the Marshall Doctrine subverted international law in order to gain control of Native American lands. He notes that the U.S. policies of extermination and assimilation of Native American populations would have succeeded, except for the fact that the ostensibly useless land to which Native Americans were consigned ironically turned out to be some of the most mineral-rich land anywhere. Even so, given the way the Bureau of Indian Affairs manages this land, Churchill points out, little of this wealth actually benefits Native Americans. By U.S. figures, Native Americans have by far the lowest annual and lifetime per-capita income of any group in the United States.

Churchill draws analogies between the U.S. expansion over the North American continent and European colonial empires, the territorial ambitions of the Axis powers (Hitler explicitly anchored his concept of "politics of living space" on the United States' treatment of American Indians), and Iraq's invasion and occupation of Kuwait. He claims that Iraq had a far better claim to Kuwait (its nineteenth province, separated from it by the British after World War I) than the U.S. government has to virtually any part of North America.

Suppose we apply Rousseau's social contract theory to relations between the U.S. government and Native Americans. Would Rousseau's theory support Churchill's contention that the U.S. government has no legitimate claim to at least half the territory it claims as its own on this continent? If so, what would this show, if anything, about the validity of Rousseau's theory?

# 25    A Discourse on the Origin and Foundation of the Inequality of Mankind

JEAN-JACQUES ROUSSEAU

## The First Part: Man in a State of Nature

. . . IT APPEARS, AT FIRST VIEW, that men in a state of nature, having no moral relations or determinate obligations one with another, could not be either good or bad, virtuous or vicious; unless we take these terms in a physical sense, and call, in an individual, those qualities vices which may be injurious to his preservation, and those virtues which contribute to it; in which case, he would have to be accounted most virtuous, who put least

check on the pure impulses of nature. But without deviating from the ordinary sense of the words, it will be proper to suspend the judgment we might be led to form on such a state, and be on our guard against our prejudices, till we have weighed the matter in the scales of impartiality, and seen whether virtues or vices preponderate among civilized men: and whether their virtues do them more good than their vices do harm; till we have discovered whether the progress of the sciences sufficiently indemnifies them for the mischiefs they do one another, in proportion as they are better informed of the good they ought to do; or whether they would not be, on the whole, in a much happier condition if they had nothing to fear or to hope from anyone, than as they are, subjected to universal dependence, and obliged to take everything from those who engage to give them nothing in return.

Above all, let us not conclude, with Hobbes, that because man has no idea of goodness, he must be naturally wicked; that he is vicious because he does not know virtue; that he always refuses to do his fellow-creatures services which he does not think they have a right to demand; or that by virtue of the right he justly claims to all he needs, he foolishly imagines himself the sole proprietor of the whole universe. Hobbes had seen clearly the defects of all the modern definitions of natural right: but the consequences which he deduces from his own show that he understands it in an equally false sense. In reasoning on the principles he lays down, he ought to have said that the state of nature, being that in which the care for our own preservation is the least prejudicial to that of others, was consequently the best calculated to promote peace, and the most suitable for mankind. He does say the exact opposite, in consequence of having improperly admitted, as a part of savage man's care for self-preservation, the gratification of a multitude of passions which are the work of society, and have made laws necessary. A bad man, he says, is a robust child. But it remains to be proved whether man in a state of nature is this robust child: and, should we grant that he is, what would he infer? Why truly, that if this man, when robust and strong, were dependent on others as he is when feeble, there is no extravagance he would not be guilty of; that he would beat his mother when she was too slow in giving him her breast; that he would strangle one of his younger brothers, if he should be troublesome to him, or bit the leg of another, if he put him to any inconvenience. But that man in the state of nature is both strong and dependent involves two contrary suppositions. Man is weak when he is dependent, and is his own master before he comes to be strong. Hobbes did not reflect that the same

cause, which prevents a savage from making use of his reason, as our jurists hold, prevents him also from abusing his faculties, as Hobbes himself allows: so that it may be justly said that savages are not bad merely because they do not know what it is to be good: for it is neither the development of the understanding nor the restraint of law that hinders them from doing ill; but the peacefulness of their passions, and their ignorance of vice. . . .

There is another principle which has escaped Hobbes; which, having been bestowed on mankind, to moderate, on certain occasions, the impetuosity of *amour-propre*, or, before its birth, the desire of self-preservation, tempers the ardour with which he pursues his own welfare, by an innate repugnance at seeing a fellow-creature suffer. I think I need not fear contradiction in holding man to be possessed of the only natural virtue, which could not be denied him by the most violent detractor of human virtue. I am speaking of compassion, which is a disposition suitable to creatures so weak and subject to so many evils as we certainly are: by so much the more universal and useful to mankind, as it comes before any kind of reflection; and at the same time so natural, that the very brutes themselves sometimes give evident proofs of it. Not to mention the tenderness of mothers for their offspring and the perils they encounter to save them from danger, it is well known that horses show a reluctance to trample on living bodies. One animal never passes by the dead body of another of its species without disquiet: some even give their fellows a sort of burial; while the mournful lowings of the cattle when they enter the slaughterhouse show the impressions made on them by the horrible spectacle which meets them. We find, with pleasure, the author of *The Fable of the Bees* obliged to own that man is a compassionate and sensible being, and laying aside his cold subtlety of style, in the example he gives, to present us with the pathetic description of a man who, from a place of confinement, is compelled to behold a wild beast tear a child from the arms of its mother, grinding its tender limbs with its murderous teeth, and tearing its palpitating entrails with its claws. What horrid agitation must not the eye-witness of such a scene experience, although he would not be personally concerned! What anguish would he not suffer at not being able to give any assistance to the fainting mother and the dying infant!

Such is the pure emotion of nature, prior to all kinds of reflection! Such is the force of natural compassion, which the greatest depravity of morals has as yet hardly been able to destroy! for we daily find at our theatres men affected, nay, shedding tears at the sufferings of a wretch who, were he in the tyrant's place, would probably even add to the torments of his enemies; like the bloodthirsty Sulla, who was so sensitive to ills he had not caused, or that Alexander of Pheros who did not dare to go and see any tragedy acted, for fear of being seen weeping with Andromache and Priam, though he could listen without emotion to the cries of all the citizens who were daily strangled at his command. . . . Mandeville well knew that, in spite of all their morality, men would have never been better than monsters, had not nature bestowed on them a sense of compassion, to aid their reason: but he did not see that from this quality alone flow all those social virtues, of which he denied man the possession. But what is generosity, clemency, or humanity but compassion applied to the weak, to the guilty, or to mankind in general? Even benevolence and friendship are, if we judge rightly, only the effects of compassion, constantly set upon a particular object: for how is it different to wish that another person may not suffer pain and uneasiness and to wish him happy? Were it even true that pity is no more than a feeling, which puts us in the place of the sufferer, a feeling obscure yet lively in a savage, developed yet feeble in civilized man; this truth would have no other consequence than to confirm my argument. Compassion must, in fact, be the stronger, the more the animal beholding any kind of distress identifies himself with the animal that suffers. Now, it is plain that such identification must have been much more perfect in a state of nature than it is in a state of reason. It is reason that engenders *amour-propre,* and reflection that confirms it: it is reason which turns man's mind back upon itself,

and divides him from everything that could disturb or afflict him. It is philosophy that isolates him, and bids him say, at sight of the misfortunes of others: "Perish if you will, I am secure." Nothing but such general evils as threaten the whole community can disturb the tranquil sleep of the philosopher, or tear him from his bed. A murder may with impunity be committed under his window; he has only to put his hands to his ears and argue a little with himself, to prevent nature, which is shocked within him, from identifying itself with the unfortunate sufferer. Uncivilized man has not this admirable talent; and for want of reason and wisdom, is always foolishly ready to obey the first promptings of humanity. It is the populace that flocks together at riots and street brawls, while the wise man prudently makes off. It is the mob and the market-women, who part the combatants, and stop decent people from cutting one another's throats.

It is then certain that compassion is a natural feeling, which, by moderating the activity of love of self in each individual, contributes to the preservation of the whole species. It is this compassion that hurries us without reflection to the relief of those who are in distress: it is this which in a state of nature supplies the place of laws, morals, and virtues, with the advantage that none are tempted to disobey its gentle voice: it is this which will always prevent a sturdy savage from robbing a weak child or a feeble old man of the sustenance they may have with pain and difficulty acquired, if he sees a possibility of providing for himself by other means: it is this which, instead of inculcating that sublime maxim of rational justice, *Do to others as you would have them do unto you,* inspires all men with that other maxim of natural goodness, much less perfect indeed, but perhaps more useful; *Do good to yourself with as little evil as possible to others.* In a word, it is rather in this natural feeling than in any subtle arguments that we must look for the cause of that repugnance, which every man would experience in doing evil, even independently of the maxims of education. Although it might belong to Socrates and other minds of the like craft to acquire virtue by reason, the human race would long since have ceased to be, had its preservation depended only on the reasonings of the individuals composing it.

With passions so little active, and so good a curb, men, being rather wild than wicked, and more intent to guard themselves against the mischief that might be done them, than to do mischief to others, were by no means subject to very perilous dissensions. They maintained no kind of intercourse with one another, and were consequently strangers to vanity, deference, esteem, and contempt; they had not the least idea of "mine" and "thine," and no true conception of justice; they looked upon every violence to which they were subjected, rather as an injury that might easily be repaired than as a crime that ought to be punished; and they never thought of taking revenge, unless perhaps mechanically and on the spot, as a god will sometimes bite the stone which is thrown at him. Their quarrels therefore would seldom have very bloody consequences; for the subject of them would be merely the question of subsistence. But I am aware of one greater danger, which remains to be noticed.

Of the passions that stir the heart of man, there is one which makes the sexes necessary to each other, and is extremely ardent and impetuous; a terrible passion that braves danger, surmounts all obstacles, and in its transports seems calculated to bring destruction on the human race which it is really destined to preserve. What must become of men who are left to this brutal and boundless rage, without modesty, without shame, and daily upholding their amours at the price of their blood?

It must, in the first place, be allowed that, the more violent the passions are, the more are laws necessary to keep them under restraint. But, setting aside the inadequacy of laws to effect this purpose, which is evident from the crimes and disorders to which these passions daily give rise among us, we should do well to inquire if these evils did not spring up with the laws themselves; for in this case, even if the laws were capable of repressing such evils, it is the least that could be expected from them, that they should check a mischief which would not have arisen without them.

Let us begin by distinguishing between the physical and moral ingredients in the feeling of love. The physical part of love is that general desire which urges the sexes to union with each other. The moral part is that which determines and fixes this desire exclusively upon one particular object; or at least gives it a greater degree of energy toward the object thus preferred. It is easy to see that the moral part of love is a factitious feeling, born of social usage, and enhanced by the women with much care and cleverness, to establish their empire, and put in power the sex which ought to obey. This feeling, being founded on certain ideas of beauty and merit which a savage is not in a position to acquire, and on comparisons which he is incapable of making, must be for him almost non-existent; for, as his mind cannot form abstract ideas of proportion and regularity, so his heart is not susceptible of the feelings of love and admiration, which are even insensibly produced by the application of these ideas. He follows solely the character nature has implanted in him, and not tastes which he could never have acquired; so that every woman equally answers his purpose.

Men in a state of nature being confined merely to what is physical in love, and fortunate enough to be ignorant of those excellences, which whet the appetite while they increase the difficulty of gratifying it, must be subject to fewer and less violent fits of passion, and consequently fall into fewer and less violent disputes. The imagination, which causes such ravages among us, never speaks to the heart of savages, who quietly await the impulses of nature, yield to them involuntarily, with more pleasure than ardour, and, their wants once satisfied, lose the desire. It is therefore incontestable that love, as well as all other passions, must have acquired in society that glowing impetuosity, which makes it so often fatal to mankind. And it is the more absurd to represent savages as continually cutting one another's throats to indulge their brutality, because this opinion is directly contrary to experience; the Caribbeans, who have as yet least of all deviated from the state of nature, being in fact the most peaceable of people in their amours, and the least subject to jealousy, though they live in a hot climate which seems always to inflame the passions.

With regard to the inferences that might be drawn, in the case of several species of animals, the males of which fill our poultry-yards with blood and slaughter, or in spring make the forests resound with their quarrels over their females; we must begin by excluding all those species, in which nature has plainly established, in the comparative power of the sexes, relations different from those which exist among us: thus we can base no conclusion about men on the habits of fighting cocks. In those species where the proportion is better observed, these battles must be entirely due to the scarcity of females in comparison with males; or, what amounts to the same thing, to the intervals during which the female constantly refuses the advances of the male: for if each female admits the male but during two months in the year, it is the same as if the number of females were five-sixths less. Now, neither of these two cases is applicable to the human species, in which the number of females usually exceeds that of males, and among whom it has never been observed, even among savages, that the females have, like those of other animals, their stated times of passion and indifference. Moreover, in several of these species, the individuals all take fire at once, and there comes a fearful moment of universal passion, tumult, and disorder among them; a scene which is never beheld in the human species, whose love is not thus seasonal. We must not then conclude from the combats of such animals for the enjoyment of the females, that the case would be the same with mankind in a state of nature: and, even if we drew such a conclusion, we see that such contests do not exterminate other kinds of animals, and we have no reason to think they would be more fatal to ours. It is indeed clear that they would do still less mischief than is the case in a state of society; especially in those countries in which, morals being still held in some repute, the jealousy of lovers and the vengeance of husbands are the daily cause of duels, murders, and even worse crimes; where the obligation of eternal fidelity only occasions adultery, and the very laws of honour and continence necessarily increase debauchery and lead to the multiplication of abortions.

Let us conclude then that man in a state of nature, wandering up and down the forests, without industry, without speech, and without home, an equal stranger to war and to all ties, neither standing in need of his fellow-creatures nor having any desire to hurt them, and perhaps even not distinguishing them one from another; let us conclude that, being self-sufficient and subject to so few passions, he could have no feelings or knowledge but such as befitted his situation; that he felt only his actual necessities, and disregarded everything he did not think himself immediately concerned to notice, and that his understanding made no greater progress than his vanity. If by accident he made any discovery, he was the less able to communicate it to others, as he did not know even his own children. Every art would necessarily perish with its inventor, where there was no kind of education among men, and generations succeeded generations without the least advance; when, all setting out from the same point, centuries must have elapsed in the barbarism of the first ages; when the race was already old, and man remained a child. . . .

## The Second Part: The Inequalities of Civilization

. . . So long as men remained content with their rustic huts, so long as they were satisfied with clothes made of the skins of animals and sewn together with thorns and fish-bones, adorned themselves only with feathers and shells, and continued to paint their bodies different colours, to improve and beautify their bows and arrows, and to make with sharp-edged stones fishing boats or clumsy musical instruments; in a word, so long as they undertook only what a single person could accomplish, and confined themselves to such arts as did not require the joint labour of several hands, they lived free, healthy, honest, and happy lives, in so far as their nature allowed, and they continued to enjoy the pleasures of mutual and independent intercourse. But from the moment one man began to stand in need of the help of another; from the moment it appeared advantageous to any one man to have enough provisions for two, equality disappeared, property was introduced, work became indispensable, and vast forests became smiling fields, which man had to water with the sweat of his brow, and where slavery and misery were soon seen to germinate and grow up with the crops.

Metallurgy and agriculture were the two arts which produced this great revolution. The poets tell us it was gold and silver, but, for the philosophers, it was iron and corn, which first civilized men, and ruined humanity. Thus both were unknown to the savages of America, who for that reason are still savage: the other nations also seem to have continued in a state of barbarism while they practised only one of these arts. One of the best reasons, perhaps, why Europe has been, if not longer, at least more constantly and highly civilized than the rest of the world, is that it is at once the most abundant in iron and the most fertile in corn.

It is difficult to conjecture how men first came to know and use iron; for it is impossible to suppose they would of themselves think of digging the ore out of the mine, and preparing it for smelting, before they knew what would be the result. On the other hand, we have the less reason to suppose this discovery the effect of any accidental fire, as mines are only formed in barren places, bare of trees and plants; so that it looks as if nature had taken pains to keep the fatal secret from us. There remains, therefore, only the extraordinary accident of some volcano which, by ejecting metallic substances already in fusion, suggested to the spectators the idea of imitating the natural operation. And we must further conceive them as possessed of uncommon courage and foresight, to undertake so laborious a work, with so distant a prospect of drawing advantage from it; yet these qualities are united only in minds more advanced than we can suppose those of these first discoverers to have been.

With regard to agriculture, the principles of it were known long before they were put in practice; and it is indeed hardly possible that men, constantly employed in drawing their subsistence from plants and trees, should not readily acquire a knowledge of the means made use of by nature for the propagation of vegetables. It was in all probability very long, however, before their industry took that turn, either because trees, which together with hunting and fishing afforded them food, did not require their attention; or because they were ignorant of the use of corn, or without instruments to cultivate it; or because they lacked foresight to future needs; or lastly, because they were without means of preventing others from robbing them of the fruit of their labour.

When they grew more industrious, it is natural to believe that they began, with the help of sharp stones and pointed sticks, to cultivate a few vegetables or roots around their huts; though it was long before they knew how to prepare corn, or were provided with the implements necessary for raising it in any large quantity; not to mention how essential it is, for [farming], to consent to immediate loss, in order to reap a future gain—a precaution very foreign to the turn of a savage's mind; for, as I have said, he hardly foresees in the morning what he will need at night.

The invention of the other arts must therefore have been necessary to compel mankind to apply themselves to agriculture. No sooner were artificers wanted to smelt and forge iron, than others were required to maintain them; the more hands that were employed in manufacturers, the fewer were left to provide for the common subsistence, though the number of mouths to be furnished with food remained the same: and as some required commodities in exchange for their iron, the rest at length discovered the method of making iron served for the multiplication of commodities. By this means the arts of [farming] and agriculture were established on the one hand, and the art of working metals and multiplying their uses on the other.

The cultivation of the earth necessarily brought about its distribution; and property, once recognized, gave rise to the first rules of justice; for, to secure each man his own, it had to be possible for each to have something. Besides, as men began to look forward to the future, and all had something to lose, everyone had reason to apprehend that reprisals would follow any injury he might do to another. This origin is so much the more natural, as it is impossible to conceive how property can come from anything but manual labour: for what else can a man add to things which he does not originally create, so as to make them his own property? It is the [farmer's] labour alone that, giving him a title to the produce of the ground he has tilled, gives him a claim also to the land itself, at least till harvest; and so, from year to year, a constant possession which is easily transformed into property. When the ancients, says Grotius, gave to Ceres the title of Legislatrix, and to a festival celebrated in her honour the name of Thesmophoria, they meant by that that the distribution of lands had produced a new kind of right: that is to say, the right of property, which is different from the right deducible from the law of nature.

In this state of affairs, equality might have been sustained, had the talents of individuals been equal, and had, for example, the use of iron and the consumption of commodities always exactly balanced each other; but, as there was nothing to preserve this balance, it was soon disturbed; the strongest did most work; the most skilful turned his labour to best account; the most ingenious devised methods of diminishing his labour: the [farmer] wanted more iron, or the smith more corn, and, while both laboured equally, the one gained a great deal by his work, while the other could hardly support himself. Thus natural inequality unfolds itself insensibly with that of combination, and the difference between men, developed by their different circumstances, becomes more sensible and permanent in its effects, and begins to have an influence, in the same proportion, over the lot of individuals.

Matters once at this pitch, it is easy to imagine the rest, I shall not detain the reader with a de-

scription of the successive invention of other arts, the development of language, the trial and utilization of talents, the inequality of fortunes, the use and abuse of riches, and all the details connected with them which the reader can easily supply for himself. I shall confine myself to a glance at mankind in this new situation.

Behold then all human faculties developed, memory and imagination in full play, *amour-propre* interested, reason active, and the mind almost at the highest point of its perfection. Behold all the natural qualities in action, the rank and condition of every man assigned him; not merely his share of property and his power to serve or injure others, but also his wit, beauty, strength or skill, merits or talents: and these being the only qualities capable of commanding respect, it soon became necessary to possess or to affect them.

It now became the interest of men to appear what they really were not. To be and to seem became two totally different things; and from this distinction sprang insolent pomp and cheating trickery, with all the numerous vices that go in their train. On the other hand, free and independent as men were before, they were now, in consequence of a multiplicity of new wants, brought into subjection as it were, to all nature, and particularly to one another; and each became in some degree a slave even in becoming the master of other men: if rich, they stood in need of the services of others; if poor, of their assistance; and even a middle condition did not enable them to do without one another. Man must now, therefore, have been perpetually employed in getting others to interest themselves in his lot, and in making them, apparently at least, if not really, find their advantage in promoting his own. Thus he must have been sly and artful in his behaviour to some, and imperious and cruel to others; being under a kind of necessity to ill-use all the persons of whom he stood in need, when he could not frighten them into compliance, and did not judge it his interest to be useful to them. Insatiable ambition, the thirst of raising their respective fortunes, not so much from real want as from the desire to surpass others, inspired all men with a vile propensity to injure one another, and with a secret jealousy, which is the more dangerous, as it puts on the mask of benevolence, to carry its point with greater security. In a word, there arose rivalry and competition on the one hand, and conflicting interests on the other, together with a secret desire on both of profiting at the expense of others. All these evils were the first effects of property, and the inseparable attendants of growing inequality.

Before the invention of signs to respect riches, wealth could hardly consist in anything but lands and cattle, the only real possessions men can have. But, when inheritances so increased in number and extent as to occupy the whole of the land, and to border on one another, one man could aggrandize himself only at the expense of another; at the same time the supernumeraries, who had been too weak or too indolent to make such acquisitions, and had grown poor without sustaining any loss, because, while they saw everything change around them, they remained still the same, were obliged to receive their subsistence, or steal it, from the rich; and this soon bred, according to their different characters, dominion and slavery, or violence and rapine. The wealthy, on their part, had no sooner begun to taste the pleasure of command, than they disdained all others, and, using their old slaves to acquire new, thought of nothing but subduing and enslaving their neighbours; like ravenous wolves, which, having once tasted human flesh, despise every other food and thenceforth seek only men to devour.

Thus, as the most powerful or the most miserable considered their might or misery, as a kind of right to the possessions of others, equivalent, in their opinion, to that of property, the destruction of equality was attended by the most terrible disorders. Usurpations by the rich, robbery by the poor, and the unbridled passions of both, suppressed the cries of natural compassion and the still feeble voice of justice, and filled men with avarice, ambition, and vice. Between the title of the strongest and that of the first occupier, there arose perpetual conflicts, which never ended but in battles and bloodshed. The new-born state of society thus gave rise to a horrible state of war; men thus harassed and depraved were no longer capable of retracing their steps or renouncing the fatal acquisitions they had made, but, labouring by the abuse of the faculties which do them honour, merely to their own confusion, brought themselves to the brink of ruin. . . .

It is impossible that men should not at length have reflected on so wretched a situation, and on the calamities that overwhelmed them. The rich, in particular, must have felt how much they suffered by a constant state of war, of which they bore all the expense; and in which, though all risked their lives, they alone risked their property. Besides, however speciously they might disguise their usurpations, they knew that they were founded on precarious and false titles; so that, if others took from them by force what they themselves had gained by force, they would have no reason to complain. Even those who had been enriched by their own industry, could hardly base their proprietorship on better claims. It was in vain to repeat: "I built this well; I gained this spot by my industry." Who gave you your standing, it might be answered, and what right have you to demand payment of us for doing what we never asked you to do? Do you not know that numbers of your fellow-creatures are starving, for want of what you have too much of? You ought to have had the express and universal consent of mankind, before appropriating more of the common subsistence than you needed for your own maintenance. Destitute of valid reasons to justify and sufficient strength to defend himself, able to crush individuals with ease, but easily crushed himself by a troop of bandits, one against all, and incapable, on account of mutual jealousy, of joining with his equals against numerous enemies united by the common hope of plunder, the rich man, thus urged by necessity, conceived at length the profoundest plan that ever entered the mind of man: this was to employ in his favour the forces of those who attacked him, to make allies of his adversaries, to inspire them with different maxims, and to give them other institutions as favourable to himself as the law of nature was unfavourable.

With this view, after having represented to his neighbours the horror of a situation which armed every man against the rest, and made their possessions as burdensome to them as their wants, and in which no safety could be expected either in riches or in poverty, he readily devised plausible arguments to make them close with his design. "Let us join," said he, "to guard the weak from oppression, to restrain the ambitious, and secure to every man the possession of what belongs to him: let us institute rules of justice and peace, to which all without exception may be obliged to conform; rules that may in some measure make amends for the caprices of fortune, by subjecting equally the powerful and the weak to the observance of reciprocal obligations. Let us, in a word, instead of turning our forces against ourselves, collect them in a supreme power which may govern us by wise laws, protect and defend all the members of the association, repulse their common enemies, and maintain eternal harmony among us."

Far fewer words to this purpose would have been enough to impose on men so barbarous and easily seduced; especially as they had too many disputes among themselves to do without arbitrators, and too much ambition and avarice to go long without masters. All ran headlong to their chains, in hopes of securing their liberty; for they had just wit enough to perceive the advantages of political institutions, without experience enough to enable them to foresee the dangers. The most capable of foreseeing the dangers were the very persons who expected to benefit by them; and even the most prudent judged it not inexpedient to sacrifice one part of their freedom to ensure the rest; as a wounded man has his arm cut off to save the rest of his body.

Such was, or may well have been, the origin of society and law, which bound new fetters on the poor, and gave new powers to the rich; which irretrievably destroyed natural liberty, eternally fixed the law of property and inequality, converted clever usurpation into unalterable right, and, for the advantage of a few ambitious individuals, subjected all mankind to perpetual labour, slavery, and wretchedness. It is easy to see how the establishment of one community made that of all the rest necessary, and how, in order to make head against united forces, the rest of mankind had to unite in turn. Societies soon multiplied and spread over the face of the earth, till hardly a corner of the world was left in which a man could escape the yoke, and withdraw his head from beneath the sword which he saw perpetually hanging over him by a thread. Civil right having thus become the common rule among the members of each community, the law of nature maintained its place only between different communities, where, under the name of the right of nations, it was qualified by certain tacit conventions, in order to make commerce practicable, and serve as a substitute for natural compassion, which lost, when applied to societies, almost all the influence it had over individuals, and survived no longer except in some great cosmopolitan spirits, who, breaking down the imaginary barriers that separate different peoples, follow the examples of our Sovereign Creator, and include the whole human race in their benevolence.

But bodies politic, remaining thus in a state of nature among themselves, presently experienced the inconveniences which had obliged individuals to forsake it; for this state became still more fatal to these great bodies than it had been to the individuals of whom they were composed. Hence arose national wars, battles, murders, and reprisals, which shock nature and outrage reason; together with all those horrible prejudices which class among the virtues the honour of shedding human blood. The most distinguished men hence learned to consider cutting each other's throats a duty; at length men massacred their fellow-creatures by thousands without so much as knowing why, and committed more murders in a single day's fighting, and more violent outrages in the sack of a single town, than were committed in the state of nature during whole ages over the whole earth. Such were the first effects which we can see to have followed the division of mankind into different communities. But let us return to their institution.

# 26    On the Social Contract

JEAN-JACQUES ROUSSEAU

## Book I

### CHAPTER I:
### SUBJECT OF THE FIRST BOOK

MAN IS BORN FREE; and everywhere he is in chains. One thinks himself the master of others, and still remains a greater slave than they. How did this change come about? I do not know. What can make it legitimate? That question I think I can answer.

If I took into account only force, and the effects derived from it, I should say: "As long as a people is compelled to obey, and obeys, it does well; as soon as it can shake off the yoke, and shakes it off, it does still better; for, regaining its liberty by the same right as took it away, either it is justified in resuming it, or there was no justification for those who took it away." But the social order is a sacred right which is the basis of all other rights. Nevertheless, this right does not come from nature, and must therefore be founded on conventions. Before coming to that, I have to prove what I have just asserted.

### CHAPTER II: THE FIRST SOCIETIES

The most ancient of all societies, and the only one that is natural, is the family: and even so the children remain attached to the father only so long as they need him for their preservation. As soon as this need ceases, the natural bond is dissolved. The children, released from the obedience they owed to the father, and the father, released from the care he owed his children, return equally to independence. If they remain united, they continue so no longer naturally, but voluntarily; and the family itself is then maintained only by convention.

This common liberty results from the nature of man. His first law is to provide for his own preservation, his first cares are those which he owes to himself; and, as soon as he reaches years of discretion, he is the sole judge of the proper means of preserving himself, and consequently becomes his own master.

The family then may be called the first model of political societies: the ruler corresponds to the father, and the people to the children; and all, being born free and equal, alienate their liberty only for their own advantage. The whole difference is that, in the family, the love of the father for his children repays him for the care he takes of them, while, in the State, the pleasure of commanding takes the place of the love which the chief cannot have for the peoples under him.

Grotius denies that all human power is established in favour of the governed, and quotes slavery as an example. His usual method of reasoning is constantly to establish right by fact.[1] It would be possible to employ a more logical method, but none could be more favourable to tyrants.

It is then, according to Grotius, doubtful whether the human race belongs to a hundred men, or that hundred men to the human race: and, throughout his book, he seems to incline to the former alternative, which is also the view of Hobbes. On this showing, the human species is divided into so many herds of cattle, each with its ruler, who keeps guard over them for the purpose of devouring them.

As a shepherd is of a nature superior to that of his flock, the shepherds of men, i.e. their rulers, are of a nature superior to that of the peoples under them. Thus, Philo tells us, the Emperor Caligula reasoned, concluding equally well either that kings were gods, or that men were beasts.

The reasoning of Caligula agrees with that of Hobbes and Grotius. Aristotle, before any of them, had said that men are by no means equal naturally, but that some are born for slavery, and others for dominion.

Aristotle was right; but he took the effect for the cause. Nothing can be more certain than that every man born in slavery is born for slavery. Slaves lose everything in their chains, even the desire of escaping from them: they love their servitude, as the comrades of Ulysses loved their brutish condition.[2] If then there are slaves by nature, it is because there have been slaves against nature. Force made the first slaves, and their cowardice perpetuated the condition.

I have said nothing of King Adam, or Emperor Noah, father of the three great monarchs who shared out the universe, like the children of Saturn, whom some scholars have recognised in them. I trust to getting due thanks for my moderation; for, being a direct descendant of one of these princes, perhaps of the eldest branch, how do I know that a verification of titles might not leave me the legitimate king of the human race? In any case, there can be no doubt that Adam was sovereign of the world, as Robinson Crusoe was of his island, as long as he was its only inhabitant; and this empire had the advantage that the monarch, safe on his throne, had no rebellions, wars, or conspirators to fear.

## CHAPTER III:
## THE RIGHT OF THE STRONGEST

The strongest is never strong enough to be always the master, unless he transforms strength into right, and obedience into duty. Hence the right of the strongest, which, though to all seemingly meant ironically, is really laid down as a fundamental principle. But are we never to have an explanation of this phrase? Force is a physical power, and I fail to see what moral effect it can have. To yield to force is an act of necessity, not of will—at the most, an act of prudence. In what sense can it be a duty?

Suppose for a moment that this so-called "right" exists. I maintain that the sole result is a mass of inexplicable nonsense. For, if force creates right, the effect changes with the cause: every

force that is greater than the first succeeds to its right. As soon as it is possible to disobey with impunity, disobedience is legitimate; and, the strongest being always in the right, the only thing that matters is to act so as to become the strongest. But what kind of right is that which perishes when force fails? If we must obey perforce, there is no need to obey because we ought; and if we are not forced to obey, we are under no obligation to do so. Clearly, the word "right" adds nothing to force: in this connection, it means absolutely nothing.

Obey the powers that be. If this means yield to force, it is a good precept, but superfluous: I can answer for its never being violated. All power comes from God, I admit; but so does all sickness: does that mean that we are forbidden to call in the doctor? A brigand surprises me at the edge of a wood: must I not merely surrender my purse on compulsion; but, even if I could withhold it, am I in conscience bound to give it up? For certainly the pistol he holds is also a power.

Let us then admit that force does not create right, and that we are obliged to obey only legitimate powers. In that case, my original question recurs.

## CHAPTER IV: SLAVERY

Since no man has a natural authority over his fellow, and force creates no right, we must conclude that conventions form the basis of all legitimate authority among men.

If an individual, says Grotius, can alienate his liberty and make himself the slave of a master, why could not a whole people do the same and make itself subject to a king? There are in this passage plenty of ambiguous words which would need explaining; but let us confine ourselves to the word *alienate*. To alienate is to give or to sell. Now, a man who becomes the slave of another does not give himself; he sells himself, at the least for his subsistence: but for what does a people sell itself? A king is so far from furnishing his subjects with their subsistence that he gets his own only from them; and, according to Rabelais, kings do not live on nothing. Do subjects then give their persons on condition that the king takes their goods also? I fail to see what they have left to preserve.

It will be said that the despot assures his subjects civil tranquility. Granted; but what do they gain, if the wars his ambition brings down upon them, his insatiable avidity, and the vexatious conduct of his ministers press harder on them than their own dissensions would have done? What do they gain, if the very tranquillity they enjoy is one of their miseries? Tranquillity is found also in dungeons; but is that enough to make them desirable places to live in? The Greeks imprisoned in the cave of the Cyclops lived there very tranquilly, while they were awaiting their turn to be devoured.

To say that a man gives himself gratuitously, is to say what is absurd and inconceivable; such an act is null and illegitimate, from the mere fact that he who does it is out of his mind. To say the same of a whole people is to suppose a people of madmen; and madness creates no right.

Even if each man could alienate himself, he could not alienate his children: they are born men and free; their liberty belongs to them, and no one but them has the right to dispose of it. Before they come to years of discretion, the father can, in their name, lay down conditions for their preservation and well-being, but he cannot give them irrevocably and without conditions: such a gift is contrary to the ends of nature, and exceeds the rights of paternity. It would therefore be necessary, in order to legitimise an arbitrary government, that in every generation the people should be in a position to accept or reject it; but, were this so, the government would be no longer arbitrary.

To renounce liberty is to renounce being a man, to surrender the rights of humanity and even its duties. For him who renounces everything no indemnity is possible. Such a renunciation is incompatible with man's nature; to remove all liberty from his will is to remove all morality from his acts. Finally, it is an empty and contradictory convention that sets up, on the one side, absolute authority, and, on the other, unlimited obedience. Is it not clear that we can be under no obligation to a person from whom we have the right to exact everything? Does not this condition alone, in the absence of equivalence or exchange, in itself involve the nullity of the act? For what right can my slave have against me, when all that he has belongs to me, and, his right being mine, this right of mine against myself is a phrase devoid of meaning?

Grotius and the rest find in war another origin for the so-called right of slavery. The victor having, as they hold, the right of killing the vanquished, the latter can buy back his life at the price of his liberty; and this convention is the more legitimate because it is to the advantage of both parties.

But it is clear that this supposed right to kill the conquered is by no means deducible from the state of war. Men, from the mere fact that, while they are living in their primitive independence, they have no mutual relations stable enough to constitute either the state of peace or the state of war, cannot be naturally enemies. War is constituted by a relation between things, and not between persons; and, as the state of war cannot arise out of simple personal relations, but only out of real relations, private war, or war of man with man, can exist neither in the state of nature, where there is no constant property, nor in the social state, where everything is under the authority of the laws.

Individual combats, duels and encounters, are acts which cannot constitute a state; while the private wars, authorised by the Establishments of Louis IX, King of France, and suspended by the Peace of God, are abuses of feudalism, in itself an absurd system if ever there was one, and contrary to the principles of natural right and to all good polity.

War then is a relation, not between man and man, but between State and State, and individuals are enemies only accidentally, not as men, nor even as citizens,[3] but as soldiers; not as members of their country, but as its defenders. Finally, each State can have for enemies only other States, and not men; for between things disparate in nature there can be no real relation.

Furthermore, this principle is in conformity with the established rules of all times and the constant practice of all civilised peoples. Declarations of war are intimations less to powers than to their subjects. The foreigner, whether king, individual, or people, who robs, kills or detains the subjects, without declaring war on the prince, is not an enemy, but a brigand. Even in real war, a just prince, while laying hands, in the enemy's country, on all that belongs to the public, respects the lives and goods of individuals: he respects rights on which his own are founded. The object of the war being the destruction of the hostile State, the other side has a right to kill its defenders, while they are bearing arms; but as soon as they lay them down and surrender, they cease to be enemies or instruments of the enemy, and become once more merely men, whose life no one has any right to take. Sometimes it is possible to kill the State without killing a single one of its members; and war gives no right which is not necessary to the gaining of its object. These principles are not those of Grotius: they are not based on the authority of poets, but derived from the nature of reality and based on reason.

The right of conquest has no foundation other than the right of the strongest. If war does not give the conqueror the right to massacre the conquered peoples, the right to enslave them cannot be based upon a right which does not exist. No one has a right to kill an enemy except when he cannot make him a slave, and the right to enslave him cannot therefore be derived from the right to kill him. It is accordingly an unfair exchange to make him buy at the price of his liberty his life, over which the victor holds no right. Is it not clear that there is a vicious circle in founding the right of life and death on the right of slavery, and the right of slavery on the right of life and death?

Even if we assume this terrible right to kill everybody, I maintain that a slave made in war, or a conquered people, is under no obligation to a master, except to obey him as far as he is compelled to do so. By taking an equivalent for his life, the victor has not done him a favour; instead of killing him without profit, he has killed him usefully. So far then is he from acquiring over him any authority in addition to that of force, that the state of war continues to subsist between them: their

mutual relation is the effect of it, and the usage of the right of war does not imply a treaty of peace. A convention has indeed been made; but this convention, so far from destroying the state of war, presupposes its continuance.

So, from whatever aspect we regard the question, the right of slavery is null and void, not only as being illegitimate, but also because it is absurd and meaningless. The words *slave* and *right* contradict each other, and are mutually exclusive. It will always be equally foolish for a man to say to a man or to a people: "I make with you a convention wholly at your expense and wholly to my advantage; I shall keep it as long as I like, and you will keep it as long as I like."

## CHAPTER V: THAT WE MUST ALWAYS GO BACK TO A FIRST CONVENTION

Even if I granted all that I have been refuting, the friends of despotism would be no better off. There will always be a great difference between subduing a multitude and ruling a society. Even if scattered individuals were successively enslaved by one man, however numerous they might be, I still see no more than a master and his slaves, and certainly not a people and its ruler; I see what may be termed an aggregation, but not an association; there is as yet neither public good nor body politic. The man in question, even if he has enslaved half the world, is still only an individual; his interest, apart from that of others, is still a purely private interest. If this same man comes to die, his empire, after him, remains scattered and without unity, as an oak falls and dissolves into a heap of ashes when the fire has consumed it.

A people, says Grotius, can give itself to a king. Then, according to Grotius, a people is a people before it gives itself. The gift is itself a civil act, and implies public deliberation. It would be better, before examining the act by which a people gives itself to a king, to examine that by which it has become a people; for this act, being necessarily prior to the other, is the true foundation of society.

Indeed, if there were no prior convention, where, unless the election were unanimous, would be the obligation on the minority to submit to the choice of the majority? How have a hundred men who wish for a master the right to vote on behalf of ten who do not? The law of majority voting is itself something established by convention, and presupposes unanimity, on one occasion at least.

## CHAPTER VI: THE SOCIAL COMPACT

I suppose men to have reached the point at which the obstacles in the way of their preservation in the state of nature show their power of resistance to be greater than the resources at the disposal of each individual for his maintenance in the state. That primitive condition can then subsist no longer; and the human race would perish unless it changed its manner of existence.

But, as men cannot engender new forces, but only unite and direct existing ones, they have no other means of preserving themselves than the formation, by aggregation, of a sum of forces great enough to overcome the resistance. These they have to bring into play by means of a single motive power, and cause to act in concert.

This sum of forces can arise only where several persons come together: but, as the force and liberty of each man are the chief instruments of his self-preservation, how can he pledge them without harming his own interest, and neglecting the care he owes to himself? This difficulty, in its bearing on my present subject, may be stated in the following terms—

"The problem is to find a form of association which will defend and protect with the whole common force the person and goods of each associate, and in which each, while uniting himself with all, may still obey himself alone, and remain as free as before." This is the fundamental problem of which the *Social Contract* provides the solution.

The clauses of this contract are so determined by the nature of the act that the slightest modification would make them vain and ineffective; so that, although they have perhaps never been formally set forth, they are everywhere the same and everywhere tacitly admitted and recog-

nised, until, on the violation of the social compact, each regains his original rights and resumes his natural liberty, while losing the conventional liberty in favour of which he renounced it.

These clauses, properly understood, may be reduced to one—the total alienation of each associate, together with all his rights, to the whole community; for, in the first place, as each gives himself absolutely, the conditions are the same for all; and, this being so, no one has any interest in making them burdensome to others.

Moreover, the alienation being without reserve, the union is as perfect as it can be, and no associate has anything more to demand: for, if the individuals retained certain rights, as there would be no common superior to decide between them and the public, each, being on one point his own judge, would ask to be so on all; the state of nature would thus continue, and the association would necessarily become inoperative or tyrannical.

Finally, each man, in giving himself to all, gives himself to nobody; and as there is no associate over whom he does not acquire the same right as he yields others over himself, he gains an equivalent for everything he loses, and an increase of force for the preservation of what he has.

If then we discard from the social compact what is not of its essence, we shall find that it reduces itself to the following terms—

"*Each of us puts his person and all his power in common under the supreme direction of the general will, and, in our corporate capacity, we receive each member as an indivisible part of the whole.*"

At once, in place of the individual personality of each contracting party, this act of association creates a moral and collective body, composed of as many members as the assembly contains votes, and receiving from this act its unity, its common identity, its life and its will. This public person, so formed by the union of all other persons formerly took the name of *city*,[4] and now takes that of *Republic* or *body politic*; it is called by its members *State* when passive, *Sovereign* when active, and *Power* when compared with others like itself. Those who are associated in it take collectively the name of *people*, and severally are called *citizens*, as sharing in the sovereign power, and *subjects,* as being under the laws of the State. But these terms are often confused and taken one for another: it is enough to know how to distinguish them when they are being used with precision.

## CHAPTER VII: THE SOVEREIGN

This formula shows us that the act of association comprises a mutual undertaking between the public and the individuals, and that each individual, in making a contract, as we may say, with himself, is bound in a double capacity; as a member of the Sovereign he is bound to the individuals, and as a member of the State to the Sovereign. But the maxim of civil right, that no one is bound by undertakings made to himself, does not apply in this case; for there is a great difference between incurring an obligation to yourself and incurring one to a whole of which you form a part.

Attention must further be called to the fact that public deliberation, while competent to bind all the subjects to the Sovereign, because of the two different capacities in which each of them may be regarded, cannot, for the opposite reason bind the Sovereign to itself; and that it is consequently against the nature of the body politic for the Sovereign to impose on itself a law which it cannot infringe. Being able to regard itself in only one capacity, it is in the position of an individual who makes a contract with himself; and this makes it clear that there neither is nor can be any kind of fundamental law binding on the body of the people—not even the social contract itself. This does not mean that the body politic cannot enter into undertakings with others, provided the contract is not infringed by them; for in relation to what is external to it, it becomes a simple being, an individual.

But the body politic or the Sovereign, drawing its being wholly from the sanctity of the contract, can never bind itself, even to an outsider, to do anything derogatory to the original act, for instance, to alienate any part of itself, or to submit to another Sovereign. Violation of the act by which it exists would be self-annihilation; and that which is itself nothing can create nothing.

As soon as this multitude is so united in one body, it is impossible to offend against one of the members without attacking the body, and still more to offend against the body without the members resenting it. Duty and interest therefore equally oblige the two contracting parties to give each other help; and the same men should seek to combine, in their double capacity, all the advantages dependent upon that capacity.

Again, the Sovereign, being formed wholly of the individuals who compose it, neither has nor can have any interest contrary to theirs; and consequently the sovereign power need give no guarantee to its subjects, because it is impossible for the body to wish to hurt all its members. We shall also see later on that it cannot hurt any in particular. The Sovereign, merely by virtue of what it is, is always what it should be.

This, however, is not the case with the relation of the subjects to the Sovereign, which, despite the common interest, would have no security that they would fulfil their undertakings, unless it found means to assure itself of their fidelity.

In fact, each individual, as a man, may have a particular will contrary or dissimilar to the general will which he has as a citizen. His particular interest may speak to him quite differently from the common interest: his absolute and naturally independent existence may make him look upon what he owes to the common cause as a gratuitous contribution, the loss of which will do less harm to others than the payment of it is burdensome to himself; and, regarding the moral person which constitutes the State as a *persona ficta,* because not a man, he may wish to enjoy the rights of citizenship without being ready to fulfil the duties of a subject. The continuance of such an injustice could not but prove the undoing of the body politic.

In order then that the social compact may not be an empty formula, it tacitly includes the undertaking, which alone can give force to the rest, that whoever refuses to obey the general will shall be compelled to do so by the whole body. This means nothing less than that he will be forced to be free; for this is the condition which, by giving each citizen to his country, secures him against all personal dependence. In this lies the key to the working of the political machine; this alone legitimises civil undertakings, which, without it, would be absurd, tyrannical, and liable to the most frightful abuses.

## CHAPTER VIII: THE CIVIL STATE

The passage from the state of nature to the civil state produces a very remarkable change in man, by substituting justice for instinct in his conduct, and giving his actions the morality they had formerly lacked. Then only, when the voice of duty takes the place of physical impulses and right of appetite, does man, who so far had considered only himself, find that he is forced to act on different principles, and to consult his reason before listening to his inclinations. Although, in this state, he deprives himself of some advantages which he got from nature, he gains in return others so great, his faculties are so stimulated and developed, his ideas so extended, his feelings so ennobled, and his whole soul so uplifted, that, did not the abuses of this new condition often degrade him below that which he left, he would be bound to bless continually the happy moment which took him from it forever, and, instead of a stupid and unimaginative animal, made him an intelligent being and a man.

Let us draw up the whole account in terms easily commensurable. What man loses by the social contract is his natural liberty and an unlimited right to everything he tries to get and succeeds in getting; what he gains is civil liberty and the proprietorship of all he possesses. If we are to avoid mistake in weighing one against the other, we must clearly distinguish natural liberty, which is bounded only by the strength of the individual, from civil liberty, which is limited by the general will; and possession, which is merely the effect of force or the right of the first occupier, from property, which can be founded only on a positive title.

We might, over and above all this, add, to what man acquires in the civil state, moral liberty, which alone makes him truly master of himself; for the mere impulse of appetite is slavery, while obedience to a law which we prescribe to ourselves is

liberty. But I have already said too much on this head, and the philosophical meaning of the word liberty does not now concern us.

## CHAPTER IX: REAL PROPERTY

Each member of the community gives himself to it, at the moment of its foundation, just as he is, with all the resources at his command, including the goods he possesses. This act does not make possession, in changing hands, change its nature, and become property in the hands of the Sovereign; but, as the forces of the city are incomparably greater than those of an individual, public possession is also, in fact, stronger and more irrevocable, without being any more legitimate, at any rate from the point of view of foreigners. For the State, in relation to its members, is master of all their goods by the social contract, which, within the State, is the basis of all rights; but, in relation to other powers, it is so only by the right of the first occupier, which it holds from its members.

The right of the first occupier, though more real than the right of the strongest, becomes a real right only when the right of property has already been established. *Every man has naturally a right to everything he needs,* but the positive act which makes him proprietor of one thing excludes him from everything else. Having his share, he ought to keep to it, and can have no further right against the community. This is why the right of the first occupier, which in the state of nature is so weak, claims the respect of every man in civil society. In this right we are respecting not so much what belongs to another as what does not belong to ourselves.

In general, to establish the right of the first occupier over a plot of ground, the following conditions are necessary: first, the land must not yet be inhabited; secondly, a man must occupy only the amount he needs for his subsistence; and, in the third place, possession must be taken, not by an empty ceremony, but by labour and cultivation, the only sign of proprietorship that should be respected by others, in default of a legal title.

In granting the right of first occupancy to necessity and labour, are we not really stretching it as far as it can go? Is it possible to leave such a right unlimited? Is it to be enough to set foot on a plot of common ground, in order to be able to call yourself at once the master of it? Is it to be enough that a man has the strength to expel others for a moment, in order to establish his right to prevent them from ever returning? How can a man or a people seize an immense territory and keep it from the rest of the world except by a punishable usurpation, since all others are being robbed, by such an act, of the place of habitation and the means of subsistence which nature gave them in common? When Nuñez Balbao, standing on the sea-shore, took possession of the South Seas and the whole of South America in the name of the crown of Castille, was that enough to dispossess all their actual inhabitants, and to shut out from them all the princes of the world? On such a showing, these ceremonies are idly multiplied, and the Catholic King need only take possession all at once, from his apartment, of the whole universe, merely making a subsequent reservation about what was already in the possession of other princes.

We can imagine how the lands of individuals, where they were contiguous and came to be united, became the public territory, and how the right of Sovereignty, extending from the subjects over the lands they held, became at once real and personal. The possessors were thus made more dependent, and the forces at their command used to guarantee their fidelity. The advantage of this does not seem to have been felt by ancient monarchs, who called themselves King of the Persians, Scythians, or Macedonians, and seemed to regard themselves more as rulers of men than as masters of a country. *Those of the present day more cleverly call themselves Kings of France, Spain, England, etc.: thus holding the land, they are quite confident of holding the inhabitants.*

The peculiar fact about this alienation is that, in taking over the goods of individuals, the community, so far from despoiling them, only assures them legitimate possession, and changes usurpation into a true right and enjoyment into proprietorship. Thus the possessors, being regarded as depositaries of the public good, and having their rights respected by all the members of the State

and maintained against foreign aggression by all its forces, have, by a cession which benefits both the public and still more themselves, acquired, so to speak, all that they gave up. This paradox may easily be explained by the distinction between the rights which the Sovereign and the proprietor have over the same estate, as we shall see later on.

It may also happen that men begin to unite one with another before they possess anything, and that, subsequently occupying a tract of country which is enough for all, they enjoy it in common, or share it out among themselves, either equally or according to a scale fixed by the Sovereign. However the acquisition be made, the right which each individual has to his own estate is always subordinate to the right which the community has over all: without this, there would be neither stability in the social tie, nor real force in the exercise of Sovereignty.

I shall end this chapter and this book by remarking on a fact on which the whole social system should rest: *i.e.* that, instead of destroying natural inequality, the fundamental compact substitutes, for such physical inequality as nature may have set up between men, an equality that is moral and legitimate, and that men, who may be unequal in strength or intelligence, become everyone equal by convention and legal right.[5]

## Book II

### CHAPTER I: THAT SOVEREIGNTY IS INALIENABLE

The first and most important deduction from the principles we have so far laid down is that the general will alone can direct the State according to the object for which it was instituted, *i.e.* the common good: for if the clashing of particular interests made the establishment of societies necessary, the agreement of these very interests made it possible. The common element in these different interests is what forms the social tie; and, were there no point of agreement between them all, no society could exist. It is solely on the basis of this common interest that every society should be governed.

I hold then that Sovereignty, being nothing less than the exercise of the general will, can never be alienated, and that the Sovereign, who is no less than a collective being, cannot be represented except by himself: the power indeed may be transmitted, but not the will.

In reality, if it is not impossible for a particular will to agree on some point with the general will, it is at least impossible for the agreement to be lasting and constant; for the particular will tends, by its very nature, to partiality, while the general will tends to equality. It is even more impossible to have any guarantee of this agreement; for even if it should always exist, it would be the effect not of art, but of chance. The Sovereign may indeed say: "I now will actually what this man wills, or at least what he says he wills"; but it cannot say: "What he wills tomorrow, I too shall will" because it is absurd for the will to bind itself for the future, nor is it incumbent on any will to consent to anything that is not for the good of the being who wills. If then the people promise simply to obey, by that very act it dissolves itself and loses what makes it a people; the moment a master exists, there is no longer a Sovereign, and from that moment the body politic has ceased to exist.

This does not mean that the commands of the rulers cannot pass for general wills, so long as the Sovereign, being free to oppose them, offers no opposition. In such a case, universal silence is taken to imply the consent of the people. This will be explained later on.

## CHAPTER II: THAT SOVEREIGNTY IS INDIVISIBLE

SOVEREIGNTY, for the same reason as makes it inalienable, is indivisible; for will either is, or is not, general;[6] it is the will either of the body of the people, or only of a part of it. In the first case, the will, when declared, is an act of Sovereignty and constitutes law: in the second, it is merely a particular will, or act of magistracy—at the most a decree.

But our political theorists, unable to divide Sovereignty in principle, divide it according to its object: into force and will; into legislative power and executive power; into rights of taxation, justice and war; into internal administration and power of foreign treaty. Sometimes they confuse all these sections, and sometimes they distinguish them; they turn the Sovereign into a fantastic being composed of several connected pieces: it is as if they were making man of several bodies, one with eyes, one with arms, another with feet, and each with nothing besides. We are told that the jugglers of Japan dismember a child before the eyes of the spectators; then they throw all the members into the air one after another, and the child falls down alive and whole. The conjuring tricks of our political theorists are very like that; they first dismember the body politic by an illusion worthy of a fair, and then join it together again we know not how.

This error is due to a lack of exact notions concerning the Sovereign authority, and to taking for parts of it what are only emanations from it. Thus, for example, the acts of declaring war and making peace have been regarded as acts of Sovereignty; but this is not the case, as these acts do not constitute law, but merely the application of a law, a particular act which decides how the law applies, as we shall see clearly when the idea attached to the word *law* has been defined.

If we examined the other divisions in the same manner, we should find that, whenever Sovereignty seems to be divided, there is an illusion: the rights which are taken as being part of Sovereignty are really all subordinate, and always imply supreme wills of which they only sanction the execution.

It would be impossible to estimate the obscurity this lack of exactness has thrown over the decisions of writers who have dealt with political right, when they have used the principles laid down by them to pass judgment on the respective rights of kings and peoples. Everyone can see, in Chapters III and IV of the First Book of Grotius, how the learned man and his translator, Barbeyrac, entangle and tie themselves up in their own sophistries, for fear of saying too little or too much of what they think, and so offending the interests they have to conciliate. Grotius, a refugee in France, ill-content with his own country, and desirous of paying his court to Louis XIII, to whom his book is dedicated, spares no pains to rob the peoples of all their rights and invest kings with them by every conceivable artifice. This would also have been much to the taste of Barbeyrac, who dedicated his translation to George I of England. But unfortunately the expulsion of James II, which he called his "abdication," compelled him to use all reserve, to shuffle and to tergiversate, in order to avoid making William out a usurper. If these two writers had adopted the true principles, all difficulties would have been removed, and they would have been always consistent; but it would have been a sad truth for them to tell, and would have paid court for them to no one save the people. Moreover, truth is no road to fortune, and the people dispenses neither ambassadorships, nor professorships, nor pensions.

## CHAPTER III: WHETHER THE GENERAL WILL IS FALLIBLE

It follows from what has gone before that the general will is always right and tends to the public advantage; but it does not follow that the deliberations of the people are always equally correct. (Our will is always for our own good, but we do not always see what that is; the people is never corrupted, but it is often deceived, and on such occasions only does it seem to will what is bad.)

There is often a great deal of difference between the will of all and the general will; the latter considers only the common interest, while the former takes private interest into account, and is no more than a sum of particular wills: but take away from these same wills the pluses and minuses that cancel one another,[7] and the general will remains as the sum of the differences.

If, when the people, being furnished with adequate information, held its deliberations, the citizens had no communication one with another, the grand total of the small differences would always give the general will, and the decision would always be good. But when factions arise, and partial associations are formed at the expense of the great association, the will of each of these associations becomes general in relation to its members, while it remains particular in relation to the State: it may then be said that there are no longer as many votes as there are men, but only as many as there are associations. The differences become less numerous and give a less general result. Lastly, when one of these associations is so great as to prevail over all the rest, the result is no longer a sum of small differences, but a single difference; in this case there is no longer a general will, and the opinion which prevails is purely particular.

It is therefore essential, if the general will is to be able to express itself, that there should be no partial society within the State, and that each citizen should think only his own thoughts:[8] which was indeed the sublime and unique system established by the great Lycurgus. But if there are partial societies, it is best to have as many as possible and to prevent them from being unequal, as was done by Solon, Numa, and Servius. These precautions are the only ones that can guarantee that the general will shall be always enlightened, and that the people shall in no way deceive itself.

## CHAPTER IV: THE LIMITS OF THE SOVEREIGN POWER

If the State is a moral person whose life is in the union of its members, and if the most important of its cares is the care for its own preservation, it must have a universal and compelling force, in order to move and dispose each part as may be most advantageous to the whole. As nature gives each man absolute power over all his members, the social compact gives the body politic absolute power over all its members also; and it is this power which, under the direction of the general will, bears, as I have said, the name of Sovereignty.

But, besides the public person, we have to consider the private persons composing it, whose life and liberty are naturally independent of it. We are bound then to distinguish clearly between the respective rights of the citizens and the Sovereign,[9] and between the duties the former have to fulfil as subjects, and the natural rights they should enjoy as men.

Each man alienates, I admit, by the social compact, only such part of his powers, goods and liberty as it is important for the community to control; but it must also be granted that the Sovereign is sole judge of what is important.

Every service a citizen can render the State he ought to render as soon as the Sovereign demands it; but the Sovereign, for its part, cannot impose upon its subjects any fetters that are useless to the community, nor can it even wish to do so; for no more by the law of reason than by the law of nature can anything occur without a cause.

The undertakings which bind us to the social body are obligatory only because they are mutual; and their nature is such that in fulfilling them we cannot work for others without working for ourselves. Why is it that the general will is always in the right, and that all continually will the happiness of each one, unless it is because there is not a man who does not think of "each" as meaning him, and consider himself in voting for all? This proves that equality of rights and the idea of justice which such equality creates originate in the preference each man gives to himself, and accordingly in the very nature of man. It proves that the general will, to be really such, must be general in its object as well as its essence; that it must both come from all and apply to all; and that it loses its natural rectitude when it is directed to some particular and determinate object, because in such a case we are judging of something foreign to us, and have no true principle of equity to guide us.

Indeed, as soon as a question of particular fact or right arises on a point not previously regulated by a general convention, the matter becomes contentious. It is a case in which the individuals concerned are one party, and the public the other, but in which I can see neither the law that ought to be followed nor the judge who ought to give the decision. In such a case, it would be absurd to propose to refer the question to an express decision of the general will, which can be only the conclusion

reached by one of the parties and in consequence will be, for the other party, merely an external and particular will, inclined on this occasion to injustice and subject to error. Thus, just as a particular will cannot stand for the general will, the general will, in turn, changes its nature, when its object is particular, and, as general, cannot pronounce on a man or a fact. When, for instance, the people of Athens nominated or displaced its rulers, decreed honours to one, and imposed penalties on another, and, by a multitude of particular decrees, exercised all the functions of government indiscriminately, it had in such cases no longer a general will in the strict sense; it was acting no longer as Sovereign, but as magistrate. This will seem contrary to current views; but I must be given time to expound my own.

It should be seen from the foregoing that what makes the will general is less the number of voters than the common interest uniting them; for, under this system, each necessarily submits to the conditions he imposes on others: and this admirable agreement between interest and justice gives to the common deliberations an equitable character which at once vanishes when any particular question is discussed, in the absence of a common interest to unite and identify the ruling of the judge with that of the party.

From whatever side we approach our principle, we reach the same conclusion, that the social compact sets up among the citizens an equality of such a kind, that they all bind themselves to observe the same conditions and should therefore all enjoy the same rights. Thus, from the very nature of the compact, every act of Sovereignty, *i.e.* every authentic act of the general will, binds or favours all the citizens equally; so that the Sovereign recognises only the body of the nation, and draws no distinctions between those of whom it is made up. What, then, strictly speaking, is an act of Sovereignty? It is not a convention between a superior and an inferior, but a convention between the body and each of its members. It is legitimate, because based on the social contract, and equitable, because common to all; useful, because it can have no other object than the general good, and stable, because guaranteed by the public force and the supreme power. So long as the subjects have to submit only to conventions of this sort, they obey no one but their own will; and to ask how far the respective rights of the Sovereign and the citizens extend, is to ask up to what point the latter can enter into undertakings with themselves, each with all, and all with each.

We can see from this that the sovereign power, absolute, sacred and inviolable as it is, does not and cannot exceed the limits of general conventions, and that every man may dispose at will of such goods and liberty as these conventions leave him; so that the Sovereign never has a right to lay more charges on one subject than on another, because, in that case, the question becomes particular, and ceases to be within its competency.

When these distinctions have once been admitted, it is seen to be so untrue that there is, in the social contract, any real renunciation on the part of the individuals, that the position in which they find themselves as a result of the contract is really preferable to that in which they were before. Instead of a renunciation, they have made an advantageous exchange: instead of an uncertain and precarious way of living they have got one that is better and more secure; instead of natural independence they have got liberty, instead of the power to harm others security for themselves, and instead of their strength, which others might overcome, a right which social union makes invincible. Their very lives, which they have devoted to the State, are by it constantly protected; and when they risk them in the State's defence, what more are they doing than giving back what they have received from it? What are they doing that they would not do more often and with greater danger in the state of nature, in which they would inevitably have to fight battles at the peril of their lives in defence of that which is the means of their preservation? All have indeed to fight when their country needs them; but then no one has ever to fight for himself. Do we not gain something by running, on behalf of what gives us our security, only some of the risks we should have to run for ourselves, as soon as we lost it? . . .

## Book IV

### CHAPTER I: THAT THE GENERAL WILL IS INDESTRUCTIBLE

As long as several men in assembly regard themselves as a single body, they have only a single will which is concerned with their common preservation and general well-being. In this case, all the springs of the State are vigorous and simple and its rules clear and luminous; there are no embroilments or conflicts of interests; the common good is everywhere clearly apparent, and only good sense is needed to perceive it. Peace, unity and equality are the enemies of political subtleties. Men who are upright and simple are difficult to deceive because of their simplicity; lures and ingenious pretexts fail to impose upon them, and they are not even subtle enough to be dupes. When, among the happiest people in the world, bands of peasants are seen regulating affairs of State under an oak, and always acting wisely, can we help scorning the ingenious methods of other nations, which make themselves illustrious and wretched with so much art and mystery?

A State so governed needs very few laws; and, as it becomes necessary to issue new ones, the necessity is universally seen. The first man to propose them merely says what all have already felt, and there is no question of factions or intrigues or eloquence in order to secure the passage into law of what everyone has already decided to do, as soon as he is sure that the rest will act with him.

Theorists are led into error because, seeing only States that have been from the beginning wrongly constituted, they are struck by the impossibility of applying such a policy to them. They make great game of all the absurdities a clever rascal or an insinuating speaker might get the people of Paris or London to believe. They do not know that Cromwell would have been put to "the bells" by the people of Berne, and the Duc de Beaufort on the treadmill by the Genevese.

But when the social bond begins to be relaxed and the State to grow weak, when particular interests begin to make themselves felt and the smaller societies to exercise an influence over the larger, the common interest changes and finds opponents: opinion is no longer unanimous; the general will ceases to be the will of all; contradictory views and debates arise; and the best advice is not taken without question.

Finally, when the State, on the eve of ruin, maintains only a vain, illusory and formal existence, when in every heart the social bond is broken, and the meanest interest brazenly lays hold of the sacred name of "public good," the general will becomes mute: all men, guided by secret motives, no more give their views as citizens than if the State had never been; and iniquitous decrees directed solely to private interest get passed under the name of laws.

Does it follow from this that the general will is exterminated or corrupted? Not at all: it is always constant, unalterable and pure; but it is subordinated to other wills which encroach upon its sphere. Each man, in detaching his interest from the common interest, sees clearly that he cannot entirely separate them; but his share in the public mishaps seems to him negligible beside the exclusive good he aims at making his own. Apart from this particular good, he wills the general good in his own interest, as strongly as anyone else. Even in selling his vote for money, he does not extinguish in himself the general will, but only eludes it. The fault he commits is that of changing the state of the question, and answering something different from what he is asked. Instead of saying, by his vote, "It is to the advantage of the State," he says, "It is of advantage to this or that man or party that this or that view should prevail." Thus the law of public order in assemblies is not so much to maintain in them the general will as to secure that the question be always put to it, and the answer always given by it.

I could here set down many reflections on the simple right of voting in every act of Sovereignty—a right which no one can take from the citizens—and also on the right of stating views, making proposals, dividing and discussing, which the government is always most careful to leave solely to its members; but this important subject would need a treatise to itself, and it is impossible to say everything in a single work.

## CHAPTER II: VOTING

It may be seen, from the last chapter, that the way in which general business is managed may give a clear enough indication of the actual state of morals and the health of the body politic. The more concert reigns in the assemblies, that is, the nearer opinion approaches unanimity, the greater is the dominance of the general will. On the other hand, long debates, dissensions and tumult proclaim the ascendancy of particular interests and the decline of the State.

This seems less clear when two or more orders enter into the constitution, as patricians and plebeians did at Rome; for quarrels between these two orders often disturbed the comitia, even in the best days of the Republic. But the exception is rather apparent than real; for then, through the defect that is inherent in the body politic, there were, so to speak, two States in one, and what is not true of the two together is true of either separately. Indeed, even in the most stormy times, the plebiscita of the people, when the Senate did not interfere with them, always went through quietly and by large majorities. The citizens having but one interest, the people had but a single will.

At the other extremity of the circle, unanimity recurs; this is the case when the citizens, having fallen into servitude, have lost both liberty and will. Fear and flattery then change votes into acclamation; deliberation ceases, and only worship or malediction is left. Such was the vile manner in which the senate expressed its views under the Emperors. It did so sometimes with absurd precautions. Tacitus observes that, under Otho, the senators, while they heaped curses on Vitellius, contrived at the same time to make a deafening noise, in order that, should he ever become their master, he might not know what each of them had said.

On these various considerations depend the rules by which the methods of counting votes and comparing opinions should be regulated, according as the general will is more or less easy to discover, and the State more or less in its decline.

There is but one law which, from its nature, needs unanimous consent. This is the social compact; for civil association is the most voluntary of all acts. Every man being born free and his own master, no one, under any pretext whatsoever, can make any man subject without his consent. To decide that the son of a slave is born a slave is to decide that he is not born a man.

If then there are opponents when the social compact is made, their opposition does not invalidate the contract, but merely prevents them from being included in it. They are foreigners among citizens. When the State is instituted, residence constitutes consent; to dwell within its territory is to submit to the Sovereign.[10]

Apart from this primitive contract, the vote of the majority always binds all the rest. This follows from the contract itself. But it is asked how a man can be both free and forced to conform to wills that are not his own. How are the opponents at once free and subject to laws they have not agreed to?

I retort that the question is wrongly put. The citizen gives his consent to all the laws, including those which are passed in spite of his opposition, and even those which punish him when he dares to break any of them. The constant will of all the members of the State is the general will; by virtue of it they are citizens and free.[11] When in the popular assembly a law is proposed, what the people is asked is not exactly whether they approve or reject the proposal, but whether it is in conformity with the general will, which is their will. Each man, in giving his vote, states his opinion on that point; and the general will is found by counting votes. When therefore the opinion that is contrary to my own prevails, this proves neither more nor less than that I was mistaken, and that what I thought to be the general will was not so. If my particular opinion had carried the day I should have achieved the opposite of what was my will; and it is in that case that I should not have been free.

This presupposes, indeed, that all the qualities of the general will still reside in the majority: when they cease to do so, whatever side a man may take, liberty is no longer possible.

In my earlier demonstration of how particular wills are substituted for the general will in public deliberation, I have adequately pointed out the practicable methods of avoiding this abuse; and I shall have more to say of them later on. I have also given the principles for determining the proportional number of votes for declaring that will. A difference of one vote destroys equality; a single opponent destroys unanimity; but between equality and unanimity, there are several grades of unequal division, at each of which this proportion may be fixed in accordance with the condition and the needs of the body politic.

There are two general rules that may serve to regulate this relation. First, the more grave and important the questions discussed, the nearer should the opinion that is to prevail approach unanimity. Secondly, the more the matter in hand calls for speed, the smaller the prescribed difference in the numbers of votes may be allowed to become: where an instant decision has to be reached, a majority of one vote should be enough. The first of these two rules seems more in harmony with the laws, and the second with practical affairs. In any case, it is the combination of them that gives the best proportions for determining the majority necessary.

NOTES

1. "Learned inquiries into public right are often only the history of past abuses; and troubling to study them too deeply is a profitless infatuation" (*Essay on the Interests of France in Relation to its Neighbours,* by the Marquis d'Argenson). This is exactly what Grotius has done.

2. See a short treatise of Plutarch's entitled "That Animals Reason."

3. The Romans, who understood and respected the right of war more than any other nation on earth, carried their scruples on this head so far that a citizen was not allowed to serve as a volunteer without engaging himself expressly against the enemy, and against such and such an enemy by name. A legion in which the younger Cato was seeing his first service under Popilius having been reconstructed, the elder Cato wrote to Popilius that, if he wished his son to continue serving under him, he must administer to him a new military oath, because, the first having been annulled, he was no longer able to bear arms against the enemy. The same Cato wrote to his son telling him to take great care not to go into battle before taking this new oath. I know that the siege of Clusium and other isolated events can be quoted against me; but I am citing laws and customs. The Romans are the people that least

often transgressed its laws; and no other people has had such good ones.

4. The real meaning of this word has been almost wholly lost in modern times; most people mistake a town for a city, and a townsman for a citizen. They do not know that houses make a town, but citizens a city. The same mistake long ago cost the Carthaginians dear. I have never read of the title of citizens being given to the subjects of any prince, not even the ancient Macedonians or the English of to-day, though they are nearer liberty than anyone else. The French alone everywhere familiarly adopt the name of citizens, because, as can be seen from their dictionaries, they have no idea of its meaning; otherwise they would be guilty in usurping it, of the crime of *lèse-majesté:* among them, the name expresses a virtue, and not a right. When Bodin spoke of our citizens and townsmen, he fell into a bad blunder in taking the one class for the other. M. d'Alembert has avoided the error, and, in his article on Geneva, has clearly distinguished the four orders of men (or even five, counting mere foreigners) who dwell in our town, of which two only compose the Republic. No other French writer, to my knowledge, has understood the real meaning of the word citizen.

5. Under bad governments, this equality is only apparent and illusory: it serves only to keep the pauper in his poverty and the rich man in the position he has usurped. In fact, laws are always of use to those who possess and harmful to those who have nothing: from which it follows that the social state is advantageous to men only when all have something and none too much.

6. To be general, a will need not always be unanimous; but every vote must be counted: any exclusion is a breach of generality.

7. "Every interest," says the Marquis d'Argenson, "has different principles. The agreement of two particular interests is formed by opposition to a third." He might have added that the agreement of all interests is formed by opposition to that of each. If there were no different interests, the common interest would be barely felt, as it would encounter no obstacle; all would go on of its own accord, and politics would cease to be an art.

8. "In fact," says Machiavelli, "there are some divisions that are harmful to a Republic and some that are advantageous. Those which stir up sects and parties are harmful; those attended by neither are advantageous. Since, then, the founder of a Republic cannot help enmities arising, he ought at least to prevent them from growing into sects" (*History of Florence,* Book vii). [Rousseau quotes the Italian.]

9. Attentive readers, do not, I pray, be in a hurry to charge me with contradicting myself. The terminology made it unavoidable, considering the poverty of the language; but wait and see.

10. This should of course be understood as applying to a free State; for elsewhere family, goods, lack of a refuge, necessity, or violence may detain a man in a country against his will; and then his dwelling there no longer by itself implies his consent to the contract or to its violation.

11. At Genoa, the word *Liberty* may be read over the front of the prisons and on the chains of the galley-slaves. This application of the device is good and just. It is indeed only malefactors of all estates who prevent the citizen from being free. In the country in which all such men were in the galleys, the most perfect liberty would be enjoyed.

# 27    Emile

## JEAN-JACQUES ROUSSEAU

### Book V

... BUT FOR HER SEX, a woman is a man; she has the same organs, the same needs, the same faculties. The machine is the same in its construction; its parts, its working, and its appearance are similar. Regard it as you will the difference is only in degree.

Yet where sex is concerned man and woman are unlike; each is the complement of the other; the difficulty in comparing them lies in our inability to decide, in either case, what is a matter of sex, and what is not. General differences present themselves to the comparative anatomist and even to the superficial observer; they seem not to be a matter of sex; yet they are really sex differences, though the connection eludes our observation. How far such differences may extend we cannot tell; all we know for certain is that where man and woman are alike we have to do with the characteristics of the species; where they are unlike, we have to do with the characteristics of sex. Considered from these two standpoints, we find so many instances of likeness and unlikeness that it is perhaps one of the greatest of marvels how nature has contrived to make two beings so like and yet so different.

These resemblances and differences must have an influence on the moral nature; this inference is obvious, and it is confirmed by experience; it shows the vanity of the disputes as to the superiority or the equality of the sexes; as if each sex, pursuing the path marked out for it by nature, were not more perfect in that very divergence than if it more closely resembled the other. A perfect man and a perfect woman should no more be alike in mind than in face, and perfection admits of neither less nor more.

In the union of the sexes each alike contributes to the common end, but in different ways. From this diversity springs the first difference which may be observed between man and woman in their moral relations. The man should be strong and active; the woman should be weak and passive; the one must have both the power and the will; it is enough that the other should offer little resistance.

When this principle is admitted, it follows that woman is specially made for man's delight. If man in his turn ought to be pleasing in her eyes, the necessity is less urgent, his virtue is in his strength, he pleases because he is strong. I grant you this is not the law of love, but it is the law of nature, which is older than love itself.

If woman is made to please and to be in subjection to man, she ought to make herself pleasing in his eyes and not provoke him to anger; her strength is in her charms, by their means she should compel him to discover and use his strength. The surest way of arousing this strength is to make it necessary by resistance. Thus pride comes to the help of desire and each exults in the other's victory. This is the origin of attack and defence, of the boldness of one sex and the timidity of the other, and even of the shame and modesty with which nature has armed the weak for the conquest of the strong.

Who can possibly suppose that nature has prescribed the same advances to the one sex as to the other, or that the first to feel desire should be the first to show it? What strange depravity of judgment! The consequences of the act being so different for the two sexes, is it natural that they should enter upon it with equal boldness? How can anyone fail to see that when the share of each is so unequal, if the one were not controlled by modesty as the other is controlled by nature, the result would be the destruction of both, and the human race would perish through the very means ordained for its continuance?

Women so easily stir a man's senses and fan the ashes of a dying passion, that if philosophy ever succeeded in introducing this custom into any unlucky country, especially if it were a warm country where more women are born than men, the men, tyrannised over by the women, would at last become their victims, and would be dragged to their death without the least chance of escape.

Female animals are without this sense of shame, but what of that? Are their desires as boundless as those of women, which are curbed by this shame? The desires of the animals are the result of necessity, and when the need is satisfied, the desire ceases; they no longer make a feint of repulsing the male, they do it in earnest. Their seasons of complaisance are short and soon over. Impulse and restraint are alike the work of nature. But what would take the place of this negative instinct in women if you rob them of their modesty?

The Most High has deigned to do honour to mankind; he has endowed man with boundless passions, together with a law to guide them, so that man may be alike free and self-controlled; though swayed by these passions man is endowed with reason by which to control them. Woman is also endowed with boundless passions; God has given her modesty to restrain them. Moreover, he has given to both a present reward for the right use of their powers, in the delight which springs from that right use of them, *i.e.,* the taste for right conduct established as the law of our behaviour. To my mind this is far higher than the instinct of the beasts.

Whether the woman shares the man's passion or not, whether she is willing or unwilling to satisfy it, she always repulses him and defends herself, though not always with the same vigour, and therefore not always with the same success. If the siege is to be successful, the besieged must permit or direct the attack. How skillfully can she stimulate the efforts of the aggressor. The freest and most delightful of activities does not permit of any real violence; reason and nature are alike against it; nature, in that she has given the weaker party strength enough to resist if she chooses; reason, in that actual violence is not only most brutal in itself, but it defeats its own ends, not only because the man thus declares war against his companion and thus gives her a right to defend her person and her liberty even at the cost of the enemy's life, but also because the woman alone is the judge of her condition, and a child would have no father if any man might usurp a father's rights.

Thus the different constitution of the two sexes leads us to a third conclusion, that the stronger party seems to be master, but is as a matter of fact dependent on the weaker, and that, not by any foolish custom of gallantry, nor yet by the magnanimity of the protector, but by an inexorable law of nature. For nature has endowed woman with a power of stimulating man's passions in excess of man's power of satisfying those passions, and thus made him dependent on her goodwill, and compelled him in his turn to endeavour to please her, so that she may be willing to yield to his superior strength. Is it weakness which yields to force, or is it voluntary self-surrender? This uncertainty constitutes the chief charm of the man's victory, and the woman is usually cunning enough to leave him in doubt. In this respect the woman's mind exactly resembles her body; far from being ashamed of her weakness, she is proud of it; her soft muscles offer no resistance, she professes that she cannot lift the lightest weight; she would be ashamed to be strong. And why? Not only to gain an appearance of refinement; she is too clever for that; she is providing herself beforehand with excuses, with the right to be weak if she chooses. . . .

The consequences of sex are wholly unlike for man and woman. The male is only a male now and again, the female is always a female, or at least all her youth; everything reminds her of her sex; the performance of her functions requires a special constitution. She needs care during pregnancy and freedom from work when her child is born; she must have a quiet, easy life while she nurses her children; their education calls for patience and gentleness, for a zeal and love which nothing can dismay; she forms a bond between father and child, she alone can win the father's love for his children and convince him that they are indeed his own. What loving care is required to preserve a united family! And there should be no question of virtue in all this, it must be a labour of love, without which the human race would be doomed to extinction.

The mutual duties of the two sexes are not, and cannot be, equally binding on both. Women do wrong to complain of the inequality of man-made laws; this inequality is not of man's making, or at any rate it is not the result of mere prejudice, but of reason. She to whom nature has entrusted the care of the children must hold herself responsible for them to their father. No doubt every breach of faith is wrong, and every faithless husband, who robs his wife of the sole reward of the stern duties of her sex, is cruel and unjust; but the faithless wife is worse; she destroys the family and breaks the bonds of nature; when she gives her husband children who are not his own, she is false both to him and them, her crime is not infidelity but treason. To my mind, it is the source of dissension and of crime of every kind. Can any position be more wretched than that of the unhappy father who, when he clasps his child to his breast, is haunted by the suspicion that this is the child of another, the badge of his own dishonour, a thief who is robbing his own children of their inheritance. Under such circumstances the family is little more than a group of secret enemies, armed against each other by a guilty woman, who compels them to pretend to love one another.

Thus it is not enough that a wife should be faithful; her husband, along with his friends and neighbours, must believe in her fidelity; she must be modest, devoted, retiring; she should have the witness not only of a good conscience, but of a good reputation. In a word, if a father must love his children, he must be able to respect their mother. For these reasons it is not enough that the woman should be chaste, she must preserve her reputation and her good name. From these principles there arises not only a moral difference between the sexes, but also a fresh motive for duty and propriety, which prescribes to women in particular the most scrupulous attention to their conduct, their manners, their behaviour. Vague assertions as to the equality of the sexes and the similarity of their duties are only empty words; they are no answer to my argument.

It is a poor sort of logic to quote isolated exceptions against laws so firmly established. Woman, you say, are not always bearing children. Granted; yet that is their proper business. Because there are a hundred or so of large towns in the world where women live licentiously and have few children, will you maintain that it is their business to have few children? And what would become of your towns if the remote country districts, with their simpler and purer women, did not make up for the barrenness of your fine ladies? There are plenty of country places where women with only four or five children are reckoned unfruitful. In conclusion, although here and there a woman may have few children,[1] what difference does it make? Is it any the less a woman's business to be a mother? And do not the general laws of nature and morality make provision for this state of things?

Even if there were these long intervals, which you assume, between the periods of pregnancy, can a woman suddenly change her way of life without danger? Can she be a nursing mother to-day and a soldier to-morrow? Will she change her tastes and her feelings as a chameleon changes his colour? Will she pass at once from the privacy of household duties and indoor occupations to the buffeting of the winds, the toils, the labours, the perils of war? Will she be now timid,[2] now brave, now fragile, now robust? If the young men of Paris finds a soldier's life too hard for them, how would a woman put up with it, a woman who has hardly ventured out of doors without a parasol and who has scarcely put a foot to the ground? Will she make a good soldier at an age when even men are retiring from this arduous business?

There are countries, I grant you, where women bear and rear children with little or no difficulty, but in those lands the men go half-naked in all weathers, they strike down the wild beast, they carry a canoe as easily as a knapsack, they pursue the chase for 700 or 800 leagues, they sleep in the open on the bare ground, they bear incredible fatigues and go many days without food. When women become strong, men become still stronger; when men become soft, women become softer; change both the terms and the ratio remains unaltered.

I am quite aware that Plato, in the *Republic,* assigns the same gymnastics to women and men. Having got rid of the family there is no place for women in his system of government, so he is forced to turn them into men. That great genius has worked out his plans in detail and has provided for every contingency; he has even provided against a difficulty which in all likelihood no one would ever have raised; but he has not succeeded in meeting the real difficulty. I am not speaking of the alleged community of wives which has often been laid to his charge; this assertion only shows that his detractors have never read his works. I refer to that political promiscuity under which the same occupations are assigned to both sexes alike, a scheme which could only lead to intolerable evils; I refer to that subversion of all the tenderest of our natural feelings, which he sacrificed to an artificial sentiment which can only exist by their aid. Will the bonds of convention hold firm without some foundation in nature? Can devotion to the state exist apart from the love of those near and dear to us? Can patriotism thrive except in the soil of that miniature fatherland, the home? Is it not the good son, the good husband, the good father, who makes the good citizen?

When once it is proved that men and women are and ought to be unlike in constitution and in temperament, it follows that their education must be different. Nature teaches us that they should work together, but that each has its own share of the work; the end is the same, but the means are different, as are also the feelings which direct them. We have attempted to paint a natural man, let us try to paint a helpmeet for him.

You must follow nature's guidance if you would walk aright. The native characters of sex should be respected as nature's handiwork. You are always saying, "Women have such and such faults, from which we are free." You are misled by your vanity; what would be faults in you are virtues in them; and things would go worse, if they were without these so-called faults. Take care that they do not degenerate into evil, but beware of destroying them.

On the other hand, women are always exclaiming that we educate them for nothing but vanity and coquetry, that we keep them amused with trifles that we may be their masters; we are responsible, so they say, for the faults we attribute to them. How silly! What have men to do with the education of girls? What is there to hinder their mothers educating them as they please? There are no colleges for girls; so much the better for them! Would God there were none for the boys, their education would be more sensible and more wholesome. Who is it that compels a girl to waste her time on foolish trifles? Are they forced, against their will, to spend half their time over their toilet, following the example set them by you? Who prevents you teaching them, or having them taught, whatever seems good in your eyes? Is it our fault that we are charmed by their beauty and delighted by their airs and graces, if we are attracted and flattered by the arts they learn from you, if we love to see them prettily dressed, if we let them display at leisure the weapons by which we are subjugated? Well then, educate them like men. The more women are like men, the less influence they will have over men, and then men will be masters indeed.

All the faculties common to both sexes are not equally shared between them, but taken as a whole they are fairly divided. Woman is worth more as a woman and less as a man; when she makes a good use of her own rights, she has the best of it; when she tries to usurp our rights, she is our inferior. It is impossible to controvert this, except by quoting exceptions after the usual fashion of the partisans of the fair sex.

To cultivate the masculine virtues in women and to neglect their own is evidently to do them an injury. Women are too clear-sighted to be thus deceived; when they try to usurp our privileges they do not abandon their own; with this result: they are unable to make use of two incompatible things, so they fall below their own level as women, instead of rising to the level of men. If you are a sensible mother you will take my advice. Do not try to make your daughter a good man in defiance of nature. Make her a good woman, and be sure it will be better both for her and us.

Does this mean that she must be brought up in ignorance and kept to housework only? Is she to be man's handmaid or his helpmate? Will he dispense with her greatest charm, her companionship? To keep her a slave will he prevent her knowing and feeling? Will he make an automaton of her? No, indeed, that is not the teaching of nature, who has given women such a pleasant easy wit. On the contrary, nature means them to think, to will, to love, to cultivate their minds as well as their persons; she puts these weapons in their hands to make up for their lack of strength and to enable them to direct the strength of men. They should learn many things, but only such things as are suitable.

When I consider the special purpose of woman, when I observe her inclinations or reckon up her duties, everything combines to indicate the mode of education she requires. Men and women are made for each other, but their mutual dependence differs in degree; man is dependent on woman through his desires; woman is dependent on man through her desires and also through her needs; he could do without her better than she can do without him. She cannot fulfil her purpose in life without his aid, without his goodwill, without his respect; she is dependent on our feelings, on the price we put upon her virtue, and the opinion we have of her charms and her deserts. Nature herself has decreed that woman, both for herself and her children, should be at the mercy of man's judgment.

Worth alone will not suffice, a woman must be thought worthy; nor beauty, she must be admired; nor virtue, she must be respected. A woman's honour does not depend on her conduct alone, but on her reputation, and no woman who permits herself to be considered vile is really virtuous. A man has no one but himself to consider, and so long as he does right he may defy public opinion; but when a woman does right her task is only half finished, and what people think of her matters as much as what she really is. Hence her education must, in this respect, be different from man's education. "What will people think" is the grave of a man's virtue and the throne of a woman's.

The children's health depends in the first place on the mother's, and the early education of man is also in a woman's hands; his morals, his passions, his tastes, his pleasures, his happiness itself, depend on her. A woman's education must therefore be planned in relation to man. To be pleasing in his sight, to win his respect and love, to train him in childhood, to tend him in manhood, to counsel and console, to make his life pleasant and happy, these are the duties of woman for all time, and this is what she should be taught while she is young. The further we depart from this principle, the further we shall be from our goal, and all our precepts will fail to secure her happiness or our own.

Every woman desires to be pleasing in men's eyes, and this is right; but there is a great difference between wishing to please a man of worth, a really lovable man, and seeking to please those foppish manikins who are a disgrace to their own sex and to the sex which they imitate. Neither nature nor reason can induce a woman to love an effeminate person, nor will she win love by imitating such a person.

If a woman discards the quiet modest bearing of her sex, and adopts the airs of such foolish creatures, she is not following her vocation, she is forsaking it; she is robbing herself of the rights to which she lays claim. "If we were different," she says, "the men would not like us." She is mistaken. Only a fool likes folly; to wish to attract such men only shows her own foolishness. If there were no frivolous men, women would soon make them, and women are more responsible for men's follies than men are for theirs. The woman who loves true manhood and seeks to find favour in its sight will adopt means adapted to her ends. Woman is a coquette by profession, but her coquetry varies with her aims; let these aims be in accordance with those of nature, and a woman will receive a fitting education.

Even the tiniest little girls love finery; they are not content to be pretty, they must be admired; their little airs and graces show that their heads are full of this idea, and as soon as they can understand they are controlled by "What will people think of you?" If you are foolish enough to try this way with little boys, it will not have the same effect; give them their freedom and their sports, and they care very little what people think; it is a work of time to bring them under the control of this law.

However acquired, this early education of little girls is an excellent thing in itself. As the birth of the body must precede the birth of the mind, so the training of the body must precede the cultivation of the mind. This is true of both sexes; but the aim of physical training for boys and girls is not the same; in the one case it is the development of strength, in the other of grace; not that these qualities should be peculiar to either sex, but that their relative values should be different. Women should be strong enough to do anything gracefully; men should be skillful enough to do anything easily. . . .

Boys and girls have many games in common, and this is as it should be; do they not play together when they are grown up? They have also special tastes of their own. Boys want movement and noise, drums, tops, toy-carts; girls prefer things which appeal to the eye, and can be used for dressing-up—mirrors, jewellery, finery, and specially dolls. The doll is the girl's special plaything; this shows her instinctive bent towards her life's work. The art of pleasing finds its physical basis in personal adornment, and this physical side of the art is the only one which the child can cultivate.

Here is a little girl busy all day with her doll; she is always changing its clothes, dressing and undressing it, trying new combinations of trimmings well or ill matched; her fingers are clumsy, her taste is crude, but there is no mistaking her bent; in this endless occupation time flies unheeded, the hours slip away unnoticed, even meals are forgotten. She is more eager for adornment than for food. "But she is dressing her doll, not herself," you will say. Just so; she sees her doll, she cannot see herself; she cannot do anything for herself, she has neither the training, nor the talent, nor the strength; as yet she herself is nothing, she is engrossed in her doll and all her coquetry is devoted to it. This will not always be so; in due time she will be her own doll. . . .

Whatever may be said by the scornful, good sense belongs to both sexes alike. Girls are usually more docile than boys, and they should be subjected to more authority, as I shall show later on, but that is no reason why they should be required to do things in which they can see neither rhyme nor reason. The mother's art consists in showing the use of everything they are set to do, and this is all the easier as the girl's intelligence is more precocious than the boy's. This principle banishes, both for boys and girls, not only those pursuits which never lead to any appreciable results, not even increasing the charms of those who have pursued them, but also those studies whose utility is beyond the scholar's present age and can only be appreciated in later years. If I object to little boys being made to learn to read, still more do I object to it for little girls until they are able to see the use of reading; we generally think more of our own ideas than theirs in our attempts to convince them of the utility of this art. After all, why should a little girl know how to read and write? Has she a house to manage? Most of them make a bad use of this fatal knowledge, and girls are so full of curiosity that few of them will fail to learn without compulsion. Possibly cyphering should come first; there is nothing so obviously useful, nothing

which needs so much practice or gives so much opportunity for error as reckoning. If the little girl does not get the cherries for her lunch without an arithmetical exercise, she will soon learn to count. . . .

Show the sense of the tasks you set your little girls, but keep them busy. Idleness and insubordination are two very dangerous faults, and very hard to cure when once established. Girls should be attentive and industrious, but this is not enough by itself; they should early be accustomed to restraint. This misfortune, if such it be, is inherent in their sex, and they will never escape from it, unless to endure more cruel sufferings. All their life long, they will have to submit to the strictest and most enduring restraints, those of propriety. They must be trained to bear the yoke from the first, so that they may not feel it, to master their own caprices and to submit themselves to the will of others. If they were always eager to be at work, they should sometimes be compelled to do nothing. Their childish faults, unchecked and unheeded, may easily lead to dissipation, frivolity, and inconstancy. To guard against this, teach them above all things self-control. Under our senseless conditions, the life of a good woman is a perpetual struggle against self; it is only fair woman should bear her share of the ills she has brought upon man. . . .

Just because they have, or ought to have, little freedom, they are apt to indulge themselves too fully with regard to such freedom as they have; they carry everything to extremes, and they devote themselves to their games with an enthusiasm even greater than that of boys. This is the second difficulty to which I referred. This enthusiasm must be kept in check, for it is the source of several vices commonly found among women, caprice and that extravagant admiration which leads a woman to regard a thing with rapture today and to be quite indifferent to it tomorrow. This fickleness of taste is as dangerous as exaggeration; and both spring from the same cause. Do not deprive them of mirth, laughter, noise, and romping games, but do not let them tire of one game and go off to another; do not leave them for a moment without restraint. Train them to break off their games and return to their other occupations without a murmur. Habit is all that is needed, as you have nature on your side.

This habitual restraint produces a docility which woman requires all her life long, for she will always be in subjection to a man, or to man's judgment, and she will never be free to set her own opinion above his. What is most wanted in a woman is gentleness; formed to obey a creature so imperfect as man, a creature often vicious and always faulty, she should early learn to submit to injustice and to suffer the wrongs inflicted on her by her husband without complaint; she must be gentle for her own sake, not his. Bitterness and obstinacy only multiply the sufferings of the wife and the misdeeds of the husband; the man feels that these are not the weapons to be used against him. Heaven did not make women attractive and persuasive that they might degenerate into bitterness, or meek that they should desire the mastery; their soft voice was not meant for hard words, nor their delicate features for the frowns of anger. When they lose their temper they forget themselves; often enough they have just cause of complaint; but when they scold they always put themselves in the wrong. We should each adopt the tone which befits our sex; a soft-hearted husband may make an overbearing wife, but a man, unless he is a perfect monster, will sooner or later yield to his wife's gentleness, and the victory will be hers. . . .

What is, is good, and no general law can be bad. This special skill with which the female sex is endowed is a fair equivalent for its lack of strength; without it woman would be man's slave, not his helpmeet. By her superiority in this respect she maintains her equality with man, and rules in obedience. She has everything against her, our faults and her own weakness and timidity; her beauty and her wiles are all that she has. Should she not cultivate both? Yet beauty is not universal; it may be destroyed by all sorts of accidents, it will disappear with years, and habit will destroy its influence. A woman's real resource is her wit; not that foolish wit which is so greatly admired in society, a wit which does nothing to make life happier; but that wit which is adapted to her condition, the art of taking advantage of our position and controlling us through our own strength. Words cannot tell how beneficial this is to man, what a charm it gives to the society of men and women, how it checks the petulant child and restrains the brutal husband; without it the home would be a scene of strife; with it, it is the abode of happiness. I know that this power is abused by the sly and the spiteful; but what is there that is not liable to abuse? Do not destroy the means of happiness because the wicked use them to our hurt.

The toilet may attract notice, but it is the person that wins our hearts. Our finery is not us; its very artificiality often offends, and that which is least noticeable in itself often wins the most attention. The education of our girls is, in this respect, absolutely topsy-turvy. Ornaments are promised them as rewards, and they are taught to delight in elaborate finery. "How lovely she is!" people say when she is most dressed up. On the contrary, they should be taught that so much finery is only required to hide their defects, and that beauty's real triumph is to shine alone. The love of fashion is contrary to good taste, for faces do not change with the fashion, and while the person remains unchanged, what suits it at one time will suit it always. . . .

Growing girls perceive at once that all this outside adornment is not enough unless they have charms of their own. They cannot make themselves beautiful, they are too young for coquetry, but they are not too young to acquire graceful gestures, a pleasing voice, a self-possessed manner, a light step, a graceful bearing, to choose whatever advantages are within their reach. The voice extends its range, it grows stronger and more resonant, the arms become plumper, the bearing more assured, and they perceive that it is easy to attract attention however dressed. Needlework and industry suffice no longer, fresh gifts are developing and their usefulness is already recognised.

I know that stern teachers would have us refuse to teach little girls to sing or dance, or to acquire any of the pleasing arts. This strikes me as absurd. Who should learn these arts—our boys? Are these to be the favourite accomplishments of men or women? Of neither, say they; profane songs are simply so many crimes, dancing is an invention of the Evil One; her tasks and her prayers are all the amusement a young girl should have. What strange amusements for a child of ten! I fear that these little saints who have been forced to spend their childhood in prayers to God will pass their youth in another fashion; when they are married they will try to make up for lost time. I think we must consider age as well as sex; a young girl should not live like her grandmother; she should be lively, merry, and eager; she should sing and dance to her heart's content, and enjoy all the innocent pleasures of youth; the time will come, all too soon, when she must settle down and adopt a more serious tone. . . .

Taste is formed partly by industry and partly by talent, and by its means that mind is unconsciously opened to the idea of beauty of every kind, till at length it attains to those moral ideas which are so closely related to beauty. Perhaps this is one reason why ideas of propriety and modesty are acquired earlier by girls than by boys, for to suppose that this early feeling is due to the teaching of the governesses would show little knowledge of their style of teaching and of the natural development of the human mind. The art of speaking stands first among the pleasing arts; it alone can add fresh charms to those which have been blunted by habit. It is the mind which not only gives life to the body, but renews, so to speak, its youth; the flow of feelings and ideas give life and variety to the countenance, and the conversation to which it gives rise arouses and sustains attention, and fixes it continuously on one object. I suppose this is why little girls so soon learn to prattle prettily, and why men enjoy listening to them even before the child can understand them; they are watching for the first gleam of intelligence and sentiment.

Women have ready tongues; they talk earlier, more easily, and more pleasantly than men. They are also said to talk more; this may be true, but I am prepared to reckon it to their credit; eyes and mouth are equally busy and for the same cause. A man says what he knows, a woman says what will please; the one needs knowledge, the other taste; utility should be the man's object; the woman speaks to give pleasure. There should be nothing in common but truth.

You should not check a girl's prattle like a boy's by the harsh question, "What is the use of that?" but by another question at least as difficult to answer, "What effect will that have?" At this early age when they know neither good nor evil, and are incapable of judging others, they should make this their rule and never say anything which is unpleasant to those about them; this rule is all the more difficult to apply because it must always be subordinated to our first rule, "Never tell a lie." . . .

If young boys must not be allowed to ask unsuitable questions, much more must they be forbidden to little girls; if their curiosity is satisfied or unskillfully evaded it is a much more serious matter, for they are so keen to guess the mysteries concealed from them and so skilful to discover them. But while I would not permit them to ask questions, I would have them questioned frequently, and pains should be taken to make them talk; let them be teased to make them speak freely, to make them answer readily, to loosen mind and tongue while it can be done without danger. Such conversation always leading to merriment, yet skilfully controlled and directed, would form a delightful amusement at this age and might instil into these youthful hearts the first and perhaps the most helpful lessons in morals which they will ever receive, by teaching them in the guise of pleasure and fun what qualities are esteemed by men and what is the true glory and happiness of a good woman.

If boys are incapable of forming any true idea of religion, much more is it beyond the grasp of girls; and for this reason I would speak of it all the sooner to little girls, for if we wait till they are ready for a serious discussion of these deep subjects we should be in danger of never speaking of religion at all. A woman's reason is practical, and therefore she soon arrives at a given conclusion, but she fails to discover it for herself. The social relation of the sexes is a wonderful thing. This relation produces a moral person of which woman is the eye and man the hand, but the two are so dependent on one another that the man teaches the woman what to see, while she teaches him what to do. If women could discover principles and if men had as good heads for detail, they would be mutually independent, they would live in perpetual strife, and there would be an end to all society. But in their mutual harmony each contributes to a common purpose; each follows the other's lead, each commands and each obeys.

As a woman's conduct is controlled by public opinion, so is her religion ruled by authority. The daughter should follow her mother's religion, the wife her husband's. Were that religion false, the docility which leads mother and daughter to submit to nature's laws would blot out the sin of error in the sight of God. Unable to judge for themselves they should accept the judgment of father and husband as that of the church. . . .

Moreover, it is as well to observe that, until the age when the reason becomes enlightened, when growing emotion gives a voice to conscience, what is wrong for young people is what those about them have decided to be wrong. What they are told to do is good; what they are forbidden to do is bad; that is all they ought to know: this shows how important it is for girls, even more than for boys, that the right people should be chosen to be with them and to have authority over them. At last there comes a time when they begin to judge things for themselves, and that is the time to change your method of education.

Perhaps I have said too much already. To what shall we reduce the education of our women if we give them no law but that of conventional prejudice? Let us not degrade so far the sex which rules over us, and which does us honour when we have not made it vile. For all mankind there is a law anterior to that of public opinion. All other laws should bend before the inflexible control of this law; it is the judge of public opinion, and only in so far as the esteem of men is in accordance with this law has it any claim on our obedience.

This law is our individual conscience. I will not repeat what has been said already; it is enough to point out that if these two laws clash, the education of women will always be imperfect. Right feeling without respect for public opinion will not give them that delicacy of soul which lends to right conduct the charm of social approval; while respect for public opinion without right feeling will only make false and wicked women who put appearances in the place of virtue.

It is, therefore, important to cultivate a faculty which serves as judge between the two guides, which does not permit conscience to go astray and corrects the errors of prejudice. That faculty is reason. But what a crowd of questions arise at this word. Are women capable of solid reason; should they cultivate it, can they cultivate it successfully? Is this culture useful in relation to the functions laid upon them? Is it compatible with becoming simplicity?

The different ways of envisaging and answering these questions lead to two extremes; some would have us keep women indoors sewing and spinning with their maids; thus they make them nothing more than the chief servant of their master. Others, not content to secure their rights lead them to usurp ours; for to make woman our superior in all the qualities proper to her sex, and to make her our equal in all the rest, what is this but to transfer to the woman the superiority which nature has given to her husband?

The reason which teaches a man his duties is not very complex; the reason which teaches a woman hers is even simpler. The obedience and fidelity which she owes to her husband, the tenderness and care due to her children, are such natural and self-evident consequences of her position that she cannot honestly refuse her consent to the inner voice which is her guide, nor fail to discern her duty in her natural inclination.

I would not altogether blame those who would restrict a woman to the labours of her sex and would leave her in profound ignorance of everything else; but that would require a standard of morality at once very simple and very healthy, or a life withdrawn from the world. In great towns, among immoral men, such a woman would be too easily led astray; her virtue would too often be at the mercy of circumstances; in this age of philosophy, virtue must be able to resist temptation; she must know beforehand what she may hear and what she should think of it.

Moreover, in submission to man's judgment she should deserve his esteem; above all she should obtain the esteem of her husband; she should not only make him love her person, she should make him approve her conduct; she should justify his choice before the world, and do honour to her husband through the honour given to the wife. But how can she set about this task if she is ignorant of our institutions, our customs, our notions of propriety, if she knows nothing of the source of man's judgment, nor the passions by which it is swayed? Since she depends both on her own conscience and on public opinion, she must learn to know and reconcile these two laws, and to put her own conscience first only when the two are opposed to each other. She becomes the judge of her own judges, she decides when she should obey and when she should refuse her obedience. She weighs their prejudices before she accepts or rejects them; she learns to trace them to their source, to foresee what they will be, and to turn them in her own favour; she is careful never to give cause for blame if duty allows her to avoid it. This cannot be properly done without cultivating her mind and reason. . . .

. . . The more modest a woman is, the more art she needs, even with her husband. Yes, I maintain that *coquetry*, kept within bounds, becomes modest and true, and out of it springs a law of right conduct.

One of my opponents has very truly asserted that virtue is one; you cannot disintegrate it and choose this and reject the other. If you love virtue, you love it in its entirety, and you close your heart when you can, and you always close your lips to the feelings which you ought not to allow. Moral truth is not only what is, but what is good; what is bad ought not to be, and ought not to be confessed, especially when that confession produces results which might have been avoided. If I were tempted to steal, and in confessing it I tempted another to become my accomplice, the very confession of my temptation would amount to a yielding to that temptation. Why do you say that

modesty makes women false? Are those who lose their modesty more sincere than the rest? Not so, they are a thousandfold more deceitful. This degree of depravity is due to many vices, none of which is rejected, vices which owe their power to intrigue and falsehood.[3]

On the other hand, those who are not utterly shameless, who take no pride in their faults, who are able to conceal their desires even from those who inspire them, those who confess their passion most reluctantly, these are the truest and most sincere, these are they on whose fidelity you may generally rely.

The only example I know which might be quoted as a recognised exception to these remarks is Mlle. de L'Enclos; and she was considered a prodigy. In her scorn for the virtues of women, she practised, so they say, the virtues of a man. She is praised for her frankness and uprightness; she was a trustworthy acquaintance and a faithful friend. To complete the picture of her glory it is said that she became a man. That may be, but in spite of her high reputation I should no more desire that man as my friend than as my mistress.

This is not so irrelevant as it seems. I am aware of the tendencies of our modern philosophy which make a jest of female modesty and its so-called insincerity; I also perceive that the most certain result of this philosophy will be to deprive the women of this century of such shreds of honour as they still possess.

On these grounds I think we may decide in general terms what sort of education is suited to the female mind, and the objects to which we should turn its attention in early youth.

As I have already said, the duties of their sex are more easily recognised than performed. They must learn in the first place to love those duties by considering the advantages to be derived from them—that is the only way to make duty easy. Every age and condition has its own duties. We are quick to see our duty if we love it. Honour your position as a woman, and in whatever station of life to which it shall please heaven to call you, you will be well off. The essential thing is to be what nature has made you; women are only too ready to be what men would have them.

The search for abstract and speculative truths, for principles and axioms in science, for all that tends to wide generalisation, is beyond a woman's grasp; their studies should be thoroughly practical. It is their business to apply the principles discovered by men, it is their place to make the observations which lead men to discover those principles. A woman's thoughts, beyond the range of her immediate duties, should be directed to the study of men, or the acquirement of that agreeable learning whose sole end is the formation of taste; for the works of genius are beyond her reach, and she has neither the accuracy nor the attention for success in the exact sciences; as for the physical sciences, to decide the relations between living creatures and the laws of nature is the task of that sex which is more active and enterprising, which sees more things, that sex which is possessed of greater strength and is more accustomed to the exercise of that strength. Woman, weak as she is and limited in her range of observation, perceives and judges the forces at her disposal to supplement her weakness, and those forces are the passions of man. Her own mechanism is more powerful than ours; she has many levers which may set the human heart in motion. She must find a way to make us desire what she cannot achieve unaided and what she considers necessary or pleasing; therefore she must have a thorough knowledge of man's mind; not an abstract knowledge of the mind of man in general, but the mind of those men who are about her, the mind of those men who have authority over her, either by law or custom. She must learn to divine their feelings from speech and action, look and gesture. By her own speech and action, look and gesture, she must be able to inspire them with the feelings she desires, without seeming to have any such purpose. The men will have a better philosophy of the human heart, but she will read more accurately in the heart of men. Woman should discover, so to speak, an experimental morality, man should reduce it to a system. Woman has more wit, man more genius; woman observes, man reasons; together they provide the clearest light and the profoundest knowledge which is possible to the unaided human mind; in a word, the surest knowledge of self and of others

of which the human race is capable. In this way art may constantly tend to the perfection of the instrument which nature has given us.

The world is woman's book; if she reads it ill, it is either her own fault or she is blinded by passion. Yet the genuine mother of a family is no woman of the world, she is almost as much of a recluse as the nun in her convent. Those who have marriageable daughters should do what is or ought to be done for those who are entering the cloisters: they should show them the pleasures they forsake before they are allowed to renounce them, lest the deceitful picture of unknown pleasures should creep in to disturb the happiness of their retreat. In France it is the girls who live in convents and the wives who flaunt in society. Among the ancients it was quite otherwise; girls enjoyed, as I have said already, many games and public festivals; the married women lived in retirement. This was a more reasonable custom and more conducive to morality. A girl may be allowed a certain amount of coquetry, and she may be mainly occupied at amusement. A wife has other responsibilities at home, and she is no longer on the look-out for a husband; but women would not appreciate the change, and unluckily it is they who set the fashion. Mothers, let your daughters be your companions. Give them good sense and an honest heart, and then conceal from them nothing that a pure eye may behold. Balls, assemblies, sports, the theatre itself; everything which viewed amiss delights imprudent youth may be safely displayed to a healthy mind. The more they know of these noisy pleasures, the sooner they will cease to desire them. . . .

If you would inspire young people with a love of good conduct avoid saying, "Be good"; make it their interest to be good; make them feel the value of goodness and they will love it. It is not enough to show this effect in the distant future, show it now, in the relations of the present, in the character of their lovers. Describe a good man, a man of worth, teach them to recognise him when they see him, to love him for their own sake; convince them that such a man alone can make them happy as friend, wife, or mistress. Let reason lead the way to virtue; make them feel that the empire of their sex and all the advantages derived from it depend not merely on the right conduct, the morality, of women, but also on that of men; that they have little hold over the vile and base, and that the lover is incapable of serving his mistress unless he can do homage to virtue. You may then be sure that when you describe the manners of our age you will inspire them with a genuine disgust; when you show them men of fashion they will despise them; you will give them a distaste for their maxims, an aversion to their sentiments, and a scorn for their empty gallantry; you will arouse a nobler ambition, to reign over great and strong souls, the ambition of the Spartan women to rule over men. A bold, shameless, intriguing woman, who can only attract her lovers by coquetry and retain them by her favours, wins a servile obedience in common things; in weighty and important matters she has no influence over them. But the woman who is both virtuous, wise, and charming, she who, in a word, combines love and esteem, can send them at her bidding to the end of the world, to war, to glory, and to death at her behest. This is a fine kingdom and worth the winning.

This is the spirit in which Sophy has been educated, she has been trained carefully rather than strictly, and her taste has been followed rather than thwarted. Let us say just a word about her person, according to the description I have given to Emile and the picture he himself has formed of the wife in whom he hopes to find happiness.

I cannot repeat too often that I am not dealing with prodigies. Emile is no prodigy, neither is Sophy. He is a man and she is a woman; this is all they have to boast of. In the present confusion between the sexes it is almost a miracle to belong to one's own sex. . . .

Needlework is what Sophy likes best; and the feminine arts have been taught her most carefully, even those you would not expect, such as cutting out and dressmaking. There is nothing she cannot do with her needle, and nothing that she does not take a delight in doing; but lacemaking is her favourite occupation, because there is nothing which requires such a pleasing attitude, nothing which calls for such grace and dexterity of finger. She has also studied all the details of housekeeping; she understands cooking and cleaning; she knows the prices of food, and also how to choose it; she can keep accounts accurately, she is her mother's housekeeper. Some day she will be the mother of a family; by managing her father's house she is preparing to manage her own; she can take the place of any of the servants and she is always ready to do so. You cannot give orders unless you can do the work yourself; that is why her mother sets her to do it. Sophy does not think of that; her first duty is to be a good daughter, and that is all she thinks about for the present. Her one idea is to help her mother and relieve her of some of her anxieties. However, she does not like them all equally well. For instance, she likes dainty food, but she does not like cooking; the details of cookery offend her, and things are never clean enough for her. She is extremely sensitive in this respect and carries her sensitiveness to a fault; she would let the whole dinner boil over into the fire rather than soil her cuffs. She has always disliked inspecting the kitchen-garden for the same reason. The soil is dirty, and as soon as she sees the manure heap she fancies there is a disagreeable smell.

This defect is the result of her mother's teaching. According to her, cleanliness is one of the most necessary of a woman's duties, a special duty, of the highest importance and a duty imposed by nature. Nothing could be more revolting than a dirty woman, and a husband who tires of her is not to blame. She insisted so strongly on this duty when Sophy was little, she required such absolute cleanliness in her person, clothing, room, work, and toilet, that use has become habit, till it absorbs one half of her time and controls the other; so that she thinks less of how to do a thing than of how to do it without getting dirty. . . .

Sophy's mind is pleasing but not brilliant, and thorough but not deep; it is the sort of mind which calls for no remark, as she never seems cleverer or stupider than oneself. When people talk to her they always find what she says attractive, though it may not be highly ornamental according to modern ideas of an educated woman; her mind has been formed not only by reading, but by conversation with her father and mother, by her own reflections, and by her own observations in the little world in which she has lived. Sophy is naturally merry; as a child she was even giddy; but her mother cured her of her silly ways, little by little, lest too sudden a change should make her self-conscious. Thus she became modest and retiring while still a child, and now that she is a child no longer, she finds it easier to continue this conduct than it would have been to acquire it without knowing why. It is amusing to see her occasionally return to her old ways and indulge in childish mirth and then suddenly check herself, with silent lips, downcast eyes, and rosy blushes; neither child nor woman, she may well partake of both.

Sophy is too sensitive to be always good humoured, but too gentle to let this be really disagreeable to other people; it is only herself who suffers. If you say anything that hurts her she does not sulk, but her heart swells; she tries to run away and cry. In the midst of her tears, at a word from her father or mother she returns at once laughing and playing, secretly wiping her eyes and trying to stifle her sobs.

Yet she has her whims; if her temper is too much indulged it degenerates into rebellion, and then she forgets herself. But give her time to come round and her way of making you forget her wrong-doing is almost a virtue. If you punish her she is gentle and submissive, and you see that she is more ashamed of the fault than the punishment. If you say nothing, she never fails to make amends, and she does it so frankly and so readily that you cannot be angry with her. She would kiss the ground before the lowest servant and would make no fuss about it; and as soon as she is forgiven, you can see by her delight and her caresses that a load is taken off her heart. In a word, she endures patiently the wrong-doing of others, and she is eager to atone for her own. This amiability is natural to her sex when unspoiled. Woman is made to submit to man and to endure even injustice at his hands. You will never bring young lads to this; their feelings rise in revolt against injustice; nature has not fitted them to put up with it. . . .

NOTES

1. Without this the race would necessarily diminish; all things considered, for its preservation each woman ought to have about four children, for about half the children born die before they can become parents, and two must survive to replace the father and mother. See whether the towns will supply them?

2. Women's timidity is yet another instinct of nature against the double risk she runs during pregnancy.

3. I know that women who have openly decided on a certain course of conduct profess that their lack of concealment is a virtue in itself, and swear that, with one exception, they are possessed of all the virtues; but I am sure they never persuaded any but fools to believe them. When the natural curb is removed from their sex, what is there left to restrain them? What honour will they prize when they have rejected the honour of their sex? Having once given the rein to passion they have no longer any reason for self-control. "Nec femina, amissa pudicitia, alia abnuerit." No author ever understood more thoroughly the heart of both sexes than Tacitus when he wrote those words.

# 28        A Vindication of the Rights of Woman

MARY WOLLSTONECRAFT

*Introduction to the First Edition*

I HAVE TURNED OVER VARIOUS BOOKS written on the subject of education, and patiently observed the conduct of parents and the management of schools; but what has been the result?—a profound conviction that the neglected education of my fellow-creatures is the grand source of the misery I deplore; and that women, in particular, are rendered weak and wretched by a variety of concurring causes, originating from one hasty conclusion. The conduct and manners of women, in fact, evidently prove that their minds are not in a healthy state; for, like the flowers which are planted in too rich a soil, strength and usefulness are sacrificed to beauty; and the flaunting leaves, after having pleased a fastidious eye, fade, disregarded on the stalk, long before the season when they ought to have arrived at maturity. One cause of this barren blooming I attribute to a false system of education, gathered from the books written on this subject by men who, considering females rather as women than human creatures, have been more anxious to make them alluring mistresses than affectionate wives and rational mothers; and the understanding of the sex has been so bubbled by this specious homage, that the civilized women of the present century, with a few exceptions, are only anxious to inspire love, when they ought to cherish a nobler ambition, and by their abilities and virtues exact respect.

In a treatise, therefore, on female rights and manners, the works which have been particularly written for their improvement must not be overlooked; especially when it is asserted, in direct terms, that the minds of women are enfeebled by false refinement; that the books of instruction, written by men of genius, have had the same tendency as more frivolous productions; and that, in the true style of Mahometanism, they are treated as a kind of subordinate beings, and not as a part of the human species, when improveable reason is allowed to be the dignified distinction which raises men above the brute creation, and puts a natural sceptre in a feeble hand.

Yet, because I am a woman, I would not lead my readers to suppose that I mean violently to agitate the contested question respecting the quality or inferiority of the sex; but as the subject lies in my way, and I cannot pass it over without subjecting the main tendency of my reasoning to misconstruction, I shall stop a moment to deliver, in a few words, my opinion. In the government of the physical world it is observable that the

female in point of strength is, in general, inferior to the male. This is the law of nature; and it does not appear to be suspended or abrogated in favour of woman. A degree of physical superiority cannot, therefore, be denied—and it is a noble prerogative! But not content with this natural pre-eminence, men endeavour to sink us still lower, merely to render us alluring objects for a moment; and women, intoxicated by the adoration which men, under the influence of their senses, pay them, do not seek to obtain a durable interest in their hearts, or to become the friends of the fellow creatures who find amusement in their society.

I am aware of an obvious inference:—from every quarter have I heard exclamations against masculine women; but where are they to be found? If by this appellation men mean to inveigh against their ardour in hunting, shooting, and gaming, I shall most cordially join in the cry; but if it be against the imitation of manly virtues, or, more properly speaking, the attainment of those talents and virtues, the exercise of which ennobles the human character, and which raise females in the scale of animal being, when they are comprehensively termed mankind;—all those who view them with a philosophic eye must, I should think, wish with me, that they may every day grow more and more masculine. . . .

## CHAPTER I
## THE RIGHTS AND INVOLVED DUTIES OF MANKIND CONSIDERED

In the present state of society it appears necessary to go back to first principles in search of the most simple truths, and to dispute with some prevailing prejudice every inch of ground. To clear my way, I must be allowed to ask some plain questions, and the answers will probably appear as unequivocal as the axioms on which reasoning is built; though, when entangled with various motives of action, they are formally contradicted, either by the words or conduct of men.

In what does man's pre-eminence over the brute creation consist? The answer is as clear as that a half is less than the whole; in Reason.

What acquirement exalts one being above another? Virtue; we spontaneously reply.

For what purpose were the passions implanted? That man by struggling with them might attain a degree of knowledge denied to the brutes; whispers Experience.

Consequently the perfection of our nature and capability of happiness, must be estimated by the degree of reason, virtue, and knowledge, that distinguish the individual, and direct the laws which bind society: and that from the exercise of reason, knowledge and virtue naturally flow, is equally undeniable, if mankind be viewed collectively. . . .

## CHAPTER 2

## THE PREVAILING OPINION OF A SEXUAL CHARACTER DISCUSSED

To account for, and excuse the tyranny of man, many ingenious arguments have been brought forward to prove, that the two sexes, in the acquirement of virtue, ought to aim at attaining a very different character; or, to speak explicitly, women are not allowed to have sufficient strength of mind to acquire what really deserves the name of virtue. Yet it should seem, allowing them to have souls, that there is but one way appointed by Providence to lead *mankind* to either virtue or happiness.

If then women are not a swarm of ephemeron triflers, why should they be kept in ignorance under the specious name of innocence? Men complain, and with reason, of the follies and caprices of our sex, when they do not keenly satirise our headstrong passions and grovelling vices. Behold, I should answer, the natural effect of ignorance! The mind will ever be unstable that has only prejudices to rest on, and the current will run with destructive fury when there are no barriers to break its force. Women are told from their infancy, and taught by the example of their mothers, that a little knowledge of human weakness, justly termed cunning, softness of temper, *outward* obedience, and a scrupulous attention to a puerile kind of propriety, will obtain for them the protection of man; and should they be beautiful, every-

thing else is needless, for at least twenty years of their lives. . . .

How grossly do they insult us who thus advise us only to render ourselves gentle, domestic brutes! For instance, the winning softness so warmly and frequently recommended, that governs by obeying. What childish expressions, and how insignificant is the being—can it be an immortal one?—who will condescend to govern by such sinister methods? . . .

Children, I grant, should be innocent; but when the epithet is applied to men, or women, it is but a civil term for weakness. For if it be allowed that women were destined by Providence to acquire human virtues, and, by the exercise of their understandings, that stability of character which is the firmest ground to rest our future hopes upon, they must be permitted to turn to the fountain of light, and not forced to shape their course by the twinkling of a mere satellite. . . .

In treating therefore of the manners of women, let us, disregarding sensual arguments, trace what we should endeavour to make them in order to cooperate, if the expression be not too bold, with the Supreme Being. . . .

. . . [T]he most perfect education, in my opinion, is such an exercise of the understanding as is best calculated to strengthen the body and form the heart. Or, in other words, to enable the individual to attain such habits of virtue as will render it independent. In fact, it is a farce to call any being virtuous whose virtues do not result from the exercise of its own reason. This was Rousseau's opinion respecting men; I extend it to women, and confidently assert that they have been drawn out of their sphere by false refinement, and not by an endeavour to acquire masculine qualities. Still the regal homage which they receive is so intoxicating, that until the manners of the times are changed, and formed on more reasonable principles, it may be impossible to convince them that the illegitimate power which they obtain by degrading themselves is a curse, and that they must return to nature and equality if they wish to secure the placid satisfaction that unsophisticated affections impart. But for this epoch we must wait—

wait perhaps till kings and nobles, enlightened by reason, and, preferring the real dignity of man to childish state, throw off their gaudy hereditary trappings; and if then women do not resign the arbitrary power of beauty—they will prove that they have *less* mind than man. . . .

. . . [T]o reason on Rousseau's ground, if man did attain a degree of perfection of mind when his body arrived at maturity, it might be proper, in order to make a man and his wife *one;* that she should rely entirely on his understanding; and the graceful ivy, clasping the oak that supported it, would form a whole in which strength and beauty would be equally conspicuous. But, alas! husbands, as well as their helpmates, are often only overgrown children—nay, thanks to early debauchery, scarcely men in their outward form,—and if the blind lead the blind, one need not come from heaven to tell us the consequences.

Many are the causes that, in the present corrupt state of society, contribute to enslave women by cramping their understandings and sharpening their senses. One, perhaps, that silently does more mischief than all the rest, is their disregard of order.

To do everything in an orderly manner is a most important precept, which women, who, generally speaking, receive only a disorderly kind of education, seldom attend to with that degree of exactness that men, who from their infancy are broken into method, observe. This negligent kind of guesswork—for what other epithet can be used to point out the random exertions of a sort of instinctive common-sense never brought to the test of reason?—prevents their generalising matters of fact; so they do to-day what they did yesterday, merely because they did it yesterday.

This contempt of the understanding in early life has more baneful consequences than is commonly supposed; for the little knowledge which women of strong minds attain is, from various circumstances, of a more desultory kind than the knowledge of men, and it is acquired more by sheer observations on real life than from comparing what has been individually observed with the results of experience generalized by speculation. Led by their dependent situation and domestic employments more into society, what they learn is rather by snatches; and as learning is with them in general only a secondary thing, they do not pursue any one branch with that persevering ardour necessary to give vigour to the faculties and clearness to the judgment. In the present state of society a little learning is required to support the character of a gentleman, and boys are obliged to submit to a few years of discipline. But in the education of women, the cultivation of the understanding is always subordinate to the acquirement of some corporeal accomplishment. Even while enervated by confinement and false notions of modesty, the body is prevented from attaining that grace and beauty which relaxed half-formed limbs never exhibit. Besides, in youth their faculties are not brought forward by emulation; and having no serious scientific study, if they have natural sagacity, it is turned too soon on life and manners. They dwell on effects and modifications, without tracing them back to causes; and complicated rules to adjust behaviour are a weak substitute for simple principles.

As a proof that education gives this appearance of weakness to females, we may instance the example of military men, who are, like them, sent into the world before their minds have been stored with knowledge, or fortified by principles. The consequences are similar; soldiers acquire a little superficial knowledge, snatched from the muddy current of conversation, and from continually mixing with society, they gain what is termed a knowledge of the world; and this acquaintance with manners and customs has frequently been confounded with a knowledge of the human heart. But can the crude fruit of casual observation, never brought to the test of judgment, formed by comparing speculation and experience, deserve such a distinction? Soldiers, as well as women, practise the minor virtues with punctilious politeness. Where is then the sexual difference, when the education has been the same? All the difference that I can discern arises from the superior advantage of liberty which enables the former to see more of life. . . .

The great misfortune is this, that they both acquire manners before morals, and a knowledge of life before they have from reflection any acquaintance with the grand ideal outline of human nature. The consequence is natural. Satisfied with common nature, they become a prey to prejudices, and taking all their opinions on credit, they blindly submit to authority. So that if they have any sense, it is a kind of instinctive glance that catches proportions, and decides with respect to manners, but fails when arguments are to be pursued below the surface, or opinions analysed.

May not the same remark be applied to women? Nay, the argument may be carried still further, for they are both thrown out of a useful station by the unnatural distinctions established in civilised life. Riches and hereditary honours have more cyphers of women to give consequence to the numerical figure; and idleness has produced a mixture of gallantry and despotism into society, which leads the very men who are the slaves of their mistresses to tyrannise over their sisters, wives, and daughters. This is only keeping them in rank and file, it is true. Strengthen the female mind by enlarging it, and there will be an end to blind obedience; but as blind obedience is ever sought for by power tyrants and sensualists are in the right when they endeavour to keep women in the dark, because the former only want slaves, and the latter a plaything. The sensualist, indeed, has been the most dangerous of tyrants, and women have been duped by their lovers, as princes by their ministers, whilst dreaming that they reigned over them. . . .

Women are therefore to be considered either as moral beings, or so weak that they must be entirely subjected to the superior faculties of men.

Let us examine this question. Rousseau declares that a woman should never for a moment feel herself independent, that she should be governed by fear to exercise her *natural* cunning, and made a coquettish slave in order to render her a more alluring object of desire, a *sweeter* companion to man, whenever he chooses to relax himself. He carries the arguments, which he pretends to draw from the indications of nature, still further, and insinuates that truth and fortitude, the corner-stones of all human virtue, should be cultivated with certain restrictions, because, with respect to the female character, obedience is the grand lesson which ought to be impressed with unrelenting rigour.

What nonsense! When will a great man arise with sufficient strength of mind to puff away the fumes which pride and sensuality have thus spread over the subject? If women are by nature inferior to men, their virtues must be the same in quality, if not in degree, or virtue is a relative idea; consequently, their conduct should be founded on the same principles, and have the same aim.

Connected with man as daughters, wives, and mothers, their moral character may be estimated by their manner of fulfilling those simple duties; but the end, the grand end, of their exertions should be to unfold their own faculties, and acquire the dignity of conscious virtue. They may try to render their road pleasant; but ought never to forget, in common with man, that life yields not the felicity which can satisfy as immortal soul. I do not mean to insinuate that either sex should be so lost in abstract reflections or distant views as to forget the affections and duties that lie before them, and are, in truth, the means appointed to produce the fruit of life; on the contrary, I would warmly recommend them, even while I assert, that they afford most satisfaction when they are considered in their true sober light. . . .

Let it not be concluded that I wish to invert the order of things. I have already granted that, from the constitution of their bodies, men seem to be designed by Providence to attain a greater degree of virtue. I speak collectively of the whole sex; but I see not the shadow of a reason to conclude that their virtues should differ in respect to their nature. In fact, how can they, if virtue has only one eternal standard? I must therefore, if I reason consequentially, as strenuously maintain that they have the same simple direction as that there is a God.

It follows then that cunning should not be opposed to wisdom, little cares to great exertions, or insipid softness, varnished over with the name of gentleness, to that fortitude which grand views alone can inspire. . . .

Women ought to endeavour to purify their heart, but can they do so when their uncultivated understandings make them entirely dependent on their senses for employment and amusement, when no noble pursuit sets them above the little vanities of the day, or enables them to curb the wild emotions that agitate a reed, over which every passing breeze has power? To gain the affections of a virtuous man, is affection necessary? Nature has given woman a weaker frame than man; but, to ensure her husband's affections, must a wife, who, by the exercise of her mind and body whilst she was discharging the duties of a daughter, wife, and mother, has allowed her constitution to retain its natural strength, and her nerves a healthy tone,— is she, I say, to condescend to use art, and feign a sickly delicacy, in order to secure her husband's affection? Weakness may excite tenderness, and gratify the arrogant pride of man; but the lordly caresses of a protector will not gratify a noble mind that pants for and deserves to be respected. Fondness is a poor substitute for friendship! . . .

. . . [T]he woman who strengthens her body and exercises her mind will, by managing her family and practising various virtues, become the friend, and not the humble dependent of her husband; and if she, by possessing such substantial qualities, merit his regard, she will not find it necessary to conceal her affection, nor to pretend to an unnatural coldness of constitution to excite her husband's passions. In fact, if we revert to history, we shall find that the women who have distinguished themselves have neither been the most beautiful nor the most gentle of their sex. . . .

To recommend gentleness, indeed, on a broad basis is strictly philosophical. A frail being should labour to be gentle. But when forbearance confounds right and wrong, it ceases to be a virtue; and, however convenient it may be found in a companion—that companion will ever be considered as an inferior, and only inspire a vapid tenderness, which easily degenerates into contempt. Still, if advice could really make a being gentle, whose natural disposition admitted not of such a fine polish, something towards the advancement of order would be attained; but if, as might quickly be demonstrated, only affection be produced by this indiscriminate counsel, which throws a stumbling-block in the way of gradual improvement, and true melioration of temper, the sex is not much benefited by sacrificing solid virtues to the attainment of superficial graces, though for a few years they may procure the individuals regal sway.

As a philosopher, I read with indignation the plausible epithets which men use to soften their insults; and, as a moralist, I ask what is meant by such heterogeneous associations, as fair defects, amiable weaknesses, etc.? If there be but one criterion of morals, but one archetype for man, women appear to be suspended by destiny, according to the vulgar tale of Mahomet's coffin; they have neither the unerring instinct of brutes, nor are allowed to fix the eye of reason on a perfect model. They were made to be loved, and must not aim at respect, lest they should be hunted out of society as masculine.

But to view the subject in another point of view. Do passive indolent women make the best wives? Confining our discussion to the present moment of existence, let us see how such weak creatures perform their part. Do the women who, by the attainment of a few superficial accomplishments, have strengthened the prevailing prejudice, merely contributed to the happiness of their husbands? Do they display their charms merely to amuse them? And have women who have early imbibed notions of passive obedience, sufficient character to manage a family or educate children? So far from it, that, after surveying the history of woman, I cannot help agreeing with the severest satirist, considering the sex as the weakest as well as the most oppressed half of the species. What does history disclose but marks of inferiority, and how few women have emancipated themselves from the galling yoke of sovereign man? So few that the exceptions remind me of an ingenious conjecture respecting Newton—that he was probably a being of superior order accidentally caged in a human body. Following the same train of thinking, I have been led to imagine that the few extraordinary women who have rushed in eccentrical directions out of the orbit prescribed to their sex, were *male* spirits, confined by mistake in female frames. But if it be not philosophical to think of sex when the soul is mentioned, the inferiority must depend on the organs; or the heavenly fire, which is to ferment the clay, and is not given in equal portions.

But avoiding, as I have hitherto done, any direct comparison of the two sexes collectively, or frankly acknowledging the inferiority of woman, according to the present appearance of things, I shall only insist that men have increased that inferiority till women are almost sunk below the standard of rational creatures. Let their faculties have room to unfold, and their virtues to gain strength, and then determine where the whole sex must stand in the intellectual scale. Yet let it be remembered, that for a small number of distinguished women I do not ask a place.

It is difficult for us purblind mortals to say to what height human discoveries and improvements may arrive when the gloom of despotism subsides, which makes us stumble at every step; but when morality shall be settled on a more solid basis, then, without being gifted with a prophetic spirit, I will venture to predict that woman will be either the friend or slave of man. We shall not, as at present, doubt whether she is a moral agent, or the link which unites man with brutes. But should it then appear that like the brutes they were principally created for the use of man, he will let them patiently bite the bridle, and not mock them with empty praise; or, should their rationality be proved, he will not impede their improvement merely to gratify his sensual appetites. He will not, with all the graces of rhetoric, advise them to submit implicitly their understanding to the guidance of man. He will not, when he treats of the education of women, assert that they ought never to have the free use of reason, nor would he recommend cunning and dissimulation to beings who are acquiring, in like manner as himself, the virtues of humanity.

Surely there can be but one rule of right, if morality has an eternal foundation, and whoever sacrifices virtue, strictly so called, to present convenience, or whose *duty* it is to act in such a manner, lives only for the passing day, and cannot be an accountable creature. . . .

These may be termed Utopian dreams. Thanks to that Being who impressed them on my soul, and gave me sufficient strength of mind to dare to exert my own reason, till, becoming dependent only on Him for the support of my virtue, I view with indignation, the mistaken notions that enslave my sex.

I love man as my fellow; but his sceptre, real or usurped, extends not to me, unless the reason of an individual demands my homage; and even then the submission is to reason, and not to man. In fact, the conduct of an accountable being must be regulated by the operations of its own reason; or on what foundation rests the throne of God?

It appears to me necessary to dwell on these obvious truths, because females have been insulated, as it were; and while they have been stripped of the virtues that should clothe humanity, they have been decked with artificial graces that enable them to exercise a short-lived tyranny. Love, in their bosoms, taking place of every nobler passion, their sole ambition is to be fair, to raise emotion instead of inspiring respect; and this ignoble desire, like the servility in absolute monarchies, destroys all strength of character. Liberty is the mother of virtue, and if women be, by their very constitution, slaves, and not allowed to breathe the sharp invigorating air of freedom, they must ever languish like exotics, and be reckoned beautiful flaws in nature.

As to the argument respecting the subjection in which the sex has ever been held, it retorts on man. The many have always been enthralled by the few; and monsters, who scarcely have shown any discernment of human excellence, have tyrannised over thousands of their fellow-creatures. Why have men of superior endowments submitted to such degradation? For, is it not universally acknowledged that kings, viewed collectively, have ever been inferior, in abilities and virtue, to the same number of men taken from the common mass of mankind—yet have they not, and are they not still treated with a degree of reverence that is an insult to reason? China is not the only country where a living man has been made a God. *Men* have submitted to superior strength to enjoy with impunity the pleasure of the moment; *women* have only done the same, and therefore till it is proved that the courtier, who servilely resigns the birthright of a man, is not a moral agent, it cannot be demonstrated that woman is essentially inferior to man because she has always been subjugated.

Brutal force has hitherto governed the world, and that the science of politics is in its infancy, is evident from philosophers scrupling to give the knowledge most useful to man that determinate distinction.

I shall not pursue this argument any further than to establish an obvious inference, that as sound politics diffuse liberty, mankind, including woman, will become more wise and virtuous.

---

## 29    Perversions of Justice: A Native-American Examination of the Doctrine of U.S. Rights to Occupancy in North America

WARD CHURCHILL

*For the nation, there is an unrequited account of sin and injustice that sooner or later will call for national retribution.*

—GEORGE CATLIN, 1844

RECOGNITION OF THE LEGAL AND MORAL rights by which it occupies whatever land base it calls its own is perhaps the most fundamental issue confronting any nation. Typically, such claims to sovereign and proprietary interest in national territorialities devolve, at least in considerable part, upon supportable contentions that the citizenry is preponderantly composed of persons directly descended from peoples who have dwelt within the geographical area claimed since "time immemorial." The matter becomes infinitely more complex in situations in which the dominant—or dominating—population comprises either the representatives of a foreign power or immigrants ("settlers") who can offer no such assertion of "aboriginal" lineage to justify their presence or ownership of property in the usual sense.

History is replete with instances in which various peoples have advanced philosophical, theological, and juridical arguments concerning their alleged entitlement to the homelands of others, only to have them rebuffed by the community of nations as lacking both moral force and sound legal principle. In such cases, the trend has been that international rejection of "imperial" pretensions has led to the inability of those nations extending such claims to sustain them. Modern illustrations of this tendency include the dissolution of the classic European empires—those of France, the Netherlands, Portugal, and Great Britain, in particular—during the post-World War II period, as well as the resounding defeat of the Axis powers' territorial ambitions during the war itself. Even more recent examples may be found in the breakup of the Soviet (Great Russian) and Yugoslavian (Serbian) states and in the extreme controversy attending maintenance of such settler states as Northern Ireland, Israel, and South Africa.

The purpose of this essay is to examine the basis upon which another contemporary settler state, the United States of America, contends that it possesses legitimate—indeed, inviolate—rights to approximately 2.25 billion acres of territory in North America. Through such scrutiny, the philosophical validity of U.S. legal claims to territorial integrity can be understood and tested against the standards of both logic and morality. This, in turn, is intended to provide a firm foundation from which readers may assess the substance of that image generated by the sweeping pronouncements so frequently offered by official America and its adherents over the years: that this is a country so essentially "peaceful," so uniquely enlightened in its commitments to the rule of law and concept of liberty, that it has inevitably emerged as the natural leader of a global drive to consolidate a "new world order" in which the conquest and occupation of the territory of any nation by another "cannot and will not stand."

## Rights to Territorial Acquisition in International Law

From the outset of the "Age of Discovery" precipitated by the Columbian voyages, the European powers, eager to obtain uncontested title to at least some portions of the lands their emissaries were encountering, quickly recognized the need to establish a formal code of juridical standards to legitimate what they acquired. To some extent, this was meant to lend a patina of "civilized"— and therefore, it was imagined, inherently superior—legality to the actions of the European Crowns in their relations with the peoples indigenous to the desired geography. More importantly, however, the system was envisioned as a necessary means of resolving disputes among the Crowns themselves, each of which was vying with the others in a rapacious battle over the prerogative to benefit from wealth accruing through ownership of given regions in the "New World." In order for any such regulatory code to be considered effectively binding by all Old World parties, it was vital that it be sanctioned by the Church.

Hence, the mechanism deployed for this purpose was a theme embodied in a series of Papal bulls begun by Pope Innocent IV during the late-13th-century First Crusade. The bulls were de-signed to define the proper ("lawful") relationship between Christians and "Infidels" in all such worldly matters as property rights. Beginning in the early 16th century, Spanish jurists in particular did much to develop this theory into what have come to be known as the "Doctrine of Discovery" and an attendant dogma, the "Rights of Conquest." Through the efforts of legal scholars such as Franciscus de Victoria and Matías de Paz, Spanish articulations of Discovery Doctrine, endorsed by the pope, rapidly evolved to hold the following as primary tenets of international law:

1. Outright ownership of land accrued to the Crown represented by a given Christian (European) discoverer only when the land discovered proved to be uninhabited (territorium res nullius).

2. Title to inhabited lands discovered by Crown representatives was recognized as belonging inherently to the indigenous people thereby encountered, but rights to acquire land from, and to trade with, the natives of the region accrued exclusively to the discovering Crown vis-à-vis other European powers. In exchange for this right, the discovering power committed itself to proselytizing the Christian gospel among the natives.

3. Acquisition of land title from indigenous peoples could occur only by their consent—by an agreement usually involving purchase—rather than through force of arms, so long as the natives did not arbitrarily decline to trade with Crown representatives, refuse to admit missionaries among them, or inflict gratuitous violence upon citizens of the Crown.

4. In the absence of these last three conditions, utilization of armed force to acquire aboriginally held territory was considered to be unjust and claims to land title accruing therefrom to be correspondingly invalid.

5. Should one or more of the three conditions be present, then it was held that the Crown had a legal right to use whatever force was required to subdue native resistance and

impound their property as compensation. Land title gained by prosecution of such "just wars" was considered valid.

Although this legal perspective was hotly debated at the time (it still is, in certain quarters), and saw considerable violation by European colonists, it was generally acknowledged as the standard against which international conduct would be weighed. By the early 17th century, the requirements of Discovery Doctrine had led the European states (England in particular) to adopt a policy of entering into formal treaties—full-fledged international instruments in which the sovereignty of the indigenous parties to such agreements were, by definition, officially recognized as equivalent to that of the respective Crowns—as an expedient to obtaining legally valid land titles from American Indian peoples, first in what is now the State of Virginia and then in areas further north. Treaties concerning trade, professions of peace and friendship, and military alliances were also quite common. Undeniably, there is a certain overweening arrogance embedded in the proposition that Europeans were somehow intrinsically imbued with an authority to unilaterally restrict the range of those to whom Native Americans might sell their property, assuming they wished to sell it at all. Nonetheless, in its recognition that indigenous peoples constituted bona fide nations holding essentially the same rights to land and sovereignty as any other, the legal posture of early European colonialism seems rather advanced and refined in retrospect. In these respects, the Doctrine of Discovery is widely viewed as one of the more important cornerstones of modern international law and diplomacy.

With its adoption of Protestantism, however, Britain had already begun to mark its independence from papal regulation by adding an element of its own to the doctrine. Usually termed the "Norman Yoke," this concept asserted that land rights devolve in large part upon the extent to which the owners demonstrate a willingness and ability to "develop" their territories in accordance with a scriptural obligation to exercise "domin-ium" over nature. In other words, a person or a people is ultimately entitled to only that quantity of real estate which he/she/they convert from "wilderness" to a "domesticated" state. By this criterion, English settlers were seen as possessing an inherent right to dispossess native people of all land other than that which the latter might be "reasonably expected" to put to such "proper" uses as cultivation. By the same token, this doctrinal innovation automatically placed the British Crown on a legal footing from which it could contest the discovery rights of any European power not adhering to the requirement of "overcoming the wilderness" per se.

This last allowed England to simultaneously "abide by the law" *and* directly confront Catholic France for ascendancy in the Atlantic regions of North America. After a series of "French and Indian Wars" beginning in the late 1600s and lasting nearly a century, the British were victorious, but at a cost more than negating the expected financial benefits to the Crown that had led it to launch its colonial venture in the first place. As one major consequence, King George II, in a move intended to preclude further warfare with indigenous nations, issued the Proclamation of 1763. This royal edict stipulated that all settlement or other forms of land acquisition by British subjects west of a line running along the Allegheny and Appalachian Mountains from Canada to the Spanish colony of Florida would be suspended indefinitely, and perhaps permanently. English expansion on the North American continent was thereby brought to an abrupt halt.

## Enter the United States

The new British policy conflicted sharply with the desires for personal gain evident among a voracious elite that had been growing within England's seaboard colonial population. Most of the colonies held some pretense of title to "western" lands, much of it conveyed by earlier Crown grant, and had planned to use it as a means of bolstering their respective economic positions. Similarly, members of the landed gentry such as George Washington,

Thomas Jefferson, John Adams, James Madison, and Anthony Wayne all possessed considerable speculative interests in land parcels on the far side of the 1763 demarcation line. The only way in which these could be converted into profit was for the parcels to be settled and developed. Vociferous contestation and frequent violation of the proclamation, eventually enforced by George III, became quite common. All in all, this dynamic became a powerful precipitating factor in the American Revolution, during which many rank-and-file rebels were convinced to fight against the Crown by promises of western land grants "for services rendered" in the event their revolt was successful.

There was, however, a catch. The United States emerged from its decolonization struggle against Britain—perhaps the most grievous offense that could be perpetrated by any subject people under then-prevailing law—as a pariah, an outlaw state that was shunned as an utterly illegitimate entity by most other countries. Desperate to establish itself as a legitimate nation, and lacking any other viable alternatives with which to demonstrate its aptitude for complying with international legality, the new government was virtually compelled to observe the strictest of protocols in its dealings with Indians. Indeed, what the Continental Congress needed more than anything at the time was for indigenous nations, already recognized as respectable sovereignties via their treaties with European states, to bestow a comparable recognition upon the fledgling United States by entering into treaties with *it*. The urgency of the matter was compounded by the fact that the Indians maintained military parity with, and in some cases superiority to, the U.S. Army all along the frontier.

As a result, both Articles of Confederation and the subsequent Constitution of the United States contained clauses explicitly and exclusively restricting relations with indigenous nations to the federal government, insofar as the former were recognized as enjoying the same politico-legal status as any other foreign power. The United States also officially renounced, in the 1789 Northwest Ordinance and elsewhere, any aggressive intent

concerning indigenous nations especially with regard to their respective land bases:

> The utmost good faith shall always be observed towards the Indians; their land and property shall never be taken from them without their consent; and in their property, rights, and liberty, they shall never be disturbed . . . but laws founded in justice and humanity shall from time to time be made, for wrongs done to them, and for peace and friendship with them.[1]

This rhetorical stance, reflecting an impeccable observance of international legality, was also incorporated into such instruments of agreement with European states as the United States was able to obtain during its formative years. For instance, in the 1803 Louisiana Purchase from France of much of North America west of the Mississippi, the federal government solemnly pledged itself to protect "the inhabitants of the ceded territory . . . in the free enjoyment of their liberty, property, and the religion they profess."[2] Other phraseology in the purchase agreement makes it clear that federal authorities understood they were acquiring from the French, not the land itself, but France's monopolistic trade rights and prerogative to buy any acreage within the area its indigenous owners wished to sell.

The same understanding certainly pertained to all unceded Indian Country claimed by Britain under Discovery Doctrine east of the Mississippi, after it was quit-claimed by George III in the Treaty of Paris concluding the Revolution. Even if English discovery rights somehow "passed" to the new republic by virtue of this royal action (an extremely dubious premise in itself), there still remained the matter of obtaining native consent to literal U.S. ownership of any area beyond the 1763 proclamation line. Hence, the securing of indigenous agreement to land cessions must be added to the impressive list of diplomatic and military reasons why treaty-making with Indians constituted the main currency of American diplomacy throughout the immediate postrevolutionary period. Moreover, the need to secure valid land title from native people through treaties far outlasted the motivations of diplomatic and military necessity, these having been greatly diminished in importance after U.S. victories over Tecumseh's alliance in 1794 and 1811, over Britain in the War of 1812, and over the Red Stick Confederacy during 1813–1814. The treaties were and remain, in substance, the basic real-estate documents anchoring U.S. claims to land title—and thus to rights of occupancy—in North America.

What was most problematic in this situation for early federal policymakers was the fact that, in gaining diplomatic recognition and land cessions from indigenous nations through treaties, the United States was simultaneously admitting not only that Indians ultimately owned virtually all of the coveted territory but also that they were really under no obligation to part with it. As William Wirt, an early attorney general, put it in 1821: "[Legally speaking,] so long as a tribe exists and remains in possession of its lands, its title and possession are sovereign and exclusive. We treat with them as separate sovereignties, and while an Indian nation continues to exist within its acknowledged limits, we have no more right to enter upon their territory than we have to enter upon the territory of a foreign prince."[3] A few years later, Wirt amplified this point:

> The point, once conceded, that the Indians are independent to the purpose of treating, their independence is to that purpose as absolute as any other nation. Being competent to bind themselves by treaty, they are equally competent to bind the party that treats with them. Such party cannot take benefit of [a] treaty with the Indians, and then deny them the reciprocal benefits of the treaty on the grounds that they are not independent nations to all intents and purposes. . . . Nor can it be conceded that their independence as a nation is a limited independence. Like all other independent nations, they have the absolute power of war and peace. Like all other independent nations, their territories are inviolate by any other sovereignty. . . . They are entirely self-governed, self-directed. They treat, or refuse to treat, at their pleasure; and there is no human power that can rightly control them in the exercise of their discretion in this respect.[4]

Such enjoyment of genuine sovereign rights and status by indigenous nations served, during the 20 years following the Revolution (roughly 1790–1810), to considerably retard the assumption of lawful possession of their land grants by revolutionary soldiers, as well as consummation of the plans of the elite caste of prerevolutionary land speculators. Over the next two decades (1810–1830), the issue assumed an ever-increasing policy importance as the matter of native sovereignty came to replace Crown policy in being construed as *the* preeminent barrier to U.S. territorial consolidation east of the Mississippi. Worse, as Chief Justice of the Supreme Court John Marshall pointed out in 1822, any real adherence to the rule of law in regard to native rights might not only block U.S. expansion but—since not all the territory therein had been secured through Crown treaties—cloud title to significant portions of the original 13 states as well. Perhaps predictably, it was perceived in juridical circles that the only means of circumventing this dilemma was through construction of a legal theory—a subterfuge, as it were—by which the more inconvenient implications of international law might be voided even while the republic maintained an appearance of holding to its doctrinal requirements.

## Emergence of the Marshall Doctrine

Not unnaturally, the task of forging the required "interpretation" of existing law fell to Marshall, who was widely considered one of the great legal minds of his time. Whatever his scholarly qualifications, the chief justice can hardly be said to have been a disinterested party, given not only his vociferous ideological advocacy of the rebel cause before and during the Revolution but also the fact that both he and his father were consequent recipients of 10,000-acre grants west of the Appalachians, in what is now the State of West Virginia. His first serious foray into land-rights law thus centered in devising a conceptual basis to secure title for his own and similar grants. In the 1810 *Fletcher v. Peck* case, he invoked the Norman Yoke tradition in a manner that far exceeded previous British applications, advancing the patently absurd contention that the areas involved were effectively "vacant" even though very much occupied—and in many instances stoutly defended—by indigenous inhabitants. On this basis, he declared that individual Euro-American deeds within recognized Indian territories might be considered valid whether or not native consent was obtained.

Although *Peck* was obviously useful from the U.S. point of view, resolving as it did a number of short-term difficulties in meeting obligations already incurred by the government vis-à-vis individual citizens, it was in itself a tactical opinion, falling far short of accommodating the country's overall territorial goals and objectives. In the 1823 *Johnson* v. *McIntosh* case, however, Marshall followed up with a more clearly strategic enunciation, reaching for something much closer to the core of what he had in mind. Here he opined that, because discovery rights purportedly constricted native discretion in disposing of property, the sovereignty of discoverers was to that extent inherently superior to that of indigenous nations. From this point of departure, he then proceeded to invert all conventional understandings of Discovery Doctrine, ultimately asserting that native people occupied land within discovered regions at the sufferance of their discoverers rather than the other way around. A preliminary rationalization was thus contrived by which to explain the fact that the United States had already begun depicting its borders as encompassing rather vast portions of unceded Indian country.

Undoubtedly aware that neither *Peck* nor *McIntosh* was likely to withstand the gaze of even minimal international scrutiny, Marshall next moved to bolster the logic undergirding his position. In the two "Cherokee Cases" of the early 1830s, he hammered out the thesis that native nations within North America were "nations like any other" in the sense that they possessed both territories they were capable of ceding and recognizable governmental bodies empowered to cede these areas through treaties. On the other hand, he argued on the basis of the reasoning deployed in *McIntosh*, they were nations of a "peculiar type," both "domestic to" and "dependent upon" the United States, and therefore possessed of a degree of sovereignty intrinsically less than that enjoyed by the United States itself. The essential idea boils down to a presumption that, although native peoples are entitled to exercise some range of autonomy in managing their affairs within their own territories, both the limits of that autonomy and the extent of the territories involved can be "naturally" and unilaterally established by the federal government. At base, this is little more than a judicial description of the classic relationship between colonizer and colonized, but it was put forth in such a way as to seem at first glance to be the exact opposite.

Although it might be contended (and has been, routinely enough) that Marshall's framing of the circumstances pertaining to the Cherokee Nation, already completely surrounded by the territorality of the United States by 1830, bore some genuine relationship to then-prevailing reality, it must be reiterated that he did not confine his observations of the situation to Cherokees, or even to native nations east of the Mississippi. Rather, he purported to articulate the legal status of *all* indigenous nations, including those west of the Mississippi—the Lakota, Cheyenne, Arapaho, Comanche, Kiowa, Navajo, and Chiricahua Apache, to name but a few—that had not yet encountered the United States in any appreciable way. Self-evidently, these nations could not have been described with the faintest accuracy as domestic to or dependent upon the United States. The clear intent belied by Marshall's formulation was that they be made so in the future. The doctrine completed with elaboration of the Cherokee Cases was thus the pivotal official attempt to rationalize and legitimate a vast campaign of conquest and colonization—absolutely contrary to the customary law of the period—upon which the United States was planning to embark in the years ahead.

A final inversion of accepted international legal norms and definitions stems from this: an outright reversal of what was meant by "just" and "unjust" warfare.[5] Within Marshall's convoluted and falsely premised reasoning, it became arguable that indigenous nations acted unlawfully whenever and wherever they attempted to physically prevent exercise of the U.S. "right" to expropriate their property. Put another way, Indians could be construed as committing "aggression" against the United States at any point when they attempted to resist the invasion of their homelands by American citizens. In this sense the United States could declare itself to be waging a "just"—and therefore lawful—war against native people on virtually any occasion when force of arms was required to realize its territorial ambitions. *Ipso facto,* all efforts of native people to defend themselves against systematic dispossession and subordination could thereby be categorized as "unjust"—and thus unlawful—by the United States.[6]

In sum, the Marshall Doctrine shredded significant elements of the existing Laws of Nations. Given the understandings of these very same legal requirements placed on record by federal judicial officials such as Attorney General Wirt and Marshall himself, not to mention the embodiment of such understandings in the Constitution and formative federal statutes, this cannot be said to have been unintentional or inadvertent. Instead, the chief justice engaged in a calculated exercise in juridical cynicism, quite deliberately confusing and deforming accepted legal principles as an expedient to "justifying" his country's pursuit of a thoroughly illegitimate course of territorial acquisition. Insofar as federal courts and policy-makers elected to adopt his doctrine as the predicate to all subsequent relations with American Indians, it may be said that he not only replicated the initial posture of the United States as an outlaw state but rendered it permanent.

## Evolution of the Marshall Doctrine

The Cherokee Cases were followed by a half-century hiatus in important judicial determinations regarding American Indians. On the foundation provided by the Marshall Doctrine, the government felt confident in entering into the great bulk of the at least 371 treaties with indigenous nations by which it professed to have gained the consent of Indians in ceding huge portions of the native land base, assured all the while that, because of its self-anointed position of superior sovereignty, it would be under "no legal obligation" to live up to its end of the various bargains struck. Well before the end of the 19th century, the United States stood in default on virtually every treaty agreement it had made with native people, and there is considerable evidence in many instances that this was intended to be so from the outset. Aside from the fraudulent nature of U.S. participation in the treaty process, there is an ample record that many of the instruments of cession were militarily coerced while the government implemented Marshall's version of "just wars" against Indians. As the U.S. Census Bureau put it in 1894:

> The Indian wars under the United States government have been about 40 in number [most of them occurring after 1835]. They have cost the lives of . . . about 30,000 Indians [at a minimum]. . . . The actual number of killed and wounded Indians must be very much greater than the number given, as they conceal, where possible, their actual loss in battle. . . . Fifty percent additional would be a safe number to add to the numbers given.[7]

The same report noted that some number "very much more" than 8,500 Indians were known to have been killed by government-sanctioned private citizen action—dubbed "individual affairs"—during the course of U.S./Indian warfare.[8] In reality, such citizen action is known to have been primarily responsible for the reduction of the native population of Texas from about 100,000 in 1828 to under 10,000 in 1880.[9] Similarly, in California, an aggregate indigenous population that still numbers approximately 300,000 had been reduced to fewer than 35,000 by 1860, mainly because of "the cruelties and wholesale massacres perpetrated by [American] miners and early settlers."[10] Either of these illustrations offers a death toll several times that officially acknowledged as having accrued through individual affairs within the whole of the 48 contiguous states.

Even while this slaughter was occurring, the government was conducting what it itself frequently described as a "policy of extermination" in its conduct of wars against those indigenous nations that proved "recalcitrant" about giving up their land and liberty. This manifested itself in a lengthy series of massacres of native people—men, women, children, and old people alike—at the hands of U.S. troops. Among the worst were those at Blue River (Nebraska, 1854), Bear River (Idaho, 1863), Sand Creek (Colorado, 1864), Washita River (Oklahoma, 1868), Sappa Creek (Kansas, 1875), Camp Robinson (Nebraska, 1878), and Wounded Knee (South Dakota, 1890). Somewhat different, but comparable, methods of destroying indigenous peoples were evidenced in the forced march of the entire Cherokee Nation along the "Trail of Tears" to Oklahoma during the 1830s (55% attrition)[11] and in the internment of the bulk of the Navajo Nation under abysmal conditions at the Bosque Redondo from 1864 to 1868 (35–50% attrition).[12] Such atrocities against humans were coupled with an equally systematic extermination of an entire animal species, the buffalo or North American bison, as part of a military strategy to starve resistant Indians into submission by "destroying their commissary."

All told, it is probable that more than a quarter-million Indians perished as a direct result of U.S. extermination campaigns directed against them.[13] By the turn of the century, only 237,196 native people were recorded by census as still being alive within the United States,[14] perhaps 2% of the total indigenous population of the U.S. portion of North America at the point of first contact with Europeans.[15] Correlating rather precisely with this genocidal reduction in the number of native inhabitants was an erosion of Indian land holdings to approximately 2.5% of the "lower 48" states.[16] Small wonder that, barely 50 years later, Adolf Hitler would explicitly anchor his concept of *lebensraumpolitik* ("politics of living space") directly upon U.S. practice against American Indians. Meanwhile, even as the 1890 census figures were being tallied, the United States had already moved beyond the "Manifest Destiny" embodied in the conquest phase of its continental expansion and was emphasizing the development of colonial administration over residual indigenous land and lives through the Bureau of Indian Affairs (BIA), a subpart of the War Department that had been reassigned for this purpose to the Department of the Interior.

This was begun as early as 1871, when Congress—having determined that the military capacity of indigenous nations had finally been sufficiently reduced by incessant wars of attrition—elected to consecrate Marshall's description of their "domestic" status by suspending further treaty-making with them. In 1885, the United States moved for the first time to directly extend its internal jurisdiction over reserved Indian territories through passage of the Major Crimes Act. When this was immediately challenged as a violation of international standards, Supreme Court Justice Samuel F. Miller rendered an opinion that consolidated and extended Marshall's earlier assertion of federal plenary power over native nations, contending that the government held an "incontrovertible right" to exercise authority over Indians as it saw fit and "for their own good." Miller also concluded that Indians lacked any legal recourse in matters of federal interest, their sovereignty being defined as whatever Congress did not remove through specific legislation. This decision opened the door to enactment of more than 5,000 statutes regulating affairs in Indian Country through the present day.

One of the first of these was the General Allotment Act of 1887, "which unilaterally negated Indian control over land tenure patterns within the reservations, forcibly replacing the traditional mode of collective use and occupancy with the Anglo-Saxon system of individual property ownership."[17] The act also imposed for the first time a formal eugenics code—dubbed "blood quantum"—by which American Indian identity would be federally defined on racial grounds rather than by native nations themselves on the basis of group membership/citizenship.[18]

The Allotment Act set forth that each American Indian recognized as such by the federal government would receive an allotment of land according to the following formula: 160 acres for family heads, eighty acres for single persons over eighteen years of age and orphans under eighteen, and forty acres for [non-orphan] children under eighteen "Mixed blood" Indians received title by fee simple patent; "full bloods" were issued "trust patents," meaning they had no control over their property for a period of twenty-five years. Once each person recognized by the government as belonging to a given Indian nation had received his or her allotment, the "surplus" acreage was "opened" to non-Indian homesteading or conversion into the emerging system of national parks, forests, and grasslands.[19]

Needles to say, there proved to be far fewer Indians identifiable as such under federal eugenics criteria than there were individual parcels available within the reserved land areas of the 1890s. Hence, "not only was the cohesion of indigenous society dramatically disrupted by allotment, and traditional government prerogatives preempted, but it led to the loss of some two-thirds of all the acreage [about 100 million of 150 million acres] still held by native people at the time it was passed."[20] Moreover, the land assigned to individual Indians during the allotment process fell overwhelmingly within arid and semi-arid locales considered to be the least productive in North America; uniformly, the best-watered and otherwise useful portions of the reservations were declared surplus and quickly stripped away. This, of course, greatly reinforced the "dependency" aspect of the Marshall thesis and led U.S. Indian Commissioner Francis Leupp to conclude approvingly that allotment should be considered as "a mighty pulverizing engine for breaking up [the last vestiges of] the tribal mass" that stood as a final barrier to complete Euro-American hegemony on the continent.

As with the Major Crimes Act, native people attempted to utilize their treated standing in federal courts to block the allotment process and corresponding erosion of the reservation land base. In the 1903 *Lonewolf* v. *Hitchcock* case, however, Justice Edward D. White extended the concept of federal plenary power to hold that the government possessed a right to unilaterally abrogate whatever portion of any treaty with Indians it found inconvenient while continuing to consider the remaining terms and provisions binding upon the Indians. In essence, this meant that the United States could point to the treaties as being the instruments that legally validated much of its North American land title while simultaneously avoiding whatever reciprocal obligations it had incurred by way of payment. White also opined that the government's plenary power over Indians lent it a "trust responsibility" over residual native property such that it might opt to "change the form" of this property—from land, say, to cash or "services"—whenever and however it chose to do so. This final consolidation of the Marshall Doctrine effectively left native people with *no* true national rights under U.S. law while voiding the remaining pittance of conformity to international standards the United States had exhibited with regard to its Indian treaties.

## The Open Veins of Native America

A little-discussed aspect of the Allotment Act is that it required each Indian, as a condition of receiving the deed to his or her land parcel, to accept U.S. citizenship. By the early 1920s, when most of the allotment the United States wished to accomplish had been completed, there were still a significant number of native people who still had not been "naturalized," either because they'd been left out of the process for one reason or another or because they'd refused to participate. Consequently, in 1924 the Congress passed a "clean-up bill" entitled the Indian Citizenship Act, which imposed citizenship upon all remaining indigenous people within U.S. borders whether they wished it or not.

> The Indian Citizenship Act greatly confused the circumstances even of many of the blooded and federally certified Indians insofar as it was held to bear legal force, and to carry legal obligations, whether or not any given Indian or group of Indians wished to be U.S. citizens. As for the host of non-certified, mixed-blood people residing in

the U.S., their status was finally "clarified"; they had been definitively absorbed into the American mainstream at the stroke of the congressional pen. And, despite the fact that the act technically left certified Indians occupying the status of citizenship within their own indigenous nation as well as the U.S. (a "dual form" of citizenship so awkward as to be sublime), the juridical door had been opened by which the weight of Indian obligations would begin to accrue more to the U.S. than to themselves.[21]

All of this—suspension of treaty-making, extension of federal jurisdiction, plenary power and "trust" prerogatives, blood quantum and allotment, and imposition of citizenship—was bound up in a policy officially designated as the compulsory assimilation of American Indians into the dominant (Euro-American) society. Put another way, U.S. Indian policy was carefully (and openly) designed to bring about the disappearance of all recognizable Indian groups, as such. The methods used included the general proscription of native languages and spiritual practices, the systematic and massive transfer of Indian children into non-Indian settings via mandatory attendance at boarding schools remote from their communities, and the deliberate suppression of reservation economic structures. As Indian Commissioner Charles Burke put it at the time, "It is not consistent with the general welfare to promote [American Indian national] characteristics and organization."[22]

The assimilationist policy trajectory culminated during the 1950s with the passage of House Concurrent Resolution 108, otherwise known as the "Termination Act of 1953," a measure through which the United States moved to unilaterally dissolve 109 indigenous nations within its borders. Termination was coupled to the "Relocation Act," a statute passed in 1956 and designed to coerce reservation residents to disperse to various urban centers around the country. As a result of the ensuing programmatic emphasis on creating an American Indian diaspora, by 1990 over half of all U.S. Indians had been severed from their respective land bases and generally acculturated to non-Indian mores. Meanwhile, the enactment of Public Law 280, placing many reservations under the jurisdiction of individual states, thereby reduced the level of native sovereignty to that held by counties or municipalities. This voided one of the last federal pretenses that Indians retained "certain characteristics of sovereign nations."

The question arises, of course, as to why, given the contours of this aspect of federal policy, the final obliteration of the indigenous nations of North America has not long since occurred. The answer, apparently, resides within something of a supreme irony: unbeknownst to the policymakers who implemented allotment policy against Indians during the late 19th century, much of the ostensibly useless land to which native people were consigned has turned out to be some of the most mineral rich on earth. It is presently estimated that as much as two-thirds of all known U.S. "domestic" uranium reserves lie beneath reservation lands, as well as perhaps a quarter of the readily accessible low-sulphur coal and about a fifth of the oil and natural gas. In addition, the reservations are now known to hold substantial deposits of copper, zinc, iron, nickel, molybdenum, bauxite, zeolites, and gold.

These facts began to surface in the early 1920s. Federal economic planners quickly discerned a distinct advantage in retaining these abundant resources within the framework of governmental trust control, an expedient to awarding extractive leases, mining licenses, and the like to preferred corporate entities in ways that might have proven impossible had the reservations been liquidated altogether. Hence, beginning in 1921, it was determined that selected indigenous nations should be maintained in some semblance of being, and Washington began to experiment with the creating of "tribal governments" intended to administer what was left of Indian Country on behalf of an emerging complex of interlocking federal/corporate interests. In 1934, this resulted in the passage of the Indian Reorganization Act (IRA), a bill that served to supplant virtually every remaining traditional indigenous government in the country, replacing them with federally designed "tribal councils" structured along the lines of corporate boards and empowered primarily to sign off on mineral leases and similar instruments.

The arrangement led to a recapitulation of the Marshall Doctrine's principle of indigenous "quasi-sovereignty" in slightly revised form: now, native nations were cast as always being sovereign enough to legitimate Euro-American mineral exploitation on their reservations but never sovereign enough to prevent it. Predictably, under such circumstances the BIA negotiated mineral leases, duly endorsed by the puppet governments it had installed, "on behalf of" its "Indian wards" that typically paid native people 15% or less of market royalty rates on minerals taken from their lands. The "superprofits" thus generated for major corporations have had a significant positive effect on U.S. economic growth since 1950, a matter amplified by the fact that the BIA also "neglected" to include land restoration and other environmental cleanup clauses into contracts pertaining to reservation land (currently, Indians are always construed as being sovereign enough to waive such things as environmental protection regulations but never sovereign enough to enforce them). One consequence of this trend is that, on reservations where uranium mining has occurred, Indian Country has become so contaminated by radioactive substances that the government has actively considered designating them as "National Sacrifice Areas" unfit for human habitation. At this juncture, planning is also afoot to utilize several reservations as dump sites for high-level nuclear wastes and toxic chemical substances that cannot be otherwise conveniently disposed of.

Further indications of the extent and virulence of the colonial system by which the United States has come to rule Native America are not difficult to find. For instance, dividing the 50-million-odd acres of land still nominally reserved for Indian use and occupancy in the United States by the approximately 1.6 million Indians the government recognized in its 1980 census reveals that native people—on paper, at least—remain the largest landholders on a per capita basis of any population sector on the continent.[23] Given this, in combination with the resources known to lie within

their land and the increasingly intensive "development" of these resources over the past 40 years, simple arithmetic strongly suggests that they should also be the wealthiest of all aggregate groups. Instead, according to the federal government's own data, Indians are far and away the poorest in terms of both annual and lifetime per capita income. Correspondingly, we suffer all the standard indices of dire poverty: North America's highest rates of infant mortality and teen suicide and of death from malnutrition, exposure, and plague. Overall, we consistently experience the highest rate of unemployment, lowest level of educational attainment, and one of the highest rates of incarceration of any group. The average life expectancy of a reservation-based American Indian male is currently less than 45 years; that of a reservation-based female, barely over 47.

In Latin America, there is a core axiom that guides understanding of the interactive dynamics between the northern and southern continents of the Western Hemisphere. "Your wealth," Latino analysts point out to their Yanqui counterparts, "is our poverty."[24] Plainly, the structure of the relationship forged by the United States vis-à-vis the indigenous nations of the northern continent itself follows exactly the same pattern of parasitic domination. The economic veins of the prostrate Native North American host have been carefully opened, their content provided lifeblood to the predatory creature that applied the knife. Such are the fruits of John Marshall's doctrine after a century and a half of continuous application to the "real world" context.

## International Sleight of Hand

It's not that the United States has ever attempted to mask the face of this reality. Indeed, in the wake of World War II, even as the United States was engaged in setting a "moral example" to all of humanity by assuming a lead role in prosecuting former Nazi leaders for having ventured down much the same road of continental conquest that the United States itself had pioneered, Congress passed what it called the Indian Claims Commission Act. The premise of the bill was that all non-consensual—and therefore illegal—seizures of native property that had transpired during the course of American history had been "errors," sometimes "tragic" ones. As a means, at least figuratively, of separating U.S. historical performance and expansionist philosophy from the more immediate manifestations of the Nazis, the new law established a commission empowered to review the basis of U.S. land title in every quarter of the country and to award retroactive monetary compensation to indigenous nations shown to have been unlawfully deprived of their lands. Tellingly, the commission was authorized to set compensation amounts only on the basis of the estimated per-acre value of illegally taken land *at the time it was taken* (often a century or more before), and was specifically disempowered from restoring land to Indian control, no matter *how* the land was taken or *what* the desires of the impacted native people might be.

Although the life of the commission was originally envisioned as being only ten years, the magnitude of the issues it encountered, and the urgency with which its mission came to be viewed by the Euro-American status quo, caused it to be repeatedly extended. When it was ultimately suspended on September 30, 1978, it still had 68 cases docketed for review, despite having heard and ostensibly "disposed of" several hundred others over a period of three decades. In the end, although its intent had been the exact opposite, it had accomplished nothing so much as to establish with graphic clarity how little of North America the United States could be said to legally own.

> The fact is that about half the land area of the country was purchased by treaty or agreement at an average price of less than a dollar an acre; another third of a [billion] acres, mainly in the West, were confiscated without compensation; another two-thirds of a [billion] acres were claimed by the United States without pretense of a unilateral action extinguishing native title.[25]

This summary, of course, says nothing at all about the approximately 44 million acres of land presently being taken from the Indians, Aleuts, and Inuits of the Arctic North under provision of the 1971 Alaska Native Claims Settlement Act, or the several million acres of Hawaii stripped away from the natives of those islands. Similarly, it says nothing of the situation in such U.S. "possessions" as Guam, Puerto Rico, the "U.S." Virgin Islands, "American" Samoa, and the Marshall Islands.

Serious challenges to commission findings have been mounted in U.S. courts, based largely in the cumulative contradictions inherent to federal Indian law. As a consequence, the Supreme Court has been compelled to resort to ever more convoluted and logically untenable argumentation as a means of upholding certain governmental assertions of "legitimate" land title. In its 1980 opinion in the Black Hills Land Claim case, for example, the high court was forced to extend the Marshall Doctrine's indigenous domesticity thesis to a ludicrous extreme, holding that the United States had merely exercised its rightful internal power of "imminent domain" over the territory of the Lakota Nation when it expropriated 90% of the latter's land a century earlier, in direct violation of the 1868 Treaty of Fort Laramie. Similarly, in the Western Shoshone Land Claim case, where the government could show no documentation that it had ever even pretended to assume title to the native land at issue, the Supreme Court let stand the Claims Commission's assignment of an arbitrary date on which a transfer supposedly took place.

During the 1970s, the American Indian Movement (AIM), an organization militantly devoted to the national liberation of Native North America, emerged in the United States. In part, the group attempted the physical decolonization of the Pine Ridge Reservation in South Dakota (home of the Oglala Lakota people) but was met with a counterinsurgency war waged by federal agencies such as the FBI and U.S. Marshalls Service and by surrogates associated with the reservation's IRA Council. Although unsuccessful in achieving a resumption of indigenous self-determination at Pine Ridge, the tenacity of

AIM's struggle (and the ferocity of the government's repression of it) attracted considerable international attention. This led, in 1980, to the establishment of a United Nations Working Group on Indigenous Populations, under auspices of the U.N. Economic and Social Council (UNESCO), an entity mandated to assess the situation of native peoples globally and produce a universal declaration of their rights as a binding element of international law.

Within this arena, the United States, joined by Canada, has consistently sought to defend its relations with indigenous nations by trotting out the Marshall Doctrine's rationalization that the United States has assumed a trust responsibility over, rather than outright colonial domination of, Native North America. Native delegates have countered, correctly, that trust prerogatives, in order to be valid under international law, must be tied to some clearly articulated time interval after which the trustee nations resume independent existence. This has been successfully contrasted to the federal (and Canadian) government's presumption that it enjoys a permanent trust authority over indigenous nations; assumption of permanent plenary authority over another nation's affairs and property is the essential definition of colonialism, it is argued, and is illegal under a number of international covenants.

The United States and Canada have responded with prevarication, contending that their relationship to Native North America cannot be one of colonialism insofar as United Nations Resolution 1541 (XV), the "Blue Water Thesis," specifies that in order to be defined as a colony a nation must be separated from its colonizer by at least 30 miles of open ocean. The representatives of both countries have also done everything in their power to delay or prevent completion of the Universal Declaration of the Rights of Indigenous Peoples, arguing, among other things, that the term "peoples," when applied to native populations, should not carry the force of law implied by its use in such international legal instruments as the Universal Declaration of Human Rights (1948), Covenant on Civil and Political Rights (1978), and the International Convention on Elimination of All Forms of Racial Discrimination (1978). The United States in particular has implied that it will not abide by any declaration of indigenous rights that runs counter to what it perceives as its own interests, a matter that would replicate its posture with regard to the authority of the International Court of Justice (the "World Court")[26] and elements of international law such as the 1948 Convention on Prevention and Punishment of the Crime of Genocide.[27]

Meanwhile, the United States has set out to "resolve things internally" through what may be intended as a capstone extrapolation of the Marshall Doctrine. This strategy has involved a drive to convince Indians to accept the premise that, rather than struggling to regain the self-determining rights to separate sovereign existence embodied in their natural histories and treaty relationships, they should voluntarily merge themselves with the U.S. polity. In this scenario, the IRA administrative apparatus created during the 1930s would assume a position as a "third level of the federal government," finally making indigenous rights within the United States inseparable from those of the citizenry as a whole. This final assimilation of native people into the "American sociopolitical mainstream" would obviously void most (or perhaps all) potential utility for Indian rights that exist or might emerge from international law over the next few years. The option is therefore being seriously pursued at this juncture by a Senate Select Committee on Indians Affairs, chaired by Hawaii Senator Daniel Inouye (who has already done much to undermine the last vestiges of rights held by the native people of his own state).

## United States Out of North America

During the fall of 1990, President George Bush stepped onto the world stage beating the drums for what he termed a "just war" to roll back the "naked aggression" of Iraq's invasion and occupation of neighboring Kuwait. Claiming to articulate "universal principles of international relations and human decency," Bush stated that such aggression "cannot stand," that "occupied territory must be liberated, legitimate governments must be reinstated, the benefits of their aggression must be denied to aggressive powers."[28] Given the tone and tenor of this Bushian rhetoric—and the undeniable fact that Iraq had a far better claim to Kuwait (its 19th province, separated from the Iraqis by the British as an administrative measure following World War I) than the United States has to virtually any part of North America[29]—one could only wait with baited breath for the American president to call airstrikes in upon his own Capitol as a means of forcing his own government to withdraw from Indian Country. Insofar as he did not, the nature of the "New World Order" [to which] his war in the Persian Gulf harkened tends to speak for itself.

The United States does not now possess, nor has it ever possessed, a legitimate right to occupancy in at least half the territory it claims as its own on this continent. It began its existence as an outlaw state, and, given the nature of its expansion to its present size, it has adamantly remained so through the present moment. In order to make things appear otherwise, its legal scholars and its legislators have persistently and often grotesquely manipulated and deformed accepted and sound legal principles, both internationally and domestically. They have done so in precisely the same fashion, and on the same basis, as the Nazi leaders they stood at the forefront in condemning for Crimes against Humanity at Nuremberg.

In no small part because of its success in consolidating its position on other people's land in North America, the United States may well continue to succeed where the Nazis failed. With the collapse of the Soviet Union, it has emerged as *the* ascendent military power on the planet during the late 20th century. As the sheer margin of its victory over Iraq has revealed, it now possesses the capacity to extend essentially the same sort of relationships it has already imposed upon American Indians to the remainder of the world. And, given the experience it has acquired in Indian Affairs over the years, it is undoubtedly capable of garb-

ing this process of planetary subordination in a legalistic attire symbolizing its deep-seated concern with international freedom and dignity, the sovereignty of other nations, and the human rights of all peoples. At a number of levels, the Marshall Doctrine reckons to become truly globalized in the years ahead.

This is likely to remain the case, unless and until significant numbers of people within the United States as well as without come to recognize the danger, and the philosophical system that underpins it, for what they are. More importantly, any genuine alternative to a consummation of the Bushian vision of world order is predicated upon these same people acting upon their insights, opposing the order implicit to the U.S. status quo both at home and abroad. Ultimately, the dynamic represented by the Marshall Doctrine must be reversed, and the structure it fostered dismantled, within the territorial corpus of the United States itself. In this, nothing can be more central than the restoration of indigenous land and indigenous national rights in the fullest sense of the term. The United States—at least as it has come to be known, and in the sense that it knows itself—must be driven from North America. In its stead resides the possibility, likely the *only* possibility, of a genuinely just and liberatory future for all humanity.

NOTES AND REFERENCES

1. 1 *Stat.* 50, 1789.
2. Quoted in Lazarus, Edward, *Black Hills, White Justice: The Sioux Nation versus the United States, 1775 to the Present,* HarperCollins, New York, 1991, p. 158.
3. Opinion rendered by the Attorney General (Op. Atty Gen.), April 26, 1821, p. 345.
4. Op. Atty. Gen., 1828, pp. 623–4. For further background, see Berman, Howard. "The Concept of Aboriginal Rights in the Early Legal History of the United States," *Buffalo Law Review,* No. 28, 1798, pp. 637–67. Also see Cohen, Felix. S., "Original Indian Land Title." *Minnesota Law Review,* No. 32, 1947, pp. 28–59.
5. For a comprehensive survey of the meanings of these terms in the international legal vernacular, see Walzer, Michael, *Just and Unjust Wars: A Moral Argu-*

*ment with Historical Illustrations,* Basic Books, New York, 1977.

6. One indicator of the pervasiveness with which this outlook has been implanted is that armed conflicts between the United States and indigenous nations are inevitably described as "Indian Wars" despite the fact that each one was demonstrably initiated by the invasion by American citizens of territory belonging to one or more native peoples. The so-called Indian Wars would thus be accurately depicted as "Settlers' Wars" (or, more appropriately yet, "Wars of Aggression by the United States").

7. U.S. Bureau of the Census, *Report on Indians Taxed and Indians Not Taxed in the United States (except Alaska) at the Eleventh U.S. Census: 1890,* U.S. Government Printing Office, Washington, D.C., 1894, pp. 637–38.

8. Ibid.

9. See Stiffarm and Lane, *op. cit.,* pp. 35–36. The government of first the Republic, and then the State of Texas maintained a bounty on Indian—*any* Indian—scalps until well into the 1870s; see Newcome, W. W., Jr., *The Indians of Texas,* University of Texas Press, Austin, 1961.

10. Mooney, James, "Population," in Frederick W. Dodge (ed.), *Handbook of the Indians North of Mexico, Vol. 2,* Bureau of American Ethnology Bulletin No. 30, Smithsonian Institution, U.S. Government Printing Office, Washington, D.C., 1910, pp. 286–87. Also see Cook, Sherburn F., *The Conflict between the California Indian and White Civilization,* University of California Press, Berkeley, 1976.

11. See Thornton, Russell, "Cherokee Population Losses during the Trail of Tears: A New Perspective and Estimate," *Ethnohistory,* No. 31, 1984, pp. 289–300.

12. See Johansson, S. Ryan, and S. H. Preston, "Tribal Demography: The Navajo and Hopi Populations as Seen through Manuscripts from the 1900 Census," *Social Science History,* No. 3, 1978, p. 26. Also see Salmon, Roberto Mario, "The Disease Complaint at Bosque Redondo (1864–1868)," *The Indian Historian,* No. 9, 1976.

13. Scholarly sources suggest the actual total may have been as high as a half-million. See Thornton, Russell, *American Indian Holocaust and Survival: A Population History since 1492,* University of Oklahoma Press, Norman, 1987, p. 49.

14. This nadir figure is reported in U.S. Bureau of the Census, *Fifteenth Census of the United States, 1930: The Indian Population of the United States and Alaska,* U.S. Government Printing Office, Washington, D.C., 1937. Barely 101,000 Canadian Indians were estimated as surviving in the same year.

15. Estimating native population figures at the point of first contact is, at best, a slippery business. Recent demographic work has, however, produced a broad consensus that the standard anthropological estimates of "about one million north of the Rio Grande" fashioned by James Mooney and Alfred Kroeber, as well as Harold Driver's subsequent upward revision of their calculations to "approximately two million," are *far* too low. The late Henry Dobyns, using more appropriate methodologies than his predecessors, computed a probable aggregate precontact North American Indian population of 18.5 million, about 15 million of them within present U.S. borders (*Their Numbers Become Thinned: Native American Population Dynamics in Eastern North America,* University of Tennessee Press, Knoxville, 1983). A somewhat more conservative successor, the Cherokee demographer Russell Thornton, counters that the figure was more likely about 12.5 million, perhaps 9.5 million of them within the United States (*American Indian Holocaust and Survival, op. cit.*). Splitting the difference between Dobyns and Thornton leaves one with an approximate 15 million North American population total, about 12.5 million in the United States. Interestingly, no matter which set of the newer estimates one uses, the overall attrition by 1900 is in the upper 90th percentile range.

16. The figure is arrived at by relying upon Royce, Charles C., *Indian Land Cessions in the United States* (2 Vols.), Bureau of American Ethnography, 18th Annual Report, 1896–97, Smithsonian Institution, Washington, D.C., 1899.

17. Ch. 119, 24 *Stat.* 388, now codified as amended at 25 U.S.C. 331 *et seq.,* better known as the "Dawes Act," after its sponsor, Massachusetts Senator Henry Dawes. The quote is from Robbins, Rebecca L., "Self-Determination and Subordination: The Past, Present, and Future of American Indian Governance," in Jaimes, *op. cit.,* p. 93.

18. See Jaimes, M. Annette, "Federal Indian Identification Policy: A Usurpation of Indigenous Sovereignty in North America," in Jaimes, *op. cit.,* pp. 123–38. It is noteworthy that official eugenics codes have been employed by very few states, mostly such unsavory examples as Nazi Germany (against the Jews), South Africa (against "Coloreds"), and Israel (against Palestinian Arabs).

19. Robbins, *op. cit.* Also see McDonnell, Janet A., *The Dispossession of the American Indian, 1887–1934,* Indiana University Press, Bloomington/Indianapolis, 1991.

20. Robbins, *op. cit.* Also see Kicking Bird, Kirk, and Karen Ducheneaux, *One Hundred Million Acres,* Macmillan, New York, 1973.

21. Jaimes, "Federal Indian Identification Policy," *op. cit.,* pp. 127–28.

22. Letter, Charles Burke to William Williamson, September 16, 1921; William Williamson Papers, Box 2, File—Indian Matters, Miscellaneous, I.D. Weeks Library, University of South Dakota, Vermillion.

Such articulation of official sensibility was hardly isolated; see Kvasnicka, Robert M., and Herman J. Viola (eds.), *The Commissioners of Indian Affairs, 1824–1977,* University of Nebraska Press, Lincoln, 1979.

23. See U.S. Bureau of the Census, *1980 Census of the Population, Supplementary Reports, Race of the Population by States, 1980,* U.S. Government Printing Office, Washington, D.C., 1981. Also see, U.S. Bureau of the Census, *Ancestry of the Population by State, 1980,* Supp. Rep. PC80-SI-10, U.S. Government Printing Office, Washington, D.C., 1983.

24. The quote is taken from Galeano, Eduardo, *The Open Veins of Latin America: Five Centuries of the Pillage of a Continent,* Monthly Review Press, New York, 1973.

25. Barsh, Russell, "Indian Land Claims Policy in the United States," *North Dakota Law Review,* No. 58, 1982, pp. 1–82.

26. In October 1985, President Ronald Reagan withdrew a 1946 U.S. declaration accepting ICJ jurisdiction in all matters of "international dispute." The withdrawal took effect in April 1986. This was in response to the ICJ determination in *Nicaragua v. United States,* the first substantive case ever brought before it to which the United States was a party. The ICJ ruled the U.S. action of mining Nicaraguan harbors in times of peace to be unlawful. The Reagan administration formally rejected the authority of the ICJ to decide the matter (but removed the mines). It is undoubtedly significant that the Reagan instrument contained a clause accepting continued ICJ jurisdiction over matters pertaining to "international commercial relationships," thus attempting to convert the world court into a mechanism of mere trade arbitration. See *U.S. Terminates Acceptance of ICJ Compulsory Jurisdiction,* Department of State Bulletin No. 86, Washington, D.C., January 1986.

27. The United States declined to ratify the Genocide Convention until 1988, 40 years after it became international law (and after more than 100 other nations had ratified it), and then only with an attached "Sovereignty Package" purporting to subordinate the convention to the U.S. Constitution (thereby seeking to protect certain aspects of genocidal conduct). The U.S. stipulation in this regard is, of course, invalid under Article 27 of the 1969 Vienna Convention on the Law of Treaties and has been protested as such by such countries as Britain, Denmark, and the Netherlands. Further, the Genocide Convention is now customary international law, meaning—according to the United States' own Nuremberg Doctrine—that it is binding upon the United States, whether Congress ratifies its terms or not. For further analysis, see LeBlanc, Lawrence J., *The United States and the Genocide Convention,* Duke University Press, Durham (N.C.)/London, 1991.

28. For the context of this rhetoric, see Chomsky, Noam, "'What We Say Goes': The Middle East in the New World Order," in Cynthia Peters (ed.), *Collateral Damage: The "New World Order" at Home and Abroad.* South End Press, Boston, 1992, pp. 49–92.

29. For further information, see Chomsky, Noam, and Eqbal Ahmed, "The Gulf Crisis: How We Got There," in Greg Bates (ed.), *Mobilizing Democracy: Changing the U.S. Role in the Middle East,* Common Courage Press, Monroe, ME. 1991, pp. 3–24.

## *Recommended Readings*

### TEXTS

Chavet, John. *The Social Problem in the Philosophy of Rousseau.* Cambridge: Cambridge University Press, 1974.

Gildin, Hilail. *Rousseau's Social Contract.* Chicago: University of Chicago Press, 1982.

Hall, J. C. *Rousseau: An Introduction to His Political Philosophy.* New York: Macmillan, 1973.

Masters, Roger D. *The Political Philosophy of Rousseau.* Princeton: Princeton University Press, 1968.

Orwin, Clifford, *The Legacy of Rousseau.* Chicago: University of Chicago Press, 1996.

Shklar, Judith. *Men and Citizens: A Study of Rousseau's Social Theory.* Cambridge: Cambridge University Press, 1969.

### FEMINIST PERSPECTIVE

Brody, Miriam. "Mary Wollstonecraft: Sexuality and Women's Rights." In *Feminist Theorists,* edited by Dale Spender. London: The Women's Press, 1983.

Canovan, Margaret. "Rousseau's Two Concepts of Citizenship." In *Women in Western Political Philosophy,* edited by Ellen Kennedy and Susan Mendus. Brighton: Wheatsheaf Books, 1987.

Schwartz, Joel. *The Sexual Politics of Jean-Jacques Rousseau.* Chicago: University of Chicago Press, 1984.

Wexler, Victor G. "'Made for Man's Delight': Rousseau as Anti-Feminist." *American Historical Review,* 81, no. 1 (1976): 266–291.

## MULTICULTURAL PERSPECTIVE

Brown, Dee. *Bury My Heart at Wounded Knee.* New York: Henry Holt, 1971.

Churchill, Ward. *Indians Are Us.* Monroe, ME: Common Courage Press, 1995.

Churchill Ward, A Little Matter of Homicide: Holocaust and Denial in the Americas, 1492 to the present. San Francisco: City Lights Press, 1997.

# VIII

# *Kant*

## Introduction

IMMANUEL KANT WAS BORN IN 1724 in Königsberg, East Prussia (now part of Russia), and he never journeyed more than forty miles from the city. Kant appears to have seriously entertained the possibility of marriage at least twice during his life. On one occasion, he was in the process of assessing his financial situation to determine whether to propose to a young widow when the woman accepted a marriage proposal from someone else. On another occasion, a Westphalian visitor to Königsberg, in whom Kant was interested, left town with her employer before Kant could make up his mind.

Kant was educated in Leibniz's philosophy but later was profoundly influenced by Hume and Rousseau. By Kant's own admission, Hume awakened him from his dogmatic slumbers. However, Rousseau seemed to have had an even stronger influence on him. When he received a copy of Rousseau's *Emile* in 1762, his rigid schedule (rising, coffee drinking, writing, lecturing, dining, walking, each at a set time) was thrown out of kilter for two whole days while he read the book.

Kant's most important work, his *Critique of Pure Reason*, was published in 1781. After that, his other famous writings followed in quick succession; he published the *Prolegomena to Any Future Metaphysics* (1783), *Groundwork of the Metaphysic of Morals* (1785), *Metaphysical First Principles of Natural Science* (1786), the second edition of *Critique of Pure Reason* (1787), *Critique of Practical Reason* (1788), *Critique of Judgment* (1790), *Theory and Practice* (1792), *Religion Within the Bounds of Reason Alone* (1793), *Perpetual Peace* (1795), and *Metaphysic of Morals* (1797).

Only once did Kant come into collision with political authority. That was in connection with his *Religion Within the Bounds of Reason Alone*. The work was approved by the theological faculty of Königsberg in 1793. But in 1794, the work was censured by Frederick William II, and Kant was forbidden to write or lecture on any religious subject. Kant accepted this censure, for which he was widely criticized.

Kant was already fifty-seven years old when he published his *Critique of Pure Reason*. Consequently, his literary production from 1781 to the time of his death in 1804 constitutes a remarkable performance. He was working on a restatement of his philosophy at the time of his death.

In the selection from *Theory and Practice,* Kant sets out his social contract justification of a civil state. He claims that a civil state ought to be founded on an original contract that satisfies the requirements of freedom (the freedom to seek happiness in whatever way one sees fit as long as one does not infringe upon the freedom of others to pursue a similar end), equality (the equal right of each person to coerce others to use their freedom in a way that harmonizes with one's own freedom), and independence (that independence of each person that is necessarily presupposed by the free agreement of the original contract).

According to Kant, the original contract, which ought to be the foundation of every civil state, does not have to "actually exist as a fact." It suffices that the laws of a civil state are such that people would agree to them under conditions in which the requirements of freedom, equality, and independence obtain. Laws that accord with this original contract would then, Kant claims, give all members of society the right to reach any degree of rank that they could earn through their labor, industry, and good fortune. Thus, the equality demanded by the original contract would not, in Kant's view, exclude a considerable amount of economic liberty.

The "union of nations" proposed by Kant in the selection from *Perpetual Peace* is close in concept to President Wilson's League of Nations and its successor, the United Nations. According to Kant, the respect for law that prevails in a republican state makes it incumbent upon its citizens and its government to establish a similar system of law in international affairs. Kant's principles of right demand that the nations agree to laws capable of peacefully settling disputes between them.

In "Kant: 'An Honest but Narrow-Minded Bourgeois'?" Susan Mendus claims that Kant regards women as passive citizens in a very strong sense. As Kant claims in the selection from the *Metaphysic of Morals,* women, unlike male passive citizens, who can attain active citizenship and the right to vote once they become sufficiently independent, can never become active citizens. This is because Kant identifies women by nature with inclination and men with reason.

Why did Kant get things so wrong? Mendus suggests that it is not simply because he was a narrow-minded bourgeois. Rather, it was because he was committed to individualism, and individualism requires that in any relationship someone must dominate and someone must be subordinated. But why should a commitment to individual human rights (individualism) require a commitment to dominant/subordinate relationships? Can you think of any good reason why this would be the case? If not, it may be that the best explanation of why Kant got things so wrong is, after all, that he was a narrow-minded bourgeois.

In his *Perpetual Peace,* Kant sketched a plan for achieving peaceful relations between nations. In "On *Satyagraha,*" Mohandas K. Gandhi sketches a nonviolent way of dealing with violent conflict. Gandhi requires that one approach violent conflict in such a way as to enable both oneself and one's opponents to progress to greater awareness of the truth. To do this, one must be willing to suffer. According to Gandhi, a willingness to suffer helps transform one's opponents by confronting them with the reality, in human terms, of their violence toward others. Only in this way can one maximize the conditions by which both sides can progress toward the truth and a peaceful resolution of conflicts. Using the practice of satyagraha or nonviolent resistance, Gandhi was able to win independence for India in 1948.

# 30    Theory and Practice

IMMANUEL KANT

## II

### ON THE RELATIONSHIP OF THEORY TO PRACTICE IN POLITICAL RIGHT

### *(Against Hobbes)*

AMONG ALL THE CONTRACTS by which a large group of men unites to form a society, . . . the contract establishing a *civil constitution* . . . is of an exceptional nature. For while, so far as its execution is concerned, it has much in common with all others that are likewise directed towards a chosen end to be pursued by joint effort, it is essentially different from all others in the principle of its constitution. . . . In all social contracts, we find a union of many individuals for some common end which they all *share*. But a union as an end in itself which they all *ought to share* and which is thus an absolute and primary duty in all external relationships whatsoever among human beings (who cannot avoid mutually influencing one another), is only found in a society in so far as it constitutes a civil state, i.e. a commonwealth. . . .

The civil state, regarded purely as a lawful state, is based on the following *a priori* principles:

1. The *freedom* of every member of society as a *human being*.
2. The *equality* of each with all the others as a *subject*.
3. The *independence* of each member of a commonwealth as a *citizen*.

These principles are not so much laws given by an already established state, as laws by which a state can alone be established in accordance with pure rational principles of external human right. Thus:

1. Man's *freedom* as a human being, as a principle for the constitution of a commonwealth, can be expressed in the following formula. No one can compel me to be happy in accordance with his conception of the welfare of others, for each may seek his happiness in whatever way he sees fit, so long as he does not infringe upon the freedom of others to pursue a similar end which can be reconciled with the freedom of everyone else within a workable general law—i.e. he must accord to others the same right as he enjoys himself. A government might be established on the principle of benevolence towards the people, like that of a father towards his children. Under such a *paternal government* . . . the subjects, as immature children who cannot distinguish what is truly useful or harmful to themselves, would be obliged to behave purely passively and to rely upon the judgement of the head of state as to how they *ought* to be happy, and upon his kindness in willing their happiness at all. Such a government is the greatest conceivable *despotism*, i.e. a constitution which suspends the entire freedom of its subjects, who thenceforth have no rights whatsoever. The only conceivable government for men who are capable of possessing rights, even if the ruler is benevolent, is not a *paternal* but a *patriotic* government. . . . A *patriotic* attitude is one where everyone in the state, not excepting its head, regards the commonwealth as a maternal womb, or the land as the paternal ground from which he himself sprang and which he must leave to his descendants as a treasured pledge. Each regards himself as authorized to protect the rights of the commonwealth by laws of the general will, but not to submit it to his personal use at his own absolute pleasure. This right of freedom belongs to each member of the commonwealth as a human being, in so far as each is a being capable of possessing rights.

2. Man's *equality* as a subject might be formulated as follows. Each member of the common-

wealth has rights of coercion in relation to all the others, except in relation to the head of state. For he alone is not a member of the commonwealth, but its creator or preserver, and he alone is authorized to coerce others without being subject to any coercive law himself. But all who are subject to laws are the subjects of a state, and are thus subject to the right of coercion along with all other members of the commonwealth; the only exception is a single person (in either the physical or the moral sense of the word), the head of state, through whom alone the rightful coercion of all others can be exercised. For if he too could be coerced, he would not be the head of state, and the hierarchy of subordination would ascend infinitely. But if there were two persons exempt from coercion, neither would be subject to coercive laws, and neither could do to the other anything contrary to right, which is impossible.

This uniform equality of human beings as subjects of a state is, however, perfectly consistent with the utmost inequality of the mass in the degree of its possessions, whether these take the form of physical or mental superiority over others, or of fortuitous external property and of particular rights (of which there may be many) with respect to others. Thus the welfare of the one depends very much on the will of the other (the poor depending on the rich), the one must obey the other (as the child its parents or the wife her husband), the one serves (the labourer) while the other pays, etc. Nevertheless, they are all equal as subjects, *before the law*, which, as the pronouncement of the general will, can only be single in form, and which concerns the form of right and not the material or object in relation to which I possess rights. For no one can coerce anyone else other than through the public law and its executor, the head of state, while everyone else can resist the others in the same way and to the same degree. No one, however, can lose this authority to coerce others and to have rights towards them except through committing a crime. And no one can voluntarily renounce his rights by a contract or legal transaction to the effect that he has no rights but only duties, for such a contract would deprive

him of the right to make a contract, and would thus invalidate the one he had already made.

From this idea of the equality of men as subjects in a commonwealth, there emerges this further formula: every member of the commonwealth must be entitled to reach any degree of rank which a subject can earn through his talent, his industry and his good fortune. And his fellow-subjects may not stand in his way by *hereditary* prerogatives or privileges of rank and thereby hold him and his descendants back indefinitely.

All right consists solely in the restriction of the freedom of others, with the qualification that their freedom can co-exist with my freedom within the terms of a general law; and public right in a commonwealth is simply a state of affairs regulated by a real legislation which conforms to this principle and is backed up by power, and under which a whole people live as subjects in a lawful state. . . . This is what we call a civil state, and it is characterised by equality in the effects and counter-effects of freely willed actions which limit one another in accordance with the general law of freedom. Thus the *birthright* of each individual in such a state (i.e. before he has performed any acts which can be judged in relation to right) is absolutely *equal* as regards his authority to coerce others to use their freedom in a way which harmonises with his freedom. Since birth is not an act on the part of the one who is born, it cannot create any inequality in his legal position and cannot make him submit to any coercive laws except in so far as he is a subject, along with all the others, of the one supreme legislative power. Thus no member of the commonwealth can have a hereditary privilege as against his fellow-subjects; and no one can hand down to his descendants the privileges attached to the rank he occupies in the commonwealth, nor act as if he were qualified as a ruler by birth and forcibly prevent others from reaching the higher levels of the hierarchy (which are *superior* and *inferior*, but never *imperans* and *subiectus*) through their own merit. He may hand down everything else, so long as it is material and not pertaining to his person, for it may be acquired and disposed of as property and may over a series of generations create considerable inequalities in wealth among the members of the commonwealth (the employee and the employer, the landowner and the agricultural servants, etc.). But he may not prevent his subordinates from raising themselves to his own level if they are able and entitled to do so by their talent, industry and good fortune. If this were not so, he would be allowed to practise coercion without himself being subject to coercive counter-measures from others, and would thus be more than their fellow-subject. No one who lives within the lawful state of a commonwealth can forfeit this equality other than through some crime of his own, but never by contract or through military force. . . . For no legal transaction on his part or on that of anyone else can make him cease to be his own master. He cannot become like a domestic animal to be employed in any chosen capacity and retained therein without consent for any desired period, even with the reservation (which is at times sanctioned by religion, as among the Indians) that he may not be maimed or killed. He can be considered happy in any condition so long as he is aware that, if he does not reach the same level as others, the fault lies either with himself (i.e. lack of ability or serious endeavour) or with circumstances for which he cannot blame others, and not with the irresistible will of any outside party. For as far as right is concerned, his fellow-subjects have no advantage over him.

3. The *independence* . . . of a member of the commonwealth as a *citizen*, i.e. as a co-legislator, may be defined as follows. In the question of actual legislation, all who are free and equal under existing public laws may be considered equal, but not as regards the right to make these laws. Those who are not entitled to this right are nonetheless obliged, as members of the commonwealth, to comply with these laws, and they thus likewise enjoy their protection (not as *citizens* but as co-beneficiaries of this protection). For all right depends on laws. But a public law which defines for everyone that which is permitted and prohibited by right, is the act of a public will, from which all right proceeds and which must not therefore itself be able to do an injustice to anyone. And this re-

quires no less than the will of the entire people (since all men decide for all men and each decides for himself). For only towards oneself can one never act unjustly. But on the other hand, the will of another person cannot decide anything for someone without injustice, so that the law made by this other person would require a further law to limit his legislation. Thus an individual will cannot legislate for a commonwealth. For this requires freedom, equality, and *unity* of the will of *all* the members. And the prerequisite for unity, since it necessitates a general vote (if freedom and equality are both present), is independence. The basic law, which can come only from the general united will of the people, is called the *original contract*.

Anyone who has the right to vote on this legislation is a *citizen* . . . (i.e. citizen of a state, not *bourgeois* or citizen of a town). The only qualification required by a citizen (apart, of course, from being an adult male) is that he must be his *own master (sui iuris)*, and must have some *property* (which can include any skill, trade, fine art or science) to support himself. In cases where he must earn his living from others, he must earn it only by *selling* that which is his,[1] and not by allowing others to make use of him; for he must in the true sense of the word *serve* no one but the commonwealth. In this respect, artisans and large or small landowners are all equal, and each is entitled to one vote only. As for landowners, we leave aside the question of how anyone can have rightfully acquired more land than he can cultivate with his own hands (for acquisition by military seizure is not primary acquisition), and how it came about that numerous people who might otherwise have acquired permanent property were thereby reduced to serving someone else in order to live at all. It would certainly conflict with the above principle of equality if a law were to grant them a privileged status so that their descendants would always remain feudal landowners, without their land being sold or divided by inheritance and thus made useful to more people; it would also be unjust if only those belonging to an arbitrarily selected class were allowed to acquire land, should the estates in fact be divided. The owner of a large estate keeps out as many smaller property owners (and their votes) as could otherwise occupy his territories. He does not vote on their behalf, and himself has only *one* vote. It should be left exclusively to the ability, industry and good fortune of each member of the commonwealth to enable each to acquire a part and all to acquire the whole, although this distinction cannot be observed within the general legislation itself. The number of those entitled to vote on matters of legislation must be calculated purely from the number of property owners, not from the size of their properties.

Those who possess this right to vote must agree *unanimously* to the law of public justice, or else a legal contention would arise between those who agree and those who disagree, and it would require yet another higher legal principle to resolve it. An entire people cannot, however, be expected to reach unanimity, but only to show a majority of votes (and not even of direct votes, but simply of the votes of those delegated in a large nation to represent the people). Thus the actual principle of being content with majority decisions must be accepted unanimously and embodied in a contract; and this itself must be the ultimate basis on which a civil constitution is established.

## CONCLUSION

This, then, is an *original contract* by means of which a civil and thus completely lawful constitution and commonwealth can alone be established. But we need by no means assume that this contract, . . . based on a coalition of the wills of all private individuals in a nation to form a common, public will for the purposes of rightful legislation, actually exists as a *fact,* for it cannot possibly be so. Such an assumption would mean that we would first have to prove from history that some nation, whose rights and obligations have been passed down to us, did in fact perform such an act, and handed down some authentic record or legal instrument, orally or in writing, before we could regard ourselves as bound by a pre-existing civil constitution. It is in fact merely an *idea* of reason, which nonetheless has undoubted practical reality; for it can oblige every legislator to frame his laws

in such a way that they could have been produced by the united will of a whole nation, and to regard each subject, in so far as he can claim citizenship, as if he had consented within the general will. This is the test of the rightfulness of every public law. For if the law is such that a whole people could not *possibly* agree to it (for example, if it stated that a certain class of *subjects* must be privileged as a hereditary *ruling class*), it is unjust; but if it is at least *possible* that a people could agree to it, it is our duty to consider the law as just, even if the people is at present in such a position or attitude of mind that it would probably refuse its consent if it were consulted. But this restriction obviously applies only to the judgement of the legislator, not to that of the subject. Thus if a people, under some existing legislation, were asked to make a judgment which in all probability would prejudice its happiness, what should it do? Should the people not oppose the measure? The only possible answer is that they can do nothing but obey. For we are not concerned here with any happiness which the subject might expect to derive from the institutions or administrations of the commonwealth, but primarily with the rights which would thereby be secured for everyone. And this is the highest principle from which all maxims relating to the commonwealth must begin, and which cannot be qualified by any other principles. No generally valid principle of legislation can be based on happiness. For both the current circumstances and the highly conflicting and variable illusions as to what happiness is (and no one can prescribe to others how they should attain it) make all fixed principles impossible, so that happiness alone can never be a suitable principle of legislation. The doctrine that *salus publica suprema civitatis lex est* retains its value and authority undiminished; but the public welfare which demands *first* consideration lies precisely in that legal constitution which guarantees everyone his freedom within the law, so that each remains free to seek his happiness in whatever way he thinks best, so long as he does not violate the lawful freedom and rights of his fellow subjects at large. If the supreme power makes laws which are primarily directed towards happiness (the affluence of the citizens, increased population etc.), this cannot be regarded as the end for which a civil constitution was established, but only as a means of *securing the rightful state,* especially against external enemies of the people. The head of state must be authorised to judge for himself whether such measures are necessary for the commonwealth's prosperity, which is required to maintain its strength and stability both internally and against external enemies. The aim is not, as it were, to make the people happy against its will, but only to ensure its continued existence as a commonwealth. The legislator may indeed err in judging whether or not the measures he adopts are *prudent,* but not in deciding whether or not the law harmonises with the principle of right. For he has ready at hand as an infallible *a priori* standard the idea of an original contract, and he need not wait for experience to show whether the means are suitable, as would be necessary if they were based on the principle of happiness. For so long as it is not self-contradictory to say that an entire people could agree to such a law, however painful it might seem, then the law is in harmony with right. But if a public law is beyond reproach (i.e. *irreprehensible*) with respect to right, it carries with it the authority to coerce those to whom it applies, and conversely, it forbids them to resist the will of the legislator by violent means. In other words, the power of the state to put the law into effect is also *irresistible,* and no rightfully established commonwealth can exist without a force of this kind to suppress all internal resistance. For such resistance would be dictated by a maxim which, if it became general, would destroy the whole civil constitution and put an end to the only state in which men can possess rights.

It thus follows that all resistance against the supreme legislative power, all incitement of the subjects to violent expressions of discontent, all defiance which breaks out into rebellion, is the greatest and most punishable crime in a commonwealth, for it destroys its very foundations. This prohibition is *absolute.* And even if the power of the state or its agent, the head of state, has violated the original contract by authorising the government to act tyrannically, and has thereby, in the eyes of the subject, forfeited the right to legislate, the subject is still not entitled to offer counter-resistance. The reason for this is that the people, under an existing civil constitution, has no longer any right to judge how the constitution should be administered. For if we suppose that it does have this right to judge and that it disagrees with the judgment of the actual head of state, who is to decide which side is right? Neither can act as judge of his own cause. Thus there would have to be another head above the head of state to mediate between the latter and the people, which is self-contradictory.—Nor can a right of necessity (*ius in casu necessitatis*) be involved here as a means of removing the barriers which restrict the power of the people; for it is monstrous to suppose that we can have a right to do wrong in the direst (physical) distress.[2] For the head of state can just as readily claim that his severe treatment of his subjects is justified by their insubordination as the subjects can justify their rebellion by complaints about their unmerited suffering, and who is to decide? The decision must rest with whoever controls the ultimate enforcement of the public law, i.e. the head of state himself. Thus no one in the commonwealth can have a right to contest his authority. . . .

NOTES

1. He who does a piece of work (*opus*) can sell it to someone else, just as if it were his own property. But guaranteeing one's labour (*praestatio operae*) is not the same as selling a commodity. The domestic servant, the shop assistant, the labourer, or even the barber, are merely labourers (*operarii*), not *artists* (*artifices*, in the wider sense) or members of the state, and are thus unqualified to be citizens. And although the man to whom I give my firewood to chop and the tailor to whom I give material to make into clothes both appear to have a similar relationship towards me, the former differs from the latter in the same way as the barber from the wig-maker (to whom I may in fact have given the requisite hair) or the labourer from the artist or tradesman, who does a piece of work which belongs to him until he is paid for it. For the latter, in pursuing his trade, exchanges his property with someone else (*opus*), while the former allows someone else to make use of him.— But I do admit that it is somewhat difficult to define the

qualifications which entitle anyone to claim the status of being his own master.

2. There is no *casus necessitatis* except where duties, i.e. an *absolute* duty and another which, however pressing, is nevertheless *relative,* come into conflict. For instance, it might be necessary for someone to betray someone else, even if their relationship were that of father and son, in order to preserve the state from catastrophe. This preservation of the state from evil is an absolute duty, while the preservation of the individual is merely a relative duty (i.e. it applies only if he is not guilty of a crime against the state). The first person might denounce the second to the authorities with the utmost unwillingness, compelled only by (moral) necessity. But if a person, in order to preserve his own life, pushes a shipwrecked fellow away from the plank he grasps, it would be quite false to say that (physical) necessity gives him a right to do so. For it is only a relative duty for me to preserve my own life (i.e. it applies only if I can do so without committing a crime). But it is an absolute duty not to take the life of another person who has not offended me and does not even make me risk my own life. Yet the teachers of general civil law are perfectly consistent in authorising such measures in cases of distress. For the authorities cannot combine *a penalty* with this prohibition, since this penalty would have to be death. But it would be a nonsensical law which threatened anyone with death if he did not voluntarily deliver himself up to death when in dangerous circumstances.

# 31    The Metaphysic of Morals

IMMANUEL KANT

## Section 45

A STATE (*civitas*) IS A UNION of an aggregate of men under rightful laws. In so far as these laws are necessary *a priori* and follow automatically from concepts of external right in general (and are not just set up by statute), the form of the state will be that of a state in the absolute sense, i.e. as the idea of what a state ought to be according to pure principles of right. This idea can serve as an internal guide (*norma*) for every actual case where men unite to form a commonwealth.

Every state contains three powers, i.e. the universally united will is made up of three separate persons (*trias politica*). These are the *ruling power* (or sovereignty) in the person of the legislator, the *executive power* in the person of the individual who governs in accordance with the law, and the *judicial power* (which allots to everyone what is his by law) in the person of the judge (*potestas legislatoria, rectoria et iudiciaria*). They can be likened to the three propositions in a practical operation of reason: the major premise, which contains the *law* of the sovereign will, the minor premise, which contains the *command* to act in accordance with the law (i.e. the principle of subsumption under the general will), and the conclusion, which contains the *legal decision* (the sentence) as to the rights and wrongs of each particular case.

## Section 46

The legislative power can belong only to the united will of the people. For since all right is supposed to emanate from this power, the laws it gives must be absolutely *incapable* of doing anyone an injustice. Now if someone makes dispositions for *another* person, it is always possible that he may thereby do him an injustice, although this is never possible in the case of decisions he makes for himself (for *volenti non fit iniuria*). Thus only the unanimous and combined will of everyone whereby each decides the same for all and all decide the same for each—in other words, the general united will of the people—can legislate.

The members of such a society (*societas civilis*) or state who unite for the purpose of legislating are known as *citizens* (*cives*), and the three rightful attributes which are inseparable from the nature of a citizen as such are as follows: firstly, lawful *freedom* to obey no law other than that to which he has given his consent; secondly, civil *equality* in recognising no one among the people as superior to himself, unless it be someone whom he is just as morally entitled to bind by law as the other is to bind him; and thirdly, the attribute of civil *independence* which allows him to owe his existence and sustenance not to the arbitrary will of anyone else among the people, but purely to his own rights and powers as a member of the commonwealth (so that he may not, as a civil personality, be represented by anyone else in matters of right).

Fitness to vote is the necessary qualification which every citizen must possess. To be fit to vote, a person must have an independent position among the people. He must therefore be not just a part of the commonwealth, but a member of it, i.e. he must by his own free will actively participate in a community of other people. But this latter quality makes it necessary to distinguish between the *active* and the *passive* citizen, although the latter concept seems to contradict the definition of the concept of a citizen altogether. The following examples may serve to overcome this difficulty. Apprentices to merchants or tradesmen, servants who are not employed by the state, minors (*naturaliter vel civiliter*), women in general and all those who are obliged to depend for their living (i.e. for food and protection) on the offices of others (excluding the state)—all of these people have no civil personality, and their existence is, so to speak, purely inherent. The woodcutter whom I employ on my premises; the blacksmith in India who goes from house to house with his hammer, anvil and bellows to do work with iron, as opposed to the European carpenter or smith who can put the products of his work up for public sale; the domestic tutor as opposed to the academic, the tithe-holder as opposed to the farmer; and so on—they are all mere auxiliaries to the commonwealth, for they have to receive orders or protection from other individuals, so that they do not possess civil independence.

This dependence upon the will of others and consequent inequality does not, however, in any way conflict with the freedom and equality of all men as *human beings* who together constitute a people. On the contrary, it is only by accepting these conditions that such a people can become a state and enter into a civil constitution. But all are not equally qualified within this constitution to possess the right to vote, i.e. to be citizens and not just subjects among other subjects. For from the fact that as passive members of the state, they can demand to be treated by all others in accordance with laws of natural freedom and equality, it does not follow that they also have a right to influence or organise the state itself as *active* members, or to co-operate in introducing particular laws. Instead it only means that the positive laws to which the voters agree, of whatever sort they may be, must not be at variance with the natural laws of freedom and with the corresponding equality of all members of the people whereby they are allowed to work their way up from their passive condition to an active one. . . .

# 32     Perpetual Peace

IMMANUEL KANT

## Section II

THE STATE OF PEACE AMONG MEN living side by side is not the natural state (*status naturalis*); the natural state is one of war. This does not always mean open hostilities, but at least an unceasing threat of war. A state of peace, therefore, must be *established*, for in order to be secured against hostility it is not sufficient that hostilities simply be not committed; and, unless this security is pledged to each by his neighbor (a thing that can occur only in a civil state), each may treat his neighbor, from whom he demands this security, as an enemy.

### FIRST DEFINITIVE ARTICLE FOR PERPETUAL PEACE

"*The Civil Constitution of Every State Should Be Republican.*" The only constitution which derives from the idea of the original compact, and on which all juridical legislation of a people must be based, is the republican. This constitution is established, firstly, by principles of the freedom of the members of a society (as men); secondly, by principles of dependence of all upon a single common legislation (as subjects); and, thirdly, by the law of their equality (as citizens). The republican constitution, therefore, is, with respect to law, the one which is the original basis of every form of civil constitution. The only question now is: Is it also the one which can lead to perpetual peace?

The republican constitution, besides the purity of its origin (having sprung from the pure source of the concept of law), also gives a favorable prospect for the desired consequence, i.e., perpetual peace. The reason is this: if the consent of the citizens is required in order to decide that war should be declared (and in this constitution it cannot but be the case), nothing is more natural than that they would be very cautious in commencing such a poor game, decreeing for themselves all the calamities of war. Among the latter would be: having to fight, having to pay the costs of war from their own resources, having painfully to repair the devastation war leaves behind, and, to fill up the measure of evils, load themselves with a heavy national debt that would embitter peace itself and that can never be liquidated on account of constant wars in the future. But, on the other hand, in a constitution which is not republican, and under which the subjects are not citizens, a declaration of war is the easiest thing in the world to decide upon, because war does not require of the ruler, who is the proprietor and not a member of the state, the least sacrifice of the pleasures of his table, the chase, his country houses, his court functions, and the like. He may, therefore, resolve on war as on a pleasure party for the most trivial reasons, and with perfect indifference leave the justification which decency requires to the diplomatic corps who are ever ready to provide it.

### SECOND DEFINITIVE ARTICLE FOR A PERPETUAL PEACE

"*The Law of Nations Shall be Founded on a Federation of Free States.*" Peoples, as states, like individuals, may be judged to injure one another merely by their coexistence in the state of nature (i.e., while independent of external laws). Each of them may and should for the sake of its own security demand that the others enter with it into a constitution similar to the civil constitution, for under such a constitution each can be secure in his right. This would be a league of nations, but it would not have to be a state consisting of nations. That would be contradictory, since a state implies the relation of a superior (legislating) to an inferior (obeying), i.e., the people, and many nations in one state would then constitute only one nation. This contradicts the presupposition, for here we have to weigh the rights of nations against each other so far as they are distinct states and not amalgamated into one.

When we see the attachment of savages to their lawless freedom, preferring ceaseless combat to subjection to a lawful constraint which they might establish, and thus preferring senseless freedom to rational freedom, we regard it with deep contempt as barbarity, rudeness, and a brutish degradation of humanity. Accordingly, one would think that civilized people (each united in a state) would hasten all the more to escape, the sooner the better, from such a depraved condition. But, instead, each state places its majesty (for it is absurd to speak of the majesty of the people) in being subject to no external juridical restraint, and the splendor of its sovereign consists in the fact that many thousands stand at his command to sacrifice themselves for something that does not concern them and without his needing to place himself in the least danger.[1] The chief difference between European and American savages lies in the fact that many tribes of the latter have been eaten by their enemies, while the former know how to make better use of their conquered enemies than to dine off them; they know better how to use them to increase the number of their subjects and thus the quantity of instruments for even more extensive wars.

When we consider the perverseness of human nature which is nakedly revealed in the uncontrolled relations between nations (this perverseness being veiled in the state of civil law by the constraint exercised by government), we may well be astonished that the word "law" has not yet been banished from war politics as pedantic, and that no state has yet been bold enough to advocate this

point of view. Up to the present, Hugo Grotius, Pufendorf, Vattel, and many other irritating comforters have been cited in justification of war, though their code, philosophically or diplomatically formulated, has not and cannot have the least legal force, because states as such do not stand under a common external power. There is no instance on record that a state has ever been moved to desist from its purpose because of arguments backed up by the testimony of such great men. But the homage which each state pays (at least in words) to the concept of law proves that there is slumbering in man an even greater moral disposition to become master of the evil principle in himself (which he cannot disclaim) and to hope for the same from others. Otherwise the word "law" would never be pronounced by states which wish to war upon one another; it would be used only ironically, as a Gallic prince interpreted it when he said, "It is the prerogative which nature has given the stronger that the weaker should obey him."

States do not plead their cause before a tribunal; war alone is their way of bringing suit. But by war and its favorable issue in victory, right is not decided, and though by a treaty of peace this particular war is brought to an end, the state of war, of always finding a new pretext to hostilities, is not terminated. Nor can this be declared wrong, considering the fact that in this state each is the judge of his own case. Notwithstanding, the obligation which men in a lawless condition have under the natural law, and which requires them to abandon the state of nature, does not quite apply to states under the law of nations, for as states they already have an internal juridical constitution and have thus outgrown compulsion from others to submit to a more extended lawful constitution according to their ideas of right. This is true in spite of the fact that reason, from its throne of supreme moral legislating authority, absolutely condemns war as a legal recourse and makes a state of peace a direct duty, even though peace cannot be established or secured except by a compact among nations.

For these reasons there must be a league of a particular kind, which can be called a league of peace (*foedus pacificum*), and which would be distinguished from a treaty of peace (*pactum pacis*) by the fact that the latter terminates only one war, while the former seeks to make an end of all wars forever. This league does not tend to any dominion over the power of the state but only to the maintenance and security of the freedom of the state itself and of other states in league with it, without there being any need for them to submit to civil laws and their compulsion, as men in a state of nature must submit.

The practicability (objective reality) of this idea of federation, which should gradually spread to all states and thus lead to perpetual peace, can be proved. For if fortune directs that a powerful and enlightened people can make itself a republic, which by its nature must be inclined to perpetual peace, this gives a fulcrum to the federation with other states so that they may adhere to it and thus secure freedom under the idea of the law of nations. By more and more such associations, the federation may be gradually extended.

We may readily conceive that a people should say, "There ought to be no war among us, for we want to make ourselves into a state; that is, we want to establish a supreme legislative, executive, and judiciary power which will reconcile our differences peaceably." But when this state says, "There ought to be no war between myself and other states, even though I acknowledge no supreme legislative power by which our rights are mutually guaranteed," it is not at all clear on what I can base my confidence in my own rights unless it is the free federation, the surrogate of the civil social order, which reason necessarily associates with the concept of the law of nations—assuming that something is really meant by the latter.

The concept of a law of nations as a right to make war does not really mean anything, because it is then a law of deciding what is right by unilateral maxims through force and not by universally valid public laws which restrict the freedom of each one. The only conceivable meaning of such a law of nations might be that it serves men right who are so inclined that they should destroy each other and thus find perpetual peace in the vast grave that swallows both the atrocities and their perpetrators. For states in their relation to each other, there cannot be any reasonable way out of the lawless condition which entails only war except that they, like individual men, should give up their savage (lawless) freedom, adjust themselves to the constraints of public law, and thus establish a continuously growing state consisting of various nations (*civitas gentium*), which will ultimately include all the nations of the world. But under the idea of the law of nations they do not wish this, and reject in practice what is correct in theory. If all is not to be lost, there can be, then, in place of the positive idea of a world republic, only the negative surrogate of an alliance which averts war, endures, spreads, and holds back the stream of those hostile passions which fear the law, though such an alliance is in constant peril of their breaking loose again. *Furor impius intus . . . fremit horridus ore cruento* (Virgil).[2]

## THIRD DEFINITIVE ARTICLE FOR A PERPETUAL PEACE

*"The Law of World Citizenship Shall Be Limited to Conditions of Universal Hospitality."* Here, as in the preceding articles, it is not a question of philanthropy but of right. Hospitality means the right of a stranger not to be treated as an enemy when he arrives in the land of another. One may refuse to receive him when this can be done without causing his destruction; but, so long as he peacefully occupies his place, one may not treat him with hostility. It is not the right to be a permanent visitor that one may demand. A special beneficent agreement would be needed in order to give an outsider a right to become a fellow inhabitant for a certain length of time. It is only a right of temporary sojourn, a right to associate, which all men have. They have it by virtue of their common possession of the surface of the earth, where, as a globe, they cannot infinitely disperse and hence must finally tolerate the presence of each other. Originally, no one had more right than another to a particular part of the earth.

Uninhabitable parts of the earth—the sea and the deserts—divide this community of all men, but the ship and the camel (the desert ship) enable them to approach each other across these unruled regions and to establish communication by using the common right to the face of the earth, which belongs to human beings generally. The inhospitality of the inhabitants of coasts (for instance, of the Barbary Coast) in robbing ships in neighboring seas or enslaving stranded travelers, or the inhospitality of the inhabitants of the deserts (for instance, the Bedouin Arabs) who view contact with nomadic tribes as conferring the right to plunder them, is thus opposed to natural law, even though it extends the right of hospitality, i.e., the privilege of foreign arrivals, no further than to conditions of the possibility of seeking to communicate with the prior inhabitants. In this way distant parts of the world can come into peaceable relations with each other, and these are finally publicly established by law. Thus the human race can gradually be brought closer and closer to a constitution establishing world citizenship.

But to this perfection compare the inhospitable actions of the civilized and especially of the commercial states of our part of the world. The injustice which they show to lands and peoples they visit (which is equivalent to conquering them) is carried by them to terrifying lengths. America, the lands inhabited by the Negro, the Spice Islands, the Cape, etc., were at the time of their discovery considered by these civilized intruders as lands without owners, for they counted the inhabitants as nothing. In East India (Hindustan), under the pretense of establishing economic undertakings, they brought in foreign soldiers and used them to oppress the natives, excited widespread wars among the various states, spread famine, rebellion, perfidy, and the whole litany of evils which afflict mankind.

China and Japan (Nippon), who have had experience with such guests, have wisely refused them entry, the former permitting their approach to their shores but not their entry, while the latter permit this approach to only one European people, the Dutch, but treat them like prisoners, not allowing them any communication with the inhabitants. The worst of this (or, to speak with the moralist, the best) is that all these outrages profit them nothing, since all these commercial ventures stand on the verge of collapse, and the Sugar Islands, that place of the most refined and cruel slavery, produces no real revenue except indirectly, only serving a not very praiseworthy purpose of furnishing sailors for war fleets and thus for the conduct of war in Europe. This service is rendered to powers which make a great show of their piety, and, while they drink injustice like water, they regard themselves as the elect in point of orthodoxy.

Since the narrow or wider community of the peoples of the earth has developed so far that a violation of rights in one place is felt throughout the world, the idea of a law of world citizenship is no high-flown or exaggerated notion. It is a supplement to the unwritten code of the civil and international law, indispensable for the maintenance of the public human rights and hence also of perpetual peace. One cannot flatter oneself into believing one can approach this peace except under the condition outlined here.

NOTES AND REFERENCES

1. A Bulgarian prince gave the following answer to the Greek emperor who good-naturedly suggested that they settle their difference by a duel: "A smith who has tongs won't pluck the glowing iron from the fire with his bare hands."

2. "Within, impious Rage, sitting on savage arms, his hands fast bound behind with a hundred brazen knots, shall roar in the ghastliness of blood-stained lips" (*Aeneid* I, 294–96, trans. H. Rushton Fairclough, "Loeb Classical Library," Cambridge: Harvard University Press, 1926).

# 33 Kant: "An Honest but Narrow-Minded Bourgeois"? [1]

SUSAN MENDUS

IN THEIR RECENT BOOK, *Women's Choices,* Mary Midgley and Judith Hughes remark that:

> When women read philosophy they tend to fall into an embarrassed habit of thinking that they ought not to criticize the ludicrous views which result, that it is unfair and anachronistic to think that people of this calibre ought to be able to avoid going into print with this sort of stuff. [2]

Nowhere is the embarrassment more keenly felt than in reading Kant's views on the nature of women and the role of women as citizens. The problem is not simply that Kant is dismissive about woman's status as a citizen (though this is in fact so), but rather that the explicit claims made in the political philosophy conflict markedly with what we might expect on the basis of reading the *Groundwork for a Metaphysic of Morals.* In *Groundwork* Kant emphasizes that the moral principles he proposes must be applicable not simply to men, nor even to human beings, but to rational beings as such. This generates the expectation that in the political philosophy women will be accorded equal status with men. Such expectations, are however, quickly disappointed, for when we reach the political philosophy, we find Kant insisting that women may be passive citizens only—never active citizens. Moreover, his reasons for insisting on this are far from clear: sometimes he gestures at reasons, sometimes he merely states baldly that this is so, but nowhere does he spell out explicitly and consistently exactly why women cannot be active citizens. The arguments of *Metaphysic of Morals, Theory and Practice* and *Anthropology* vacillate uneasily between the philosophic and the homespun, and frequently Kant simply appears to indulge in an unthinking endorsement of the prejudices of his day and an uncritical acceptance

of the dogma of others—notably Rousseau. However, it would be wrong to suggest or imply that it is only in the treatment of women as citizens that the expectations of the moral philosophy are disappointed: many commentators have remarked upon Kant's Janus-faced attitude in his political writings generally. Thus Rheinhold Aris notes that, "he [Kant] attacked serfdom and defended the exclusion of the unpropertied members of society from all essential political rights almost in the same breath, in both cases in the name of reason." [3]

Similarly, Kant's general disapproval of revolution is hard to square with his fulsome praise of the French Revolution as "a moral cause," and this vacillation between adherence to the status quo and enthusiasm for change is amongst the most perplexing features of his political philosophy and the most difficult to analyse. Commentators have described these tensions variously as tensions between conservatism and radicalism; idealism and pragmatism; rationalism and empiricism; and as an aspect of the phenomena–noumena distinction of the *First Critique.* That the tensions exist, then, is not in doubt; what must be questioned is *why* they exist and how deep they run. We have seen already that Aris believed Kant to be simply incapable of spotting the inconsistencies of his own arguments. By contrast, Howard Williams, in his book *Kant's Political Philosophy,* interprets the tensions simply as a recognition by Kant of the limits of political endeavour; thus, "at times, he appears to be advocating the most radical of political changes (when donning his philosophical hat), and, at others, he appears to be advocating the most cautious of conservatism (when donning his everyday, realist hat)." [4]

For Williams, however, the tensions are simply a recognition of the limits of what is practically possible. Kant's radicalism expresses what he believes to be ideal; his conservatism expresses what he believes to be prudent and practical. A further diagnosis is provided by Cohen in his article "A critique of Kant's philosophy of law." Cohen suggests that the conflict in Kant's writings may be resolved only by ascribing to reason factors which are merely contingent and variable. "Kant assumes," he says, "that reason dictates that men can transmit their titles of nobility to their wives, but not conversely . . . This approach to the problem reduces Kant's position to such an absurdity that one may wonder how such a powerful mind could have been led to it even in old age."[5] This criticism of Kant—that he confuses the dictates of reason with the merely contingent and socially determined—provides a third diagnosis of the difficulty involved in giving a coherent picture of his political philosophy. It must be repeated, however, that these are quite general difficulties involved in interpreting the political philosophy and in determining its relation to the moral philosophy, particularly the moral philosophy of the *Groundwork*. What is needed, therefore, is a general diagnosis of the cause of the tensions together with an inquiry into whether they explain Kant's view on the position of women; for it may be that there are specific problems involved in his account of women, over and above the general tensions mentioned here. In what follows I shall firstly try to elucidate Kant's stated views on the nature of women and their status as citizens, I shall then go on to say something about what accounts for these views, bearing in mind the three interpretations mentioned above. Finally, I shall attempt a reconstruction of Kant's doctrines to see whether there is anything in his moral and political thought which could give cause for optimism amongst feminists. I began with Kant's theses about citizenship and the criteria for being a citizen.

## Citizenship

The main texts in which Kant expounds his theory of citizenship are *Theory and Practice* and the *Metaphysic of Morals*. John Ladd, in his Introduction to Part I of *Metaphysic of Morals*, "The Meta-

physical Elements of Justice," points to an important difficulty in Kant's text. He notes that Kant has been criticized both for being a "radical revolutionary" and for being an "unregenerate reactionary."

However, he defends Kant by urging that:

> far from ignoring this seeming paradox, Kant makes it the central theme of his inquiry. The whole book may be regarded as an extended philosophical commentary on the relation between what is and what ought to be, both in politics and law. In order to follow the various discussions in the book, it is essential to realize that at times he is discussing actual states and actual obligations, whereas at other times he is discussing the ideal.[6]

Sadly for us, Kant rarely states explicitly when he is indulging in idealism and when he is being pragmatic: it is therefore left to the reader to disentangle these strands, and this task is an extremely difficult one. At the moment, I can do no more than mention this problem, and make no attempt to resolve it. However, it is a point to which I shall return later.

In *Metaphysic of Morals* Kant identifies three characteristics or attributes which, he says, are "inseparable from the nature of a citizen as such."[7] In *Theory and Practice* these are referred to as "three principles by which a state can alone be established in accordance with pure rational principles of external human right."[8] They are:

1. The *freedom* of every member of society as a human being.
2. The *equality* of each with all the others as a subject.
3. The *independence* of each member of a commonwealth as a citizen.[9]

However, having stated these three principles, and having insisted, in *Theory and Practice*, that they are not laws given by an already established state but rather the laws by which alone a state may be established, Kant immediately goes on to insist that not everyone within the state will in fact have the independence requisite for being a citizen. Although all will be free as human beings, and all will be equal as subjects, nevertheless not all will be independent as citizens. Not all will have a hand in framing the law, even though all will be equal as subjects under the law. Kant is emphatic on this, urging that:

> all are not equally qualified within this constitution to possess the right to vote, i.e. to be citizens and not just subjects among other subjects. For from the fact that as passive members of the state, they can demand to be treated by all others in accordance with laws of natural freedom and equality, *it does not follow* that they also have a right to influence or organise the state itself as *active* members, or to co-operate in introducing particular laws.[10]

The distinction between active and passive citizenship is therefore crucial for Kant and problematic for him, since it serves to justify the disenfranchisement of whole groups within society. We must therefore consider the criteria which Kant offers for distinguishing between active and passive citizens and try to establish whether the distinction can be made good and what it tells us about the assumptions of Kant's political philosophy.

In *Metaphysic of Morals,* Kant himself expresses a certain unease about proposing two classes of citizen, since this, he confesses, "seems to contradict the definition of the concept of a citizen altogether."[11] However, he then proceeds to provide examples of both active and passive citizens which, he says, "may serve to overcome the difficulty." His conclusion is that passive citizens are "mere auxiliaries of the commonwealth, for they have to receive orders or protection from other individuals, so that they do not possess civil independence." What is crucial for active citizenship, therefore, is being one's own master or being independent of the will of others, and such independence cannot be attributed to any servant (other than a servant of the state) or to anyone who sells merely his labour rather than the product of his labour. Those who must take orders from, or receive protection from, others cannot count as independent in this sense, and therefore cannot be granted the status of active citizen. To clarify yet further, Kant goes on to list passive citizens as:

apprentices to merchants or tradesmen, servants who are not employed by the state, minors (*naturaliter vel civiliter*), women in general, and all those who are obliged to depend for their living (i.e. for food and protection) on the offices of others (excluding the state)—all of these people have no civil personality, and their existence is, so to speak, purely inherent. The woodcutter, whom I employ on my premises; the blacksmith in India who goes from house to house with his hammer, anvil and bellows to do work with iron, as opposed to the European carpenter or smith who can put the products of his work up for public sale; the domestic tutor as opposed to the academic, the tithe-holder as opposed to the farmer and so on—they are all mere auxiliaries to the commonwealth.[12]

Several points emerge here to which I would like to draw attention: firstly, that Kant construes independence very literally, arguing that no one can serve two masters and that anyone who is any sort of servant (other than a servant of the state) must, *for that reason,* be denied active citizenship. Presumably, his thought here is that if servants are allowed the vote, they may become the mere mouthpiece of their masters: economic servitude may become political servitude and economic mastery may lead to political coercion. I shall say more about this later.

The second point is that in this formulation of the independence criterion it might be thought purely contingent that women count as passive citizens only. For here Kant is anxious to emphasize the differences which might be relative to a given society. Thus the blacksmith in India is merely a passive citizen, whereas the European smith is an active citizen. This because the latter, unlike the former, is not merely a servant, does not sell merely his labour but sells the products of his labour to the public. Such distinctions between societies make a difference to whether any one individual within the society may be accorded the status of active citizen. Reading this, one might think that Kant would be prepared to allow that in some societies, even if not in eighteenth-century Germany, women might indeed be active citizens. Superficially, it appears to be simply a function of eighteenth-century German society that women were not independent in the requisite sense. Here then, in *Metaphysic of Morals,* the status of women as passive citizens appears to be merely contingent: it just so happens that women in that time in that country lacked civil independence, just as Indian smiths lacked independence, but circumstances might alter and there need be no objection in principle to women aspiring to the status of active citizenship. A final point emerges in the immediately following paragraph, when Kant argues that:

> Whatever might be the kind of laws to which the citizens agree, these laws must not be incompatible with the natural laws of freedom and with the equality that accords with this freedom, namely, that everyone be able to work up from this passive status to an active status.[13]

The implication of this passage is that even the Indian smith, the apprentice and the domestic servant, might be allowed the opportunity to advance to active citizenship—to obtain the economic and social independence which bring with them civil independence. So the political status of the smith may vary from one society to another, but even the servant, who presumably counts as a passive citizen in *every* society, must be allowed the opportunity to "better himself" by becoming something other than a servant. Even he must not be prevented from aspiring to an occupation which carries civil independence and active citizenship with it. Kant insists that *"everyone* be able to work up from this passive status to an active status," and we would hope that "everyone" includes women.

It would seem, therefore, that although the situation of women is one of subordination and inferiority, there is nevertheless no principled objection to women being active citizens. At any rate, nothing which has been said so far precludes this possibility. However, if we turn from *Metaphysic of Morals* to *Theory and Practice,* we find that Kant offers different reasons for denying women the status of active citizens. Here he says that "the only qualification required by a citizen (apart, of

course, from being an adult male) is that he must be his own master (*sui-juris*) and must have some property (which can include any skill, trade, fine art or science) to support himself."[14] In this stipulation it appears to be not merely contingent that women lack active citizenship; rather, women are ruled out from the start. By contrast with the formulation in *Metaphysic of Morals,* we are invited *first* to enquire into the sex of the individual and *then,* if the individual is male, to ask whether he satisfies the independence criterion. Of course, in this way, women, so to speak, never get past the starting post. They become, not persons occupying particular social positions but occupants of the position "woman" which, by definition, fits them only for passive citizenship—and, unlike servants, they cannot hope to occupy a different position in the future. Thus they are eternally denied that possibility of advancement, which is open even to the lowliest of men. So, in *Theory and Practice* the exclusion of women is not contingent, but principled, and to understand why Kant might favour the exclusion of women as a matter of principle we shall need to look at his discussion of marriage in the *Metaphysical Elements of Justice* (Part I of *Metaphysic of Morals*). Before embarking on that, however, I shall digress briefly and say a little more about the independence criterion generally. This is necessary in order, ultimately, to assess the causes of the tensions in Kant's political philosophy.

We have seen already that Kant takes the term "independent" very literally: he requires that citizens should serve no master other than the state, and that, for him, involves having something other than one's own labour to sell—the citizen must see "that which is his," and not "allow others to make use of him."[15] Now this insistence that the citizen sell only what is his (where "what is his" must be something other than his labour) needs explanation, which Kant proceeds to provide in an extended footnote:

> guaranteeing one's labour is not the same as selling a commodity . . . although the man to whom I give my firewood to chop and the tailor to whom I give material to make into clothes both appear to have a similar relationship toward me,

the former differs from the latter in the same way as the barber from the wig-maker (to whom I may in fact have given the requisite hair) or the labourer from the artist or tradesman, who does a piece of work which belongs to him until he is paid for it. For the latter, in pursuing his trade, exchanges his property with someone else, while the former allows someone else to make use of him. But I do admit that it is somewhat difficult to define the qualifications which entitle anyone to claim the status of being his own master.[16]

In this passage Kant employs two apparently separable criteria: first, he argues that to be an active citizen a man must sell that which is his—he must sell his alienable property, where merely guaranteeing one's labour is not something alienable. (In this context Kant assumes a sharp distinction between one's labour and the product of one's labour. Thus, the barber merely sells his labour, the wig-maker sells the product of his labour). Second, however, he insists that it is in this way alone that a man may be his own master: where he guarantees only his labour, he effectively allows himself to be used by others as a means to the fulfilment of their plans and purposes. These, however, are surely distinct features of the case, for from the fact that the barber takes instruction from, or serves his customers, it does not follow that the customer is his master in any sense which need affect the ability to attain the status of active citizen. Moreover, if the barber takes instructions from, and serves, his customer, it is surely also true that the wig-maker similarly serves and takes instructions from his client. Kant's desire to distinguish between active and passive citizens rests upon the belief that only those who are independent should have a hand in framing the law. Now it is indeed important that those who frame the law should not be coerced by others. They need to be their own masters and not the political tools of others. However, Kant construes as independent all and only those who have some skill or property to sell—and this is surely wrong, for the wig-maker is no more immune from coercion than the barber, and the tailor to whom I give material is just as much my servant as the wood-chopper. Of

course, the social status of the wig-maker is higher than that of the barber, and the social status of the tailor is higher than that of the wood-chopper. But we need not believe, as Kant appears to, that fitness to vote is a function of social status.

By emphasizing these difficulties in the independence criterion we may see the source of the complaint that Kant is simply an honest but narrow-minded bourgeois, anxious to justify and strengthen the social status of his own class and fumbling ineffectively for reasons which will ground the justification. The discussion of the independence criterion, together with the earlier discussions, now give us three kinds of objection to Kant's treatment of women as citizens:

1. Women are relegated to the status of passive citizens and in the *Metaphysic of Morals* this move appears to be justified by appeal to the independence criterion. However, on inspection, the independence criterion appears to make social status the test of fitness to vote, and it is far from clear why this should be accepted. So it seems the independence criterion fails in general and, *a fortiori,* fails to justify the exclusion of women from active citizenship.

2. Even if the independence criterion were coherent and plausible, still it is not invariably Kant's stated reason for the exclusion of women. In *Theory and Practice* women appear to be, by definition, incapable of independence.

3. This definitional exclusion of women makes them worse off than any male passive citizen, since it denies them any opportunity of advancing to active citizenship. This is a sinister and far-reaching implication of Kant's political thought; for, as we have seen, the opportunity to advance to active citizenship is a requirement of equality. Again, "Whatever might be the kind of laws to which the citizens agree, these laws must not be incompatible with the natural laws of freedom and with the equality that accords with this freedom, namely, that

everyone be able to work up from this passive status to an active status."[17]

But if women are to be denied the possibility of advancement to the status of active citizens, then it is at least *prima facie* the case that they are also denied the equality which belongs to all men, whether active or passive citizens. And if this is so, then Kant appears not merely to be denying women a hand in framing the law, but worse, he is denying them the equality which he has already said belongs to all as subjects.

Why then are women denied the possibility of advancement, and what are the implications for Kant's view of women generally? To understand this we must turn to his treatment of the topic of marriage, to his doctrine of equality, and to his account of the nature of the sexes.

## Marriage

Kant's views about the nature of the marriage relationship are advanced in Part I of the *Metaphysic of Morals,* "The Metaphysical Elements of Justice." His treatment of the topic is notorious, an embarrassment to moral philosophers and philosophers of law alike. Few have found a good word to say about it, and at least one commentator has described Kant's views as "shallow and repulsive."[18] The salient features are these: Kant's view of sex is that it is basically animal, ultimately incompatible with the dignity of man and man's worth as a moral being. Even when contained within the confines of monogamous marriage, sex is still fundamentally animal and sexual love is not properly called love at all: "it is a unique kind of pleasure (*sui generis*), and the passion really has nothing in common with moral love, though it can enter into close union with it under the limiting conditions of practical reason."[19] Indeed, Kant insists that yielding to the desire for sexual gratification is worse even than suicide:

> the man who defiantly casts off the burden of life is at least not making a feeble surrender to animal impulse in throwing himself away; self-murder requires courage. . . . But unnatural vice, which is complete abandonment of oneself to animal inclination, makes man not only an object of enjoyment, but still further an unnatural thing, i.e. a loathsome object, and so deprives him of all reverence for himself.[20]

This denial of one's own humanity is, however, permissible within the context of a monogamous marriage, where the relationship between the partners is reciprocal.

This conception of sex—as a form of mutual exploitation for which one must pay the price of marriage—has the ironic consequence that it turns one feminist objection on its head. In Kant's eyes, sex represents just as much an exploitation of the man by the woman as of the woman by the man:

> The feminist complains that the man treats the woman as a sexual object. Kant suggests that the complaint is more deep-lying than this. According to him, both the man and the woman treat each other as things. This suggests that the feminist argument that sex takes on an exploitative form in modern society might best be reformulated not as an instance of the inhumanity of man towards woman, but as an instance of the general inhumanity of man (i.e. human beings in general) towards man.[21]

The exploitative and dehumanizing nature of sex is thus legitimized to some extent by the reciprocity involved in monogamous marriage. Yet Kant's appeal to reciprocity is both puzzling and misleading—puzzling because it is a central tenet of *Groundwork* that all employment of persons as things is immoral, and it is hard to see how that immorality can be modified or translated merely by the addition of reciprocity. "Man is not a thing—not something used *merely* as a means."[22] What separates man from mere things is precisely that persons, unlike things, are not to be used as mere means. Talk of reciprocity may also be misleading because it suggests that the marriage relationship is one of equality. However, as we shall see, reciprocity does not imply equality, and Kant never departs from his belief that man is naturally superior to woman, nor does he question the concomitant right of the husband to command the wife. I shall look at these points separately: first, the claim that the reciprocal nature of the monogamous marriage legitimizes that exploitation of one by the other which is involved in sex. It is important to note that Kant does not believe that sex within marriage is any less animal than fornication or adultery. The reciprocity is simply a guarantee for the wife that she will not be treated as a chattel or slave. In polygamous or adulterous relationships the woman's rights over the man are unequal and thus her position is reduced to one of servitude. The demand for reciprocity cannot therefore transform sex into something human, it can only ensure that the bargain struck is an equal one; that the exploitation of the woman by the man is matched by the exploitation of the man by the woman. Opportunities are equalized, but they are, nevertheless, opportunities to do what is fundamentally denaturing.

But doesn't reciprocity—so understood—imply equality? It does not. Kant's willingness to invest the wife with rights greater than those of a servant or chattel does not amount to a willingness to grant her equality, and he is quite clear that the natural superiority of the husband brings with it the right to command on his part, and the duty to obey on her part. Moreover, the marriage contract is one which ensures that the woman's position is one of subordination, for Kant tells us that by entering into marriage the woman, unlike the man, renounces her civil independence. Why should she do this? Why should a free and equal human being enter a contract that *always* places her in subjection and subordination to a male individual? To understand this we need to look more closely at Kant's account of equality.

## Equality

Kant is quite clear that the actual position of woman in marriage is not one of equality with her husband. However, he is ambivalent as to whether this *de facto* inequality is grounded in natural inequality. Sometimes he argues that wife and husband are naturally equal, but that the wife forgoes her equality for the sake of the common household good:

> juridical law cannot be considered as contradicting the equality of the couple. Consequently, that domination has the sole objective of asserting, in the realisation of the common interest of the family, the natural superiority of the husband over the wife.[23]

Here the argument appears to be that superiority does not necessarily imply natural inequality: although the husband is superior to the wife, nevertheless she is his equal. However, recognizing his superiority over her, and mindful of what is in the interest of the family as a whole, she renounces her natural equality and submits to her husband. At other times, however, Kant claims that husband and wife (man and woman) are naturally *unequal,* but argues that this inequality is justified because reciprocal: in return for her lack of political power, the wife secures domestic domination; "he loves domestic peace and readily submits to her regime."[24] In this argument it is the chivalry of the man, not the self-denial of the woman, which explains the *de facto* inequality between them.

Either way, there is no reason for the married woman to be dissatisfied with her lot in life: if she has *voluntarily* renounced her equality, then she has no cause for complaint; equally, if she has exchanged subordination in one sphere for domination in another, she still has no cause for complaint. The two arguments, although divided on the question of woman's natural equality, both point to the same conception of woman's nature. The former argument, premised on the existence of natural equality which is voluntarily renounced, makes reference to a greater good than the equality of each with all others. In particular it implies that women are not ends in themselves, but are fully realized as women only when they submit to becoming means to some further social end— the unit and coherence of the family. The latter argument, premised on the assumption of natural inequality, makes explicit reference to woman's distinct and singular nature, and this appeal to the different nature of woman is fleshed out in Kant's claim that marriage is the means whereby woman obtains her genuine freedom and man loses his. The crucial point then is that, whether or not woman is formally equal with man, her nature is different from man's nature. This difference justifies her different status (as [a] passive rather than active citizen) and explains why she becomes free by marrying, whereas the man loses freedom.

Summarizing, we may present Kant's views about woman's status as follows. Woman may be accorded the status of passive citizen only. Unlike a male passive citizen, she may not, by self-improvement or advancement, aspire to the status of active citizen. This is because of her intrinsic nature as exemplified in the marriage contract. By the marriage contract woman relinquishes her equality and allows the man to dominate in political life in exchange for her own domination in domestic life. It is fitting that a woman should do this, since she, unlike a man, gains her true freedom by entering into marriage. It is in woman's nature that her freedom should best be obtained by marrying. What, then, is woman's nature? And why is it so different from man's nature that the three characteristics of freedom, equality and independence are either denied woman altogether or reinterpreted in their application to her?

## Woman's Nature

The discussion "Of the nature of the Sexes" is to be found in the *Anthropology*. Here Kant's mind, almost wholly uncluttered by any actual experience, is laid bare and the prejudice and bigotry are revealed. A great deal of what he has to say about the inherent nature of woman is merely ludicrous. For example:

> By extending favours towards men, the feminine character lays claim to freedom and simultaneously to the conquest of the entire male species. Although this inclination is in ill-repute, under the name of coquetry, it is not without a real justifiable basis. A young wife is always in danger

of becoming a widow, and this leads her to distribute her charms to all men whose fortunes make them marriageable; so that, if this should occur, she would not be lacking in suitors.[25]

And again:

> In marriage the husband woos only his own wife, but the wife has an inclination for all men. Out of jealousy she dresses up only for the eyes of her own sex, in order to outdo other women in charm or pretended distinguished appearance. The man, on the other hand, dresses up only so far as not to shame his wife by his clothes. The man judges feminine mistakes leniently, whereas the woman judges very severely (in public); and young ladies, if they had the choice to have their trespasses judged by a male or female jury, would certainly choose a male jury for their judge.[26]

And so it grinds on. One implausible remark following upon another. Most important here, however, is not this parade of blind prejudices or pretence to have discovered the intrinsic nature of woman as such. What is important, I believe, is the assertion in this same chapter that woman is to be identified with inclination and man with reason. Thus:

> the woman should reign and the man should rule; because inclination reigns and reason rules.[27]

It might be argued that it is wrong to place too much emphasis on this somewhat throwaway line, buried in a late and minor work. However, remarks made elsewhere do nothing to gainsay this observation in the *Anthropology*: we have already seen the desperate attempts to justify woman's status as passive citizen only; to explain the subordination of woman within the marriage relationship and her effective exclusion from all political life. Against this background, the identification of woman with inclination and of man with reason, even if not required, is hardly a bolt from the blue. Moreover, other aspects of Kant's philosophy of law mesh in with this final dismissal of woman. As Cohen notes, Kant seems to believe that the obedience of wife to husband is a requirement of natural law.[28] The honest but narrow-minded bourgeois in Kant fails to distinguish between what is merely conventional and accepted in his society and what is a command of reason. (This failure, it should be noted, is not confined to Kant's treatment of women: his view that life tenure for competent officials was a dictate of reason provides further evidence of his inability to distinguish the contingent and circumstantial from the *a priori*.)

From the beginning of the paper with the disappointing but not wholly surprising revelation that Kant will not enfranchise women, we have come a long way. The lack of independence of women is certainly not merely contingent in the way an apprentice's lack of independence may be thought to be contingent. Thus woman is denied not only the vote but also all hope of aspiring to it. Independence is eternally withheld from her. Then her freedom and equality are also threatened: the former by the radical dichotomy between woman's freedom and man's; the latter by a reinterpretation of the notion of equality as it applies to women (or, alternatively, by insistence that woman's equality is not denied, but merely voluntarily given up for practical purposes). Finally, it is denied—fleetingly and indirectly, but nevertheless denied—that woman's nature has a connection with reason. Woman's nature is identified with inclination, and it is for this reason that she must submit herself to man. It would appear that in the kingdom of rational beings there are only adult males. Kant even goes so far as to deny that there can be "scholarly women": "As for the scholarly woman, she uses her books in the same way as her watch, for example, which she carries so that people will see that she has one, though it is usually not running or not set by the sun."[29]

In general, then, women are loquacious, quarrelsome, jealous and possessed of an overpowering inclination to dominate. It would be foolish and imprudent to allow them any power or authority in political matters since, Kant comes close to saying, they are not strictly rational. The downward

spiral has brought us close to a situation in which it is hard to see what exactly distinguishes women from serfs or even animals, despite the lip-service Kant pays to the equality of women in marriage and the reciprocity of the marriage relationship.

What accounts for this massive underestimation of the value of women and suspicion of woman's nature? For even if the situation is not quite as bad as I have suggested, and as the texts quietly imply, nevertheless there can be little doubt that Kant took an extremely dim view of woman's nature and abilities. I have mentioned several times the excuse that Kant is merely a child of his time. Penned up in the narrow confines of Königsberg, starved of the company of women, it is surely, the argument goes, absurd to expect any more than this of him. It is not. At the beginning of this paper I quoted a remark from Mary Midgley and Judith Hughes's book *Women's Choices,* in which this comment upon the embarrassment which overcomes us when we read the views of the great dead philosophers on the subject of women. They comment too on the feeling that it is unfair and anachronistic to criticize the philosophers involved, but go on to conclude that even if excuses may be made for Aquinas, say, or Aristotle, nevertheless, "When we get to the eighteenth century all such excuses fail, and it is important to say plainly that things went very badly wrong. Unthinking conformism was replaced by positive reactionary efforts to resist and reverse change."[30]

Can we now say plainly that Kant's response to the question of women's status as citizens is rather more than mere unthinking prejudice, rather more than the reflections of an "honest but narrow-minded bourgeois"? I think we can, and must. In this way, we may, I hope, find more far-reaching and useful lessons than the simple and by now unsurprising one that Kant "got it wrong," for there is little point in establishing that he got it wrong without, at the same time, seeing how we might do better and without questioning whether the wrong done to women does not spring from a source which also involves doing wrong to others. In other words, is the wrong done to women simply the manifestation of a more deep-rooted and systematically misguided way of thinking? I now turn to these questions. My responses to them will be very partial and speculative. I recognize this and wish it were not so, but even a partial response may be better than nothing and I hope that what I say will suggest some lines of further inquiry.

At the beginning of the paper I noted the tensions in Kant's political philosophy and three accounts of the source of these tensions. Howard Williams' claim is that the tensions are merely part of Kant's general conservatism; his recognition that there are limits to what is practically possible in political life. Similarly, John Ladd's Introduction to the *Metaphysical Elements of Justice* suggests that the tensions represent a shrewd awareness of the gap between what is and what ought to be. That there is an element of this is undeniable; the most striking example of Kant's conservatism is perhaps his instruction always to obey the sovereign and his abhorrence of revolution. Thus he prefers to risk despotism rather than advocate the disobedience which would, he fears, result in chaos and strife. Other examples of conservatism are not hard to find in Kant's political philosophy and indeed in his own life (note, for example, his undertaking to Frederick William II not to mention religious matters either in his writings or in his lectures). However, it is difficult to see any element of compromise of this sort in his attitude to women; nowhere does he apologize for the low status he accords women. Far from it. In *Anthropology* he goes so far as to suggest that in civilized society woman's status is improved far beyond what it is in primitive society and even warns against the dangers of allowing women too much education. The same attitude is manifested in a series of letters concerning Maria von Herbert. This young woman had written to Kant about a romantic problem which was causing her great worry and unhappiness. Kant replied to the letters in stern moralistic tones and also sent them to Elizabeth Motherby, the daughter of an English friend, as a warning of what happens to women when they think too much and fail to control their

fantasies![31] So even if the conservatism and caution are present in Kant's political philosophy, they cannot, I think account for his treatment of women. For the problem here is precisely that there are no tensions at all: there is no radicalism or idealism to set against the pragmatism and conservatism, and it is this which distinguishes the treatment of women from, say, the discussion of revolution generally and the French Revolution in particular.

A second interpretation of Kant attributes the tensions in his political philosophy to straightforward failure to spot inconsistencies and contradictions. Thus Aris holds that Kant "attacked serfdom and defended the exclusion of the unproperitied members of society from all essential political rights almost in the same breath, in both cases in the name of reason."[32] This is true, but again not the whole truth. What is wrong with Kant's political philosophy in so far as it concerns the status of women is not simply that it expresses a cautious conservatism and eagerness to defend the status quo. Rather, the elevation of contingent practices to the status of requirements of reason represents a categorical denial on Kant's part that anything other than the status quo might be either feasible or permissible, and that is justified by appeal to pure reason. Thus the whole-hearted defence of capitalism, requiring that everything, even the marriage relationship, be understood in socio-economic terms; the defence of individualism generating the "shallow and repulsive" concept of marital relations, are all construed as demands of reason, not merely variable and changeable customs. Here we find a resistance to change which goes far beyond mere conservatism and elevates the principles and practices of eighteenth-century Germany to the level of undeniable and indubitable truth.

Still, the distinction between contingent practices and dictates of reason may not be quite as sharp as I have so far implied: in defending the status quo, Kant is not simply doing that. He is also defending his own individualism in *Groundwork*, and the difficulties he encounters are not, I think, peculiar to him, but are general difficulties which infect all individualist theories. In discussing Kant's views on woman's equality, I noted that he appears to be torn between, on the one hand, the belief that men and women are naturally equal, but that women must renounce her natural equality for the common household good, and, on the other, the belief that men and women are *not* naturally equal: woman's singular nature renders inappropriate an equal division of authority and power. However, the problem here is a deep one— not only for Kant, but for individualism generally and for feminist individualism in particular. In all its forms, individualism runs the risk of failing to do justice to the facts of our social lives. Caird makes this point with particular reference to Kant's philosophy, pointing out that in distinguishing between monogamous marriage and concubinage Kant alludes to a social unity between two persons which quite contradicts his original idea of right:

> If we keep strictly to the category of reciprocity, and refuse to go on to the higher category of organic community, each person would have to be regarded as means to the other, and neither as end. This would answer to the case of sensual indulgence in which each individual was a means to the pleasure of the other, and no higher end was sought on either side. But Kant really points to a higher social relation in which each individual loses himself to find himself again in the common life to which he contributes.[33]

All individualist theories share this difficulty: in construing persons as essentially independent, free and equal, they support an atomistic model which cannot readily accommodate those social units, such as the family, which transcend mere atomism. The choice then is between abandoning individualism and construing the family as itself a single unit, with the husband as the head and decision-maker. The dilemma is explained thus by Elizabeth Wolgast:

> Husband and wife are different individuals with wills of their own. One would think that, in the last determination, they form a small organisation which has to make decisions in its own way, for

which its members are jointly responsible. But this would conflict with the atomistic model: from the point of view of society, the parties would then neither be fully individuals, nor together be one. It is simpler to say that the husband will represent them: that saves the surface features of atomism. Like a single person, the head of the family speaks for an atomic unit.[34]

And so it is with Kant: "If a union is to be harmonious and indissoluble, it is not enough for two people to associate as they please; one party must be *subject* to the other."[35] Against this background Kant appeals to woman's nature to justify his claim that it is she who should be subject; he who should dominate. At this point, the honest but narrow-minded bourgeois appears, for it is undeniable that here the contingent facts of eighteenth-century German society are elevated to the status of eternal truths. Nevertheless, the dilemma is thrown up by individualism itself, which dictates, as a central tenet, that *someone* must dominate, *someone* must give way. Even in Mill (champion of the emancipation of women), this problem arises, forcing him to appeal to woman's nature as a guarantee against the destruction of the patriarchal family. When individualism is feminist individualism, it still cannot escape its own internal demands. Thus the modern feminist may insist that at least sometimes the head of the family may be female, but is never in doubt that *someone* must be the head and decision-maker. The language of domination and subordination is central to individualism and cannot be dispensed with except by abandoning individualism itself. Hence the charge that individualist feminism would turn women into pseudo-men.

In conclusion, then, it may well be that Kant is an honest but narrow-minded bourgeois, unable to see beyond the social conventions of his time. Nevertheless, we must beware of swapping one set of conventions for another: to abandon eighteenth-century German values for twentieth-century British values is not necessarily an improvement, particularly if the philosophical model underpinning both is faulty. The battle between individualist feminists and individualist misogynists will not be resolved satisfactorily until the implications of individualism are fully explained. As Kant himself says, in a different context:

> As impartial umpires, we must leave aside the question whether it is for the good or the bad cause that the contestants are fighting. They must be left to decide the issue for themselves. After they have rather exhausted than injured one another, they will perhaps themselves perceive the futility of their quarrel, and part good friends.[36]

NOTES AND REFERENCES

I am very grateful to John Horton and Peter Nicholson for their extensive and helpful comments on an earlier draft of this paper.

1. The quotation is taken from Rheinhold Aris, *History of Political Thought in Germany, 1789–1815* (Frank Cass and Co., 1965) p. 87.

2. Mary Midgley and Judith Hughes, *Women's Choices* (Weidenfeld and Nicolson, 1983) p. 45.

3. Aris, p. 98. (Perhaps Aris exaggerates somewhat here: the denial of political rights to some members of society does not necessarily amount to applauding serfdom, as he suggests.)

4. Howard Williams, *Kant's Political Philosophy* (Blackwell, 1983) p. 179.

5. Morris R. Cohen, "A critique of Kant's philosophy of law," in G. T. Whitney and D. F. Bowers (eds.) *The Heritage of Kant* (Russell and Russell, 1962) p. 296.

6. *The Metaphysical Elements of Justice,* trans. John Ladd (Bobbs-Merrill, 1965) p. xxix.

7. *Metaphysic of Morals,* sect. 46, in H. Reiss (ed.), trans. H. Nisbet, *Kant's Political Writings* (Cambridge University Press, 1970), p. 139. All page references to *Metaphysic of Morals* and *Theory and Practice* are to the Reiss edition, unless otherwise stated.

8. *Theory and Practice* p. 74.

9. Ibid.

10. *Metaphysic of Morals,* sect. 46, p. 140.

11. Ibid., p. 139.

12. Ibid., pp. 139–40.

13. Ibid., p. 140.

14. *Theory and Practice,* p. 78.

15. Ibid.

16. Ibid.

17. *Metaphysic of Morals,* sect. 46, p. 140.

18. Aris, p. 102.

19. *The Doctrine of Virtue* (Part II of *Metaphysic of Morals*), trans. M. Gregor (Harper and Row, 1964) p. 90.

20. *The Doctrine of Virtue,* p. 89.

21. Howard Williams, p. 118.

22. *Groundwork for a Metaphysic of Morals,* Ak. 427–9.

23. *Metaphysical Elements of Justice,* Ch. III., sect. 26, as quoted in B. Edelman, *The Ownership of the Image* (Routledge and Kegan Paul, 1979).

24. *Anthropology from a Pragmatic Point of View,* trans. M. Gregor (Martinus Nijhoff, The Hague, 1974) p. 167.

25. Ibid., p. 168.

26. Ibid., p. 170.

27. Ibid., p. 172.

28. Ibid., p. 285.

29. Ibid., p. 171.

30. Midgley and Hughes, pp. 45–6.

31. *Kant: Philosophical Correspondence,* 1759–99. ed. Arnulf Zweig (University of Chicago, 1967), p. 204 and Introduction, pp. 25–6.

32. Aris, p. 98.

33. E. Caird, *The Critical Philosophy of Kant* (James Maclehose and Sons, 1889), vol. II, 361, n.1.

34. Elizabeth H. Wolgast, *Equality and the Rights of Women* (Cornell University, 1980) pp. 145–6.

35. *Anthropology* p. 167.

36. *Critique of Pure Reason,* trans. N. Kemp Smith (Macmillan, 1929) A423/B451.

# 34    On *Satyagraha*

## MOHANDAS K. GANDHI

### Soul-Force and Tapasya

THE FORCE DENOTED by the term "passive resistance" and translated into Hindi as *nishkriya pratirodha* is not very accurately described either by the original English phrase or by its Hindi rendering. Its correct description is "*satyagraha*." *Satyagraha* was born in South Africa in 1908. There was no word in any Indian language denoting the power which our countrymen in South Africa invoked for the redress of their grievances. There was an English equivalent, namely, "passive resistance," and we carried on with it. However, the need for a word to describe this unique power came to be increasingly felt, and it was decided to award a prize to anyone who could think of an appropriate term. A Gujarati-speaking gentleman submitted the word "*satyagraha*," and it was adjudged the best.

"Passive resistance" conveyed the idea of the Suffragette Movement in England. Burning of houses by these women was called "passive resistance" and so also their fasting in prison. All such acts might very well be "passive resistance" but they were not "*satyagraha*." It is said of "passive resistance" that it is the weapon of the weak, but the power which is the subject of this article can be used only by the strong. This power is not "passive" resistance; indeed it calls for intense activity. The movement in South Africa was not passive but active. The Indians of South Africa believed that Truth was their object, that Truth ever triumphs, and with this definiteness of purpose they persistently held on to Truth. They put up with all the suffering that this persistence implied. With the conviction that Truth is not to be renounced even unto death, they shed the fear of death. In the cause of Truth, the prison was a palace to them and its doors the gateway to freedom.

*Satyagraha* is not physical force. A *satyagrahi* does not inflict pain on the adversary; he does not seek his destruction. A *satyagrahi* never resorts to firearms. In the use of *satyagraha*, there is no ill-will whatever.

*Satyagraha* is pure soul-force. Truth is the very substance of the soul. That is why this force is called *satyagraha*. The soul is informed with knowledge. In it burns the flame of love. If someone gives us pain through ignorance, we shall win him through love. "Non-violence is the supreme *dharma*" [*Ahimsa paramo Dharma*] is the proof of this power of love. Non-violence is a dormant state. In the waking state, it is love. Ruled by love, the world goes on. In English there is a saying, "Might is Right." Then there is the doctrine of the survival of the fittest. Both these ideas are contradictory to the above principle. Neither is wholly true. If ill-will were the chief motive-force, the world would have been destroyed long ago; and neither would I have had the opportunity to write this article nor would the hopes of the readers be fulfilled. We are alive solely because of love. We are all ourselves the proof of this. Deluded by modern western civilization, we have forgotten our ancient civilization and worship the might of arms.

We forget the principle of non-violence, which is the essence of all religions. The doctrine of arms stands for irreligion. It is due to the sway of that doctrine that a sanguinary war is raging in Europe.

In India also we find worship of arms. We see it even in that great work of Tulsidas. But it is seen in all the books that soul-force is the supreme power.

Rama stands for the soul and Ravana for the non-soul. The immense physical might of Ravana is as nothing compared to the soul-force of Rama. Ravana's ten heads are as straw to Rama. Rama is a *yogi*, he has conquered self and pride. He is "placid equally in affluence and adversity," he has "neither attachment, nor greed nor the intoxication of status." This represents the ultimate in *satyagraha*. The banner of *satyagraha* can again fly in the Indian sky and it is our duty to raise it. If we take recourse to *satyagraha*, we can conquer our conquerors the English, make them bow before our tremendous soul-force, and the issue will be of benefit to the whole world.

It is certain that India cannot rival Britain or Europe in force of arms. The British worship the war-god and they can all of them become, as they are becoming, bearers of arms. The hundreds of millions in India can never carry arms. They have made the religion of non-violence their own. It is impossible for the *varnashrama* system to disappear from India.

The way of *varnashrama* is a necessary law of nature. India, by making a judicious use of it derives much benefit. Even the Muslims and the English in India observe this system to some extent. Outside of India, too, people follow it without being aware of it. So long as this institution of *varnashrama* exists in India, everyone cannot bear arms here. The highest place in India is assigned to the *brahmana dharma*—which is soul-force. Even the armed warrior does obeisance to the *Brahmin*. So long as this custom prevails, it is vain for us to aspire for equality with the West in force of arms.

It is our Kamadhenu.[1] It brings good both to the *satyagrahi* and his adversary. It is ever victorious. For instance, Harishchandra was a *satyagrahi*, Prahlad was a *satyagrahi*, Mirabai was a *satyagrahi*. Daniel, Socrates and those Arabs who hurled themselves on the fire of the French artillery were all *satyagrahis*. We see from these examples that a *satyagrahi* does not fear for his body, he does not give up what he thinks is Truth; the word "defeat" is not to be found in his dictionary, he does not wish for the destruction of his antagonist, he does not vent anger on him; but has only compassion for him.

A *satyagrahi* does not wait for others, but throws himself into the fray, relying entirely on his own resources. He trusts that when the time comes, others will do likewise. His practice is his precept. Like air, *satyagraha* is all-pervading. It is infectious, which means that all people—big and small, men and women—can become *satyagrahis*. No one is kept out from the army of *satyagrahis*. A *satyagrahi* cannot perpetrate tyranny on anyone; he is not subdued through application of physical force; he does not strike at anyone. Just as anyone can resort to *satyagraha*, it can be resorted to in almost any situation.

People demand historical evidence in support of *satyagraha*. History is for the most part a record of armed activities. Natural activities find very little mention in it. Only uncommon activities strike us with wonder. *Satyagraha* has been used always and in all situations. The father and the son, the man and the wife are perpetually resorting to *satyagraha*, one towards the other. When a father gets angry and punishes the son, the son does not hit back with a weapon, he conquers his father's anger by submitting to him. The son refuses to be subdued by the unjust rule of his father but he puts up with the punishment that he may incur through disobeying the unjust father. We can similarly free ourselves of the unjust rule of the Government by defying the unjust rule and accepting the punishments that go with it. We do not bear malice towards the Government. When we set its fears at rest, when we do not desire to make armed assaults on the administrators, nor to unseat them from power, but only to get rid of their injustice, they will at once be subdued to our will.

The question is asked why we should call any rule unjust. In saying so, we ourselves assume the function of a judge. It is true. But in this world, we always have to act as judges for ourselves. That is why the *satyagrahi* does not strike his adversary with arms. If he has Truth on his side, he will win, and if his thought is faulty, he will suffer the consequences of his fault.

What is the good, they ask, of only one person opposing injustice; for he will be punished and destroyed, he will languish in prison or meet an untimely end through hanging. The objection is not valid. History shows that all reforms have begun with one person. Fruit is hard to come by without *tapasya*. The suffering that has to be undergone in *satyagraha* is *tapasya* in its purest form. Only when the *tapasya* is capable of bearing fruit do we have the fruit. This establishes the fact that when there is insufficient *tapasya,* the fruit is delayed. The *tapasya* of Jesus Christ, boundless though it was, was not sufficient for Europe's need. Europe has disapproved Christ. Through ignorance, it has disregarded Christ's pure way of life. Many Christs will have to offer themselves as sacrifice at the terrible altar of Europe, and only then will realization dawn on that continent. But Jesus will always be the first among these. He has been the sower of the seed and his will therefore be the credit for raising the harvest. . . .

## Non-Violence and Non-Retaliation

It has become the fashion these days to say that society cannot be organized or run on non-violent lines. I join issue on that point. In a family, when a father slaps his delinquent child, the latter does not think of retaliating. He obeys his father not because of the deterrent effect of the slap but because of the offended love which he senses behind it. That in my opinion is an epitome of the way in which society is or should be governed. What is true of family must be true of society which is but a larger family. It is man's imagination that divides the world into warring groups of enemies and friends. In the ultimate resort it is the power of love that acts even in the midst of the clash and sustains the world. . . .

## Non-Violence of the Strong and of the Weak

Hence, I ask you, is our non-violence the non-violence of the coward, the weak, the helpless, the timid? In that case, it is of no value. A weakling is a born saint. A weak person is obliged to become

a saint. But we are soldiers of non-violence, who, if the occasion demands, will lay down their lives for it. Our non-violence is not a mere policy of the coward. But I doubt this. I am afraid that the non-violence we boast of might really be only a policy. It is true that, to some extent, non-violence works even in the hands of the weak. And, in this manner, this weapon has been useful to us. But, if one makes use of non-violence in order to disguise one's weakness or through helplessness, it makes a coward of one. Such a person is defeated on both the fronts. Such a one cannot live like a man and the Devil he surely cannot become. It is a thousand times better that we die trying to acquire the strength of the arm. Using physical force with courage is far superior to cowardice. At least we would have attempted to act like men. That was the way of our forefathers. That is because some people hold the view that the ancestors of the human race were animals. I do not wish to enter into the controversy whether Darwin's theory is tenable or not. However, from one standpoint we must all have originally been animals. And I am ready to believe that we are evolved from the animal into the human state. That is why physical strength is called brute force.

We are born with such strength, hence if we used it we could be, to say the least, courageous. But we are born as human beings in order that we may realize God who dwells within our hearts. This is the basic distinction between us and the beasts. . . .

Man is by nature non-violent. But he does not owe his origin to non-violence. We fulfil our human life when we see the *atman*, and when we do so we pass the test. Now is the time for our test. God-realization means seeing Him in all beings. Or, in other words, we should learn to become one with every creature. This is man's privilege and that distinguishes him from the beasts. This can happen only when we voluntarily give up the use of physical force and when we develop the non-violence which lies dormant in our hearts. It can be awakened only through real strength. . . .

Non-violence is an active principle of the highest order. It is soul-force or the power of the godhead within us. Imperfect man cannot grasp the whole of that Essence—he would not be able to bear its full blaze—but even an infinitesimal fraction of it, when it becomes active within us, can work wonders. The sun in the heavens fills the whole universe with its life-giving warmth. But if one went too near it, it would consume him to ashes. Even so is it with godhead. We become godlike to the extent we realize non-violence; but we can never become wholly God. Non-violence is like radium in its action. An infinitesimal quantity of it imbedded in a malignant growth, acts continuously, silently, and ceaselessly till it has transformed the whole mass of the diseased tissue into a healthy one. Similarly, even a tiny grain of true non-violence acts in a silent, subtle, unseen way and leavens the whole society.

It is self-acting. The soul persists even after death, its existence does not depend on the physical body. Similarly, non-violence or soul-force too, does not need physical aids for its propagation or effect. It acts independently of them. It transcends time and space.

It follows, therefore, that if non-violence becomes successfully established in one place, its influence will spread everywhere. So long as a single dacoity takes place in Utmanzai, I will say that our non-violence is not genuine.

The basic principle on which the practice of non-violence rests is that what holds good in respect of yourself holds good equally in respect of the whole universe. All mankind in essence are alike. . . .

## Non-Violence and Bravery

Just as one must learn the art of killing in the training for violence, so one must learn the art of dying in the training for non-violence. Violence does not mean emancipation from fear, but discovering the means of combating the cause of fear. Non-violence, on the other hand, has no cause for fear. The votary of non-violence has to cultivate the capacity for sacrifice of the highest type in order to be free from fear. He recks not if he should lose his land, his wealth, his life. He who has not overcome all fear cannot practise *ahimsa* to perfection. The votary of *ahimsa* has only one fear, that is of God. He who seeks refuge in God ought to have a glimpse of the *atman* that transcends the body; and the moment one has a glimpse of the Imperishable *atman* one sheds the love of the perishable body. Training in non-violence is thus diametrically opposed to training in violence. Violence is needed for the protection of things external, non-violence is needed for the protection of the *atman*, for the protection of one's honour.

This non-violence cannot be learnt by staying at home. It needs enterprise. In order to test ourselves we should learn to dare danger and death, mortify the flesh and acquire the capacity to endure all manner of hardships. He who trembles or takes to his heels the moment he sees two people fighting is not non-violent, but a coward. A non-violent person will lay down his life in preventing such quarrels. The bravery of the non-violent is vastly superior to that of the violent. The badge of the violent is his weapon—spear, or sword, or rifle. God is the shield of the non-violent.

This is not a course of training for one intending to learn non-violence. But it is easy to evolve one from the principles I have laid down.

It will be evident from the foregoing that there is no comparison between the two types of bravery. The one is limited, the other is limitless. There is no such thing as out-daring or outfighting non-violence. Non-violence is invincible. There need be no doubt that this non-violence can be achieved. . . .

## The Acid Test

Indeed the acid test of non-violence is that one thinks, speaks and acts non-violently, even when there is the gravest provocation to be violent. There is no merit in being non-violent to the good and the gentle. Non-violence is the mightiest force in the world capable of resisting the greatest imaginable temptation. Jesus knew "the generation of vipers," minced no words in describing them, but pleaded for mercy for them before the Judgment Throne, "for they knew not what they were doing."

I gave the company chapter and verse in support of the statements I made. I regard myself as a friend of the missionaries. I enjoy happy relations with many of them. But my friendships have never been blind to the limitations of my friends or the systems or methods they have supported.

False notions of propriety or fear of wounding susceptibilities often deter people from saying what they mean and ultimately land them on the shores of hypocrisy. But if non-violence of thought is to be evolved in individuals or societies or nations, truth has to be told, however harsh or unpopular it may appear to be for the moment. And mere non-violent action without the thought behind it is of little value. It can never be infectious. It is almost like a whited sepulchre. Thought is the power and the life behind it. We hardly know that thought is infinitely greater than action or words. When there is correspondence between thought, word and deed, either is a limitation of the first. And the third is a limitation of the second. Needless to say that here I am referring to the living thought which awaits translation into speech and action. Thoughts without potency are airy nothings and end in smoke. . . .

The way of peace is the way of truth. Truthfulness is even more important than peacefulness. Indeed, lying is the mother of violence. A truthful man cannot long remain violent. He will perceive in the course of his search that he has no need to be violent and he will further discover that so long as there is the slightest trace of violence in him, he will fail to find the truth he is searching.

There is no half way between truth and non-violence on the one hand and untruth and violence on the other. We may never be strong enough to be entirely non-violent in thought, word and deed. But we must keep non-violence as our goal and make steady progress towards it. The attainment of freedom, whether for a man, a nation or the world, must be in exact proportion to the attainment of non-violence by each. Let those, therefore, who believe in non-violence as the only method of achieving real freedom, keep the lamp of non-violence burning bright in the midst of the present impenetrable gloom. The truth of a few will count, the untruth of millions will vanish even like chaff before a whiff of wind.

NOTES AND REFERENCES

1. Mythical cow that yielded whatever one wished. Copyright © Navajivan Trust 1986/1987. Reprinted from *The Moral and Political Writings of Mahatma Gandhi*, edited by Ragharan Iyer, vol. 2 (1986) and vol. 3 (1987) by permission of Oxford University Press.

## Recommended Readings

### TEXTS

Allison, Henry. *Kant's Theory of Freedom*. Cambridge: Cambridge University Press, 1990.

Arendt, Hannah. *Lectures on Kant's Political Philosophy*. Chicago: University of Chicago Press, 1982.

Beiner, Ronald *Kant and Political Philosophy* New Haven: Yale University Press, 1993.

Korsgaard, Christine, *Creating the Kingdom of Ends*. Cambridge: Harvard University Press, 1996.

Reiss, Hans, ed. *Kant's Political Writings*. Cambridge: Cambridge University Press, 1970.

### FEMINIST PERSPECTIVE

Blum, Lawrence A. "Kant's and Hegel's Moral Rationalism: A Feminist Perspective." *Canadian Journal of Philosophy* 12, no. 2 (182): 287–302.

Cartwright, David. "Kant's View of the Moral Significance of Kindhearted Emotions and the Moral Insignificance of Kant's View." *The Journal of Value Inquiry* 21 (1987): 291–304.

MULTICULTURAL PERSPECTIVE

Bondurant, Joan V. *Conquest of Violence: The Gandhian Philosophy of Conflict.* Princeton: Princeton University Press, 1988.
Holmes, Robert L. *Nonviolence in Theory and Practice.* Belmont, CA: Wadsworth, 1990.

# IX

# *Mill and Harriet Taylor*

## Introduction

JOHN STUART MILL WAS BORN IN LONDON IN 1806. He was educated at home by his father, James Mill, a prominent economist, and Jeremy Bentham. The two men were eager for a subject on whom to test their utilitarian educational theories. At three, Mill learned Greek, at six, Latin—all the while being treated to an intensive regimen of mathematics and logic. Later, when he was twenty, Mill experienced a deep depression. He came to recognize that his education had provided him with little opportunity for emotional development. He turned to Wordsworth and Coleridge, the great Romantic poets, and in other ways tried to compensate for this lack.

In 1823, Mill became a clerk with the East India Company and rose to the office of chief examiner. In 1830, he was introduced to Harriet Taylor, then married with two children. She became his closest friend and confidante, and Mill credits her with inspiring much of his own thinking and writing. This unconventional relationship, which lasted twenty years, estranged Mill from his family and most of their friends. In 1851, two years after Harriet Taylor's husband died, they were married. Seven years later, she died from tuberculosis, probably contracted from Mill, who was suffering from the disease. In 1865, Mill was elected to Parliament, despite his refusal to campaign, and served one term.

Mill published *On Liberty* in 1859, claiming that more than anything he had written, this book was a joint production with Harriet Taylor. In 1863, he published *Utilitarianism*, and in 1869, *The Subjection of Women*. Harriet Taylor's *Enfranchisement of Women* was published earlier, in 1851.[1] Cared for in his last years by his stepdaughter Helen, Mill died in Avignon in 1873 and was buried alongside Harriet.

In the selection from *Utilitarianism*, Mill argues that actions are right in direct proportion to how they tend to promote happiness and wrong as they tend to produce the reverse of happiness. By happiness, Mill means pleasure and the absence of pain; by unhappiness, pain and the privation of pleasure. Mill differs from Bentham in maintaining

1 For the discussion of the authorship of this work, see Alice Rossi's introductory essay to John Stuart Mill and Harriet Taylor Mill, *Essays on Sex Equality* (Chicago: University of Chicago Press, 1970), p. 41ff.

that pleasures can be evaluated in terms of quality as well as quantity. According to Mill, the more desirable pleasures are those that would be preferred by competent judges who have experienced the alternatives. Applying this standard for evaluating pleasures, Mill contends that it is better to be a human being dissatisfied than a pig satisfied. While most people tend to share Mill's preference for being human here, it is not clear how that preference could be supported by a competent judge who had experienced both alternatives. Experiencing what it is like to be a pig is not the same as imagining what it is like to be a human trapped in a pig's body!

In the selection from *On Liberty,* Mill is concerned with how much liberty there should be in society, or with what is the other side of the coin, what are the limits of legitimate authority in society. Mill thinks that the rise of popular governments presents a special problem for securing liberty in society. The problem is that the popularity of these governments prevents people from noticing the extent to which they are denying people freedom. To deal with this problem, Mill proposes the principle that the exercise of power over members of society should be limited to what is necessary to prevent harm to others. This principle, Mill claims, is ultimately justified in terms of utility.

In the selections from *The Subjection of Women,* Mill contends that the subjection of women was never justified but was imposed upon them because they were physically weaker than men and that later this subjection was confirmed by law. Mill argues that society must remove the legal restrictions that deny women the same opportunities enjoyed by men in society. However, Mill does not consider whether, because of past discrimination against women, it may be necessary to do more than simply remove legal restrictions to provide women with the same opportunities that men now enjoy. He doesn't consider whether positive assistance may also be required.

But usually it is not enough simply to remove unequal restrictions to make a competition fair among those who have been participating. Positive assistance to those who have been disadvantaged in the past may also be required, as would be the case if one were running a race in which one was unfairly impeded by having to carry a 10-pound weight. Similarly, positive assistance, such as affirmative action programs, may be necessary if women, who have been disadvantaged in the past, are now for the first time to enjoy equal opportunity with men.

In *The Subjection of Women,* Mill does not see any need to compensate women for the work they do in the home, but in the selection from her *Enfranchisement of Women,* Taylor does see such a need. She contends that it would be preferable "if women both earned and had a right to possess, a part of the income of the family." In this work, Taylor also speaks out more strongly in favor of married women having a life and career of their own. In these respects, Taylor is clearly more in accord with present-day feminism than Mill is.

In her "Marital Slavery and Friendship," Mary Lyndon Shanley reviews the arguments that some critics have advanced against Mill's feminism. While some critics believe Mill did not go far enough in advancing the cause of women, Shanley argues that such attacks fail to acknowledge the significant achievements of Mill's feminism, especially concerning his call for an equality-based, mutually rewarding friendship between the sexes in marriage.

Mo Tzu was born in 470 B.C.E., shortly after Confucius's death, and he founded a rival school of philosophy known as Moism. In the selection from Mo Tzu's *Universal Love,* the similarities to utilitarianism are striking. In Moism, as in utilitarianism, actions are evaluated in terms of their overall consequences. Mo Tzu argues that the best overall consequences are achieved through the practice of universal mutual love. He goes on to consider various objections to the practice of universal mutual love and finds them wanting. There are also obvious similarities between Moism and the later Christian doctrine of universal love.

Historically, however, Moism did not fare very well. Up until the beginning of the Han Empire, Moism, and its doctrine of universal mutual love, was the main rival to Confucianism, with its emphasis on particular duties to particular people, but after the third century B.C.E., other views, such as Taoism, sprang up to rival Confucianism, and Moism all but disappeared. Two factors that contributed to the decline of Moism were the turning of Confucianism into a state cult during the Han Dynasty and Moism's uncompromising condemnation of war, which obviously did not endear it to the powers that be. Yet despite its historical decline, it could be argued that Moism, given its similarities to utilitarianism, deserves a better fate.

# 35    Utilitarianism

JOHN STUART MILL

## Chapter 1: General Remarks

THERE ARE FEW CIRCUMSTANCES among those which make up the present condition of human knowledge more unlike what might have been expected, or more significant of the backward state in which speculation on the most important subjects still lingers, than the little progress which has been made in the decision of the controversy respecting the criterion of right and wrong. From the dawn of philosophy, the question concerning the *summum bonum,* or, what is the same thing, concerning the foundation of morality, has been accounted the main problem in speculative thought, has occupied the most gifted intellects and divided them into sects and schools carrying on a vigorous warfare against one another. And after more than two thousand years the same discussions continue, philosophers are still ranged under the same contending banners, and neither thinkers nor mankind at large seem nearer to being unanimous on the subject than when the youth Socrates listened to the old Protagoras and asserted (if Plato's dialogue be grounded on a real conversation) the theory of utilitarianism against the popular morality of the so-called sophist.

It is true that similar confusion and uncertainty and, in some cases, similar discordance exist respecting the first principles of all the sciences, not excepting that which is deemed the most certain of them—mathematics, without much impairing, generally indeed without impairing at all, the trustworthiness of the conclusions of those sciences. An apparent anomaly, the explanation of which is that the detailed doctrines of a science are not usually deduced from, nor depend for their evidence upon, what are called its first principles. Were it not so, there would be no science more precarious, or whose conclusions were more insufficiently made out, than algebra, which derives none of its certainty from what are commonly taught to learners as its elements, since these, as laid down by some of its most eminent teachers, are as full of fictions as English law, and of mysteries as theology. The truths which are ultimately accepted as the first principles of a science are really the last results of metaphysical analysis practiced on the elementary notions with which the science is conversant; and their relation to the science is not that of foundations to an edifice, but of roots to a tree, which may perform their office equally well though they be never dug down to and exposed to light. But though in science the particular truths precede the general theory, the contrary might be expected to be the case with a practical art, such as morals or legislation. All action is for the sake of some end, and rules of action, it seems natural to suppose, must take their whole character and color from the end to which they are subservient. When we engage in a pursuit, a clear and precise conception of what we are pursuing would seem to be the first thing we need, instead of the last we are to look forward to. A test of right and wrong must be the means, one would think, of ascertaining what is right or wrong, and not a consequence of having already ascertained it.

The difficulty is not avoided by having recourse to the popular theory of a natural faculty, a sense of instinct, informing us of right and wrong. For—besides that the existence of such a moral instinct is itself one of the matters in dispute—those believers in it who have any pretensions to philosophy have been obliged to abandon the idea that it discerns what is right or wrong in the particular case in hand, as our other senses discern the sight or sound actually present. Our moral faculty, according to all those of its interpreters who are entitled to the name of thinkers, supplies us only with the general principles of moral judgments; it is a branch of our reason, not of our sensitive faculty, and must be looked to for the abstract doctrines of morality, not for perception of it in the concrete. The intuitive, no less than what may be termed the inductive, school of ethics insists on the necessity of general laws. They both agree that the morality of an individual action is not a question of direct perception, but of the application of a law to an individual case. They recognize also, to a great extent, the same moral laws, but differ as to their evidence and the source from which they derive their authority. According to the one opinion, the principles of morals are evident *a priori,* requiring nothing to command assent except that the meaning of the terms be understood. According to the other doctrine, right and wrong, as well as truth and falsehood, are questions of observation and experience. But both hold equally that morality must be deduced from principles; and the intuitive school affirms as strongly as the inductive that there is a science of morals. Yet they seldom attempt to make out a list of the *a priori* principles which are to serve as the premises of the science; still more rarely do they make any effort to reduce those various principles to one first principle or common ground of obligation. They either assume the ordinary precepts of morals as of *a priori* authority, or they lay down as the common groundwork of those maxims some generality much less obviously authoritative than the maxims themselves, and which has never succeeded in gaining popular acceptance. Yet to support their pretensions there ought either to be some one fundamental principle or law at the root of all morality, or, if there be several, there should be a determinate order of precedence among them; and the one principle, or the rule for deciding between the various principles when they conflict, ought to be self-evident.

To inquire how far the bad effects of this deficiency have been mitigated in practice, or to what extent the moral beliefs of mankind have been vitiated or made uncertain by the absence of any distinct recognition of an ultimate standard, would imply a complete survey and criticism of past and present ethical doctrine. It would, however, be easy to show that whatever steadiness or consistency these moral beliefs have attained has been mainly due to the tacit influence of a standard not recognized. Although the nonexistence of an acknowledged first principle has made ethics not so much a guide as a consecration of men's actual sentiments, still, as men's sentiments, both of favor and of aversion, are greatly influenced by what they suppose to be the effects of things upon their happiness, the principle of utility, or, as Bentham latterly called it, the greatest happiness principle, has had a large share in forming the moral doctrines even of those who most scornfully reject its authority. Nor is there any school of thought which refuses to admit that the influence of actions on happiness is a most material and even predominant consideration in many of the details of morals, however unwilling to acknowledge it as the fundamental principle of morality and the source of moral obligation. I might go much further and say that to all those *a priori* moralists who deem it necessary to argue at all, utilitarian arguments are indispensable. It is not my present purpose to criticize these thinkers; but I cannot help referring, for illustration, to a systematic treatise by one of the most illustrious of them, the *Metaphysics of Ethics* by Kant. This remarkable man, whose system of thought will long remain one of the landmarks in the history of philosophical speculation, does, in the treatise in question, lay down a universal first principle as the origin and ground of moral obligation; it is this: "So act that the rule on which thou actest would admit of being adopted as a law by all rational beings." But when he begins to deduce from this precept any of the actual duties of morality, he fails, almost grotesquely, to show that there would be any contradiction, any logical (not to say physical) impossibility, in the adoption by all rational beings of the most outrageously immoral rules of conduct. All he shows is that the *consequences* of their universal adoption would be such as no one would choose to incur.

On the present occasion, I shall, without further discussion of the other theories, attempt to contribute something toward the understanding and appreciation of the "utilitarian" or "happiness" theory, and toward such proof as it is susceptible of. It is evident that this cannot be proof in the ordinary and popular meaning of the term. Questions of ultimate ends are not amenable to direct proof. Whatever can be proved to be good must be so by being shown to be a means to something admitted to be good without proof. The medical art is proved to be good by its conducing to health; but how is it possible to prove that health is good? The art of music is good, for the reason, among others, that it produces pleasure; but what proof is it possible to give that pleasure is good? If, then, it is asserted that there is a comprehensive formula, including all things which are in themselves good, and that whatever else is good is not so as an end but as a means, the formula may be accepted or rejected, but is not a subject of what is commonly understood by proof. We are not, however, to infer that its acceptance or rejection must depend on blind impulse or arbitrary choice. There is a larger meaning of the word "proof," in which this question is as amenable to it as any other of the disputed questions of philosophy. The subject is within the cognizance of the rational faculty; and neither does that faculty deal with it solely in the way of intuition. Considerations may be presented capable of determining the intellect either to give or withhold its assent to the doctrine; and this is equivalent to proof.

We shall examine presently of what nature are these considerations; in what manner they apply to the case, and what rational grounds, therefore, can be given for accepting or rejecting the utilitarian formula. But it is a preliminary condition of rational acceptance or rejection that the formula should be correctly understood. I believe that the very imperfect notion ordinarily formed of its meaning is the chief obstacle which impedes its reception, and that, could it be cleared even from only the grosser misconceptions, the question would be greatly simplified and a large proportion of its difficulties removed. Before, therefore, I attempt to enter into the philosophical grounds which can be given for assenting to the utilitarian standard, I shall offer some illustrations of the doctrine itself, with the view of showing more clearly what it is, distinguishing it from what it is not, and disposing of such of the practical objections to it as either originate in, or are closely connected with, mistaken interpretations of its meaning. Having thus prepared the ground, I shall afterwards endeavor to throw such light as I can call upon the question considered as one of philosophical theory.

## Chapter II: What Utilitarianism Is

A passing remark is all that needs be given to the ignorant blunder of supposing that those who stand up for utility as the test of right and wrong use the term in that restricted and merely colloquial sense in which utility is opposed to pleasure. An apology is due to the philosophical opponents of utilitarianism for even the momentary appearance of confounding them with anyone capable of so absurd a misconception; which is the more extraordinary, in as much as the contrary accusation, of referring everything to pleasure, and that, too, in its grossest form, is another of the common charges against utilitarianism: and, as has been pointedly remarked by an able writer, the same sort of persons, and often the very same persons, denounce the theory "as impracticably dry when the word 'utility' precedes the word 'pleasure,' and as too practicably voluptuous when the word 'pleasure' precedes the word 'utility.'" Those who know anything about the matter are aware that every writer, from Epicurus to Bentham, who maintained the theory of utility meant by it, not something to be contradistinguished from pleasure, but pleasure itself, together with exemption from pain; and instead of opposing the useful to the agreeable or the ornamental, have always declared that the useful means these, among other things. Yet the common herd, including the herd of writers, not only in newspapers and periodicals, but in books of weight and pretension, are perpetually falling into this shallow mistake. Having caught up the word "utilitarian," while knowing nothing whatever about it but its sound, they habitually express by it the rejection or the neglect of pleasure in some of its forms: of beauty, of ornament, or of amusement. Nor is the term thus ignorantly misapplied solely in disparagement, but occasionally in compliment, as though it implied superiority to frivolity and the mere pleasures of the moment. And this perverted use is the only

one in which the word is popularly known, and the one from which the new generation are acquiring their sole notion of its meaning. Those who introduced the word, but who had for many years discontinued it as a distinctive appellation, may well feel themselves called upon to resume it if by doing so they can hope to contribute anything toward rescuing it from this utter degradation.[1]

The creed which accepts as the foundation of morals "utility" or the "greatest happiness principle" holds that actions are right in proportion as they tend to promote happiness; wrong as they tend to produce the reverse of happiness. By happiness is intended pleasure and the absence of pain; by unhappiness, pain and the privation of pleasure. To give a clear view of the moral standard set up by the theory, much more requires to be said; in particular, what things it includes in the ideas of pain and pleasure, and to what extent this is left an open question. But these supplementary explanations do not affect the theory of life on which this theory of morality is grounded—namely, that pleasure and freedom from pain are the only things desirable as ends; and that all desirable things (which are as numerous in the utilitarian as in any other scheme) are desirable either for pleasure inherent in themselves or as means to the promotion of pleasure and the prevention of pain.

Now such a theory of life excites in many minds, and among them in some of the most estimable in feeling and purpose, inveterate dislike. To suppose that life has (as they express it) no higher end than pleasure—no better and nobler object of desire and pursuit—they designate as utterly mean and groveling, as a doctrine worthy only of swine, to whom the followers of Epicurus were, at a very early period, contemptuously likened; and modern holders of the doctrine are occasionally made the subject of equally polite comparisons by its German, French, and English assailants.

When thus attacked, the Epicureans have always answered that it is not they, but their accusers, who represent human nature in a degrading light, since the accusation supposes human beings to be capable of no pleasures except those of which swine are capable. If this supposition were true, the charge could not be gainsaid, but would then be no longer an imputation; for if the sources of pleasure were precisely the same to human beings and to swine, the rule of life which is good enough for the one would be good enough for the other. The comparison of the Epicurean life to that of beasts is felt as degrading, precisely because a beast's pleasures do not satisfy a human being's conception of happiness. Human beings have faculties more elevated than the animal appetites and, when once made conscious of them, do not regard anything as happiness which does not include their gratification. I do not, indeed, consider the Epicureans to have been by any means faultless in drawing out their scheme of consequences from the utilitarian principle. To do this in any sufficient manner, many Stoic, as well as Christian, elements require to be included. But there is no known Epicurean theory of life which does not assign to the pleasures of the intellect, of the feelings and imagination, and of the moral sentiments a much higher value as pleasures than to those of mere sensation. It must be admitted, however, that utilitarian writers in general have placed the superiority of mental over bodily pleasures chiefly in the greater permanency, safety, uncostliness, etc., of the former—that is, in their circumstantial advantages rather than in their intrinsic nature. And on all these points utilitarians have fully proved their case; but they might have taken the other and, as it may be called, higher ground with entire consistency. It is quite compatible with the principle of utility to recognize the fact that some kinds of pleasure are more desirable and more valuable than others. It would be absurd that, while in estimating all other things quality is considered as well as quantity, the estimation of pleasure should be supposed to depend on quantity alone.

If I am asked what I mean by difference of quality in pleasures, or what makes one pleasure more valuable than another, merely as a pleasure, except its being greater in amount, there is but one possible answer. Of two pleasures, if there be one to which all or almost all who have experience of both give a decided preference, irrespective of any feeling of moral obligation to prefer it, that is the more desirable pleasure. If one of the two is, by those who are competently acquainted with both, placed so far above the other that they prefer it, even though knowing it to be attended with a greater amount of discontent, and would not resign it for any quantity of the other pleasure which their nature is capable of, we are justified in ascribing to the preferred enjoyment a superiority in quality so far outweighing quantity as to render it, in comparison, of small account.

Now it is an unquestionable fact that those who are equally acquainted with and equally capable of appreciating and enjoying both do give a most marked preference to the manner of existence which employs their higher faculties. Few human creatures would consent to be changed into any of the lower animals for a promise of the fullest allowance of a beast's pleasures; no intelligent human being would consent to be a fool, no instructed person would be an ignoramus, no person of feeling and conscience would be selfish and base, even though they should be persuaded that the fool, the dunce, or the rascal is better satisfied with his lot than they are with theirs. They would not resign what they possess more than he for the most complete satisfaction of all the desires which they have in common with him. If they ever fancy they would, it is only in cases of unhappiness so extreme that to escape from it they would exchange their lot for almost any other, however undesirable in their own eyes. A being of higher faculties requires more to make him happy, is capable probably of more acute suffering, and certainly accessible to it at more points, than one of an inferior type; but in spite of these liabilities, he can never really wish to sink into what he feels to be a lower grade of existence. We may give what explanation we please of this unwillingness; we may attribute it to pride, a name which is given indiscriminately to some of the most and to some of the least estimable feelings of which mankind are capable; we may refer it to the love of liberty and personal independence, an appeal to which was with the Stoics one of the most effective means for the inculcation of it; to the love of power or to the love of excitement, both of which do really enter into and contribute to it; but its most appropriate appellation is a sense of dignity, which all human beings possess in one form or other, and in some, though by no means in exact, proportion to their higher faculties, and which is so essential a part of the happiness of those in whom it is strong that nothing which conflicts with it could be otherwise than momentarily an object of desire to them. Whoever supposes that this preference takes place at a sacrifice of happiness—that the superior being, in anything like equal circumstances, is not happier than the inferior—confounds the two very different ideas of happiness and content. It is indisputable that the being whose capacities of enjoyment are low has the greatest chance of having them fully satisfied; and a highly endowed being will always feel that any happiness which he can look for, as the world is constituted, is imperfect. But he can learn to bear its imperfections, if they are at all bearable; and they will not make him envy the being who is indeed unconscious of the imperfections, but only because he feels not at all the good which those imperfections qualify. It is better to be a human being dissatisfied than a pig satisfied; better to be Socrates dissatisfied than a fool satisfied. And if the fool, or the pig, are of a different opinion, it is because they only know their own side of the question. The other party to the comparison knows both sides.

It may be objected that many who are capable of the higher pleasures occasionally, under the influence of temptation, postpone them to the lower. But this is quite compatible with a full appreciation of the intrinsic superiority of the higher. Men often, from infirmity of character, make their election for the nearer good, though they know it to be the less valuable; and this no less when the choice is between two bodily pleasures than when it is between bodily and mental. They pursue sensual indulgences to the injury of health, though perfectly aware that health is the greater good. It may be further objected that many who begin with youthful enthusiasm for everything noble, as they advance in years, sink into indolence and selfishness. But I do not believe that those who undergo this very common change voluntarily choose the lower description of pleasures in preference to the higher. I believe that, before they devote themselves exclusively to the one, they have already become incapable of the other. Capacity for the nobler feelings is in most natures a very tender plant, easily killed, not only by hostile influences, but by mere want of sustenance; and in the majority of young persons it speedily dies away if the occupations to which their position in life has devoted them, and the society into which it has thrown them, are not favorable to keeping that higher capacity in exercise. Men lose their high aspirations as they lose their intellectual tastes, because they have not time or opportunity for indulging them; and they addict themselves to inferior pleasures, not because they deliberately prefer them, but because they are either the only ones to which they have access or the only ones which they are any longer capable of enjoying. It may be questioned whether anyone who has remained equally susceptible to both classes of pleasures ever knowingly and calmly preferred the lower, though many, in all ages, have broken down in an ineffectual attempt to combine both.

From this verdict of the only competent judges, I apprehend there can be no appeal. On a question which is the best worth having of two pleasures, or which of two modes of existence is the most grateful to the feelings, apart from its moral attributes and from its consequences, the judgment of those who are qualified by knowledge of both, or, if they differ, that of the majority among them, must be admitted as final. And there needs be the less hesitation to accept this judgment respecting the quality of pleasures, since there is no other tribunal to be referred to even on the question of quantity. What means are there of determining which is the acutest of two pains, or the intensest of two pleasurable sensations, except the general suffrage of those who are familiar with both? Neither pains nor pleasures are homogeneous, and pain is always heterogeneous with pleasure. What is there to decide whether a particular pleasure is worth purchasing at the cost of a particular pain, except the feelings and judgment of the experienced? When, therefore, those feelings and judgment declare the pleasures derived from the higher faculties to be preferable *in kind,* apart from the question of intensity, to those of which the animal nature, disjoined from the higher faculties, is susceptible, they are entitled on this subject to the same regard.

I have dwelt on this point as being a necessary part of a perfectly just conception of utility or happiness considered as the directive rule of human conduct. But it is by no means an indispensable condition to the acceptance of the utilitarian standard; for that standard is not the agent's own greatest happiness, but the greatest amount of happiness altogether; and if it may possibly be doubted whether a noble character is always the happier for its nobleness, there can be no doubt that it makes other people happier, and that the world in general is immensely a gainer by it. Utilitarianism, therefore, could only attain its end by the general cultivation of nobleness of character, even if each individual were only benefited by the nobleness of others, and his own, so far as happiness is concerned, were a sheer deduction from the benefit. But the bare enunciation of such an absurdity as this last renders refutation superfluous.

According to the greatest happiness principle, as above explained, the ultimate end, with reference to and for the sake of which all other things are desirable—whether we are considering our own good or that of other people—is an existence exempt as far as possible from pain, and as rich as possible in enjoyments, both in point of quantity and quality; the test of quality and the rule for measuring it against quantity being the preference felt by those who, in their opportunities of experience, to which must be added their habits of self-consciousness and self-observation, are best furnished with the means of comparison. This, being according to the utilitarian opinion the end of human action, is necessarily also the standard of morality, which may accordingly be defined "the rules and precepts for human conduct," by the observance of which an existence such as has been described might be, to the greatest extent possible, secured to all mankind; and not to them only, but, so far as the nature of things admits, to the whole sentient creation.

Against this doctrine, however, arises another class of objectors who say that happiness, in any form, cannot be the rational purpose of human life and action; because in the first place, it is unattainable; and they contemptuously ask, What right hast thou to be happy?—a question which Mr. Carlyle clinches by the addition, What right, a short time ago, hadst thou even *to be?* Next they say that men can do *without* happiness; that all noble human beings have felt this, and could not have become noble but by learning the lesson of *Entsagen,* or renunciation; which lesson, thoroughly learned and submitted to, they affirm to be the beginning and necessary condition of all virtue.

The first of these objections would go to the root of the matter were it well founded; for if no happiness is to be had at all by human beings, the attainment of it cannot be the end of morality or of any rational conduct. Though, even in that case, something might still be said for the utilitarian theory, since utility includes not solely the pursuit of happiness, but the prevention or mitigation of unhappiness; and if the former aim be chimerical, there will be all the greater scope and more imperative need for the latter, so long at least as mankind think fit to live and do not take refuge in the simultaneous act of suicide recommended under certain conditions by Novalis. When, however, it is thus positively asserted to be impossible that human life should be happy, the assertion, if not something like a verbal quibble, is at least an exaggeration. If by happiness be meant a continuity of highly pleasurable excitement, it is evident enough that this is impossible. A state of exalted pleasure lasts only moments or in some cases, and with some intermissions, hours or days, and is the occasional brilliant flash of enjoyment, not its permanent and steady flame. Of this the philosophers who have taught that happiness is the end of life were as fully aware as those who taunt them. The happiness which they meant was not a life of rapture, but moments of such, in an existence made up of few and transitory pains, many and various pleasures, with a decided predominance of the active over the passive, and having as the foundation of the whole not to expect more from life than it is capable of bestowing. A life thus composed, to those who have been fortunate enough to obtain it, has always appeared worthy of the name of happiness. And such an existence is even now the lot of many during some considerable portion of their lives. The present wretched education and wretched social arrangements are the only real hindrance to its being attainable by almost all.

The objectors perhaps may doubt whether human beings, if taught to consider happiness as the end of life, would be satisfied with such a moderate share of it. But great numbers of mankind have been satisfied with much less. The main constituents of a satisfied life appear to be two, either of which by itself is often found sufficient for the purpose: tranquillity and excitement. With much tranquillity, many find that they can be content with very little pleasure; with much excitement, many can reconcile themselves to a considerable quantity of pain. There is assuredly no inherent impossibility of enabling even the mass of mankind to unite both, since the two are so far from being incompatible that they are in natural alliance, the prolongation of either being a preparation for, and exciting a wish for, the other. It is only those in whom indolence amounts to a vice that do not desire excitement after an interval of repose; it is only those in whom the need of excitement is a disease that feel the tranquillity which follows excitement dull and insipid, instead of pleasurable in direct proportion to the excitement which preceded it. When people who are tolerably fortunate in their outward lot do not find in life sufficient enjoyment to make it valuable to them, the cause generally is caring for nobody but themselves. To those who have neither public nor private affections, the excitements of life are much curtailed, and in any case dwindle in value as the time approaches when all selfish interests must be terminated by death; while those who leave after them objects of personal affection, and especially those who have also cultivated a fellow-feeling with the collective interests of mankind,

retain as lively an interest in life on the eve of death as in the vigor of youth and health. Next to selfishness, the principal cause which makes life unsatisfactory is want of mental cultivation. A cultivated mind—I do not mean that of a philosopher, but any mind to which the fountains of knowledge have been opened, and which has been taught, in any tolerable degree, to exercise its faculties—finds sources of inexhaustible interest in all that surrounds it: in the objects of nature, the achievements of art, the imaginations of poetry, the incidents of history, the ways of mankind, past and present, and their prospects in the future. It is possible, indeed, to become indifferent to all this, and that too without having exhausted a thousandth part of it, but only when one has had from the beginning no moral or human interest in these things and has sought in them only the gratification of curiosity.

Now there is absolutely no reason in the nature of things why an amount of mental culture sufficient to give an intelligent interest in these objects of contemplation should not be the inheritance of everyone born in a civilized country. As little is there an inherent necessity that any human being should be a selfish egotist, devoid of every feeling or care but those which center in his own miserable individuality. Something far superior to this is sufficiently common even now, to give ample earnest of what the human species may be made. Genuine private affections and a sincere interest in the public good are possible, though in unequal degrees, to every rightly brought up human being. In a world in which there is so much to interest, so much to enjoy, and so much also to correct and improve, everyone who has this moderate amount of moral and intellectual requisites is capable of an existence which may be called enviable; and unless such a person, through bad laws or subjection to the will of others, is denied the liberty to use the sources of happiness within his reach, he will not fail to find this enviable existence, if he escapes the positive evils of life, the great sources of physical and mental suffering—such as indigence, disease, and the unkindness, worthlessness, or premature loss of objects of affection. The main stress of the problem lies, therefore, in the contest with these calamities from which it is a rare good fortune entirely to escape; which, as things now are, cannot be obviated, and often cannot be in any material degree mitigated. Yet no one whose opinion deserves a moment's consideration can doubt that most of the great positive evils of the world are in themselves removable, and will, if human affairs continue to improve, be in the end reduced within narrow limits. Poverty, in any sense implying suffering, may be completely extinguished by the wisdom of society combined with the good sense and providence of individuals. Even that most intractable of enemies, disease, may be indefinitely reduced in dimensions by good physical and moral education and proper control of noxious influences, while the progress of science holds out a promise for the future of still more direct conquests over this detestable foe. And every advance in that direction relieves us from some, not only of the chances which cut short our own lives, but, what concerns us still more, which deprive us of those in whom our happiness is wrapt up. As for the vicissitudes of fortune and other disappointments connected with worldly circumstances, these are principally the effect either of gross imprudence, of ill-regulated desires, or of bad or imperfect social institutions. All the grand sources, in short, of human suffering are in a great degree, many of them almost entirely, conquerable by human care and effort; and though their removal is grievously slow—though a long succession of generations will perish in the breach before the conquest is completed, and this world becomes all that, if will and knowledge were not wanting, it might easily be made—yet every mind sufficiently intelligent and generous to bear a part, however small and inconspicuous, in the endeavor will draw a noble enjoyment from the contest itself, which he would not for any bribe in the form of selfish indulgence consent to be without.

And this leads to the true estimation of what is said by the objectors concerning the possibility and the obligation of learning to do without happiness. Unquestionably it is possible to do without happiness; it is done involuntarily by nineteen-twentieths of mankind, even in those parts of our present world which are least deep in barbarism; and it often has to be done voluntarily by the hero or the martyr, for the sake of something which he prizes more than his individual happiness. But this something, what is it, unless the happiness of others or some of the requisites of happiness? It is noble to be capable of resigning entirely one's own portion of happiness, or chances of it; but, after all, this self-sacrifice must be for some end; it is not its own end; and if we are told that its end is not happiness but virtue, which is better than happiness, I ask, would the sacrifice be made if the hero or martyr did not believe that it would earn for others immunity from similar sacrifices? Would it be made if he thought that his renunciation of happiness for himself would produce no fruit for any of his fellow creatures, but to make their lot like his and place them also in the condition of persons who have renounced happiness? All honor to those who can abnegate for themselves the personal enjoyment of life when by such renunciation they contribute worthily to increase the amount of happiness in the world; but he who does it or professes to do it for any other purpose is no more deserving of admiration than the ascetic mounted on his pillar. He may be an inspiriting proof of what men *can* do, but assuredly not an example of what they *should*.

Though it is only in a very imperfect state of the world's arrangements that anyone can best serve the happiness of others by the absolute sacrifice of his own, yet, so long as the world is in that imperfect state, I fully acknowledge that the readiness to make such a sacrifice is the highest virtue which can be found in man. I will add that in this condition of the world, paradoxical as the assertion may be, the conscious ability to do without happiness gives the best prospect of realizing such happiness as is attainable. For nothing except that consciousness can raise a person above the chances of life by making him feel that, let fate and fortune do their worst, they have not power to subdue him; which, once felt, frees him from excess of anxiety concerning the evils of life and enables him, like many a Stoic in the worst times of the Roman Empire, to cultivate in tranquillity the sources of satisfaction accessible to him, without concerning himself about the uncertainty of their duration any more than about their inevitable end.

Meanwhile, let utilitarians never cease to claim the morality of self-devotion as a possession which belongs by as good a right to them as either to the Stoic or to the Transcendentalist. The utilitarian morality does recognize in human beings the power of sacrificing their own greatest good for the good of others. It only refuses to admit that the sacrifice is itself a good. A sacrifice which does not increase or tend to increase the sum total of happiness, it considers as wasted. The only self-renunciation which it applauds is devotion to the happiness, or to some of the means of happiness, of others, either of mankind collectively or of individuals within the limits imposed by the collective interests of mankind.

I must again repeat what the assailants of utilitarianism seldom have the justice to acknowledge, that the happiness which forms the utilitarian standard of what is right in conduct is not the agent's own happiness but that of all concerned. As between his own happiness and that of others, utilitarianism requires him to be as strictly impartial as a disinterested and benevolent spectator. In the golden rule of Jesus of Nazareth, we read the complete spirit of the ethics of utility. "To do as you would be done by," and "to love your neighbor as yourself," constitute the ideal perfection of utilitarian morality. As the means of making the nearest approach to this ideal, utility would enjoin, first, that laws and social arrangements should place the happiness or (as, speaking practically, it may be called) the interest of every individual as nearly as possible in harmony with the interest of the whole; and, secondly, that education and opinion, which have so vast a power over human character, should so use that power as to establish in the mind of every individual an indissoluble association between his own happiness and the good of the whole, especially between his own happiness and the practice of such modes of conduct, negative and positive, as regard for the universal happiness prescribes; so that not only he may be unable to conceive the possibility of happiness to himself, consistently with conduct opposed to the general good, but also that a direct impulse to promote the general good may be in every individual one of the habitual motives of action, and the sentiments connected therewith may fill a large and prominent place in every human being's sentient existence. If the impugners of the utilitarian morality represented it to their own minds in this its true character, I know not what recommendation possessed by any other morality they could possibly affirm to be wanting to it; what more beautiful or more exalted developments of human nature any other ethical system can be supposed to foster, or what springs of action, not accessible to the utilitarian, such systems rely on for giving effect to their mandates.

The objectors to utilitarianism cannot always be charged with representing it in a discreditable light. On the contrary, those among them who entertain anything like a just idea of its disinterested character sometimes find fault with its standard as being too high for humanity. They say it is exacting too much to require that people shall always act from the inducement of promoting the general interests of society. But this is to mistake the very meaning of a standard of morals and confound the rule of action with the motive of it. It is the business of ethics to tell us what are our duties, or by what test we may know them; but no system of ethics requires that the sole motive of all we do shall be a feeling of duty; on the contrary, ninety-nine hundredths of all our actions are done from other motives, and rightly so done if the rule of duty does not condemn them. It is the more unjust to utilitarianism that this particular misapprehension should be made a ground of objection to it, inasmuch as utilitarian moralists have gone beyond almost all others in affirming that the motive has nothing to do with the morality of the action, though much with the worth of the agent. He who saves a fellow creature from drowning does what is morally right, whether his motive be duty or the hope of being paid for his trouble; he who betrays the friend that trusts him is guilty of a crime, even if his object be to serve another friend to whom he is under greater obligations.[2] But to speak only of actions done from the motive of duty, and in direct obedience to principle: it is a misapprehension of the utilitarian mode of thought to conceive it as implying that people should fix their minds upon so wide a generality as the world, or society at large. The great majority of good actions are intended not for the benefit of the world, but for that of individuals, of which the good of the world is made up; and the thoughts of the most virtuous man need not on these occasions travel beyond the particular persons concerned, except so far as is necessary to assure himself that in benefiting them he is not violating the rights, that is, the legitimate and authorized expectations, of anyone else. The multiplication of happiness is, according to the utilitarian ethics, the object of virtue: the occasions on which any person (except one in a thousand) has it in his power to do this on an extended scale—in other words, to be a public benefactor—are but exceptional; and on these occasions alone is he called on to consider public utility; in every other case, private utility, the interest or happiness of some few persons, is all he has to attend to. Those alone the influence of whose actions extends to society in general need concern themselves habitually about so large an object. In the case of abstinences indeed—of things which people forbear to do from moral considerations, though the consequences in the particular case might be beneficial—it would be unworthy of an intelligent agent not to be consciously aware that the action is of a class which, if practiced generally, would be generally injurious, and that this is the ground of the obligation to abstain from it. The amount of regard for the public interest implied in this recognition is no greater than is demanded by every system of morals, for they all enjoin to abstain from whatever is manifestly pernicious to society.

The same considerations dispose of another reproach against the doctrine of utility, founded on a still grosser misconception of the purpose of a standard of morality and of the very meaning of the words "right" and "wrong." It is often affirmed that utilitarianism renders men cold and unsympathizing; that it chills their moral feelings toward individuals; that it makes them regard only the dry and hard consideration of the consequences of actions, not taking into their moral estimate the qualities from which those actions emanate. If the assertion means that they do not allow their judgment respecting the rightness or wrongness of an action to be influenced by their opinion of the qualities of the person who does it, this is a complaint not against utilitarianism, but against any standard of morality at all; for certainly no known ethical standard decides an action to be good or bad because it is done by a good or a bad man, still less because done by an amiable, a brave, or a benevolent man, or the contrary. These considerations are relevant, not to the estimation of actions, but of persons; and there is nothing in the utilitarian theory inconsistent with the fact that there are other things which interest us in persons besides the rightness and wrongness of their actions. The Stoics, indeed, with the paradoxical misuse of language which was part of their system, and by which they strove to raise themselves above all concern about anything but virtue, were fond of saying that he who has that has everything; that he, and only he, is rich, is beautiful, is a king. But no claim of this description is made for the virtuous man by the utilitarian doctrine. Utilitarians are quite aware that there are other desirable possessions and qualities besides virtue, and are perfectly willing to allow to all of them their full worth. They are also aware that a right action does not necessarily indicate a virtuous character, and that actions which are blamable often proceed from qualities entitled to praise. When this is apparent in any particular case, it modifies their estimation, not certainly of the act, but of the agent. I grant that they are, notwithstanding, of the opinion that in the long run the best proof of a good character is good actions; and resolutely refuse to consider any mental disposition as good of which the predominant tendency is to produce bad conduct. This makes them unpopular with many people, but it is an unpopularity which they must share with everyone who regards the distinction between right and wrong in a serious light; and the reproach is not one which a conscientious utilitarian need be anxious to repel.

If no more be meant by the objection than that many utilitarians look on the morality of actions, as measured by the utilitarian standards, with too exclusive a regard, and do not lay sufficient stress upon the other beauties of character which go toward making a human being lovable or admirable, this may be admitted. Utilitarians who have cultivated their moral feelings, but not their sympathies, nor their artistic perceptions, do fall into this mistake; and so do all other moralists under the same conditions. What can be said in excuse for other moralists is equally available for them, namely, that, if there is to be any error, it is better that it should be on that side. As a matter of fact, we may affirm that among utilitarians, as among adherents of other systems, there is every imaginable degree of rigidity and of laxity in the application of their standard; some are even puritanically rigorous, while others are as indulgent as can possibly be desired by sinner or by sentimentalist. But on the whole, a doctrine which brings prominently forward the interest that mankind have in the repression and prevention of conduct which violates the moral law is likely to be inferior to no other in turning the sanctions of opinion against such violations. It is true, the question "What does violate the moral law?" is one on which those who recognize different standards of morality are likely now and then to differ. But difference of opinion on moral questions was not first introduced into the world by utilitarianism, while that doctrine does supply, if not always an easy, at all events a tangible and intelligible, mode of deciding such differences.

It may not be superfluous to notice a few more of the common misapprehensions of utilitarian ethics, even those which are so obvious and gross that it might appear impossible for any person of candor and intelligence to fall into them; since persons, even of considerable mental endowment, often give themselves so little trouble to understand the bearings of any opinion against which they entertain a prejudice, and men are in general

so little conscious of this voluntary ignorance as a defect that the vulgarest misunderstandings of ethical doctrines are continually met with in the deliberate writings of persons of the greatest pretensions both to high principle and to philosophy. We not uncommonly hear the doctrine of utility inveighed against as a *godless* doctrine. If it be necessary to say anything at all against so mere an assumption, we may say that the question depends upon what idea we have formed of the moral character of the Deity. If it be a true belief that God desires, above all things, the happiness of his creatures, and that this was his purpose in their creation, utility is not only not a godless doctrine, but more profoundly religious than any other. If it be meant that utilitarianism does not recognize the revealed will of god as the supreme law of morals, I answer that a utilitarian who believes in the perfect goodness and wisdom of *God* necessarily believes that whatever God has thought fit to reveal on the subject of morals must fulfill the requirements of utility in a supreme degree. But others besides utilitarians have been of the opinion that the Christian revelation was intended, and is fitted, to inform the hearts and minds of mankind with a spirit which should enable them to find for themselves what is right, and incline them to do it when found, rather than to tell them, except in a very general way, what it is; and that we need a doctrine of ethics, carefully followed out, to *interpret* to us the will of God. Whether this opinion is correct or not, it is superfluous here to discuss; since whatever aid religion, either natural or revealed, can afford to ethical investigation is as open to the utilitarian moralist as to any other. He can use it as the testimony of God to the usefulness or hurtfulness of any given course of action by as good a right as others can use it for the indication of a transcendental law having no connection with usefulness or with happiness.

Again, utility is often summarily stigmatized as an immoral doctrine by giving it the name of "expediency," and taking advantage of the popular use of that term to contrast it with principle. But the expedient, in the sense in which it is opposed to the right, generally means that which is expedient for the particular interest of the agent himself; as when a minister sacrifices the interests of his country to keep himself in place. When it means anything better than this, it means that which is expedient for some immediate object, some temporary purpose, but which violates a rule whose observance is expedient in a much higher degree. The expedient, in this sense, instead of being the same thing with the useful, is a branch of the hurtful. Thus it would often be expedient, for the purpose of getting over some momentary embarrassment, or attaining some object immediately useful to ourselves or others, to tell a lie. But inasmuch as the cultivation in ourselves of a sensitive feeling on the subject of veracity is one of the most useful, and the enfeeblement of that feeling one of the most hurtful, things to which our conduct can be instrumental; and inasmuch as any, even unintentional, deviation from truth does that much toward weakening the trustworthiness of human assertion, which is not only the principal support of all present social well-being, but the insufficiency of which does more than any one thing that can be named to keep back civilization, virtue, everything on which human happiness on the largest scale depends—we feel that the violation, for a present advantage, of a rule of such transcendent expediency is not expedient, and that he who, for the sake of convenience to himself or to some other individual, does what depends on him to deprive mankind of the good, and inflict upon them the evil, involved in the greater or less reliance which they can place in each other's word, acts the part of one of their worst enemies. Yet that even this rule, sacred as it is, admits of possible exceptions is acknowledged by all moralists; the chief of which is when the withholding of some fact (as of information from a malefactor, or of bad news from a person dangerously ill) would save an individual (especially an individual other than oneself) from great and unmerited evil, and when the withholding can only be effected by denial. But in order that the exception may not extend itself beyond the need, and may have the least possible effect in weakening reliance on veracity, it ought to be recognized and, if possible, its limits defined; and, if the principle of utility is good for anything, it must be good for weighing these conflicting utilities against one another and marking out the region within which one or the other preponderates.

Again, defenders of utility often find themselves called upon to reply to such objections as this—that there is not time, previous to action, for calculating and weighing the effects of any line of conduct on the general happiness. This is exactly as if anyone were to say that it is impossible to guide our conduct by Christianity because there is not time, on every occasion on which anything has to be done, to read through the Old and New Testaments. The answer to the objection is that there has been ample time, namely, the whole past duration of the human species. During all that time mankind has been learning by experience the tendencies of actions; on which experience all the prudence as well as all the morality of life are dependent. People talk as if the commencement of this course of experience had hitherto been put off, and as if, at the moment when some man feels tempted to meddle with the property or life of another, he had to begin considering for the first time whether murder and theft are injurious to human happiness. Even then I do not think that he would find the question very puzzling; but, at all events, the matter is now done to his hand. It is truly a whimsical supposition that, if mankind were agreed in considering utility to be the test of morality, they would remain without any agreement as to what *is* useful, and would take no measures for having their notions on the subject taught to the young and enforced by law and opinion. There is no difficulty in proving any ethical standard whatever to work ill if we suppose universal idiocy to be conjoined with it; but on any hypothesis short of that, mankind must by this time have acquired positive beliefs as to the effects of some actions on their happiness; and the beliefs which have thus come down are the rules of morality for the multitude, and for the philosopher until he has succeeded in finding better. That philosophers might easily do this, even now, on many subjects; that the received code of ethics is by no means of divine right; and that mankind have still much to learn as to the effects of actions on the general happiness, I admit or rather earnestly maintain. The corollaries from the principle of utility, like the precepts of every practical art, admit of indefinite improvement, and, in a progressive state of the human mind, their improvement is perpetually going on. But to consider the rules of morality as improvable is one thing; to pass over the intermediate generalization entirely and endeavor to test each individual action directly by the first principle is another. It is a strange notion that the acknowledgment of a first principle is inconsistent with the admission of secondary ones. To inform a traveler respecting the place of his ultimate destination is not to forbid the use of landmarks and direction-posts on the way. The proposition that happiness is the end and aim of morality does not mean that no road ought to be laid down to that goal, or that persons going thither should not be advised to take one direction rather than another. Men really ought to leave off talking a kind of nonsense on this subject, which they would neither talk nor listen to on other matters of practical concernment. Nobody argues that the art of navigation is not founded on astronomy because sailors cannot wait to calculate the Nautical Almanac. Being rational creatures, they go to sea with it already calculated; and all rational creatures go out upon the sea of life with their minds made up on the common questions of right and wrong, as well as on many of the far more difficult questions of wise and foolish. And this, as long as foresight is a human quality, it is to be presumed they will continue to do. Whatever we adopt as the fundamental principle of morality, we require subordinate principles to apply it by; the impossibility of doing without them, being common to all systems, can afford no argument against anyone in particular; but gravely to argue as if no such secondary principles could be had, and as if mankind had remained till now, and always must remain, without drawing any general conclusions from the experience of human life is as high a pitch, I think, as absurdity has ever reached in philosophical controversy.

The remainder of the stock arguments against utilitarianism mostly consist in laying to its charge the common infirmities of human nature, and the general difficulties which embarrass conscientious persons in shaping their course through life. We are told that a utilitarian will be apt to make his own particular case an exception to moral rules, and, when under temptation, will see a utility in the breach of a rule, greater than he will see in its observance. But is utility the only creed which is able to furnish us with excuses for evil-doing and means of cheating our own conscience? They are afforded in abundance by all doctrines which recognize as a fact in morals the existence of conflicting considerations, which all doctrines do that have been believed by sane persons. It is not the fault of any creed, but of the complicated nature of human affairs, that rules of conduct cannot be so framed as to require no exceptions, and that hardly any kind of action can safely be laid down as either always obligatory or always condemnable. There is no ethical creed which does not temper the rigidity of its laws by giving a certain latitude, under the moral responsibility of the agent, for accommodation to peculiarities of circumstances; and under every creed, at the opening thus made, self-deception and dishonest casuistry get in. There exists no moral system under which there do not arise unequivocal cases of conflicting obligation. These are the real difficulties, the knotty points both in the theory of ethics and in the conscientious guidance of personal conduct. They are overcome practically, with greater or with less success, according to the intellect and virtue of the individual; but it can hardly be pretended that anyone will be the less qualified for dealing with them, from possessing an ultimate standard to which conflicting rights and duties can be referred. If utility is the ultimate source of moral obligations, utility may be invoked to decide between them when their demands are incompatible. Though the application of the standard may be difficult, it is better than none at all; while in other systems, the moral laws all claiming independent authority, there is no common umpire entitled to interfere between them; their claims to precedence one over another rest on little better than sophistry, and, unless determined, as they generally are, by the unacknowledged influence of consideration of utility, afford a free scope for the action of personal desires and partialities. We must remember that only in these cases of conflict between secondary principles is it requisite that first principles should be appealed to. There is no case of moral obligation in which some secondary principle is not involved; and if only one, there can seldom be any real doubt which one it is, in the mind of any person by whom the principle itself is recognized.

### NOTES

1. The author of this essay has reason for believing himself to be the first person who brought the word "utilitarian" into use. He did not invent it, but adopted it from a passing expression in Mr. Galt's *Annals of the Parish*. After using it as a designation for several years, he and others abandoned it from a growing dislike to anything resembling a badge or watchword of sectarian distinction. But as a name for one single opinion, not a set of opinions—to denote the recognition of utility as a standard, not any particular way of applying it—the term supplies a want in the language, and offers, in many cases, a convenient mode of avoiding tiresome circumlocution.

2. An opponent, whose intellectual and moral fairness it is a pleasure to acknowledge (the Rev. J. Llewellyn Davies), has objected to this passage, saying, "Surely the rightness or wrongness of saving a man from drowning does depend very much upon the motive with which it is done. Suppose that a tyrant, when his enemy jumped into the sea to escape from him, saved him from drowning simply in order that he might inflict upon him more exquisite tortures, would it tend to clearness to speak of that rescue as 'a morally right action'? Or suppose again, according to one of the stock illustrations of ethical inquiries, that a man betrayed a trust received from a friend, because the discharge of it would fatally injure that friend himself or someone belonging to him, would utilitarianism compel one to call the betrayal 'a crime' as much as if it had been done from the meanest motive?"

I submit that he who saves another from drowning in order to kill him by torture afterwards does not differ only in motive from him who does the same thing from duty or benevolence; the act itself is different. The rescue of the man is, in the case supposed, only the necessary first step of an act far more atrocious than leaving him to drown would have been. Had Mr. Davies said, "The rightness or wrongness of saving a man from drowning does depend very much"—not upon the motive, but—"upon the *intention*," no utilitarian would have differed from him. Mr. Davies, by an oversight too common not to be quite venial, has in this case confounded the very different ideas of Motive and Intention. There is no point which utilitarian thinkers (and Bentham pre-eminently) have taken more pains to illustrate than this. The morality of the action depends entirely upon the intention—that is, upon what the agent *wills to do*. But the motive, that is, the feeling which makes him will so to do, if it makes no difference in the act, makes none in the morality: though it makes a great difference in our moral estimation of the agent, especially if it indicates a good or a bad habitual *disposition*—a bent of character from which useful, or from which hurtful actions are likely to arise.

# 36    On Liberty

## JOHN STUART MILL

### *Chapter I. Introductory*

The subject of this Essay is not the so-called Liberty of the Will, so unfortunately opposed to the misnamed doctrine of Philosophical Necessity; but Civil, or Social Liberty: the nature and limits of the power which can be legitimately exercised by society over the individual. A question seldom stated and hardly ever discussed, in general terms, but which profoundly influences the practical controversies of the age by its latent presence, and is likely soon to make itself recognised as the vital question of the future. It is so far from being new, that, in a certain sense, it has divided mankind, almost from the remotest ages; but in the stage of progress into which the more civilised portions of the species have now entered, it presents itself under new conditions, and requires a different and more fundamental treatment.

The struggle between Liberty and Authority is the most conspicuous feature in the portions of history with which we are earliest familiar, particularly in that of Greece, Rome, and England. But in old times this contest was between subjects, or some classes of subjects, and the Government. By liberty, was meant protection against the tyranny of the political rulers. The rulers were conceived (except in some of the popular governments of Greece) as in a necessarily antagonistic position to the people whom they ruled. They consisted of a governing One, or a governing tribe or caste, who derived their authority from inheritance or conquest, who, at all events, did not hold it at the pleasure of the governed, and whose supremacy men did not venture, perhaps did not desire, to contest, whatever precautions might be taken against its oppressive exercise. Their power was regarded as necessary, but also as highly dangerous; as a weapon which they would attempt to use against their subjects, no less than against external enemies. To prevent the weaker members of the community from being preyed upon by innumerable vultures, it was needful that there should be an animal of prey stronger than the rest, commissioned to keep them down. But as the king of the vultures would be no less bent upon preying on the flock than any of the minor harpies, it was indispensable to be in a perpetual attitude of defence against his beak and claws. The aim, therefore, of patriots was to set limits to the power which the ruler should be suffered to exercise over the community; and this limitation was what they meant by liberty. It was attempted in two ways. First, by obtaining a recognition of certain immunities, called political liberties or rights, which it was to be regarded as a breach of duty in the ruler to infringe, and which if he did infringe, specific

resistance, or general rebellion, was held to be justifiable. A second, and generally a later expedient, was the establishment of constitutional checks, by which the consent of the community, or of a body of some sort, supposed to represent its interests, was made a necessary condition to some of the more important acts of the governing power. To the first of these modes of limitation, the ruling power, in most European countries, was compelled, more or less, to submit. It was not so with the second; and, to attain this, or when already in some degree possessed, to attain it more completely, became everywhere the principal object of the lovers of liberty. And so long as mankind were content to combat one enemy by another, and to be ruled by a master, on condition of being guaranteed more or less efficaciously against his tyranny, they did not carry their aspirations beyond this point.

A time, however, came, in the progress of human affairs, when men ceased to think it a necessity of nature that their governors should be an independent power, opposed in interest to themselves. It appeared to them much better that the various magistrates of the State should be their tenants or delegates, revocable at their pleasure. In that way alone, it seemed, could they have complete security that the powers of government would never be abused to their disadvantage. By degrees this new demand for elective and temporary rulers became the prominent object of the exertions of the popular party, wherever any such party existed; and superseded, to a considerable extent, the previous efforts to limit the power of rulers. As the struggle proceeded for making the ruling power emanate from the periodical choice of the ruled, some persons began to think that too much importance had been attached to the limitation of the power itself. *That* (it might seem) was a resource against rulers whose interests were habitually opposed to those of the people. What was now wanted was, that the rulers should be identified with the people; that their interest and will should be the interest and will of the nation. The nation did not need to be protected against its own will. There was no fear of its tyrannising over itself. Let the rulers be effectually responsible to it, promptly removable by it, and it could afford to trust them with power of which it could itself dictate the use to be made. Their power was but the nation's own power, concentrated, and in a form convenient for exercise. This mode of thought, or rather perhaps of feeling, was common among the last generation of European liberalism, in the Continental section of which it still apparently predominates. Those who admit any limit to what a government may do, except in the case of such governments as they think ought not to exist, stand out as brilliant exceptions among the political thinkers of the Continent. A similar tone of sentiment might by this time have been prevalent in our own country, if the circumstances which for a time encouraged it, had continued unaltered.

But, in political and philosophical theories, as well as in persons, success discloses faults and infirmities which failure might have concealed from observation. The notion, that the people have no need to limit their power over themselves, might seem axiomatic, when popular government was a thing only dreamed about, or read of as having existed at some distant period of the past. Neither was that notion necessarily disturbed by such temporary aberrations as those of the French Revolution, the worst of which were the work of a usurping few, and which, in any case, belonged, not to the permanent working of popular institutions, but to a sudden and convulsive outbreak against monarchical and aristocratic despotism. In time, however, a democratic republic came to occupy a large portion of the earth's surface, and made itself felt as one of the most powerful members of the community of nations; and elective and responsible government became subject to the observations and criticisms which wait upon a great existing fact. It was now perceived that such phrases as 'self-government,' and 'the power of the people over themselves,' do not express the true state of the case. The 'people' who exercise the power are not always the same people with those over whom it is exercised; and the 'self-government' spoken of is not the government of each by himself, but of each by all the rest. The will of the people, moreover, practically means the will of the most numerous or the most active *part* of the people; the majority, or those who succeed in making themselves accepted as the majority; the people, consequently *may* desire to oppress a part of their number; and precautions are as much needed against this as against any other abuse of power. The limitation, therefore, of the power of government over individuals loses none of its importance when the holders of power are regularly accountable to the community, that is, to the strongest party therein. This view of things, recommending itself equally to the intelligence of thinkers and to the inclination of those important classes in European society to whose real or supposed interests democracy is adverse, has had no difficulty in establishing itself; and in political speculations 'the tyranny of the majority' is now generally included among the evils against which society requires to be on its guard.

Like other tyrannies, the tyranny of the majority was at first, and is still vulgarly, held in dread, chiefly as operating through the acts of the public authorities. But reflecting persons perceived that when society is itself the tyrant—society collectively over the separate individuals who compose it—its means of tyrannising are not restricted to the acts which it may do by the hands of its political functionaries. Society can and does execute its own mandates: and if it issues wrong mandates instead of right, or any mandates at all in things with which it ought not to meddle, it practises a social tyranny more formidable than many kinds of political oppression, since, though not usually upheld by such extreme penalties, it leaves fewer means of escape, penetrating much more deeply into the details of life, and enslaving the soul itself. Protection, therefore, against the tyranny of the magistrate is not enough: there needs protection also against the tyranny of the prevailing opinion and feeling; against the tendency of society to impose, by other means than civil penalties, its own ideas and practices as rules of conduct on those who dissent from them; to fetter the development, and, if possible, prevent the formation, of any individuality not in harmony with its ways and compels all characters to fashion themselves upon the model of its own. There is a limit to the legitimate interference of collective opinion with individual independence: and to find that limit, and maintain it against encroachment, is as indispensable to a good condition of human affairs, as protection against political despotism.

. . .

The object of this Essay is to assert one very simple principle, as entitled to govern absolutely the dealings of society with the individual in the way of compulsion and control, whether the means used be physical force in the form of legal penalties, or the moral coercion of public opinion. That principle is, that the sole end for which mankind are warranted, individually or collectively, in interfering with the liberty of action of any of their number, is self-protection. That the only purpose for which power can be rightfully exercised over any member of a civilised community, against his will, is to prevent harm to others. His own good, either physical or moral, is not a sufficient warrant. He cannot rightfully be compelled to do or forbear because it will be better for him to do so, because it will make him happier, because, in the opinions of others, to do so would be wise, or even right. These are good reasons for remonstrating with him, or reasoning with him, or persuading him, or entreating him, but not for compelling him, or visiting him with any evil in case he do otherwise. To justify that, the conduct from which it is desired to deter him must be calculated to produce evil to someone else. The only part of the conduct of anyone, for which he is amenable to society, is that which concerns others. In the part which merely concerns himself, his independence is, of right, absolute. Over himself, over his own body and mind, the individual is sovereign.

It is, perhaps, hardly necessary to say that this doctrine is meant to apply to human beings in the maturity of their faculties. We are not speaking of children, or of young persons below the age which the law may fix as that of manhood or womanhood. Those who are still in a state to require being taken care of by others, must be protected against their own actions as well as against external injury. For the same reason, we may leave out of consideration those backward states of society in which the race itself may be considered as in its nonage. The early difficulties in the way of spontaneous progress are so great, that there is seldom any choice of means for overcoming them; and a ruler full of the spirit of improvement is warranted in the use of any expedients that will attain an end, perhaps otherwise unattainable. Despotism is a legitimate mode of government in dealing with barbarians, provided the end be their improvement, and the means justified by actually effecting that end. Liberty, as a principle, has no application to any state of things anterior to the time when mankind have become capable of being improved by free and equal discussion. Until then, there is nothing for them but implicit obedience to an Akbar or a Charlemagne, if they are so fortunate as to find one. But as soon as mankind have attained the capacity of being guided to their own improvement by conviction or persuasion (a period long since reached in all nations with whom we need here concern ourselves), compulsion, either in the direct form or in that of pains and penalties for non-compliance, is no longer admissible as a means to their own good, and justifiable only for the security of others.

It is proper to state that I forego any advantage which could be derived to my argument from the idea of abstract right, as a thing independent of utility. I regard utility as the ultimate appeal on all ethical questions; but it must be utility in the largest sense, grounded on the permanent interests of a man as a progressive being. Those interests, I contend, authorise the subjection of individual spontaneity to external control, only in respect to those actions of each, which concern the interest of other people. If anyone does an act hurtful to others, there is a *prima facie* case for punishing him, by law, or, where legal penalties are not safely applicable, by general disapprobation. There are also many positive acts for the benefit of others, which he may rightfully be compelled to perform; such as to give evidence in a court of justice; to bear his fair share in the common defence, or in any other joint work necessary to the interest of the society of which he enjoys the protection; and to perform certain acts of individual beneficence, such as saving a fellow-creature's life, or interposing to protect the defenseless against ill-usage, things which whenever it is obviously a man's duty to do, he may rightfully be made responsible to society for not doing. A person may cause evil to others not only by his actions but by his inaction, and in either case he is justly accountable to them for the injury. The latter case, it is true, requires a much more cautious exercise of compulsion than the former. To make anyone answerable for doing evil to others is the rule; to make him answerable for not preventing evil is, comparatively speaking, the exception. Yet there are many cases clear enough and grave enough to justify that exception. In all things which regard the external relations of the individual, he is *de jure* amenable to those whose interests are concerned, and, if need be, to society as their protector. There are often good reasons for not holding him to the responsibility; but these reasons must arise from the special expediencies of the case: either because it is a kind of case in which he is on the whole likely to act better, when left to his own discretion, than when controlled in any way in which society has it in its power to control him; or because the attempt to exercise control would produce other evils, greater than those which it would prevent. When such reasons as these preclude the enforcement of responsibility, the conscience of the agent himself should step into the vacant judgment seat, and protect those interests of others which have no external protection; judging himself all the more rigidly, because the case does not admit of his being made accountable to the judgment of his fellow-creatures.

But there is a sphere of action in which society, as distinguished from the individual, has, if any, only an indirect interest; comprehending all that portion of a person's life and conduct which affects only himself, or if it also affects others, only with their free, voluntary, and undeceived consent and participation. When I say only himself, I mean directly, and in the first instance; for whatever affects himself, may affect others through himself; and the objection which may be grounded on this contingency, will receive consideration in the sequel. This, then, is the appropriate region of human liberty. It comprises, first, the inward domain of consciousness; demanding liberty of conscience in the most comprehensive sense; liberty of thought and feeling; absolute freedom of opinion and sentiment on all subjects, practical or speculative, scientific, moral, or theological. The liberty of expressing and publishing opinions may seem to fall under a different principle, since it belongs to that part of the conduct of an individual which concerns other people; but, being almost of as much importance as the liberty of thought itself, and resting in great part on the same reasons, is practically inseparable from it. Secondly, the principle requires liberty of tastes and pursuits; of framing the plan of our life to suit our own character; of doing as we like, subject to such consequences as may follow: without impediment from our fellow-creatures, so long as what we do does not harm them, even though they should think our conduct foolish, perverse, or wrong. Thirdly, from this liberty of each individual, follows the liberty, within the same limits, of combination among individuals; freedom to unite, for any purpose not involving harm to others: the persons combining being supposed to be of full age, and not forced or deceived.

No society in which these liberties are not, on the whole, respected, is free, whatever may be its form of government; and none is completely free in which they do not exist absolute and unqualified. The only freedom which deserves the name, is that of pursuing our own good in our own way, so long as we do not attempt to deprive others of theirs, or impede their efforts to obtain it. Each is the proper guardian of his own health, whether bodily, *or* mental and spiritual. Mankind are greater gainers by suffering each other to live as seems good to themselves, than by compelling each to live as seems good to the rest.

Though this doctrine is anything but new, and, to some persons, may have the air of a truism, there is no doctrine which stands more directly opposed to the general tendency of existing opinion and practice. Society has expended fully as much effort in the attempt (according to its lights) to compel people to conform to its notions of personal as of social excellence. The ancient commonwealths thought themselves entitled to practise, and the ancient philosophers countenanced, the regulation of every part of private conduct by public authority, on the ground that the State had a deep interest in the whole bodily and mental discipline of every one of its citizens; a mode of thinking which may have been admissible in small republics surrounded by powerful enemies, in constant peril of being subverted by foreign attack or internal commotion, and to which even a short interval of relaxed energy and self-command might so easily be fatal that they could not afford to wait for the salutary permanent effects of freedom. In the modern world, the greater size of political communities, and, above all, the separation between spiritual and temporal authority (which placed the direction of men's consciences in other hands than those which controlled their worldly affairs), prevented so great an interference by law in the details of private life; but the engines of moral repression have been wielded more strenuously against divergence from the reigning opinion in self-regarding, than even in social matters; religion, the most powerful of the elements which have entered into the formation of moral feeling, having almost always been governed either by the ambition of a hierarchy, seeking control over every department of human conduct, or by the spirit of Puritanism. And some of those modern reformers who have placed themselves in strongest opposition to the religions of the past, have been in no way behind either churches or sects in their assertion of the right of spiritual domination: M. Comte, in particular, whose social system, as unfolded in his *Système de Politique Positive,* aims at establishing (though by moral more than by legal appliances) a despotism of society over the individual, surpassing anything contemplated in the political ideal of the most rigid disciplinarian among the ancient philosophers.

Apart from the peculiar tenets of individual thinkers, there is also in the world at large an increasing inclination to stretch unduly the powers of society over the individual, both by the force of opinion and even by that of legislation; and as the tendency of all the changes taking place in the world is to strengthen society, and diminish the power of the individual, this encroachment is not one of the evils which tend spontaneously to disappear, but, on the contrary, to grow more and more formidable. The disposition of mankind, whether as rulers or as fellow-citizens, to impose their own opinions and inclinations as a rule of conduct on others, is so energetically supported by some of the best and by some of the worst feelings incident to human nature, that it is hardly ever kept under restraint by anything but want of power; and as the power is not declining, but growing, unless a strong barrier of moral conviction can be raised against the mischief, we must expect, in the present circumstances of the world, to see it increase.

It will be convenient for the argument, if, instead of at once entering upon the general thesis, we confine ourselves in the first instance to a single branch of it, on which the principle here stated is, if not fully, yet to a certain point, recognised by the current opinions. This one branch is the Liberty of Thought: from which it is impossible to separate the cognate liberty of speaking and of writing. Although these liberties, to some considerable amount, form part of the political morality of all countries which profess religious toleration and free institutions, the grounds, both philosophical and practical, on which they rest, are perhaps not so familiar to the general mind, nor so thoroughly appreciated by many even of the leaders of opinion, as might have been expected. Those grounds, when rightly understood, are of much wider application than to only one division of the subject, and a thorough consideration of this part of the question will be found the best introduction to the remainder. Those to whom nothing which I am about to say will be new, may therefore, I hope, excuse me, if on a subject which for now three centuries has been so often discussed, I venture on one discussion more.

# 37     The Subjection of Women

JOHN STUART MILL

## Chapter 1

THE OBJECT OF THIS ESSAY is to explain as clearly as I am able, the grounds of an opinion which I have held from the very earliest period when I had formed any opinions at all on social or political matters, and which, instead of being weakened or modified, has been constantly growing stronger by the progress of reflection and the experience of life: That the principle which regulates the existing social relations between the two sexes— the legal subordination of one sex to the other— is wrong in itself, and now one of the chief hindrances to human improvement; and that it ought to be replaced by a principle of perfect equality, admitting no power or privilege on the one side, nor disability on the other.

The very words necessary to express the task I have undertaken show how arduous it is. But it would be a mistake to suppose that the difficulty of the case must lie in the insufficiency or obscurity of the grounds of reason on which my conviction rests. The difficulty is that which exists in all cases in which there is a mass of feeling to be contended against. So long as an opinion is strongly rooted in the feelings, it gains rather than loses in stability by having a preponderating weight of argument against it. For if it were accepted as a result of argument, the refutation of the argument might shake the solidity of the conviction; but when it rests solely on feeling, the worse it fares in argumentative contest, the more persuaded its adherents are that their feeling must have some deeper ground, which the arguments do not reach; and while the feeling remains, it is always throwing up fresh intrenchments of argument to repair any breach made in the old. And there are so many causes tending to make the feelings connected with this subject the most intense and most

deeply-rooted of all those which gather round and protect old institutions and customs, that we need not wonder to find them as yet less undermined and loosened than any of the rest by the progress of the great modern spiritual and social transition; nor suppose that the barbarisms to which men cling longest must be less barbarisms than those which they earlier shake off. . . .

In the first place, the opinion in favour of the present system, which entirely subordinates the weaker sex to the stronger, rests upon theory only; for there never has been trial made of any other; so that experience, in the sense in which it is vulgarly opposed to theory, cannot be pretended to have pronounced any verdict. And in the second place, the adoption of this system of inequality never was the result of deliberation, or forethought, or any social ideas, or any notion whatever of what conducted to the benefit of humanity or the good order of society. It arose simply from the fact that from the very earliest twilight of human society, every woman (owing to the value attached to her by men, combined with her inferiority in muscular strength) was found in a state of bondage to some man. Laws and systems of polity always begin by recognising the relations they find already existing between individuals. They convert what was a mere physical fact into a legal right, give it the sanction of society, and principally aim at the substitution of public and organized means of asserting and protecting these rights, instead of the irregular and lawless conflict of physical strength. Those who had already been compelled to obedience became in this manner legally bound to it. Slavery, from being a mere affair of force between the master and the slave, became regularized and a matter of compact among the masters, who, binding themselves to one another for common protection, guaranteed by their collective strength the private possessions of each, including his slaves. In early times, the great majority of the male sex were slaves, as well as the whole of the female. And many ages elapsed, some of them ages of high cultivation, before any thinker was bold enough to question the rightfulness and the absolute social necessity, either of the one slavery or of the other. . . .

If people are mostly so little aware how completely, during the greater part of the duration of our species, the law of force was the avowed rule of general conduct, any other being only a special and exceptional consequence of peculiar ties— and from how very recent a date it is that the affairs of society in general have been even pretended to be regulated according to any moral law; as little do people remember or consider, how institutions and customs which never had any ground but the law of force, last on into ages and states of general opinion which never would have permitted their first establishment. Less than forty years ago, Englishmen might still by law hold human beings in bondage as saleable property; within the present century they might kidnap them and carry them off, and work them literally to death. This absolutely extreme case of the law of force, condemned by those who can tolerate almost every other form of arbitrary power, and which, of all others, presents features the most revolting to the feelings of all who look at it from an impartial position, was the law of civilized and Christian England within the memory of persons now living: and in one half of Anglo-Saxon America three or four years ago, not only did slavery exist, but the slave trade, and the breeding of slaves expressly for it, was a general practice between slave states. Yet not only was there a greater strength of sentiment against it, but, in England at least, a less amount either of feeling or of interest in favour of it, than of the other of the customary abuses of force: for its motive was the love of gain, unmixed and undisguised; and those who profited by it were a very small numerical fraction of the country, while the natural feeling of all who were not personally interested in it was unmitigated abhorrence. So extreme an instance makes it almost superfluous to refer to any other; but consider the long duration of absolute monarchy. In England at present it is the almost universal conviction that military despotism is a case of the law of force having no other origin or justification. Yet in all the great nations of Europe except England it either still exists, or has only just ceased to exist, and has even now a strong party favourable to it in all ranks of the people, especially among persons of station and consequence. Such is the power of an established system, even when far from universal, when not only in almost every period of history there have been great and well-known examples of the contrary system, but these have almost invariably been afforded by the most illustrious and most prosperous communities. In this case, too, the possessor of the undue power, the person directly interested in it, is only one person, while those who are subject to it and suffer from it are literally all the rest. The yoke is naturally and necessarily humiliating to all persons, except the one who is on the throne, together with, at most, the one who expects to succeed to it. How different are these cases from that of the power of men over women! I am not now prejudging the question of its justifiableness. I am showing how vastly more permanent it could not but be, even if not justifiable, than these other dominations which have nevertheless lasted down to our own time. Whatever gratification of pride there is in the possession of power, and whatever personal interest in its exercise, is in this case not confined to a limited class, but common to the whole male sex. Instead of being, to most of its supporters, a thing desirable chiefly in the abstract, or, like the political ends usually contended for by factions, of little private importance to any but the leaders; it comes home to the person and hearth of every male head of a family, and of everyone who looks forward to being so. The clodhopper exercises, or is to exercise, his share of the power equally with the highest nobleman. And the case is that in which the desire of power is the strongest: for everyone who desires power, desires it most over those who are nearest to him, with whom his life is passed, with whom he has most concerns in common, and in whom any independence of his authority is oftenest likely to interfere with his individual preferences. If in the other cases specified, power manifestly grounded only on force, and having so much less to support them, are so slowly and with so much difficulty got rid of, much more must it be so with this, even if it rests on no better foundation than those. We must consider, too, that the possessors of the power have facilities in this case, greater than in any other, to prevent any uprising against it. Every one of the subjects lives under the very eye, and almost, it may be said, in the hands of one of the masters—in closer intimacy with him than with any of her fellow-subjects; with no means of combining against him, no power of even locally overmastering him, and, on the other hand, with the strongest motives for seeking his favour and avoiding to give him offence. In struggles for political emancipation, everybody knows how often its champions are bought off by bribes, or daunted by terrors. In the case of women, each individual of the subject-class is in a chronic state of bribery and intimidation combined. In setting up the standard of resistance, a large number of the leaders, and still more of the followers, must make an almost complete sacrifice of the pleasures or the alleviations of their own individual lot. If ever any system of privilege and enforced subjection had its yoke tightly riveted on the necks of those who are kept down by it, this has. . . .

But, it will be said, the rule of men over women differs from all these others in not being a rule of force: it is accepted voluntarily; women make no complaint, and are consenting parties to it. In the first place, a great number of women do not accept it. Ever since there have been women able to make their sentiments known by their writings (the only mode of publicity which society permits to them), an increasing number of them have recorded protests against their present social condition: and recently many thousands of them, headed by the most eminent women known to the public, have petitioned Parliament for their admission to the Parliamentary Suffrage. The claim of women to be educated as solidly, and in the same branches of knowledge, as men, is urged with growing intensity, and with a great prospect of success; while the demand for their admission into professions and occupations hitherto closed against them, becomes every year more urgent. Though there are not in this country, as there are in the United States, periodical Conventions and an organized party to agitate for the Rights of Women, there is a numerous and active Society organized and managed by women, for the more limited object of obtaining the political franchise. Nor is it only in our own country and in America that women are beginning to protest, more or less collectively, against the disabilities under which they labour. France, and Italy, and Switzerland, and Russia now afford examples of the same thing. How many more women there are who silently cherish similar aspirations, no one can possibly know; but there are abundant tokens how many *would* cherish them, were they not so strenuously taught to repress them as contrary to the proprieties of their sex. It must be remembered, also, that no enslaved class ever asked for complete liberty at once. When Simon de Montfort called the deputies of the commons to sit for the first time in Parliament, did any of them dream of demanding that an assembly, elected by their constituents, should make and destroy ministries, and dictate to the king in affairs of state? No such thought entered into the imagination of the most ambitious of them. The nobility had already these pretensions; the commons pretended to nothing but to be exempt from arbitrary taxation, and from the gross individual oppression of the king's officers. It is a political law of nature that those who are under any power of ancient origin, never begin by complaining of the power itself, but only of its oppressive exercise. There is never any want of women who complain of ill usage by their husbands. There would be infinitely more, if complaint were not the greatest of all provocatives to a repetition and increase of the ill usage. It is this which frustrates all attempts to maintain the power but protect the woman against its abuses. In no other case (except that of a child) is the person who has been proved judicially to have suffered an injury, replaced under the physical power of the culprit who inflicted it. Accordingly wives, even in the most extreme and protracted cases of bodily ill usage, hardly ever dare avail themselves of the laws made for their protection: and if, in a moment of irrepressible indignation, or by the interference of neighbours, they are induced to do so, their whole effort afterwards is to disclose as little as they can, and to beg off their tyrant from his merited chastisement.

All men, except the most brutish, desire to have, in the woman most nearly connected with them, not a forced slave but a willing one, not a slave merely, but a favourite. They have therefore put everything in practice to enslave their minds. The masters of all other slaves rely, for maintaining obedience, on fear; either fear of themselves, or religious fears. The masters of women wanted more than simple obedience, and they turned the whole force of education to effect their purpose. All women are brought up from the very earliest years in the belief that their ideal of character is the very opposite to that of men; not self-will, and government by self-control, but submission, and yielding to the control of others. All the moralities tell them that it is the duty of women, and all the current sentimentalities that it is their nature, to live for others; to make complete abnegation of themselves, and to have no life but in their affections. And by their affections are meant the only ones they are allowed to have—those to the men with whom they are connected, or to the children who constitute an additional and indefeasible tie between them and a man. When we put together three things—first, the natural attraction between opposite sexes; secondly, the wife's entire dependence on the husband, every privilege or pleasure she has being either his gift, or depending entirely on his will; and lastly, that the principal object of human pursuit, consideration, and all objects of social ambition, can in general be sought or obtained by her only through him, it would be a miracle if the object of being attractive to men had not become the polar star of feminine education and formation of character. And, this great means of influence over the minds of women having been

acquired, an instinct of selfishness made men avail themselves of it to the utmost as a means of holding women in subjection, by representing to them meekness, submissiveness, and resignation of all individual will into the hands of a man, as an essential part of sexual attractiveness. Can it be doubted that any of the other yokes which mankind have succeeded in breaking, would have subsisted till now if the same means had existed, and had been as sedulously used, to bow down their minds to it? If it had been made the object of the life of every young plebeian to find personal favour in the eyes of some patrician, of every young serf with some seigneur; if domestication with him, and a share of his personal affections, had been held out as the prize which they all should look out for, the most gifted and aspiring being able to reckon on the most desirable prizes; and if, when this prize had been obtained, they had been shut out by a wall of brass from all interests not centering in him, all feelings and desires but those which he shared or inculcated; would not serfs and seigneurs, plebeians and patricians, have been as broadly distinguished at this day as men and women are? and would not all but a thinker here and there, have believed the distinction to be a fundamental and unalterable fact in human nature?

The preceding considerations are amply sufficient to show that custom, however universal it may be, affords in this case no presumption, and ought not to create any prejudice, in favour of the arrangements which place women in social and political subjection to men. But I may go farther, and maintain that the course of history, and the tendencies of progressive human society, afford not only no presumption in favour of this system of inequality of rights, but a strong one against it; and that, so far as the whole course of human improvement up to this time, the whole stream of modern tendencies, warrants any inference on the subject, it is, that this relic of the past is discordant with the future, and must necessarily disappear.

For, what is the peculiar character of the modern world—the difference which chiefly distinguishes modern institutions, modern social ideas, modern life itself, from those of times long past?

It is, that human beings are no longer born to their place in life, and chained down by an inexorable bond to the place they are born to, but are free to employ their faculties, and such favourable chances as offer, to achieve the lot which may appear to them most desirable. Human society of old was constituted on a very different principle. All were born to a fixed social position, and were mostly kept in it by law, or interdicted from any means by which they could emerge from it. As some men are born white and others black, so some were born slaves and others freemen and citizens; some were born patricians, others plebeians; some were born feudal nobles, others commoners and *roturiers*. A slave or serf could never make himself free, nor, except by the will of his master, become so. In most European countries it was not till towards the close of the middle ages, and as a consequence of the growth of regal power, that commoners could be ennobled. Even among nobles, the eldest son was born the exclusive heir to the paternal possessions, and a long time elapsed before it was fully established that the father could disinherit him. Among the industrious classes, only those who were born members of a guild, or were admitted into it by its members, could lawfully practise their calling within its local limits; and nobody could practise any calling deemed important, in any but the legal manner—by processes authoritatively prescribed. Manufacturers have stood in the pilory for presuming to carry on their business by new and improved methods. In modern Europe, and most in those parts of it which have participated most largely in all other modern improvements, diametrically opposite doctrines now prevail. Law and government do not undertake to prescribe by whom any social or industrial operation shall or shall not be conducted, or what modes of conducting them shall be lawful. These things are left to the unfettered choice of individuals. Even the laws which required that workmen should serve an apprenticeship, have in this country been repealed: there being ample assurance that in all cases in which an apprenticeship is necessary, its necessity will suffice to enforce it. The old theory was, that the least possible should be left to the choice of the individual agent; that all he had to do should, as far as practicable, be laid down for him by superior wisdom. Left to himself he was sure to go wrong. The modern conviction, the fruit of a thousand years of experience is, that things in which the individual is the person directly interested, never go right but as they are left to his own discretion; and that any regulation of them by authority, except to protect the rights of others, is sure to be mischievous. This conclusion, slowly arrived at, and not adopted until almost every possible application of the contrary theory had been made with disastrous result, now (in the industrial department) prevails universally in the most advanced countries, almost universally in all that have pretensions to any sort of advancement. It is not that all processes are supposed to be equally good, or all persons to be equally qualified for everything; but that freedom of individual choice is now known to be the only thing which procures the adoption of the best processes, and throws each operation into the hands of those who are best qualified for it. Nobody thinks it necessary to make a law that only a strong-armed man shall be a blacksmith. Freedom and competition suffice to make blacksmiths strong-armed men, because the weak-armed can earn more by engaging in occupations for which they are more fit. In consonance with this doctrine, it is felt to be an overstepping of the proper bounds of authority to fix beforehand, on some general presumption, that certain persons are not fit to do certain things. It is now thoroughly known and admitted that if some such presumptions exist, no such presumption is infallible. Even if it be well grounded in a majority of cases, which it is very likely not to be, there will be a minority of exceptional cases in which it does not hold; and in those it is both an injustice to the individuals, and a detriment to society, to place barriers in the way of their using their faculties for their own benefit and for that of others. In the cases, on the other hand, in which the unfitness is real, the ordinary motives of human conduct will on the whole suffice to prevent the incompetent person from making, or from persisting in, the attempt.

If this general principle of social and economical science is not true; if individuals, with such help as they can derive from the opinion of those who know them, are not better judges than the law and the government, of their own capacities and vocation; the world cannot too soon abandon this principle, and return to the old system of regulations and disabilities. But if the principle is true, we ought to act as if we believed it, and not to ordain that to be born a girl instead of a boy, any more than to be born black instead of white, or a commoner instead of a nobleman, shall decide the person's position through all life—shall interdict people from all the more elevated social positions, and from all, except a few, respectable occupations. Even were we to admit the utmost that is ever pretended as to the superior fitness of men for all the functions now reserved to them, the same argument applies which forbids a legal qualification for members of Parliament. If only once in a dozen years the conditions of eligibility exclude a fit person, there is a real loss, while the exclusion of thousands of unfit persons is no gain; for if the constitution of the electoral body disposes them to choose unfit persons, there are always plenty of such persons to choose from. In all things of any difficulty and importance, those who can do them well are fewer than the need, even with the most unrestricted latitude of choice; and any limitation of the field of selection deprives society of some chances of being served by the competent, without ever saving it from the incompetent.

At present, in the more improved countries, the disabilities of women are the only case, save one, in which laws and institutions take persons at their birth, and ordain that they shall never in all their lives be allowed to compete for certain things. . . .

The social subordination of women thus stands out an isolated fact in modern social institutions; a solitary breach of what has become their fundamental law; a single relic of an old world of thought and practice exploded in everything else, but retained in the one thing of most universal interest. . . .

The least that can be demanded is that the question should not be considered as prejudged by existing fact and existing opinion, but open to discussion on its merits, as a question of justice and expediency; the decision on this, as on any of the other social arrangements of mankind, depending on what an enlightened estimate of tendencies and consequences may show to be most advantageous to humanity in general without distinction of sex. And the discussion must be a real discussion, descending to foundations, and not resting satisfied with vague and general assertions. It will not do, for instance, to assert in general terms, that the experience of mankind has pronounced in favour of the existing system. Experience cannot possibly have decided between two courses, so long as there has only been experience of one. If it be said that the doctrine of the equality of the sexes rests only on theory, it must be remembered that the contrary doctrine also has only theory to rest upon. All that is proved in its favour by direct experience, is that mankind have been able to exist under it, and to attain the degree of improvement and prosperity which we now see; but whether that prosperity has been attained sooner, or is now greater, than it would have been under the other system, experience does not say. On the other hand, experience does say, that every step in improvement has been so invariably accompanied by a step made in raising the social position of women, that historians and philosophers have been led to adopt their elevation or debasement as on the whole the surest test and most correct measure of the civilization of a people or an age. Through all the progressive period of human history, the condition of women has been approaching nearer to equality with men. This does not of itself prove that the assimilation must go on to complete equality; but it assuredly affords some presumption that such is the case.

Neither does it avail anything to say that the *nature* of the two sexes adapts them to their present functions and position, and renders these appropriate to them. Standing on the ground of common sense and the constitution of the human mind, I deny that anyone knows, or can know, the nature of the two sexes, as long as they have only been seen in their present relation to one another. If men had ever been found in society without women, or women without men, or if there had been a society of men and women in which the women were not under the control of the men, something might have been positively known about the mental and moral differences which may be inherent in the nature of each. What is now called the nature of women is an eminently artificial thing—the result of forced repression in some directions, unnatural stimulation in others. It may be asserted without scruple, that no other class of dependents have had their character so entirely distorted from its natural proportions by their relation with their masters; for, if conquered and slave races have been, in some respects, more forcibly repressed, whatever in them has not been crushed down by an iron heel has generally been let alone, and if left with any liberty of development, it has developed itself according to its own laws; but in the case of women, a hot-house and stove cultivation has always been carried on of some of the capabilities of their nature, for the benefit and pleasure of their masters. . . .

Hence, in regard to that most difficult question, what are the natural differences between the two sexes—a subject on which it is impossible in the present state of society to obtain complete and correct knowledge—while almost everybody dogmatizes upon it, almost all neglect and make light of the only means by which any partial insight can be obtained into it. This is, an analytic study of the most important department of psychology, the laws of the influences of circumstances on character. For, however great and apparently ineradicable the moral and intellectual differences between men and women might be, the evidence of their being natural differences could only be negative. Those only could be inferred to be natural which could not possibly be artificial—the residuum, after deducting every characteristic of either sex which can admit of being explained from education or external circumstances. The profoundest knowledge of the laws of the formation of character is indispensable to entitle anyone to affirm even

that there is any difference, much more what the difference is, between the two sexes considered as moral and rational beings; and since no one, as yet, has that knowledge (for there is hardly any subject which, in proportion to its importance, has been so little studied), no one is thus far entitled to any positive opinion on the subject. Conjectures are all that can at present be made; conjectures more or less probable, according as more or less authorized by such knowledge as we yet have of the laws of psychology, as applied to the formation of character.

Even the preliminary knowledge, what the differences between the sexes now are, apart from all questions as to how they are made what they are, is still in the crudest and most incomplete state. . . .

One thing we may be certain of—that what is contrary to women's nature to do, they never will be made to do by simply giving their nature free play. The anxiety of mankind to interfere in behalf of nature, for fear lest nature should not succeed in effecting its purpose, is an altogether unnecessary solicitude. What women by nature cannot do, it is quite superfluous to forbid them from doing. What they can do, but not so well as the men who are their competitors, competition suffices to exclude them from; since nobody asks for protective duties and bounties in favour of women; it is only asked that the present bounties and protective duties in favour of men should be recalled. If women have a greater natural inclination for some things than for others, there is no need of laws or social inculcation to make the majority of them do the former in preference to the latter. Whatever women's services are most wanted for, the free play of competition will hold out the strongest inducements to them to undertake. And, as the words imply, they are most wanted for the things for which they are most fit; by the apportionment of which to them, the collective faculties of the two sexes can be applied on the whole with the greatest sum of valuable result.

The general opinion of men is supposed to be, that the natural vocation of a woman is that of a wife and mother. I say, is supposed to be, because, judging from acts—from the whole of the present constitution of society—one might infer that their opinion was the direct contrary. They might be supposed to think that the alleged natural vocation of women was of all things the most repugnant to their nature; insomuch that if they are free to do anything else—if any other means of living, or occupation of their time and faculties, is open, which has any chance of appearing desirable to them—there will not be enough of them who will be willing to accept the condition said to be natural to them. If this is the real opinion of men in general, it would be well that it should be spoken out. I should like to hear somebody openly enunciating the doctrine (it is already implied in much that is written on the subject)—"It is necessary to society that women should marry and produce children. They will not do so unless they are compelled. Therefore it is necessary to compel them." The merits of the case would then be clearly defined. It would be exactly that of the slaveholders of South Carolina and Louisiana. "It is necessary that cotton and sugar should be grown. White men cannot produce them, Negroes will not, for any wages which we choose to give, *Ergo* they must be compelled." An illustration still closer to the point is that of impressment. Sailors must absolutely be had to defend the country. It often happens that they will not voluntarily enlist. Therefore there must be the power of forcing them. How often has this logic been used! and, but for one flaw in it, without doubt it would have been successful up to this day. But it is open to the retort—First pay the sailors the honest value of their labour. When you have made it as well worth their while to serve you, as to work for other employers, you will have no more difficulty than others have in obtaining their services. To this there is no logical answer except "I will not": and as people are now not only ashamed, but are not desirous, to rob the labourer of his hire, impressment is no longer advocated. Those who attempt to force women into marriage by closing all other doors against them, lay themselves open to a sim-

ilar retort. If they mean what they say, their opinion must evidently be, that men do not render the married condition so desirable to women, as to induce them to accept it for its own recommendations. It is not a sign of one's thinking the boon one offers very attractive, when one allows only Hobson's choice, "that or none." And here, I believe, is the clue to the feelings of those men, who have a real antipathy to the equal freedom of women. I believe they are afraid, not lest women should be unwilling to marry, for I do not think that anyone in reality has that apprehension; but lest they should insist that marriage should be on equal conditions; lest all women of spirit and capacity should prefer doing almost anything else, not in their own eyes degrading, rather than marry, when marrying is giving themselves a master, and a master too of all their earthly possessions. And truly, if this consequence were necessarily incident to marriage, I think that the apprehension would be very well founded. I agree in thinking it probable that few women, capable of anything else, would, unless under an irresistible *entrainement,* rendering them for the time insensible to anything but itself, choose such a lot, when any other means were open to them of filling a conventionally honourable place in life: and if men are determined that the law of marriage shall be a law of despotism, they are quite right, in point of mere policy, in leaving to women only Hobson's choice. But, in that case, all that has been done in the modern world to relax the chain on the minds of women, has been a mistake. They never should have been allowed to receive a literary education. Women who read, much more women who write, are, in the existing constitution of things, a contradiction and a disturbing element: and it was wrong to bring women up with any acquirements but those of an odalisque, or of a domestic servant. . . .

## Chapter IV

There remains a question, not of less importance than those already discussed, and which will be asked the most importunately by those opponents whose conviction is somewhat shaken on the main point. What good are we to expect from the changes proposed in our customs and institutions? Would mankind be at all better off if women were free? If not, why disturb their minds, and attempt to make a social revolution in the name of an abstract right?

It is hardly to be expected that this question will be asked in respect to the change proposed in the condition of women in marriage. The sufferings, immoralities, evils of all sorts, produced in innumerable cases by the subjection of individual women to individual men, are far too terrible to be overlooked. Unthinking or uncandid persons, counting those cases alone which are extreme, or which attain publicity, may say that the evils are exceptional; but no one can be blind to their existence, nor, in many cases, to their intensity. And it is perfectly obvious that the abuse of power cannot be very much checked while the power remains. It is a power given, or offered, not to good men, or to decently respectable men, but to all men; the most brutal, and the most criminal. There is no check but that of opinion, and such men are in general within the reach of no opinion but that of men like themselves. If such men did not brutally tyrannize over the one human being whom the law compels to bear everything from them, society must already have reached a paradisiacal state. There could be no need any longer of laws to curb men's vicious propensities. Astraea must not only have returned to earth, but the heart of the worst man must have become her temple. The law of servitude in marriage is a monstrous contradiction to all the principles of the modern world, and to all the experience through which those principles have been slowly and painfully worked out. It is the sole case, now that negro slavery has been abolished, in which a human being in the plenitude of every faculty is delivered up to the tender mercies of another human being, in the hope forsooth that this other will use the power solely for the good of the person subjected to it. Marriage is the only actual bondage

known to our law. There remain no legal slaves, except the mistress of every house.

It is not, therefore, on this part of the subject, that the question is likely to be asked, *Cui bono?*[1] We may be told that the evil would outweigh the good, but the reality of the good admits of no dispute. In regard, however, to the larger question, the removal of women's disabilities—their recognition as the equals of men in all that belongs to citizenship—the opening to them of all honourable employments, and of the training and education which qualifies for those employments—there are many persons for whom it is not enough that the inequality has no just or legitimate defence; they require to be told what express advantage would be obtained by abolishing it.

To which let me first answer, the advantage of having the most universal and pervading of all human relations regulated by justice instead of injustice. The vast amount of this gain to human nature, it is hardly possible, by any explanation or illustration, to place in a stronger light than it is placed by the bare statement, to anyone who attaches a moral meaning to words. All the selfish propensities, the self-worship, the unjust self-preference, which exist among mankind, have their source and root in, and derive their principal nourishment from, the present constitution of the relation between men and women. Think what it is to a boy, to grow up to manhood in the belief that without any merit or any exertion of his own, though he may be the most frivolous and empty or the most ignorant and stolid of mankind, by the mere fact of being born a male he is by right the superior of all and everyone of an entire half of the human race: including probably some whose real superiority to himself he has daily or hourly occasion to feel; but even if in his whole conduct he habitually follows a woman's guidance, still, if he is a fool, he thinks that of course she is not, and cannot be, equal in ability and judgment to himself; and if he is not a fool, he does worse—he sees that she is superior to him, and believes that, notwithstanding her superiority, he is entitled to command and she is bound to obey. What must be the effect on his character, of this lesson? And men of the cultivated classes are often not aware how deeply it sinks into the immense majority of male minds. For, among right-feeling and well-bred people, the inequality is kept as much as possible out of sight; above all, out of sight of the children. As much obedience is required from boys to their mother as to their father: they are not permitted to domineer over their sisters, nor are they accustomed to see these postponed to them, but the contrary; the compensations of the chivalrous feeling being made prominent, while the servitude which requires them is kept in the background. Well brought-up youths in the higher classes thus often escape the bad influences of the situation in their early years, and only experience them when, arrived at manhood, they fall under the dominion of facts as they really exist. Such people are little aware, when a boy is differently brought up, how early the notion of his inherent superiority to a girl arises in his mind; how it grows with his growth and strengthens with his strength; how it is inoculated by one schoolboy upon another; how early the youth thinks himself superior to his mother, owing her perhaps forbearance, but no real respect; and how sublime and sultan-like a sense of superiority he feels, above all, over the woman whom he honours by admitting her to a partnership of his life. Is it imagined that all this does not pervert the whole manner of existence of the man, both as an individual and as a social being? It is an exact parallel to the feeling of a hereditary king that he is excellent above others by being born a king, or a noble by being born a noble. The relation between husband and wife is very like that between lord and vassal, except that the wife is held to more unlimited obedience than the vassal was. However the vassal's character may have been affected, for better and for worse, by his subordination, who can help seeing that the lord's was affected greatly for the worse? whether he was led to believe that his vassals were really superior to himself, or to feel that he was placed in command over people as good as himself, for no merits or labours of his

own, but merely for having, as Figaro says, taken the trouble to be born. The self-worship of the monarch, or of the feudal superior is matched by the self-worship of the male. Human beings do not grow up from childhood in the possession of unearned distinctions, without pluming themselves upon them. Those whom privileges not acquired by their merit, and which they feel to be disproportioned to it, inspire with additional humility, are always the few, and the best few. The rest are only inspired with pride, and the worst sort of pride, that which values itself upon accidental advantages, not of its own achieving. Above all, when the feeling of being raised above the whole of the other sex is combined with personal authority over one individual among them; the situation, if a school of conscientious and affectionate forbearance to those whose strongest points of character are conscience and affection, is to men of another quality a regularly constituted Academy or Gymnasium for training them in arrogance and overbearingness; which vices, if curbed by the certainty of resistance in their intercourse with other men, their equals, break out towards all who are in a position to be obliged to tolerate them, and often revenge themselves upon the unfortunate wife for the involuntary restraint which they are obliged to submit to elsewhere.

The example afforded, and the education given to the sentiments, by laying the foundation of domestic existence upon a relation contradictory to the first principles of social justice, must, from the very nature of man, have a perverting influence of such magnitude, that it is hardly possible with our present experience to raise our imaginations to the conception of so great a change for the better as would be made by its removal. All that education and civilization are doing to efface the influences on character of the law of force, and replace them by those of justice, remains merely on the surface, as long as the citadel of the enemy is not attacked. The principle of the modern movement in morals and politics, is that conduct, and conduct alone, entitles to respect: that not what men are, but what they do, constitutes their claim to deference;

that, above all, merit, and not birth, is the only rightful claim to power and authority. If no authority, not in its nature temporary, were allowed to one human being over another, society would not be employed in building up propensities with one hand which it has to curb with the other. The child would really, for the first time in man's existence on earth, be trained in the way he should go, and when he was old there would be a chance that he would not depart from it. But so long as the right of the strong to power over the weak rules in the very heart of society, the attempt to make the equal right of the weak the principle of its outward actions will always be an uphill struggle; for the law of justice, which is also that of Christianity, will never get possession of men's inmost sentiments; they will be working against it, even when bending to it. . . .

Any society which is not improving, is deteriorating: and the more so, the closer and more familiar it is. Even a really superior man almost always begins to deteriorate when he is habitually (as the phrase is) king of his company: and in his most habitual company the husband who has a wife inferior to him is always so. While his self-satisfaction is incessantly ministered to on the one hand, on the other he insensibly imbibes the modes of feeling, and of looking at things, which belong to a more vulgar or a more limited mind than his own. This evil differs from many of those which have hitherto been dwelt on, by being an increasing one. The association of men with women in daily life is much closer and more complete than it ever was before. Men's life is more domestic. Formerly, their pleasures and chosen occupations were among men, and in men's company: their wives had but a fragment of their lives. At the present time, the progress of civilization, and the turn of opinion against the rough amusements and convivial excesses which formerly occupied most men in their hours of relaxation—together with (it must be said) the improved tone of modern feeling as to the reciprocity of duty which binds the husband towards the wife—have thrown the man very much more upon home and its inmates, for his personal and social pleasures: while the kind and degree of improvement which has been made in women's education, has made them in some degree capable of being his companions in ideas and mental tastes, while leaving them, in most cases, still hopelessly inferior to him. His desire of mental communication is thus in general satisfied by a communion from which he learns nothing. An unimproving and unstimulating companionship is substituted for (what he might otherwise have been obliged to seek) the society of his equals in powers and his fellows in the higher pursuits. We see, accordingly, that young men of the greatest promise generally cease to improve as soon as they marry, and, not improving, inevitably degenerate. If the wife does not push the husband forward, she always holds him back. He ceases to care for what she does not care for; he no longer desires, and ends by disliking and shunning, society congenial to his former aspirations, and which would now shame his falling-off from them; his higher faculties both of mind and heart cease to be called into activity. And this change coinciding with the new and selfish interests which are created by the family, after a few years he differs in no material respect from those who have never had wishes for anything but the common vanities and the common pecuniary objects.

What marriage may be in the case of two persons of cultivated faculties, identical in opinions and purposes, between whom there exists that best kind of equality, similarity of powers and capacities with reciprocal superiority in them—so that each can enjoy the luxury of looking up to the other, and can have alternately the pleasure of leading and of being led in the path of development—I will not attempt to describe. To those who can conceive it, there is no need; to those who cannot, it would appear the dream of an enthusiast. But I maintain, with the profoundest conviction, that this, and this only, is the ideal of marriage; and that all opinion, customs, and institutions which favour any other notion of it, or turn the conceptions and aspirations connected with it into any other direction, by whatever pretences they may be coloured, are relics of primitive barbarism. The moral regeneration of mankind will only really commence, when the most fundamental of the social relations is placed under the rule of equal justice, and when human beings learn to cultivate their strongest sympathy with an equal in rights and in cultivation.

NOTE

1. "For the good of whom?"

---

# 38    Enfranchisement of Women

HARRIET TAYLOR

. . . CONCERNING THE FITNESS, THEN, OF WOMEN for politics, there can be no question: but the dispute is more likely to turn upon the fitness of politics for women. When the reasons alleged for excluding women from active life in all its higher departments are stripped of their garb of declamatory phrases, and reduced to the simple expression of a meaning, they seem to be mainly three: first, the incompatibility of active life with maternity, and with the cares of a household; secondly, its alleged hardening effect on the character; and thirdly, the inexpediency of making an addition to the already excessive pressure of competition in every kind of professional or lucrative employment.

The first, the maternity argument, is usually laid most stress upon: although (it needs hardly be said) this reason; if it be one, can apply only to mothers. It is neither necessary nor just to make imperative on women that they shall be either mothers or nothing; or that if they have been mothers once, they shall be nothing else during the whole remainder of their lives. Neither women nor men need any law to exclude them from an occupation, if they have undertaken another which is incompatible with it. No one proposes to exclude the male sex from Parliament because a man may be a soldier or sailor in active service, or a merchant whose business requires all his time and energies. Nine-tenths of the occupations of men exclude them *de facto* from public life, as effectually as if they were excluded by law; but that is no reason for making laws to exclude even the nine-tenths, much less the remaining tenth. The reason of the case is the same for women as for men. There is no need to make provision by law that women shall not carry on the active details of a household, or of the education of children, and at the same time practise a profession, or be elected to parliament. Where incompatibility is real, it will take care of itself: but there is gross injustice in making the incompatibility a pretence for the exclusion of those in whose case it does not exist. And these, if they were free to choose, would be a very large proportion. The maternity argument deserts its supporters in the case of single women, a large and increasing class of the population; a fact which, it is not irrelevant to remark, by tending to diminish the excessive competition of numbers, is calculated to assist greatly the prosperity of all. There is no inherent reason or necessity that all women should voluntarily choose to devote their lives to one animal function and its consequences. Numbers of women are wives and mothers only because there is no other career open to them, no other occupation for their feelings or their activities. Every improvement in their education, and enlargement of their faculties, everything which renders them more qualified for any other mode of life, increases the number of those to whom it is an injury and an oppression to be denied the choice. To say that women must be excluded from active life because maternity disqualifies them for it, is in fact to say, that every other career should be forbidden them in order that maternity may be their only resource.

But secondly, it is urged, that to give the same freedom of occupation to women as to men, would be an injurious addition to the crowd of competitors, by whom the avenues to almost all kinds of employment are choked up, and its remuneration depressed. This argument, it is to be observed, does not reach the political question. It gives no excuse for withholding from women the rights of citizenship. The suffrage, the jury-box, admission to the legislature and to office, it does not touch. It bears only on the industrial branch of the subject. Allowing it, then, in an economical point of view, its full force; assuming that to lay open to women the employments now monopolized by men, would tend, like the breaking down of other monopolies, to lower the rate of remuneration in those employments; let us consider what is the amount of this evil consequence, and what the compensation is for it. The worst ever asserted, much worse than is at all likely to be realized, is that if women competed with men, a man and a woman could not together earn more than is now earned by the man alone. Let us make this supposition, the most unfavourable supposition possible: the joint income of the two would be the same as before, while the woman would be raised from the position of a servant to that of a partner. Even if every woman, as matters now stand, had a claim on some man for support, how infinitely preferable is it that part of the income should be of the woman's earning, even if the aggregate sum were but little increased by it, rather than that she should be compelled to stand aside in order that men may be the sole earners, and the sole dispensers of what is earned. Even under the present laws respecting the property of women, a woman

who contributes materially to the support of the family, cannot be treated in the same contemptuously tyrannical manner as one who, however she may toil as a domestic drudge, is a dependent on the man for subsistence.[1] As for the depression of wages by increase of competition, remedies will be found for it in time. Palliatives might be applied immediately; for instance, a more rigid exclusion of children from industrial employment, during the years in which they ought to be working only to strengthen their bodies and minds for later life. Children are necessarily dependent, and under the power of others; and their labour, being not for themselves but for the gain of their parents, is a proper subject for legislative regulation. With respect to the future, we neither believe that improvident multiplication, and the consequent excessive difficulty of gaining a subsistence, will always continue, nor that the division of mankind into capitalists and hired labourers, and the regulation of the reward of labourers mainly by demand and supply, will be for ever, or even much longer, the rule of the world. But so long as competition is the general law of human life, it is tyranny to shut out one-half of the competitors. All who have attained the age of self-government have an equal claim to be permitted to sell whatever kind of useful labour they are capable of, for the price which it will bring.

The third objection to the admission of women to political or professional life, its alleged hardening tendency, belongs to an age now past, and is scarcely to be comprehended by people of the present time. There are still, however, persons who say that the world and its avocations render men selfish and unfeeling; that the struggles, rivalries, and collisions of business and of politics make them harsh and unamiable; that if half the species must unavoidably be given up to these things, it is the more necessary that the other half should be kept free from them; that to preserve women from the bad influences of the world, is the only chance of preventing men from being wholly given up to them.

There would have been plausibility in this argument when the world was still in the age of violence; when life was full of physical conflict, and every man had to redress his injuries or those of others, by the sword or by the strength of his arm. Women, like priests, by being exempted from such responsibilities, and from some part of the accompanying dangers, may have been enabled to exercise a beneficial influence. But in the present condition of human life, we do not know where those hardening influences are to be found, to which men are subject and from which women are at present exempt. Individuals now-a-days are seldom called upon to fight hand to hand, even with peaceful weapons; personal enmities and rivalries count for little in worldly transactions; the general pressure of circumstances, not the adverse will of individuals, is the obstacle men now have to make head against. That pressure, when excessive, breaks the spirit, and cramps and sours the feelings, but not less of women than of men, since they suffer certainly not less from its evils. There are still quarrels and dislikes, but the sources of them are changed. The feudal chief once found his bitterest enemy in his powerful neighbour, the minister or courtier in his rival for place: but opposition of interest in active life, as a cause of personal animosity, is out of date; the enmities of the present day arise not from great things but small, from what people say of one another, more than from what they do; and if there are hatred, malice, and all uncharitableness, they are to be found among women fully as much as among men. In the present state of civilization, the notion of guarding women from the hardening influences of the world, could only be realized by secluding them from society altogether. The common duties of common life, as at present constituted, are incompatible with any other softness in women than weakness. Surely weak minds in weak bodies must ere long cease to be even supposed to be either attractive or amiable.

But, in truth, none of these arguments and considerations touch the foundations of the subject. The real question is, whether it is right and expedient that one-half of the human race should pass through life in a state of forced subordination to the other half. If the best state of human society is that of being divided into two parts, one consisting of persons with a will and a substantive existence, the other of humble companions to these persons, attached, each of them to one, for the purpose of bringing up *his* children, and making *his* home pleasant to him; if this is the place assigned to women, it is but kindness to educate them for this; to make them believe that the greatest good fortune which can befall them, is to be chosen by some man for this purpose; and that every other career which the world deems happy or honourable, is closed to them by the law, not of social institutions, but of nature and destiny.

When, however, we ask why the existence of one-half the species should be merely ancillary to that of the other—why each woman should be a mere appendage to a man, allowed to have no interests of her own, that there may be nothing to compete in her mind with his interests and his pleasure; the only reason which can be given is, that men like it. It is agreeable to them that men should live for their own sake, women for the sake of men: and the qualities and conduct in subjects which are agreeable to rulers, they succeed for a long time in making the subjects themselves consider as their appropriate virtues. Helvetius has met with much obloquy for asserting, that persons usually mean by virtues the qualities which are useful or convenient to themselves. How truly this is said of mankind in general, and how wonderfully the ideas of virtue set afloat by the powerful, are caught and imbibed by those under their dominion, is exemplified by the manner in which the world were once persuaded that the supreme virtue of subjects was loyalty to kings, and are still persuaded that the paramount virtue of womanhood is loyalty to men. Under a nominal recognition of a moral code common to both, in practice self-will and self-assertion form the type of what are designated as manly virtues, while abnegation of self, patience, resignation, and submission to power, unless when resistance is commanded by other interests than their own, have been stamped by general consent as preeminently the duties and graces required of women. The meaning being merely, that power makes itself the centre of moral obligation, and that a man likes to have his own will, but does not like that his domestic companion should have a will different from his. . . .

NOTE

1. The truly horrible effects of the present state of the law among the lowest of the working population, is exhibited in those cases of hideous maltreatment of their wives by working men, with which every newspaper, every police report, teems. Wretches unfit to have the smallest authority over any living thing, have a helpless woman for their household slave. These excesses could not exist if women both earned, and had the right to possess, a part of the income of the family.

# 39        Marital Slavery and Friendship: John Stuart Mill's *The Subjection of Women*

MARY LYNDON SHANLEY

JOHN STUART MILL'S ESSAY *The Subjection of Women* was one of the nineteenth century's strongest pleas for opening to women opportunities for suffrage, education, and employment. Although hailed by women's rights activists in its own day, it was rarely treated with much seriousness by Mill scholars and political theorists until feminists, beginning in the 1970s, demonstrated the centrality of its themes for feminist theory and political thought. Many feminists have, however, been ambivalent about the legacy of *The Subjection of Women,* seeing in it a brief for "equal rights," and questioning the efficacy of merely striking down legal barriers against women as the way to establish equality between the sexes. Mill's failure to extend his critique of inequality to the division of labor in the household, and his confidence that most women would choose marriage as a "career," in this view, subverted his otherwise egalitarian impulses.[1]

While fully acknowledging the limitations of "equal rights feminism," I argue in this essay that *The Subjection of Women* was not solely about equal opportunity for women. It was also, and more fundamentally, about the corruption of male–female relationships and the hope of establishing friendship in marriage. Such friendship was not only desirable for emotional satisfaction, it was crucial if marriage were to become, as Mill desired, a "school of genuine moral sentiment."[2] The fundamental assertion of *The Subjection of Women* was not that equal opportunity would ensure the liberation of women, but that male–female equality, however achieved, was essential to marital friendship and to the progression of human society.

Mill's vision of marriage as a locus of sympathy and understanding between autonomous adults not only reforms our understanding of his feminism, but also draws attention to an often submerged or ignored aspect of liberal political thought. Liberal individualism is attacked by Marxists and neo-conservatives alike as wrongly encouraging the disintegration of affective bonds and replacing them with merely self-interested economic and contractual ties. Mill's essay, however, emphasizes the value of noninstrumental relationships in human life. His depictions of both corrupt and well-ordered marriage traces the relationship of family order to right political order.

His vision of marriage as a locus of mutual sympathy and understanding between autonomous adults stands as an unrealized goal for those who believe that the liberation of women requires not only formal equality of opportunity but measures which will enable couples to live in genuine equality, mutuality, and reciprocity.

## The Perversion of Marriage by the Master–Slave Relationship

Mill's reconstruction of marriage on the basis of friendship was preceded by one of the most devastating critiques of male domination in marriage in the history of Western philosophy. In *The Subjection of Women* Mill repeatedly used the language of "master and slave" or "master and servant" to describe the relationship between husband and wife. In the first pages of the book, Mill called the dependence of women on men "the primitive state of slavery lasting on." [3] Later he said that despite the supposed advances of Christian civilization, "the wife is the actual bond-servant of her husband: no less so, as far as legal obligation goes, than slaves commonly so called." [4] Still later he asserted that "there remain no legal slaves, except the mistress of every house." [5] The theme of women's servitude was not confined to *The Subjection of Women*. In his speech on the Reform Bill of 1867, Mill talked of that "obscure feeling" which members of parliament were "ashamed to express openly" that women had no right to care about anything except "how they may be the most useful and devoted servants of some man." [6] To Auguste Comte he wrote comparing women to "domestic slaves" and noted that women's capacities were spent "seeking happiness not in their own life, but exclusively in the favor and affection of the other sex, which is only given to them on the condition of their dependence." [7]

But what did Mill mean by denouncing the "slavery" of married women? How strongly did he wish to insist on the analogy between married women and chattel slaves? While middle-class Victorian wives were clearly not subject to the suffer-

ing of chattel slaves, Mill chose the image quite deliberately to remind his readers that by marriage a husband assumed legal control of his wife's property and her body. [8] The social and economic system gave women little alternative except to marry; once married, the legal personality of the woman was subsumed in that of her husband; and the abuses of human dignity—including rape—permitted by custom and law within marriage were egregious.

In Mill's eyes, women were in a double bind: they were not free within marriage, and they were not truly free not to marry. [9] What could an unmarried woman do? Even if she were of the middle or upper classes, she could not attend any of the English universities, and thus she was barred from a systematic higher education. If somehow she acquired a professional education, the professional associations usually barred her from practicing her trade. "No sooner do women show themselves capable of competing with men in any career, than that career, if it be lucrative or honorable, is closed to them." [10] Mill's depiction of the plight of Elinor Garrett, sister of Millicent Garrett Fawcett, the suffrage leader, is telling:

> A young lady, Miss Garrett, . . . studied the medical profession. Having duly qualified, she . . . knocked successively at all the doors through which, by law, access is obtained into the medical profession. Having found all other doors fast shut, she fortunately discovered one which had accidentally been left ajar. The Society of Apothecaries, it seems, had forgotten to shut out those who they never thought would attempt to come in, and through this narrow entrance this young lady found her way into the profession. But so objectionable did it appear to this learned body that women should be the medical attendants even of women, that the narrow wicket through which Miss Garrett entered has been closed after her. [11]

Working-class women were even worse off. In the *Principles of Political Economy*, Mill argued that their low wages were due to the "prejudice" of society which "making almost every woman, socially speaking, an appendage of some man, enables men to take systematically the lion's share of whatever belongs to both." A second cause of low wages for women was the surplus of female labor for unskilled jobs. Law and custom ordained that a woman has "scarcely any means open to her of gaining a livelihood, except as a wife and mother."[12] Marriage was, as Mill put it, a "Hobson's choice" for women, "that or none."[13]

Worse than the social and economic pressure to marry, however, was women's status within marriage. Mill thoroughly understood the stipulations of the English common law which deprived a married woman of a legal personality independent of that of her husband. The doctrine of coverture or spousal unity, as it was called, was based on the Biblical notion that "a man [shall] leave his father and his mother, and shall cleave to his wife, and they shall be one flesh" (Genesis 2:24). If "one flesh," then, as Blackstone put it, "by marriage, the husband and wife are one person in law." And that "person" was represented by the husband. Again Blackstone was most succinct: "The very being or legal existence of the woman is suspended during the marriage, or at least is incorporated and consolidated into that of the husband."[14] One of the most commonly felt injustices of the doctrine of spousal unity was the married woman's lack of ownership of her own earnings. As the matrimonial couple was "one person," the wife's earnings during marriage were owned and controlled by her husband.[15] During his term as a member of parliament, Mill supported a Married Women's Property Bill, saying that its opponents were men who thought it impossible for "society to exist on a harmonious footing between two persons unless one of them has absolute power over the other," and insisting that England has moved beyond such a "savage stage."[16] In *The Subjection of Women* Mill argued that the "wife's position under the common law of England [with respect to property] is worse than that of slaves in the laws of many countries: by the Roman law, for example, a slave might have his peculium, which to a certain extent the law guaranteed to him for his exclusive use."[17] Similarly, Mill regarded the husband's ex-

clusive guardianship over the married couple's children as a sign of the woman's dependence on her husband's will.[18] She was, in his eyes, denied any role in life except that of being "the personal body-servant of a despot."[19]

The most egregious aspects of both common and statute law, however, were those which sanctioned domestic violence. During the parliamentary debates on the Representation of the People Bill in 1867, Mill argued that women needed suffrage to enable them to lobby for legislation which would punish domestic assault:

> I should like to have a Return laid before this house of the number of women who are annually beaten to death, or trampled to death by their male protectors; and, in an opposite column, the amount of sentence passed. . . . I should also like to have, in a third column, the amount of property, the wrongful taking of which was . . . thought worthy of the same punishment. We should then have an arithmetical value set by a male legislature and male tribunals on the murder of a woman.[20]

But the two legal stipulations which to Mill most demonstrated "the assimilation of the wife to the slave" were her inability to refuse her master "the last familiarity" and her inability to obtain a legal separation from her husband unless he added desertion or extreme cruelty to his adultery. Mill was appalled by the notion that no matter how brutal a tyrant a husband might be, and no matter how a woman might loathe him, "he can claim from her and enforce the lowest degradation of a human being," which was to be made the instrument of "an animal function contrary to her inclination."[21] A man and wife being one body, rape was by definition a crime which a married man could not commit against his own wife. By law a wife could not leave her husband on account of this offense without being guilty of desertion, nor could she prosecute him. The most vicious form of male domination of women according to Mill was rape within marriage; it was particularly vicious because it was legal. Mill thus talked not of individual masters and wives as aberrations, but of a legally sanctioned system of domestic slavery which shaped the character of marriage in his day.[22]

Mill's depiction of marriage departed radically from the majority of Victorian portrayals of home and hearth. John Ruskin's praise of the home in *Sesame and Lilies* reflected the feelings and aspirations of many: "This is the true nature of home— it is the place of Peace; the shelter, not only from all injury, but from all terror, doubt and division. . . . It is a sacred place, a vestal temple, a temple of the hearth watched over by Household Gods."[23] Walter Houghton remarked that the title of Coventry Patmore's poem, *The Angel in the House,* captured "the essential character of Victorian love," and reflected "the exaltation of family life and feminine character" characteristic of the mid-nineteenth century.[24] James Fitzjames Stephen, who wrote that he disagreed with *The Subjection of Women* "from the first sentence to the last," found not only Mill's ideas but his very effort to discuss the dynamics of marriage highly distasteful. "There is something—I hardly know what to call it; indecent is too strong a word, but I may say unpleasant in the direction of indecorum—in prolonged and minute discussions about the relations between men and women, and the character of women as such."[25]

*The Subjection of Women* challenged much more than Victorian decorum, however; it was a radical challenge to one of the most fundamental and preciously held assumptions about marriage in the modern era, which is that it was a relationship grounded on the consent of the partners to join their lives. Mill argued to the contrary that the presumed consent of women to marry was not, in any real sense, a free promise, but one socially coerced by the lack of meaningful options. Further, the laws of marriage deprived a woman of many of the normal powers of autonomous adults, from controlling her earnings, to entering contracts, to defending her bodily autonomy by resisting unwanted sexual relations. Indeed, the whole notion of a woman "consenting" to the marriage "offer" of a man implied from the outset a hierarchical relationship. Such a one-way offer did not reflect the relationship which should exist between those who were truly equal, among beings who should be able to create together by free discussion and mutual agreement an association to govern their lives together.

In addition, Mill's view of marriage as slavery suggested a significantly more complicated and skeptical view of what constituted a "free choice" in society than did either his own earlier works or those of his liberal predecessors. Hobbes, for example, regarded men as acting "freely" even when moved by fear for their lives. Locke disagreed, but he in turn talked about the individual's free choice to remain a citizen of his father's country, as if emigration were a readily available option for all. In other of his works Mill himself seemed overly sanguine about the amount of real choice enjoyed, for example, by wage laborers in entering a trade. Yet Mill's analysis of marriage demonstrated the great complexity of establishing that any presumed agreement was the result of free volition, and the fatuousness of presuming that initial consent could create perpetual obligation. By implication, the legitimacy of many other relationships, including supposedly free wage and labor agreements and the political obligation of enfranchised and unenfranchised alike, was thrown into question. *The Subjection of Women* exposed the inherent fragility of traditional conceptualizations of free choice, autonomy, and self-determination so important to liberals, showing that economic and social structures were bound to limit and might coerce any person's choice of companions, employment, or citizenship.

Mill did not despair of the possibility that marriages based on true consent would be possible. He believed that some individuals even in his own day established such associations of reciprocity and mutual support. (He counted his own relationship with Harriet Taylor Mill as an example of a marriage between equals.)[26] But there were systematic impediments to marital equality. To create conditions conducive to a marriage of equals rather than one of master and slave, marriage law itself would have to be altered, women would have to be provided equal educational and employment opportunity, and both men and women would have to become capable of sustaining genuinely equal and reciprocal relationships within marriage. The last of these, in Mill's eyes, posed the greatest challenge.

## The Fear of Equality

Establishing legal equality in marriage and equality of opportunity would require, said Mill, that men sacrifice those political, legal, and economic advantages they enjoyed "simply by being born male." Mill therefore supported such measures as women's suffrage, the Married Women's Property Bills, the Divorce Act of 1857, the repeal of the Contagious Diseases Acts, and the opening of higher education and the professions to women. Suffrage, Mill contended, would both develop women's faculties through participation in civic decisions and enable married women to protect themselves from male-imposed injustices such as lack of rights to child custody and to control of their income. Access to education and jobs would give women alternatives to marriage. It would also provide a woman whose marriage turned out badly some means of self-support if separated or divorced. The Divorce Act of 1857, which established England's first civil divorce courts, would enable women and men to escape from intolerable circumstances (although Mill rightly protested the sexual double standard ensconced in the Act by which men might divorce their wives for adultery, but women had to prove their husbands were guilty of incest, bigamy or cruelty as well as adultery). And for those few women with an income of their own, a Married Women's Property Act would recognize their independent personalities and enable them to meet their husbands more nearly as equals.

However, Mill's analysis went further. He insisted that the subjection of women could not be ended by law alone, but only by law and the reformation of education, of opinion, of social inculcation, of habits, and finally of the conduct of family life itself. This was so because the root of much of men's resistance to women's emancipation was not simply their reluctance to give up their position of material advantage, but many men's fear of living with an equal. It was to retain marriage as "a law of despotism" that men shut all other occupations to women, Mill contended.[27] Men who "have a real antipathy to the equal freedom of women" were at bottom afraid "lest [women] should insist that marriage be on equal conditions."[28] One of Mill's central assertions in *The Subjection of Women* was that "[women's disabilities [in law] are only clung to in order to maintain their subordination in domestic life: *because the generality of the male sex cannot yet tolerate the idea of living with an equal*" (emphasis added).[29] The public discrimination against women was a manifestation of a disorder rooted in family relationships.

Mill did not offer any single explanation or account of the origin of men's fear of female equality. Elsewhere, he attributed the general human resistance to equality to the fear of the loss of privilege, and to apprehensions concerning the effect of levelling on political order.[30] But these passages on the fear of spousal equality bring to a twentieth-century mind the psychoanalytic works about human neuroses and the male fear of women caused by the infant boy's relationship to the seemingly all-powerful mother, source of both nurturance and love and of deprivation and punishment.[31] Mill's own account of the fear of equality was not psychoanalytic. He did, however, undertake to depict the consequences of marital inequality both for the individual psyche and for social justice. The rhetorical purpose of *The Subjection of Women* was not only to convince men that their treatment of women in law was unjust, but also that their treatment of women in the home was self-defeating, even self-destructive.

Women were those most obviously affected by the denial of association with men on equal footing. Women's confinement to domestic concerns was a wrongful "forced repression."[32] Mill shared Aristotle's view that participation in civic life was an enriching and ennobling activity, but Mill saw that for a woman, no spirited dimension to her life was possible. There was no impetus to consider with others the principles which were to govern their common life, no incentive to conform to principles which defined their mutual activity for the common good, no possibility for the self-development which comes from citizen activity.[33] The cost to women was obvious; they were dull or petty, or unprincipled.[34] The cost to men was less apparent but no less real; in seeking a reflection of themselves in the consciousness of these stunted women, men deceived, deluded, and limited themselves.

Mill was convinced that men were corrupted by their dominance over women. The most corrupting element of male domination of women was that men learned to "worship their own will as such a grand thing that it is actually the law for another rational being."[35] Such self-worship arises at a very tender age, and blots out a boy's natural understanding of himself and his relationship to others.

A boy may be "the most frivolous and empty or the most ignorant and stolid of mankind," but "by the mere fact of being born a male" he is encouraged to think that "he is by right the superior of all and everyone of an entire half of the human race: including probably some whose real superiority he has daily or hourly occasion to feel."[36] By contrast, women were taught "to live for others" and "to have no life but in their affections," and then further to confine their affections to "the men with whom they are connected, or to the children who constitute an additional indefeasible tie between them and a man."[37] The result of this upbringing was that what women would tell men was not, could not be, wholly true; women's sensibilities were systematically warped by their subjection. Thus the reflections were not accurate and men were deprived of self-knowledge.

The picture which emerged was strikingly similar to that which Hegel described in his passages on the relationship between master and slave in *The Phenomenology of Mind*.[38] The lord who sees himself solely as master, wrote Hegel, cannot obtain an independent self-consciousness. The master thinks he is autonomous, but in fact he relies totally upon his slaves, not only to fulfill his needs

and desires, but also for his identity: "Without slaves, he is no master." The master could not acquire the fullest self-consciousness when the "other" in whom he viewed himself was in the reduced human condition of slavery: to be *merely* a master was to fall short of full self-consciousness, and to define himself in terms of the "thing" he owns. So for Mill, men who have propagated the belief that all men are superior to all women have fatally affected the dialectic involved in knowing oneself through the consciousness others have of one. The present relationship between the sexes produced in men that "self-worship" which "all privileged persons, and all privileged classes" have had. That distortion deceived men and other privileged groups as to both their character and their self-worth.

No philosopher prior to Mill had developed such a sustained argument about the corrupting effects on men of their social superiority over and separation from women. Previous philosophers had argued either that the authority of men over women was natural (Aristotle, Grotius), or that while there was no natural dominance of men over women prior to the establishment of families, in any civil society such preeminence was necessary to settle the dispute over who should govern the household (Locke), or the result of women's consent in return for protection (Hobbes), or the consequence of the development of the sentiments of nurturance and love (Rousseau).[39] None had suggested that domestic arrangements might diminish a man's ability to contribute to public debates in the *agora* or to the rational governing of a democratic republic. Yet Mill was determined to show that the development of the species was held in check by that domestic slavery produced by the fear of equality, by spousal hierarchy, and by a lack of the reciprocity and mutuality of true friendship.

## The Hope of Friendship

Mill's remedy for the evils generated by the fear of equality was his notion of marital friendship. The topic of the rather visionary fourth chapter of *The Subjection of Women* was friendship, "the ideal of marriage."[40] That ideal was, according to Mill, "a union of thoughts and inclinations" which created a "foundation of solid friendship" between husband and wife.[41]

Mill's praise of marital friendship was almost lyrical, and struck resonances with Aristotle's, Cicero's, and Montaigne's similar exaltations of the pleasures as well as the moral enrichment of this form of human intimacy. Mill wrote:

> When each of two persons, instead of being a nothing, is a something; when they are attached to one another, and are not too much unlike to begin with; the constant partaking of the same things, assisted by their sympathy, draws out the latent capacities of each for being interested in the things . . . by a real enriching of the two natures, each acquiring the tastes and capacities of the other in addition to its own.[42]

This expansion of human capacities did not, however, exhaust the benefits of friendship. Most importantly, friendship developed what Montaigne praised as the abolition of selfishness, the capacity to regard another human being as fully as worthy as oneself. Therefore friendship of the highest order could only exist between those equal in excellence.[43] And for precisely this reason, philosophers from Aristotle to Hegel had consistently argued that women could not be men's friends, for women lacked the moral capacity for the highest forms of friendship. Indeed, it was common to distinguish the marital bond from friendship not solely on the basis of sexual and procreative activity, but also because women could not be part of the school of moral virtue which was found in friendship at its best.

Mill therefore made a most significant break with the past in adopting the language of friendship in his discussion of marriage. For Mill, no less than for any of his predecessors, "the true virtue of human beings is the fitness to live together as equals." Such equality required that individuals "[claim] nothing for themselves but what they as freely concede to everyone else," that they regard command of any kind as "an exceptional necessity," and that they prefer whenever possible "the society of those with whom leading and following can be alternate and reciprocal."[44] This picture of reciprocity, of the shifting of leadership according to need, was a remarkable characterization of family life. Virtually all of Mill's liberal contemporaries accepted the notion of the natural and inevitable complimentariness of male and female personalities and roles. Mill, however, as early as 1833 had expressed his belief that "the highest masculine and the highest feminine" characters were without any real distinction.[45] That view of the androgynous personality lent support to Mill's brief for equality within the family.

Mill repeatedly insisted that his society had no general experience of "the marriage relationship as it would exist between equals," and that such marriages would be impossible until men rid themselves of the fear of equality and the will to domination.[46] The liberation of women, in other words, required not just legal reform but a reeducation of the passions. Women were to be regarded as equals not only to fulfill the demand for individual rights and in order that they could survive in the public world of work, but also in order that women and men could form ethical relations of the highest order. Men and women alike had to "learn to cultivate their strongest sympathy with an equal in rights and in cultivation."[47] Mill struggled, not always with total success, to talk about the quality of such association. For example, in *On Liberty*, Mill explicitly rejected von Humbolt's characterization of marriage as a contractual relationship which could be ended by "the declared will of either party to dissolve it." That kind of dissolution was appropriate when the benefits of partnership could be reduced to monetary terms. But marriage involved a person's expectations for the fulfillment of a "plan of life," and created "a new series of moral obligations . . . toward that person, which may possibly be overruled, but cannot be ignored."[48] Mill was convinced that difficult though it might be to shape the law to recognize the moral imperatives of such a relationship, there were ethical communities which transcended and were not reducible to their individual components.

At this juncture, however, the critical force of Mill's essay weakened, and a tension developed between his ideal and his prescriptions for his own society. For all his insight into the dynamics of domestic domination and subordination, the only specific means Mill in fact put forward for the fostering of this society of equals was providing equal opportunity to women in areas outside the family. Indeed, in *On Liberty* he wrote that "nothing more is needed for the complete removal of [the almost despotic power of husbands over wives] than that wives should have the same rights and should receive the same protection of law in the same manner, as all other persons."[49] In the same vein, Mill seemed to suggest that nothing more was needed for women to achieve equality than that "the present duties and protective bounties in favour of men should be recalled."[50] Moreover, Mill did not attack the traditional assumption about men's and women's different responsibilities in an ongoing household, although he was usually careful to say that women "chose" their role or that it was the most "expedient" arrangement, not that it was theirs by "nature."

Mill by and large accepted the notion that once they marry, women should be solely responsible for the care of the household and children, men for providing the family income: "When the support of the family depends . . . on earnings, the common arrangement, by which the man earns the income and the wife superintends the domestic expenditure, seems to be in general the most suitable division of labour between the two persons."[51] He did not regard it as "a desirable custom, that the wife should contribute by her labour to the income of the family."[52] Mill indicated that women alone would care for any children of the marriage; repeatedly he called it the "care which . . . nobody else takes," the one vocation in which there is "nobody to compete with them." and the occupation which "cannot be fulfilled by others."[53] Further, Mill seemed to shut the door on combining household duties and a public life: "like a man when he chooses a profession, so, when a woman marries, it may be in general understood that she makes a choice of the manage-

ment of a household, and the bringing up of a family, as the first call upon her exertions . . . and that she renounces . . . all [other occupations] which are not consistent with the requirements of this."[54]

Mill's acceptance of the traditional gender-based division of labor in the family has led some critics to fault Mill for supposing that legal equality of opportunity would solve the problem of women's subjection, even while leaving the sexual division of labor in the household intact. For example, Julia Annas, after praising Mill's theoretical arguments in support of equality, complains that Mill's suggestions for actual needed changes in sex roles are "timid and reformist at best. He assumes that most women will in fact want only to be wives and mothers."[55] Leslie Goldstein agrees that "the restraints which Mill believed should be imposed on married women constitute a major exception to his argument for equality of individual liberty between the sexes—an exception so enormous that it threatens to swallow up the entire argument."[56] But such arguments, while correctly identifying the limitations of antidiscrimination statues as instruments for social change, incorrectly identify Mill's argument for equal opportunity as the conclusion of his discussion of male–female equality.[57] On the contrary, Mill's final prescription to end the subjection of women was not equal opportunity but spousal friendship; equal opportunity was a means whereby such friendship could be encouraged.

The theoretical force of Mill's condemnation of domestic hierarchy has not yet been sufficiently appreciated. Mill's commitment to equality in marriage was of a different theoretical order than his acceptance of a continued sexual division of labor. On the one hand, Mill's belief in the necessity of equality as a precondition to marital friendship was a profound theoretical tenet. It rested on the normative assumption that human relationships between equals were of a higher, more enriching order than those between unequals. Mill's belief that equality was more suitable to friendship than inequality was as unalterable as his conviction that democracy was a better system of government than despotism; the human spirit could not develop its fullest potential when living in absolute subordination to another human being or to government.[58] On the other hand, Mill's belief that friendship could be attained and sustained while women bore nearly exclusive responsibility for the home was a statement which might be modified or even abandoned if experience proved it to be wrong. In this sense it was like Mill's view that the question of whether socialism was preferable to capitalism could not be settled by verbal argument alone but must "work itself out on an experimental scale, by actual trial."[59] Mill believed that marital equality was a moral imperative; his view that such equality might exist where married men and women moved in different spheres of activity was a proposition subject to demonstration. Had Mill discovered that managing the household to the exclusion of most other activity created an impediment to the friendship of married women and men, *The Subjection of Women* suggests that he would have altered his view of practicable domestic arrangements, but not his commitment to the desirability of male–female friendship in marriage.

The most interesting shortcomings of Mill's analysis are thus not found in his belief in the efficacy of equal opportunity, but rather in his blindness to what other conditions might hinder or promote marital friendship. In his discussion of family life, for example, Mill seemed to forget his own warning that women could be imprisoned not only "by actual law" but also "by custom equivalent to law."[60] Similarly, he overlooked his own cautionary observation that in any household "there will naturally be more potential voice on the side, whichever it is, that brings the means of support."[61] And although he had brilliantly depicted the narrowness and petty concerns of contemporary women who were totally excluded from political participation, he implied that the mistresses of most households might content themselves simply with exercising the suffrage (were it to be granted), a view hardly consistent with his arguments in other works for maximizing the level of political discussion and participation whenever possible. More significantly, however,

Mill ignored the potential barrier between husband and wife which such different adult life experiences might create, and the contribution of shared experience to building a common sensibility and strengthening the bonds of friendship.

Mill also never considered that men might take any role in the family other than providing the economic means of support. Perhaps Mill's greatest oversight in his paean of marital equality was his failure to entertain the possibilities that nurturing and caring for children might provide men with useful knowledge and experience, and that shared parenting would contribute to the friendship between spouses which he so ardently desired. Similarly, Mill had virtually nothing to say about the positive role which sex might play in marriage. The sharp language with which he condemned undesired sexual relations as the execution of "an animal function" was nowhere supplemented by an appreciation of the possible enhancement which sexuality might add to marital friendship. One of the striking features of Montaigne's lyrical praise of friendship was that it was devoid of sensuality, for Montaigne abhorred "the Grecian license," and he was adamant that women were incapable of the highest forms of friendship. Mill's notion of spousal friendship suggested the possibility of a friendship which partook of both a true union of minds and of a physical expression of the delight in one's companion, a friendship which involved all of the human faculties. It was an opportunity which (undoubtedly to the relief of those such as James Fitzjames Stephen) Mill himself was not disposed to use, but which was nonetheless implicit in his praise of spousal friendship.[62]

One cannot ask Mill or any other theorist to "jump over Rhodes" and address issues not put forward by conditions and concerns of his own society.[63] Nevertheless, even leaving aside an analysis of the oppression inherent in the class structure (an omission which would have to be rectified in a full analysis of liberation), time has made it clear that Mill's prescriptions alone will not destroy the master–slave relationship which he so detested. Women's aspirations for equality will not be met by insuring equal civic rights and equal access to jobs outside the home. To accomplish that end would require a transformation of economic and public structures which would allow wives and husbands to share those domestic tasks which Mill assigned exclusively to women. In their absence it is as foolish to talk about couples choosing the traditional division of labor in marriage as it was in Mill's day to talk about women choosing marriage: both are Hobson's choices, there are no suitable alternatives save at enormous costs to the individuals involved.

Mill's feminist vision, however, transcends his own immediate prescriptions for reform. *The Subjection of Women* is not only one of liberalism's most incisive arguments for equal opportunity, but it embodies as well a belief in the importance of friendship for human development and progress. The recognition of individual rights is important in Mill's view because it provides part of the groundwork for more important human relationships of trust, mutuality and reciprocity. Mill's plea for an end to the subjection of women is not made, as critics such as Gertrude Himmelfarb assert, in the name of "the absolute primacy of the individual," but in the name of the need of both men and women for community. Mill's essay is valuable both for its devastating critique of the corruption of marital inequality, and for its argument, however incomplete, that one of the aims of a liberal polity should be to promote the conditions which will allow friendship, in marriage and elsewhere, to take root and flourish.

NOTES

1. Contemporary authors who criticize Mill's analysis of equal opportunity for women as not far-reaching enough are Julia Annas, "Mill and the Subjection of Women," *Philosophy*, 52, 1977, pp. 179–94; Leslie F. Goldstein, "Mill, Marx, and Women's Liberation," *Journal of the History of Philosophy*, 18, 1980, pp. 319–34; Richard Krouse, "Patriarchal Liberalism and Beyond: From John Stuart Mill to Harriet Taylor," in *The Family in Political Thought*, ed. Jean Bethke Elshtain (Amherst: University of Massachusetts Press, 1982), pp. 145–72; Susan Moller Okin, *Women in Western Political Thought* (Princeton: Princeton University Press,

1979). From a different perspective, Gertrude Himmelfarb, *On Liberty and Liberalism: The Case of John Stuart Mill* (New York: Alfred Knopf, 1974) criticizes Mill's doctrine of equality as being too absolute and particularly takes issue with modern feminist applications of his theory.

2. J. S. Mill, *The Subjection of Women* (1869) in *Essays on Sex Equality*, ed. Alice Rossi (Chicago: University of Chicago Press, 1970), ch. 2, p. 173.

3. Ibid., ch. 1, p. 130.

4. Ibid., ch. 2, p. 158.

5. Ibid., ch. 4, p. 217.

6. Hansard, *Parliamentary Debates*, series 3, vol. 187 (May 20, 1867), p. 820.

7. Letter to August Comte, October, 1843, in *The Collected Works of John Stuart Mill*, vol. XIII, *The Earlier Letters*, ed. Francis C. Mineka (Toronto: University of Toronto Press, 1963), p. 609, my translation.

8. For an assessment of black slave women's possession by their masters, see Jacqueline Jones, *Labor of Love, Labor of Sorrow: Black Women, Work, and the Family from Slavery to the Present* (New York: Basic Books, 1985).

9. Mill's analysis of women's choices of marriage as a state of life reminds one of Hobbes's discussion of some defeated soldier giving his consent to the rule of a conquering sovereign. Women, it is true, could decide which among several men to marry, while Hobbes's defeated yeoman had no choice of master. But what could either do but join the only protective association available to each?

10. Hansard, vol. 187 (May 20, 1867), p. 827.

11. Ibid. In the United States, one well-documented case in which a woman was prohibited from practicing law was *Bradwell v Illinois*, 83 US (16 Wall) 130 (1873).

12. J. S. Mill, *The Principles of Political Economy* (1848) in *Collected Works*, vol. II, p. 394, and vol. III, pp. 765–6.

13. *Subjection of Women*, ch. 1, p. 156. Tobias Hobson, a Cambridge carrier commemorated by Milton in two Epigraphs, would only hire out the horse nearest the door of his stable, even if a client wanted another. *Oxford English Dictionary*, II, p. 369.

14. William Blackstone, *Commentaries on the Laws of England* (4 vols, Oxford: Clarendon Press, 1765–69), Book I, ch XV, p. 430.

15. The rich found ways around the common law's insistence that the management and use of any income belonged to a woman's husband, by setting up trusts which were governed by the laws and courts of equity. A succinct explanation of the law of property as it affected married women in the nineteenth century is found in Erna Reiss, *Rights and Duties of Englishwomen* (Manchester: Sheratt and Hughes, 1934), pp. 20–34.

16. Hansard, vol 192 (June 10, 1868), p. 1371. Several Married Women's Property Bills, which would have given married women possession of their earnings, were presented in parliament beginning in 1857, but none was successful until 1870.

17. *Subjection of Women*, ch. 2, pp. 158–9.

18. Ibid., p. 160.

19. Ibid., p. 161.

20. Hansard, vol. 187 (May 20, 1867), p. 826.

21. *Subjection of Women*, ch. 2, pp. 160–1.

22. For a full discussion of the legal disabilities of married women in Mill's day see Mary Lyndon Shanley, *Feminism, Marriage and the Law in Victorian England, 1850–1895* (Princeton: Princeton University Press, 1989).

23. John Ruskin, "Of Queen's Gardens," in *Works*, ed. E. T. Cook and A. D. C. Wedderburn (39 vols. London: G. Allen, 1902–12), vol. XVIII, p. 122.

24. Walter E. Houghton, *The Victorian Frame of Mind* (New Haven: Yale University Press, 1957), p. 344.

25. James Fitzjames Stephen, *Liberty, Equality, Fraternity* (New York: Henry Holt, n.d.), p. 206.

26. On the relationship between John Stuart Mill and Harriet Taylor see F. A. Hayek, *John Stuart Mill and Harriet Taylor; Their Correspondence and Subsequent Marriage* (Chicago: University of Chicago Press, 1951); Michael St. John Packe, *The Life of John Stuart Mill* (New York: Macmillan, 1954); Alice Rossi, "Sentiment and Intellect," in *Essays on Sex Equality*, ed. Rossi; and Himmelfarb, *On Liberty and Liberalism*, pp. 187–238.

27. *Subjection of Women*, ch. 1, p. 156.

28. Ibid.

29. Ibid., ch. 3 p. 181.

30. For a discussion of Mill's views on equality generally, see Dennis Thompson, *John Stuart Mill and Representative Government* (Princeton: Princeton University Press, 1976), pp. 158–73.

31. For a reading of Mill from this perspective which challenges my own, see Christine Di Stefano, "Rereading J. S. Mill: Interpolations from the (M)Otherworld," in *Discontented Discourses: Feminism/Textual Intervention/Psychoanalysis*, ed. M. Barr and R. Feldstein (Urbana: University of Illinois Press, 1989). See also Linda Zerilli, *"Women" in Political Theory: Agents of Culture and Chaos* (Madison: University of Wisconsin, 1990).

32. *Subjection of Women*, ch. 1, p. 148.

33. See also Mill's *Considerations on Representative Government* (1861), in *Collected Works*, vol XIX, pp. 399–400, 411. During his speech on the Reform Bill of 1867, Mill argued that giving women the vote would provide "that stimulus to their faculties . . .

which the suffrage seldom fails to produce." Hansard, vol. 189 (May 20, 1867), p. 824.

34. *Subjection of Women*, ch. 2 p. 168, and ch. 4, p. 238.

35. Ibid., ch. 2, p. 172.

36. Ibid., ch. 4, p. 218.

37. Ibid., ch. 1, p. 141.

38. G. W. F. Hegel, *The Phenomenology of Mind*, trans. J. B. Baillie (New York: Harper and Row, 1969). This paragraph is indebted to the excellent study of the *Phenomenology* by Judith N. Shklar, *Freedom and Independence* (Cambridge: Cambridge University Press, 1976), from which the quote is taken, p. 61. Mill's analysis also calls to mind Simone de Beauvoir's discussion of "the Other" and its role in human consciousness in *The Second Sex*, trans. H. M. Parshley (New York: Random House, Vintage Books, 1974), pp. xix ff.

39. For studies of the views of each of these authors on women (except for Grotius) see Okin. Grotius' views can be found in his *De Juri Belli et Pacis Libri Tres (On the Law of War and Peace)* (1625), trans. Francis W. Kelsey (Oxford: Clarendon Press, 1925), Book II, ch. 5, section i, p. 231.

40. *Subjection of Women*, ch. 4. pp. 233, 235.

41. Ibid., pp. 231, 233.

42. Ibid., p. 233.

43. Montaigne's essay, "Of Friendship" in *The Complete Works of Montaigne*, trans. Donald M. Frame (Stanford: Stanford University Press, 1948), pp. 135–44.

44. *Subjection of Women*, ch. 4, pp. 174–5.

45. Letter to Thomas Carlyle, October 5, 1833, in *Collected Works*, vol. XII, *Earlier Letters*, p. 184.

46. Letter to John Nichol, August 1869, in *Collected Works*, vol. XVII, *The Later Letters*, ed. Francis C. Mineka and Dwight N. Lindley (Toronto: University of Toronto Press, 1972), p. 1634.

47. *Subjection of Women*, ch. 4, p. 236.

48. *Collected Works*, vol. XVIII, p. 300. Elsewhere Mill wrote, "My opinion on Divorce is that . . . nothing ought to be rested in, short of entire freedom on both sides to dissolve this like any other partnership" (letter to an unidentified correspondent, November 1855, *Collected Works*, vol. XIV, *Later Letters*, p. 500). But against this letter was the passage from *On Liberty*, and his letter to Henry Rusden of July 1870 in which he abjured making any final judgments about what a proper divorce law would be "until women have an equal voice in making it." He denied that he advocated that marriage should be dissoluble "at the will of either party," and stated that no well-grounded opinion could be put forward until women first achieved equality under the laws and in married life. *Collected Works*, vol. XVII, *Later Letters*, pp. 1750–1.

49. *Collected Works,* vol. XVIII, p. 301.

50. *Subjection of Women,* ch. 1, p. 154.

51. Ibid., ch. 2, p. 178.

52. Ibid., ch. 2, p. 179.

53. Ibid., ch. 2, p. 178; ch. 3, p. 183; ch. 4, p. 241.

54. Ibid., ch. 1, p. 179.

55. Annas, "Mill and the Subjection of Women," p. 189.

56. Goldstein, "Mill, Marx and Women's Liberation," p. 328.

57. Richard Krouse points out that Mill's own "ideal of a reformed family-life, based upon a full non-patriarchal marriage bond," requires "on the logic of his own analysis . . . [the] rejection of the traditional division of labor between the sexes." Krouse, "Patriarchal Liberalism," p. 39.

58. *Considerations on Representative Government,* in *Collected Works,* vol. XIX, pp. 399–403.

59. *Chapters on Socialism* (1879), in *Collected Works,* vol. V, p. 736.

60. *Subjection of Women,* ch. 4, p. 241.

61. Ibid., ch. 2, p. 170.

62. Throughout his writings Mill displayed a tendency to dismiss or deprecate the erotic dimension of life. In his *Autobiography* he wrote approvingly that his father looked forward to an increase in freedom in relations between the sexes, freedom which would be devoid of any sensuality "either of a theoretical or of a practical kind." His own 20-year friendship with Harriet Taylor before their marriage was "one of strong affection and confidential intimacy only." *Autobiography of John Stuart Mill* (New York: Columbia University Press, 1944), pp. 75, 161. In *The Principles of Political Economy* Mill remarked that in his own day "the animal instinct" occupied a "disproportionate preponderance in human life." *Collected Works,* vol. III, p. 766.

63. G. W. F. Hegel, *The Philosophy of Right,* ed. T. M. Knox (London: Oxford University Press, 1952), p. 11, quoted in Krouse, "Patriarchal Liberalism," p. 40.

# 40      Universal Love

MO TZU

## *Chapter 1*

IT IS THE BUSINESS OF THE SAGES to effect the good government of the world. They must know, therefore, whence disorder and confusion arise, for without this knowledge their object cannot be effected. We may compare them to a physician who undertakes to cure men's diseases:—he must ascertain whence a disease has arisen, and then he can assail it with effect, while, without such knowledge, his endeavors will be in vain. Why should we except the case of those who have to regulate disorder from this rule? They must know whence it has arisen, and then they can regulate it.

It is the business of the sages to effect the good government of the world. They must examine therefore into the cause of disorder; and when they do so they will find that it arises from the want of mutual love. When a minister and a son are not filial to their sovereign and their father, this is what is called disorder. A son loves himself, and does not love his father;—he therefore wrongs his father, and seeks his own advantage: a younger brother loves himself and does not love his elder brother;—he therefore wrongs his elder brother, and seeks his own advantage: a minister loves himself, and does not love his sovereign;—he therefore wrongs his sovereign, and seeks his own advantage:—all these are cases of what is called disorder. Though it be the father who is not kind to his son, or the elder brother who is not kind to his younger brother, or the sovereign who is not gracious to his minister:—the case comes equally under the general name of disorder. The father loves himself, and does not love his son:—he therefore wrongs his son, and seeks his own advantage: the elder brother loves himself, and does not love his younger brother;—he therefore wrongs his younger brother, and seeks his own advantage: the sovereign loves himself, and does not love his minister;—he therefore wrongs his minister, and seeks his own advantage. How do these things come to pass? They all arise from the want of mutual love. Take the case of any thief or robber:—it is just the same with him. The thief loves his own house, and does not love his neighbour's house:—he therefore steals from his neighbour's house to benefit his own: the robber loves his own person, and does not love his neighbour;—he therefore does violence to his neighbour to benefit himself. How is this? It all arises from the want of mutual love. Come to the case of great officers throwing each other's Families into confusion, and of princes attacking one another's States:—it is just the same with them. The great officer loves his own Family, and does not love his neighbour's;—he therefore throws the neighbour's Family into disorder to benefit his own: the prince loves his own State, and does not love his neighbour's;—he therefore attacks his neighbour's State to benefit his own. All disorder in the kingdom has the same explanation. When we examine into the cause of it, it is found to be the want of mutual love.

Suppose that universal, mutual love prevailed throughout the kingdom;—if men loved others as they love themselves, disliking to exhibit what was unfilial. . . . And moreover would there be those who were unkind? Looking on their sons, younger brothers, and ministers as themselves, and disliking to exhibit what was unkind . . . the want of filial duty would disappear. And would there be thieves and robbers? When every man regarded his neighbour's house as his own, who would be found to steal? When everyone regarded his neighbour's person as his own, who would be found to rob? Thieves and robbers would disappear. And would there be great officers throwing one another's Families into confusion, and princes attacking one another's States? When officers re-garded the families of others as their own, what one would make confusion? When princes regarded other States as their own, what one would begin an attack? Great officers throwing one another's Families into confusion, and princes attacking one another's States, would disappear.

If, indeed, universal, mutual love prevailed throughout the kingdom; one State not attacking another, and one Family not throwing another into confusion; thieves and robbers nowhere existing; rulers and ministers, fathers and sons, all being filial and kind:—in such a condition the nation would be well governed. On this account, how many sages, whose business it is to effect the good government of the kingdom, do but prohibit hatred and advise to love? On this account it is affirmed that universal mutual love throughout the country will lead to its happy order, and that mutual hatred leads to confusion. This was what our master, the philosopher Mo, meant, when he said, "We must above all inculcate the love of others."

## Chapter II

Our Master, the philosopher Mo, said, "That which benevolent men consider to be incumbent on them as their business, is to stimulate and promote all that will be advantageous to the nation, and to take away all that is injurious to it. This is what they consider to be their business."

And what are the things advantageous to the nation, and the things injurious to it? Our master said, "The mutual attacks of State on State; the mutual usurpation of Family on Family; the mutual robberies of man on man; the want of kindness on the part of the ruler and of loyalty on the part of the minister; the want of tenderness and filial duty between father and son and of harmony between brothers:—these, and such as these, are the things injurious to the kingdom."

And from what do we find, on examination, that these injurious things are produced? Is it not from the want of mutual love?

Our Master said, "Yes, they are produced by the want of mutual love. Here is a prince who only knows to love his own State, and does not love his neighbour's;—he therefore does not shrink from raising all the power of his State to attack his neighbour. Here is the chief of a Family who only knows to love it, and does not love his neighbour's;—he therefore does not shrink from raising all his powers to seize on that other Family. Here is a man who only knows to love his own person, and does not love his neighbour's;—he therefore does not shrink from using all his resources to rob his neighbour. Thus it happens, that the princes, not loving one another, have their battle-fields; and the chiefs of Families, not loving one another, have their mutual usurpations; and men, not loving one another, have their mutual robberies; and rulers and ministers, not loving one another, become unkind and disloyal; and fathers and sons, not loving one another, lose their affection and filial duty; and brothers, not loving one another, contract irreconcilable enmities. Yea, men in general not loving one another, the strong make prey of the weak; the rich do despite to the poor; the noble are insolent to the mean; and the deceitful impose upon the stupid. All the miseries, usurpations, enmities, and hatreds in the world, when traced to their origin, will be found to arise from the want of mutual love. On this account, the benevolent condemn it."

They may condemn it; but how shall they change it?

Our Master said, "They may change it by the law of universal mutual love and by the interchange of mutual benefits."

How will this law of universal mutual love and the interchange of mutual benefits accomplish this?

Our Master said, "It would lead to the regarding another's kingdom as one's own: another's family as one's own: another's person as one's own. That being the case, the princes, loving one another, would have no battle-fields; the chiefs of families, loving one another, would attempt no usurpations; men, loving one another, would commit no robberies; rulers and ministers, loving one another, would be gracious and loyal; fathers and sons, loving one another, would be kind and filial; brothers, loving one another, would be harmonious and easily reconciled. Yea, men in general loving one another, the strong would not make prey of the weak; the many would not plunder the few; the rich would not insult the poor; the noble would not be insolent to the mean; and the deceitful would not impose upon the simple. The way in which all the miseries, usurpations, enmities, and hatreds in the world, may be made not to arise, is universal mutual love. On this account, the benevolent value and praise it."

Yes; but the scholars of the kingdom and superior men say, "True; if there were this universal love, it would be good. It is, however, the most difficult thing in the world."

Our Master said, "This is because the scholars and superior men simply do not understand the advantageousness of the law, and to conduct their reasonings upon that. Take the case of assaulting a city, or of a battle-field, or of the sacrificing one's life for the sake of fame:—this is felt by the people everywhere to be a difficult thing. Yet, if the ruler be pleased with it, both officers and people are able to do it:—how much more might they attain to universal mutual love, and the interchange of mutual benefits, which is different from this! When a man loves others, they respond to and love him; when a man benefits others, they respond to and benefit him; when a man injures others, they respond to and injure him; when a man hates others, they respond to and hate him:—what difficulty is there in the matter? It is only that rulers will not carry on the government on this principle, and so officers do not carry it out in their practice. . . ."

Yes; but now the officers and superior men say, "Granted; the universal practice of mutual love would be good; but it is an impracticable thing. It is like taking up the T'ai mountain, and leaping with it over the Ho or the Chi."

Our Master said, "That is not the proper comparison for it. To take up the T'ai mountain and leap with it over the Ho or the Chi, may be called an exercise of most extraordinary strength; it is, in fact, what no one, from antiquity to the present time, has ever been able to do. But how widely different from this is the practice of universal mutual love, and the interchange of mutual benefits!

"Anciently, the sage kings practised this. . . ."

If, now, the rulers of the kingdom truly and sincerely wish all in it to be rich, and dislike any being poor; if they desire its good government, and dislike disorder; they ought to practise universal mutual love, and the interchange of mutual benefits. This was the law of the sage kings; it is the way to effect the good government of the nation; it may not but be striven after.

## Chapter III

Our Master, the philosopher Mo, said, "The business of benevolent men requires that they should strive to stimulate and promote what is advantageous to the kingdom, and to take away what is injurious to it."

Speaking, now, of the present time, what are to be accounted the most injurious things to the kingdom? They are such as the attacking of small States by great ones; the inroads on small Families by great ones; the plunder of the weak by the strong; the oppression of the few by the many; the scheming of the crafty against the simple; the insolence of the noble to the mean. To the same class belong the ungraciousness of rulers, and the disloyalty of ministers; the unkindness of fathers, and the want of filial duty on the part of sons. Yea, there is to be added to these the conduct of the mean men, who employ their edged weapons and poisoned stuff, water and fire, to rob and injure one another.

Pushing on the inquiry now, let us ask whence all these injurious things arise. Is it from loving others and advantaging others? It must be answered "No"; and it must likewise be said, "They arise clearly from hating others and doing violence to others." If it be further asked whether those who hate and do violence to others hold the principle of loving all, or that of making distinctions, it must be replied, "They make distinctions." So then, it is the principle of making distinctions between man and man, which gives rise to all that is most injurious in the kingdom. On this account we conclude that the principle is wrong.

Our Master said, "He who condemns others must have means whereby to change them." To condemn men, and have no means of changing them, is like saving them from fire by plunging them in water. A man's language in such a case must be improper. On this account our Master said, "There is the principle of loving all, to take the place of that which makes distinctions." If, now, we ask, "And how is it that universal love can change the consequences of that other principle which makes distinctions?" the answer is, "If princes were as much for the States of others as for their own, what one among them would raise the forces of his State to attack that of another?—he is for that other as much as for himself. If they were for the capitals of others as much as for their own, what one would raise the forces of his capital to attack that of another?—he is for that as much as for his own. If chiefs regarded the families of others as their own, what one would lead the power of his Family to throw that of another into confusion?—he is for that other as much as for himself. If, now, States did not attack, nor holders of capitals smite, one another, and if Families were guilty of no mutual aggressions, would this be injurious to the kingdom, or its benefit? It must be replied, "This would be advantageous to the kingdom." Pushing on the inquiry, now, let us ask whence all these benefits arise. Is it from hating others and doing violence to others? It must be answered, "No"; and it must likewise be said, "They arise clearly from loving others and doing good to others." If it be further asked whether those who love others and do good to others hold the principle of making distinctions between man and man, or that of loving all, it must be replied, "They love all." So then it is this principle of universal mutual love which really gives rise to all that is most beneficial to the nation. On this account we conclude that that principle is right.

Our Master said, a little while ago, "The business of benevolent men requires that they should strive to stimulate and promote what is advantageous to the kingdom, and to take away what is injurious to it." We have now traced the subject up, and found that it is the principle of universal love which produces all that is most beneficial to the kingdom, and the principle of making distinctions which produces all that is injurious to it. On this account what our Master said, "The principle of making distinctions between man and man is wrong, and the principle of universal love is right," turns out to be correct as the sides of a square.

If, now, we just desire to promote the benefit of the kingdom, and select for that purpose the principle of universal love, then the acute ears and piercing eyes of people will hear and see for one another; and the strong limbs of people will move and be ruled for one another; and men of principle will instruct one another. It will come about that the old, who have neither wife nor children, will get supporters who will enable them to complete their years; and the young and weak, who have no parents, will yet find helpers that shall bring them up. On the contrary, if this principle of universal love is held not to be correct, what benefits will arise from such a view? What can be the reason that the scholars of the kingdom, whenever they hear of this principle of universal love, go on to condemn it? Plain as the case is, their words in condemnation of this principle do not stop;—they say "It may be good, but how can it be carried into practice?"

Our Master said, "Supposing that it could not be practiced, it seems hard to go on likewise to condemn it. But how can it be good, and yet incapable of being put into practice?"

Let us bring forward two instances to test the matter—Let anyone suppose the case of two individuals, the one of whom shall hold the principle of making distinctions, and the other shall hold the principle of universal love. The former of these will say, "How can I be for the person of my friend as much as for my own person? How can I be for the parents of my friend as much as for my own parents?" Reasoning in this way, he may see his friend hungry, but he will not feed him; cold, but he will not clothe him; sick, but he will not nurse him; dead, but he will not bury him. Such will be the language of the individual holding the principle of distinction, and such will be his conduct. He will say, "I have heard that he who wishes to play a lofty part among men, will be for the person of his friend as much as for his own person, and for the parents of his friend as much as for his

own parents. It is only thus that he can attain his distinction?" Reasoning in this way, when he sees his friend hungry, he will feed him; cold, he will clothe him; sick, he will nurse him; dead, he will bury him. Such will be the language of him who holds the principle of universal love, and such will be his conduct.

The words of the one of these individuals are a condemnation of those of the other, and their conduct is directly contrary. Suppose now that their words are perfectly sincere, and that their conduct will be carried out,—that their words and actions will correspond like the parts of a token, every word being carried into effect; and let us proceed to put the following questions on the case:—Here is a plain in the open country, and an officer, with coat of mail, gorget, and helmet, is about to take part in a battle to be fought in it, where the issue, whether for life or death, cannot be foreknown; or here is an officer about to be dispatched on a distant commission from Pa to Yüeh, or from Ch'i to Ching, where the issue of the journey, going and coming, is quite uncertain—on either of these suppositions, to whom will the officer entrust the charge of his house, the support of his parents, and the care of his wife and children?—to one who holds the principle of universal love? or to one who holds that which makes distinctions? I apprehend there is no one under heaven, man or woman, however stupid, though he may condemn the principle of universal love, but would at such a time make one who holds it the subject of his trust. This is in words to condemn the principle, and when there is occasion to choose between it and the opposite, to approve it;—words and conduct are here in contradiction. I do not know how it is that throughout the kingdom scholars condemn the principle of universal love, whenever they hear it.

Plain as the case is, their words in condemnation of it do not cease, but they say, "This principle may suffice perhaps to guide in the choice of an officer, but it will not guide in the choice of a sovereign."

Let us test this by taking two illustrations:—Let anyone suppose the case of two sovereigns, the one of whom shall hold the principle of mutual love, and the other shall hold the principle which makes distinctions. In this case, the latter of them will say, "How can I be as much for the persons of all my people as for my own? This is much opposed to human feelings. The life of man upon the earth is but a very brief space; it may be compared to the rapid movement of a team of horses whirling past a small chink." Reasoning in this way, he may see his people hungry, but he will not feed them; cold, but he will not clothe them; sick, but he will not nurse them; dead, but he will not bury them. Such will be the language of the sovereign who holds the principle of distinctions, and such will be his conduct. Different will be the language and conduct of the other who holds the principle of universal love. He will say, "I have heard that he who would show himself a virtuous and intelligent sovereign, ought to make his people the first consideration, and think of himself only after them." Reasoning in this way, when he sees any of the people hungry, he will feed them; cold he will clothe them; sick, he will nurse them; dead, he will bury them. Such will be the language of the sovereign who holds the principle of universal love, and such his conduct. If we compare the two sovereigns, the words of the one are condemnatory of those of the other, and their actions are opposite. Let us suppose that their words are equally sincere, and that their actions will make them good—that their words and actions will correspond like the parts of a token, every word being carried into effect; and let us proceed to put the following questions on the case:—Here is a year when a pestilence walks abroad among the people; many of them suffer from cold and famine; multitudes die in the ditches and water-channels. If at such a time they might make an election between the two sovereigns whom we have supposed, which would they prefer? I apprehend there is no one under heaven, however stupid, though he may condemn the principle of universal love, but would at such a time prefer to be under the sovereign who holds it. This is in words to condemn the principle, and, when there is occasion to choose between it and the opposite, to approve it;—words and conduct are here in contradiction. . . .

. . . How is that the scholars throughout the kingdom condemn this universal love, whenever they hear of it? Plain as the case is, the words of those who condemn the principle of universal love do not cease. They say, "It is not advantageous to the entire devotion to parents which is required:—it is injurious to filial piety." Our Master said, "Let us bring this objection to the test:—A filial son, having the happiness of his parents at heart, considers how it is to be secured. Now, does he, so considering, wish men to love and benefit his parents? or does he wish them to hate and injure his parents?" On this view of the question, it must be evident that he wishes men to love and benefit his parents. And what must he himself first do in order to gain this object? If I first address myself to love and benefit men's parents, will they for that return love and benefit to my parents? or if I first address myself to hate men's parents, will they for that return love and benefit to my parents? It is clear that I must first address myself to love and benefit men's parents, and they will return to me love and benefit to my parents. The conclusion is that a filial son has no alternative.—He must address himself in the first place to love and do good to the parents of others. If it be supposed that this is an accidental course, to be followed on emergency by a filial son, and not sufficient to be regarded as a general rule, let us bring it to the test to what we find in the Books of the ancient kings.—It is said in the Ta Ya,

> Every word finds its answer;
> Every action its recompense
> He threw me a peach;
> I returned him a plum.

These words show that he who loves others will be loved, and that he who hates others will be hated. How is it that the scholars throughout the kingdom condemn the principle of universal love, when they hear it?. . . .

. . . And now, as to universal mutual love, it is an advantageous thing and easily practiced—beyond all calculation. The only reason why it is not practised is, in my opinion, because superiors do not take pleasure in it. If superiors were to take pleasure in it, stimulating men to it by rewards and praise, and awing them from opposition to it by punishments and fines, they would, in my opinion, move to it—the practice of universal mutual love, and the interchange of mutual benefits—as fire rises upwards, and as water flows downwards:—nothing would be able to check them. This universal love was the way of the sage kings; it is the principle to secure peace for kings, dukes, and great men; it is the means to secure plenty of food and clothes for the myriads of the people. The best course for the superior man is to well understand the principle of universal love, and to exert himself to practice it. It requires the sovereign to be gracious, and the minister to be loyal; the father to be kind and the son to be filial; the elder brother to be friendly, and the younger to be obedient. Therefore the superior man,—with whom the chief desire is to see gracious sovereigns and loyal ministers; kind fathers and filial sons; friendly elder brothers and obedient younger ones—ought to insist on the indispensableness of the practice of universal love. It was the way of the sage kings; it would be the most advantageous thing for the myriads of the people.

## Recommended Readings

### TEXTS

Berger, Fred. *Happiness, Justice and Freedom.* Berkeley: University of California Press, 1985.

Brittain, Karl. *John Stuart Mill.* Harmondsworth: Penguin, 1953.

Donner, Wendy. *The Liberal Self: John Stuart Mill's Moral and Political Philosophy.* Ithaca, NY: Cornell University Press, 1991.

Gorowitz, S., ed. *Utilitarianism and Critical Essays.* Indianapolis: Bobbs-Merrill, 1971.

Gray, John. *Mill on Liberty: A Defence.* London: Routledge, 1983.

Plamenatz, John. *The English Utilitarians.* Oxford: Blackwell, 1949.

Radcliff, Peter, ed. *Limits of Liberty.* Belmont, CA: Wadsworth, 1966.

Ryan, Alan. *Mill.* London: Routledge, 1974.

Thomas, William. *J. S. Mill.* Oxford University Press, 1985.

### FEMINIST PERSPECTIVE

Annas, Julia. "Mill and the Subjection of Women," *Philosophy* 52 (1977).

Boralevi, Lea Campos. "Utilitarianism and Feminism." In *Women in Western Political Philosophy,* edited by Ellen Kennedy and Susan Mendus. Brighton: Wheatsheaf Books, 1987.

Held, Virginia. "Justice and Harriet Taylor." *The Nation* (October 25, 1971): 405–406.

Mill, John Stuart, and Harriet Taylor. *Essays on Sex Equality,* edited by Alice S. Rossi. Chicago: University of Chicago Press, 1970.

Morales, Maria. *Perfect Equality: John Stuart Mill on Well-Constituted Communities.* New York: Rowman and Littlefield, 1996.

### MULTICULTURAL PERSPECTIVE

DeGrazia, Sebastian, ed. *Masters of Chinese Political Thought.* New York: Viking Press, 1973.

Thomas, Edward. *Chinese Political Thought.* New York: Greenwood Press, 1968.

# X

## *Marx and Engels*

## Introduction

K ARL MARX WAS BORN IN TRIER in the Rhineland, then part of Prussia, in 1818. His father, a well-known lawyer, became a Christian to avoid the restrictions then being placed on Jews in Germany. In 1835, Marx went to the University of Bonn to study law, transferring first to Berlin and then to Jena. There, he received a doctorate for his thesis on the ancient Greek atomists. Barred from a university position for his liberal political views, Marx became an editor for a newspaper in Cologne, which was soon suppressed by the Prussian government. In 1842, he married Jenny von Westphen, whom he had courted for several years and in whose honor he had written three volumes of poetry. In 1843, Marx moved to Paris to edit a new journal. There, he began his lifelong collaboration with Friedrich Engels.

Engels was born in 1820 in Barmen, a village in the Rhineland. Family financial reversals forced him to interrupt his liberal education and take a position in one of his father's commercial firms in England. In 1844, Engels visited Paris and contributed two articles to the journal Marx was editing in Paris.

Working together, Marx and Engels completed *German Ideology* in 1846, and they published *The Communist Manifesto* in 1848. After the 1848 French Revolution, Marx was forced to leave Paris and went to London, which was to become his home for the rest of his life. Marx's financial situation in London was desperate for many years. He had no regular source of income except what Engels was able to provide. By 1856, three of Marx's six children had died. In 1867, Marx published the first volume of *Das Kapital (Capital)*. Marx's *Critique of the Gotha Program* was published by Engels in 1891. In 1883, Marx died and was buried next to his wife, who had died two years earlier. Engels died in 1895.

Engels referred to *The Origin of the Family, Private Property, and the State* as "the execution of a bequest," and "a debt I owe to Marx." In the winter of 1880–1881, Marx had read Lewis Morgan's *Ancient Society or Researches in the Lines of Human Progress from Savagery, Through Barbarism to Civilization* (1877) and was struck by its relevance to his own view. However, ill health prevented him from doing more than taking ninety-eight pages of notes on Morgan's work. Engels worked from these notes and, in 1884, published the book that Marx had apparently wished to write.

In *The Communist Manifesto,* Marx and Engels maintain that the abolition of bourgeois property and bourgeois family structure is a necessary first requirement for building a society based upon the political ideal of equality. In *Critique of the Gotha Program,* Marx provides a much more positive view of what is required. In such a society, Marx claims, the distribution of social goods must conform, at least initially, to the principle "from each according to his ability, to each according to his contribution." But when the highest stage of communist society has been reached, Marx adds, distribution will conform to the principle "from each according to his ability, to each according to his need."

In *The Origin of the Family, Private Property, and the State,* Engels claims that women's oppression originated in the introduction of private property, an institution that obliterated whatever equality the human community had previously enjoyed. Private ownership of the means of production by relatively few persons, originally all male, inaugurated a class system whose contemporary manifestations are corporate capitalism and imperialism. Reflection on this state of affairs suggests that even more than patriarchy (those large social systems that privilege men over women), capitalism is the cause of women's oppression. If all women, not just the relatively privileged or exceptional ones, are ever to be liberated, the capitalist system must be replaced by a socialist system in which the means of production belong to one and all. Because, under socialism, no one would be economically dependent on anyone else, women would be economically freed from men. So freed, Engels claims, women would enter into sexual relations and/or marriage relations with men for one reason only: their own desire to do so.

In "The Unhappy Marriage of Marxism and Feminism: Towards a More Progressive Union," Heidi Hartmann maintains that although the categories of Marxist analysis—for example, "class," "reserve army of labor," "wage laborer"—help explain the generation of a particular occupational structure, they leave unexplained why it is *women* rather than men who play the subordinate and submissive roles both in the workplace and in the home. If we are to understand women's relation to men as well as workers' relation to capital, says Hartmann, a Marxist analysis of capitalism needs to be complemented with a feminist analysis of patriarchy. Through the sexual division of labor, patriarchy maintains the subordinate status of women both in the workplace and in the home. In a workplace that is divided into high-paying, male-dominated jobs and low-paying, female-dominated jobs, women earn $.70 for every $1.00 men earn. In the home, working women (but not working men) experience the stresses and strains of the "double day." Study after study shows that the husbands of working women do not do much more work around the house than the husbands of stay-at-home housewives. Hartmann concludes that men's desire to control women is at least as strong as capital's desire to control workers. Capitalism and patriarchy must be fought simultaneously.

In "Buddhist Economics," E. F. Schumacher contrasts modern economics with what he calls Buddhist economics. The contrast is primarily with capitalist economics since it is in capitalism that work is seen primarily as a means to income and not as rewarding in itself. But there is a contrast with Marxist economics as well because neither Marxism nor capitalism distinguished between renewable and nonrenewable resources, nor has either faced the issue of long-term sustainability.

# 41    The Communist Manifesto

KARL MARX AND FRIEDRICH ENGELS

A SPECTRE IS HAUNTING EUROPE—the spectre of Communism. All the Powers of old Europe have entered into a holy alliance to exorcise this spectre: Pope and Czar, Metternich and Guizot, French Radicals and German police-spies.

Where is the party in opposition that has not been decried as Communistic by its opponents in power? Where is the Opposition that has not hurled back the branding reproach of Communism, against the more advanced opposition parties, as well as against its reactionary adversaries?

Two things result from this fact.

I. Communism is already acknowledged by all European Powers to be itself a Power.

II. It is high time that Communists should openly, in the face of the whole world, publish their views, their aims, their tendencies, and meet this nursery tale of the Spectre of Communism with a Manifesto of the party itself. . . .

## The Communist Program

The Communists do not form a separate party opposed to other working-class parties.

They have no interests separate and apart from those of the proletariat as a whole.

They do not set up any sectarian principles of their own, by which to shape and mould the proletarian movement.

The Communists are distinguished from the other working-class parties by this only: (1) In the national struggles of the proletarians of the different countries, they point out and bring to the front the common interests of the entire proletariat, independently of all nationality. (2) In the various stages of development which the struggle of the working class against the bourgeoisie has to pass through they always and everywhere represent the interests of the movement as a whole.

The Communists, therefore, are on the one hand, practically, the most advanced and resolute section of the working-class parties of every country, that section which pushes forward all others; on the other hand, theoretically, they have over the great mass of the proletariat the advantage of clearly understanding the line of march, the conditions, and the ultimate general results of the proletarian movement.

The immediate aim of the Communists is the same as that of all the other proletarian parties: formation of the proletariat into a class, overthrow of the bourgeois supremacy, conquest of political power by the proletariat.

The theoretical conclusions of the Communists are in no way based on ideas or principles that have been invented, or discovered, by this or that would-be universal reformer.

They merely express, in general terms, actual relations springing from an existing class struggle, from a historical movement going on under our very eyes. The abolition of existing property relations is not at all a distinctive feature of Communism.

All property relations in the past have continually been subject to historical change consequent upon the change in historical conditions.

The French Revolution, for example, abolished feudal property in favour of bourgeois property.

The distinguishing feature of Communism is not the abolition of property generally, but the abolition of bourgeois property. But modern bourgeois private property is the final and most complete expression of the system of producing and appropriating products, that is based on class antagonisms, on the exploitation of the many by the few.

In this sense, the theory of the Communists may be summed up in the single sentence: Abolition of private property.

We Communists have been reproached with the desire of abolishing the right of personally acquiring property as the fruit of man's own labour, which property is alleged to be the groundwork of all personal freedom, activity and independence.

Hard-won, self-acquired, self-earned property! Do you mean the property of the petty artisan and of the small peasant, a form of property that preceded the bourgeois form? There is no need to abolish that; the development of industry has to a great extent already destroyed it, and is still destroying it daily.

Or do you mean modern bourgeois private property?

But does wage-labour create any property for the labourer? Not a bit. It creates capital, *i.e.,* that kind of property which exploits wage-labour, and which cannot increase except upon condition of begetting a new supply of wage-labour for fresh exploitation. Property, in its present form, is based on the antagonism of capital and wage-labour. Let us examine both sides of this antagonism.

To be capitalist, is to have not only a purely personal, but a social *status* in production. Capital is a collective product, and only by the united action of many members, nay, in the last resort, only by the united action of all members of society, can it be set in motion.

Capital is, therefore, not a personal, it is a social power.

When, therefore, capital is converted into common property, into the property of all members of society, personal property is not thereby transformed into social property. It is only the social character of the property that is changed. It loses its class-character.

Let us now take wage-labour.

The average price of wage-labour is the minimum wage, *i.e.,* that quantum of the means of subsistence, which is absolutely requisite to keep the labourer in bare existence as a labourer. What, therefore, the wage-labourer appropriates by means of his labour, merely suffices to prolong and reproduce a bare existence. We by no means intend to abolish this personal appropriation of the products of labour, an appropriation that is made for the maintenance and reproduction of human life, and that leaves no surplus wherewith to command the labour of others. All that we want to do away with, is the miserable character of this appropriation, under which the labourer lives merely to increase capital, and is allowed to live only in so far as the interest of the ruling class requires it.

In bourgeois society, living labour is but a means to increase accumulated labour. In Communist society, accumulated labour is but a means to widen, to enrich, to promote the existence of the labourer.

In bourgeois society, therefore, the past dominates the present; in Communist society, the present dominates the past. In bourgeois society capital is independent and has individuality, while the living person is dependent and has no individuality.

And the abolition of this state of things is called by the bourgeois, abolition of individuality and freedom! And rightly so. The abolition of bourgeois independence, and bourgeois freedom is undoubtedly aimed at.

By freedom is meant, under the present bourgeois conditions of production, free trade, free selling and buying.

But if selling and buying disappears, free selling and buying disappears also. This talk about free selling and buying, and all the other "brave words" of our bourgeoisie about freedom in general, have a meaning, if any, only in contrast with restricted selling and buying, with the fettered traders of the Middle Ages, but have no meaning when opposed to the Communistic abolition of buying and selling, of the bourgeois conditions of production, and of the bourgeoisie itself.

You are horrified at our intending to do away with private property. But in your existing society, private property is already done away with for nine-tenths of the population; its existence for the few is solely due to its non-existence in the hands of those nine-tenths. You reproach us, therefore, with intending to do away with a form of property, the necessary condition for whose existence is the non-existence of any property for the immense majority of society.

In one word, you reproach us with intending to do away with your property. Precisely so; that is just what we intend.

From the moment when labour can no longer be converted into capital, money, or rent, into a social power capable of being monopolised, *i.e.*, from the moment when individual property can no longer be transformed into bourgeois property, into capital, from that moment, you say, individuality vanishes.

You must, therefore, confess that by "individual" you mean no other person than the bourgeois, than the middle-class owner of property. This person must, indeed, be swept out of the way, and made impossible.

Communism deprives no man of the power to appropriate the products of society; all that it does is to deprive him of the power to subjugate the labour of others by means of such appropriation.

It has been objected that upon the abolition of private property all work will cease, and universal laziness will overtake us.

According to this, bourgeois society ought long ago to have gone to the dogs through sheer idleness; for those of its members who work, acquire nothing, and those who acquire anything, do not work. The whole of the objection is but another expression of the tautology: that there can no longer be any wage-labour when there is no longer any capital.

All objections urged against the Communistic mode of producing and appropriating material products, have, in the same way, been urged against the Communistic modes of producing and appropriating intellectual products. Just as, to the bourgeois, the disappearance of class property is the disappearance of production itself, so the disappearance of class culture is to him identical with the disappearance of all culture.

That culture, the loss of which he laments, is, for the enormous majority, a mere training to act as a machine.

But don't wrangle with us so long as you apply, to our intended abolition of bourgeois property, the standard of your bourgeois notions of freedom, culture, law, [and so on]. Your very ideas are but the outgrowth of the conditions of your bourgeois production and bourgeois property, just as your jurisprudence is but the will of your class made into a law for all, a will, whose essential character and direction are determined by the economical conditions of existence of your class.

The selfish misconception that induces you to transform into eternal laws of nature and reason, the social forms springing from your present mode of production and form of property—historical relations that rise and disappear in the progress of production—this misconception you share with every ruling class that has preceded you. What you see clearly in the case of ancient property, what you admit in the case of feudal property, you are of course forbidden to admit in the case of your own bourgeois form of property.

Abolition of the family! Even the most radical flare up at this infamous proposal of the Communists.

On what foundation is the present family, the bourgeois family, based? On capital, on private gain. In its completely developed form this family exists only among the bourgeoisie. But this state of things finds its complement in the practical absence of the family among the proletarians, and in public prostitution.

The bourgeois family will vanish as a matter of course when its complement vanishes, and both will vanish with the vanishing of capital.

Do you charge us with wanting to stop the exploitation of children by their parents? To this crime we plead guilty.

But, you will say, we destroy the most hallowed of relations, when we replace home education by social.

And your education! Is not that also social, and determined by the social conditions under which you educate, by the intervention, direct or indirect, of society, by means of schools, [and so on]? The Communists have not invented the intervention of society in education; they do but seek to alter the character of that intervention, and to rescue education from the influence of the ruling class.

The bourgeois clap-trap about the family and education, about the hallowed co-relation of parent and child, becomes all the more disgusting, the more, by the action of Modern Industry, all family ties among the proletarians are torn asunder, and their children transformed into simple articles of commerce and instruments of labour.

But you Communists would introduce community of women, screams the whole bourgeoisie in chorus.

The bourgeois sees in his wife a mere instrument of production. He hears that the instruments of production are to be exploited in common, and, naturally, can come to no other conclusion than that the lot of being common to all will likewise fall to the women.

He has not even a suspicion that the real point aimed at is to do away with the status of women as mere instruments of production.

For the rest, nothing is more ridiculous than the virtuous indignation of our bourgeois at the community of women which, they pretend, is to be openly and officially established by the Communists. The Communists have no need to introduce community of women; it has existed almost from time immemorial.

Our bourgeois, not content with having the wives and daughters of their proletarians at their disposal, not to speak of common prostitutes, take the greatest pleasure in seducing each other's wives.

Bourgeois marriage is in reality a system of wives in common and thus, at the most, what the Communists might possibly be reproached with, is that they desire to introduce, in substitution for a hypocritically concealed, an openly legalised community of women. For the rest, it is self-evident that the abolition of the present system of production must bring with it the abolition of the community of women springing from that system, *i.e.,* of prostitution both public and private.

The Communists are further reproached with desiring to abolish countries and nationality.

The working men have no country. We cannot take from them what they have not got. Since the proletariat must first of all acquire political supremacy, must rise to be the leading class of the nation, must constitute itself *the* nation, it is, so

far, itself national, though not in the bourgeois sense of the word.

National differences and antagonisms between peoples are daily more and more vanishing, owing to the development of the bourgeoisie, to freedom of commerce, to the world-market, to uniformity in the mode of production and in the conditions of life corresponding thereto.

The supremacy of the proletariat will cause them to vanish still faster. United action, of the leading civilised countries at least, is one of the first conditions for the emancipation of the proletariat.

In proportion as the exploitation of one individual by another is put an end to, the exploitation of one nation by another will also be put an end to. In proportion as the antagonism between classes within the nation vanishes, the hostility of one nation to another will come to an end.

The charges against Communism made from a religious, a philosophical, and, generally, from an ideological standpoint, are not deserving of serious examination.

Does it require deep intuition to comprehend that man's ideas, views, and conceptions, in one word, man's consciousness, changes with every change in the conditions of his material existence, in his social relations and in his social life?

What else does the history of ideas prove, than that intellectual production changes its character in proportion as material production is changed? The ruling ideas of each age have ever been the ideas of its ruling class.

When people speak of ideas that revolutionise society, they do but express the fact, that within the old society, the elements of a new one have been created, and that the dissolution of the old ideas keeps even pace with the dissolution of the old conditions of existence.

When the ancient world was in its last throes, the ancient religions were overcome by Christianity. When Christian ideas succumbed in the 18th century to rationalist ideas, feudal society fought its death battle with the then revolutionary bourgeoisie. The ideas of religious liberty and freedom of conscience merely gave expression to the sway of free competition within the domain of knowledge.

"Undoubtedly," it will be said, "religious, moral, philosophical and juridical ideas have been modified in the course of historical development. But religion, morality, philosophy, political science, and law, constantly survived this change."

"There are, besides, eternal truths, such as Freedom, Justice, etc., that are common to all states of society. But Communism abolishes eternal truths, it abolishes all religion, and all morality, instead of constituting them on a new basis; it therefore acts in contradiction to all past historical experience."

What does this accusation reduce itself to? The history of all past society has consisted in the development of class antagonisms, antagonisms that assumed different forms at different epochs.

But whatever form they may have taken, one fact is common to all past ages, *viz.*, the exploitation of one part of society by the other. No wonder, then, that the social consciousness of past ages, despite all the multiplicity and variety it displays, moves within certain common forms, or general ideas, which cannot completely vanish except with the total disappearance of class antagonisms.

The Communist revolution is the most radical rupture with traditional property relations; no wonder that its development involves the most radical rupture with traditional ideas.

But let us have done with the bourgeois objections to Communism.

We have seen above, that the first step in the revolution by the working class, is to raise the proletariat to the position of ruling class, to win the battle of democracy.

The proletariat will use its political supremacy to wrest, by degrees, all capital from the bourgeoisie, to centralise all instruments of production in the hands of the State, *i.e.*, of the proletariat organised as the ruling class; and to increase the total of production forces as rapidly as possible.

Of course, in the beginning, this cannot be effected except by means of despotic inroads on the rights of property, and on the conditions of bourgeois production; by means of measures, there-fore, which appear economically insufficient and untenable, but which, in the course of the movement, outstrip themselves, necessitate further inroads upon the old social order, and are unavoidable as a means of entirely revolutionising the mode of production.

These measures will of course be different in different countries.

Nevertheless in the most advanced countries, the following will be pretty generally applicable.

1. Abolition of property in land and application of all rents of land to public purposes.
2. A heavy progressive or graduated income tax.
3. Abolition of all right of inheritance.
4. Confiscation of the property of all emigrants and rebels.
5. Centralisation of credit in the hands of the State, by means of a national bank with State capital and an exclusive monopoly.
6. Centralisation of the means of communication and transport in the hands of the State.
7. Extension of factories and instruments of production owned by the State; the bringing into cultivation of waste-lands, and the improvement of the soil generally in accordance with a common plan.
8. Equal liability of all to labour. Establishment of industrial armies, especially for agriculture.
9. Combination of agriculture with manufacturing industries; gradual abolition of the distinction between town and country, by a more equable distribution of the population over the country.
10. Free education for all children in public schools. Abolition of children's factory labour in its present form. Combination of education with industrial production [and so on].

When, in the course of development, class distinctions have disappeared, and all production has been concentrated in the hands of a vast association of the whole nation, the public power will lose its political character. Political power, properly so called, is merely the organised power of one class for oppressing another. If the proletariat during its contest with the bourgeoisie is compelled, by the force of circumstances, to organise itself as a class, if, by means of a revolution, it makes itself the ruling class, and, as such, sweeps away by force the old conditions of production, then it will, along with these conditions, have swept away the conditions for the existence of class antagonisms and of classes generally, and will thereby have abolished its own supremacy as a class.

In place of the old bourgeois society, with its classes and class antagonisms, we shall have an association, in which the free development of each is the condition for the free development of all. . . .

# 42     Critique of the Gotha Program

KARL MARX

IN PRESENT-DAY SOCIETY, the instruments of labour are the monopoly of the capitalist class; the resulting dependence of the working class is the cause of misery and servitude in all its forms.

This sentence, borrowed from the Statutes of the International, is incorrect in this "improved" edition.

In present-day society the instruments of labour are the monopoly of the landowners (the monopoly of property in land is even the basis of the monopoly of capital) *and* the capitalists. In the passage in question, the Statutes of the International do not mention by name either the one or the other class of monopolists. They speak of the "*monopoly of the means of labour, that is the sources of life.*" The addition, "*sources of life*" makes it sufficiently clear that land is included in the instruments of labour.

The correction was introduced because Lassalle, for reasons now generally known, attacked *only* the capitalist class and not the landowners. In England, the capitalist is usually not even the owner of the land on which his factory stands.

The emancipation of labour demands the promotion of the instruments of labour to the common property of society, and the co-operative regulation of the total labour with equitable distribution of the proceeds of labour.

"Promotion of the instruments of labour to the common property" ought obviously to read, their "conversion into the common property," but this only in passing.

What are the "proceeds of labour"? The product of labour or its value? And in the latter case, is it the total value of the product or only that part of the value which labour has newly added to the value of the means of production consumed?

The "proceeds of labour" is a loose notion which Lassalle has put in the place of definite economic conceptions.

What is "equitable distribution"?

Do not the bourgeois assert that the present-day distribution is "equitable"? And is it not, in fact, the only "equitable" distribution on the basis of the present-day mode of production? Are economic relations regulated by legal conceptions or do not, on the contrary, legal relations arise from economic ones? Have not also the socialist sectarians the most varied notions about "equitable" distribution?

To understand what idea is meant in this connection by the phrase "equitable distribution," we must take the first paragraph and this one together. The latter implies a society wherein "the instruments of labour are common property, and the total labour is co-operatively regulated," and from the first paragraph we learn that "the proceeds of labour belong undiminished with equal right to all members of society."

"To all members of society"? To those who do not work as well? What remains then of the "undiminished proceeds of labour"? Only to those members of society who work? What remains then of the "equal right" of all members of society?

But "all members of society" and "equal right" are obviously mere phrases. The kernel consists in this, that in this communist society every worker must receive the "undiminished" Lassallean "proceeds of labour."

Let us take first of all the words "proceeds of labour" in the sense of the product of labour, then the co-operative proceeds of labour are the *total social product*.

From this is then to be deducted:

*First,* cover for replacement of the means of production used up.

*Secondly,* additional portion for expansion of production.

*Thirdly,* reserve or insurance fund to provide against mis-adventures, disturbances through natural events, etc.

These deductions from the "undiminished proceeds of labour" are an economic necessity and their magnitude is to be determined by available means and forces, and partly by calculation of probabilities, but they are in no way calculable to equity.

There remains the other part of the total product, destined to serve as means of consumption.

Before this is divided among the individuals, there has to be deducted from it:

*First, the general costs of administration not belonging to production.*

This part will, from the outset, be very considerably restricted in comparison with present-day society and it diminishes in proportion as the new society develops.

*Secondly, that which is destined for the communal satisfaction of needs, such as schools, health services, etc.*

From the outset this part is considerably increased in comparison with present-day society and it increases in proportion as the new society develops.

*Thirdly, funds for those unable to work, etc.,* in short, what is included under so-called official poor relief today.

Only now do we come to the "distribution" which the programme, under Lassallean influence, alone has in view in its narrow fashion, namely that part of the means of consumption which is divided among the individual producers of the co-operative society.

The "undiminished proceeds of labour" have already quietly become converted into the "diminished" proceeds, although what the producer is deprived of in his capacity as a private individual benefits him directly or indirectly in his capacity as a member of society.

Just as the phrase "undiminished proceeds of labour" has disappeared, so now does the phrase "proceeds of labour" disappear altogether.

Within the co-operative society based on common ownership of the means of production, the producers do not exchange their products; just as little does the labour employed on the products appear here *as the value* of these products, as a material quality possessed by them, since now, in contrast to capitalist society, individual labour no longer exists in an indirect fashion but directly as a component part of the total labour. The phrase "proceeds of labour," objectionable even today on account of its ambiguity, thus loses all meaning.

What we have to deal with here is a communist society, not as it has *developed* on its own foundations, but, on the contrary, as it *emerges* from capitalist society; which is thus in every respect, economically, morally and intellectually, still stamped with the birthmarks of the old society from whose womb it emerges. Accordingly the individual producer receives back from society—after the deductions have been made—exactly what he gives to it. What he has given to it is his individual amount of labour. For example, the social working day consists of the sum of the individual labour hours; the individual labour time of the individual producer is the part of the social labour day contributed by him, his share in it. He receives a certificate from society that he has furnished such and such an amount of labour (after deducting his labour for the common fund), and with this certificate he draws from the social stock of means of consumption as much as the same amount of labour costs. The same amount of labour which he has given to society in one form, he receives back in another.

Here obviously the same principle prevails as that which regulates the exchange of commodities, as far as this is exchange of equal values. Content and form are changed, because under the altered circumstances no one can give anything except his labour, and because, on the other hand, nothing can pass into the ownership of individuals except individual means of consumption. But, as far as the distribution of the latter among the individual producers is concerned, the same principle prevails as in the exchange of commodity-equivalents, so much labour in one form is exchanged for an equal amount of labour in another form.

Hence, *equal right* here is still in principle—*bourgeois right*, although principle and practice are no longer in conflict, while the exchange of equivalents in commodity exchange only exists on the *average* and not in the individual case.

In spite of this advance, this *equal right* is still stigmatised by a bourgeois limitation. The right of the producers is *proportional* to the labour they supply; the equality consists in the fact that measurement is made with an *equal standard,* labour.

But one man is superior to another physically or mentally and so supplies more labour in the same time, or can labour for a longer time; and labour, to serve as a measure, must be defined by its duration or intensity, otherwise it ceases to be a standard of measurement. This *equal* right is an unequal right for unequal labour. It recognises no class differences, because everyone is only a worker like everyone else; but it tacitly recognises unequal individual endowment and thus productive capacity as natural privileges. *It is therefore a right of inequality in its content, like every right.* Right by its very nature can only consist in the application of an equal standard; but unequal individuals (and they would not be different individuals if they were not unequal) are only measurable by an equal standard in so far as they are brought under an equal point of view, are taken from one *definite* side only, *e.g.,* in the present case are regarded *only as workers,* and nothing more seen in them, everything else being ignored. Further, one worker is married, another not; one has more children than another and so on and so forth. Thus with an equal output, and hence an equal share in the social consumption fund, one will in fact receive more than another, one will be richer than another, and so on. To avoid all these defects, right, instead of being equal, would have to be unequal.

But these defects are inevitable in the first phase of communist society as it is when it has just emerged after prolonged birth pangs from capitalist society. Right can never be higher than the economic structure of society and the cultural development thereby determined.

In a higher phase of communist society, after the enslaving subordination of individuals under division of labour, and therewith also the antithesis between mental and physical labour, has vanished; after labour, from a mere means of life, has itself become the prime necessity of life; after the productive forces have also increased with the all-round development of the individual, and all the springs of co-operative wealth flow more abundantly—only then can the narrow horizon of bourgeois right be fully left behind and society inscribe on its banners: from each according to his ability, to each according to his needs!

I have dealt more at length with the "undiminished proceeds of labour" on the one hand, and with "equal right" and "equitable distribution" on the other, in order to show what a crime it is to attempt, on the one hand, to force on our party again, as dogmas, ideas which in a certain period had some meaning but have now become obsolete rubbishy phrases, while on the other, perverting the realistic outlook, which has cost so much effort to instill into the party, but which has now taken root in it, by means of ideological nonsense about "right" and other trash common among the democrats and French Socialists.

Quite apart from the analysis so far given, it was in general incorrect to make a fuss about so-called "*distribution*" and put the principal stress on it.

The distribution of the means of consumption at any time is only a consequence of the distribution of the conditions of production themselves. The latter distribution, however, is a feature of the mode of production itself. The capitalist mode of production, for example, rests on the fact that the material conditions of production are in the hands of non-workers in the form of property in capital and land, while the masses are only owners of the personal condition of production, *viz.,* labour power. Once the elements of production are so distributed, then the present-day distribution of the means of consumption results automatically. If the material conditions of production are the co-operative property of the workers themselves, then this likewise results in a different distribution of the means of consumption from the present one. Vulgar socialism (and from it in turn a section of democracy) has taken over from the bourgeois economists the consideration and treatment of distribution as independent of the mode of production and hence the presentation of socialism as turning principally on distribution. After the real position has long been made clear, why go back again?

# 43 The Origin of the Family, Private Property, and the State

FRIEDRICH ENGELS

THE STUDY OF PRIMITIVE HISTORY reveals conditions where the men live in polygamy and their wives in polyandry at the same time, and their common children are therefore considered common to them all—and these conditions in their turn undergo a long series of changes before they finally end in monogamy. The trend of these changes is to narrow more and more the circle of people comprised within the common bond of marriage, which was originally very wide, until at last it includes only the single pair, the dominant form of marriage today.

Reconstructing thus the past history of the family, Morgan, in agreement with most of his colleagues, arrives at a primitive stage when unrestricted sexual freedom prevailed within the tribe, every woman belonging equally to every man and every man to every woman. . . .

According to Morgan, from this primitive state of promiscuous intercourse there developed, probably very early:

## 1. The Consanguine Family, the First Stage of the Family

Here the marriage groups are separated according to generations: all the grandfathers and grandmothers within the limits of the family are all husbands and wives of one another; so are also their children, the fathers and mothers; the latter's children will form a third circle of common husbands and wives; and their children, the great-grandchildren of the first group, will form a fourth. In this form of marriage, therefore, only ancestors and progeny, and parents and children, are excluded from the rights and duties (as we should say) of marriage with one another. Brothers and sisters, male and female cousins of the first, second, and more remote degrees, are all brothers and sisters of one another, and *precisely for that reason* they are all husbands and wives of one another. At this stage the relationship of brother and sister also includes as a matter of course the practice of sexual intercourse with one another. In its typical form, such a family would consist of the descendants of a single pair, the descendants of these descendants in each generation being again brothers and sisters, and therefore husbands and wives, of one another.

The consanguine family is extinct. Even the most primitive peoples known to history provide no demonstrable instance of it. But that it *must* have existed, we are compelled to admit; for the Hawaiian system of consanguinity still prevalent today throughout the whole of Polynesia expresses degrees of consanguinity which could only arise in this form of family; and the whole subsequent development of the family presupposes the existence of the consanguine family as a necessary preparatory stage.

## 2. The Punaluan Family

If the first advance in organization consisted in the exclusion of parents and children from sexual intercourse with one another, the second was the exclusion of sister and brother. On account of the greater nearness in age, this second advance was infinitely more important, but also more difficult, than the first. It was effected gradually, beginning probably with the exclusion from sexual intercourse of one's own brothers and sisters (children of the same mother) first in isolated cases and then by degrees as a general rule (even in this century exceptions were found in Hawaii), and ending with the prohibition of marriage even between collateral brothers and sisters, or, as we should say,

between first, second, and third cousins. It affords, says Morgan, "a good illustration of the operation of the principle of natural selection." There can be no question that the tribes among whom inbreeding was restricted by this advance were bound to develop more quickly and more fully than those among whom marriage between brothers and sisters remained the rule and the law. How powerfully the influence of this advance made itself felt is seen in the institution which arose directly out of it and went far beyond it—the gens, which forms the basis of the social order of most, if not all, barbarian peoples of the earth and from which in Greece and Rome we step directly into civilization.

After a few generations at most, every original family was bound to split up. The practice of living together in a primitive communistic household which prevailed without exception till late in the middle stage of barbarism set a limit, varying with the conditions but fairly definite in each locality, to the maximum size of the family community. As soon as the conception arose that sexual intercourse between children of the same mother was wrong, it was bound to exert its influence when the old households split up and new ones were founded (though these did not necessarily coincide with the family group). One or more lines of sisters would form the nucleus of the one household and their own brothers the nucleus of the other. It must have been in some such manner as this that the form which Morgan calls the punaluan family originated out of the consanguine family. According to the Hawaiian custom, a number of sisters, natural or collateral (first, second or more remote cousins) were the common wives of their common husbands, from among whom, however, their own brothers were excluded. These husbands now no longer called themselves brothers, for they were no longer necessarily brothers, but *punalua*—that is, intimate companion, or partner. Similarly, a line of natural or collateral brothers had a number of women, *not* their sisters, as common wives, and these wives called one another *punalua*. This was the classic form of family structure [*Familienformation*], in which later a number of variations was possible, but whose essential feature was the mutually common possession of husbands and wives within a definite family circle, from which, however, the brothers of the wives—first one's own and later also collateral—and conversely also the sisters of the husbands, were excluded. . . .

In all forms of group family, it is uncertain who is the father of a child; but it is certain who its mother is. Though she calls *all* the children of the whole family her children and has a mother's duties toward them, she nevertheless knows her own children from the others. It is therefore clear that in so far as group marriage prevails, descent can only be proved on the *mother's* side and that therefore only the *female* line is recognized. And this is in fact the case among all peoples in the period of savagery or in the lower stage of barbarism. . . .

If we now take one of the two standard groups of the punaluan family, namely a line of natural and collateral sisters (that is, one's own sisters' children in the first, second or more remote degree), together with their children and their own collateral brothers on the mother's side (who, according to our assumption, are *not* their husbands), we have the exact circle of persons whom we later find as members of a gens, in the original form of that institution. They all have a common ancestral mother, by virtue of their descent from whom the female offspring in each generation are sisters. The husbands of these sisters, however, can no longer be their brothers and therefore cannot be descended from the same ancestral mother; consequently, they do not belong to the same consanguine group, the later gens. The children of these sisters, however, do belong to this group, because descent on the mother's side alone counts, since it alone is certain. As soon as the ban had been established on sexual intercourse between all brothers and sisters, including the most remote collateral relatives on the mother's side, this group transformed itself into a gens—that is, it constituted itself as a firm circle of blood relations in the female line between whom marriage was prohibited; and henceforward by other common institutions of a social and religious character, it increasingly consolidated and differentiated itself from the other gentes of the same tribe (more of this later). When we see, then, that the development of the gens follows, not only necessarily, but also perfectly naturally from the punaluan family, we may reasonably infer that at one time this form of family almost certainly existed among all peoples among whom the presence of gentile institutions can be proved—that is, practically all barbarians and civilized peoples. . . .

## 3. The Pairing Family

A certain amount of pairing, for a longer or shorter period, already occurred in group marriage or even earlier; the man had a chief wife among his many wives (one can hardly yet speak of a favorite wife), and for her he was the most important among her husbands. This fact has contributed considerably to the confusion of the missionaries, who have regarded group marriage sometimes as promiscuous community of wives, sometimes as unbridled adultery. But these customary pairings were bound to grow more stable as the gens developed and the classes of "brothers" and "sisters" between whom marriage was impossible became more numerous. The impulse given by the gens to the prevention of marriage between blood relatives extended still further. Thus among the Iroquois and most of the other Indians at the lower stage of barbarism, we find that marriage is prohibited between *all* relatives enumerated in their system—which includes several hundred degrees of kinship. The increasing complication of these prohibitions made group marriages more and more impossible; they were displaced by the *pairing family*. In this stage, one man lives with one woman, but the relationship is such that polygamy and occasional infidelity remain the right of the men, even though for economic reasons polygamy is rare, while from the woman the strictest fidelity is generally demanded throughout the time she lives with the man and adultery on her part is cruelly punished. The marriage tie can, however, be easily dissolved by either partner; after separation, the children still belong as before to the mother alone. . . .

Thus the history of the family in primitive times consists in the progressive narrowing of the circle, originally embracing the whole tribe, within which the two sexes have a common conjugal relation. The continuous exclusion, first of nearer, then of more and more remote relatives, and at last even of relatives of marriage, ends by making any kind of group marriage practically impossible. Finally, there remains only the single, still loosely linked pair, the molecule with whose dissolution marriage itself ceases. This in itself shows what a small part individual sex love, in the modern sense of the word, played in the rise of monogamy. Yet stronger proof is afforded by the practice of all peoples at this stage of development. Whereas in the earlier forms of the family, men never lacked women but, on the contrary, had too many rather than too few, women had now become scarce and highly sought after. Hence it is with the pairing marriage that there begins the capture and purchase of women—widespread *symptoms,* but no more than symptoms, of the much deeper change that had occurred. . . .

The pairing family, itself too weak and unstable to make an independent household necessary or even desirable, in no ways destroys the communistic household inherited from earlier times. Communistic housekeeping, however, means the supremacy of women in the house; just as the exclusive recognition of the female parent, owing to the impossibility of recognizing the male parent with certainty, means that the women—the mothers—are held in high respect. One of the most absurd notions taken over from 18th century enlightenment is that in the beginning of society woman was the slave of man. Among all savages and all barbarians of the lower and middle stages, and to a certain extent of the upper stage also, the position of women is not only free, but honorable. As to what it still is in the pairing marriage, let us hear the evidence of Ashur Wright, for many years missionary among the Iroquois Senecas:

As to their family system, when occupying the old long houses [communistic households comprising several families], it is probable that some one clan [gens] predominated, the women taking in husbands, however, from the other clans [gentes]. . . . Usually, the female portion ruled the house. . . . The stores were in common; but woe to the luckless husband or lover who was too shiftless to do his share of the providing. No matter how many children, or whatever goods he might have in the house, he might at any time be ordered to pick up his blanket and budge; and after such orders it would not be healthful for him to attempt to disobey. The house would be too hot for him; and . . . he must retreat to his own clan [gens]; or, as was often done, go and start anew matrimonial alliance in some other. The women were the great power among the clans [gentes]; as everywhere else. They did not hesitate, when occasion required, "to knock off the horns," as it was technically called, from the head of a chief, and send him back to the ranks of the warriors.

The communistic household, in which most or all of the women belong to one and the same gens, while the men came from various gentes, is the material foundation of that supremacy of the women which was general in primitive times, and which it is Bachofen's third great merit to have discovered. The reports of travelers and missionaries, I may add, to the effect that women among savages and barbarians are overburdened with work in no way contradict what has been said. The division of labor between the two sexes is determined by quite other causes than by the position of woman in society. Among peoples where the women have to work far harder than we think suitable, there is often much more real respect for women than among our Europeans. The lady of civilization, surrounded by false homage and estranged from all real work, has an infinitely lower social position than the hard-working woman of barbarism, who was regarded among her people as a real lady (lady, *frowa, Frau*—mistress) and who was also a lady in character. . . .

The first beginnings of the pairing family appear on the dividing line between savagery and barbarism; they are generally to be found already at the upper stage of savagery, but occasionally not until the lower stage of barbarism. The pairing family is the form characteristic of barbarism, as group marriage is characteristic of savagery and monogamy of civilization. To develop it further, to strict monogamy, other causes were required than those we have found active hitherto. In the single pair the group was already reduced to its final unit, its two-atom molecule: one man and one woman. Natural selection, with its progressive exclusions from the marriage community, had accomplished its task; there was nothing more for it to do in this direction. Unless new, *social* forces came into play, there was no reason why a new form of family should arise from the single pair. But these new forces did come into play.

We now leave America, the classic soil of the pairing family. No sign allows us to conclude that a higher form of family developed here or that there was ever permanent monogamy anywhere in America prior to its discovery and conquest. But not so in the Old World.

Here the domestication of animals and the breeding of herds had developed a hitherto unsuspected source of wealth and created entirely new social relations. Up to the lower stage of barbarism, permanent wealth had consisted almost solely of house, clothing, crude ornaments and the tools for obtaining and preparing food—boat, weapons, and domestic utensils of the simplest kind. Food had to be won afresh day by day. Now, with their herds of horses, camels, asses, cattle, sheep, goats, and pigs, the advancing pastoral peoples—the Semites on the Euphrates and the Tigris, and the Aryans in the Indian country of the Five Streams (Punjab), in the Ganges region, and in the steppes then much more abundantly watered by the Oxus and the Jaxartes—had acquired property which only needed supervision and the rudest care to reproduce itself in steadily increasing quantities and to supply the most abundant food in the form of milk and meat. All former means of procuring food now receded into the background; hunting, formerly a necessity, now became a luxury.

But to whom did this new wealth belong? Originally to the gens, without a doubt. Private property in herds must have already started at an early period, however. Is it difficult to say whether the author of the so-called first book of Moses regarded the patriarch Abraham as the owner of his herds in his own right as head of a family community or by right of his position as actual hereditary head of a gens. What is certain is that we must not think of him as a property owner in the modern sense of the word. And it is also certain that at the threshold of authentic history we already find the herds everywhere separately owned by heads of families, as are the artistic products of barbarism (metal implements, luxury articles and, finally, the human cattle—the slaves).

For now slavery had also been invented. To the barbarian of the lower stage, a slave was valueless. Hence the treatment of defeated enemies by the American Indians was quite different from that at a higher stage. The men were killed or adopted as brothers into the tribe of the victors; the women were taken as wives or otherwise adopted with their surviving children. At this stage human labor power still does not produce any considerable surplus over and above its maintenance costs. That was no longer the case after the introduction of cattle breeding, metalworking, weaving and, lastly, agriculture. Just as the wives whom it had formerly been so easy to obtain had now acquired an exchange value and were bought, so also with labor power, particularly since the herds had definitely become family possessions. The family did not multiply so rapidly as the cattle. More people were needed to look after them; for this purpose use could be made of the enemies captured in war, who could also be bred just as easily as the cattle themselves.

Once it had passed into the private possession of families and there rapidly begun to augment, this wealth dealt a severe blow to the society founded on pairing marriage and the matriarchal gens. Pairing marriage had brought a new element into the family. By the side of the natural mother of the child it placed its natural and attested father with a better warrant of paternity, probably, than that of many a "father" today. According to the division of labor within the family at that time, it was the man's part to obtain food and the instruments of labor necessary for the purpose. He therefore also owned the instruments of labor, and in the event of husband and wife separating, he took them with him, just as she retained her household goods. Therefore, according to the social custom of the time, the man was also the owner of the new source of subsistence, the cattle, and later of the new instruments of labor, the slaves. But according to the custom of the same society, his children could not inherit from him. For as regards inheritance, the position was as follows:

At first, according to mother right—so long, therefore, as descent was reckoned only in the female line—and according to the original custom of inheritance within the gens, the gentile relatives inherited from a deceased fellow member of their gens. His property had to remain within the gens. His effects being insignificant, they probably always passed in practice to his nearest gentile relations—that is, to his blood relations on the mother's side. The children of the dead man, however, did not belong to his gens, but to that of their mother; it was from her that they inherited, at first conjointly with her other blood-relations, later perhaps with rights of priority; they could not inherit from their father because they did not belong to his gens within which his property had to remain. When the owner of the herds died, therefore, his herds would go first to his brothers and sisters and to his sister's children, or to the issue of his mother's sisters. But his own children were disinherited.

Thus on the one hand, in proportion as wealth increased it made the man's position in the family more important than the woman's, and on the other hand created an impulse to exploit this strengthened position in order to overthrow, in favor of his children, the traditional order of inheritance. This, however, was impossible so long as descent was reckoned according to mother right. Mother right, therefore, had to be overthrown, and overthrown it was. This was by no means so difficult as it looks to us today. For this revolution—one of the most decisive ever experienced by humanity—could take place without disturbing a single one of the living members of a gens. All could remain as they were. A simple decree sufficed that in the future the offspring of the male members should remain within the gens, but that of the female should be excluded by being transferred to the gens of their father. The reckoning of descent in the female line and the matriarchal law of inheritance were thereby overthrown, and the male line of descent and the paternal law of inheritance were substituted for them. As to how and when this revolution took place among civilized peoples, we have no knowledge. It falls entirely within prehistoric times. But that it *did* take place is more than sufficiently proved by the abundant traces of mother right which have been collected. . . .

The overthrow of mother right was the world historical defeat of the female sex. The man took command in the home also; the woman was degraded and reduced to servitude; she became the slave of his lust and a mere instrument for the production of children. This degraded position of the woman, especially conspicuous among the Greeks of the heroic and still more of the classical age, has gradually been palliated and glossed over, and sometimes clothed in a milder form; in no sense has it been abolished.

The establishment of the exclusive supremacy of the man shows its effects first in the patriarchal family, which now emerges as an intermediate form. . . .

Its essential features are the incorporation of unfree persons and paternal power; hence the perfect type of this form of family is the Roman. The original meaning of the word "family" (*familia*) is not that compound of sentimentality and domestic strife which forms the ideal of the present-day philistine; among the Romans it did not at first even refer to the married pair and their children but only to the slaves. *Famulus* means domestic slave, and *familia* is the total number of slaves belonging to one man. . . . The term was invented by the Romans to denote a new social organism whose head ruled over wife and children and a number of slaves, and was invested under Roman paternal power with rights of life and death over them all. . . .

Such a form of family shows the transition of the pairing family to monogamy. In order to make certain of the wife's fidelity and therefore of the paternity of the children, she is delivered over unconditionally into the power of the husband; if he kills her, he is only exercising his rights. . . .

## 4. The Monogamous Family

It develops out of the pairing family, as previously shown, in the transitional period between the upper and middle stages of barbarism; its decisive victory is one of the signs that civilization is beginning. It is based on the supremacy of the man, the express purpose being to produce children of undisputed paternity; such paternity is demanded because these children are later to come into their father's property as his natural heirs. It is distinguished from pairing marriage by the much greater strength of the marriage tie, which can no longer be dissolved at either partner's wish. As a rule, it is now only the man who can dissolve it and put away his wife. The right of conjugal infidelity also remains secured to him, at any rate of custom. . . .

We meet this new form of the family in all its severity among the Greeks. While the position of the goddesses in their mythology, as Marx points out, refers to an earlier period when the position of women was freer and more respected, in the heroic age we find the woman already being humiliated by the domination of the man and by competition from girl slaves. Note how Telemachus in the *Odyssey* silences his mother. In Homer young women are booty and are handed over to the pleasure of the conquerors, and the handsomest being picked by the commanders in order of rank; the entire *Iliad*, it will be remembered, turns on the quarrel of Achilles and Agamemnon over one of these slaves. If a hero is of any importance, Homer also mentions the captive girl with whom he shares his tent and his bed. These girls were also taken back to Greece and brought under the same roof as the wife, as Cassandra was brought by Agamemnon in Aeschylus; the sons begotten of them received a small share of the paternal inheritance and had the full status of freemen. Teucer, for instance, is a natural son of Telamon by one of these slaves and has the right to use his father's name. The legitimate wife was expected to put up with all this, but herself to remain strictly chaste and faithful. In the heroic age a Greek woman is, indeed, more respected than in the period of civilization, but to her husband she is after all nothing but the mother of his legitimate children and heirs, his chief housekeeper and the supervisor of his female slaves, whom he can and does take as concubines if he so fancies. It is the existence of slavery side by side with monogamy, the presence of young, beautiful slaves belonging unreservedly to the *man*, that stamps monogamy from the very beginning with its specific character of monogamy *for the woman only*, but not for the man. And that is the character it still has today. . . .

In *Euripides* [Orestes] a woman is called an *oikurema*, a thing (the word is neuter) for looking after the house, and, apart from her business of bearing children, that was all she was for the Athenian—his chief female domestic servant. The man had his athletics and his public business from which women were barred; in addition, he often had female slaves at his disposal and during the most flourishing days of Athens an extensive system of prostitution which the state at least favored. It was precisely through this system of prostitution that the only Greek women of personality were able to develop, and to acquire that intellectual and artistic culture by which they stand out as high above the general level of classic womanhood as the Spartan women by their qualities of character. But that a woman had to be a *hetaera* before she could be a woman is the worst condemnation of the Athenian family. . . .

This is the origin of monogamy as far as we can trace it back among the most civilized and highly developed people of antiquity. It was not in any way the fruit of individual sex love, with which it had nothing whatever to do; marriages remained as before marriages of convenience. It was the first form of the family to be based not on natural but on economic conditions—on the victory of private property over primitive, natural communal property. The Greeks themselves put the matter quite frankly: the sole exclusive aims of monogamous marriage were to make the man supreme in the family and to propagate, as the future heirs to his wealth, children indisputably his own. Otherwise, marriage was a burden, a duty which had to be performed whether one liked it or not to gods, state, and one's ancestors. In Athens the law exacted from the man not only marriage but also the performance of a minimum of so-called conjugal duties.

Thus when monogamous marriage first makes its appearance in history, it is not as the reconciliation of man and woman, still less as the highest form of such a reconciliation. Quite the contrary, monogamous marriage comes on the scene as the subjugation of the one sex by the other; it announces a struggle between the sexes unknown throughout the whole previous prehistoric period. In an old unpublished manuscript written by Marx and myself in 1846, I find the words: "The first division of labor is that between man and woman for the propagation of children." And today I can add: The first class opposition that appears in history coincides with the development of the antagonism between man and woman in monogamous marriage, and the first class oppression coincides with that of the female sex by the male. Monogamous marriage was a great historical step forward; nevertheless, together with slavery and private wealth, it opens the period that has lasted until today in which every step forward is also relatively a step backward, in which prosperity and development for some is won through the misery and frustration of others. It is the cellular form of civilized society in which the nature of the

oppositions and contradictions fully active in that society can be already studied. . . .

If monogamy was the only one of all the known forms of the family through which modern sex love could develop, that does not mean that within monogamy modern sexual love developed exclusively or even chiefly as the love of husband and wife for each other. That was precluded by the very nature of strictly monogamous marriage under the rule of the man. Among all historically active classes—that is, among all ruling classes—matrimony remained what it had been since the pairing marriage, a matter of convenience which was arranged by the parents. The first historical form of sexual love as passion, a passion recognized as natural to all human beings (at least if they belonged to the ruling classes), and as the highest form of the sexual impulse—and that is what constitutes its specific character—this first form of individual sexual love, the chivalrous love of the middle ages, was by no means conjugal. Quite the contrary, in its classic form among the Provençals, it heads straight for adultery, and the poets of love celebrated adultery. The flowers of Provençal love poetry are the Albas [songs of dawn], in German, *Tagelieder*. They describe in glowing colors how the knight lies in bed beside his love—the wife of another—while outside stands the watchman who calls to him as soon as the first gray of dawn (*alba*) appears so that he can get away unobserved; the parting scene then forms the climax of the poem. The northern French and also the worthy Germans adopted this kind of poetry together with the corresponding fashion of chivalrous love. . . . Sex love in the relationship with a woman becomes and can only become the real rule among the oppressed classes, which means today among the proletariat—whether this relation is officially sanctioned or not. But here all the foundations of typical monogamy are cleared away. Here there is no property, for the preservation and inheritance of which monogamy and male supremacy were established; hence there is no incentive to make this male supremacy effective. What is more, there are no means of making it so. Bourgeois law, which protects this supremacy, exists only for the possessing class and their dealings with the proletarians. The law costs money and, on account of the worker's poverty, it has no validity for his relation to his wife. Here quite other personal and social conditions decide. And now that large-scale industry has taken the wife out of the home onto the labor market and into the factory, and made her often the breadwinner of the family, no basis for any kind of male supremacy is left in the proletarian household, except, perhaps, for something of the brutality toward women that has spread since the introduction of monogamy. The proletarian family is therefore no longer monogamous in the strict sense, even where there is passionate love and firmest loyalty on both sides and maybe all the blessings of religious and civil authority. Here, therefore, the eternal attendants of monogamy, hetaerism and adultery, play only an almost vanishing part. The wife has in fact regained the right to dissolve the marriage, and if two people cannot get on with one another, they prefer to separate. In short, proletarian marriage is monogamous in the etymological sense of the word, but not at all in its historical sense.

Our jurists, of course, find that progress in legislation is leaving women with no further ground of complaint. Modern civilized systems of law increasingly acknowledge first, that for a marriage to be legal it must be a contract freely entered into by both partners and secondly, that also in the married state both partners must stand on a common footing of equal rights and duties. If both these demands are consistently carried out, say the jurists, women have all they can ask.

This typically legalist method of argument is exactly the same as that which the radical republican bourgeois uses to put the proletarian in his place. This labor contract is to be freely entered into by both partners. But it is considered to have been freely entered into as soon as the law makes both parties equal on *paper*. The power conferred on the one party by the difference of class position, the pressure thereby brought to bear on the other party—the real economic position of both—that is not the law's business. Again, for the duration of the labor contract, both parties are to have equal rights in so far as one or the other does not expressly surrender them. That economic relations compel the worker to surrender even the last semblance of equal rights—here again, that is no concern of the law.

In regard to marriage, the law, even the most advanced, is fully satisfied as soon as the partners have formally recorded that they are entering into the marriage of their own free consent. What goes on in real life behind the juridical scenes, how this free consent comes about—that is not the business of the law and the jurist. And yet the most elementary comparative jurisprudence should show the jurist what this free consent really amounts to. In the countries where an obligatory share of the paternal inheritance is secured to the children by law and they cannot therefore be disinherited—in Germany, in the countries with French law and elsewhere—the children are obliged to obtain their parents' consent to their marriage. In the countries with English law, where parental consent to a marriage is not legally required, the parents on their side have full freedom in the testamentary disposal of their property and can disinherit their children at their pleasure. It is obvious that in spite and precisely because of this fact, freedom of marriage among the classes with something to inherit is in reality not a whit greater in England and America than it is in France and Germany.

As regards the legal equality of husband and wife in marriage, the position is no better. The legal inequality of the two partners bequeathed to us from earlier social conditions is not the cause but the effect of the economic oppression of the woman. In the old communistic household, which comprised many couples and their children, the task entrusted to the women of managing the household was as much a public, a socially necessary industry as the procuring of food by the men. With the patriarchal family and still more with the single monogamous family, a change came. Household management lost its public character. It no longer concerned society. It became a *private service;* the wife became the head servant, excluded from all participation in social production. Not until the coming of modern large-scale industry was the road to social production opened to her again—and then only to the proletarian wife. But it was opened in such a manner that, if she carries out her duties in the private service of her family, she remains excluded from public production and unable to earn; and if she wants to take part in public production and earn independently, she cannot carry out family duties. And the wife's position in the factory is the position of women in all branches of business, right up to medicine and the law. The modern individual family is founded on the open or concealed domestic slavery of the wife, and modern society is a mass composed of these individual families as its molecules.

In the great majority of cases today, at least in the possessing classes, the husband is obliged to earn a living and support his family, and that in itself gives him a position of supremacy without any need for special legal titles and privileges. Within the family he is the bourgeois, and the wife represents the proletariat. In the industrial world, the specific character of the economic oppression burdening the proletariat is visible in all its sharpness only when all special legal privileges of the capitalist class have been abolished and complete legal equality of both classes established. The democratic republic does not do away with the opposition of the two classes; on the contrary, it provides the clear field on which the fight can be fought out. And in the same way, the peculiar character of the supremacy of the husband over the wife in the modern family, the necessity of creating real social equality between them and the way to do it, will only be seen in the clear light of day when both possess legally complete equality of rights. Then it will be plain that the first condition for the liberation of the wife is to bring the whole female sex back into public industry, and that this in turn demands that the characteristic of the monogamous family as the economic unit of society be abolished. . . .

We are now approaching a social revolution in which the economic foundations of monogamy as they have existed hitherto will disappear just as surely as those of its complement—prostitution.

Monogamy arose from the concentration of considerable wealth in the hands of a single individual—a man—and from the need to bequeath this wealth to the children of that man and of no other. For this purpose, the monogamy of the woman was required, not that of the man, so this monogamy of the woman did not in any way interfere with open or concealed polygamy on the part of the man. But by transforming by far the greater portion, at any rate, of permanent, heritable wealth—the means of production—into social property, the coming social revolution will reduce to a minimum all this anxiety about bequeathing and inheriting. Having arisen from economic causes, will monogamy then disappear when these causes disappear?

One might answer, not without reason: far from disappearing, it will on the contrary begin to be realized completely. For with the transformation of the means of production into social property there will disappear also wage labor, the proletariat, and therefore the necessity for a certain—statistically calculable—number of women to surrender themselves for money. Prostitution disappears; monogamy, instead of collapsing, at last becomes a reality—also for men.

In any case, therefore, the position of men will be very much altered. But the position of women, of *all* women, also undergoes significant change. With the transfer of the means of production into common ownership, the single family ceases to be the economic unit of society. Private housekeeping is transformed into a social industry. The care and education of the children becomes a public affair; society looks after all children alike, whether they are legitimate or not. This removes all the anxiety about the "consequences," which today is the most essential social—moral as well as economic—factor that prevents a girl from giving herself completely to the man she loves. Will not that suffice to bring about the gradual growth of unconstrained sexual intercourse and with it a more tolerant public opinion in regard to a maiden's honor and a woman's shame? And finally, have we not seen that in the modern world monogamy and prostitution are indeed contradictions, but inseparable contradictions, poles of the same state of society? Can prostitution disappear without dragging monogamy with it into the abyss?

Here a new element comes into play, an element which at the time when monogamy was developing existed at most in embryo—individual sexual love. . . .

As sexual love is by its nature exclusive—although at present this exclusiveness is fully realized only in the woman—the marriage based on sexual love is by its nature individual marriage. . . . If now the economic considerations disappear which made women put up with the habitual infidelity of their husbands—concern for their own means of existence and still more for their children's future—then, according to all previous experience, the equality of woman thereby achieved will tend infinitely more to make men really monogamous than to make women polyandrous.

But what will quite certainly disappear from monogamy are all the features stamped upon it through its origin in property relations; these are, in the first place, supremacy of the man and secondly, the indissolubility of marriage. The supremacy of the man in marriage is the simple consequence of his economic supremacy, and with the abolition of the latter will disappear of itself. The indissolubility of marriage is partly a consequence of the economic situation in which monogamy arose, partly tradition from the period when the connection between this economic situation and monogamy was not yet fully understood and was carried to extremes under a religious form. Today it is already broken through at a thousand points. If only the marriage based on love is moral, then also only the marriage is moral in which love continues. But the intense emotion of individual sex love varies very much in duration from one individual to another, especially among men, and if affection definitely comes to an end or is supplanted by a new passionate love, separation is a benefit for both partners as well as for society—only people will then be spared having to wade through the useless mire of a divorce case.

What we can now conjecture about the way in which sexual relations will be ordered after the impending overthrow of capitalist production is mainly of a negative character, limited for the most part to what will disappear. But what will there be new? That will be answered when a new generation has grown up: a generation of men who never in their lives have known what it is to buy a woman's surrender with money or any other social instrument of power; a generation of women who have never known what it is to give themselves to a man from any other considerations than real love or to refuse to give themselves to their lover from fear of the economic consequences. When these people are in the world, they will care precious little what anybody today thinks they ought to do; they will make their own practice and their corresponding public opinion about the practice of each individual—and that will be the end of it.

# 44     The Unhappy Marriage of Marxism and Feminism: Towards a More Progressive Union

HEIDI HARTMANN

THE "MARRIAGE" OF MARXISM AND FEMINISM has been like the marriage of husband and wife depicted in English common law: marxism and feminism are one, and that one is marxism. Recent attempts to integrate marxism and feminism are unsatisfactory to us as feminists because they subsume the feminist struggle into the "larger" struggle against capital. To continue our simile further, either we need a healthier marriage or we need a divorce.

The inequalities in this marriage, like most social phenomena, are no accident. Many marxists typically argue that feminism is at best less important than class conflict and at worst divisive of the working class. This political stance produces an analysis that absorbs feminism into the class struggle. Moreover, the analytic power of marxism with respect to capital has obscured its limitations with respect to sexism. We will argue here that while marxist analysis provides essential insight into the laws of historical development, and those of capital in particular, the categories of marxism are sex-blind. Only a specifically feminist analysis reveals the systemic character of relations between men and women. Yet feminist analysis by itself is inadequate because it has been blind to history and insufficiently materialist. Both marxist analysis, particularly its historical and materialist method, and feminist analysis, especially the identification of patriarchy as a social and historical structure, must be drawn upon if we are to understand the development of western capitalist societies and the predicament of women within them. In this essay we suggest a new direction for marxist feminist analysis. . . .

## I. Marxism and the Woman Question

The woman question has never been the "feminist question." The feminist question is directed at the causes of sexual inequality between women and men, of male dominance over women. Most marxist analyses of women's position take as their question the relationship of women to the economic system, rather than that of women to men, apparently assuming the latter will be explained in their discussion of the former. Marxist analysis of the woman question has taken several forms. All see women's oppression in our connection (or lack of it) to production. Defining women as part of the working class, these analyses consistently subsume women's relation to men under workers' relation to capital. . . .

All attempt to include women in the category working class and to understand women's oppression as another aspect of class oppression. In doing so all give short shrift to the object of feminist analysis, the relations between women and men. While our "problems" have been elegantly analyzed, they have been misunderstood. The focus of marxist analysis has been class relations; the object of marxist analysis has been understanding the laws of motion of capitalist society. While we believe marxist methodology *can* be used to formulate feminist strategy, these marxist feminist approaches discussed above clearly do not do so; their marxism clearly dominates their feminism.

As we have already suggested, this is due in part to the analytical power of marxism itself. Marxism is a theory of the development of class society, of the accumulation process in capitalist societies, of the reproduction of class dominance, and of the development of contradictions and class struggle. Capitalist societies are driven by the demands of the accumulation process, most succinctly summarized by the fact that production is oriented to exchange, not use. In a capitalist system production is important only insofar as it contributes to the making of profits, and the use value of products is only an incidental consideration. Profits derive from the capitalists' ability to exploit labor power, to pay laborers less than the value of what they produce. The accumulation of profits systematically transforms social structure as it transforms the relations of production. The reserve army of labor, the poverty of great numbers of people and the near-poverty of still more, these human reproaches to capital are by-products of the accumulation process itself. From the capitalist's point of view, the reproduction of the working class may "safely be left to itself." At the same time, capital creates an ideology, which grows up along side it, of individualism, competitiveness, domination, and in our time, consumption of a particular kind. Whatever one's theory of the genesis of ideology one must recognize these as the dominant values of capitalist societies.

Marxism enables us to understand many aspects of capitalist societies: the structure of production, the generation of a particular occupational structure, and the nature of the dominant ideology. Marx's theory of the development of capitalism is a theory of the development of "empty places." Marx predicted, for example, the growth of the proletariat and the demise of the petit bourgeoisie. More precisely and in more detail, Braverman among others has explained the creation of the "places" clerical worker and service worker in advanced capitalist societies. Just as capital creates these places indifferent to the individuals who fill them, the categories of marxist analysis, class, reserve army of labor, wage-laborer, do not explain why particular people fill particular places. They give no clues about why *women* are subordinate to *men* inside and outside the family and why it is not the other way around. *Marxist categories, like capital itself, are sex-blind.* The categories of marxism cannot tell us who will fill the empty places. Marxist analysis of the woman question has suffered from this basic problem. . . .

## II. Radical Feminism and Patriarchy

The great thrust of radical feminist writing has been directed to the documentation of the slogan "the personal is political." Women's discontent, radical feminists argued, is not the neurotic lament of the maladjusted, but a response to a social structure in which women are systematically dominated, exploited, and oppressed. Women's inferior position in the labor market, the male-centered emotional structure of middle class marriage, the use of women in advertising, the so-called understanding of women's psyche as neurotic—popularized by academic and clinical psychology—aspect after aspect of women's lives in advanced capitalist society was researched and analyzed. The radical feminist literature is enormous and defies easy summary. At the same time, its focus on psychology is consistent. The New York Radical Feminists' organizing document was "The Politics of the Ego." "The personal is political" means for radical feminists, that the original and basic class division is between the sexes, and that the motive force of history is the striving of men for power and domination over women, the dialectic of sex.

Accordingly, Firestone rewrote Freud to understand the development of boys and girls into men and women in terms of power. Her characterizations of what are "male" and "female" character traits are typical of radical feminist writing. The male seeks power and domination; he is egocentric and individualistic, competitive and pragmatic; the "technological mode," according to Firestone, is male. The female is nurturant, artistic, and philosophical; the "aesthetic mode" is female.

No doubt, the idea that the aesthetic mode is female would have come as quite a shock to the ancient Greeks. Here lies the error of radical feminist analysis: the dialectic of sex as radical feminists present it projects male and female characteristics as they appear in the present back into all of history. Radical feminist analysis has its greatest strength in its insights into the present. Its greatest weakness is a focus on the psychological which blinds it to history.

The reason for this lies not only in radical feminist method, but also in the nature of patriarchy itself, for patriarchy is a strikingly resilient form of social organization. Radical feminists use patriarchy to refer to a social system characterized by male domination over women. Kate Millett's definition is classic:

> our society . . . is a patriarchy. The fact is evident at once if one recalls that the military, industry, technology, universities, science, political offices, finances—in short, every avenue of power within the society, including the coercive force of the police, is entirely in male hands.[1]

This radical feminist definition of patriarchy applies to most societies we know of and cannot distinguish among them. The use of history by radical feminists is typically limited to providing examples of the existence of patriarchy in all times and places. For both marxist and mainstream social scientists before the women's movement, patriarchy referred to a system of relations between men, which formed the political and economic outlines of feudal and some pre-feudal societies, in which hierarchy followed ascribed characteristics. Capitalist societies are understood as meritocratic, bureaucratic, and impersonal by bourgeois social scientists; marxists see capitalist societies as systems of class domination. For both kinds of social scientists neither the historical patriarchal societies nor today's western capitalist societies are understood as systems of relations between men that enable them to dominate women.

## TOWARDS A DEFINITION OF PATRIARCHY

We can usefully define patriarchy as a set of social relations between men, which have a material base, and which, though hierarchical, establish or create interdependence and solidarity among men that enable them to dominate women. Though patriarchy is hierarchical and men of different classes, races, or ethnic groups have different places in the patriarchy, they also are united in their shared relationship of dominance over their women; they are dependent on each other to maintain that domination. Hierarchies "work" at least in part because they create vested interests in the status quo. Those at the higher level can "buy off" those at the lower levels by offering them power over those still lower. In the hierarchy of patriarchy, all men, whatever their rank in the patriarchy, are bought off by being able to control at least some women. There is some evidence to suggest that when patriarchy was first institutionalized in state societies, the ascending rulers literally made men the heads of their families (enforcing their control over their wives and children) in exchange for the men's ceding some of their tribal resources to the new rulers. Men are dependent on one another (despite their hierarchical ordering) to maintain their control over women.

The material base upon which patriarchy rests lies most fundamentally in men's control over women's labor power. Men maintain this control by excluding women from access to some essential production resources (in capitalist societies, for example, jobs that pay living wages) and by restricting women's sexuality. Monogamous heterosexual marriage is one relatively recent and efficient form that seems to allow men to control both these areas. Controlling women's access to

resources and their sexuality, in turn, allows men to control women's labor power, both for the purpose of serving men in many personal and sexual ways and for the purpose of rearing children. The services women render men, and which exonerate men from having to perform many unpleasant tasks (like cleaning toilets) occur outside as well as inside the family setting. Examples outside the family include the harassment of women workers and students by male bosses and professors as well as the common use of secretaries to run personal errands, make coffee, and provide "sexy" surroundings. Rearing children, whether or not the children's labor power is of immediate benefit to their fathers, is nevertheless a crucial task in perpetuating patriarchy as a system. Just as class society must be reproduced by schools, work places, consumption norms, etc., so must patriarchal social relations. In our society children are generally reared by women at home, women socially defined and recognized as inferior to men, while men appear in the domestic picture only rarely. Children raised in this way generally learn their places in the gender hierarchy well. Central to this process, however, are the areas outside the home where patriarchal behaviors are taught and the inferior position of women enforced and reinforced: churches, schools, sports, clubs, unions, armies, factories, offices, health centers, the media, etc.

The material base of patriarchy, then, does not rest solely on childrearing in the family, but on all the social structures that enable men to control women's labor. The aspects of social structures that perpetuate patriarchy are theoretically identifiable, hence separable from their other aspects. Gayle Rubin has increased our ability to identify the patriarchal element of these social structures enormously by identifying "sex/gender systems":

> a "sex/gender system" is the set of arrangements by which a society transforms biological sexuality into products of human activity, and in which these transformed sexual needs are satisfied.[2]

We are born female and male, biological sexes, but we are created woman and man, socially recognized genders. *How* we are so created is that second aspect of the *mode* of production of which

Engels spoke, "the production of human beings themselves, the propagation of the species."

How people propagate the species is socially determined. If, biologically, people are sexually polymorphous, and society were organized in such a way that all forms of sexual expression were equally permissible, reproduction would result only from some sexual encounters, the heterosexual ones. The strict division of labor by sex, a social invention common to all known societies, creates two very separate genders and a need for men and women to get together for economic reasons. It thus helps to direct their sexual needs toward heterosexual fulfillment, and helps to ensure biological reproduction. In more imaginative societies, biological reproduction might be ensured by other techniques, but the division of labor by sex appears to be the universal solution to date. Although it is theoretically possible that a sexual division of labor not imply inequality between the sexes, in most known societies, the socially acceptable division of labor by sex is one which accords lower status to women's work. The sexual division of labor is also the underpinning of sexual subcultures in which men and women experience life differently; it is the material base of male power which is exercised (in our society) not just in not doing housework and in securing superior employment, but psychologically as well.

How people meet their sexual needs, how they reproduce, how they inculcate social norms in new generations, how they learn gender, how it feels to be a man or a woman—all occur in the realm Rubin labels the sex/gender system. Rubin emphasizes the influence of kinship (which tells you with whom you can satisfy sexual needs) and the development of gender-specific personalities via childrearing and the "oedipal machine." In addition, however, we can use the concept of the sex/gender system to examine all other social institutions for the roles they play in defining and reinforcing gender hierarchies. Rubin notes that theoretically a sex/gender system could be female dominant, male dominant, or egalitarian, but declines to label various known sex/gender systems or to periodize history accordingly. We choose to label our present sex/gender system patriarchy,

because it appropriately captures the notion of hierarchy and male dominance which we see as central to the present system.

Economic production (what marxists are used to referring to as *the* mode of production) and the production of people in the sex/gender sphere both determine "the social organization under which the people of a particular historical epoch and a particular country live," according to Engels. The whole of society, then, can be understood by looking at both these types of production and reproduction, people and things. There is no such thing as "pure capitalism," nor does "pure patriarchy" exist, for they must of necessity coexist. What exists is patriarchal capitalism, or patriarchal feudalism, or egalitarian hunting/gathering societies, or matriarchal horticultural societies, or patriarchal horticultural societies, and so on. There appears to be no necessary connection between *changes* in the one aspect of production and changes in the other. A society could undergo transition from capitalism to socialism, for example, and remain patriarchal. Common sense, history, and our experience tell us, however, that these two aspects of production are so closely intertwined, that change in one ordinarily creates movement, tension, or contradiction in the other.

Racial hierarchies can also be understood in this context. Further elaboration may be possible along the lines of defining color/race systems, arenas of social life that take biological color and turn it into a social category, race. Racial hierarchies, like gender hierarchies, are aspects of our social organization, of how people are produced and reproduced. They are not fundamentally ideological; they constitute that second aspect of our mode of production, the production and reproduction of people. It might be most accurate then to refer to our societies not as, for example, simply capitalist, but as patriarchal capitalist white supremacist. In Part III below, we illustrate one case of capitalism adapting to and making use of racial orders and several examples of the interrelations between capitalism and patriarchy.

Capitalist development creates the places for a hierarchy of workers, but traditional marxist categories cannot tell us who will fill which places.

Gender and racial hierarchies determine who fills the empty places. *Patriarchy is not simply hierarchical organization,* but hierarchy in which *particular* people fill *particular* places. It is in studying patriarchy that we learn why it is women who are dominated and how. While we believe that most known societies have been patriarchal, we do not view patriarchy as a universal, unchanging phenomenon. Rather patriarchy, the set of interrelations among men that allow men to dominate women, has changed in form and intensity over time. It is crucial that the hierarchy among men, and their differential access to patriarchal benefits, be examined. Surely, class, race, nationality, and even marital status and sexual orientation, as well as the obvious age, come into play here. And women of different class, race, national, marital status, or sexual orientation groups are subjected to different degrees of patriarchal power. Women may themselves exercise class, race, or national power, or even patriarchal power (through their family connections) over men lower in the patriarchal hierarchy than their own male kin.

To recapitulate, we define patriarchy as a set of social relations which has a material base and in which there are hierarchical relations between men and solidarity among them which enable them in turn to dominate women. The material base of patriarchy is men's control over women's labor power. That control is maintained by excluding women from access to necessary economically productive resources and by restricting women's sexuality. Men exercise their control in receiving personal service work from women, in not having to do housework or rear children, in having access to women's bodies for sex, and in feeling powerful and being powerful. The crucial elements of patriarchy as we *currently* experience them are: heterosexual marriage (and consequent homophobia), female childrearing and housework, women's economic dependence on men (enforced by arrangements in the labor market), the state, and numerous institutions based on social relations among men—clubs, sports, unions, professions, universities, churches, corporations, and armies. All of these elements need to be examined if we are to understand patriarchal capitalism.

Both hierarchy and interdependence among men and the subordination of women are *integral* to the functioning of our society; that is, these relationships are *systemic*. We leave aside the question of the creation of these relations and ask, can we recognize patriarchal relations in capitalist societies? Within capitalist societies we must discover those same bonds between men which both bourgeois and marxist social scientists claim no longer exist or are, at the most, unimportant leftovers. Can we understand how these relations among men are perpetuated in capitalist societies? Can we identify ways in which patriarchy has shaped the course of capitalist development?

## III. The Partnership of Patriarchy and Capital

How are we to recognize patriarchal social relations in capitalist societies? It appears as if each woman is oppressed by her own man alone; her oppression seems a private affair. Relationships among men and among families seem equally fragmented. It is hard to recognize relationships among men, and between men and women, as *systematically* patriarchal. We argue, however, that patriarchy as a system of relations between men and women exists in capitalism, and that in capitalist societies a healthy and strong partnership exists between patriarchy and capital. Yet if one begins with the concept of patriarchy and an understanding of the capitalist mode of production, one recognizes immediately that the partnership of patriarchy and capital was not inevitable; men and capitalists often have conflicting interests, particularly over the use of women's labor power. Here is one way in which this conflict might manifest itself: the vast majority of men might want their women at home to personally service them. A smaller number of men, who are capitalists, might want most women (not their own) to work in the wage labor market. In examining the tensions of this conflict over women's labor power historically, we will be able to identify the material base of patriarchal relations in capitalist societies, as well as the basis for the partnership between capital and patriarchy.

## INDUSTRIALIZATION AND THE DEVELOPMENT OF FAMILY WAGES

Marxists made quite logical inferences from a selection of the social phenomena they witnessed in the nineteenth century. But marxists ultimately underestimated the strength of the preexisting patriarchal social forces with which fledgling capital had to contend and the need for capital to adjust to these forces. The industrial revolution was drawing all people into the labor force, including women and children; in fact the first factories used child and female labor almost exclusively. That women and children could earn wages separately from men both undermined authority relations (as discussed in Part I above) and kept wages low for everyone. Kautsky, writing in 1892, describes the process this way:

> [Then with] the wife and young children of the working-man . . . able to take care of themselves, the wages of the male worker can safely be reduced to the level of his own personal needs without the risk of stopping the fresh supply of labor power.
>
> The labor of women and children, moreover, affords the additional advantage that these are less capable of resistance than men [sic]; and their introduction into the ranks of the workers increases tremendously the quantity of labor that is offered for sale in the market.
>
> Accordingly, the labor of women and children . . . also diminishes [the] capacity [of the male worker] for resistance in that it overstocks the market; owning to both these circumstances it lowers the wages of the working-man.[3]

The terrible effects on working class family life of low wages and of forced participation of all family members in the labor force were recognized by marxists. Kautsky wrote:

> The capitalist system of production does not in most cases destroy the single household of the working-man, but robs it of all but its unpleasant features. The activity of woman today in industrial pursuits . . . means an increase of her former burden by a new one. *But one cannot serve two masters.* The household of the working-man suffers whenever his wife must help to earn the daily bread.[4]

Working men as well as Kautsky recognized the disadvantages of female wage labor. Not only were women "cheap competition" but working women were their very wives, who could not "serve two masters" well.

Male workers resisted the wholesale entrance of women and children into the labor force, and sought to exclude them from union membership and the labor force as well. In 1846 the *Ten Hours' Advocate* stated:

> It is needless for us to say, that all attempts to improve the morals and physical condition of female factory workers will be abortive, unless their hours are materially reduced. Indeed we may go so far as to say, that married females would be much better occupied in performing the domestic duties of the household, than following the never-tiring motion of machinery. We therefore hope the day is not distant, when the husband will be able to provide for his wife and family, without sending the former to endure the drudgery of a cotton mill.[5]

In the United States in 1854 the National Typographical Union resolved not to "encourage by its act the employment of female compositors." Male unionists did not want to afford union protection to women workers; they tried to exclude them instead. In 1879 Adolph Strasser, president of the Cigarmakers International Union, said: "We cannot drive the females out of the trade, but we can restrict their daily quota of labor through factory laws."

While the problem of cheap competition could have been solved by organizing the wage earning women and youths, the problem of disrupted family life could not be. Men reserved union protection for men and argued for protective labor laws for women and children. Protective labor laws, while they may have ameliorated some of the worst abuses of female and child labor, also limited the participation of adult women in many "male" jobs. Men sought to keep high wage jobs for themselves and to raise male wages generally.

They argued for wages sufficient for their wage labor alone to support their families. This "family wage" system gradually came to be the norm for stable working class families at the end of the nineteenth century and the beginning of the twentieth. Several observers have declared the non-wage-working wife to be part of the standard of living of male workers. Instead of fighting for equal wages for men and women, male workers sought the family wage, wanting to retain their wives' services at home. In the absence of patriarchy a unified working class might have confronted capitalism, but patriarchal social relations divided the working class, allowing one part (men) to be bought off at the expense of the other (women). Both the hierarchy between men and the solidarity among them were crucial in this process of resolution. Family wages may be understood as a resolution of the conflict over women's labor power which was occurring between patriarchal and capitalist interests at that time.

Family wages for most adult men imply men's acceptance, and collusion in, lower wages for others, young people, women and socially defined inferior men as well (Irish, blacks, etc., the lowest groups in the patriarchal hierarchy who are denied many of the patriarchal benefits). Lower wages for women and children and inferior men are enforced by job segregation in the labor market, which in turn is maintained by unions and management as well as by auxiliary institutions like schools, training programs, and even families. Job segregation by sex, by insuring that women have the lower paid jobs, both assures women's economic dependence on men and reinforces notions of appropriate spheres for women and men. For most men, then, the development of family wages, secured the material base of male domination in two ways. First, men have the better jobs in the labor market and earn higher wages than women. The lower pay women receive in the labor market both perpetuates men's material advantage over women and encourages women to choose wifery as a career. Second, then, women do housework, childcare, and perform other services at home which benefit men directly. Women's home responsibilities in turn reinforce their inferior labor market position.

The resolution that developed in the early twentieth century can be seen to benefit capitalist interests as well as patriarchal interests. Capitalists, it is often argued, recognized that in the extreme conditions which prevailed in the early nineteenth century industrialization, working class families could not adequately reproduce themselves. They realized that housewives produced and maintained healthier workers than wage-working wives and that educated children became better workers than noneducated ones. The bargain, paying family wages to men and keeping women home, suited the capitalists at the time as well as the male workers. Although the terms of the bargain have altered over time, it is still true that the family and women's work in the family serve capital by providing a labor force and serve men as the space in which they exercise their privilege. Women, working to serve men and their families, also serve capital as consumers. The family is also the place where dominance and submission are learned, as Firestone, the Frankfurt School, and many others have explained. Obedient children become obedient workers; girls and boys each learn their proper roles.

While the family wage shows that capitalism adjusts to patriarchy, the changing status of children shows that patriarchy adjusts to capital. Children, like women, came to be excluded from wage labor. As children's ability to earn money declined, their legal relationship to their parents changed. At the beginning of the industrial era in the United States, fulfilling children's need for their fathers was thought to be crucial, even primary, to their happy development; fathers had legal priority in cases of contested custody. As children's ability to contribute to the economic well-being of the family declined, mothers came increasingly to be viewed as crucial to the happy development of their children, and gained legal priority in cases of contested custody. Here patriarchy adapted to the changing economic role of children: when children were productive, men claimed them; as children became unproductive, they were given to women.

## THE FAMILY AND THE FAMILY WAGE TODAY

We argued above, that, with respect to capitalism and patriarchy, the adaptation, or mutual accommodation, took the form of the development of the family wage in the early twentieth century. The family wage cemented the partnership between patriarchy and capital. Despite women's increased labor force participation, particularly rapid since World War II, the family wage is still, we argue, the cornerstone of the present sexual division of labor—in which women are primarily responsible for housework and men primarily for wage work. Women's lower wages in the labor market (combined with the need for children to be reared by someone) assure the continued existence of the family as a necessary income pooling unit. The family, supported by the family wage, thus allows the control of women's labor by men both within and without the family.

Though women's increased wage work may cause stress for the family (similar to the stress Kautsky and Engels noted in the nineteenth century), it would be wrong to think that as a consequence, the concepts and the realities of the family and of the sexual division of labor will soon disappear. The sexual division of labor reappears in the labor market, where women work at women's jobs, often the very jobs they used to do only at home—food preparation and service, cleaning of all kinds, caring for people, and so on. As these jobs are low-status and low-paying patriarchal relations remain intact, though their material base shifts somewhat from the family to the wage differential, from family-based to industrially based patriarchy.

Industrially based patriarchal relations are enforced in a variety of ways. Union contracts which specify lower wages, lesser benefits, and fewer advancement opportunities for women are not just atavistic hangovers—a case of sexist attitudes or male supremacist ideology—they maintain the material base of the patriarchal system. While some would go so far as to argue that patriarchy is already absent from the family (see, for example, Stewart Ewen, *Captains of Consciousness*), we

would not. Although the terms of the compromise between capital and patriarchy are changing as additional tasks formerly located in the family are capitalized, and the location of the deployment of women's labor power shifts, it is nevertheless true, as we have argued above, that the wage differential caused by extreme job segregation in the labor market reinforces the family, and, with it, the domestic division of labor, by encouraging women to marry. The "ideal" of the family wage—that a man can earn enough to support an entire family—may be giving way to a new ideal that both men and women contribute through wage earning to the cash income of the family. The wage differential, then, will become increasingly necessary in perpetuating patriarchy, the male control of women's labor power. The wage differential will aid in *defining* women's work as secondary to men's at the same time it necessitates women's actual continued economic dependence on men. The sexual division of labor in the labor market and elsewhere should be understood as a manifestation of patriarchy which serves to perpetuate it.

Many people have argued that though the partnership between capital and patriarchy exists now, it may *in the long run* prove intolerable to capitalism; capital may eventually destroy both familial relations and patriarchy. The argument proceeds logically that capitalist social relations (of which the family is not an example) tend to become universalized, that women will become increasingly able to earn money and will increasingly refuse to submit to subordination in the family, and that since the family is oppressive particularly to women and children, it will collapse as soon as people can support themselves outside it.

We do not think that the patriarchal relations embodied in the family can be destroyed so easily by capital, and we see little evidence that the family system is presently disintegrating. Although the increasing labor force participation of women has made divorce more feasible, the incentives to divorce are not overwhelming for women. Women's wages allow very few women to support themselves and their children independently and adequately. The evidence for the decay of the traditional family is weak at best. The divorce rate has not so much increased, as it has evened out among classes; moreover, the remarriage rate is also very high. Up until the 1970 census, the first-marriage age was continuing its historic decline. Since 1970 people seem to have been delaying marriage and child-bearing, but most recently, the birth rate has begun to increase again. It is true that larger proportions of the population are now living outside traditional families. Young people, especially, are leaving their parents' homes and establishing their own households before they marry and start traditional families. Older people, especially women, are finding themselves alone in their own households, after their children are grown and they experience separation or death of a spouse. Nevertheless, trends indicate that the new generations of young people will form nuclear families at some time in their adult lives in higher proportions than ever before. The cohorts, or groups of people, born since 1930 have much higher rates of eventual marriage and childrearing than previous cohorts. The duration of marriage and childrearing may be shortening, but its incidence is still spreading.

The argument that capital destroys the family also overlooks the social forces which make family life appealing. Despite critiques of nuclear families as psychologically destructive, in a competitive society the family still meets real needs for many people. This is true not only of long-term monogamy, but even more so for raising children. Single parents bear both financial and psychic burdens. For working class women, in particular, these burdens make the "independence" of labor force participation illusory. Single parent families have recently been seen by policy analysts as transitional family formations which become two-parent families upon remarriage.

It could be that the effects of women's increasing labor force participation are found in a declining sexual division of labor within the family, rather than in more frequent divorce, but evidence for this is also lacking. Statistics on who does housework, even in families with wage-earning wives, show little change in recent years; women still do most of it. The double day is a reality for wage-working women. This is hardly surprising since the sexual division of labor outside the family, in the labor market, keeps women financially dependent on men—even when they earn a wage themselves. The future of patriarchy does not, however, rest solely on the future of familial relations. For patriarchy, like capital, can be surprisingly flexible and adaptable.

Whether or not the patriarchal division of labor, inside the family and elsewhere, is "ultimately" intolerable to capital, it is shaping capitalism now. As we illustrate below, patriarchy both legitimates capitalist control and delegitimates certain forms of struggle against capital.

## IDEOLOGY IN THE TWENTIETH CENTURY

Patriarchy, by establishing and legitimating hierarchy among men (by allowing men of all groups to control at least some women), reinforces capitalist control, and capitalist values shape the definition of patriarchal good. . . .

If we examine the characteristics of men as radical feminists describe them—competitive, rationalistic, dominating—they are much like our description of the dominant values of capitalist society.

The "coincidence" may be explained in two ways. In the first instance, men, as wage laborers, are absorbed in capitalist social relations at work, driven into the competition these relations prescribe, and absorb the corresponding values. The radical feminist description of men was not altogether out of line for capitalist societies. Secondly, even when men and women do not actually behave in the way sexual norms prescribe, men *claim for themselves* those characteristics which are valued in the dominant ideology. So, for example, the authors of *Crestwood Heights* found that while the men, who were professionals, spent their days manipulating subordinates (often using techniques that appeal to fundamentally irrational motives to elicit the preferred behavior), men and women characterized men as "rational and pragmatic." And while the women devoted great energies to studying scientific methods of childrearing and child development, men and women in Crestwood Heights characterized women as "irrational and emotional."

This helps to account not only for "male" and "female" characteristics in capitalist societies, but for the particular form sexist ideology takes in capitalist societies. Just as women's work serves the dual purpose of perpetuating male domination and capitalist production, so sexist ideology serves the dual purpose of glorifying male characteristics/capitalist values, and denigrating female characteristics/social need. If women were degraded or powerless in other societies, the reasons (rationalizations) men had for this were different. Only in a capitalist society does it make sense to look down on women as emotional or irrational. As epithets, they would not have made sense in the renaissance. Only in a capitalist society does it make sense to look down on women as "dependent." "Dependent" as an epithet would not make sense in feudal societies. Since the division of labor ensures that women as wives and mothers in the family are largely concerned with the production of use values, the denigration of these activities obscures capital's inability to meet socially determined need at the same time that it degrades women in the eyes of men, providing a rationale for male dominance. An example of this may be seen in the peculiar ambivalence of television commercials. On one hand, they address themselves to the real obstacles to providing for socially determined needs: detergents that destroy clothes and irritate skin, shoddily made goods of all sorts. On the other hand, concern with these problems must be denigrated; this is accomplished by mocking women, the workers who must deal with these problems.

A parallel argument demonstrating the partnership of patriarchy and capitalism may be made about the sexual division of labor in the work force. The sexual division of labor places women in low-paying jobs, and in tasks thought to be appropriate to women's role. Women are teachers, welfare workers, and the great majority of workers in the health fields. The nurturant roles that women play in these jobs are of low status because

capitalism emphasizes personal independence and the ability of private enterprise to meet social needs, emphases contradicted by the need for collectively provided social services. As long as the social importance of nurturant tasks can be denigrated because women perform them, the confrontation of capital's priority on exchange value by a demand for use values can be avoided. In this way, it is not feminism, but sexism that divides and debilitates the working class.

## IV. Towards a More Progressive Union

Many problems remain for us to explore. Patriarchy as we have used it here remains more a descriptive term than an analytic one. If we think marxism alone inadequate, and radical feminism itself insufficient, then we need to develop new categories. What makes our task a difficult one is that the same features, such as the division of labor, often reinforce both patriarchy and capitalism, and in a thoroughly patriarchal capitalist society, it is hard to isolate the mechanisms of patriarchy. Nevertheless, this is what we must do. We have pointed to some starting places: looking at who benefits from women's labor power, uncovering the material base of patriarchy, investigating the mechanisms of hierarchy and solidarity among men. The questions we must ask are endless. . . .

### FEMINISM AND THE CLASS STRUGGLE

. . . The struggle against capital and patriarchy cannot be successful if the study and practice of the issues of feminism is abandoned. A struggle aimed only at capitalist relations of oppression will fail, since their underlying supports in patriarchal relations of oppression will be overlooked. And the analysis of patriarchy is essential to a definition of the kind of socialism useful to women. While men and women share a need to overthrow capitalism they retain interests particular to their gender group. It is not clear—from our sketch, from history, or from male socialists—that the socialism being struggled for is the same for both men and women. For a humane socialism would require not only consensus on what the new society should look like and what a healthy person should look like, but more concretely, it would require that men relinquish their privilege.

As women we must not allow ourselves to be talked out of the urgency and importance of our tasks, as we have so many times in the past. We must fight the attempted coercion, both subtle and not so subtle, to abandon feminist objectives.

This suggests two strategic considerations. First, a struggle to establish socialism must be a struggle in which groups with different interests form an alliance. Women should not trust men to liberate them after the revolution, in part, because there is no reason to think they would know how; in part, because there is no necessity for them to do so. In fact their immediate self-interest lies in our continued oppression. Instead we must have our own organizations and our own power base. Second, we think the sexual division of labor within capitalism has given women a practice in which we have learned to understand what human interdependence and needs are. While men have long struggled *against* capital, women know what to struggle *for*. As a general rule, men's position in patriarchy and capitalism prevents them from rec-

ognizing both human needs for nurturance, sharing, and growth, and the potential for meeting those needs in a nonhierarchical, nonpatriarchal society. But even if we raise their consciousness, men might assess the potential gains against the potential losses and choose the status quo. Men have more to lose than their chains.

As feminist socialists, we must organize a practice which addresses both the struggle against patriarchy and the struggle against capitalism. We must insist that the society we want to create is a society in which recognition of interdependence is liberation rather than shame, nurturance is a universal, not an oppressive practice, and in which women do not continue to support the false as well as the concrete freedoms of men.

NOTES

1. Kate Millett, *Sexual Politics* (New York: Avon Books, 1971), p. 25.

2. Gayle Rubin, "The Traffic in Women," in *Anthropology of Women,* ed. Reiter, p. 159.

3. Karl Kautsky, *The Class Struggle* (New York: Norton, 1971), pp. 25–26.

4. We might add, "outside the household," Kautsky, *Class Struggle*, p. 26, our emphasis.

5. Cited in Neil Smelser, *Social Change and the Industrial Revolution* (Chicago: University of Chicago Press, 1959), p. 301.

# 45     Buddhist Economics

E. F. SCHUMACHER

"RIGHT LIVELIHOOD" is one of the requirements of the Buddha's Noble Eightfold Path. It is clear, therefore, that there must be such a thing as Buddhist economics.

Buddhist countries have often stated that they wish to remain faithful to their heritage. So

Burma: "The New Burma sees no conflict between religious values and economic progress. Spiritual health and material well-being are not enemies: they are natural allies."[1] Or: "We can blend successfully the religious and spiritual values of our heritage with the benefits of modern technology."[2] Or: "We Burmans have a sacred duty to conform both our dreams and our acts to our faith. This we shall ever do."[3]

All the same, such countries invariably assume that they can model their economic development plans in accordance with modern economics, and they call upon modern economists from so-called advanced countries to advise them, to formulate the policies to be pursued, and to construct the grand design for development, the Five-Year Plan or whatever it may be called. No one seems to think that a Buddhist way of life would call for Buddhist economics, just as the modern materialist way of life has brought forth modern economics.

Economists themselves, like most specialists, normally suffer from a kind of metaphysical blindness, assuming that theirs is a science of absolute and invariable truths, without any presuppositions. Some go as far as to claim that economic laws are as free from "metaphysics" or "values" as the law of gravitation. We need not, however, get involved in arguments of methodology. Instead, let us take some fundamentals and see what they look like when viewed by a modern economist and a Buddhist economist.

There is universal agreement that a fundamental source of wealth is human labour. Now, the modern economist has been brought up to consider "labour" or work as little more than a necessary evil. From the point of view of the employer, it is in any case simply an item of cost, to be reduced to a minimum if it cannot be eliminated altogether, say, by automation. From the point of view of the workman, it is a "disutility"; to work is to make a sacrifice of one's leisure and comfort, and wages are a kind of compensation for the sacrifice. Hence, the ideal from the point of view of the employer is to have output without employees, and the ideal from the point of view of the employee is to have income without employment.

The consequences of these attitudes both in theory and in practice are, of course, extremely far-reaching. If the ideal with regard to work is to get rid of it, every method that "reduces the work load" is a good thing. The most potent method, short of automation, is the so-called "division of labour" and the classical example is the pin factory eulogised in Adam Smith's *Wealth of Nations*.[4] Here it is not a matter of ordinary specialisation, which mankind has practised from time immemorial, but of dividing up every complete process of production into minute parts, so that the final product can be produced at great speed without anyone having had to contribute more than a totally insignificant and, in most cases, unskilled movement of his limbs.

The Buddhist point of view takes the function of work to be at least threefold: to give a man a chance to utilise and develop his faculties; to enable him to overcome his egocentredness by joining with other people in a common task; and to bring forth the goods and services needed for a becoming existence. Again, the consequences that flow from this view are endless. To organise work in such a manner that it becomes meaningless, boring, stultifying, or nerve-racking for the worker would be little short of criminal; it would indicate a greater concern with goods than with people, an evil lack of compassion and a soul-destroying degree of attachment to the most primitive side of this worldly existence. Equally, to strive for leisure as an alternative to work would be considered a complete misunderstanding of one of the basic truths of human existence, namely that work and leisure are complementary parts of the same living process and cannot be separated without destroying the joy of work and the bliss of leisure.

From the Buddhist point of view, there are therefore two types of mechanisation which must be clearly distinguished: one that enhances a man's skill and power and one that turns the work of man over to a mechanical slave, leaving man in a position of having to serve the slave. How to tell the one from the other? "The craftsman himself," says Ananda Coomaraswamy, a man equally competent to talk about the modern west as the ancient east, "can always, if allowed to, draw the delicate distinction between the machine and the tool. The carpet loom is a tool, a contrivance for holding warp threads at a stretch for the pile to be woven round them by the craftsmen's fingers; but the power loom is a machine, and its significance as a destroyer of culture lies in the fact that it does the essentially human part of the work."[5] It is clear, therefore, that Buddhist economics must be very different from the economics of modern materialism, since the Buddhist sees the essence of civilisation not in a multiplication of wants but in the purification of human character. Character, at the same time, is formed primarily by a man's work. And work, properly conducted in conditions of human dignity and freedom, blesses those who do it and equally their products. The Indian philosopher and economist J. C. Kumarappa sums the matter up as follows:

"If the nature of the work is properly appreciated and applied, it will stand in the same relation to the higher faculties as food is to the physical body. It nourishes and enlivens the higher man and urges him to produce the best he is capable of. It directs his free will along the proper course and disciplines the animal in him into progressive channels. It furnishes an excellent background for man to display his scale of values and develop his personality."[6]

If a man has no chance of obtaining work he is in a desperate position, not simply because he lacks an income but because he lacks this nourishing and enlivening factor of disciplined work which nothing can replace. A modern economist may engage in highly sophisticated calculations on whether full employment "pays" or whether it might be more "economic" to run an economy at less than full employment so as to ensure a greater mobility of labour, a better stability of wages, and so forth. His fundamental criterion of success is simply the total quantity of goods produced during a given period of time. "If the marginal urgency of goods is low," says Professor Galbraith in *The Affluent Society*, "then so is the urgency of employing the last man or the last million men in the labour force."[7] And again: "If . . . we can afford some unemployment in the interest of stability—a proposition, incidentally, of impeccably conservative antecedents—then we can afford to give those who are unemployed the goods that enable them to sustain their accustomed standard of living."

From a Buddhist point of view, this is standing the truth on its head by considering goods as more important than people and consumption as more important than creative activity. It means shifting the emphasis from the worker to the product of work, that is, from the human to the sub-human, a surrender to the forces of evil. The very start of Buddhist economic planning would be a planning for full employment, and the primary purpose of this would in fact be employment for everyone who needs an "outside" job: it would not be the maximisation of employment nor the maximisation of production. Women, on the whole, do not need an "outside" job, and the large-scale employment of women in offices or factories would be considered a sign of serious economic failure. In particular, to let mothers of young children work in factories while the children run wild would be as uneconomic in the eyes of a Buddhist economist as the employment of a skilled worker as a soldier in the eyes of a modern economist.

While the materialist is mainly interested in goods, the Buddhist is mainly interested in liberation. But Buddhism is "The Middle Way" and therefore in no way antagonistic to physical well-being. It is not wealth that stands in the way of liberation but the attachment to wealth; not the enjoyment of pleasurable things but the craving for them. The keynote of Buddhist economics, therefore, is simplicity and non-violence. From an economist's point of view, the marvel of the Buddhist way of life is the utter rationality of its pattern—amazingly small means leading to extraordinarily satisfactory results.

For the modern economist this is very difficult to understand. He is used to measuring the "standard of living" by the amount of annual consumption, assuming all the time that a man who consumes more is "better off" than a man who consumes less. A Buddhist economist would consider this approach excessively irrational: since consumption is merely a means to human well-being, the aim should be to obtain the maximum of well-being with the minimum of consumption. Thus, if the purpose of clothing is a certain amount of temperature comfort and an attractive appearance, the task is to attain this purpose with the smallest possible effort, that is, with the smallest annual destruction of cloth and with the help of designs that involve the smallest possible input of toil. The less toil there is, the more time and strength is left for artistic creativity. It would be highly uneconomic, for instance, to go in for complicated tailoring, like the modern west, when a much more beautiful effect can be achieved by the skilful draping of uncut material. It would be the height of folly to make material so that it should wear out quickly and the height of barbarity to make anything ugly, shabby or mean. What has just been said about clothing applies equally to all other human requirements. The ownership and the consumption of goods is a means to an end, and Buddhist economics is the systematic study of how to attain given ends with the minimum means.

Modern economics, on the other hand, considers consumption to be the sole end and purpose of all economic activity, taking the factors of production—land, labour, and capital—as the means. The former, in short, tries to maximise human satisfactions by the optimal pattern of consumption, while the latter tries to maximise consumption by the optimal pattern of productive effort. It is easy to see that the effort needed to sustain a way of life which seeks to attain the optimal pattern of consumption is likely to be much smaller than the effort needed to sustain a drive for maximum consumption. We need not be surprised, therefore, that the pressure and strain of living is very much less in, say, Burma than it is in the United States, in spite of the fact that the amount of labour-saving machinery used in the former country is only a minute fraction of the amount used in the latter.

Simplicity and non-violence are obviously closely related. The optimal pattern of consumption, producing a high degree of human satisfaction by means of a relatively low rate of consumption, allows people to live without great pressure and strain and to fulfil the primary injunction of Buddhist teaching: "Cease to do evil; try to do good." As physical resources are everywhere limited, people satisfying their needs by means of a modest use of resources are obviously less likely to be at each other's throats than people depending upon a high rate of use. Equally, people who live in highly self-sufficient local communities are less likely to get involved in large-scale violence than people whose existence depends on worldwide systems of trade.

From the point of view of Buddhist economics, therefore, production from local resources for local needs is the most rational way of economic life, while dependence on imports from afar and the consequent need to produce for export to unknown and distant peoples is highly uneconomic and justifiable only in exceptional cases and on a small scale. Just as the modern economist would admit that a high rate of consumption of transport services between a man's home and his place of work signifies a misfortune and not a high standard of life, so the Buddhist economist would hold that to satisfy human wants from faraway sources rather than from sources nearby signifies failure rather than success. The former tends to take statistics showing an increase in the number of ton/miles per head of the population carried by a country's transport system as proof of economic progress, while to the latter—the Buddhist economist—the same statistics would indicate a highly undesirable deterioration in the *pattern* of consumption.

Another striking difference between modern economics and Buddhist economics arises over the use of natural resources. Bertrand de Jouvenel, the eminent French political philosopher, has characterised "western man" in words which may be taken as a fair description of the modern economist:

"He tends to count nothing as an expenditure, other than human effort; he does not seem to mind how much mineral matter he wastes and, far worse, how much living matter he destroys. He does not seem to realise at all that human life is a dependent part of an ecosystem of many different forms of life. As the world is ruled from towns where men are cut off from any form of life other than human, the feeling of belonging to an ecosystem is not revived. This results in a harsh and improvident treatment of things upon which we ultimately depend, such as water and trees."[8]

The teaching of the Buddha, on the other hand, enjoins a reverent and non-violent attitude not only to all sentient beings but also, with great emphasis, to trees. Every follower of the Buddha ought to plant a tree every few years and look after it until it is safely established, and the Buddhist economist can demonstrate without difficulty that the universal observation of this rule would result in a high rate of genuine economic development independent of any foreign aid. Much of the economic decay of south-east Asia (as of many other parts of the world) is undoubtedly due to a heedless and shameful neglect of trees.

Modern economics does not distinguish between renewable and non-renewable materials, as its very method is to equalise and quantify everything by means of a money price. Thus, taking various alternative fuels, like coal, oil, wood, or water-power: the only difference between them recognised by modern economics is relative cost per equivalent unit. The cheapest is automatically the one to be preferred, as to do otherwise would be irrational and "uneconomic." From a Buddhist point of view, of course, this will not do; the essential difference between non-renewable fuels like coal and oil on the one hand and renewable fuels like wood and water-power on the other cannot be simply overlooked. Non-renewable goods must be used only if they are indispensable, and then only with the greatest care and the most meticulous concern for conservation. To use them heedlessly or extravagantly is an act of violence, and while complete non-violence may not be attainable on this earth, there is nonetheless an ineluctable duty on man to aim at the ideal of non-violence in all he does.

Just as a modern European economist would not consider it a great economic achievement if all European art treasures were sold to America at attractive prices, so the Buddhist economist would insist that a population basing its economic life on non-renewable fuels is living parasitically, on capital instead of income. Such a way of life could have no permanence and could therefore be justified only as a purely temporary expedient. As the world's resources of non-renewable fuels—coal,

oil and natural gas—are exceedingly unevenly distributed over the globe and undoubtedly limited in quantity, it is clear that their exploitation at an ever-increasing rate is an act of violence against nature which must almost inevitably lead to violence between men.

This fact alone might give food for thought even to those people in Buddhist countries who care nothing for the religious and spiritual values of their heritage and ardently desire to embrace the materialism of modern economics at the fastest possible speed. Before they dismiss Buddhist economics as nothing better than a nostalgic dream, they might wish to consider whether the path of economic development outlined by modern economics is likely to lead them to places where they really want to be. Towards the end of his courageous book *The Challenge of Man's Future*, Professor Harrison Brown of the California Institute of Technology gives the following appraisal:

> Thus we see that, just as industrial society is fundamentally unstable and subject to reversion to agrarian existence, so within it the conditions which offer individual freedom are unstable in their ability to avoid the conditions which impose rigid organisation and totalitarian control. Indeed, when we examine all of the foreseeable difficulties which threaten the survival of industrial civilisation, it is difficult to see how the achievement of stability and the maintenance of individual liberty can be made compatible.[9]

Even if this were dismissed as a long-term view there is the immediate question of whether "modernisation," as currently practised without regard to religious and spiritual values, is actually producing agreeable results. As far as the masses are concerned, the results appear to be disastrous—a collapse of the rural economy, a rising tide of unemployment in town and country, and the growth of a city proletariat without nourishment for either body or soul.

It is in the light of both immediate experience and long-term prospects that the study of Buddhist economics could be recommended even to those who believe that economic growth is more important than any spiritual or religious values. For it is not a question of choosing between "modern growth" and "traditional stagnation." It is a question of finding the right path of development, the Middle Way between materialist heedlessness and traditionalist immobility, in short, of finding "Right Livelihood."

## NOTES

1. *The New Burma* (Economic and Social Board, Government of the Union of Burma, 1954)

2. Ibid.

3. Ibid.

4. *Wealth of Nations* by Adam Smith

5. *Art and Swadeshi* by Ananda K. Coomaraswamy (Ganesh & Co., Madras)

6. *Economy of Permanence* by J. C. Kumarappa (Sarva-Seva Sangh Publication, Rajghat, Kashi, 4th edn., 1958)

7. *The Affluent Society* by John Kenneth Galbraith (Penguin Books Ltd., 1962)

8. *A Philosophy of Indian Economic Development* by Richard B. Gregg (Navajivan Publishing House, Ahmedabad, 1958)

9. *The Challenge of Men's Future* by Harrison Brown (The Viking Press, New York, 1954)

## Recommended Readings

### TEXTS

Avineri, Shlomo. *The Social and Political Thought of Karl Marx.* Cambridge: Cambridge University Press, 1968.

Bottomore, Tom, ed. *Karl Marx.* Oxford: Blackwell, 1979.

Buchanan, A. *Marx and Justice: The Radical Critique of Liberalism.* Totowa, NJ: Rowman and Allanheld, 1982.

Elster, Jon. *Making Sense of Marx.* Cambridge: Cambridge University Press, 1985.

Lukes, S. *Marxism and Morality.* Oxford: Oxford University Press, 1984.

Tucker, R. C. *The Marxian Revolutionary Idea.* London: Allen & Unwin, 1970.

Wood, Alan. *Karl Marx.* London: Routledge, 1981.

### FEMINIST PERSPECTIVE

Barrett, Michele. *Women's Oppression Today: Problems in Marxist Feminist Analysis.* London: New Left Books, 1980.

Delmar, Rosalyn. "Looking Again at Engels." In *The Rights and Wrongs of Women,* edited by J. Mitchell and A. Oakley. Harmondsworth: Penguin, 1976.

MacKinnon, Catherine. "Marxism, Feminism, Method and the State," Parts I and II. *Signs,* 7, no. 3 (1983) and 8, no. 4 (1984).

### MULTICULTURAL PERSPECTIVE

Ross, Nancy. *Buddhism: A Way of Life and Thought.* New York: Vintage, 1980.

Schumacher, E. F. *Small Is Beautiful.* New York: Harper & Row, 1973.

# XI

# *Rawls and Hospers*

## Introduction

J OHN RAWLS WAS BORN IN BALTIMORE IN 1921. He received his Ph.D. in philosophy from Princeton in 1950. He taught at Cornell University and MIT before going to Harvard University in 1962. In 1971, he published his best-known work, *A Theory of Justice*. It has been translated into every major European language as well as Chinese, Japanese, and Korean. Rawls was named James Bryant Conant University Professor in 1979. In 1993, he published *Political Liberalism*. Most recently, he published *The Law of Peoples* in 1999, and *Justice as Fairness: A Restatement* in 2001.

In *Justice as Fairness: A Restatement*, Rawls, like Immanuel Kant before him, argues that principles of justice are those principles that free and rational persons who are concerned to advance their own interests would accept in an initial position of equality. Yet Rawls goes beyond Kant by interpreting the conditions of his "original position" to explicitly require a "veil of ignorance." This veil of ignorance, he claims, requires that we discount certain knowledge about ourselves in order to reach fair agreements. Rawls now reformulates the principles of justice that he claims would be chosen in the original position somewhat differently, as follows:

1. Each person has the same indefeasible claim to a fully adequate scheme of equal basic liberties, which scheme is compatible with the same scheme of liberties for all.
2. Social and economic inequalities are to satisfy two conditions: First, they are to be attached to offices and positions open to all under conditions of fair equality of opportunity; second, they are to be to the greatest benefit of the least advantaged members of society (the difference principle).

What is significantly different in Rawls's current theory of justice is how he now argues for these two principles from the perspective of the original position. In his earlier work, *A Theory of Justice*, Rawls had defended his principles of justice primarily by appealing to the *maximin* strategy. By contrast, in *Justice as Fairness: A Restatement* Rawls defends his principles of justice by making two comparisons, one of which does not appeal to the maximin strategy at all. In the first comparison, the two principles taken as a unit are compared with the principle of average utility. In the second comparison, the two principles taken as a unit are compared with an alternative formed by substituting for the difference principle the principle of average utility combined with a stipulated social minimum. In the first comparison, Rawls holds that his two principles of justice would be chosen over the principle of average utility because persons in the original position would find it reasonable to follow the conservative dictates of the maximin strategy and <u>maximize</u> the <u>minimum</u> payoff primarily because they fear that the principle of average utility could require that the basic rights and liberties of some be restricted to secure greater benefits for others. In the second comparison, however, Rawls holds that the difference principle would be favored over the principle of average utility combined with a stipulated social minimum primarily because the difference principle expresses an ideal of reciprocity absent from the principle of average utility, even with a stipulated social minimum.

John Hospers was born in Pella, Iowa, in 1918. He received his Ph.D. in philosophy from Columbia University in 1946. He taught at Columbia University, the University of Minnesota, and Brooklyn College of the City University of New York before joining the faculty at the University of Southern California in 1966. Among his numerous publications, those books most relevant to social and political philosophy are *Human Conduct*, third edition (1995), *Libertarianism* (1971), and *Will Capitalism Survive?* (1980). He is a contributing editor of the *Libertarian Review* and the *Journal of Libertarian Studies* and editor of the *Pacific Philosophical Quarterly*. In 1971, he was the first Libertarian Party candidate for U.S. president.

In "The Libertarian Manifesto," John Hospers explores various ways of understanding the basic libertarian thesis, which also has Kantian roots, that every person is the owner of his or her life. According to Hospers, such ownership is said to be limited to the retaliatory use of force against those who have initiated its use. All other possible roles for government, such as protecting individuals against themselves or requiring people to help one another, are regarded as illegitimate. Hospers does not deny that it would be a good thing for people to have sufficient resources to meet at least their basic nutritional needs, but he denies that any government has a duty to provide for those needs. Hence, Hospers thinks that the poor have no right to welfare.

A basic difficulty with Hospers's view is his claim that rights to life and property are understood so as to exclude a right to welfare derive from an ideal of liberty. Surely, such a right to property might well justify a rich person's depriving a poor person of the liberty to acquire the goods and resources necessary for meeting his or her basic nutritional needs. But how could we appeal to an ideal of liberty to justify such a deprivation? Libertarians like Hospers argue that we can, but welfare liberals like Rawls disagree.[1]

In "Justice as Fairness—For Whom?" Susan M. Okin also examines the capacity of Rawls's theory of justice to deal with gender-structured roles of our society. Noting Rawls's failure to apply his original position–type thinking to family structures, Okin is skeptical about the possibility of using a welfare liberal ideal of fairness to support feminist justice. She contends that in a gender-structured society like our own, male philosophers cannot achieve the sympathetic imagination required to see things from the standpoint of women. In a gender-structured society, Okin claims, male philosophers cannot do the original position–type thinking required by Rawls's ideal of justice as fairness because they lack the ability to put themselves in the position of women.

1 This question is taken up later in the Concluding Philosophical Postscript.

Yet at the same time that Okin despairs of doing original position–type thinking in a gender-structured society, like our own, she herself purportedly does a considerable amount of just that type of thinking. For example, she claims that Rawls's principles of justice "would seem to require a radical rethinking not only of the division of labor within families but also of all the nonfamily institutions that assume it." She also claims that "the abolition of gender seems essential for the fulfillment of Rawls's criterion of political justice."

But which is it? Can we or can we not do the original position–type thinking required by Rawls's ideal of justice as fairness? I think that Okin's own work, as well as my own, demonstrates that we can do such thinking and that her reasons for thinking that we cannot are not persuasive. For to do original position–type thinking, it is not necessary that everyone be able to put themselves imaginatively in the position of everyone else. All that is necessary is that some people be able to do so. Some people may not be able to do original position–type thinking because they have been deprived of a proper moral education. Others may be able to do original position–type thinking only after they have been forced to mend their ways and live morally for a period of time.

Moreover, in putting oneself imaginatively in the place of others, one need not completely replicate the experience of others. For example, one need not actually feel what it is like to be a murderer to adequately take into account the murderer's perspective. Original position–type thinking with respect to a particular issue requires only a general appreciation of the benefits and burdens that accrue to people affected by that issue. So with respect to feminist justice, we need to be able to generally appreciate what women and men stand to gain and lose when moving from a nonandrogynous or gendered society to an androgynous or gender-free society.

Of course, even among men and women in our gendered society who are in a broad sense capable of a sense of justice, some may not presently be able to do such original position–type thinking about the proper relationships between men and women; these men and women may be able to do so only after the laws and social practices in our society have significantly shifted toward a more gender-free society. But this inability of some to do original position-type thinking does not render it impossible for others, who have effectively used the opportunities for moral development available to them to achieve the sympathetic imagination necessary for original position-type thinking with respect to the proper relationships between men and women.[2]

Despite their differences, the political views of Rawls, Hospers, and Okin have more in common with each other than they do with the view that Abu'l A'la Mawdudi defends in "The Political Theory of Islam." A'la Mawdudi explains that the first principle of Islamic political theory is that authority rests with Allah; no one has any right to command in his or her own right. Nor does the right to interpret the law of Allah rightfully rest with any priestly class. Every Muslim is entitled to interpret the law of Allah when such interpretation becomes necessary. In so-called Western democracies, with their separation of politics and religion, those who come to power usually do not have the best interests of the great mass of common people at heart. To make matters worse, the great mass of common people are frequently incapable of perceiving their own true interests. That is why it is appropriate that Allah has laid down limits to human freedom. For example,

2 Interestingly, when Rawls finally takes up the question of justice in the family in *Restatement,* a question that he neglected in virtually all of his previous work, he agrees with the positive requirements that Okin suggests can be derived from his theory.

while a right to private property is recognized, it is qualified by the obligation to pay *zakah* (poor dues) and the prohibition of interest, gambling, and speculation. Similarly, the law of God has prohibited the unrestricted intermingling of the sexes and recognized man's guardianship of women for the betterment of all. A'la Mawdudi further maintains that the lives, property, and honor of nonbelievers are protected within an Islamic state; it is just that they are not allowed to influence the basic policies of the state. Moreover, in an Islamic state everyone is equal by nature; the only true criterion of superiority is religious piety.

Obviously, while the specific interpretation of the laws of God may be different, there are clear points of similarity between what A'la Mawdudi describes as an Islamic state and the kind of state many fundamentalist Christians want to establish in the West.

# 46    Justice as Fairness: A Restatement

JOHN RAWLS

## The Idea of the Original Position

. . . Let us begin with how we might be led to the original position and the reasons for using it. The following line of thought might lead us to it: we start with the organizing idea of society as a fair system of cooperation between free and equal persons. Immediately the question arises as to how the fair terms of cooperation are specified. For example: Are they specified by an authority distinct from the persons cooperating, say, by God's law? Or are these terms recognized by everyone as fair by reference to a moral order of values,[1] say, by rational intuition, or by reference to what some have viewed as "natural law"? Or are they settled by an agreement reached by free and equal citizens engaged in cooperation, and made in view of what they regard as their reciprocal advantage, or good?

Justice as fairness adopts a form of the last answer: the fair terms of social cooperation are to be given by an agreement entered into by those engaged in it. One reason it does this is that, given the assumption of reasonable pluralism, citizens cannot agree on any moral authority, say a sacred text or a religious institution or tradition. Nor can

they agree about a moral order of values or the dictates of what some view as natural law. So what better alternative is there than an agreement between citizens themselves reached under conditions that are fair for all?

Now this agreement, like any other, must be entered into under certain conditions if it is to be a valid agreement from the point of view of political justice. In particular, these conditions must situate free and equal persons fairly and must not permit some to have unfair bargaining advantages over others. Further, threats of force and coercion, deception and fraud, and so on must be ruled out. So far, so good. These considerations are familiar from everyday life. But agreements in everyday life are made in determinate situations within the background institutions of the basic structure; and the particular features of these situations affect the terms of the agreements reached. Clearly, unless those situations satisfy the conditions for valid and fair agreements, the terms agreed to will not be regarded as fair.

Justice as fairness hopes to extend the idea of a fair agreement to the basic structure itself. Here we face a serious difficulty for any political conception of justice that uses the idea of contract, whether or not the contract is social. The difficulty is this: we must specify a point of view from which a fair agreement between free and equal persons can be reached; but this point of view must be removed from and not distorted by the particular features and circumstances of the existing basic structure. The original position, with the feature I have called the "veil of ignorance" (*Theory,* 824) specifies this point of view. In the original position, the parties are not allowed to know the social positions or the particular comprehensive doctrines of the persons they represent. They also do not know persons' race and ethnic group, sex, or various native endowments such as strength and intelligence, all within the normal range. We express these limits on information figuratively by saying the parties are behind a veil of ignorance.[2]

One reason why the original position must abstract from the contingencies—the particular features and circumstances of persons—within the basic structure is that the conditions for a fair agreement between free and equal persons on the first principles of justice for that structure must eliminate the bargaining advantages that inevitably arise over time within any society as a result of cumulative social and historical tendencies. "To persons according to their threat advantage" (or their de facto political power, or wealth, or native endowments) is not the basis of political justice. Contingent historical advantages and accidental influences from the past should not affect an agreement on principles that are to regulate the basic structure from the present into the future.[3]

The idea of the original position is proposed, then, as the answer to the question of how to extend the idea of a fair agreement to an agreement on principles of political justice for the basic structure. That position is set up as a situation that is fair to the parties as free and equal, and as properly informed and rational. Thus any agreement made by the parties as citizens' representatives is fair. Since the content of the agreement concerns the principles of justice for the basic structure, the agreement in the original position specifies the fair terms of social cooperation between citizens regarded as such persons. Hence the name: justice as fairness.

Observe that, as stated in *Theory,* the original position generalizes the familiar idea of the social contract (*Theory,* §3). It does so by making the object of agreement the first principles of justice for the basic structure, rather than a particular form of government, as in Locke. The original position is also more abstract: the agreement must be regarded as both hypothetical and nonhistorical.

(i) It is hypothetical, since we ask what the parties (as described) could, or would, agree to, not what they have agreed to.

(ii) It is nonhistorical, since we do not suppose the agreement has ever, or indeed ever could actually be entered into. And even if it could, that would make no difference.

The second point (ii) means that what principles the parties would agree to is to be decided by analysis. We characterize the original position by various stipulations—each with its own reasoned backing—so that the agreement that would be reached can be worked out deductively by reasoning from how the parties are situated and described, the alternatives open to them, and from what the parties count as reasons and the information available to them.

Here there may seem to be a serious objection: since hypothetical agreements are not binding at all, the agreement of the parties in the original position would appear to be of no significance.[4] In reply, the significance of the original position lies in the fact that it is a device of representation or, alternatively, a thought-experiment for the purpose of public- and self-clarification. We are to think of it as modeling two things:

First, it models what we regard—here and now—as fair conditions under which the representatives of citizens, viewed solely as free and equal persons, are to agree to the fair terms of cooperation whereby the basic structure is to be regulated.

Second, it models what we regard—here and now—as acceptable restrictions on the reasons on the basis of which the parties, situated in fair conditions, may properly put forward certain principles of political justice and reject others.

Thus if the original position suitably models our convictions about these two things (namely, fair conditions of agreement between citizens as free and equal, and appropriate restrictions on reasons), we conjecture that the principles of justice the parties would agree to (could we properly work them out) would specify the terms of cooperation that we regard—here and now—as fair and supported by the best reasons. This is because, in that case, the original position would have succeeded in modeling in a suitable manner what we think on due reflection are the reasonable considerations to ground the principles of a political conception of justice.

To illustrate regarding fair conditions: the parties are symmetrically situated in the original position. This models our considered conviction that in matters of basic political justice citizens are equal in all relevant respects: that is, that they possess to a sufficient degree the requisite powers of moral personality and the other capacities that enable them to be normal and fully cooperating members of society over a complete life. Thus, in accordance with the precept of formal equality that those equal (similar) in all relevant respects are to be treated equally (similarly), citizens' representatives are to be situated symmetrically in the original position. Otherwise we would not think that position fair to citizens as free and equal.

To illustrate regarding appropriate restrictions on reasons: if we are reasonable, it is one of our considered convictions that the fact that we occupy a particular social position, say, is not a good reason for us to accept, or to expect others to accept, a conception of justice that favors those in that position. If we are wealthy, or poor, we do not expect everyone else to accept a basic structure favoring the wealthy, or the poor, simply for that reason. To model this and other similar convic-tions, we do not let the parties know the social position of the persons they represent. The same idea is extended to other features of persons by the veil of ignorance.

In short, the original position is to be understood as a device of representation. As such it models our considered convictions as reasonable persons by describing the parties (each of whom is responsible for the fundamental interests of a free and equal citizen) as fairly situated and as reaching an agreement subject to appropriate restrictions on reasons for favoring principles of political justice. . . .

## The Original Position: The Setup

[This section] considers two main topics in this order: the setup of the original position and the argument from the original position for the two principles of justice. This argument is divided into two fundamental comparisons: the first fundamental comparison and the second fundamental comparison. Since we have already discussed the original position as a device of representation, I focus here on a few details about how it is set up.[5]

Keep in mind throughout that, as a device of representation, the original position models two things.

First, it models what we regard—here and now—as fair conditions under which the representatives of citizens, viewed solely as free and equal persons, are to agree to the fair terms of social cooperation (as expressed by principles of justice) whereby the basic structure is to be regulated.

Second, it models what we regard—here and now—as acceptable restrictions on the reasons on the basis of which the parties (as citizens' representatives), situated in those fair conditions, may properly put forward certain principles of justice and reject others.

Keep in mind also that the original position serves other purposes as well. As we have said, it provides a way to keep track of our assumptions. We can see what we have assumed by looking at the way the parties and their situation have been described. The original position also brings out the combined force of our assumptions by uniting them into one surveyable idea that enables us to see their implications more easily.

I now turn to matters of detail. Note first the similarity between the argument from the original position and arguments in economics and social theory. The elementary theory of the consumer (the household) contains many examples of the latter. In each case we have rational persons (or agents) making decisions, or arriving at agreements, subject to certain conditions. From these persons' knowledge and beliefs, their desires and interests, and the alternatives they face, as well as the likely consequences they expect from adopting each alternative, we can figure out what they will decide, or agree to, unless they make a mistake in reasoning or otherwise fail to act sensibly. If the main elements at work can be modeled by mathematical assumptions, it may be possible to prove what they will do, ceteris paribus.

Despite the similarity between familiar arguments in economics and social theory and the argument from the original position, there are fundamental differences. One difference is that our aim is not to describe and explain how people actually behave in certain situations, or how institutions actually work. Our aim is to uncover a public basis for a political conception of justice, and doing this belongs to political philosophy and not social theory. In describing the parties we are not describing persons as we find them. Rather, the parties are described according to how we want to model rational representatives of free and equal citizens. In addition, we impose of the parties certain reasonable conditions as seen in the symmetry of their situation with respect to one another and the limits of their knowledge (the veil of ignorance).

Here again we distinguish between the rational and the reasonable, a distinction that parallels Kant's distinction between the hypothetical imperative and the categorical imperative. Kant's cat-

egorical imperative procedure subjects an agent's rational and sincere maxim (drawn up in the light of the agent's empirical practical reason) to the reasonable constraints contained in that procedure, and thus constrains the agent's conduct by the requirements of pure practical reason. Similarly, the reasonable conditions imposed on the parties in the original position constrain them in reaching a rational agreement on principles of justice as they try to advance the good of those they represent. In each case the reasonable has priority over the rational and subordinates it absolutely. This priority expresses the priority of right; and justice as fairness resembles Kant's view in having this feature.[6]

The terms "reasonable" and "rational" will not be explicitly defined. We gather their meaning by how they are used and by attending to the contrast between them. Yet a remark may help: the reasonable is viewed as a basic intuitive moral idea; it may be applied to persons, their decisions and actions, as well as to principles and standards, to comprehensive doctrines and to much else. We are concerned at first with reasonable principles of justice for the basic structure. These are principles it would be reasonable for free and equal citizens to accept as specifying the fair terms of their social cooperation. Justice as fairness conjectures that the principles that will seem reasonable for this purpose, all things considered, are the same principles that rational representatives of citizens, when subject to reasonable constraints, would adopt to regulate their basic institutions. What constraints, though, are reasonable? We say: those that arise from situating citizens" representatives symmetrically when they are represented solely as free and equal, and not as belonging to this or that social class, or as possessing these or those native endowments, or this or that (comprehensive) conception of the good. While this conjecture may have an initial plausibility, only its detailed elaboration can show how far it is sound.

We should like the argument from the original position to be, so far as is possible, a deductive one, even if the reasoning we actually give falls short of this standard.[7] The point in aiming for this is that we do not want the parties' accepting the two principles to depend on psychological hypotheses or social conditions not already included in the description of the original position. Consider the proposition in economics that the agent for the household buys the commodity-bundle indicated by the (unique) point in commodity-space at which the budget line is tangent to the (highest) in-difference curve touching that line. This proposition follows deductively from the premises of demand theory. The necessary psychology is already included in those premises. Ideally we want the same to be true of the argument from the original position: we include the necessary psychology in the description of the parties as rational representatives who are moved to secure the good of those they represent, as this good is specified by the account of primary goods. As such, the parties are artificial persons, merely inhabitants of our device of representation: they are characters who have a part in the play of our thought-experiment.

With respect to the alternatives available to the parties, we do not try to say what principles they would think of as possible alternatives. To do so would be a complicated business and a distraction from our practical aim. Rather, we simply hand the parties a list of principles, a menu, as it were. Included on the list are the more important conceptions of political justice found in our tradition of political philosophy, together with several other alternatives we want to examine. The parties must agree on one alternative on this menu.

The principles of justice agreed to are not, then, deduced from the conditions of the original position: they are selected from a given list. The original position is a selection device: it operates on a familiar family of conceptions of justice found in, or shaped from, our tradition of political philosophy. If it is objected that certain principles are not on the list, say libertarian principles of justice,[8] those principles must be added to it. Justice as fairness then argues that the two principles of justice would still be agreed to. Should this argument

succeed, libertarians must object to the setup of the original position itself as a device of representation. For example, they must say that it fails to represent considerations they regard as essential, or that it represents them in the wrong way. The argument continues from there.

To argue from a given list cannot, of course, establish what is the most appropriate conception of justice among all possible alternatives, the best conception, as it were. It may, however, suffice for our first and minimum objective: namely, to find a conception of political justice that can specify an appropriate moral basis of democratic institutions and can hold its own against the known existing alternatives.

## The Circumstances of Justice

We are to think of the circumstances of justice as reflecting the historical conditions under which modern democratic societies exist. These include what we may call the objective circumstances of moderate scarcity and the necessity of social cooperation for all to have a decent standard of life. Also especially important are the circumstances that reflect the fact that in a modern democratic society citizens affirm different, and indeed incommensurable and irreconcilable, though reasonable, comprehensive doctrines in the light of which they understand their conceptions of the good. This is the fact of reasonable pluralism. There is no politically practicable way to eliminate this diversity except by the oppressive use of state power to establish a particular comprehensive doctrine and to silence dissent, the fact of oppression. This seems evident not only from the history of democratic states but also from the development of thought and culture in the context of free institutions. We take this pluralism to be a permanent feature of a democratic society, and view it as characterizing what we may call the subjective circumstances of justice.

One role of political philosophy is to help us reach agreement on a political conception of justice, but it cannot show, clearly enough to gain general and free political agreement, that any single reasonable comprehensive doctrine, with its conception of the good, is superior. It does not follow (and justice as fairness as a political conception of justice does not say, and must not say) that there is no true comprehensive doctrine, or no best conception of the good. It only says that we cannot expect to reach a workable political agreement as to what it is. Since reasonable pluralism is viewed as permanent condition of a democratic culture, we look for a conception of political justice that takes that plurality as given. Only in this way can we fulfill the liberal principle of legitimacy: when constitutional essentials are involved, political power, as the power of free and equal citizens, is to be exercised in ways that all citizens as reasonable and rational might endorse in the light of their common human reason. Social unity is based on citizens' accepting a political conception of justice and uses ideas of the good fitting within it. It is not based on a complete conception of the good rooted in a comprehensive doctrine.

The parties, as representatives of free and equal citizens, act as trustees or guardians. Thus, in agreeing to principles of justice, they must secure the fundamental interests of those they represent. This does not mean that the parties are self-interested, much less selfish, as these words are normally used. Nor does it mean this when applied to citizens in society for whom the parties are responsible. True, the parties take no direct interest in the interests of persons represented by other parties. But whether people are self-interested, or even selfish, depends on the content of their final ends; on whether these are interests in themselves, in their own wealth and position, in their own power and prestige. In acting responsibly as trustees to secure persons' fundamental interests in their freedom and quality—in the conditions adequate for the development and exercise of their moral powers and the effective pursuit of their conception of the good on fair terms with others—the parties are not viewing those they represent as selfish, or self-interested. Certainly we

expect and indeed want people to care about their liberties and opportunities so that they can achieve their good. We think they would show a lack of self-respect and weakness of character in not doing so.

That the parties take no direct interest in the interests of those represented by the other parties reflects an essential aspect of how citizens are quite properly moved when questions of political justice arise about the basic structure. Deep religious and moral conflicts characterize the subjective circumstances of justice. Those engaged in these conflicts are surely not in general self-interested, but rather, see themselves as defending their basic rights and liberties which secure their legitimate and fundamental interests. Moreover, these conflicts can be the most intractable and deeply divisive, often more so than social and economic ones.

Similarly, without an appreciation of the depth of the conflict between comprehensive doctrines as they enter the political domain, the case for formulating a reasonable political conception of justice with its idea of public reason is less likely to seem convincing. But this is getting ahead.

Once again recall that the original position is a device of representation: it models, first, what we regard (here and now) as fair conditions for the terms of social cooperation to be agreed to (reflected in the symmetry of the parties' situation); and second, it models what we regard (here and now) as reasonable restrictions on reasons that may be used in arguing for principles of justice to regulate the basic structure. Various formal constraints of the concept of right are modeled in the original position by requiring the parties to evaluate principles of justice from a suitably general point of view. However rational it might be for the parties to favor principles framed to promote the determinate and known interests of those they represent, should they have the opportunity, the constraints of right, joined with the limits on information (modeled by the veil of ignorance), make that impossible.[9]

It is a commonplace of moral philosophy to require first principles to be general and universal.

Principles are general when it is possible to state them without the use of proper names or rigged definite descriptions. They are universal when they can be applied without inconsistency or self-defeating incoherence to all moral agents, in our case, to all citizens in the society in question. Justice as fairness also requires, and this is much less common, that first principles of political justice be public. This condition is applied to political conceptions, not to moral conceptions generally; whether it applies to the latter is a separate question. In the case of political conceptions for the basic structure the publicity condition seems appropriate. It means that in evaluating principles the parties in the original position are to take into account the consequences, social and psychological, of public recognition by citizens that these principles are mutually acknowledged and that they effectively regulate the basic structure. These consequences are important in the argument from the original position, as we see in due course.

## Formal Constraints of the Veil of Ignorance

Although the argument from the original position could be presented formally, I use the idea of the original position as a natural and vivid way to convey the kind of reasoning the parties may engage in. Many questions about the original position answer themselves if we remember this and see it is a device of representation modeling reasonable constraints that limit the reasons that the parties as rational representatives may appeal to. Is that position a general assembly which includes at one moment every one who lives at some time? No. Is it a gathering of all actual or possible persons? Plainly not. Can we enter it, so to speak, and if so when? We can enter it at any time. How? Simply by reasoning in accordance with the modeled constraints, citing only reasons those constraints allow.

It is essential that the parties as rational representatives be led to the same judgment as to which

principles to adopt. This allows that a unanimous agreement can be reached. The veil of ignorance achieves this result by limiting the parties to the same body of general facts (the presently accepted facts of social theory) and to the same information about the general circumstances of society: that it exists under the circumstances of justice, both objective and subjective, and that reasonably favorable conditions making a constitutional democracy possible obtain.

Along with other conditions on the original position, the veil of ignorance removes differences in bargaining advantages, so that in this and other respects the parties are symmetrically situated. Citizens are represented solely as free and equal persons: as those who have to the minimum sufficient degree the two moral powers and other capacities enabling them to be normal cooperating members of society over a complete life. By situating the parties symmetrically, the original position respects the basic precept of formal equality, or Sidgwick's principle of equity: those similar in all relevant respects are to be treated similarly. With this precept satisfied, the original position is fair.

We suppose that the parties are rational, where rationality (as distinguished from reasonableness) is understood in the way familiar from economics. Thus the parties are rational in that they can rank their final ends consistently; they deliberate guided by such principles as: to adopt the most effective means to one's ends; to select the alternative most likely to advance those ends; to schedule activities so that, ceteris paribus, more rather than less of those ends can be fulfilled.

There is, be it noted, one important modification in this idea of rationality in regard to certain special psychologies.[10] These include a liability to envy and spite, a peculiarly high aversion to risk and uncertainty, and a strong will to dominate and exercise power over others. The parties (in contrast to persons in society) are not moved by such desires and inclinations. Remember it is up to us, you and me, who are setting up justice as fairness, to describe the parties (as artificial persons in our device of representation) as best suits our aims in developing a political conception of justice. Since envy, for instance, is generally regarded as something to be avoided and feared, at least when it becomes intense, it seems desirable that, if possible, the choice of principles should not be influenced by this trait.[11] So we stipulate that the parties are not influenced by these psychologies as they try to secure the good of those they represent.

Since the veil of ignorance prevents the parties from knowing the (comprehensive) doctrines and conceptions of the good of the persons they represent, they must have some other grounds for deciding which principles to select in the original position. Here we face a serious problem: unless we can set up the original position so that the parties can agree on principles of justice moved by appropriate grounds, justice as fairness cannot be carried through.

To solve this problem is one reason we introduced the idea of primary goods and enumerated a list of items falling under this heading. As we saw, these goods are identified by asking which things are generally necessary as social conditions and all-purpose means to enable citizens, regarded as free and equal, adequately to develop and fully exercise their two moral powers, and to pursue their determinate conceptions of the good. Primary goods, we said, are things persons need as citizens, rather than as human beings apart from any normative conception. Here the political conception, and not a comprehensive moral doctrine, helps to specify these needs and requirements. . . .

## Two Principles of Justice

[V]iewing society as a fair system of cooperation between citizens regarded as free and equal, what principles of justice are most appropriate to specify basic rights and liberties, and to regulate social and economic inequalities in citizens' prospects over a complete life? These inequalities are our primary concern.

To find a principle to regulate these inequalities, we look to our firmest considered convic-

tions about equal basic rights and liberties, the fair value of the political liberties as well as fair equality of opportunity. We look outside the sphere of distributive justice more narrowly construed to see whether an appropriate distributive principle is singled out by those firmest convictions once their essential elements are represented in the original position as a device of representation. This device is to assist us in working out which principle, or principles, the representatives of free and equal citizens would select to regulate social and economic inequalities in these prospects over a complete life when they assume that the equal basic liberties and fair opportunities are already secured.

The idea here is to use our firmest considered convictions about the nature of a democratic society as a fair system of cooperation between free and equal citizens—as modeled in the original position—to see whether the combined assertion of those convictions so expressed will help us to identify an appropriate distributive principle for the basic structure with its economic and social inequalities in citizens' life-prospects. Our convictions about principles regulating those inequalities are much less firm and assured; so we look to our firmest convictions for guidance where assurance is lacking and guidance is needed (*Theory*, §§4, 20). . . .

To try to answer our question, let us turn to a revised statement of the two principles of justice discussed in *Theory*, §§11–14. They should now read:[12]

(a) Each person has the same indefeasible claim to a fully adequate scheme of equal basic liberties, which scheme is compatible with the same scheme of liberties for all; and

(b) Social and economic inequalities are to satisfy two conditions: first, they are to be attached to offices and positions open to all under conditions of fair equality of opportunity; and second, they are to be to the greatest benefit of the least-advantaged members of society (the difference principle).[13]

## First Fundamental Comparison

The preceding survey completes a brief account of the setup of the original position. We now start on the second topic of this part, the reasoning of the parties for the two principles of justice. This reasoning is organized as two fundamental comparisons.[14] Doing this enables us to separate the reasons that lead the parties to select the difference principle from the reasons that lead them to select the principle of the basic equal liberties. Despite the formal resemblance between the difference principle as a principle of distributive justice and the maximin rule as a rule of thumb for decisions under uncertainty, the reasoning for the difference principle does not rely on this rule. The formal resemblance is misleading.[15]

To proceed: we assume that the parties reason by comparing alternatives two at a time. They begin with the two principles of justice and compare those principles with the other available alternatives on the list. If the two principles are supported by a stronger balance of reasons in each such comparison, the argument is complete and those principles are adopted. In any comparison there may be reasons, possibly strong ones, for and against each of the two alternatives. Still, it may be clear that the balance of reasons favors one alternative over the other. Plainly an argument for the two principles depends on judgment—on judging the balance of reasons—and is also relative to a given list. We do not claim that the two principles would be agreed to from a complete, or any possible, list.[16] To claim that would be excessive and I attempt no general argument.

The two comparisons we will discuss are, then, but a small part of the argument that would be required to provide a reasonably conclusive argument for the two principles of justice. This is because the two principles are compared, each time in a different way, with the principle of average utility, and the comparison shows at best their superiority over that principle. The first comparison, which gives the reasoning for the first principle, is,

I think, quite conclusive; the second comparison, which gives the reasoning for the difference principle, is less conclusive. It turns on a more delicate balance of less decisive considerations. Nevertheless, despite the limited scope of this two-part argument, it is instructive in suggesting how we can proceed in other comparisons to bring out the merits of the two principles.

The two comparisons arise as follows. In the history of democratic thought two contrasting ideas of society have a prominent place: one is the idea of society as a fair system of social cooperation between citizens regarded as free and equal; the other is the idea of society as a social system organized so as to produce the most good summed over all its members, where this good is a complete good specified by a comprehensive doctrine. The tradition of the social contract elaborates the first idea, the utilitarian tradition is a special case of the second.

Between these two traditions there is a basic contrast: the idea of society as a fair system of social cooperation is quite naturally specified so as to include the ideas of equality (the equality of basic rights, liberties, and fair opportunities) and of reciprocity (of which the difference principle is an example). By contrast, the idea of society organized to produce the most good expresses a maximizing and aggregative principle of political justice. In utilitarianism, the ideas of equality and of reciprocity are accounted for only indirectly, as what is thought to be normally necessary to maximize the sum of social welfare. The two comparisons turn on this contrast: the first brings out the advantage of the two principles with respect to equality, the second their advantage with respect to reciprocity, or mutuality.

As I said above, presenting the case for the two principles by way of these two comparisons separates the reasons that particularly favor the equal basic liberties from the reasons that particularly favor the difference principle. Given this separation, the situation is not as one might have thought. The first comparison, which uses the guidelines of the maximin rule for decisions under uncertainty, is quite decisive in supporting the equal basic rights and liberties; but those guidelines lend little support to the difference principle. In fact, when we formulate the second comparison they are not used at all.

In the first comparison the two principles of justice, taken as a unit are compared with the principle of average utility as the sole principle of justice. The principle of average utility says that the institutions of the basic structure are to be arranged so as to maximize the average welfare of the members of society, beginning now and extending into the foreseeable future.

The second fundamental comparison is that in which the two principles, again taken as a unit, are compared with an alternative formed by substituting for the difference principle the principle of average utility (combined with a stipulated social minimum). In all other respects the two principles of justice are unchanged. In the second comparison, then, the principles prior to the difference principle are already accepted and the parties are selecting a principle for regulating economic and social inequalities (differences in citizens' prospects over a complete life) for a society in which those prior principles are assumed to be effective in regulating the basic structure. This means that people already view themselves as free and equal citizens of a democratic society, and the parties must take that into account.

The first comparison is the more fundamental because the aim of justice as fairness is to work out an alternative conception of political justice to those found in utilitarianism, perfectionism, and intuitionism (the first has been particularly dominant in our political tradition), while at the same time finding a more appropriate moral basis for the institutions of a modern democratic society. Should the two principles win in the first comparison, this aim is already in good part achieved; but should they lose, all is lost. The first comparison is also essential in replying to recent libertarian views, as we may call them, of Buchanan, Gauthier, and Nozick, the first two being explicitly contractarian.

The first comparison with the principle of average utility is important for another reason: it illustrates how arguments from the original position

proceed, and it provides a fairly simple case which displays the nature of those arguments. Surveying them prepares us for the second comparison, which turns on a less decisive balance of reasons.

## The Structure of the Argument and the Maximin Rule

First, a statement of the maximin rule: it tells us to identify the worst outcome of each available alternative and then to adopt the alternative whose worst outcome is better than the worst outcomes of all the other alternatives. To follow this rule in selecting principles of justice for the basic structure we focus on the worst social positions that would be allowed when that structure is effectively regulated by those principles under various circumstances. What this means will become clearer by looking at the argument from the original position in the first comparison.[17]

The argument can be described as follows:

(i) If there are certain conditions in which it is rational to be guided by the maximin rule when agreeing to principles of justice for the basic structure, then under those conditions the two principles of justice would be agreed to rather than the principle of average utility.

(ii) There are certain conditions, three in particular, such that, when they obtain, it is rational to be guided by the maximin rule when agreeing to principles of justice for the basic structure.

(iii) These three conditions obtain in the original position.

(iv) Therefore, the two principles would be agreed to by the parties rather than the principle of average utility.

While each of the premises (i)–(iii) might be disputed, for the time being let's assume that (i) is acceptable. It is (iii) that calls for the most explanation; but (ii) also requires comment, so let's start with (ii).

Let us review the three conditions referred to in (ii) above.[18]

(a) Since the maximin rule takes no account of probabilities, that is, of how likely it is that the circumstances obtain for their respective worst outcomes to be realized, the first condition is that the parties have no reliable basis for estimating the probabilities of the possible social circumstances that affect the fundamental interests of the persons they represent. This condition fully obtains when the concept of probability does not even apply.

(b) Since the maximin rule directs the parties to evaluate the alternatives only by their worst possible outcomes, it must be rational for the parties as trustees not to be much concerned for what might be gained above what can be guaranteed (for those they represent) by adopting the alternative whose worst outcome is better than the worst outcomes of all the other alternatives. Let's call this best worst outcome the "guaranteeable level." The second condition obtains, then, when the guaranteeable level is itself quite satisfactory. It fully obtains when this level is completely satisfactory.

(c) Since the maximin rule directs the parties to avoid alternatives whose worst outcomes are below the guaranteeable level, the third condition is that the worst outcomes of all the other alternatives are significantly below the guaranteeable level. When those outcomes are far below that level and altogether intolerable, and must, if possible, be avoided, the third condition fully obtains.

Three comments about these conditions: First, being guided by the maximin rule in these conditions is compatible with the familiar principle of maximizing the fulfillment of one's interests, or (rational) good. The parties' use of the rule to organize their deliberations in no way violates this familiar principle of rationality. Rather, they use the rule to guide them in deciding in accordance with that principle in the highly unusual, if not unique, circumstances of the original position when the matter at hand is of such fundamental significance.

Note, however, this caveat: the argument guided by the rule fits with the idea that rational agents maximize their expected utility, but only if

that expected utility is understood to have no substantive content. That is, it does not mean expected pleasure, or agreeable consciousness (Sidgwick), or satisfaction. Expected utility is a purely formal idea specified by a rule or a mathematical function. As such, the rule or function simply represents the order, or ranking, in which the alternatives are judged better and worse in meeting the agent's fundamental interests, which are in this case the interests of citizens as free and equal.

A second point is that it is not necessary that all, or any, of the three conditions fully obtain for the maximin rule to be a sensible way to organize deliberation. For should the third condition fully obtain, this suffices to bring the maximin rule into play, provided that the guaranteeable level is reasonably satisfactory, so long as the first condition at least partially obtains. However, in the first comparison the first condition has a relatively minor role. As we shall see, what is crucial is that the second and third conditions should obtain to a high degree.

Finally, it is not essential for the parties to use the maximin rule in the original position. It is simply a useful heuristic device. Focusing on the worst outcomes has the advantage of forcing us to consider what our fundamental interests really are when it comes to the design of the basic structure. This is not a question that we would often, if ever, ask ourselves in ordinary life. Part of the point of the original position is that it forces us to ask that question and moreover to do so in a highly special situation which gives it a definite sense.

Let us now review why the second and third conditions obtain to a high degree for the parties given their situation in the original position.

The second condition obtains because the guaranteeable level is quite satisfactory. What is this level? It is the situation of the least-advantaged members of the well-ordered society that results from the full realization of the two principles of justice (given reasonably favorable conditions). Justice as fairness claims that a well-ordered society paired with the two principles of justice is a highly satisfactory political and social world. . . . This basic point about the guaranteeable level is crucial for the argument.[19]

The third condition obtains given the assumption we make that there are realistic social circumstances, even with reasonably favorable conditions, under which the principle of utility would require, or allow, that the basic rights and liberties of some be in various ways restricted, or even denied altogether, for the sake of greater benefits for others or for society as a whole. These circumstances are among the possibilities that the parties must guard against on behalf of those they represent.

Utilitarians may question this assumption. But to support it we need not invoke such drastic infringements of liberty as slavery and serfdom, or oppressive religious persecution. Consider instead a possible balance of social advantages to a sizable majority from limiting the political liberties and religious freedoms of small and weak minorities.[20] The principle of average utility seems to allow possible outcomes that the parties, as trustees, must regard as altogether unacceptable and intolerable. So the third condition obtains to a high degree. . . .

In this comparison, we do not stress the first condition: we assume it to hold, not fully, but only to some significant degree. This we do because the first condition raises difficult points in the theory of probability that so far as possible we want to avoid. Hence we stipulate that knowledge and well-founded beliefs about probabilities must be based on at least some established facts or well-supported beliefs about the world. This fits any interpretation of probability except a general subjectivist (or Bayesian) one. We then say the parties lack the requisite information, and so cannot have well-founded probabilities in selecting among alternatives.

The point is this: the parties know the general commonsense facts of human psychology and political sociology. They also know that the society in question exists in the circumstances of justice under reasonably favorable conditions. These are conditions that, provided the political will exists, make a constitutional regime possible. Yet whether the political will exists depends on a society's political culture and traditions, its religious and ethnic composition, and much else. Favorable conditions may exist when the political will does not.[21] Thus the knowledge that reasonably favorable conditions exist is far too little for the parties to specify a well-grounded probability distribution over the forms of political culture and tradition that might exist. History tells of more aristocracies and theocracies, dictatorships and class-states, than democracies. Of course, the parties don't have this particular knowledge. In any case, does that make those outcomes more likely than democracy? Surely such speculation is far beyond the reach of common sense, or uncommon sense, for that matter. About the first condition of the maximin rule, we claim, then, only that it holds sufficiently so that the argument of the first comparison emphasizing the second and third conditions is not put in doubt.

The argument emphasizing the second and third conditions is essentially as follows: if it is indeed the case that a well-ordered society regulated by the two principles of justice is a highly satisfactory form of political society that secures the basic rights and liberties equally for all (and thus represents a highly satisfactory guaranteeable level), and if the principle of utility may sometimes permit or else require the restriction or suppression of the rights and liberties of some for the sake of a greater aggregate of social well-being, then the parties must agree to the two principles of justice. Only in this way (in the first comparison) can they act responsibly as trustees: that is, effectively protect the fundamental interests of the person each represents, and at the same time make sure to avoid possibilities the realization of which would be altogether intolerable.

This argument rests on the parties' assuming that, given the capacity of those they represent to be free and equal persons and fully cooperating members of society over a complete life, those persons would never put their basic rights and liberties in jeopardy so long as there was a readily available and satisfactory alternative. What aim could the parties suppose those persons might have for doing that? Do they wish to take a chance on having ever more adequate material means to fulfill their ends? But the parties as representatives of citizens regarded as free and equal cannot for that purpose jeopardize citizens' basic rights and liberties. Their responsibility as trustees for citizens so regarded does not allow them to gamble with the basic rights and liberties of those citizens. . . .

## Second Fundamental Comparison

We have now completed our survey of the first fundamental comparison: the reasoning favoring the two principles of justice (as a unit) over the principle of average utility (as the sole principle of justice). While the outcome of that comparison achieves the most fundamental aim of justice as fairness, it does not give much support to the difference principle. The most it shows is that this principle adequately secures the general all-purpose means we need to take advantage of our basic freedoms. But other principles may be superior to it on that count.

To explore this question let us now discuss a second fundamental comparison in which the two principles of justice taken as a unit are compared to an alternative exactly the same as those principles except in one respect. The principle of average utility, combined with a suitable social minimum, is substituted for the difference principle. A minimum must be included, for the parties will always insist on some insurance of that kind: the question is how much is appropriate. The basic structure is, then, to be arranged so as to maximize average utility consistent, first, with guaranteeing the equal basic liberties (including their fair value) and fair equality of opportunity, and second, with maintaining a suitable social minimum. We refer to this mixed conception as the principle of restricted utility.[22]

The second comparison is fundamental for this reason: among the conceptions of justice in which the principle of utility has a prominent role, the principle of restricted utility would seem to be the strongest rival to the two principles of justice. Should these principles still be favored in this

comparison, then it would appear that other forms of the restricted utility principle would also be rejected. Their role would be that of subordinate norms regulating social policies within the limits allowed by more fundamental principles.

Note that the third condition of the maximin rule no longer obtains since both alternatives ensure against the worst possibilities, not only against the denial or restriction of the basic liberties and of fair equality of opportunity, but also, given the social minimum in the utility principle, against the more serious losses of well-being. Since we do not want to put any weight on the first condition of that rule, we exclude probability arguments entirely. We assume that there are two groups in society, the more and the less advantaged; and then we try to show that both would favor the difference principle over that of restricted utility. In effect, we argue that the second condition of the maximin rule is fully satisfied, or nearly enough so to provide an independent argument for the two principles. . . .

## Grounds Falling under Reciprocity

[T]he fact that the difference principle includes an idea of reciprocity distinguishes it from the restricted utility principle. The latter is a maximizing aggregative principle with no inherent tendency toward either equality or reciprocity; any such tendency depends on the consequences of applying it in given circumstances, which vary from case to case. The two fundamental comparisons exploit this fact: as we have said, the first brings out the advantage of the two principles with respect to equality (the equal basic liberties), the second with respect to reciprocity.

To simplify matters, let us assume that there are only two groups in society, the more and the less advantaged, and focus on inequalities of income and wealth alone. In its simplest form, the difference principle regulates these inequalities. Since the parties in the original position are symmetrically situated and know (from the common content of the two alternatives) that the principle adopted will apply to citizens viewed as free and

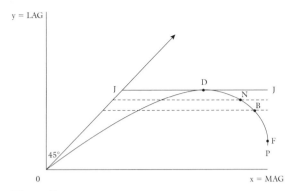

**Figure 1**

equal, they take equal division of income and wealth (equal life-prospects as indexed by those primary goods) as the starting point. They then ask: are there good reasons for departing from equal division, and if so, which inequalities arising in what ways are acceptable?

A political conception of justice must take into account the requirements of social organization and economic efficiency. The parties would accept inequalities in income and wealth when these work effectively to improve everyone's situation starting from equal division. This suggests the difference principle: taking equal division as the benchmark, those who gain more are to do so on terms acceptable to those who gain less, and in particular to those who gain the least.

We get that principle, then, by taking equal division as the starting point, together with an idea of reciprocity. The principle selects the highest point on the (most efficient) OP curve; and we saw that this point is the efficient point closest to the 45° line, which line represents equality and preserves equal division (see Figure 1). The idea of reciprocity implicit in the difference principle selects a natural focal point between the claims of efficiency and equality.[23]

To see one way the parties might arrive at the difference principle, consider Figure 1. Imagine they have agreed to move from O to D, as everyone gains in the segment OD and D is the first (Pareto) efficient point.

At D the parties ask whether they should proceed from D to B, which is on the southeast-sloping part of the OP curve to the right of D. B is the Bentham point at which average utility (so far as it depends on income and wealth) is maximized (subject to the constraints). The points in the segment D to B and on to the point F (the feudal point), where the utility of the most advantaged is maximized, are also efficient points: movements along that segment can raise the index of one group only by lowering the index of the other. The segment DF is the conflict segment in contrast to the segment OD along which everyone benefits by moving northeast.

The difference principle represents an agreement to stop at D and not to enter the conflict segment. D is the only point on the (highest) OP curve that meets the following reciprocity condition: those who are better off at any point are not better off to the detriment of those who are worse off at that point. Since the parties represent citizens as free and equal, and thus take equal division as the appropriate starting point, we say this is an (not the only) appropriate reciprocity condition. We haven't shown there is no other such condition. But it is hard to imagine what it might be.

To sum up: the difference principle expresses the idea that, starting from equal division, the more advantaged are not to be better off at any point to the detriment of the less well off. But since the difference principle applies to the basic structure, a deeper idea of reciprocity implicit in it is that social institutions are not to take advantage of contingencies of native endowment, or of initial social position, or of good or bad luck over the course of life, except in ways that benefit everyone, including the least favored. This represents a fair undertaking between the citizens seen as free and equal with respect to those inevitable contingencies.

Recall what we said earlier: the better endowed (who have a place in the distribution of native endowments they do not morally deserve) are encouraged to seek still further benefits—they are already favored by their fortunate place in the distribution—provided they train their endowments and use them in ways that contribute to the good of all, and in particular to the good of the least endowed (who have a less fortunate place in the distribution, a place they also do not morally deserve). This idea of reciprocity is implicit in the idea of regarding the distribution of native endowments as a common asset. Parallel but not identical considerations hold for the contingencies of social position and of good and bad luck. . . .

NOTES

1. This order I assume to be viewed as objective as in some form of moral realism. [Notes renumbered.—ED.]

2. [See Rawls, *Political Liberalism* (New York: Columbia University Press, 1993), pp. 24–25.]

3. This is an essential feature of justice as fairness as a form of the contract doctrine. It differs from Locke's view in this respect, and also from the contract views of Robert Nozick in *Anarchy, State, and Utopia* (New York: Basic Books, 1974), of James Buchanan in *The Limits of Liberty* (Chicago: University of Chicago Press, 1975), and of David Gauthier in *Morals by Agreement* (Oxford: Oxford University Press, 1986). In these three works citizens basic rights, liberties, and opportunities, as secured by the basic structure, depend on contingencies of history, and social circumstance and native endowment, in ways excluded by justice as fairness. We come back to this in §16.1.

4. This question is discussed by Ronald Dworkin in §1 of his critical review entitled Justice and Rights," *University of Chicago Law Review* (1973), reprinted in *Taking Rights Seriously* (Cambridge, Mass.: Harvard University Press, 1977), as chap. 6. I have discussed his interpretation briefly in "Justice as Fairness: Political Not Metaphysical," *Philosophy and Public Affairs* 14 (Summer 1985): 236f., n. 19; reprinted in Rawls, *Collected Papers*, ed. Samuel Freeman (Cambridge, Mass.: Harvard University Press, 1999), 400f., n. 19.

5. See *Theory*, §§20–25.

6. Here I correct a remark in *Theory*, §3: 15 and §9: 47 (1st ed.), where it is said that the theory of justice is a part of the theory of rational choice. From what we have just said, this is simply a mistake, and would imply that justice as fairness is at bottom Hobbesian (as Hobbes is often interpreted) rather than Kantian. What should have been said is that the account of the parties, and of their reasoning, uses the theory of rational choice (decision), but that this theory is itself part of a political conception of justice, one that tries to give an account of reasonable principles of justice. There is no thought

of deriving those principles from the concept of rationality as the sole normative concept.

7. See *Theory*, §20: 104f.

8. See Nozick's formulation of them in *Anarchy, State, and Utopia*, p. 151.

9. *Theory* doesn't use the phrase "a device of representation," but at various places makes the points in this paragraph. See *Theory*, §4: 16f., 18f.; §20: 104f.; §24: 119f., §78: 453. §87: 514.

10. See *Theory*, §25: 123ff.

11. [See *Theory*, §80: 465.]

12. This section summarizes some points from "The Basic Liberties and Their Priority, *Tanner Lectures on Human Values,* vol. 3, ed. Sterling McMurrin (Salt Lake City: University of Utah Press, 1982), §I, reprinted in *Political Liberalism*. In that essay I try to reply to what I believe are two of the more serious objections to my account of liberty in *Theory* raised by H. L. A. Hart in his splendid critical review essay, "Rawls on Liberty and Its Priority," *University of Chicago Law Review* 40 (Spring 1973): 551–555, reprinted in his *Essays in Jurisprudence and Philosophy* (Oxford: Oxford University Press, 1983). No changes made in justice as fairness in this restatement are more significant than those forced by Hart's review.

13. Instead of "the difference principle," many writers prefer the term "the maximin principle," or simply "maximin justice," or some such locution. See, for example, Joshua Cohen's very full and accurate account of the difference principle in "Democratic Equality," *Ethics* 99 (July 1989): 727–751. But I still use the term "difference principle" to emphasize first, that this principle and the maximin rule for decision under uncertainty (§28.1) are two very distinct things; and second, that in arguing for the difference principle over other distributive principles (say a restricted principle of (average) utility, which includes a social minimum), there is no appeal at all to the maximin rule for decision under uncertainty. The widespread idea that the argument for the difference principle depends on extreme aversion to uncertainty is a mistake, although a mistake unhappily encouraged by the faults of exposition in *Theory,* faults to be corrected in Part III of this restatement.

14. This way of organizing the reasoning for both principles was first sketched in "Reply to Alexander and Musgrave," *Quarterly Journal of Economics* 88 (November 1974), §§III–VI, pp. 639–653, reprinted in *Collected Papers*.

15. The failure to explain this was a serious fault in *Theory*.

16. See *Theory*, §87: 509.

17. *Theory*, §26: 132–135. As the account of this and later sections shows, the maximin rule was never proposed as the general principle of rational decision in all cases of risk and uncertainty, as some seem to have

thought. For example, see J. C. Harsanyi, in his review essay, "Can the Maximin Principle Serve as a Basis for Morality?" *American Political Science Review* 69 (1975): 594–606, and reprinted in his *Essays on Ethics, Social Behavior, and Scientific Explanation* (Dordrecht: D. Reidel Pub. Co., 1976). Such a proposal would be simply irrational, as Harsanyi argues, pp. 39f. On this point there was, and is, no disagreement. The only question is whether, given the highly special, indeed unique, conditions of the original position, the maximin rule is a useful heuristic rule of thumb for the parties to use to organize their deliberations.

18. Here we follow William Fellner, *Probability and Profit* (Homewood, Ill.: R. D. Irwin, 1965), pp. 140–142.

19. This important point about the guaranteeable level, while perhaps obvious, is never expressly stated in *Theory*. The failure to do so led some to think of the guaranteeable level as a natural, nonsocial, level below which individual utility drops precipitously to minus infinity, as it were. Thus they hoped to explain why *Theory* used the maximin rule even though they rejected the idea of such a natural, nonsocial level. But, as the text shows, this was not the intention. See the discussion by Joshua Cohen in "Democratic Equality," pp. 733f.

20. To block this kind of argument some utilitarians have imposed restrictions on the kind of advantages to individuals relevant to their utility function. For example, Harsanyi in his essay "Morality and the Theory of Rational Behavior," in *Utilitarianism and Beyond*, ed. Sen and Williams, p. 56, excludes what he calls antisocial preferences, for example, malice, envy, resentment, and the pleasures of cruelty. Now this is a funda-

mental departure from the classical (and traditional) utilitarian view in which all pleasures, or the satisfaction of actual preferences, regardless of their source, are intrinsically good. When Harsanyi abandons that view (a view he held in 1955 in his "Cardinal Welfare, Individualistic Ethics, and Interpersonal Comparisons," *Journal of Political Economy* 63 (1955): 309–321, reprinted in *Essays on Ethics, Social Behavior, and Scientific Explanation*, pp. 18ff.), he owes us an explanation of the grounds for counting certain pleasures, or satisfactions, for naught. Calling them antisocial is not enough. We need to know where his restrictions on entries in utility functions come from and how they are justified. Until these questions are answered within a suitably specified framework that is recognizably utilitarian, we cannot decide whether Harsanyi is entitled to impose them. One might ask whether a theory of basic rights and liberties, or a nonutilitarian ideal, lies in the background, tacit and unexpressed.

21. Germany between 1870 and 1945 is an example of a country where reasonably favorable conditions existed—economic, technological and no lack of resources, an educated citizenry and more—but where the political will for a democratic regime was altogether lacking. One might say the same of the United States today, if one decides our constitutional regime is largely democratic in form only.

22. For mixed conceptions, see *Theory*, §21: 107.

23. See E. S. Phelps, "Taxation of Wage Income for Economic Justice," *Quarterly Journal of Economics* 87 (1973), §1. The idea of a focal point is due to Thomas Schelling, *Strategy of Conflict* (Cambridge, Mass.: Harvard University Press, 1960), e.g., pp. 57f.

# 47     The Libertarian Manifesto

JOHN HOSPERS

The political philosophy that is called libertarianism (from the Latin *libertas,* liberty) is the doctrine that every person is the owner of his own life, and that no one is the owner of anyone else's life: and that consequently every human being has the right to act in accordance with his own choices, unless those actions infringe on the equal liberty of other human beings to act in accordance with their choices.

There are several other ways of stating the same libertarian thesis:

1. *No one is anyone else's master, and no one is anyone else's slave.* Since I am the one to de-

cide how my life is to be conducted just as you decide about yours, I have no right (even if I had the power) to make you my slave and be your master, nor have you the right to become the master by enslaving me. Slavery is *forced* servitude, and since no one owns the life of anyone else, no one has the right to enslave another. Political theories past and present have traditionally been concerned with who should be the master (usually the king, the dictator, or government bureaucracy) and who should be the slaves, and what the extent of the slavery should be. Libertarianism holds that no one has the right to use force to enslave the life of another, or any portion or aspect of that life.

2. *Other men's lives are not yours to dispose of.* I enjoy seeing operas; but operas are expensive to produce. Opera-lovers often say, "The state (or the city, etc.) should subsidize opera, so that we can all see it. Also it would be for people's betterment, cultural benefit, etc." But what they are advocating is nothing more or less than legalized plunder. They can't pay for the productions themselves, and yet they want to see opera, which involves a large number of people and their labor; so what they are saying in effect is, "Get the money through legalized force. Take a little bit more out of every worker's paycheck every week to pay for the operas we want to see." But I have no right to take by force from the workers' pockets to pay for what I want.

Perhaps it would be better if he *did* go to see opera—then I should try to convince him to go voluntarily. But to take the money from him forcibly, because in my opinion it would be good for *him*, is still seizure of his earnings, which is plunder.

Besides, if I have the right to force him to help pay for my pet projects, hasn't he equally the right to force me to help pay for his? Perhaps he in turn wants the government to subsidize rock-and-roll, or his new car, or a house in the country? If I have the right to milk him, why hasn't he the right to milk me? If I can be a moral cannibal, why can't he too?

We should beware of the inventors of utopias. They would remake the world according to their vision—with the lives and fruits of the labor of *other* human beings. Is it someone's utopian vision that others should build pyramids to beautify the landscape? Very well, then other men should provide the labor; and if he is in a position of political power, and he can't get men to do it voluntarily, then he must *compel* them to "cooperate"—i.e., he must enslave them.

A hundred men might gain great pleasure from beating up or killing just one insignificant human being; but other men's lives are not theirs to dispose of. "In order to achieve the worthy goals of the next five-year-plan, we must forcibly collectivize the peasants . . ."; but other men's lives are not theirs to dispose of. Do you want to occupy, rent-free, the mansion that another man has worked for twenty years to buy? But other men's lives are not yours to dispose of. Do you want operas so badly that everyone is forced to work harder to pay for their subsidization through taxes? But other men's lives are not yours to dispose of. Do you want to have free medical care at the expense of other people, whether they wish to provide it or not? But this would require them to work longer for you whether they want to or not, and other men's lives are not yours to dispose of. . . .

3. *No human being should be a nonvoluntary mortgage on the life of another.* I cannot claim your life, your work, or the products of your effort as mine. The fruit of one man's labor should not be fair game for every freeloader who comes along and demands it as his own. The orchard that has

been carefully grown, nurtured, and harvested by its owner should not be ripe for the plucking for any bypasser who has a yen for the ripe fruit. The wealth that some men have produced should not be fair game for looting by government, to be used for whatever purposes its representatives determine, no matter what their motives in so doing may be. The theft of your money by a robber is not justified by the fact that he used it to help his injured mother.

It will already be evident that libertarian doctrine is embedded in a view of the rights of man. Each human being has the right to live his life as he chooses, compatibly with the equal right of all other human beings to live their lives as they choose.

All men's rights are implicit in the above statement. Each man has the right to life: any attempt by others to take it away from him, or even to injure him, violates this right, through the use of coercion against him. Each man has the right to liberty: to conduct his life in accordance with the alternatives open to him without coercive action by others. And every man has the right to property: to work to sustain his life (and the lives of whichever others he chooses to sustain, such as his family) and to retain the fruits of his labor.

People often defend the rights of life and liberty but denigrate property rights, and yet the right to property is as basic as the other two: indeed, without property rights no other rights are possible. Depriving you of property is depriving you of the means by which you live. . . .

I have no right to decide how *you* should spend your time or your money. I can make that decision for myself, but not for you, my neighbor. I may deplore your choice of life-style, and I may talk with you about it provided you are willing to listen to me. But I have no right to use force to change it. Nor have I the right to decide how you should spend the money you have earned. I may appeal to you to give it to the Red Cross, and you may pre-

fer to go to prize-fights. But that is your decision, and however much I may chafe about it I do not have the right to interfere forcibly with it, for example by robbing you in order to use the money in accordance with *my* choices. (If I have the right to rob you, have you also the right to rob me?)

When I claim a right, I carve out a niche, as it were, in my life, saying in effect, "This activity I must be able to perform without interference from others. For you and everyone else, this is off limits." And so I put up a "no trespassing" sign, which marks off the area of my right. Each individual's right is his "no trespassing" sign in relation to me and others. I may not encroach upon his domain any more than he upon mine, without my consent. Every right entails a duty, true—but the duty is only that of *forbearance*—that is, of *refraining* from violating the other person's right. If you have a right to life, I have no right to take your life; if you have a right to the products of your labor (property), I have no right to take it from you without your consent. The nonviolation of these rights will not guarantee you protection against natural catastrophes such as floods and earthquakes, but it will protect you against the aggressive activities *of other men*. And rights, after all, have to do with one's relations to other human beings, not with one's relations to physical nature.

Nor were these rights created by government; governments—some governments, obviously not all—*recognize* and *protect* the rights that individuals already have. Governments regularly forbid homicide and theft; and, at a more advanced stage, protect individuals against such things as libel and breach of contract.

The *right to property* is the most misunderstood and unappreciated of human rights, and it is one most constantly violated by governments. "Property" of course does not mean only real estate; it includes anything you can call your own—your clothing, your car, your jewelry, your books and papers.

The right of property is not the right to just *take* it from others, for this would interfere with *their* property rights. It is rather the right to work for it, to obtain non-coercively, the money or services which you can present in voluntary exchange.

The right to property is consistently underplayed by intellectuals today, sometimes even frowned upon, as if we should feel guilty for upholding such a right in view of all the poverty in the world. But the right to property is absolutely basic. It is your hedge against the future. It is your assurance that what you have worked to earn will still be there and be yours, when you wish or need to use it, especially when you are too old to work any longer.

Government has always been the chief enemy of the right to property. The officials of government, wishing to increase their power, and finding an increase of wealth an effective way to bring this about, seize some or all of what a person has earned—and since government has a monopoly of physical force within the geographical area of the nation, it has the power (but not the right) to do this. When this happens, of course, every citizen of that country is insecure: he knows that no matter how hard he works the government can swoop down on him at any time and confiscate his earnings and possessions. A person sees his life savings wiped out in a moment when the tax-collectors descend to deprive him of the fruits of his work; or, an industry which has been fifty years in the making and cost millions of dollars and millions of hours of time and planning, is nationalized overnight. Or the government, via inflation, cheapens the currency, so that hard-won dollars aren't worth anything any more. The effect of such actions, of course, is that people lose hope and incentive: if no matter how hard they work the government agents can take it all away, why bother to work at all, for more than today's needs? Depriving people of property is *depriving them of the means by which they live*—the freedom of the individual citizen to do what he wishes with his own life and to plan for the future. Indeed only if property rights are respected is there any point to planning for the future and working to achieve one's goals. *Property rights are what makes long-range planning possible*—the kind of planning

which is a distinctively human endeavor, as opposed to the day-by-day activity of the lion who hunts, who depends on the supply of game tomorrow but has no real insurance against starvation in a day or a week. Without the right to property, the right to life itself amounts to little: how can you sustain your life if you cannot plan ahead? and how can you plan ahead if the fruits of your labor can at any moment be confiscated by government? . . .

Indeed, the right to property may well be considered second only to the right to life. Even the freedom of speech is limited by considerations of property. If a person visiting in your home behaves in a way undesired by you, you have every right to evict him; he can scream or agitate elsewhere if he wishes, but not in your home without your consent. Does a person have a right to shout obscenities in a cathedral? No, for the owners of the cathedral (presumably the Church) have not allowed others on their property for that purpose; one may go there to worship or to visit, but not just for any purpose one wishes. Their property right is prior to your or my wish to scream or expectorate or write graffiti on their building. Or, to take the stock example, does a person have a right to shout "Fire!" falsely in a crowded theater? No, for the theater owner has permitted others to enter and use his property only for a specific purpose, that of seeing a film or watching a stage show. If a person heckles or otherwise disturbs other members of the audience, he can be thrown out. (In fact, he can be removed for any reason the owner chooses, provided his admission money is returned.) And if he shouts "Fire!" when there is no fire, he may be endangering other lives by causing a panic or a stampede. The right to free speech doesn't give one the right to say anything anywhere; it is circumscribed by property rights.

Again, some people seem to assume that the right to free speech (including written speech) means that they can go to a newspaper publisher and demand that he print in his newspaper some propaganda or policy statement for their political party (or other group). But of course they have no right to the use of his newspaper. Ownership of the newspaper is the product of his labor, and he has a right to put into his newspaper whatever he wants, for whatever reason. If he excludes material which many readers would like to have in, perhaps they can find it in another newspaper or persuade him to print it himself (if there are enough of them, they will usually do just that). Perhaps they can even cause his newspaper to fail. But as long as he owns it, he has the right to put in it what he wishes; what would a property right be if he could not do this? They have no right to place their material in his newspaper without his consent—not for free, nor even for a fee. Perhaps other newspapers will include it, or perhaps they can start their own newspaper (in which case they have a right to put in it what they like). If not, an option open to them would be to mimeograph and distribute some handbills.

In exactly the same way, no one has a right to "free television time" unless the owner of the television station consents to give it; it is his station, he has the property rights over it, and it is for him to decide how to dispose of his time. He may not decide wisely, but it is his right to decide as he wishes. If he makes enough unwise decisions, and courts enough unpopularity with the viewing public or the sponsors he may have to go out of business; but as he is free to make his own decisions, so is he free to face their consequences. (If the government owns the television station, then government officials will make the decisions, and there is no guarantee of *their* superior wisdom. The difference is that when "the government" owns the station, you are forced to help pay for its upkeep through your taxes, whether the bureaucrat in charge decides to give you television time or not.)

"But why have *individual* property rights? Why not have lands and houses owned by everybody together?" Yes, this involves no violation of individual rights, as long as everybody consents to this arrangement and no one is forced to join it. The parties to it may enjoy the communal living enough (at least for a time) to overcome certain inevitable problems: that some will work and some not, that some will achieve more in an hour than others can do in a day, and still they will all get the same income. The few who do the most will in the end consider themselves "work-horses" who do the work of two or three or twelve, while the others will be "freeloaders" on the efforts of these few. But as long as they can get out of the arrangement if they no longer like it, no violation of rights is involved. They got in voluntarily, and they can get out voluntarily; no one has used force.

"But why not say that everybody owns everything" That we *all* own everything there is?"

To some this may have a pleasant ring—but let us try to analyze what it means. If everybody owns everything, then everyone has an equal right to go everywhere, do what he pleases, take what he likes, destroy if he wishes, grow crops or burn them, trample them under, and so on. Consider what it would be like in practice. Suppose you have saved money to buy a house for yourself and your family. Now suppose that the principle, "everybody owns everything," becomes adopted. Well then, why shouldn't every itinerant hippie just come in and take over, sleeping in your beds and eating in your kitchen and not bothering to replace the food supply or clean up the mess? After all, it belongs to all of us, doesn't it? So we have just as much right to it as you, the buyer, have. What happens if we *all* want to sleep in the bedroom and there's not room for all of us? Is it the strongest who wins?

What would be the result? Since no one would be responsible for anything, the property would soon be destroyed, the food used up, the facilities nonfunctional. Beginning as a house that *one* family could use, it would end up as a house that *no one* could use. And if the principle continued to be adopted, no one would build houses any more—or anything else. What for? They would only be occupied and used by others, without remuneration.

Suppose two men are cast ashore on an island, and they agree that each will cultivate half of it. The first man is industrious and grows crops and builds a shelter, making the most of the situation with which he is confronted. The second man, perhaps thinking that the warm days will last forever, lies in the sun, picks coconuts while they last, and does a minimum of work to sustain himself. At the time of harvest, the second man has nothing to harvest, nor does he assist the first man in his labors. But later when there is a dearth of food on the island, the second man comes to the first man and demands half of the harvest as his right. But of course he has no right to the product of the first man's labors. The first man may freely choose to give part of his harvest to the second out of charity rather than see him starve; but that is just what it is—charity, not the second man's right.

How can any of man's rights be violated? Ultimately, only by the use of force. I can make suggestions to you, I can reason with you, entreat you (if you are willing to listen), but I cannot *force* you without violating your rights; only by forcing you do I cut the cord between your free decisions and your actions. Voluntary relations between individuals involve no deprivation of rights, but murder, assault, and rape do, because in doing these things I make you the unwilling victim of my actions. A man's beating his wife involves no violation of rights if she *wanted* to be beaten. *Force is behavior that requires the unwilling involvement of other persons.*

Thus the use of force need not involve the use of physical violence. If I trespass on your property or dump garbage on it, I am violating your property rights, as indeed I am when I steal your watch; although this is not force in the sense of violence, it *is* a case of your being an unwilling victim of my action. Similarly, if you shout at me so that I cannot be heard when I try to speak, or blow a siren in my ear, or start a factory next door which pollutes my land, you are again violating my rights (to free speech, to property); I am, again, an unwilling victim of your actions. Similarly, if you steal a manuscript of mine and publish it as your own, you are confiscating a piece of my property and thus violating my right to keep what is the product of my labor. Of course, if I give you the manuscript with permission to sign your name to it and keep the proceeds, no violation of rights is involved—any more than if I give you permission to dump garbage on my yard.

According to libertarianism, the role of government should be limited to the retaliatory use of force against those who have initiated its use. It should not enter into any other areas, such as religion, social organization, and economics.

## Government

Government is the most dangerous institution known to man. Throughout history it has violated the rights of men more than any individual or group of individuals could do: it has killed people, enslaved them, sent them to forced labor and concentration camps, and regularly robbed and pillaged them of the fruits of their expended labor. Unlike individual criminals, government has the power to arrest and try; unlike individual criminals, it can surround and encompass a person totally, dominating every aspect of one's life, so that one has no recourse from it but to leave the country (and in totalitarian nations even that is prohibited). Government throughout history has a much sorrier record than any individual, even that of a ruthless mass murderer. The signs we see on bumper stickers are chillingly accurate: "Beware: the Government Is Armed and Dangerous."

The only proper role of government, according to libertarians, is that of the protector of the citizen against aggression by other individuals. The government, of course, should never initiate aggression; its proper role is as the embodiment of the *retaliatory* use of force against anyone who initiates its use.

If each individual had constantly to defend himself against possible aggressors, he would have to spend a considerable portion of his life in target practice, karate exercises, and other means of self-defense, and even so he would probably be helpless against groups of individuals who might try to kill, maim, or rob him. He would have little time for cultivating those qualities which are essential to civilized life, nor would improvements in science, medicine, and the arts be likely to occur. The function of government is to take this responsibility off his shoulders: the government undertakes to defend him against aggressors and to punish them if they attack him. When the government is effective in doing this, it enables the citizen to go about his business unmolested and without constant fear for his life. To do this, of course, government must have physical power—the police, to protect the citizen from aggression within its borders, and the armed forces, to protect him from aggressors outside. Beyond that, the government should not intrude upon his life, either to run his business, or adjust his daily activities, or prescribe his personal moral code.

Government, then, undertakes to be the individual's protector; but historically governments have gone far beyond this function. Since they already have the physical power, they have not hesitated to use it for purposes far beyond that which was entrusted to them in the first place. Undertaking initially to protect its citizens against aggression, it has often itself become an aggressor—a far greater aggressor, indeed, than the criminals against whom it was supposed to protect its citizens. Governments have done what no private citizen can do: arrest and imprison individuals without a trial and send them to slave labor camps. Government must have power in order to be effective—and yet the very means by which alone it can be effective make it vulnerably to the abuse of power, leading to managing the lives of individuals and even inflicting terror upon them.

What then should be the function of government? In a word, the *protection of human rights.*

1. *The right to life:* libertarians support all such legislation as will protect human beings against the use of force by others, for example, laws against killing, attempting killing, maiming, beating, and all kinds of physical violence.
2. *The right to liberty:* there should be no laws compromising in any way freedom of speech, of the press, and peaceable assembly. There should be no censorship of ideas, books, films, or of anything else by government.
3. *The right to property:* libertarians support legislation that protects the property rights of individuals against confiscation, nationalization, eminent domain, robbery, trespass, fraud and misrepresentation, patent and copyright, libel and slander.

Someone has violently assaulted you. Should he be legally liable? Of course. He has violated one of your rights. He has knowingly injured you and since he has initiated aggression against you he should be made to expiate.

Someone has negligently left his bicycle on the sidewalk where you trip over it in the dark and injure yourself. He didn't do it intentionally; he didn't mean you any harm. Should he be legally liable? Of course; he has, however unwittingly, injured you, and since the injury is caused by him and you are the victim, he should pay.

Someone across the street is unemployed. Should you be taxed extra to pay for his expenses? Not at all. You have not injured him, you are not responsible for the fact that he is unemployed (unless you are a senator or bureaucrat who agitated for further curtailing of business, which legislation passed, with the result that your neighbor was laid off by the curtailed business). You may voluntarily wish to help him out, or better still, try to get him a job to put him on his feet again; but since you have initiated no aggressive act against him, and neither purposely nor accidentally injured him in any way, you should not be legally penalized for the fact of his unemployment. (Actually, it is just such penalties that increase unemployment.)

One man, A, works hard for years and finally earns a high salary as a professional man. A second man, B, prefers not to work at all, and to spend wastefully what money he has (through inheritance), so that after a year or two he has nothing left. At the end of this time he has a long siege of illness and lots of medical bills to pay. He demands that the bills be paid by the government—that is, by the taxpayers of the land, including Mr. A.

But of course B has no such right. He chose to lead his life in a certain way—that was his voluntary decision. One consequence of that choice is that he must depend on charity in case of later need. Mr. A chose not to live that way. (And if everyone lived like Mr. B, on whom would he depend in case of later need?) Each has a right to live in the way he pleases, but each must live with the consequences of his own decision (which, as always, fall primarily on himself). He cannot, in time of need, claim A's beneficence as his right.

If a house-guest of yours starts to carve his initials in your walls and break up your furniture, you have a right to evict him, and call the police if he makes trouble. If someone starts to destroy the machinery in a factory, the factory-owner is also entitled to evict him and call the police. In both cases, persons other than the owner are permitted on the property only under certain conditions, at the pleasure of the owner. If those conditions are violated, the owner is entitled to use force to set things straight. The case is exactly the same on a college or university campus: if a campus demonstrator starts breaking windows, occupying the president's office, and setting fire to a dean, the college authorities are certainly within their rights to evict him forcibly; one is permitted on the college grounds only under specific conditions, set by the administration: study, peaceful student activity, even political activity if those in charge choose to permit it. If they do not choose to permit peaceful political activity on campus, they may be unwise, since a campus is after all a place where all sides of every issue should get discussed, and the college that doesn't permit this may soon lose its reputation and its students. All the same, the college official who does not permit it is quite within his rights; the students do not own the campus, nor do the hired trouble-makers imported from elsewhere. In the case of a privately owned college, the owners, or whoever they have delegated to administer it, have the right to make the decisions as to who shall be permitted on the campus and under what conditions. In the case of a state university or college, the ownership problem is more complex: one could say that the "government" owns the campus or that "the people" do since they are the taxpayers who support it; but in either case, the university administration has the delegated task of keeping order, and until they are removed by the state administration or the taxpayers, it is theirs to decide who shall be permitted on campus, and what nonacademic activities will be permitted to their students on the premises.

Property rights can be violated by physical trespass, of course, or by anyone entering on your property for any reason without your consent. (If you *do* consent to having your neighbor dump garbage on your yard, there is no violation of your rights.) But the physical trespass of a person is only a special case of violation of property rights. Property rights can be violated by sound-waves, in the form of a loud noise, or the sounds of your neighbor's hi-fi set while you are trying to sleep. Such violations of property rights are of course the subject of action in the courts.

But there is another violation of property rights that has not thus far been honored by the courts; this has to do with the effects of *pollution* of the atmosphere.

> From the beginnings of modern air pollution, the courts made a conscious decision not to protect, for example, the orchards of farmers from the smoke of nearby factories or locomotives. They said, in effect, to the farmers: yes, your private property is being invaded by this smoke, but we hold that "public policy" is more important than private property, and public policy holds factories and locomotives to be good things. These goods were allowed to override the defense of property rights—with our consequent headlong rush into pollution disaster. The remedy is both "radical" and crystal clear, and it has nothing to do with multibillion dollar palliative programs at the expense of the taxpayers which do not even meet the real issue. The remedy is simply to enjoin anyone from injecting pollutants into the air, and thereby invading the rights of persons and property. Period. The argument that such an injunction prohibition would add to the costs of industrial production is as reprehensible as the pre-Civil War argument that the abolition of slavery would add to the costs of growing cotton, and therefore should not take place. For this means that the polluters are able to impose the high costs of pollution upon those whose property rights they are allowed to invade with impunity.[1]

What about automobiles, the chief polluters of the air? One can hardly sue every automobile owner. But one can sue the manufacturers of automobiles who do not install anti-smog devices on the cars which they distribute—and later (though this is more difficult), owners of individual automobiles if they discard the equipment or do not keep it functional.

The violation of rights does not apply only to air-pollution. If someone with a factory upstream on a river pollutes the river, anyone living downstream from him, finding his water polluted, should be able to sue the owner of the factory. In this way the price of adding the anti-pollutant devices will be the owner's responsibility, and will probably be added to the cost of the products which the factory produces and thus spread around among all consumers, rather than the entire cost being borne by the users of the river in the form of polluted water, with the consequent impossibility of fishing, swimming, and so on. In each case, pollution would be stopped at the source rather than having its ill effects spread around to numerous members of the population.

What about property which you do not work to earn, but which you *inherit* from someone else? Do you have a right to that? You have no right to it until someone decides to give it to you. Consider the man who willed it to you; it was his, he had the right to use and dispose of it as *he* saw fit; and if he decided to give it to you, this is a windfall for you, but it was only the exercise of *his* right. Had the property been seized by the government at the man's death, or distributed among numerous other people designated by the government, it *would* have been a violation of his rights: for he, who worked to earn and sustain it, would not have been able to dispose of it according to his own judgment. If he doesn't have the right to determine who shall have it, who does?

What about the property status of your intellectual activity, such as inventions you may devise and books you write? These, of course, are your property also; they are the products of your mind; you worked at them, you created them. Prior to that, they did not exist. If you worked five years to write a book, and someone stole it and published it as his own, receiving royalties from its sales, he would have stolen your property just as surely as if he had robbed your home. The same is true if someone used and sold without your permission an invention which was the product of your labor and ingenuity.

The role of government with respect to this issue, at least most governments of the Western world, is a proper one: government protects the products of your labor from the moment they materialize. Copyright law protects your writings from piracy. In the United States, one's writings are protected for a period of twenty-seven years, and another twenty-seven if one applies for renewal of the copyright. In most other countries, they are protected for a period of fifty years after the author's death, permitting both himself and his surviving heirs to reap the fruits of his labor. After that they enter the "public domain"—that is, anyone may reprint them without your or your heir's permission. Patent law protects your inventions for a limited period, which varies according to the type of invention. In no case are you forced to avail yourself of this protection; you need not apply for patent or copyright coverage if you do not wish to do so. But the protection of your intellectual property is there in case you wish to use it.

What about the property status of the airwaves? Here the government's position is far more questionable. The government now claims ownership of the airwaves, leasing them to individuals and corporations. The government renews leases or refuses them depending on whether the programs satisfy authorities in the Federal Communications Commission. The official position is that "we all own the airwaves": but since only one party can broadcast on a certain frequency at a certain time without causing chaos, it is simply a fact of reality that "everyone" cannot use it. In fact the government decides who shall use the airwaves and one courts its displeasure only at the price of a revoked license. One can write without government approval, but one cannot use the airwaves without the approval of government.

What policy should have been observed with regard to the airwaves? Much the same as the policy that was followed in the case of the Homestead Act, when the lands of the American West were opening up for settlement. There was a policy of "first come, first served," with the government parcelling out a certain acreage for each individual who wanted to claim the land as his own. There was no charge for the land, but if a man had not used it and built a dwelling during the first two-year period, it was assumed that he was not homesteading and the land was given to the next man in line. The airwaves too could have been given out on a "first come, first served" basis. The first man who used a given frequency would be its owner, and the government would protect him in the use of it against trespassers. If others wanted to use the same frequency, they would have to buy it from the first man, if he was willing to sell, or try to buy another, just as one now does with the land.

Laws may be classified into three types: (1) laws protecting individuals against themselves, such as laws against fornication and other sexual behavior, alcohol, and drugs; (2) laws protecting individuals against aggressions by other individuals, such as laws against murder, robbery, and fraud; (3) laws requiring people to help one another; for example, all laws which rob Peter to pay Paul, such as welfare.

Libertarians reject the first class of laws totally. Behavior which harms no one else is strictly the individual's own affair. Thus, there should be no laws against becoming intoxicated, since whether or not to become intoxicated is the individual's own decision: but there should be laws against driving while intoxicated, since the drunken driver is a threat to every other motorist on the highway (drunken driving falls into type 2). Similarly, there should be no laws against drugs (except the prohibition of sale of drugs to minors) as long as the taking of these drugs poses no threat to anyone else. Drug addiction is a psychological problem to which no present solution exists. Most of the social harm caused by addicts, other than to themselves, is the result of thefts which they perform in order to continue their habit—and then the *legal* crime is the theft, not the addiction. The actual cost of heroin is about ten cents a shot; if it were legalized, the enormous traffic in illegal sale and purchase of it would stop, as well as the accompa-

nying proselytization to get new addicts (to make more money for the pusher) and the thefts performed by addicts who often require eighty dollars a day just to keep up the habit. Addiction would not stop, but the crimes would: it is estimated that 75 percent of the burglaries in New York City today are performed by addicts, and all these crimes could be wiped out at one stroke through the legalization of drugs. (Only when the taking of drugs could be shown to constitute a threat to *others,* should it be prohibited by law. It is only laws protecting people against *themselves* that libertarians oppose.)

Laws should be limited to the second class only: aggression by individuals against other individuals. These are laws whose function is to protect human beings against encroachment by others; and this, as we have seen, is (according to libertarianism) the sole function of government.

Libertarians also reject the third class of laws totally: no one should be forced by law to help others, not even to tell them the time of day if requested, and certainly not to give them a portion of one's weekly paycheck. Governments, in the guise of humanitarianism, have given to some by taking from others (charging a "handling fee" in the process, which, because of the government's waste and inefficiency, sometimes is several hundred percent). And in so doing they have decreased incentive, violated the rights of individuals and lowered the standard of living of almost everyone.

All such laws constitute what libertarians call *moral cannibalism*. A cannibal in the physical sense is a person who lives off the flesh of other human beings. A *moral* cannibal is one who believes he has a right to live off the "spirit" of other human beings—who believes that he has a moral claim on the productive capacity, time, and effort expended by others.

It has become fashionable to claim virtually everything that one needs or desires as one's *right*. Thus, many people claim that they have a right to a job, the right to free medical care, to free food and clothing, to a decent home, and so on. Now if one asks, apart from any specific context, whether it would be desirable if everyone had these things, one might well say yes. But there is a gimmick attached to each of them: *At whose expense?* Jobs, medical care, education, and so on, don't grow on trees. These are goods and services *produced only by men.* Who then is to provide them, and under what conditions?

If you have a right to a job, who is to supply it? Must an employer supply it even if he doesn't want to hire you? What if you are unemployable, or incurably lazy? (If you say "the government must supply it," does that mean that a job must be created for you which no employer needs done, and that you must be kept in it regardless of how much or little you work?) If the employer is forced to supply it at his expense even if he doesn't need you, then isn't *he* being enslaved to that extent? What ever happened to *his* right to conduct his life and his affairs in accordance with his choices?

If you have a right to free medical care, then, since medical care doesn't exist in nature as wild apples do, some people will have to supply it to you for free: that is, they will have to spend their time and money and energy taking care of you whether they want to or not. What ever happened to *their* right to conduct their lives as they see fit? Of do you have a right to violate theirs? Can there be a right to violate rights?

All those who demand this or that as a "free service" are consciously or unconsciously evading the fact that there is in reality no such thing as free services. All man-made goods and services are the result of human expenditure of time and effort. There is no such thing as "something for nothing" in this world. If you demand something free, you are demanding that other men give their time and effort to you without compensation. If they voluntarily choose to do this, there is no problem; but if you demand that they be *forced* to do it, you are interfering with their right not to do it if they so choose. "Swimming in this pool ought to be free! says the indignant passerby. What he means is that others should build a pool, others should provide the material, and still others should run it and keep it in functioning order, so that *he* can use it without fee. But what right has he to the expenditure of *their* time and effort? To expect something "for free" is to expect it *to be paid for by others* whether they choose to or not.

Many questions, particularly about economic matters, will be generated by the libertarian account of human rights and the role of government. Should government have a role in assisting the needy, in providing social security, in legislating minimum wages, in fixing prices and putting a ceiling on rents, in curbing monopolies, in erecting tariffs, in guaranteeing jobs, in managing the money supply? To these and all similar questions the libertarian answers with an unequivocal no.

"But then you'd let people go hungry!" comes the rejoinder. This, the libertarian insists, is precisely what would not happen; with the restrictions removed, the economy would flourish as never before. With the controls taken off business, existing enterprises would expand and new ones would spring into existence satisfying more and more consumer needs; millions more people would be gainfully employed instead of subsisting on welfare, and all kinds of research and production, released from the stranglehold of government, would proliferate, fulfilling man's needs and desires as never before. It has always been so whenever government has permitted men to be free traders on a free market. But *why* this is so, and how the free market is the best solution to all problems relating to the material aspect of man's life, is another and far longer story.

NOTE

1. Murray Rothbard, "The Great Ecology Issue," *The Individualist,* 2, no. 2 (Feb. 1970), p. 5.

# 48    Justice as Fairness—For Whom?

SUSAN MOLLER OKIN

THEORIES OF JUSTICE are centrally concerned with whether, how, and why persons should be treated differently from each other. Which initial or acquired characteristics or positions in society, they ask, legitimize differential treatment of persons by social institutions, laws and customs? In particular, how should beginnings affect outcomes? Since we live in a society in whose past the innate characteristic of sex has been regarded as one of the clearest legitimizers of different rights and restrictions, both formal and informal, the division of humanity into two sexes would seem to provide an obvious subject for such inquiries. But the deeply entrenched social institutionalization of sexual difference, which I will refer to as "the gender system" or simply "gender," has rarely been subjected to the tests of justice. When we turn to the great tradition of Western political thought with questions about the justice of gender in mind, it is to little avail.[1] Except for rare exceptions, such as John Stuart Mill, those who hold central positions in the tradition almost never questioned the justice of the subordination of women. When we turn to contemporary theories of justice, however, we might expect to find more illuminating and positive contributions to the subject of gender and justice. In this essay, I turn to John Rawls's extremely influential *A Theory of Justice,* to see not only what it says explicitly on the subject but also what undeveloped potential it has as we try to answer the question "How just is gender?"[2]

There is little indication throughout most of *A Theory of Justice* that the modern liberal society to which the principles of justice are to be applied is deeply and pervasively gender structured. Thus an ambiguity runs throughout the work, which is continually noticeable to anyone reading it from a feminist perspective. On the one hand, as I shall argue below, a consistent and wholehearted application of Rawls's liberal principles of justice can lead us to challenge fundamentally the gender system of our society. On the other hand, in his own account of his theory, this challenge is barely hinted at, much less developed. The major reason is that throughout most of the argument, it is assumed (as throughout almost the entire liberal tradition) that the appropriate subjects of political theories are not all adult individuals, but heads of families. As a result, although Rawls indicates on several occasions that a person's sex is a morally arbitrary and contingent characteristic, and although he states initially that the family itself is one of those basic social institutions to which the principles of justice must apply, his theory of justice develops neither of these convictions.

Rawls, like almost all political theorists until very recent years, employs in *A Theory of Justice* supposedly generic male terms of reference.[3] "Men," "mankind," "he" and "his" are interspersed with gender-neutral terms of reference such as "individual" and "moral person." Examples of intergenerational concern are worded in terms of "fathers" and "sons," and the difference principle is said to correspond to "the principle of fraternity."[4] This linguistic usage would perhaps be less significant if it were not for the fact that Rawls is self-consciously a member of a long tradition of moral and political philosophy that has used in its arguments either such supposedly generic male terms, or even more inclusive terms of reference ("human beings," "persons," "all rational beings as such"), only to exclude women from the scope of the conclusions reached. Kant is a clear example.[5] But when Rawls refers to the generality and universality of Kant's ethics, and when he compares the principles chosen in his own original position to those regulative of Kant's kingdom of ends, "acting from [which] expresses our nature as free and equal rational persons,"[6] he does not mention the fact that women were not included in that category of "free and equal rational persons" to which Kant meant his moral theory to apply. Again, in a brief discussion of Freud's account of moral development, Rawls presents Freud's theory of the formation of the male superego in largely gender-neutral terms, without mentioning the fact that Freud considered women's moral development to be sadly deficient, on account of their incomplete resolution of the Oedipus complex.[7] Thus there is a certain blindness to the sexism of the tradition in which Rawls is a participant, which tends to render his terms of reference even more ambiguous than they might otherwise be. A feminist reader finds it difficult not to keep asking: "Does this theory of justice apply to women, or not?"

This question is not answered in the important passages listing the characteristics that persons in the original position are not to know about themselves in order to formulate impartial principles of justice. In a subsequent article, Rawls has made it clear that sex *is* one of those morally irrelevant contingencies that are hidden by the veil of ignorance.[8] But throughout *A Theory of Justice*, while the list of things unknown by a person in the original position includes "his place in society, his class position or social status . . . his fortune in the distribution of natural assets and abilities, his intelligence and strength, and the like . . . his conception of the good, the particulars of his rational plan of life, [and] even the special features of his psychology . . ."[9] "his" sex is not mentioned. Since the parties also "know the general facts about human society,"[10] presumably including the fact that it is gender structured both by custom and still in some respects by law, one might think that whether or not they knew their sex might matter enough to be mentioned. Perhaps Rawls means to cover it by his phrase "and the like," but it is also possible that he did not consider it significant.

The ambiguity is exacerbated by the statement that those free and equal moral persons in the original position who formulate the principles of justice are to be thought of not as "single individuals," but as "heads of families" or "representatives of families."[11] Rawls says that it is not necessary to think of the parties as heads of families, but that he will generally do so. The reason he does this, he explains, is to ensure that each person in the original position cares about the well-being of some persons in the next generation. These "ties of sentiment" between generations, which Rawls regards as important in the establishment of his just savings principle, would otherwise constitute a problem, because of the general assumption that the parties in the original position are mutually disinterested.[12] In spite of the ties of sentiment *within* families, then, "as representatives of families their interests are opposed as the circumstances of justice imply."[13]

The head of a family need not necessarily, of course, be a man. Certainly in the US, at least, there has been a striking growth in the proportion of "female-headed households" during the last several decades. But the very fact that, in common usage, the term "female-headed household" is used *only* in reference to households without resident adult males implies the assumption that any present male takes precedence over a female as the household or family head. Rawls does nothing to contest this impression when he says of those in the original position that "imagining themselves to be fathers, say, they are to ascertain how much they should set aside for their sons by noting what they would believe themselves entitled to claim of their fathers."[14] Although the "heads of families" assumption is made in order to address the issue of intergenerational justice, and is presumably not intended to be sexist, Rawls is effectively trapped by it into the traditional mode of thinking that life within the family and relations between the sexes are not properly to be regarded as part of the subject matter of a theory of social justice.

Before I go on to argue this, I must first point out that Rawls, for good reason, states at the outset of his theory that the family *is* part of the subject matter of a theory of social justice. "For us," he says, "the primary subject of justice is the basic structure of society . . . the political constitution and the principal economic and social arrangements." These are basic because "taken together as one scheme, [they] define men's rights and duties and influence their life prospects, what they can expect to be and how well they can hope to do. The basic structure is the primary subject of justice because its effects are so profound and present from the start."[15] Rawls specifies "the monogamous family" as an example of such major social institutions, together with the political constitution, the legal protection of essential freedoms, competitive markets, and private property. This initial inclusion of the family as a basic social institution to which the principles of justice should apply, although a break with earlier liberal thought, seems unavoidable given the stated criteria for inclusion in the basic structure. Different family structures, and different distributions of rights and duties within families, clearly affect men's "life prospects, what they can expect to be and how well they can hope to do," and even more clearly affect the life prospects of women. There is no doubt, then, that in Rawls's initial definition of the sphere of social justice, the family is included. However, it is to a large extent ignored, though assumed, in the rest of the theory.[16]

The two principles of justice that are derived and defended in part 1—the principle of equal basic liberty, and the difference principle combined with the requirement of fair equality of opportunity—are intended to apply to the basic structure of society. They are "to govern the assignment of rights and duties and to regulate the distribution of social and economic advantages."[17] Whenever in these basic institutions there are differences in authority, in responsibility, in the distribution of resources such as wealth or leisure, these differences must be both to the greatest benefit of the least advantaged, and attached to positions accessible to all under conditions of fair equality of opportunity.

In part 2, Rawls discusses at some length the application of his principles of justice to almost all of the major social institutions listed at the beginning of the book. The legal protection of liberty of thought and conscience is defended, as are democratic constitutional institutions and procedures; competitive markets feature prominently in the discussion of the just distribution of income; the issue of the private or public ownership of the means of production is explicitly left open, since Rawls argues that his principles of justice might be compatible with certain versions of either. But throughout all these discussions, he never raises the question of whether the monogamous family, in either its traditional or any other form, is just. When he announces that "the sketch of the system of institutions that satisfy the two principles of justice is now complete,"[18] Rawls has still paid no attention at all to the internal justice of the family. In fact, apart from passing references, the family appears in *A Theory of Justice* in only three contexts: as the link between generations necessary for the just savings principle; as an obstacle to fair equality of opportunity—on account of the inequalities among families; and as the first school of moral development. It is in the third of these contexts that Rawls first specifically mentions the family as a just institution. He mentions it, however, not to *consider* whether the family "in some form" is just but to *assume* it.[19]

Clearly, however, by Rawls's own reasoning about the social justice of major social institutions, this assumption is unwarranted, and this has serious significance for the theory as a whole. The central tenet of the theory, after all, is that justice as fairness characterizes institutions whose members could hypothetically have agreed to their structure and rules from a position in which they did not know which place in the structure they were to occupy. The argument of the book is designed to show that the two principles of justice are those that individuals in such a hypothetical situation would agree to. But since those in the original position are only the heads or representatives of families, they are *not in a position to determine questions of justice within families*.[20] As far as children are concerned, Rawls makes a convincing argument from paternalism for their temporary inequality. But wives (or whichever adult member[s] of a family are *not* its "head") go completely unrepresented in the original position. If families are just, as is assumed, then they must become just in some different way (unspecified by Rawls) than other institutions, for it is impossible to see how the viewpoint of their less advantaged members ever gets to be heard.

There are two occasions when Rawls seems either to depart from his assumption that those in the original position are "family heads," or to assume that a "head of a family" is equally likely to be a woman as a man. In the assignment of the basic rights of citizenship, he argues, favoring men over women is "justified by the difference principle . . . only if it is to the advantage of women and acceptable from their standpoint."[21] Later, he seems to imply that the injustice and irrationality of racist doctrines are also characteristic of sexist ones.[22] But in spite of these passages, which appear to challenge formal sex discrimination, the discussions of institutions in part 2 implicitly rely, in a number of respects, on the assumption that the parties formulating just institutions are (male) heads of (fairly traditional) families, and are therefore not concerned with issues of just distribution within the family or between the sexes. Thus the "heads of families" assumption, far from being neutral or innocent, has the effect of banishing a large sphere of human life—and a particularly large sphere of most women's lives—from the scope of the theory.

One example of this occurs during the discussion of the distribution of wealth. Here Rawls seems to assume that all the parties in the original position expect, once the veil of ignorance is removed, to be participants in the paid labor market. Distributive shares are discussed in terms of household income, but reference to "individuals" is interspersed into this discussion as if there were no difference between the advantage or welfare of a household and that of an individual.[23] This confusion obscures the fact that wages are paid to employed members of the labor force, but that in societies characterized by gender (all current societies) a much larger proportion of women's than men's labor is unpaid, and is often not even acknowledged to be labor. It obscures the fact

that the resulting disparities in the earnings of men and women, and the economic dependence of women on men, are likely to affect power relations within the household, as well as access to leisure, prestige, political power, and so on, among its adult members. Any discussion of justice *within* the family would have to address these issues.

Later, too, in his discussion of the obligations of citizens, Rawls's assumption that justice is agreed on by heads of families in the original position seems to prevent him from considering an issue of crucial importance to women—their exemption from the draft. He concludes that military conscription is justifiable in the case of defense against an unjust attack on liberty, so long as institutions "try to make sure that the risks of suffering from these imposed misfortunes are more or less evenly shared by all members of society over the course of their life, and that there is no avoidable *class* bias in selecting those who are called for duty."[24] However, the issue of the complete exemption of women from this major interference with the basic liberties of equal citizenship is not even mentioned.

In spite of two explicit rejections of the justice of formal sex discrimination in part 1, then, Rawls seems in part 2 to be so heavily influenced by his "family heads" assumption that he fails to consider as part of the basic structure of society the greater economic dependence of women and the sexual division of labor within the typical family, or any of the broader social ramifications of this basic gender structure. Moreover, in part 3, where he *assumes* the justice of the family "in some form" as a given, he does not discuss any alternative forms, but sounds very much as though he is thinking in terms of traditional, gendered family structure and roles. The family he says, is "small association, normally characterized by a definite hierarchy, in which each member has certain rights and duties." The family's role as moral teacher is achieved partly through parental expectations of "the virtues of a good son or a good daughter."[25] In the family and in other associations such as schools, neighborhoods, and peer groups, Rawls continues, one learns various moral virtues and ideals, leading to those adopted in the various statuses, occupations, and family positions of later life: "The content of these ideals is given by the various conceptions of a good wife and husband, a good friend and citizen, and so on."[26] Given these unusual departures from the supposedly generic male terms of reference used throughout the rest of the book, it seems likely that Rawls means to imply that the goodness of daughters is distinct from the goodness of sons, and that of wives from that of husbands. A fairly traditional gender system seems to be assumed.

However, despite this, not only does Rawls "assume that the basic structure of a well-ordered society includes the family *in some form*"; he adds to this the comment that "in a broader inquiry the institution of the family might be questioned, and other arrangements might indeed prove to be preferable."[27] But why should it require a broader inquiry than the colossal task engaged in *A Theory of Justice* to raise questions about the institution and the form of the family? Surely Rawls is right at the outset when he names it as one of those basic social institutions that most affects the life chances of individuals. The family is not a private association like a church or a university, which vary considerably in type and in degree of commitment expected, and which one can join and leave voluntarily. For although one has some choice (albeit a highly constrained one) about marrying into a gender-structured family, one has no choice at all about whether to be born into one. Given this, Rawls's failure to subject the structure of the family to his principles of justice is particularly serious in the light of his belief that a theory of justice must take account of "how [individuals] get to be what they are" and "cannot take their final aims and interests, their attitudes to themselves and their life, as given."[28] For the gendered family, and female parenting in particular, are clearly crucial determinants in the different socialization of the two sexes—in how men and women "get to be what they are."

If Rawls were to assume throughout the construction of his theory that all human adults are participants in what goes on behind the veil of ignorance, he would have no option but to require that the family, as a major social institution affecting the life chances of individuals, be constructed in accordance with the two principles of justice. I shall develop this positive potential of Rawls's theory in the final section of this essay. But first I shall turn to a major problem for the theory that results from its failure to address the issue of justice within the family—its placing in jeopardy Rawls's account of how one develops a sense of justice.

## Gender, the Family, and the Development of a Sense of Justice

Apart from being briefly mentioned as the link between generations necessary for Rawls's "savings principle," and as an obstacle to fair equality of opportunity, the family appears in Rawls's theory in only one context—albeit one of considerable importance—as the earliest school of moral development. Rawls argues, in a much neglected section of part 3 of *A Theory of Justice,* that a just, well-ordered society will be stable only if its members continue to develop a sense of justice—"a strong and normally effective desire to act as the principles of justice require."[29] He specifically turns his attention to the question of childhood moral development, aiming to indicate the major steps by which a sense of justice is acquired.

It is in the context of early moral development, in which families play a fundamental role, that Rawls *assumes* that they are just. In these supposedly just families, the love of parents for their children, coming to be reciprocated in turn by the child, is important in the development of a sense of self-worth. By loving the child and being "worthy objects of his admiration . . . they arouse in him a sense of his own value and the desire to become the sort of person that they are."[30] Next, Rawls argues that healthy moral development in early life depends on love, trust, affection, example and guidance.[31]

Later in moral development, at the stage he calls "the morality of association," Rawls perceives the family, which he describes in gendered and hierarchial terms, as the first of many associations in which, by moving through a sequence of roles and positions, our moral understanding increases. The crucial aspect of the sense of fairness that is learned during this stage is the capacity to take up the points of view of others and to see things from their perspectives. We learn to perceive from what they say and do what other people's ends, plans and motives are. Without this experience, Rawls says, "we cannot put ourselves into another's place and find out what we would do in his position," which we need to be able to do in order "to regulate our own conduct in an appropriate way by reference to it."[32] Participation in different roles in the various associations of society leads to the development of a person's "capacity for fellow feeling" and to "ties of friendship and mutual trust."[33] Rawls says that, just as in the first stage certain natural attitudes develop towards the parents, "so here ties of friendship and confidence grow up among associates. In each case certain natural attitudes underlie the corresponding moral feelings: a lack of these feelings would manifest the absence of these attitudes."[34]

This whole account of moral development is strikingly unlike that of Kant, whose ideas are so influential in other respects on Rawls's thinking about justice. For Kant, any feelings that did not follow from independently established moral principles were morally suspect.[35] But Rawls clearly acknowledges the importance of feelings, first nurtured within supposedly just families, in the development of the capacity for moral thinking. In accounting for his third and final stage of moral development, where persons are supposed to become attached to the principles of justice themselves, Rawls says that "the sense of justice is continuous with the love of mankind."[36] At the same time, he allows for the fact that we have particularly strong feelings about those to whom we are closely attached, and says that this is rightly reflected in our moral judgements: even though "our moral sentiments display an independence from the accidental circumstances of our world . . . our natural attachments to particular persons and

groups still have an appropriate place."[37] He indicates clearly that empathy, or imagining oneself into the place of others, plays a major role in moral development, and he turns from Kant to other philosophers—such as Adam Smith and Elizabeth Anscombe—who have paid more attention to such aspects of moral learning, in developing his ideas about the moral emotions or sentiments.[38]

Rawls believes that three psychological laws of moral development help account for the development of a sense of justice. The three laws, Rawls says, are: "not merely principles of association or of reinforcement . . . [but] assert that the active sentiments of love and friendship, and even the sense of justice, arise from the manifest intention of other persons to act for our good. Because we recognize that they wish us well, we care for their well being in return . . ."[39] Each of the laws of moral development, as set out by Rawls, depends on the one before it, and the first assumption of the first law is: "given that family institutions are just . . ." Thus Rawls frankly admits that the whole of moral development rests at base on the loving ministrations of those who raise small children from the earliest stages, and on the moral character—in particular the *justice*—of the environment in which this takes place. At the foundation of the development of the sense of justice, then, are an activity and a sphere of life that—though by no means necessarily so—have throughout history been predominantly the activity and the sphere of women.

Rawls does not explain the basis of his assumption that family institutions are just. If gendered family institutions are *not* just, but are, rather, a relic of caste or feudal societies in which roles, responsibilities and resources are distributed not in accordance with the two principles of justice, but in accordance with innate differences that are imbued with enormous social significance, then Rawls's whole structure of moral development seems to be built on uncertain ground. Unless the households in which children are first nurtured and see their first examples of human interaction are based on equality and reciprocity rather than on dependence and domination, how can whatever love they receive from their parents make up for the injustice they see before their eyes in the relationship between these same parents? How, in hierarchial families in which sex roles are rigidly assigned, are we to learn to "put ourselves into another's place and find out what we would do in his position"? Unless they are parented equally by adults of both sexes, how will children of both sexes come to develop a sufficiently similar and well-rounded moral psychology to enable them to engage in the kind of deliberation about justice that is exemplified in the original position? Rawls's neglect of justice within the family is clearly in tension with his own theory of moral development, which *requires* that families be just.

## What Can Rawls's Theory of Justice Contribute to Feminism?

The significance of Rawls's central, brilliant idea, the original position, is that it forces one to question and consider traditions, customs, and institutions from all points of view, and ensures that the principles of justice are acceptable to everyone, regardless of what position "he" ends up in. The critical force of the original position is clear from the fact that some of the most creative critiques of Rawls's theory have resulted from others interpreting the original position more radically or broadly than he did.[40] For feminist readers, the problem of the theory as stated by Rawls himself is encapsulated in that ambiguous "he." While Rawls briefly rules out formal, legal discrimination on the grounds of sex, he fails entirely to address the justice of the gender system, which, with its roots in the sex roles of the family, is one of the fundamental structures of our society. If, however, we read Rawls in such a way as to take seriously both the notion that those behind the veil of ignorance are sexless persons, and the requirement that the family and the gender system, as basic social institutions, are to be subject to scrutiny, then constructive feminist criticism of these contemporary institutions follows. So also, however, do hidden difficulties for the application of a Rawlsian theory of justice in a gendered society.

Both the critical perspective and the incipient problems of a feminist reading of Rawls can be illuminated by a description of a cartoon I saw a few years ago. Three elderly, robed male justices are depicted looking down with astonishment at their very pregnant bellies. One says to the others, without further elaboration: "Perhaps we'd better reconsider that decision." This illustration points to several things. First, it graphically demonstrates the importance, in thinking about justice, of a concept like Rawls's original position, which makes us adopt the positions of others—especially positions that we ourselves could never be in. Second, it suggests that those thinking in such a way might well conclude that more than formal legal equality of the sexes is required if justice is to be done. As we have seen in recent years, it is quite possible to institutionalize the formal legal equality of the sexes and at the same time to enact laws concerning pregnancy, abortion, maternity leave, and so on, that in effect discriminate against women, not as women *per se,* but as "pregnant persons."[41] One of the virtues of the cartoon is its suggestion that one's thinking on such matters is likely to be affected by the knowledge that one might become "a pregnant person." Finally, however, the illustration suggests the limits of our abilities to think ourselves into the original position as long as we live in a gender-structured society. While the elderly male justices can, in a sense, imagine *themselves* pregnant, what is much more difficult is whether, in constructing principles of justice, they can imagine themselves *women.* This raises the question whether, in a society structured by gender, sex *is* a morally irrelevant and contingent characteristic.

Let us first assume that sex is contingent in this way, though I shall later question this assumption. Let us suppose that it is possible, as Rawls clearly considers that it is, to hypothesize the moral thinking of representative human beings who are ignorant of their sex. Although Rawls does not do so, we must consistently take the relevant positions of both sexes into account in formulating and applying principles of justice. In particular, those in the original position must take special account of the perspective of women, since their knowledge of "the general facts about human society" must include the knowledge that women have been and continue to be the less advantaged sex in a great number of respects. In considering the basic institutions of society, they are more likely to pay special attention to the family than virtually to ignore it, since its customary unequal assignment of responsibilities and privileges to the two sexes and its socialization of children into sex roles make it, in its current form, a crucial institution for the perpetuation of sex inequality.

In innumerable ways, the principles of justice that Rawls arrives at are inconsistent with a gender-structured society and with traditional family roles. The critical impact of a feminist application of Rawls's theory comes chiefly from his second principle, which requires that inequalities be both "to the greatest benefit of the least advantaged" and "attached to offices and positions open to all."[42] This means that if any roles or positions analogous to our current sex roles, including those of husband and wife, mother and father, were to survive the demands of the first requirement, the second requirement would prohibit any linkage between these roles and sex. Gender, with its ascriptive designation of positions and expectations of behavior in accordance with the inborn characteristic of sex, could no longer form a legitimate part of the social structure, whether inside or outside the family. Three illustrations will help to link this conclusion with specific major requirements that Rawls makes of a just or well-ordered society.

First, after the basic political liberties, one of the most essential liberties is "the important liberty of free choice of occupation."[43] This liberty is obviously compromised by the customary expectation, central to our gender system, that women take far greater responsibility for housework and childcare, whether or not they also work for wages outside the home. In fact, both the assignment of these responsibilities to women—resulting in their economic dependence of men—and also the related responsibility of husbands to support their wives, compromise the liberty of choice of occupation of both sexes. But the current roles of the two sexes inhibit women's choices over the

courses of a lifetime far more severely than those of men; it is much easier to switch from being a wageworker to a domestic role than to do the reverse. While Rawls has no objection to some aspects of the division of labor, he asserts that in a well-ordered society, "no one need be servilely dependent on others and made to choose between monotonous and routine occupations which are deadening to human thought and sensibility"; work can and should be "meaningful for all."[44] These conditions are far more likely to be met in a society that does not assign family responsibilities in a way that makes women into a marginal sector of the paid workforce and renders likely their economic dependence on men.

Second, the abolition of gender seems essential for the fulfillment of Rawls's criterion for political justice. For he argues that not only would equal formal political liberties be espoused by those in the original position, but that any inequalities in the *worth* of these liberties (for example, the effects on them of factors like poverty and ignorance) must be justified by the difference principle. Indeed, "the constitutional process should preserve the equal representation of the original position to the degree that this is practicable."[45] While Rawls discusses this requirement in the context of *class* differences, stating that those who devote themselves to politics should be "drawn more or less equally from all sectors of society,"[46] it is just as clearly and importantly applicable to sex differences. The equal political representation of women and men, especially if they are parents, is clearly inconsistent with our gender system.[47]

Finally, Rawls argues that the rational moral persons in the original position would place a great deal of emphasis on the securing of self-respect or self-esteem. They "would wish to avoid at almost any cost the social conditions that undermine self-respect," which is "perhaps the most important" of all the primary goods.[48] In the interests of this primary value, if those in the original position did not know whether they were to be men or women, they would surely be concerned to establish a thoroughgoing social and economic equality between the sexes that would preserve either from the need to pander to or servilely provide for the pleasures of the other. They would be highly motivated, for example, to find a means of regulating pornography that did not seriously compromise freedom of speech, and would be unlikely to tolerate basic social institutions that asymmetrically either forced or gave strong incentives to members of one sex to serve as sex objects for the other.

There is, then, implicit in Rawls's theory of justice a potential critique of gender-structured social institutions which can be developed by taking seriously the fact that those formulating the principles of justice do not know their sex. At the beginning of my brief account of this feminist critique, however, I made an assumption that I said would later be questioned—that a person's sex is, as Rawls at times indicates, a contingent and morally irrelevant characteristic, such that human beings really can hypothesize ignorance of this fact about them. First, I shall explain why, unless this assumption is a reasonable one, there are likely to be further feminist ramifications for a Rawlsian theory of justice in addition to those I have just sketched out. I shall then argue that the assumption is very probably not plausible in any society that is structured along the lines of gender. The conclusion I reach is that not only is gender incompatible with the attainment of social justice, in practice, for members of both sexes, but that the disappearance of gender is a prerequisite for the *complete* development of a nonsexist, fully human *theory* of justice.

Although Rawls is clearly aware of the effects on individuals of their different places in the social system, he regards it as possible to hypothesize free and rational moral persons in the original position who, temporarily freed from the contingencies of actual characteristics and social circumstances, will adopt the viewpoint of the "representative human being." He is under no illusions about the difficulty of this task, which requires a great shift in perspective from the way we think about fairness in everyday life. But with the help of the veil of ignorance, he believes that we can "take up a point of view that everyone can adapt on an equal footing," so that "we share a common

standpoint along with others and do not make our judgments from a personal slant."[49] The result of this rational impartiality or objectivity, Rawls argues, is that—all being convinced by the same arguments—agreement about the basic principles of justice will be unanimous.[50] He does not mean that those in the original position will agree about *all* moral or social issues—"ethical differences are bound to remain"—but that complete agreement will be reached on all basic principles, or "essential understandings."[51] However, it is a crucial assumption of this argument for unanimity that all the parties have similar motivations and psychologies (for example, he assumes mutually disinterested rationality and an absence of envy), and that they have experienced similar patterns of moral development, and are thus presumed capable of a shared sense of justice. Rawls regards these assumptions as the kind of "weak stipulations" on which a general theory can safely be founded.[52]

The coherence of Rawls's hypothetical original position, with its unanimity of representative human beings, however, is placed in doubt if the kinds of human beings we actually become in society not only differ in respect of interests, superficial opinions, prejudices, and points of view that we can discard for the purpose of formulating principles of justice, but also differ in our basic psychologies, conceptions of the self in relation to others, and experiences of moral development. A number of feminist theorists have argued in recent years that in a gender-structured society the different life experiences of females and males from the start in fact affect their respective psychologies, modes of thinking, and patterns of moral development in significant ways.[53] Special attention has been paid to the effects on the psychological and moral development of both sexes of the fact that children of both sexes are primarily reared by women. It has been argued that the experience of individuation—of separating oneself from the nurturer with whom one is originally psychologically fused—is a very different experience for girls than for boys, leaving the members of each sex with a different perception of themselves and of their relations with others. In addition, it has been argued that the experience of *being* primary nur-turers (and of growing up with this expectation) also affects the psychological and moral perspec-tive of women, as does the experience of growing up in society in which members of one's sex are in many ways subordinate to the other. Feminist the-orists' scrutiny and analysis of the different experi-ences that we encounter as we develop, from our actual lived lives to our absorption of their ideo-logical underpinnings, have in valuable ways filled out de Beauvoir's claim that "one is not born, but rather becomes, a woman."[54]

What is already clearly indicated by these stud-ies, despite their incompleteness so far, is that *in a gender-structured society* there is such a thing as the distinct standpoint of women, and that this standpoint cannot be adequately taken into ac-count by male philosophers doing the theoretical equivalent of the elderly male justices in the car-toon. The very early formative influence on chil-dren of female parenting, especially, seems to sug-gest that sex difference in a gendered society is more likely to affect one's thinking about justice than, for example, racial difference in a society in which race has social significance, or class differ-ence in a class society. The notion of the stand-point of women (while not without its own prob-lems) suggests, first, that a fully human moral or political theory can be developed only with the full participation of both sexes. At the very least, this will require that women take their place with men in the dialogue in approximately equal num-bers and in positions of comparable influence. In a society structured along the lines of gender, this cannot happen.

In itself, moreover, this is insufficient for the complete development of a fully human theory of justice. For if principles of justice are to be adopted unanimously by representative human beings ignorant of their particular characteristics and positions in society, they must be persons whose psychological and moral development is in all essentials identical. This means that the social factors influencing the differences presently found between the sexes—from female parenting to all the manifestations of female subordination and

dependence—would have to be replaced by gen-derless institutions and customs. Only when men participate equally in what have been principally women's realms of meeting the daily material and psychological needs of those close to them, and when women participate equally in what have been principally men's realms of larger scale pro-duction, government, and intellectual and creative life, will members of both sexes be able to develop a more complete *human* personality than has hith-erto been possible. Whereas Rawls and most other philosophers have assumed that human psychol-ogy, rationality, moral development and so on are completely represented by the males of the spe-cies, this assumption itself has now been exposed as part of the male-dominated ideology of our gendered society.

It is not feasible to consider here at any length what effect the consideration of women's stand-point might have on Rawls's theory of justice. I would suggest, however, that it might place in doubt some assumptions and conclusions, while reinforcing others. For example, the discussion of rational plans of life and primary goods might be focussed more on relationships and less exclu-sively on complex activities if it were to encompass the traditionally more female parts of life.[55] On the other hand, those aspects of Rawls's theory, such as the difference principle, that require a far greater capacity to identify with others than is normally characteristic of liberal theory might well be strengthened by reference to conceptions of re-lations between self and others that seem in gen-dered society to be more predominantly female, but that would in a gender-free society be more or less evenly shared by members of both sexes.[56]

The arguments of this essay, while critical of some aspects of Rawls's theory of justice, suggest the potential usefulness of the theory from a fem-inist viewpoint. Rawls himself neglects gender and, despite his initial inclusion of the family in the basic structure, he does not consider issues having to do with justice *within* the family. In recent work, moreover, he suggests that the family be-longs with those "private" and therefore non-political associations for which the principles of justice are not appropriate. He does this, moreover, despite the fact that his own theory of moral development rests centrally on the early experience of persons within a family environment that is both loving and just. Thus the theory as it stands contains an internal paradox. Because of his assumptions about gender, he has not applied the principles of justice to the realm of human nurturance which is so crucial for the achievement and the maintenance of justice.

On the other hand, I have argued that the feminist *potential* of Rawls's method of thinking and his conclusions is considerable. The original position, with the veil of ignorance hiding from its participants their sex as well as their other particular characteristics, their talents, circumstances and aims, is a powerful concept for challenging the gender structure. In particular—notwithstanding the difficulties for those socialized in a gender society of thinking in the original position—it provides a viewpoint from which we can think about how to achieve justice within the family.

NOTES

1. I have analyzed some of the ways in which theorists in the tradition have avoided considering the justice of gender, in "Are Our Theories of Justice Gender Neutral?" in *The Moral Foundations of Civil Rights,* ed. Robert Fullinwider and Claudia Mills (Totowa, NJ: Rowman and Littlefield, 1986), pp. 125–43.

2. John Rawls, *A Theory of Justice* (Cambridge, Mass.: Harvard University Press, 1971).

3. This is no longer the case in his most recent writings. See for example "Justice as Fairness: Political not Metaphysical," *Philosophy and Public Affairs,* 14(3), summer 1985, pp. 223–51.

4. Rawls, *Theory,* pp. 105–6, 208–9, 288–9.

5. See my "Women and the Making of the Sentimental Family," *Philosophy and Public Affairs,* 11(1), winter 1982, pp. 65–88, at pp. 78–82; Carole Pateman, *The Sexual Contract* (Stanford: Stanford University Press, 1988), pp. 168–73.

6. Rawls, *Theory,* pp. 251, 256. See also "Kantian Constructivism in Moral Theory," *The Journal of Philosophy,* 77(9), September 1980, pp. 515–72.

7. *Theory,* p. 459.

8. John Rawls, "Fairness to Goodness," *Philosophical Review,* 84, 1975, p. 537.

9. *Theory,* p. 137; see also p. 12.

10. Ibid. Numerous commentators on *Theory* have pointed out how controversial some of these "facts" are.

11. Ibid., pp. 128, 146.

12. As I have argued elsewhere, this assumption has frequently been misinterpreted by those of Rawls's critics who consider it in isolation from other crucial components of the original position, especially the veil of ignorance. See my "Reason and Feeling in Thinking about Justice," *Ethics,* 99(2), January 1989, pp. 229–49.

13. *Theory,* p. 128; see also p. 292.

14. Ibid., p. 289.

15. Ibid., p. 7.

16. It is noteworthy that in a subsequent paper on the subject of why the basic structure is the primary subject of justice, Rawls does *not* mention the family as part of the basic structure. See "The Basic Structure as Subject," *American Philosophical Quarterly,* 14(2), April 1977, p. 159. More significantly, whereas at the beginning of *Theory* he explicitly distinguishes the institutions of the basic structure from other "private associations," "less comprehensive social groups," and "various informal conventions and customs of everyday life" (p. 8), for which he suggests the principles of justice might be less appropriate or relevant, in two recent papers he classifies the family as belonging *with* such private, nonpolitical associations. See "Justice as Fairness," at p. 245; "The Priority of Right and Ideas of the Good," *Philosophy and Public Affairs,* 17(4), fall 1988, pp. 251–76, at p. 263.

17. *Theory,* p. 61.

18. Ibid., p. 303.

19. Ibid., pp. 463, 490. See Deborah Kearns, "A Theory of Justice—and Love; Rawls on the Family," *Politics (Australasian Political Studies Association Journal),* 18(2), November 1983, pp. 36–42, at pp. 39–40, for an interesting discussion of the significance for Rawls's theory of moral development of his failure to address the justice of the family.

20. As Jane English says, "By making the parties in the original position heads of families rather than individuals, Rawls makes the family opaque to claims of justice." "Justice between Generations," *Philosophical Studies,* 31(2), 1977, pp. 91–104, at p. 95.

21. *Theory,* p. 99.

22. Ibid., p. 149.

23. Ibid., pp. 270–4, 304–9.

24. Ibid., pp. 380–1 (emphasis added).

25. Ibid., p. 467.

26. Ibid., p. 468.

27. Ibid., p. 463 (emphasis added).

28. Rawls, "Basic Structure as Subject," p. 160.

29. *Theory,* p. 454.

30. Ibid., p. 465.

31. Ibid., p. 466.

32. Ibid., p. 469.

33. Ibid., p. 470.

34. Ibid., p. 471.

35. See Okin, "Reason and Feeling."

36. *Theory*, p. 476.

37. Ibid., p. 475.

38. Ibid., pp. 479ff.

39. Ibid., p. 494; see also pp. 490–1.

40. Charles Beitz, for example, argues that there is no justification for not extending its application to the population of the entire world, which would lead to challenging virtually everything that is currently assumed in the dominant "statist" conception of international relations. *Political Theory and International Relations* (Princeton: Princeton University Press, 1979).

41. The US Supreme Court decided in 1976, for example that "an exclusion of pregnancy from a disability benefits plan . . . providing general coverage is not a gender-based discrimination at all." *General Electric v. Gilbert*, 429 US 125 (1976).

42. *Theory*, p. 302.

43. Ibid., p. 274.

44. Ibid., p. 529.

45. Ibid., p. 222; see also pp. 202–5, 221–8.

46. Ibid., p. 228.

47. The paltry numbers of women in high political office is an obvious indication of this. As of 1987, 41 out of the 630 members of the British House of Commons were women. Since 1789, over 10,000 men have served in the US House of Representatives, but only 107 women; some 1,140 men have been senators, compared with 15 women.

48. *Theory*, pp. 440, 396; see also pp. 178–9.

49. Ibid., pp. 516–17.

50. Ibid., pp. 139–41.

51. Ibid., p. 517.

52. Ibid., p. 149.

53. Major works contributing to this thesis are Jean Baker Miller, *Toward a New Psychology of Women* (Boston: Beacon Press, 1976); Dorothy Dinnerstein, *The Mermaid and the Minotaur* (New York: Harper and Row, 1977); Nancy Chodorow, *The Reproduction of Mothering* (Berkeley: University of California Press, 1978): Carol Gilligan, *In a Different Voice* (Cambridge, Mass.: Harvard University Press, 1982); Nancy Hartsock, *Money, Sex, and Power* (New York: Longmans, 1983). Important individual papers are Jane Flax, "The Conflict between Nurturance and Autonomy in Mother–Daughter Relationships and within Feminism," *Feminist Studies*, 4(2), summer 1978; Sara Ruddick, "Maternal Thinking," *Feminist Studies,* 6(2), summer 1980. Summaries and/or analyses are presented in Alison Jaggar, *Feminist Politics and Human Nature* (Totowa, NJ: Rowman and Allenheld, 1983), ch. 11; Jean Grimshaw, *Philosophy and Feminist Thinking* (Minneapolis: University of Minnesota Press, 1986), chs. 5–8; Susan Moller Okin, "Thinking Like a Woman," in Deborah Rhode, ed., *Theoretical Perspectives on Sexual Difference* (New Haven: Yale University Press, 1990); Joan Tronto, "Women's Morality: Beyond Gender Difference to a Theory of Care," *Signs,* 12(4), summer 1987, pp. 644–63.

54. Simone de Beauvoir, *The Second Sex,* trans. H. M. Parshley (New York: Vintage Books, 1952), p. 301.

55. Brian Barry has made a similar, though more general, criticism of Rawls's focus on complex and challenging practices—the "Aristotelian Principle"—in *The Liberal Theory of Justice* (Oxford: Oxford University Press, 1973), pp. 27–30.

56. I have developed this argument in "Reason and Feeling."

# 49    The Political Theory of Islam

## ABU'L A'LA MAWDUDI

WITH CERTAIN PEOPLE it has become a sort of fashion to somehow identify Islam with one or the other system of life in vogue at the time. So at this time also there are people who say that Islam is democracy, and by this they mean to imply that there is no difference between Islam and the democracy as in vogue in the West. Some others suggest that Communism is but the latest and revised version of Islam and it is in the fitness of things that Muslims imitate the Communist experiment of Soviet

Russia. Still some others whisper that Islam has the elements of dictatorship in it and we should revive the cult of "obedience to the *Amir*" (the leader). All these people, in this misinformed and misguided zeal to serve what they hold to be the cause of Islam, are always at great pains to prove that Islam contains within itself the elements of all types of contemporary social and political thought and action. Most of the people who indulge in this prattle have no clear idea of the Islamic way of life. They have never made nor try to make a systematic study of the Islamic political order—the place and nature of democracy, social justice, and equality in it. Instead they behave like the proverbial blind men who gave altogether contradictory descriptions of an elephant because one had been able to touch only its tail, the other its legs, the third its belly and the fourth its ears only. Or perhaps they look upon Islam as an orphan whose sole hope for survival lies in winning the patronage and the sheltering care of some dominant creed. That is why some people have begun to present apologies on Islam's behalf. As a matter of fact, this attitude emerges from an inferiority complex, from the belief that we as Muslims can earn no honor or respect unless we are able to show that our religion resembles the modern creeds and it is in agreement with most of the contemporary ideologies. These people have done a great disservice to Islam; they have reduced the political theory of Islam to a puzzle, a hotchpotch. They have turned Islam into a juggler's bag out of which can be produced anything that holds a demand! Such is the intellectual plight in which we are engulfed. Perhaps it is a result of this sorry state of affairs that some people have even begun to say that Islam has no political or economic system of its own and anything can fit into its scheme.

In these circumstances it has become essential that a careful study of the political theory of Islam should be made in a scientific way, with a view to grasp its real meaning, nature, purpose and significance. Such a systematic study alone can put an end to this confusion of thought and silence those who out of ignorance proclaim that there is nothing like Islamic political theory, Islamic social order and Islamic culture. I hope it will also bring to the world groping in darkness the light that it urgently needs, although it is not yet completely conscious of such a need. . . .

## First Principle of Islamic Political Theory

The belief in the Unity and the sovereignty of Allah is the foundation of the social and moral system propounded by the Prophets. It is the very starting-point of the Islamic political philosophy. The basic principle of Islam is that human beings must, individually and collectively, surrender all rights of overlordship, legislation and exercising of authority over others. No one should be allowed to pass orders or make commands *in his own right* and no one ought to accept the obligation to carry out such commands and obey such orders. None is entitled to make laws on his own authority and none is obliged to abide by them. This right vests in Allah alone:

> The Authority rests with none but Allah. He commands you not to surrender to any one save Him. This is the right way (of life). (Qur'ān 12:40)

> They ask: "have we also got some authority?" Say: "all authority belongs to God alone." (3:154)

> Do not say wrongly with your tongues that this is lawful and that is unlawful. (16:116)

> Whoso does not establish and decide by that which Allah has revealed, such are disbelievers. (5:44)

According to this theory, sovereignty belongs to Allah. He alone is the law-giver. No man, even if he be a Prophet, has the right to order others *in his own right* to do or not to do certain things. The Prophet himself is subject to God's commands:

> I do not follow anything except what is revealed to me. (6:50)

Other people are required to obey the Prophet because he enunciates not his own but God's commands:

> We sent no messenger save that he should be obeyed by Allah's command. (4:64)

They are the people to whom We gave the Scripture and Command and Prophethood. (6:90)

It is not (possible) for any human being to whom Allah has given the Scripture and the Wisdom and the Prophethood that he should say to people: Obey me instead of Allah. Such a one (could only say): be solely devoted to the Lord. (3:79)

Thus the main characteristics of an Islamic state that can be deduced from these express statements of the Holy Qur'ān are as follows:—

1. No person, class or group, not even the entire population of the state as a whole, can lay claim to sovereignty. God alone is the real sovereign; all others are merely His subjects;

2. God is the real law-giver and the authority of absolute legislation vests in Him. The believers cannot resort to totally independent legislation nor can they modify any law which God has laid down, even if the desire to effect such legislation or change in Divine laws is unanimous; and

3. An Islamic state must, in all respects, be founded upon the law laid down by God through His Prophet. The government which runs such a state will be entitled to obedience in its capacity as a political agency set up to enforce the laws of God and only in so far as it acts in that capacity. If it disregards the law revealed by God, its commands will not be binding on the believers.

## The Islamic State

### ITS NATURE AND CHARACTERISTICS

The preceding discussion makes it quite clear that Islam, speaking from the view-point of political philosophy, is the very antithesis of secular Western democracy. The philosophical foundation of Western democracy is the sovereignty of the people. In it, this type of absolute powers of legislation—of the determination of values and of the norms of behavior—rest in the hands of the people. Law-making is their prerogative and legislation must correspond to the mood and temper of their opinion. If a particular piece of legislation is desired by the masses, howsoever ill-conceived it may be from a religious and moral viewpoint, steps have to be taken to place it on the statute book; if the people dislike any law and demand its abrogation, howsoever just and rightful it might be, it has to be expunged forthwith. This is not the case in Islam. On this count, Islam has no trace of Western democracy. Islam, as already explained, altogether repudiates the philosophy of popular sovereignty and rears its polity on the foundations of the sovereignty of God and the viceregency (*Khilāfah*) of man.

A more apt name for the Islamic polity would be the "kingdom of God" which is described in English as a "theocracy." But Islamic theocracy is something altogether different from the theocracy of which Europe has had a bitter experience wherein a priestly class, sharply marked off from the rest of the population, exercises unchecked domination and enforces laws of its own making in the name of God, thus virtually imposing its own divinity and godhood upon the common people. Such a system of government is satanic rather than divine. Contrary to this, the theocracy built up by Islam is not ruled by any particular religious class but by the whole community of Muslims including the rank and file. The entire Muslim population runs the state in accordance with the Book of God and the practice of His Prophet. If I were permitted to coin a new term, I would describe this system of government as a "theo-democracy," that is to say a divine democratic government, because under it the Muslims have been given a limited popular sovereignty under the suzerainty of God. The executive under this system of government is constituted by the general will of the Muslims who have also the right to depose it. All administrative matters and all questions about which no explicit injunction is to be found in the *shariah* are settled by the consensus of opinion among the Muslims.[1] Every Muslim who is capable and qualified to give a sound opinion on matters of Islamic law, is entitled to interpret the law of God when such interpretation becomes necessary. In this sense the Islamic polity is a democracy. But, as has been explained above, it is a theocracy in the sense that where an explicit command of God or His Prophet already exists, no Muslim leader or legislature, or any religious scholar can form an independent judgment, not even all the Muslims of the world put together have any right to make the least alteration in it.

Before proceeding further, I feel that I should put in a word of explanation as to why these limitations and restrictions have been placed upon popular sovereignty in Islam, and what is the nature of these limitations and restrictions. It may be said that God has, in this manner, taken away the liberty of the human mind and intellect instead of safeguarding it as I was trying to prove. My reply is that God has retained the right of legislation in His own hand not in order to deprive man of his natural freedom but to safeguard that very freedom. His purpose is to save man from going astray and inviting his own ruin.

One can easily understand this point by attempting a little analysis of the so-called Western secular democracy. It is claimed that this democracy is founded on popular sovereignty. But everybody knows that the people who constitute a state do not all of them take part either in legislation or in its administration. They have to delegate their sovereignty to their elected representatives so that the latter may make and enforce laws on their behalf. For this purpose, an electoral system is set up. But as a divorce has been effected between politics and religion, and as a result of this secularization, the society and particularly its politically active elements have ceased to attach much or any importance to morality and ethics. And this is also a fact that only those persons generally come to the top who can dupe the masses by their wealth, power, and deceptive propaganda. Although these representatives come into power by the votes of the common people, they soon set themselves up as an independent authority and assume the position of overlords (*ilāhs*). They often make laws not in the best interest of the people who raised them to power but to further their own sectional and class interests. They impose their will on the people by virtue of the authority delegated to them by those

over whom they rule. This is the situation which besets people in England, America and in all those countries which claim to be the haven of secular democracy.

Even if we overlook this aspect of the matter and admit that in these countries laws are made according to the wishes of the common people, it has been established by experience that the great mass of the common people are incapable of perceiving their own true interests. It is the natural weakness of man that in most of the affairs concerning his life he takes into consideration only some one aspect of reality and loses sight of other aspects. His judgments are usually one-sided and he is swayed by emotions and desires to such an extent that rarely, if ever, can he judge important matters with the impartiality and objectivity of scientific reason. Quite often he rejects the plea of reason simply because it conflicts with his passions and desires. I can cite many instances in support of this contention but to avoid prolixity I shall content myself with giving only one example: the Prohibition Law of America. It had been rationally and logically established that drinking is injurious to health, produces deleterious effects on mental and intellectual faculties and leads to disorder in human society. The American public accepted these facts and agreed to the enactment of the Prohibition Law. Accordingly the law was passed by the majority vote. But when it was put into effect, the very same people by whose vote it had been passed, revolted against it. The worst kinds of wine were illicitly manufactured and consumed, and their use and consumption became more widespread than before. Crimes increased in number, and eventually drinking was legalized by the vote of the same people who had previously voted for its prohibition. This sudden change in public opinion was not the result of any fresh scientific discovery or the revelation of new facts providing evidence against the advantages of prohibition, but because the people had been completely enslaved by their habit and could not forgo the pleasures of self-indulgence. They delegated their own sovereignty to the evil spirit in them and set up their own desires and passions as their *ilāhs* (gods) at whose call they all went in for the repeal of the very law they had passed after having been convinced of its rationality and correctness. There are many other similar instances which go to prove that man is not competent to become an absolute legislator. Even if he secures deliverance from the service of other *ilāhs*, he becomes a slave to his own petty passions and exalts the devil in him to the position of a supreme Lord. Limitations on human freedom, provided they are appropriate and do not deprive him of all initiative, are absolutely necessary in the interest of man himself.

That is why God has laid down those limits which, in Islamic phraseology, are termed "divine limits." These limits consist of certain principles, checks and balances and specific injunctions in different spheres of life and activity, and they have been prescribed in order that man may be trained to lead a balanced and moderate life. They are intended to lay down the broad framework within which man is free to legislate, decide his own affairs and frame subsidiary laws and regulations for his conduct. These limits he is not permitted to overstep and if he does so, the whole scheme of his life will go awry.

Take for example man's economic life. In this sphere God has placed certain restrictions on human freedom. The right to private property has been recognized, but it is qualified by the obligation to pay *Zakāh* (poor dues) and the prohibition of interest, gambling and speculation. A specific law of inheritance for the distribution of property among the largest number of surviving relations on the death of its owner has been laid down and certain forms of acquiring, accumulating and spending wealth have been declared unlawful. If people observe these just limits and regulate their affairs within these boundary walls, on the one hand their personal liberty is adequately safeguarded and, on the other, the possibility of class war and domination of one class over another, which begins with capitalist oppression and ends in working-class dictatorship, is safely and conveniently eliminated.

Similarly in the sphere of family life, God has prohibited the unrestricted intermingling of the sexes and has prescribed *Pardah*, recognized man's guardianship of woman, and clearly defined the rights and duties of husband, wife and children.[2] The laws of divorce and separation have been clearly set forth, conditional polygamy has been permitted and penalties for fornication and false accusations of adultery have been prescribed. He has thus laid down limits which, if observed by man, would stabilize his family life and make it a haven of peace and happiness. There would remain neither that tyranny of male over female which makes family life an inferno of cruelty and oppression, nor that satanic flood of female liberty and licence which threatens to destroy human civilization in the West.

In like manner, for the preservation of human culture and society God has, by formulating the law of *Qisyāsy* (Retaliation) commanding to cut off the hands for theft, prohibiting wine-drinking, placing limitations on uncovering of one's private parts and by laying down a few similar permanent rules and regulations, closed the door of social disorder forever. I have no time to present to you a complete list of all the divine limits and show in detail how essential each one of them is for maintaining equilibrium and poise in life. What I want to bring home to you here is that through these injunctions God has provided a permanent and immutable code of behavior for man, and that it does not deprive him of any essential liberty nor does it dull the edge of his mental faculties. On the contrary, it sets a straight and clear path before him, so that he may not, owing to his ignorance and weaknesses which he inherently possesses, lose himself in the maze of destruction and instead of wasting his faculties in the pursuit of wrong ends, he may follow the road that leads to success and progress in this world and the hereafter. If you have ever happened to visit a mountainous region, you must have noticed that in the winding mountain paths which are bounded by deep caves on the one side and lofty rocks on the other, the border of the road is barricaded and protected in such a way as to prevent travelers from straying towards the abyss by mistake. Are these barricades intended to deprive the wayfarer of his liberty? No, as a matter of fact, they are meant to protect him from destruction; to warn him at every bend of the dangers ahead and to show him the path leading to his destination. That precisely is the purpose of the restrictions which God has laid down in His revealed Code. These limits determine what direction man should take in life's journey and they guide him at every turn and pass and point out to him the path of safety which he should steadfastly follow.

As I have already stated, this code, enacted as it is by God, is unchangeable. You can, if you like, rebel against it, as some Muslim countries have done. But you cannot alter it. It will continue to be unalterable till the last day. It has its own avenues of growth and evolution, but no human being has any right to tamper with it. Whenever an Islamic State comes into existence, this code would form its fundamental law and will constitute the mainspring of all its legislation. Everyone who desires to remain a Muslim is under an obligation to follow the Qur'ān and the Sunnah which must constitute the basic law of an Islamic State.

## THE PURPOSE OF
## THE ISLAMIC STATE

The purpose of the state that may be formed on the basis of the Qur'ān and the *Sunnah* has also been laid down by God. The Qur'ān says:

> We verily sent Our messengers with clear proofs, and revealed with them the Scripture and the Balance, that mankind may observe right measure; and We revealed iron, wherein is mighty power and (many) uses for mankind. (57:25)

In this verse steel symbolizes political power and the verse also makes it clear that the mission of the Prophets is to create conditions in which the mass of people will be assured of social justice in accordance with the standards enunciated by God in His Book which gives explicit instructions for a well-disciplined mode of life. In another place God has said:

> (Muslims are) those who, if We give them power in the land, establish the system of worship and poor dues and enjoin virtue and forbid evil and inequity. (22:41)

> You are the best community sent forth to mankind; you enjoin the Right conduct and forbid the wrong; and you believe in Allah. (3:110)

It will readily become manifest to anyone who reflects upon these verses that the purpose of the state visualized by the Holy Qur'ān is not negative but positive. The object of the state is not merely to prevent people from exploiting each other, to safeguard their liberty and to protect its subjects from foreign invasion. It also aims at evolving and developing that well-balanced system of social justice which has been set forth by God in His Holy Book. Its object is to eradicate all forms of evil and to encourage all types of virtue and excellence expressly mentioned by God in the Holy Qur'ān. For this purpose political power will be made use of as and when the occasion demands; all means of propaganda and peaceful persuasion will be employed; the moral education of the people will also be undertaken; and social influence as well as the force of public opinion will be harnessed to the task.

## ISLAMIC STATE IS UNIVERSAL
## AND ALL-EMBRACING

A state of this sort cannot evidently restrict the scope of its activities. Its approach is universal and all-embracing. Its sphere of activity is coextensive with the whole of human life. It seeks to mould every aspect of life and activity in consonance with its moral norms and program of social reform. In such a state no one can regard any field of his affairs as personal and private. Considered from this aspect the Islamic state bears a kind of resemblance to the Fascist and Communist states. But you will find later on that, despite its all-inclusiveness, it is something vastly and basically different from the modern totalitarian and authoritarian states. Individual liberty is not suppressed under it nor is there any trace of dictatorship in it. It presents the middle course and embodies the best that the human society has ever evolved. The excellent balance and moderation that characterize the Islamic system of government and the precise distinctions made in it between right and wrong—elicit from all men of honesty and intelligence the admiration and the admission that such a balanced system could not have been framed by anyone but the Omniscient and All-Wise God.

## ISLAMIC STATE IS AN IDEOLOGICAL STATE

Another characteristic of the Islamic State is that it is an ideological state. It is clear from a careful consideration of the Qur'ān and the *Sunnah* that the state in Islam is based on an ideology and its objective is to establish that ideology. The state is an instrument of reform and must act likewise. It is a dictate of this very nature of the Islamic State that such a state should be run only by those who believe in the ideology on which it is based and in the Divine Law which it is assigned to administer. The administrators of the Islamic state must be those whose whole life is devoted to the observance and enforcement of this Law, who not only agree with its reformatory program and fully believe in it but thoroughly comprehend its spirit and are acquainted with its details. Islam does not recognize any geographical, linguistic or colour bars in this respect. It puts forward its code of guidance and the scheme of its reform before all men. Whoever accepts this program, no matter to what race, nation or country he may belong, can join the community that runs the Islamic state. But those who do not accept it are not entitled to have any hand in shaping the fundamental policy of the State. They can live within the confines of the State as non-Muslim citizens (*Dhimmis*). Specific rights and privileges have been accorded to them in the Islamic Law. A *Dhimmi's* life, property and honor will be fully protected, and if he is capable of any service, his services will also be made use of. He will not, however, be allowed to influence the basic policy of this ideological state. The Islamic state is based on a particular ideology and it is the community which believes in the Islamic ideology which pilots it. Here again, we notice some sort of resemblance between the Islamic

and the Communist states. But the treatment meted out by the Communist states to persons holding creeds and ideologies other than its own bears no comparison with the attitude of the Islamic state. Unlike the Communist state, Islam does not impose its social principles on others by force, nor does it confiscate their properties or unleash a reign of terror by mass executions of the people and their transportation to the slave camps of Siberia. Islam does not want to eliminate its minorities, it wants to protect them and give them the freedom to live according to their own culture. The generous and just treatment which Islam has accorded to non-Muslims in an Islamic state and the fine distinction drawn by it between justice and injustice and good and evil will convince all those who are not prejudiced against it, that the prophets sent by God accomplish their task in an altogether different manner—something radically different and diametrically opposed to the way of the false reformers who strut about here and there on the stage of history.

## The Theory of the Caliphate and the Nature of Democracy in Islam

I will now try to give a brief exposition of the composition and structure of the Islamic state. I have already stated that in Islam, God alone is the real sovereign. Keeping this cardinal principle in mind, if we consider the position of those persons who set out to enforce God's law on earth, it is but natural to say that they should be regarded as representatives of the Supreme Ruler. Islam has assigned precisely this very position to them. Accordingly the Holy Qur'ān says:

> Allah has promised to those among you who believe and do righteous deeds that He will assuredly make them to succeed (the present rulers) and grant them viceregency in the land just as He made those before them to succeed (others).

The verse illustrates very clearly the Islamic theory of state. Two fundamental points emerge from it.

1. The first point is that Islam uses the term "viceregency" (*Khilāfah*) instead of sovereignty. Since, according to Islam, sovereignty belongs to God alone, anyone who holds power and rules in accordance with the laws of God would undoubtedly be the viceregency of the Supreme Ruler and would not be authorized to exercise any powers other than those delegated to him.

2. The second point stated in the verse is that the power to rule over the earth has been promised to *the whole community of believers;* it has not been stated that any particular person or class among them will be raised to that position. From this it follows that all believers are repositories of the Caliphate. The Caliphate granted by God to the faithful is the popular viceregency and not a limited one. There is no reservation in favor of any family, class or race. Every believer is a Caliph of God in his individual capacity. By virtue of this position he is individually responsible to God. The Holy Prophet has said: "Everyone of you is a ruler and everyone is answerable for his subjects." Thus one Caliph is in no way inferior to another.

This is the real foundation of democracy in Islam. The following points emerge from an analysis of this conception of popular viceregency.

(a) A society in which everyone is a Caliph of God and an equal participant in this Caliphate, cannot tolerate any class divisions based on distinctions of birth and social position. All men enjoy equal status and position in such a society. The only criterion of superiority in this social order is personal ability and character. This is what has been repeatedly and explicitly asserted by the Holy Prophet:

> No one is superior to another except in point of faith and piety. All men are descended from Adam and Adam was made of clay.

> An Arab has no superiority over a non-Arab nor a non-Arab over an Arab; neither does a white man possess any superiority over a black man nor a black man over a white one, except in point of piety.

After the conquest of Mekka, when the whole of Arabia came under the domination of the Is-

lamic state, the Holy Prophet addressing the members of his own clan, who in the days before Islam enjoyed the same status in Arabia as the Brahmins did in ancient India, said:

> O people of Quraysh! Allah has rooted out your haughtiness of the days of ignorance and the pride of ancestry. O men, all of you are descended from Adam and Adam was made of clay. There is no pride whatever in ancestry; there is no merit in an Arab as against a non-Arab nor in a non-Arab against an Arab. Verily the most meritorious among you in the eyes of God is he who is the most pious.

(b) In such a society no individual or group of individuals will suffer any disability on account of birth, social status, or profession that may in any way impede the growth of his faculties or hamper the development of his personality.

Every one would enjoy equal opportunities of progress. The way would be left open for him to make as much progress as possible according to his inborn capacity and personal merits without prejudice to similar rights of other people. Thus, unrestricted scope for personal achievement has always been the hallmark of Islamic society. Slaves and their descendants were appointed as military officers and governors of provinces, and noble men belonging to the highest families did not feel ashamed to serve under them. Those who used to stitch and mend shoes rose in the social scale and became leaders of highest order (*imāms*); weavers and cloth-sellers became judges and jurists and to this day they are reckoned as the heroes of Islam. The Holy Prophet has said:

> Listen and obey even if a negro is appointed as a ruler over you.

(c) There is no room in such a society for the dictatorship of any person or group of persons since everyone is a Caliph of God herein. No person or group of persons is entitled to become an absolute ruler by depriving the rank and file of their inherent right of Caliphate. The position of a man who is selected to conduct the affairs of the state is no more than this; that all Muslims (or, technically speaking, all Caliphs of God) delegate their Caliphate to him for administrative purposes. *He is answerable to God on the one hand and on the other to his fellow "Caliphs" who have delegated their authority to him.* Now, if he raises himself to the position of an irresponsible absolute ruler, that is to say a dictator, he assumes the character of a usurper rather than a Caliph, because dictatorship is the negation of popular vice regency. No doubt the Islamic state is an all-embracing state and comprises within its sphere all departments of life, but this all-inclusiveness and universality are based upon the universality of Divine Law which an Islamic ruler has to observe and enforce. The guidance given by God about every aspect of life will certainly be enforced in its entirety. But an Islamic ruler cannot depart from these instructions and adopt a policy of regimentation on his own. He cannot force people to follow or not to follow a particular profession; to learn or not to learn a special art; to use or not to use a certain script; to wear or not to wear a certain dress and to educate or not to educate their children in a certain manner. The powers which the dictators of Russia, Germany and Italy have appropriated or which Ataturk has exercized in Turkey have not been granted by Islam to its leader. Besides this, another important point is that in Islam *every individual is held personally answerable to God.* This personal responsibility cannot be shared by anyone else. Hence, an individual enjoys full liberty to choose whichever path he likes and to develop his faculties in any direction that suits his natural gifts. If the leader obstructs him or obstructs the growth of his personality, he will himself be punished by God for this tyranny. That is precisely the reason why there is not the slightest trace of regimentation in the rule of the Holy Prophet and of his Rightly-Guided Caliphs; and

(d) In such a society every sane and adult Muslim, male or female, is entitled to express his or her opinion, for each one of them is the repository of the Caliphate. God has made this Caliphate conditional, not upon any particular standard of wealth or competence but only upon faith and good conduct. Therefore all Muslims have equal freedom to express their opinions.

## EQUILIBRIUM BETWEEN INDIVIDUALISM AND COLLECTIVISM

Islam seeks to set up, on the one hand, this superlative democracy and on the other it has put an end to that individualism which militates against the health of the body politic. The relations between the individual and the society have been regulated in such a manner that neither the personality of the individual suffers any diminution, or corrosion as it does in the Communist and Fascist social system, nor is the individual allowed to exceed his bounds to such an extent as to become harmful to the community, as happens in the Western democracies. In Islam, the purpose of an individual's life is the same as that of the life of the community, namely, the execution and enforcement of Divine Law and the acquisition of God's pleasure. Moreover, Islam has, after safeguarding the rights of the individual, imposed upon him certain duties towards the community. In this way requirements of individualism and collectivism have been so well harmonized that the individual is afforded the fullest opportunity to develop his potentialities and is thus enabled to employ his developed faculties in the service of the community at large.

These are, briefly, the basic principles and essential features of the Islamic political theory.

### NOTES

1. [*Qur'anic* commands, together with the *Sunnah* (which means custom and refers to whatever Muhammad said or did) constitute the *shari'ah* ("basic laws").—ED.]

2. [*Pardah* refers to practices of secluding women, such as veiling—ED.]

## *Recommended Readings*

TEXTS

Barry, Brian. *Justice as Impartiality.* Oxford: Oxford University Press, 1995.

Daniels, N., ed. *Reading Rawls.* Oxford: Basic Blackwell, 1975.

Hosper, John. *Libertarianism.* Los Angeles: Nash, 1971.

Machan, Tibor and Rasmussen, Douglas. *Liberty for the 21st Century.* Lanham: Rowman and Littlefield, 1995.

Neal, P. "Justice as Fairness: Political or Metaphysical?" *Political Theory* 18:24–50.

Sandel, M. *Liberalism and the Limits of Justice.* Cambridge, MA: Harvard University Press, 1982.

Sterba, James P. *The Demands of Justice.* Notre Dame: University of Notre Dame Press, 1980.


FEMINIST PERSPECTIVE

Brown, Wendy. "Reproductive Freedom and the 'Right to Privacy': A Paradox for Feminists." In *Families, Politics, and Public Policy: A Feminist Dialogue on Women and the State,* edited by Irene Diamond. New York: Longman, 1983.

Pitkin, Hanna. "Justice: On Relating Public and Private." *Political Theory* 9, no. 3 (1981).

Waylen, Georgina. "Women and Neo-Liberalism." In *Feminism and Political Theory,* edited by Judith Evans. London: Sage, 1986.


MULTICULTURAL PERSPECTIVE

Ajijola, Adeleke *The Islamic Concept of Social Justice.* Yahore, Islamic Publications, 1977.

Johnson, James ed. *Cross, Cresent and the Sword.* (New York: Greenwood Press, 1990).

# XII

# *Habermas and Foucault*

## Introduction

J ÜRGEN HABERMAS WAS BORN IN 1929 in Düsseldorf, Germany. He married Ute Wesselhoeft, a teacher, in 1955, and they have three children, Judith, Rebekka, and Tilmann. Habermas attended the University of Goettingham and the University of Zurich, and received a Ph.D. from the University of Bonn in 1954. He taught at the University of Heidelberg from 1961–1964 and Frankfurt on Main from 1964–1971. He has taught at the Max Planck Institute since 1974.

In the early 1960s, Habermas was a leading spokesperson for the student movement. However, by the late 1960s, he had become estranged from the movement's leading groups. He became critical of what he saw as their departure from their original democratic and nonauthoritarian goals. The students in turn criticized Habermas for failing to become involved in actual struggles and for retreating into theoretical reflection. Since that time, Habermas appears to have put less emphasis on the practical implications of his work.

Some of Habermas's principal works are *Knowledge and Human Interests* (1968), *The Legitimation Crisis* (1973), *The Theory of Communicative Action* (1981), *Moral Consciousness and Communicative Action* (1983), and *Justification and Application: Remarks on Discourse Ethics* (1993).

At least since the publication of *The Theory of Communicative Action,* Habermas's work has tended to focus on the philosophical underpinnings of a critical theory of society. In our selection from *Moral Consciousness and Communicative Action,* Habermas seeks to justify a principle of universalization from which the central principle of his discourse ethics can be derived.

Habermas's principle of universalization maintains that

> All affected can freely accept the consequences and the side effects that the general observance of the proposed norm can be expected to have for the satisfaction of everyone's interests.

The central principle of discourse ethics that Habermas thinks can be derived from his principle of universalization is

Only those norms can claim to be valid that meet (or could meet) with the approval of all affected in their capacity as participants in a practical discourse.

Unlike Rawls, Habermas maintains that the valid norms for a society must be actually accepted, not just hypothetically accepted, by all the members of a society.

The justification that Habermas hopes to provide for his principle of universalization is to show that the principle is implied by the presuppositions of argumentation itself.

One formulation of these presuppositions of argumentation, which Habermas endorses, is as follows:

1. Every subject with the competence to speak and act is allowed to take part in a discourse.
2. Everyone is allowed to question any assertion whatsoever.
   a. Everyone is allowed to introduce any assertion whatsoever into the discourse.
   b. Everyone is allowed to express his or her attitudes, desires, and needs.
3. No speaker may be prevented, by internal or external coercion, from exercising his or her rights as laid down in (1) and (2).

Habermas thinks that these presuppositions along with the claim that one should not prejudge any issue entail the principle of universalization, from which the principle of discourse ethics follows.

In brief, what Habermas wants to show is that fair rules of argumentation entail a requirement that norms affecting everyone should be acceptable (i.e., ought to be accepted) by everyone. What is not so clear, however, is whether Habermas's argument has force for people who are not committed to fair rules of argumentation.

Michel Foucault was born in 1926 in Poitiers, France. He died in 1984 of a neurological disorder. He attended École Normale Supérieure and the Sorbonne, University of Paris, from which he received licenses in 1948 and 1950 and a diploma in 1952. He taught philosophy and French literature at the universities of Lille, Warsaw, Hamburg, Clermont-Ferrand, São Paulo, Tunis, and Paris. From 1970 to 1984, he was chair of the History of Systems Thought at the Collège de France.

Foucault's major works include *Madness and Civilization* (1961), *The Archaeology of Knowledge* (1966), *Discipline and Punish: The Birth of the Prison* (1975), *The History of Sexuality* (1976), *Power/Knowledge* (1980), and *The Use of Pleasure* (1984).

In our selection from *Power/Knowledge*, Foucault claims that while the traditional role of theories of right from medieval times until the present has been to fix the legitimacy of power, we should seek to determine how such theories have also been the instruments of domination. To do this, Foucault recommends that we follow a certain methodological strategy.

1. Examine systems of power and right as they reveal themselves in their more regional and local forms, such as prisons and asylums.
2. Examine how systems of power and right, whatever the professed intentions of their practitioners, succeed in constituting their subjects.
3. Recognize how systems of power and right diffuse power throughout a society so that many individuals both exercise power and are subjected to it.
4. Recognize that systems of power and right cannot help but bring into existence forms of knowledge that are more than ideologies, which help sustain those systems in place.

Sandra Lee Bartky, in "Foucault, Femininity and the Modernization of Patriarchal Power," criticizes Foucault for writing as though there is no difference between the bodily experiences of men and women and as if men and women bear the same relationship to the characteristic institutions of modern life. Bartky details our current image of women as feminine, touching on body size and configuration, gestures, postures, styles of movement, and styles of ornamentation. She also describes the "disciplinary practices" or forms of subjection (e.g., dieting, exercise, skin care, hair care, makeup) women undergo to produce this image—all for the sake of being attractive to men. Since this image of femininity is impossible to ever fully achieve, or achieve for very long, real women may live much of their lives feeling inadequate about their body. And even when some real women do achieve this image, they may gain attention and some admiration, but little respect and rarely any social power as a result. According to Bartky,

> This system aims at turning women into the docile and compliant companions of men just as surely as the army aims to turn its raw recruits into soldiers.

If Bartky is correct, then Foucault's analysis of power must be broadened to expose the ways in which men and women are treated differently in society.

In "Philosophy, Politics, and Power: An Afro-American Perspective," Cornel West looks at modern philosophy and, in particular, the work of Foucault from an Afro-American perspective. West thinks that it is possible to use Foucault's method of analyzing power to provide a genealogy of modern racism, in particular, by showing how modern discourse excludes the idea of black equality in beauty, culture, and character. However, West maintains, Foucault's focus on power relations must be supplemented with a commitment to a revolutionary future.

# 50    Discourse Ethics

JÜRGEN HABERMAS

## I   *Propaedeutic Considerations . . .*

### 4 THE MORAL PRINCIPLE OR THE CRITERION OF GENERALIZING MAXIMS OF ACTION

. . . THE PRINCIPLE OF UNIVERSALIZATION is by no means exhausted by the requirement that moral norms must take the *form* of unconditionally universal "ought" statements. The *grammatical form* of normative statements alone, which does not permit such sentences to refer to or be addressed to particular groups or individuals, is not a sufficient condition for valid moral commands, for we could give such universal form to commands that are plainly immoral. What is more, in some respects the requirement of formal universality may well be too restrictive; it may make sense to submit nonmoral norms of action, whose range of jurisdictions is socially and spatiotemporally limited, to a practical discourse (restricted in this case to those concerned, and hence relative), and to test them for generalizability.

Other philosophers subscribe to a less formalistic view of the consistency required by the principle of universality. Their aim is to avoid the contraditions that occur when equal cases are treated unequally and unequal ones equally. R. M. Hare has given this requirement the form of a semantic postulate. As we do when we attribute descriptive predicates (". . . is red"), so we should attribute normative predicates (". . . is of value," ". . . is good," ". . . is right") in *conformity with a rule,* using the same linguistic expression in all cases that are the same in the respects relevant to the particular case. Applied to moral norms, Hare's consistency postulate comes to this: Every individual, before making a particular norm the basis for his moral judgment, should test if he can will the adoption of this norm by every other individual in a comparable situation. However, this, or another similar postulate is suitable to serve as a moral principle only if it is conceived as a warrant of impartiality in the process of judging. But one can hardly derive the meaning of impartiality from the notion of consistent language use.

Kurt Baier[1] and Bernard Gert[2] come closer to this meaning of the principle of universalization when they argue that valid moral norms must be generally teachable and publicly defendable. The same is true of Marcus Singer[3] when he proposes the requirement that norms are valid only if they ensure equality of treatment. Just as, however, an empirical check to see that allowance for disagreement has been made does not guarantee an impartial process of judging, so a norm cannot be considered the expression of the common interest of all who might be affected simply because it seems acceptable to some of them under the condition that it be applied in a nondiscriminatory fashion. The intuition expressed in the idea of the generalizability of maxims intends something more than this—namely, that valid norms must *deserve* recognition by *all* concerned. It is not sufficient, therefore, for *one person* to test

- whether he can will the adoption of a contested norm in consideration of the consequences and the indirect effects that would occur if all persons followed that norm; or
- whether every other person in an identical position could will the adoption of such a norm.

In both cases the process of judging is relative to the vantage point and perspective of *some* and not *all* concerned. True impartiality pertains only to that standpoint from which precisely those norms are generalizable that can count on universal assent because they perceptibly embody an interest common to all concerned. It is these norms that deserve intersubjective recognition. Thus the impartiality of judgment is expressed in a principle that constrains *all* concerned to adopt the perspectives of *all others* in the balancing of interests. The principle of universalization is intended to compel the *universal exchange of roles* that G. H. Mead called "ideal role-taking" or "universal discourse."[4] Thus every valid norm has to fulfill the condition

> that *all* concerned can accept the consequences and the side effects its *universal* observance can be anticipated to have for the satisfaction of *everyone's* interests (and that these consequences are preferred to those of known alternative possibilities for regulation).[5]

We should not, however, mistake this principle of universalization for a principle already containing the distinctive idea of an ethics of discourse. According to discourse ethics, a norm may claim validity only if all who might be affected by it reach (or would reach), *as participants in a practical discourse,* agreement that this norm is valid. This principle of discourse ethics (D), to which I will return after offering my justification for the principle of universalization (U), already *presupposes* that we *can* justify our choice of a norm. At this point in my argument that presupposition is what is at issue. I have introduced "U" as a rule of argumentation which makes agreement in practical discourses possible whenever matters of concern to all are open to regulation in the equal interest of everyone. Once this bridging principle has been justified, we will be able to make the transition to discourse ethics. I have, however, formulated "U" in a way that precludes a monological application of this principle: "U" regulates only argumentation among a plurality of participants; it even suggests the perspective of real-life argumentations in which all concerned are admitted as participants.

In this respect, our universalization principle differs from the one John Rawls proposes.

Rawls wants to ensure impartial consideration of all affected interests by putting the moral judge into a fictitious "original position" where differences of power are eliminated, equal freedoms for all are guaranteed, and the individual is left in a condition of ignorance with regard to the position he might occupy in a future social order. Like Kant, Rawls operationalizes the standpoint of impartiality in such a way that every individual can undertake to justify basic norms on his own. The same holds for the moral philosopher himself. It is only logical, therefore, that Rawls views the substantive parts of his study (e.g., the principle of average utility), not as the *contribution* of a participant in argumentation to a process of discursive will-formation regarding the basic institutions of late capitalist society, but as the outcome of a "theory of justice" which he, as an expert, is qualified to construct.

If we keep in mind the action-coordinating function that normative validity claims play in the communicative practice of everyday life, we see why the problems to be resolved in moral argumentation cannot be handled monologically but require a cooperative effort. By entering into a process of moral argumentation, the participants continue their communicative action in a reflexive attitude, with the aim of restoring a consensus that has been disrupted. Moral argumentation thus serves to settle conflicts of action by consensual means. Conflicts in the domain of norm-guided interaction can be traced directly to some disruption of a normative consensus. Repairing a disrupted consensus can mean one of two things: restoring intersubjective recognition to a validity claim after it has become controversial, or assuring intersubjective recognition for a new claim to validity which is a substitute for the old one. Agreement of this kind expresses a *common will*. If moral argumentation is to produce this kind of agreement, however, it is not enough for the individual to reflect on whether he can assent to a norm. It is not even enough for *all* individuals, each one on his own, to reflect in this way and then to register their votes. What is needed is a "real" process of argumentation in which the individuals concerned cooperate. Only an intersubjective process of reaching understanding can produce an agreement that is reflexive in nature; only it can give the participants the knowledge that they have collectively become convinced of something.

From this viewpoint, the categorical imperative needs to be reformulated as follows:

> Rather than ascribing as valid to all others any maxim that I can will to be a universal law, I must submit my maxim to all others for purposes of discursively testing its claim to universality. The emphasis shifts from what each can will without contradiction to be a general law, to what all can will in agreement to be a universal norm.[6]

This version of the universality principle does in fact entail the idea of a cooperative process of argumentation. For one thing, nothing prevents the perspectively conditioned distortion of one's own interests by others better than his actual participation. It is in this pragmatic sense that the individual is the last court of appeal for judging what is in his best interest. On the other hand, the descriptive terms in which each individual perceives his interests must be open to criticism by others. Needs and wants are interpreted in the light of cultural values. Since cultural values are always components of traditions we share intersubjectively, the revision of the values used to interpret needs and wants cannot be a matter for individuals to handle monologically. . . .[7]

## III    Discourse Ethics and Its Bases in Action Theory

. . . (b) We must, then, return to the justification of the principle of universalization. We are now in a position to specify the role that the transcendental-pragmatic argument can play in this process. Its function is to help to show that the principle of universalization, which acts as a rule of argumentation, is implied by the presuppositions of argumentation in general. This requirement is met if it can be shown that

- every person who accepts the universal and necessary communicative presuppositions of argumentative speech, and who knows what it means to justify a norm of action, implicitly presupposes as valid the principle of universalization (whether in the form I gave it above or in an equivalent form).

It makes sense to distinguish three levels of presuppositions of argumentation, along the lines suggested by Aristotle: those at the logical level of products, those at the dialectical level of procedures, and those at the rhetorical level of processes.[8] First, reasoning or argumentation is designed to *produce* intrinsically cogent arguments with which we can redeem or repudiate claims to validity. This is the level on which I would situate the rules of a "minimal logic" currently being discussed by the Popperians for example, or the consistency requirements proposed by Hare and others. For simplicity's sake, I will follow the catalogue of presuppositions of argumentation drawn up by R. Alexy.[9] For the logical-semantic level, the following rules[10] can serve as *examples:*

(1.1) No speaker may contradict himself.

(1.2) Every speaker who applies predicate F to object A must be prepared to apply F to all other objects resembling A in all relevant aspects.

(1.3) Different speakers may not use the same expression with different meanings.

The presuppositions of argumentation at this level are logical and semantic rules that have no ethical content. They are not a suitable point of departure for a transcendental-pragmatic argument.

In *procedural* terms, arguments are processes of reaching understanding that are ordered in such a way that proponents and opponents, having assumed a hypothetical attitude and being relieved of the pressures of action and experience, can test validity claims that have become problematic. At this level are located the pragmatic presuppositions of a special form of interaction, namely, everything necessary for a search for truth organized in the form of a competition. Examples would include recognition of the accountability

and truthfulness of all participants in the search. At this level we also situate general rules of jurisdiction and relevance that regulate themes for discussion, contributions to the argument, etc.[11] Again, I shall cite a few examples from Alexy's catalogue of rules:

(2.1) Every speaker may assert only what he really believes.

(2.2) A person who disputes a proposition or norm not under discussion must provide a reason for wanting to do so.

Some of these rules obviously have an ethical import. At this level, presuppositions come to the fore that are common to both discourses and action oriented to reaching understanding as such, e.g., presuppositions about relations of mutual recognition.

But to fall back directly here on argumentation's basis in action theory would be to put the cart before the horse. The presuppositions of an unrestrained competition for better arguments are, however, relevant to our purpose in that they are irreconcilable with traditional ethical philosophies which have to protect a dogmatic core of fundamental convictions from all criticism.

Finally, in *process* terms, argumentative speech is a process of communication which, given its goal of reaching a rationally motivated agreement, must satisfy improbable conditions. In argumentative speech we see the structures of a speech situation that is immune to repression and inequality in a particular way: it presents itself as a form of communication that adequately approximates ideal conditions. This is why I tried at one time to describe the presuppositions of argumentation as the defining characteristics of an ideal speech situation.[12] I cannot undertake here the elaboration, revision, and clarification that my earlier analysis would require, and accordingly, the present essay is rightly characterized as a "sketch" or a "proposal." The intention of my earlier analysis still seems correct to me, namely, the reconstruction of the general symmetry conditions that every competent speaker who believes he is engaging in an argumentation must presuppose as adequately fulfilled. The presupposition of something like an "unrestricted communication community," an idea that Apel developed following Peirce and Mead, can be demonstrated through systematic analysis of performative contradictions. Participants in argumentation cannot avoid the presupposition that the structure of their communication, owing to certain characteristics that require formal description, rules out all external or internal coercion other than the force of the better argument, and thereby also neutralizes all motives other than that of the cooperative search for truth. Following my analysis, R. Alexy has suggested the following rules of discourse for this level: [13]

(3.1) Every subject with the competence to speak and act is allowed to take part in a discourse.
(3.2) a. Everyone is allowed to question any assertion whatever.
b. Everyone is allowed to introduce any assertion whatever into the discourse.
c. Everyone is allowed to express his attitudes, desires, and needs.[14]
(3.3) No speaker may, by internal or external coercion, be prevented from exercising his rights as laid down in (3.1) and (3.2).

A few explanations are in order here. Rule (3.1) defines the set of potential participants. It includes all subjects without exception who have the capacity to take part in argumentation. Rule (3.2) guarantees all participants equal opportunity to contribute to the argumentation and to put forth their own arguments. Rule (3.3) sets down conditions under which the right to universal access and the right to equal participation can be enjoyed equally by all, that is, without the possibility of repression, be it ever so subtle or covert.

If these considerations are to amount to something more than a definition favoring an ideal form of communication and thus prejudging everything else, we must show that our rules of discourse are not mere *conventions* but inescapable presuppositions.

The presuppositions themselves are identified by convincing* a person who contests the hypothetical reconstructions offered that he is caught up in performative contradictions. In this process, I must appeal to the intuitive preunderstanding which every subject competent in speech and action brings to a process of argumentation. At this point I shall be content to discuss a few examples, indicating what such an analysis might actually look like.

(1) "Using good reasons, I finally convinced H that p" can be read as someone's report on the outcome of a discourse. In this discourse, the speaker, by using reasons, motivated the hearer to accept the truth claim connected with the assertion "p," that is, to consider "p" true. Central to the meaning of the word "convince" is the notion that a subject other than the speaker adopts a view on the basis of good reasons.
Which is why the statement

(1)+ "Using lies, I finally convinced H that p" is nonsensical.

It can be revised to state:

(2) "Using lies, I finally talked H into believing that p."

I can refer someone to a dictionary to look up the meaning of the verb "to convince." But that will not explain *why* statement (1)+ is a semantic paradox that can be resolved by statement (2). To explain that, I can start with the internal connection between the expressions "to convince someone of something" and "to come to a reasoned agreement about something." In the *final* analysis, convictions rest on a consensus that has been attained discursively. Now, statement (1)+ implies that H has formed his conviction under conditions which

* In what follows, Habermas contrasts *überzeugen* and *überreden*, here translated as "convince" vs. "talk into." The contrast is more emphatic in German than in English; *überzeugen* implies the use of argument, while "to cause to believe by argument" is one but not the only meaning of "convince."—TRANS.

simply do not permit the formation of convictions. Such conditions contradict the pragmatic presuppositions of argumentation as such (in this case rule 2.1). This presupposition holds not only for particular instances but inevitably for every process of argumentation. I can prove this, furthermore, by making a proponent who defends the truth of statement (1)+ aware that he thereby gets himself into a performative contradiction. For as soon as he cites a reason for the truth of (1)+, he enters a process of argumentation and has thereby accepted the presupposition, among others, that he can never *convince* an opponent of something by resorting to lies: at most, he can talk him into believing something to be true. But then the content of the assertion to be justified contradicts one of the presuppositions the proponent must operate with if his statement is to be regarded as a justification.

Similarly, performative contradictions can be demonstrated in the statements of a proponent who tried to justify the following sentence:

(3)+   "Having excluded persons A, B, C . . . from the discussion by silencing them or by foisting our interpretation on them, we were able to convince ourselves that N is justified."

Here A, B, C . . . shall be assumed to be (a) among the persons who would be affected by putting norm N into effect, and (b) are indistinguishable in their capacity as *participants in argumentation* in all relevant respects from the other participants. In any attempt to justify statement (3)+, a proponent would necessarily put himself in contradiction with the presuppositions set out in rules (3.1) to (3.3).

In giving these presuppositions the form of rules, Alexy may well be promoting the misconception that all actual discourses must conform to these rules. In many cases this is clearly not so, and in all cases we have to be content with approximations. This misconception may have something to do with the ambiguity of the word "rule." "Rules of discourse," in Alexy's sense, are not *constitutive*

of discourses in the sense in which chess rules are constitutive of real chess games. Whereas chess rules *determine* the playing of actual chess games, discourse rules are merely the *form* in which we present the implicitly adopted and intuitively known pragmatic presuppositions of a special type of speech, presuppositions that are adopted implicitly and known intuitively. If one wanted to make a serious comparison between argumentation and playing chess, one would find that the closest equivalents to the rules of chess are the rules pertaining to the construction and exchange of arguments. It is these rules that must be followed in *actual fact* if error-free argumentation is to take place in real life. By contrast, the discourse rules (3.1) to (3.3) state only that participants in argumentation must assume these conditions to be approximately realized, or realized in an approximation adequate enough for the purpose of argumentation, regardless of whether and to what extent these assumptions are counterfactual in a given case or not.

Discourses take place in particular social contexts and are subject to the limitation of time and space. Their participants are not Kantian intelligible characters but real human beings driven by other motives in addition to the one permissible motive of the search for truth. Topics and contributions have to be organized. The opening, the adjournment, and resumption of discussions must be arranged. Given all this, institutional measures are needed to neutralize empirical limitations and avoidable internal and external interference sufficiently that the idealized conditions always already presupposed by participants in argumentation can at least be adequately approximated. The need to *institutionalize discourses,* trivial though it may be, does not contradict the partly counterfactual content of the presuppositions of discourse. To the contrary, attempts at institutionalization are subject in turn to normative conceptions of their goal, which spring *spontaneously* from our intuitive grasp of what argumentation is. This assertion can be verified empirically by studying the authorizations, exemptions, and procedural rules that have been used to institutionalize theoretical discourse in science or practical discourse in parliamentary activity.[15] To avoid the fallacy of misplaced concreteness, one must differentiate carefully between rules of discourse and conventions serving the institutionalization of discourses, conventions, that is, which help to actualize the ideal content of the presuppositions of argumentation under empirical conditions.

If, after these cursory remarks and pending a more detailed analysis, we accept the rules tentatively set down by Alexy, we have at our disposal, in conjunction with a weak idea of normative justification (i.e., one that does not prejudge the matter) premises that are strong enough for the derivation of the universalization principle "U."

If every person entering a process of argumentation must, among other things, make presuppositions whose content can be expressed in rules (3.1) to (3.3), and if, further, we understand what it means to discuss hypothetically whether norms of action ought to be adopted, then everyone who seriously tries to redeem normative claims to validity in a *discursive* way intuitively accepts procedural conditions which amount to an implicit acknowledgment of "U." It follows from the aforementioned rules of discourse that a contested norm cannot meet with the consent of the participants in a practical discourse unless "U" holds true, that is,

- unless the consequences and the side effects which the *general* observance of a controversial norm can be expected to have for the satisfaction of the interests of *each individual* can be *freely* accepted by all.

But once it has been shown that "U" can be grounded upon the presuppositions of argumentation through a transcendental-pragmatic derivation, discourse ethics itself can be formulated in terms of the economical principle "D," which stipulates

- that only those norms can claim to be valid that meet (or could meet) with the approval of all concerned in their capacity as participants in a practical discourse.[16]

The justification of discourse ethics outlined here avoids confusions in the use of the term "moral principle." The only moral principle here is the universalization principle given above, which is conceived as a rule of argumentation and is part of the logic of practical discourses. "U" must be carefully distinguished from

- substantive principles or basic norms, which can only be the *subject-matter* of moral argumentation;
- the normative content of the presuppositions of argumentation, which can be expressed in terms of rules (as in 3.1 to 3.3);
- "D," the principle of discourse ethics, which stipulates the basic idea of a moral theory but does not form part of a logic of argumentation.

Previous attempts to ground discourse ethics were flawed because they tended to collapse *rules, contents,* and *presuppositions* of argumentation and in addition confused all of these with "moral principles" in the sense of principles of philosophical ethics. "D" is the assertion that the philosopher as moral theorist finally seeks to justify. The program of justification I have outlined in this essay describes what I regard as the most promising *road* to that goal. This road is the transcendental-pragmatic justification of a rule of argumentation with normative content. This rule is selective, to be sure, but it is also formal. It is not compatible with all substantive legal and moral principles, but it does not prejudge substantive regulations, as it is a rule of argumentation only. All contents, no matter how fundamental the action norm involved may be, must be made dependent on real discourses (or advocatory discourses conducted as substitutes for them). The moral theorist may take part in one of them as one of "those concerned," perhaps even as an expert, but he may not conduct such discourses by *himself alone.* To the extent to which a moral theory touches on substantive areas—as Rawls's theory of justice does, for example—it must be understood as a contribution to a discourse among citizens.

NOTES

1. A. MacIntyre, *After Virtue* (London, 1981), p. 52; M. Horkheimer, *Eclipse of Reason* (New York, 1974), ch. 1, pp. 3–57

2. R. Wimmer, *Universalisierung in der Ethik* (Frankfurt, 1980).

3. W. K. Frankena, *Ethics* (Englewood Cliffs, N.J., 1973), ch. 6.

4. J. Habermas, *Theory of Communicative Action*, vol. 1 (Boston, 1984), ch. 3. "Social Action, Purposive Activity, and Communication," p. 273ff.

5. At most we could compare theories, as higher-level systems of propositions, with norms. But it is debatable whether theories can be said to be true or false in the same sense as the descriptions, predictions, and explanations we derive from them, whereas norms for their part are right or wrong in the same sense as the actions that satisfy them.

6. J. Habermas, "Legitimation Problems in the Modern State," in Habermas, *Communication and the Evolution of Society* (Boston, 1979), pp. 178ff. On the relation between justification of norms, their being put into effect, and their being accepted, see also W. Kuhlmann, "Ist eine philosophische Letztbegründung von Normen möglich?" in *Funkkolleg Ethik*, Studienbegleitbrief 8, (Weinheim, 1981), p. 32.

7. *The Uses of Argument* (Cambridge, 1958).

8. J. Habermas, "Wahrheitstheorien," in H. Fahrenbach, ed., *Festschrift für W. Schulz* (Pfullingen, 1973), pp. 211ff; J. Habermas, *The Theory of Communicative Action*, vol. 1 (Boston, 1984), pp. 22ff.

9. On the logic of practical discourse, see T. McCarthy, *The Critical Theory of Jürgen Habermas* (Cambridge, MA, 1978), pp. 310ff.

10. Wimmer (1980), pp. 174ff.

11. G. Patzig, *Tatsachen, Normen, Sätze* (Stuttgart, 1980), p. 162.

12. K. Baier, *The Moral Point of View* (London, 1958).

13. B. Gert, *Moral Rules* (New York, 1976).

14. M. Singer, *Generalization in Ethics* (New York, 1961).

15. G. H. Mead, "Fragments on Ethics," in *Mind, Self, and Society* (Chicago, 1934), pp. 379ff. See also H. Joas, *G. H. Mead: A Contemporary Reexamination of His Thought* (Cambridge, MA, 1985); J. Habermas, *The Theory of Communicative Action*, vol. 2 (Boston 1987), pp. 92ff.

16. With reference to B. Gert's *Moral Rules*, p. 72, G. Nunner-Winkler has raised the objection that "U" is unable to single out from among the norms that fulfill the stated conditions those that are moral in the narrow sense and to exclude others (e.g., "you ought to smile when you say hello to people"). This objection is met when one proposes to call moral only those norms that are strictly universalizable, i.e., those that are invariable over historical time and across social groups. This usage of the moral theorist does not of course coincide with that of the sociologist or historian who tends to describe epoch-specific and culture-specific rules as moral rules, if they are accepted as such by the members of the group under study.

# 51    Power/Knowledge

MICHEL FOUCAULT

*Lecture Two: 14 January 1976*

THE COURSE OF STUDY that I have been following until now—roughly since 1970/71—has been concerned with the *how* of power. I have tried, that is, to relate its mechanisms to two points of reference, two limits: on the one hand, to the rules of right that provide a formal delimi- tation of power; on the other, to the effects of truth that this power produces and transmits, and which in their turn reproduce this power. Hence we have a triangle: power, right, truth.

Schematically, we can formulate the traditional question of political philosophy in the following terms: how is the discourse of truth, or quite sim- ply, philosophy as that discourse which *par excel-*

*lence* is concerned with truth, able to fix limits to the rights of power? That is the traditional question. The one I would prefer to pose is rather different. Compared to the traditional, noble and philosophic question it is much more down to earth and concrete. My problem is rather this: what rules of right are implemented by the relations of power in the productions of discourses of truth? Or alternatively, what type of power is susceptible of producing discourses of truth that in a society such as ours are endowed with such potent effects? What I mean is this: in a society such as ours, but basically in any society, there are manifold relations of power which permeate, characterise and constitute the social body, and these relations of power cannot themselves be established, consolidated nor implemented without the production, accumulation, circulation and functioning of a discourse. There can be no possible exercise of power without a certain economy of discourses of truth which operates through and on the basis of this association. We are subjected to the production of truth through power and we cannot exercise power except through the production of truth. This is the case for every society, but I believe that in ours the relationship between power, right and truth is organised in a highly specific fashion. If I were to characterise, not its mechanism itself, but its intensity and constancy, I would say that we are forced to produce the truth of power that our society demands, of which it has need, in order to function: we *must* speak the truth; we are constrained or condemned to confess or to discover the truth. Power never ceases its interrogation, its inquisition, its registration of truth: it institutionalises, professionalises and rewards its pursuit. In the last analysis, we must produce truth as we must produce wealth, indeed we must produce truth in order to produce wealth in the first place. In another way, we are also subjected to the truth in the sense in which it is truth that makes the laws, that produces the true discourse which, at least partially, decides, transmits and itself extends upon the effects of power. In the end, we are judged, condemned, classified, determined in our undertakings, destined to a certain

mode of living or dying, as a function of the true discourses which are the bearers of the specific effects of power.

So, it is the rules of right, the mechanisms of power, the effects of truth or if you like, the rules of power and the powers of true discourses, that can be said more or less to have formed the general terrain of my concern, even if, as I know full well, I have traversed it only partially and in a very zig-zag fashion. I should like to speak briefly about this course of research, about what I have considered as being its guiding principle and about the methodological imperatives and precautions which I have sought to adopt. As regards the general principle involved in a study of the relations between right and power, it seems to me that in Western societies since Medieval times it has been royal power that has provided the essential focus around which legal thought has been elaborated. It is in response to the demands of royal power, for its profit and to serve as its instrument or justification, that the juridical edifice of our own society has been developed. Right in the West is the King's right. Naturally everyone is familiar with the famous, celebrated, repeatedly emphasised role of the jurists in the organisation of royal power. We must not forget that the re-vitalisation of Roman Law in the twelfth century was the major event around which, and on whose basis, the juridical edifice which had collapsed after the fall of the Roman Empire was reconstructed. This resurrection of Roman Law had in effect a technical and constitutive role to play in the establishment of the authoritarian, administrative, and, in the final analysis, absolute power of the monarchy. And when this legal edifice escapes in later centuries from the control of the monarch, when, more accurately, it is turned against that control, it is always the limits of this sovereign power that are put in question, its prerogatives that are challenged. In other words, I believe that the King remains the central personage in the whole legal edifice of the West. When it comes to the general organisation of the legal system in the West, it is essentially with the King, his rights, his power and its eventual limitations, that one is dealing. Whether the jurists were the King's henchmen or his adversaries, it is of royal power that we are speaking in every case when we speak of these grandiose edifices of legal thought and knowledge.

There are two ways in which we do so speak. Either we do so in order to show the nature of the juridical armoury that invested royal power, to reveal the monarch as the effective embodiment of sovereignty, to demonstrate that his power, for all that it was absolute, was exactly that which befitted his fundamental right. Or, by contrast, we do so in order to show the necessity of imposing limits upon this sovereign power, of submitting it to certain rules of right, within whose confines it had to be exercised in order for it to remain legitimate. The essential role of the theory of right, from medieval times onwards, was to fix the legitimacy of power; that is the major problem around which the whole theory of right and sovereignty is organised.

When we say that sovereignty is the central problem of right in Western societies, what we mean basically is that the essential function of the discourse and techniques of right has been to efface the domination intrinsic to power in order to present the latter at the level of appearance under two different aspects: on the one hand, as the legitimate rights of sovereignty, and on the other, as the legal obligation to obey it. The system of right is centred entirely upon the King, and it is therefore designed to eliminate the fact of domination and its consequences.

My general project over the past few years has been, in essence, to reverse the mode of analysis followed by the entire discourse of right from the time of the Middle Ages. My aim, therefore, was to invert it, to give due weight, that is, to the fact of domination, to expose both its latent nature and its brutality. I then wanted to show not only how right is, in a general way, the instrument of this domination—which scarcely needs saying—but also to show the extent to which, and the forms in which, right (not simply the laws but the whole complex of apparatuses, institutions and regulations responsible for their application) transmits and puts in motion relations that are not relations of sovereignty, but of domination. More-

over, speaking of domination I do not have in mind that solid and global kind of domination that one person exercises over others, or one group over another, but the manifold forms of domination that can be exercised within society. Not the domination of the King in his central position, therefore, but that of his subjects in their mutual relations: not the uniform edifice of sovereignty, but the multiple forms of subjugation that have a place and function within the social organism.

The system of right, the domain of the law, are permanent agents of these relations of domination, these polymorphous techniques of subjugation. Right should be viewed, I believe, not in terms of a legitimacy to be established, but in terms of the methods of subjugation that it instigates.

The problem for me is how to avoid this question, central to the theme of right, regarding sovereignty and the obedience of individual subjects in order that I may substitute the problem of domination and subjugation for that of sovereignty and obedience. Given that this was to be the general line of my analysis, there were a certain number of methodological precautions that seemed requisite to its pursuit. In the very first place, it seemed important to accept that the analysis in question should not concern itself with the regulated and legitimate forms of power in their central locations, with the general mechanisms through which they operate, and the continual effects of these. On the contrary, it should be concerned with power at its extremities, in its ultimate destinations, with those points where it becomes capillary, that is, in its more regional and local forms and institutions. Its paramount concern, in fact, should be with the point where power surmounts the rules of right which organise and delimit it and extends itself beyond them, invests itself in institutions, becomes embodied in techniques, and equips itself with instruments and eventually even violent means of material intervention. To give an example: rather than try to discover where and how the right of punishment is founded on sovereignty, how it is presented in the theory of monarchical right or in that of democratic right, I have tried to see in what ways punishment and the power of punishment are effectively embodied in a certain number of local, regional, material institutions, which are concerned with torture or imprisonment, and to place these in the climate—at once institutional and physical, regulated and violent—of the effective apparatuses of punishment. In other words, one should try to locate power at the extreme points of its exercise, where it is always less legal in character.

A second methodological precaution urged that the analysis should not concern itself with power at the level of conscious intention or decision; that it should not attempt to consider power from its internal point of view and that it should refrain from posing the labyrinthine and unanswerable question: "Who then has power and what has he in mind? What is the aim of someone who possesses power?" Instead, it is a case of studying power at the point where its intention, if it has one, is completely invested in its real and effective practices. What is needed is a study of power in its external visage, at the point where it is in direct and immediate relationship with that which we can provisionally call its object, its target, its field of application, there—that is to say—where it installs itself and produces its real effects.

Let us not, therefore, ask why certain people want to dominate, what they seek, what is their overall strategy. Let us ask, instead, how things work at the level of on-going subjugation, at the level of those continuous and uninterrupted processes which subject our bodies, govern our gestures, dictate our behaviours etc. In other words, rather than ask ourselves how the sovereign appears to us in his lofty isolation, we should try to discover how it is that subjects are gradually, progressively, really and materially constituted through a multiplicity of organisms, forces, energies, materials, desires, thoughts, etc. We should try to grasp subjection in its material instance as a constitution of subjects. This would be the exact opposite of Hobbes' project in *Leviathan,* and of that, I believe, of all jurists for whom the problem is the distillation of a single will—or rather, the constitution of a unitary, singular body animated by the spirit of sovereignty—from the particular wills of

a multiplicity of individuals. Think of the scheme of *Leviathan:* insofar as he is a fabricated man, Leviathan is no other than the amalgamation of a certain number of separate individualities, who find themselves reunited by the complex of elements that go to compose the State; but at the heart of the State, or rather, at its head, there exists something which constitutes it as such, and this is sovereignty, which Hobbes says is precisely the spirit of Leviathan. Well, rather than worry about the problem of the central spirit, I believe that we must attempt to study the myriad of bodies which are constituted as peripheral *subjects* as a result of the effects of power.

A third methodological precaution relates to the fact that power is not to be taken to be a phenomenon of one individual's consolidated and homogeneous domination over others, or that of one group or class over others. What, by contrast, should always be kept in mind is that power, if we do not take too distant a view of it, is not that which makes the difference between those who exclusively possess and retain it, and those who do not have it and submit to it. Power must be analysed as something which circulates, or rather as something which only functions in the form of a chain. It is never localised here or there, never in anybody's hands, never appropriated as a commodity or piece of wealth. Power is employed and exercised through a net-like organisation. And not only do individuals circulate between its threads; they are always in the position of simultaneously undergoing and exercising this power. They are not only its inert or consenting target; they are always also the elements of its articulation. In other words, individuals are the vehicles of power, not its point of application.

The individual is not to be conceived as a sort of elementary nucleus, a primitive atom, a multiple and inert material on which power comes to fasten or against which it happens to strike, and in so doing subdues or crushes individuals. In fact, it is already one of the prime effects of power that certain bodies, certain gestures, certain discourses, certain desires, come to be identified and constituted as individuals. The individual, that is, is not the *vis-à-vis* of power; it is, I believe, one of its prime effects. The individual is an effect of power, and at the same time, or precisely to the extent to which it is that effect, it is the element of its articulation. The individual which power has constituted is at the same time its vehicle.

There is a fourth methodological precaution that follows from this: when I say that power establishes a network through which it freely circulates, this is true only up to a certain point. In much the same fashion we could say that therefore we all have a fascism in our heads, or, more profoundly, that we all have a power in our bodies. But I do not believe that one should conclude from that that power is the best distributed thing in the world, although in some sense that is indeed so. We are not dealing with a sort of democratic or anarchic distribution of power through bodies. That is to say, it seems to me—and this then would be the fourth methodological precaution—that the important thing is not to attempt some kind of deduction of power starting from its centre and aimed at the discovery of the extent to which it permeates into the base, of the degree to which it reproduces itself down to and including the most molecular elements of society. One must rather conduct an *ascending* analysis of power, starting, that is, from its infinitesimal mechanisms, which each have their own history, their own trajectory, their own techniques and tactics, and then see how these mechanisms of power have been— and continue to be—invested, colonised, utilised, involuted, transformed, displaced, extended, etc., by ever more general mechanisms and by forms of global domination. It is not that this global domination extends itself right to the base in a plurality of repercussions: I believe that the manner in which the phenomena, the techniques and the procedures of power enter into play at the most basic levels must be analysed, that the way in which these procedures are displaced, extended and altered must certainly be demonstrated; but above all what must be shown is the manner in which they are invested and annexed by more global phenomena and the subtle fashion in which more general powers or economic interests are

able to engage with these technologies that are at once both relatively autonomous of power and act as its infinitesimal elements. In order to make this clearer, one might cite the example of madness. The descending type of analysis, the one of which I believe one ought to be wary, will say that the bourgeoisie has, since the sixteenth or seventeenth century, been the dominant class; from this premise, it will then set out to deduce the internment of the insane. One can always make this deduction, it is always easily done and that is precisely what I would hold against it. It is in fact a simple matter to show that since lunatics are precisely those persons who are useless to industrial production, one is obliged to dispense with them. One could argue similarly in regard to infantile sexuality—and several thinkers, including Wilhelm Reich have indeed sought to do so up to a certain point. Given the domination of the bourgeois class, how can one understand the repression of infantile sexuality? Well, very simply— given that the human body had become essentially a force of production from the time of the seventeenth and eighteenth century, all the forms of its expenditure which did not lend themselves to the constitution of the productive forces—and were therefore exposed as redundant—were banned, excluded and repressed. These kinds of deduction are always possible. They are simultaneously correct and false. Above all they are too glib, because one can always do exactly the opposite and show, precisely by appeal to the principle of the dominance of the bourgeois class, that the forms of control of infantile sexuality could in no way have been predicted. On the contrary, it is equally plausible to suggest that what was needed was sexual training, the encouragement of a sexual precociousness, given that what was fundamentally at stake was the constitution of a labour force whose optimal state, as we well know, at least at the beginning of the nineteenth century, was to be infinite: the greater the labour force, the better able would the system of capitalist production have been to fulfil and improve its functions.

I believe that anything can be deduced from the general phenomenon of the domination of the bourgeois class. What needs to be done is something quite different. One needs to investigate historically, and beginning from the lowest level, how mechanisms of power have been able to function. In regard to the confinement of the insane, for example, or the repression and interdiction of sexuality, we need to see the manner in which, at the effective level of the family, of the immediate environment, of the cells and most basic units of society, these phenomena of repression or exclusion possessed their instruments and their logic, in response to a certain number of needs. We need to identify the agents responsible for them, their real agents (those which constituted the immediate social *entourage,* the family, parents, doctors, etc.), and not be content to lump them under the formula of a generalised bourgeoisie. We need to see how these mechanisms of power, at a given moment, in a precise conjuncture and by means of a certain number of transformations, have begun to become economically advantageous and politically useful. I think that in this way one could easily manage to demonstrate that what the bourgeoisie needed, or that in which its system discovered its real interests, was not the exclusion of the mad or the surveillance and prohibition of infantile masturbation (for, to repeat, such a system can perfectly well tolerate quite opposite practices), but rather, the techniques and procedures themselves of such an exclusion. It is the mechanisms of that exclusion that are necessary, the apparatuses of surveillance, the medicalisation of sexuality, of madness, of delinquency, all the micro-mechanisms of power, that came, from a certain moment in time, to represent the interests of the bourgeoisie. Or even better, we could say that to the extent to which this view of the bourgeoisie and of its interests appears to lack content, at least in regard to the problems with which we are here concerned, it reflects the fact that it was not the bourgeoisie itself which thought that madness had to be excluded or infantile sexuality repressed. What in fact happened was that the mechanisms of the exclusion of madness, and of the surveillance of infantile sexuality, began from a particular point in time, and for reasons which

need to be studied, to reveal their political usefulness and to lend themselves to economic profit, and that as a natural consequence, all of a sudden, they came to be colonised and maintained by global mechanisms and the entire State system. It is only if we grasp these techniques of power and demonstrate the economic advantages or political utility that derives from them in a given context for specific reasons, that we can understand how these mechanisms come to be effectively incorporated into the social whole.

To put this somewhat differently: the bourgeoisie has never had any use for the insane; but the procedures it has employed to exclude them have revealed and realised—from the nineteenth century onwards, and again on the basis of certain transformations—a political advantage, on occasion even a certain economic utility, which have consolidated the system and contributed to its overall functioning. The bourgeoisie is interested in power, not in madness, in the system of control of infantile sexuality, not in that phenomenon itself. The bourgeoisie could not care less about delinquents, about their punishment and rehabilitation, which economically have little importance, but it is concerned about the complex of mechanisms with which the delinquency is controlled, pursued, punished and reformed, etc.

As for our fifth methodological precaution: it is quite possible that the major mechanisms of power have been accompanied by ideological productions. There has, for example, probably been an ideology of education, an ideology of the monarchy, an ideology of parliamentary democracy, etc.; but basically I do not believe that what has taken place can be said to be ideological. It is both much more and much less than ideology. It is the production of effective instruments for the formation and accumulation of knowledge—methods of observation, techniques of registration, procedures for investigation and research, apparatuses of control. All this means that power, when it is exercised through these subtle mechanisms, cannot but evolve, organise and put into circulation a knowledge, or rather apparatuses of knowledge, which are not ideological constructs.

By way of summarising these five methodological precautions, I would say that we should direct our researches on the nature of power not towards the juridical edifice of sovereignty, the State apparatuses and the ideologies which accompany them, but towards domination and the material operators of power, towards forms of subjection and the inflections and utilisations of their localised systems, and towards strategic apparatuses. We must eschew the model of *Leviathan* in the study of power. We must escape from the limited field of juridical sovereignty and State institutions, and instead base our analysis of power on the study of the techniques and tactics of domination.

This in its general outline, is the methodological course that I believe must be followed, and which I have tried to pursue in the various researches that we have conducted over recent years on psychiatric power, on infantile sexuality, on political systems, etc. Now as one explores these fields of investigation, observing the methodological precautions I have mentioned, I believe that what then comes into view is a solid body of historical fact, which will ultimately bring us into confrontation with the problems of which I want to speak this year.

This solid, historical body of fact is the juridical-political theory of sovereignty of which I spoke a moment ago, a theory which has had four roles to play. In the first place, it has been used to refer to a mechanism of power that was effective under the feudal monarchy. In the second place, it has served as instrument and even as justification for the construction of the large-scale administrative monarchies. Again, from the time of the sixteenth century and more than ever from the seventeenth century onwards, but already at the time of the wars of religion, the theory of sovereignty has been a weapon which has circulated from one camp to another, which has been utilised in one sense or another, either to limit or else to re-inforce royal power: we find it among Catholic monarchists and Protestant anti-monarchists, among Protestant and more-or-less liberal monarchists, but also among Catholic partisans of regicide or dynastic transformation. It functions both in the hands of

aristocrats and in the hands of parliamentarians. It is found among the representatives of royal power and among the last feudatories. In short, it was the major instrument of political and theoretical struggle around systems of power of the sixteenth and seventeenth centuries. Finally, in the eighteenth century, it is again this same theory of sovereignty, re-activated through the doctrine of Roman Law, that we find in its essentials in Rousseau and his contemporaries, but now with a fourth role to play: now it is concerned with the construction, in opposition to the administrative, authoritarian and absolutist monarchies, of an alternative model, that of parliamentary democracy. And it is still this role that it plays at the moment of the Revolution.

Well, it seems to me that if we investigate these four roles there is a definite conclusion to be drawn: as long as a feudal type of society survived, the problems to which the theory of sovereignty was addressed were in effect confined to the general mechanisms of power, to the way in which its forms of existence at the higher level of society influenced its exercise at the lowest levels. In other words, the relationship of sovereignty, whether interpreted in a wider or a narrower sense, encompasses the totality of the social body. In effect, the mode in which power was exercised could be defined in its essentials in terms of the relationship sovereign–subject. But in the seventeenth and eighteenth centuries, we have the production of an important phenomenon, the emergence, or rather the invention, of a new mechanism of power possessed of highly specific procedural techniques, completely novel instruments, quite different apparatuses, and which is also, I believe, absolutely incompatible with the relations of sovereignty.

This new mechanism of power is more dependent upon bodies and what they do than upon the Earth and its products. It is a mechanism of power which permits time and labour, rather than wealth and commodities, to be extracted from bodies. It is a type of power which is constantly exercised by means of surveillance rather than in a discontinuous manner by means of a system of levies or obligations distributed over time. It presupposes a tightly knit grid of material coercions rather than the physical existence of a sovereign. It is ultimately dependent upon the principle, which introduces a genuinely new economy of power, that one must be able simultaneously both to increase the subjected forces and to improve the force and efficacy of that which subjects them.

This type of power is in every aspect the antithesis of that mechanism of power which the theory of sovereignty described or sought to transcribe. The latter is linked to a form of power that is exercised over the Earth and its products, much more than over human bodies and their operations. The theory of sovereignty is something which refers to the displacement and appropriation on the part of power, not of time and labour, but of goods and wealth. It allows discontinuous obligations distributed over time to be given legal expression but it does not allow for the codification of a continuous surveillance. It enables power to be founded in the physical existence of the sovereign, but not in continuous and permanent systems of surveillance. The theory of sovereignty permits the foundation of an absolute power in the absolute expenditure of power. It does not allow for a calculation of power in terms of the minimum expenditure for the maximum return.

This new type of power, which can no longer be formulated in terms of sovereignty, is, I believe, one of the great inventions of bourgeois society. It has been a fundamental instrument in the constitution of industrial capitalism and of the type of society that is its accompaniment. This non-sovereign power, which lies outside the form of sovereignty, is disciplinary power. Impossible to describe in the terminology of the theory of sovereignty from which it differs so radically, this disciplinary power ought by rights to have led to the disappearance of the grand juridical edifice created by that theory. But in reality, the theory of sovereignty has continued not only to exist as an ideology of right, but also to provide the organising principle of the legal codes which Europe acquired in the nineteenth century, beginning with the Napoleonic Code.

Why has the theory of sovereignty persisted in this fashion as an ideology and an organising prin-

ciple of these major legal codes? For two reasons, I believe. On the one hand, it has been, in the eighteenth and again in the nineteenth century, a permanent instrument of criticism of the monarchy and of all the obstacles that can thwart the development of disciplinary society. But at the same time, the theory of sovereignty, and the organisation of a legal code centred upon it, have allowed a system of right to be superimposed upon the mechanisms of discipline in such a way as to conceal its actual procedures, the element of domination inherent in its techniques, and to guarantee to everyone, by virtue of the sovereignty of the State, the exercise of his proper sovereign rights. The juridical systems—and this applies both to their codification and to their theorisation—have enabled sovereignty to be democratised through the constitution of a public right articulated upon collective sovereignty, while at the same time this democratisation of sovereignty was fundamentally determined by and grounded in mechanisms of disciplinary coercion.

To put this in more rigorous terms, one might say that once it became necessary for disciplinary constraints to be exercised through mechanisms of domination and yet at the same time for their effective exercise power to be disguised, a theory of sovereignty was required to make an appearance at the level of the legal apparatus, and to reemerge in its codes. Modern society, then, from the nineteenth century up to our own day, has been characterised on the one hand, by a legislation, a discourse, an organisation based on public right, whose principle of articulation is the social body and the delegative status of each citizen; and, on the other hand, by a closely linked grid of disciplinary coercions whose purpose is in fact to assure the cohesion of this same social body. Though a theory of right is a necessary companion to this grid, it cannot in any event provide the terms of its endorsement. Hence these two limits, a right of sovereignty and a mechanism of discipline, which define, I believe, the arena in which power is exercised. But these two limits are so heterogeneous that they cannot possibly be reduced to each other. The powers of modern society are exercised through, on the basis of, and by virtue of, this very heterogeneity between a public right of sovereignty and a polymorphous disciplinary mechanism. This is not to suggest that there is on the one hand an explicit and scholarly system of right which is that of sovereignty, and, on the other hand, obscure and unspoken disciplines which carry out their shadowy operations in the depths, and thus constitute the bedrock of the great mechanism of power. In reality, the disciplines have their own discourse. They engender, for the reasons of which we spoke earlier, apparatuses of knowledge (*savoir*) and a multiplicity of new domains of understanding. They are extraordinarily inventive participants in the order of these knowledge-producing apparatuses. Disciplines are the bearers of a discourse, but this cannot be the discourse of right. The discourse of discipline has nothing in common with that of law, rule, or sovereign will. The disciplines may well be the carriers of a discourse that speaks of a rule, but this is not the juridical rule deriving from sovereignty, but a natural rule, a norm. The code they come to define is not that of law but that of normalisation. Their reference is to a theoretical horizon which of necessity has nothing in common with the edifice of right. It is human science which constitutes their domain, and clinical knowledge their jurisprudence.

In short, what I have wanted to demonstrate in the course of the last few years is not the manner in which at the advance front of the exact sciences the uncertain, recalcitrant, confused dominion of human behaviour has little by little been annexed to science: it is not through some advancement in the rationality of the exact sciences that the human sciences are gradually constituted. I believe that the process which has really rendered the discourse of the human sciences possible is the juxtaposition, the encounter between two lines of approach, two mechanisms, two absolutely heterogeneous types of discourse: on the one hand there is the re-organisation of right that invests sovereignty, and on the other, the mechanics of the coercive forces whose exercise takes a disciplinary form. And I believe that in our own times

power is exercised simultaneously through this right and these techniques and that these techniques and these discourses, to which the disciplines give rise invade the area of right so that the procedures of normalisation come to be ever more constantly engaged in the colonisation of those of law. I believe that all this can explain the global functioning of what I would call a *society of normalisation*. I mean, more precisely, that disciplinary normalisations come into ever greater conflict with the juridical systems of sovereignty: their incompatibility with each other is ever more acutely felt and apparent; some kind of arbitrating discourse is made ever more necessary, a type of power and of knowledge that the sanctity of science would render neutral. It is precisely in the extension of medicine that we see, in some sense, not so much the linking as the perpetual exchange, or encounter of mechanisms of discipline with the principle of right. The developments of medicine, the general medicalisation of behaviours, conducts, discourses, desires, etc., take place at the point of intersection between the two heterogeneous levels of discipline and sovereignty. For this reason, against these usurpations by the disciplinary mechanisms, against this ascent of a power that is tied to scientific knowledge, we find that there is no solid recourse available to us today, such being our situation, except that which lies precisely in the return to a theory of right organised around sovereignty and articulated upon its ancient principle. When today one wants to object in some way to the disciplines and all the effects of power and knowledge that are linked to them, what is it that one does, concretely, in real life, what do the Magistrates Union[1] or other similar institutions do, if not precisely appeal to this canon of right, this famous, formal right, that is said to be bourgeois, and which in reality is the right of sovereignty? But I believe that we find ourselves here in a kind of blind alley: it is not through recourse to sovereignty against discipline that the effects of disciplinary power can be limited, because sovereignty and disciplinary mechanisms are two absolutely integral constituents of the general mechanism of power in our society.

If one wants to look for a non-disciplinary form of power, or rather, to struggle against disciplines and disciplinary power, it is not towards the ancient right of sovereignty that one should turn, but towards the possibility of a new form of right, one which must indeed be anti-disciplinarian, but at the same time liberated from the principle of sovereignty. It is at this point that we once more come up against the notion of repression, whose use in this context I believe to be doubly unfortunate. On the one hand, it contains an obscure reference to a certain theory of sovereignty, the sovereignty of the sovereign rights of the individual, and on the other hand, its usage introduces a system of psychological reference points borrowed from the human sciences, that is to say, from discourses and practices that belong to the disciplinary realm. I believe that the notion of repression remains a juridical-disciplinary notion whatever the critical use one would make of it. To this extent the critical application of the notion of repression is found to be vitiated and nullified from the outset by the two-fold juridical and disciplinary reference it contains to sovereignty on the one hand and to normalisation on the other.

NOTE

1. This Union, established after 1968, has adopted a radical line on civil rights, the law and the prisons.

# 52 Foucault, Femininity and the Modernization of Patriarchal Power

SANDRA LEE BARTKY

## I

IN A STRIKING CRITIQUE OF MODERN SOCIETY, Michel Foucault has argued that the rise of parliamentary institutions and of new conceptions of political liberty was accompanied by a darker countermovement, by the emergence of a new and unprecedented discipline directed against the body. More is required of the body now than mere political allegiance or the appropriation of the products of its labor: the new discipline invades the body and seeks to regulate its very forces and operations, the economy and efficiency of its movements.

The disciplinary practices Foucault describes are tied to peculiarly modern forms of the army, the school, the hospital, the prison, and the manufactory; the aim of these disciplines is to increase the utility of the body, to augment its forces:

What was then being formed was a policy of coercions that act upon the body, a calculated manipulation of its elements, its gestures, its behaviour. The human body was entering a machinery of power that explores it, breaks it down and rearranges it. A "political anatomy," which was also a "mechanics of power," was being born; it defined how one may have a hold over others' bodies, not only so that they may do what one wishes, but so that they may operate as one wishes, with the techniques, the speed and the efficiency that one determines. Thus, discipline produces subjected and practiced bodies, "docile" bodies.[1]

The production of "docile bodies" requires that an uninterrupted coercion be directed to the very processes of bodily activity, not just their result; this "micro-physics of power" fragments and partitions the body's time, its space, and its movements.

The student, then, is enclosed within a classroom and assigned to a desk he cannot leave; his ranking in the class can be read off the position of his desk in the serially ordered and segmented space of the classroom itself. Foucault tells us that "Jean-Baptiste de la Salle dreamt of a classroom in which the spatial distribution might provide a whole series of distinctions at once, according to the pupil's progress, worth, character application, cleanliness and parents' fortune." The student must sit upright, feet upon the floor, head erect; he may not slouch or fidget; his animate body is brought into a fixed correlation with the inanimate desk.

The minute breakdown of gestures and movements required of soldiers at drill is far more relentless:

> Bring the weapon forward. In three stages. Raise the rifle with the right hand, bringing it close to the body so as to hold it perpendicular with the right knee, the end of the barrel at eye level, grasping it by striking it with the right hand, the arm held close to the body at waist height. At the second stage, bring the rifle in front of you with the left hand, the barrel in the middle between the two eyes, vertical, the right hand grasping it at the small of the butt, the arm outstretched, the triggerguard resting on the first finger, the left hand at the height of the notch, the thumb lying along the barrel against the moulding. At the third stage. . . .[2]

These "body-object articulations" of the soldier and his weapon, the student and his desk effect a "coercive link with the apparatus of production." We are far indeed from older forms of control that "demanded of the body only signs or products, forms of expression or the result of labour."

The body's time, in these regimes of power, is as rigidly controlled as its space: the factory whistle and the school bell mark a division of time into discrete and segmented units that regulate the various activities of the day. The following timetable, similar in spirit to the ordering of my grammar school classroom, is suggested for French "écoles mutuelles" of the early nineteenth century:

8:45 entrance of the monitor, 8:52 the monitor's summons, 8:56 entrance of the children and prayer, 9:00 the children go to their benches 9:04 first slate, 9:08 end of dictation, 9:12 second slate, etc.

Control this rigid and precise cannot be maintained without a minute and relentless surveillance.

Jeremy Bentham's design for the Panopticon, a model prison, captures for Foucault the essence of the disciplinary society. At the periphery of the Panopticon, a circular structure; at the center, a towel with wide windows that opens onto the inner side of the ring. The structure on the periphery is divided into cells, each with two windows, one facing the windows of the tower, the other facing the outside, allowing an effect of backlighting to make any figure visible within the cell. "All that is needed, then, is to place a supervisor in a central tower and to shut up in each cell a madman, a patient, a condemned man, a worker or a schoolboy." Each inmate is alone, shut off from effective communication with his fellows, but constantly visible from the tower. The effect of this is "to induce in the inmate a state of conscious and permanent visibility that assures the automatic functioning of power"; each becomes to himself his own jailor. This "state of conscious and permanent visibility" is a sign that the tight, disciplinary control of the body has gotten a hold on the mind as well. In the perpetual self-surveillance of the inmate lies the genesis of the celebrated "individualism" and heightened self-consciousness that are hallmarks of modern times. For Foucault, the structure and effects of the Panopticon resonate throughout society: Is it surprising that "prisons resemble factories, schools, barracks, hospitals, which all resemble prisons"?

Foucault's account in *Discipline and Punish* of the disciplinary practices that produce the "docile bodies" of modernity is a genuine *tour de force,* incorporating a rich theoretical account of the ways in which instrumental reason takes hold of the body with a mass of historical detail. But Foucault treats the body throughout as if it were one, as if the bodily experiences of men and women did not differ and as if men and women bore the same relationship to the characteristic institutions of modern life. Where is the account of the disciplinary practices that engender the "docile bodies" of women, bodies more docile than the bodies of men? Women, like men, are subject to many of the same disciplinary practices Foucault describes. But he is blind to those disciplines that produce a modality of embodiment that is peculiarly feminine. To overlook the forms of subjection that engender the feminine body is to perpetuate the silence and powerlessness of those upon whom these disciplines have been imposed. Hence, even though a liberatory note is sounded in Foucault's critique of power, his analysis as a whole reproduces that sexism which is endemic throughout Western political theory.

We are born male or female, but not masculine or feminine. Femininity is an artifice, an achievement, "a mode of enacting and reenacting received gender norms which surface as so many styles of the flesh." In what follows, I shall examine those disciplinary practices that produce a body which in gesture and appearance is recognizably feminine. I consider three categories of such practices: those that aim to produce a body of a certain size and general configuration; those that bring forth from this body a specific repertoire of gestures, postures, and movements; and those that are directed toward the display of this body as an ornamented surface. I shall examine the nature of these disciplines, how they are imposed and by whom. I shall probe the effects of the imposition of such discipline on female identity and subjectivity. In the final section I shall argue that these disciplinary practices must be understood in the light of the modernization of patriarchal domination, a modernization that unfolds historically according to the general pattern described by Foucault.

## II

Styles of the female figure vary over time and across cultures: they reflect cultural obsessions and preoccupations in ways that are still poorly understood. Today, massiveness, power, or abundance in a woman's body is met with distaste. The current body of fashion is taut, small-breasted, narrow-hipped, and of a slimness bordering on emaciation; it is a silhouette that seems more appropriate to an adolescent boy or a newly pubescent girl than to an adult woman. Since ordinary women have normally quite different dimensions, they must of course diet.

Mass-circulation women's magazines run articles on dieting in virtually every issue. The *Ladies' Home Journal* of February 1986 carries a "Fat Burning Exercise Guide," while *Mademoiselle* offers to "Help Stamp Out Cellulite" with "Six Sleek-Down Strategies." After the diet-busting Christmas holidays and, later, before summer bikini season, the titles of these features become shriller and more arresting. The reader is now addressed in the imperative mode: Jump into shape for summer! Shed ugly winter fat with the all-new Grapefruit Diet! More women than men visit diet doctors, while women greatly outnumber men in such self-help groups as Weight Watchers and Overeaters Anonymous—in the case of the latter, by well over 90 percent.

Dieting disciplines the body's hungers: appetite must be monitored at all times and governed by an iron will. Since the innocent need of the organism for food will not be denied, the body becomes one's enemy, an alien being bent on thwarting the disciplinary project. Anorexia nervosa, which has now assumed epidemic proportions, is to women of the late twentieth century what hysteria was to women of an earlier day: the crystallization in a pathological mode of a widespread cultural obsession. A survey taken recently at UCLA is astounding: of 260 students interviewed, 27.3 percent of women but only 5.8 percent of men said they were "terrified" of getting fat; 28.7 percent of women but only 7.5 percent of men said they were obsessed or "totally preoccupied" with food. The body images of women and men are strikingly different as well: 35 percent of women but only 12.5 percent of men said they felt fat though other people told them they were thin. Women in the survey wanted to weigh ten pounds less than their average weight; men felt they were within a pound of their ideal weight. A total of 5.9 percent of women and no men met the psychiatric criteria for anorexia or bulimia.

Dieting is one discipline imposed upon a body subject to the "tyranny of slenderness"; exercise is another. Since men as well as women exercise, it is not always easy in the case of women to distinguish what is done for the sake of physical fitness from what is done in obedience to the requirements of femininity. Men as well as women lift weights and do yoga, calisthenics, and aerobics, though "jazzercise" is a largely female pursuit. Men and women alike engage themselves with a variety of machines, each designed to call forth from the body a different exertion: there are Nautilus machines, rowing machines, ordinary and motorized exercycles, portable hip and leg cycles, belt massagers, trampolines, treadmills, and arm and leg pulleys. However, given the widespread female obsession with weight, one suspects that many women are working out with these apparatuses in the health club or at the gym with an aim in mind and in a spirit quite different from men's.

But there are classes of exercises meant for women alone, these designed not to firm or to reduce the body's size overall, but to resculpture its various parts on the current model. M. J. Saffon, "international beauty expert," assures us that his twelve basic facial exercises can erase frown lines, smooth the forehead, raise hollow cheeks, banish crow's feet, and tighten the muscles under the chin. There are exercises to build the breasts and exercises to banish "cellulite," said by "figure consultants" to be a special type of female fat. There is "spot-reducing," an umbrella term that covers dozens of punishing exercises designed to reduce "problem areas" like thick ankles or "saddlebag" thighs. The very idea of "spot-reducing" is both scientifically unsound and cruel, for it raises expectations in women that can never be realized—the pattern in which fat is deposited or removed is known to be genetically determined.

It is not only her natural appetite or unreconstructed contours that pose a danger to woman: the very expressions of her face can subvert the disciplinary project of bodily perfection. An expressive face lines and creases more readily than an inexpressive one. Hence, if women are unable to suppress strong emotions, they can at least learn to inhibit the tendency of the face to register them. Sophia Loren recommends a unique solution to this problem: a piece of tape applied to the forehead or between the brows will tug at the skin when one frowns and act as a reminder to relax the face. The tape is to be worn whenever a woman is home alone.

## III

There are significant gender differences in gesture, posture, movement, and general bodily comportment: women are far more restricted than men in their manner of movement and in their spatiality. In her classic paper on the subject, Iris Young observes that a space seems to surround women in imagination that they are hesitant to move beyond: this manifests itself both in a reluctance to reach, stretch, and extend the body to meet resistances of matter in motion—as in sport or in the performance of physical tasks—and in a typically constricted posture and general style of movement. Woman's space is not a field in which her bodily intentionality can be freely realized but an enclosure in which she feels herself positioned and by which she is confined. The "loose woman" violates these norms: her looseness is manifest not only in her morals, but in her manner of speech and quite literally in the free and easy way she moves.

In an extraordinary series of over two thousand photographs, many candid shots taken in the street, the German photographer Marianne Wex has documented differences in typical masculine and feminine body posture. Women sit waiting for trains with arms close to the body, hands folded together in their laps, toes pointing straight ahead or turned inward, and legs pressed together. The women in these photographs make themselves small and narrow, harmless; they seem tense; they take up little space. Men, on the other hand, expand into the available space; they sit with legs far apart and arms flung out at some distance from the body. Most common in these sitting male figures is what Wex calls the "proffering position": the men sit with legs thrown wide apart, crotch visible, feet pointing outward, often with an arm and a casually dangling hand resting comfortably on an open, spread thigh.

In proportion to total body size, a man's stride is longer than a woman's. The man has more spring and rhythm to his step; he walks with toes pointed outward, holds his arms at a greater distance from his body and swings them farther; he tends to point the whole hand in the direction he is moving. The women holds her arms closer to her body, palms against her sides; her walk is circumspect. If she has subjected herself to the additional constraint of high-heeled shoes, her body is thrown forward and off balance; the struggle to walk under these conditions shortens her stride still more.

But women's movement is subjected to a still finer discipline. Feminine faces, as well as bodies, are trained to the expression of deference. Under male scrutiny, women will avert their eyes or cast them downward; the female gaze is trained to abandon its claim to the sovereign status of seer. The "nice" girl learns to avoid the bold and unfettered staring of the "loose" woman who looks at whatever and whomever she pleases. Women are trained to smile more than men, too. In the economy of smiles, as elsewhere, there is evidence that women are exploited, for they give more than they receive in return; in a smile elicitation study, one researcher found that the rate of smile return by women was 93 percent, by men only 67 percent. In many typical women's jobs, graciousness, deference, and the readiness to serve are part of the work; this requires the worker to fix a smile on her face for a good part of the working day, whatever her inner state. The economy of touching is out of balance, too: men touch women more often and on more parts of the body than women touch men: female secretaries, factory workers, and waitresses report that such liberties are taken routinely with their bodies.

Feminine movement, gesture, and posture must exhibit not only constriction, but grace and a certain eroticism restrained by modesty: all three. Here is a field for the operation of a whole new training: a woman must stand with stomach pulled in, shoulders thrown slightly back and chest out, this to display her bosom to maximum advantage. While she must walk in the confined fashion appropriate to women, her movements must, at the same time, be combined with a subtle but provocative hiproll. But too much display is taboo: women in short, low-cut dresses are told to avoid bending over at all, but if they must, great care must be taken to avoid an unseemly display of breast or rump. From time to time, fashion magazines offer quite precise instructions on the proper way of getting in and out of cars. These instructions combine all three imperatives of women's movement: a woman must not allow her arms and legs to flail about in all directions; she must try to manage her movements with the appearance of grace—no small accomplishment when one is climbing out of the backseat of a Fiat—and she is well-advised to use the opportunity for a certain display of leg.

All the movements we have described so far are self-movements; they arise from within the woman's own body. But in a way that normally goes unnoticed, males in couples may literally steer a woman everywhere she goes: down the street, around corners, into elevators, through doorways, into her chair at the dinner table, around the dance floor. The man's movement "is not necessarily heavy and pushy or physical in an ugly way; it is light and gentle but firm in the way of the most confident equestrians with the best trained horses."

## IV

We have examined some of the disciplinary practices a woman must master in pursuit of a body of the right size and shape that also displays the proper styles of feminine motility. But woman's body is an ornamented surface too, and there is much discipline involved in this production as well. Here, especially in the application of makeup and the selection of clothes, art and discipline converge, though, as I shall argue, there is less art involved than one might suppose.

A woman's skin must be soft, supple, hairless, and smooth; ideally, it should betray no sign of wear, experience, age, or deep thought. Hair must be removed not only from the face but from large surfaces of the body as well, from legs and thighs, an operation accomplished by shaving, buffing with fine sandpaper, or applying foul-smelling depilatories. With the new high-leg bathing suits and leotards, a substantial amount of pubic hair must be removed too. The removal of facial hair can be more specialized. Eyebrows are plucked out by the roots with a tweezer. Hot wax is sometimes poured onto the mustache and cheeks and then ripped away when it cools. The woman who wants a more permanent result may try electrolysis: this involves the killing of a hair root by the passage of an electric current down a needle that has been inserted into its base. The procedure is painful and expensive.

The development of what one "beauty expert" calls "good skincare habits" requires not only attention to health, the avoidance of strong facial expressions, and the performance of facial exercises, but the regular use of skincare preparations, many to be applied more often than once a day: cleansing lotions (ordinary soap and water "upsets the skin's acid and alkaline balance"), wash-off cleansers (milder than cleansing lotions), astringents, toners, makeup removers, night creams, nourishing creams, eye creams, moisturizers, skin balancers, body lotions, hand creams, lip pomades, suntan lotions, sunscreens, and facial masks. Provision of the proper facial mask is complex: there are sulfur masks for pimples; oil or hot masks for dry areas; if these fail, then tightening masks; conditioning masks; peeling masks; cleansing masks made of herbs, cornmeal, or almonds; and mudpacks. Black women may wish to use "fade creams" to "even skin tone." Skincare preparations are never just sloshed onto the skin, but applied according to precise rules: eye cream is dabbed on gently in movements toward, never away from, the nose; cleansing cream is applied in outward directions only, straight across the forehead, the upper lip, and the chin, never up but straight down the nose and up and out on the cheeks.

The normalizing discourse of modern medicine is enlisted by the cosmetics industry to gain credibility for its claims. Dr. Christiaan Barnard lends his enormous prestige to the Glycel line of "cellular treatment activators"; these contain "glycosphingolipids" that can "make older skin behave and look like younger skin." The Clinique computer at any Clinique counter will select a combination of preparations just right for you. Ultima II contains "procollagen" in its anti-aging eye cream that "provides hydration" to "demoralizing lines." "Biotherm" eye cream dramatically improves the "biomechanical properties of the skin." The Park Avenue clinic of Dr. Zizmor, "chief of dermatology at one of New York's leading hospitals," offers not only such medical treatment as derma-brasion and chemical peeling, but "total deep skin cleansing" as well.

Really good skincare habits require the use of a variety of aids and devices: facial steamers, faucet filters to collect impurities in the water, borax to soften it, a humidifier for the bedroom, electric massagers, backbrushes, complexion brushes, loofahs, pumice stones, and blackhead removers. I will not detail the implements or techniques involved in the manicure or pedicure.

The ordinary circumstances of life as well as a wide variety of activities cause a crisis in skincare and require a stepping-up of the regimen as well as an additional laying-on of preparations. Skincare discipline requires a specialized knowledge: a woman must know what to do if she has been skiing, taking medication, doing vigorous exercise, boating, or swimming in chlorinated pools: or if she has been exposed to pollution, heated rooms, cold, sun, harsh weather, the pressurized cabins on airplanes, saunas, or steam rooms, fatigue, or stress. Like the schoolchild or prisoner, the woman mastering good skincare habits is put on a timetable: Georgette Klinger requires that a shorter or longer period of attention be paid to the complexion at least four times a day. Haircare, like skincare, requires a similar investment of time, the use of a wide variety of preparations, the mastery of a set of techniques, and, again, the acquisition of a specialized knowledge.

The crown and pinnacle of good haircare and skincare is, of course, the arrangement of the hair and the application of cosmetics. Here the regimen of haircare, skincare, manicure, and pedicure is recapitulated in another mode. A woman must learn the proper manipulation of a large number of devices—the blow dryer, styling brush, curling iron, hot curlers, wire curlers, eyeliner, lipliner, lipstick brush, eyelash curler, and mascara brush. And she must learn to apply a wide variety of products—foundation, toner, covering stick, mascara, eyeshadow, eyegloss, blusher, lipstick, rouge, lip gloss, hair dye, hair rinse, hair lightener, hair "relaxer," and so on.

In the language of fashion magazines and cosmetic ads, making-up is typically portrayed as an aesthetic activity in which a woman can express her individuality. In reality, while cosmetic styles change every decade or so, and while some variation in makeup is permitted depending on the occasion, making-up the face is, in fact, a highly stylized activity that gives little rein to self-expression. Painting the face is not like painting a picture; at best, it might be described as painting the same picture over and over again with minor variations. Little latitude is permitted in what is considered appropriate makeup for the office and for most social occasions; indeed, the woman who uses cosmetics in a genuinely novel and imaginative way is liable to be seen not as an artist but as an eccentric. Furthermore, since a properly made-up face is, if not a card of entree, at least a badge of acceptability in most social and professional contexts, the woman who chooses not to wear cosmetics at all faces sanctions of a sort that will never be applied to someone who chooses not to paint a watercolor.

## V

Are we dealing in all this merely with sexual *difference*? Scarcely. The disciplinary practices I have described are part of the process by which the ideal body of femininity–and hence the feminine body-subject—is constructed; in doing this, they produce a "practiced and subjected" body, that is, a body on which an inferior status has been inscribed. A woman's face must be made-up, that is

to say, made-over, and so must her body: she is ten pounds overweight; her lips must be made more kissable, her complexion dewier, her eyes more mysterious. The "art" of makeup is the art of disguise, but this presupposes that a woman's face, unpainted, is defective. Soap and water, a shave, and routine attention to hygiene may be enough for *him;* for *her* they are not. The strategy of much beauty-related advertising is to suggest to women that their bodies are deficient; but even without such more or less explicit teaching, the media images of perfect female beauty that bombard us daily leave no doubt in the minds of most women that they fail to measure up. The technologies of femininity are taken up and practiced by women against the background of a pervasive sense of bodily deficiency: this accounts for what is often their compulsive or even ritualistic character.

The disciplinary project of femininity is a "setup": it requires such radical and extensive measures of bodily transformation that virtually every woman who gives herself to it is destined in some degree to fail. Thus, a measure of shame is added to a woman's sense that the body she inhabits is deficient: she ought to take better care of herself; she might after all have jogged that last mile. Many women are without the time or resources to provide themselves with even the minimum of what such a regimen requires, for example, a decent diet. Here is an additional source of shame for poor women, who must bear what our society regards as the more general shame of poverty. The burdens poor women bear in this regard are not merely psychological, since conformity to the prevailing standards of bodily acceptability is a known factor in economic mobility.

The larger disciplines that construct a "feminine" body out of a female one are by no means race- or class-specific. There is little evidence that women of color or working-class women are in general less committed to the incarnation of an ideal femininity than their more privileged sisters: this is not to deny the many ways in which factors of race, class, locality, ethnicity, or personal taste can be expressed within the kinds of practices I have described. The rising young corporate executive may buy her cosmetics at Bergdorf-Goodman, while the counter-server at McDonald's gets hers at the Kmart; the one may join an expensive "upscale" health club, while the other may have to make do with the $9.49 GFX Body-Flex II Home-Gym advertised in the *National Enquirer*: both are aiming at the same general result.

In the regime of institutionalized heterosexuality, woman must make herself "object and prey" for the man: it is for him that these eyes are limpid pools, this cheek baby-smooth. In contemporary patriarchal culture, a panoptical male connoisseur resides within the consciousness of most women: they stand perpetually before his gaze and under his judgment. Woman lives her body as seen by another, by an anonymous patriarchal Other. We are often told that "women dress for other women." There is some truth in this: who but someone engaged in a project similar to my own can appreciate the panache with which I bring it off? But women know for whom this game is played: they know that a pretty young woman is likelier to become a flight attendant than a plain one, and that a well-preserved older woman has a better chance of holding onto her husband than one who has "let herself go."

Here it might be objected that performance for another in no way signals the inferiority of the performer to the one for whom the performance is intended: the actor, for example, depends on his audience but is in no way inferior to it; he is not demeaned by his dependency. While femininity is surely something enacted, the analogy to theater breaks down in a number of ways. First, as I argued earlier, the self-determination we think of as requisite to an artistic career is lacking here: femininity as spectacle is something in which virtually ever woman is required to participate. Second, the precise nature of the criteria by which women are judged, not only the inescapability of judgment itself, reflects gross imbalances in the social power of the sexes that do not mark the relationship of artists and their audiences. An aesthetic of femininity, for example, that mandates fragility and a lack of muscular strength produces female bodies

that can offer little resistance to physical abuse, and the physical abuse of women by men, as we know, is widespread. It is true that the current fitness movement has permitted women to develop more muscular strength and endurance than was heretofore allowed; indeed, images of women have begun to appear in the mass media that seem to eroticize this new muscularity. But a woman may by no means develop more muscular strength than her partner: the bride who would tenderly carry her groom across the threshold is a figure of comedy, not romance.

Under the current "tyranny of slenderness" women are forbidden to become large or massive; they must take up as little space as possible. The very contours a woman's body takes on as she matures—the fuller breasts and rounded hips—have become distasteful. The body by which a woman feels herself judged and which by rigorous discipline she must try to assume is the body of early adolescence, slight and unformed, a body lacking flesh or substance, a body in whose very contours the image of immaturity has been inscribed. The requirement that a woman maintain a smooth and hairless skin carries further the theme of inexperience, for an infantilized face must accompany her infantilized body, a face that never ages or furrows its brow in thought. The face of the ideally feminine woman must never display the marks of character, wisdom, and experience that we so admire in men.

To succeed in the provision of a beautiful or sexy body gains a woman attention and some admiration but little real respect and rarely any social power. A woman's effort to master feminine body discipline will lack importance just because she does it: her activity partakes of the general depreciation of everything female. In spite of unrelenting pressure to "make the most of what she has," women are ridiculed and dismissed for their interest in such "trivial" things as clothes and makeup. Further, the narrow identification of woman with sexuality and the body in a society that has for centuries displayed profound suspicion toward both does little to raise her status. Even the most adored female bodies complain routinely of their situation in ways that reveal an implicit understanding that there is something demeaning in the kind of attention they receive. Marilyn Monroe, Elizabeth Taylor, and Farrah Fawcett have all wanted passionately to become actresses-artists—and not just "sex objects."

But it is perhaps in their more restricted motility and comportment that the inferiorization of women's bodies is most evident: women's typical body-language, a language of relative tension and constriction, is understood to be a language of subordination, when it is enacted by men in male status hierarchies. In groups of men, those with higher status typically assume looser and more relaxed postures: the boss lounges comfortably behind the desk, while the applicant sits tense and rigid on the edge of his seat. Higher-status individuals may touch their subordinates more than they themselves get touched; they initiate more eye contact and are smiled at by their inferiors more than they are observed to smile in return. What is announced in the comportment of superiors is confidence and ease, especially ease of access to the Other. Female constraint in posture and movement is no doubt overdetermined: the fact that women tend to sit and stand with legs, feet, and knees close or touching may well be a coded declaration of sexual circumspection in a society that still maintains a double standard, or an effort, albeit unconscious, to guard the genital area. In the latter case, a woman's tight and constricted posture must be seen as the expression of her need to ward off real or symbolic sexual attack. Whatever proportions must be assigned in the final display to fear or deference, one thing is clear: woman's body language speaks eloquently, though silently, of her subordinate status in a hierarchy of gender.

## VI

If what we have described is a genuine discipline—a system of "micropower" that is "essentially non-egalitarian and asymmetrical"—who then are the disciplinarians? Who is the top sergeant in the disciplinary regime of femininity? Historically, the law has had some responsibility for enforcement: in times gone by, for example, individuals who appeared in public in the clothes of the other sex could be arrested. While cross-dressers are still liable to some harassment, the kind of discipline we are considering is not the business of the police or the courts. Parents and teachers, of course, have extensive influence, admonishing girls to be demure and ladylike, to "smile pretty," to sit with their legs together. The influence of the media is pervasive, too, constructing as it does an image of the female body as spectacle, nor can we ignore the role played by "beauty experts" or by emblematic public personages such as Jane Fonda and Lynn Redgrave.

But none of these individuals—the skincare consultant, the parent, the policeman—does in fact wield the kind of authority that is typically invested in those who manage more straightforward disciplinary institutions. The disciplinary power that inscribes femininity in the female body is everywhere and it is nowhere; the disciplinarian is everyone and yet no one in particular. Women regarded as overweight, for example, report that they are regularly admonished to diet, sometimes by people they scarcely know. These intrusions are often softened by reference to the natural prettiness just waiting to emerge: "People have always said that I had a beautiful face and 'if you'd only lose weight you'd be really beautiful.'" Here, "people"—friends and casual acquaintances alike—act to enforce prevailing standards of body size.

Foucault tends to identify the imposition of discipline upon the body with the operation of specific institutions, for example, the school, the factory, the prison. To do this, however, is to overlook the extent to which discipline can be institutionally *unbound* as well as institutionally bound. The anonymity of disciplinary power and its wide dispersion have consequences that are crucial to a proper understanding of the subordination of women. The absence of a formal institutional structure and of authorities invested with the power to carry out institutional directives creates the impression that the production of femininity is either entirely voluntary or natural. The several senses of "discipline" are instructive here. On the one hand, discipline is something imposed on subjects of an "essentially non-egalitarian and asymmetrical" system of authority. Schoolchildren, convicts, and draftees are subject to discipline in this sense. But discipline can be sought voluntarily as well—for example, when an individual seeks initiation into the spiritual discipline of Zen Buddhism. Discipline can, of course, be both at once: the volunteer may seek the physical and occupational training offered by the army without the army's ceasing in any way to be the instrument by which he and other members of his class are kept in disciplined subjection. Feminine bodily discipline has the dual character: on the one hand, no one is marched off for electrolysis at gunpoint, nor can we fail to appreciate the initiative and ingenuity displayed by countless women in an attempt to master the rituals of beauty. Nevertheless, insofar as the disciplinary practices of femininity produce a "subjected and practiced," an inferiorized, body, they must be understood as aspects of a far larger discipline, an oppressive and inegalitarian system of sexual subordination. This system aims at turning women into the docile and compliant companions of men just as surely as the army aims to turn its raw recruits into soldiers.

Now the transformation of oneself into a properly feminine body may be any or all of the following: a rite of passage into adulthood, the adoption and celebration of a particular aesthetic, a way of announcing one's economic level and social status, a way to triumph over other women in the competition for men or jobs, or an opportunity for massive narcissistic indulgence. The social construction of the feminine body is all these things, but at its base it is discipline, too, and discipline of the inegalitarian sort. The absence of formally identifiable disciplinarians and of a public schedule of sanctions only disguises the extent to which the imperative to be "feminine" serves the interest

of domination. This is a lie in which all concur: making-up is merely artful play; one's first pair of high-heeled shoes is an innocent part of growing up, not the modern equivalent of foot-binding.

Why aren't all women feminists? In modern industrial societies, women are not kept in line by fear of retaliatory male violence; their victimization is not that of the South African black. Nor will it suffice to say that a false consciousness engendered in women by patriarchal ideology is at the basis of female subordination. This is not to deny that women are often subject to gross male violence or that women and men alike are ideologically mystified by the dominant gender arrangements. What I wish to suggest instead is that an adequate understanding of women's oppression will require an appreciation of the extent to which not only women's lives but their very subjectivities are structured within an ensemble of systematically duplicitous practices. The feminine discipline of the body is a case in point: the practices that construct this body have an overt aim and character far removed, indeed, radically distinct, from their covert function. In this regard, the system of gender subordination, like the wage-bargain under capitalism, illustrates in its own way the ancient tension between what-is and what-appears: the phenomenal forms in which it is manifested are often quite different from the real relations that form its deeper structure.

## VII

The lack of formal public sanctions does not mean that a woman who is unable or unwilling to submit herself to the appropriate body discipline will face no sanctions at all. On the contrary, she faces a very severe sanction indeed in a world dominated by men: the refusal of male patronage. For the heterosexual woman, this may mean the loss of a badly needed intimacy; for both heterosexual women and lesbians, it may well mean the refusal of a decent livelihood.

As noted earlier, women punish themselves too for the failure to conform. The growing literature on women's body size is filled with wrenching confessions of shame from the overweight:

> I felt clumsy and huge. I felt that I would knock over furniture, bump into things, tip over chairs, not fit into VW's, especially when people were trying to crowd into the backseat. I felt like I was taking over the whole room. . . . I felt disgusting and like a slob. In the summer I felt hot and sweaty and I knew people saw my sweat as evidence that I was too fat.

> I feel so terrible about the way I look that I cut off connection with my body. I operate from the neck up. I do not look in mirrors. I do not want to spend time buying clothes. I do not want to spend time with make-up because it's painful for me to look at myself.[3]

> I can no longer bear to look at myself. . . . Whenever I have to stand in front of a mirror to comb my hair I tie a large towel around my neck. Even at night I slip my nightgown on before I take off my blouse and pants. But all this has only made it worse and worse. It's been so long since I've really looked at my body.[4]

The depth of these women's shame is a measure of the extent to which all women have internalized patriarchal standards of bodily acceptability. A fuller examination of what is meant here by "internalization" may shed light on a question posed earlier: Why isn't every woman a feminist?

Something is "internalized" when it gets incorporated into the structure of the self. By "structure of the self" I refer to those modes of perception and of self-perception that allow a self to distinguish itself both from other selves and from things that are not selves. I have described elsewhere how a generalized male witness comes to structure woman's consciousness of herself as a bodily being. This, then, is one meaning of "internalization." The sense of oneself as a distinct and valuable individual is tied not only to the sense of how one is perceived, but also to what one knows, especially to what one knows how to do; this is a second sense of "internalization." Whatever its ultimate effect, discipline can provide the individual upon whom it is imposed with a sense of mastery as well as a secure sense of iden-

tity. There is a certain contradiction here: while its imposition may promote a larger disempowerment, discipline may bring with it a certain development of a person's powers. Women, then, like other skilled individuals, have a stake in the perpetuation of their skills, whatever it may have cost to acquire them and quite apart from the question whether, as a gender, they would have been better off had they never had to acquire them in the first place. Hence, feminism, especially a genuinely radical feminism that questions the patriarchal construction of the female body, threatens women with a certain de-skilling, something people normally resist: beyond this, it calls into question that aspect of personal identity that is tied to the development of a sense of competence.

Resistance from this source may be joined by a reluctance to part with the rewards of compliance; further, many women will resist the abandonment of an aesthetic that defines what they take to be beautiful. But there is still another source of resistance, one more subtle, perhaps, but tied once again to questions of identity and internalization. To have a body felt to be "feminine"—a body socially constructed through the appropriate practices—is in most cases crucial to a woman's sense of herself as female and, since persons currently can *be* only as male or female, to her sense of herself as an existing individual. To possess such a body may also be essential to her sense of herself as a sexually desiring and desirable subject. Hence, any political project that aims to dismantle the machinery that turns a female body into a feminine one may well be apprehended by a woman as something that threatens her with desexualization, if not outright annihilation.

The categories of masculinity and femininity do more than assist in the construction of personal identities; they are critical elements in our informal social ontology. This may account to some degree for the otherwise puzzling phenomenon of homophobia and for the revulsion felt by many at the sight of female bodybuilders; neither the homosexual nor the muscular woman can be assimilated easily into the categories that structure everyday life. The radical feminist critique of femininity, then, may pose a threat not only to a woman's sense of her own identity and desirability but to the very structure of her social universe.

Of course, many women *are* feminists, favoring a program of political and economic reform in the struggle to gain equality with men. But many "reform," or liberal, feminists (indeed, many orthodox Marxists) are committed to the idea that the preservation of a woman's femininity is quite compatible with her struggle for liberation. These thinkers have rejected a normative femininity based upon the notion of "separate spheres" and the traditional sexual division of labor, while accepting at the same time conventional standards of feminine body display. If my analysis is correct, such a feminism is incoherent. Foucault has argued that modern bourgeois democracy is deeply flawed in that it seeks political rights for individuals constituted as unfree by a variety of disciplinary micropowers that lie beyond the realm of what is ordinarily defined as the "political." "The man described for us whom we are invited to free," he says, "is already in himself the effect of a subjection much more profound than himself." If, as I have argued, female subjectivity is constituted in any significant measure in and through the disciplinary practices that construct the feminine body, what Foucault says here of "man" is perhaps even truer of "woman." Marxists have maintained from the first the inadequacy of a purely liberal feminism: we have reached the same conclusion through a different route, casting doubt at the same time on the adequacy of traditional Marxist prescriptions for women's liberation as well. Liberals call for equal rights for women, traditional Marxists for the entry of women into production on an equal footing with men, the socialization of housework, and proletarian revolution: neither calls for the deconstruction of the categories of masculinity and femininity. Femininity as a certain "style of the flesh" will have to be surpassed in the direction of something quite different—not masculinity, which is in many ways only its mirror opposite, but a radical and as yet unimagined transformation of the female body.

## VIII

Foucault has argued that the transition from traditional to modern societies has been characterized by a profound transformation in the exercise of power, by what he calls "a reversal of the political axis of individualization." In older authoritarian systems, power was embodied in the person of the monarch and exercised upon a largely anonymous body of subjects; violation of the law was seen as an insult to the royal individual. While the methods employed to enforce compliance in the past were often quite brutal, involving gross assaults against the body, power in such a system operated in a haphazard and discontinuous fashion; much in the social totality lay beyond its reach.

By contrast, modern society has seen the emergence of increasingly invasive apparatuses of power: these exercise a far more restrictive social and psychological control than was heretofore possible. In modern societies, effects of power "circulate through progressively finer channels, gaining access to individuals themselves, to their bodies, their gestures and all their daily actions." Power now seeks to transform the minds of those individuals who might be tempted to resist it, not merely to punish or imprison their bodies. This requires two things: a finer control of the body's time and of its movements—a control that cannot be achieved without ceaseless surveillance and a better understanding of the specific person, of the genesis and nature of his "case." The power these new apparatuses seek to exercise requires a new knowledge of the individual: modern psychology and sociology are born. Whether the new modes of control have charge of correction, production, education, or the provision of welfare, they resemble one another; they exercise power in a bureaucratic mode—faceless, centralized, and pervasive. A reversal has occurred: power has now become anonymous, while the project of control has brought into being a new individuality. In fact, Foucault believes that the operation of power constitutes the very subjectivity of the subject. Here, the image of the Panopticon returns: knowing that he may be observed from the tower at any time, the inmate takes over the job of policing himself. The gaze that is inscribed in the very structure of the disciplinary institution is internalized by the inmate: modern technologies of behavior are thus oriented toward the production of isolated and self-policing subjects.

Women have their own experience of the modernization of power, one that begins later but follows in many respects the course outlined by Foucault. In important ways, a woman's behavior is less regulated now than it was in the past. She has more mobility and is less confined to domestic space. She enjoys what to previous generations would have been an unimaginable sexual liberty. Divorce, access to paid work outside the home, and the increasing secularization of modern life have loosened the hold over her of the traditional family and, in spite of the current fundamentalist revival, of the church. Power in these institutions was wielded by individuals known to her. Husbands and fathers enforced patriarchal authority in the family. As in the ancient régime, a woman's body was subject to sanctions if she disobeyed. Not Foucault's royal individual but the Divine Individual decreed that her desire be always "unto her husband," while the person of the priest made known to her God's more specific intentions concerning her place and duties. In the days when civil and ecclesiastical authority were still conjoined, individuals formally invested with power were charged with the correction of recalcitrant women whom the family had somehow failed to constrain.

By contrast, the disciplinary power that is increasingly charged with the production of a properly embodied femininity is dispersed and anonymous; there are no individuals formally empowered to wield it; it is, as we have seen, invested in everyone and in no one in particular. This disciplinary power is peculiarly modern: it does not rely upon violent or public sanctions, nor does it seek to restrain the freedom of the female body to move from place to place. For all that, its invasion of the body is well-nigh total: the female body enters "a machinery of power that explores it, breaks it down and rearranges it." The disciplinary techniques through which the "docile bodies" of women are constructed aim at a regulation that is perpetual and exhaustive—a regulation of the body's size and contours, its appetite, posture, gestures and general comportment in space, and the appearance of each of its visible parts.

As modern industrial societies change and as women themselves offer resistance to patriarchy, older forms of domination are eroded. But new forms arise, spread, and become consolidated. Women are no longer required to be chaste or modest, to restrict their sphere of activity to the home, or even to realize their properly feminine destiny in maternity: normative femininity is coming more and more to be centered on woman's body—not its duties and obligations or even its capacity to bear children, but its sexuality, more precisely, its presumed heterosexuality and its appearance. There is, of course, nothing new in women's preoccupation with youth and beauty. What is new is the growing power of the image in a society increasingly oriented toward the visual media. Images of normative femininity, it might be ventured, have replaced the religiously oriented tracts of the past. New too is the spread of this discipline to all classes of women and its deployment throughout the life cycle. What was formerly the specialty of the aristocrat or courtesan is now the routine obligation of every woman, be she a grandmother or a barely pubescent girl.

To subject oneself to the new disciplinary power is to be up-to-date, to be "with-it"; as I have argued, it is presented to us in ways that are regularly disguised. It is fully compatible with the current need for women's wage labor, the cult of youth and fitness, and the need of advanced capitalism to maintain high levels of consumption. Further, it represents a saving in the economy of enforcement: since it is women themselves who practice this discipline on and against their own bodies, men get off scot-free.

The woman who checks her makeup half a dozen times a day to see if her foundation has caked or her mascara has run, who worries that the wind or the rain may spoil her hairdo, who looks frequently to see if her stockings have bagged at the ankle or who, feeling fat, monitors everything she eats, has become, just as surely as the inmate of the Panopticon, a self-policing subject, a self committed to a relentless self-surveillance. This self-surveillance is a form of obedience to patriarchy. It is also the reflection in woman's consciousness of the fact that *she* is under surveillance in ways that *he* is not, that whatever else she may become, she is importantly a body designed to please or to excite. There has been induced in many women, then, in Foucault's words, "a state of conscious and permanent visibility that assures the automatic functioning of power." Since the standards of female bodily acceptability are impossible fully to realize, requiring as they do a virtual transcendence of nature, a woman may live much of her life with a pervasive feeling of bodily deficiency. Hence a tighter control of the body has gained a new kind of hold over the mind.

Foucault often writes as if power constitutes the very individuals upon whom it operates:

> The individual is not to be conceived as a sort of elementary nucleus, a primitive atom, a multiple and inert material on which power comes to fasten or against which it happens to strike. . . . In fact, it is already one of the prime effects of power that certain bodies, certain gestures, certain discourses, certain desires, come to be identified and constituted as individuals.[5]

Nevertheless, if individuals were wholly constituted by the power-knowledge regime Foucault describes, it would make no sense to speak of resistance to discipline at all. Foucault seems sometimes on the verge of depriving us of a vocabulary in which to conceptualize the nature and meaning of those periodic refusals of control that, just as much as the imposition of control, mark the course of human history.

Peter Dews accuses Foucault of lacking a theory of the "libidinal body," that is, the body upon which discipline is imposed and whose bedrock impulse toward spontaneity and pleasure might perhaps become the locus of resistance. Do women's "libidinal" bodies, then, not rebel against the pain, constriction, tedium, semistarvation, and

constant self-surveillance to which they are currently condemned? Certainly they do, but the rebellion is put down every time a woman picks up her eyebrow tweezers or embarks upon a new diet. The harshness of a regimen alone does not guarantee its rejection, for hardships can be endured if they are thought to be necessary or inevitable.

While "nature," in the form of a "libidinal" body, may not be the origin of a revolt against "culture," domination (and the discipline it requires) are never imposed without some cost. Historically, the forms and occasions of resistance are manifold. Sometimes, instances of resistance appear to spring from the introduction of new and conflicting factors into the lives of the dominated: the juxtaposition of old and new and the resulting incoherence or "contradiction" may make submission to the old ways seem increasingly unnecessary. In the present instance, what may be a major factor in the relentless and escalating objectification of women's bodies—namely, women's growing independence—produces in many women a sense of incoherence that calls into question the meaning and necessity of the current discipline. As women (albeit a small minority of women) begin to realize an unprecedented political, economic, and sexual self-determination, they fall ever more completely under the dominating gaze of patriarchy. It is this paradox, not the "libidinal body," that produces, here and there, pockets of resistance.

In the current political climate, there is no reason to anticipate either widespread resistance to currently fashionable modes of feminine embodiment or joyous experimentation with new "styles of the flesh"; moreover, such novelties would face profound opposition from material and psychological sources identified earlier in this essay (see Section VII). In spite of this, a number of oppositional discourses and practices have appeared in recent years. An increasing number of women are "pumping iron," a few with little concern for the limits of body development imposed by current canons of femininity. Women in radical lesbian communities have rejected hegemonic images of femininity and are struggling to develop a new female aesthetic. A striking feature of such communities is the extent to which they have overcome the oppressive identification of female beauty and desirability with youth: here, the physical features of aging—"character" lines and graying hair—not only do not diminish a woman's attractiveness, they may even enhance it. A popular literature of resistance is growing, some of it analytical and reflective, like Kim Chernin's *The Obsession,* some oriented toward practical self-help, like Marcia Hutchinson's recent *Transforming Body Image, Learning to Love the Body You Have.* This literature reflects a mood akin in some ways to that other and earlier mood of quiet desperation to which Betty Friedan gave voice in *The Feminine Mystique.* Nor should we forget that a mass-based women's movement is in place in this country that has begun a critical questioning of the meaning of femininity, if not yet in the corporeal presentation of self, then in other domains of life. We women cannot begin the re-vision of our own bodies until we learn to read the cultural messages we inscribe upon them daily and until we come to see that even when the mastery of the disciplines of femininity produces a triumphant result, we are still only women.

NOTES

1. Michel Foucault, *Discipline and Punish: The Birth of the Prison,* trans. Alan Sheridan (New York: Vintage Books, 1979), p. 138.
2. Ibid., p. 28.
3. Millman, *Such a Pretty Face,* pp. 80, 195.
4. Chernin, *The Obsession,* p. 53.
5. Foucault, *Power/Knowledge,* p. 98. In fact, Foucault is not entirely consistent on this point. For an excellent discussion of contending Foucault interpretations and for the difficulty of deriving a consistent set of claims from Foucault's work generally, see Nancy Fraser. "Michel Foucault: A 'Young Conservative'?" *Ethics* 96 (October 1985): 165–84.

---

## 53     Philosophy, Politics, and Power: An Afro-American Perspective

CORNEL WEST

IS IT A MERE COINCIDENCE that the major philosophical thinkers in the modern West—Marx, Kierkegaard, and Nietzsche in the nineteenth century and Wittgenstein, Heidegger, and Derrida in the twentieth century—call for an end to philosophy? What do these post-philosophical voices have to do with Afro-Americans engaged in the philosophical enterprise?

I suggest that the calls for an end to philosophy are symptomatic of fundamental cultural transformations in the modern West. These transformations primarily consist of three salient developments in modern Western culture. First, the demythologizing of the institution of science—still in its rudimentary stage—renders the status of philosophy problematic. This demythologizing is not a discrediting of the achievements of science, but an undermining of its legitimacy regarding its alleged monopoly on truth and reality. Second, the demystifying of the role of authority makes the function of philosophy suspect. This demystifying is not simply a revolt against intellectual, social, and political authority, it calls into question the very notion of and need for authority. Third, the disclosure of a deep sense of impotence tends to support the view that philosophy is superfluous. This disclosure is not only a recognition of dominant ironic forms of thinking and narcissistic forms of living, but a pervasive despair about the present and lack of hope for the future.

These three developments require that philosophy—both as a professional discipline and as a mode of thinking—either redefine itself or bring itself to an end. In this historical moment, Afro-Americans engaged in the philosophical enterprise can contribute to the redefining of philosophy principally by revealing why and showing how philosophy is inextricably linked to politics and power—to structures of domination and mechanisms of control. This important task does not call for an end to philosophy. Rather it situates philosophical activity in the midst of personal and collective struggles in the present.

## Revaluations of the Philosophical Past

In order to understand the prevailing crisis of philosophy in the modern West, it is necessary to examine the beginning of modern Western philosophy. Modern philosophy emerged alongside modern science. The basic aim of modern philosophy was to promote and encourage the legitimacy of modern science. Descartes, the famous mathematician and scientist, was the father of modern philosophy. He tried to show that modern science not merely provides more effective ways of coping with the world, but also yields objective, accurate, value-free copies of the world. Descartes attempted to do this by putting forward rational foundations for knowledge independent of theological grounds and moral concerns. For the first time, epistemological matters became the center around which philosophical reflection revolved. Henceforth, the principal thrust of modern philosophy would be toward the justification of and rationale for belief. Modern philosophy became a disinterested quest for certainty regulated by a conception of truth that stands outside the world of politics and power—a prop that undergirds the claims of modern science.

The emergence of the capitalist mode of production, with its atomistic individualism and profit-oriented dispositions toward nature and people, partly accounts for the way in which Descartes chose to defend modern science. This defense takes the form of a justification of knowledge that starts with the self-consciousness of the individual, the immediate awareness of the subject, the *cogitatio* of the ego. Descartes' methodological doubt, a search for certainty that begins in radical doubt, rests upon the only mental activity that cannot be doubted: the activity of doubt itself. In his view, such doubting presupposes an agent who doubts, that is, a thinking individual, subject, or ego. Only by validly inferring from this indubitable activity of doubting—the only certainty available—can claims about God, the world, and the bodily self be justified. Like the new literary genre of early capitalist culture—the novel—Descartes' viewpoint supports the notion that we have access to, arrive at, and acquire knowledge of the world through the autonomous individual. Therefore, the primacy of the individual, subject, or ego who accurately copies the world or validly makes inferences about the world serves as the foundation of knowledge, the philosophical basis of modern science.

The obsession of the early modern philosophers with science (especially Newton) partly explains the empiricist twist given to Descartes' subjectivist turn in philosophy. For Locke, Berkeley, and Hume, the primacy of the thinking individual, subject, or ego remained, but experience (understood as sensations and perceptions) became the major candidate for the foundation of knowledge. Yet this ambitious project faltered. When Berkeley rejected the substantial self—the subject to which attributes are attached—and called on God to ground it as spirit, philosophical havoc set in. Hume, who had little philosophical use for God, explicitly articulated the skeptical result: the idea that knowledge has no empirical foundation. Instead, knowledge is but the (philosophically unjustifiable) imaginative constructs enacted by thinking individuals, subjects, or egos. Yet these thinking individuals, subjects, or egos are but themselves bundles of sensations and perceptions. Hence the subject and object of knowledge is rendered problematic—and modern philosophy found itself in a quandary.

Kant, the first modern professional philosopher in the West, rescued modern philosophy by providing transcendental grounds for knowledge and science. He reenacted the quest for certainty—the situating of the grounds for truth outside of politics and power—by locating the justification of what we know in the conditions for the possibility of knowing. These conditions are neither deductively arrived at nor empirically grounded. Rather they are transcendental in that they consist of the universal and necessary conceptual scheme people employ in order to know and hence have experience. Although Kant rejected the rationalist inference-making activity of Descartes, he deepened Descartes' subjectivist turn by locating the universal and necessary conceptual scheme in the thinking activity of the subject. Although Kant criticized the empiricist perspectives of Locke, Berkeley, and especially Hume, he accepted Hume's skepticism by holding that the universal and necessary conceptual scheme constitutes an objective world, but not the real world. In addition, Kant's architectonic project tried to link science, morals and aesthetics—Truth, Goodness, and Beauty—while arguing for their different foundations.

With the appearance of Hegel, modern philosophy drifted into a deep crisis. This was so primarily because of the emergence of historical consciousness. This consciousness was threatening to modern philosophy because it acknowledged the historical character of philosophy itself. This acknowledgement presented a major challenge to modern philosophy because it implied that the very aim of modern philosophy—the quest for certainty and search for foundations of knowledge—was an ahistorical enterprise. Hegel's historicizing of Kant's universal and necessary conceptual scheme questioned the very content and character of modern philosophy.

It is no accident that the first modern calls for the end of philosophy were made by the two major thinkers who labored under the shadow of Hegel: Kierkegaard and Marx. Both accepted Hegel's historicizing of the subjectivist turn in philosophy, his emphasis on activity, development, and process, his dialectical approach to understanding and transforming the world, and his devastating critiques of Cartesian and Kantian notions of substance, subject, and the self. Kierkegaard rejected Hegel's intellectualist attempt to link thought to concrete, human existence and put forward a profound existential dialectic of the self. Marx discarded Hegel's idealistic project of resolving the dominant form of alienation in the existing order and presented a penetrating materialistic dialectic of capitalist society. Both Kierkegaard and Marx understood philosophy as an antiquated, outmoded form of thinking, a mere fetter that impeded their particular praxis-oriented projects of redemption. Kierkegaard noted that, "philosophy is life's dry nurse, it can stay with us but not give milk." And Marx stated that, "philosophy stands in the same relation to the study of the actual world as masturbation to sexual love."

Afro-American philosophers should take heed of the radical antiphilosophical stances of Kierkegaard and Marx, not because they are right but rather because of the concerns that motivate their viewpoints. Both stress the value-laden character of philosophical reflection; the way in which such reflection not only serves particular class and personal interests, but also how it refuses to see itself as a form of praxis-in-the-world-of-politics-and-power. This refusal conceals the complex linkages of philosophical reflection to politics and power by defining itself as above and outside politics and power. By viewing itself as the queen of the disciplines that oversee the knowledge-claims of other disciplines, modern philosophy elides its this-worldly character, its role and function in the world of politics and power.

Despite Hegel's historicizing efforts, academic philosophers managed to overthrow Hegelianism, ignore Kierkegaard and Marx (both nonacademics!), and replace Hegelianism either with the analytical realism of Bertrand Russell and G. E. Moore in England; the diverse forms of returns to Kant (neo-Kantianisms) and Descartes (phenomenology) in Germany; and the various modes of vitalism (Bergson) and religious-motivated conventionalism (Pierre Duhem) in France. The only kind of professional philosophizing that took Hegel seriously was Dewey's version of American pragmatism, yet even Dewey wrote as if Kierkegaard and Marx never lived. In short, the professionalization of modern philosophy in the West shielded the academy from the powerful antiphilosophical perspectives of post-Hegelian figures, especially that of Nietzsche.

Since Nietzsche is first and foremost a philosopher of power—who links philosophy to power, truth to strategic linguistic tropes, and thinking to coping techniques—he has never been welcomed in the philosophical academy. This is so primarily because—like Kierkegaard and Marx—his understanding of the power dimensions of knowledge and the political aspects of philosophy calls into question the very conception of philosophy that legitimates philosophical reflection in the academy. Ironically, the recent developments in philosophy and literary theory—antirealism in ontology, antifoundationalism in epistemology, and the detranscendentalizing of the subject—were prefigured by Nietzsche.[1] Yet the relation of these developments to politics and power is ignored.

## Repetition in the Post-Philosophical Present

The contemporary philosophical scene can be viewed as a repetition of Hegel's historicizing efforts—but with a difference. This crucial difference primarily consists of retranslating Hegel's stress on History as an emphasis on Language. The Hegelian notions of origins and ends of history, of homogeneous continuities in and overarching totalizing frameworks for history, are replaced by beginnings and random play of differences within linguistic systems, heterogeneous discontinuities in and antitotalizing deconstructions of linguistic discourses. This repetition of Hegel—the replacement of history with language—is mediated by three central-European processes in this century: the nihilistic Death-of-God perspective conjoined with Sausurean linguistics, which radically questions the meaning and value of human life (best portrayed in contemporary literature); the rise of fascism and totalitarianism, which tempers efforts for social change; and the sexual revolution, which unleashes hedonistic and narcissistic sensibilities on an unprecedented scale. These three processes circumscribe the repetition of Hegel within the perimeters of philosophical nihilism, political impotence, and hedonistic fanfare. Professional philosophy finds itself either radically historicized and linguisticized hence vanishing or holding on to the Kantian tradition for dear life.[2]

On a philosophical plane, the repetition of Hegel takes the form of an antirealism in ontology, antifoundationalism in epistemology, and a detranscendentalizing of the Kantian subject. The antirealism in ontology leaves us with changing descriptions and versions of the world, which come from various communities as responses to problematics, as fallible attempts to overcome specific situations and as means to satisfy particular needs and interests. The antifoundationalism in epistemology precludes notions of privileged representations that correctly correspond to the world, hence ground our knowledge; it leaves us with sets of transient social practices that facilitate our survival as individuals and members of society. The detranscendentalizing of the Kantian subject—the historical and linguistic situating of ourselves as knowers and doers—focuses our attention no longer on the mental activity of thinking individuals, but rather on the values and norms of historical and linguistic groups, Kierkegaard and Marx, like their master Hegel, held such antirealist, antifoundationalist, detranscendentalist views, but they did so with a sense of engagement in the present and hope for the future. The repetition of Hegel holds similar post-philosophical views yet despairs of the present and has little hope, if any, for the future.

This post-philosophical despair and hopelessness—with its concomitant forms of ironic and apocalyptic thinking and narcissistic living—is inextricably linked to the fundamental cultural transformations I noted earlier: the demythologizing of the institution of science, the demystifying of the role of authority, and the disclosure of a deep sense of impotence. Since modern philosophy at its inception was the handmaiden to modern science, it is not surprising that the demythologizing of science occurs alongside the vanishing of modern philosophy. Just as the Enlightenment era witnessed the slow replacement of the authority of the church with that of science, so we are witnessing a displacement of science, but there is no replacement as of yet. The *philosophes* of the Enlightenment—the propagandists for science and ideologues for laissez-faire capitalism—had a vision of the future; whereas the professional avant-gardists—propagandists against "bourgeois" science and ideologues against monopoly capitalism—rarely present a project for the future. The neo-Marxist Frankfurt School, including Max Horkheimer, Theodor Adorno, and Herbert Marcuse, along with creative followers like Stanley Aronowitz and Michel Foucault, are pioneers of this novel perspective of philosophy.[3] Yet, with the exception of Aronowitz and Marcuse at times, the hopelessness for the future is overwhelming. Nevertheless, these figures are much further along than their contemporaries, as illustrated by Quine's outdated neo-positivist veneration of physics or Rorty's nostalgic longing for preprofessional humanistic "conversation" among men and women of letters.

The demystifying of the role of authority—promoted by the "hermeneutics of suspicion" of Marx, Nietzsche, and Freud and encouraged by the antifoundationalism in contemporary philosophy—can be traced to the more general problem of the deep crisis of legitimacy in post-modern capitalist civilization. Of course, the breakdown of scientific, technocratic culture also affects the socialist world, but the crisis of legitimacy is in many ways a phenomenon rooted in the process of monopoly capitalist societies. By undermining traditional forms of authority—church, family, school—owing to the profit-motivated promo-

tion of hedonistic sensibilities, capitalist societies can legitimate themselves principally by satisfying the very needs it helps activate. These societies keep the populace loyal to its authority primarily by "delivering the goods," often luxury consumer goods that are rendered attractive by means of ingenious advertising. These goods do not merely pacify the populace; they also come to be viewed as the basic reason, in contrast to moral, religious or political reasons, that people have for acquiescence to capitalist authority. Hence, the crisis of legitimacy—the undermining of the work ethic, the collapse of the family, anarchy in public schools, and the proliferation of sexually-oriented advertisements, commercials, movies, and television shows—becomes part and parcel of the very legitimizing processes of monopoly capitalist societies.

The disclosure of a deep sense of impotence sits at the center of the post-philosophical present: the sense of reaching an historical dead end with no foreseeable way out and no discernible liberating projects or even credible visions in the near future. This disclosure is related to the detranscendentalizing of the Kantian subject in the sense that the emergence of the transcendental subject—the creative and conquering romantic hero—signifies the sense of optimistic triumph of early modern capitalist civilization. The detranscendentalizing of the subject portrays the sense of pessimistic tragedy of post-modern capitalist civilization, with the primary redemptive hope for this civilization, Marx's collective subject, the proletariat, remaining relatively dormant and muted.

The dominant forms of intellectual activity, especially philosophical reflection, enact this sense of impotence: analytical philosophy makes a fetish of technical virtuosity and uses it as a measure to regulate the intense careerism in the profession; antiacademic professional avant-gardists fiercely assault fellow colleagues and fervently attack notions of epistemological privilege yet remain relatively silent about racial, sexual, and class privilege in society at large; and poststructuralists perennially decenter prevailing discourses and dismantle philosophical and literary texts yet valorize a barren, ironic disposition by deconstructing, hence disarming and discarding, any serious talk about praxis. In this way, the repetition of Hegel is, from an Afro-American perspective, meretricious: attractive on a first glance but much less substantive after careful examination.

## Recommendations for a Revolutionary Future

The principal task of the Afro-American philosopher is to keep alive the idea of a revolutionary future, a better future different from the deplorable present, a state of affairs in which the multifaceted oppression of Afro-Americans (and others) is, if not eliminated, alleviated. Therefore the Afro-American philosopher must preserve the crucial Hegelian (and deeply Christian) notions of negation and transformation of what is in light of a revolutionary not-yet.[4] The notions of negation and transformation—the pillars of the Hegelian process of *Aufhebung*—promote the activity of resistance to what is and elevate the praxis of struggle against existing realities. In this way, Afro-American philosophers must wage an intense intellectual battle in the form of recovering the revolutionary potential of Hegel against the ironic repetition of Hegel, which dilutes and downplays this potential. The revolutionary potential of Hegel—indigenously grounded in the prophetic religious and progressive secular practices of Afro-Americans—can be promoted by a serious confrontation with the Marxist tradition and, among others, the recent work of Michel Foucault.

Foucault's exorbitant reaction to his former vulgar Marxism and past Communist allegiances often leads him to embody the worst of the repetition of Hegel: precluding any talk about a better future and downplaying the activity of resistance and struggle in the present. Despite these limitations, certain aspects of Foucault's work can contribute to a revolutionary future, notably his attempt to construct "a new politics of truth." For Foucault, the Western will to truth has not been truthful about itself. Only with the appearance of

Hegel and later Kierkegaard, Marx, and Nietzsche, has the this-worldly character of truth—its rootedness in politics and power—been disclosed and dissected. Foucault, who views his own work as "philosophical fragments put to work in a historical field of problems," begins his philosophical reflections with two basic questions: How are the conditions for the possibility of knowledges—the rules, conventions, and operations that circumscribe fields of discourse wherein notions, metaphors, categories, and ideas are rendered intelligible and comprehensible—ensconced in particular sets of power-relations? How are these conditions articulated in discursive practices and elaborated (in the sense in which Antonio Gramsci defines this crucial term) in nondiscursive formations? These questions are answered neither by abstract philosophical arguments nor by systematic theoretical treatises, but rather by detailed analytical descriptions—containing arguments and explanations—that constitute a genealogy of moral and political technologies, a genealogy that lays bare the workings of structures of domination and mechanisms of control over human bodies. Foucault's genealogical approach eschews the philosophical past and shuns the ironic repetition of Hegel in the present; he writes a subversive history of this past and present by discerning and detaching "the power of truth from the forms of hegemony, social, economic, and cultural, within which it operates."[5]

Foucault's perspective can be valuable for Afro-American philosophers whose allegiance is to a revolutionary future. With the indispensable aid of sophisticated neo-Marxist analysis, Foucault's viewpoint can be creatively transformed and rendered fruitful for a genealogy of modern racism, in both its ideational and material forms. This genealogy would take the form of detailed, analytical descriptions of the battery of notions, categories, metaphors, and concepts that regulate the inception of modern discourse, a discourse that constituted the idea of white supremacy in a particular way (e.g., inaugurated the category of "race") and excluded the idea of black equality in beauty, culture, and character from its discursive field.[6] Unlike Foucault, this Afro-American genealogical approach also would put forward an Afro-American counter-discourse, in all its complexity and diversity, to the modern European racist discourse and examine and evaluate how the Afro-American response promotes or precludes a revolutionary future.[7] In addition, a more refined effort would even delve into the political content of Afro-American everyday life and disclose the multivarious Afro-American cultural elements that debilitate or facilitate an Afro-American revolutionary future.

If Afro-American philosophers are to make a substantive contribution to the struggle for Afro-American freedom, it is imperative that we critically revaluate the grand achievements of the past philosophical figures in the West and avoid falling into their alluring ahistorical traps, traps that disarm Afro-American philosophers and render us mere colorful presences in the glass menagerie of the academy in monopoly capitalist USA. Afro-American philosophers must understand the repetition of Hegel in the present time as inescapable yet of highly limited value owing to its nihilistic outlooks; outlooks that implicitly presuppose luxury and explicitly preclude any serious talk about a future better than the inferno-like present. Lastly, Afro-American philosophers must articulate and elaborate recommendations for a revolutionary future. This articulation and elaboration requires a recovery of the revolutionary potential of Hegel, a deepening of the Marxist tradition, and a concrete grounding in the indigenous prophetic and progressive practices of Afro-Americans. This calling of Afro-American philosophers—this vocation of service—permits us to take our place alongside, not above, other committed Afro-Americans who continue to hold up the blood-stained banner, a banner that signifies the Afro-American struggle for freedom.

## NOTES

1. Cornel West, "Nietzsche's Prefiguration of Postmodern American Philosophy," *Boundary 2: A Journal of Postmodern Literature*, Special Nietzsche issue, vols. 9, 10, nos. 1, 3, (Fall-Winter 1980–81), pp. 241–270.

2. The most penetrating and provocative examination of these two options for contemporary philosophy is Richard Rorty's *Philosophy and the Mirror of Nature* (Princeton, 1979). For a sympathetic yet biting critique of this book, see my review in *Union Seminary Quarterly Review*, vol, 37, nos. 1, 2, (Fall-Winter 1981–82).

3. The central works on this subject are Max Horkheimer and Theodor Adorno, *Dialectic of Enlightenment* (New York, 1972); Herbert Marcuse, *One-Dimensional Man: Studies in the Ideology of Advanced Industrial Society* (Boston, 1964); Stanley Aronowitz, *The Crisis in Historical Materialism: Class, Politics and Culture in Marxist Theory* (New York, 1981); Michel Foucault, *Discipline and Punish: The Birth of the Prison*, trans. Alan Sheridan (New York, 1977).

4. For a brief treatment of these two basic notions as a basis for prophetic Christian and progressive Marxist praxis, see Cornel West, *Prophesy Deliverance! An Afro-American Revolutionary Christianity* (Philadelphia, 1982), "Introduction: The Sources and Tasks of Afro-American Critical Thought."

5. Michel Foucault, *Power/Knowledge: Selected Interviews & Other Writings 1972–1977* (New York, 1980), p. 133.

6. For a rudimentary effort at such a genealogical approach, see Cornel West, *Prophesy Deliverance! An Afro-American Revolutionary Christianity* (Philadelphia, 1982), Chapter 2.

7. For a humble attempt at such a project, see Cornel West, "Philosophy and the Afro-American Experience," *The Philosophical Forum*, vol. IX, nos. 2–3 (Winter-Spring 1977–78), pp. 117–148, and, with additions and revisions, Cornel West, *Prophesy Deliverance! An Afro-American Revolutionary Christianity* (Philadelphia, 1982), Chapter 3.

## Recommended Readings

TEXTS

Best, Steven, and Douglas Kellner. *Postmodern Theory*. New York: The Guilford Press, 1991.
Dreyfus, Hubert, and Paul Rabinow. *Michel Foucault: Beyond Structuralism and Hermeneutics*.
   Chicago: University of Chicago, 1983.

Foucault, Michel. *The Archaeology of Knowledge.* New York: Pantheon, 1972.

Giddens, A. "Jürgen Habermas." In *The Return of Grand Theory in the Human Sciences,* edited by Q. Skinner, 121–139. Cambridge: Cambridge University Press, 1985.

Habermas, Jürgen. *Between Facts and Norms.* Cambridge: MIT, 1996.

Ingram, D. *Habermas and the Dialectic of Reason.* New Haven, CT: Yale University Press, 1987.

McCarthy, T. *The Critical Theory of Jürgen Habermas.* Cambridge, MA: MIT Press, 1978.

Rabinow, Paul, ed. *Foucault Reader.* New York: Pantheon Books, 1984.

White, S. K. *The Recent Work of Jürgen Habermas: Reason, Justice, and Modernity.* Cambridge: Cambridge University Press, 1989.

### FEMINIST PERSPECTIVE

Fraser, N. "What's Critical about Critical Theory? The Case of Habermas and Gender." In *Feminism as Critique: On the Politics of Gender,* edited by S. Benhabib and D. Cornell. Minneapolis, MN: University of Minnesota Press, 1987.

Sawicki, Jana. "Foucault and Feminism." *Hypatia* (1990).

### MULTICULTURAL PERSPECTIVE

Allen Norm, ed. *African-American Humanism.* Buffalo: Prometheus Books, 1991.

Harris, Leonard, ed. *Philosophy Born of Struggle.* Dubuque: Kendall/Hunt, 1983.

# XIII

---

# *MacIntyre and Charles Taylor*

## Introduction

ALASDAIR MACINTYRE WAS BORN IN GLASGOW, SCOTLAND, IN 1929. He holds degrees from the University of London, Manchester University, and Oxford University. He has taught at Princeton, Oxford, Brandeis, Boston, Wesleyan, Vanderbilt, Yale, and Duke universities. He is currently Senior Research Professor at the University of Notre Dame. *After Virtue,* his most important book, was published in 1981. Subsequently, he published *Whose Justice? Which Rationality?* (1988), *Three Rival Versions of Moral Enquiry* (1990), and *Dependent Rational Animals* (1999).

Alasdair MacIntyre sees his political theory as rooted in Aristotelian moral theory, but one that has been refurbished in certain respects. Specifically, MacIntyre claims that Aristotelian moral theory must, first of all, reject any reliance on a metaphysical biology. Instead of appealing to a metaphysical biology, MacIntyre proposes to ground Aristotelian moral theory on a conception of a practice. A practice, for MacIntyre, is "any coherent and complex form of socially established cooperative human activity through which goods internal to that form of activity are realized in the course of trying to achieve those standards of excellence which are appropriate to and partially definitive of that form of activity, with the result that human powers to achieve excellence, and human conceptions of the ends and goods involved are systematically extended." As examples of practices, MacIntyre cites arts, sciences, games, and the making and sustaining of family life.

MacIntyre then partially defines the virtues in terms of practices. A virtue, such as courage, justice, or honesty, is "an acquired human quality the possession and exercise of which tends to enable us to achieve those goods which are internal to practices and the lack of which prevents us from achieving any such goods." However, MacIntyre admits that the virtues that sustain practices can conflict (e.g., courage can conflict with justice) and that practices so defined are not themselves above moral criticism.

Accordingly, to further ground his account, MacIntyre introduces the conception of a *telos* or good of a whole human life conceived as a unity. It is by means of this conception that MacIntyre proposes to morally evaluate practices and resolve conflicts between virtues. For MacIntyre, the telos of a whole human life is a life spent in seeking that telos; it is a quest for the good human life, and it proceeds with only partial knowledge of what is sought. Nevertheless, this quest is never undertaken in isolation but always within some shared tradition. Moreover, such a tradition provides additional resources for evaluating practices and for resolving conflicts while remaining open to moral criticism itself.

MacIntyre's characterization of the human telos in terms of a quest undertaken within a tradition marks a second respect in which he wants to depart from Aristotle's view. This historical dimension to the human telos, which MacIntyre contends is essential for a rationally acceptable communitarian account, is absent from Aristotle's view.

A third respect in which MacIntyre's account departs from Aristotle's concerns the possibility of tragic moral conflicts. As MacIntyre points out, Aristotle only recognized moral conflicts that are the outcome of wrongful or mistaken action. Yet MacIntyre, following Sophocles, wants to recognize the possibility of additional conflicts between rival moral goods that are rooted in the very nature of things.

Rather than drawing out the particular requirements of his own political theory, MacIntyre usually defends his theory by attacking rival theories, and, by and large, he has focused his attacks on liberal political theories. In "The Political and Social Structures of the Common Good," Alasdair MacIntyre argues that for independent practical reasoners Marx's principle for a socialist society—to each according to his or her contribution—is appropriate, but between those capable of giving and those who are most dependent, it is Marx's principle for a communist society—from each according to his or her ability to each according to his or her need—that is appropriate. MacIntyre further argues that these requirements for a common good cannot be secured by either the nation state or the nuclear family. The nation-state is too large, and the interests operating in it too conflicted, to provide such a common good, and families generally lack the self-sufficiency to provide it. Only through the intermediate institutions of the local community, MacIntyre argues, can this common good characterized by a just generosity and other virtues of acknowledged dependence be achieved. To understand how best to achieve this common good of local community, MacIntyre suggests that we do well to study the different types of local community that currently exist or have existed in the past, such as fishing communities in New England, Welsh mining communities, farming cooperatives in Donegal, Mayan towns in Guatemala, and Mexico and city states from a more distant past.

Charles Taylor was born in 1931 in Montreal. He received a B.A. degree from McGill University in 1952 and a Ph.D. in philosophy (D.Phil.) from Oxford University in 1961. He was formerly Chichele Professor of Social and Political Theory at Oxford University and has taught at many universities, among them Princeton University and the University of Montreal. He is now professor at McGill University. Among his books are *Hegel* (1975), *Philosophical Papers* (1985), and *Sources of the Self* (1989), *The Ethics of Authenticity* (1992).

Taylor primarily defends his own political theory by criticizing rival liberal theories. In "Atomism," he criticizes such theories for affirming the primacy of rights over obligations, particularly for affirming the primacy of rights over any obligation to belong to or contribute to a society. The problem is that liberals affirm the rights they do for the sake of achieving certain human goods. These goods, however, cannot be achieved unless societies are formed and structured in certain ways. So, Taylor claims, by affirming the rights they do, liberals are required to affirm a corresponding obligation to belong and contribute to society so as to make the achievement of the related human goods possible. According to Taylor, what liberals fail to see is that you can't endorse liberal rights without endorsing the means necessary for securing those rights. What liberals fail to see is that rights and obligations are equally primary.

Interpreted one way, liberals cannot help but agree with Taylor here. This is because it is generally recognized that rights entail obligations, so that even a right of noninterference entails an obligation on the part of others not to interfere in certain ways. So if Taylor's claim about the equal primacy of rights and obligations is interpreted in this sense, liberals would have no difficulty affirming that the affirmation of rights entail obligations of a certain sort on the part of others.

What is not so clear is that if we affirm a right for the sake of achieving certain human goods, we are thereby obligated to do whatever is necessary to achieve those human goods. Rights of noninterference are one means necessary for achieving the good of autonomy, and if one affirms such rights, one is thereby committed to recognizing an obligation not to interfere with others in certain ways that help protect and secure their autonomy. But rights of noninterference alone are usually not enough to ensure that others will be autonomous. Other means are also needed, and the question is, if we are under an obligation to provide the one means, must we be under an obligation to provide other means as well? Taylor assumes that we are, and so criticizes liberals for not recognizing the extent of their obligations to others.

But it is not so clear that liberals (or we) must accept these additional obligations. Surely, if liberals see themselves as obligated to provide one of the means necessary to secure a certain human good (e.g., the good of autonomy), they must think that the other means necessary for securing that good will generally be provided. Otherwise, their contribution, through noninterference, would be to no avail. In this regard, some liberals (e.g., libertarians) believe that provided that rights of noninterference are secured, mutual advantage and other personal attachments and commitments generally will be enough to secure the relevant goods, and in cases where they will not, it would be too burdensome to further obligate people to provide those goods. Other liberals (e.g., welfare liberals) believe that in such cases where the other means are lacking, people are further obligated to provide the relevant goods. But neither group of liberals holds that just because we recognize an obligation to provide one means that is necessary for achieving certain human goods, we are thereby obligated to provide all the means that are necessary for achieving those goods, as Taylor seems to be arguing.

The general view endorsed by philosophers like MacIntyre and Taylor has been called communitarian because of its emphasis on the common good and on the way we are constituted by the society that we live in. In "Feminism and Modern Friendship: Dislocating the Community," Marilyn Friedman finds communitarianism both attractive and problematic from a feminist perspective. According to Friedman, communitarianism is attractive because it emphasizes the contribution of communities and social relationships to one's self-identity. It is problematic because it tends to uncritically accept just those found communities of family, neighborhood, and nation that feminists have been wont to criticize and transform, and because it does not direct our attention to the kinds of chosen communities that would serve to foster feminist values and goals.

In "Ancient Futures," Helena Norberg-Hodge is critical of the dominant emphasis on economic growth and technological development in existing societies. She suggests that we have much to learn from certain traditional societies, particularly the Ladakhis, a Buddhist community located near Tibet, about how we should live.

In Ladakh, power is decentralized and the economy is regionally based and sustainable. Children grow up in extended families rather than nuclear families. People are able to put down roots and feel attached to a place rather than, as in Western industrialized societies, move as many as six different times while their children are growing up. Norberg-Hodge also maintains that the role of women in traditional Ladakh society is actually preferable to the roles of women in Western industrial societies. Could she be right, then, that our most promising future lies in rediscovering our ancient past?

# 54     The Political and Social Structures of the Common Good

ALASDAIR MACINTYRE

WHAT ARE THE TYPES OF POLITICAL AND SO-cial society that can embody those relationships of giving and receiving through which our individual and common goods can be achieved? They will have to satisfy three conditions. First they must afford expression to the political decision-making of independent reasoners on all those matters on which it is important that the members of a particular community be able to come through shared rational deliberation to a common mind. So there will have to be institutionalized forms of deliberation to which all those members of the community who have proposals, objections and arguments to contribute have access. And the procedures of decision-making will have to be generally acceptable, so that both deliberation and decisions are recognizable as the work of the whole.

Secondly, in a community in which just generosity is counted among the central virtues the established norms of justice will have to be consistent with the exercise of this virtue. No single simple formulation will be capable of capturing the different kinds of norm that will be necessary for different kinds of just relationship. Between in-

dependent practical reasoners the norms will have to satisfy Marx's formula for justice in a socialist society, according to which what each receives is proportionate to what each contributes. Between those capable of giving and those who are most dependent and in most need of receiving—children, the old, the disabled—the norms will have to satisfy a revised version of Marx's formula for justice in a communist society, "From each according to her or his ability, to each, so far as is possible, according to her or his needs' (*Critique of the Gotha Program*, I). Marx of course understood his second formula as having application only in an as yet unrealizable future. And we must recognize that limited economic resources allow only for its application in imperfect ways. But without its application, even if imperfectly, even if *very* imperfectly, we will be unable to sustain a way of life characterized both by effective appeals to desert and by effective appeals to need, and so by justice to and for both the independent and the dependent.

Thirdly, the political structures must make it possible both for those capable of independent practical reason and for those whose exercise of reasoning is limited or nonexistent to have a voice in communal deliberation about what these norms of justice require. And the only way in which the latter can have a voice is if there are others who are able and prepared to stand proxy for them and if the role of proxy is given a formal place in the political structures.

What I am trying to envisage then is a form of political society in which it is taken for granted that disability and dependence on others are something that all of us experience at certain times in our lives and this to unpredictable degrees, and that consequently our interest in how the needs of the disabled are adequately voiced and met is not a special interest, the interest of one particular group rather than of others, but rather the interest of the whole political society, an interest that is integral to their conception of their common good. What kind of society might possess the structures necessary to achieve a common good thus conceived?

If at this point we turn for assistance to recent social and political philosophy, we will be for the most part disappointed, since with rare exceptions work in that area ignores questions about the common goods of associations and relationships that are intermediate between on the one hand the nation-state and on the other the individual and the nuclear family. Yet it is with just this intermediate area that we shall need to be concerned, since those whose relationships embody both a recognition of the independence of practical reasoners and an acknowledgment of the facts of human dependence, and for whom therefore the virtue of just generosity is a key virtue, presuppose in their activities, explicitly, or more usually implicitly, the sharing of a common good that is constitutive of a type of association that can be realized neither in the forms of the modern state nor in those of the contemporary family.

Why not? What is it about the modern state and the contemporary family that renders them incapable of providing the kind of communal association within which this type of common good can be achieved? Let me consider each in turn. Modern nation-states are governed through a series

of compromises between a range of more or less conflicting economic and social interests. What weight is given to different interests varies with the political and economic bargaining power of each and with its ability to ensure that the voices of its protagonists are heard at the relevant bargaining tables. What determines both bargaining power and such ability is in key part money, money used to provide the resources to sustain political power: electoral resources, media resources, relationships to corporations. This use of money procures very different degrees and kinds of political influence for different interests. And the outcome is that although most citizens share, although to greatly varying extents, in such public goods as those of a minimally secure order, the distribution of goods by government in no way reflects a common mind arrived at through widespread shared deliberation governed by norms of rational enquiry. Indeed the size of modern states would itself preclude this. It does not follow that relationships to the nation-state, or rather to the various agencies of government that collectively compose it, are unimportant to those who practice the politics of the virtues of acknowledged dependence. No one can avoid having some significant interest in her or his relationships to the nation-state just because of its massive resources, its coercive legal powers, and the threats that its blundering and distorted benevolence presents. But any rational relationship of the governed to the government of modern states requires individuals and groups to weigh any benefits to be derived from it against the costs of entanglement with it, at least so far as that aspect of states is concerned in which they are and present themselves as giant utility companies.

There is of course another aspect of the modern state in which it presents itself as the guardian of our values and from time to time invites us to die for it. This invitation is one issued by every ruling power that asserts its legitimate and justifiable political and legal sovereignty over its subjects. For no state can justify that assertion unless it is able to provide at least minimal security for its subjects from external aggression and from internal criminality. And the provision of such security generally requires that there be police officers, firefighters, and soldiers prepared, if need arise—and it does arise remarkably often—to give up their lives in the course of their duties. But the importance of the good of public security, although it is a good served by this admirable devotion, and although it is a good without which none of us in our various local communities could achieve our common goods, must not be allowed to obscure the fact that the shared public goods of the modern nation-state are not the common goods of a genuine nationwide community and, when the nation-state masquerades as the guardian of such a common good, the outcome is bound to be either ludicrous or disastrous or both. For the counterpart to the nation-state thus misconceived as itself a community is a misconception of its citizens as constituting a *Volk*, a type of collectivity whose bonds are simultaneously to extend to the entire body of citizens and yet to be as binding as the ties of kinship and locality. In a modern, large scale nation-state no such collectivity is possible and the pretense that it is is always an ideological disguise for sinister realities. I conclude then that insofar as the nation-state provides necessary and important public goods, these must not be confused with the type of common good for which communal recognition is required by the virtues of acknowledged dependence, and that insofar as the rhetoric of the nation-state presents it as the provider of something that is indeed, in this stronger sense, a common good, that rhetoric is a purveyor of dangerous fictions.

The virtues of acknowledged dependence and the virtues of independence require for their practice a very different kind of shared pursuit of a common good. Where the virtues of acknowledged dependence are practiced, there will have to be a common mind as to how responsibilities for and to dependent others are allocated and what standards of success or failure in discharging these responsibilities are appropriate. And, where the virtues of independent practical reasoning are practiced, such a common mind will have to emerge from shared deliberation, so that social agreement on responsibilities will not only be, but be seen to be rationally justified. Hence those who practice both sets of virtues will have a double attitude to the nation-state. They will recognize that it is an ineliminable feature of the contemporary landscape and they will not despise the resources that it affords. It may and on occasion does provide the only means for removing obstacles to humane goals and we all have reason, for example, to be very grateful indeed to those who secured the passage of the Americans with Disabilities Act and to those who have used its provisions constructively and creatively. But they will also recognize that the modern state cannot provide a political framework informed by the just generosity necessary to achieve the common goods of networks of giving and receiving.

If then the nation-state cannot provide a form of association directed towards the relevant type of common good, what of the family? Families at their best are forms of association in which children are first nurtured, and then educated for and initiated into the activities of an adult world in which their parents' participatory activities provide them both with resources and models. It follows that the quality of life of a family is in key part a function of the quality of the relationships of the individual members of the family to and in a variety of other institutions and associations: workplaces, schools, parishes, sports clubs, trade union branches, adult education classes, and the like. And it is insofar as children learn to recognize and to pursue as their own, and parents and other adult members of the family continue to recognize and to pursue, the goods internal to the practices of which such associations and institutions are the milieu that the goods of family life are realized. The family flourishes only if its social environment also flourishes. And since the social environments of families vary a great deal, so do the modes of flourishing of families. All happy families are not alike and only a very great novelist could have got away with telling us otherwise. And as it is with the strengths and achievements of family life, so it is also with its weaknesses and failures. They too are inseparable from features of the social environment of the family. (I do not want to suggest by this that families cannot sometimes flourish in highly unfavorable conditions. They can and do. But, when they can and do, it is always because the family members and more especially the parents have been able to construct for that family a range of activities and opportunities that substitute for those of a more favorable social environment. So, for example, for a family living successfully in conditions of extreme isolation, perhaps a hundred miles from their nearest neighbors, the activity of workplace, of school, of parish, and of play may all become activities of the household. That household will have become a microcosm of community and not only a family. Yet this must clearly be an exceptional type of case.)

Generally and characteristically then the goods of family life are achieved in and with the goods of various types of local community. And generally and characteristically the common good of a family can only be achieved in the course of achieving the common goods of the local community of which it is a part. It is because of the family's lack of self-sufficiency that the type of common good recognition of which is required by the virtues of acknowledged dependence cannot be achieved within the family, at least insofar as the family is conceived of as a distinct and separate social unit. Yet families are of course key and indispensable constituents of local community and there are many areas of family life in which the exercise of the virtues of acknowledged dependence is called for. Indeed, as I suggested earlier, the relationships of parents to young children and of adults to their elderly parents are both paradigm cases of relationships that can be sustained only by those virtues. And so is the relationship of the able and independent members of a family to other members who are temporarily or permanently disabled and largely or wholly dependent.

Neither the state nor the family then is the form of association whose common good is to be both served and sustained by the virtues of acknowledged dependence. It must instead be some form of local community within which the activities of families, workplaces, schools, clinics, clubs dedicated to debate and clubs dedicated to games and sports, and religious congregations may all find a place. What kind of place then are those who are temporarily or permanently disabled able to have in such a community? What kind of recognition is

the recognition required to sustain respect both for them and for those not disabled, as well as their self-respect? It will build upon that regard for each individual, however badly disabled, that I characterized earlier. But it will add to that regard a recognition that each member of the community is someone from whom we may learn and may have to learn about our common good and our own good, and who always may have lessons to teach us about those goods that we will not be able to learn elsewhere. It is not primarily because others find what we achieve worthwhile that we are owed this respect. For even at those times when we are disabled so that we cannot engage in worthwhile projects we are still owed by others and we still owe to others that attentive care without which neither we nor they can learn what we have to teach each other. . . .

Political reasoning at the level of practice is not a special kind of reasoning, one distinct from ordinary practical reasoning. One cannot generally become an effective practical reasoner without becoming in some measure a political reasoner, and this for two reasons. First, because participants in networks of giving and receiving are only able to identify their individual goods in the course of identifying their common goods, and because their identification of those common goods can only be achieved by contributing to and learning from shared deliberation with those others whose common goods they are, an ability to reason practically about the common good is indispensable. But to reason together about the common good is to reason politically.

Secondly, so many of our goods, individual as well as common, are shared goods that generally my decisions about what part certain goods are to play in my life will not be and cannot be independent of our decisions about what part those goods are to play in the life of our community. I will not be able to find a place, whether a larger or smaller place, for dramatic art in my own life—as amateur or professional actor, as director or stagehand, as a member of the orchestra or the audience—in a community in which the goods of theater are not given a certain priority in the allocation of communal resources. It is in and through political decisions about these priorities that we determine the range of possibilities open for the shaping of our individual lives and, if we exclude ourselves or are excluded by others from contributing to such political decision-making, we diminish the scope and effectiveness of our decision-making.

This suggests that the account advanced so far of the prerequisites for a political community whose common good would be that of social networks of giving and receiving badly needs to be supplemented, if it is not to be misleading. For I have asked what attitudes of regard we should take to each other, whether able or disabled, if we are to satisfy the requirements of such virtues as that of just generosity, as though we could first answer that question and only then as a secondary matter enquire what kinds of political structures might give expression to such attitudes. But it now becomes clear that these attitudes of regard must be understood from the outset as political attitudes. To treat someone else as someone for whom we have a regard because of what, one way or another, they contribute to our shared education in becoming rational givers and receivers is to accord them political recognition. It is to treat them as someone whom it would be wrong to ignore or to exclude from political deliberation.

This conception of political reasoning as one aspect of everyday practical reasoning has as its counterpart a conception of political activity as one aspect of the everyday activity of every adult capable of engaging in it. The contrast is with the conception of political activity embodied in the modern state, according to which there is a small minority of the population who are to make politics their active occupation and preoccupation, professional and semiprofessional politicians, and a huge largely passive majority who are to be mobilized only at periodic intervals, for elections or national crises. Between the political elites on the one hand and the larger population on the other there are important differences, as in, for example, how much or how little information is required and provided for each. A modern electorate can only function as it does, so long as it has only a highly simplified and impoverished account of the issues that are presented to it. And the modes of presentation through which elites address electorates are designed to conceal as much as to reveal.

These are not accidental features of the politics of modern states any more than is the part that money plays in affording influence upon the decision-making process. The sometimes revolutionary struggles of the past that broke down the barriers to achieving modern citizenship—to abolish slavery, to extend the suffrage, especially to women, to secure for the labor movement defenses against capitalist exploitation and victimization—involved degrees and kinds of effective political participation that are quite as alien to the democratic forms of the politics of the contemporary state as they are to nondemocratic forms. It is not at all, as I have already stressed, that the politics of the state have become unimportant. There are numerous crucial needs of local communities that can only be met by making use of state resources and invoking the interventions of state agencies. But it is the quality of the politics of local communities that will be crucial in defining those needs adequately and in seeing to it that they are met.

It is therefore a mistake, the communitarian mistake, to attempt to infuse the politics of the state with the values and modes of participation in local community. It is a further mistake to suppose that there is anything good about local community as such. The relatively small-scale character and the face-to-face encounters and conversations of local community are necessary for the shared achievement of the common goods of those who participate in the rational deliberation needed to sustain networks of giving and receiving, but, absent the virtues of just generosity and of shared deliberation, local communities are always open to corruption by narrowness, by complacency, by prejudice against outsiders and by a whole range of other deformities, including those that arise from a cult of local community.

This is one point at which the discussions of moral and political philosophers benefit from becoming historical and sociological. We need to set side by side for comparative study examples of different types of local community, examples of such communities at their best and at their worst, and most of all examples of communities that have been or are open to alternative possibilities and that sometimes move towards the better and sometimes towards the worse. So it would be instructive to look at the history of some fishing communities in New England over the past hundred and fifty years and to examine the different ways in which at different times their virtues have enabled them to cope with the stress of adversity and with the stress of prosperity. And it would be similarly instructive to examine the history of Welsh mining communities and of a way of life informed by the ethics of work at the coal face, by a passion for the goods of choral singing and of rugby football and by the virtues of trade union struggle against first coal-owners and then the state. Such examples can be multiplied: farming cooperatives in Donegal, Mayan towns in Guatemala and Mexico, some city-states from a more distant past.

What such comparative studies will bring home to us is both the variety of social forms within which networks of giving and receiving can be institutionalized and the variety of ways in which such networks can be sustained and strengthened or weakened and destroyed. Different conditions pose different threats that in turn require different responses. Yet the tasks that have to be undertaken to meet those threats share a great deal in common. So it is, for example, with the tasks of providing for the security of a local community from internal crime or external aggression, tasks that can never safely be handed over completely to the agencies of the state. (On occasion it is the danger presented by just those agencies that has to be guarded against.) Those who perform such tasks on behalf of the community are asked by the community to be prepared, if necessary, to risk their lives, but to ask this can only be justified, if those who accept this risk can be confident that they, if disabled, or their dependents, if they die, will receive adequate care. The defense of a community whose structures are governed by norms of relatively uncalculated giving and receiving, if it is in good order, will itself be similarly structured. Yet the forms taken by those structures will vary with the culture and the history of the community.

What extended comparative study of the varying characteristics of communities that embody networks of giving and receiving may teach us is how better to identify what relationships of the relevant kinds of giving and receiving already exist in our own local community and how perhaps to greater extent than we have realized there is already a degree of shared recognition of the common good. About such communities we will need to bear in mind three things. First, even when they are at their best, the exercise of shared deliberative rationality is always imperfect and what should impress us is not so much the mistakes made and the limitations upon its exercise at any particular stage as the ability through time and conflict to correct those mistakes and to move beyond those limitations. The exercise of practical relationships in communities always has a history and it is the direction of that history that is important.

Secondly, the politics of such communities, when they are at their best or are at least moving in the right direction, is not a politics of competing interests in the way in which the politics of the modern state is. For the basic political question is what resources each individual and group needs, if it is to make its particular contribution to the common good, and, insofar as the community if in good order, it is to the interest of all that each should be able to make its contribution. Of course because local communities are always to some degree imperfect, competing interests are always apt to emerge. And it is therefore important that, so far as is possible, communities are structured so as to limit such emergence. Economically what matters is that there should be relatively small inequalities of income or wealth. For gross inequality of income or wealth is by itself always liable to generate conflicts of interests and to obscure the possibility of understanding one's social relationships in terms of a common good.

This is of course only one example of how economic considerations will have to be subordinated to social and moral considerations, if a local community that is a network of giving and receiving is to survive, let alone thrive. There may have to be self-imposed limits to labor mobility for the sake of the continuities and the stabilities of families and other institutions. There will have to be what from an economic point of view is disproportionate investment in types of education of children that are not economically productive. Everyone, so far as is possible, will have to take their turn in performing the tedious and the dangerous jobs, in order to avoid another disruptive form of social inequality. These are of course Utopian standards, not too often realized outside Utopia, and only then, as I have already suggested, in flawed ways. But trying to live by Utopian standards is not Utopian, although it does involve a rejection of the economic goals of advanced capitalism. For the institutional forms through which such a way of life is realized, although economically various, have this in common: they do not promote economic growth and they require some significant degree of insulation from and protection from the forces generated by outside markets. Most importantly, such a society will be inimical to and in conflict with the goals of a consumer society. But to take note of this directs our attention to the extent to which these norms are to some extent already accepted in a variety of those settings—households, workplaces, schools, parishes—in which resistance to the goals and norms of a consumer society is recurrently generated. And, where such resistance is found, it is characteristically within groups whose social relationships are those of giving and receiving.

Thirdly, among the distinguishing marks of communities thus structured is the importance that they attach to the needs of children and the needs of the disabled. Partly this is a matter of the allocation of attention and other resources. Children are never able to constitute an interest group in the modern sense of that word. And what children need can rarely be adequately supplied only by their own families. They are therefore cared for adequately only when the care that they receive, although inevitably constrained by the limits of the community's resources, is not constrained by predictions about how much those children will one day give in return. And as it is with the care needed by children, so it is too with the care needed by the old and the mentally and physically infirm. What matters is not only that in this kind of community children and the disabled are objects of care and attention. It matters also and correspondingly that those who are no longer children recognize in children what they once were, that those who are not yet disabled by age recognize in the old what they are moving towards becoming, and that those who are not ill or injured recognize in the ill and injured what they often have been and will be and always may be. It matters also that these recognitions are not a source of fear. For such recognitions are a condition of adequate awareness of both the common needs and the common goods that are served by networks of giving and receiving and by the virtues, both of independence and of acknowledged dependence. Yet that awareness cannot itself be achieved without those same virtues.

# 55    Atomism

## CHARLES TAYLOR

I WOULD LIKE TO EXAMINE THE ISSUE of political atomism, or at least to try to clarify what this issue is. I want to say what I think atomist doctrines consist in, and to examine how the issue can be joined around them—this is, how they might be proved or disproved, or at least cogently argued for or against, and what in turn they may be used to prove.

The term "atomism" is used loosely to characterize the doctrines of social-contract theory which arose in the seventeenth century and also successor doctrines which may not have made use of the notion of social contract but which inherited a vision of society as in some sense constituted by individuals for the fulfillment of ends which were primarily individual. Certain forms of utilitarianism are successor doctrines in this sense. The term is also applied to contemporary doctrines which hark back to social-contract theory, or which try to defend in some sense the priority of the individual and his rights over society, or which present a purely instrumental view of society.

Of course, any term loosely used in political discourse can be defined in a host of ways. And perhaps one should even leave out of philosophical discourse altogether those terms which tend to be branded as epithets of condemnation in the battle between different views. One might well argue that "atomism" is one such, because it seems to be used almost exclusively by its enemies. Even extreme individualists like Nozick don't seem to warm to this term, but tend to prefer others, like "individualism."

Perhaps I am dealing with the wrong term. But there is a central issue in political theory which is eminently worth getting at under some description. And perhaps the best way of getting at it is this: what I am calling atomist doctrines underlie the seventeenth-century revolution in the terms of normative discourse, which we associate with the names of Hobbes and Locke.

These writers, and others who presented social-contract views, have left us a legacy of political thinking in which the notion of rights plays a central part in the justification of political structures and action. The central doctrine of this tradition is an affirmation of what we could call the primacy of rights.

Theories which assert the primacy of rights are those which take as the fundamental, or at least a fundamental, principle of their political theory the ascription of certain rights to individuals and which deny the same status to a principle of belonging or obligation, that is a principle which states our obligation as men to belong to or sustain society, or a society of a certain type, or to obey authority or an authority of a certain type. Primacy-of-right theories in other words accept a principle ascribing rights to men as binding unconditionally,[1] binding, that is, on men as such. But they do not accept as similarly unconditional a principle of belonging or obligation. Rather our obligation to belong to or sustain a society, or to obey its authorities, is seen as derivative, as laid on us conditionally, through our consent, or through its being to our advantage. The obligation to belong is derived in certain conditions from the more fundamental principle which ascribes rights.[2]

The paradigm of primacy-of-right theories is plainly that of Locke. But there are contemporary theories of this kind, one of the best known in recent years being that of Robert Nozick.[3] Nozick too makes the assertion of rights to individuals fundamental and then proceeds to discuss whether and in what conditions we can legitimately demand obedience to a state.

Primacy-of-right theories have been one of the formative influences on modern political consciousness. Thus arguments like that of Nozick have at least a surface plausibility for our contemporaries and sometimes considerably more. At the very least, opponents are brought up short, and have to ponder how to meet the claims of an argument which reaches conclusions about political obedience which lie far outside the common sense of our society; and this because the starting-point in individual rights has an undeniable *prima facie* force for us.

This is striking because it would not always have been so. In an earlier phase of Western civilization, of course, not to speak of other civilizations, these arguments would have seemed wildly eccentric and implausible. The very idea of starting an argument whose foundation was the rights of the individual would have been strange and puzzling—about as puzzling as if I were to start with the premise that the Queen rules by divine right. You might not dismiss what I said out of hand, but you would expect that I should at least have the sense to start with some less contentious premiss and argue up to divine right, not take it as my starting-point.

Why do we even begin to find it reasonable to start a political theory with an assertion of individual rights and to give these primacy? I want to argue that the answer to this question lies in the hold on us of what I have called atomism. Atomism represents a view about human nature and the human condition which (among other things) makes a doctrine of the primacy of rights plausible; or, to put it negatively, it is a view in the absence of which this doctrine is suspect to the point of being virtually untenable.

How can we formulate this view? Perhaps the best way is to borrow the terms of the opposed thesis—the view that man is a social animal. One of the most influential formulations of this view is Aristotle's. He puts the point in terms of the notion of self-sufficiency (*autarkeia*). Man is a social animal, indeed a political animal, because he is not self-sufficient alone, and in an important sense is not self-sufficient outside a *polis*. Borrowing this term then, we could say that atomism affirms the self-sufficiency of man alone or, if you prefer, of the individual.

That the primacy-of-rights doctrine needs a background of this kind may appear evident to some; but it needs to be argued because it is vigorously denied by others. And generally proponents of the doctrine are among the most vigorous deniers. They will not generally admit that the assertion of rights is dependent on any particular view about the nature of man, especially one as difficult to formulate and make clear as this. And to make their political theory dependent on a thesis formulated in just this way seems to be adding insult to injury. For if atomism means that man is self-sufficient alone, then surely it is a very questionable thesis. . . .

The claim I am trying to make could be summed up in this way. (1) To ascribe the natural (not just legal) right of X to agent A is to affirm that A commands our respect, such that we are normally bound not to interfere with A's doing or enjoying of X. This means that to ascribe the right is far more than simply to issue the injunction: don't interfere with A's doing or enjoying X. The injunction can be issued, to self or others, without grounds, should we so choose. But to affirm the right is to say that a creature such as A lays a moral claim on us not to interfere. It thus also asserts something about A: A is such that this injunction is somehow inescapable.

(2) We may probe further and try to define what it is about A which makes the injunction inescapable. We can call this, whatever it is, A's essential property or properties, E. Then it is E (in our case, the essentially human capacities) which defines not only who are the bearers of rights but what they have rights to. A has a natural right to X, if doing or enjoying X is essentially part of manifesting E (e.g., if E is being a rational life-form, then A's have a natural right to life and also to the unimpeded development of rationality); or if X is a causally necessary condition of manifesting E (e.g., the ownership of property, which has been widely believed to be a necessary safeguard of life or freedom, or a living wage).

(3) The assertion of a natural right, while it lays on us the injunction to respect A in his doing or enjoying of X, cannot but have other moral consequences as well. For if A is such that this injunction is inescapable and he is such in virtue of E, then E is of great moral worth and ought to be fostered and developed in a host of appropriate ways, and not just not interfered with.

Hence asserting a right is more than issuing an injunction. It has an essential conceptual background, in some notion of the moral worth of certain properties or capacities, without which it would not make sense. Thus, for example, our position would be incomprehensible and incoherent if we ascribed rights to human beings in respect of the specifically human capacities (such as the right to one's own convictions or to the free choice of one's life-style or profession) while at the same time denying that these capacities ought to be developed, or if we thought it a matter of indifference whether they were realized or stifled in ourselves or others.

From this we can see that the answer to [the] question . . . why do we ascribe these rights to men and not to animals, rocks, or trees . . . is quite straightforward. It is because men and women are the beings who exhibit certain capacities which are worthy of respect. The fact that we ascribe rights to idiots, people in a coma, bad men who have irretrievably turned their back on the proper development of these capacities, and so on, does not show that the capacities are irrelevant. It shows only that we have a powerful sense that the status of being a creature defined by its potential for these capacities cannot be lost. This sense has been given a rational account in certain ways, such as, for instance, by the belief in an immortal soul. But it is interestingly enough shared even by those who have rejected all such traditional rationales. We sense that in the incurable psychotic there runs a current of human life, where the definition of "human" may be uncertain but relates to the specifically human capacities; we sense that he has feelings that only a human being, a language-using animal, can have, that his dreams and fantasies are those which only a human can have. Pushed however deep, and however distorted, his humanity cannot be eradicated.

If we look at another extreme case, that of persons in a terminal but long-lasting coma, it would seem that the sense that many have that the life-support machines should be disconnected is based partly on the feeling that the patients themselves, should they *per impossible* be able to choose, would not want to continue, precisely because the range of human life has been shrunk here to zero.

How does the notion then arise that we can assert rights outside of a context of affirming the worth of certain capacities? The answer to this question will take us deep into the issue central to the modern thought of the nature of the subject. We can give but a partial account here. There clearly are a wide number of different conceptions of the characteristically human capacities and thus differences too in what are recognized as rights. I will come back to this in another connection later.

But what is relevant for our purposes here is that there are some views of the properly human which give absolutely central importance to the freedom to choose one's own mode of life. Those who hold this ultra-liberal view are chary about allowing that the assertion of right involves any affirmation about realizing certain potentialities; for they fear that the affirming of any obligations will offer a pretext for the restriction of freedom. To say that we have a right to be free to choose our life-form must be to say that any choice is equally compatible with this principle of freedom and that no choices can be judged morally better or worse by this principle—although, of course, we might want to discriminate between them on the basis of other principles.

Thus if I have a right to do what I want with my property, then any disposition I choose is equally justifiable from the point of view of this principle: I may be judged uncharitable if I hoard it to myself and won't help those in need, or uncreative if I bury it in the ground and don't engage in interesting enterprises with it. But these latter criticisms arise from our accepting other moral standards, quite independent from the view that we have a right to do what we want with our own.

But this independence from a moral obligation of self-realization cannot be made good all around. All choices are equally valid; but they must be *choices*. The view that makes freedom of choice this absolute is one that exalts choice as a human capacity. It carries with it the demand that we become beings capable of choice, that we rise to the level of self-consciousness and autonomy where we can exercise choice, that we not remain enmired through fear, sloth, ignorance, or superstition in some code imposed by tradition, society, or fate which tells us how we should dispose of what belongs to us. Ultra-liberalism can only appear unconnected with any affirmation of worth and hence obligation of self-fulfillment, where people have come to accept the utterly facile moral psychology of traditional empiricism, according to which human agents possess the full capacity of choice as a given rather than as a potential which has to be developed.

If all this is valid, then the doctrine of the primacy of rights is not as independent as its proponents want to claim from considerations about human nature and the human social condition. For the doctrine could be undermined by arguments which succeeded in showing that men were not self-sufficient in the sense of the above argument—that is, that they could not develop their characteristically human potentialities outside of society or outside of certain kinds of society. The doctrine would in this sense be dependent on an atomist thesis, which affirms this kind of self-sufficiency.

The connection I want to establish here can be made following the earlier discussion of the background of rights. If we cannot ascribe natural rights without affirming the worth of certain human capacities, and if this affirmation has other normative consequences (i.e., that we should foster and nurture these capacities in ourselves and others), then any proof that these capacities can only develop in society or in a society of a certain kind is a proof that we ought to belong to or sustain society or this kind of society. But then, provided a social (i.e., an anti-atomist) thesis of the right kind can be true, an assertion of the primacy of rights is impossible; for to assert the rights in question is to affirm the capacities, and, granted the social thesis is true concerning these capacities, this commits us to an obligation to belong. This will be as fundamental as the assertion of rights, because it will be inseparable from it. So it would be incoherent to try to assert the rights, while denying the obligation or giving it the status of an optional extra which we may or may not contract; this assertion is what the primacy doctrine makes.

The normative incoherence becomes evident if we see what it would be to assert the primacy of rights in the face of such a social thesis. Let us accept, for the sake of this argument, the view that men cannot develop the fullness of moral autonomy—that is, the capacity to form independent moral convictions—outside a political culture sustained by institutions of political participation and guarantees of personal independence. In fact, I do not think this thesis is true as it stands, although I do believe that a much more compli-

cated view, formed from this one by adding a number of significant reservations, is tenable. But, for the sake of simplicity, let us accept this thesis in order to see the logic of the arguments.

Now if we assert the right to one's own independent moral convictions, we cannot in the face of this social thesis go on to assert the primacy of rights, that is, claim that we are not under obligation "by nature" to belong to and sustain a society of the relevant type. We could not, for instance, unreservedly assert our right in the face of, or at the expense of, such a society; in the event of conflict we should have to acknowledge that we were legitimately pulled both ways. For in undermining such a society we should be making the activity defended by the right assertion impossible of realization. But if we are justified in asserting the right, we cannot be justified in our undermining; for the same considerations which justify the first condemn the second.

In whatever way the conflict might arise it poses a moral dilemma for us. It may be that we have already been formed in this culture and that the demise of this mode of society will not deprive us of this capacity. But in asserting our rights to the point of destroying the society, we should be depriving all those who follow after us of the exercise of the same capacity. To believe that there is a right to independent moral convictions must be to believe that the exercise of the relevant capacity is a human good. But then it cannot be right, if no over-riding considerations intervene, to act so as to make this good less available to others, even though in so doing I could not be said to be depriving them of their rights.

The incoherence of asserting primacy of rights is even clearer if we imagine another way in which the conflict could arise: that, in destroying the society, I would be undermining my own future ability to realize this capacity. For then, in defending my right, I should be condemning myself to what I should have to acknowledge as a truncated mode of life, in virtue of the same considerations that make me affirm the right. And this would be a paradoxical thing to defend as an affirmation of my rights—in the same way as it would be paradoxical for me to offer to defend you against those who menace your freedom by hiding you in my deep freeze. I would have to have misunderstood what freedom is all about; and similarly, in the above case, I should have lost my grasp of what affirming a right is.

We could put the point in another way. The affirmation of certain rights involves us in affirming the worth of certain capacities and thus in accepting certain standards by which a life may be judged full or truncated. We cannot then sensibly claim the morality of a truncated form of life for people on the ground of defending their rights. Would I be respecting your right to life if I agreed to leave you alive in a hospital bed, in an irreversible coma, hooked up to life-support machines? Or suppose I offered to use my new machine to erase totally your personality and memories and give you quite different ones? These questions are inescapably rhetorical. We cannot take them seriously as genuine questions because of the whole set of intuitions which surround our affirmation of the right to life. We assert this right because human life has a certain worth; but exactly wherein it has worth is negated by the appalling conditions I am offering you. That is why the offer is a sick joke, the lines of the mad scientist in a B movie.

It is the mad scientists's question, and not the question whether the person in the coma still enjoys rights, which should be decisive for the issue of whether asserting rights involves affirming the worth of certain capacities. For the latter question just probes the conditions of a right being valid; whereas the former shows us what it is to respect a right and hence what is really being asserted in a rights claim. It enables us to see what else we are committed to in asserting a right.

How would it do for the scientist to say, "Well, I have respected his right to *life,* it is other rights (free movement, exercise of his profession, etc.) which I have violated"? For the separation in this context is absurd. True, we do sometimes enumerate these and other rights. But the right to life could never have been understood as excluding all these activities, as a right just to biological non-death in a coma. It is incomprehensible how any-

one could assert a right to life meaning just this. "Who calls that living?" would be the standard reaction. We could understand such an exiguous definition of life in the context of forensic medicine, for instance, but not in the affirmation of a right to life. And this is because the right-assertion is also an affirmation of worth, and this would be incomprehensible on behalf of this shadow of life.

If these arguments are valid, then the terms of the arguments are very different from what they are seen to be by most believers in the primacy of rights. Nozick, for instance, seems to feel that he can start from our intuitions that people have certain rights to dispose, say, of what they own so long as they harm no one else in doing so; and that we can build up (or fail to build up) a case for legitimate allegiance to certain forms of society and/or authority from this basis, by showing how they do not violate the rights. But he does not recognize that asserting rights itself involves acknowledging an obligation to belong. If the above considerations are valid, one cannot just baldly start with such an assertion of primacy. We would have to show that the relevant potentially mediating social theses are not valid; or, in other terms, we would have to defend a thesis of social atomism, that men are self-sufficient outside of society. We would have to establish the validity of arguing from the primacy of right.

But we can still try to resist this conclusion, in two ways. We can resist it first of all in asserting a certain schedule of rights. Suppose I make the basic right I assert that to life, on the grounds of sentience. This I understand in the broad sense that includes also other animals. Now sentience, as was said above, is not a capacity which can be realized or remain undeveloped; living things have it, and in dying they fail to have it; and there is an end to it. This is not to say that there are not conditions of severe impairment which constitute an infringement on sentient life, short of death. And clearly a right to life based on sentience would rule out accepting the mad scientist's offer just as much as any other conception of this right. But sentient life, while it can be impaired, is not a potential which we must develop and frequently fail to develop, as is the capacity to be a morally autonomous agent, or the capacity for self-determining freedom, or the capacity for the full realization of our talents.

But if we are not dealing with a capacity which can be underdeveloped in this sense, then there is no room for a thesis about the conditions of its development, whether social or otherwise. No social thesis is relevant. We are sentient beings whatever the social organization (or lack of it) of our existence; and if our basic right is to life, and the grounds of this right concern sentience (being capable of self-feeling, of desire and its satisfaction/frustration, of experiencing pain and pleasure), then surely we are beings of this kind in any society or none. In this regard we are surely self-sufficient.

I am not sure that even this is true—that is, that we really are self-sufficient even in regard to sentience. But it certainly is widely thought likely that we are. And therefore it is not surprising that the turn to theories of the primacy of rights goes along with an accentuation of the right to life which stresses life as sentience. For Hobbes our attachment to life is our desire to go on being agents of desire. The connection is not hard to understand. Social theories require a conception of the properly human life which is such that we are not assured it by simply being alive, but it must be developed and it can fail to be developed; on this basis they can argue that society or a certain form of society is the essential condition of this development. But Hobbesian nominalism involves rejecting utterly all such talk of forms or qualities of life which are properly human. Man is a being with desires, all of them on the same level. "Whatsoever is the object of any man's desire . . . that is it which he for his part calleth good."[4] At one stroke there is no further room for a social thesis; and at the same time the right to life is interpreted in terms of desire. To be alive now in the meaning of the act is to be an agent of desires.

So we can escape the whole argument about self-sufficiency, it would seem, by making our schedule of rights sparse enough. Primacy-of-rights talk tends to go with a tough-mindedness which dismisses discussion of the properly human life-form as empty and metaphysical. From within its philosophical position, it is impregnable; but this does not mean that it is not still open to objection.

For the impregnability is purchased at a high price. To affirm a right for man merely *qua* desiring being, or a being feeling pleasure and pain, is to restrict his rights to those of life, desire-fulfillment, and freedom from pain. Other widely claimed rights, like freedom, enter only as means to these basic ones. If one is a monster of (at least attempted) consistency, like Hobbes, then one will be willing to stick to this exiguous conception of rights regardless of the consequences. But even then the question will arise of what on this view is the value of human as against animal life; and of whether it really is not a violation of people's rights if we transform them, unknown to themselves, into child-like lotus-eaters, say, by injecting them with some drug.

In fact, most of those who want to affirm the primacy of rights are more interested in asserting the right of freedom, and moreover, in a sense which can only be attributed to humans, freedom to choose life plans, to dispose of possessions, to form one's own convictions and within reason act on them, and so on. But then we are dealing with capacities which do not simply belong to us in virtue of being alive—capacities which at least in some cases can fail to be properly developed; thus, the question of the proper conditions for their development arises.

We might query whether this is so with one of the freedoms mentioned above—that to dispose of one's own possessions. This is the right to property which has figured prominently with the right to life in the schedules put forward by defenders of primacy. Surely this right, while not something we can attribute to an animal, does not presuppose a capacity which could fail to be developed, at least for normal adults! We all are capable of possessing things, of knowing what we possess, and of deciding what we want to do with these possessions.

This right does not seem to presuppose a capacity needing development, as does the right to profess independent convictions, for instance.

But those who assert this right almost always are affirming a capacity which we can fail to develop. And this becomes evident when we probe the reason for asserting this right. The standard answer, which comes to us from Locke, is that we need the right to property as an essential underpinning of life. But this is patently not true. Men have survived very well in communal societies all the way from paleolithic hunting clans through the Inca empire to contemporary China. And if one protests that the issue is not under what conditions one would not starve to death, but rather under what conditions one is independent enough of society not to be at its mercy for one's life, then the answer is that, if the whole point is being secure in my life, then I would be at less risk of death from agents of my own society in the contemporary Chinese commune than I would be in contemporary Chile. The property regime is hardly the only relevant variable.

But the real point is this: supposing a proponent of the right to property were to admit that the above was true—that the right to property does not as such secure life—would he change his mind? And the answer is, in the vast majority of cases, no. For what is at stake for him is not just life, but life in freedom. My life is safe in a Chinese commune, he might agree, but that is so only for so long as I keep quiet and do not profess heterodox opinions; otherwise the risks are very great. Private property is seen as essential, because it is thought to be an essential part of a life of genuine independence. But realizing a life of this form involves developing the capacity to act and choose in a genuinely independent way. And here the issue of whether a relevant social thesis is not valid can arise.

Hence this way of resisting the necessity of arguing for self-sufficiency (by scaling down one's schedules of rights to mere sentience or desire) is hardly likely to appeal to most proponents of primacy—once they understand the price they pay. For it involves sacrificing the central good of freedom, which it is their principal motive to safeguard.

There remains another way of avoiding the issue. A proponent of primacy could admit that the question arises of the conditions for the development of the relevant capacities; he could even agree that a human being entirely alone could not possibly develop them (this is pretty hard to contest: wolf-boys are not candidates for properly human freedoms), and yet argue that society in the relevant sense was not necessary.

Certainly humans need others in order to develop as full human beings, he would agree. We must all be nurtured by others as children. We can only flourish as adults in relationship with friends, mates, children, and so on. But all this has nothing to do with any obligations to belong to political society. The argument about the state of nature should never have been taken as applying to human beings alone in the wilderness. This is a Rousseauian gloss, but is clearly not the conception of the state of nature with Locke, for instance. Rather it is clear that men must live in families (however families are constituted); that they need families even to grow up human; and that they continue to need them to express an important part of their humanity.

But what obligations to belong does this put on them? It gives us obligations in regard to our parents. But these are obligations of gratitude, and are of a different kind, for when we are ready to discharge these obligations our parents are no longer essential conditions of our human development. The corresponding obligations are to our children, to give them what we have been given; and for the rest we owe a debt to those with whom we are linked in marriage, friendship, association, and the like. But all this is perfectly acceptable to a proponent of the primacy of rights. For all obligations to other adults are freely taken on in contracting marriage, friendships, and the like; there is no natural obligation to belong. The only involuntary associations are those between generations: our obligations to our parents and to those children (if we can think of these as involuntary associations, since no one picks his children in the process of natural generation). But these are obligations to specific people and do not necessarily involve continuing associations; and they are neither of them cases where the obligation arises in the way it does in the social thesis, that is that we must maintain the association as a condition of our continued development.

Hence we can accommodate whatever is valid in the social thesis without any danger to the primacy of rights. Family obligations and obligations of friendship can be kept separate from any obligations to belong.

I do not think that this argument will hold. But I cannot really undertake to refute it here, not just on the usual cowardly grounds of lack of space, but because we enter here precisely on the central issue of the human condition which divides atomism from social theories. And this issue concerning as it does the human condition cannot be settled in a knockdown argument. My aim in this paper was just to show that it is an issue, and therefore has to be addressed by proponents of primacy. For this purpose I would like to lay out some considerations to which I subscribe, but of which I can do no more than sketch an outline in these pages.

The kind of freedom valued by the protagonists of the primacy of rights, and indeed by many others of us as well, is a freedom by which men are capable of conceiving alternatives and arriving at a definition of what they really want, as well as discerning what commands their adherence or their allegiance. This kind of freedom is unavailable to one whose sympathies and horizons are so narrow that he can conceive only one way of life, for whom indeed the very notion of a way of life which is *his* as against everyone's has no sense. Nor is it available to one who is riveted by fear of the unknown to one familiar lifeform, or who has been so formed in suspicion and hate of outsiders that he can never put himself in their place. Moreover, this capacity to conceive alternatives must not only be available for the less important choices of one's life. The greatest bigot or the narrowest

xenophobe can ponder whether to have Dover sole or Wiener schnitzel for dinner. What is truly important is that one be able to exercise autonomy in the basic issues of life, in one's most important commitments.

Now, it is very dubious whether the developed capacity for this kind of autonomy can arise simply within the family. Of course, men may learn, and perhaps in part must learn, this from those close to them. But my question is whether this kind of capacity can develop within the compass of a single family. Surely it is something which only develops within an entire civilization. Think of the developments of art, philosophy, theology, science, of the evolving practices of politics and social organization, which have contributed to the historic birth of this aspiration to freedom, to making this ideal of autonomy a comprehensible goal men can aim at—something which is in their universe of potential aspiration (and it is not yet so for all men, and may never be).

But this civilization was not only necessary for the genesis of freedom. How could successive generations discover what it is to be an autonomous agent, to have one's own way of feeling, of acting, of expression, which cannot be simply derived from authoritative models? This is an identity, a way of understanding themselves, which men are not born with. They have to acquire it. And they do not in every society; nor do they all successfully come to terms with it in ours. But how can they acquire it unless it is implicit in at least some of their common practices, in the ways that they recognize and treat each other in their common life (for instance, in the acknowledgement of certain rights), or in the manner in which they deliberate with or address each other, or engage in economic exchange, or in some mode of public recognition of individuality and the worth of autonomy?

Thus we live in a world in which there is such a thing as public debate about moral and political questions and other basic issues. We constantly forget how remarkable that is, how it did not have to be so, and may one day no longer be so. What would happen to our capacity to be free agents if this debate should die away, or if the more specialized debate among intellectuals who attempt to define and clarify the alternatives facing us should also cease, or if the attempts to bring the culture of the past to life again as well as the drives to cultural innovation were to fall off? What should there be left to choose between? And if the atrophy went beyond a certain point, could we speak of choice at all? How long would we go on understanding what autonomous choice was? Again, what would happen if our legal culture were not constantly sustained by a contact with our traditions of the rule of law and a confrontation with our contemporary moral institutions? Would we have as sure a grasp of what the rule of law and the defence of rights required?

In other words, the free individual or autonomous moral agent can only achieve and maintain his identity in a certain type of culture, some of whose facets and activities I have briefly referred to. But these and others of the same significance do not come into existence spontaneously each successive instant. They are carried on in institutions and associations which require stability and continuity and frequently also support from society as a whole—almost always the moral support of being commonly recognized as important, but frequently also considerable material support. These bearers of our culture include museums, symphony orchestras, universities, laboratories, political parties, law courts, representative assemblies, newspapers, publishing houses, television stations, and so on. And I have to mention also the mundane elements of infrastructure without which we could not carry on these higher activities: buildings, railroads, sewage plants, power grids, and so on. Thus the requirement of a living and varied culture is also the requirement of a complex and integrated society, which is willing and able to support all these institutions.[5]

I am arguing that the free individual of the West is only what he is by virtue of the whole society and civilization which brought him to be and which nourishes him; that our families can only form us up to this capacity and these aspirations because they are set in this civilization; and that a family alone outside of this context—the real old patriarchal family—was a quite different animal which never tended these horizons. And I want to claim finally that all this creates a significant obligation to belong for whoever would affirm the value of this freedom; this includes all those who want to assert rights either to this freedom or for its sake.

One could answer this by saying that the role of my civilization in forming me is a thing of the past; that, once adult, I have the capacity to be an autonomous being; and that I have no further obligation arising out of the exigencies of my development to sustain this civilization. I doubt whether this is in fact true; I doubt whether we could maintain our sense of ourselves as autonomous beings or whether even only a heroic few of us would succeed in doing so, if this liberal civilization of ours were to be thoroughly destroyed. I hope never to have to make the experiment. But even if we could, the considerations advanced a few pages back would be sufficient here: future generations will need this civilization to reach these aspirations; and if we affirm their worth, we have an obligation to make them available to others. This obligation is only increased if we ourselves have benefited from this civilization and have been enabled to become free agents ourselves.

But then the proponent of primacy could answer by questioning what all this has to do with political authority, with the obligation to belong to a polity or to abide by the rules of a political society. Certainly, we could accept that we are only what we are in virtue of living in a civilization and hence in a large society, since a family or clan could not sustain this. But this does not mean that we must accept allegiance to a polity.

To this there are two responses. First, there is something persuasive about this objection in that it seems to hold out the alternative of an anarchist civilization—one where we have all the benefits of wide association and none of the pains of politics. And indeed, some libertarians come close to espousing an anarchist position and express sympathy for anarchism, as does Nozick. Now it is perfectly true that there is nothing in principle which excludes anarchism in the reflection that we owe our identity as free men to our civilization. But the point is that the commitment we recognize in affirming the worth of this freedom is a commitment to this civilization whatever are the conditions of its survival. If these can be assured in conditions of anarchy, that is very fortunate. But if they can only be assured under some form of representative government to which we all would have to give allegiance, then this is the society we ought to try to create and sustain and belong to. For this is by hypothesis the condition of what we have identified as a crucial human good, by the very fact of affirming this right. (I have, of course, taken as evident that this civilization could not be assured by some tyrannical form of government, because the civilization I am talking about is that which is the essential milieu for free agency.)

The crucial point here is this: since the free individual can only maintain his identity within a society/culture of a certain kind, he has to be concerned about the shape of this society/culture as a whole. He cannot, following the libertarian anarchist model that Nozick sketched,[6] be concerned purely with his individual choices and the associations formed from such choices to the neglect of the matrix in which such choices can be open or closed, rich or meagre. It is important to him that certain activities and institutions flourish in society. It is even of importance to him what the moral tone of the whole society is—shocking as it may be to libertarians to raise this issue—because freedom and individual diversity can only flourish in a society where there is a general recognition of their worth. They are threatened by the spread of bigotry, but also by other conceptions of life—for example, those which look on originality, innovation, and diversity as luxuries which society can ill afford given the need for efficiency, productivity, or growth, or those which in a host of other ways depreciate freedom.

Now, it is possible that a society and culture propitious for freedom might arise from the spontaneous association of anarchist communes. But it seems much more likely from the historical record that we need rather some species of political society. And if this is so then we must acknowledge an obligation to belong to this kind of society in affirming freedom. But there is more. If realizing our freedom partly depends on the society and culture in which we live, then we exercise a fuller freedom if we can help determine the shape of this society and culture. And this we can only do through instruments of common decision. This means that the political institutions in which we live may themselves be a crucial part of what is necessary to realize our identity as free beings.

This is the second answer to the last objection. In fact, men's deliberating together about what will be binding on all of them is an essential part of the exercise of freedom. It is only in this way that they can come to grips with certain basic issues in a way which will actually have an effect in their lives. Those issues, which can only be effectively decided by a society as a whole and which often set the boundary and framework for our lives, can indeed be discussed freely by politically irresponsible individuals wherever they have license to do so. But they can only be truly *deliberated* about politically. A society in which such deliberation was public and involved everyone would realize a freedom not available anywhere else or in any other mode.

Thus, always granted that an anarchist society is not an available option, it is hard to see how one can affirm the worth of freedom in this sense of the exercise of autonomous deliberation and at the same time recognize no obligation to bring about and sustain a political order of this kind.

The argument has gone far enough to show how difficult it is to conclude here. This is because we are on a terrain in which our conception of freedom touches on the issue of the nature of the human subject, and the degree and manner in which this subject is a social one. To open this up is to open the issue of atomism, which is all I hoped to do in this paper. I wanted to show that there is an issue in the "self-sufficiency" or not of man outside political society and that this issue cannot be side-stepped by those who argue from natural rights. This issue, as we can see, leads us very deep, and perhaps we can see some of the motivation of those who have wanted to side-step it. It seems much easier and clearer to remain on the level of our intuitions about rights.

For we can now see more clearly what the issue about atomism is, and how uncommonly difficult it is. It concerns self-sufficiency, but not in the sense of the ability to survive north of Great Slave Lake. That is a question whether we can fulfil certain causal conditions for our continued existence. But the alleged social conditions for the full development of our human capacities are not causal in the same sense. They open another set of issues altogether: whether the condition for the full development of our capacities is not that we achieve a certain identity, which requires a certain conception of ourselves; and more fundamentally whether this identity is ever something we can attain on our own, or whether the crucial modes of self-understanding are not always created and sustained by the common expression and recognition they receive in the life of the society.

Thus the thesis just sketched about the social conditions of freedom is based on the notion, first, that developed freedom requires a certain understanding of self, one in which the aspirations to autonomy and self-direction become conceivable; and, second, that this self-understanding is not something we can sustain on our own, but that our identity is always partly defined in conversation with others or through the common understanding which underlies the practices of our society. The thesis is that the identity of the autonomous, self-determining individual requires a social matrix, one, for instance, which through a series of practices recognizes the right to autonomous decision and which calls for the individual having a voice in deliberation about public action.

The issue between the atomists and their opponents therefore goes deep; it touches the nature of freedom, and beyond this what it is to be a human subject; what is human identity, and how it is defined and sustained. It is not surprising therefore that the two sides talk past each other. For atomists the talk about identity and its conditions in social practice seems impossibly abstruse and speculative. They would rather find themselves on the clear and distinct intuition which we all share (all of us in this society, that is) about human rights.

For non-atomists, however, this very confidence in the starting-point is a kind of blindness, a delusion of self-sufficiency which prevents them from seeing that the free individual, the bearer of rights, can only assume this identity thanks to his relationship to a developed liberal civilization; that there is an absurdity in placing this subject in a state of nature where he could never attain this identity and hence never create by contract a society which respects it. Rather, the free individual who affirms himself as such *already* has an obligation to complete, restore, or sustain the society within which this identity is possible.

It is clear that we can only join this issue by opening up questions about the nature of man. But it is also clear that the two sides are not on the same footing in relationship to these questions. Atomists are more comfortable standing with the intuitions of common sense about the rights of individuals and are not at all keen to open these wider issues. And in this they derive support in those philosophical traditions which come to us from seventeenth century and which started with the postulation of an extensionless subject, epistemologically a *tabula rasa* and politically a presuppositionless bearer of rights. It is not an accident that these epistemological and political doctrines are often found in the writings of the same founding figures.

But if this starting-point no longer appears to us self-evident, then we have to open up questions about the nature of the subject and the conditions of human agency. Among these is the issue about atomism. This is important for any theory of rights, but also for a great deal else besides. For the issue about atomism also underlies many of our discussions about obligation and the nature of freedom, as can already be sensed from above.

That is why it is useful to put it again on our agenda.

NOTES

1. The words "conditional/unconditional" may mislead, because there are certain theories of belonging, to use this term for them, which hold that our obligation to obey, or to belong to a particular society, may in certain circumstances be inoperative. For instance, medieval theories which justified tyrannicide still portrayed man as a social animal and were thus theories of belonging in the sense used here. But they allowed that in certain circumstances our obligation to obey that authority by which our society cohered was abrogated, and that when the ruler was a tyrant he might be killed. In this sense we could say that the obligation to obey was "conditional." But this is not the same as a theory of the primacy of right. For in theories of belonging it is clear that men *qua* men have an obligation to belong to and sustain society. There may be a restriction on what kind of society would fulfil the underlying goal, and from this a licence to break with perverted forms; but the obligation to belong itself was fundamental and unconditional; it held "by nature." In primacy-of-right theories the notion is that simply by nature we are under no obligation to belong whatever; we have first to contract such an obligation.

2. This may not be true of all doctrines which found a political theory on an affirmation of natural right. For the new doctrine of human rights which Professor Macpherson envisages in, for example *Democratic Theory: Essays in Retrieval* (Oxford, 1973), 236, and which would free itself of "the postulate of the inherent and permanent contentiousness of men," would seem to involve an affirmation of individual rights which presuppose society, rather than merely setting the boundary conditions of its possible legitimacy.

3. R. Nozick, *Anarchy, State and Utopia* (Cambridge, Mass., 1974).

4. T. Hobbes, *Leviathan,* pt. I, ch. 6.

5. This is what makes so paradoxical the position of someone like Robert Nozick. He presents (*Anarchy, State and Utopia,* particularly ch. 10) the model of an ideal society where within the framework of the minimal state individuals form or join only those associations which they desire and which will admit them. There is no requirement laid down concerning the overall pattern that will result from this. But can we really do without this? The aim of Nozick's utopian framework is to enable people to give expression to their real diversity. But what if the essential cultural activities which make a great diversity conceivable to people begin to falter? Or are we somehow guaranteed against this? Nozick does not discuss this; it is as though the conditions of a creative, diversifying freedom were given by nature. In this respect the standard utopian literature, which as Nozick says is concerned with the character of the ideal community and not just with a framework for any community, is more realistic. For it faces the question of what kind of community we need in order to be free men, and then goes on to assume that this is given noncoercively.

6. Ibid, ch. 10.

# 56    Feminism and Modern Friendship: Dislocating the Community

MARILYN FRIEDMAN

A PREDOMINANT THEME in much recent feminist thought has been the critique of the abstract individualism which underlies some important versions of liberal political theory.[1] Abstract individualism considers individual human beings as social atoms, abstracted from their social contexts, and disregards the role of social relationships and human community in constituting the very identity and nature of individual human beings. Sometimes the individuals of abstract individualism are posited as rationally self-interested utility maximizers.[2] Sometimes, also, they are theorized to form communities based fundamentally on competition and conflict among persons vying for scarce resources, communities which represent no deeper social bond than that of instrumental relations based on calculated self-interest.[3]

Against this abstractive individualist view of the self and of human community, many feminists have asserted a conception of what might be called the "social self."[4] This conception fundamentally acknowledges the role of social relationships and human community in constituting both self-identity and the nature and meaning of the particulars of individual lives.[5] The modified conception of the self has carried with it an altered conception of community. Conflict and competition are no longer considered to be the basic human relationships; instead they are being replaced by alternative visions of the foundation of human society derived from nurturance, caring attachment, and mutual interestedness.[6] Some feminists, for example, recommend that the mother–child relationship be viewed as central to human society, and they project major changes in moral theory from such a revised focus.[7]

Some of these anti-individualist developments emerging from feminist thought are strikingly similar to other theoretical developments which are not specifically feminist. Thus, the "new communitarians," to borrow Amy Gutmann's term,[8] have also reacted critically to various aspects of modern liberal thought, including abstract individualism, rational egoism, and an instrumental conception of social relationships. The communitarian self, or subject, is also not a social atom but is instead a being constituted and defined by its attachments, including the particularities of its social relationships, community ties, and historical context. Its identity cannot be abstracted from community or social relationships.

With the recent feminist attention to values of care, nurturance, and relatedness—values that psychologists call "communal"[9] and which have been amply associated with women and women's moral reasoning[10]—one might anticipate that communitarian theory would offer important insights for feminist reflection. There is considerable

power to the model of the self as deriving its identity and nature from its social relationships, from the way it is intersubjectively apprehended, from the norms of the community in which it is embedded.

However, communitarian philosophy as a whole is a perilous ally for feminist theory. Communitarians invoke a model of community which is focused particularly on families, neighbourhoods, and nations. These sorts of communities have harboured social roles and structures which have been highly oppressive for women, as recent feminist critiques have shown. But communitarians seem oblivious to those criticisms and manifest a troubling complacency about the moral authority claimed or presupposed by these communities in regard to their members. By building on uncritical references to those sorts of communities, communitarian philosophy can lead in directions which feminists should not wish to follow.

This article is an effort to redirect communitarian thought so as to avoid some of the pitfalls which it poses, in its present form, for feminist theory and feminist practice. In the first part of the article, I develop some feminist-inspired criticisms of communitarian philosophy as it is found in writings by Michael Sandel and Alasdair Mac–Intyre.[11] My brief critique of communitarian thought has the aim of showing that communitarian theory, in the form in which it condones or tolerates traditional communal norms of gender subordination, is unacceptable from any standpoint enlightened by feminist analysis. This does not preclude agreeing with certain specific communitarian views, for example, the broad metaphysical conception of the individual, self, or subject as constituted by its social relationships and communal ties, or the assumption that traditional communities have some value. But the aim of the first section is critical: to focus on the communitarian disregard of gender-related problems with the norms and practices of traditional communities.

In the second part of the article, I will delve more deeply into the nature of different types of community and social relationship. I will suggest that friendships, on the one hand, and urban relationships and communities, on the other, offer an important clue toward a model of community which usefully counterbalances the family–neighbourhood–nation complex favoured by communitarians. With that model in view, we can begin to transform the communitarian vision of self and community into a more congenial ally for feminist theory.

## The Social Self, in Communitarian Perspective

. . . Despite the feminist concern with a social conception of the self and the importance of social relationships, at least three features of the communitarian version of these notions are troubling from a feminist standpoint. First, a relatively minor point: the communitarian's metaphysical conception of an inherently social self has little usefulness for normative analysis; in particular, it will not support a specifically feminist critique of individualist personality. Second, communitarian theory fails to acknowledge that many communities make illegitimate moral claims on their members, linked to hierarchies of domination and subordination. Third, the specific communities of family, neighbourhood, and nation so commonly invoked by communitarians are troubling paradigms of social relationship and communal life. I will discuss each of these points in turn.

First, the communitarian's metaphysical conception of the social self will not support feminist critiques of ruggedly individualist personality or its associated attributes: the avoidance of intimacy, nonnurturance, social distancing, aggression, or violence. Feminist theorists have often been interested in developing a critique of the norm of a highly individualistic, competitive, aggressive personality type, seeing that personality type as more characteristically male than female and as an important part of the foundation for patriarchy.

Largely following the work of Nancy Chodorow, Dorothy Dinnerstein, and, more recently, Carol Gilligan,[12] many feminists have theorized that the processes of psycho-gender development, in a society in which early infant care is the primary responsibility of women but not men, result in a radical distinction between the genders in the extent to which the self is constituted by, and self-identifies with, its relational connections to others. Males are theorized to seek and value autonomy, individuation, separation, and the moral ideals of rights and justice which are thought to depend on a highly individuated conception of persons. By contrast, females are theorized to seek and value connection, sociality, inclusion, and moral ideals of care and nurturance.

From this perspective, highly individuated selves have been viewed as a problem. They are seen as incapable of human attachments based on mutuality and trust, unresponsive to human needs, approaching social relationships merely as rationally self-interested utility maximizers, thriving on separation and competition, and creating social institutions which tolerate, even legitimize, violence and aggression.

However, a metaphysical view that all human selves are constituted by their social and communal relationships does not itself entail a critique of these highly individualistic selves or yield any indication of what degree of psychological attachment to others is desirable. On metaphysical grounds alone, there would be no reason to suppose that caring, nurturant, relational, sociable selves were better than more autonomous, individualistic, and separate selves. All would be equivalently socially constituted at a metaphysical level. Abstract individualism's failure would be, not that it has produced asocial selves, for, on the communitarian view, such beings are metaphysically impossible, but, rather, that it has simply failed theoretically to acknowledge that selves are inherently social. And autonomy, independence, and separateness would become just a different way of being socially constituted, no worse nor better than heteronomy, dependence, or connectedness.

The communitarian conception of the social self, if it were simply a metaphysical view about the constitution of the self (which is what it seems to be), thus provides no basis for regarding nurturant, relational selves as morally superior to those who are highly individualistic. For that reason, it appears to be of no assistance to feminist theorists seeking a normative account of what might be wrong or excessive about competitive self-seeking behaviours or other seeming manifestations of an individualistic perspective. The communitarian "social self," as a metaphysical account of the self, is largely irrelevant to the array of normative tasks which many feminist thinkers have set for a conception of the self.

My second concern about communitarian philosophy has to do with the legitimacy of the moral influences which communities exert over their members and which are supposed to define the moral starting-points of those members. As a matter of moral psychology, it is common for subjects to regard or presume as binding the moral claims made upon them by the norms of their communities. However, this point about moral psychology does not entail an endorsement of those moral claims, and it leaves open the question of whether, and to what extent, those claims might "really" be morally binding. Unfortunately, the new communitarians seem sometimes to go beyond the point of moral psychology to a stronger view, namely, that the moral claims of communities really are morally binding, at least as 'moral starting-points.' MacIntyre refers to the "debts, inheritances, *rightful* expectations and obligations" which we "inherit" from family, nation, and so forth.[13]

But such inheritances are enormously varied and troubling. Many communities are characterized by practices of exclusion and suppression of non-group members, especially outsiders defined by ethnicity and sexual orientation.[14] If the new communitarians do not recognize legitimate "debts, inheritances, rightful expectations and obligations" across community lines, then their views have little relevance for our radically heterogeneous modern society. If people have "rightful expectations and obligations" across community lines, if, for example, whites have debts to blacks

and Native Americans for histories of exploitation, if Germany owed reparations to non-Germans for genocidal practices, and so on, then "the" community as such, that is, the relatively bounded and local network of relationships which forms a subject's primary social setting, would not singularly determine the legitimate moral values or requirements which rightfully constitute the self's moral commitments or self-definition.

Besides excluding or suppressing outsiders, the practices and traditions of numerous communities are exploitative and oppressive towards many of their own members. This problem is of special relevance to women. Feminist theory is rooted in a recognition of the need for change in all the traditions and practices which show gender differentiation; many of these are located in just the sorts of communities invoked by communitarians, for example, family practices and national political traditions. The communitarian emphasis on communities unfortunately dovetails too well with the current popular emphasis on "the family" and seems to hark back to the repressive world of what some sociologists call communities of "place," the world of family, neighbourhood, school, and church, which so intimately enclosed women in oppressive gender politics—the peculiar politics which it has been feminism's distinctive contribution to uncover. Any political theory which appears to support the hegemony of such communities and which appears to restore them to a position of unquestioned moral authority must be viewed with grave suspicion. I will come back to this issue when I turn to my third objection to communitarian philosophy.

Thus, while admitting into our notion of the self the important constitutive role played by social communal relationships, we, from a standpoint independent of some particular subject, are not forced to accept as binding on that subject the moral claims made by the social and communal relationships in which that subject is embedded or by which she is identified. Nor are we required to say that any particular subject is herself morally obliged to accept as binding the moral claims made on her by any of the communities which constitute or define her. To evaluate the moral identities conferred by communities on their members, we need a theory of communities, of their interrelationships, of the structures of power, dominance, and oppression within and among them. Only such a theory would allow us to assess the legitimacy of the claims made by communities upon their members by way of their traditions, practices, and conventions of "debts, inheritances . . . expectations, and obligations."

The communitarian approach suggests an attitude of celebrating the attachments which one finds oneself unavoidably to have, the familial ties and so forth. But some relationships compete with others, and some relationships provide standpoints from which other relationships appear threatening or dangerous to oneself, one's integrity, or one's well-being. In such cases, simple formulas about the value of community provide no guidance. The problem is not simply to appreciate community *per se* but, rather, to reconcile the conflicting claims, demands, and identity-defining influences of the variety of communities of which one is a part.

It is worth recalling that liberalism has always condemned, in principle if not in practice, the norms of social hierarchy and political subordination based on inherited or ascribed status. Where liberals historically have applied this tenet at best only to the public realm of civic relationships, feminism seeks to extend it more radically to the "private" realm of family and other communities of place. Those norms and claims of local communities which sustain gender hierarchies have no intrinsic legitimacy from a feminist standpoint. A feminist interest in community must certainly aim for social institutions and relational structures which diminish and, finally, erase gender subordination.

Reflections such as these characterize the concerns of the modern self, the self who acknowledges no a priori loyalty to any feature of situation or role, and who claims the right to question the moral legitimacy of any contingent moral claim.[15]

We can agree with the communitarians that it would be impossible for the self to question all her contingencies at once, yet at the same time, unlike the communitarians, still emphasize the critical importance of morally questioning various communal norms and circumstances.

A third problem with communitarian philosophy has to do with the sorts of communities evidently endorsed by communitarian theorists. Human beings participate in a variety of communities and social relationships, not only across time, but at any one time. However, when people think of "community," it is common for them to think of certain particular social networks, namely, those formed primarily out of family, neighbourhood, school, and church.[16] MacIntyre and Sandel both emphasize family specifically. MacIntyre cites neighbourhood along with clan, tribe, city, and nation, while Sandel includes "nation or people . . . bearers of this history . . . sons and daughters of that revolution . . . citizens of this republic."[17]

But where, one might ask, is the International Ladies Garment Workers' Union, the Teamsters, the Democratic Party, Alcoholics Anonymous, or the Committee in Solidarity with the People of El Salvador?

The substantive examples of community listed by MacIntyre and Sandel fall largely into two groups: one, governmental communities which constitute our civic and national identities in a public world of nation-states, and two, local communities centered around family and neighbourhood. Although MacIntyre does mention professions and, rather archaically, "guilds,"[18] these references are anomalous in his work, which, for the most part, ignores such communities as trade unions, political action groups, associations of hobbyists, and so forth.

Some of the communities cited by MacIntyre and Sandel will resonate with the historical experiences of women, especially the inclusive communities of family and neighbourhood. However, it should not be forgotten that governing communities have, until only recently, excluded the legitimate participation of women. It would seem to follow that they have accordingly not historically constituted the identities of women in profound ways. As "daughters" of the American Revolution, looking back to the "fathers of our country," we find that we have inconveniently been deprived of the self-identifying heritage of our cultural mothers. In general, the contribution made to the identities of various groups of people by governing communities is quite uneven, given that they are communities to which many are subject but in which far fewer actively participate.

At any rate, there is an underlying commonality to most of the communities which MacIntyre and Sandel cite as constitutive of self-identity and definitive of our moral starting-points. Sandel himself explicates this commonality when he writes that, for people "bound by a sense of community," the notion of community describes *not a relationship they choose (as in a voluntary association) but an attachment they discover,* not merely an attribute but a constituent of their identity." [19] Not voluntary but "discovered" relationships and communities are what Sandel takes to define subjective identity for those who are bound by a "sense of community." It is the communities to which we are involuntarily bound to which Sandel accords metaphysical pride of place in the constitution of subjectivity. What are important are not simply the "associations" in which people "co-operate" but the "communities" in which people "participate," for these latter "describe a form of life in which the members find themselves commonly situated 'to begin with,' their commonality consisting less in relationships they have entered than in attachments they have found." [20] Thus, the social relationships which one finds, the attachments which are discovered and not chosen, become the points of reference for self-definition by the communitarian subject.

For the child maturing to self-consciousness in her community of origin, typically the family–neighbourhood–school–church complex, it seems uncontroversial, that "the" community is found, not entered, discovered, not created. But this need not be true of an adult's communities of

mature self-identification. Many of these adult communities are, for at least some of their members, communities of choice to a significant extent: labour unions, philanthropic associations, political coalitions, and, if one has ever moved or migrated, even the communities of neighbourhood, church, city, or nation-state might have been chosen to an important extent. One need not have simply discovered oneself to be embedded in them in order that one's identity or the moral particulars of one's life be defined by them. Sandel is right to indicate the role of found communities in constituting the unreflective, "given" identity which the self discovers when *first* beginning to reflect on itself. But, for mature self-identity, we should also recognize a legitimate role for communities of choice, supplementing, if not displacing, the communities and attachments which are merely found.

Moreover, the discovered identity constituted by one's original community of place might be fraught with ambivalences and ambiguities. Thus, poet Adrienne Rich writes about her experiences growing up with a Christian mother, a Jewish father who suppressed his ethnicity, and a family community which taught Adrienne Rich contempt for all that was identified with Jewishness. In 1946, while still a high-school student, Rich saw, for the first time, a film about the Allied liberation of Nazi concentration camps. Writing about this experience in 1982, she brooded: "I feel belated rage that I was so impoverished by the family and social worlds I lived in, that I had to try to figure out by myself what this did indeed mean for me. That I had never been taught about resistance, only about passing. That I had no language for anti-Semitism itself." [21] As a student at Radcliffe in the late forties, Rich met "real" Jewish women who inducted her into the lore of Jewish background and customs, holidays and foods, names and noses. She plunged in with trepidation: "I felt I was testing a forbidden current, that there was danger in these revelations. I bought a reproduction of a Chagall portrait of a rabbi in striped prayer shawl and hung it on the wall of my room.

I was admittedly young and trying to educate myself, but I was also doing something that *is* dangerous: I was flirting with identity." [22] And she was doing it apart from the family community from which her ambiguous ethnic identity was originally derived.

For Sandel, Rich's lifelong troubled reflections on her ethnic identity might seem compatible with his theory. In his view, the subject discovers the attachments which are constitutive of its subjectivity through reflection on a multitude of values and aims, differentiating what is self from what is not-self. He might say that Rich discriminated among the many loyalties and projects which defined who she was in her original community, that is, her family, and discerned that her Jewishness appeared "essential" [23] to who she was. But it is not obvious, without question begging, that her original community really defined her as essentially Jewish. Indeed, her family endeavoured to suppress loyalties and attachments to all things Jewish. Thus, one of Rich's quests in life, so evidently not inspired by her community of origin alone, was to re-examine the identity found in that original context. The communitarian view that found communities and social attachments constitute self-identity does not, by itself, explicate the source of such a quest. It seems more illuminating to say that her identity became, in part, "chosen," that it had to do with social relationships and attachments which she sought out, rather than merely found, created as well as discovered.

Thus, the commitments and loyalties of our found communities, our communities of origin, may harbour ambiguities, ambivalences, contradictions, and oppressions which complicate as well as constitute identity and which have to be sorted out, critically scrutinized. And since the resources for such scrutiny may not be found in all "found" communities, our theories of community should recognize that resources and skills derived from communities which are not merely found or discovered may equally well contribute to the constitution of identity. The constitution of identity and moral particularity, for the modern self, may well require radically different communities from those so often invoked by communitarians.

The whole tenor of communitarian thinking would change once we opened up the conception of the social self to encompass chosen communities, especially those which lie beyond the typical original community of family–neighbourhood–school–church. No longer would communitarian thought present a seemingly conservative complacency about the private and local communities of place which have so effectively circumscribed, in particular, the lives of most women.

In the second part of this article, I will explore more fully the role of communities and relationships of "choice," which point the way toward a notion of community more congenial to feminist aspirations.

## Modern Friendship, Urban Community, and Beyond

My goals are manifold: to retain the communitarian insights about the contribution of community and social relationship to self-identity, yet open up for critical reflection the moral particulars imparted by those communities, and identify the sorts of communities which will provide non-oppressive and enriched lives for women.

Toward this end, it will be helpful to consider models of human relationship and community which contrast with those cited by communitarians. I believe that friendship and urban community can offer us crucial insights into the social nature of the modern self. It is in moving forward from these relationships that we have the best chance of reconciling the communitarian conception of the social self with the longed-for communities of feminist aspiration.

Both modern friendship and the stereotypical urban community share an important feature which is either neglected or deliberately avoided in communitarian conceptions of human relationship. From a liberal, or Enlightenment, or modernist standpoint, this feature would be characterized as voluntariness: those relationships are based partly on choice.

Let us first consider friendship as it is understood in this culture. Friends are supposed to be people whom one chooses on one's own to share activities and intimacies. No particular people are assigned by custom or tradition to be a person's friends. From among the larger number of one's acquaintances, one moves toward closer and more friendlike relationships with some of them, motivated by one's own needs, values, and attractions. No consanguineous or legal connections establish or maintain ties of friendship. As this relationship is widely understood in our culture, its basis lies in voluntary choice.

In this context, "voluntary choice" refers to motivations arising out of one's own needs, desires, interests, values, and attractions, in contrast to motivations arising from what is socially assigned, ascribed, expected, or demanded. This means that friendship is more likely than many other relationships, such as those of family and neighbourhood, to be grounded in and sustained by shared interests and values, mutual affection. and possibilities for generating mutual respect and esteem.

In general, friendship has had an obvious importance to feminist aspirations as the basis of the bond which is (ironically) called "sisterhood." [24] Friendship is more likely than many other close personal relationships to provide social support for people who are idiosyncratic, whose unconventional values and deviant life-styles make them victims of intolerance from family members and others who are unwillingly related to them. In this regard, friendship has socially disruptive possibilities, for out of the unconventional living which it helps to sustain there often arise influential forces for social change. Friendship among women has been the cement not only of the various historical waves of the feminist movement, but as well of numerous communities of women throughout history who defied the local conventions for their gender and lived lives of creative disorder. [25] In all these cases, women moved out of their given or found communities into new attachments with

other women by their own choice, that is, motivated by their own needs, desires, attractions, and fears rather than, and often in opposition to, the expectations and ascribed roles of their found communities.

Like friendship, many urban relationships are also based more on choice than on socially ascribed roles, biological connections, or other nonvoluntary ties. Voluntary associations, such as political action groups, support groups, associations of co-hobbyists, and so on, are a common part of modern urban life, with its large population centres and the greater availability of critical masses of people with special interests or needs. But while friendship is almost universally extolled, urban communities and relationships have been theorized in wildly contradictory ways. Cities have sometimes been taken as "harbingers" of modern culture *per se* [26] and have been particularly associated with the major social trends of modern life, such as industrialization and bureaucratization. [27] The results of these trends are often thought to have been a fragmentation of "real" community and the widely lamented alienation of modern urban life: people seldom know their neighbours; population concentration generates massive psychic overload; [28] fear and mutual distrust, even outright hostility, generated by the dangers of urban life, may dominate most daily associations. Under such circumstances, meaningful relationships are often theorized to be rare, if at all possible.

But is this image a complete portrait of urban life? It is probably true, in urban areas, that communities of place are diminished in importance; neighbourhood plays a far less significant role in constituting community than it does in non-urban areas. [29] But this does not mean that the social networks and communities of urban dwellers are inferior to those of non-urban residents.

Much evidence suggests that urban settings do not, as commonly stereotyped, promote only alienation, isolation, and psychic breakdown. The communities available to urban dwellers are different from those available to non-urban dwellers, but not necessarily less gratifying or fulfilling.[30] Communities of place are relatively non-voluntary; one's extended family of origin is given or ascribed, and the relationships found as one grows. Sociological research has shown that urban dwellers tend to form their social networks, their communities, out of people who are brought together for reasons other than geographical proximity. As Sociologist Claude Fischer has stated it, in urban areas "population concentration stimulates allegiances to subcultures based on more significant social traits" than common locality or neighbourhood.[31] Communities of place, centred around the family–neighbourhood–church–school web, are more likely, for urban dwellers, to be supplanted by other sorts of communities, resulting in what the sociologist Melvin Webber has called "community without propinquity."[32] But most important for our purposes, these are still often genuine communities, and not the cesspools of "Rum, Romanism, and Rebellion" sometimes depicted by anti-urbanists.

Literature reveals that women writers have been both repelled and inspired by cities. The city, as a concentrated centre of male political and economic power, seems to exclude women altogether.[33] However, as literary critic Susan Merrill Squier points out, the city can provide women not only with jobs, education, and the cultural tools with which to escape imposed gender roles, familial demands, and domestic servitude, but can also bring women together, in work or in leisure, and lay the basis for bonds of sisterhood.[34] The quests of women who journey to cities leaving behind men, home, and family are subversive, writes literary critic Blanche Gelfant, and may well be perceived by others "as assaults upon society."[35] Thus, cities open up for women possibilities of supplanting communities of place with relationships and communities of choice. These chosen communities can provide the resources for women to surmount the moral particularities of family and place which define and limit their moral starting-points.

Social theorists have long decried the interpersonal estrangement of urban life, an observation which seems predominantly inspired by the public world of conflict between various subcultural groups. Urbanism does not create interpersonal estrangement within subcultures but, rather, tends to promote social involvement.[36] This is especially true for people with special backgrounds and interests, for people who are members of small minorities, and for ethnic groups. Fischer has found that social relationships in urban centres are more "culturally specialized: urbanites were relatively involved with associates in the social world they considered most important and relatively uninvolved with associates, if any, in other worlds."[37] As Fischer summarizes it, "Urbanism . . . fosters social involvement in the subculture(s) of *choice,* rather than the subculture(s) of circumstances."[38] This is doubtless reinforced by the recent more militant expression of group values and group demands for rights and respect on the parts of urban subcultural minorities.

We might describe urban relationships as being characteristically "modern" to signal their relatively greater voluntary basis. We find, in these relationships and the social networks formed of them, not a loss of community but an increase in importance of community of a different sort from that of family–neighbourhood–church–school complexes. Yet these more voluntary communities may be as deeply constitutive of the identities and particulars of the individuals who participate in them as are the communities of place so warmly invoked by communitarians.

Perhaps it is more illuminating to say that communities of choice foster not so much the constitution of subjects but their reconstitution. They may be sought out as contexts in which people relocate the various constituents of their identities, as Adrienne Rich sought out the Jewish community in her college years. While people in a community of choice may not share a common history, their shared values or interests are likely to manifest backgrounds of similar experiences, as, for example, among the members of a lesbian community. The modern self may seek new communities whose norms and relationships stimulate and develop her identity and self-understanding more adequately than her unchosen community of origin, her original community of place.

In case it is chosen communities which help us to define ourselves, the project of self-definition would not be arising from communities in which we merely found or discovered our immersion. It is likely that chosen communities, lesbian communities, for example, attract us in the first place because they appeal to features of ourselves which, though perhaps merely found or discovered, were inadequately or ambivalently sustained by our unchosen families, neighbourhoods, schools, or churches. Thus, unchosen communities are sometimes communities which we can, and should, leave, searching elsewhere for the resources to help us discern who we really are.

Our communities of origin do not necessarily constitute us as selves who agree or comply with the norms which unify those communities. Some of us are constituted as deviants and resisters by our communities of origin, and our defiance may well run to the foundational social norms, which ground the most basic social roles and relationships upon which those communities rest. The feminist challenge to sex/gender arrangements is precisely of this foundational sort.

A community of choice might be a community of people who share a common oppression. This is particularly critical in those instances in which the shared oppression is not concentrated within certain communities of place, as it might be, for example, in the case of ethnic minorities, but, rather, is focused on people who are distributed throughout social and ethnic groupings and who do not themselves constitute a traditional community of place. Women are a prime example of such a distributed group. Women's communities are seldom the original, non-voluntary, found communities of their members.

To be sure, non-voluntary communities of place are not without value. Most lives contain mixtures of relationships and communities, some given/found/discovered and some chosen/created. Most people probably are, to some extent,

ineradicably constituted by their communities of place, the community defined by some or all of their family, neighbourhood, school, or church. It is noteworthy that dependent children, elderly persons, and all other individuals whose lives and well-being are at great risk need the support of communities whose other members do not or cannot choose arbitrarily to leave. Recent philosophical investigation into communities and relationships not founded or sustained by choice has brought out the importance of these social networks for the constitution of social life.[39] But these insights should not obscure the additional need for communities of choice to counter oppressive and abusive relational structures in those nonvoluntary communities by providing models of alternative social relationships as well as standpoints for critical reflection on self and community.

Having attained a critically reflective stance toward one's communities of origin, one's community of place, toward family, neighbourhood, church, school, and nation, one has probably at the same time already begun to question and distance oneself from aspects of one's "identity" in that community and, therefore, to have embarked on the path of personal redefinition. From such a perspective, the uncritically assumed communities of place invoked by the communitarians appear deeply problematic. We can concede the influence of those communities without having unreflectively to endorse it. We must develop communitarian thought beyond its complacent regard for the communities in which we once found ourselves toward (and beyond) an awareness of the crucial importance of dislocated communities, communities of choice.

NOTES

1. Cf. C. Pateman, *The Problem of Political Obligation: A Critique of Liberal Theory* (Berkeley, Calif., 1979); Z. Eisenstein, *The Radical Future of Liberal Feminism* (New York, 1981); N. C. M. Hartsock, *Money, Sex, and Power* (Boston, 1983); A. M. Jaggar, *Feminist Politics and Human Nature* (Totowa, NJ,

1983); N. Scheman, "Individualism and the Objects of Psychology," in S. Harding and M. B. Hintikka (eds.), *Discovering Reality* (Dordrecht, 1983), 225–44; J. Flax, "Political Philosophy and the Patriarchal Unconscious: A Psychoanalytic Perspective on Epistemology and Metaphysics," in Harding and Hintikka (eds.), *Discovering Reality*, pp. 245–81; and S. Benhabib, "The Generalized and the Concrete Other: The Kohlberg–Gilligan Controversy and Moral Theory," in E. F. Kittay and D. T. Meyers (eds.), *Women and Moral Theory* (Totowa, NJ, 1987), 154–77.

2. Cf. D. Gauthier, *Morals by Agreement* (Oxford, 1986).

3. Cf. G. Homans, *Social Behavior: Its Elementary Forms* (New York, 1961); and P. Blau, *Exchange and Power in Social Life* (New York, 1974).

4. Cf. my "Autonomy in Social Context," in J. Sterba and C. Peden (eds.), *Freedom, Equality, and Social Change: Problems in Social Philosophy Today* (Lewiston, NY, 1989).

5. Cf. D. Cornell, "Toward a Modern/Postmodern Reconstruction of Ethics," *University of Pennsylvania Law Review*, 133 (1985), 291–380.

6. Cf. A. Baier, "Trust and Antitrust," *Ethics*, 96 (1986), 231–60; and O. Flanagan and K. Jackson, "Justice, Care, and Gender: The Kohlberg–Gilligan Debate Revisited," *Ethics*, 97 (1987), 622–37.

7. Cf. Hartsock, *Money, Sex, and Power*, pp. 41–2; and V. Held, "Non-Contractual Society," in M. Hanen and K. Nielsen (eds.), *Science, Morality and Feminist Theory* (*Canadian Journal of Philosophy*, 13, suppl. (1987), 111–38).

8. A. Gutmann, "Communitarian Critics of Liberalism," *Philosophy and Public Affairs*, 14 (1985), 308–22.

9. Cf. A. H. Eagly and V. J. Steffen, "Gender-Stereotypes Stem from the Distribution of Women and Men into Social Roles," *Journal of Personality and Social Psychology*, 46 (1984), 735–54.

10. Cf. C. Gilligan, *In a Different Voice* (Cambridge, Mass., 1989).

11. In particular, M. Sandel, *Liberalism and the Limits of Justice* (Cambridge, 1982); A. MacIntyre, *After Virtue* (Notre Dame, Ind., 1981).

12. D. Dinnerstein, *The Mermaid and the Minotaur: Sexual Arrangements and Human Malaise* (New York, 1976); N. Chodorow, *The Reproduction of Mothering* (Berkeley, Calif., 1978); and Gilligan, *In a Different Voice*.

13. MacIntyre, *After Virtue*, p. 205 (emphasis added).

14. A similar point is made by I. Young, "The Ideal of Community and the Politics of Difference," *Social Theory and Practice*, 12 (1986), 12–13.

15. Cf. Cornell, "Toward a Modern/Postmodern Reconstruction of Ethics," p. 323.

16. This point is made by Young, "The Ideal of Community," p. 12.

17. MacIntyre, *After Virtue*, p. 204; Sandel, *Liberalism and the Limits of Justice*, p. 179.

18. MacIntyre, *After Virtue*, p. 204.

19. Sandel, *Liberalism and the Limits of Justice*, p. 150 (emphasis added).

20. Ibid. 151–2.

21. A. Rich, "Split at the Root: An Essay on Jewish Identity," in her *Blood, Bread, and Poetry* (New York, 1986), 107; repr. from Evelyn Torton Beck (ed.), *Nice Jewish Girls: A Lesbian Anthology* (Trumansburg, NY, 1982), 67–84.

22. Ibid. 108.

23. This term is used by Sandel, *Liberalism and the Limits of Justice*, p. 180.

24. Martha Ackelsberg points out the ironic and misleading nature of this use of the term "sisterhood" in "'Sisters' or 'Comrades'? The Politics of Friends and Families," in I. Diamond (ed.), *Families, Politics, and Public Policy* (New York, 1983), 339–56.

25. Cf. J. Raymond, *A Passion for Friends* (Boston, 1986), esp. chs. 2 and 3.

26. C. Fischer, *To Dwell among Friends* (Chicago, 1982). I.

27. Cf. R. Sennett, "An Introduction," in R. Sennett (ed.), *Classic Essays on the Culture of Cities* (New York, 1969), 3–22.

28. Cf. S. Milgram, "The Experience of Living in Cities," *Science*, 167 (1970), 1461–8.

29. Fischer, *To Dwell among Friends*, pp. 97–103.

30. Ibid. 193–232.

31. Ibid. 273.

32. M. Webber, "Order in Diversity: Community without Propinquity," in R. Gutman and D. Popenoe (eds.), *Neighbourhood, City and Metropolis* (New York, 1970), 792–811.

33. Cf. the essays in C. Stimpson *et al.* (eds.), *Women and the American City* (Chicago, 1980, 1981); and the special issue on "Women in the City," *Urban Resources*, 3. 2 (Winter 1986).

34. Introduction to S. M. Squier (ed.), *Women Writers and the City* (Knoxville, Tenn., 1984), 3–10.

35. B. Gelfant, "Sister to Faust: The City's 'Hungry' Woman as Heroine," in Squier (ed.), *Women Writers and the City*, p. 267.

36. Fischer, *To Dwell among Friends*, pp. 247–8.

37. Ibid. 230.

38. Ibid.

39. Cf. Baier, "Trust and Antitrust"; Held, "Non-Contractual Society"; and Pateman, *The Problem of Political Obligation*.

# 57     Ancient Futures

HELENA NORBERG-HODGE

IT SEEMS TO ME that Western society today is moving in two distinct and opposing directions. On the one hand, mainstream culture led by government and industry moves relentlessly toward continued economic growth and technological development, straining the limits of nature and all but ignoring fundamental human needs. On the other hand, a counter-current, comprising a wide range of groups and ideas, has kept alive the ancient understanding that all life is inextricably connected.

At present, this is only a minority voice, but it is growing in strength as more and more people begin to question the whole notion of progress. The formation of Green parties and the rise in membership in environmental organizations indicate widespread commitment to environmental protection. Individual consumers are beginning to realize their power to bring about change in the economic system, and businesses are competing with each other to appear "environmentally friendly." Governments and major international agencies are under pressure to place the environment high on the political agenda.

We still have an opportunity to steer our society toward social and ecological balance. But if we are to do more than simply treat symptoms, it is important that we understand the systemic nature of the crises facing us. Under the surface even such seemingly unconnected problems as ethnic violence, pollution of the air and water, broken families, and cultural disintegration are closely interlinked. Understanding that the problems are interrelated can make them seem overwhelming, but finding the points at which they converge can, in fact, make our attempts to tackle them a great deal more effective. It is then just a question of pulling the right threads to affect the entire fabric, rather than having to deal with each problem individually.

The fabric of industrial society is to a great extent determined by the interaction of science, technology, and a narrow economic paradigm—an interaction that is leading to ever-greater centralization and specialization. Since the Industrial Revolution, the perspective of the individual has become more limited while political and economic units have grown larger. I have become convinced that we need to decentralize our political and economic structures and broaden our approach to knowledge if we are to find our way to a more balanced and sane society. In Ladakh, I have seen how human-scale structures nurture intimate bonds with the earth and an active and participatory democracy, while supporting strong and vital communities, healthy families, and a greater balance between male and female. These structures in turn provide the security needed for individual well-being and, paradoxically, for a sense of freedom.

The changes that we need to make can greatly enrich our lives. Yet they are often treated, even within the environmental movement, as sacrifices. The emphasis is on giving things up and making do with less, rather than recognizing how much we stand to gain. We forget that the price for never-ending economic growth and material prosperity has been spiritual and social impoverishment, psychological insecurity, and the loss of cultural vitality. We think of ourselves as "having everything," and are surprised when young people turn to drugs or strange gurus to fill the void in their lives.

Perhaps the most important lesson of Ladakh has to do with happiness. It was a lesson that I was slow to learn. Only after many years of peeling away layers of preconceptions did I begin to see the joy and laughter of the Ladakhis for what it really was: a genuine and unhindered appreciation of life itself. In Ladakh I have known a people who regard peace of mind and joie de vivre as their unquestioned birthright. I have seen that community and a close relationship to the land can enrich human life beyond all comparison with material wealth or technological sophistication. I have learned that another way is possible.

At the moment, the emerging global economy and the growing domination of science and technology are not only severing our connection to nature and to one another but also breaking down natural and cultural diversity. In so doing, we are threatening our very existence. In the natural world, diversity is an inescapable fact of life. We are just beginning to discover how important even the most "insignificant" insect or plant can be for our survival. The alarming rate at which we are eradicating species of plant and animal life has, in fact, become a major issue. Biologists are now corroborating the life-sustaining importance of species diversity, and some are speaking out about the danger of erasing it for the sake of short-term gain. Individuals throughout the world are organizing themselves to protect endangered species of plants and animals. In addition to safeguarding the future of wild animals, people are now breeding threatened strains of goats, sheep, ponies, and other domestic animals. Some apple farmers are choosing to propagate traditional local varieties before they are all replaced by a single hybrid such as Golden Delicious.

In a modern setting it is easy to believe that economic development has increased diversity. Efficient transportation and communication bring together a vast array of foods and products from different cultures. However, the very system that facilitates these multicultural experiences is helping to erase them and to eliminate local cultural differences throughout the world. Lingonberry and pineapple juice are giving way to Coca Cola, woolen robes and cotton saris to blue jeans, yaks and highland cattle to Jersey cows. Diversity does not mean having the choice between ten different kinds of blue jeans all made by the same company.

Cultural diversity is as important as diversity in the natural world and, in fact, follows directly from it. Traditional cultures mirrored their particular environments, deriving their food, clothing, and shelter primarily from local resources. Even in the West today, there are still remnants of local adaptation to diversity. In the American Southwest, you find flat-roofed adobe houses, which are ideally suited to the extremes of the desert climate, while in New England, the houses are made of wood and have pointed roofs designed to shed the rain and snow. The cuisines of different cultures still reflect local food sources, from the olive oil prevalent in Mediterranean cooking to the oatmeal and kippered herring on the Scotsman's breakfast table.

Without retreating into cultural or economic isolationism, we can nourish the traditions of our own region. A true appreciation of cultural diversity means neither imposing our own culture on others, nor packaging, exploiting, and commercializing exotic cultures for our own consumption.

One of the most effective ways of reviving cultural differences would be to lobby for a reduction in unnecessary trade. At the moment, our taxpayers' money is going to expand transport infrastructures and to increase trade for the sake of trade. We are transporting across whole continents a vast range of products, from milk to apples to furniture, that could just as easily be produced in their place of destination. What we should be doing instead is reinforcing and diversifying local economies. By reducing and eliminating subsidies for transportation, we would cut waste and pollution, improve the position of small farmers, and strengthen communities in one fell swoop.

What exactly is "local," and what is "necessary" as opposed to "unnecessary" trade, are issues that cannot be defined in absolute terms. But the crucial point is that the *principle* of heavily subsidized international trade is one that needs critical reassessment—not with the goal of encouraging protectionism, but so as to allow for the sustainable and equitable use of natural resources world-wide. It is in robust, local-scale economies that we find genuinely "free" markets; free of the corporate manipulation, hidden subsidies, waste, and immense promotional costs that characterize today's global market.

The trend toward a globalization of the market not only concentrates power and resources in ever-fewer hands, but contributes directly to ever-greater dependence on urban centers. Even though the numbers of people living in many Western cities may actually be falling, the pull to the center is increasing. Commuters are travelling farther and farther, while whole regions suffer severe decline as economic and political power is increasingly focused in a few large cities. Living and working outside the reach of these centers is becoming increasingly difficult.

It is often said that there are too many people and not enough land for a demographic shift into rural areas. But in many unseen ways, today's centralized systems take up much more space. The relationship between the vast urban centers of today and their physical requirements is analogous to the way we use more land the higher up on the food chain we eat. A beef cow does not take up nearly as much room in itself as a vegetable garden, but when you take into account the fields of grain to feed the cow, the water to irrigate the fields, and the land that dried up because of the diversion of that water, it is clear that a cow actually takes up much more land. A large city takes up less physical space than the same population dispersed into small communities, but it lives higher on the energy chain; and per capita consumption in the cities is also higher. The freeways, the transport, the used-car lots, the oil fields, the food-processing plants, the pollution of air, water, and land mean that contemporary urban centers use more resources and ultimately more space than decentralized communities closer to nature.

The process of decentralization would involve a succession of changes in the whole socioeconomic system. It is important to remember, however, that we are not talking about dismantling a static entity but rather about steering in the direction of change. The scale of our society is growing year by year, and the logic of centralization is progressively being carried to new extremes. The pace is such that we would need to actually implement plans for decentralization simply to stay where we are now. That alone would be a significant achievement.

The need to belong to a group is in itself an important reason for human-scale social units. Here we can learn directly from Ladakh, where families are large, but communities small. Children are nurtured by people of different generations, benefiting particularly from the special bond with their grandparents. Though the relationships in this larger family are close, they are not so intense as those of the nuclear family. Each individual is supported in a web of intimate relationships, and no one relationship has to bear too much weight. In Ladakh, I have never observed anything approaching the needy attachment or the guilt and rejection that are so characteristic of the nuclear family.

While there are clearly exceptions, the extended family generally provides more space and flexibility and far less pressure on each individual, both emotionally and in terms of responsibility. It is particularly beneficial for the elderly and for women and children. Within the extended family, older people are appreciated for their wisdom and experience, and their slower pace does not prevent them from making an important contribution to the community. In our society, by contrast, technological change is so rapid that experience has less and less value. We have transformed the world around us so dramatically that older people have little to offer from their lifetime. Ladakhis who have traveled to the West tell horror stories about the neglect old people suffer, living alone with no one to talk to. "Grandmothers wait for months to see their grandchildren for a few short hours," Gyelong Paldan remarked, "and then get only a small peck on the cheek."

At the same time as the nuclear family excludes old people, it imprisons women. In traditional societies, women do not have to choose between home and work, since the household is the center of the economy and the two realms are one. By contrast, women with families in the modern world have two choices, neither of which is an easy option. They can stay at home with children, not valued for the work they do, or they can do two jobs, typically with no more than token help from their husbands.

All the signs tell us that the nuclear family is not working. The divorce rate, the alienation of adolescents from their parents, the shocking extent of domestic violence and sexual abuse within the family are examples of this breakdown. Psychologists now describe the "dysfunctional family" as the typical family. Even as recently as fifty years ago, the family in the industrial world was healthier and more supportive than it is today. Once, Grandmother lived next door, and there were cousins and aunts nearby; connections to the larger community were stronger and longer-lasting. Now, as the economic arena expands, it is not unusual for a family to live in as many as six different homes while the children are growing up. There's no room for Grandmother anymore: physically, economically, or psychologically.

Often when I talk about family with people in the West, they say, "Having my mother living with us is a nice idea, but it just wouldn't work. We'd all go crazy after two or three days." They are right—it wouldn't work very well at the moment. Because of the way our society is structured, having aging parents in the house becomes a burden. But it could work, if we changed our political priorities to give more attention to fundamental human needs.

In stark contrast to the nuclear family, which tends to seal itself off from the outside world, relationships within the Ladakhi family naturally extend themselves into the broader community. It is sometimes hard to say where family ends and community begins. Any woman old enough to be your mother is called "Mother," anyone of the right age to be your brother is called "Brother." We still see remnants of this in industrial society. In the more traditional parts of Sweden and Russia, for example, a child will call any familiar adult "Uncle" or "Auntie."

Most Westerners would agree that we have lost our sense of community. Our lives are fragmented, and in spite of the number of people with whom we come into contact in the course of a day, we are often left feeling sadly alone, not even knowing our neighbors. In Ladakh, people are part of a community that is spiritually, socially, and economically interdependent.

Decentralization is a prerequisite for the rekindling of community in Western society. Mobility erodes community, but as we put down roots and feel attachment to a place, our human relationships deepen, become more secure, and—as they continue over time—more reliable.

The broader sense of self in traditional Ladakhi society contrasts with the individualism of Western culture. A Ladakhi's identity is to a great extent molded by close bonds with other people, and is reinforced by the Buddhist emphasis on interconnectedness. People are supported in a network of relationships that spread in concentric circles around them—family, farm, neighborhood, village. In the West we pride ourselves on our individualism, but sometimes individualism is a euphemism for isolation. We tend to believe that a person should be completely self-sufficient, that he or she should not need anybody else. I have a friend who was divorced the same year her only child left home for school. She was quite naturally unhappy. But she felt that her misery was a sign of weakness, that she should learn to like being on her own, to feel at peace in her empty house.

The closely knit relationships in Ladakh seem liberating rather than oppressive, and have forced me to reconsider the whole concept of freedom. This is not as surprising as it might appear. Psychological research is verifying the importance of intimate, reliable, and lasting relations with others in creating a positive self-image. We are beginning to recognize how this in turn is the foundation for healthy development. Ladakhis score very highly in terms of self-image. It is not something conscious; it is perhaps closer to a total absence of self-doubt, a profound sense of security. This inner security breeds tolerance and an acceptance of others with all their differences.

One summer, when I was doing a study of child development and child care practices in the Zanskar Valley, I asked a group of mothers if they ever worried when a child was late in learning to walk. They roared with laughter: "Why should we worry about a thing like that? They'll learn to walk when they are ready." In mainstream Western culture, we keep increasingly careful percentile charts of our babies' height and weight because we live in a society that is growing ever more insecure and competitive. A generation ago, mothers were told to feed their newborn babies according to a strict schedule, so as not to "spoil" them. A friend of mine tells me that when her baby daughter was crying in her crib from hunger, she would be sitting in the next room, crying too, until she was allowed by the clock to feed her.

The Western monoculture exerts tremendous pressure to conform. At a bus stop in Sweden I was standing next to two little boys who were comparing their sport shoes. One of them was in tears while desperately pulling at the inside of his shoe, looking for the label that would show he had the right brand. The damage is obviously on a deeper level when it is our sex, skin color, or age that is not the right brand. In the commercial mass culture the young white male is the cultural ideal. As a result women, minorities, and old people are disadvantaged. We do not have as much individual freedom as we think we have. While decentralization is the most necessary structural change we must make, it needs to be accompanied by a corresponding change in world view. Increasing ecological distress has clearly demonstrated wide-reaching interconnections in natural systems, but most academic institutions continue to perpetuate ever more narrowly focused specialization. This reductionist perspective is, in fact, one of the root causes of the malaise of industrial culture. Paradoxically, a trend toward smaller-scale political and economic units would help us to develop a broader world view—one based on interconnectedness. Instead of narrowing our vision,

an intimate connection to community and place would encourage an understanding of interdependence. When you are dependent on the earth under your feet and the community around you for your survival, you experience interdependence as a fact of daily life. Such a deep experiential understanding of interconnectedness—feeling yourself a part of the continuum of life—contrasts starkly with the analytic, fragmented, and theoretical thinking of modern society.

We need to return to a more empathetic relationship with the living world and learn to see broader patterns, process, and change. Nowadays, one biologist does not speak the same language as another, unless they are both studying the same kind of fruit fly. How can we understand life by breaking it into fragments and freezing it in time? Our static and mechanistic world view has reached its limits, and some scientists—particularly quantum physicists—now speak of a paradigm shift away from the old "building block" view of reality to a more organic one. In direct opposition to the trend in mainstream culture toward greater specialization, we need to actively promote the generalist—the one who sees connections and makes links across different disciplines. In this regard, one of the most hopeful trends is the increasing respect for more feminine values and ways of thinking.

Research into women's thought patterns is substantiating the assertion that the feminine point of view places greater emphasis on relationship and connections, both in terms of empathy and abstract thinking. Such a perspective is obviously not the exclusive property of women, and in recent years men have begun to value more consciously the feminine side of themselves. But for hundreds of years, this more contextual way of thinking and being has been not only neglected, but undermined by industrial culture. The dominant perspective of our society is now out of balance. A shift toward the feminine is long overdue.

This shift would also bring with it an emphasis on experiential knowledge. To a much greater extent than men, women can be said to form their abstractions from personal experience. Interestingly enough, the same can be said of the Ladakhis and many traditional and non-Western cultures. To understand the complexities of the natural world, theory must be grounded in experience. Experiential learning is based in messy reality, with all its paradox and untidiness, its ever-changing pattern, its refusal to conform to our expectations. As such, it inevitably leads to humility. If our studies were conducted less in the laboratory and more in the field—in the fields, in fact—scientific advance would proceed more cautiously. If we learned to examine the potential effects of new technologies in context, over time, we would be less likely to set off destructive chains of unintended effects.

In the West, we tend to live our lives at one remove from reality, relying on images and concepts. As Tashi Rabgyas said after spending a few months in England, "It's amazing how indirect everything is here. They write about the beauty of nature, they talk about it, and everywhere there are potted plants and plastic plants, and pictures of trees on the wall. And all the time television programs about nature. But they don't ever seem to have contact with the real thing."

On my most recent visit to Sweden, I had lunch with my friend Karin in her garden outside Stockholm. A successful lawyer and the mother of two teenage daughters, she had been a volunteer with the Ladakh Project the previous summer and we had become friends.

"Ladakh came home with me," she said. "I keep discovering how deeply it affected me." On her return to Sweden, she had realized the need to make changes in her life. She cut back on her legal practice to do voluntary work for an environmental organization. She slowed her pace, planted a vegetable garden, and started spending more time with her children.

Karin is by no means alone. A movement to build eco-villages is sweeping Sweden: two hundred are already planned, all of them based on renewable energy and the recycling of waste. Increasing numbers of people are choosing to buy organic food and are strengthening the local economy by buying from farmers close to home.

The government has committed itself to establishing an environmental accounting system in which the destruction of natural resources will be subtracted from the gross national product.

These changes in Sweden reflect a crucial shift in direction. Throughout the industrial world, people are searching for a better balance with nature. In the process, they are starting to mirror traditional cultures. In fields as diverse as hospice care for the dying and mediation as a way of settling disputes, striking parallels are emerging between the most ancient and the most modern cultures. Just as Ladakhi villagers have always done, increasing numbers of people are making the kitchen the center of their household activity, eating whole foods that are grown naturally, and using age-old natural remedies for their health problems. Even in more subtle ways, such as a reawakened interest in storytelling, a renewed appreciation for physical work, and the use of natural materials for clothing and construction, the direction of change is clear. We are spiraling back to an ancient connection between ourselves and the earth.

The process, however, is often an unconscious one. Our mainstream culture encourages a linear view of progress, one in which the goal is to free ourselves from our past and from the laws of nature. The modern-day mantra "we cannot go back, we cannot go back" is deeply ingrained in our thinking. Of course we could not go back, even if we wanted to, but our search for a future that works is inevitably bringing us back to certain fundamental patterns that are in greater harmony with nature—including human nature.

In our attempts to find ways of living that correspond more closely with our inner selves, some of the greatest advances have been in the area of child rearing. Could this be because it is here that the woman's viewpoint is most strongly felt? Thankfully, the practice of clock-controlled feeding has been abandoned as we have returned to a greater respect for natural instincts; and now both mothers and fathers carry their babies around next to their bodies in postindustrial papooses. We are beginning to learn what the traditional Ladakhis never forgot—that every human being is born deserving unconditional love, and that children can only really flourish in a family system in which there is no need to prove yourself, no need to earn the right to be who you are.

Around the world, in every sphere of life, from psychology to physics, from farming to the family kitchen, there is a growing awareness of the interconnectedness of all life. New movements are springing up, committed to living on a human scale, and to more feminine and spiritual values. The numbers are growing, and the desire for change is spreading. These trends are often labeled "new," but, as I hope Ladakh has shown, in an important sense they are very old. They are, in fact, a rediscovery of values that have existed for thousands of years—values that recognize our place in the natural order, our indissoluble connection to one another and to the earth.

## Recommended Readings

TEXTS

Barry, B. "Social Criticism and Political Philosophy." *Philosophy and Public Affairs* 19, no. 4 (1990): 360–373.

Bell, Daniel. *Communitarianism and its Critics*. Oxford: Clarendon Press, 1993.

Buchanan, A. "Assessing Communitarian Critique of Liberalism." *Ethics* 99 (1989): 852–882.

Dopplet, G. "Is Rawls's Kantian Liberalism Coherent and Defensible?" *Ethics* 99, no. 4 (1989): 815–852.

Galston, W. "Moral Personality and Liberal Theory: John Rawls's Dewey Lectures." *Political Theory* 10 (1982): 492–519.

Kymlika, W. *Liberalism, Community and Culture*. Oxford: Oxford University Press, 1989.

Larmore, C. *Patterns of Moral Complexity*. Cambridge: Cambridge University Press, 1987.

MacIntyre, A. *After Virtue*. London: University of Notre Dame Press, 1981.

———. *Whose Justice, Which Rationality?* London: University of Notre Dame Press, 1989.

Raz, J. "Liberalism, Autonomy and the Politics of Neutral Concern." *Midwest Studies in Philosophy* 7 (1982): 89–120.

———. *The Morality of Freedom*. Oxford: Oxford University Press, 1986.

Rorty, R. "The Priority of Democracy to Philosophy." In *The Virginia Statute for Religious Freedom*, edited by M. Peterson and R. Vaughan. Madison: University of Wisconsin Press, 1988.

Sandel, M. *Liberalism and the Limits of Justice*. Cambridge: Cambridge University Press, 1982.

Taylor, Charles. *Sources of the Self: The Making of Modern Identity*. Cambridge: Cambridge University Press, 1989.

Walzer, M. "The Communitarian Critique of Liberalism." *Political Theory* 18, no. 1 (1990): 6–23.


FEMINIST PERSPECTIVE

Baier, A. "Trust and Anti-Trust." *Ethics* 96 (1986): 231–260.

Young, Iris. *Justice and the Politics of Difference*. Princeton: Princeton University Press, 1990.


MULTICULTURAL PERSPECTIVE

Sale, Kirpatrick. *Dwellers in the Land*. Santa Cruz: New Society, 1991.

Shiva, Vandana. *Ecology and the Politics of Survival*. London: Sage, 1991.

# XIV

---

# *Cornel West and Martha Nussbaum*

## Introduction

CORNEL WEST WAS BORN IN 1953 in Tulsa, Oklahoma. His father was a civilian air force administrator and his mother an elementary schoolteacher. West reported that at age eight, Theodore Roosevelt was his earliest role model. "Teddy was very close to me because we both had asthma and would stay awake at night with our backs propped up by a pillow. But he overcame it, went to Harvard, and became a great speaker. So I decided I had to go to Harvard, too, although at eight I didn't know exactly what it was." West did go to Harvard, graduating in 1973 with an A.B. degree in Near Eastern languages and literature, and then later to Princeton, receiving a Ph.D. degree in 1980. He has taught at Union Theological Seminary and Yale University and is currently returning to the Afro-American Studies Department of Princeton University after a stint at Harvard. He published his first book, *Prophecy Deliverance! An Afro-American Revolutionary Christianity* in 1982, edited with John Rajchman, *Post-Analytic Philosophy* in 1985, *Prophetic Fragments* in 1988, *The American Evasion of Philosophy: A Genealogy of Pragmatism* in 1989, *The Ethical Dimensions of Marxist Thought* in 1991, and *Race Matters* in 1993. It was this last book that brought him to the attention of the mainstream media.

West has been described as "a lanky easygoing man with a folksy drawl and a penchant for three-piece suits." He does not conform to the stereotype of the stuffy academician and is reported to have once turned down a position at Harvard because the Boston stations don't play enough Black music although he later joined the African American studies department there for a number of years. According to his brother Clifton, "Cornel has always liked to go to two or three parties every weekend, but only after reading two or three books. He's been like that since he was a kid."

In "The Politics of American Neo-Pragmatism," West argues that the neo-pragmatism advocated most recently by Richard Rorty needs to be broadened and given a political and cultural turn. While Rorty develops an antifoundational, nonreductionist critique of academic philosophy, West argues, he does not extend this critique to the political and cultural practices of society. It is a critique that "fervently attacks epistemological privilege but remains relatively silent about political, economic, racial and sexual privilege."

To be successful, West argues, neopragmatism needs to extend its critique beyond academic philosophy to the political and cultural practices of society.

Martha Nussbaum was born in 1947 in New York City. She attended Wellesley College and graduated from New York University with a B.A. in 1969. She received a Ph.D. in philosophy from Harvard University in 1975. Nussbaum has taught at Harvard University, Wellesley College, and Brown University and is currently professor of Law and Ethics at the University of Chicago. Her major works in ethics are *The Fragility of Goodness* (1986), *The Therapy of Desire: Theory and Practice in Hellenistic Ethics* (1994), *Poetic Justice* (1996), *Sex and Social Justice* (1998), and *Women and Human Development* (2000).

In "The Future of Feminist Liberalism," which was her presidential address for the Central Division of the American Philosophical Association, Martha Nussbaum focuses on two areas where liberalism, even in its strongest forms, has not yet given satisfactory answers to deep problems exposed by feminist thinkers. These two areas are the need for care in times of extreme dependency and the political role of the family. Nussbaum criticizes John Rawls, in particular, for not making care giving and dependency central to his political philosophy. Rejecting Kantian liberalism, Nussbaum argues for an Aristotelian liberalism that uses a suitable list of human capabilities, differently shared by people, and then designs institutions for securing those capabilities as far as possible. She also criticizes Rawls for maintaining that his principles of justice do not "apply directly to the internal life of families." While Nussbaum thinks that her Aristotelian approach and Rawls's Kantian approach would support many of the same laws to protect women and children, she also thinks that Rawls's approach, unlike her own, would find it difficult to oppose certain practices, such as the dowery system in India, because Rawls treats the family as a prepolitical institution with which the state should generally not interfere. Yet surprisingly, neither Rawls nor Nussbaum have much to say to libertarians, like John Hospers, in defense of the amount of interference with people's lives they both sanction.

# 58     The Politics of American Neo-Pragmatism

CORNEL WEST

Pragmatism could be characterized as the doctrine that all problems are at bottom problems of conduct, that all judgments are, implicitly, judgments of value, and that, as there can be ultimately no valid distinction of theoretical and practical, so there can be no final separation of questions of truth of any kind from questions of the justifiable ends of action.

C. I. Lewis, *Collected Papers*

I revelled in the keen analysis of William James, Josiah Royce and young George Santayana. But it was James with his pragmatism . . . that turned me from the lovely but sterile land of philosophic speculation to the social sciences.

W. E. B. Du Bois, *Autobiography*

IN THE EYES of many, we live among the ruins of North Atlantic civilization. Major philosophical figures such as Hannah Arendt, Walter Benjamin, Martin Heidegger, Alasdair MacIntyre and Ludwig Wittgenstein echo this Spenglerian theme. Possible nuclear holocaust hovers over us. Rampant racism, persistent patriarchy, extensive class inequality, brutal state repression, subtle bureaucratic surveillance, and technological abuse of nature pervade capitalist, communist, and neocolonial countries. The once vital tradition of bourgeois humanism has become vapid and sterile. The emancipatory intent of revolutionary Marxism has been aborted and discredited. The shock effect of Catastrophic nihilism is now boring and uninteresting. As we approach the end of the twentieth century, the rich intellectual resources of the West are in disarray and a frightening future awaits us.

The most terrifying aspects of this contemporary situation fail to affect the discourses and practices of most American intellectuals—principally owing to unique geographical isolation, recent professional insularity, and relative economic prosperity. This is especially so in regard to American philosophers. Under the spell of Viennese-style logical positivism (whose major proponents migrated here), Oxford-inspired linguistic analysis, Continental phenomenology, and existentialism, and homespun naturalism, post-World War II American philosophy became a legitimate academic discipline and respectable professional career. Similar to the singular roles of New Criticism in literary studies and structural-functionalism in the social sciences, these philosophical "schools of thought" not only produced intense intellectual activity, they also provided stable and secure self-images for new arrivals in the then-expanding stratum of university and college professors. This unprecedented expansion was regulated by professional norms and habits: easy transmittance of techniques, routine evaluation of performance, and widespread agreement on pertinent problems.

By the late fifties, the voices of something new could be heard. Thoroughly trained in the predominant paradigm of Anglo-American philosophy—diverse forms of atomism, reductionism, and empiricism loosely dubbed "logical positiv-

ism"—Willard Van Orman Quine, Nelson Goodman, and Wilfred Sellars reached conclusions which threatened the basic presuppositions of the paradigm. To put it crudely, logical positivism rested upon three basic assumptions. First, it assumed a form of *sentential atomism* which correlates isolated sentences with either possible empirical confirmation, logical necessity, or emotion. Second, it emerged with a kind of *phenomenalist reductionism* which translates sentences about physical objects into sentences about actual and possible sensations. Third, it presupposed a version of *analytical empiricism* which holds observational evidence to be the criterion for cognitively meaningful sentences and hence the final court of appeal in determining valid theories about the world. These independent yet interrelated doctrines—held at various times by Rudolf Carnap, Carl Hempel, and other logical positivists—were guided by distinctions between the analytical and the synthetic, the linguistic and the empirical, theory and observation.[1]

Quine's breakthrough, by far the most influential, accented an *epistemological holism* which shifted the basic units of empirical significance from isolated sentences to systems of sentences or theories; a *methodological monism* that abandoned the analytic-synthetic distinction; and a *naturalism* which rejected a first philosophy prior to science.[2] Goodman's project promoted a *logical conventionalism* which replaced accurate pictorial depiction with acceptable verbal description as the end and aim of constructing versions of the world; a *postempiricist antireductionism* that highlighted the theory-laden character of observation; and an *ontological pluralism* which relegated the notion of truth to that of fitness and encouraged diverse, even conflicting, true versions of the world instead of a fixed world and unique truth.[3] Sellars' major move was toward an *anti-foundationalism* in epistemology which undermined attempts to invoke self-justifying, intrinsically credible, theory-neutral or noninferential elements in experience which provide foundations for other knowledge-claims and serve as the final terminating points for chains of epistemic justification. Furthermore, his *psychological nominalism* held that knowledge begins with the ability to justify—the capacity to use words—and since language is public and inter-subjective, all "given" elements which purportedly ground knowledge are matters of social practice.[4] The common theme in the perspectives of these three American philosophers recovers and reiterates Charles Peirce's "first rule of reason": Do not block the way of inquiry.[5]

The major contributions of Quine, Goodman, and Sellars, though related in complex and sometimes conflicting ways and still quite controversial in some philosophical circles, signified the Americanization of analytical philosophy—like abstract expressionism Americanized modern art—and set the terms of the debate in contemporary humanistic studies. A distinctive feature of the various philosophical positions reached by Quine, Goodman, and Sellars was their elective affinities with the viewpoints of American pragmatists. Their conscious and often unconscious revival of aspects of American pragmatism opened new avenues in present-day philosophy.

Notoriously popularized by Thomas Kuhn in *The Structure of Scientific Revolutions* (1962) and controversially formulated by Richard Rorty in *Philosophy and the Mirror of Nature* (1979), epistemological holism led to a "distrust of the whole epistemological enterprise."[6] Quine quickly quipped that such scrapping of his underdetermined yet minimally foundational "observation sentences" results in "epistemological nihilism" which he unequivocably rejects.[7] For Kuhn and Rorty, methodological monism yielded a rapacious antirealism in ontology against which Sellars revolted and of which Quine recanted. Last, monocosmic naturalism blossomed into a polycosmic pluralism—dethroning the authority of science as the monopoly on truth and knowledge—which radically called into question Quine's ontological allegiance to physics and Sellars' neo-Tractarian defense of the correspondence theory of truth.[8] The patriarchal trio of postmodern American philosophy bickered among themselves, with Goodman and Quine (along with the brilliant, though then vacillating, Hilary Putnam) do-

ing so quite publicly in their historic sessions on the third floor of Emerson Hall at Harvard. Yet, despite such fruitful disagreements, Pandora's box had been opened—and pragmatism returned with a vengeance.

The great contribution of Richard Rorty is that he constructs a powerful narrative of modern North Atlantic philosophy in light of the Quine-Goodman-Sellars contributions and boldly draws the threatening implications for philosophy as a discipline. His *Philosophy and the Mirror of Nature* brings to light the deep sense of crisis within the profession of academic philosophy. Rorty's provocative and often profound meditations impel philosophers to examine the problematic status of their subject-matter—only to discover that modern North Atlantic philosophy has come to an end.

Rorty credits Wittgenstein, Heidegger, and Dewey for having "brought us into a period of 'revolutionary' philosophy" by undermining the prevailing Cartesian and Kantian paradigms and advancing new conceptions of philosophy.[9] And these monumental figures surely inspire Rorty. Yet, Rorty's philosophical debts—the actual sources of his particular anti-Cartesian and anti-Kantian arguments—are Quine's holism, Goodman's pluralism, and Sellars' anti-foundationalism. In short, despite his adamant attack on analytical philosophy—the last stage of modern Euro-American philosophy—Rorty feels most comfortable with the analytical form of philosophical argumentation.

From the disparate figures of Wittgenstein, Heidegger, and Dewey, Rorty gets a historicist directive: to eschew the quest for certainty and the search for foundations.

> These writers have kept alive the suggestion that, even when we have justified true belief about everything we want to know, we may have no more than conformity to the norms of the day. They have kept alive the historicist sense that this century's "superstition" was the last century's triumph of reason, as well as the relativist sense that the latest vocabulary, borrowed from the latest scientific achievement, may not express privileged

representations of essences, but be just another of the potential infinity of vocabularies in which the world can be described.[10]

For Rorty, the Western philosophical tradition can be overcome principally by holding at arm's length the ahistorical philosophical notions of necessity, universality, rationality, objectivity, and transcendentality. Instead, we should speak historically about transient practices, contingent descriptions, and revisable theories.

The basic lesson Rorty learns from Quine, Goodman, and Sellars is an antireductionist one: to refuse to privilege one language, language-game, morality, or society over another solely by appealing to philosophical criteria. For the results will more than likely be apologetics, "attempts to eternalize a certain contemporary language-game, social practice, or self-image."[11] In cases of conflict and disagreement, we should either support our prevailing practices, reform them, or put forward realizable alternatives to them—without appealing to ahistorical philosophical criteria or standards. In short, Rorty rejects philosophical discourse as the privileged mode of resolving intellectual disagreements.

Rorty strikes a deathblow to modern North Atlantic philosophy by telling a story about the emergence, development, and decline of its primary props: the correspondence theory of truth, the notion of privileged representations, and the idea of a self-reflective transcendental subject. Rorty's fascinating tale—his-story—is regulated by three Quine-Goodman-Sellars shifts which he delineates in detail and promotes in principle: the move toward antirealism in ontology, the move toward anti-foundationalism in epistemology and the move toward dismissing the mind as a sphere of philosophical inquiry.[12]

The move toward antirealism in ontology leaves no room for a correspondence theory of truth (of any importance) in that it undermines the very distinctions upon which such a theory rests: the distinctions between ideas and objects, words and things, language and the world, propositions and states of affairs, theories and facts. The result is not a form of idealism because the claim is not that ideas create objects, words create things, language creates the world, and so forth. Nor is the result a form of Kantianism because the claim is not that ideas constitute objects, words constitute things, language constitutes the world, and so on. Rather the result is a form of pragmatism because the claim is that evolving descriptions and ever-changing versions of objects, things, and the world issue forth from various communities as responses to certain problematics, as attempts to overcome specific situations and as means to satisfy particular needs and interests. To put it crudely, ideas, words, and language are not mirrors which copy the "real" or "objective" world but rather tools with which we cope with "our" world.

In a more philosophical vein—and as more pointedly argued in Rorty's influential essay "The World Well Lost"—the theory-laden character of observations relativizes talk about the world such that realist appeals to "the world" as a final court of appeal to determine what is true can only be viciously circular.[13] We cannot isolate "the world" from theories of the world, then compare these theories of the world with a theory-free world. We cannot compare theories with anything that is not a product of another theory. So any talk about "the world" is relative to the theories available.

The second move, toward anti-foundationalism in epistemology, takes the form of an attack on prelinguistic awareness and various notions of intuition.[14] This move precludes the notion of privileged representations because it views knowledge as a relation to propositions rather than as privileged relations to the objects certain propositions are about.

> If we think in the first way, we will see no need to end the potentially infinite regress of propositions-brought-forward-in-defense-of-other-propositions. It would be foolish to keep conversation on the subject going once everyone, or the majority, or the wise, are satisfied, but of course we *can*. If we think of knowledge in the second way, we will want to get behind rea-

sons to causes, beyond argument to compulsion from the object known, to a situation in which argument would be not just silly but impossible, for anyone gripped by the object in the required way will be *unable* to doubt or to see an alternative. To reach that point is to reach the foundations of knowledge.[15]

For Rorty, the search for such foundations expresses a need to be gripped, grasped, and compelled. This holds for Plato's Eye of the Soul perceiving the World of Being, Descartes' Eye of the Mind turned inward grasping clear and distinct mental representations, or Locke's Eye of the Mind turned outward seeing "singular presentations of sense" as bases for our knowledge. All such models view ahistorical, terminal confrontation—rather than historical, fluid conversation—as the determinant of human belief. In short, the philosophical privileging of representations principally rests upon epistemological attempts to escape from history and put a closure upon human practices. Therefore Rorty concludes:

> When Sellars's and Quine's doctrines are purified, they appear as complementary expressions of a single claim: that no "account of the nature of knowledge" can rely on a theory of representations which stand in privileged relations to reality. The work of these two philosophers enables us . . . to make clear why an "account of the nature of knowledge" can be, at most, a description of human behavior.[16]

The third move, toward dismissing the mind as a sphere of inquiry or detranscendentalizing the transcendental subject, relies, in part, on Gilbert Ryle's logical behaviorism in *The Concept of Mind* (1949) and Quine's radical behaviorism in *Word and Object* (1960). Rorty's own epistemological behaviorism links Ryle's attack on the Cartesian disembodied ego and Quine's assault on the Kantian transcendental subject (and Husserlian nonempirical ego) to a wholesale rejection of ocular metaphors in epistemology.

> A behavioristic approach to episodes of "direct awareness" is not a matter of antimentalistic polemic, but a distrust of the Platonic quest for that

special sort of certainty associated with visual perception. The image of the Mirror of Nature—a mirror more easily and certainly seen than that which it mirrors—suggests, and is suggested by, the image of philosophy as such a quest.[17]

Two crucial consequences flow from Rorty's historicist, antireductionist project. First, the distinction between the "soft" human sciences and the "hard" natural sciences collapses. The basic difference between the *Geisteswissenschaften* and the *Naturwissenschaften* is neither the self-defining character of the former nor the context-free facts of the latter. Rather the difference is between the relative stability of normal vocabularies in the natural sciences and the relative instability of normal vocabularies in the human sciences. And the irreducibility of one vocabulary to another does not imply an ontological distinction—only a functional difference.

> As Kuhn says in connection with a smaller, though obviously related issue, we cannot differentiate scientific communities by "subject matter," but rather by "examining patterns of education and communication."[18]

Needless to say, this rudimentary demythologizing of the natural sciences is of immense importance for literary critics, artists, and religious thinkers who have been in retreat and on the defensive since the Enlightenment. And the sparks generated by such a novel viewpoint in our technocentric culture are only beginning to fly.

Second, the conception of philosophy is no longer that of a tribunal of pure reason which defends or debunks claims to knowledge made by science, morality, art, or religion. Rather the voice of the philosopher is but one voice—that of the informed dilettante or polypragmatic, Socratic thinker—among others in a grand Conversation. Rorty's deconstruction of philosophy as a subject, a *Fach,* a field of professional inquiry results in equalizing (or depriviling) the voice of the philosopher in this grand Conversation.

> In this conception, "philosophy" is not a name for a discipline which confronts permanent issues,

and unfortunately keeps misstating them, or attacking them with clumsy dialectical instruments. Rather, it is a culture genre, a "voice in the conservation of mankind" (to use Michael Oakeshott's phrase), which centers on one topic rather than another at some given time not by dialectical necessity but as a result of various things happening elsewhere in the conservation (the New Science, the French Revolution, the modern novel) or of individual men of genius who think of something new (Hegel, Marx, Frege, Freud, Wittgenstein, Heidegger), or perhaps of the resultant of several such forces. Interesting philosophical change (we might say "philosophical progress," but this would be question-begging) occurs not when a new way is found to deal with an old problem but when a new set of problems emerges and the old ones begin to fade away.[19]

Rorty's historicist, antireductionist perspective amounts to a self-styled neo-pragmatism. His plausible yet objectionable uses of Wittgenstein, Heidegger, and Dewey and his creative misreadings of Quine, Goodman, and Sellars yield the most adversarial position in American academic philosophy since the fervent antiprofessionalism of William James. His controversial viewpoint is a move back not simply to American pragmatism, but more fundamentally, to Ralph Waldo Emerson, in that we are left with no philosophically authoritative traditions with which to re-create and redescribe ourselves and the world.[20] Even Dewey's historically-derived authority of science is rendered suspect—thanks to Thomas Kuhn and especially Paul Feyerabend—hence merely one tradition among others.

> Pragmatism . . . does not erect Science as an idol to fill the place once held by God. It views science as one genre of literature—or, put the other way around, literature and the arts as inquiries, on the same footing as scientific inquiries. Thus it sees ethics as neither more "relative" or "subjective" than scientific theory, nor as needing to be made "scientific." Physics is a way of trying to cope with various bits of the universe; ethics is a matter of trying to cope with other bits. Mathematics helps physics do its job; literature and the arts help ethics do its. Some of these inquiries come

up with propositions, some with narratives, some with paintings. The question of what propositions to assert, which pictures to look at, what narratives to listen to and comment on and retell, are all questions about what will help us get what we want (or about what we *should* want).[21]

For Rorty, we are Emersonian sailors, self-rebegetting creatures, adrift on Neurath's boat—forever inventing and creating new self-images, vocabularies, techniques, and instruments in light of a useful backdrop of mortal beliefs and values which have no philosophical foundation or transhistorical justification. To put it bluntly, we are North Atlantic ethnocentrists in solidarity with a civilization (or set of contemporary tribal practices)—and possibly a decaying and declining one—which has no philosophical defense. In this sense, Rorty's neo-pragmatism is a form of ethnocentric posthumanism. He is unashamedly ethnocentric in that he holds that no other civilization is worth choosing over the modern West. Yet his viewpoint differs from Matthew Arnold's bourgeois humanism and John Dewey's plebeian humanism because he believes no philosophical case can be made for this civilization.

Rorty's neo-pragmatism ingeniously echoes the strident antihumanist critiques—such as those of Martin Heidegger, Jacques Derrida, and Michel Foucault—of a moribund bourgeois humanism. Yet his brand of neo-pragmatism domesticates these critiques in a smooth and witty Attic prose and, more importantly, dilutes them by refusing to push his own project toward cultural and political criticisms of the civilization he (and, in varying degrees, we) cherishes. In this way, Rorty circumscribes his ethnocentric posthumanism within a practical arena of bourgeois humanism.

Yet, from an ethical point of view—the central point of view for pragmatists—what is the difference that makes a difference here? Does Rorty's neo-pragmatism only kick the philosophical props from under bourgeois capitalist societies and require no change in our culture and political practices? What are the ethical and political consequences of adopting his neo-pragmatism? On the macrosocietal level, there simply are none. In this sense, Rorty's neo-pragmatism is, in part, a self-conscious post-philosophical ideological project to promote the basic practices of bourgeois capitalist societies while discouraging philosophical defenses of them. Rorty's insouciance toward philosophy is coupled with his vigilance toward bourgeois American practices. In short, he throws the ball back into the leftist or rightist courts.

But, on the microinstitutional level, Rorty's neo-pragmatism makes a difference. This difference is that his viewpoint has immense antiprofessional implications for the academy—as enacted in his departure from, and refusal to be appointed in, an academic philosophy department. On his view, academic philosophers can neither justify their specialized activities nor legitimate their narrow results without the very philosophical defenses he undermines. In this way, Rorty's neo-pragmatism provides not an earth-shaking perspective for the modern West but rather is a symptom of the crisis in the highly specialized professional stratum of educational workers in the philosophical departments of universities and colleges. Rorty's antiepistemological radicalism and belletristic antiacademicism are welcome in a discipline deeply entrenched in a debased insularity and debilitating isolation. Yet, ironically, his project, though pregnant with rich possibilities, remains polemical and hence barren. It refuses to give birth to the offspring it conceives. Rorty leads philosophy to the complex world of politics and culture, but confines his engagement to transformation in the academy and apologetics for the modern West.

This political narrowness is exemplified in Rorty's seductive interpretation of the Western philosophical tradition in general and the Anglo-American analytical tradition in particular. This interpretation is itself symptomatic of the ahistorical character of Anglo-American philosophy. Rorty's historicist sense remains too broad, too thin—devoid of the realities of power; his ethnocentric posthumanism is too vague, too nonchalant—and unmindful of the decline of liberalism. Furthermore, Rorty's demythologizing of philosophy seems to retreat into the philosophical

arena as soon as pertinent sociohistorical issues are raised.

For instance, is there a link between the emerging antirealism in ontology and the crisis of intellectual authority within our learned professional academies and educational institutions? Is there a relation between the anti-foundationalism in epistemology and the crisis of legitimacy among those subjected to our intellectual authority? Does the detranscendentalizing of the subject express the deep sense of impotence in contemporary capitalist societies, the sense of reaching a dead end with no foreseeable way out or no discernible liberating projects in the near future—hence the proliferation of prevailing apocalyptic forecasts, narcissistic living, and self-indulgent, ironic forms of thinking? If science is, as Rorty notes, a "value-laden enterprise,"[22] is there an ideological character intrinsic to the very methods of the natural sciences owing to an agreed-upon conception of and disposition toward nature which may promote the domination not only of our environment but also those people subsumed under the rubric "nature" such as women, non-Europeans and even "earthy" workers?

The central concern underlying these rhetorical yet crucial questions is that it is impossible to historicize philosophy without partly politicizing (in contrast to vulgarly ideologizing) it. Surely, the relation of philosophy to history and politics is complex. Yet embarking on a historicist project which demystifies philosophy entails dragging-in the complexities of politics and culture. To tell a tale about the historical character of philosophy while eschewing the political content, role, and function of philosophy in various historical periods is to promote an ahistorical approach in the name of history. To undermine the privileged notions of objectivity, universality, and transcendentality without acknowledging and accenting the oppressive deeds done under the aegis of these notions is to write a thin, i.e., intellectual and homogeneous, history—a history which fervently attacks epistemological privilege but remains relatively silent about political, economic, racial, and sexual privilege. Such a history which surreptitiously suppresses certain histories even raises the sinister possibility that the antiepistemological radicalism of neo-pragmatism—much like the antimetaphysical radicalism of poststructuralism—may be an emerging form of ideology in late capitalist societies which endorses the existing order while undergirding sophisticated antiepistemological and antimetaphysical tastes of postmodern avant-gardists.

Indeed, the relativist, even nihilist, implications of neo-pragmatism upset mainstream realists and old-style humanists. So the narrow though noteworthy battle within the academy between the professional avant-gardists and professional establishmentarians will continue to be intense. Yet after the philosophical smoke clears, the crucial task is to pursue thick, i.e., social and heterogeneous, historical accounts for the emergence, development, sustenance, and decline of vocabularies and practices in the natural and human sciences against the background of dynamic changes in specific (and often coexisting) modes of production, political conflicts, cultural configurations, and personal turmoil.

Rorty is highly suspicious of thick historical accounts. For example, when a provisional explanation—even a speculative one—seems appropriate for the centrality of ocular metaphors in Western thought, he asserts that:

> there was, we moderns may say with the ingratitude of hindsight, no particular reason why this ocular metaphor seized the imagination of the founders of Western thought.[23]

And when he contemplates questions about the acceptance and performance of modern science and moral consciousness in the West, he concludes that "in no case does anyone know what might count as a good answer."[24]

In light of such pessimism regarding historical accounts, one wonders whether Rorty takes his own neo-pragmatic viewpoint seriously. Is a "good answer" something more than a particular insightful interpretation based on an emerging, prevailing, or declining social consensus put to a specific purpose? Is not Rorty's narrative itself a "good answer" to Cartesians, Kantians, and analytic philosophers? In short, Rorty's neo-pragmatism has no place for ahistorical philosophical justifications, yet his thin historicism rests content with intellectual historical narratives and distrusts social historical narratives. This thin historicism—linked to the narrow ethical and political consequences of his narrative—is clearly illustrated in his frequent use of an all-encompassing and undifferentiated conception of society.

> Explaining rationality and epistemic authority by reference to what society lets us say, rather than the latter by the former, is the essence of what I shall call "epistemological behaviorism."[25]

It should be clear that Rorty's thin historicism needs Marx, Durkheim, Weber, de Beauvoir, and Du Bois; that is, his narrative needs a more subtle historical and sociological perspective.

Despite the limitations, Rorty's neo-pragmatism can serve as a useful springboard for a more engaged, even subversive, philosophical perspective. This is so primarily because it encourages the cultivation of critical attitudes toward all philosophical traditions. This crucial shift in the subject matter of philosophers from the grounding of beliefs to the scrutiny of groundless traditions—from epistemology to ethics, truth to practices, foundations to consequences—can lend itself to emancipatory ends in that it proposes the tenuous self-images and provisional vocabularies that undergird past and present social orders as central objects of criticism, as the primary subject matter for neo-pragmatic philosophers.

Rorty's perspective creates new discursive space—especially in the academy—for those on the underside of history. Its explicit ethnocentrism—of which there is much to preserve and reject—solicits critiques from those victimized by the North Atlantic conversation which often excludes them and by the North Atlantic societies which usually oppress them. These marginal voices and peoples are excluded and oppressed not because they have a monopoly on truth which frightens the dominant culture—though there is much to learn from marginal peoples—but rather because the historical development of the structural societal mechanisms, such as class exploitation, state repression, patriarchy, and racism, reproduce and reinforce such marginality.[26] Alienated intellectuals from marginal groups and subaltern classes often forget that their relative exclusion from the dominant conversation is a by-product of these mechanisms—not a personal conspiracy to silence their eager voices. Rorty's neo-pragmatism is significant for marginal intellectuals principally because oppressed peoples have more at stake than others in focusing on the tenuous self-images and provisional vocabularies which have had and do have hegemonic status in past and present societies.

Rorty's project should not be viewed as a nostalgic call for a pristine form of pragmatism nor a nativistic move toward Americanism in philosophy. Yet, as I noted earlier, his cosmopolitan conversation presupposes the fruits of bourgeois humanism: North Atlantic ethnocentrism. In this sense, his viewpoint resembles the earlier forms of American pragmatism. Like the first great pragmatists, Charles Peirce and William James, Rorty demystifies science—but he does not share their interest in updating religion. He shuns Peirce's attempt to save the notion of Reality by means of a communal eschatology and rejects James' obsession with the irreducibility of individuality and the mystery of plurality. Similar to John Dewey—the first world-historical figure in American philosophy—Rorty historicizes philosophy and Americanizes history. He frees philosophy from its illusions of transcendental quests and delusions of detached autonomy. Philosophy becomes an enabling device to enhance the capacity of men and women to create new and better self-images and vocabularies. Rorty and Dewey herald community and solidarity and reject nihilism, skepticism, and pessimism. Yet Rorty's neo-pragmatism contains neither the creative ambition nor the engaged activism of Dewey's historical theory of inquiry and reflective intelligence which is, in part, a theory of social reform and amelioration. Last, Rorty and Dewey both Americanize history in that for them the march of freedom in modern history is exemplified in the march of the best in America and the march of America in history is to be viewed critically in light of the best in American democracy. In this way, Dewey's libertarian democratic socialism and Rorty's revisionist liberalism view history through an American lens.[27]

If American neo-pragmatism is to put forward an acceptable philosophic vision and project for contemporary North Atlantic civilization, it must build upon the Quine-Goodman-Sellers contributions, refine the conceptions of philosophy put forward by Dewey and Rorty and encounter more fully the classical and contemporary discourses in social theory, cultural criticism, and historiography. American neo-pragmatic philosophers should not settle simply for shedding old self-images and breaking out of professional modes; they also can contribute to the making of a new and better global civilization.

NOTES

1. The classic essays on the philosophical refinement and rejection of these various doctrines are Carl G. Hempel, "Empiricist Criteria of Cognitive Significance: Problems and Changes" and "The Theoretician's Dilemma: A Study in the Logic of Theory Construction" in his *Aspects of Scientific Explanation and Other Essays in the Philosophy of Science* (New York: Free Press, 1965), p. 101–122; 173–226.

2. For the powerful and often persuasive arguments for Quine's epistemological holism and methodological monism, see his classic essay, "Two Dogmas of Empiricism" in *From a Logical Point of View* (New York: Harper & Row, 1963), pp. 20–46 and his more personal reflections in "The Pragmatists' Place in Empiricism," in Robert J. Mulvaney and Philip M. Zeltner, eds., *Pragmatism: Its Sources and Prospects* (Columbia: University of South Carolina Press, 1981), pp. 23–39. For Quine's naturalism, especially his conception of philosophy as being continuous with science, see "Epistemology Naturalized" and "Natural Kinds" in *Ontological Relativity and Other Essays* (New York: Columbia University Press, 1969), pp. 69–90; 114–138.

3. Nelson Goodman arrived at his logical conventionalism after his long and tortuous struggle with Rudolf Carnap's *The Logical Construction of the World* as portrayed in the revision of his Harvard dissertation, *The Structure of Appearance* (Cambridge: Harvard University Press, 1951). Goodman's postempiricist antire-

ductionism is best seen in his powerful essay, "The Test of Simplicity" and his classic piece, "The Way the World Is," in *Problems and Projects* (New York: Bobbs-Merrill, 1972), 279–294, pp. 24–32 respectively. His full-blown ontological pluralism is put forward in his *Ways of Worldmaking* (Indianapolis: Hackett, 1978).

4. Sellars' classic statement is "Empiricism and the Philosophy of Mind" in Herbert Feigel and Michael Scriven, eds. *Minnesota Studies in the Philosophy of Science*, vol. 1 (Minneapolis: University of Minnesota Press, 1956), pp. 253–329.

5. *Collected Papers of Charles Sanders Peirce*, Charles Hartshorne, Paul Weiss, and Arthur Burks, eds. (Cambridge: Harvard University Press, 1933–58), 1:135.

6. Richard Rorty, *Philosophy and the Mirror of Nature* (Princeton: Princeton University Press, 1979), p. 181.

7. For Quine's defense of observation sentences and the intimation that Kuhn is an epistemological nihilist and cultural relativist, see Quine, *Ontological Relativity and Other Essays*, pp. 86–90.

8. For Sellars' neo-Tractarian theory of "logical picturing," see his *Science and Metaphysics* (New York: Humanities Press, 1968), pp. 116–150, 169–174. For Quine's full-scale defense of what he calls his "ontological line of naive and unregenerate realism" and "robust realism"—which recants his earlier pragmatic claims in "On What There Is" in Quine, *From a Logical Point of View*, pp. 1–19—see *The Roots of Reference* (Lasalle, Canada: Open Court, 1973) and *Theories and Things* (Cambridge: Harvard University Press, 1981), especially his responses to Donald Davidson, Nelson Goodman, Saul Kripke, Grover Maxwell, and David Armstrong, pp. 38–42; 96–99; 173–178; 182–184.

9. Richard Rorty, *Philosophy and the Mirror of Nature*, p. 6.

10. *Ibid.*, p. 367.

11. *Ibid.*, p. 10.

12. I have explored these shifts in detail in Cornel West, "Nietzsche's Prefiguration of Postmodern American Philosophy," *Boundary* 2, special Nietzsche issue, Daniel O'Hara, ed., (Spring-Fall 1981), 9(10):241–270.

13. Richard Rorty, "The World Well Lost," in *Consequences of Pragmatism* (Minneapolis: University of Minnesota Press: 1982), pp. 3–18. This essay first appeared in *The Journal of Philosophy*, (1972), 69:649–665.

14. For Rorty's more direct and technical attacks on the various forms of intuition, see his important essays, "Intuition" in the *Encyclopedia of Philosophy*, vol. 4, pp. 204–212; "Wittgenstein, Privileged Access, and Incommunicability," *American Philosophical Quarterly* (1970), 7:192–205; and "Criteria and Necessity," *Nous* (1973), 7:313–329. It also should be noted that Rorty

learned historicist and antireductionist lessons from and in response to his early teachers at the University of Chicago, Richard McKeon and Robert Brumbaugh, and his thesis adviser at Yale, Paul Weiss. His first two major essays, published in 1961, bear witness to such lessons: "The Limits of Reductionism" in Irwin C. Lied, ed., *Experience, Existence, and The Good: Essays in Honor of Paul Weiss* (Carbondale: University of Illinois Press, 1961), pp. 100–116 and "Pragmatism, Categories, and Language" in *Philosophical Review* (1961), 70:197–223. The impact of Rorty's maternal grandfather, Walter Rauschenbusch, the great social gospel advocate, upon his neo-pragmatism remains unexplored.

15. Richard Rorty, *Philosophy and the Mirror of Nature, op. cit.*, p. 159.

16. *Ibid.*, p. 182.

17. *Ibid.*, p. 181.

18. *Ibid.*, p. 331. Rorty's quote from Kuhn is in Thomas S. Kuhn's *The Essential Tension* (Chicago: University of Chicago Press, 1977), p. xvi.

19. *Ibid.*, p. 264

20. Rorty's neo-pragmatism also is of an Emersonian sort in that poetic activity tends to regulate his conception of human redescription and constitute the most noble of human practices. For his constant praise of self-redescription, see Rorty, *Philosophy and the Mirror of Nature*, pp. 358–359, 362, 367, and 378. This Emersonian theme should come to the fore in Rorty's book on Heidegger that will appear in the Cambridge University Press *Modern European Philosophy* series. In his unpublished essay, "Heidegger Against the Pragmatists," Emerson already has an absent presence.

21. Rorty, *Consequences of Pragmatism*, p. xliii.

22. Rorty, *Philosophy and the Mirror of Nature*, p. 341.

23. *Ibid.*, p. 38.

24. *Ibid.*, p. 341.

25. *Ibid.*, p. 174.

26. The most intellectually underdeveloped state of academic philosophical articulation among marginal peoples may be that of Afro-Americans and Africans—owing to severe conversational exclusion and societal oppression. But presently black philosophical voices are emerging with power and perspicacity. Note the collection of essays on "Philosophy and the Black Experience" in *The Philosophical Forum*, vol. 9, nos. 2–3 (Winter 1977–78) and those in Leonard Harris, ed. *Philosophy Born of Struggle: Anthology of Afro-American Philosophy from 1917* (Dubuque, Iowa: Kendall/Hunt, 1983.). For exemplary African texts, see Kwasi Wiredu, *Philosophy and an African Culture* (Cambridge: Cambridge University Press, 1980); Paulin J. Hountondji, *African Philosophy: Myth and Reality* (Bloomington: Indiana University Press, 1983); and Theophilus Okere, *African Philosophy: A Historico-Hermeneutical*

*Investigation of the Conditions of Its Possibility* (New York: University Press of America, 1983).

27. American pragmatism has moved beyond such lens primarily in the philosophical journalism of Max Eastman in the late twenties and thirties, the sophisticated pragmatic Marxism of Sidney Hook in the thirties and moments in the eclectic yet learned texts of Richard Bernstein. Eastman was the first noteworthy left pragmatist but ultimately became captive to a vulgar Americanism. Hook has fought the major ideological battles of this century, holding his social democratic ground, taking a few courageous stands yet making major mistakes. His Americanism retains a tempered and hardly discernible critical cutting edge. Bernstein writes well about the major philosophical minds of our time, yet he is reluctant to specify in any detail his progressive politics. Yet he, along with the early Eastman and Hook, provide inspiration to young left neopragmatist philosophers. Of course, this holds for high moments in Dewey.

# 59      The Future of Feminist Liberalism [1]

MARTHA NUSSBAUM

*Giribala, at the age of fourteen, then started off to make her home with her husband. Her mother put into a bundle the pots and pans that she would be needing. Watching her doing that, Aulchand remarked, "Put in some rice and lentils too. I've got a job at the house of the babu. Must report to work the moment I get back. . . ."*

*Giribala picked up the bundle of rice, lentils, and cooking oil and left her village, walking a few steps behind him. He walked ahead, and from time to time asked her to walk faster, as the afternoon was starting to fade.*

—MAHASWETA DEVI, "GIRIBALA," 1982 [2]

*It will be seen how in place of the wealth and poverty of political economy come the rich human being and rich human need. The rich human being is . . . the human being in need of a totality of human life-activities.*

—MARX, *ECONOMIC AND PHILOSOPHICAL MANUSCRIPTS OF 1844*

## I. Liberalism and Feminism

During the 1950's and 1960's, it was widely believed that political philosophy had come to a stop. The normative tradition of theorizing about justice that extended, in Western thought, from Plato through Sidgwick and T. H. Green was con-demned as "nonsense" by those under the sway of positivism, since it pursued neither conceptual analysis nor empirical factual inquiry. Young American philosophers were discouraged from pursuing projects in this area, unless they confined themselves to analyzing the function of moral and political language.

By now all this has dramatically changed. Theorizing about justice is one of the most fertile areas of work for young philosophers, and there is virtually no department that would condemn all such work as soft and unphilosophical. Two distinct sources of creativity in this area must be credited with the shift, and it is the tense relationship between them that I wish to consider.

On the one hand, writers in the tradition of Kantian liberalism must surely be given much of the credit for the turn back to substantive political philosophy. John Rawls and Jürgen Habermas, in particular, have become central points of reference, and both must surely be counted as among the most distinguished philosophers of our century.

On the other hand, the most creative movement in the revival of theorizing about justice, I would argue, has been feminist philosophy, which has put new questions on the agenda of moral, political, and legal thought, and has pursued those questions with a prophetic sense of urgency that can be lacking in our sometimes all too detached profession. Important though issues of gender justice are now agreed to be, they were simply not addressed in most major works of political philosophy in the Western tradition; or, as in the case of Rousseau, they were addressed in a perverse and unhelpful manner. Plato and Mill are major exceptions; Mill's *The Subjection of Women* is still one of the major works in the subject, alongside the writings of Mary Wollstonecraft and other feminist women who wrote philosophy before the late-twentieth century feminist movement.[3] But systematic investigation of justice in the family, of domestic violence and child abuse, of sexual harassment and full workplace equality—all these awaited the modern feminist movement, and have been illuminated by its insights.[4]

As the names of Wollstonecraft and Mill indicate, liberalism and feminism have not always been at odds in our philosophical tradition.[5] Even today, some of our most influential feminist philosophers are liberals.[6] But on the whole liberalism has not fared well in feminist circles. Leading feminists have denounced liberalism as a theoretical approach with insufficient radical potential to expose the roots of women's subordination or to articulate principles for a society of gender justice.[7]

I have argued in the past that some of these feminist criticisms are based on a misunderstanding of the deepest and most appealing liberal conceptions, and that other criticisms, while based on an adequate understanding, should themselves be rejected in favor of liberal conceptions by those who seek full justice for the world's women.[8] Here I shall not return to those arguments. Instead, I shall investigate two areas of political thought in which liberalism, even in its strongest forms, has not yet given satisfactory answers to deep problems exposed by feminist thinkers.[9] Those areas are: the need for care in times of extreme dependency; and the political role of the family. I shall argue that the failure of current liberal theories to solve these problems does not mean that we should reject liberalism; it does mean, however, that we need to recast it in some major ways. I'll conclude that a form of liberalism based on ideas of human functioning and capability can carry us further than we have been able to go so far.

## II.   Need and Dependency

All theories of justice and morality based on the idea of a social contract adopt a fictional hypothesis that appears innocent, but that ultimately has problematic consequences. This is the fiction of competent adulthood. Whatever differences there are among the different founders of that tradition, all accept the basic Lockean conception of a contract among parties who, in the state of nature, are "free, equal, and independent."[10] Thus for Kant persons are characterized by both freedom and equality, and the social contract is defined as an agreement among persons so characterized. Contemporary contractarians explicitly adopt this hypothesis. For David Gauthier, people of unusual need are "not party to the moral relationships grounded by a contractarian theory."[11] Similarly, the citizens in Rawls's Well Ordered Society are "fully cooperating members of society over a complete life."[12]

Life, of course, is not like that. Real people begin their lives as helpless infants, and remain in a state of extreme, asymmetrical dependency, both physical and mental, for anywhere from ten to twenty years. At the other end of life, those who are lucky enough to live on into old age are likely to encounter another period of extreme dependency, either physical or mental or both, which may itself continue in some form for as much as twenty years. During the middle years of life, many of us encounter periods of extreme dependency, some of which involve our mental powers and some our bodily powers only, but all of which may put us in need of daily, even hourly, care by others. Finally, and centrally, there are many citizens who never have the physical and/or mental powers requisite for independence. These citizens are dependent in different ways. Some have high intellectual capabilities but are unable to give and receive love and friendship; some are capable of love, but unable to learn basic intellectual skills. Some have substantial emotional and intellectual capabilities, but in a form or at a level that requires special care. These lifelong states of asymmetrical dependency are in many respects isomorphic to the states of infants and the elderly.

In short, any real society is a caregiving and care-receiving society, and must therefore discover ways of coping with these facts of human neediness and dependency that are compatible with the self-respect of the recipients and do not exploit the caregivers. This is a central issue for feminism since, in every part of the world, women do a large part of this work, usually without pay, and often without recognition that it is work. They are often thereby handicapped in other functions of life.[13]

It must be said at the outset that in this particular area a Kantian starting point is likely to give bad guidance. For Kant, human dignity and our moral capacity, dignity's source, are radically separate from the natural world. Morality certainly has the task of providing for human neediness, but the idea that we are at bottom split beings, both

rational persons and animal dwellers in the world of nature, never ceases to influence Kant's way of thinking about how these deliberations about our needs will go.

What's wrong with the split? Quite a lot. First, it ignores the fact that our dignity just is the dignity of a certain sort of animal. It is the animal sort of dignity, and that very sort of dignity could not be possessed by a being who was not mortal and vulnerable, just as the beauty of a cherry tree in bloom could not be possessed by a diamond. If it makes sense to think of God as having dignity (I'm not sure—magnificence and awe-inspiringness seem more appropriate attributes), it is emphatically not dignity of that type.[14] Second, the split wrongly denies that animality can itself have a dignity; thus it leads us to slight aspects of our own lives that have worth, and to distort our relation to the other animals.[15] Third, it makes us think of the core of ourselves as self-sufficient, not in need of the gifts of fortune; in so thinking we greatly distort the nature of our own morality and rationality, which are thoroughly material and animal themselves; we learn to ignore the fact that disease, old age, and accident can impede the moral and rational functions, just as much as the other animal functions. Fourth, it makes us think of ourselves as a-temporal. We forget that the usual human lifecycle brings with it periods of extreme dependency, in which our functioning is very similar to that enjoyed by the mentally or physically handicapped throughout their lives.

It is important to notice that the split goes wrong in both directions: it suggests, as I have said, that our rationality is independent of our vulnerable animality; and it also suggests that animality, and non-human animals, lack intelligence, are just brutish and "dumb." Both implications of the split should, of course, be called into question: in nature we find a rich continuum of types of intelligence, and of practical capacities of many types; we cannot understand ourselves well without situating ourselves within that continuum.[16]

Political thought in the Kantian social-contract tradition (to stick with the part of the tradition I find deepest and most appealing) suffers from the conception of the person with which it begins. Rawls's contracting parties are fully aware of their need for material goods. Here Rawls diverges from Kant, building need into the foundations of the theory.[17] But he does so only to a degree: for the parties are imagined throughout as competent contracting adults, roughly similar in need, and capable of a level of social cooperation that makes them able to make a contract with others. Such a hypothesis seems required by the very idea of a contract for mutual advantage.

In so conceiving of persons, Rawls explicitly omits from the situation of basic political choice the more extreme forms of need and dependency human beings may experience. His very concept of social cooperation is based on the idea of reciprocity between rough equals, and has no explicit place for relations of extreme dependency. Thus, for example, Rawls refuses to grant that we have any duties of justice to animals, on the grounds that they are not capable of reciprocity (TJ 17,504–5); they are owed "compassion and humanity," but "[t]hey are outside the scope of the theory of justice, and it does not seem possible to extend the contract doctrine so as to include them in a natural way" (TJ 512). This makes a large difference to his theory of political distribution. For his account of the primary goods, introduced, as it is, as an account of the needs of citizens who are characterized by the two moral powers and by the capacity to be "fully cooperating," has no place for the need of many real people for the kind of care we give to people who are not independent.[18]

Now of course Rawls is perfectly aware that his theory focuses on some cases and leaves others to one side. He insists that, although the need for care for people who are not independent is "a pressing practical question," it may reasonably be postponed to the legislative stage, after basic political institutions are designed:

> So let's add that all citizens are fully cooperating members of society over the course of a complete life. This means that everyone has sufficient intellectual powers to play a normal part in society, and no one suffers from unusual needs that are especially difficult to fulfill, for example, unusual and costly medical requirements. Of course, care for those with such requirements is a pressing practical question. But at this initial stage, the fundamental problem of social justice arises between those who are full and active and morally conscientious participants in society, and directly or indirectly associated together throughout a complete life. Therefore, it is sensible to lay aside certain difficult complications. If we can work out a theory that covers the fundamental case, we can try to extend it to other cases later. (DL 546)

This reply seems inadequate. Care for children, the elderly, and the mentally and physically handicapped is a major part of the work that needs to be done in any society, and in most societies it is a source of great injustice. Any theory of justice needs to think about the problem from the beginning, in the design of the most basic level of institutions, and particularly in its theory of the primary goods.[19]

More generally, variations and asymmetries in physical need are simply not isolated or easily isolable cases: they are a pervasive fact of human life: pregnant or lactating women need more nutrients than non-pregnant persons, children need more protein than adults; and the very young and very old need more care than others in most areas of their lives. Even within the clearly recognized terrain of the "fully cooperating," then, the theory of primary goods seems flawed if it does not take such variations into account in measuring who is and is not the least well off, rather than, as the theory recommends, determining that status by income and wealth alone.[20] Amartya Sen has used the example of a person in a wheelchair, who will certainly need more resources to be fully mobile than will a person whose limbs work well.[21] With the same amount of income and wealth, this person will actually be much worse off than someone whose limbs work well.[22] Rawls can't consistently exclude this person, who surely has the mental and moral powers. But even if he should exclude these physical disabilities, as some of his remarks suggest,[23] the problem of variation in need is pervasive. So even in order to take account of the physical needs of non-disabled citizens—which the theory seems bound, even on its own terms, to take account of[24]—Rawls will need a way of measuring well-being that does not rely on income and wealth alone, but looks at the abilities of citizens to engage in a wide range of human activities.

Thomas Scanlon confronts these problems facing a Kantian contract doctrine much more directly than does Rawls. I am unable here to discuss the subtleties of his view, which in any case is a moral and not a political contract doctrine, and which does not employ a hypothetical initial contract situation as does Rawls's theory. But, taking cognizance of the problem posed for such a theory by people with various handicaps, and by non-human animals, he concludes that we may recognize facts of extreme dependency in such a doctrine in one of two ways. Either we may persist in our pursuit of the contract doctrine, and say that the contracting parties are also trustees for those who are incapable of participating in that process; or we may say that the contract doctrine offers an account of only one part of morality: we will need a different account to cope with the facts of extreme dependency.[25] Applied to the Rawlsian project of selecting principles of justice that will form the basic structure of society,[26] this would mean that we either take the parties in the Original Position to be trustees for the interests of all dependent members of society, as they currently are trustees for future generations—or else we should grant that the Original Position is not a complete device for designing political justice, and that other approaches are also required.

The first solution seems unsatisfactory. To make the "fully cooperating" trustees in a hypothetical original situation slights the dignity of physically and mentally handicapped people, suggesting that they are worthy of respect in the design of basic political institutions only on account of some relationship in which they stand to so-called "fully cooperating" people. The bargain, after all, is a bargain for mutual advantage, and it assumes a rough equality among its participants; the dependents enter the bargain not because they are equipped to participate in such a bargain, but only because a contracting party cares about their interests. Furthermore, the move also means making the "fully cooperating" trustees for their own infancy and senility, and perhaps other stages of their own lives. Gauthier puts the problem most starkly, when he says that the elderly have paid for their care by earlier periods of productive activity, but the handicapped have not.[27] In other words, for the contractarian only productivity justifies, ultimately, a claim to support, and the elderly get support only because at one time they were not elderly. Animality and human neediness all on their own cannot justify a claim to support. Rawls's theory, though more subtle than Gauthier's, still suffers from something like this problem. To require of the parties that they split their thinking in this way, conceiving of themselves as made up of two parts, the rational and the animal, is to force into their thinking a Kantian splitting that may well prejudice their thinking about the dignity of animality in themselves. Are we not in effect saying that animality gets support only in virtue of its contingent link to "fully cooperating" adulthood? And doesn't this slight the dignity and worth that needy human animals surely possess even when they are not fully cooperating? Surely, if it is not necessary to require such split thinking, we should avoid it.

Thus I prefer the second solution: the contract doctrine does not provide a complete ethical theory. But this reply, which would be fine for Scanlon, because he is doing ethical theory, employs no hypothetical initial situation, and makes no claims to completeness, creates large problems for the contract doctrine in the area of political theory. Any approach to the design of basic political institutions must aim at a certain degree of completeness and finality, as Rawls's doctrine explicitly does.[28] We are designing the basic structure of society, those institutions that influence all citizens' life-chances pervasively and from the start. So it is not open to us to say: we have done one part of that task, but of course other parts, equally basic, based on completely different principles, will come along later. If we leave for another day not only our relations to the non-human animals, but also the needs entailed by our own animality, that would leave huge areas of political justice up for grabs and would entail the recognition of much indeterminacy in the account of basic justice as so far worked out.

What, then, can be done to give the problem of care and dependency sufficient prominence in a theory of justice? The first thing we might try, one that has been suggested by Eva Kittay in her fine book, is to add the need for care during periods of extreme and asymmetrical dependency to the Rawlsian list of primary goods, thinking of care as among the basic needs of citizens.[29]

This suggestion, if we adopt it, would lead us to make another modification: for care is hardly a commodity, like income and wealth, to be measured by the sheer amount of it citizens have. Thus adding care to the list would cause us to notice that Rawls's list of primary goods is already quite heterogeneous in its structure. Some of its members are thing-like items such as income and wealth; but some are already more like human capabilities to function in various ways: the liberties, opportunities, and powers, and also the social basis of self-respect. Along with this suggestion, we might propose understanding the entire list of primary goods as a list not of things but of basic capabilities.[30] This change would not only enable us to deal better with people's needs for various types of love and care as elements of the list, but would also answer the point that Sen has repeatedly made all along about the unreliability of income and wealth as indices of well-being. The well-being of citizens will now be measured not by the sheer amount of income and wealth they have, but by the degree to which they have the various capabilities on the list. One may be well off in terms of income and wealth, and yet unable to function well in the workplace, because of burdens of caregiving at home.[31]

If we accepted these two changes, we would surely add a third, highly relevant to our thoughts about infancy and old age. We would add other capability-like items to the list of basic goods: for example the social basis of health, and the social basis of imagination and emotional well-being.[32]

Suppose, then, we do make these three changes in the list of primary goods: we add care in times of extreme dependency to the list of primary goods; we reconfigure the list as a list of capabilities; and we add other pertinent items to the list as well. Have we done enough to salvage the contract doctrine as a way of generating basic political principles? I believe that there is still room for doubt. Consider the role of primary goods in Rawls's theory. The account of primary goods is introduced in connection with the Kantian political conception of the person, as an account of what citizens characterized by the two moral powers need.[33] Thus, we have attributed basic importance to care only from the point of view of our own current independence. It is good to be cared for only because care subserves moral personality, understood in a Kantian way as conceptually quite distinct from need and animality. This seems like another more subtle way of making our animality subserve our humanity, where humanity is understood to exclude animality. The idea is that because we are dignified beings capable of political reciprocity, therefore we had better provide for times when we are not that, so we can get back to being that as quickly as possible. I think that this is a dubious enough way to think about illnesses in the prime of life; but it surely leads us in the direction of a contemptuous attitude toward infancy and childhood, and, a particular danger in our society, toward elderly disability. Finally, it leads us strongly in the direction of not fully valuing those with lifelong mental disabilities: somehow or other, care for them is supposed to be valuable only for the sake of what it does for the "fully cooperating." They are, it would seem, being used as means for someone else's ends, and their full humanity is still being denied.

So I believe that we need to delve deeper, redesigning the political conception of the person, bringing the rational and the animal into a more intimate relation with one another, and acknowledging that there are many types of dignity in the world, including the dignity of mentally disabled children and adults, the dignity of the senile demented elderly, and the dignity of babies at the breast. We want the picture of the parties who design political institutions to build these facts in from the start. The kind of reciprocity in which we humanly engage has its periods of symmetry, but also, of necessity, its periods of more or less extreme asymmetry—and this is part of our lives that we bring into our situation as parties who design just institutions. And this may well mean that the theory cannot be a contractarian theory at all.

Such a conclusion should be reached with caution. Rawls's theory has often been wrongly criticized, because critics have not noticed that his model of the person in the Original Position is complex: his account of the person is not simply the account of the rationality of the parties, but that account *combined with* the account of the veil of ignorance, which is a complex way of modeling benevolence. Thus it is incorrect to say that he has not included concern for others in the conception of the person that forms the foundation of his theory—as he has noted, discussing Schopenhauer's similar critique of Kant.[34] What this mistake shows us is that the contract doctrine has many ways of modeling the person; so we should not rule out the possibility that some device may be found through which a doctrine basically contractarian in spirit could model need and animality, just as it has modeled benevolence.[35] There is, however, some reason to doubt that this can be done. For any such model would still involve a split of just the sort I've objected to, one that makes our rationality trustee, in effect, for our animality. And that, as I've argued, is inadequate for the kind of dignity and centrality we want to give to the problems of asymmetrical need.

Thus, while not denying that some determined contractarian might possibly solve this problem, I think it best to proceed as if it has not been solved. When we add to our worries the fact that Rawls's contract doctrine uses a political concept of the person at a number of different points, most of them not in association with the complex model of the original position, we have even more reason to want the political concept of the person to be one that does justice to temporality and need.

So I believe we need to adopt a political conception of the person that is more Aristotelian than Kantian,[36] one that sees the person from the start as both capable and needy—"in need of a rich plurality of life-activities," to use Marx's phrase, whose availability will be the measure of well-being. Such a conception of the person, which builds growth and decline into the trajectory of human life, will put us on the road to thinking well about what society should design. We don't have to contract for what we need by producing; we have a claim to support in the dignity of our human need itself. Since this is not just an Aristotelian idea, but one that corresponds to human experience, there is good reason to think that it can command a political consensus in a pluralistic society. If we begin with this conception of the person and with a suitable list of the central capabilities as primary goods, we can begin designing institutions by asking what it would take to get citizens up to an acceptable level on all these capabilities.

In *Women and Human Development* I therefore propose that the idea of central human capabilities be used as the analogue of Rawlsian primary goods, and that the guiding political conception of the person should be an Aristotelian/Marxian conception of the human being as in need of a rich plurality of life-activities, to be shaped by both practical reason and affiliation. I argue that these interlocking conceptions can form the core of a political conception that is a form of political liberalism, close to Rawls's in many ways. The core of the political conception is endorsed for political purposes only, giving citizens a great deal of space to pursue their own comprehensive conceptions of value, whether secular or religious. Yet more room for a reasonable pluralism in conceptions of the good is secured by insisting that the appropriate political goal is capability only: citizens should be given the option, in each area, of functioning in accordance with a given capability or not so functioning. To secure a capability to a citizen it is not enough to create a sphere of non-interference: the public conception must design the material and institutional environment so that it provides the requisite affirmative support for all the relevant capabilities.[37] Thus care for physical and mental dependency needs will enter into the conception at many points, as part of what is required to secure to citizens one of the capabilities on the list.[38]

My solution to these problems lies, then, squarely within the liberal tradition. But Kittay suggests that we should go further, departing from that tradition altogether. She holds that Western political theory must be radically reconfigured to put the fact of dependency at its heart. The fact, she says, that we are all "some mother's child," existing in intertwined relations of dependency, should be the guiding image for political thought.[39] Such a care-based theory, she thinks, will be likely to be very different from any liberal theory, since the liberal tradition is deeply committed to goals of independence and liberty. Although Kittay supplies few details to clarify the practical meaning of the difference, I think her idea is that the care-based theory would support a type of politics that provides comprehensive support for need throughout all citizens' lives, as in some familiar ideals of the welfare state—but a welfare state in which liberty is far less important than security and well-being.

Kittay is not altogether consistent on this point. At times she herself uses classic liberal arguments, saying that we need to remember that caregivers have their own lives to lead, and to support policies that give them more choices.[40] But on the whole she rejects, in the abstract, solutions that emphasize freedom as a central political goal. The concrete measures she favors do not seem to have such sweeping anti-liberal implications. The restoration and expansion of Aid to Families with Dependent Children; expansion of the Family and Medical Leave Act of 1993; various educational measures promoting the dignity of the disabled, through a judicious combination of "mainstreaming" and separate education[41]—all these are familiar liberal policies, which can be combined with an emphasis on choice and liberty as important social goals. Kittay's most controversial proposal, that of a direct non-means-tested payment to those who care for family dependents at home—clearly has, or could have, a liberal rationale: that of ensuring that these people are seen as active, dignified workers rather than passive non-contributors.

Indeed, if we adopt all the changes I have proposed, we will still have a theory that is basically liberal. For theories that take their start from an idea of human capability and functioning emphasize the importance of giving all citizens the chance to develop the full range of human powers, at whatever level their condition allows, and to enjoy the sort of liberty and independence their condition allows. Would we do better to reject this theory in favor of Kittay's idea, rejecting independence as a major social goal and conceiving of the state as a universal mother? To be sure, nobody is ever self-sufficient; the independence we enjoy is always both temporary and partial, and it is good to be reminded of that fact by a theory that also stresses the importance of care in times of dependency. But is being "some mother's child" a sufficient image for the citizen in a just society? I think we need a lot more: liberty and opportunity, the chance to form a plan of life, the chance to learn and imagine on one's own.

These goals are as important for the mentally handicapped as they are for others, though much more difficult to achieve. Although Kittay's daughter Sesha will never live on her own (and although Kittay is right to say that independence should not be seen as a necessary condition of dignity for all mentally disabled people),[42] many others do aspire to hold a job, and vote, and tell their own story. Michael Bérubé ends his compelling account of his son's life with the hope that Jamie, too, will write a book about himself, as two adults with Down Syndrome recently have.[43] One day Jamie's kindergarten class went round the room, asking the children what they wanted to be when they grew up. They said the usual things: basketball star, ballet dancer, fireman. The teacher wasn't sure Jamie would understand the question, so she asked it very clearly. Jamie just said, "Big." And his literal answer, said the teacher, taught them all something about the question. Bérubé too wants, simply, a society in which his son will be able to be "big": healthy, educated, loving, active, seen as a particular person with something distinctive to contribute, rather than as "a retarded child."

For that to happen, his dependencies must be understood and supported. But so too must his need to be distinct and an individual: and at this point Bérubé refers sympathetically to Rawls. He argues that the idea at the heart of the Individuals With Disabilities Education Act (IDEA)—the idea that every child has the right to an "appropriate education" in the "least restrictive environment" possible, based on an "Individualized Education Plan"—is a profoundly liberal idea, an idea about individuality and freedom. One of the most important kinds of support mentally disabled children need is the support required to be free choosing adults, each in his or her own way. Insofar as Kittay suggests that we downplay or marginalize such liberal notions in favor of a conception of the state that makes it the parental supporter of its "children"'s needs, I think she goes too far, misconceiving what justice would be for both the disabled and the elderly. Even for Sesha, who will never vote or write, doesn't a full human life involve a kind of freedom and individuality, namely, a space in which to exchange love and enjoy light and sound, free from confinement and mockery?

So I believe that the problem we have investigated shows us that liberal theory needs to question some of its most traditional starting points—questioning, in the process, the Kantian notion of the person. But that does not disable liberalism: it just challenges us all to produce a new form of liberalism, more attentive to need and its material and institutional conditions. The liberal ideas of freedom and of the human need for various types of liberty of action are precious ideas that feminist philosophers, it seems to me, should cherish and further develop, creating theories that make it possible for all citizens to have the support they need for the full development of their human capabilities.

## III.    Justice in the Family

The most difficult problem liberal theory faces in the area of women's equality is the problem of the family.[44] On the one hand, the family is among the most significant arenas in which people pursue their own conceptions of the good, and transmit them to the next generation. This fact suggests that a liberal society should give people considerable latitude to form families as they choose. On the other hand, the family is one of the most nonvoluntary and pervasively influential of social institutions, and one of the most notorious homes of sex hierarchy, denial of equal opportunity, and sex-based violence and humiliation. These facts suggest that a society committed to equal justice for all citizens, and to securing for all citizens the social bases of liberty, opportunity, and self-respect, must constrain the family in the name of justice. Most liberal theories (Mill being the honorable exception) have simply neglected this problem, or have treated the family as a "private" sphere into which political justice should not meddle.[45] As Catharine MacKinnon has observed, the public-private distinction has typically functioned to protect *male* privacy, and not female privacy, and thence the unlimited sway of men over women in a protected domain; thus liberal rhetoric about the sanctity of privacy should strike us as "an injury got up as a gift."[46] Rawls from the first has denied that the family is a space exempt from the claims of justice, by asserting that it is part of society's basic structure, ergo one of those institutions to which principles of justice would apply.[47] But, having granted this, he then has to solve one of the most difficult of problems: how to render this institution compatible with justice.[48]

In "The Idea of Public Reason Revisited,"[49] Rawls has finally addressed the problem. He makes two claims, which are difficult to render consistent. On the one hand, he asserts that the family forms part of society's basic structure (788). At the same time, however, he claims that the two principles of justice, while they apply directly to the basic structure, do not "apply directly to the internal life of families" (788–9). In fact, he continues, the principles apply to families in just the way that they apply to society's many voluntary associations, such as churches and universities (789). That is, the principles supply external constraints on what the associations can do, but they do not regulate their internal workings. A university, for example, cannot violate basic provisions of the criminal law, or of political justice more generally; but it may assign functions in accordance with its own criteria, whatever they are. So too with the family: the principles of justice do supply real constraints, by specifying the basic rights of equal citizens. The family cannot violate these rights. "The equal rights of women and the basic rights of their children as future citizens are inalienable and protect them wherever they are. Gender distinctions limiting those rights and liberties are excluded" (791). And yet, citizens are not required to raise their children in accordance with liberal principles; we may have to allow for some traditional gendered division of labor in families, "provided it is fully voluntary and does not result from or lead to injustice" (792)—words that are honorable, but difficult to apply to reality.[50]

In practical terms, Rawls thinks that we cannot make rules for the division of labor in families, or penalize those who don't comply. But at the legislative stage we can introduce laws that protect women's full equality as citizens, for example divorce laws of the sort favored by Susan Okin: "It seems intolerably unjust that a husband may depart the family taking his earning power with him and leaving his wife and children far less advantaged than before. . . . A society that permits this does not care about women, much less about their equality, or even about their children, who are its future" (793).[51]

These proposals raise three large questions. First of all, if the family is part of the basic structure, how can it also be a voluntary institution, analogous to a church or a university?[52] The institutions of the basic structure are those whose influence is pervasive and present from the start of a human life. The family is such an institution; universities, and churches (except as extensions of families) are not. For adult women, membership in a family may be voluntary (though this is not always clear), and Rawls's protection of their exit options may suffice to ensure their full equality. But children are simply hostages to the family in which they grow up, and their participation in its

gendered structure is by no means voluntary. Granted, it is not terribly clear what it would mean to apply the principles of justice to the family *as part of the basic structure:* for surely the principles apply to the basic structure taken as a whole, and this does not entail that they apply piecemeal to every institution that forms part of the basic structure.[53] And yet the fact that the family is part of the basic structure and universities, etc., are not ought to make *some* difference in the way in which the principles apply; Rawls ought to have given us some account of that difference.

Second, Rawls does not acknowledge the parochial character of the Western nuclear family. Surprisingly, he still seems to regard some such unit as having a quasi-natural status, and as characterized by what he continues to call "natural affections"; although he has broadened his account to include non-traditional nuclear groupings, such as same-sex couples, he nowhere acknowledges the parochial character of the whole idea of raising children in a nuclear family. Village groups, extended families, women's collectives, kibbutzim, these and other groups have been involved in raising children; the contracting parties, not knowing where they are in place and time, should not give preference to a Western bourgeois form over other possible forms. They should look at the issues of justice with an open mind, giving favor to those groupings that seem most capable of rearing children, compatibly with other requirements of justice.

Third, Rawls does not recognize the extent to which, in all modern societies, the "family" is a creation of state action, enjoying a very different status from that of a church or a university. People associate in many different ways, live together, love each other, have children. Which of these will get the name "family" is a legal and political matter, never one to be decided simply by the parties themselves. The state constitutes the family structure through its laws, defining which groups of people can count as families, defining the privileges and rights of family members, defining what marriage and divorce are, what legitimacy and parental responsibility are, and so forth. This difference makes a difference: the state is present in the family from the start, in a way that is less clearly the case with the religious body or the university; it is the state who says what this thing *is* and controls how one becomes a member of it.[54]

To see this more clearly, let us consider the rituals that define a person as a member of an association: in the (private) University, matriculation (and, later, the granting of a degree); in a religious body, baptism, conversion, or some analogous entrance rite; in the family, marriage. Now it is evident that the State has some connection with university matriculation/graduation and with religious baptism/conversion: it polices these rites on the outside, by defining the institution as enjoying tax-free status, by preventing the use of cruelty or other illegalities in the ritual, and so forth. But marriage is from the start a public, state-administered rite. There are state laws defining it, which restrict entry into that privileged domain. The state does not police marriage on the outside, it marries people. Other similar people who don't meet the state's test cannot count as married, even if they satisfy all private and even religious criteria for marriage. (Thus, same-sex couples whose unions have been solemnized by some religious body still are not married, because the state has not granted them a license.) All human associations are shaped by laws and institutions, which either favor or disfavor them, and structure them in various ways. But the family is shaped by law in a yet deeper and more thoroughgoing way, in the sense that its very definition is legal and political; individuals may call themselves "a family" if they wish, but they only get to be one, in the sense that is socially significant, and that yields a wide range of social recognitions and benefits,[55] if they satisfy legal tests. In short, the political sphere cannot avoid directly shaping the family structure, by recognizing some and not other groupings as families. Rawls tends to treat the family as an organization that has an extrapolitical existence, and to ask how far the state may interfere with it. If, instead, he had recognized the foundational character of the state's presence in the family, he might have granted that it makes good sense for principles of justice to recognize and favor any units, traditional or non-traditional, that perform the functions associated with family in ways that are compatible with political justice.

My feeling is that in this delicate area Rawls has been too ready to recognize what are, in effect, group rights: the right of families, conceived of as pre-political, to protection against state action. Put another way, his distinction between external and internal regulation re-creates the problematic features of the very distinction he questions, the distinction between the public and the private sphere. If we really acknowledge the equal worth of all citizens, and the profound vulnerability of children in families, we should, I believe, conceive of the entire issue in a subtly different way: by thinking how we may balance adult freedom of association, and other important interests in pursuing one's own conception of the good, against the liberties and opportunities of children as future citizens.

Once again, beginning from citizens' needs for a wide range of human capabilities puts the problem on a subtly different footing from the start and enables us to move forward. No group gets special privileges qua group. But all persons deserve support for a wide range of capabilities—prominently including not only the capabilities of freedom of religion and freedom of association, but also the capability to form relationships of affection and care.[56]

If we proceed in this way, and recognize in addition that there is no group that exists "by nature," and that the family is more a state creation than most other associations, then the natural question will be: What forms of state action, and what forms of privilege given to certain groupings, will best protect the liberties and opportunities of women and children, within limits set by the protection of adult freedom of association and other important liberties? In posing this question, we do not assume that any one affiliative grouping is prior or central in promoting those capabilities. People have needs for love and care, for reproduction, for sexual expression; children have needs for love, support, and education; and people also enjoy a wide range of associational liberties. But at this point I believe we need to look and see how different groupings of persons do in promoting these capabilities. In some nations, for example India, women's collectives play a valuable role in giving women love and friendship, in caring for children, and in fostering the other capabilities. Conventional families often do less well. Sometimes a women's collective appears to be more truly a child's family than its nuclear home, as when, as often happens, women's collectives protect children from sexual abuse, or arrange for children at risk of abuse, or child marriage, to be protected through state-run schools. There need not even be a presumption that all the functions we now associate with family will be bundled under a single institution. Thus France has acted wisely, I believe, when it asks why the definition of household for the purposes of inheritance should be at all the same as the account of who gets to adopt and raise children. Brothers and sisters who live in the same house may be a household for the former purpose but not for the latter.[57] My approach would urge that such decisions be contextual, asking how, in the given history and circumstances, public policy can best promote the claims of the human capabilities. The only thing that stops state intervention is the person and the various liberties and rights of the person, including associative liberties, the right to be free from unwarranted search and seizure, and so forth. The family has no power to stop this intervention on its own, as though it were a mystical unity over and above the lives of its members.

Similarly, my approach urges us to question whether the distinctions relied upon by Rawls's current position—distinctions between external and internal regulation, and between state action and inaction, are really coherent. Laws governing marriage, divorce, compulsory education, inheritance—all are as internal as anything can be in the family. Nor should the criminal justice system know a distinction between inside and outside, in the definition and ranking of criminal offenses: it should treat rape as rape, battery as battery, coercion as coercion, wherever they occur. To let things take their status quo ante course is to choose a course of action, not to be completely neutral. In short, the state's interest in protecting the dignity, integrity, and well-being of each citizen never simply leads to external constraints on the family structure, whatever appearances may be; it always leads to positive constructing of the family institution. This constructing should be done in ways that are compatible with political justice.[58]

In practical terms, my approach in terms of the promotion of capabilities and Rawls's approach, which views the two principles of justice as supplying external constraints on the family, will give many of the same answers. Laws against marital rape, laws protecting marital consent, laws mandating compulsory education, laws banning child marriage and child labor, laws ensuring an appropriate material recognition of the wife's economic contribution to the family, laws providing child care to support working mothers, laws promoting the nutrition and health of girl children—all these laws, I think, we would both support as appropriate expressions of state concern for citizens and future citizens. But the grounds on which we will support them will be subtly different. Rawls sees the laws as supplying external constraints on something that has its own form, the way laws constrain a university or a church; I see them as contributing to the constitution of an institution that is in the most direct sense a part of the basic structure of society.

Furthermore, my approach, like Rawls's, would permit the state to give conventional family groupings certain special privileges and protections, just as it gives religious bodies certain privileges and protections. It will probably do so in many cases, since the family does promote the rearing of children, as well as serving other needs of citizens. Thus parents may be given certain limited kinds of deference in making choices regarding their children. And tax breaks for family units are not ruled out, insofar as these units promote human capabilities. But for me, the reason the state will choose such policies is to protect the central capabilities of individuals; the definition of family, and the policies chosen, should be chosen with this aim in view. Rawls does not ask how "family" should be defined, nor does he make it clear on what basis it should have special privileges, although the state's interest in its future citizens would appear to be one such basis.[59]

Most important of all, because Rawls takes the family as given, he does not ask what my approach urges us to ask at all times: what other affective and associational ties deserve public protection and support? It is not at all clear, then, what role non-traditional affective groupings such as Indian women's collectives, or French Pacts of Civil Solidarity, could play in his account of society's basic structure. And yet he proceeds as if, at the level of the Original Position, the account is historically neutral, not biased in favor of the status quo in any given place and time. In my approach, at that basic level we have only the capabilities to consider,[60] and we may consider any institutional grouping that can promote them. At a later, more concrete level—corresponding to Rawls's constitutional and legislative stages—such inquiries will rightly become contextual, although even at that point this will not mean that the traditional form of a practice will have exclusive privileges.

Notice, then, that my approach leaves for fine-tuned contextual judgment certain matters that Kantian liberalism wishes to settle in a definite way before launching into the currents of history, including the all-important question what forms of human organization shall be favored for the care and education of children. I urge that these questions be left to the contextual deliberation of citizens, in the light of their history and their current problems, and in the light of the capability list, which remains relatively constant over time. Such an approach will strike the Rawlsian as dangerously "intuitionistic"; and yet we should not purchase definiteness at the price of falsehood, by stating or implying that a parochial grouping is ahistorical and universal.[61]

Again, my approach would forbid certain types of interference with the family structure that Rawls's approach would also forbid. For me as for Rawls, it is wrong for the state to mandate the equal division of domestic labor or equal decision-making in the household. But again, the reasons for this shared conclusion will differ. Rawls judges that it is wrong to interfere with the internal workings of a particular institution, deemed to exist

apart from the state—whereas I judge simply that there are associational liberties of individuals, and liberties of speech, that should always be protected for citizens, no matter where they occur. (Rawls might have reached a result similar to the one he does reach by relying on the priority of liberty; but, significantly, he does not use that argument.) It just seems an intolerable infringement of liberty for the state to get involved in dictating how people do their dishes. But for me, dubious conduct gets less prima facie protection if it is in the family than if it is in a purely voluntary association, since the family (for children at any rate) is a non-voluntary institution that influences citizens' life chances pervasively and from the start.

In a wide range of areas, our approaches will support different choices of public policy. In my approach, the central capabilities always supply a compelling interest for purposes of government action. Thus it will be all right to render dowry illegal in India (as has been done), given the compelling evidence that the dowry system is a major source of women's capability failure.[62] I believe that Rawls would have a difficult time justifying this law—because he is thinking of the family as pre-political, and dowry as one of the choices it makes in its pre-political state. For me, by contrast, the family is constituted by laws and institutions, and one of the questions to be asked is whether dowry-giving is one of the things it should be in the business of doing. Permitting dowry is not neutral state inaction toward an autonomous private entity; it is another (alternative) way of constituting a part of the public sphere. Again, interference with traditional decision-making patterns in the family will be much easier to justify on my approach than on Rawls's. Consider the Mahila Samakhya project in Andhra Pradesh, in southern India. This project, funded and run by the national government, is explicitly aimed at increasing women's confidence and initiative, and empowering them in their dealings with employers, government officials, and husbands, and extending a wide range of life options to their female children. There is no doubt at all that the government is attempting to reconstruct the family by altering social norms and perceptions. No community and no individual is forced to join, and this is a reservation I would support. Nonetheless, it seems likely that there is more in the way of endorsing a particular conception of family governance than Rawls would consider acceptable. Apart from the content of the teaching, the very existence of the women's collectives as a focus for women's affective lives transforms the family profoundly, making it no longer the sole source of personal affiliation. It seems likely that Rawls would oppose government support for such collectives on that account, thinking of it as the endorsement of one conception of the good over another—for much the same reason that he has opposed government support for music and the arts. For me, the fact that women's capabilities are in a perilous state, together with the fact that empowerment programs have succeeded in giving them greater control over their material and political environment, gives government a compelling interest in introducing such programs.

Or consider governmental programs that focus on giving women access to credit and economic self-sufficiency, together with education in confidence and leadership.[63] (Such programs are common in developing countries; at least some such programs are governmental.) I surmise that for Rawls such programs would be an impermissible interference by government into the family structure. The very idea that government would support an all-women's bank, for example, would be highly suspect. For me, while I think it's very important for a program like this to be non-coercive, it seems quite all right for government to act in ways that aim at changing social norms that shape the family, and at promoting capabilities in those who lack them. For after all, and this is the crux of the matter, government is already in the business of constructing an institution that is part of the basic structure of society. It had better do this job well.

The largest difference in the two approaches will be in the treatment of female children. It is here, especially, that my approach recognizes the pervasive and non-voluntary nature of family membership, and gives the state broad latitude in shaping perception and behavior to promote the development of female children to full adult capability in the major areas. This means not only the abolition of child marriage and (where practically possible) child labor, and (where practically possible) compulsory primary and secondary education for all children. Rawls would presumably also favor these changes. It also means encouraging the public perception that women are suited for many different roles in life, something that Rawls is likely to see as too much promoting of a definite conception of the good. Thus the content of public education should include information about options for women, and about resistance to women's inequality.[64] In addition to regular schooling, the Indian government also supports residential programs for young girls who are at risk for child marriage, to remove them from home and give them education and job training. Rawls would be likely to see this as too much state intervention, even if the mothers consent to the girls going away: after all, government is saying, "I will support you if you leave this dangerous structure." My approach judges that the protection of girls' capabilities warrants an interventionist strategy.

Rawls's approach to the family and mine are very close. Both of us take our bearings from the idea of the dignity and worth of humanity, and the idea that no human being shall be used as a mere means for the ends of others. Both of us define the person as the basis of distribution; both of us see an important role for liberties of association and self-definition; both of us recognize the intrinsic value of love and care. But Rawls, while rejecting the public/private distinction, remains half-hearted in that rejection. I have tried to show how an approach through the central capabilities would capture the value of family love and care, while nonetheless rejecting more consistently a distinction that has disfigured the lives of girls and women through the ages.[65]

## IV.  A Liberal Future?

Liberal political thought has not yet realized its full potential. In two areas crucial to women's equality, there are basic problems with liberal doctrines as so far developed. These difficulties give us good reason to try out new liberal alternatives; one that deserves a hearing is a neo-Aristotelian liberalism based on an idea of human capabilities as central political goals.

It seems clear that a theory basically liberal in spirit can meet the problems of need and dependency. The difficulties pertaining to the family raise more troubling issues: for they seem to threaten the very project of a political liberalism, an approach committed both to respecting each person as an end and to respecting the fact of reasonable pluralism among comprehensive views of life. There is no doubt that some of the major comprehensive views of what gives life meaning are dead set against the kind of revisionary treatment of family structure that my approach sees required by political justice. Extending the privileges of marriage to previously unrecognized couples is at least on our political agenda; radical rethinking of the institutions of marriage and family will be much more difficult to achieve, although nations such as France and India have been able to go further. It is no accident that in a sphere that is the home both of intimate self-definition and also of egregious wrongdoing the search for liberal justice should encounter difficulties: for liberal justice is committed both to protecting spheres of self-definition and to ending the wrongful tyranny of some people over others.

But the failure to have a fully satisfactory solution to these difficulties is not a failure of liberal justice, because the liberal is right. Self-definition is important, and it is also important to end wrongful tyranny. The tension that results from these twin principles is at the heart of liberalism, but it is a valuable and fruitful tension, not one that shows confusion or moral failure. In general, tension within a theory does not necessarily show that it is defective; it may simply show that it is in touch with the difficulty of life. And that, I believe, is the case here. Reflection on the tension ought to lead us, over time, to figure out how to design a society that balances these competing values as well as they can be balanced, and to provide institutional protections for women and children who currently suffer from unresolved conflicts between them.

This effort would do well to begin by imagining and studying the many ways in which groups of people of many different types have managed, in different places at different times, to care for one another and to raise children with both love and justice.

## Appendix: The Central Human Capabilities (as in Women and Human Development, 2000)

1. *Life.* Being able to live to the end of a human life of normal length; not dying prematurely, or before one's life is so reduced as to be not worth living.

2. *Bodily Health.* Being able to have good health, including reproductive health; to be adequately nourished; to have adequate shelter.

3. *Bodily Integrity.* Being able to move freely from place to place; to be secure against violent assault, including sexual assault and domestic violence; having opportunities for sexual satisfaction and for choice in matters of reproduction.

4. *Senses, Imagination, and Thought.* Being able to use the senses, to imagine, think, and reason—and to do these things in a "truly human" way, a way informed and cultivated by an adequate education, including, but by no means limited to, literacy and basic mathematical and scientific training. Being able to use imagination and thought in connection with experiencing and producing works and events of one's own choice, religious, literary, musical, and so forth. Being able to use one's mind in ways protected by guarantees of freedom of expression with respect to both political and artistic speech, and freedom of religious exercise. Being able to have pleasurable experiences and to avoid non-beneficial pain.

5. *Emotions.* Being able to have attachments to things and people outside ourselves; to love those who love and care for us, to grieve at their absence; in general, to love, to grieve, to experience longing, gratitude, and justified anger. Not having

one's emotional development blighted by fear and anxiety. (Supporting this capability means supporting forms of human association that can be shown to be crucial in their development.)

6. *Practical Reason.* Being able to form a conception of the good and to engage in critical reflection about the planning of one's life. (This entails protection for the liberty of conscience and religious observance.)

7. *Affiliation.* A. Being able to live with and toward others, to recognize and show concern for other human beings, to engage in various forms of social interaction; to be able to imagine the situation of another. (Protecting this capability means protecting institutions that constitute and nourish such forms of affiliation, and also protecting the freedom of assembly and political speech.)

B. Having the social bases of self-respect and non-humiliation; being able to be treated as a dignified being whose worth is equal to that of others. This entails provisions of non-discrimination on the basis of race, sex, sexual orientation, ethnicity, caste, religion, national origin.

8. *Other Species.* Being able to live with concern for and in relation to animals, plants, and the world of nature.

9. *Play.* Being able to laugh, to play, to enjoy recreational activities.

10. *Control over one's Environment.* A. *Political.* Being able to participate effectively in political choices that govern one's life; having the right of political participation, protections of free speech and association.

B. *Material.* Being able to hold property (both land and movable goods), and having property rights on an equal basis with others; having the right to seek employment on an equal basis with others; having the freedom from unwarranted search and seizure. In work, being able to work as a human being, exercising practical reason and entering into meaningful relationships of mutual recognition with other workers.

## NOTES

1. I am grateful to Ann Cudd, John Deigh, Dolores Dooley, Chad Flanders, Jill Hasday, Eva Kittay, Charles Larmore, Peter Cicchino, Thomas Scanlon, David Strauss, and Cass Sunstein for comments on a previous draft and to Geof Sayre McCord, Tom Hill, Jr., and other members of the Research Triangle Ethics discussion group for extremely helpful discussion of these issues. This Address is dedicated to the memory of Peter Cicchino, gifted law professor, feminist, and courageous social activist, who died of cancer on July 8, 2000, at the age of 39. I discuss Peter's views about Aristotle in section II below.

2. Translated from the Bengali by Kalpana Bardhan, in *Of Women, Outcastes, Peasants, and Rebels* (Berkeley and Los Angeles: University of California Press, 1990). The story (originally published in 1982) concerns Giribala's arranged marriage to a man both improvident and corrupt, who eventually sells two of their daughters into prostitution to get spending money for himself. The story ends as Giribala leaves with the two remaining children. Its final sentence: "She just kept walking."

3. John Stuart Mill, *The Subjection of Women* (1869), ed. Susan M. Okin (Indianapolis: Hackett, 1988); Mary Wollstonecraft, *A Vindication of the Rights of Woman* (1792) (London and New York: Penguin, 1992). Seventeenth century feminists Mary Astell and Damaris Lady Masham are helpfully discussed in Margaret Atherton, "Cartesian Reason and Gendered Reason," in *A Mind of One's Own: Feminist Essays on Reason and Objectivity,* ed. Louise M. Antony and Charlotte Witt (Boulder, CO: Westview Press, 1993). Harriet Taylor (Mill)'s *The Enfranchisement of Women* (1851) is an important contribution to the nineteenth century debate: see edition in John Stuart Mill and Harriet Taylor Mill, *Essays on Sex Equality,* ed. Alice S. Rossi (Chicago: University of Chicago Press, 1970); for a good treatment of the Mills' views on these issues, see Gail Tulloch, *Mill and Sexual Equality* (Hemel Hempstead, Hertfordshire and Boulder, CO: Harvester Wheatsheaf and Lynne Rienner, 1989). Another prominent woman in Utilitarian circles was Anna Doyle Wheeler, who co-authored with economist William Thompson the *Appeal of One-Half the Human Race, Women, Against the Pretensions of the Other Half, Men, to Retain Them in Political and Thence in Civil and Domestic Slavery* (London: Longmans, 1825); on her writings, see Dolores Dooley, *Equality in Community: Sexual Equality in the Writings of William Thompson and Anna Doyle Wheeler* (Cork, Ireland: Cork University Press, 1996). On nineteenth century feminist thought about domestic violence and marital rape, see Jill Elaine Hasday, "Contest and Consent: A Legal History of Marital Rape," *California Law Review* 88 (2000). Many other examples could be added. From a very different philosophical tradition, a major influence on modern feminism has been Simone de Beauvoir, *The Second Sex,* trans. H. Parshley (New York: Bantam, 1953); much of her work is compatible with liberalism.

4. Again, however, one should remember that these themes were central in nineteenth century feminism as well: see, for example, Hasday (above n. 3), and Reva B. Siegel, "'The Rule of Love': Wife Beating as Prerogative and Privacy," *Yale Law Journal* 105 (1996), 2117–2207.

5. See also the works of Harriet Taylor and Anna Doyle Wheeler, cited in n. 3 above.

6. Barbara Herman, Onora O'Neill, Sharon Lloyd, and the late Jean Hampton (all students of John Rawls) write feminist philosophy in the Kantian liberal tradition. See Herman, "Could It Be Worth Thinking About Kant on Sex and Marriage?" in *A Mind of One's Own* (above n. 3), 49–68; O'Neill, "Justice, Gender, and International Boundaries," in *The Quality of Life,* ed. M. Nussbaum and A. Sen (Oxford: Clarendon Press, 1993), 303–35; Lloyd, "Family Justice and Social Justice," *Pacific Philosophical Quarterly* 75 (1994), 353–71; Hampton, "Feminist Contractarianism," in *A Mind of One's Own* (above n. 3), 227–56, and "The Case for Feminism" and "Hampton's Reply" in *The Liberation Debate,* ed. M. Leahy and D. Cohn-Sherbok (London: Routledge, 1996), 3–24, 41–45; in this same category see also the first feminist critique of Rawls, in Jane English, "Justice Between Generations," *Philosophical Studies* 31 (1977), 91–104. Susan Moller Okin, surely one of the most influential contemporary feminists, is, though a critic of Rawls, clearly in the liberal tradition, and a particular admirer of Mill: see *Women in Western Political Thought* (Princeton: Princeton University Press, 1978); "Justice and Gender," *Philosophy and Public Affairs* 16 (1987), 42–72; "Reason and Feeling in Thinking About Justice," *Ethics* 99 (1989a), 229–49; *Justice, Gender, and the Family* (New York: Basic Books, 1989); "*Political Liberalism,* Justice, and Gender," *Ethics* 105, 23–43; *Is Multiculturalism Bad For Women?* (Princeton: Princeton University Press, 1999). Two other liberal feminists whose views lie closer to those of Mill (and T. H. Green?) than to any other earlier figure in the tradition are Elizabeth Anderson and Candace Vogler: see Anderson, *Value in Ethics and Economics* (Cambridge, MA: Harvard University Press, 1993), and "John Stuart Mill and Experiments in Living," *Ethics* 102 (1991), 4–26; Vogler, *John Stuart Mill's Deliberative Landscape,* Garland Dissertation Series, ed. R. Nozick, forthcoming 2000, and "Philosophical Feminism, Feminist Philosophy," *Philosophical Topics* 23 (1995), 295–319. The work of Jürgen Habermas has been a major influence on the writings of Seyla Benhabib, whom I think it would be correct to count as a liberal feminist: see *Situating the Self: Gender, Community, and Postmodernism in Contemporary Ethics* (New York: Routledge, 1992); an anthology of feminist writing in the Habermasian tradition is *Feminists Read Habermas,* ed. Johanna Meehan (New York: Routledge, 1995). Another feminist prominently influenced by Habermas, Iris Young, is probably not correctly classified as a liberal: see "The Ideal of Community and the Politics of Difference," in *Feminism and Postmodernism,* ed. Linda Nicholson (New York: Routledge, 1990), and *Justice and the Politics of Difference* (Princeton: Princeton University Press, 1990), and *Throwing Like a Girl and Other Essays in Feminist Philosophy and Social Theory* (Bloomington: Indiana University Press, 1990). Finally, on the continent, a prominent liberal feminist influenced by both Rawls and Habermas, as well as by the work of Okin and other liberal feminists, is Herlinde Pauer-Studer, *Das Andere der Gerechtigkeit: Moraltheorie im Kontext der Geschlechterdifferenz* (Berlin: Akademie Verlag, 1996). In India (though the *word* "liberal" would be avoided, since there it means "libertarian") most prominent feminist political thinkers are liberal social-democrats of some type: see Bina Agarwal, *A Field of One's Own: Gender and Land Rights in South Asia* (Cambridge: Cambridge University Press, 1994), and "'Bargaining' and Gender Relations: Within and Beyond the Household," *Feminist Economics* 3 (1997), 1–51; Zoya Hasan, "Introduction" and essay "Minority Identity, State Policy and the Political Process" (59–73) in Hasan, ed., *Forging Identities: Gender, Communities, and the State in India* (Boulder, CO: Westview, 1994); Roop Rekha Verma, "Femininity, Equality, and Personhood," in *Women, Culture, and Development,* ed. M. Nussbaum and J. Glover (Oxford: Clarendon Press, 1995), 433–43; and one should of course include in this category the feminist writings of Amartya Sen, to be discussed in both text and notes below. Once again: this list is very incomplete.

7. Some influential such critiques have been Alison Jaggar, *Feminist Politics and Human Nature* (Totowa, NJ: Rowman and Allanheld, 1983, repr. 1988), esp. 27–50, 173–206; Carole Pateman, *The Problem of Political Obligation: A Critique of Liberal Theory* (Berkeley: University of California Press, 1979), and *The Sexual Contract* (Stanford, CA: Stanford University Press, 1988); Nancy C. M. Hartsock, *Money, Sex, and Power* (Boston: Northeastern University Press, 1983); Catharine MacKinnon, *Toward a Feminist Theory of the State* (Cambridge, MA: Harvard University Press, 1989), especially chs. 3 and 8, and *Feminism Unmodified* (Cambridge, MA: Harvard University Press, 1987), esp. chs. 2 and 8. In "The Feminist Critique" I argue that MacKinnon's primary target is a type of neutralist liberalism that is quite common in legal circles, but that her critique can be met by the strongest forms of contemporary liberal philosophy, including, on some topics, at least, the views of Rawls. See section III below for her valuable critique of liberalism on the public-private distinction.

8. "The Feminist Critique of Liberalism," chapter 2 of *Sex and Social Justice* (New York: Oxford University

Press, 1999), 55–80; also published as a Lindley Lecture, 1997, University of Kansas Press.

9. In "Rawls and Feminism," forthcoming in *The Cambridge Companion to Rawls,* ed. Samuel Freeman (Cambridge: Cambridge University Press, 2000), I argue that liberal views have not yet provided an adequate account of global justice, and that global justice is a central feminist issue because women in poorer nations are especially likely to be deprived of basic human goods, including education, health, bodily integrity, and life. Securing to women the basic necessary conditions of a decent life is the central theme of my *Women and Human Development: The Capabilities Approach* (Cambridge: Cambridge University Press, 2000), hereafter WHD; thinking globally about the need for redistribution of wealth from richer to poorer nations is the central concern of *The Cosmopolitan Tradition* (the Castle Lectures at Yale University, 2000, and under contract to Yale University Press).

10. Locke, *Second Treatise on Government,* chapter 8.

11. David Gauthier, *Morals By Agreement* (New York: Oxford University Press, 1986), p. 18, speaking of all "persons who decrease th[e] average level" of well-being in a society.

12. In the subsequent discussion I shall refer to the following works of Rawls: *A Theory of Justice* (Cambridge, MA: Harvard University Press, 1971), hereafter TJ; *Political Liberalism,* expanded paperback edition (New York: Columbia University Press, 1996), hereafter PL; the Dewey Lectures, *Kantian Constructivism in Moral Theory, The Journal of Philosophy* 77 (1980), 515–71. References to citizens as "fully cooperating" occur frequently in DL and PL, for example DL 546, PL 183.

13. This is a major theme in recent feminist work: see especially Eva Kittay, *Love's Labor: Essays on Women, Equality, and Dependency* (New York: Routledge, 1999); Nancy Folbre, "Care and the Global Economy," background paper prepared for the *Human Development Report 1999,* United Nations Development Programme (New York: Oxford University Press, 1999), and, based largely on Folbre, chapter 3 of *Human Development Report 1999;* Joan Williams, *Unbending Gender: Why Family and Work Conflict and What to Do About It* (New York: Oxford University Press, 2000); Mona Harrington, *Care and Equality* (New York: Knopf, 1999). Earlier influential work in this area includes: Martha A. Fineman, *The Illusion of Equality* (Chicago: University of Chicago Press, 1991), and *The Neutered Mother, the Sexual Family and Other Twentieth Century Tragedies* (New York: Routledge, 1995); Sarah Ruddick, *Maternal Thinking* (New York: Beacon Press, 1989); Joan Tronto, *Moral Boundaries: A Political Argument for an Ethic of Care* (New York: Routledge, 1993); Virginia Held, *Feminist Morality: Transforming Culture, Society, and Politics* (Chicago: University of

Chicago Press, 1993); Robin West, *Caring for Justice* (New York: New York University Press, 1997). For an excellent collection of articles from diverse feminist perspectives, see *Justice and Care: Essential Readings in Feminist Ethics,* ed. Virginia Held (Boulder, CO: Westview Press, 1995).

14. This problem is exacerbated, of course, by Kant's focus on some aspects of our humanity and not others as what particularly constitutes its worth and dignity.

15. For one particularly valuable treatment of this theme, see James Rachels, *Created From Animals: The Moral Implications of Darwinism* (New York: Oxford University Press, 1990). Two wonderful pictures of the animal sort of dignity: Barbara Smuts, untitled reply to J. M. Coetzee, in *The Lives of Animals,* ed. Amy Gutmann (Princeton: Princeton University Press, 1999), and, my favorite, George Pitcher, *The Dogs Who Came to Stay* (New York: G. Putnam, 1995). I discuss the implications of recognizing the dignity of non-human animals in a review article about Steven M. Wise's *Rattling the Cage: Toward Legal Rights for Animals* (Cambridge, MA: Perseus Books, 2000), forthcoming in *The Harvard Law Review.* See also Alasdair MacIntyre, *Dependent Rational Animals: Why Human Beings Need the Virtues* (Peru, IL: Open Court Publishing, 1999).

16. See especially Rachels and MacIntyre (above n. 15).

17. I do not mean to deny that Kant gives need an important role in his theory: for just one good treatment of this aspect of Kant's thought, see Allen Wood, *Kant's Ethical Theory* (Cambridge: Cambridge University Press, 1999). What I mean is that whereas for Kant personality and animality are conceptually independent, and personality is not itself understood in terms of need, for Rawls these two elements are more thoroughly integrated, and the person is understood from the first as in need of material and other goods.

18. As Eva Kittay has argued in an excellent discussion (*Love's Labor,* pp. 88–99, and see also "Human Dependency and Rawlsian Equality," in *Feminists Rethink the Self,* ed. Diana T. Meyers (Boulder, CO: Westview, 1997), 219–66), there are five places in Rawls's theory where he fails to confront facts of asymmetrical neediness that might naturally have been confronted. (1) His account of the "circumstances of justice" assumes a rough equality between persons, such that none could dominate all the others; thus we are not invited to consider relations of justice that might obtain between an adult and her infants, or her senile demented parents. (2) Rawls's idealization of citizens as "fully cooperating" etc. puts to one side the large facts about extreme neediness I have just mentioned. (3) His conception of social cooperation, again, is based on the idea of reciprocity between equals, and has no

explicit place for relations of extreme dependency. (4) His account of the primary goods, introduced, as it is, as an account of the needs of citizens who are characterized by the two moral powers and by the capacity to be "fully cooperating," has no place for the need of many real people for the kind of care we give to people who are not independent. And (5) his account of citizens' freedom as involving the concept of being a self-authenticating source of valid claims (e.g. PL 32) fails to make a place for any freedom that might be enjoyed by someone who is not independent in that sense.

19. See Kittay, *Love's Labor*, p. 77: "Dependency must be faced from the beginning of any project in egalitarian theory that hopes to include all persons within its scope." For a remarkable narrative of a particular life that shows exactly how many social structures play a part in the life of a mentally handicapped child from the very beginning, see Michael Bérubé, *Life As We Know It: A Father, A Family, and An Exceptional Child* (New York: Vintage, 1996).

20. This point has been repeatedly made by Amartya Sen in recommending an approach based on capability and functioning over the Rawlsian approach to primary goods; for the classic original statement, see Sen, "Equality of What?", in Sen, *Choice, Welfare, and Measurement* (Oxford: Basil Blackwell, 1982), 353–69; other good accounts of the approach are in Sen, "Capability and Well–Being," in *The Quality of Life*, ed. M. Nussbaum and A. Sen (Oxford: Clarendon Press, 1993), 30–53; "Gender Inequality and Theories of Justice," in *Women, Culture and Development*, ed. M. Nussbaum and J. Glover (Oxford: Clarendon Press, 1995), and *Inequality Reexamined* (New York: Russell Sage, 1992), esp. chs. 1, 3, 5.

21. Sen, "Equality of What?"

22. Two further problems not raised by Sen: First, even if we were to give more income and wealth to the person in a wheelchair, this would not solve the problem: for making this person mobile requires public action (construction of wheelchair ramps, accessible buses, etc.) that individuals cannot achieve on their own. Second, even if the person in the wheelchair were equally well off with regard to economic well-being, there is a separate issue of dignity and self-respect. By measuring relative social positions by income and wealth alone, Rawls ignores the possibility that a group may be reasonably well-off economically, but suffer grave disabilities with regard to the social bases of self-respect. One might argue that gays and lesbians in our society are in precisely that position; but certainly the physically and mentally handicapped will be in that position, unless society makes a major and fundamental commitment to inclusion and respect.

23. At times, as in the passage from the DL cited in the text above, Rawls suggest leaving aside all severe or expensive physical illness, as well as mental disability:

see also PL 272 n. 10. At other times (e.g. PL 302) he treats possession of the two moral powers as a sufficient, as well as a necessary, condition of fully cooperating status.

24. Rawls proposes taking account of it at the legislative stage: see PL 183–6; but given the pervasive role of political institutions in shaping the life chances of such citizens from the very beginning of a human life, this seems an inadequate reply. The concrete strategems adopted to address issues of disability (laws mandating wheel chair ramps, laws such as the Individuals with Disabilities Education Act) could well be left until this stage; but the fact that citizens experience such needs for care must be recognized from the start, and a commitment made to address these concerns.

25. Scanlon, *What We Owe to Each Other* (Cambridge, MA: Harvard University Press, 1999). pp. 177–87. I am very grateful to Scanlon for correspondence that makes the complexity of his approach to these cases clear. Because this is a paper about the basic structure of a political conception, I shall hope to take up his views elsewhere.

26. Once again, it is very important to stress the fact that this is Rawls's project, not Scanlon's, and that Scanlon does not recommend applying it in this way.

27. *Morals by Agreement*, p. 18 n. 30.

28. See for example TJ 135, where finality is a formal condition on political principles, and 175–8, in the argument for the two principles where it is made clear that the agreement "is final and made in perpetuity" and that "there is no second chance" (176). Rawls's opposition to intuitionism focuses on this issue: see for example TJ 35–6.

29. Kittay, *Love's Labor*, 102–3.

30. Like Sen, I defend this idea, in WHD, chapter 1; unlike Sen, I propose an actual list of the central capabilities, analogous to primary goods. WHD ch. I discusses in detail the relationship of my approach to Rawls's.

31. On this point see especially Williams, *Unbending Gender* (above n. 13).

32. See my discussion of this point in WHD ch. 1.

33. In TJ primary goods were characterized as all-purpose means to the pursuit of one's own conception of the good, whatever it is; in DL and PL, the interpretation shifts, and Rawls acknowledges that they are means with regard to the Kantian political conception of the person: see PL 187–90.

34. I discuss this issue in detail in "Rawls and Feminism," with respect to both Rawls's text and the most prominent feminist critiques. See, for example, Seyla Benhabib, "The Generalized and the Concrete Other,' in *Situating the Self*, pp. 148–77; Marilyn Friedman, *What Are Friends For? Feminist Perspectives on Personal Relationships and Moral Theory* (Ithaca: Cornell University Press, 1993).

35. I owe this point to Geof Sayre-McCord, who pointed out that I myself have criticized feminists who don't see the Veil of Ignorance as part of the model of the person: see "Rawls and Feminism."

36. As Peter Cicchino eloquently put this point, Aristotle's conception is not deductive or a priori: it respects widely held views about human reality, but takes experience as its source and guide. Second, it takes seriously the materiality of human beings—their need for food, shelter, friendship, care, what might be called their basic dependency. Third, it is epistemologically modest—it does not claim to have the exactitude of mathematics, but rather is content to look for "such precision as accords with the subject-matter" (Cicchino, "Building of Foundational Myths: Feminism and the Recovery of 'Human Nature': A Response to Martha Fineman," April 15, 1999).

37. In that way my view is close to the type of liberalism defended (against Lockean contractarianism) by T. H. Green, though my form is not perfectionistic, but is, rather, a form of political liberalism. I have found very illuminating the discussion of the liberal tradition in John Deigh, "Liberalism and Freedom," forthcoming in *Social and Political Philosophy: Contemporary Perspectives,* ed. James Sterba (London: Routledge, forthcoming 2001).

38. I attach the current version of the capabilities list as an Appendix. The view is further debated in a symposium on my political philosophy in *Ethics,* fall 2000; see in particular the paper by Richard Arneson, which takes me up on the question of capability and functioning, arguing that a more robust perfectionism that makes actual functioning the goal is required in areas such as health. I dispute this, defending my form of political liberalism, in "Aristotle, Politics, and Human Capabilities: A Response to Antony, Arneson, Charlesworth, and Mulgan," *Ethics* 111 (2000), 102–40.

39. Kittay, *Love's Labor,* ch. 1. Part III, on political strategies, is entitled "Some Mother's Child."

40. For passages that focus on the need of the individual for choice and independence, see for example 34–5, 53, 98, 192 n. 32.

41. Kittay, *Love's Labor,* ch. 5.

42. See Kittay, *Love's Labor,* ch. 6, a beautiful and lucid account of her daughter's life.

43. Bérubé, *Life As We Know It,* p. 264: "For I have no sweeter dream than to imagine—aesthetically and ethically and parentally—that Jamie will someday be his own advocate, his own author, his own best representative." The book he mentions is Mitchell Levitz and Jason Kingsley, *Count Us In: Growing Up With Down Syndrome* (New York: Harcourt Brace, 1994).

44. The ideas in this section are developed at greater length in WHD chapter 4.

45. Or, as in the case of Rousseau (see my remarks in section 1) and Hegel (if one should call either of them liberals), they have treated the topic in a rather unhelpful way.

46. MacKinnon, "Privacy v. Equality: Beyond Roe v. Wade," in *Feminism Unmodified,* p. 100; cf. *Feminist Theory of the State* p. 191 (above n. 7).

47. The development of Rawls's ideas about the family is traced in detail in my "Rawls and Feminism." For the family as part of the basic structure, see for example TJ 4, 462, PL 258. At this point already, Rawls alludes to problems of justice within the family, thinking of inequalities of opportunities between children because of unequal parental treatment: see TJ 74, 301, and especially 511: "Is the family to be abolished then? Taken all by itself and given a certain primacy, the idea of equality of opportunity inclines in this direction."

48. The most influential critique of Rawls on this point is that of Susan Okin, in "Justice and Gender," and *Justice, Gender, and the Family* (above n. 6).

49. Rawls, "The Idea of Public Reason Revisited," *University of Chicago Law Review* 64 (1997, 765–807, now reprinted in Rawls, *The Law of Peoples* (Cambridge, MA: Harvard University Press, 1999), 129–80; my page references are to the law review version.

50. Rawls understands the fact that it is chosen on the basis of one's religion as a sufficient condition of voluntariness, in background conditions that are fair (792 and n. 68); he notes that the question needs a fuller discussion.

51. See the related defense of the Rawlsian position in Lloyd (above n. 6).

52. On this tension see also G. A. Cohen, "Where the Action Is: On the Site of Distributive Justice," *Philosophy and Public Affairs* 26 (1997), 3–30.

53. See the good comments on this point in Lloyd (above n. 6).

54. See Martha Minow, "All in the Family and In All Families: Membership, Loving, and Owing," in *Sex, Preference, and Family: Essays on Law and Nature,* ed. D. Estlund and M. Nussbaum (New York: Oxford University Press, 1997), 249–76, with many fascinating examples of how the INS uses definitions of "family" to restrict immigration; Frances Olsen, "The Family and the Market: A Study of Ideology and Legal Reform," *Harvard Law Review* 96 (1983), 1497–1577, and Olsen, "The Myth of State Intervention in the Family," *University of Michigan Journal of Law Reform* 18 (1985), 1497–1577.

55. In *Baehr v. Lewin,* 852 P.2d 44 (Hawaii SC 1993), the Hawaii Supreme Court gave the following list of the political and social benefits of marriage:

1. a variety of state income tax advantages, including deductions, credits, rates, exemptions, and estimates;
2. public assistance from and exemptions relating to the Department of Human Services;

3. control, division, acquisition, and disposition of community property;
4. rights relating to dower, curtesy, and inheritance;
5. rights to notice, protection, benefits, and inheritance under the Uniform Probate Code;
6. award of child custody and support payments in divorce proceedings;
7. the right to spousal support;
8. the right to enter into premarital agreements;
10. the right to file a nonsupport action;
11. post-divorce rights relating to support and property division;
12. the benefit of the spousal privilege and confidential marital communications;
13. the benefit of the exemption of real property from attachment or execution;
14. the right to bring a wrongful death action.

And this list is far from complete: to get even close, we need to add: the right of next of kin in hospital visitation and decisions about medical treatment and burial; immigration advantages; and there are many other discounts and privileges available to married couples on a local basis. Finally, there are issues in the area of the "social bases of self-respect," to use Rawls's excellent phrase: public recognition of one's union as on a par with, having a dignity equal to that of, others is a major social good.

56. This is the approach that I develop more fully in WHD chapter 4.

57. See the good discussion in Michael Warner, *The Trouble with Normal: Sex, Politics, and the Ethics of Queer Life* (New York: The Free Press, 1999), and Claudia Card, "Against Marriage and Motherhood," Hypatia vol. 11, no. 3 (Summer 1996), 1–23.

58. Similarly, one should question standard distinctions between state action and inaction in this sphere:

the state is acting as much when it supports conventional heterosexual marriage as when it extends similar privileges to nontraditional groups.

59. Many comparisons become difficult to make at this point, because my approach has no sequence analogous to the Rawlsian four-stage sequence.

60. At their most general level the capabilities are taken to be neutral across time as well as place, though their more concrete specifications (literacy, for example, as a concrete specification of an educational capability) are held to be relatively time-specific.

61. See further remarks on this issue in WHD chs. 3 and 4.

62. For relevant background information focusing on India, see WHD Introduction and chs. 1 and 4.

63. Again, these programs are described in WHD, especially Introduction.

64. In WHD chapter 31 discuss *Wisconsin v. Yoder,* where Amish parents won the right to remove their children from two years of required public education. I consider this case a very hard case for my approach, and I recommend a balancing approach (based on the Religious Freedom Restoration Act of 1993) that would surely not satisfy the Rawlsian's demand for principles that are final, fully general, and ordered in advance.

65. For related observations about the public/private distinction, see my "Is Privacy Good for Women? What the Indian Constitutional Tradition Can Teach Us About Sex Equality," *The Boston Review* 25 (April/May 2000), 42–47; a longer article on the same topic is forthcoming as "Sex Equality, Liberty, and Privacy: A Comparative Approach to the Feminist Critique," in *Constitutional Ideas and Political Practices: Fifty Years of the Republic,* E. Sridharan, R. Sudarshan, and Z. Hasan, eds., forthcoming from Oxford University Press, Delhi.

## Recommend Readings

West, Cornel. *The American Evasion of Philosophy: A Genealogy of Pragmatism.* Madison: University of Wisconsin Press, 1989.

———. *The Ethical Dimensions of Marxist Thought.* Monthly Review Press, 1991.

———. *Race Matters.* Boston: Beacon Press, 1993.

——— and John Rajchman, eds. *Post-Analytic Philosophy.* New York: Columbia University Press, 1985.

Nussbaum, Martha, *The Fragility of Goodness.* New York: Cambridge University Press, 1986.

———. *Poetic Justice.* Boston: Beacon Press, 1995.

———. *Sex and Social Justice.* New York: Oxford University Press, 1999.

———. *Women and Human Development.* New York: Cambridge University Press, 2000.

# XV

## Concluding Philosophical Postscript

## Reconciling Social and Political Ideals[*]

JAMES P. STERBA

IT IS WIDELY BELIEVED that alternative social and political ideals are incommensurable such that no nonarbitrary reason can be given for accepting one social and political ideal over another. So we find libertarians with their ideal of liberty endorsing the practical requirements of a minimal state, welfare liberals with their ideal of fairness endorsing the practical requirements of a welfare state, and socialists with their ultimate ideal of equality endorsing the practical requirements of a socialist state, and so on. Each political ideal is said to lead to different practical requirements, yet there is no nonarbitrary way to determine which ideal to accept. Alasdair MacIntyre seemed to champion this view, but even an opponent of MacIntyre like John Rawls in his recent work seems to grant that the ideal that he favors is rooted in a prior acceptance of modern social democratic traditions, from which many have concluded that without a prior and seemingly arbitrary acceptance of those traditions, one would not be led to endorse Rawls's social and political ideal.

[*] An earlier version of this paper was presented as a symposium paper at the 1992 Central Division American Philsophical meeting held in Louisville, Kentucky. Alison Jaggar and Jan Narveson were the commentators.

For a number of years now I have argued that this incommensurability thesis is mistaken and that alternative social and political ideals in their most defensible contemporary formulations are not, in fact, incommensurable but can be shown to lead to the same practical requirements.[1] Thus I claim that libertarianism with its ideal of liberty, welfare liberalism with its ideal of fairness, socialism with its ideal of equality, communitarianism with its ideal of the common good and feminism with its ideal of androgyny can all be seen to support the same practical requirements, specifically, the practical requirements that are usually associated with a welfare liberal ideal, namely, a right to welfare and a right to equal opportunity. Since most people endorse one or another of these social and political ideals, to reach agreement in practice it should suffice to show them that all these conceptions support the same practical requirements of a right to welfare and a right to equal opportunity.[2] Nevertheless, to make my practical reconciliation argument even more compelling, I further argue that the conception of rationality required by rational egoism leads at least to the libertarian ideal, which, in turn, has been shown to lead to the same practical requirements as the other four ideals. So I argue that there is no escaping my practical reconciliation of alternative social and political ideals by rejecting morality altogether and endorsing rational egoism.

Now obviously, I cannot in this paper lay out my entire practical reconciliation argument. What I propose to do then is to focus on two related parts of my argument where I attempt to show that libertarians and feminists should endorse the same practical requirements of a right to welfare and a right to equal opportunity. In setting out these two parts of the argument, I will try to make the argument more perspicuous than I have in the past and relate the argument to recent work done by libertarians and feminists.

## A Libertarian Social and Political Ideal

Now libertarians have interpreted their ideal of liberty in basically two different ways. Some libertarians, following Herbert Spencer, have (1) taken a right to liberty as basic and (2) derived all other rights from this right to liberty. Other libertarians, following John Locke, have (1) taken a set of rights, including typically a right to life and a right to property, as basic and (2) defined liberty as the absence of constraints in the exercise of these rights. Now both groups of libertarians regard liberty as the ultimate social and political ideal, but they do so for different reasons. For Spencerian libertarians, liberty is the ultimate social and political ideal because all other rights are derived from a right to liberty. For Lockean libertarians, liberty is the ultimate social and political ideal because liberty just is the absence of constraints in the exercise of people's fundamental rights.

## Spencerian Libertarians

Let us begin by considering the view of Spencerian libertarians, who take a right to liberty to be basic and define all other rights in terms of this right to liberty. According to this view, liberty is usually interpreted as being unconstrained by other persons from doing what one wants or is able to do. Interpreting liberty this way, libertari-

ans like to limit constraints to positive acts (that is, acts of commission) that prevent people from doing what they otherwise want or are able to do. By contrast, welfare liberals and socialists interpret constraints to include, in addition, negative acts (acts of omission) that prevent people from doing what they otherwise want or are able to do. In fact, this is one way to understand the debate between defenders of "negative liberty" and defenders of "positive liberty." This is because defenders of negative liberty interpret constraints to include only positive acts of others that prevent people from doing what they otherwise want or are able to do, while defenders of positive liberty interpret constraints to include both positive and negative acts of others that prevent people from doing what they otherwise want or are able to do.

In order not to beg the question against libertarians, suppose we interpret constraints in the manner favored by libertarians to include only positive acts by others that prevent people from doing what they otherwise want or are able to do. Libertarians go on to characterize their social and political ideal as requiring that each person should have the greatest amount of liberty commensurate with the same liberty for all. From this ideal, libertarians claim that a number of more specific requirements, in particular a right to life, a right to freedom of speech, press, and assembly, and a right to property can be derived.

Here it is important to observe that the libertarian's right to life is not a right to receive from others the goods and resources necessary for preserving one's life; it is not a right to welfare: it is simply a right not to be killed unjustly. Correspondingly, the libertarian's right to property is not a right to receive from others the goods and resources necessary to meet one's basic needs, but rather a right to acquire goods and resources either by initial acquisitions or by voluntary agreements.

Of course, libertarians would allow that it would be nice of the rich to share their surplus resources with the poor. Nevertheless, libertarians deny that government has a duty to provide for such needs. Some good things, such as the provision of welfare to the needy, are requirements of charity rather than justice, libertarians claim. Accordingly, failure to make such provisions is neither blameworthy nor punishable. As a consequence, libertarians contend that such acts of charity should not be coercively required. For this reason, libertarians are opposed to any coercively supported welfare program.

For a similar reason, libertarians are opposed to coercively supported opportunity programs. This is because the basic opportunities one has under a libertarian ideal are primarily a function of the property one controls; and since unequal property distributions are taken to be justified under a libertarian ideal, unequal basic opportunities are also regarded as justified.

## Lockean Libertarians

The same opposition to coercively supported welfare and equal opportunity programs characterizes the Lockean libertarians who take a set of rights, typically including a right to life and a right to property, as basic and then interpret liberty as being unconstrained by other persons from doing what one has a right to do. For according to this view, a right to life is simply a right not to be killed unjustly; it is not a right to receive welfare. Correspondingly, a right to property is a right to acquire property either by initial acquisitions or by voluntary transactions; it is not a right to receive from others whatever goods and resources one needs to maintain oneself. Understanding a right to life and a right to property in this way, libertarians reject both coercively supported welfare programs and equal opportunity programs as a violation of liberty.

## Spencerian Libertarians and the Problem of Conflict

To evaluate the libertarian view, let us begin with the ideal of liberty as defended by Spencerian libertarians and consider a typical conflict situation between the rich and the poor. In this situation, the rich have more than enough resources to satisfy their basic needs. By contrast, the poor lack the resources to meet their most basic needs even though they have tried all the means available to

them that Spencerian libertarians regard as legitimate for acquiring such resources. Under circumstances like these, libertarians usually maintain that the rich should have the liberty to use their resources to satisfy their luxury needs if they so wish. Spencerian libertarians recognize that this liberty might well be enjoyed at the expense of the satisfaction of the most basic needs of the poor; they just think that liberty always has priority over other social and political ideals, and since they assume that the liberty of the poor is not at stake in such conflict situations, it is easy for them to conclude that the rich should not be required to sacrifice their liberty so that the basic needs of the poor may be met.

Of course, Spencerian libertarians allow that it would be nice of the rich to share their surplus resources with the poor. Nevertheless, according to Spencerian libertarians, such acts of charity cannot be required because the liberty of the poor is not thought to be at stake in such conflict situations.

In fact, however, the liberty of the poor is at stake in such conflict situations. What is at stake is the liberty of the poor not to be interfered with in taking from the surplus possessions of the rich what is necessary to satisfy their basic needs.[3]

Needless to say, Spencerian libertarians would want to deny that the poor have this liberty. But how could they justify such a denial? As this liberty of the poor has been specified, it is not a positive right to receive something, but a negative right of noninterference. Nor will it do for Spencerian libertarians to appeal to a right to life or a right to property to rule out such a liberty because, on the Spencerian view, liberty is basic and all other rights are derived from a right to liberty. Clearly, what Spencerian libertarians must do is recognize the existence of such a liberty, and then claim that it conflicts with other liberties of the rich. But when Spencerian libertarians see that this is the case, they are often genuinely surprised, one might even say rudely awakened, for they had not previously seen the conflict between the rich and the poor as a conflict of liberties.

Now when the conflict between the rich and the poor is viewed as a conflict of liberties, we can either say that the rich should have the liberty not to be interfered with in using their surplus resources for luxury purposes, or we can say that the poor should have the liberty not to be interfered with in taking from the rich what they require to meet their basic needs. If we choose one liberty, we must reject the other. What needs to be determined, therefore, is which liberty is morally preferable: the liberty of the rich or the liberty of the poor.

## TWO PRINCIPLES

In order to see that the liberty of the poor not to be interfered with in taking from the surplus resources of the rich what is required to meet their basic needs is morally preferable to the liberty of the rich not to be interfered with in using their surplus resources for luxury purposes, we need to appeal to one of the most fundamental principles of morality, one that is common to all political perspectives. This is

> The "Ought" Implies "Can" Principle: People are not morally required to do what they lack the power to do or what would involve so great a sacrifice that it would be unreasonable to ask them to perform such an action, and/or in the case of severe conflicts of interest, unreasonable to require them to perform such an action.[4]

For example, suppose I promised to attend a departmental meeting on Friday, but on Thursday I am involved in a serious car accident that leaves me in a coma. Surely, it is no longer the case that I ought to attend the meeting now that I lack the power to do so. Or suppose instead that on Thursday I develop a severe case of pneumonia for which I am hospitalized. Surely, I could legitimately claim that I cannot attend the meeting on the grounds that the risk to my health involved in attending is a sacrifice that it would be unreasonable to ask me to bear. Or suppose the risk to my health from having pneumonia is not so serious that it would be unreasonable to ask me to attend the meeting (a supererogatory request), it might still be serious enough to be unreasonable to require my attendance at the meeting (a demand that is backed up by blame or coercion).

What is distinctive about this formulation of the "ought" implies "can" principle is that it claims that the requirements of morality cannot, all things considered, be unreasonable to ask, and/or in cases of severe conflict of interest, unreasonable to require people to abide by. The principle claims that reason and morality must be linked in an appropriate way, especially if we are going to be able to justifiably use blame or coercion to get people to abide by the requirements of morality. It should be noted, however, that while major figures in the history of philosophy, and most philosophers today, including virtually all libertarian philosophers, accept this linkage between reason and morality, this linkage is not usually conceived to be part of the "ought" implies "can" principle. Nevertheless, I claim that there are good reasons for associating this linkage between reason and morality with the "ought" implies "can" principle, namely our use of the word *can* as in the example just given, and the natural progression from logical, physical, and psychological possibility found in the traditional "ought" implies "can" principle to the notion of moral possibility found in this formulation of the "ought" implies "can" principle. In any case, the acceptability of this formulation of the "ought" implies "can" principle is determined by the virtual universal acceptance of its components and not by the manner in which I have proposed to join those components together.[5]

Now applying this principle to the case at hand, it seems clear that the poor have it within their power willingly to relinquish such an important liberty as the liberty not to be interfered with in taking from the rich what they require to meet their basic needs. Nevertheless, it would be unreasonable to ask or require them to make so great a sacrifice. In the extreme case, it would involve asking or requiring the poor to sit back and starve to death. Of course, the poor may have no real alternative to relinquishing this liberty. To do anything else may involve worse consequences for themselves and their loved ones and may invite a painful death. Accordingly, we may expect that the poor would acquiesce, albeit unwillingly, to a political system that denied them the right to welfare supported by such a liberty, at the same time that we recognize that such a system imposed an unreasonable sacrifice upon the poor—a sacrifice that we could not morally blame the poor for trying to evade.[6] Analogously, we might expect that a woman whose life was threatened would submit to a rapist's demands, at the same time that we recognize the utter unreasonableness of those demands.

By contrast, it would not be unreasonable to ask and require the rich to sacrifice the liberty to meet some of their luxury needs so that the poor can have the liberty to meet their basic needs.[7] Naturally, we might expect that the rich, for reasons of self-interest and past contribution, might be disinclined to make such a sacrifice. We might even suppose that the past contribution of the rich provides a good reason for not sacrificing their liberty to use their surplus for luxury purposes. Yet, unlike the poor, the rich should not claim that relinquishing such a liberty involved so great a sacrifice that it would be unreasonable to ask and require them to make it; unlike the poor, the rich could be morally blameworthy for failing to make such a sacrifice.

Notice that in virtue of the "ought" implies "can" principle this argument establishes that

1a. Since it would be unreasonable to ask or require the poor to sacrifice the liberty not to be interfered with when taking from the surplus resources of the rich what is necessary to meet their basic needs, 1b) it is not the case that the poor are morally required to make such a sacrifice.

2a. Since it would not be unreasonable to ask and require the rich to sacrifice the liberty not to be interfered with when using their surplus resources for luxury purposes, 2b) it may be the case that the rich are morally required to make such a sacrifice.

What the argument does not establish is that it is the case that the rich are *morally required* to sacrifice (some of) their surplus so that the basic needs of the poor can be met. To clearly establish that conclusion, we need to appeal to a principle, which is, in fact, simply the contrapositive of the "ought" implies "can" principle. It is

The Conflict Resolution Principle: What people are morally required to do is what is either reasonable to ask everyone affected to accept, or in the case of severe conflicts of interest, reasonable to require everyone affected to accept.

While the "ought" implies "can" principle claims that if any action is *not reasonable to ask or require* a person to do, all things considered, that action is *not morally required* for that person, all things considered [$-R(A \text{ v } Re) \; -> \; -MRe$], the conflict resolution principle claims that if any action is *morally required* for a person to do, all things considered, that action is *reasonable to ask or require* that person to do, all things considered [$MRe \; -> \; R(A \text{ v } Re)$].

This conflict resolution principle accords with the generally accepted view of morality as a system of reasons for resolving interpersonal conflicts of interest. Of course, morality is not limited to such a system of reasons. Most surely it also includes reasons of self-development. All that is being claimed by the principle is that moral resolutions of interpersonal conflicts of interest cannot be contrary to reason to ask everyone affected to accept, or in the case of severe interpersonal conflicts of interest, unreasonable to require everyone affected to accept. The reason for the distinction between the two kinds of cases is that when interpersonal conflicts of interest are not severe, moral resolutions must still be reasonable to ask everyone affected to accept, but they need not be reasonable to *require* everyone affected to accept. This is because not all moral resolutions can be justifiably enforced; only moral resolutions of severe interpersonal conflicts of interest can and *should* be justifiably enforced. Furthermore, the reason why moral resolutions of severe interpersonal conflicts of interest should be enforced is that if the parties are simply asked but not required to abide by a moral resolution in such cases of conflict, then it will be morally permissible, and even likely, that the stronger party will violate the resolution and that would be unreasonable to ask or require the weaker party to accept.

Now applying the conflict resolution principle to our example of severe conflict between the rich and the poor, there are three possible moral resolutions:

I. A moral resolution that would require the rich to sacrifice the liberty not to be interfered with when using their surplus resources for luxury purposes so that the poor can have the liberty not to be interfered with when taking from the surplus resources of the rich what is necessary to meet their basic needs.

II. A moral resolution that would require the poor to sacrifice the liberty not to be interfered with when taking from the surplus resources of the rich what is necessary to meet their basic needs so that the rich can have the liberty not to be interfered with when using their surplus resources for luxury purposes.

III. A moral resolution that would require the rich and the poor to accept the results of a power struggle in which both the rich and the poor are at liberty to appropriate and use the surplus resources of the rich.

Applying our previous discussion of the "ought" implies "can" principle to these three possible moral resolutions, it is clear that Ia (it would be unreasonable to ask or require the poor . . .) rules out II, but 2a (it would not be unreasonable to ask and require the rich . . .) does not rule out I. But what about III? Some libertarians have contended that III is the proper resolution of severe conflicts of interest between the rich and the poor.[8] But a resolution, like III, that sanctions the results of a power struggle between the rich and the poor, by and large, favors the rich over the poor. So all things considered, it would be no more reasonable to require the poor to accept III than it would be to require them to accept II. This means that only I satisfies the conflict resolution principle by being reasonable to require everyone affected to accept it. Consequently, if we assume that however else we specify the requirements of morality, they cannot violate the "ought" implies "can" principle or the conflict resolution principle, it fol-

lows that, despite what Spencerian libertarians claim, the basic right to liberty endorsed by them, as determined by a weighing of the relevant competing liberties according to these two principles, actually favors the liberty of the poor over the liberty of the rich.

Yet couldn't Spencerian libertarians object to this conclusion, claiming that it would be unreasonable to require the rich to sacrifice the liberty to meet some of their luxury needs so that the poor could have the liberty to meet their basic needs? As has been pointed out, libertarians don't usually see the situation as a conflict of liberties, but suppose they did. How plausible would such an objection be? Not very plausible at all.

Consider: What are Spencerian libertarians going to say about the poor? Isn't it clearly unreasonable to require the poor to sacrifice the liberty to meet their basic needs so that the rich can have the liberty to meet their luxury needs? Isn't it clearly unreasonable to require the poor to sit back and starve to death? If it is, then, there is no resolution of this conflict that would be reasonable to require both the rich and the poor to accept. But that would mean that libertarians could not be putting forth a moral resolution because according to the conflict resolution principle, in cases of severe conflict of interest, a moral resolution resolves conflicts of interest in ways that it would be reasonable to require everyone affected to accept. Therefore, as long as libertarians think of themselves as putting forth a moral resolution for cases of severe conflict of interest, they cannot allow that it would be unreasonable *both* to require the rich to sacrifice the liberty to meet some of their luxury needs in order to benefit the poor and to require the poor to sacrifice the liberty to meet their basic needs in order to benefit the rich. But I submit that if one of these requirements is to be judged reasonable, then, by any neutral assessment, it must be the requirement that the rich sacrifice the liberty to meet some of their luxury needs so that the poor can have the liberty to meet their basic needs; there is no other plausible resolution, if libertarians intend to put forth a moral resolution.

## Lockean Libertarians and the Problem of Conflict

The same conclusions can be established against Lockean libertarians who take a set of rights, typically including a right to life and a right to property, as basic and then interpret liberty as being unconstrained by other persons from doing what one has a right to do. In this context, the "ought" implies "can" principle and the conflict resolution principle can be shown, as I have argued elsewhere, to favor a conditional right to property over an unconditional right to property.[9] Consequently, if we assume that however else we specify the requirements of morality, they cannot violate these two principles, it follows that, despite what Lockean libertarians claim, the right to life and the right to property endorsed by them actually support a right to welfare.

Now it might be objected that the rights that this argument establishes from libertarian premises are not the same as the rights to welfare endorsed by welfare liberals and socialists. This is correct. We could mark this difference by referring to the rights that this argument establishes as "negative welfare rights" and by referring to the rights endorsed by welfare liberals and socialists as "positive welfare rights." The significance of this difference is that a person's negative welfare rights can be violated only when other people through acts of commission interfere with their exercise, whereas a person's positive welfare rights can be violated not only by such acts of commission but by acts of omission as well. Nonetheless, this difference will have little practical import. For once libertarians come to recognize the legitimacy of negative welfare rights, then in order not to be subject to the discretion of rightholders in choosing when and how to exercise these rights, libertarians will tend to favor the only morally legitimate way of preventing the exercise of such rights: they will institute adequate positive welfare rights that will then take precedence over the exercise of negative welfare rights. Accordingly, if libertarians adopt this morally legitimate way of preventing the exercise of such rights: they will end up endorsing the same sort of welfare institutions favored by welfare liberals and socialists.

## A RIGHT TO EQUAL OPPORTUNITY

It is possible that libertarians convinced to some extent by the above arguments might want to accept a right to welfare but then deny that there is a right to equal opportunity. Such a stance, however, is only plausible if we restrict the class of morally legitimate claimants to those within a given (affluent) society, for only then would a right to equal opportunity require something different from a right to welfare—which entails a right to the basic opportunities necessary for the satisfaction of one's basic needs.[10]

Consider: At present, there is probably a sufficient worldwide supply of goods and resources to meet the normal costs of satisfying the basic nutritional needs of all existing persons. According to former U.S. Secretary of Agriculture, Bob Bergland,

> For the past 20 years, if the available world food supply had been evenly divided and distributed, each person would have received more than the minimum number of calories.[11]

Other authorities have made similar assessments of the available world food supply.

Needless to say, the adoption of a policy of supporting a right to welfare for all existing persons would necessitate significant changes, especially in developed countries. For example, the large percentage of the U.S. population whose food consumption clearly exceeds even an adequately adjusted poverty index would have to substantially alter their eating habits. In particular, they would have to reduce their consumption of beef and pork in order to make more grain available for direct human consumption. (Presently the amount of grain-fed American livestock is as much as all the people of China and India eat in a year.) Thus, at least the satisfaction of some of the nonbasic needs of the more advantaged in developed countries would have to be forgone if the basic nutritional needs of all existing persons in developing and underdeveloped countries are to be met. Furthermore, to raise the standard of living in developing and underdeveloped countries will require substantial increases in the consumption of energy and other resources. But such an increase would have to be matched by a substantial decrease in the consumption of these goods in developing countries, otherwise global ecological disaster would result from increased global warming, ozone depletion, and acid rain, lowering virtually everyone's standard of living.[12]

In addition, once the basic nutritional needs of future generations are also taken into account, the satisfaction of the nonbasic needs of the more advantaged in developed countries would have to be further restricted in order to preserve the fertility of cropland and other food-related natural resources for the use of future generations. Obviously, the only assured way to guarantee the energy and resources necessary for the satisfaction of the basic needs of future generations is by setting aside resources that would otherwise be used to satisfy the nonbasic needs of existing generations. And once basic needs other than nutritional needs are taken into account as well, still further restrictions would be required. For example, it has been estimated that presently a North American uses fifty times more resources than an Indian. This means that in terms of resource consumption the North American continent's population is the equivalent of 12.5 billion Indians. Obviously, this would have to be radically altered if the basic needs of distant peoples and future generations are to be met. Accordingly, recognizing a right to welfare applicable both to distant peoples and future generations would significantly affect the right to equal opportunity that people can be guaranteed.

Now the form of equal opportunity that Rawls defends in *A Theory of Justice* requires that persons who have the same natural assets and the same willingness to use them have an equal chance to occupy roles and positions in society commensurate with their natural assets.[13] So construed, equal opportunity provides two sorts of benefits. It benefits society as a whole by helping to ensure that the most talented people will fill the most re-

sponsible roles and positions in society. It benefits individuals by ensuring that they will not be discriminated against with respect to filling the roles and positions in society for which they are qualified, thereby giving them a fair chance of securing whatever benefits attach to those roles and positions in society.

I have argued, however, that once it is recognized that the class of morally legitimate claimants includes distant peoples and future generations, then guaranteeing a right to welfare to all morally legitimate claimants would lead to a state of affairs in which few resources are available for directly meeting nonbasic needs, although such needs may still be met indirectly through the satisfaction of basic needs. As a consequence, there won't be greater benefits attaching to certain roles and positions in society, since people can only expect to have their basic needs directly met in whatever roles and positions they happen to occupy. Of course, we will still want the most talented people occupying the most responsible roles and positions in society; it's just that occupying those roles and positions will not secure greater benefits to those who occupy them. Therefore, to ensure that the most talented people occupy roles and positions that are commensurate with their abilities, we will need to do something like the following. First, borrowing an idea from socialist justice, we will need to make the roles and positions people occupy as intrinsically rewarding as possible. Second, we will need to convince the more talented that they have a moral responsibility to the less talented and to society as a whole to use their talents to the fullest. Consequently, the equal opportunity that will be guaranteed to everyone in society will only be a fair means of ensuring that everyone's basic needs are met, not a means of providing differential rewards or of directly meeting nonbasic needs.

Accordingly, my practical reconciliation argument fails to guarantee a right to equal opportunity that provides greater benefits to the talented, enabling them to directly meet nonbasic as well as basic needs. But the failure to guarantee this sort of equal opportunity is no objection to my argument, given that having this sort of equal opportunity is incompatible with the more fundamental requirement of meeting everyone's basic needs. On this account, both libertarians, and welfare liberals would come to endorse the same right to equal opportunity—an equal right not to be discriminated against in filling the roles and positions in a society that satisfies its obligations to meet everyone's basic needs.

What these arguments show, therefore, is that a libertarian ideal supports the same practical requirements as a welfare liberal ideal. Both favor a right to welfare and a right to equal opportunity. This is not to deny, of course, that there won't be disagreements concerning how to interpret a right to welfare understood as a right to the resources necessary for meeting one's basic needs and a right to equal opportunity understood as an equal right not to be discriminated against in filling the roles and positions in a society that satisfies its obligations to meet everyone's basic needs, but there is no reason to think that libertarians will disagree with welfare liberals any more than welfare liberals will disagree with themselves over the interpretation of these rights, especially over what is required for meeting people's basic needs.[14] Recall that it is generally thought that what divides welfare liberals from libertarians is that the former are committed to rights to welfare and equal opportunity whereas the latter reject both of these rights. It is quite evident that libertarians want to reject rights to welfare and equal opportunity because they think (wrongly) that to endorse these rights is to abandon their ideal of liberty. No libertarian has argued that it will do just as well to grant such rights and then disagree as to how these rights are to be interpreted. Thus, given my argument that both libertarians and welfare liberals are required to endorse a right to welfare understood as a right to the resources necessary for meeting one's basic needs and a right to equal opportunity understood as an equal right not to be discriminated against in filling the roles and positions in a society that satisfies its obligations to meet everyone's basic needs, it is implausible for us to think that comparable differences will now

emerge between libertarians and welfare liberals over the interpretation of these rights. Differences between welfare liberals and libertarians over what constitutes a basic needs minimum are likely to be no greater than differences among welfare liberals themselves over what constitutes such a minimum. Moreover, once libertarians and welfare liberals have taken the first practical steps to implement a right to welfare and a right to equal opportunity for distant peoples and future generations, they will both be in an even better position to know what is required for meeting people's basic needs. This is because sincerely attempting to live out one's practical moral commitments helps one to interpret them better, just as failing to live out one's practical moral commitments makes interpreting them all that more difficult.

In brief, what I have argued is that a libertarian ideal supports the same rights to welfare and equal opportunity as endorsed by a welfare liberal ideal.

## Libertarian Objections

In his recent book, *Individuals and Their Rights,* Tibor Machan criticizes the above argument that a libertarian ideal of liberty leads to a right to welfare, accepting its theoretical thrust but denying its practical significance.[15] He appreciates the force of the argument enough to grant that if the type of conflict cases that we have described between the rich and the poor actually obtained, the poor would have a right to welfare. But he denies that such cases—in which the poor have done all that they legitimately can to satisfy their basic needs in a libertarian society—actually obtain. "Normally," he writes, "persons do not lack the opportunities and resources to satisfy their basic needs."[16]

But this response virtually concedes everything that the above argument intended to establish. For the poor's right to welfare is not claimed to be unconditional. Rather it is said to be conditional principally upon the poor doing all that they legitimately can to meet their own basic needs. So it follows that only when the poor lack sufficient opportunity to satisfy their own basic needs would their right to welfare have any practical moral force. Accordingly, on libertarian grounds, Machan has conceded the legitimacy of just the kind of right to welfare that the above argument hoped to establish.

The only difference that remains is a practical one. Machan thinks that virtually all of the poor have sufficient opportunities and resources to satisfy their basic needs and that therefore, a right to welfare has no practical moral force. In contrast, I would think that many of the poor do not have sufficient opportunities and resources to satisfy their basic needs and that, therefore, a right to welfare has considerable practical moral force.

But isn't this practical disagreement resolvable? For who could deny that most of the 1.2 billion people who are currently living in conditions of absolute poverty "lack the opportunities and resources to satisfy their basic needs"?[17] And even within our own country, it is estimated that some 32 million Americans live below the official poverty index, and that one fifth of American children are growing up in poverty.[18] Surely, it is impossible to deny that many of these Americans also "lack the opportunities and resources to satisfy their basic needs." Given the impossibility of reasonably denying these factual claims, Machan would have to concede that the right to welfare, which he grants can be theoretically established on libertarian premises, also has practical moral force.[19]

More recently, different objections to my attempt to derive a right to welfare from libertarian premises have been raised by John Hospers.[20] First, Hospers contends that I am committed to distributing welfare too broadly, to the undeserving poor as well as to the deserving poor. Second, Hospers contends that the taxes on the wealthy that I defend, in effect, commit me to killing the goose that lays the golden egg, because the poor would be worse off under a tax-supported welfare system than they would be in a completely libertarian society.

In response to the first objection Hospers raises, I have in a number of places made it clear that I am defending a right to welfare only for the deserving poor, that is, the poor who have exhausted all of their legitimate opportunities for meeting their basic needs. Hosper's second objection, however, questions whether even the deserving poor would be better off demanding welfare, even if they have a right to it. Hospers cites the example of Ernst Mahler, an entrepreneurial genius who employed more than 100,000 and produced newsprint and tissue products that are now used by more than 2 billion people. Hospers suggests that requiring Mahler to contribute to a welfare system for the deserving poor would not only "decrease his own wealth but that of countless other people."

In response to this objection, I contend that if the more talented members of a society provided sufficient employment opportunities and voluntary welfare assistance to enable the poor to meet their basic needs, then the conditions for invoking a right to welfare would not arise, since the poor are first required to take advantage of whatever employment opportunities and voluntary welfare assistance are available to them before they can legitimately invoke such a right. Consequently, when *sufficient* employment opportunities and voluntary welfare assistance obtain, there would be no practical differences in this regard between a libertarian society and a welfare or socialist state, since neither would justify invoking a right to welfare. Only when *insufficient* employment opportunities and voluntary welfare assistance obtain would there be a practical difference between a libertarian society and a welfare or socialist state, and then it would clearly benefit the poor to be able to invoke the right to welfare. Consequently, given the practical possibility, and in most cases, the actuality of insufficient employment opportunities and voluntary welfare assistance obtaining, there is no reason to think that the poor would be better off without the enforcement of such a right.

Now one might think that once the rich realize that the poor should have the liberty not be interfered with when taking from the surplus possessions of the rich what they require to satisfy their basic needs, they should stop producing any surplus whatsoever. This appears to be what Hospers is suggesting by citing the example of Ernst

Mahler. Yet it would be in the interest of the rich to stop producing a surplus only if (a) they did not enjoy producing a surplus, (b) their recognition of the rightful claims of the poor would exhaust their surplus, and (c) the poor would never be in a position to be obligated to repay what they appropriated from them. Fortunately for the poor, not all of these conditions are likely to obtain.[21] But suppose they all did. Wouldn't the poor be justified in appropriating, or threatening to appropriate, even the nonsurplus possessions of those who can produce more in order to get them to do so?[22] Surely this would not be an unreasonable imposition on those who can produce more because it would not be unreasonable to require them to be a bit more productive when the alternative is requiring the poor to forego meeting their basic needs. Surely if we have no alternative, requiring those who can produce more to be a bit more productive is less of an imposition than requiring the poor to forego meeting their basic needs.

This is an important conclusion in our assessment of the libertarian ideal, because it shows that ultimately the right of the poor to appropriate what they require to meet their basic needs does not depend, as many have thought, upon the talented having sufficient self-interested incentives to produce a surplus. All that is necessary is that the talented can produce a surplus and that the (deserving) poor cannot meet their basic needs in any other way.

It might be objected, however, that if the talented can be required to produce a surplus so that the (deserving) poor can meet their basic needs, then why can't the poor be required to sterilize themselves as a condition for receiving that surplus. What the objection rightly points to is the need for the poor and everyone else as well to take steps to control population growth. What the objection wrongly maintains is that the poor would have a greater obligation to limit their procreation than the rich would have to limit theirs. Surely population can be brought under control by a uniform policy that imposes the same requirements on both rich and poor. There is no need or justification for a population policy that comes

down harder on the poor. I turn now to a consideration of a feminist social and political ideal.

## A Feminist Social and Political Ideal

Contemporary feminists almost by definition seek to put an end to male domination and to secure women's liberation. To achieve these goals, many feminists support the social and political ideal of a gender-free or androgynous society.[23] According to these feminists, all assignments of rights and duties are ultimately to accord with the ideal of a gender-free or androgynous society.

## The Ideal of Androgyny

But how is this ideal to be interpreted? A gender-free or genderless society is one where basic rights and duties are not assigned on the basis of a person's biological sex. Being male or female is not the grounds for determining what basic rights and duties a person has in a gender-free society. But this is to characterize the feminist ideal only negatively. It tells us what we need to get rid of, not what we need to put in its place. A more positive characterization is provided by the ideal of androgyny. Putting the feminist ideal more positively in terms of the ideal of androgyny also helps to bring out why men should be attracted to feminism.

In a well-known article, Joyce Trebilcot distinguishes two forms of androgyny.[24] The first form postulates the same ideal for everyone. According to this form of androgyny, the ideal person "combines characteristics usually attributed to men with characteristics usually attributed to women." Thus, we should expect both nurturance and mastery, openness and objectivity, and compassion and competitiveness from each and every person who has the capacities for these traits.

By contrast, the second form of androgyny does not advocate the same ideal for everyone but rather a variety of options from "pure" femininity to "pure" masculinity. As Trebilcot points out, this form of androgyny shares with the first the view that biological sex should not be the basis for determining the appropriateness of gender characterization. It differs in that it holds that "all alternatives with respect to gender should be equally available to and equally approved for everyone, regardless of sex."

It would be a mistake, however, to sharply distinguish between these two forms of androgyny. Properly understood, they are simply two facets of a single ideal. For, as Mary Ann Warren has argued, the second form of androgyny is appropriate *only* "with respect to feminine and masculine traits which are largely matters of personal style and preference and which have little direct moral significance."[25] However, when we consider so-called feminine and masculine *virtues*, it is the first form of androgyny that is required because, then, other things being equal, the same virtues are appropriate for everyone.

We can even formulate the ideal of androgyny more abstractly so that it is no longer specified in terms of so-called feminine and masculine traits. We can specify the ideal as requiring no more than that the traits that are truly desirable and distributable in society be equally available to both women and men, or in the case of virtues, equally expected of both women and men.

There is a problem, of course, in determining which traits of character are virtues and which traits are largely matters of personal style and preference. To make this determination, Trebilcot has suggested that we seek to bring about the second form of androgyny, where people have the option of acquiring the full range of so-called feminine and masculine traits.[26] But surely when we already have good grounds for thinking that certain traits are virtues (such as courage and compassion, fairness and openness) there is no reason to adopt such a laissez-faire approach to moral education. Although, as Trebilcot rightly points out, proscribing certain options will involve a loss of freedom, nevertheless, we should be able to determine at least with respect to some character traits when a gain in virtue is worth the loss of freedom. It may even be the case that the loss of freedom suffered by an individual now will be compensated for by a gain of freedom to that same individual in the future once the relevant virtue or virtues have been acquired.

So understood, the class of virtues will turn out to be those desirable and distributable traits that can be reasonably expected of both women and men. Admittedly, this is a restrictive use of the term *virtue*. In normal usage, "virtue" is almost synonymous with the term "desirable trait."[27] But there is good reason to focus on those desirable traits that can be reasonably expected of both women and men, and, for present purposes, I will refer to this class of desirable traits as virtues.

Unfortunately, many of the challenges to the ideal of androgyny fail to appreciate how the ideal can be interpreted to combine an expected set of virtues with equal choice from among other desirable traits. For example, some challenges interpret the ideal as attempting to achieve "a proper balance of moderation" among opposing feminine and masculine traits and then question whether traits like feminine gullibility or masculine brutality could ever be combined with opposing gender traits to achieve such a balance.[28] Other challenges interpret the ideal as permitting unrestricted choice of personal traits and then regard the possibility of Total Women and Hell's Angels androgynes as a *reductio ad absurdum* of the ideal.[29] But once it is recognized that the ideal of androgyny cannot only be interpreted to expect of everyone a set of virtues (which need not be a mean between opposing extreme traits), but can also be interpreted to limit everyone's choice to desirable traits, then such challenges to the ideal clearly lose their force.

Actually, the main challenge raised by feminists to the ideal of androgyny is that the ideal is self-defeating in that it seeks to eliminate sexual stereotyping of human beings at the same time that it is formulated in terms of the very same stereotypical concepts it seeks to eliminate.[30] Or as Warren has put it, "Is it not at least mildly paradoxical to urge people to cultivate both feminine and masculine virtues, while at the same time holding that virtues ought not to be sexually stereotyped?"

But in response to this challenge, it can be argued that to build a better society we must begin where we are now, and where we are now people still speak of feminine and masculine character traits. Consequently, if we want to easily refer to such traits and to formulate an ideal with respect to how they should be distributed in society it is plausible to refer to them in the way that people presently refer to them, that is, as feminine or masculine traits.

Alternatively, to avoid misunderstanding altogether, the ideal could be formulated in the more abstract way I suggested earlier so that it no longer specifically refers to so-called feminine or masculine traits. So formulated, the ideal requires that the traits that are truly desirable and distributable in society be equally available to both women and men, or in the case of virtues, equally expected of both women and men. So formulated, the ideal would, in effect, expect that men and women have in the fullest sense an equal right of self-development. The ideal requires this because an equal right to self-development can only be effectively guaranteed by expecting the same virtues of both women and men and by making other desirable traits equally available to both women and men.

So characterized, the ideal of androgyny represents neither a revolt against so-called feminine virtues and traits nor their exaltation over so-called masculine virtues and traits.[31] Accordingly, the ideal of androgyny does not view women's liberation as *simply* the freeing of women from the confines of traditional roles, thus making it possible for them to develop in ways heretofore reserved for men. Nor does the ideal view women's liberation as *simply* the revaluation and glorification of so-called feminine activities like housekeeping or mothering or so-called feminine modes of thinking as reflected in an ethic of caring. The first perspective ignores or devalues genuine virtues and desirable traits traditionally associated with women, while the second ignores or devalues genuine virtues and desirable traits traditionally associated with men. By contrast, the ideal of androgyny seeks a broader-based ideal for both women and men that combines virtues and desirable traits traditionally associated with women and

those virtues and desirable traits traditionally associated with men. Nevertheless, the ideal of androgyny will clearly reject any so-called virtues or desirable traits traditionally associated with women or men that have been supportive of discrimination or oppression against women or men. In general, the ideal of androgyny substitutes a socialization based on natural ability, reasonable expectation, and choice for a socialization based on sexual difference.

Of course, in proposing to characterize a feminist ideal in terms of the ideal of a gender-free or androgynous society, I recognize that not all feminists start off endorsing this ideal. Christina Sommers, for example, has attracted attention recently by distinguishing liberal feminism which she endorses from androgynous feminism which she opposes.[32] But as one gets clearer and clearer about the liberal feminism that Sommers endorses, it begins to look more and more like the androgynous feminism that she says she opposes. There is nothing surprising about this, however. We cannot have the genuine equal opportunity for men and women that Sommers wants without reforming the present distribution of gender traits. Women cannot be passive, submissive, dependent, indecisive, and weak and still enjoy the same opportunities enjoyed by men who are aggressive, dominant, independent, decisive, and strong. So I contend that liberal feminism and androgynous feminism go together because genuine equal opportunity requires the feminist ideal of a gender-free or androgynous society.

It also seems that those who claim that we cannot escape a gendered society are simply confused about what a gender-free society would be like.[33] For they seem to agree with those who favor a gender-free or androgynous society that the assignments of roles in society should be based on (natural) ability, rational expectation, and choice. But what they also hold is that some of these assignments will be based on sex as well because some of the natural abilities that people have will be determined by their sex. But even assuming this is the case, it wouldn't show that society was gendered in the sense that its roles in society are based on sex *rather than* being based on (natural) ability, rational expectation, and choice. And this is the only sense of gendered society to which defenders of a feminist ideal would be objecting.[34] So once the notion of a gender-free society is clarified, there should be widespread agreement that the assignments of roles in society should be based on (natural) ability, rational expectation, and choice. The ideal of androgyny simply specifies this notion of a gender-free society a bit further by requiring that the traits that are truly desirable in society be equally open to (equally qualified) women and men, or in the case of virtues, equally expected of (equally capable) women and men.

Of course, insofar as natural abilities are a function of sexual difference, there will be differences in the desirable traits and virtues that women and men acquire even in a gender-free or androgynous society. And some contend that these differences will be substantial.[35] But given that we have been slow to implement the degree of equal opportunity required by the ideal of a gender-free or androgynous society, it is difficult to know what differences will emerge that are both sex based and natural ability based. What we can be sure of is that given the variety and types of discrimination employed against women in existing societies, a gender-free or androgynous society will look quite different from the societies that we know.

## Defenses of Androgyny

Now there are various contemporary defenses of the ideal of androgyny. Some feminists have attempted to derive the ideal from a welfare liberal ideal. Others have attempted to derive the ideal from a socialist political ideal. Here I will only consider the attempt to derive the ideal of androgyny from a welfare liberal idea.[36]

In attempting to derive the ideal of androgyny from a welfare liberal ideal, feminists have tended to focus on the right to equal opportunity which is a central requirement of such an ideal. Of course, equal opportunity could be interpreted minimally as providing people only with the same legal rights of access to all advantaged positions in society for which they are qualified. But this is not the interpretation given the right by welfare liberals. In a welfare liberal ideal, equal opportunity is interpreted to require in addition the same prospects for success for all those who are relevantly similar, where relevant similarity involves more than simply present qualifications. For example, Rawls claims that persons in his original position would favor a right to "fair equality of opportunity" which means that persons who have the same natural assets and the same willingness to use them would have the necessary resources to achieve similar life prospects.[37]

Yet any attempt to derive the feminist ideal of androgyny from the right to equal opportunity endorsed by welfare liberals can only be partially successful because the ideal still transcends this right by requiring not only that desirable traits be equally available to both women and men but also that the same virtues be equally inculcated in both women and men. Of course, part of the rationale for inculcating the same virtues in both women and men is to support a right to equal opportunity. And if support for such a right is to be fairly allocated, the virtues needed to support this right must be equally inculcated in both women and men. Nevertheless, to hold that the virtues required to support a right to equal opportunity must be equally inculcated in both women and men is different from claiming, as the ideal of androgyny does, that human virtues, sans phrase, should be equally inculcated in both women and men. Thus, the ideal of androgyny clearly requires an inculcation of virtues beyond what is necessary to support a right to equal opportunity. What additional virtues are required by the ideal obviously depends upon what other rights should be recognized. In this regard, the ideal of androgyny is somewhat open ended. Feminists who endorse the ideal would simply have to go along with the best arguments for additional rights and corresponding virtues.

In particular, I would claim that they would have to support a right to welfare that is necessary for meeting the basic needs of all legitimate claimants given the strong case that can be made for such a right from welfare liberal, socialist, and libertarian perspectives.

Obviously, in order to provide all legitimate claimants with the resources necessary for meeting their basic needs, there has to be a limit on the resources that will be available for each individual, and this limit will definitely have an effect upon the implementation of the ideal of androgyny. Of course, some feminists would want to pursue various possible technological transformations of human biology in order to implement their ideal. For example, they would like to make it possible for women to inseminate other women and for men to lactate and even to bring fertilized ova to term. But bringing about such possibilities would be very costly indeed.[38] Consequently, since the means selected for meeting basic needs must be provided to all legitimate claimants, including distant peoples and future generations, it is unlikely that such costly means could ever be morally justified. Rather it seems preferable to radically equalize the opportunities that are conventionally provided to women and men and wait for such changes to ultimately have their effect on human biology as well. Of course, if any "technological fixes" for achieving androgyny should prove to be cost efficient as a means for meeting people's basic needs, then obviously there would be every reason to utilize them.

## Androgyny and the Family

Now the primary locus for the radical restructuring required by the ideal of androgyny is the family. Here two fundamental changes are needed. First, all children irrespective of their sex must be given the same type of upbringing consistent with their native capabilities. Second, mothers and fathers must also have the same opportunities for education and employment consistent with their native capabilities.

Yet at least in the United States this need to radically modify traditional family structures to guarantee equal opportunity confronts a serious problem. Given that a significant proportion of the available jobs are at least 9 to 5, families with pre-

school children require day-care facilities if their adult members are to pursue their careers. Unfortunately, for many families such facilities are simply unavailable. In New York City, for example, more than 144,000 children under the age of six are competing for 46,000 full-time slots in day-care centers. In Seattle, there is licensed day-care space for 8,800 of the 23,000 children who need it. In Miami, two children, 3 and 4 years old, were left unattended at home while their mother worked. They climbed into a clothes dryer while the timer was on, closed the door and burned to death.[39]

Moreover, even the available day-care facilities are frequently inadequate either because their staffs are poorly trained or because the child/adult ratio in such facilities is too high. At best, such facilities provide little more than custodial care; at worst, they actually retard the development of those under their care. What this suggests is that at least under present conditions if preschool children are to be adequately cared for, frequently, one of the adult members of the family will have to remain at home to provide that care. But since most jobs are at least 9 to 5, this will require that the adult members who stay at home temporarily give up pursuing a career.

However, such sacrifice appears to conflict with the equal opportunity requirement of a feminist ideal. Now families might try to meet this equal opportunity requirement by having one parent give up pursuing a career for a certain period of time and the other give up pursuing a career for a subsequent (equal) period of time. But there are problems here too. Some careers are difficult to interrupt for any significant period of time, while others never adequately reward latecomers. In addition, given the high rate of divorce and the inadequacies of most legally mandated child support, those who first sacrifice their careers may find themselves later faced with the impossible task of beginning or reviving their careers while continuing to be the primary caretaker of their children.[40] Furthermore, there is considerable evidence that children will benefit more from equal rearing from both parents.[41] So the option of having just one parent doing the child-rearing for any length of time is, other things being equal, not optimal.

It would seem therefore, that to truly share child-rearing within the family, what is needed are flexible (typically part-time) work schedules that also allow both parents to be with their children for a significant period every day. Now some flexible job schedules have already been tried by various corporations. But if equal opportunity is to be a reality in our society, the option of flexible job schedules must be guaranteed to all those with preschool children. Of course, to require employers to guarantee flexible job schedules to all those with preschool children would place a significant restriction upon the rights of employers, and it may appear to move the practical requirements of feminism closer to those of socialism. But if the case for flexible job schedules is grounded on a right to equal opportunity, then at least defenders of welfare liberalism will have no reason to object. This is clearly one place where feminism with its focus on equal opportunity within the family tends to drive welfare liberalism and socialism closer together in their practical requirements.

## Feminist Objections

In her recent book, *Justice, Gender and the Family*, Susan Okin also examines the capacity of a welfare liberal ideal to support the ideal of a gender-free society, which I take to be the same as an androgynous society.[42] Noting Rawls's failure to apply his original position–type thinking to family structures, Okin is skeptical about the possibility of using a welfare liberal ideal of fairness to support a feminist ideal. She contends that in a gender-structured society like our own, male philosophers cannot achieve the sympathetic imagination required to see things from the standpoint of women. In a gender-structured society, Okin claims, male philosophers cannot do the original position–type thinking required by the welfare liberal ideal of fairness because they lack the ability to put themselves in the position of women. As Okin puts it,

> For if principles of justice are to be adopted unanimously by representative human beings ignorant of their particular characteristics and positions in society, they must be persons whose psychological and moral development is in all essentials identical. This means that the social factors influencing the differences presently found between the sexes—from female parenting to all the manifestations of female subordination and dependence—would have to be replaced by genderless institutions and customs.[43]

So, according to Okin, original position–type thinking can only really be achieved in a gender-free society.

Yet at the same time that Okin despairs of doing original position–type thinking, in a gender-structured society, like our own, she herself purportedly does a considerable amount of just that type of thinking. For example, she claims that Rawls's principles of justice "would seem to require a radical rethinking not only of the division of labor within families but also of all the nonfamily institutions that assume it."[44] She also claims that "the abolition of gender seems essential for the fulfillment of Rawls's criterion of political justice."[45] More specifically, she contends that

> if those in the original position did not know whether they were to be men or women, they would surely be concerned to establish a thoroughgoing social and economic equality between the sexes that would protect either sex from the need to pander to or servilely provide for the pleasures of the other. They would emphasize the importance of girls' and boys' growing up with an equal sense of respect for themselves and equal expectations of self-definition and development. They would be highly motivated, too, to find a means of regulating pornography that did not seriously compromise freedom of speech. In general, they would be unlikely to tolerate basic social institutions that asymmetrically either forced or gave strong incentives to members of one sex to serve as sex objects for the other.[46]

But which is it? Can we or can we not do the original position–type thinking required by a welfare liberal ideal of fairness? I think that Okin's own work, as well as the work of others, demonstrates that we can do such thinking and that her reasons for thinking that we cannot are not persuasive. For to do original position–type thinking, it is not necessary that everyone be able to put themselves imaginatively in the position of everyone else. All that is necessary is that some people be able to do so. For some people may not be able to do original position–type thinking because they have been deprived of a proper moral education. Others may be able to do original position–type thinking only after they have been forced to mend their ways and live morally for a period of time.

Moreover, in putting oneself in the place of others, one need not completely replicate the experience of others. For example, one need not actually feel what it is like to be a murderer to adequately take into account the murderer's perspective. Original position–type thinking with respect to a particular issue only requires a general appreciation of the benefits and burdens that accrue to people affected by that issue. So with respect to feminist justice, we need to be able to generally appreciate what women and men stand to gain and lose when moving from a nonandrogynous or gendered society to an androgynous or gender-free society.

Of course, even among men and women in our gendered society who are in a broad sense capable of a sense of justice, some may not presently be able to do such original position-type thinking with respect to the proper relationships between men and women; these men and women may only be able to do so after the laws and social practices in our society have significantly shifted toward a more gender-free society. But this inability of some to do original position-type thinking does not render it impossible for others, who have effectively used the opportunities for moral development available to them to achieve the sympathetic imagination necessary for original position–type thinking with respect to the proper relationships between men and women. Accordingly, Okin has not provided any compelling reason to reject my previous argument that a welfare liberal ideal of fairness supports the ideal of androgyny.[47]

In sum, what I have argued in this paper is that a libertarian political ideal and a feminist political ideal support the practical requirements that are usually associated with a welfare liberal political idea, namely, a right to welfare and a right to equal opportunity. I have also attempted to show that recent work done by libertarians and feminists neither undercuts nor is incompatible with this argument for reconciling political ideals.

NOTES

1. See "Neolibertarianism," *American Philosophical Quarterly* (1978); *The Demands of Justice* (Notre Dame: University of Notre Dame Press, 1980); "The Welfare Rights of Distant Peoples and Future Generations: Moral Side-Constraints on Social Policy," *Social Theory and Practice* (1981); "Recent Work on Alternative Conceptions of Justice," *American Philosophical Quarterly* (1986); "Justifying Morality: The Right and the Wrong Ways," *Synthese* (1987); *How to Make People Just* (Totowa: NJ, Rowman & Littlefield, 1988); "Feminist Justice and the Family," reprinted in my anthology, *Justice: Alternative Political Perspectives*, 2d ed. (Belmont, CA: Wadsworth, 1991).

2. It is interesting to note that in his recent work Alasdair MacIntyre has significantly qualified his commitment to the incommensurability thesis with which he is so widely associated. MacIntyre now allows that while alternative political ideals are incommensurable, it is still possible for a sensitive interpreter to come to adequately understand competing ideals so as to raise problems for those ideals that should lead either to their abandonment or their modification. MacIntyre credits Aquinas with being a sensitive interpreter of Aristotelianism and Augustianianism who showed the need to modify each perspective to produce a more adequate synthesis. In his most recent work, MacIntyre sees himself as being the sensitive interpreter of two views he calls the encyclopaedist (which he apparently thinks contains the core view of liberalism) and the genealogist (which represents an ugly form of relativism). MacIntyre then attempts to show that both of these views are plagued with internal contradictions which he takes to provide support for the Augustinian-Aristotelian synthesis that he derives from Aquinas. Obviously, I welcome MacIntyre's newly stated recognition that it is possible to argue nonarbitrarily with respect to alternative political ideals. Nevertheless, I think that while MacIntyre in his most recent work may have correctly refuted the genealogist, the liberalism he criticizes is only a caricature of contemporary liberalism. Ironically, it turns out that contemporary liberalism, correctly understood, is in fact one variant of the general Augustianian-Aristotelian synthesis that MacIntyre derives from Aquinas! (See Alasdair MacIntyre, *Three Rival Versions of Moral Enquiry* (Notre Dame: University of Notre Dame Press, 1990).

3. It is not being assumed here that the surplus possessions of the rich are either justifiably or unjustifiably possessed by the rich. Moreover, according to

Spencerian libertarians, it is an assessment of the liberties involved that determines whether the possession is justifiable or not.

4. I first appealed to this interpretation of the "ought" implies "can" principle to bring libertarians around to the practical requirements of welfare liberalism in an expanded version of an article entitled "Neo-Libertarianism," which appeared in the fall of 1979. In 1982, T. M. Scanlon, in "Contractualism and Utilitarianism," appealed to much the same standard to arbitrate the debate between contractarians and utilitarians. In my judgment, however, this standard embedded in the "ought" implies "can" principle can be more effectively used in the debate with libertarians than in the debate with utilitarians, because sacrifices libertarians standardly seek to impose on the less advantaged are more outrageous and, hence, more easily shown to be contrary to reason.

5. I am indebted to Alasdair MacIntyre for helping me make this point clearer.

6. See James P. Sterba, "Is There a Rationale for Punishment?" *American Journal of Jurisprudence* (1984).

7. By the liberty of the rich to meet their luxury needs I continue to mean the liberty of the rich not to be interfered with when using their surplus possessions for luxury purposes. Similarly, by the liberty of the poor to meet their basic needs I continue to mean the liberty of the poor not to be interfered with when taking what they require to meet their basic needs from the surplus possessions of the rich.

8. See, for example, Eric Mack, "Individualism, Rights and the Open Society," *The Libertarian Alternative,* edited by Tibor Machan (Chicago: Nelson Hall, 1974) and "Libertarianism Untamed," *Journal of Social Philosophy,* special issue (1991).

9. For a sketch of this argument, see *How To Make People Just,* pp. 92–97.

10. Moreover, libertarians have not restricted the class of morally legitimate claimants in this fashion. After all, the fundamental rights recognized by libertarians are universal rights, that is, rights possessed by all people not just those who live in certain places or at certain times. Of course, to claim that these rights are universal does not mean that they are universally recognized. Obviously, the fundamental rights that flow from the libertarian ideal have not been universally recognized. Rather to claim that they are universal rights, despite their spotty recognition, implies only that they ought to be recognized at all times and places by people who have or could have had good reasons to recognize these rights, whether or not they actually did or do so.

Nor need these universal rights be unconditional. This is particularly true in the case of the right to welfare, which, I have argued, is conditional on people doing all that they legitimately can to provide for themselves. In addition, this right is conditional on there being sufficient resources available so that everyone's welfare needs can be met. So where people do not do all that they can to provide for themselves or where there are not sufficient resources available, people simply do not have a right to welfare.

Yet even though libertarians have claimed that the rights they defend are universal rights in the manner I have just explained, it may be that they are simply mistaken in this regard. Even when universal rights are stripped of any claim to being universally recognized or unconditional, still it might be argued that there are no such rights, that is, that there are no rights that all people ought to recognize.

But how would one argue for such a view? One couldn't argue from the failure of people to recognize such rights because we have already said that such recognition is not necessary. Nor could one argue that not everyone ought to recognize such rights because some lack the capacity to do so. This is because "ought" does imply "can" here, so that the obligation to recognize certain rights only applies to those who actually have or have had at some point the capacity to do so. Thus, the existence of universal rights is not ruled out by the existence of individuals who have never had the capacity to recognize such rights. It would only be ruled out by the existence of individuals who could recognize these rights but for whom it would be correct to say that they ought, all things considered, not to do so. But we have just seen that even a minimal libertarian moral ideal supports a universal right to welfare. And I have also argued elsewhere that when "ought" is understood prudentially rather than morally a nonquestion-begging conception to rationality favors morality over prudence. (See *How to Make People Just,* Chapter 11.) So for those capable of recognizing universal rights, it simply is not possible to argue that they, all things considered, ought not to do so.

11. Bob Bergland, "Attacking the Problem of World Hunger," *The National Forum 69,* no. 2 (1979): 4.

12. For a discussion of these causal connections, see Cheryl Silver, *One Earth One Future* (Washington, D.C.: National Academy Press, 1990); Bill McKibben, *The End of Nature* (New York: Random, 1989); Jeremy Leggett, ed., *Global Warming* (New York: Oxford University Press, 1990); Lester Brown, ed., *The World Watch Reader* (New York: W. W. Norton & Co., 1991).

13. John Rawls, *A Theory of Justice* (Cambridge: Harvard University Press, 1971), chapter 2.

14. For further discussion of a basic needs minimum, see *How To Make People Just,* 45–48.

15. Tibor Machan, *Individuals and Their Rights* (La Salle: Open Court, 1989) 100–111.

16. Ibid., 107.

17. Alan Durning, "Life on the Brink," *World Watch 3,* no. 2 (1990): 24.

18. Ibid., 29.

19. In *Individuals and Their Rights* and in correspondence, Machan has distinguished between poverty and hunger that results from natural causes and poverty and hunger that results from "political tyrannies" or from other human causes. Machan suggests that only the first sort of poverty and hunger need concern libertarians. But unless the victims are morally responsible for their fate, then, it seems to me, others will have at least a prima facie obligation not to interfere with relief efforts, even when those relief efforts happen to be utilizing their own surplus possessions.

20. John Hospers, "Some Unquestioned Assumptions," *Journal of Social Philosophy,* 22 (1991), 42–51.

21. Although given what I have said about the welfare rights of distant peoples and future generations, it would seem that (b) and (c) are unlikely to obtain.

22. Actually, the possessions in question are not truly nonsurplus since those who have them could relatively easily produce a surplus.

23. See, for example, Ann Ferguson, "Androgyny as An Ideal for Human Development." In *Feminism and Philosophy,* edited by Mary Vetterling-Braggin and others (Totowa, Rowman & Littlefield, 1977), 45–69; Mary Ann Warren, "Is Androgyny the Answer to Sexual Stereotyping?" In *"Femininity," "Masculinity," and "Androgyny,"* edited by Mary Vetterling-Braggin (Totowa, NJ: Rowman & Littlefield, 1982), 170–186; A. G. Kaplau and J. Bean, eds. *Beyond Sex-Role Stereotypes: Reading Towards a Psychology of Androgyny* (Totowa, NJ: Rowman & Littlefield, 1976); Andrea Dworkin, *Women Hating* (New York: Dutton, 1974), Part IV. Carol Gould, "Privacy Rights and Public Virtues: Women, the Family and Democracy." In Carol Gould, *Beyond Domination* (Totowa, NJ, Rowman & Littlefield, 1983), 3–18; Carol Gould, "Women and Freedom," *The Journal of Social Philosophy* (1984) 20–34; Linda Lindsey, *Gender Roles* (Englewood Cliffs, NJ: Prentice-Hall, 1990); Marilyn Friedman, "Does Sommers Like Women?" *Journal of Social Philosophy* (1991) 75–90.

24. Joyce, Trebilcot, "Two Forms of Androgynism." Reprinted in *Feminism and Philosophy,* Mary Vetterling-Braggin, Frederick Ellison, and Jane English (Totowa, NJ: Rowman & Littlefield, 1977), 70–78.

25. Ibid., 178–179.

26. Ibid., 74–77.

27. On this point, see Edmund Pincoffs, *Quandaries and Virtue* (Lawrence: University of Kansas, 1986) Chapter 5.

28. See, for example, Kathryn Paula Morgan, "Androgyny: A Conceptual Critique," *Social Theory and Practice* (1982), 256–257.

29. See, for example, Mary Daly, *Gyn-Ecology: The Meta-Ethics of Radical Feminism* (Boston: Beacon, 1978), xi.

30. Margrit Erchler, *The Double Standard* (New York, St. Martin's Press, 1980), 69–71; Elizabeth Lane Beardsley, "On Curing Conceptual Confusion." In *"Femininity," "Masculinity" and "Androgyny,"* 197–202; Mary Daly, "The Qualitative Leap Beyond Patriarchal Religion," *Quest* I (1975): 20–40; Janice Raymond, "The Illusion of Androgyny," *Quest 2* (1975): 57–66.

31. For a valuable discussion and critique of these two viewpoints see Iris Young, "Humanism, Gynocentrism and Feminist Politics," *Women's Studies International Forum* (1985) 8, no. 3: 173–183.

32. See Christina Sommers, "Philosophers Against the Family." In George Graham and Hugh LaFollette, *Person to Person* (Philadelphia: Temple University Press, 1989), 82–105; "Do These Feminists Like Women?" *Journal of Social Philosophy* (1990), 66–74; "Argumentum Ad Feminam," *Journal of Social Philosophy* (1991), 5–19.

33. Elizabeth Wolgast, *Equality and the Rights of Women* (Ithaca, NY: Cornell University Press, 1980).

34. Moreover, given that the basic rights that we have in society (e.g., a right to equal opportunity), are equal for all citizens and are not based on our differing natural abilities, these rights are not even in this derivative sense based on one's sex.

35. Anne Moir and David Jessel, *Brain Sex* (New York, 1991).

36. For an attempt to derive the ideal of androgyny from a socialist ideal, see "Feminist Justice and the Family," 319–320.

37. John Rawls, *A Theory of Justice* (Cambridge, 1971), 73.

38. See Barbara Katz Rothman, "How Science Is Redefining Parenthood," *Ms* (August 1982), 154–158.

39. *New York Times,* November 25, 1987.

40. See Lenore Weitzman, *The Divorce Revolution: The Unexpected Social and Economic Consequences for Women and Children in America* (New York: Free Press, 1985).

41. Dorothy Dinnerstein, *The Mermaid and the Minotaur* (New York: Harper and Row, 1977); Nancy Chodorow, *Mothering: Psychoanalysis and the Sociology of Gender* (Berkeley, University of California Press, 1978).

42. Susan Okin, *Justice, Gender and the Family* (New York: Basic Books, 1989), Chapter 5.

43. Ibid., 107.

44. Ibid., 104.

45. Ibid., 104.

46. Ibid., 104–105.

47. It is worth pointing out that my previous argument for androgyny actually benefited from criticisms raised by Okin in private correspondence in 1987.